CW00520414

1 MONTH OF
FREE
READING
at
www.ForgottenBooks.com

By purchasing this book you are eligible for one month membership to ForgottenBooks.com, giving you unlimited access to our entire collection of over 700,000 titles via our web site and mobile apps.

To claim your free month visit:

www.forgottenbooks.com/free183889

* Offer is valid for 45 days from date of purchase. Terms and conditions apply.

ISBN 978-0-483-27394-8
PIBN 10183889

This book is a reproduction of an important historical work. Forgotten Books uses state-of-the-art technology to digitally reconstruct the work, preserving the original format whilst repairing imperfections present in the aged copy. In rare cases, an imperfection in the original, such as a blemish or missing page, may be replicated in our edition. We do, however, repair the vast majority of imperfections successfully; any imperfections that remain are intentionally left to preserve the state of such historical works.

Forgotten Books is a registered trademark of FB &c Ltd.
Copyright © 2017 FB &c Ltd.
FB &c Ltd, Dalton House, 60 Windsor Avenue, London, SW19 2RR.
Company number 08720141. Registered in England and Wales.

For support please visit www.forgottenbooks.com

FISHER'S

COLONIAL MAGAZINE

AND JOURNAL OF

TRADE, COMMERCE, AND BANKING.

[C.9 Ser. 2]

NEW SERIES—1844.

VOL. I.

"FAR AS THE BREEZE CAN BEAR THE BILLOW'S FOAM,
SURVEY OUR EMPIRE, AND BEHOLD OUR HOME."

236490
17.10.29

FISHER, SON, & CO.,
THE CAXTON PRESS, ANGEL STREET-NEWGATE STREET, LONDON;
POST-OFFICE PLACE, LIVERPOOL; AND 93, PICCADILLY, MANCHESTER.

HC
259
F45
Ser. 2
v.1

PREFACE.

A Colonial Magazine, like class-legislation, being circumscribed in its objects, must ever be conducted with less private profit than public advantage. Having reached the verge of green old age, encouraged, as we passed, by the approbation of the wise and patriotic portion of society,—finding increase of strength simultaneous with added years,—we decided upon acknowledging the gift by gratitude to the givers. For this purpose, that is, to extend our sphere of usefulness, and to remit taxation to those who have contributed to support our infant steps, we have reduced the price of our monthly number from half-a-crown to *one shilling;* accompanied by a reduction in the quantity of matter considerably less, however, than the abated cost would have justified. Nor shall the diminished number of our pages detract from the real value of our labours,—since it is one of our maxims to give an extra sheet, or sheets, whenever the surpassing interest of an article, its present importance, or the desirableness of retaining it in an undivided form, shall render such additional space desirable. Closed, by high cost, against those whose means were moderate, or whose curiosity extended no further than to some one particular article in a number, our pages are now, and have been since the commencement of this year (1844), thrown open to the utmost limits to which commercial enterprise can wisely venture. Our principles remain unchanged; our practice, we trust, is improved: self-respect recommends the one—self-interest the other.

In the economy of our publication, the same liberality which elicited approbation and deserved patronage, is still maintained; and new energies are exerted, to procure with speed and certainty the most authentic intelligence from every colony.

We request our subscribers' attention—their re-perusal, in some instances, of articles which have appeared in these pages during the vanished year. We appeal to several of them in evidence of the dispassionate opinions set forth by us on the most momentous questions. One of our earliest numbers pressed upon the British commercial public the vast importance of a railroad or canal across the Isthmus of Panama. The French have anticipated us,—our warning voice was unhappily neglected. We hailed the system of sheep-boiling in the Australian colonies, even at the risk of displeasing the *Sydney Herald,* by naming a wrong man in a right cause, (no bad man, however, in very many respects,) and we now congratulate ourselves on seeing tallow one of the chief exports of that great colony.—While New Zealand sank under the injuries of a negligent administration, we raised our voice in her behalf, and its tones have at length opened the ears of those who have the power to alleviate her sufferings. There may be different opinions as to the origin, growth, conduct, &c., of the Company; there can be but one as to the humanity of protecting the lives and properties of our fellow-citizens, whose emigration to that land of cannibalism has left more room at home for us.—There are two other articles in the volume now closed, the value of which is permanent and sterling: one, "Sir Charles Metcalfe in Canada," written by an eminent public character, foretold the policy since pursued by the Canadian government; the other, "the System of Crown-Land-Granting in Canada," by a sixteen-years resident, is entitled to the most serious consideration. Its doctrines are not precisely new, but they are so distinctly and honestly expressed and maintained, that they become almost irresistible. They are not in accordance with the principle of joint-stock land-companies, nor of wholesale systems of emigration by government or communities; they are based on those feelings of independence which have rendered British yeomen—British peasants—the British people—the envy and admiration of the world. These principles are,—let every man find food, clothing, and education for himself and his offspring; let the government see that he has fair play.

P. S.—An early number in the ensuing year will contain the first parts of two interesting serials; one relating to the Cape of Good Hope—the other to the Island of Trinidad.

London, December, 1844.

CONTENTS OF VOL. I.

CONTENTS.

INDEX.

CITY AND BAY OF PANAMA.

FISHER'S

COLONIAL MAGAZINE.

On the Use and the Practicability of the Construction of

A CANAL OR OTHER COMMUNICATION FROM THE ATLANTIC TO THE PACIFIC.

We are appalled in taking up our pen to treat of this vast subject; but, while we are constrained into becoming diffidence by its peculiar character, we shall endeavour to express our sentiments on it with the earnestness which its very great importance to society in general, and to the commercial world in particular, demands. Were we about to offer our sentiments on the formation of a canal of even larger extent than any now existing, either for internal communication, or between rivers, lakes, channels, or even seas, we might call to our aid a tolerable quantum of resolution; but, when on the brink of considering the feasibility of uniting two vast oceans, and that by crossing through a portion of the most stupendous range of mountains on our earth, we become sensible of our relative pigmy weakness in attempting, perhaps rashly attempting, to modify, by human art, the vast works of an all-intelligent, all-powerful, and beneficent Creator. Weak, however, as we are, in comparison with an all-efficient Providence, yet have we been formed acute and strong for the obtainment of our own social convenience and happiness, and been permitted to know all that is necessary for enabling us to arrive at their enjoyment, an enjoyment which we are not allowed to pluck at the reach of our fingers'-ends, but must be the fruit of vigorous and persevering application of that activity and exertion, both bodily and mental, with which we have been endued for our preservation and edification, and for the proper and effectual use of which we are accountable to their great Giver. And, as an useful object is the primary and most important feature in any undertaking, we will first consider, in that point of view, the construction of a canal, from the Atlantic to the Pacific Ocean, across the continent of America; and, having established its utility, we will then offer our affirmative opinion of its practicability, and our recommendation as to the place where it could most conveniently and beneficially be carried into effect; after which, we will touch upon points which will naturally arise out of our discussion of the matter, namely, whether, instead of an entire canal-communication, a passage had, or had not, better be made, partly by canal, and partly by rail or other road, or altogether by railroad; and, in the event of all these modes of transit being now not profitably practicable, whether even a good carriage-road could not, at present, be constructed at a comparatively trifling expense, and alone be of immense saving and advantage, not only to the immediate inhabitants of the place, but to intermundane commerce and communication in general.

The idea of a communication between the Atlantic and Pacific Oceans, is not a new or recent one. It did not escape the keen imagination of Columbus, the last days of whose eventful, ever-active, and vastly-useful life, were devoted to the deep contemplation of the work. His great mind did not rest satiated, as well it might have been, with discovering for his fellow-men a new and mighty continent; but, like all master-minds born to improve their species, an achievement gained, was to him the foundation upon which he lifted himself towards the accomplishment of others. But he had already done more than is commonly allotted to man, and, unfortunately for mankind, the great design was left by him for the precarious accomplishment of subsequent ages. After his death, the scheme had attractions for the bold and daring aspirations of the early Spaniards, to whose habits of enterprising adventure, the vastness and sublimity of the project were congenial; but nothing was effected. We are not surprised at little having been done in later times, during the dominion in South America of the Spanish government; for what could be expected from the dullest political and scientific apathy, but a stagnation of all that is good and profitable to man in his social condition? Beyond a solitary survey, made by order of the government, it would seem, solely and only for the embellishment of the archives of the city of Guatimala, and which was, in truth, most religiously confined to its musty dormitory until the South Americans cast off their galling yoke, the matter was hardly thought of. Since the achievement of their freedom, however, the republics of Venezuela and New Granada, and of Central America, have not been idle; amid their young flutterings for stability of government, they have found time to do much, by investigation, towards removing the imagined obstacles in the way of the accomplishment of the undertaking, having bestowed much pains in procuring those exact surveys, and other data, which are essential to a careful and accurate consideration of its accomplishment.

It would, we believe, be almost a work of supererogation, to enter seriously upon the elucidation of the surpassing importance, and great profitable benefit, that would be derived from a canal connecting the two Oceans, if we addressed exclusively mariners and such merchants as trade with places abroad, for we think that the matter is to them as clear as it is to us; but, as our subject is comparatively unknown to the great body of the inhabitants of those parts of the world, which are remote from the regions where its practicability has naturally been most agitated and discussed, namely, South and Central America, it cannot fail to be interesting to them, while we shall endeavour to make it profitable to all.

We will here request the reader to place before him now a map of the world, and cast his eye over it, calling to mind the important commercial and other relations of the various countries on its face, and considering the difficulties of intercommunication which at present exist, he will perceive that, along with many facilities, there are great drawbacks; and that, while we have overcome many impediments, great ones still stand in our way. The reader will perceive, that when, as in that of Europe, a continent is opened by inlets of the ocean of great extent, such as the Mediterranean and Baltic seas; or when, like Asia, its coast is broken by deep bays advancing far into the country, such as the Black Sea, and the Gulfs of Arabia, of Persia, of Bengal, of Siam, and of Tonquin; when the circumjacent seas are filled with large and fertile islands, and the continent itself is watered with a variety of navigable rivers, such a region may be said to possess whatever can facilitate its progress in commerce and general improvement; but, when a continent is formed, as is Africa, of one vast wide extent, unbroken by arms of the sea penetrating into its interior, with few large rivers, and those flowing at a considerable distance from each other, the greater part of it seems destined to remain imperfectly civilized, and to be debarred from an active or very much enlarged communication with the rest of mankind; and that hence, principally, may be deduced its present very insignificant place in the scale of advancement. Its having been made the hot-bed of slavery, has not been, as might be supposed, its chief retardment in the race of improvement, but only a secondary one; although one certainly, it must be allowed, but too powerful in palsying its, at best, weakly energies: that incubus, however, having now in a great measure been removed, it is to be expected that it will begin to move on, according to whatever pace it may be capable of, under its very great natural disadvantages.

On turning to America, however, we are struck with the conviction that it will bear a comparison with the most gifted quarters of our globe. The Gulf of Mexico, and the Caribbean Sea, which flow in between North and South America, may be considered as a second Mediterranean Sea, which opens a maritime commerce with all the fertile countries by which it is encircled. The islands scattered in them are inferior only to those in the East Indian Archipelago, in number, in magnitude, and in value. As we stretch along the northern division of the American hemisphere, the Bay of Chesapeak presents a spacious inlet, which conducts the navigator far into the interior parts of regions no less fertile than extensive; and, when the greater progress of culture and population shall have mitigated the extreme rigour of the climate in the more northern districts of America, Hudson's Bay may become as subservient to commercial intercourse in that part of the globe, as the Baltic is in Europe. The other great portion of the New World is encompassed on every side by the sea, except at one narrow neck, which separates the Atlantic from the Pacific Ocean; and, though it be not opened by spacious bays or arms of the sea, its inland places are rendered accessible by a number of large rivers, fed by so many auxiliary tributary streams, flowing in such various directions, that already, almost without any aid from the hand of industry and art, an inland navigation may be carried on through all the provinces from the River De la Plata to the Gulf of Paria; and thence, with comparatively trifling artificial appliances, as far as the Gulf of Mexico. Nor is this bounty of Nature confined to the southern division of America, its northern continent abounds no less in rivers, which are navigable almost to their sources; and, by its immense chain of lakes, provision is made for an internal water-communication, surpassing, in extent and convenience, that in any other quarter of the globe. The countries extending from the Gulf of Darien on one side, to that of California on the other, which form the chain which binds the two great portions of the American continent together, are not destitute of peculiar advantages. Their coast is on one side washed by the Atlantic Ocean, and on the other by the Pacific; while some of their rivers flow into the former, others run into the latter, and afford them some of the commercial benefits that may be derived from a communication with both.

We have thus seen that the New World is in itself naturally of a form eminently favourable to commercial enterprise; but, it is clearly also susceptible of great artificial improvement, and particularly and prominently so as respects the subject of our present article; a subject affecting not only that vast hemisphere itself, but of immeasurable account to the other quarters of the globe. Were a water-communication, by means of a canal for ships, effected across the Isthmus of Darien, through Central America, or even Mexico, it is obvious that the harshest features of our present navigation would be softened down, and that also vast countries abounding in natural resources and wealth, would be soon quickened into active commercial life. Instead of the now precarious and perilous voyage by the Cape of Good Hope to the East Indies and China, and their neighbouring islands, and also Australia, a safe one, occupying much less time, could be effected; not, however, because of their being any great difference of direct distance, but on account of extremely advantageous winds, tides, and weather. In place of the still more hazardous and trying route round Cape Horn, through icy seas, and along inhospitable coasts, to the western shores of America—every day rising in commercial and political consequence—and the islands of the Pacific, now assuming a prominent importance, and also to the whale-fisheries in that ocean, an opening through the continent of America, would furnish both a fearless and an infinitely shorter voyage than that so frequently ruinously disastrous one. In short, a glance over the map of the world will make it evident, better than any description that can be given, that the execution of this great work would send over our globe a flood of commercial light, the effects of which would benefit not only Europe, but every part of the habitable earth. It would most emphatically and decidedly advantage those magnificent countries through which it would pass; Europe and North America, unquestionably so, in an eminent degree; Asia would be vastly benefited by it, and even dormant Africa would feel its awakening, enlivening influence.

The much agitated question of the practicability of a communication between the Atlantic and Pacific Oceans, is now no longer a matter of speculation, if any seeming ground for doubt was ever involved in it, such has been now quite dissipated, for competent men, from actual survey, have confirmed what has been always our opinion, the admissibility of its accomplishment, at not only one, but at several places—

although the work has certainly appeared to us to be one of great difficulty, and also of distant and very uncertain fulfilment; necessarily difficult, from the very great magnitude of the work; and remote and precarious, from paucity of inhabitants and want of sufficient capital and enterprise in the states immediately concerned in bringing about its execution: but now that other governments seem to be taking up the matter, we may look for the early fruition of this unspeakable benefit to commerce and civilization.

As many as four places have been supposed eligible for effecting this junction. It has been proposed that the Gulf of Mexico should be united to the Gulf of Tehuantépec, in the Pacific, by means of a canal, which should join the sources of the river Chimilapa to those of the Rio del Passo. The distance, however, being as great as thirty-eight leagues, added to other unfavourable local circumstances, renders this plan by no means an advisable one; and then, its being so much to the north, would also detract from its merit; besides, its realization is of more moment to the state of Mexico, than to the general interests of the whole commercial world. The second plan proposes a line of communication across Central America by passing from the Atlantic up the river San Juan, into the lake of Nicaragua, and thence by a canal to the Pacific. This project has great recommendations, and, we think, is even preferable to any other, which we shall endeavour to make apparent, after having stated the merits of the two most popular ones; the third and fourth plans, which contemplate a passage through the Isthmus of Panama, and have occupied more attention than any of the others: an account of the features, both topographical and statistical of the locality, is essential to an explanation of the subject.

The Isthmus of Panama, a name which must not be confounded with a province having the same designation in New Granada, is that remarkable ligature, neck, or link of land, more properly speaking, which connects the continents of North and South America. It is sometimes also called the Isthmus of Darien, a name which is, however, now much out of use, and ought to be expunged, on that account, from geographical works. It extends from about the meridian of 77° to that of 81° west of Greenwich Its breadth at the narrowest part, which is opposite the city of Panama, which is situated on the Pacific Ocean, is not less than thirty miles; and it swells out more or less at either extremity, where it blends with the parent continental portions of the New World. The continuity of the great Andesian chain of mountains, which, for the most part, traverses the whole continent of America, is twice interrupted, if not entirely broken, within the limits above defined. The northern Cordillera exhibits the first indication of depression in the province of Nicaragua; but it again rears itself in the province of Veragua, where it expands and forms into a very fine table-land. In the eastern part of the last-named province it breaks into detached mountains of considerable elevation, and of a most abrupt and rugged formation, until, still further to the east, numerous conical hills make their appearance, raised not more than three or four hundred feet high, and having their bases skirted by extensive plains and savannas. These finally disappear, and the country becomes almost uninterruptedly level, until the conical mountains again thicken, and, becoming connected, form a small Cordillera, which runs from about opposite Porto-Bello on the Atlantic side, to the Bay of Mandingo on the Pacific, and in the country of that name to the north-east, where the second break occurs. The land there continues low for a considerable distance, and abounds in rivers—those on the north side flowing to the Gulf of Uraba, or Darien, and those on the south to that of San Miguel, beyond which point the Cordillera again raises itself on an extended scale, and enters South America. The general bearing of the mountains in the vicinity of Panama is north-east and south-west. They vary elsewhere, and appear to have a relation to the line of coast, although their course is not always parallel to it. Their height is not considerable; near Panama, their elevation is not more than 1,000 to 1,100 feet; east of Porto-Bello, however, they are considerably higher, and are generally covered with that dense and almost impenetrable forest and vegetation, which can only grow on a soil of great depth and amazing fertility, under the prolific action of great heat and moisture.

The present very limited communication across the Isthmus is maintained chiefly by two lines of road, one from Panama to Porto-Bello, and another equally from Panama by way of the town of Cruces to Gorgona, down the river Chagres to the seaport of the same name, at its mouth. There are some others in use, but little known, and, under the Spaniards, their improvement and multiplication were much discouraged. The present roads are exceedingly bad, and they traverse a mountainous part of the country. That between Panama and Porto-Bello is infinitely the worst of the two principal ones, being in many places almost impassable in the rainy season, from the steepness of the ascents and descents. But the roads to Cruces and Gorgona also lead across a mountainous country, and are extremely difficult in bad weather—a considerable part of the latter, indeed, being merely the bed of what is in winter a large stream.

The Isthmus of Panama is divided into two provinces, namely, Panama, which includes Darien and Veragua; these again are divided into cantons, each having a certain number of parishes. By a census taken in 1822, the following was the state of the population in the two provinces: that of Panama contained 66,188, and that of Veragua 35,367 inhabitants—making the population of the whole isthmus, for that year, 101,550, an amount which has not since materially altered. The people are composed of white and coloured, as in the other parts of South and Central America, and are given up to indolence and want of industry, although strong and enduring under occasional fatigue; they are, in point of civilization, less advanced than their neighbours of the same continent. The extreme fertility of the soil, together with their great destitution of moral enlightenment, are the chief causes of their general indolence, as, in the absence of the good impulses of civilization, a man can there, notwithstanding, for a small expenditure of desultory labour, procure a sufficient subsistence for himself and family. They are, however, like other persons, quite susceptible of steadily practising habits of industry, when proper incentives and sufficient stimulents are powerful enough to call forth their energies. There are within the province several regiments of militia, formed of the lower classes of people and Indians, and there are also excellent workmen in felling timber and clearing ground, and not inapt in acquiring any mechanical trade or art. They are, moreover, exceedingly simple in their habits, and are easily maintained, so that, in the projected work of a communication between the Pacific and Atlantic Oceans, some workmen may be obtained at a tolerably moderate rate of wages—a circumstance of much importance in assisting the success of the undertaking, which we will here state must be principally the work of foreign labourers, as we shall explain in its proper place.

The site of Panama, the capital of the Isthmus, has been once changed. The old city stood about three miles east from the present situation. The name is supposed to be derived from the Indian word *panama*, signifying "much fish," from its great abundance along the coast. The first city was originally a village inhabited by Indians, at the invasion by the Spaniards in 1515. The present city of Panama is situated in latitude 8° 57′ north, and longitude 79° 30′ west from Greenwich, on a rocky tongue of land, shaped nearly like a spear-head, and extending a considerable way into the sea. Its harbour is protected by a number of islands lying at a little distance from the mainland, and some of which are of considerable size, and highly cultivated. Its anchorage is good, and it has a plentiful supply of water and provisions. Its great advantages in regard to situation will, no doubt, be one day turned to great commercial profit. The population amounts, according to some, to not more than 12,000, but others make it to contain nearer 25,000 inhabitants, which seems the more probable estimate. It is tolerably healthy, notwithstanding its high temperature, if we except during the months of August and September, when its increased warmth engenders frightful epidemics.

Panama is protected by some fortifications, and is divided into the high and low towns, the last, called Varal, being the most densely peopled. Its streets are narrow, dark, and filthy. The houses, for the most part, are built of wood, and covered with a thatch; they are of three stories high in general, and are much neglected in their interior arrangements. It has a large open square, but, through the inattention of the authorities, this is overgrown with weeds, and encumbered with the fallen ruins of a great many buildings, and particularly of the college of Jesuits. Here is a college, in which are professorships for Spanish and Latin grammar, philosophy, theology, and public and canon law. The churches and convents, which are still numerous, are built of stone: the cathedral and the hospital are very fine buildings. The roadsted of Panama is extensive, but rendered dangerous by the prevailing north winds, which are violent. There is so little depth of water along the shore, that goods can only be landed at one place, and that by using flat-bottomed boats and piraguas. Hence large vessels are obliged to come to at the islands Perico and Flaminco, two miles out; but nevertheless there is a good deal of traffic carried on, principally with the English at Jamaica and the United States of America. The annual exportation of pearls alone amounts to 40,000 dollars. A good deal of commercial spirit is manifest; the stores for ships'-goods are spacious, and well filled with merchandise. Every year there is a well-frequented fair. English fashions and customs have the ascendant; and even the *cuisine* of Old England is allowed supremacy. The women wear no head-covering, and parade statelily with their long black tresses flowing down their shoulders. The environs of the city are planted with bananas, oranges, figs, and limes; and the tamarind and cocoa-nut trees are beautifully conspicuous in their majestic height. Our readers will remember that Panama was a most flourishing port when the commerce of South America with Spain was carried on by means of the *galleons;* it was then the *entrepôt* of the commerce of America, Asia, and Europe. Its importance since then has greatly decreased.

Porto-Bello is situated in latitude 9° 34″ 35′ north, and longitude

77° 45′ west, close to the sea, at the foot of immense mountains which surround the whole of the port. It is, from its situation, most unhealthy, for the heat is exceedingly oppressive; and the town being encompassed by mountains, the freshness of the sea-breezes cannot gain admittance as a relief, while the country being uncleared of wood, and there being a great deal of, nay, almost constant, rain and damp, the uninviting features of the place are rendered most repulsive, although some 2,000 mortals contrive to exist in it. Chagres and Porto-Bello are the only towns or villages on the Atlantic shore of the Isthmus. About nine miles east from Chagres is the Bay of Simon, also called Navy Bay, which is large and spacious, being as much as three miles wide at the entrance. The other towns of Panama are of trifling importance. Gatun is only a small hamlet; Gorgona is somewhat larger, and is a point at which passengers going to Panama frequently land. Cruces, however, is of more consequence—it is the place to which goods are always conveyed. It is agreeably situated on a fine open plain, upon the left or southern bank of the river Chagres, about thirty-four miles from its mouth, and eight hours' journey on mule-back from Panama. The inhabitants of these places are, for the most part, owners of canoes or mules for the purposes of transport, or are storekeepers for taking charge of the custody of goods and merchandise; or *logas*, that is, persons employed in working canoes. Cruces and Gorgona are also places of resort in the dry season or summer, as watering places for the inhabitants of Panama; for they are considered extremely salubrious, a reputation likewise enjoyed by the town of Chorrera, situated upon the river of that name.

The, at present, very limited trade on the Atlantic shore of the Isthmus, is maintained with Jamaica by a British man-of-war, which sails monthly for the purpose of conveying letters and specie; with Carthagena, by government vessels twice a month, and also with the same place and a few other points by private trading-vessels, which bring freight to Chagres, and there exchange or sell it. Its commerce on the Pacific is, however, more extensive, embracing all parts of the coast, both north and south, which find it their interest to communicate with Europe by this way. Specie is conveyed across the Isthmus to be embarked at Chagres at an expense of ten dollars and two rials for every 5,000 dollars; besides which there is a transit duty of three per cent. on silver, and one per cent. on gold. In return, goods are brought to Panama, where they are lodged in the custom-house immediately on their arrival. When for exportation, they pay a duty of two per cent, but if for home consumption, one is imposed according to the nature of each particular article. Limited as the trade of the Isthmus is, it is yet somewhat improving. The receipts of the treasury of the government of Panama in the year 1827, we are assured, by good authority, amounted in round numbers to 250,000 dollars, of which was left a balance in the public chest of nearly 3,000 dollars, after providing for all the exigencies of the state; and there is reason to suppose that since that period the finances of the territory have improved. The receipts are not one-third, it is true, of what they were in the year 1812, when Panama was a colony of Spain; but this we are not surprised at, when we consider the grinding, exclusive system of dealing which was universally adopted by that unfortunate government. It is important to mention, that by the last arrangement affecting the territorial distribution of this country, it became the north-western boundary of New Granada, one of the three republics into which Colombia was divided in the year 1832.

Now, in considering the merits of the Isthmus of Panama as a point at which to attempt the junction of the two oceans, we must not allow our judgment to be led aside by a circumstance which is no doubt calculated to render us liable to be warped from an impartial view of the matter; we mean this: the Isthmus presents the narrowest barrier to the meeting of the two mighty waters, whose conjunctive commercial assistance we are so anxious for. That is not all,—not only its form, but its peculiarly convenient position with respect to the civilized world, seems to draw us, as it were, instinctively towards it, as to a place which nature has formed and destined expressly for the great purpose of aiding man in beneficial intercourse with his fellow-man, and has therefore, it would appear, legibly written in its lineaments a powerful appeal to him to model it to his necessities. The land retiring on either side seems only the more to woo on the embrace, while even its stern hills stoop in encouraging aid of the longed-for union. Nature, however, does not send things out of her laboratory so nicely adjusted to our hand, but has wisely left much to give play to our mental exercise and industrial perseverance; and has taught us, and that too frequently by dear-bought experience, that the most encouraging appearances are but the meretricious lures of empty insubstantiality. But, reader, a canal across the Isthmus of Panama *could* be effected—we mean a ship canal—yet in the present social condition of that country such an undertaking is altogether impracticable, as we shall endeavour to explain in a future number of this Magazine.

NICARAGUENSIS.

LATE AFFRAY AT CLOUDY BAY, IN COOK'S STRAITS, NEW ZEALAND.

In various articles in which reference has been made to the settlements in these straits, great stress has been laid on the fact that the company's settlements have been founded without the presence, or even the show of a soldier; but there appears to have been a determination on the part of the local government, and indeed the authorities in Downing-street, that this state of things should not remain.

Mr. Patrick Matthew, in his very able little work entitled "Emigration Fields," devotes a chapter* to forming a half-labouring and half-military corps. This could not be done without expense—that, and the continued hostility of the Downing-street authorities, prevented his advice being taken.

Governor Fitzroy, in the account of his voyages in the Adventure and Beyle surveying-ships, advised an "overawing European force, maintained by the show, not physical action of that force, until the natives see the wonderful effects of a changed system."

Governor Hobson took soldiers with him, and continually wrote for more:† "an augmentation of the military is absolutely necessary; it must never be overlooked that the native population are a warlike race, well armed, and ever ready to use those arms on the slightest provocation."

Although Colonel Wakefield and his companions founded the colony in Cook's Straits upon the most friendly terms with the natives,‡ still no sooner was the council of the provincial government constituted, in consequence of the home authorities having declared New Zealand an independent state, than the following agreement was entered into, "that all the persons, parties to this agreement, shall submit themselves to be mustered and drilled under the directions of persons to be appointed as hereinafter mentioned."§

Had this system been allowed to remain, all would have been safe and well, without the adoption of the exceedingly wise plan proposed by Mr. Matthew, or the imposing force recommended by Governor

* Chapter xi. p. 150.

† P. 83, Par. Papers, p. 83, May 11th, 1841; his letter is dated 15th June, 1840.

‡ See his despatch in Ward's Supplementary Information respecting New Zealand.

§ The constitution of the provisional government, of which this forms a part, may be found in No. 2, of the 18th of April, 1840, of the *New Zealand Gazette.*

Fitzroy, or the military force which Governor Hobson wrote for; but it furnished no dignity to the station which he filled; and although he was unable to defend the settlers in case of attack, he would not allow them to attain the means of defending themselves. The settlers and the natives went on so harmoniously together, and with the appearance of the races amalgamating, and the Maori being led gradually to speak the languagé of the Anglo-Saxon race,* so that the want of a military force was almost forgotten. The sovereignty of our queen was proclaimed, and the granting of the charter to the company known at Port Nicholson, and then the following address was voted to Governor Hobson :—

"We the undersigned, holding the office of magistrates in New Zealand, avail ourselves of the present opportunity of offering our congratulations to your Excellency, upon the independent position in which the colony entrusted to your government is now placed; and, at the same time, we take the liberty of offering some suggestions with regard to the future government of the colony, which appear to us of the utmost importance.

"We have long deeply regretted that any circumstances should have arisen, tending to disturb those amicable arrangements between your Excellency and the settlers at Port Nicholson, which, for the interests of the colony and the honour of the crown, it is most desirable to maintain; and we rejoice at the intelligence recently received from England, because it appears to afford the means of establishing these relations upon a firm basis, and of enabling your Excellency to rally round your government the entire British population of these islands. We are most anxious that any misconception that may have arisen, as to the feelings or intentions of your Excellency, should be removed, and that the government and the colonists should combine to give the utmost development to the vast natural resources of the colony. We are willing to believe that whatever difference of opinion may exist as to the means by which this result is to be attained, there is on the part of your Excellency a sincere desire to advance the general interests of the colony; and that no sacrifice on your part will be deemed too great, if it be found necessary for that purpose. We do not presume to question the eligibility of the spot selected by your Excellency for the seat of government, in reference to the objects for which it was originally chosen. If no settlement of British subjects had been established in New Zealand, it is possible that the town of Aucland might have advantageously formed the capital of the country, and the centre from which colonization should spread. We however venture to submit, that the actual circumstances of the colony must neutralize, to a very great extent,

* The reader is particularly referred to a most able and benevolent public document, the Report of E. Halswell, Esq., a magistrate of the county of Middlesex, who went out as protector of the aborigines on the part of the company, for whom Governor Hobson felt so much respect as to nominate him a magistrate and member of his council. This Report is dated November 11th, 1841, and will be found in vol. iii. *New Zealand Journal,* p. 111, being No. 61, 14th of May, 1842.

whatever advantages may belong to that position, and must render the establishment of the seat of government there, inconvenient to the governor, and injurious to the vast majority of those whose interests it is the duty, and, we are assured, no less the desire of your Excellency to protect.* The most weighty and numerous functions of government will in such case be exercised in ignorance of the state of three-fourths of the British population of the islands; and while the proceedings, both of the legislative and executive, will often be seriously impeded by this circumstance, it cannot but happen that the interests of the settlers in this district must suffer deeply from the same cause.

"The recent negotiations in England between her majesty's principal secretary of state for the colonies, and the directors of the New Zealand Company, have placed the settlers at Port Nicholson in an entirely different position from that which they formerly occupied, (this was the grant of the charter, and the award of Mr. Pennington). They are no longer an assemblage of individuals irregularly establishing themselves in a foreign country, beyond the protection or control of Great Britain; nor are they squatters upon government land, liable to be dispossessed of their property, and having no claim to recognition by government. They form at this moment a recognized community, at least six times more numerous than any other in New Zealand, holding their lands, under a title from the crown, having contributed largely to the public revenue, and, above all, forming the nucleus of the only extensive and systematic scheme for covering with an active and industrious population, the fertile wastes of the island.

"The arrangements of the New Zealand Company are so far matured, that within the course of the next twelve months, at least 5,000 additional settlers will be landed at Port Nicholson,† whilst it is not too much to assert, that within the same period, not one-tenth of that number will immigrate, either from Great Britain or from the neighbouring colonies, to any other port.‡ In every particular,

* This is borne out by a letter of Bishop Selwyn's, dated at sea off Kapiti, November 3rd, 1842, to the Society for the Propagation of the Gospel. London: published by Rivington, 1843.

The bishop states the population of Wellington at 2,500; Petine, 700; Total, 3 200 at Port Nicholson. Nelson, 2,100; Wanguani, Petre, 100; Taranaki, near Plymouth, 900; Total, 6,300 in the Company's settlements. Aucland, 400 miles from them, 2,100; Kororarika (Bay of Islands), 300; Windsor, near Aucland, 100; Total, 2,500: but this includes soldiers, (barracks being built at Aucland,) and all officials and their dependants, clergy, and missionaries.

† So far from these expectations being fulfilled, the New Zealand Company were obliged to stop their proceedings, waiting to learn that the local government at the antipodes had carried into execution the engagements of Lord John Russell, in putting Mr. Pennington's award into execution; but so far from Governor Hobson paying it any attention, he advertised to seduce the labourers to Aucland, by the lure of higher wages, who had been sent out by the company to their settlements. It is believed that this has been redressed by the colonial minister at home, as far as the mere payment of passage-money is concerned, but it raised the price of labour throughout the settlements, and who can return to the colonists the extra money that they thus paid?

‡ The Government Emigration Commissioners sent some colonists out from the Clyde to Aucland. The surgeon-superintendant, Dr. Thompson, states that

therefore, they are entitled to expect from government a consideration proportioned to their numbers. Especially are they entitled to expect that the local legislature shall be established in that part of the island where the greatest interests are at stake, and that the members of that legislature who are not officers of the crown, should be selected from their body. It would be invidious, and could hardly fail to result in injustice, if the concerns of a community of 8,000 persons should be subject to the control of individuals, selected from a population of less than 300,* ignorant of their wants, and having different, and perhaps opposite interests. The present position of the settlers at Port Nicholson is changed moreover in another most important respect. A few months since it appeared as though all communication between that harbour and the fertile districts of the West Coasts must take place by water, the hills surrounding the Port were regarded as impassable barriers, over which no practicable road could be carried, and thus it was assumed that Port Nicholson, whatever its other advantages, was ill adapted to form a centre from which the settlers might radiate. Recent investigations have disproved this assumption, and a road is now nearly completed to Porirua, which brings the settlers immediately upon that rich belt of land at the base of the Tararua and Tengariro mountains, including the whole Taranaki district, and watered by numerous rivers, two of which, the Wanguani and Manaioutu, are hardly inferior in importance to the Thames itself. Not merely is it important for the sake of the settlers at Port Nicholson, but we would suggest that the honour of your Excellency, which is deeply involved in the tranquillity and progress of the colony, equally requires that the seat of government should be established at Port Nicholson. The relations between the British settlers and the native population are at present in an undefined and uncertain state; there is no question connected with New Zealand, in which the interests of humanity are more deeply concerned, and none, perhaps, which is more likely to excite the attention of the British public; but it is obvious, that these relations, which may be expected every day to become more complicated, cannot be superintended by your Excellency at a distance of some hundred miles, with no certain or regular means of communication between Port Nicholson and the present seat of government.† The settlers are already brought into contact with a native population of probably 20,000 persons,‡ without the presence of some controlling power, which may challenge the respect and submission of the natives, and may at the same time inspire them with confidence, that they shall

---

when they landed, there was no place of shelter, no work—a more miserable account could hardly be given—how different to those who emigrated under the company's auspices, and who, on leaving their ships, were found house, food, and work, until employed by the settlers.

* This was the population of Aucland when this address was presented.

† This is fully confirmed by Bishop Selwyn in his letter to the Society for the Propagation of the Gospel, p. 6. "The Bishop of Australia, at Sydney, is in a better position for communicating with Wellington and Nelson than I, when I am at Aucland." Will the colonial minister pay no attention to this?

‡ This is an error. See Deiffenbach, vol. i. p. 195, for a statistical table of the name of all the tribes, their location, &c., from Taranaki to Cook's Straits, and to both shores of them, in consequence of a personal examination subsequent to this address; he makes them 6,490.

be maintained in the full enjoyment of their lawful rights, it is impossible to assert that the peaceful intercourse, hitherto so happily maintained, will be permanent. If from the absence of such a power, any dissension should unfortunately arise, the presence of your Excellency will be imperatively required; but it may then be too late to cure the evils which an early residence in this place might have prevented—deep-seated distrust, and enduring hostility may take the place of the kindness and confidence at present existing; and such feelings, while they would give a serious check to the progress of settlement in every part of New Zealand, could only result in the destruction of the native population, or their being driven from the present seats of their tribes, to take refuge in the mountains of the interior. Such results every humane and just man, and none more than your Excellency, must be anxious at any cost to avoid, but no effectual safeguard against their occurrence can be found other than the establishment of the seat of government at this port.

"We would further venture to suggest, that the terms accorded by the home-government to the New Zealand Company, afford to your Excellency an opportunity of freeing yourself from the invidious duties of Land Commissioner, and of devoting your undivided attention to the discharge of the higher functions of government. We may even express our belief, that in according these terms, it was the intention of her majesty's ministers, as far as possible, without creating an absolute monopoly, to place the disposal of the waste lands in New Zealand in the hands of that company, subject undoubtedly to the supervision of the governor of the colony. This arrangement would place your Excellency in the most advantageous position for protecting the interests of the settlers, and for guiding the progress of settlement. Instead of a rivalry undignified, if not absolutely injurious, between the colonial government and a private but powerful company, there would be a combination of effects for the one great object of colonizing, in the briefest period, and in the most advantageous mode, the islands of New Zealand. In this work there would be due subordination, the operations of the company being performed under the eye of your Excellency; but this advantage can only be obtained by making Port Nicholson the seat of government. We entreat you to believe that in thus addressing you, we are actuated by a sincere desire to see your Excellency's government established upon a prosperous and permanent footing.

"(Signed) W. WAKEFIELD, HENRY ST. HILL,
R. DAVIS HANSON, GEORGE HUNTER,
GEO. SAMUEL EVANS, ED. DANIELL."

These gentlemen had been put into the commission of the peace by Sir George Gipps, the governor of Australia, when New Zealand was considered an appendage to that colony; previously to this, a public meeting of the inhabitants of the district of Port Nicholson had taken place at Wellington, on July the 1st; Colonel Wakefield was called to the chair, and opened the meeting by reading the following address of the council of the provisional government, of which he had been the president:—

"Although willing to admit, to the fullest extent, the power and the right of the English government to exercise the sovereignty within the islands, whenever it may please the legislature of England to assert that right, yet it appeared to the council that under the recent proclamations of the Governor of New South Wales, the English government had formally disclaimed the existence of any right of sovereignty in the crown of England; and had, in the amplest manner, recognized the independent sovereignty of the native chiefs of the islands. As that proclamation contains a reference to the acquisition, by purchase, of the sovereign rights of the chiefs, the council believe and hope, that ere long, the authority of the English crown will be established in this place."

His whole speech was worthy of the man who led his companions to form the colony; want of space prevents its being copied, the following extract cannot well be passed by:—

"Allegiance was not a duty which could be laid down and taken up at pleasure; he thought that the time was now arrived when they should make a demonstration of their loyalty; and he urged it upon them, from no fear of shrinking from the responsibility of past acts; neither denying or retracting any act or word to which he had been a party; and prove, that although, whilst left to themselves, they knew how to maintain law and order, they seized the first opportunity to claim the protection of the government, whose authority they had never disputed, and in whose support they were as ready as ever, notwithstanding what may have been said to the contrary, to tender their cordial and dutiful services."

Dr. Evans then moved the following address:—

"Port Nicholson, July 1, 1840.

"To His Excellency Governor Hobson—We, the undersigned, inhabitants of the district of Port Nicholson, avail ourselves of the opportunity presented by the arrival of the Colonial Secretary with sufficient means for the protection of life and property, to express to your Excellency those sentiments of respect for yourself, and loyalty to the crown, in which we yield to none other of her Majesty's subjects in these islands. The peculiar circumstances in which we were placed before the establishment here of British authority, and the false reports which have been made to your Excellency, and of which we have heard with equal surprise and indignation, render it necessary for us to be the more explicit in our declarations of attachment to the crown and constitution of England, and to assure your Excellency that we took no steps but such as we thought consistent with our allegiance as British subjects, and justified by the necessity of the case. That such were our real feelings, and that our arrangements for the preservation of order were adopted by us as merely provisional, is proved by the acclamation with which the British flag was welcomed, as well as by the cordial support which has been rendered by all classes to the Colonial Secretary and the magistrates, of which they themselves are the most competent witnesses. We might add, that in planning the surveys of our future town, we had as far as possible anticipated the wants of the government, and set apart the most valuable sections of land for the convenience of the public offices, and the personal accommodation of your Excellency, feeling assured, as we do, that sooner or later, this must become the seat of government for these islands. Should this prove the case, your Excellency may rest assured, that you would be welcomed here by the largest body of her Majesty's subjects in New Zealand, unanimous in their loyalty, and desirous of promoting by every means in their power the comfort of your private life, as well as the authority and dignity of your public administration."*

This was the answer of "the demagogues,"† and for whom he sent fetters by the policemen under Lieutenant Smart.‡ Colonel Wakefield was deputed to present this address to Governor Hobson, which he did at the Bay of Islands; but it had no effect. Governor Hobson, instead of going, or even looking at Port Nicholson, proceeded to the spot now called Aucland, where he formed a colony of thirty-five acres of land, building barracks and a government-house. The address produced no effect; the personal communication between Colonel Wakefield and Governor Hobson was equally unheeded; the settlers in Cook's Straits were left without any crown-title to the land; they were, in point of fact, squatters, forbid to defend themselves, after Shortland's visit, and left at the mercy of an aborigines' population, of whom Hobson himself had written, "it must never be overlooked, that the native population are a warlike race, well armed, and ever ready to use their arms on the slightest provocation;" he however overlooked it, as it regarded the settlers on Cook's Straits; the only communication he held with them was that of taxing them, and drawing money from them, for the payment of his dignity at Aucland, and seducing the settlers' labourers. It is due to Lord Stanley, to say that he reprobated the jobbing in the lots of land by Governor Hobson's officials; and he blamed the seduction of the labourers.

It would have been more in order, if an account of this public address had been given previous to that of the six magistrates, with which this article almost commenced. The latter was adopted in consequence of the neglect which the first received; it is now become a document recorded in our parliamentary reports,§ and for this the sincere thanks of every Anglo-New-Zealander is due; since it has been written with almost Delphic wisdom, and has exactly portrayed the lamentable circumstances which have lately occurred. It was a warning to prevent

* A minute account of this meeting is reported in the *New Zealand Gazette*, printed at Wellington, July the 4th, 1840.

† The term given to them by Governor Hobson, in his public despatch of the 25th of May, 1840, and printed in the Parliamentary Papers of the 11th of May, 1841, at page 16.

‡ See Heaphy's Narrative of a Residence in New Zealand, chap. ii., p. 9, entitled the Early Progress of the Colony. This little book furnishes truthful materials for the future historian of these settlements.

§ It is printed at page 109 of Parliamentary Papers, of the 12th of August, 1842; and at page 210 of the 2d volume of the *New Zealand Journal*.

them. Attention to it would have saved many a life; it would have prevented the ruin of many a settler.

We must, as briefly as possible, continue the narrative. Governor Hobson never deigned to visit Wellington, until August, 1841; *a year and a quarter after* this wise and precious document had been delivered to him; he took with him the lay-agent of the Church of England Missionary Society, and appointed him chief protector of the aborigines; he officially granted a certain quantity of land to the Company; but there was an under-current at work. Up to this time, the natives and the settlers were upon the best of terms, as far as Port Nicholson was concerned; the former were perfectly contented with the treaty which they had made with the Company's agent,* and a very intelligent observer states—

"That there exists already a numerous and deserving population of natives, who perfectly understand that they have become English citizens, and are aware of their duties and rights as such. It is pleasing to reflect, that the first serious attempt will be made in New Zealand to civilize what has been termed a horde of savages, to amalgamate their interests with that of Europeans, and to make them participate in the hereditary immunities and privileges of British subjects. The natives are the national wards of England, and it seems possible to prevent another blot appearing on the pages of history regarding the intercourse of civilized nations with savage tribes."†

This same writer, who witnessed all that passed up to Hobson's arrival, observes—"Up to the present time, nearly three years since the purchase, there has not been a single serious misunderstanding between the natives and the settlers."‡ It is with great affliction we state, that since the arrival of the agent of the Church Missionary Society in Wellington, many of the natives have become worse than restless and discontented. We cannot doubt but that the report which he made to Governor Hobson has in some way been made known to them, and what is it but a denial of the treaty which Colonel Wakefield made with the aborigines? Of course there is no space in a Magazine to copy such documents at length; but it is hoped that influential and public men will examine it,§ and it will be found that the promise made of thwarting the colonization of New Zealand was not a vain one. More than this, Mr. Clark was not an uninterested person as to Cook's Straits; he was the intimate friend of eleven individuals who laid claim to 96,219 acres in the northern part of the island.‖ But, independent

* See Deiffenbach, vol. i., p. 67. † Ibid vol. i. 20. ‡ Ibid, vol. i., p. 94.

§ At page 171 of Parliamentary Papers, ordered to be printed the 12th of August, 1842.

‖ For the names and details, see Deiffenbach's table, vol. ii., p. 168.

of Mr. Clark, it is to be perceived that Governor Hobson himself was anxious to raise any quibble as to title, which would give the settlers trouble, in his despatch of the 15th of December, 1841 :—*

"It appears that, in 1839, Colonel Wakefield visited the country, and bought a considerable proportion of it from the few Nagati-awas who had resumed their habitations on the retreat of Te-whero-whero; now Te-whero-whero claims the country as by right of conquest."

He then goes on to say, "Te-whero-whero certainly has a claim to the land, and I referred him to Colonel Wakefield;" adding, that the case was the type of a hundred others; and, since Governor Hobson encouraged this claim, it is necessary to show who this barbarian is, and how he claims a compensation :—

"About ten years ago (speaking of a native village), it was taken, after a long siege, by the Waikati, and nearly 500 of the inhabitants were slaughtered; 50 of them by the hand of Te-whero-whero, who at present is a great Mikanene, as the natives call those who have adopted Christianity, from the word missionary, and lives at Waitemata, or Manukao; the rest of the population was carried into slavery."†

We appeal to such men as Sir Thomas Fowel Buxton, Dr. Hodgskins, &c., all real abolitionists of slavery; will you not interfere, and assist to turn these savage customs into a different channel? will you support such claims? Be no longer dazzled with the name of Chief; read with attention Mr. Montefiore's evidence, on oath, before the House of Lords;‡ and you will exert yourselves to relieve suffering humanity, by assisting in blending the native with the European. It is not believed, that in any instance an aborigines can be degraded by amalgamating with an European; but, if he should be, the individuals are so few, that it cannot for one moment be placed in comparison with the benefit which the mass would receive. Why did those inhabiting Cook's Straits invite the settlers to establish themselves? It was because they were subject to be attacked by such savage barbarians as Te-whero-whero. Does not Governor Hobson tell you that there were a hundred such claimants? Did you never read of the horse attacked with the claws of the tiger, and butted by the stag with his horns? The tiger was too strong for him, the stag too fleet; he turned to man, and prayed his assistance. The inhabitants of Cook's Straits, of Wanguani, of Taranaki, of Cloudy Bay, &c., were exactly in the position of the horse, and he bought his safety by parting with some of his freedom.

* Page 188 of Parliamentary Papers, 12th of August, 1842.

† Deiffenbach, vol. i., p. 162.

‡ Parliamentary Papers, 8th of August 1838, page 55.

He has since been subject to the curb and the saddle, and the Te-whero-wheros of New Zealand must yield the law of the tomahawk in exchange for national freedom; he must not be allowed to turn upon his benefactor, and kick at the curb which has been imposed on him. No right is borne down, no injustice is incurred, by civilized man settling on the land; the greater part of the islands are the unappropriated domain of nature; the greater part, over which a human foot has never trod. There is the authority of Governor Hobson, that "the native chiefs have neither power over the soil, nor authority over those who reside on it."* The missionary reign has been unfortunate, but well-intentioned: the population, if the accounts are correct, has diminished to one fourth of what it was when it was established. It is accounted for by two very able writers, Patrick Matthew,† and by Dr. Deiffenbach, in a chapter on the diseases of the natives.‡ A most powerful writer in the *Times* newspaper of the 15th of April, 1843, says—

> "It is the glory of the missionary, that he plants no other standard than that of Christ; he crosses the frontiers of barbarous empires; he enters the confines of unknown lands—but he claims no sovereignty but that of his Master, and he establishes no law but that of the Church of God. At times, he may derive assistance from the accidental combinations of human politics; more frequently, he has to contend against the suspicion or the hostility of the powers of this world: but these are not the circumstances which daunt or encourage his exertions;—all that the true missionary requires at the hands of man, is liberty of teaching the Word; and, we confess, that when we find a missionary society setting up a claim to spiritual rights, almost amounting to exclusive civil jurisdiction, we are led to suspect, that such rights and powers are exercised for purposes not altogether of a spiritual character."

Now this is exactly what the brave settlers on Cook's Straits have had to contend with: a splendid bureaucracy in London, struggling with the government itself—doling out permissions to take possession of the waste lands of the crown, as if they had been clothed with the power of making grants; and sending revenues of immense extent to their agents in New Zealand. The Church Missionary Society, in 1840-41, sent 14,232*l.* 13s. 7d.; the Wesleyan Missionary Society, in 1839-41, sent 3,885*l.* 11s. 11d.; and this, divided amongst 8 clergymen of the Church of England, 16 catechists, and 16 clergymen of the Wesleyans.§ With such splendid incomes, it is not to be wondered at that eleven of them should aim to attain 91,000 acres of land. Some of them were employed by Governor Hobson as political agents.

* Parliamentary Papers, 11th of May, 1841.

† Fields of Emigration, page 131.

‡ Vol. ii., p. 13.

§ Terry's New Zealand, pp. 189—191.

The readers of the *Colonial Magazine* may rely that everything which appears under this signature is drawn from authentic sources, and that the real state of New Zealand, without favour or affection, is described. Nothing is more important than to distinguish between cant and philanthropy; the former requires only to be exposed, to be despised; the latter will shine the brighter, the more it is known. The true policy of the Colonial Minister is not to check, but to utterly destroy all missionary interference at home or abroad, and plant the Church of England at the antipodes, through the medium of the New Zealand Church of England Society and Bishop Selwyn. That kind-hearted, affectionate, and accomplished man, will never lend his advice to such a wretch as Te-whero-whero, under pretence of his being a missionary. The good bishop received some excellent hints upon the subject from his friend Lord Seaton, which would not have been known, had he not publicly mentioned them. There will be found in the Life of Lord Sydenham, the opinions of that very considerable man upon the same subject.

Since the article was written which appeared in the December number of the old series of this magazine, information has been received, which it is the duty of the writer to lay before those who interest themselves in the settlements; and they shall be detailed in their order.

1st. A letter from Wellington, dated 24th of April, on which entire confidence may be placed, describing the uninhabited plains of Wairarapu, of being not only of boundless extent, but of surpassing fertility; but that the encouragement which had been given to native claims ever since Governor Hobson's visit, had been attended with the most injurious effect. The aborigines had been advised to make a demand for new payments for the land, not merely those who had been perfectly contented, but that new claimants arrived. The writer thought the natives would obey whatever was determined on, but that the government turned it over to the Company's agent, upon whom demand after demand was made, with which it was impossible for him to comply, but that he relied on a remonstrance to Lord Stanley.

2nd. A letter from William Fox, Esq., the barrister, dated June 3d, who sailed in the spring. He found the country equal to all which had been said of it. He had been into the plains of Wairarapu, where there was not a living soul, but that there were natives making claims which it was impossible to satisfy. His observation is, that the government officers yield no assistance, but stand perfectly aloof. He had been refused by the chief justice to practise, without making a declaration which was incompatible with a gentleman, and degrading to his profession. Just before quitting England Mr. Fox had been called to the bar by the Society of the Inner Temple, the benchers of which court, no doubt, will feel an interest in defending him, and we know that it has been brought before Lord Stanley.

3rd. The *New Zealand Gazette* to the 10th of June have been received, the contents of which are most lamentable. The government, the Company, and their indefatigable agent, had become the continued object of attack from the settlers on this question of title. It is grievous to observe the settlers almost falling out amongst themselves. They have been most ill treated, but not by the company. It was the duty of the local government to have carried into execution Mr. Pennington's award. The agent of the London Missionary Society should never have been allowed to question the original treaty between the Company's agent and the natives; having done so, the local government will yield him no assistance, but tells him to extinguish the native title. In the *New Zealand Gazette* of the 31st of May, there is a long and very able article on the ordinances passed by the council at Aucland, which is composed chiefly of aliens to the settlers.

On the Ordinances of New Zealand.—The Legislative Council of New Zealand is constituted by the colonial charter, and the subsequent instructions of the 9th December, 1840. In addition to the Governor or Lieutenant-governor, it consists of six members, three of whom, the Colonial Secretary, Colonial Treasurer, and Attorney-General, are councillors by virtue of their offices; the other three are the justices of the peace, whose names for the time being stand first upon the commission, and who hold no government-post of emolument. The three members first referred to, cannot be supposed to have any very deep or abiding interest in the colony. They are gentlemen who would probably have consented to reside in any place where appointments as good as those they hold might have been offered to them; and we have no reason to imagine that it was any peculiar preference for this colony above others which brought them amongst us. The three justices of peace are removable from the commission, and by consequence from the council, at the pleasure of the governor; and it may be supposed that their votes will never be much at variance with his wishes.

"The absence of a legislative body elected by the people who are to be governed by the laws enacted by it, is a very serious practical evil. The laws passed by a non-elective body seldom if ever represent the wishes of the people, or are calculated to meet in any great degree their real and immediate wants. They are too often framed with no other view than the maintenance and extension of the power of the executive branch of the government; or if they have any more general and philanthropic object, it is probably an attempt to carry out some Utopian system, which has been devised in the closet of a theorist, ignorant of the whole business of life, and practically unacquainted with the feelings and wants of his fellow-men. The deliberations of non-elective bodies (if they do deliberate) are also carried on in secret, and their measures are passed and brought into operation without any of that free and open discussion, which, while it aids the legislator in obtaining clear views of his subject, satisfies the public mind, by laying bare the ground on which the laws rest, and makes the people willing to obey enactments, of the reasonableness of which they have been satisfied before they were passed."

What is here copied is the mere preamble to this excellent essay, which should be attentively read by the colonial minister; and, if some redress be not attempted, it must be brought before parliament. When the council was first formed, Governor Hobson enrolled Colonel Wakefield's name amongst its first members; but since he had, first, duties to perform at Wellington, he declined going to Aucland to attend it, and begged his name might be erased; and thus he has had nothing to do with their ill-digested legislative enactments. Whenever the council is held at Wellington, the Anglo-New-Zealand public in England will never be satisfied, if he is not a member of it.

June 7th.—Is an account of a public meeting to form an agricultural society, Colonel Wakefield in the chair. He was requested to become its president; to which he consented, on the condition, that at the end of the first year the presidency should be elective.

June 10th, the following paragraph appears :—

"What with the government and their friendly actions on the one part, the apathy displayed by the company on the other, and the rascally behaviour of certain missionaries, verily the Wellingtonians are placed in a pretty pickle. Here we are in the middle of the fourth year, and the second of the land-question, and it is not yet settled. The energies of the settlers have been cramped, and they have had to struggle against difficulties which cannot be conceived by any one who has not lived on the spot. We trust, however, the day of settlement will soon arrive, and the colonists then be enabled, though at the eleventh hour, to prove the capabilities of their location; and that when the present exorbitant claims of the Maories shall have been set at rest, they will receive treatment as British subjects, and the lives and properties of their white neighbours be protected from aggression, and the natives themselves obtain the salutary benefits of the civil law."

The following letter which appeared in the *Times* of the 4th of December, will further show the state into which the local government has brought the colony :—

Extract from the letter of a settler, dated Wanguani, May 26, 1843.

"Since the government land-agent left, the Maoris have been much more troublesome than before, turning off several parties whom they had allowed to settle in their sections, and in some instances burning down the houses (Maori ones) they had erected, but in no case using any violence, saying that they were determined not to let any person whatever settle on the land until the payment for the whole had been received; indeed, I believe that if they thought they could do it with impunity, they would attempt to turn us off the town sections, but they know well enough they dare not do this; but still, as no notice is taken of their continual annoyances, there is no telling how far they may be induced to venture. What is most vexing is, that not the slightest notice is taken of these things, or attempt made to put a stop to them, either by the Company's agent here or by the magistrates, although in many instances the Maoris have been unjustifiably aggressors. I am convinced, that had we only the permission to do so, we could at once put a stop to further injustice, and be held in proper estimation by them, and this without fear of bloodshed, as they are not the people to fight for what is to them an useless piece of land, and are besides, I think I may safely say, without exception, the greatest cowards in existence. Only a short time ago almost every one of them went up the river upon the bare report that 200 Waihatos were coming down the coast; and yet here are about 100 English capable of bearing arms bounced by every fellow calling himself a chief, who can muster two or three more to help him to bully, knowing as he does that he can do it with impunity. No longer than a week ago three fellows came down and turned out five English from a place where no Maoris ever thought of going before, and which the party had been in quiet possession of for some months, and no notice was taken of it. I cannot think either that the Company at home or the government know what we have to put up with, or I think we should get justice from one or the other."

After this there is the news *viâ* Sydney, of the dreadful affray in Cloudy Bay—of the municipality of Wellington having called upon the acting governor at Aucland for protection—of having sent to Sydney for military. It must be obvious to all who have examined the subject, that the peaceable state of this flourishing and important colony has been risked by the unauthorized and unjustifiable interference of missionary interest in Downing Street, as well as at the antipodes.

The speech of the Hon. Francis Baring on the 19th of June, 1838, should have received greater attention. The correspondence between the Company and the Colonial Minister has been examined with great care.—Lord Stanley was correct as regarded the attempted sale of the Chatham Islands; but his retaining Governor Hobson, and not carrying into execution his own letter of the 13th of May, 1842, are incomprehensible.—

"You will acquaint the inhabitants of Wellington, from whom this address and petition proceed, that I have laid them before the Queen, who was pleased to receive them very graciously; and that her Majesty has been pleased to command me to express her sense of the efforts which they have made, and the success which appears to have attended them in the formation of a thriving settlement, and to assure them that she has issued such instructions to her representative in the colony, as will secure to them the advantages which they desire, in the administration of justice and the management of their local affairs." *

Now, mark the date of this, and the state of the colony at the last

* Parliamentary Papers, 12th August, 1842, p. 179.

advices. We have omitted to state one circumstance in the late papers. Settlers had been attacked with impunity by the natives, and they called on the Company's agent to repay the damage; his answer was, that it was the duty of the local government to defend them—that government, instead of doing so, said the Company must extinguish the main claims by another payment. Both these circumstances, however desirable, are impossible—no money can satisfy the aborigines; the more they receive, the more they demand. Money, but for missionary advice, would never have been sought. They not merely might have been, but were led to prefer the arts of civilization, and many at Wellington continue to pursue it—it is there beyond the influence of its magic powers—who are ignorantly attacking the settlers. The local government, not content with the mischievous alliance which it had made with the political landowners, who wore the cloke of missionaries, destroyed the system of a national guard, which had been formed by Colonel Wakefield and his council; and substituted no protection in its stead. It taxed the inhabitants of Wellington and Nelson—had the money sent to Aucland, and suffered the commonest police-officers and pilots to remain unpaid. In your December number, Mr. Editor, a confidence was expressed in Governor Fitzroy. That which creates anxiety at this time is, that the afflicting occurrences of which we have lately heard, took place immediately after his quitting England in the Bangalore; but he was to go to Sydney, and no doubt would take troops with him to Cook's Straits. A new interest has arisen, at least has become more conspicuous—missionary and Company sink before it. The Queen's authority is at stake—her magistrates have been fired on—the proclamations in the name of the British crown have been despised. Our country is a great and mighty nation, but its greatest glory is, that it puts forth its shield, and protects the meanest individual in the farthermost part of the world, whoever with the breath of life owed it allegiance. It is in Cook's Straits that the government of England is now called upon to vindicate, not merely her name, but her wisdom This is but a transitory affair—whether of a week, a month, or a year, this will be done. But for the future.

Advice is seldom welcome, particularly to public men; but Lord John Russell and Lord Stanley, you have laid the Anglo-New-Zealanders under obligation to you. There are 8,000 of them on Cook's Straits—their connections and friends at home are numerous; there are also many owners of land in the islands, who are not gone out—these are holders of the stock of the Company. Altogether, there is a mass of persons on whom the charter conferred a deep obligation. The unheeded instructions to Governor Hobson by Lord John Russell, amongst which was one of forming a national guard, in principle the same as this insane governor put down at Wellington, and, above all, the publications of the Blue Books of the 11th of May, 1841, and 12th of August, 1842, are not to be forgotten. All this emboldens the writer of this to suggest the adoption of Mr. Patrick Matthew's proposals for raising a peace force,* with perhaps some little change. None but married men should be enlisted; one such queen's ship as the Cyclops would carry out sufficient, and perhaps ultimately the settling them upon the plan of Prince Eugene's military cordons between Hungary and Turkey, an immense plan of defence which has never cost the government a shilling. It is hoped that advices will be received previous to printing the next number, which will gratify our readers with more cheering prospects. W.

January, 1844, *Blois*.

Extract from the Sydney Herald, 28th August, 1843.

This melancholy affair, the massacre at Cloudy Bay was solely consequent to the reckless conduct of the local government in passing over a grievous catalogue of native aggressions without punishment, and in having screened the aborigines, when Europeans—insulted, and robbed, and otherwise maltreated, have sought for justice, and the cruel sentences pronounced on the latter, even when roused, to have recourse to self-defence. We have not the remotest doubt but that the *fair fame* of the two ruthless chiefs will be insisted on by a body ycleped "Protectors of the Aborigines." We do not wholly blame the natives in burning the rush huts, as they were careful in placing in safety the property found in them; but their brutal use of victory cannot surely be defended. When Makatu, the chief who murdered Mrs. Robertson, previously committing another crime of equal turpitude, and, further, murdering her two children, hurling a third into the sea from a steep perpendicular cliff, and firing the house to consume his victims, the government never interfered in capturing him—he was sought after by two of the townsmen of Kororarika, who delivered him up to the local magistrate. Despite the horrid crimes committed in cold blood by this young chief, (for he was not twenty,) the Protector of Aborigines did all that lay in his power to prevent his suffering the penalty of his crimes.

In brief, anarchy between the colonists and aborigines, and native war, has resulted from the conduct of the local government. A Mr. Gunner, of Maunganni, lately tried to obtain a warrant from the police magistrate of the Bay of Islands and Aucland, to apprehend a native who was caught robbing, but was unsuccessful in both cases. The magistrate of Aucland excused himself, the aggression not being committed in his district. Outrages must increase, aggressions will continue to be committed, and will be permitted without redress until the incubus of the Protectorate is wholly subverted. The intelligent New Zealanders require no such functionaries. Their sagacity and enlarged mental powers are too well known to fear the much longer continuation in office of such a body of apologists for native misdemeanors. They are perfectly aware that when aggrieved, the police magistrate is their best authority to apply to for redress. We believe, with the exception of Mr. Halswell, of Port Nicholson, not one of the corps has any legal knowledge.

---

* Fields of Emigration, p. 137.

ON HOGGING OF SHIPS, AND ON DOCK-GATES.

FROM THE MS. WORKS OF CAPTAIN J. N. TAYLER, R.N.

THE maritime works contemplated by Napoleon, and now vigorously carrying out by the King of the French, are every way adapted to awaken the full attention of the nation at large to the importance of our own maritime improvements. In the short period of eight years, a naval port was formed by digging into the live rock at Cherbourg; it was capable of containing forty-five ships-of-the-line, a proportionate number of frigates and steamers, with several ships, together with the requisite accommodations for building, repairing, and fitting out; in short, it possesses everything that might be expected in so important a creation of art, and is justly considered to be one of the noblest monuments of Napoleon's reign. He had determined on constructing a second or inward port, to receive thirty ships-of-the-line, with thirty covered docks for thirty sail-of-the-line, to be in constant readiness to put to sea.

Such is the formation of the coast of France opposite Great Britain, that these laborious artificial works are required, to form harbours; whilst the natural and magnificent inlets we are happily favoured with, well protected and defended, from our rivers running into the country, give us a decided advantage. The splendid harbour of Hamoaze, where our ships have been laid up in ordinary, free from fire, for ages, and where, if such a calamity should take place, would most probably be confined to *a solitary* ship;—*this was evinced by the destruction of the Captain at her moorings.* But, with all these natural advantages, what evil genius could have suggested the formation of a basin for the purpose of huddling our ships together in the centre of a dockyard, admitted to be too small for the duties of the yard? The confined situation of Cherbourg compelled *them* to form a basin; not so with *us;* Providence has been abundantly bountiful. The fire which not long since took place in the dockyard, seemed to be ordained by Providence as a salutary warning to let well alone. This piece of land, with the increased work from steamers, was most valuable to the yard; and the fruits of this enormous outlay for excavations and pile-driving, appears to have necessitated the application to parliament for funds to purchase an extension of land for our dockyards.

The plan which I had the honour to submit to the Admiralty, March

7th, 1839, would have prevented this enormous outlay, and placed our demonstration ships always ready. Twenty sail-of-the-line, if required, might have been ready at a moment's notice, in the splendid natural basin of Hamoaze, and the men kept efficient in every nautical pursuit; and the system of gunnery, as established on board the San Josef with such success, might have been carried out on board every ship, creating a spirit of emulation so much required in the service, and checked under the plea of interfering with the Excellent. However, we rejoice that the system Captain Tayler introduced, of instructing the seamen and boys in gunnery and seamanship, has been transferred to the Excellent, and the thanks of the Admiralty fully given to this officer on the termination of her period of service in the command of the Plymouth ordinary, on the recommendation of the commander-in-chief, Admiral Sir Graham More, G.C.B. In reference to the beacon, will it be prudent to keep the men on board the ten sail-of-the-line, or must they have hulks at a distance? The sails in the ships in Hamoaze might be kept bent, covered with painted waterproof canvass, so that the men, by constant exercise, would be made efficient, in every acceptation of the word, and the vessels approach nearly to sea-going ships. The simultaneous attacks we must expect from steamers, forcibly points out that such a system must be pursued; and every British sailor made a gunner.

Steamers must be the advance-post; and Cawsand Bay, with a floating breakwater at Vinter Point, would present an excellent advance station. The following extracts from Captain Tayler's forthcoming work will show with what ease ships might have been kept in a state of readiness, and their beautiful symmetry maintained free from hogging; also his plan of forming coffer-dams and making docks accessible at all times of tide, at Devonport.

"The enormous expense of executing submarine works, and its consequent delay in preventing many improvements, induce me to suggest the following. For all submarine work, the surface should be first levelled by artificial means, and a good covering of puddled-clay placed over the entire surface, projecting beyond the intended submarine work. This will prevent air-holes, and the foundation being sapped. In a line with the intended work, I drive or fix piles about twelve feet asunder, against which I lower my feather-edge guide, which is made of iron, fitted with a chain at each end; this rests against the piles, in its place, to receive the iron coffer, which is made with a spring, to deposit the stone or compos resting on a piece of iron, which fits on the spring inside the box, and is deposited with the contents of the box. The compos is made with the local materials. When there is a difficulty of obtaining it, I prepare it of coal-ashes, lime, and coal-tar, boiled an hour, and sprinkled over with a coat of pulverized granite—this is prepared by calcination. After lowering the feather-edge guide, I lower the coffer-box to slide down it, and, by raising the lever, deposit a solid block, six feet long and one wide. After completing several feet, I sink inside four rows, in one solid line ; over this, I lower transverse blocks, and, when brought up to its height, I leave a space of four feet between the parallel lines, and lay down a second line of blocks in a similar manner, filling in between with puddled clay ; this prevents air-holes, as compressed air from the force of the sea is most detrimental to stone-work. After forming this breakwater or cofferdam water-tight, I pump out the water, and fix shores, as preventers, where there may be a great weight of water, and commence the excavation. At Hamoaze, it is necessary to carry out the jetties, to enable our large ships to go alongside at all times, and it is the first work to proceed with. The bottom outside our docks is composed of slate, and the water deepens suddenly. After carrying out the jetty to its intended situation, formed as described, I place across the intended entrance to the dock, coffers filled with clay, and fitted with rings and chains, to be easily removed. The stone-work, on the water being pumped out, can be built with cement-stone facing.

Thus submarine work can be built without cofferdams of piles, and in one-third the time ; my moveable pile, as used with the short ground pile, not requiring to be drawn to sap the foundation, but driven down. This mode of laying artificial blocks may be used for breakwaters, the same as the loose stone submarine break, brought up within eight feet of low-water mark, and my floating breakwater moored outside, to receive the top sea. I also claim in my patent the right of fixing, in particular localities, upon these submarine breakwaters, a framework of open wood-work, or metal, to receive the top sea, similar to the top of the breakwater, and filled in with stone, as weight, to keep it in its place.

PLAN FOR PREVENTING SHIPS BEING HOGGED.

"In my official inspection of the ships placed under my command in ordinary, I have been induced, by experiments and frequent observations, to conclude, from the number of broken-back ships, that the system adopted for many years of placing a quantity of ballast in the centre of a ship, to prevent her being hogged, or broken, has a direct tendency to the contrary ; and, in lieu of preventing this injury, so repugnant to science, greatly accelerates it.

The weight which a body has when it is immersed in water is always the weight of as much of that water as is equal in bulk to itself; that is, a vessel displaces a volume of water equal to its own immersed bulk; consequently, the stern, quarters, rudder, &c., not receiving any support from the fluid, naturally fall, and cause what is nautically termed "a broken back."

Many line-of-battle ships in ordinary have on board seven hundred tons of iron ballast, being about four hundred tons more than is required for her trim; and, when a ship is ordered into commission, she goes alongside the jetty to take out this centre weight, which considerably retards her equipment; and it must be obvious to every one, if a vessel requires seven hundred tons for this specific purpose, the sudden removal of it from the centre, and more particularly when alongside the jetty in high tides, with the mooring-chain on the quarters and bow-port pressing her down, considerably accelerates this weakening of her frame. This was clearly demonstrated by the appearance of the copper of the Implacable; she had five hundred tons of iron ballast amidships, and when it was taken out, the copper became ruffled, and she evidently showed every indication of being broken; for when placed in dock on the blocks, it was partly removed, but on coming out of dock it immediately assumed its former appearance. It is therefore abundantly clear, that the ballast placed in the centre, with a view of preventing a ship from being broken, acts diametrically opposite on its sudden removal, and occasions this visible weakness.

It will, I presume, be admitted, that vessels, when first taken out of dock, naturally fall at the stern, from the projecting weight being unsupported by the fluid; this want of bearing from the buoyancy of the ship is attempted to be counteracted by five hundred tons of iron ballast, to prevent her rising in the centre, although it is the extremes falling which cause the mischief. What, then, must be the sudden impulse upon displacing a weight intended to counterpoise a rising force, by removing a pressure of five hundred tons!

In the operation of bringing a ship down to her sea-bearings, she actually undergoes three distinct disjointings, commonly called "a broken frame," and which weakness she never recovers. To prevent this serious injury, by being hogged, I would propose that temporary caissoons of iron or wood, as bearing-pieces (as in plate M., 8, fig. 1. in Captain Tayler's work on "Naval Tactics"), should be placed under the quarters of all ships, previous to their being immersed in the water. This would prevent the extremes falling, which alone is the cause of a ship being hogged, from want of support; and then ships need not take in more than their proper quantity of ballast, with their tanks, and all their shot and anchors. This would enable ships, when ordered into commission, to go alongside the sheer-hulk, and get in their masts, in lieu of going alongside the jetty to get out and restow their ballast. The caissoons are so fixed to their respective vessels, that they can be removed in an hour; merely fitted into a dovetailed slide under, and secured to the counter by screw-bolts above the copper.

If ships are intended to remain long in ordinary, the timber boards might be kept open, and a portion of ballast and tanks placed accordingly; this would expedite the equipment of demonstration ships, as well as prevent this broken-back system; which, like a dislocation of the spine, is never recovered. A ship might be docked at half-tide by these caissoons fixed under her quarters.

Since I verbally made a communication on this subject, I have had ocular demonstration of its effects on board the Implacable and other vessels; I would therefore suggest, before a ship of any class leaves the stocks, she should be braced or trussed in the following manner:— a strong chain (part of her intended cable) is to be laid loose fore and aft, parallel with the keelson, (as in fig. 3, vide Captain Tayler's work on "Naval Tactics,") according to the class of ship; let the chains (as in fig. 4,) be attached fore and aft, rising from the surface of the keelson, and of each deck, (as in fig. 5.) Erect strong blocking on the keelson fore and aft, to receive the shores which support the chains; the said shores being about one-fourth the entire length of the vessel distant from the stern or the stern-post; they are rounded at the bottom, and shod with iron, to work into corresponding sockets on the head of each shore. Let these chains be swayed up in succession, and the shores wedged up so as to bring the centre or main-chain to the greatest possible state of tension. Suppose the main chain to be sixty feet long between the shores, or points of suspension, then one ton of iron ballast suspended from the centre will give a strain on each bridle-chain of thirty tons, at whatever angle the same be attached to the stem or stern; hence, all the top-weight at the stem and stern of ships, when laying in ordinary, or without their equipment, may be transferred to their centre, without extra ballast; the pendent weight in the centre of each main-chain will regulate their expansion and contraction under any change of temperature.

When ships are intended to be laid up in ordinary for a considerable period, my caissoon should be used to prevent their hogging, placed under each quarter (see plate in "Naval Tactics"), at the light draught of water, extending about one foot below her bearings, or floating water-line, when dismantled; from this platform or stage there are chocks, which carry the weight of the stern, frame, &c. As an additional support to ships with heavy hanging sterns, intended to be placed in ordinary, I propose to construct sheet-iron caissoons, so as to combine the greatest strength with the least possible weight. These are floated under the counter on each side, and to which they are secured by iron fastenings; and on pumping out the water they contain, by a pump inserted through an air-tight stop-water plug, they will support the ship's quarters equal to the buoyancy required.

In the event of a vessel getting on shore, or severely damaged in action, or otherwise becoming weak and leaky, she could be trussed together by these means, fore and aft and athwart ship, with trussing binders, brought through the ports to a chain-cable—forming a complete frame-work round the ship, and thus preventing her working and foundering. This powerful purchase is founded on the well-known principle, that if you heave a strain on the centre or bight of a rope or chain, previously stretched, that the lateral tension may be increased 100 fold, and that any amount of force may be thus obtained. These plans would be most useful in ships laid up long in a state of ordinary, more particularly when the masts are left standing as demonstration ships. In order to clear the pumps, the main-chain may be doubled and expanded where necessary.

Letter from Captain Tayler to ———, on Dock-Gates.

"I beg to express my acknowledgments for the candid manner you have treated my endeavours to accomplish an object which the recent calamity seemed to render requisite; and I feel greatly obliged for the opportunity afforded me to explain away the objections which I apprehend have arisen from a misunderstanding on the part of the military engineer.

"It was generally admitted at the fire in the dock-yard, that if the dock-gates could have been opened, the Minden would not have suffered from the fire. This led me to engage my attention how, in such an emergency, that desideratum might be accomplished; and, having done so, I submitted the model in question, which has been admitted by the engineer to be an "ingenious plan," but at the same time, "impracticable for use, very liable to get out of order, and complicated in the mode of working." To these objections I feel it my duty to reply, the more especially as the extra-expense in fitting would be so trivial, (about £100); and if a line-of-battle ship could be saved by so small an outlay, it is presumed to be worthy of farther consideration. I beg distinctly to declare, that neither of my gates will be subjected to more pressure than those fitted on the old plan, for when they are used for the ordinary purposes of docking and undocking, they are governed by the same principle.

"Atmospheric pressure is fifteen pounds to the square inch, which would be more than one's hand could support, were it not equally supported on its opposite side. The same with water—it finds its level, and the pressure is equal on both sides, for the gates are never opened till it is so, except in cases of emergency; when No. 2 gate, being hung on a sliding gate-post, traversing upon a railway into the pier, is allowed to be screwed back, and should be eased off by a chain, and the eddy water running round the inclined surface of No. 1 gate, which is also secured by a chain, the pressure would be of no consequence on No. 2 gate, which opens both ways, and in every way the same as No. 1, and there is not so much pressure thrown upon the pier. When necessary to close the gates, the same power now used will be sufficient. The model shows that the sill should be composed of metal. The wedge-sill of No. 2 gate always adjusts itself, and is not so liable to have anything in the way as the sill on the opposite side; for in shutting No. 1 gate, it pushes everything before it against the sill; not so by No. 2 gate, and it is much easier to clean out, but should silt get into the groves, it will only render it more water-tight than otherwise.

"As to the supposed difficulty in making the two rods for raising the moveable sill act together, I conceive it to be no more than lifting a penstock or miller's hatch; and if two screws would cause it to work parallel, I do not conceive that there can be any objection to its being fitted in that way.

"As to a platform being necessary to work the screws, I must observe, that all canal-hatches are worked by racks upon the gates; but if platforms are found to be necessary, the bridges now used might be fitted to answer that as well as their present purposes.

"In reference to the groove and tongue spoken of, there is an error, for the model shows it to be a ruled joint, and admirably adapted for the purpose of preventing a leak between the gates. The wedge alluded to as an abutment, can act on the bottom of the gates as well as the top, and the rack-and-pinion might be fitted at the top, centre, or bottom if requisite—but the gate running on a railway does not require so much power.

"I do not apprehend that the shores to support the gate No. 1 will be necessary; as there will be no unequal pressure, the water will find its level on each side the gate, before the sill is raised or the gate drawn back.

"As to the necessity for increasing the width between the entrance of the dock-piers, it must be borne in mind that both gates would fall into a recess; but in allusion to shorter ships or longer docks, a reply is hardly necessary, for it is evident that longer docks are at present required for the new class of ships, and it would be a great oversight to fit new docks without remedying this evil, either by putting the gates further back or altering the head of the docks, so as to allow abundance of room for shipping rudders, and erecting stern frame-work, which is not the case in any of our docks.

"There is no difficulty in fitting dock-gates to run wholly back on railways by this principle; indeed, the pressure on the convex side would force a gate back, if fitted with rollers or railroad conductors. If, as it is stated, the dock can be filled with water in half an hour, why was it *not done at the late fire?** and, I might add, are not those who are conversant on the subject fully aware that no water can be let into the dock until *after half-tide?* But if my plan for bringing water into the docks be adopted, they could be filled at any time, and a great flow of water would carry out a ship, when she might be otherwise left in the dock, and consequently burned. The plan adverted to is connected with my method of making the docks accessible at all times of tide, and to do away with the necessity of a basin, which had the one now in progress been completed, and had there been ships in it, the recent fire would have consumed them, and, in all probability, destroyed the whole yard. The expense which would attend my proposition in this respect would not amount to so much as that of driving piles for coffer-dams, and that noble piece of ground in the centre of the yard would have been spared from destruction.

"In reference to the latter part of the engineer's letter, wherein he expresses a hope that my plan may be submitted to some practical man of more experience *than himself,* I must observe, that I could appreciate his modesty and acknowledged want of experience had he not previously passed a decided opinion totally at variance with the construction of the gate, and carried out his objections contrary to established principles in science. These objections were subsequently withdrawn."

---

* In Devonport dockyard.

A VOICE FROM TRINIDAD.*

CHAP. III.—MR. BURNLEY'S SCHEME OF EMIGRATION A REMEDY FOR THE ILLS OF TRINIDAD, CONSIDERED.

MR. BURNLEY having to *his own satisfaction* fully proved the points just discussed, viz., the awful demoralization* of the labouring popu-

* To *disprove* this unwarrantable assertion of Mr. Burnley's, we will give the following quotations from his *own* report on the condition of Trinidad:—

"The labourers are generally quiet and orderly throughout the district. The number of labourers on my estates have nearly doubled since the abolition of apprenticeship."—*Vide* Dr. Philip's Evidence.

"The condition of the labouring class is much improved since their emancipation. We work generally six days in the week. Two tasks can easily be done from six in the morning by eleven A.M. I have two women on the estate who do *three* tasks per day with ease. The labourer can easily save six or seven dollars a week; the two women of whom I speak save as much. We have three liberated Africans on the estate; they work extremely well; I have 100 dollars belonging to one of them in my possession."—*Vide* Frederick Maxwell's Evidence, overseer to Dr. Philip.

"The population of the town of San Fernando has *trebled* since emancipation. They are generally orderly and peaceable, and improved within these two years; and from my general acquaintance with the proprietors of estates, I am of opinion that agriculture is in general in a state of prosperity in the three quarters in which I practise."—*Vide* Dr. Meikleham's Evidence.

"I think that the industry of the labourers has generally improved since emancipation. Their circumstances are very comfortable, and I know that many of them are saving money; this is the case generally with all the emigrants."—*Vide* The Rev. Mr. Mühlhausser's Evidence.

"There has been a very considerable immigration of labourers into the colony since the emancipation, and it seems to become more steady and regular every day, and I find in general the women work much more steadily than I expected." —*Vide* Mr. Darling's Evidence.

"Since my arrival, I have had an opportunity of visiting the several estates on which the immigrants are settled. Some masons and carpenters said they could do better in Sierra Leone than in Trinidad. The mischief which I apprehend might result from immigration from Africa is, that foreigners might *pretend* to follow our example, and embark a number of Africans as immigrants for the Brazils and Cuba, and *make slaves of them* on arrival; and I deprecate the proceeding, as a continuance of the slave-trade indeed. The very discussion on this subject involves a *revolting discussion* regarding human flesh; and no results, however desirable, can be justified, if arrived at by the sacrifice of feelings, which should be cherished by human nature."—*Vide* Evidence of Wm. Hamilton, Esq.

* Continued from p. 470, vol. iv. old series.

lation, the utter and immediate ruin of the agricultural interests,† and as a natural consequence, supposing the foregoing to be correct, the complete failure of emancipation, which promised such benefits to the

† We will now see how far the "utter and immediate ruin of the agricultural interests" is to be feared, from this "awful demoralization of the labourers."

"I think the state of the labouring classes is generally improving, both physically and morally; but, unfortunately, *they receive too much rum from the planters,* which frequently renders them unable to attend divine service, and indifferent to improving their minds.

"With respect to marriage, their improvement has been very great; in 1836, I united only one couple; 1837, three; in 1838, seven; in 1839, fifteen; in 1840, twenty-nine; and, with *one* exception, they are all living happily together.

"For the further improvement of the labouring population, I think it would be very advantageous, if the practice of *paying the people on Sundays* were entirely done away with, as it frequently interferes with their attendance on divine service; also the discontinuance of *carting produce on a Sunday.* The circumstances of the labouring classes composing my flock are very comfortable, and many of them are saving money.

"There is no hospital in San Fernando for the use of my district, which is a great deficiency; and frequently the captains of droghers, and the steamer, will not take the sick up to Port of Spain (the capital), as it would deter other passengers from embarking. I have been obliged to pay as high as seven dollars to get a sick person conveyed to town."—*Vide* the Rev. Mr. Mühlhausser's Evidence.

"In the four districts under my spiritual charge, the population has increased since emancipation, and is daily increasing. Three large villages have sprung up, on the line of road to Arima, and settlers are establishing themselves everywhere. The number attending the ministry of the church of England may amount to about 1,500 adults.

"Considering their recent emancipation, and the benighted state in which it found them, added to the very high rate of wages they receive, I think there is more industry among them than we could reasonably have anticipated. With regard to their sobriety, *the large quantity of rum gratuitously distributed to them on the estates,* presents a temptation to inebriety which they cannot resist; and as their opportunities of religious improvement are now increased, I have every hope, when the evils alluded to meet the attention of government, that these difficulties will be gradually removed.

"The planters have invariably admitted, that this practice (of distributing rum) is demoralizing and pernicious, but complain of a *want of unanimity* in endeavouring to put it down. I do not consider the labourers, as a body, would object to the withdrawal of the allowance of rum, whether effected through a government order, or otherwise, provided they received an equivalent in money.

"In general the labouring class are never in want of employment, and are in a state of great prosperity.

"From a residence of many years in most of the Leeward Islands, I ascribe the moral superiority among them, to more attention having been paid to their moral and religious instruction, than in Trinidad; both in early years, and after life, and from the means of religious instruction being easily accessible to all slave, as well as advantages to his master; from a free-labour system, he hastens to develope his scheme for the correction of the errors of

---

classes; and I am of opinion, that this colony does not furnish the same facilities for religious instruction as the old Islands.

"Independent of the gratuitous distribution of rum by the planters, I have reason to believe that the payment of wages on a Sunday, is unfavourable to the moral improvement of the labourers."—*Vide* the Rev. J. H. Hamilton's Evidence.

"With a sufficiency of labour, and proper cultivation, I consider that 5,000 lbs. of sugar per acre is not an uncommon return for good soil in South Naparima, without manure and only two weedings; and I believe from the richness and extent of the sugar-soil in Trinidad, that this island is capable of producing more than a sufficiency of sugar for the consumption of Great Britain, and as cheaply as in any other part of the world. Cane pieces have been pointed out to me which have been *forty years* in cultivation, and are still perfectly good.

"With fair and reasonable exertion, a labourer can perform two tasks per day with ease, and this is frequently done; three tasks are very generally performed by the Americans. In addition to 50 cents, or 2s. 2d. sterling for weeding, we give in allowance half a pound of cod-fish, and one or two glasses of rum per task."—*Vide* Mr. Darling's Evidence.

"As a magistrate, the cases of assault among the labourers are rarely of a serious nature, only one of that description having occurred since my first appointment. This I may attribute to the general good conduct and orderly behaviour of the labourers; and when I have occasion to fine them, not one in ten is committed in default of payment.

"In regard to the present practice of giving rum to the labourers, judging from the nature of the cases which come before me, I think it a very bad practice, and the great majority of such cases which come before me, result from drunken quarrels. The mischief is increasing every day; it is now becoming more prevalent than formerly among the women; and if the practice is continued for two or three years longer, it *will demoralize the whole labouring population*."—*Vide* Mr. Guiseppi's Evidence.

"With reference to the principal effect which Emancipation appears to have had upon the moral conduct and deportment of the peasantry among the British Islands, I am of opinion, that Emancipation has had the most favourable effects upon their general conduct and behaviour, particularly in a religious point of view.

"In March, 1841, when I was in St. Lucia, wages were at from 1s. 3d. to 1s. 8d. sterling per day, with houses and gardens provided for the labourers; a day's work was considered to be from nine to ten hours, exclusive of the time required for meals, and I was credibly informed, that the labourers worked quite as well, as at any time during slavery or apprenticeship.

"With reference to the question whether the Immigrants who have arrived in Trinidad are more moral or better behaved than the native labourers, I am of opinion, from my own observations, and from what I have heard from gentlemen of the highest respectability, that they are *decidedly not*, but give the preference to the natives of the Island."—*Vide* Evidence of the Right Rev. Dr. Smith, Lord Bishop of Agra, &c,

that measure. In doing so, we observe the old and determined slave-holder, assuming the garb and language of one deeply intent on the suppression of the slave trade, and the civilization of Afric's sons.

There is, however, this trifling difference between *his* plan and the views of others in the field long before; that while it promises good to the Africans, it holds out no hope for his unfortunate country. It is only to the exiled negro, torn from his father-land, his kindred, and his home, that Mr. Burnley's civilizing efforts would be directed. Such a proposition appears to me to have much more selfishness and cruelty in it than of kindness. Coming from the party it does, it would be very surprising to find it based on any other principles.

But the Trinidad planters "claim to be allowed a share in the promotion of the welfare of the African race, upon a plan which they believe better calculated to promote its eventual success," than any other yet devised. "They ask for a calm and fair examination of their proposal, and if, after deliberate inquiry, it should be found to promise no better success than other schemes, which he takes for granted have proved failures, they will then be prepared to renounce it." This seems remarkably candid, and it would be unfair to refuse them such a reasonable request. Nothing on earth can be more desirable, than the discovery which these gentlemen appear to have made, should its results prove as satisfactory as they are led to suppose. There is an old saying, "Send a rogue to catch a rogue," and it may so turn out in this case. The "decisive measures" proposed by Mr. Burnley for the speedy accomplishment of the extinction of the slave-trade, are deserving of consideration, coming, as they do, from an experienced individual. Should they ultimately prove efficient, the Trinidad planters will have done much to restore their characters as men possessed of human feelings. Indeed, they wish even at this early stage of their experiment, to make that impression, by requesting to be allowed a share in the sacred enterprise of civilizing the Africans. Were a crusade to be established for that high and holy purpose, I doubt not but an army of West Indian planters would be found marshalled under the chairman of the "Agricultural Society," and foremost in the field, provided they be allowed to remove the spoils to certain localities, there to accomplish the moral elevation of the captives.

In examining the proposition of Mr. Burnley, it will be of vast importance to keep in mind, not only the deep sympathy expressed by that gentleman for the elevation of the long-neglected Africans, but also that expressed for the moral condition of the emancipated negroes of the British West Indies, in connection with the distressed condition of the agricultural proprietors. The scheme emanating from the "Trinidad Agricultural Society" must be viewed as based upon these three particulars. To allow it to rest upon the needy state of the planters, might do them an injustice, as their scheme would then appear the offspring of the rankest selfishness and avarice; and, on the other hand, to give these gentlemen credit for a pure and disinterested spirit of philanthropy, in their apparent concern for the degraded moral state, either of the uncivilized African, or for our emancipated negroes, would be awarding to them more of purity of heart, than their past career would warrant.

We shall at the first consider, whether it is likely, that the ignorant and uncivilized condition of the Africans, taken in conjunction with the awful picture given by Mr. Burnley of the West Indian labourers, would have possessed sufficient influence over the commiseration o him and his party, apart from the other consideration of the agricultural distress so prominently set forth, as to induce such costly efforts on their parts, for the moral improvement of these parties as are now proposed to meet the case of all three unitedly? On looking over the past history of the planters, as a body, nothing can be gathered to encourage such a hope. The evidence of the agricultural party in Trinidad, furnishes no ground to suppose that any measures would be adopted to meet the moral destitution, save the importation of the African in all his native barbarity, and when here, *a general distribution amongst the dissipated and awfully demoralized emancipated labourers.* Seeing that such a measure would only meet the necessities of the planters, without at all benefiting the moral condition of either our labourers, or those who might be introduced to the colony, it is no injustice to these gentlemen to suspect the soundness of all their lamentations for the darkness and ignorance of the negro, whether here or in Africa; and to give them credit for being actuated only by the most sordid and selfish principles. Assuming the character of philanthropists, while prompted by the most interested motives, they have rendered themselves doubly contemptible in the eyes of those who formerly looked upon them in no very favourable light. Their efforts to establish a claim to consideration, as the abettors of the true and holy principles of humanity, at the expense of the characters of our labouring population, places the Trinidad planters in the most pitiful position.

Mr. Burnley seems disposed to give the preference to a free labour, over that of a slave system, provided the former can be rendered, by some "moral force of necessity" pressing upon the labourers, *less expensive than the latter.* In order that such may be the case, to the extent that would satisfy his party, a variety of circumstances must combine to compel the labourer to constant employment, upon *any* terms proposed to him. A superabundant population, a rigorous climate, an oppressive tax, and coercive enactments, are amongst the chief inducements to industry, according to the hypothesis of Mr. Burnley. Where one or more of these is wanting, the labouring class will not be over-anxious to devote themselves steadily to their immediate calling. In the absence of all, according to this view of the case, the lower class would degenerate into a semi-barbarous state, and retire to the woods from the light of civilization, there to herd with the inferior animals of creation. Or if induced to adopt the duties of labour, it must be by brute force being exercised over them, according to Mr. Burnley's well-known doctrine, that "negroes would never labour without the whip."

In the West Indies, and particularly in Trinidad, there is neither a redundant population, a rigorous climate, nor heavy taxation, to urge the people to steady industry. If the foregoing theory be correct, the labouring population must be fully as idly disposed, and as reluctant to labour, as Mr. Burnley and the planters would make it appear. Should it be proved that the opposite is the case, which I think has already been shown, then it becomes us to account for this disposition to labour, in a way which Mr. Burnley keeps in the back ground. Self-interest has urged on certain planters, with Mr. Burnley at their head, to manifest every disposition to seek their own aggrandizement. Schemes highly indicative of the most earnest concern for their own well-being, have emanated from them. If they have been compelled, by the "moral force of necessity," the effects of which would prove so very salutary in regulating the conduct of the labourers, it must be for their advantage to be placed under such circumstances; according to their own views, therefore, to be delivered from such "necessity," might only be productive of an entire disregard to their interests, except some more powerful motive could be discovered. Mr. Burnley, with his princely fortune, will not pretend to urge "necessity" as the great moving principle by which *he* is actuated in all his schemes for the prosperity of himself and the planters of Trinidad. A principle deeply implanted in the breast of every man of sane mind, whether he be of high or low descent, whether he be wealthy or needy, operates alike upon the mind of Mr. Burnley and of the meanest labourer of the colony. The principle of self-interest—a noble principle of our nature, if not leagued with debasing covetousness—is strong in the breasts of all men, and will act powerfully in regulating their conduct regarding industry. Every individual should be allowed full scope for exercising it, either in this way or that, whichever may appear to him more to his advantage. This is his birthright. To overreach, or deprive him in any way, of the privilege of benefiting himself or his family in any lawful way, *amounts to slavery.* The man thus hedged in, and made subservient to the interests of another party, enjoys but a nominal freedom. To reduce the labourers of Trinidad to such a pinching state of "necessity," as to meet the wishes of the planters, by depriving them of their present facilities to further their interests, and thereby confine them in penury and want to the cultivation of the soil, can only be done artificially, and, if accomplished, must be attended with the blackest guilt on the part of those, who, urged on by a spirit of covetousness—not self-interest or necessity—recommend it.

In countries where a dense natural population already exists, pinching "necessity" will urge many individuals to adopt occupations, in which they would not otherwise engage. This distress arises from a *natural* cause, with which those who benefit by cheap labour, are not wont to complain, and in whom it is kind and humane to afford employment at any rate of remuneration. To murmur at this, would be to accuse the Moral Governor of the universe, and an aggravated crime even on the part of the subjects of distress, except produced by positive mislegislation.

To subject the lower classes of every country by artificial means to the same condition of distress, for the sole benefit of a few capitalists, would be the very essence of cruelty to the unfortunate sufferers. When human suffering is relieved, and the objects of misery soothed, angels rejoice; and fallen humanity, so mercifully engaged, bears some resemblance to the "Father of mercies." To contrive means for depriving the unfortunate poor of their small measure of happiness, and render them and their infant race the subjects of poverty and distress all their days, is as fiendish a scheme as that carried out on our first parents, when they and their numerous posterity became the subjects of suffering and sorrow.

The planters may succeed in adding to our population, and imposing a system of taxation grievously oppressive, through the consent of her Majesty's government, but they can effect no change in the state of the climate. According to their view, therefore, the population should be the more increased, and the taxation oppressive in proportion, in order to counterbalance the state of climate; to accomplish which all their efforts are now being turned. The introduction of English laws, so much desired, and, to a certain extent, so desirable, will no doubt be followed by some "stringent" enactment intended to bear upon the labouring population of Trinidad.

If we examine, however, the principles by which men are actuated, in the most densely-populated countries, and under climates the most rigorous, we shall find, where no species of slavery exists, that men follow such occupations as favour their interests most. They are generally found pursuing that course for which nature and education, or a want of it, has fitted them. To abandon it, let it be ever so mean, in favour of any other, would be to injure their already blighted prospects; therefore, they adhere to the calling, or something on a level with it, which they first embraced, and all for the want of a better. Here, self-interest urges them to adopt a particular mode of life, be it what it may, and also induces them to continue it, be it ever so unprofitable. I have been supposing all through, that their condition is produced by natural causes, which none could avert. If the lower classes be thus reduced to bitter distress, either by partial or positive mislegislation, the guilt of their suffering must rest with others, while 'tis theirs to bear all their distress with patience. All "necessity" without any interest, can only be produced by brute force, as in the state of slavery; if caused in any other way, it generally saps the foundation of all cheerful industry, and not unfrequently drives men to desperation. That employment which yields the largest remuneration, is very likely to be adopted, if in other respects it be congenial; and that mode of speculation by the capitalist, which will secure the greatest returns. For the latter to attempt to increase these returns beyond the fair and natural profits of capital, at the expense of the interests of his more needy fellow—to whom he may be indebted for profitably investing his money, and on whom he may be depending for all his profits—is not only ungrateful, but grossly unjust and oppressive. Should the condition of employers become so embarrassed as to render them unable to meet the demands of the employed as to wages, no steps should be taken to compel the latter to comply with the offers of such employers, more than the principle of self-interest within them. If it can be seen by the employed that it will be more to their advantage to turn their attention to some other mode of life, rather than to accept of the terms of their employers, no obstacle should be placed in their way; even though they should mistake their interest, and be ultimately injured, the consequences rest with themselves. This is necessary to perfect freedom. If individual interests were not allowed to rise and sink according to circumstances, we had been no further now in the march of improvement than our Saxon forefathers. Our West Indian colonies had been now two hundred years in advance of their present condition, *were it not for the withering effects of slavery*, and the perfect security the planters experienced from any pressure.

What has led to the great improvements of England during the last fifty years?—A desire to lessen the price of labour was one great object in view. Why are the agriculturists of our West India colonies so slow to follow the example of British capitalists in devising similar schemes for their benefit?—Simply because they have ever found a disposition on the part of the British government to support their interests at the expense of almost every other. It is now high time they should be placed on a footing with others of her Majesty's subjects. Palatable and desirable as the productions of the West are to the people of England, they should not forget, that there are at this moment 800,000 individuals who, from a long servitude, understand the whole process of raising and preparing them all, and who possess sufficient industry, if proper encouragement were afforded them, to supply all the wants of Britain at no higher rates than are now paid, independently of the present race of planters. Are they to be encouraged, or are the principles of industry to be stifled in their bosoms? Are they to be held for ever as the cultivators of a soil, in which they possess no interest—to be eternally the slaves of the planters—shut out from every chance of elevating their condition, except by the miserable remuneration they may receive? Certainly such was not the purpose for which they were liberated. That both the Wakefield system of allotments adopted in Trinidad at the recommendation of the planters, and Mr. Burnley's scheme of African immigration, are based on oppressive and unjust principles, cannot be denied.

The great question involved, is not the benefit resulting to the African by transporting him to Trinidad or elsewhere, nor is it the relief the planters would experience by an increased labour-population; that at issue is, the injustice to our emancipated negroes of these colonies. First, in shutting them out from all hope—as in Trinidad, of a participation in the soil, and thus confine them to labour in the cane-piece, or at some unsettled employment, during life;* and,

* Vide *Trinidad Standard* of May 16th, 1842.

secondly, in reducing their wages, by the introduction of some thousands of Africans, to a mere trifle, and, consequently, our labourers to great distress. Such a line of conduct would be a gross breach of national faith, which for its turpitude could be only equalled by a Russian despot. Britain should be the faithful guardian of her negro subjects in the west, during their helpless condition, and preserve them from the base and avaricious designs of those who too long held them in degradation. Neither the barbarous condition of the native African, nor the distress of which West Indian planters complain, would warrant such a deep and permanent injury, as the proposition of Mr. Burnley would inflict on our emancipated labouring population. To better the deplorable state of the rude African in any measure, would be, 'tis true, a work of mercy, but one in which neither Mr. Burnley nor his fellow-planters would be likely to embark, if not urged on by other than purely philanthropic motives. To relieve the present distressed state of the planters, or any other class of men similarly circumstanced, none would be opposed, if it could be accomplished without positive injury to another and far more numerous class of our fellow-men, equally entitled to consideration. Why they should be made to suffer for the mismanagement and prodigality of the proprietors of the soil, I have yet to learn. Believing it to be wholly within the power of the planters to improve their condition very materially, by following out the hints contained in the previous observations, without having recourse to any of the plans proposed by them, the doing of evil and the production of misery to relieve their distress, appear to me far the less justifiable.

The only object the Trinidad Agricultural Committee have in view, or rather Mr. Burnley, who suggested its formation, is to increase our labouring population, by opening a direct communication with any part of the west coast of Africa for immigration purposes. The boldness of this proposition at once characterizes the parties from whom it emanates. After the universal condemnation passed by Britain on the traffic in slaves, either in or out of her dependencies, it is matter of surprise that any subject of hers, over whom her flag of liberty waves, should be so audacious as to propose such a scheme for consideration. The well-merited indignation of the whole empire should follow such a proposition.

Mr. Burnley, however, seems to view the matter in another light, for he says,—

"The plans proposed for liberating African slaves, and conveying them to a British colony, there to enjoy freedom and the benefits of civilization, is calculated to diminish immediately, and at no very distant period entirely to extinguish, the slave-trade; and that, consequently, it cannot prove so objectionable to a wise and humane legislature, as to decline its adoption."

This seems remarkably kind on the part of the planters of Trinidad, and will no doubt be considered so by the friends of Africa. To extinguish the slave-trade is that for which Europe has been exerting herself for years, with Britain at the head of the other powers. Could Mr. Burnley suppress that horrible traffic in the short space of time he states, he would deserve to be crowned with laurels, and his name descend to posterity, not as the cruel and rigorous slaveholder, but as the benefactor and deliverer of the African tribes.

It is sometimes customary, in case of great and extensive conflagration, to employ gunpowder as a means of suppressing the flames. Can Mr. Burnley have borrowed his idea of extinguishing the slave-trade by purchasing the slaves, from this custom? The demand for sugar in Europe does not tend to suppress the desire of our planters to yield a supply, neither does the demand for British merchandise in our colonies, render our home and colonial merchants more inert or careless in attending to it.

How an increased demand for slaves on the coast of Africa can effect the extinction of the slave-trade, remains for the sophistry and logic of Mr. Burnley to show:—

"I firmly believe the most advantageous mode of proceeding, would be to tear up all our treaties for the suppression of the slave-trade, withdraw our cruisers from the coast of Africa, and allow *all* who pleased to procure labourers to work in Cuba and the Brazils and elsewhere, under the impulse of the whip."

Such was the opinion of Mr. Burnley at a meeting held in Trinidad, in February, 1841.

(To be continued.)

THE ANTI-CORN LEAGUE, AND SYSTEMATIC COLONIZATION.

THE London *Times* of the 18th of November, in one of the most powerful leaders which has ever appeared in that paper, has shown how much the obstinacy of our public men has added to the power of the League. Perhaps it may be of some interest to look back to the infliction of a duty on corn imported from abroad. Burke, so much admired by the aristocracy—so beloved by all who had the happiness to know him personally—where great good sense is so generally admitted, has left amongst his works a sort of protest against such a duty; but it was not a protest unattended with reason, for when in 1815, Mr. Robinson, (now Lord Ripon,) introduced the bill to the Commons, he was met by Mr. Alexander Baring, (now Lord Ashburton,) who appeared to be his match. In the Upper House there was a triumvirate of talent; there was Lord Grenville, Lord Wellesley, Lord Grey—but their voices were unheeded—some said, and it was not entirely without cause, that the horse-guards passed it. Many who had been the best friends to constitutional liberty amongst the Whigs, supported it with vehemence; it was, in fact, only part and parcel of the artificial system which had been produced by the long war. Bank restriction—that fatal act—an immense paper circulating-medium enhanced prices. The rent of land did not stand still between the years 1798 and 1815, it had trebled. It was Francis Horner who first exposed the disease with which the country was infected; landowners would not believe it, but parliament was saturated with landowners. Vansittart, (now Lord Bexley, with a great pension,) found no difficulty in persuading the Commons to affirm the truth of a most notorious falsehood, whilst the government was buying up the gold-coin for the payment of the Peninsular army. The Commons passed a resolution that a pound-note and one shilling were of equal value with a guinea; the Commons voted it, but nobody believed it, and thousands practically knew that it was false. The landlords meant by that resolution to vote a continuation of their enhanced rents, notwithstanding which, a little fear lurked behind; there was a feeling that peace might create an abatement; there was a want of confidence in Vansittart's prescription, it was notoriously false, and although so little understood as not to require the horse-guards to pass it, still its falsity led many to think that some Robert Peel might arise, and overturn this system. To preserve rents, it was absolutely necessary to have another prop, and thus a duty was to be placed upon the importation of foreign corn, and the landowners were to have the monopoly of the home-market; the artificial enhanced rents were to form the basis of all marriage-settlements—landlords were to calculate upon their fixity—their expenditure was calculated accordingly—mortgages were created without a doubt of paying the interest from increased rents. The Irish landowners were universally in favour of this monopoly; the mass of the people felt no interest in the question, knew nothing about it; their food was not corn, they were destined to exist, or, to speak truly, to starve, on potatoes—the lazy root, as Drennan called it; it is the landowners, not the people, who are interested in that part of the empire in the price of corn; all this is artificial, for Nature never destined Ireland for a corn-growing country; nothing but price—high price—price attained by a market of monopoly, keeps the greater part of it under tillage; this price goes exclusively into the pockets of the landlords; it is their voices that are heard, and of course nothing can be more unpopular amongst them than the slightest movement towards diminishing the price. No tax which ever was imposed answered the purpose of Irish landlords so well as that which tended to prevent the importation of foreign corn; so in England, the same men who deprecate taxation generally, cheer the minister when he imposes one which shall assist to raise the price of that commodity whence their income is derived. Burke, Grenville, Wellesley, and Grey, wrote, spoke, entered a protest in the lords against it; but, as the *Times* then said, it was "Corn and Currency," "Currency and Corn," —they are Siamese Twins—you may artificially keep one alive, but it cannot last. Sir Robert Peel cannot be too much praised for the manly way in which he disappointed many of his friends, and attacked the former. Let him but act from his own conviction, untrammelled by party, and he will get rid of the other. Falling back, as Mr. Attwood wishes, into the ditch from which the courageous baronet has extracted us, would be suicide indeed. The mire in which we had lain, still adheres to the state—will he have the courage to wash us clean, or will he leave it to the Corn-Law League to effect that operation? the fear is, that in them the patient will have a sort of rough Abernethian surgeon, who may half kill by the violence of his remedy. The Corn-Law question, as it is called, notwithstanding the immensity which has been said and written upon it, lies in a small compass. We are speaking for the whole people, and not for this interest, or that.

Is it safest for the food of the people to depend on a small area, the United Kingdom—or upon a large one, the whole world? But then, say the patrons of high prices—you must send gold out of the country for it? Agreed. But then arises the question—how did it get in? but one answer can be given—In exchange for British labour, of one sort or kind, turned into manufactures, ships, or something or other. If gold from Mexico is exchanged for corn from Poland, the transferer gains by both exchanges. To have done, however, with theories—what is the actual state of the matter? Is not the League rendering every man a politician? Is that a trifling matter not worth attention? But listen to the able editor of the *Times*, and when that has been attentively read, a few more observations will be submitted:—

"There are few political maxims more strongly warranted by the experience of ages, than that which recommends timely concessions to the fair wishes of intelligent and moderate men. It too frequently happens that statesmen defer the important season of change, till remonstrance has been stimulated into clamour, and earnestness warmed into vehemence—till measures which would have been received with thankfulness if granted sooner, are rejected by the indignation of slighted zeal or powerful faction; and those whose gratitude for a well-timed boon might have assuaged the tempest of popular demands, and soothed the fury of popular wrath, are themselves swept along in the full tide of general discontent, helpless, inactive, and desponding.

"We are at the present moment spectators of such a scene. We are witnesses of the effects—sad effects, we honestly believe—which are chargeable upon the pride of unconceding stubbornness. We have for fifteen years seen petitions and remonstrances against a sliding scale—we have ourselves given our hearty support to these petitions and remonstrances, coming as they did from the most opulent the most intelligent, the best versed in commercial affairs amongst our English merchants—we have seen these pouring in session after session into the House of Commons—we have heard them advocated by no contemptible eloquence, and supported by the authority of no slight experience—we have seen the influence of the great mercantile classes, the reasoning of theorists, the deductions of plain practical men, all embattled against a system of duties which has been universally pronounced to be as injurious in its operations on commerce as it is absurd and indefensible in argument; yet the system has been continued—the petitions slighted — the remonstrances treated with indifference — the nuisance unredressed.

"And what has been the issue of this? That which alone could have been expected to ensue—that which all men, acquainted either with the organization of parties or the tempers of their fellow-men, should have been prepared to see; and seeing which, they have no right to feel or profess surprise. The moderate men, whose wishes, whose experience, whose sagacity were all set at nought—who, years ago, said, 'Let us have a fixed duty on corn; do away with these shifting, up-and-down, bothering scales, which only serve to enrich a few speculators, whilst they ruin hundreds'—who petitioned Parliament to this effect—who waited on Ministers—who held meetings, until they were sick and tired of speaking and petitioning on the subject—these men at last combined to effect by an organization of numbers that which their isolated efforts had failed to compass. But when, in the history of kingdoms, or of parties, was any combination of men limited to its original elements or its proposed objects? There is a gravitation in the social as in the physical world. No one mass can long exist separate or independent of other bodies. It attracts, consolidates, and conforms. Each successive particle, while it adds to the density and increases the force of the primary body, changes also its character, its direction, and its velocity. Individual tendencies and personal interests become subject to new laws of action; and the collective force of such a combination is felt in far different directions, and in very different degrees, from those which a knowledge of its constituent particles would suggest. That men whose business was hampered, and whose interests were injured, by the working of the corn duties, would unite sooner or later to procure their modification, was within the range of ordinary conjecture; but who, unaccustomed to trace the progress of opinions and the vicissitudes of party, could have argued the rise, the advance, the present power, of the Anti-Corn Law League?

"The League is a great fact. It would be foolish—nay, rash to deny its importance. It is a great fact that there should have been created in the homesteads of our manufactures a confederacy devoted to the agitation of one political question, persevering at it year after year, shrinking from no trouble, dismayed by no danger, making light of every obstacle. It demonstrates the hearty strength of purpose—the indomitable will—by which Englishmen, working together for a great object, are armed and animated. It is a great fact that at one meeting at Manchester, more than forty manufacturers should subscribe on the spot each *at least* £100, some £300, some 400, some £500, for the advancement of a measure which, right or wrong, just or unjust, expedient or injurious, they at least believe it to be their duty or their interest, or both, to advance in every possible way.

"These are facts important and worthy of consideration. No moralist can disregard them; no politician can sneer at them; no statesman can undervalue them. He who collects opinions must chronicle them. He who frames laws, must to some extent consult them.

"These things are so. It matters not that you tell us—as you may tell us with truth—that the League has another character, and other objects than those which it now professes. The League may be a hypocrite, a great deceiver, a huge Trojan horse of sedition. Be it so. But we answer—the League exists. You may tell us, and with truth, that there are men in the League sworn foes to church and crown—to peers and dignities—to bishops and to judges: that, now speaking and declaiming, and begging, and taxing, and, an' you like, plundering men to resist the corn-laws, this monster-being will next raise its head and subdue all laws beneath it. You may tell us, that its object is not to open the ports, to facilitate commerce, to enrich England, but to ruin our aristocracy, whom Leaguers envy and detest. You may tell us, that no men of honesty or intelligence could, consistently with their honour and their knowledge, seek to rifle an embarrassed State of that just subsidy which all States impose upon articles of the most necessary consumption. You may tell us, that, whatever be the specious pretext which they hold out, or the disguise under which they work, they can really only look forward to that disastrous crisis in the annals of a kingdom, when indiscriminate plunder consummates the work of hopeless and inextricable confusion. You may tell us, that the League has whined and canted about the sufferings of the poor; that its orators wink with malicious cunning at the 'point' they make about the miserable victims of landlord legislation. In all this there is, doubtless, much truth.

"But, we ask, tell us this:—Who created the League? Who found the ribs and planks of this "*infandum monstrum*?" Who filled it with armed men, and introduced its perilous presence within the walls of the Constitution? We answer—experience set at nought—advice derided—warnings neglected—these brought the League into existence—these gave it power, and motion, and vital energy—these gave it an easy and unresisted ingress into the very sanctuaries of our domestic life—'Scandit fatalis machina muros,' &c. A new power has arisen in the State; and maids and matrons flock to theatres, as though it were but a new 'translation from the French.'

"Let no man say that we are blind to the possible mischiefs of such a state of things. We acknowledge that we dislike gregarious collections of cant and cotton-men. We cannot but know that—whatever be the end of this agitation—it will expire only to bequeath its violence and its turbulence to some successor. We fear that though to-day men clamour for cheap bread, next year they may riot for cheap gold. This year the cry is 'No tax on bread,' next year it may be 'No tax on anything.' To limit the objects of popular desires, or to measure the sweep of popular excitement, is to foreknow every whim which may stimulate the ambition, or fire the passion, or tickle the vanity of future ages. We turn from the contemplation of probabilities with apprehension and alarm. We turn to the present only because it is less fearful than the future.

"That the past may have taught its lesson, we fondly hope; but dare we hope that the lesson has not been learned too late? There is a stern retribution that awaits legislative stubbornness. The Nemesis who haunts the precincts of a Statesman's cabinet, is as fleet as she is sure. The wisdom of the moderate, the authority of the old, the influence of the rich, are frail and tottering barriers against the impetuosity of thoughtless and incensed myriads. The madness of the multitude palliates its excesses by the indifference which was repaid to the admonitions of temperate, and the scorn which was heaped on the remonstrances of wise, men: and when the trembling Minister, at the 11th hour, calls out 'Take the boon now,'—there is but one reply which greets him, 'It is too late.'"

It is to avert, if possible, the result which the *Times* fears, that this article is written. Will the League cease and dissolve itself, if the minister brings in a bill for a low fixed duty, say 7s. a quarter on wheat, and other grain in proportion, with a sliding scale, declining 1s. every year, until all duty ceased? Whatever blame may have been incurred by having created such a duty, the effects of it stare us in the face as much as the League—the one is a fact as much as the other. Examine what this effect has been; it has not merely raised prices, but it has created a confidence that prices would always continue high. Seven years would allow many marriage-settlements to die. With the prospects of a gradual decrease in the price of corn, at any rate there would be seven years of prudent marriage-settlements. But away with such selfish stuff! Does our legislature assemble only to make laws for the small class who execute marriage-settlements? No, No. It has other duties to discharge. The duty on foreign corn has brought thousands, ay, millions of acres of land into cultivation, which cannot be maintained in it. If prices permanently fall, all this is artificial; do not let it be argued that this has been a misfortune to the owners, in the name of rent. They have received the value of the fee-simple of the land, and that in many instances over and over again. The owner of poor lands, the owner of lands where the climate forbids cultivation, is not only to be considered, but the population, farmer, labourer, manufacturer, and tradesman, dependent on them, and these are no inconsiderable number; millions who have nothing to do with marriage-settlements. Retfordise the duty on corn, break the whole down at once, and it would be on a par with clearing an Irish estate of its population; in point of fact, it would be doing the same thing in a different form. If the minister adopts this suggestion, he will put the League in the wrong. Can Sir Robert Peel do it? Undoubtedly. His declared principle is expediency; he assailed a paper circulating-medium; his friends, his party, were angry, but they have since supported him. He emancipated the Catholic; his party were equally adverse, but they have since supported him. Let him assail the remaining monster; they may be angry, but in all probability will support him. But what if they do not, and he goes out, can they continue the fight? Let them try. Sir Robert Peel would soon become the umpire between the parties, and both must yield to his advice. But putting aside men, League, or Peel, or Lord Melbourne's madmen. The duty is in a bad way. What is to become of the people, of all classes, who have been created, in consequence of these artificial rents? What provision can be made, but systematic colonization, and that upon a larger scale than has ever yet been contemplated? To those who have property on such lands, we say, Gather it up before it is melted, and invest in a way that a free passage will be found for the labourers. If some such safety-valve, as this now chalked out, is not adopted, we fear the most awful consequences. Sir Robert Peel at Litchfield and at Tamworth, Lord Stanley at Liverpool, made some pretty speeches; their hearers were easily pleased, but it is hardly to be imagined, that they either of them seriously thought, that what they recommended, would be adopted upon a scale to secure the marriage-settlements of their companions; it was a pretty little pastime, the amusement of the moment.

It was at one of these agricultural meetings, about two years since, that Sir Robert Peel gave to intended emigrants, a little wholesome advice, much in the same manner as he did to young farmers. Still the subject does not appear to have made that strong impression upon him which it merits; there is something in his disposition, which renders it necessary to relate the same thing many times before he takes it up; but, in two great circumstances of his life, Currency and Catholic emancipation; he has proved himself open to reason and conviction: again, the sentiments he lately avowed relative to Postal communication did him great credit; one or two more parliamentary discussions like that which took place upon Mr. Buller's motion, and he probably will be amongst the most forward in adopting systematic colonization as the true combination for preventing, rather than relieving distress at home, and planting in the Southern Ocean a modern Britain.

W.

REVIEWS OF NEW BOOKS.

ART. I.—*The Life and Speeches of the Hon. Henry Clay.* Edited by DANIEL MALLORY. Two vols. 8vo. New York: Bixby. London: Fisher, Son, & Co.

As Mr. Clay's political life is terminated, there is nothing indelicate or premature in laying before his country, and the world, those bursts of impassioned eloquence, with which he enlightened the American senate, and those just views of legislation which may be studied with the highest advantage by all political economists. Born in a country where the art of oratory is little understood—where turgidity and bombast are mistaken for eloquence—and living under a form of government known not to be congenial, at all events, and even suspected of being inimical, to oratorical excellence, Mr. Clay attained to the highest rank amongst the public speakers of his own country, and to no inferior one amongst those of other countries who speak the English language. His style is classical and ornate; his arrangement always perspicuous; and his replies always pointed, terse, and antithetical. A pardonable pride has led his countrymen to compare him to the celebrated Irish orator, statesman, and philosopher, Edmund Burke; but he rather resembles Lord Brougham in his early and brilliant career in the Lower House, than the unequalled Hibernian Cicero. In either case, however, the talents of the American senator are not depreciated.

The author of these inestimable speeches was born in 1777, and the premature death of his father, a Baptist minister, left him without the means of acquiring a sound rudimental education. His boyhood was spent in a manner not unlike that of the first Sir Robert Peel:—one carried the milk of the farm to the neighbouring village every day; the other rode daily to the mill, seated on a sack thrown across the back of his horse. A desire for something more intellectual induced him to seek service in a druggist's shop, from which he migrated to a lawyer's office, and there laid the foundation of those legal and literary acquirements by which he has deserved a name amongst men. His character as an advocate became quickly ascertained and highly appreciated; and the urbanity of his manners and benevolence of his disposition, contributed to bring to his chambers all those who were in the deepest and most inextricable difficulties. His defence of a lady who shot her sister under suspicious circumstances, and his appeal in favour of two Germans, father and son, indicted for murder, are amongst his ablest efforts in advocacy.

But to attempt an enumeration of the subjects with which the comprehensive mind of Mr. Clay did not hesitate to grapple, would be vain; it will be sufficient, as it will also be just to his fame, to state, that he was the uncompromising asserter of the rights of man—the strenuous advocate for mercy—and the benevolent promoter of all humane institutions. Amongst the valuable collection of his public speeches accessible through these interesting volumes, we find his wise views and humane policy on the subjects of slavery, British impressment of seamen, encouragement of home manufactures, relief to agriculture, reciprocal commercial liberty, and, lastly, the American banking system, and the currency question.

A sketch even of the *Times* of Mr. Clay would extend inevitably over a moderate-sized volume, as he was the contemporary of Pitt, Castlereagh, Canning, Wellington, Peel, &c., and rode in the whirlwind of revolution that swept over the world from France. But it is due to his political renown to mention, that he has been even here firm, consistent, and liberal. In the characteristic volumes before us, we meet some few startling items, such as the deliberate system of duelling, in which he was occasionally an actor, and from which he wanted moral courage to emancipate himself. And we have also to make allowance for the paralyzing effect which his senatorial appeals are sometimes said to have produced upon his hearers. If the narration of his over-eloquent biographer be not rather highly coloured, Mr. Clay must indeed have been a perfect master of elocution, and of the histrionic art itself—for, a graceful movement of his hand is represented as having silenced the clamour of the Assembly—a look, to have *fixed* his adversary to the spot—an emphatic word, to have drawn forth an involuntary tear. We are assured (speaking of Webster and Clay,) "that the collision of these intellectual giants was inconceivably grand. The eloquence of Webster was the majestic roar of a strong and steady blast pealing through the forest; but that of Clay was the tone of a god-like instrument, sometimes visited by an angel-touch, and swept anon by all the fury of the raging elements." This is quite enough in the way of eulogy; amongst more sober reasoners perhaps too much, but the hyperbole in which his enthusiastic biographer has indulged should not, indeed it cannot, detract from the value of the admirable political and commercial essays which are included in this collection. Our readers may not perhaps be aware that Mr. Clay is still living, and that, like Washington in days of yore, he has retired from public life, and now enjoys an honoured leisure in his country villa.

The best mode of enabling our readers to judge of the oratorical merits of Mr. Clay is by a few extracts from his speeches; and the best evidence of his philanthropy, liberality, and political acumen is afforded by the opinions he repeatedly expressed in his place in the parliament of his country. Speaking of the neutrality of the United States in the war between Spain and her colonies, he said,—

Nine or ten British disbanded officers had formed in Europe the resolution to unite themselves with the Spanish patriots in the contest existing between them and Spain; that, to carry into effect this intention, they had sailed from Europe, and in their transit to South America had touched at the port of Philadelphia; that during their residence in Philadelphia, wearing perhaps the arms and habiliments of military men, making no disguise of their intention to participate in the struggle, they took passage in a vessel bound to some port in South America; that a knowledge of this fact having come to the ears of the public authorities, or, perhaps, at the instigation of some agent of the Spanish government, a prosecution was commenced against these officers, who, from their inability to procure bail, were confined in prison. If, said Mr. Clay, the circumstances attending this transaction be correctly stated, it becomes an imperious duty in the house to institute the inquiry contemplated by the amendment which I have proposed. That this was an extraordinary case, was demonstrated by the fact of the general sensation which it had excited on the subject, in the place where it had occurred. Filled, as that respectable and populous city is, with men who differ widely on political topics, and entertaining various views of public affairs, but one sentiment prevailed on this subject, which was favourable to the persons thus arraigned. With regard to the conduct of the court on this occasion, he would say nothing. The respect which, whilst he had a seat on this floor, he should always show to every branch of the government, the respect he entertained for the honourable judge who had presided, forbade him from pronouncing the decision of that court to have been unwarranted by law. But he felt himself perfectly sustained in saying, that if the proceeding was warranted by the existing law, it was the imperious duty of congress to alter the law in this respect. For what, he asked, was the neutral obligation which one nation owed to another engaged in war? The essence of it is this; that the belligerent means of the neutral shall not be employed in the war in favour of either of the parties. That is the whole of the obligation of a third party in a war between two others; it certainly does not require of one nation to restrain the belligerent means of other nations. If those nations choose to permit their means to be employed in behalf of either party, it is their business to look to it, and not ours. Let the conduct of the persons prosecuted be regarded in the most unfavourable light; let it be considered as the passage of troops through our country, and there was nothing in our neutral obligations forbidding it. The passage of troops through a neutral country, according to his impressions, was a question depending on the particular interest, quiet, or repose of the country traversed, and might be granted or refused at its discretion, without in any degree affecting the obligations of the neutral to either of the parties engaged in the controversy. But, surely, this was not a case of the passage of troops; the persons apprehended not being in sufficient number, nor organized or equipped in such manner, as, under any construction, to constitute a military corps.

His speech on the encouragement of domestic manufactures is more startling in its assertions and opinions, and is the fruit of reflection upon a question both delicate and difficult.—

In considering the subject, the first important inquiry that we should make is, whether it be desirable that such a portion of the capital and labour of the country should be employed in the business of manufacturing, as would furnish a supply of our necessary wants? Since the first colonization of America, the principal direction of the labour and capital of the inhabitants, has been to produce raw materials for the consumption or fabrication of foreign nations. We have always had, in great abundance, the means of subsistence, but we have derived chiefly from other countries our clothes, and the instruments of defence. Except during those interruptions of commerce arising from a state of war, or from measures adopted for vindicating our commercial rights, we have experienced no very great inconvenience heretofore from this mode of supply. The limited amount of our surplus produce, resulting from the smallness of our numbers, and the long and arduous convulsions of Europe, secured us good markets for that surplus in her ports, or those of her colonies. But those convulsions have now ceased, and our population has reached nearly ten millions. A new epoch has arisen; and it becomes us deliberately to contemplate our own actual condition, and the relations which are likely to exist between us and the other parts of the world. The actual state of our population, and the ratio of its progressive increase, when compared with the ratio of the increase of the population of the countries which have hitherto consumed our raw produce, seem, to me, alone to demonstrate the necessity of diverting some portion of our industry from its accustomed channel. We double our population in about the term of twenty-five years. If there be no change in the mode of exerting our industry, we shall double, during the same term, the amount of our exportable produce. Europe, including such of her colonies as we have free access to, taken altogether, does not duplicate her population in a shorter term, probably, than one hundred years. The ratio of the increase of her capacity of consumption, therefore, is, to that of our capacity of production, as one is to four. And it is manifest, from the simple exhibition of the powers of the consuming countries, compared with those of the supplying country, that the former are inadequate to the latter. It is certainly true, that a portion of the mass of our raw produce, which we transmit to her, reverts to us in a fabricated form, and that this return augments with our increasing population. This is, however, a very inconsiderable addition to her actual ability to afford a market for the produce of our industry.

I believe that we are already beginning to experience the want of capacity in Europe to consume our surplus produce. Take the articles of cotton, tobacco, and bread-stuffs. For the latter we have scarcely any foreign demand. And is there not reason to believe, that we have reached, if we have not passed, the maximum of the foreign demand for the other two articles? Considerations connected with the cheapness of cotton, as a raw material, and the facility with which it can be fabricated, will probably make it to be more and more used as a substitute for other materials. But, after you allow to the demand for it the utmost extension of which it is susceptible, it is yet quite *limited*—limited by the number of persons who use it, by their wants and their ability to supply them. If we have not reached, therefore, the maximum of the foreign demand, (as I believe we have,) we must soon fully satisfy it. With respect to tobacco, that article affording an enjoyment not necessary, as food and clothes are, to human existence, the foreign demand for it is still more precarious, and I apprehend that we have already passed its limits. It appears to me, then, that, if we consult our interest merely, we ought to encourage home manufactures. But there are other motives to recommend it, of not less importance.

These extracts have exhausted our paper but not our patience, for we shall resume our notice of Mr. Clay's second volume in our succeeding number.

ART. II.—*The People's Gallery of Engravings*, after Originals by Turner, Lawrence, Stanfield, Prout, Roberts, Allom, Chalons, Hayter, Parris, Maclise, Stephanoff, Pickersgill, Cattermole, Bartlett, Leitch, &c. With Letter-press Descriptions of the Plates, by the REV. G. N. WRIGHT, M.A. Quarto.—London: Fisher, Son & Co., Newgate-street and Angel-street.

Scientific improvements adopted by printers, and a widely-extended taste for general literature, have enabled enterprising publishers to scatter wholesome works of history, and fiction, and science, over the land. The great cost of engraving, especially on steel, has hitherto sealed all portfolios of well-executed prints against the middle and the lower classes. That barrier would now appear to be broken down, for we have now before us a quarto number of "The People's Gallery," containing *five* first-rate engravings, and eight pages of descriptive matter, all for the price of one shilling! Now, to avert misconception, we premise, that this beautiful quarto does not intrude itself on the plea of cheapness, because nothing that is bad can be cheap, but solely and entirely on that of the high excellence of the engravings—by which is meant the ability of the original design, when the subject is historic; the truth of the portrait and landscape, when they are stated to be from nature; and the finish of the engravings, in both instances. The first plate in the first number is deserving of a half-guinea frame; the fourth, Chatsworth, has been carried away from us already, to illuminate a MS. account of her Majesty's tour in the Midland Counties; but the portrait of that splendid soldier Lynedoch, we shall never part with. "Lynedoch is a name," said the speaker, "never to be mentioned in our military annals, without the strongest expressions of respect and admiration."

"The People's Gallery," allowing the first number, by synecdoche, to stand for the whole, is the best general album ever published, exclusive of all consideration of its miraculously moderate cost. The letter-press contains a memoir of Lord Lynedoch, a rather minute and careful description of Chatsworth, and a very pleasing poem by L. E. L.

ART. III.—*Waverley Novels.* Abbotsford Edition. Vol. IV.
London: Houlston & Stoneman. Edinburgh: Cadell.

This magnificent, yet popular edition, of the favourite fictions of the age, progresses with the same spirit that was at first breathed upon it. Admirable taste, unsparing enterprise, and a firm resolve to win public patronage, were amongst the sentiments that influenced its publishers; and the harvest that we understand has been reaped, is eminently deserved by the indefatigable and meritorious labourers. This volume includes the Bride of Lammermoor, Legend of Montrose, and Ivanhoe; the last, one of the most fascinating novels ever produced. The illustrations include eleven engravings on steel, and about two hundred wood-cuts. Stanfield and Leitch, who have furnished most of the drawings for the steel engravings, are both names familiar to the public, and both men of the scenic school. In this particular instance, the senior scholar has evidently the advantage; let his view from "Fast Castle" be referred to for the truth of this assertion; and even after this, "The Temple Church" supports his claim to precedence of his co-adjutors in these exquisite illustrations. It was a politic and prudent thought, to enrich the tales of Scott with actual views of the scenes he has so vividly, yet faithfully described, because this gives a reality to his stories, which the enemies of fiction have always pleaded as an argument for their exclusion from the domestic circle. Indeed, even the historic illustrations, such as Franklin has designed for Ivanhoe, although they do not represent what does now exist, are faithful records of costume; and, in fact, more instructive, from the truth of their details, and the quality of the information they convey, than bird's-eye views of Aberdeen, or Aberdour. But, descriptions both give completeness to the work, and tend to remove the only objection which the most fastidious have been able to concoct; and both are very wisely given in the varied embellishments of Messrs. Houlston and Stoneman's edition of the Waverley Novels.

ART. IV.—*The History of British India.* By EDWARD THORNTON, Esq. Vol. V., Part VI. London: Allen & Co., Leadenhall-street.

This is the last occasion on which we shall have the pleasure of noticing Mr. Thornton's impartial and valuable history, because, for the present, it is concluded. Many a time and oft, have we, *ex cathedrâ*, pronounced our deliberate conviction, that a history compiled so elaborately as we know this to have been—by one to whom the archives of our Indian parliament were so accessible; by one who demonstrated the wisdom of throwing open those records to him, from the discretion and ability with which he has used them—could not have failed in acquiring and retaining public confidence. Part VI., the finale, is entirely occupied by an index; and, from its fulness and accuracy, which we had occasion recently to test, gives an increased value to the work. The administration of the late Marquis Wellesley in India will shortly, we understand, be given to the world by an ardent admirer of that statesman's learning, and talents for governing. Now, we too have sentiments of our own upon that very question—"An Analysis of the Wellesley Administration in India"—which we prefer suppressing for the present, because, if our conclusions be mistaken, they would give offence where none was deserved or intended; and if otherwise, even, they will form a part of history sufficiently early. Meanwhile, we recommend Mr. Thornton's straightforward narrative of that eventful era in Anglo-Indian history, to the attentive perusal of those who will doubtless peruse with avidity the threatened biography of the Marquis Wellesley.

ART. V.—*The Sequential System of Musical Notation.* By ARTHUR WALLBRIDGE. London: W. Strange, Paternoster-row.

The human voice, the most flexible and feeling of all instruments, is subjected to an arbitrary arrangement of sounds, rendering change of key difficult and inconvenient; from which circumstance it principally arises that so few attain, or even attempt to acquire perfection in singing. Mr. Wallbridge has discovered a system, which he denominates the Sequential, that supersedes this arbitrary imposition, enabling the composer to write music irrespectively of all artificial considerations, and the performer to play it, unfettered by any conventional agreements, beyond those which the particular instrument necessarily implies. The more general any system can be rendered, the more valuable; it becomes not only more easy of acquisition, but more extended in its application and advantages. We have, perhaps, a very remote prospect of extinguishing the Chinese language, and inducing those prejudiced antiquaries to adopt our own; but we have no such distant prospects as to music, any more than painting—both being susceptible of rapid circulation, as universal languages. The Chinese principle in painting is wrong; this they will soon discover from our views of their country; and, correcting their perspective, their exquisite colours will be better employed than before; and, as like causes produce like effects, we shall then understand Chinese views as they are meant. Music is sister to painting, and certainly its acquisition is impeded by change of key, as well as change of instrument. Mr. Wallbridge will confer a lasting benefit on society, if he can so generalize the language of music, that wherever his pages are presented, they will be both intelligible and practicable.

Art. VI.—*Domestic Scenes in Greenland and Iceland.* London: Van Voorst, Paternoster-row. 18mo., pp. 114.

Perhaps this is one of the neatest and most delicately got up books for children that has ever appeared. It is intended for those of tender years alone, and the chapters or tales, containing useful truths only, are progressive in difficulty both of expression and meaning. The wood-cuts are of a superior description, the publisher justly concluding that, as the mind is most susceptible of impressions in infancy, we should be the more cautious not to make false or foolish ones upon it; and the same principle has operated in his choice of subjects, which are all of a rational, instructive kind, instead of the Mother-Goose-Cap or Punch-and-Judy family, with which our juvenile books are so mischievously filled. The admirable taste of the publisher, with which his confreres are all familiar, has been most meritoriously employed in endeavouring to save our infant population from the corruption of books carelessly printed and illustrated, productions that slander nature and inculcate falsehood. "Domestic Scenes" is an example for all books of amusement for children.

SONNET—THE RAILROAD.

Noonday in our far-east Metropolis
Saw me an exil'd wight;—when, swift desire
Yearning for *Home* did all my soul inspire,
For Memory's wing had wafted its last kiss.
And wondrous agency fulfill'd my bliss;
A car, instinct with warring flood and fire,
Whose flame-fed steed no course, no haste can tire,
Tho' pant his brazen maw, and boil, and hiss.
At eve, from that strange transport I alighted
In the dear distant region of the west,
And many a well-known face with joy was lighted
To welcome back the straggler to his nest;
Who, smiling, thus the travel-thought indited,
And thank'd the *Railroad* for effect so blest.

C. J. C.

G. W. R. Second Class.
24th December, 1843.

COLONIAL AND COMMERCIAL STATISTICS.

Regulations of the Government of Hayti with America.—The following laws, bearing upon the North American commerce, recently enacted by the Government of Hayti, to take effect from and after the 11th day of September, 1843, were received from the United States Commercial Agent at Cape Haytien, at the Department of State, Washington, October 7th, 1843, and are published officially in the Madisonian, as follows:

The tonnage duty heretofore exacted on foreign vessels, at one dollar, Spanish, per ton, is increased to two dollars, Spanish, per ton, (consequently American vessels pay two dollars and twenty cents per ton.)

All foreign vessels going from one port to another, in this Island, will pay for each port visited, an additional duty of one hundred dollars, Haytien currency, on vessels under one hundred and fifty tons.

Vessels from one hundred and fifty to two hundred tons, pay one hundred and fifty dollars.

Vessels of two hundred tons and upwards, pay two hundred Haytien dollars.

The duties on wharfage, and weighage on merchandise *imported*, are increased to double their former rates.

The "Territorial" duty on exports is still in force; but the duty of exportation is reduced, which reduces the export duty on coffee from twenty dollars, Haytien currency, per one thousand pounds, to twelve dollars.

Cocoa from ten dollars to four, per one thousand pounds.

Tobacco, in leaf, from fifteen dollars per one thousand pounds, to five dollars. Logwood, from seven dollars per one thousand pounds, to two dollars.

Mahogany, from twenty-two dollars to twelve dollars per thousand feet. Hides, of all kinds, are free of export duty.

The wharfage and the weighing and measuring are to be added to the foregoing quantities as follows:—On coffee, one dollar, Haytien currency. Cocoa, one dollar. Tobacco, one dollar. Logwood, one dollar. Mahogany, one dollar. Hides are charged one cent, Haytien, each.

The present value of a Haytien dollar is two-fifths (2-5ths) of a Spanish or American dollar, or sixty per cent. below their par.

Retirement of Sir Henry Pottinger.—Mr. Davis, formerly, for a short time, successor to Lord Napier, in China, has been selected to relieve Sir Henry Pottinger, as governor of Hong-Kong.

East Indies and China.—In consequence of the extension of our possessions in the East Indies, and the opening of the various ports in the Chinese seas, acquired by the late treaty with the Emperor of China, which has occasioned an extensive demand for our manufactures, a very large supply of shipping, for the export of the various commodities, has been advertised at Lloyd's during the previous week, to be ready to start for their respective foreign ports in the course of the ensuing month. The number of ships announced to leave the various docks adjoining the Thames and Gravesend, for Madras, Calcutta, Bombay, Australia, China, Hong-Kong, and other parts of the East, amounts to above 60, whose tonnage varies, each vessel from 300 to 1,000 and upwards. Of these, one firm, whose establishment is at Newcastle-upon-Tyne, furnishes nine vessels (five of them being above 1,000 tons each, and which collectively amount to 7,150). Another firm, in London, sends out five ships (of these three carry above 1,000 tons, and the five collectively 4,850 tons).

Programme of the French Steam Ships.—The starting of the French transatlantic steamships, in May 1844, will form a new era in steam navigation. The following appears to be the programme; and the first great line, we have reason for believing, is to start in May, from Havre to New York:

First great line—from Havre to New York. Four steamships are to be placed on this line; the departures are to take place once a fortnight. Fifteen days are allowed for each passage, and ten days at New York—in all, forty days. Twenty days are to be allowed to each vessel at Cherbourg, between every voyage, to rest the crew, and repair the vessel and engines.

Second great line—from Bordeaux to Martinique. Three steamers are to be placed on this line; the departures are to take place once a month. Two days are allowed for the passage from Bordeaux to Corunna, and ten hours' stay there; five days twelve hours for the passage from Corunna to the Azores, and one day's stay there; twelve days sixteen hours for the passage from the Azores to Martinique; the steamers to remain ten days at Martinique. Twenty days are allowed for the return passage from Martinique to Bordeaux—in all, forty days' sailing, and eleven days and a half stoppages. Thirty-seven days are allowed between every voyage, at Rochefort or Bordeaux, for repairs and stoppages.

Third great line—from Marseilles to Martinique. Three steamers are to be placed on this line; the departures are to take place once a month. From Marseilles to Barcelona, one day, and four hours' stay; from Barcelona to Cadiz, three days, and twenty-four hours' stay; from Cadiz to Madeira, three days, and twenty-four hours' stay; from Madeira to Martinique, fourteen days. The steamer is to remain ten days at Martinique. Twenty-one days are allowed for the return voyage from Martinique to Marseilles—in all, forty-two days' sailing, and fourteen and a half days' stoppages. Thirty-three days are to be allowed at Toulon or Marseilles, between every voyage, for repairs and repose.

Fourth great line—from St. Nazaire to Rio Janeiro. Four steamers are to be placed on this line; the departures are to take place once a month. From St. Nazaire to Lisbon, three days and a half, twenty-four hours' stay; thence to Goree, eight days, three days' stay; from Goree to Pernambuco, eight days sixteen hours, four days' stay; from Pernambuco to Bahia, one day twenty-two hours, four hours' stay; from Bahia to Rio Janeiro, three days nineteen hours. The steamer is to remain eleven days fourteen hours at Rio Janeiro. Twenty-five days twenty-one hours are allowed for the return voyage from Rio Janeiro to St. Nazaire. Forty-eight days are allowed between every voyage, at St. Nazaire or L'Orient, for rest and repairs.

First secondary line—from Martinique to Havana. This line is omitted by the *Journal des Debats*, from which we quote. There are to be three steamers placed on it; the departures are to take place once a fortnight. Seventeen days are allowed at Martinique, for rest and repairs.

Second secondary line—from Havana to Vera Cruz. One steamer is to be placed on this line; and the departures to take place once a month. From Havana to Vera Cruz, three days eighteen hours, and twenty-four hours' stay; from Vera Cruz to Tampico, one day, and four hours' stay; from Tampico to Galveston, two days and four hours' stay; from Galveston to New Orleans, one day six hours, and twelve hours' stay; from New Orleans to Havana, two days fourteen hours—in all, ten days fourteen hours' sailing, and one day twenty hours' stoppages.

Third secondary line—from Martinique to the ports of the Spanish main. One steamer is to be placed on this line; the departures are to be monthly. From Martinique to Chagres, six days, and twelve hours' stay; from Chagres to Carthagena, one day twelve hours, and four hours' stay; from Carthagena to Santa Martha, twelve hours, and four hours' stay; from Santa Martha to La Guayra, two days twelve hours, and twelve hours' stay; from La Guayra to Martinique, two days sixteen hours—in all, thirteen days four hours' sailing, and one day eight hours' stoppages.

Fourth secondary line—from Rio Janeiro to the ports on La Plata. One steamer is to be placed on this line; the departures are be monthly. From Rio Janeiro to Montevideo, five days six hours, and five hours' stay; thence to Buenos Ayres, thirteen hours; return direct in six days.

THE FALKLAND ISLANDS EMIGRATION ASSOCIATION. *In re G. T. Whitington.*—To us, who have so often enjoyed public applause through the aid of Mr. Whitington's talents and liberality, the close of his persecution is a subject of sincere gratification. The judge felt, as we have always done, that he had been too sanguine in his expectations of bringing Government to consider the hardship of his position, and of releasing a man, so eminently qualified for the colonizing of a maritime position, from difficulties, in which generosity and misplaced confidence had involved him. With more than ordinary satisfaction, we make the following extract from the *Chronicle* of the 17th ult., in which Commissioner Fonblanque placed the conduct of the bankrupt in that pure light, in which an impartial tribunal must inevitably have done, and yet did no more than discharge the high duties of his office.

"This case," said the Commissioner, "has been frequently discussed before me since the month of June last; and in my opinion no fraud is attributable to the bankrupt, as to the Admiralty order, nor to Messrs. Abbott, nor to any one else. Indeed, taking all the objections urged against the bankrupt, I see nothing, certainly, of fraud; and more, nothing other than the results of a very sanguine mind. No person has ventured here to say, much less to swear, that he has lost even by any one false representation of the bankrupt; and I should feel it my duty to enter very fully into the whole of the transactions brought under the notice of the court in this case, were it not that I had entered very fully into their consideration upon the bankrupt's passing his final examination. All that I have, therefore, now to add is, that it is the opinion of the court that the bankrupt should have his certificate forthwith."

The certificate was granted accordingly.

It is but justice to the bankrupt to state that he alleges, on the face of his balance-sheet, that if the Government settle with him as they have done with the New Zealand Company, he will have a considerable surplus, after paying 20s. in the pound; and that the expenses which he had incurred by sending ships out to the islands with emigrants, was for the purpose of enabling the then-existing Government to lay claim to them as a colony.

DISTRIBUTION OF THE BRITISH ARMY.

[Where two places are mentioned, the last named is that at which the Depôt of the Regiment is stationed.]

1st Life Guards—Windsor
2d Regent's Park
Royal Horse Guards—Hyde Park
1st Dragoon Guards—Canterbury
2d Ballincollig
3d Dublin
4th Longford
5th Dundalk
6th Piershill
7th Cape of Good Hope; Maidstone
1st Dragoons—Newbridge
2d Ipswich
3d Bengal—Maidstone
4th Exeter
6th Nottingham
7th Hussars—Brighton
8th York
9th Lancers—Bengal, Maidstone
10th Hussars—Cahir
11th Dublin
12th Lancers—Manchester
13th Light Dragoons—Hounslow
14th Bombay; Maidstone
15th Hussars—Madras; Maidstone
16th Lancers—Bengal; Canterbury
17th Birmingham
Grenadier Guards (1st batt.) The Tower
(2d batt) Portman-street
(3d batt) Windsor
Coldstream Guards (1st batt.)—Wellington bks.
(2d batt.) St. John's Wood
Scotch Fusileer Guards (1st batt.)—Winchester
(2d batt.) St. George's Barracks
1st Foot (1st batt.)—Gibraltar; Tralee
(2d batt.) Barbadoes; Londonderry
2d Foot—Bombay; Chatham
3d Bengal; Chatham
4th Madras; Chatham
5th Dublin
6th Chester
7th Gibraltar; Brecon
8th Bolton
9th Bengal; Chatham
10th Bengal; Chatham
11th Kilkenny
12th Mauritius; Isle of Wight—Reserve batt. Mauritius
13th Bengal; Chatham
14th Canada; Armagh
15th Templemore
16th Birr
17th Aden; Chatham
18th China; Chatham
19th Corfu; Jersey
20th Bermuda; Isle of Wight—Reserve batt. Bermuda
21st Bengal; Chatham
22d Bombay; Chatham
23d Barbadoes; Isle of Wight—Reserve batt. Canada
24th Dublin
25th Madras; Chatham
26th Edinburgh
27th Cape of Good Hope; Drogheda
28th Bombay; Chatham
29th Bengal; Chatham
30th All at Cork
31st Bengal; Chatham
32d Manchester
33d Halifax, N. S. Limerick
34th Dublin
35th Mauritius, Templemore
36th Dublin
37th Newcastle-on-Tyne
38th Gibraltar, Hull
39th Bengal, Chatham
40th Bengal, Chatham
41st Canterbury
42d Malta, Isle of Wight—Reserve batt. Malta
43d Canada, Cashel
44th Gosport
45th Cape of G. Hope, Isle of Wight—Reserve batt. Gibraltar*
46th Barbadoes, Boyle
47th Gosport
48th Gibraltar, Guernsey
49th Portsmouth
50th Bengal, Chatham
51st Van Dieman's Land, Chatham
52d New Brunswick, Nenagh
53d Newry
54th Athlone
55th China, Chatham
56th Cork
57th Madras, Chatham
58th Chatham
59th Portsmouth
60th (1st batt.) Dublin—(2d batt.) Jamaica Belturbet
61st Limerick
62d Bengal, Chatham
63d Madras, Chatham
64th Weedon
65th Mullingar
66th Belfast
67th Manchester
68th Canada, Chatham
69th Castlebar
70th Leeds
71st Barbadoes, Isle of Wight—Reserve batt. Canada
72d Fermoy
73d Newport (South Wales)
74th Canada, Kinsale
75th Plymouth
76th Devonport
77th Jamaica, Dover
78th Bengal, Chatham
79th Gibraltar, Aberdeen
80th New South Wales, Chatham
81st Canada, Buttevant
82d Quebec, Clare Castle
83d Northampton
84th Madras, Chatham
85th Antigua, Newbridge
86th Bombay, Chatham
87th Glasgow
88th Malta, Stirling
89th Canada, Cork
90th Ceylon, Carlow
91st Cape G. Hope and St. Helena, Isle of Wight—Reserve batt. Cape Good Hope
92d Barbadoes, Dundee
93d Canada, Carlisle
94th Bombay, Chatham
95th Ceylon, Dover
96th Van Dieman's Land, Chatham
97th Corfu, Isle of Wight—Reserve batt. Corfu
98th China, Chatham
99th New South Wales, Chatham
Rifle Brigade (1st batt.) Corfu—(2d batt.) Halifax, N.S., Isle of Wight—Reserve batt. Halifax

COLONIAL CORPS.

1st West India Regiment, Demarara, &c.
2d Ditto, Jamaica and Sierra Leone
3d Ditto, Sierra Leone
Ceylon Rifle Regiment, Ceylon
Cape Mounted Riflemen, Cape of Good Hope
Royal Canadian Rifle Regiment, Canada
Royal Newfoundland Veteran Cos. Newfound.
Royal Malta Fencibles, Malta
St. Helena Regiment, St. Helena

* On passage to Gibraltar.

OBITUARY.

Bellingham, Lady Francis, on January 10th, at Dunany-house, Ireland, in her 81st year.

Bethune, Colonel Drinkwater, on Jan. 16th, at Thorncroft, near Leatherhead, aged 81.

Burdett, Sophia, the lady of Sir Francis Burdett, bart., and youngest daughter of the late Mr. Coutts, the banker, on Jan. 13th, at St. James's Place, London.

Burdett, Sir Francis, bart., M.P, on Jan. 23rd, at London, aged 74 years. The deceased baronet was a man of very ancient descent, the possessor of an old baronetcy, the owner of a splendid fortune, the representative of a great county, the head of an honourable family; a man most carefully educated, of considerable attainments, of great natural endowments and of very popular talents, of generous feelings, whatever may be thought of his wisdom and discretion, of dignified manners, of winning address, invested with almost every personal advantage, and prompted by the most benevolent impulses; it can occasion therefore no surprise that he should have enjoyed a remarkable degree of popularity. In 1796, Sir Francis first came into parliament for Boroughbridge; in 1807, was first returned for Westminster, which he represented for nearly 30 years; and in 1837 took his place in parliament for North Wilts. On the 5th of Aug., 1793, he married Sophia, the youngest daughter of Mr. Coutts, the banker, (whom he only survived ten days,) by whom he had several children, the eldest of whom, Lieutenant-Colonel Burdett, now 48 years of age, succeeds to his father's title, and, no doubt, to the bulk of his estates.

Champion, Commander Charles, Royal Navy, on Jan. 14th, at Kingsland, in his 72d year.

Davies, the Rev. Peter, master of the Grammar School at Carmarthen, South Wales, and formerly Unitarian minister at Belper, Derbyshire, on Jan. 13th, suddenly at Carmarthen.

Fitz-Gerald, Vice-Admiral Sir Robert Lewis, K.C.H., on Jan. 17th, at Bath, in the 69th year of his age.

Guyon, Commander John, Royal Navy, on Jan. 15th, at Richmond, Surrey, in his 77th year.

Haliburton, Robert, Esq., only surviving son of the late General Haliburton, of the Madras establishment, on January 7th, at Barbourne Cottage, Worcester, deeply and deservedly lamented.

Hastings, the most noble the Marquis of, on Jan. 13th, at Southampton, in the 36th year of his age. The deceased, George Augustus Francis Rawdon Hastings, was Marquis of Hastings, Earl of Rawdon, Vicount Loudoun, and Baron Botreaux, Hungerford, Molines, Hastings, Moels of Cadbury, Newmarch, Peverill, De Homet, and Rawdon, in the peerage of the United Kingdom; Earl of Moira, county Down, and Baron Rawdon of Moira, in the Irish peerage; was second son of Francis, first Marquis, the distinguished Governor-General and Commander-in-Chief of India, [*vide* Wright's Life of Wellington, *passim*]; by Flora Muir Campbell, in her own right Countess of Loudoun, who died in 1841 He married on the 1st of August, 1831, Barbara Yelverton, in her own right Baroness Grey de Ruthyn, by whom his lordship leaves issue one son (Paulyn Reginald Serlo, Earl of Rawdon, born June 2d, 1832, who of course becomes Marquis of Hastings), and four daughters.

Johnston, Major-General, F. J. T., C.B., only brother of the Right Hon. Sir Alexander Johnston of Carnsallock, Dumfriesshire, on Jan. 5th.

Kyon, Captain John Howard, many years a brave officer in the East India Company's Bengal Cavalry, distinguished for his loyalty and undaunted courage, Jan. 17th, aged 66.

Lowe, Sir Hudson, on January 10th. As the Governor of St. Helena, the name of Sir Hudson Lowe is sure of being ever remembered in connection with that of Napoleon Bonaparte. Because it will ever be believed, that from his hands, and through his means, indignities were attempted to be inflicted upon greatness, genius, and glory, that were combined in the fallen emperor of France. It is affirmed of Sir Hudson Lowe, that he merely obeyed the orders he received from his superiors in his treatment of Napoleon. As a soldier this is sufficient excuse for him; but not so as a man, and a Christian.

Maber, the Rev. G. M., M.A., of St. John's College, Cambridge, and Rector of Merthyr Tydfil, South Wales, on Jan. 8th, at Swansea, aged 77.

Peel, Lieutenant J. H., Royal Navy, on Jan. 13th, at Lake, in the Isle of Wight, aged 47.

Strutt, Joseph, Esq., on Jan. 16th, at Derby. The deceased was the third son of Mr. Jedediah Strutt, the ingenious inventor of the frame for making ribbed stockings, a partner of Sir Richard Arkwright, and a man distinguished for integrity, industry, and ingenuity. The deceased belonged to a family which has been by their public and private acts, their great enterprise in business, their upright and honourable dealings, and their general benevolence, held in the highest respect throughout the neighbourhood of Derby. Literature and the fine arts found in Mr Joseph Strutt a munificent patron; and throughout his whole career he was the firm friend and liberal supporter of institutions having for their object the promotion of useful knowledge; in short, he will long be considered the benefactor of his native town, and the friend of mankind. He was born in 1765, married in 1793, and left a widower in 1802. He was for some time Colonel of the Belper regiment of local militia, a Deputy-Lieutenant of the county, an alderman and a magistrate of the borough of Derby, and first mayor under the municipal corporation act.

Taylor, John Edward, Esq., proprietor and principal editor of the *Manchester Guardian*, on Jan. 6th, at Beech Hill, Cheetham, near Manchester, aged 53 years.

LONDON: FISHER, SON, AND CO, PRINTERS.

FISHER'S

COLONIAL MAGAZINE.

NEW AUSTRALIAN EXPORT—TALLOW.

It was Napoleon who exclaimed, when a thousand victories had shed their lustre on his military name, "I want ships, colonies, and commerce;" and never was there uttered a sentence more comprehensive or momentous, by the ablest statesman Europe ever saw. Now, as none ever doubted the wisdom and foresight of this modern Justinian, the objects of his wishes are allowed to be of paramount value; and these inestimable treasures, for which he sighed so often and in vain, Great Britain possesses in the amplest degree. But, does she fully appreciate the blessing, and employ her talent in the most remunerative manner? Are her colonies governed by sage, experienced, independent men—are the just and reasonable complaints of her colonists heard and redressed, or treated with coldness and indifference—does any comprehensive system exist, uniting the colonies and parent state in one common bond of union—is justice equally administered in the colonies to all bearing the name of British citizens—and is the hope of encouragement, or the hand of help, held out to the struggling colonist?

How melancholy the echo! Last session of parliament was not propitious to colonial affairs,—let us see whether "the signs of the times" are more exhilarating as the present opens. Already have Indian bungling and partiality attracted the attention, and called into action, the purest spirits in the atmosphere of parliament; and since distance is no longer a disqualification in the estimation of the senate, may not our Australasian possessions still cherish a hope that they will be remembered? But the personal condition of the parent will compel her to extend kindness to her issue; the colonial interest is a momentous thing—it is irresistibly forcing itself upon the notice of those who have the power to regulate, but hesitate to exercise it. To disguise the fact that the future progressive movements of this country are wound up with those of our colonies, is futile; the truth is written on the walls of parliament as with a sunbeam. 'Tis true, and thanks are given that it is so, that

> A fairer Isle than Britain
> Never sun saw in his wide career,—

but how limited her area, how restricted therefore the means of subsistence and employment for those multitudes—"the forestalled of nature," by the introduction of scientific inventions, and invention of substitutes for manual labour? England is but a spot "on this great empire which the sun ever beholds"—but a fraction in the great territorial account, although certainly the head from which thought and action emanate, and are infused into those far-extended members. England is the metropolis of that immense state, the empire of Victoria, which has now extended its language, laws, and limits into every part of the habitable globe. It has been most dispassionately examined into, and the conclusion arrived at by competent and impartial analysts is, that the strength of the empire is to be sought for in her colonies; and that as a paralysis in the members disables the body, however sound the head remains—decay in our colonies may debilitate us, without diminishing the consciousness of our sufferings or our loss. Commerce entering as a chief ingredient into the constitution of happiness and prosperity, (and those who are indifferent to colonial subjects are fully alive to the truth of this assertion); if, therefore, we can show the colonies to be the most abundant fountain of commercial adventure, we have a right to demand the adhesion of the hesitating, indifferent, and even ignorant, amongst their opponents.——From the year 1802 to 1835 the trade of Great Britain with the continent of Europe declined from 65 to 48, from which Mr. Alison justly inferred "that our true policy is to be found in cultivating, with the most assiduous care, our colonial dependencies, in our intercourse with which we employ only our own shipping, and in our commercial dealings with which we experience the benefit of a trade, sharing in the rapid extension and luxuriant growth of these vigorous offshoots of the empire." From Porter's Statistical Tables it appears, that the annual value of British produce and manufactures exported to the colonies and to the United States (a recreant child of Great Britain), amounts to £25,000,000; while, if the amount of population be taken into the calculation, the result will appear infinitely more palpable, as showing the superior advantages of her colonial trade over that with the European continent. Amongst the latter, France is the best customer (the anarchy of Spain and ingratitude of Portugal operating most injuriously upon her relations with the Peninsula), and, she only imports British goods to the amount of 11d. per head per annum; whilst our colonies consume, in proportion to their population, to the value of £1. 11s. 6d. to £11. 15s. 0d. per head—the whole of the colonial trade being done in British bottoms.

We are about to plead protection for Australia, more particularly in this article, but think we can adduce a powerful evidence of the indifference of the legislature to our imperial commerce, in the shade of the once majestic India. There, one hundred millions of our fellow-subjects have been so totally excluded from the sphere of civilized intercourse. by the apathy or meanness of our executive, that they do not consume of British manufactures beyond the rate of sixpence per head per annum; while, if they could be induced to increase their consumption until it amounted to one-tenth of the quantity absorbed by the negro-population of the West Indies, it would give an increase of £72,000,000 to the general export-trade of the United Kingdom.

Hence it follows, that it is the highest duty, the best interest, of the parent-state, to foster and protect colonial commerce; and Great Britain seems to have been destined for the task of civilizing and peopling the rude regions of the globe. The trust is honourable and important to human happiness, and the English are better disposed to submit to human institutions, and possess a greater propensity for organization, than any other people that we know of. Our population, like the flood that bursts its banks, is now pouring out upon the surface of the world; let us guide these waters into a safe and profitable channel, so that we may at once reap the fruits of those benefits which their ultimate rest will confer upon some new scene of industry. Our rulers must undertake this political engineering; they must not shrink from the responsibility; they must not permit the waters to escape, and contribute to benefit a hostile soil;—they cannot, for there is a moral power at work, that will alarm the indifferent, and punish the obstinate. We might here press the necessity for colonization, to which our arguments lead so imperceptibly and conclusively, but we purposely turn to the protection of those that have gone into honourable exile, and to the encouragement of their conspicuous efforts for the establishment of a wholesome, remunerative, constant commerce.

In all infant states, a pastoral life is the first that presents itself;

and, if the increase of population and luxurious habits of society did not multiply our wants, to this arcadian happiness a large portion of our race would undoubtedly adhere. However, those days of innocence have passed away, and pastoral cares only occupy the mind until it can emancipate itself from a course so simple. The wealth of Australia may yet perhaps consist in flocks, and it is of paramount consequence to the colony, and therefore to the country of which it is a colony, to obtain a sale for this peculiar produce of the land. We have endeavoured, in a recent number of our former series, to point out the successful issue of the project for salting beef; we shall here detail the progress of a second attempt to establish another staple for export, (tallow,) which is even more meritorious; and, as opposing the Russian trade solely, while the export of salted beef opposes an Irish trade, is therefore the rather entitled to legislative protection, and the especial fostering care of our Colonial Office.

It was the unanimous opinion of the Committee of Council on Immigration, at the latter end of the year 1842, that "one grand cause of the depression in the pastoral interests of New South Wales, was the want of sale for the surplus stock." The fleece alone, from the relative dearness of labour, did not yield a remunerative profit; whilst the increase from breeding—which had previously been all clear gain—had become so utterly useless, that most of the settlers during the preceding two years, prevented their flocks from multiplying. The natural increase of sheep throughout the colony far exceeding the consumption of mutton, while the only vent for that increase, the demand of newly-arrived capitalists, having totally ceased, it was the interest of the sheep-owner to check, rather than promote, the increase of his flocks. Had this crooked policy still prevailed, which had, in fact, been pursued for three years up to September, 1842, in 1846 all the sheep in Australia would have been old, and their numbers diminished and diminishing. The prosperity of the colony would have been retarded by such a proceeding for an incalculable period; and the children's children of the first colonists would feel its ruinous impoverishing consequences.

Mortgages, discounts, and other destructive expedients were adopted, to obviate the approaching ruin to the pastoral cause, but without benefit to the settler, whose sheep could only procure a shilling a head for him in Sydney. At this moment of darkness, a light appeared in the atmosphere of hope—genius, industry, and perseverance, the inheritance of Britons, succeeded in the discovery of a mode of converting much of the sheep's carcass into tallow, in a short period, and with productive results. The discovery in a moment of time, doubled the value of every flock, stayed the annihilation of the sheep, which this plague of despondence was just about to create, and restored the rapidly declining commerce of Australia, by adding a new and most valuable staple to those already firmly established—wool and salted beef. It is not the least remarkable point in this new project, that the ravages of rot amongst sheep are no longer apprehended by the owner: ointments, washes, doctors, and fees, are henceforth superseded by the knife and the cauldron, to which he resorts the moment disease appears amongst his flocks.

Sheep-boiling is one of the most fortunate hits that colonial experimentalists have ever made: the want of a market for their sheep was foremost amongst the objections of the small capitalists who contemplated emigrating, and engaging in the easy life of shepherds; and its removal will open a flood-gate, and let in a considerable amount of capital, accompanied in all cases by respectable *bonâ fide* settlers. From actual experiment made by Mr. Henry O'Brien, it was ascertained, that by boiling down the entire carcass, the skin and hams excepted, there may be extracted on the average from 25 to 30 pounds of tallow from each sheep, which, at the moderate valuation of 3½d. per pound, is worth 7s. 3½d. to 8s. 9d., or upwards of a hundred per cent more than has of late been realized by the sale of the living animal. But, adding to this the value of the wool, skin, mutton, hams, &c., the sum total yielded by this novel process, is no less than 14s. 3½d. per sheep. If this result be thought too flattering, let the odd 4s. 3½d. be taken off; and even then, it is demonstrated that, in the very depth of winter, when the fleece is in the worst possible state, the intrinsic value of a sheep is 10s.; and even deducting twenty per cent from this, we have still the cheering minimum of 8s. Contrasted with the *nominal* value which sheep hitherto bore.

The quotations of *ox* tallow in the home-market, for the last six years, from which an average may be taken, are as follow:—In 1837, 41s. 3d. per cwt.; 1838, 52s.; 1839, 49s. 7d.; 1840, 50s. 1d.; 1841, 47s. 7½d.; 1842, 48s. 2d.—average of the six years, 48s. 1¼d. per cwt. This average is rather more than 5d. per pound. In the previous estimate, the price was taken at 3½d., which was full thirty per cent below the mark. The above quotations, however, relate to *ox* tallow, which is of less value than mutton tallow by £5 per ton.*

* Beef suet consists of stearine, margarine, and oleine; mutton and goat suet contain a little hircine. In ox fat there are 76 parts of stearine, in sheep fat rather more.

To show that in the home-market the supply does not exceed the demand, we mention the fact, that, according to a parliamentary document, the entire quantity imported in the year 1841, amounting to 1,241,278 cwts., was kept for home-consumption. And that the demand for home-consumption is increasing, and is likely to increase, appears not only from the increase of population, but also from its own extended application, in combined forms, to making candles, soap, dressing leather, and various processes in the arts.*

It may, therefore, be safely assumed, that for all the tallow the Australians can produce, whether from oxen or from sheep, they will find in England a sure and steady market, and remunerative prices.

Our native supply is estimated at 120,000 tons; 60,000 tons are annually imported, the principal part of which is brought from Russia, which pays a duty of 3s. 2d. per cwt., while colonial tallow is only subject to 3d.—why is it subject to any duty? The illiberality of Russia should render us less scrupulous in reducing the amount of their exports; and that they can afford to sustain a slight shock, may be reasonably concluded, from the estimated value of tallow shipped from St. Petersburgh in one year, £2,306,150; of this 3,600,000 poods were exported to Great Britain (63 poods are equal to an English ton). Other countries participate but slightly in this valuable trade; the proportion may be judged with sufficient accuracy from the return of 1829, which was as follows:—From Russia, 1,164,180 cwts.; from the United States, 6,143 cwts.; from Turkey, 3,799 cwts.; from France, 1,992 cwts.; from Sweden, 1,626 cwts.; a small quantity is also imported from the South American States on the La Plata, and from Sicily. Tallow is an article of speculation, the price ranging from 35s. to 51s., but averaging, upon an estimate of returns for upwards of twenty years, 42s. per cwt. Town tallow is higher priced.

From the imperfect mode in which some hundred sheep were at first boiled down—from their wretched condition at the time of the experiment—from the opposition of usurers, who did not wish that the creditor should get on his feet again, by getting his property once more into his hands—and from the hostility of the butchers generally—the whole speculation has been grossly misrepresented. Now, as those of

* Tallow imported into the United Kingdom in 1836—1,186,364 cwts., 1 qr., 4 lbs. Retained for home consumption, 1,318,678 cwts. 1 qr. 25 lbs. Duty, £208,284.

Tallow imported into the United Kingdom in 1837—1,308,734 cwts. 1 qr. 4 lbs. Retained for home-consumption, 1,294,009 cwts. 2 qrs. 21 lbs. Duty, £204,377.

our readers who are just on the wing for another clime, may be desirous to have an authentic statement of an actual experiment in this way, we give the report of Mr. Robertson, of Keilor, which appeared in the *Port Philip Gazette*, and is attested by the editor.

Statement on rendering down Sheep for Tallow.—"Weight of a barren aged ewe, boiled down by Jas. Robertson, of Upper Keilor, Salt Water River. The ewe was small and fine-woolled, of the Merino breed; the carcase was boiled about twenty hours, and the produce is as follows:—

Weight of carcase after taking out the kidney tallow	...46 lbs.	
Weight of hind legs, kept for hams, taken off	.... 12 lbs.	
Boiled down with head and feet	..........34 lbs.	
Weight of tallow from inside	..........11½ lbs.	
From carcase boiled down	..........10½ lbs.	
	22 lbs. at 3d.	..........5s. 6d.
Wool taken off skin after washing, 1 lb. 14 ounces, at 1s. per lb.		.........1s. 10½d.
12 lbs. of hams, at 2d. per lb.		..........2s.
		9s. 4½d.

"The above trial of a single sheep I consider to be rather under what might be rendered from a number of the same quality, as the boiler I had was small, and boiled over at times, causing some loss; and I think there would not be so much waste in proportion on a large quantity boiled, as on a single sheep. I am of opinion, boiling down will do well with old ewes in particular, as they cannot be sold at present, and by boiling they can be turned into cash in a very short time, and will bring a fair price, if the market for tallow continue good."

Besides the reduction of decaying sheep to profitable tallow, the conversion of a mortgaged estate to an unencumbered property, of an oppressed and disheartened people to a relieved and hoping one, nothing can or will be more instrumental in restoring confidence at home, than those constant discoveries in these new countries, of profitable commodities for export. Already suggestions, the origin of occupation, order, and prosperity, flow in, and animate the hitherto desponding colonists. Those who have fairly averaged the remuneration of 12s. per head for boiled-down sheep, the tallow being brought to the London market, still look for further profits and further modes of vesting capital and employing labourers, in the curing of mutton-hams, converting the lean pieces of mutton into palatable soup, as they do in Germany and France; grinding the bones for manure and for exportation; preparing the smaller intestines for harp-strings, besides manufacturing glue and size.

Enough has been stated, to show that the energies of the Australians are not prostrated, that British industry lives in their hearts, and that wherever an honourable livelihood is attainable by mental and physical efforts, there the original Briton will prosper. The discussion upon the sheep-boiling had subsided, the process was in full operation at the latest departures from Sydney and Port Philip. The principal sheep-proprietors were then diligently employed in an important part of their duty, one which an experienced shepherd should alone undertake, that of culling the flock. Setting apart those fit for breeding, and those only adapted for the tallow-trade; he should be careful in all cases not to reduce the stock below the probable amount of lambs which the ensuing season would afford; for, after all, in her flocks the true treasures of Australia consist.

DUTCH SETTLEMENTS IN ASIA.

ORGANIZATION OF THE COLONIAL GOVERNMENT—RELATIONS OF THE GOVERNOR-GENERAL WITH THE TRIBUTARY PRINCES—DUTCH-INDIAN ARMY—INDUSTRIOUS AND AGRICULTURAL PURSUITS OF THE JAVANESE—COMMERCIAL COMPANY, NAMED HANDEL-MAATSCHAPPY—INCOME OF THE ISLAND OF JAVA. *

SINCE the moment when the Dutch government succeeded (in 1795) to the Indian Company, in all its possessions, a supreme government, armed with the most extensive powers, has exercised sovereign functions, according to the laws, customs, and high commission of the home-government; but, nevertheless, its authority has not far exceeded that of the king of Holland in Europe.

This government is assisted in its important duties by the Indian Council, a sort of Council of State, whose attributes at the present moment are simply and purely deliberative, and whose discussions reach no other subjects than those of a political nature, or those relating to interior affairs. The army and navy are under the entire control of the governor-general, who is sole arbiter and judge in these depart-

* This highly-interesting article is extracted from the Journal of M. E. Dubruzet, who was attached to the expedition of the sloops Astrolabe and La Zélée.

ments; but he is compelled to communicate everything relating to the superior and political government to each of the members of the Indian Council; these give their opinions in writing, on the back of each document, but the solution of these difficulties devolves upon the governor-general, who is empowered, even when their opinions are contrary to his own, to take no notice of their advice. It is only within a few years that the governor-general has enjoyed powers thus extensive; the home-government appearing to have armed him with such powers, as an indemnity for the little liberty which the present colonial minister has thought fit to leave him; for it is in Holland that the initiative of nearly all important measures is taken, by those who constitute by themselves the exercise of the sovereignty.

The governor-general has under his direction a director-general of finance, whose duty consists in the due administration of the revenues and expenses of the colony, and who ranks immediately after the Indian Council; below him again, in the Indianarchy, are the commander-general of the forces, the rear-admiral, head of the naval department; the attorney-general, of the supreme court; the director of the interior, who is charged with the system of internal police; and the government state-secretary, from whom orders emanate, and whose signatures are attached to all decrees.

The administration of justice is confided to the judges, who bear the title of counsellors. These counsellors form two courts of justice, of different natures; the one, denominated the *supreme court*, fulfils the duties of a court of appeal, and chief court, in the last instance, in all cases, both civil and criminal. Europeans, however, are always at liberty to appeal from these decisions to the supreme court of Holland; but, in consequence of the enormous expense and the interminable delays, cases are seldom or ever transmitted to Europe, except in instances of the most complicated nature, when the judgment rendered has been disputed amongst the members of the colonial court themselves.

The other courts, which are minor ones, consist of three, established in Batavia, Sanderang, and Soucabaya; they divide betwixt them all the provinces of the island; their jurisdiction extends to all cases, civil or criminal, without the assistance of a jury. The Europeans are judged according to the Dutch laws; but, in cases where the causes are those of the Javanese, the judges are assisted by the regent of the country, and the high priest of Java; in these cases, the punishments administered are conformable to the doctrines of the Koran and the primitive laws of the country, so long as these punishments do not exhibit too much contradiction against the laws of Holland, and are not of that cruel nature abolished by the Dutch government.

In each province, the resident presides over a court of justice, composed of the secretary to the residency, of the native regent, who commands under his orders, and of the principal Mussulman priest; the attributes of this court are mid-way betwixt those of the justices of the peace and the first court of tribunal. This court is charged with adjudicating upon crimes and offences of a graver nature, and transmitting such information to the counsellor or judge, who, every three months, takes a journey into the province, to regulate all criminal affairs, and to send the results of his investigation, as well as the criminal, to the court, which alone can sit in judgment on him. Happily, crime is scarce in Java; the most common offence is that of thieving, and murder is seldom committed, save when caused by an excess of jealousy on the part of a husband, who thus avenges himself upon the seducer of his wife; and, it is remarked in such cases, that, with few exceptions, the party surrenders himself a prisoner. The punishment inflicted upon the murderer is that of the convict's labours on the forced agricultural work, a punishment much lighter than that of confinement in our bagnios. Banishment is seldom inflicted, save upon rebels, or those who have had a hand in some seditious movement.

Each province has a resident at the head of its administration, who fills the office of governor, and who overlooks the conduct of the chiefs, and executes the laws; beneath him is a powerful native chief, called a regent, who in his turn commands other chiefs as subalterns, whose province is to transmit his orders to the natives, to superintend the payment due to the state by the peasantry, and to preserve by the police good order in all parts. The resident has also a body of troops at his command, to enforce obedience and command respect, especially where his district includes fortified posts.

The Dutch wisely seem to make as little military display as possible; in the interior provinces the residents often prefer even the total absence of the military, finding it much easier to govern without them, for we can easily imagine how much these men, their vocation being inert, embarrass and annoy the government by their insolence towards the inhabitants; always acting and thinking themselves the masters of the conquered nation. In the interior of Java, such is the state of the people, that a population of upwards of 500,000 persons, having but two Europeans to govern them, display a degree of readiness and obedience perfectly astonishing. Such an example as this speaks, is one worthy of imitation in colonial government, where the conqueror renders his presence the least offensive to a population strange to their masters by their customs, their manners, and their religion. Certainly, it is true, that a people so submissive as the Javanese is not often found, to make such a trial of.

All the functionaries hitherto mentioned, with the exception of the Indian Council, are removable at the will of the governor-general. It is he also who makes promotions in the army to the rank of colonel inclusive. This, be it understood, is totally distinct from the Dutch army in Europe. Promotion takes place according to seniority, but the governor-general is able to pass the term of any officer who, by his conduct, may have given umbrage: it is easy to conceive that, armed with such prerogatives, his authority is redoubtable, and that these functionaries, whose very existence depends upon him, dare scarcely permit themselves to express the least disapprobation of his acts. Complaints made to Holland respecting the governor's administration, have caused many years of disgrace to one of the most elevated officers of state, for making them public, and allowing their transmission. The richest commercial strangers, whom the governor-general may force to quit the colony with scarce any delay, dare hardly trust themselves audibly with the least observation upon the abuse of a power thus unlimited, for fear of compromising themselves. During our stay, the functionaries did not cease eulogizing the administrative system of Java, in terms of evident exaggeration; for, however great may be the results produced, however extensive the revenue Holland has derived from this colony, this species of government is not the less subject to well-founded criticism, at least in respect to the principle which forms its basis.

The revolt of the regent of the empire of Solo, which took place in 1826, and which caused great uneasiness to the Dutch, offered them, when once overcome, the finest possible opportunity of consolidating their power and increasing their territory, by the total dependence under which they placed the sultans of Surakatra and Djocokatra, and opened a smooth path for the accomplishment of their desired object—the absolute conquest of the whole island; to this end their views had always tended, their diplomacy always been directed. The sovereigns of these two kingdoms, already tied by treaties, before this epoch, to the Dutch government, which gave the Dutch the right to appoint out of their families a successor to the throne, to occupy military positions in their territories, and to have always a detachment of their troops to surround their persons, yet preserved sufficient influence with their people to render them intractable, and to excite the defiance of their allies; but at this time, the late treaties have completely prostrated them at the feet of Holland; a portion of their possessions has been given as an appendage to a prince, who, formerly one of their vassals, was thus rewarded for his services during the war. These sovereigns, who receive salaries from Holland to a large amount, as pensions in reparation for the loss of their authority, retain nothing more than a nominal rule over their subjects; and are simply instruments whom the Dutch yet find necessary to their own purposes, but are becoming daily more onerous, and from whom, upon the first opportunity, they will entirely free themselves.

The government draws largely upon its right to nominate a successor to the title out of the house of each prince, and takes especial care to choose such as are the least warlike in character, and who show the most surety of submission and devotedness to their supreme wills. Surrounded by the greatest honours in his palace, the fousounan, or emperor of Solo, is nothing but a prisoner, since he cannot go out without informing in advance the Dutch resident, who is charged with the inspection of all his acts, and the duty of watching that the terms of the treaties are fulfilled. An instance of what occurred some years since to the young emperor, who is now an exile at Amboine, and who was deposed instantly for having, during the night, without the necessary notice being given to the resident, gone to pray at the tombs of his fathers, is a good proof of the severity exercised towards these princes by their conquerors, in later times. The measure, it is true, was considered extremely severe by the greater part of the Javanese planters. The young emperor, who comports himself in his exile with much dignity, renders himself agreeable in the extreme by his distinguished manners, his liveliness, and his knowledge; he has completely adopted the European manners, and acknowledges the superiority of our civilization; even by this he perhaps inspires the watchfulness of the government, which fears some day he might apply it to his profit. The fidelity he displayed during the war of Java, when by allying himself to the rebels he might have caused much evil, merited a trifling indulgence for so light a fault; but such ideas of generosity are incompatible with a dominion so strange as that which a handful of Europeans exercise over nearly nine millions of Javanese.

In their intercourse with the general government, the princes, all sovereigns as they are, hold rank totally dependent upon its authority; they make use of the singular appellation of *grandfather*, and the government in their diplomatic relations with them always addresses them as, my *grandson*. These terms are obligatory in the court-language of Java, between a prince vassal and his suzerain, and are reciprocal. The Javanese language, which appears to be derived from the Sanscrit, is remarkable from this circumstance, that it is entirely different when spoken to a superior and when addressed to an inferior; there are such expressions in the conversation of the upper circles, as a man belonging to the people never permits himself to make use of. It may also be remarked, that the Polynesians have in their tongue expressions of a peculiar construction when speaking to a chief, which are forbidden to men of the inferior classes when they talk together.

European and native troops, composed entirely of soldiers from the different Malayan isles and of Africans, all equally strangers to Java, are, following the policy adopted, garrisoned in the sea-coast towns, as well as occupying an immense number of inland military stations. With this army, which consists of about 30,000 men for all the Dutch-Indian possessions, and of whom from 8,000 to 10,000 are Europeans, the Dutch consider themselves absolute masters of the country, and as having no cause of dread from the interior; but, at the same time, the Batavian government is not without some uneasiness from the circumstance of the English possessions entirely surrounding theirs, to which they augur that we covet the annexation of this island, on the score of our ignorance of its value when we ceded it to Holland.

Every effort of the government at the present day is directed to the concentration of its forces in the interior, to the formation of an inland capital, and the creation of military positions beyond the places of landing, with the view of rendering itself capable to hold their vassals in submission, to await with firmness the enemy after having allowed them to expend their fury in guerilla warfare, and partially forced them to submit, before bringing into play the main body of the Dutch forces, liable to be considerably weakened by the diseases incidental to the coast, and which maladies, so devastating in their effects on the European constitution, form one of the most powerful barriers nature has given them to repel foreign aggression. This system of self-defence appears perfectly rational, inasmuch as the ease with which Java was taken and captured in 1811, proves that the system then followed was totally useless; that now established is intended to balance, in cases of hostility, the inequality which exists between the Dutch marine and that of England, who could at any time she wished land numbers of troops at any point whatever upon the coast of this important island.

Since the rapid acquirement of Dutch territory already mentioned, considerable progress has been made in the cultivation of this island, and its products have been treble the quantity raised twenty years since. The attention of the government has been carefully turned to this subject, and for this purpose liberal advances were made to the colonists willing to establish themselves here, and clear these new lands, which cultivation has rendered of unexampled fertility.

Acting on this principle, every Hollander bringing guarantees as to his fitness, who was willing to consecrate his labour and industry to the raising of crops, received from government, not only a grant of lands for twenty years, but considerable pecuniary advances also, which he was required to invest in raising sugar-plantations; thereby creating vast property, without the least capital being looked for from him. The sole condition imposed upon him being to remit to the government his productions of sugar or coffee, at a certain price fixed by a reasonable tariff, although below that of the island. The repayment of the advances made to him were at first pre-levied upon the price of the crops of the first year, and no interest was required from him for the use of these advances. It is easy to conceive that, with such encouragements, the industrious Dutchman soon grew rich at Java; and numbers were, above all, drawn thither by the immense and rapid fortunes made by those who first acceded to these terms. Latterly the tariff of productions has materially diminished, and has reduced the benefits of the cultivators in augmenting those of the government; hence arise the immense revenues which it draws from the island of Java, which previously was to them of no worth; and here is the source of the augmentation, upon a large scale, of the productions of this island, of which a great portion is still waste, despite its immense population. Now it has become more difficult to obtain grants of lands; the advances made by government are comparatively insignificant; and the colonists must possess sufficient capital to enable them to undertake the expenses of their establishments; now that the first movement has been made, there is no lack of people to invest their capital, and undertake parallel enterprises; and the government, without running any risks, reaps the fruit of the golden seed it has so wisely and skilfully sown. Than this, nothing can be more just, provided it is done in moderation; but, unhappily, it is reproached at the present moment with making its monopoly most injurious to the interests of the country, by the immense reduction which it has effected in the tariff of prices at which it purchases the various provisions. As to how far these reproaches are merited, it is not possible to say.

Let us now glance at the power at the disposal of the colonists for the culture of the lands thus granted to them. However large the population of Java might be, the inhabitants have so few wants, and the soil is so truly prolific, that the enticements of gain could not persuade them to shake off their habitual indolence, and to labour more than was actually necessary to supply their animal wants. Whilst under the authority of their chiefs, who were the entire proprietors of the soil, and to whom they were attached as so many glebe serfs, they cultivated the land for the profit of their lords, receiving from them only the necessaries indispensable to the subsistence of themselves and their families. These chiefs enjoyed a power, a caprice, totally unlimited, and could dispose of everything belonging to the peasant, without the latter, habituated to this tie of slavery, rebelling against his authority, or appealing by remonstrance. The lord of the soil but rarely abused this authority; the mildness with which he exacted obedience rendered it an easy task; contenting himself with little, he required but little from his serfs. The peasant laboured then conscientiously, and the earth was bringing forth but little of what it was capable of producing. The Javanese, to whom there wanted in this social organization the stimulating life of the spirit of ownership, did but deliver themselves up with more gusto to the delights of that idleness, to which the inhabitants of equatorial countries are so much inclined, where prolific nature requires so little from the toil of man to provide abundantly for the first wants of existence. But the Dutch, whose aim, in establishing themselves upon this island, was to draw from it every species of colonial produce that could be raised in a large quantity, perceived, after a lengthened essay, that in this they should never succeed by adopting the same mode that these chiefs had used, of making use of a portion of the produce by way of impost, and by creating an easy poll-tax. This might succeed perfectly in meeting the expenditure of their occupation of the island, but would not create an extensive commerce; for the Javanese cultivated nothing but rice, and a small quantity of other vegetables, that they consumed; and produced no more yearly than was strictly necessary for their means of subsistence, and payment of their tribute. They attempted to arrive at their ends at first, by imposing upon the harvest the exorbitant impost of one-third of its produce; but this measure was but little calculated to encourage agriculture. The labourer, deprived of a large portion of the fallow-ground, was not willing to take the trouble of cultivating for another party; and the capitalists were but little disposed to place their funds in agricultural enterprises, in which the government were to be such large gainers.

[To be continued.]

WESTERN AUSTRALIA; HER CALUMNIATORS AND HER CHAMPIONS.

We are ever disposed to set our face against the system of puffing, but we are equally alive to the necessity of publicity; and the false statements disseminated by the former course, are no more to be deplored, and not more mischievous in their results, than the ignorance which prevails in the absence of the latter. We do not wish to draw invidious comparisons, and shall therefore abstain from enumerating instances of the ill effects of puffing; but we may certainly point to Western Australia, in proof of the necessity of publicity. In natural advantages far superior to many of its neighbours, its progress has been but slow, simply because the public were never made aware of their existence; and because, in the absence of such information, they were induced and encouraged to believe that it did not possess them; and this colony, with its fine climate and advantageous situation, with fruitful soil, and bays well stocked with whales, is, in the fifteenth year of its existence, scarcely known to be a dependency of Britain. Hence we seldom meet with its name even in colonial newspapers, and never hear its progress rightly stated; hence the impunity with which rival interests have spread statements prejudicial to it, and hence its slow progress and small population. But better days, we think we can predict, are now dawning on it. We do not mean that the colonial body at home have taken any pains to obtain a correct view of its state and prospects—*that* the colonists had no right to expect. The public are always prone to adopt the general belief, and content to take to the ready-made opinions put forth by those who are supposed to have means of forming a correct estimate, without inquiring whether they have an interest in blinding themselves, and deceiving others; and, therefore, the *ex-parte* announcements which exalted other colonies at the expense of poor undefended Western Australia, gained general belief. Of course they were true, (so the public argued,) because the colonists themselves could not—or, at all events, did not—deny them. If they were false, why did they not expose their falsehood? But the public entirely overlooked the probabilities, that those who were prompted to invent these fictions, would take care that they should not fall into the hands of any who were likely to reply to them; and that, even if they were seen and refuted by the colonists, but one of the refutations would find its way, where fifty of the original mischievous statements had been seen.

We have lately received a private letter, brought by the last arrival from Perth, in which the writer, speaking of a recent calumniator of the colony, says, "If ever I felt wrathful in my life, I do against the author of 'New Holland.' I knew him well, knew every circumstance of his residence here, the feelings by which he was influenced, the extent of his knowledge; and all these convince me, that he was, perhaps, of all others of our visitors, the very worst qualified to write our history. The worst of it," he adds, "is, that before we can defend ourselves, all the mischief will be done, and that, all late in the day as it will be, few will ever see the antidote." So it has been, to the cost of the colony, while her settlers expected that their fellow-subjects, in this country, would take the trouble to inquire into the truth of what they read; but they have now discovered, that the emigrating classes will not *inquire*, but must be *told;* and have learned, by the gall and wormwood of experience, that it has grown into an actual business, and amounts to an almost constant fund of employment, to reply to falsehoods founded on interest or ignorance. Like weeds which are unattended to, these untruths have grown and spread—one falsity springing and issuing from another; really honest, truth-seeking writers taking them for granted, and lending their aid in increasing them, and interested ones taking advantage of them, and extending their baneful influence with alacrity. To stem this torrent, the "Western Australian Society" has been formed at Perth, and has already corrected many false impressions, and put forth as many correct ones. Its views have been forwarded by some zealous friends of the colony in England, and particularly by the publication in London of a neat little periodical called the *Swan River News,* which is designed to furnish accurate information on the state and prospects of the colony. So far as we can judge from the contents of the first two numbers of this work, the colony is in a healthy condition. The ingenuity of the settlers has discovered several new articles of export, but none appear to us to be so promising as the prospects of a future extensive exportation of wine. Our readers will be enabled to obtain a better idea of the condition of the colony, if we extract a few paragraphs from the last number of the *Swan River News,* which seems to contain a very useful selection of information, and presents many interesting details of the past progress, present state, and future prospects, of Western Australia. The first extract which we shall make is an abstract of the Governor's important observations on the revenue:—

On the subject of the colonial revenue and expenditure of the year 1842-3, and the estimated finances for 1844-5, the Governor made the following remarks at the council-meeting of the 20th July:

The Revenue of 1842-3.

	£	s.	d.
The receipts during the past years, 1842-3, have been......	£9,544	0	1
The receipts for the previous years, 1841-2, were......	10,080	18	7
Showing a diminution of	£536	18	6

This has been principally caused by a falling off in the land sales of 1,366*l.* 15*s.* 6*d.*; for, although deficiencies do appear in the duty on wines of 380*l.* 1*s.*, in the repayment of loans of 149*l.* 1*s.* 6*d.*, in the fees of public offices of 44*l.* 1*s.* 6*d.*, in the duty on goods sold by auction of 38*l.* 6*s.* 4*d.*, with some trifling amounts as respects other items; yet these have been more than counterbalanced by an increase of 415*l.* 3*s.* 3*d.* in the *ad valorem* duty on imported goods; of 263*l.* 10s. in licenses to sell spirits; of 228*l.* 12*s.* for warehouse rent of spirits in bond; of 218*l.* 7s. in the duty on imported spirits; of 110*l.* 8*s.* 1*d.* in the duty on tobacco; of 92*l.* 11*s.* 7*d.* in the Post-office receipts; and of a few smaller sums, under other heads: showing that the main sources from which we look for an income to supply the wants of the colony are unimpaired.

With regard to the expenditure of the same period, his Excellency says;—

	£	s.	d.
The total expenditure, including outstanding liabilities to the 1st of April, but without reckoning the sum paid for labour, has been, during the past year	£10,246	15	11
The amount of the estimate sanctioned by the Council was	9,958	12	6
Shewing an overdraft of.................	£288	3	5

Which has arisen from the excess in payments on account of the following services: Public buildings, such as the erection of a bonded store at Fremantle, addition to the gaol at Albany and court-house at York, and repair of the court-house and government-house at Perth; 341*l.* 5*s.* 7*d.*; the conveyance of mails, under which head are included the stamps and bags for the several post-offices throughout the country, together with the boxes for the foreign mails made up in Perth, extra mails to and from Fremantle, and assistant in the Perth post-office, 185*l.* 0*s.* 9*d.* On a former occasion, I stated it to be my intention to discontinue the distributions, as a regular practice, of flour to the Aborigines, and to restrain the expense on their account to the maintenance and establishment of schools, and the allowance to native constables. The large sum which appears as here set down beyond the estimate, has been required chiefly on account of arrears of supplies of flour furnished by the commissariat, some of as old standing as December, 1841, but which have only been brought in for payment to the Government in the course of the past year, 132*l.* 3*s.* 3d. Surveys and explorations, being exigencies of the service, 126*l.* 16*s.* 5*d.* Roads and bridges, 100*l.*; this is an advance which will be deducted from the sum borne upon the estimate under the same head for the current year. Pilot establishment, for the laying down of additional buoys, 76*l.* 15*s.* 8*d.* Police establishment, being an addition to the mounted police force at Albany and Toodyay, and a superintendent of police in Wellington and Sussex districts, 64*l.* 10*s.* 6*d.* Miscellaneous, 66*l.* 5*s.* 5*d.* Colonial Hospital, 12*l.* 3*s.* 11*d.* Constable at Albany, 5*l.*; this is an error in the estimate, the salary being 20*l.*, whereas it is only set down at 15*l.* Postmaster at the Vasse, 15*l.*; a new appointment consequent on the mail being now regularly conveyed to that station. Surveyor General's office, 3*l.* 6*s.* 8*d.* And lastly, a trifling sum of 7*s.* 7*d.*, overdrawn on account of the collection of revenue, a charge which depends in a great measure on the number of vessels which may visit our ports, and the time they may remain there.

The next point is an estimate of the anticipated revenue and expenditure for the finance year ending 1845, on which his Excellency says :—

I have set down the probable receipts for that period at	£10,395	0	0
The total collection last year having been	9,544	0	1
Shewing an anticipated increase of............	£850	19	11

In this calculation I have omitted, because of their extreme fluctuations and uncertainty, all sums likely to be received for land sales, which last year realized 647*l.*; but I look to an increase of about 400*l.* from the new duties on imported spirits; of about 150*l.* on wines and tobacco; of 50*l.* on goods sold by auction; of 150*l.* on fees of public offices arising out of the increased rate of charges in the Registry office, which I shall have occasion to submit to you; of 50*l.* for the warehouse rent of spirits in bond; of 100*l.* in the Post-office receipts, which, from the strict and regular system now prevailing in that department, are likely, I trust, to become annually more productive, and more equal to the heavy charge for the conveyance of mails which appears upon the estimates.

The sum voted by the Council in the course of the last session for the wants of the current year, and by which, with the sanction of the Council, I regulated the expenses of the year just concluded, was	£9,958	12	6
The total of the sums which I now have to propose for the expenditure of the ensuing year amount to	10,169	19	2
Making an increase of.................	£211	6	8

This results either from the proposed additional allowances or new appointments.

The additional allowances are—

For two assistant surveyors	£23	6	8
For second clerk Colonial Secretary's Office	25	0	0
For Postmaster General, Perth	50	0	0
For Postmaster, Guildford	5	0	0
For Surgeon, Fremantle	50	0	0
For Constable, Albany	5	0	0
For Public Buildings	150	0	0

The new appointments are—

A Clerk in the Audit-office	100	0	0
Postmaster, Vasse	15	0	0
Do. Pinjarrah	5	0	0
Do. Canning	15	0	0
Chaplain on Upper Swan	100	0	0
Clerk in the office of Registrar of Deeds	100	0	0
Tidewaiter at Perth	50	0	0
Do. Vasse	35	0	0
Constable, Australind	10	0	0
	£738	6	8

Against which is to be set off the following diminution in the expenditure—

Allowance to acting Advocate-General	£100			
Administration of justice	100			
Conveyance of mails	7			
Pilot establishment and furniture for public offices which are both to be paid out of the miscellaneous fund	120			
Miscellaneous	200			
		527	0	0
The actual increase of the estimate now brought forward over that of the present year is therefore		£211	6	8

The last division of His Excellency's observations is explanatory of the payments on the introduction of labour:—

	£	s.	d.
The balance of the labour fund on the 1st of April, 1842, was	£4,550	1	4
The receipts in the course of the year 1842-3, from sales of crown lands, fines, rents, and transfer duty amounted to	763	7	6
Making a total of	5,313	8	10
Out of which there has been paid bounty on account of immigrants introduced by private parties	72	0	0
Gratuities to the officers of the ship *Simon Taylor* ...	172	17	7
Repayment of a fine on country land disallowed by Secretary of State	45	2	6
Supplies to immigrants by the *Simon Taylor*, whilst in the depôt at Fremantle, from the 20th of August to the 19th of October, 1842	266	3	5
Portion of the passage-money of immigrants by the *Simon Taylor*	1,000	0	0
Total payments to be deducted	1,556	3	5
	5,313	8	10
Leaving a balance due to the labour fund on the 1st April, 1843, of	£3,757	5	5

Further payments have, however, been made since the commencement of the present year, consisting of—

	£	s.	d.
The remainder of the passage-money of the immigrants by the *Simon Taylor*	£1,000	0	0
Gratuities to the officers of the ship *Success*	112	10	3
Repayment of deposits for which we have received a credit in England	22	0	0

And there still remains to be paid for—

	£	s.	d.
The passage of 108 adult immigrants by the *Success* ...	1,395	18	0
Pay of Acting Superintendent of depôt at Fremantle ...	32	0	6
Supplies to immigrants by *Success* whilst in the depôt at Fremantle, about	120	0	0
Sundry expenses at Fremantle	20	18	2
Total to be deducted	2,703	6	11
From the balance above stated of	3,757	5	5
Leaving actually due to the labour fund	£1,053	18	6

But I must apprise you that, although this sum is due, and ought to be forthcoming for the supply of labour, I have been compelled to make use of it to meet the urgent demands on other accounts; and it is because of the necessity I have found myself under of having recourse to this fund, that I was so anxious to obtain the sanction of the Council to the act lately passed for imposing an additional duty on imported spirits. I now give notice of my intention to move the first reading of the ordinance for a supplementary estimate to cover the extra expenses of the past year, and to meet the proposed amount of expenditure for the year ending the 31st of March, 1845.

The next article from which we shall extract, gives a history of the origin and purposes of the Western Australian Society.

It was on the suggestion of an anonymous correspondent in the *Inquirer*, signing himself "Colonicus," that a general meeting of the colonists took place at the Court-house, Perth, in May, 1842, and formed themselves into a society, for the purpose of giving publicity to the affairs of the colony, and attracting public attention to the progress of its settlers. At the head of this society, and foremost among its members, the Governor, the Colonial Secretary, Surveyor-General, Advocate-General, Colonial Chaplain, Colonial Surgeon, and most of the influential inhabitants, were instantly enrolled, and funds raised for carrying out the intentions of its founders. The purposes to which these subscriptions were to be applied, are detailed in the prospectus as being "the insertion in the metropolitan and provincial journals, of informational paragraphs and advertisements, giving an outline of the state of the colony and its resources, with a view to attracting to it the attention of capitalists and of the labouring classes." This has been designated by a contemporary, "puffing," but no reasonable person can consider it as such a course. The statements proposed to be published are no exaggerations, but simply fair details of the qualifications of the colony, in the matters of climate, soil, and situation, and plain accounts of its past slow but steady course, and its present unostentatious but solvent state. At the first meeting of the society, upwards of fifty pounds were subscribed for this purpose, and the sum speedily remitted to England, where it was expended in advertisements which went the round of the London and provincial papers, and in circulars freely distributed throughout the empire. Whether those advertisements were of as much service as was anticipated, we are not in a position to state; but we have every reason to believe, that even these first scarcely organized operations of the society were productive of much benefit, in showing that the colonists were aroused to activity, and in exciting sympathetic energy among their friends in England. But we believe they had even still more direct tendencies, and that on the strength of the statements thus put forth, several persons, both of the labouring and of the higher classes, have been induced to emigrate.

"We have frequently seen paragraphs in the public papers which betray the grossest ignorance, not only of the state and resources, but actually of the position and extent of Western Australia; we have seen even in a London paper devoted to colonial interests, Swan River designated a "colony," and Western Australia a "settlement," the latter a portion of the former; we have smiled at a list of ships' arrivals, as given in the leading journal of Europe, at *Perth*, a town inaccessible to shipping, and have heard of Fremantle as the "capital of the colony." It is expedient that those who are daily dispensing information to the millions, should be first furnished with accurate information themselves; and it is far more politic to direct such, through the channels by which the mass is supplied, than to attempt at once to scatter it over the entire community, where it would be but as a drop in the ocean. If the press be rightly informed, the people to whom it conveys its intelligence will also be rightly informed, and, to furnish correct information to the press is the only means by which we can hope, extensively or effectually, to furnish correct information to the body of the people. It will, therefore, be proper occasionally to enlighten British journalists on Western Australian matters, and this is a department in which the society can be made to effect much good. We also have another project in contemplation, which we trust to realize in a few months—to publish in a future number of our journal, a succinct and impartial account of the colony, showing its qualifications and resources, honestly and without exaggeration, and so condensed as not to trespass too much upon our space, and yet to omit no important detail touching upon the climate, the state of agriculture, and of society, the situation and natural productions of the colony, and stating the rates of passage-money for every class of emigrants. This impression we shall circulate throughout the empire, taking care that the principal hotels of the rural districts are furnished with a copy, and that it has an extensive and desirable circulation; and should we succeed in this, we have other projects in *embryo*, which we hope will be of equal benefit."

With the following observations on the subject of colonial distillation, we fully concur, believing that the prohibition on the manufacture of brandy is a great impediment to the progress of the colony.

"From our summary of the proceedings of the Legislative Council, it will be seen, that the subject of distillation is engaging the attention of the Western Australians, and as this is a question of much importance, we shall give an outline of its details.

"Three years ago, the Legislative Council, on the motion of the Governor and the advice of the Home Government, passed an act prohibiting distillation in the colony, but the cultivation of the vine having since been extensively entered upon, the evils of this prohibition are beginning to become apparent. For the repeal of this act, so far as it related to brandy, Mr. Mackie presented a petition to the council on the 6th of July, signed by Mr. McDermott, on behalf of the Vineyard Society, the substance of which was, that the restriction was oppressive and injurious; that it rendered the colonists dependent on foreign countries, and compelled the colonial cultivators to waste the marc or refuse of the vine; that the act, if not repealed, would curtail the operations of the society; that distillation would not reduce the revenue, but would render the people better able to pay its taxes; and, lastly, that it would prevent the increase of vice, by substituting the consumption of domestic wine for foreign imported spirits. It appeared from this petition that the society only prayed for the distillation of brandy to be used in the manufacture of wine, and not of any other spirit, or for any other purpose. On the 13th of July, Mr. Mackie brought the subject under notice of the council, by moving for a bill "to permit the distillation of brandy from the products of vineyards within the colony." He enlarged upon the arguments of the petitioners, and contended that the wishes of the society were neither extravagant nor irrational. The colonial secretary warmly seconded the motion, but urged for a more extensive permission of distillation. The Governor opposed the motion on three grounds; firstly, that it would cause a falling off of the revenue, as the additional necessary expense of an excise establishment, and the decrease of receipts in duties on imported spirits, would far exceed the revenue arising from the grants of distillation licenses; secondly, that the measure would be premature, as the vineyard cultivation was not in a sufficiently advanced state to demand it; and thirdly, because internal distillation would render the colonists a community of drunkards. [We may here pause to state, that the whole of these objections were anticipated, and previously refuted by Mr. Mackie, although the Governor did not in any case allude to that gentleman's remarks. On the matter of excise, Mr. Mackie suggested that, as few persons in the colony possessed the means of entering upon distillery, it would be confined to one or two capitalists, and thus the excise establishment would be proportionately small. He also suggested that the government residents, who were already collectors of customs, could also be appointed collectors of excise, and thus any additional appointments obviated. With regard to the motion being premature, Mr. Mackie very reasonably observed, that if they were to await the increase of vineyards, the repeal of the act would be indefinitely postponed, as, while it was in force, it was not likely that vineyards would increase to any extent; and, lastly, in reply to the expected temperance point of objection, he contended that, if so disposed, the colonists could as well indulge to excess in imported as in internally manufactured spirits.] His Excellency was followed, on the same side, by the Advocate-General, and the debate was now unaccountably extended to the subject of *general* distillation, which Mr. Moore opposed on exactly the same grounds as the Governor. He admitted that "distillation would be carried on by some two or three capitalists," and yet declared that "a whole train of excise officers, and a whole army of collectors, would have to be provided."

"Now, comparing these passages, in which the calculations appear to us rather inconsistent with each other, we should apprehend that, if an excise establishment became necessary on such an extensive scale, the "one or two distilleries" which these "whole trains and armies" were to attend to, would stand a fair chance of being inundated. The honourable gentleman also appeared to apprehend danger from the quality of the article likely to be produced, as he feared that spirits of an injurious nature would be manufactured, to suit the tastes of inveterate drunkards; but surely it would be the duty of some of the large establishments which its opposers fear the repeal would render necessary, to test the strength and quality of the liquor, and prevent the sale of deleterious spirit. The advocate-general concluded by stating that he considered the use of brandy to be totally unnecessary in the manufacture of wine, but this statement was distinctly denied by the next speaker, Mr. Leake, who declared that if alcohol were *not* introduced, the state of the atmosphere or a thunder-storm would materially injure the production of a season; and he quoted several authorities in corroboration of his assertion. Mr. Leake further declared his conviction that no loss would accrue to the revenue, but, granting the probability, he urged that it was no justification for an act of private injustice. He suggested that certain restrictions might be imposed, and concluded by supporting Mr. Mackie's motion. The surveyor-general briefly opposed it, but on precisely the same ground as the governor. Mr. Tanner, although opposed to distillation at present, was anxious for a full investigation, and, with the view of promoting inquiry, supported the motion. Major Irwin disapproved of the proposed measure, in the conviction that its benefits, if any, would be far less than the evils which it would entail. Mr. Mackie ably summed up the arguments and replied, after which the council divided, and his motion was lost, the numbers being equal, and four members voting on each side.—We cannot but look at this issue of the question with considerable regret, believing, as we firmly do, that the permission of distillation would be a great boon to the colony. To detail our reasons for this conviction would be but to repeat the arguments set forth in the petition, and we are the more confirmed in it by finding that, throughout the debate, not one tenable objection was brought against it. The objections of the governor appear at a first glance plausible and correct; but Mr. Mackie's remarks, in which he anticipates *every one* of those objections, at once cancel their effect, and we cannot but feel surprised at his Excellency persisting in them after they had been so clearly proved to be groundless. As for the opposition of the other members, it was a mere echo of the governor's, and on reviewing the entire discussion, we do not find a single original reason given for the continuance of the prohibition, which was not open to, and entirely answered by, Mr. Mackie's pre-refutation. Even in the light of financial policy, we consider the matter to have been wrongly disposed of, for surely a measure which is for the benefit of the tax-payers must, in the end, be beneficial to the exchequer. We are, however, glad that the question has been agitated, and that the opposition to it is far from powerful; and we trust that, ere long, that opposition will be diminished by the facts forced upon them by experience, and that they will assent to the repeal of the prohibition before its action shall have destroyed the promising cultivation of the vine, which is yet in its infancy, and awaits only the removal of that impediment, to become general, extensive, and profitable.

"We are the more encouraged in the hope, by finding that the matter was not allowed to drop at the conclusion of the debate, and that the last accounts leave the question still *in statu quo*. Mr. Leake, at the meeting of Council on the 20th of July, moved the appointment of a select committee to inquire into the subject of colonial distillation, and himself, conjointly with Messrs. Mackie, Tanner, and Moore, were then named without opposition. On the 2d August, that committee brought up its report, signed by Mr. Moore as chairman, in which they state their opinion that it is not at present expedient to sanction *general* distillation, but that distillation limited to the products of vineyards is not open to the same objections. They report their apprehension that a prohibition of the manufacture of brandy may discourage the investment of capital in vine cultivation; as, under the present system, the marc and lees of the vine are useless to the grower. They then state that during the year ending 31st March, 1843, 17,000 gallons of spirits were imported, which was an increase on former years, and deduce from authentic calculations that before the colonists could distil that quantity, they must possess 850 acres of vineyards; this they mention in proof of the groundlessness of any fear that the revenue would be materially injured by the loss of import duties; and, farther to remove loss beyond possibility, they suggest that the distiller, in addition to paying a heavy fee for his license, should be subject to the same duty as the importer; this would still leave him an advantage over the latter of freight and shipping charges only. The committee advise that the existing prohibition should be continued until thirty acres of land are under vine cultivation throughout the colony, in parcels of not less than one acre each; and that then it should be partially relaxed, on petition of the vineyard proprietors; that the manufacture of brandy should be allowed only in towns, or where the governor may permit; that responsible sureties be given by every licensee; that the officers of customs and magistrates have free access to all distilleries by day and night; that the finding on the premises of any article, except products of the vine, from which spirits may be extracted, subject the distiller to a heavy fine; that the licensee shall not sell a less quantity than twenty gallons; that every sale be recorded before a collector of customs or magistrate; and that no spirits be removed from the premises without a permit, or until the duty thereon is paid. This report appears rather favourable to the petitioners' views than otherwise, but defers the required relief until vineyard cultivation is farther advanced. The vine-growers have now therefore a goal to look forward to, and it is for them to strive their utmost to put the required number of acres into cultivation; and then to demand the promised repeal on the conditions proposed by the committee."

We must now close our extracts, for the present, from these interesting details of Western Australia; but shall take occasional opportunities of reporting the progress of the colony from the same sources.

THE DISMEMBERMENT OF SPAIN AND HER COLONIES.*

When Charles V., the grandson of the Emperor Maximilian I., and the heir through him of the vast dominions of the house of Hapsburg, entered in childhood upon the inheritance which descended from his ancestors on the mother's side, his first great duty was to consolidate from the disjointed materials which were scattered around him—from Castile, which fell into his hands through his grandmother Isabella, and from Arragon and Navarre, the possessions of his grandfather Ferdinand—the united kingdom of Spain. Under his domains were included (in part through marriage, in part through conquest), the Netherlands, Naples, Sicily, Sardinia, Malta, and the Balearic Islands, containing a surface of 220,740 square miles. During a reign of forty years, Charles V. had so used and nurtured the great resources committed to his charge, that at the time of his resignation, the kingdom of Spain, with its dependencies, had arisen to the first rank among European nations. By the conquest of the dukedom of Milan, and through the acquisition of those immense tracts of country which were then included within Mexico, Peru, and Chili, the Spanish territory in Europe was swollen to 222,000, in America to 3,560,000 square miles; and, with an army the best disciplined in the world, with a navy the most extensive, the Spanish emperor became possessed of a degree of political power which, since Charlemagne, has been unequalled.

Never was there a monarch more fitted than Philip II., both on account of his sleepless energy, his crafty politics, his personal power, for the inferior management of so great a charge. For forty-two years he continued on the throne in full possession of his remarkable faculties; he was supported by the most distinguished statesmen and generals of his age; he was enriched by the most inexhaustible mines of wealth; his domains, by the extinction of the male branch of the royal family of Portugal, were swollen by the accession of that powerful country, with its American dependencies—and yet, when he left the throne, he left it with its internal strength dissipated. *He had mistaken the spirit of the age;* he had broken where he had meant to bend; by the daring irritation of his tyranny, he had stimulated one portion of his people to rebellion—he had degraded the other into imbecility; and, when he died, the Netherlands were independent, and Spain exhausted.

* *Vide* Vol. iv., (Old Series), page 257.

From the date of Philip II., Spain has suffered irreparable losses, which have not only diminished her population and shrunk her territory, but have destroyed her internal prosperity and her external trade. From Philip III. the acknowledgment of the independence of the Netherlands was finally wrung; and a treaty, which never from the iron hand of Philip II. could have been drawn, was executed; by which Spain lost 8,560 square miles. His successor, Philip IV., lost, in 1640, the kingdom of Portugal (34,400 square miles), with its colonial possessions (3,660,000 square miles), together with the island of Jamaica (5,380 square miles); in 1655 and in 1659, by the Pyrenean peace, the countries of Roussillon and Artois, a part of Charolais, and a number of forts in Flanders, Nemours, and Hennegan. Under Charles II., the last and most feeble of the Spanish line of the house of Hapsburgh (1665—1700), Spain, through the entire inefficiency of her plans, and the utter weakness of her exertions, sunk without an effort into the second rank of European powers. Through the peace of Aix-la-Chapelle (1668), she lost the remainder of her Netherland reservations, together with half of Saint Domingo; and, by the peace of Nymwegen, the whole of Franche Comte. Through the twelve years' war of the Spanish succession, between the houses of Bourbon and Hapsburg, a fresh dismemberment took place. The house of Hapsburg, after being recompensed with the Spanish territories north of the Pyrenees, and, seven years later, with the island of Sardinia, was forced to cede to the house of Savoy the kingdom of Sicily; by which process Spain lost a territory amounting to 67,100 square miles. Under the Bourbon-Anjou ascendancy, which commenced with the reign of Philip V. (1713—1746), Gibraltar and the island of Minorca were ceded to Great Britain, amounting together to 305 square miles. Under the new dynasty, the Spanish dominions, which at its accession amounted in Europe to 168,640 square miles, and in America to 4,720,000 square miles, remained for fifty years undiminished: because, in the first place, France, from an hereditary rival, had become a family ally; and because, in the second place, the Netherlands, and the kingdoms of Lombardy and of Naples, which had become the theatre of war, had long ceased to be parts of the Spanish king's heritage. On the establishment of the Bourbons on the throne of the Two Sicilies (1735), and of Parma and Piacenza (1748), it was agreed upon by the contracting powers, as an indispensable requisite to their consent, that on no contingency of descent should the crowns of the two newly-established families be allowed to unite with that of the Spanish Bourbons. On the death, without heirs, therefore, of Ferdinand VI.

(1746, d. August 15, 1759), Charles III., king of Naples, being called to the Spanish throne, his second son, Charles, following him to Spain as Prince of the Asturias, on account of the idiocy of his elder brother, the third son, Ferdinand, then eight years old, was proclaimed king of the Two Sicilies.

During the reign of Charles III., Spain lifted herself to a level in some degree commensurate with her great resources. The acquisition of Louisiana, the conquests among the Portuguese possessions in South America, the recovery of Florida, the re-conquest of Minorca (1782), valuable as they were, were far inferior to the advantages which arose from the restoration of trade, the establishment of manufactures, and the regulation, under Aranda, Compomanes, and the Duke of Herida Blanca, the most eminent statesman of their day, of the disordered finances of the realm. But, promising as was the revival of Spanish power under auspices so happy, it was soon overbalanced by a succession of misfortunes which took their origin in the vacillatory and indolent character of Charles IV. Stretching over a period of twenty years (13th December, 1788—abdicating 19th March, 1808), and encountering in its lapse the shock of the French revolution, it is not to be wondered that the reign of that unfortunate monarch should have been productive of consequences most grave and disastrous. From the treaty of Basle (July 22, 1795), by which a strict alliance with France was clenched, Spain was exposed to the most lawless incursions, both from the allies whom she acquired, and the enemies she provoked. Fleet after fleet was lost on the high seas; cargoes of gold and silver, fresh from South America, were captured within the sight of ports to which they were bound; a navy, once the most mighty, and then the most cumbrous in Europe, was swept from the ocean; the islands of Trinidad (February 18, 1797) and Minorca (November 15, 1798) were successfully conquered by the English; and the entire foreign and colonial trade annihilated. By the continental peace, concluded at Amiens on March 17, 1802, a temporary reprieve was obtained, as a price for which, Spain ceded Trinidad to England, and to France the State of Louisiana.

On the renewal of hostilities between France and Great Britain, Spain paid at the commencement (from October 30, 1803, to December 12, 1804,) a monthly subsidy of 4,000,000 francs, as a price of neutrality. It was not long before the internal dissensions broke out, which led to the overthrow of the reigning family. The seaboard was rent with open rebellion; the interior was distracted with secret intrigue; and the court, whose attention should have been absorbed with the great emergency it was soon to meet, was occupied in the constant bickerings which were taking place between the blind and feeble king and prince Ferdinand of the Asturias. The three-century bond between Spain and the American colonies was ruptured. The reign of Joseph Napoleon (from January 6, 1808, to December 8, 1813,) produced nothing more than a temporary influence on the reigning dynasty, as Ferdinand VII. was recognized by the treaty of Paris (1814) as occupying the same throne from which he had been driven by the Emperor of France, 1808. Melancholy, however, was the change between Spain after the restoration, and Spain before the invasion. The American colonies were irrevocably lost—in part by conquest, in part by revolution; and though Ferdinand VII. attempted on his return to recover his alienated possessions, he found his arms too weak to effect so great an enterprise. So exhausted was the strength of the once giant empire of Spain, that after the formal renunciation of Guatimala, (July 1, 1823); after the defeat of the Spanish army at Ayacucho, (December 9, 1824,) and the consequential evacuation of Peru; after the surrender of St. Juan de Ulloa, (Nov. 18, 1825,) by which the last fortress in America was lost; the mother-country gave up all hopes of retaining her ancient authority over her rich but apostate children. Her territories had lost under the two last-mentioned reigns more than 4,600,000 square miles of land, which had been endowed by nature with the most diversified and inexhaustible treasures, and all that remained from a dominion once almost universal in the New World was the Island of Cuba,* (46,000 square miles,) called by Ferdinand VII., when all else had deserted him, the "faithful and true;" and St. Juan de Puerto Rico,† (3,780 square miles,) with a few of the smaller islands that form part of the great western Archipelago. The colonies in the other hemisphere are still more unimportant. In Asia, Spain still possesses the Manila, or Philippine Islands, with a part of the surrounding clusters, which are more remarkable for the amount of their territory (48,400 square miles) than for the wealth of their trade, or the number of their inhabitants. In Africa, there still remains the first and most historical of the Spanish conquests—the cities of Ceuta, Melilla, Pennon de Velez, and Alhuzemas, with a territory cramped by invasions within

* In 1834, the annual value of the united exports and imports were still about thirty-five million piastres, and the income of the island about ten million piastres.

† In 1834, the exports were about five million piastres, and the government income upwards of two million piastres.

30 square miles, which formed, centuries ago, the battle-ground where Christians and Moors met in that deadly shock which drove the crescent from the south of Spain and the north of Africa. As the European territory of Spain, as settled by the Versailles treaty, amounts to 168,940 square miles, 272,080 square miles may be taken as forming the present measure of her possessions in the hemispheres together.

On the accession of Maria Isabella II., on September 29th, 1833, the kingdom was left to experience, under the imbecile government of an infant queen, those accumulated disasters which the misgovernment of three centuries had produced. In the words of Schubert, one of the most frigid of the German historians, the horrors which have been experienced in the intestine wars that succeeded, have surpassed in terror the utmost atrocities of the dark ages. G. T. W.

COLONIAL STATISTICS.

[NEW SERIES.]

THE ISLAND OF JAMAICA.

Geography.—Jamaica, standing in the first rank of British colonies, is the largest of the West India islands, and the principal of the Leeward Islands. It is situated 4,000 miles south-west of England, in latitude 17° 56′ north, Kingston, longitude 76° 53′ west. In extent, Jamaica is 165 miles east to west; in breadth, 40 miles. The extreme altitude is 8,184 feet; area, 6,400 square miles, or 4,080,000 acres. Jamaica is divided into three counties, and twenty-one parishes, viz., Middlesex (centre), 9 parishes; Surrey (east), 7 parishes; Cornwall (west), 5 parishes. Chief towns, Kingston, St. Jago de la Vega, or Spanish Town, Port Royal, Old Harbour.

Face of the Country.—Mountainous; the elevation of the celebrated Blue Mountains at the Peak is 7,150 feet (some authorities assert that it is 8,000 feet at the highest point). What are termed the Blue Mountains cross the country from east to west, and are intersected themselves by other ridges running from north to south. The mountains are covered by many kinds of trees. Jamaica is watered by numerous streams (see *Rivers*), none of them, however, navigable, except for boats; the vallies are most fertile. Great numbers of wildfowl are met with, and rice-birds, esteemed great delicacies. In the vallies are such a variety of fruit-trees, as to make the country look like a paradise. Of the 4,000,000 acres given to the island, Jamaica is stated to contain only 1,907,089 acres held under grants from the crown in 1789; and of this extent only 1,059,000 were under culture, of which 639,000 (710 estates, averaging about 900 acres each) were occupied with sugar-plantations; 280,000 taken up by cattle-breeding farms, and 140,000 in cotton, indigo, coffee, pimento, ginger, &c. The parliamentary report of 1839 states that 3,403,359 acres have been granted by the crown. The recent emancipation of the negroes has tended to subdivide the land, and few estates now comprise more than 1,200 acres.

History.—This island was discovered by Columbus, on his second voyage, 3d May, 1494. It was settled by the Spaniards in 1503, and captured by Admiral Penn for the British in 1655. A remarkable feature in the history of the West Indies is the emancipation of the negroes, effected by the philanthropy of the British legislature. West India proprietors have termed the act of emancipation a vital injury to these colonies, but a parliamentary committee of inquiry (see *Parliamentary Report,* dated July, 1842) have effectually contraverted the opinion.

Climate.—The medium temperature near Kingston ranges between 70° and 80°; Major Tulloch (in his reports on the health of the army) gives the mean highest temperature, in the shade, at 88°, and the mean lowest temperature at 73° 1′. At an elevation of 2,000 feet, the temperature ranges between 60° and 84°, according to the above excellent authority. Little differences of elevation have a wonderful effect over the temperature and salubrity of the climate. The north side of the island is considered more healthy than the south, where less rain falls, and the temperature is higher.* The inhabitants are accustomed to four seasons—1st, the vernal, or moderate rains, April and May; 2d, hot and dry, June, July, and August; 3d, hurricane months, September, October, and November; 4th, serene and cool, December, January, February, and March. Longevity is not uncommon in Jamaica.

Rivers and Springs.—Upwards of 200 in number; the Black River is navigable about 30 miles. There are several springs of a medicinal nature in Vere and Portland; the most celebrated is one of a sulphureous nature. There are also cold and hot springs.

Geology.—The island contains no active volcanoes, but the traces of former volcanic action are obvious. Micaceous schist, quartz, and

* West India Manual.

rock spar are common; limestone, containing numerous shells, the most prevalent formation. The turf-clad hills on the north side are chiefly composed of a chalky marl; elsewhere, the soil is frequently of a deep chocolate colour, or a warm yellow or hazel; the latter, called the Jamaica *brick* mould, retaining a good deal of moisture, and is amongst the best adapted for the sugar-cane.

Minerals.—Argentiferous lead, copper, iron, and antimony ores.

Productions.—Staples: sugar, rum, molasses, coffee, cotton,* ginger, pimento, maize; guinea-corn and rice are the principal grains cultivated. A considerable falling off in the produce of this island took place just after the passing of the emancipation act, but in 1842-3 the exports improved amazingly. In 1839, the principal exports were as follow: sugar, unrefined, 765,078 cwts.; rum, 1,654,232 gallons; molasses, 52 cwts; coffee,† 9,423,197 lbs.; cotton, 116,705 lbs.; ginger, 6,054 cwts; pimento, 1,071,503 lbs.; arrow-root, 89,970 lbs.; indigo, 11,826 lbs.; succades, 28,403 lbs.; logwood, 5,908 lbs. Comparative account of the shipments of produce from Jamaica in the years 1841 and 1842: 1841—sugar, hhds., 22,691; rum, puncheons, 8,298; coffee, tierces, 7,570. 1842—sugar, 36,012; rum, 12,148; coffee, 8,803. Increase, sugar, 13,321; rum, 3,830; coffee, 1,233. The total value of imports has generally averaged, of late years, 1,600,000*l.* per annum; exports, 2,827,833*l.* The stock on the island is about 20,000 horses and mules, and 165,000 horned cattle, besides sheep, goats, &c.

Population.—Estimated, in 1836, at 385,000; of which about 35,000 are Europeans. The compensation, under the emancipation act, amounted to 6,161,927*l.*; the average value of a slave, from 1822 to 1830, having been 44*l.* 15*s.* 2*d.*

Language.—The English language is principally spoken by the Europeans; the native language in common use is African.

Cities.—St. Jago, population 6,000; Kingston (founded 1693, incorporated 1803), population 35,000. Kingston engrosses by far the largest portion of the trade of the island.

---

* The cultivation of cotton, which at one time formed one of the principal staples of the island, ceased upon the introduction of the cane and coffee plants. Hundreds and thousands of acres along the coast, which used to be profitably employed in its cultivation, have been suffered to lie waste; but, lately, a Mr. Geurgnes has come forward, and shown that the land might again be made available and profitable. 3,000 weight of sea island seed-cotton, grown and ginned at Aranfuiz pen, in the parish of St. Andrew, arrived (1843) in England.

† The tariff regulates the import of coffee, the produce of British possessions, at a duty of 4d.; all foreign coffee to pay 8d. (add 5 per cent) The duties on sugar and molasses were continued to July, 1843, by statute.

Gaols.—Three. Debtors are allowed 2s. 6d. per day; free criminals, 1s. 3d. per day; and apprentice criminals, 5s. per week. In 1836, there were 1,213 prisoners confined in the three gaols, 85 of whom only were females.

Education.—In 1837, the number of children receiving instruction in the various public, Sunday, and day schools, was 38,754. The expenditure for schools between 1832 and 1836 was 50,000*l.*

Church Establishment.—The total expenditure of the church establishment from 1832 to 1836 was 217,410*l.*. The outlay of the Jamaica government for religious purposes averages nearly 25,000*l.* per annum. The salary of the bishop is 4,000*l.*; that of the archdeacon, 2,000*l.* There are 21 rectors, 57 clergymen of the Established Church; 4 Scotch clergy; 24 Wesleyan; 16 Baptist; 8 Moravian. The established religion is Episcopalian. In 1842, an act was passed to provide for the increase of the number of bishoprics and archdeaconries in the West Indies.

Government.—The government is one of the richest, next to that of Ireland, in the disposal of the crown. The Council consists of 12 members, and an Assembly of 45. St. Jago de la Vega, or Spanish Town, is the seat of government; but Kingston (incorporated by charter in 1803) is the capital.

Since 1728, the Assembly and Council have been the originators of all laws for the government of the island, the power of legislation having been then conferred, and a permanent revenue of 10,000*l.* guaranteed by the colony to the crown. The salary of the governor is 5,500*l.* per annum. The present governor (1844) is the Earl of Elgin.

Government Officers.—Governor, the Earl of Elgin; A.D.C. Capt. Hon. R. Bruce, Grenadier Guards; Commander of the Forces, Major-General Berkeley; Assistant Military Secretary, Captain Carden, 60th foot; A. D. C. Captain Cavan, 30th foot; Bishop, Right Rev. C. Lipscombe, D.D.; Archdeacon, Rev. E. Pope, D.D.; Government Secretaries, Messrs. J. Higginson, W. Stewart; Chief Justice, Sir Joshua Rowe, Kt.; Registrar and Surrogate, W. King, Esq.; Advocate-General, W. C. M'Dougall, Esq.; Deputy-Judge Advocate, Capt. B. Campbell, 2d W. I. regiment; Attorney-General, D. O'Reilley, Esq.; Clerk of the Crown, Sir M. Nepean, Bart.; Provost-Marshal, J. A. Sullivan, Esq.; Registrar in Chancery, Hon. R. Cargill; Clerk, J. G. Vidal, Esq.; Receiver-General, of Revenue, J. Edwards, Esq.; Collector of Customs, J. G. Swainson, Esq.; Comptoller, W. Freeman, Esq.; Deputy Postmaster-General, J. Wilson, Esq.; Crown Officer, Royal Artillery, Lieut.-Col. Rudyard; Crown Officer, Engineers, Major Gossett; Deputy Adjutant-General, Lieut.-Col. W. Turnor; Deputy Quartermaster-General, Lieut.-Col. S. R. Warren; Inspector-General of Hospitals, Sir J. Adolphus, M.D.; Agent in London, W. Burge, Esq., Q.C. The last navy estimates (1844) show a reduction of salary, as affects the crown officer of engineers.

Revenue.—The revenue, which is raised by custom-duties, sale of crown lands, taxes, &c., averages nearly 500,000*l.* annually. The annual cost to the United Kingdom of Jamaica, Bahamas, Honduras, and the Cayman Islands, was, according to the parliamentary return of 1836, 232,427*l.* The total annual income of all the parishes in Jamaica, was estimated in 1841 at 840,624*l.* The value of the maritime trade of Jamaica to Great Britain is nearly 2,800,000*l.*

Currency.—The ordinary currency of the United Kingdom has recently been adopted in Jamaica.

Shipping.—Inwards and outwards, 231,000 tons annually, of which 114,000 tons are from the mother-country. In 1840, 697 ships were entered inward in the United Kingdom, as employed in the West India trade, and 855 vessels were entered as cleared outwards.

Harbours.—Sixteen in number, and 30 bays, roads, or shipping stations, affording good anchorage. Kingston harbour is a land-locked basin, in which ships of the largest burden may anchor in perfect safety. It is strongly fortified. The depth of water in the centre of channel leading to the harbour is, where most shallow, four fathoms, and in the harbour itself it varies from six to ten fathoms.

Principal Ports (*free.*)—South: Kingston, Port Royal, Morant, Black River, and Savannah la Mar. North: Lucea and Montego Bay, Falmouth, St. Ann, Ports Maria and Antonio, and Annotto Bay.

Buildings.—They are principally of brick, most of the houses having piazzas or arcades in front. An extensive parade or square occupies the higher part of the town of Kingston, in the north of which are situated the government barracks. There are two handsome churches, and several dissenting chapels, two synagogues, an hospital, and numerous other charitable institutions. A free school was established in 1729, with an endowment of 1,500*l.* per year. There are also a workhouse, a jail, commercial subscription rooms, an athenæum, a society of agriculture, arts, and science, a savings' bank, and a theatre.

Troops.—Battalions of the 60th and 77th foot are stationed in Jamaica, and also part of the 2d West India regiment, a colonial corps. The military forces of Jamaica and Honduras consist of about 2,500 European regulars, 200 colonial regulars, and 12,000 colonial militia.

Naval Force on the West India Station (1844).—Two ships, two frigates, eighteen sloops, and eight steamers—Albatros, Antelope (convict hulk), Dromedary, Electra, Eurydice, Fair Rosamond, Galatea, (coal depôt, Jamaica); Gleaner, (steamer); Griffin, Hermes, (steamer); Hornet, Illustrious, (72); Flag-ship, Imaum, (72); (receiving ship, Jamaica); Inconstant, Lark, Pickle, Pique, Resolute, Ringdove, Romney, Rose, Royal Oak, Scylla, Spartan, Tenedos, Thunder, Wasp, Weymouth, (receiving hulk).—Numerous steam-packets, belonging to the West India Steam-Packet Company, run to the various ports of the West Indies, from Southampton, on the 1st and 15th of every month. The rate of passage is 52*l.* each person; return-passage, the same. From Jamaica to all West India ports, the passage-rate varies from 7*l.* to 28*l.* Home letters, not exceeding half an ounce, for Jamaica, are charged with a postage of 1s., with or without prepayment.

The Arms of Jamaica.—The escutcheon represents the British monarch upon the throne, receiving from the hands of a kneeling slave a salver of West India fruits. The motto runs as follows: *Duro de cortice fructus quam dulci.* At the left corner of the field is a small coat of arms, representing a minor escutcheon, supported by two slaves. The heraldry appears to have a local application.

A VOICE FROM TRINIDAD.*

CHAPTER IV.

"Of all the vices, avarice is the most apt to taint and corrupt the heart."—JUNIUS.
"Liberal sensations find no entrance into a barbarous contracted heart."—IBID.

THE comments of Mr. Hamilton, immigration agent at Sierre Leone for the colony of Trinidad, on the subject of Mr. Burnley's suggestion "to tear up all our treaties for the suppression of the slave-trade, the withdrawing of our cruisers from the coast of Africa, and allowing all who pleased to procure labourers to work in Cuba, the Brazils, and elsewhere, under the impulse of the whip," are of importance. Mr. Hamilton says—

"Such a suggestion or example to slave-holding nations, would soon be prostituted to the basest purposes of slave-dealing; and the most extensive slave-dealing not only renewed, but legalized. The British emigration agent, and the foreign slave-dealer would be contending, in zealous rivalry, with bribes and presents to

* Continued from Number 1, page 48.

the chiefs. Africans must then be supplied for the markets, whether *as slaves*, or as emigrants; while the individuals, if left to themselves, *might prefer Africa*, without the advantages of civilization."

Lord Normanby, in a despatch to Governor Light, of Demerara, seems to have taken a most correct view of the case, when he said—"No precaution which has been, or could be devised, could prevent such a measure from giving a stimulus to the *internal slave-trade on the African continent.*" All men of sane minds would come unhesitatingly to a similar conclusion. Mr. Burnley, in his infatuation, dreams of extinguishing the flame, by increasing the fuel. This is not the only instance of glaring inconsistency indulged in by that gentleman and his fellow-planters. The evidence on which he and they base all their observations and recommendations teem with them. Mr. Burnley and the "Agricultural Committee,"* however, are so confident in the

* Sir,—You will allow one who feels deeply interested in the well-being of this portion of her Majesty's empire, in every sense of the word, to offer a few thoughts on some of the past and present movements in reference to West Indian affairs. Amongst this group of colonies, there is not one which has attracted greater attention, both at home and in its own immediate neighbourhood, than Trinidad. Over and over again has its condition been represented as quite peculiar, and in one breath have its distresses and unparalleled capabilities been urged upon the serious attention of the home government. That the matter might be placed in the strongest possible light in Downing-street, some half-dozen blustering attorneys, two or three influential planters, with our island organs of information, took it into their heads to constitute themselves the "Trinidad Agricultural and Immigration Society;" and further formed themselves into a "Board," purporting to receive all the impartial evidence that might be offered for their and the home-government's information respecting the state of affairs in this island. The Hon. William Burnley, who was the original *schemer* of the whole, was chosen chairman, and most assiduously did he perform his part. The mass of evidence adduced has long since appeared in print, prefaced by about forty pages of conclusions drawn from it, and suggestions offered by the honourable gentleman who called the whole into being. You have no doubt read it, perhaps with surprise and deep concern at the *facts* it revealed. There is, however, this redeeming circumstance in it, that nearly all the discoveries they pretended to have made were known to few in the colony, besides the parties concerned in getting up this mock examination of witnesses. The whole of the evidence given is quite *ex parte*, and the individuals affording it form a class. It is hardly necessary to exclude the clergymen, who figured as witnesses on the occasion referred to, from this accusation, they being more or less interested in falling in with the views of the committee before whom they appeared. Except to themselves, the place and time for receiving evidence were quite unknown to the public, until the proceedings of each sitting were published in the colonial papers after it was terminated. Evidence received on such exclusive principles appears to me to be entitled to little respect or attention. The views held by the honourable chairman for years before were those which appeared throughout the

success of their scheme, if adopted, that they undertake to reason upon it, absurd as it is. "The sole stimulus that can be applied to the

whole evidence, though it was attempted to represent them as of a later origin. A new scheme of slavery was contemplated by the originator of the "Agricultural Society," if he could succeed in establishing certain positions as true, on which to base his future propositions to the secretary for the colonies. The favourable reception of his views at the Colonial Office depended much, indeed altogether, upon previously proving the demoralized and inefficient state of the emancipated labouring population. Could he establish this point, in connexion with the almost ruined state of the sugar-growers, he conceived he should have a strong claim on the home government for some concessions to mitigate their distress. For this purpose the above-named "Board" was formed, and evidence received. You must have observed these two particulars much dwelt upon in the questions from the chair, and the same occupying a very prominent place in the plan proposed for the consideration of the Colonial Society. The scheme of emancipation, they said, having so signally failed, in having produced nothing but disorder and confusion, dissipation and general distress throughout the colony, they conceived they could reasonably claim from the British government, as the authors of the whole, some consideration in return for their blind legislation. With perfect astonishment I read from time to time in the colonial papers of the evidence establishing the general distress of the colony, while I read in the same organs of the increased value of imports, and the doubling of the colonial revenue in a few years. The rising up of decent villages in all directions, and the clearing out and cultivating of land, fully satisfied me that the distress complained of was but partial, if it existed at all: and that, however a few individuals might have suffered, general prosperity characterized the island. Nor was it with less surprise I saw an attempt made to establish the oft-told tale, that the negroes will not work, while the island exports flatly contradicted the whole tissue of falsehood upon which it was based. The great demoralization of the labourers set forth in the evidence, and to prove which particular pains were taken, seemed to lean, after all, upon the "gratuitous supply of rum dealt out by the very planters" who were endeavouring to rob the emancipated labourers of their well-merited reputation for general good conduct. The party engaged in this disgraceful affair seemed to stop at no right, no matter how dear or sacred, in order to carry out, if possible, their darling scheme of African immigration—that is, to purchase humanity, or trepan human beings. The "ignorant and docile African, who had never been degraded and demoralized by freedom, nor deteriorated by moral and religious tuition, would, according to Mr. Burnley, and his trumpet, Mr. H. Maxwell, answer the purposes of the planter much better than any others to be found. This was the height of their ambition; nor had they the slightest apprehension as to the results of large importations, morally considered, provided they were distributed among the "dissipated" native labourers of the colony. Observe the consistency of these men! Many a time do they cut their own throats. Having completed the whole design, they hastened to inform the secretary for the colonies of the unparalleled capabilities of Trinidad, if properly developed; entered into details respecting its physical appearance,—fine levels, fertile valleys, and numerous rivers; and after this fine gilding, dwelt upon the much-to-be-lamented degradation and inefficiency slave-trade, is the profits it affords," says the Committee; and, therefore, "if the profits can be diminished, that trade will be reduced and

---

of the labouring population, and all—every word—founded on the most satisfactory evidence. Then follows the most audacious prescription, as a cure for all the woes with which they—certainly not the island—were afflicted, viz., a free communication for *coerced voluntary emigration* from the west coast of Africa. I need hardly assure you that in Trinidad there are thousands of living witnesses to testify to the utter falsity of most of the evidence upon which such a recommendation is based. You may be surprised that no attempt was made by them at giving a contradiction to such false charges at the time. Had there been an organ in which confidence could be placed, it would have been the case instantaneously; but the newspapers here being both the creatures of the planters, that could not be expected. And further, the party and the proceedings were viewed with such unqualified contempt, because of their base attacks on the defenceless labourers, who were, at that very time, faithfully performing their duties on the estates of their calumniators, that many who would have solicited an opportunity to offer evidence of a contradictory character, condescended not to mix up with the affair, conceiving that the whole production of the Committee, when presented to the secretary for the colonies, would be treated with that inattention which it deserved. I find both the resolutions passed by the Committee of the House of Commons, and the report of the " Land and Immigration Committees," to whom this evidence was submitted by Lord Stanley, have fully exonerated the emancipated labourers of this island from the aspersions cast upon them. The latter document, in particular, was remarkably explicit on this point, pronouncing as inconclusive and unsatisfactory the very evidence that was intended to form the foundation of every future proposition. Notwithstanding this, I observe, the government appear disposed to comply, in some measure, with the demands of West India planters, though the very great necessity for such a compliance remains to be shown. If reference be had to the clearing and cultivation of the whole of this fine island, then I would say 50,000 or 60,000 souls might be introduced; but if to the properties under cultivation at present, an abundance of labour is at this moment in the market. This cannot be denied.

To introduce the thousands called for by the planters, while they stop up every channel of egress from the cane piece, will, I much fear, be followed by untold misery and oppression to the labourers already in the field. I may venture to affirm, that most of the estates in the island have as many hands as they require. Several of the conductors have informed me on this point. You will think it not a little remarkable, that some estates are always ill supplied with labour, though they generally draw more largely than most others from immigrant vessels arriving here. The secret lies here—either the people find the localities unhealthy, or, experience less encouragement to remain than other properties present; hence nearly the whole stream of immigration is kept open, in the first instance, for the sole benefit of such estates. I doubt much, whether the condition of such properties will ever be improved, even should other localities be amply stocked, except from bitter necessity on the part of a too dense labouring population, which is exactly the state into which Mr. Burnley and a few others would reduce them. I observe from the *Port of Spain Gazette* a long letter from Mr. B., extinguished when these are completely destroyed." At first sight, this appears very plausible. Mr Burnley, in this instance, reasons like a mercantile man; in supposing the slave-trade to be extinguished by increasing the demand, like a novice. The first thing to be proved, however, is the real principle upon which the slave-trade rests. If upon the profits of the trade, as in cases of mercantile transactions, Mr. Burnley's conclusion is about correct; but if upon another principle, peculiar only to itself, his reasoning is fallacious. I am disposed to think the continuation of the trade, and the profits derived from it, have no relation whatever; though the latter may tend to give an impetus to it. In a very unsatisfactory way, Mr. Burnley has undertaken to prove, that an increased demand will tend to reduce the profits of the slave-seller, which is of a piece with his expressed opinion, that the trade will be ultimately suppressed, by establishing depôts along the coast of Africa for purchasing slaves. This is too absurd to deserve any attempt at refutation.

That the existence of the slave-trade does not in any way depend upon the profits to be derived from it, though it may be encouraged by them, will be evident from the fact, that slaves are disposed of on the coast of Africa for a mere trifle, thirty dollars, according to Mr. Burnley, which sum appears to satisfy the chiefs, and which sum, in addition to the expense of transporting them, can be easily paid by any West India planter, under his most distressing circumstances. The great profits of the slave-trade do not go to the chiefs who furnish the supply, consequently a reduction in these profits cannot effect him, or it, to any extent. It is to the dealers who purchase from these chiefs, and pass the slaves on to the planters, that the profits go. A slave purchased from a chief for twenty or thirty dollars at most, will bring perhaps from two hundred to three hundred dollars, when disposed of from the ship.*

According to Mr. Burnley, our free-labour system, being so much

---

defending himself against your observations in reference to the locking up of immigrants in the yard of Messrs. Losh, Spiers, and Co. He quotes from a pamphlet, published by him in 1823, as a proof of his sincerity in emancipating his slaves; but were you to consult the whole of that production, I doubt not other and opposite principles would be found to prevail. His whole conduct is tortuous. I forward you a copy of the *Gazette*, containing his letter and the slave-holding principles of the editor. My next, for I beg again shortly to trouble you, shall be strictures on Mr. B.'s evidence before the Committee of the House of Commons, contrasting it with the real state of affairs here, and proving that four-fifths of the whole is not founded in fact.—*Letter from Trinidad.*

* We may safely say five hundred dollars at Cuba and Porto Rico.

more economical than that of slavery—a truth he resisted long—the British West India sugar-growers will be able to undersell those of foreign colonies, and thereby render the latter unable to purchase slaves at this high rate; and which reduction in price must, he thinks, affect the profits of the slave-dealer on the coast of Africa, and throw all that trade into the hands of our planters, who, it is presumed, could alone afford the trade any encouragement. This is all very fine, but not quite clear. As it has been already shown, the last selling price of the slave must be very considerably reduced, before the dealers acting between the chief and the agriculturist will be driven to make any reduction upon the original cost. A fall in the price of produce, rendering the agriculturists unable to pay the hitherto high prices for slaves, will be easily understood by the parties from whom they purchase, and who will prefer accommodating themselves to a change of circumstances, and a consequent reduction of their profits, rather than to suppress that trade altogether, by insisting on prices the planters can no longer meet. It is well known the profits of this trade are enormous, and that the severest reverses the planters may experience will not have any effect in discouraging, or ultimately suppressing the traffic. Slave merchants can afford to bear large reductions in their profits, before such reductions need affect the chiefs, or tend to limit the supply of slaves. Under any circumstances in which the planters of Cuba and Brazil may be placed, they can afford as high a price on the coast of Africa, under their present mode of procuring slaves, as ever can be met by British planters.

Were foreign planters so pressed as to be altogether unable to afford these slave-dealers any profits on their trade, they would then have the same advantage on the coast as our West India planters. They could go and purchase at the original prices, and have the slaves conveyed according to Mr. Burnley's plan, at so much per head, dispensing altogether with the intermediate merchants. But to this they will never be driven, while their slave system continues. Any fall that may take place—and I anticipate little—in the price of sugars, through an increased supply from the British colonies by Mr. Burnley's scheme, can never affect the foreign sugar-grower to that extent. The reverses he may experience can be easily borne by those middlemen, which will ease the planter, without limiting or stopping his supply of slaves, and thus enable him to compete with our colonies. Should Mr. Burnley's plan of unrestricted emigration be adopted, foreign sugars should, from that date, be admitted into England as from the colonies. In this view of the case, the supply of slaves on the coast of Africa would not in any way be decreased, even though it should be found to depend on the profits realized by the chiefs; but, on the contrary, according to Lord Normanby's opinion, very much encouraged in proportion to the increased demand from the British West Indies.*

---

* The noble Lord Stanley may say that he is borne out by the decision of two Parliamentary Committees as to the necessity which exists for the supply of African labour to the British colonies, and that such supply can be obtained, without stimulating the slave-trade, either internal or external, with Africa. We take the liberty of denying these assumptions. No proof whatever exists that such a supply of labour as that complained of by the planters is wanted; or that, if wanted, it might not be obtained without a resort to Africa. What really is wanted in the British colonies, is capital to secure the labour which is already there—the economical management of estates by resident proprietors—and the fair and honourable treatment of the labourers. Let these be found, and we fear not that, as the population increases by natural means, and by spontaneous emigration, the resources of the colonies would be developed, and that they would be able to compete both in the home market, and the foreign markets to which they might have access, with the growers of tropical produce by slave-labour. But were it proved that the colonies actually wanted the immense supply of labour stated, we contend that it could not be obtained from Africa without stimulating the slave-trade. As to free African labour, except to a limited extent at Sierra Leone and the Gambia, we feel satisfied that it cannot be gotten, notwithstanding the confident assertions to the contrary. The Kroos and Fishmen, who will be invited to go to the West Indies when the supply from Sierra Leone is exhausted, are not free in such a sense as to constitute them voluntary agents in their engagements with the government or the planters. Their chiefs must be consulted, and presents given, before they will consent to their departure from their homes; and then their wives and children will be retained in pawn until their return, when it is more than probable the chiefs will come in for the lion's share of their earnings. This is the case now. Moreover, we are satisfied, that, when the chiefs have assented, compulsion will be used to make the Kroos, who prefer the coast of Africa to the West Indies, willing to go whithersoever the agent may appoint.

Lord Stanley may pledge his responsibility that this shall not be the case. We beg to tell the noble Lord that we cannot accept the pledge in the present case. The public eye will not be on the agent in Africa, the public voice cannot control his movements. His instructions may be perfect; but that is no guarantee that they will be faithfully observed. Besides, Lord Stanley agrees that the Kroos may resort to the colonies unaccompanied by their wives and families, or by any females whatsoever. The horrible results of such an arrangement may be imagined, but decency forbids their mention. Is the noble Lord prepared, as a Christian man, to bear this responsibility on his conscience; or, having admitted the arrangement to hold good as it respects the introduction of Coolies into Mauritius, does he feel himself bound, in consistency, to admit it in reference to the importation of Kroos into the West Indies? We sicken at the contemplation of these things.

Looking, however, beyond the mere effect of African emigration on the Africans

Should Mr. Burnley's scheme, for enabling the British planters to compete with those of foreign colonies, be adopted, and prove as successful as he seems to anticipate, in driving foreign sugar out of the European markets, and thus so reducing the means of slave-holding planters, by the triumph of what he is pleased to term a *free-labour system, with purchased slaves,* as to drive them from the slave-market also; were this altogether improbable change to follow from the adoption of the above plan, it, after all, becomes a query, whether it would have any tendency to suppress the slave-trade. All this would not affect the source and soul of the traffic, so long as British depôts were established, and British capital at command, for that express purpose. It would be matter of perfect indifference to the continental slave-dealers, with whom they traded; indeed, it is more than probable they would prefer British customers. If Mr. Burnley's plan should succeed in extinguishing the foreign slave-trade, it must also accomplish the ruin of the planters, as he supposes; which would throw all the trade or nearly so, into the hands of our West India agriculturists, a circumstance that would no doubt afford Mr. Burnley much gratification, but which would require an equal number of African slaves to labour for its supply. To those desirous to accomplish in reality the suppression

---

themselves, whom it is proposed to benefit by the change, we again venture to ask, whether the course about to be pursued by Lord Stanley will not be soon followed by Brazil, Spain, and other slave-holding countries? In addition to Senegal and Goree, France is about establishing three forts or block-houses on the western coast of Africa; these may become depôts for labourers for the French colonies. The Portuguese settlements, south of the line, on the same coast, may easily become receptacles for negroes for Brazil; and Spain may now think it worth while to occupy Fernando Po, with a view to the supply of Cuba and Puerto Rico with *free* labourers. The slave-trade may thus assume a new form, and be perpetuated in spite of all the efforts of the British Government to suppress it. Is Lord Stanley prepared for this? can he adduce any argument against it that a clever diplomatist might not easily evade or overcome? Depend on it, Lord Stanley's scheme will put a weapon in the hands of the slaveholders, with which they will wound the dearest interests of humanity, and from the keen edge of which no shield can be opposed with success.

Lord Normanby, when at the head of the Colonial Office, foresaw the use which would be made of African emigration to the West Indies, and manfully opposed it, as he did also Coolie emigration to the Mauritius. His lordship said—

"With regard to the introduction of labourers from India, more than enough has already passed to render her Majesty's government decidedly hostile to every such project. * * * We are not less opposed to the plan of recruiting the negro population of the West Indies from Africa. No precautions which have been, or which could be devised, would prevent such a measure from giving a stimulus to the internal slave-trade on that continent, or from bringing discredit on the sincerity of the efforts made by this nation for the suppression of that system of guilt and misery."

of that traffic on the coast of Africa, and in the interior of that continent, it can make little difference as to the parties by whom it is encouraged, and for whose benefit it may be continued. So long as the abominable custom is perpetuated, and the dark deeds necessary to its continuance perpetrated, it cannot in the least alter their purpose, to be told, that the chief and only instigators of the sufferings of unfortunate Africa, are civilized and enlightened British subjects. If the supply of purchased slaves bear any proportion to the increased demand for the productions of our West India colonies, which would undoubtedly take place if Mr. Burnley succeed in crippling foreign sugar-growers, and which demand our British West India planters would no doubt endeavour to meet, who can tell, or even conceive, the amount of suffering that must be inflicted on the helpless tribes of Africa, to accomplish such an object? Revolting as is the present condition of Africa, when British subjects are denied any participation in that trade, I shudder to contemplate the atrocities that must of necessity be committed, to satisfy the rapacious desires of our "Agricultural Society," should all restrictions be removed by the home-government. The British lion would be found to rush with tenfold impetuosity on his powerless victim, and would react, in 1844 and the following years, the black catalogue of crimes which put Britain to the blush in 1838. Whether the energies of foreign planters would or would not be crippled by Mr. Burnley's proposition, is of no consequence to the question. Should such not be the case, which is more likely by a great deal, the competition of British agents on the African coast could have no other effect than to stimulate the internal slave-trade to a fearful extent. Should that trade pass altogether into the hands of British planters, the same impetus must of necessity be given, as not only an equal, but a much greater number of the unfortunate beings will be required, to furnish the European demand for sugar, &c., &c. But we will suppose, for the sake of argument, that the profits of the slave-dealer are considerably reduced, and that he comes to the chief, and solicits his slaves at a reduced price. The price of a slave on the coast, and in the interior, is generally paid in goods; and that is the highest price given which happens to please the fancy of the chief the best; though it may be far from the nominal value of the slave, even in the African market. This fact all slave-dealers are up to, and take advantage of the tastes and dispositions of these chiefs, to their own profit. In this way, the slave-dealer may save himself from the effects of any reverses experienced by the foreign planter, and also secure a continued supply of slaves at reduced rates.

Should the value of each slave be even paid the chief in specie, according to a certain standard, it is not improbable that he would consent to a reduction in the customary price, rather than allow the traffic to close. This idea is upon the supposition that British agents would not require the whole of the supply of slaves furnished by the chiefs. If the latter should be prepared to pay the full price of thirty dollars per head for the whole supply brought to market, of course the traders from foreign colonies who could not afford it, would have no share in the traffic, which would be transferred to the highest bidder. But, so long as the number of slaves captured for the market was greater than the supply required for the British colonies, foreign agents might purchase the remainder for almost any price they chose to offer. Were the competitors in the slave-market to combine for the reduction of the original cost of slaves, they might bring it down to a mere trifle. It is in the power of the dealer, now that there is no competitor, to do the same thing, which I make no doubt is frequently the case, and to which the chiefs and others are obliged to submit. If, under these circumstances, an ample supply of slaves is furnished for exportation, what may it not be, when a warm and hearty spirit of competition would enliven the market?

(To be continued.)

NEW ZEALAND.

[September 2, 1843.]

The excitement caused by the Wairau Massacre has not abated in the slightest degree, but seems, on the contrary, to have awoke the settlers to a somewhat painful sense of their situation. Hitherto, they panoplied themselves in the superiority of their modes of observing peace and making war, and in the moral results of this advantage amongst the cannibals of New Zealand; they now seem to fall back upon the simple calculation of physical strength, and stand almost paralyzed, like the hunter whose escape from the next bound of the tiger is hopeless. Having only received the Supplement of the *New Zealand Gazette* as our last pages were going to press, we have only time to prefix these few words of introduction, and only space to admit the petition of the settlers to the Queen:—

To her most gracious Majesty VICTORIA, Queen of Great Britain and Ireland, Defender of the Faith, the humble Petition of the undersigned Inhabitants of the Borough of Wellington, in New Zealand, and the neighbourhood,

Sheweth,—That the European population of New Zealand amounts to about 13,000 persons:

That about 10,000 of these reside on the shores of Cook's Straits and the southern part of the Northern Island, so near together as to possess a common interest, and to form one community:

That the other 3,000 persons are resident at Aucland, Hokianga, the Bay of Islands, and other places from 400 to 500 miles northward of Cook's Straits; that they have scarcely any common interests with the settlers in Cook's Straits, and cannot be regarded as the same community:

That the only means of communicating between Cook's Straits and Aucland is by sea, and that the voyage there and back occupies from one to two months, rendering the distance between the two equivalent in practice to between 2,000 and 3,000 miles at the ordinary rate of travel:

That the settlements in Cook's Straits were founded first; and that Aucland was not selected as the seat of government till more than a year afterwards:

That it is impossible that the settlements in Cook's Straits should be well governed by an Executive government resident at Aucland, and a Legislative Council in which they have no representative:

That the community in Cook's Straits have contributed in taxes to the expense of the Colonial Government, at the rate of nearly £12,000 a year, nearly the whole of which has been carried to Aucland and there expended, without any advantage being derived from its expenditure by those who contributed it:

That certain disputes relating to the title to lands have arisen between the settlers and the natives :

That a Commission was appointed by your Majesty in the year 1841, to adjudicate on the disputed claims:

That in the neighbourhood of Aucland upwards of 600 claims have been disposed of, but not one in the neighbourhood of Cook's Straits:

That in consequence thereof, the settlers on the shores of Cook's Straits have been prevented from cultivating the lands they purchased before leaving England, and have been obliged to live on the produce of foreign countries, while their capital has been wasted, and themselves nearly ruined:

That a Police Magistrate in the act of executing a lawful warrant, and upwards of twenty other persons lawfully aiding him therein (among whom were several Magistrates of the territory, a Crown Prosecutor, a Chief Constable, a Commander in your Majesty's Navy, and a Captain in your Majesty's Army), have recently been massacred on the shores of Cook's Straits, by an armed body of Aborigines resisting your Majesty's lawful authority:

That previously to the late massacre it was known to your Majesty's Government, at home and in the colony, that differences had arisen and aggressions been threatened by the natives:

That notwithstanding this, all the military forces in the colony were kept at Aucland, where no hostile demonstration had been made by the natives, and not one soldier was afforded for the protection of Cook's Straits:

That had a military force, however small, accompanied the Police Magistrate who fell in the massacre, it is generally believed that that event would not have happened:

That your Majesty's principal Secretaries of State for the Colonies have sanctioned and encouraged the formation of a Militia and an armed Police Force in this colony, but that the Local Government has taken no steps towards the execution of these views:

That the only Police Force in Cook's Straits consists of a few petty Constables in each settlement (in Wellington twelve in number), who are not the slightest protection against the natives:

That the primary cause of all the evils under which your Petitioners suffer, and of the late massacre, has been the non-settlement of the Land Claims, and the want of an independent government:

That the annual expense of the Protectorship of the Aborigines is about £3,000 a year, while not one penny is expended in protecting the settlers against the natives:

That your Petitioners believe that not one instance can be adduced of any aggression committed by settlers in Cook's Straits upon a native:

That the Protector and Sub-Protectors are persons totally unfit for the offices they fill, and that instead of having contributed to the mutual harmony of the two races, they have exercised an influence over the natives, which we believe to have led, in a great degree, to the hostile state of feeling now existing, and the late unhappy events:

That immediately after the late massacre, the settlement of Wellington was threatened with an attack from the tribes who had been engaged in it, and that in consequence a body of Volunteers was enrolled, armed and trained to military exercises, under the express direction of the Police Magistrate, the Mayor of the Borough, and several of the Magistrates of the territory:

That, in a month afterwards, a Proclamation was issued by the Police Magistrate, stigmatizing these musters as illegal, and threatening to disperse them:

That this charge of their illegality has been retracted, and admitted to be false:

That erroneous accounts of the massacre were promulgated by the Police Magistrate, which have also been retracted, and admitted to be false:

That a Proclamation has been issued by the Chief Protector of the Aborigines, containing false statements, which has not yet been retracted:

That when the false statements alluded to were promulgated, the parties who promulgated them had in their possession true accounts of the events they referred to:

That a Proclamation has been issued by the Officer administering the Government, which was calculated to act as an official invitation to the natives to commence further aggressions, which, with the Proclamation in their hands, they have actually done, and driven industrious settlers, in consequence, off their lands:

That your Petitioners have always been and will continue loyal subjects of your Majesty, and will endeavour, as their fellow-settlers endeavoured at Wairau, to support and maintain your Majesty's lawful authority in these islands:

That your Petitioners therefore pray that your Majesty will be pleased to inquire into the true state of this colony, to vindicate the memory of the dead, and the character of the living, from the obloquy which has been cast upon them; to visit with just punishment them who have broken the law, or abused the offices to which your Majesty has appointed them; and to take such measures for the protection of your Petitioners and the advancement of their welfare, as to your Majesty may seem wise and expedient:

And your Petitioners will ever pray, &c.

REVIEWS OF NEW BOOKS.

ART. I.—*Adam Clarke Portrayed.* By JAMES EVERETT. Vol. I., 12mo. London: Hamilton, Adams, & Co., Paternoster-row.

The memoirs of this apostle of Wesleyanism abound in practical moral lessons, encouraging examples, and profitable conclusions. The style is simple and pleasing; the author's information full and authentic; and, with a caution too often neglected by biographers, he has not suffered the warmth of friendship to encroach upon his judgment or his candour. The story of such a life as Adam Clarke's should be adopted as a library companion in every family, for the energy of his youth, the virtues of his manhood, and the usefulness of his mature years, present a splendid portrait of a happy and exemplary Christian life. Mr. Everett has employed the rich materials placed at his disposal with so much address, that his volume will be recommended to every young man, as a text-book of precepts, upon his entering society; and he will one day enjoy the gratifying reflection of having done justice to the memory of a good and great man, and, at the same time, conferred an important benefit upon society, by the publication of a volume so truly profitable for instruction. Nor are the features of Adam Clarke's memoirs confined to his religious, moral, or literary character only; they extend over many a field of general and pleasant excursion. The public men he became acquainted with, the public duties he discharged, the amazing talent for pointed, pithy, spirited repartee in which he indulged, divested however of anything that could offend the most sensitive—these, and many other light and pleasant attractions, will recommend the great linguist's portrait to the study of those who may at first only come to hear, but afterwards remain to pray.

The very lowly origin of Adam Clarke, however human vanity may desire to disguise such things, renders his subsequent elevation almost as solitary as singular in modern biography. A hundred instances might be quoted, of men who have reached the bench of bishops and of barristers from small beginnings, but no one now living, nor contemporary with him, was either so humbly born, or so poor from his very childhood: he belonged also to an unpopular part of the United Kingdom, and was the disciple of a religion discountenanced by that of the state.

"A thatched cabin" in the village of Moybeg, in the north of Ireland, was the birth-place of Adam Clarke, and his inheritance was the universal dispensation of his country—"poverty." The labours of the field added strength to a frame by nature vigorous; and the most meagre system of education, that any civilized country ever extended to its people, was his intellectual lot. But this state of things did not appear to obstruct his destiny; on the contrary, his easy victory over all difficulties throws out his character into a bolder relief. The following recapitulation of his boyhood's years, being general in its expression, may be here advantageously quoted:—

Let the reader pause a moment, and bend the mind's eye upon the ground over which he has been brought, and let him select a few particulars from what has been advanced. He will soon perceive, that when concentrated in "little Adam Clarke," they will form so many scattered rays of light brought into a focus, all contributing, less or more, to point him out as a luminary emerging from obscurity, and ordained to shine beautifully bright with other stars, either singly, or amid the galaxy, contributing to the splendour of the midnight heavens. There is scarcely anything ordinary in his movements, even in ordinary cases and circumstances. His parents, though dignified in ancestry, and respectably connected with the living, are in a comparatively humble station in life, in consequence of which he labours under many disadvantages. They, nevertheless, direct their attention to the cultivation of his mind and of his morals,—the father severely intent upon the improvement of the former, and the mother sedulously engaged in grounding and perfecting the latter. But however well qualified for their separate tasks, they find, that while their tyro manifests good moral feeling, and amazing precocity for other things, he evinces, till some time after other children have made considerable progress in letters and figures, an utter inaptitude to take in the commonest elementary principles of education. Suddenly, a change takes place—a change somewhat analagous in letters to that which is styled a "new creation" in religion; after which he strides along the path of knowledge, like Asahel over the plains and mountains of Judea, who "was light of foot as a wild roe." Continuing to fix our eye upon him, we trace him through the several gradations of childhood, boyhood, and youth, and frequently find unobtrusive intimations of something extraordinary in character: he is inured to hardness, so as to be almost impervious to cold;—industry and early rising are settled down into the form of a habit;—amusement is indulged, only so far as it connects itself with the harmless, in juvenile pastimes, and the useful in fishing; he has a nature possessed of exquisite sensibility and tenderness, and though liberal in the extreme, is so much of the economist as to mourn over needless indulgence; blessed with regularity of conduct and respect for religion, he preserves the most rigid attention to moral, while ignorant of evangelical truth;—favoured with a buoyancy of spirit which might have proved fatal to others, he is preserved in the midst of it, from intoxication at the fountain of human delight;—an insatiable thirst after knowledge is perceived, often seeking to gratify itself in the profound and mysterious, being especially inquisitive about every thing that seemed to connect itself with the invisible world and the soul of man, subjecting himself to pain, and fear, and inconvenience in its acquisition;—a taste for the classics is acquired;—judgment commences its decisions, in passing sentence upon, and in attempting to improve the literary defects of others;—improvements are grafted on experience with the wisdom of age;—a memory is discernible, which stoops and picks up the smallest particles of an incident, conversation, or passing event, bearing about the whole, through every changing scene of life;—early prejudices are seen to strike their roots, which will afterwards be found to be not only serviceable to him, but to constitute some of the excellencies and peculiarities of his manhood;—a partiality for the *antique* is visible, at a period when a love of *novelty* is the predominant passion;—books are prized above rubies;—not satisfied with philosophizing on natural objects beneath his feet, he elevates his eye to heaven, and is enamoured with the pure azure and host of stars above his head. Here we have stirring, some of the elements, the peculiarities, the characteristics of genius; and there is scarcely anything allied to the useful, the excellent, and the good, in the great man, in which he did not excel. As the sapling oak *virtually* possesses the trunk, the foliage, and the acorn-fruit of the mature tree, towards which it is perpetually growing and putting forth its strength, and at which, if its vegetable life is spared, it will eventually arrive; so Adam the younger, bids fair to be all that was actually beheld and admired in Adam the elder; —being the subject of a special providence, as if spared for important public purposes, in the accomplishment of which, he was to flourish, and tower above his fellows!

Adam Clarke having attained the age of nineteen, was admitted, through the kindness of John Wesley, to a place in Kingswood College, near Bristol, where he added but little to his stock of learning; but it was here, while digging in the garden, that he turned up a golden half-guinea, which he laid out in the purchase of a Hebrew Grammar. And it was in this trifling, accidental circumstance, much more than in his meeting with the founder of Methodism, that the acquirements and fame of Dr. Clarke originated; for, however his learned Commentary may excite admiration, and preserve his name amongst the celebrated divinity scholars of the age, it is, and ever will be, for the variety and extent of his knowledge of Oriental languages and literature, that he will be longest had in remembrance. And the foundation of this great fabric was the Hebrew Grammar of which he became the owner so fortuitously. There are many anecdotes in this volume of biography calculated both to instruct and amuse, which we would gladly transfer, if the fair limits of criticism or notice did not prohibit; but we cannot refrain from extracting Whitfield's testimony to his rival's merits, which we do not remember to have seen anywhere before. "Wesley," said this bold reformer, "has given laws, and so has retained what he won: I have not, and therefore cannot keep the people who have been brought to the truth by my ministry." The state of the societies of the separate leaders, at the present day, fulfils conspicuously this prophecy.

There is something approaching the romantic, in the extraordinary elevation to which Adam Clarke attained by the unaided force of his natural talent, independence of mind, and immoveable fixity of principle. It is almost a public benefit to disclose the simple, honest roads which alone he trod in life, that minds less generous and fearless may derive hope, under their still greater inability to labour in the vineyard.

Art. II.—*Thirty Years from Home; or, A Voice from the Main Deck.* By Samuel Leech. London: Wiley & Putnam. Boston: Tappan & Dennet.

This is no literary fraud, but the downright genuine production of a jolly tar who for six long years whistled at the tiller. It is rich, racy, and refreshing in every page and story, and conveys many a wholesome sentiment from which youth and age might both derive instruction. Those who have had the gratification of reading Lieutenant Shipp's autobiography, will find less difficulty than others in understanding the possibility, the practicability, of an agreeable, profitable, and original work being written by a genuine member of the *profanum vulgus.* Like all truants, Leech desired to shake off the trammels of school discipline; and, provided with the usual motto of all confirmed dunces—

"Was'nt the sea made for the free,"—

thought, spoke, dreamt of nothing else but emancipation from books, and the full enjoyment of that entire devotion to doing nothing at all, which this race of beings so erroneously imagine to be the life of a sailor on sea and ashore. Having accomplished his wish, like many a fondly-reared boy, whose distaste for home seems to increase with the growth of his parent's affection for himself, Leech was not to be diverted from the water by anything the earth could offer, and accordingly was shipped on board a man-of-war. Upon this interesting point, the observations of Sam Leech, dictated by an experience of thirty years, are particularly deserving of those striplings, who vainly imagine that they are competent to select an occupation for themselves, or that they in the least degree understand the true character of a sailor's life and duties:—

My time flew very rapidly and pleasantly away for two or three years, until, like most children, I began to sigh for deliverance from the restraints of home. I had already left school, and for some time, being now about thirteen years of age, had been employed in the pleasure-grounds of Blenheim Palace. This, however, was too tame a business for a lad of my spirits. I had heard tales of the sea from my cousins; my mother had filled my mind with the exploits of my grandfather; my imagination painted a life on the great deep in the most glowing colours; my mind grew uneasy; every day, my ordinary pursuits became more and more irksome, and I was continually talking about going to sea; indeed, I had made myself unhappy by being so discontented.

Little do lads and young men know of the difference between the comfort of a parent's roof, and the indifference, unkindness, and trouble they invariably experience, who go out into the world, until they have made the experiment. They paint everything in bright colours; they fancy the future to be all sunshine, all sweets, all flowers, but are sure to be wofully disappointed, when once away from the fireside of their infancy. Let me advise young people, if they wish to escape hardships, to be contented, to remain quietly at home, abiding the openings of providence, obeying the wishes of their parents, who not only have their best good at heart, but, however they may think to the contrary, who actually know what is most for their advantage.

My passion for a seaman's life was not a little increased by a soldier, who was sergeant to a company in Lord Francis Spencer's regiment of cavalry. Seated by my father's hearth-side, this old soldier, who had once been a sailor, would beguile many an evening hour with his endless tale, while I sat listening in enrapt attention. My mother, too, heedlessly fanned the flame by her descriptions of the noble appearance of the ships she had seen when at Brighton. Besides this, a footman at Blenheim House used to sing a song called "the poor little sailor boy;" which, although somewhat gloomy in its descriptions, only served to heighten the flame of desire within me, until I could think of nothing else, day or night, but of going to sea.

Having gone to sea, Sam saw something of a sailor's duty, being afloat while Decatur adorned the American navy, and while England and France disputed the supremacy of the waves; and the language of the heart in which he describes some of the most brilliant but bloody actions in that protracted war, is highly creditable to his feelings. For all those touches of his address in the graphic art, we must refer our readers to his stirring pages. But, before we ourselves bid him farewell, we must take leave to quote a main-deck-man's description of a flogging, as an illustration of the rank which we have assigned to him in literature:—

The boatswain's mate is ready, with coat off and whip in hand. The captain gives the word. Carefully spreading the cords with the fingers of his left hand, the executioner throws the cat over his right shoulder: it is brought down upon the now uncovered herculean shoulders of the MAN. His flesh creeps—it reddens as if blushing at the indignity; the sufferer groans; lash follows lash, until the first mate, wearied with the cruel employment, gives place to a second. Now two dozen of these dreadful lashes have been inflicted; the lacerated back looks inhuman; it resembles roasted meat burnt nearly black before a scorching fire; yet still the lashes fall; the captain continues merciless. Vain are the cries and prayers of the wretched man. "I would not forgive the Saviour," was the blasphemous reply of one of these naval demi-gods, or rather demi-fiends, to a plea for mercy. The executioners keep on. Four dozen strokes have cut up his flesh, and robbed him of all self-respect; there he hangs, a pitied, self-despised, groaning, bleeding wretch; and now the captain cries, forbear! His shirt is thrown over his shoulders—the seizings are loosed—he is led away, staining his path with red drops of blood, and the hands, "piped down" by the boatswain, sullenly return to their duties.

Such was the scene witnessed on board the Macedonian, on the passage from London to Spithead; such, substantially, is every punishment scene at sea—only carried, sometimes, to a greater length of severity. Sad and sorrowful were my feelings on witnessing it; thoughts of the friendly warnings of my old acquaintance filled my mind, and I inwardly wished myself once more under the friendly roof of my father, at Bladen. Vain wish! I should have believed the warning voice when it was given. Believe me, young man, you will often breathe that wish, if ever you wander from a father's house.

Flogging in the navy is more severe than in the army, though it is too bad to be tolerated there, or indeed anywhere. Other modes of punishment might be successfully substituted, which would deter from misconduct, without destroying the self-respect of the man. I hope the day will come, when a captain will no more be allowed to use the "cat" than he is now to use poison. It should be an interdicted weapon.

ART. III.—*Travels in the Great Western Prairies, the Anahuac and Rocky Mountains, and in the Oregon Territory.* By THOMAS J. FARNHAM. London: Wiley & Putnam.

In the second and third volume of this Magazine for the year 1843, our anticipation of the proximate differences between Great Britain and America is distinctly stated, and our own opinion of our claims to the Oregon Territory emphatically enforced. In an article on the "Fur-Trade between North America and China," also in "British Enterprise—American Aggression," we have stated the grounds on which England rests her claims to the Oregon, and, as we believe, shown that priority of discovery and occupation belong to her. These proved statements were dispassionately replied to, in these pages, and with our consent, by a minister of the United States government, and there, *pro illâc vice*, the question remained. Again, however, American inquietude—we would, perhaps, be justified in calling it discontent—has disturbed the international arrangement, and the right of occupancy can no longer continue undecided, whatever value may result from the decision. To confirm his countrymen in their pertinacity of opinion, and tenacity of grasp, Mr. Farnham has come to the rescue, with some two hundred pages of closely-printed matter, eminently valuable as a topographical accession, and abundantly useful to the future commissioners who are to decide the claim to a territory not bestowed originally upon either of the disputants, but merely an object of their cupidity. Intending, in an early number, to resume our consideration of this disputed question, we shall therefore postpone any remarks upon the tendency of Mr. Farnham's travels in that respect, for the present, contenting ourselves with an extract from his pages, describing the operations, resources, and prospects of the Hudson's Bay Company:—

The trade of Oregon is limited entirely to the operations of the British Hudson Bay Company. A concise account of this association is therefore deemed apposite in this place.

A charter was granted by Charles II. in 1670, to certain British subjects associated under the name of "The Hudson Bay Company," in virtue of which they were allowed the exclusive privilege of establishing trading factories on the Hudson Bay and its tributary rivers. Soon after the grant, the company took possession of the territory, and enjoyed its trade without opposition till 1787, when was organized a powerful rival under the title of the "North-west Fur Company of Canada." This company was chiefly composed of Canadian-born subjects—men whose native energy, and thorough acquaintance with the Indian character, peculiarly qualified them for the dangers and hardships of a fur-trader's life in the frozen regions of British America. Accordingly we soon find the Northwesters outreaching in enterprize and commercial importance their less active neighbours of Hudson Bay; and the jealousies naturally arising between parties so situated, leading to the most barbarous battles, and the sacking and burning of each others' posts. This state of things in 1821 arrested the attention of parliament; and an act was passed consolidating the two companies into one, under the title of "The Hudson Bay Company."

This association is now, under the operation of their charter, in sole possession of all that vast tract of country bounded north by the northern Arctic Ocean; east, by the Davis Straits and the Atlantic Ocean; south and south-westwardly, by the northern boundary of the Canadas and a line drawn through the centre of Lake Superior, and thence north westwardly to the Lake of the Wood, and thence west on the 49th parallel of north latitude to the Rocky Mountains, and along those mountains of the 54th parallel, and thence westwardly on that line to a point nine marine leagues from the Pacific Ocean; and on the west by a line commencing at the last-mentioned point, and running northwardly parallel to the Pacific coast, till it intersects the 141st parallel of longitude west from Greenwich, England, and thence due north to the Arctic Sea.

They have also leased for twenty years, commencing in March, 1840, all of Russian America, except the post of Sitka; the lease renewable at the pleasure of the H.B.C. They are also in possession of Oregon under treaty stipulations between Britain and the United States. The stockholders of this company are British capitalists, resident in Great Britain. From these are elected a board of managers, who hold their meetings and transact their business at "The Hudson Bay House" in London. This board buy goods and ship them to their territory, sell the furs for which they are exchanged, and do all other business connected with the company's transactions, except the execution of their own orders, the actual business of collecting furs, in their territory. This duty is entrusted to a class of men who are called partners, but who, in fact. receive certain portions of the annual nett profits of the company's business, as a compensation for their services.

These gentlemen are divided by their employers into different grades. The first of these is the governor-general of all the company's posts in North America. He resides at York Factory, on the west shore of Hudson Bay. The second class are chief factors; the third chief traders;

the fourth traders. Below these is another class, called clerks. These are usually younger members of respectable Scottish families. They are not directly interested in the company's profits, but receive an annual salary of £100, food, suitable clothing, and a body servant, during an apprenticeship of seven years. At the expiration of this term they are eligible to the traderships, factorships, &c., that may be vacated by death or retirement from the service. While waiting for advancement they are allowed from £80 to £120 per annum. The servants employed about their posts and in their journeyings are half breed Iroquois, and Canadian Frenchmen. These they enlist for five years, at wages varying from 68 dollars to 80 dollars per annum.

An annual council composed of the governor-general, chief factors, and chief traders, is held at York Factory. Before this body are brought the reports of the trade of each district; propositions for new enterprises, and modifications of old ones; and all these and other matters deemed important, being acted upon, the proceedings had thereon, and the reports from the several districts, are forwarded to the Board of Directors in London, and subjected to its final order.

This shrewd company never allow their territory to be overtrapped. If the annual return from any well-trapped district be less in any year than formerly, they order a less number still to be taken, until the beaver and other fur-bearing animals have time to increase. The income of the company is thus rendered uniform, and their business perpetual.

The nature and annual value of the Hudson Bay Company's business in the territory which they occupy, may be learned from the following table, extracted from Bliss's work on the trade and industry of British America, in 1831.—

SKINS.	No.		£.	s.	d.		£.	s.	d.
Beaver...	126,944	each	1	5	0	....	158,680	0	0
Muskrat...........	375,731	....	0	0	6	....	9,393	5	6
Lynx	58,010	....	0	8	0	....	23,204	0	0
Wolf................	5,947	...	0	8	0	....	2,378	16	0
Bear...........	3,850	....	1	0	0	....	3,850	0	0
Fox.................	8,765	...	0	10	0	...	4,382	10	0
Mink	9,298	....	0	2	0	....	929	16	0
Raccoon............	325	....	0	1	6	....	24	7	6
Tails...........	2,290	....	0	1	0	....	114	10	0
Wolverine...........	1,744	....	0	3	0	....	261	12	0
Deer....	645	....	0	3	0	....	96	15	0
Weasel..............	34	....	0	0	6	....	00	16	0
							£203,316	9	0

Some idea may be formed of the nett profit of this business, from the facts that the shares of the company's stock, which originally cost £100, are at 100 per cent. premium, and that the dividends range from ten per cent. upward; and this too while they are creating out of the nett proceeds an immense reserve fund, to be expended in keeping other persons out of the trade.

In 1805 the Missouri Fur Company established a trading-post on the head waters of the Saptin. In 1806 the Northwest Fur Company of Canada established one on Frazer's Lake, near the northern line of Oregon. In March of 1811, the American Pacific Fur Company built Fort Astoria, near the mouth of the Columbia. In July of the same year a partner of the Northwest Fur Company of Canada descended the great northern branch of the Columbia to Astoria. This was the first appearance of the British fur traders in the valleys drained by this river.

On the 16th of October, 1813, while war was raging between England and the States, the Pacific Fur Company sold all its establishments in Oregon to the Northwest Fur Company of Canada. On the 1st of December following, the British sloop of war Raccoon, Captain Black commanding, entered the Columbia, took formal possession of Astoria, and changed its name to Fort George. On the 1st of October, 1818, Fort George was surrendered by the British government to the government of the States, according to a stipulation in the treaty of Ghent. By the same treaty British subjects were granted the same rights of trade and settlement in Oregon as belonged to the citizens of the Republic, for the term of ten years; under the condition that, as both nations claimed Oregon, the occupancy thus authorized, should in no form affect the question as to the title to the country. This stipulation was, by treaty of London, August 6th, 1827, indefinitely extended, under the condition that it should cease to be in force twelve months from the date of a notice of either of the contracting powers to the other, to annul and abrogate it; provided such notice should not be given till after the 20th of October, 1828. And thus stands the matter at this day. And this is the manner in which the British Hudson Bay Company, after its union with the Northwest Fur Company of Canada, came into Oregon.

It has now in the territory the following trading posts: Fort Vancouver, on the north bank of the Columbia, ninety miles from the ocean, in latitude 45 1.2°, longitude 122° 30′; Fort George, (formerly Astoria,) near the mouth of the same river; Fort Nasqually, on Puget's Sound, latitude 47°; Fort Langly, at the outlet of Fraser's River, latitude 49° 25′; Fort McLaughlin, on the Mill-bank Sound, latitude 52°; Fort Simpson, on Dundas Island, latitude 54 1.2°. Frazer's Fort, Fort James, McLeod's Fort, Fort Chilcotin, and Fort Alexandria, on Frazer's river and its branches between the 51st and 54½ parallels of latitude; Thompson's Fort, on Thompson's River, a tributary of Frazer's River, putting into it in latitude 50 degrees and odd minutes; Kootania Fort, on Flatbow River; Flathead Fort, on Flathead River; Forts Hall and Boisais, on the Saptin: Forts Colville, and Oakanagan, on the Columbia, above its junction with the Saptin; Fort Nez Perces, or Wallawalla, a few miles below the junction; Fort McKay, at the mouth of Umqua River, latitude 43° 30′, and longitude 124°.

They also have two migratory trading and trapping establishments of fifty or sixty men each, The one traps and trades in Upper California: the other in the country lying west, south, and east of Fort Hall. They also have a steam-vessel, heavily armed, which runs along the coast, and among its bays and inlets, for the twofold purpose of trading with the natives in places where they have no post, and of outbidding and underselling any American vessel that attempts to trade in those seas. They likewise have five sailing vessels, measuring from 100 to 500 tons burden, and armed with cannon, muskets, cutlasses, &c. These are employed a part of the year in various kinds of trade about the coast and the islands of the North Pacific, and the remainder of the time in bringing goods from London, and bearing back the furs for which they are exchanged.

One of these ships arrives at Fort Vancouver in the spring of each year, laden with coarse woollens, cloths, baizes, and blankets; hardware and cutlery; cotton cloths, calicos, and cotton handkerchiefs; tea, sugar, coffee, and cocoa; rice, tobacco, soap, beads, guns, powder, lead, rum, wine, brandy, gin, and playing-cards; boots, shoes, and ready-made clothing, &c.; also every description of sea-stores, canvass, cordage, paints, oils, chains, and chain-cables, anchors, &c. Having discharged these "supplies," it takes a cargo of lumber to the Sandwich Islands, or of flour and goods to the Russians at Sitka or Kamskatka—returns in August—receives the furs collected at Fort Vancouver, and sails again for England.

The value of peltries annually collected in Oregon by the Hudson Bay Company, is about 140,000 dollars in the London or New York market. The prime cost of the goods exchanged for them is about 20,000 dollars. To this must be added the wages and food, &c., of about 400 men, the expense of shipping to bring supplies of goods and take back the returns of furs, and two years' interest on the investments. The nett profit of the business in the Oregon district to the stockholders, does not vary far from 10,000 dollars per annum. The company made arrangements in 1839 with the Russians at Sitka and at other ports, about the sea of Kamskatka, to supply them with flour and goods at fixed prices. And as they are opening large farms on the Cowelitz, the Umqua, and in other parts of the territory, for the production of wheat for that market; and as they can afford to sell goods purchased in England under a contract of fifty years standing, 20 or 30 per cent. cheaper than American merchants can, there seems a certainty that this powerful company will engross the entire trade of the North Pacific, as it has that of Oregon.

Soon after the union of the Northwest and Hudson Bay Companies, the British parliament passed an act extending the jurisdiction of the Canadian courts over the territories occupied by these fur traders, whether it were "owned" or "claimed by Great Britain." Under this act, certain gentlemen of the fur company were appointed justices of the peace, and empowered to entertain prosecutions for minor offences, arrest and send to Canada criminals of a higher order, and try, render judgment, and grant execution in civil suits where the amount in issue should not exceed £200; and in case of non-payment, to imprison the debtor at their own forts, or in the jails of Canada.

ART. IV.—*The Emigrants' Hand-Book of Facts, concerning Canada, New Zealand, Australia, Cape of Good Hope, &c.* By SAMUEL BUTLER. Glasgow: W.R.M'Phun; London: N. H. Cotes.

If implicit faith is to be placed in this little book of 240 pages, any discussion as to emigration to the Western World may be at once dismissed; since, in the 11th page of the introduction, the author quotes from the recent work upon

America, by Mr. Buckingham, the ex-member for Sheffield, that—"*It is ascertained as a fact, that more than one-third of the emigrants from Europe die within the first three years of their residence in this country (Anglo-America), though they generally come out in the full vigour of life!*" This is a most afflicting statement; but it is to be feared it is too true; as the relations of America, by Captain Marryat, go far to confirm it. There are few subjects more fatally misunderstood, than that of emigration to the Western World; the sea-passage, generally in bad ships, is in itself bad enough; if in American bottoms, which is generally the case, they leave the shores of the United Kingdom uncontrolled by the regulations of Lord Stanley's passengers' act. Poor Irish emigrants are carried by them at 30s. a head: the ship's-owner finding (as it is called) "fire and water;" that is, sufficient fresh-water for the voyage, and fire to cook their food. In many instances, these conditions are by no means fulfilled; the wretched emigrant, in the recklessness of despair, carries as many potatoes as he fancies will last the voyage, and, with the great bulk of them, nothing can exceed their sufferings. The sea between Europe and Northern America is a boisterous one, and it appears by the official report of the government agent for Canada, that the voyage is one of fifty-seven days—but this is only the beginning of the voyage; landed at New York, or Quebec—it is having passed, as it were, the bridge of waters—this is but a small part of the real journey; the emigrant has to find his way to the far west. Thousands every year never attempt it; but no sooner landed, than they begin to beg the means of returning. Those who have the means, go on; and then death from fatigue, severity of climate, &c. begins, and the result is what Mr. Buckingham describes. Canada is but the stepping-stone to the United States; it has more months of winter than of summer; during winter the country is under snow. This is the case also at New York, and the severity is such as is almost unknown to the inhabitants of the United Kingdom; the heat in summer excessive—painfully so. Then, politically speaking, from its having been founded by the French, and conquered by us, it is a country peopled by two races—people of different languages, habits, laws, and opinions—creating continual jealousies and disputes. And then we have the opinion of the man who best knows the United States, the Canadas, and Great Britain, the sagacious Lord Ashburton, that the Canadas will not remain twenty-five years longer under the dominion of Great Britain. Compare this with emigration to New Zealand: the average voyage is, in point of time, as far as the sea is concerned, just about double, or one hundred and twenty days, instead of fifty-seven; but then the emigrant lands where he is to finally settle. As for the voyage itself, the sea, by running down to the coast of the Brazils, and then taking the benefit of the trade-winds, which blow steadily nine months out of the twelve, and going far to the southward of the Cape of Good Hope, the voyage is generally a delightful one. And then no little pains is taken, by means of the cabin-passengers, that a due proportion of capital should go out with the labouring people. On arrival, the Company, for those who emigrate to their settlements, finds them house, rations of meat and bread, and pays them for work on the roads, until they can do better under the settlers. In point of fact, it is all the difference between emigration and colonization—between forethought and mere chance. The great object of Irish landlords is to get rid of the false population, the creation of which they encouraged for political purposes; and, now their aim is clearing their estates, whether the unfortunate wretch and his family suffer much or little, their object is attained. But emigration from the west of England is another matter. The good Earl Devon and his coadjutors have adopted wise measures for sending out capital and labour, to combine it with some of the most fertile land in the world, and in a climate which has not its equal anywhere. A philosophical politician may well look on and exclaim—this will be the Britain of the South!

ORIGINAL CORRESPONDENCE.

To the Editor of the Colonial Magazine.

GOVERNMENT BANKING, ETC., AT ALGOA BAY, (EASTERN AFRICA.)

MUCH interest and confidence being now raised in the above Colony in consequence of the new Secretary, Mr. Montague, having undertaken the task of disposing of the public debt, and of public road-making, about which so much despondency and complaint have existed, I am induced to furnish some brief particulars with which I have been favoured from Graham's Town, under date of the 30th November, 1843. In advising on these subjects, my informant states: first, in reference to Mr. Montague, "this shows the great advantage of aptitude to office, a consideration quite overlooked before in the selection of public officers here." Secondly. In reference to the Debt itself, some difference of opinion of course exists as to charging the district colonists at all with the Debt, because the sums originally forming it, have been in a great measure repaid by the parties to whom it was originally lent, and again re-issued by the Government, who have alone benefited thereby in the following extraordinary manner, viz: the rix-dollar which then passed current in the Colony for four shillings, was reduced in granting bills on the treasury, first to 3s. 6d., then 3s., 2s. 6d., and finally 1s. 6d., where it has permanently remained since; so that a person, wishing to draw a treasury bill for £100, had in the

First stage of depreciation to pay			£127	10s.
Second	ditto	ditto	175	0
Third	ditto	ditto	202	10
Fourth	ditto	ditto	235	15

in Colonial currency or notes, besides the premium on the bill, which would nearly bring it to what Mr. Ross stated, 180 per cent., or £280 for every £100, and all this time the Commissariat re-issued these rix-dollar notes in exchange for Colonial produce, rated or considered at their market value of four shillings. In this way, the British government must have realized large sums, or, to make it clear, for a load of wool value four dollars or sixteen shillings, they in the

First stage of depreciation only paid four dollars at 3s. 6d., or			14s.
Second	ditto	ditto	only 12
Third	ditto	ditto	only 10
Fourth	ditto	ditto	only 8
Fifth	ditto	ditto	only 6

and so for every thing else. This simple illustration makes the business pretty clear, and shows that they must have gained largely in the value of their purchases for many years, on the re-issue of these notes, to the extent (as shown here) of 166 per cent.

Thirdly. In reference to roads. The plan now adopted for redeeming the above debt is so far good as leaving the revenue unshackled, so that a portion of the latter, it is hoped, may in future be applied towards road-making, on which point one example will suffice: "Being in the suburbs of Graham's Town, and to the southward too, the horrible state of that main road quite surprised me, being interlaced (something like a chess-board) with ruts, longitudinally and transversely, in every direction, and some of them several feet in depth and breadth. There were at the time two loaded waggons coming in; the first got over tolerably, with a vast deal of whipping and cracking, shouting and hallooing; not so the second; the wheel stuck fast, nor could all the exertions of the driver succeed in persuading the oxen to move on. In this dilemma, the team was loosed from the first waggon and put on, but in vain, although twenty-four beasts, now yoked, exerted all their strength. The cattle were so jaded by the exertion, that the driver was obliged to outspan here, and *I suppose* the next morning succeeded in getting his load to market. On these facts comment is needless, beyond simply remarking that the British government appears here also to have, through the medium of its jackals, pretty well played the game of fleecing and exhausting, and then neglecting the industrious colonists.

G. T. W.

COMMERCE OF THE UNITED STATES, 1842.

The following table exhibits a comparative view of the commerce of the United States with the principal nations of the world. It will be seen that nearly one half of the commerce is with England and her colonies, that the balance of trade was last year in favour of the United States, and that the balance against them in Spain, Russia, America, and China, is made up by England, France, Holland, and the Hanse Towns, and numerous other places where the trade is comparatively small:—

	Imports. Dollars.	Exports. Dollars.	Excess Imp. Dollars.	Excess Exp. Dollars.
Great Britain and British Depend.,	38,613,000	42,500,000	....	3,900,000
France and her Dependencies.....	17,233,000	18,738,000	....	1,500,000
Spain " "	13,450,000	6,300,000	7,150,000	....
Russia.....	1,350,000	836,000	500,000	....
America, other than United States,	13,000,000	7,000,000	6,000,000	....
China.........	5,000,000	1,500,000	3,500,000	....
Holland	1,000,000	3,500,000	2,500,000	....
Hanse Towns................ ...	2,200,000	4,400,000	....	4,500,000
TOTAL.............	100,161,000	104,691,000	....	4,050,000

COLONIAL INTELLIGENCE.

India.—The news from India is various and important, of which the following are extracts from the papers under date of Jan. 1st. British India is tranquil, and likely to continue so, for its disaffected have discovered that their turbulence would turn to no use, and that ultimately they would have to endure the evils which they wish to inflict on others. The news from the kingdom of the Sikhs represents that country as far from being tranquillized. It appears that Golab Singh, the elder brother of Dhyan Singh, old Runjeet's favourite Minister, who was assassinated in September last, had come from his mountain fastnesses to Lahore, under pretence of supporting his nephew Heera Singh, who now governs there, under the name of the young sovereign Dhuleep, and that his arrival had not produced the expected results. The young Minister is described as giving large sums of money to the common soldiers, in order to retain them in some order, while his uncles are busy in plundering the treasures of the Sikh Government, and carrying away the jewels and articles of value to the mountains. An attempt was made by his own maternal uncle to carry away the young Rajah, and place him under the protection of the British, but it was not successful. Care is taken by the present chiefs to occupy the fords across the rivers, so that even the refugees are detained. The state of the country is described as bordering upon anarchy. Many of the petty chiefs are anxious to proclaim their independence, and are ready for an insurrection. The Affghan government is as feeble as ever in the hands of Dost Mahomed, and intrigues are afloat of various kinds. In the midst of these intrigues, Dost Mahomed appears to be unable to make the contemplated attack on Peshawur, although it is no longer defended by the European generals of the Lion of Lahore. All the French officers have left the service of the Sikhs, so that it is highly probable the boasted prowess of those troops will soon become little more than the courage of rabble, if ever Akhbar Khan, who is governing Jellalabad with the greatest cruelty, should dare to attack the Sikh provinces to the west of the Indus. It is doubted by the Affghans themselves whether Dost Mahomed, or his notorious son, will make any attempt on Peshawur, as much from their dread of the British influence, as from their own inability to govern the tribes in the neighbourhood of Cabul.

The great clamour against Lord Ellenborough had subsided, and his Lordship, the nature of whose measures was becoming clear to the very commonest understanding, was growing popular. With the army he is still a special favourite. In the meantime, the arrangements of his lordship for the subjugation of the state of Gwalior have been highly successful. He left Calcutta on the 25th of November, and, travelling in a carriage of the palanquin kind, which was propelled, and not, as usual in India, borne by men, arrived at Allahabad on the 3d of December, where a short halt was made. He reached Cawnpore on the 7th, and, proceeding direct to Agra, arrived in that city on the 11th. Instead of proceeding to the palace prepared for his reception, his lordship remained in his tent. As his intentions are unknown, in consequence of his keeping his own secrets, it is not certain whether his lordship will declare the country to be altogether a British province, and appoint collectors and other officers to administer it, or whether he will content himself in taking a portion of it to defray the expenses of the armament, and leave the remainder to the tender care of the "brutal government of the young Rajah's adherents." Every one acquainted with the state of India knows, notwithstanding the grievances of which the natives complain under the systematic rule of the Hon. Company, that those Indians who are not subject to that rule look upon it as Elysium in comparison to the yoke of a native Rajah's oppression. The Army of Exercise was ready near Agra, under the orders of the Commander-in-Chief, Sir Hugh Gough. The first brigade, led by General Valiant, was ordered to move towards Dhoolpoor, half way to Gwalior; it marched on the 12th, and the rest of the army moved in the same direction on the following days. The Commander-in-Chief and the Governor-General set out on the 16th. The intelligence reached Gwalior, and produced alarm, and a council was held on the 15th, at which the principal officers and generals attended, and debated in the presence of the Bhaee, or "young Queen."

The success of Lord Ellenborough at Gwalior will, it is expected, lead him soon to settle the intricate question of the Punjaub. Whether the care shown by the present Chiefs of Lahore to prevent any immediate outbreak may continue to have the effect for many months longer was considered doubtful. It is said that it is by money alone that Heera Singh has kept the Sikh soldiers quiet. It cannot be supposed that his funds for that purpose will last long, and therefore another revolution is anticipated there.

The sickness in Scinde continued to be the source of much comment to the opponents of the policy of Lord Ellenborough; they seemed to attribute the sickness to himself individually, as if he was the grand cause of it. A great number of medical officers had been despatched thither from Bombay. The Government appeared resolved on retaining the country, which is now tranquil; and it was said that several regiments from the Madras Presidency would be sent there in order to assist the Bombay troops, who were rather exhausted from several campaigns. Sir Charles Napier and General Simpson enjoyed good health, and were active in their arrangements for keeping the country quiet.

At Sukkur there had been much sickness, but it appeared to be diminishing. The hint had been thrown out, of the utility of having moveable barracks, with iron roofs, and wooden compartments, which would afford facilities for changing the localities, a great advantage in India, where the earth, once saturated with animal matter, and moistened either by the rain, or, what is worse, by the sea water, always produces the most fatal effects. It is therefore hoped, that the Hon. Company will take into consideration the great advantages of having such edifices prepared of iron in England, and of teak or other hard wood in India.

China.—The intelligence from China comes down to the 1st December. Little had occurred worthy of notice subsequent to the fires which consumed the factories on the 25th. of October, by which the Danish, Spanish, and a part of the French factories, were destroyed. The British Consulate was also consumed. The markets at Canton had become rather more favourable. A proclamation had been issued by the Imperial Commissioner declaring that the warehouses belonging to the new merchants (outside men) are to stand on an equal footing with the old (Hong) merchants, and that henceforth there shall be no difference between the two warehouses. The supplementary treaty, of which a copy had been sent to Pekin, was forwarded also to Bombay, and was to come by the mail to England. The British Consuls had arrived at Amoy and Shanghae, where trade was dull, as the arrangements were not then completed. The Chinese authorities at Ningpo declined granting permission for the importation of goods there until the Consul had arrived and the duties were settled. They are said to have been alarmed by an Imperial chop, which they had received from Pekin, ordering that no business should be carried on unless the Consul was there. At Chusan the British system of governing without squeezing the inhabitants had conciliated their attachment, and they appeared to regret the approaching departure of the British troops. Some Americans, as if courting a cause of quarrel with the Chinese, had ventured upon excursions into the interior: this practice had procured from the British Plenipotentiary a declaration to the Chinese Commissioner, that he should by no means countenance such proceedings, and that orders should be given to the Consuls to have all such foreigners arrested and sent to Hong Kong. The death of Major Eldred Pottinger, which occurred at Hong Kong, was greatly deplored. Colonel Knowles, of the Artillery, and assistant-surgeons Grahame and Dill, have also fallen victims to the prevalent malady. Rumour spoke of some differences between Sir H. Pottinger and the British Admiral and General. The Plenipotentiary is said to be anxious to return to Europe. The Admiral was about to sail for Calcutta. The American frigate and Minister had gone to China from Bombay and Colombo, at both of which places he had been fêted.

Letters to India and Hong Kong.—The following important notice was issued at the General Post-office, St. Martin's-le-Grand:—"General Post-office, February, 1844.—On and from the 15th February, the postage on letters posted in the United Kingdom and addressed to India, marked to be forwarded *via* Southampton, may be paid in advance or not, at the option of the sender. This regulation applies only to letters from places within the territories of the Hon. East India Company conveyed by packet, *via* Southampton, the postage on all other letters addressed to India, *via* France, as well as on all letters addressed to countries beyond India, (the colony of Hong Kong excepted,) by whatever route they may be forwarded, must be paid in advance as at present, or the letters cannot be forwarded. By command,

"W. L. Maberly, Secretary."

Tahiti.—The following are extracts of a letter announcing the deposition of Queen Pomare by the French. On the 5th of November the following order appeared:—

"'The Vice-Admiral in command of the station of the Pacific Ocean informs the commanding officers and crews of vessels in the roads of Papaiti, that the Queen Pomare refusing obstinately to recognize the treaty concluded on the 9th of September, 1842, and ratified by His Majesty Louis Philippe, he is compelled to declare that the Queen Pomare has ceased to reign over the Society Islands and their inhabitants, and to take possession of the islands in the name of the King of France. In consequence the frigate Uranie will debark to-morrow morning, at 6 o'clock, the company of marine artillery, and the men dependent on that service,' &c."

The writer of the letter, Eugene Gosse, then explains at great length the circumstances which have changed the position of the respective parties to the last treaty.

"In the night the orders were changed. The Admiral wished to act as long as possible with indulgence. He thought that the order of the day published in the day would have been sufficient to have set aside the suggestions of Mr. Pritchard and his colleagues, and to point out to the poor queen the precipice on which she stood. A delay was granted. Noon was the time fixed at which the tri-coloured flag should be hoisted by order of the queen, and France would then content herself with the execution of the other clauses of the treaty. If this was not done, the dethronement of Queen Pomare was to be declared, and her flag replaced by our own. Serious interests were thus attached to the hoisting of a flag. The quarter-decks of all the vessels in the roadstead, including that of the English frigate, were crowded with officers; all their telescopes were directed towards the Queen's Palace, and men were posted in the tops on the look out. The hour past; the flag of Pomare was still waving; Pomare—the blind, the obstinate Pomare—refused to yield to our demands. 200 artillery and marines were landed, with 300 or 400 sailors, and surrounded the queen's house, in which everything was silent—the flag of Pomare was removed; M. Aubigny, the Governor of Tahiti, exclaimed, "Officers, soldiers, and sailors, and you inhabitants of these islands, to whom we bring justice and peace, in the name of the King our august master, I take possession of this country. We shall all be content to die for the defence of the glorious tri-coloured flag. Hoist the flag.' This order was executed amidst the rolling of the drums, and cries of '*Vive le Roi.*' Queen Pomare has ceased to reign, and we now stand on French soil.

"The flag of the English Consulate was immediately struck. In the evening the town had resumed its usual tranquillity; the men smoked their cigars with the same carelessness, and the women grinned and showed their white teeth, as though they had not in the morning been present at a revolution.

"The Governor-General was installed on the 8th, and proclaimed the Council of the Government, which was composed of M. D'Aubigny, captain of the corvette, Lieutenant Clon, and M. Morenhout, ex-Consul of France.

"A proclamation, addressed to the inhabitants, assured them security for their persons and their property, and the free exercise of their religious worship.

"Papaiti is declared a free port; no anchorage dues will be claimed, nor any custom-house duties; pilot dues will alone be demanded."

Cape of Good Hope.—Papers to the 21st of December have been received. They give very little interesting intelligence. It would, however, appear from a statement they contain that the English are not likely to retain undisturbed possession of Natal, since it seems that the disaffected Boer Mocke had, with his force, seized and imprisoned several of the emigrant farmers who were on their way from the Orange river to Pietermauritzberg to tender their allegiance to Colonel Cloete. The crops in the neighbourhood of the Cape continued to bear a promising appearance, and the locusts, though numerous, were less troublesome, the late floods having cleared many thousands away. Quarterly fairs are to be established at Uitenhage, for the sale of live stock and agricultural produce, prizes being awarded for the best exhibitions, according to a graduated scale published in the journals. The depredations of the Tamboohie and other tribes are alluded to as increasing, and the thefts of cattle are not always free from encounters, which generally end in the shedding of the blood of the natives.

The regulations contained in the government notice of the 24th July, 1843, to provide for the due collection and expenditure of the public revenue of the colony having been found, in some respects, insufficient, additional regulations have been approved by his Excellency the governor, and published for the information and guidance of the officers of the government of the Cape of Good Hope.

West Indies.—The West India mail brings dates from Jamaica to the 24th of January. The papers received state that the governor had returned to Spanish town to be present at an ecclesiastical ceremony, after which he was about to take a tour through the north-side parishes. Loud complaints are made of excessive drought in Manchester and Elizabeth, and so scarce was water that the wants of the population could not be properly satisfied. The corn crops had failed, and provisions were advancing in price. Much distress prevailed, and should the dry weather continue, great fears were entertained for the result. With respect to business at Jamaica, it is represented as exceedingly dull, and money is stated to be scarce.

The Jamaica House of Assembly has evinced, by a unanimous grant of 300 guineas for a tablet to be erected in the cathedral church of Spanish Town to the memory of Lady Elgin, the high opinion entertained of her ladyship by the members of that house.

The weather at Barbadoes had been very oppressive till within a few days of the 20th ult., when a change took place, and cold and chilly winds were experienced, and then the shock of an earthquake was felt, which being a severe one, although doing no damage, spread a good deal of alarm throughout the colony. Rain had followed, which, it was hoped, would do some good to the plantations, and prepare the ground for agricultural operations. The trial of Mr. Thomas for the robbery at the Colonial Bank in that island had been delayed, for the presence of material witnesses. In all the islands the Christmas holidays had passed over quietly, and the conduct of the negro population on this occasion is alluded to as completely satisfactory.

Some statistics in these papers give the produce of Trinidad and St. Lucia up to this year. The sugar exported last year from Trinidad amounted to 22,615 hhds. 1,327 tierces, and 4,836 barrels, against 19,176 hhds. 1,401 tierces and 3,783 barrels in 1842. The coffee exported was 124,583lb. against 398,363lb. in 1842. The exports of sugar from St. Lucia last year was 5,095,195lb. against 6,405,365lb. in 1842. Coffee showed a greater decline, the exports last year being only 26,795lb. against 144,441lb. in 1842. The shock of an earthquake had been felt in St. Vincent's, St. Lucia, Dominica, and the neighbouring islands, but without serious effect. At St. Lucia the weather was highly favourable to the crops, though not so favourable for road-making. The planters of Dominica had commenced cutting their canes, the yield of which was superior to previous years, while the season was fine, and the sugar manufactured of good quality. At Trinidad a vessel had arrived with 216 emigrants from Rio de Janeiro, 93 of whom were women, and all being young and in health. They found when landed immediate employment. Another vessel with 300 more was shortly looked for from the same quarter.

Canada.—By a proclamation in the *Canada Gazette* of the 13th January, the provincial Parliament stands further prorogued until the 24th February. Sir Charles Metcalfe has given 500 dollars as a contribution to the fund raising to enable the Canadian convicts to return from New South Wales. It was reported at Toronto that the Hon. H. Stawood had been appointed Solicitor-General.

Major-General the Hon. Frederick George Heriot, K.B. and C.B., died on the 30th of December, at Comfort Hall, Drummondville. He entered the service at the age of 15, and attained the rank of lieutenant-colonel at 27, after having been engaged in all the stirring events in these provinces from 1801 to 1806; his whole service to the sovereign has been in Canada. He was born in the island of Jersey on the 11th of January, 1786.

United States.—The accounts received from the United States do not throw any additional light upon the important question of the probable amount of the cotton crop. The following are the comparative receipts up to the latest dates received, with those published at the corresponding period of last year, and the year 1842:—

Receipts in 1844, 840,823; ditto in 1843, 1,128,709; ditto in 1842, 773,453. It is right to observe, however, that the returns this year from New Orleans are 10 days, and from Mobile a week in arrear. If brought down to the same period as those for the two preceding years, they would probably show a total receipt approaching 900,000 bales, and indicating a total crop of about 1,900,000 bales. Few of the estimates from the cotton districts, however, exceed 1,800,000 to 1,850,000 bales, and the majority are below even the former amount. Meanwhile, the stocks of cotton in the different ports are rapidly accumulating. The exports both to Great Britain and France have fallen off very greatly; and prices are still too high to admit of profitable shipment to this country. So completely has the export been checked, that it is said there are now only six cotton vessels known to have cleared for Great Britain, and not arrived, whilst at the corresponding period of last year the number was 95; and the number loading for England, at the date of the last advices, was only 46 against 126 last year. Under these circumstances, notwithstanding the falling-off in the receipts at the ports, the stock continues to accumulate; amounting to about 525,000 bales. It is peculiarly fortunate for the spinners of this country that there is still a very heavy stock of American cotton remaining on hand, amounting (probably with the stocks in the interior) to nearly 200,000 bales more than at the corresponding period of last year. This large stock gives time to wait the result of the struggle upon the other side of the Atlantic, the existence of which, whatever might have been its termination, would otherwise have placed them in an exceedingly unfavourable position. On the whole, the recent advices tend to keep the price of cotton in this country tolerably steady.

Exports of Tea.—Exports of tea from Canton to the United States, from June 30th, 1842, to June 4th, 1843, stated in chests:—

Young Hyson	77,299
Hyson	14,885
Hyson Skin	15,992
Twankay	4,101
Gunpowder	9,869
Imperial	7,573
Congo	2,718
Souchong	34,774
Powchong	8,648
Pekoe	1,028
Orange Pekoe	560
Bohea	757
Total Chests	178,204

Pongees	packages	7,875
Canton Silk	cases	67
Rhubarb	boxes	666
Sweetmeats	boxes	2,026
Cassia	piculs	8,535

IMPERIAL PARLIAMENT.

House of Lords, Thurday, Feb. 1.

Her Majesty this day opened in person the fourth session of the 14th Parliament of the "United Kingdom" of Great Britain and Ireland, with the following Speech from the throne :—

My Lords, and Gentlemen,

It affords me great satisfaction again to meet you in Parliament, and to have the opportunity of profiting by your assistance and advice.

I entertain a confident hope that the general peace, so necessary for the happiness and prosperity of all nations, will continue uninterrupted.

My friendly relations with the King of the French, and the good understanding happily established between my government and that of his Majesty, with the continued assurances of the peaceful and amicable dispositions of all princes and states, confirm me in this expectation.

I have directed that the treaty which I have concluded with the Emperor of China shall be laid before you; and I rejoice to think that it will in its results prove highly advantageous to the trade of this country.

Throughout the whole course of my negociations with the government of China, I have uniformly disclaimed the wish for any exclusive advantages.

It has been my desire that equal favour should be shown to the industry and commercial enterprize of all nations.

The hostilities which took place during the past year in Scinde have led to the annexation of a considerable portion of that country to the British possessions in the East.

In all the military operations, and especially in the battles of Meeanee and Hydrabad, the constancy and valour of the troops, native and European, and the skill and gallantry of their distinguished commander, have been most conspicuous.

I have directed that additional information explanatory of the transactions in Scinde shall be forthwith communicated to you.

Gentlemen of the House of Commons,

The estimates for the ensuing year will be immediately laid before you.

They have been prepared with a strict regard to economy, and at the same time with a due consideration of those exigencies of the public service which are connected with the maintenance of our maritime strength, and the multiplied demands on the naval and military establishments from the various parts of a widely extended empire.

My Lords, and Gentlemen,

I congratulate you on the improved condition of several important branches of the trade and manufactures of the country.

I trust that the increased demand for labour has relieved, in a corresponding degree, many classes of my faithful subjects from sufferings and privations which at former periods I have had occasion to deplore.

For several successive years the annual produce of the revenue fell short of the public expenditure.

I confidently trust that in the present year the public income will be amply sufficient to defray the charges upon it.

I feel assured that, in considering all matters connected with the financial concerns of the country, you will bear in mind the evil consequences of accumulating debt during the time of peace, and that you will firmly resolve to uphold that public credit, the maintenance of which concerns equally the permanent interests and the honour and reputation of a great country.

In the course of the present year the opportunity will occur of giving notice to the Bank of England on the subject of the revision of its charter.

It may be advisable that during this session of Parliament, and previously to the arrival of the period assigned for the giving of such notice, the state of the law with regard to the privileges of the Bank of England and to other banking establishments should be brought under your consideration.

At the close of the last session of Parliament I declared to you my firm determination to maintain inviolate the Legislative Union between Great Britain and Ireland.

I expressed at the same time my earnest desire to co-operate with Parliament in the adoption of all such measures as might tend to improve the social condition of Ireland, and to develope the natural resources of that part of the United Kingdom.

I am resolved to act in strict conformity with this declaration.

I forbear from observation on events in Ireland, in respect to which proceedings are pending before the proper legal tribunal.

My attention has been directed to the state of the law and practice with regard to the occupation of land in Ireland.

I have deemed it advisable to institute extensive local inquiries into a subject of so much importance, and have appointed a commission with ample authority to conduct the requisite investigation.

I recommend to your early consideration the enactments at present in force in Ireland concerning the registration of voters for members of Parliament.

You will probably find that a revision of the law of registration, taken in conjunction with other causes at present in operation, would produce a material diminution of the number of county voters, and that it may be advisable on that account to consider the state of the law, with a view to an extension of the country franchise in Ireland.

I commit to your deliberate consideration the various important questions of public policy which will necessarily come under your review, with full confidence in your loyalty and wisdom, and with an earnest prayer to Almighty God to direct and favour your efforts to promote the welfare of all classes of my people.

At the conclusion of the speech the Commons withdrew, and the house adjourned during pleasure.

OBITUARY.

Besborough, the Right Hon. the Earl of, on 3d Feb. at Cranford House, Dorchester, aged 86 years. His Lordship is succeeded in his titles and estates by his eldest son, Viscount Duncannon, county of Wexford, Baron Besborough, of Besborough, county of Kilkenny, Ireland, Lord Ponsonby, Baron Ponsonby of Sysonby, in England, and Vice-Admiral of Munster, was born on the 26th of Jan 1758, and succeeded his father in 1793. His Lordship was married in 1780 to Henrietta Frances Spencer, daughter of John, first Earl Spencer, by whom (who died in 1821) he had issue, John William, Viscount Duncannon, the present Earl. His Lordship's second son, Sir Frederick Cavendish Ponsonby, died in 1837; and his Lordship's third son, William Francis Spencer Ponsonby, was created Baron de Mauley, by patent in 1838. His Lordship's only daughter, Caroline, was married to the present Viscount Melbourne, and died in 1828.

Dickson, Vice-Admiral Sir E. S., January 28th. This gallant officer entered the service in 1772, in his seventh year, and was present in the Actæon at the attack of Charleston, where she was destroyed by the batteries of Sullivan's Island, under which she grounded; transferred to the Bristol, he was at the capture of New York, and afterwards joined the Æolus, in which he assisted at the capture of the Prudente French frigate. In 1780 he was made a lieutenant at the unprecedented and early age of fifteen, and appointed to the Artois. In the Sampson he assisted at the relief of Gibraltar, and was in the battle of the combined fleets. He was wounded on the glorious 1st of June, while second lieutenant of the Cæsar, which led the van; and in the West Indies, while commanding the Frederick cutter, beat off a privateer of very superior force, which gained his promotion as commander to the Victorieuse. Stationed off Trinidad, he led in the fleet which reduced this important colony in 1797. In convoying the trade to St. Kitt's, he encountered off Guadaloupe two republican privateers, who laid him alongside, one of which he captured, and the other escaped. The immortal Picton, then Governor of Trinidad, with the English inhabitants, acknowledged these services by presenting him with a sword worth 100 guineas, while Earl Spencer rewarded him with the post rank. In 1804 he recaptured, while in the Inconstant, the island of Goree, on the coast of Africa, with a garrison of 400 men, and in the same ship, on the Guernsey station, commanded a squadron for the blockade of St. Malo. In the Stately he commanded the naval forces at the siege of Tariffa, and received the thanks of the Admiralty. In the Rivoli, on the escape of Napoleon from Elba, he was most actively employed in the Mediterranean. With unabated vigilance he prevented the escape of Napoleon's mother and sister Pauline from Castel de Mare, and captured at his own risk the Melpomene frigate, after a spirited resistance, bearing the tri-coloured flag, sent by Napoleon to convey them to France. Selected by Lord Exmouth from among his captains at Naples to command the expedition against the fortress of Porto Ferrajo, he reduced the island of Elba, and thus had the singular honour of striking the first and last tri-coloured flag of the 100 days' war. In 1831 he received the rank of rear-admiral, which terminated his active service.

Glentworth, the Right Hon. Lord, on 16th Feb. at London. The deceased Edmond Henry Lord Glentworth was eldest son of the late Lord, who died in 1837, and grandson and heir of the Earl of Limerick. He was born 3d of March, 1809, and married 8th of October, 1836, Miss Eve Maria Villebois, second daughter of Mr. H. Villebois, by whom, we believe, his Lordship leaves a young family.

Goodman, Major-General, C.B., K.H., January 2nd, at British Guiana. He entered the army in 1794, as ensign in the 48th regiment of foot; Lieutenant, 1795; Captain, 1803; Major and Lieutenant-Colonel, 1813; Colonel, 1830; and Major-General, 1842. Few soldiers in the British service were more actively engaged than General Goodman. He shared in most of the battles of the Peninsula, and at Waterloo. In 1821, he was appointed to the then lucrative situation of Vendue-Master of Demerara and Essequibo, in the discharge of the duties of which post he continued till his death.

Nedham, Major-General William, Colonel of the late 4th Veteran battalion, Feb. 13th, at Worthing, aged 74.

Saxe Coburg and Gotha, his royal highness the duke of, uncle and father-in-law of Her Majesty, father of Prince Albert, and eldest brother of the duchess of Kent and the king of the Belgians, Feb. —, aged 60 years. He succeeded his father, Duke Francis of Saxe Coburg and Saalfeld, in the year 1806.

Sidmouth, the Right Hon. Henry Addington, Viscount Sidmouth, Feb. 15th, at Richmond Park, aged 87 years. The father of the deceased nobleman was an eminent physician in Berkshire, through whose practice in the family of the celebrated Lord Chatham the path of distinction was smoothed to the son. He first sat in parliament for the borough of Devizes, and was made speaker of the House of Commons by Mr. Pitt, which office he filled from May, 1789, to March, 1801; First Lord of the Treasury, and Chancellor of the Exchequer, from March, 1801, to May, 1804; Lord President of the Council, 1805; Lord Privy Seal, 1806; and Secretary of State for the Home Department, from 1812 to 1822.

Wright, Lieutenant-Colonel John Alexander, late commandant of the St. Helena Regiment, East India Company's service, Dec. at St. Helena. This officer had seen much service, having been employed with the St. Helena Regiment at the expedition to South America, afterwards served with his regiment in India, and was subsequently at the taking of the Cape of Good Hope. He had retired from the service previous to the disbandment of the St. Helena Regiment by Her Majesty's Government.

LONDON: FISHER, SON, AND CO, PRINTERS.

FISHER'S

COLONIAL MAGAZINE.

ENGLAND'S BEST REFUGE LIES IN WISELY HUSBANDING HER RESOURCES.

THE "ocean" and the "earth" alike conspire in shedding around the British islands advantages, of which, in their rare accumulation, few other localities are possessed.

Setting aside their vast possessions on foreign soils, subject to all the various geographical climates of our globe, the treasures of their native soil, their numerous ports and harbours, and secure havens, surrounding our entire country, our comparatively mild atmosphere, capacitate us for the enjoyment of very extensive blessings, unimpaired by debts and pecuniary embarassments.

But England, spite of every advantage which a synchronism of fortunate events has shed around her, is, at this present moment, loaded with debts, mortgages, and financial perplexity and distress.

How shall we account for these anomalies and discrepancies? How are we to account for the apparent anomaly of a nation, possessing the elements of plenty and comfort, exhibiting, among a large portion of their denizens, distress, and want, and the wailings of discontent? How, but by assuming that our advantages of situation, and the peculiar sources of profit which we possess, over other nations, are not made the most of;—how, but by supposing negligence or supineness on the part of our governors;—how, but by supposing the constant existence of a disposition in our rulers, to legislate for certain privileged classes, in preference to the great common weal; how, but that many of those who legislate for England's prosperity, either do not understand her best interests, or, like the patricians, even in the time of the old Roman republic, are habitually prone to exalt their own weal, and depress that of their empire;—how, but by causes, such as these, are we to account for it? And yet the extraordinary fact is acknowledged and deplored on all hands.

Many other causes, it is true, have been sought for, and triumphantly cited, as contributing at least to heighten, if they were not the sole operating agents in producing these difficulties and embarrassments. It has often been argued, that the state of the currency has had a large share in the distresses of the country. That an excess in the circulating medium, a facility, or a license of paper-coinage, to an unlimited extent, that over-trading, and the mania of speculation, has often proved ruinous to our commerce. But however insisted on, the supporters of these theses have failed in making it intelligible to plain understandings, that the distresses complained of are in general attributable to them.

The Anti-Corn Law League has, meanwhile, grown into colossal power and consequence. Like a huge lion, then, it now attracts notice from its magnitude; and has enrolled among its supporters a great proportion of the mercantile and trading ranks throughout the country, with not a few of the more aristocratic.

The "League" has, beyond all question, been pushed on to its present importance, by the uncompromising spirit with which some of the just claims of the people have been met by those, whose constitutional duty it was to have paid them every calm and deliberate attention. It is natural for a suffering people to remonstrate, when, as they conceive, unjust or inadequate burdens are laid upon them; and when such remonstrances are disregarded, it is equally natural for them to look to other expedients for redress. The Americans, under George III., petitioned against their grievances, until it almost became a by-word and a subject of scoffing; when at length, under Washington, they taught Great Britain a memorable lesson, which it will not be wise in her to neglect. The rising winds do not at once, with their concentrating force, dash the ocean into fury; but once agitated, the restless surges will not immediately subside with the element which was instrumental in producing them. The discontents of a nation, which judicious and timely concessions might allay, through a course of pertinacious opposition grow into powerful faction, whose wide-spreading and contagious influence is not to be put down by after-concessions.

The present rulers of the destinies of England will act wisely not to be unmindful of truths which all history has proclaimed, and which must still continue to operate upon the great masses of society in a free country; but if they should, they alone of all mankind are responsible for the consequences.

England, occupying a position in one of the northern corners of Europe, is peculiarly fitted for commerce. As Europe is, and has ever been, the most civilized quarter of the globe, so the localities of England are pre-eminently privileged to maintain first-rate ascendancy as a nautical and a trading power.

But, in order to make all her high resources simply available to raise her above her difficulties, it is unquestionable that she wants among her legislators more of that stern patriotism, which raised the old Roman republic above all the other powers of the world, and taught each citizen to sacrifice private aggrandisement to the public weal; that private animosities, political partisanship, and the madness of party, should yield place to a steady aim at the integral prosperity of the empire.

Why should not England, indeed, highly gifted as she is with all local advantages, with a judicious application of them, outlast the period which has limited the grandeur and the enterprize of other states, renowned in other days for their vast trade, but whose ephemeral greatness has passed away.

Tyre, Rhodes, Carthage, Alexandria, Byzantium, Colchis, in ancient times, filled the world with their renown; the riches of civilized nations were conducted into their ports. Venice, Genoa, Holland, in modern days, have shone forth in splendour as the emporium of commerce, famous for their riches, splendour, and maritime enterprise. England has now for the last hundred years borne away the palm from all other countries of Europe in her commercial transactions with all parts of the earth. Shall her ascendancy in commerce, and in enterprise, recede before a more powerful rival? Shall the genius of her extensive and far-reaching influence sink before more fortunate competitors? Shall her immense facilities for lucrative intercourse with all parts of the civilized world, her exhaustless fisheries, her rich colonies of almost unbounded extent, her active and intelligent population, not lend all their aid respectively towards her continuance in that high and palmy state which she has so long held in Europe.

But unless they respectively do, unless each and all of her high resources are applied with that discriminative judgment which, under the use of some master intelligence they might be, she will recede from this high and palmy state. For no specious reasoning on a one-sided view of the question, can set aside the truth of the aphorism of Adam

Smith—that it is the same with a nation as with a family. Riches may abound in certain quarters to an overflowing excess; our great metropolis may present the bustle and aspect of a vast trade, but this will not alter the grand predicament in which England now remains. And this grand predicament is one of peril, unless economy, vigilance, and a mature judgment, be exercised over the various departments of her state. The subject has frequently had its illustrators; the process of pointing out its imminent dangers is no new task. Her political economists have, for the last half century, been loud in their oracular warnings connected with England's weal.—With one of the finest positions, then, on the globe, for the interchange of traffic with all nations, England stands at the present moment in an eventful and alarming crisis in her financial prospects and relations. For dangers there are in her relative position, which are neither slight nor imaginary. Though those dangers have frequently been dilated on in various shapes and by powerful pens, yet grave thoughts connected with England's statistics cannot be too often adverted to.

Her resources, and the true interests of her commerce as a manufacturing nation, have not by any means been always consulted by those at the head of the state—by those who have wielded her resources and directed her laws.

A dominant party has of late prevailed in our senatorial councils, which has ruled, that the commerce of this country is subordinate to its landed interests; that is, its true weal, its sheet-anchor, lies not in its foreign traffic with the other nations of the earth, and all its reciprocal relations, but in certain restrictive duties laid on the importation of foreign corn for the protection of British landowners.

To enter into all the fallacies (a thousand times refuted) of this system, with a view of exposing them, forms no part of the object of the present paper; but it may be esteemed a circumstance of most pernicious tendency when an impression of this kind rules triumphant in our councils.

"To abolish all distinctions of party," says a distinguished writer of the last century, "may not be practicable, perhaps not desirable;" but, on the other hand, when party has run high in the supreme councils of a nation, it must be esteemed prejudicial to the public interests, and derogatory to that true patriotism which is a pre-requisite in a legislator.

Many philosophers and jurists have at various periods of history occupied themselves with tracing a system of perfect government, which should be exempt from the practical evils and inconveniences which have been found to creep into all existing forms which have, in turn, succeeded each other among mankind. Plato, in his "Republic;" Sir Thomas More, in his ingenious "Utopia;" Sir Francis Bacon, in "The New Atlantis;" Harrington, in his well-known "Oceana;" Lord Erskine, in the "Armata"—have each amused themselves with tracing ideal models of what they esteemed such a system of government.

But the misfortune in all these systems has been, that they proceed on the supposition of human nature being better than it has been found to be in the experience of all ages. If the agents who carried out these ingeniously delineated models were as perfect as some of the heroes of romance are made, the working of these imaginary republics might be as happy as their conception.—Bolingbroke, again, has left us his model of a patriot king, wherein the virtues of the monarch appear not more conspicuous than the graces of language with which the writer has delineated him. Hume has left us his idea of a perfect commonwealth, wherein he also interposes a variety of barriers against the prevailing inroads of self-interest and corruption; but, however ingenious the arguments of the last, and his provisions of checks and counter-checks to fortify his imaginary republic against these inroads; however admirable the character of a chief magistrate, as drawn by the pen of the first, may appear, yet the march of human propensities is continually prone to wander from the beau-ideal of judicial excellence.

"In all places," says Sir Thomas More, at the close of his 'Utopia,' after delineating the political and domestic order of things in this famous romance—

"In all other places," says he, "it is visible that whereas people talk of a common wealth, every man only seeks his own wealth; but there, where no man has any property, all men do zealously pursue the good of the public; and, indeed, it is no wonder to see men act so differently, for in other commonwealths every man knows that unless he provides for himself, how flourishing soever the commonwealth may be, he must die of hunger; so that he sees the necessity of preferring his own concerns to the public."

How often, and how signally have these truths been illustrated in our own political history? The periods have been, wherein private views have given way to a stern and inflexible regard to the public weal. The voice of faction may, in their days, frequently have been heard in our senatorial deliberations; but, in the present day, a determination seems predominant to preserve the interests of the few, even at the sacrifice of that of the many—a principle which, when uniformly operating, may be thought fatally disastrous to the public service.

Reflections such as these will sometimes strike the mind, while contemplating the manner in which the prejudice of party, and its all-absorbing spirit, still maintain their influence in the great council of the nation. Did not they rule about the time of the close of the twenty years' war, when, after the general pacification of Europe, the famous corn-restriction laws of 1815 were passed—laws which would seem effectually opposed to our prosperity as a manufacturing power? Did not our national assembly betray a gross leaning to party, when, with the exception of one man, they rose up to do homage to our plenipotentiary (Lord Castlereagh), on his return from Ghent, where he had, amidst the assembled powers and potentates of Europe, represented the interests of Great Britain; while that assembly knew, or ought to have known, that some of the great points which England might have carried of right, were either tardily ceded, or entirely overlooked?

The intelligent author of a late publication says—

"Every member of the House of Commons representing trading and manufacturing districts, should have followed the example of Mr. Wilberforce (the member alluded to), and have told his lordship that he had neglected other and vital interests of his country."

"The continental powers," as the same author goes on to remark, "were not long in taking advantage of this disregard of the commerce of Great Britain. The ink with which the treaties of Vienna were signed was scarce dry, ere Russia, to which an immense trade used to be carried on in woollens, prohibited the importation of all coarse cloth by enormous duties. The king of Sardinia, who had his Italian dominions restored to him by British valour, and Genoa, with its rich territories and fine seaports, added to his kingdom, not only deprived us of the great privileges we formerly enjoyed, but imposed almost prohibitory duties on the importation of British manufactures, not only into his own kingdom, but into those territories which were added to his kingdom. The emperor of Austria prohibited the entrance of our woollens and cottons into his empire, including also his newly-acquired Italian States, Lombardy, the Milanese, Venice, &c., &c., which formerly took large quantities of our goods. And other governments acted in a similar manner."*

These facts, and these prohibitions, under the continued influence of which the trade of England languishes, prove that our best legislation has sometimes been directed to class-interests. And were not these interests too uppermost in the minds of the dominant party in the same house, when upon another occasion it voted an excessive grant to the West India planters, when a modified sum would, upon every possible ground of agreement, have met their just claims? As the same intelligent writer has observed—

---

* Mr. Wilberforce was right when he complained that Lord Castlereagh neglected this high question (the abolition of the slave-trade); but England had other high causes to complain of his neglect.

"The interests of our manufacturers and merchants were again lost sight of, when the abolition of slavery was purchased at the cost of twenty millions sterling, given to the West India proprietors. That money (he continues) was well spent; the object was most noble; it removed a foul and disgraceful stain from the British character; would to God it were removed from every other country, and particularly from that which assumes to herself the title of the freest country in the world;—but twenty millions sterling would, at that time, have purchased the slaves and the fee-simple of the whole soil of the West Indies, depressed and depreciated as they were; and, in giving that most unexpected boon, and in redeeming them almost from bankruptcy, the trade in sugar, coffee, and other productions might, and ought, to have been thrown open; and thus those articles would not only have been obtained at about half the price we have paid for them, but the great and important markets of South America would have been secured to us. Thus having lost the near markets of Europe, our more distant markets are placed in jeopardy."

These considerations, then, with others which legitimately flow out of them, not lost sight of by this intelligent writer, abundantly prove, that as, on the one hand, ruinous and reckless expenditure has too frequently formed an item in our legislative code; so, on the other, a monopolizing bias to class-interests, has impeded our onward march, and still presses heavily upon our springs of industry.

Soon after the general pacification of Europe in 1815, other powers, less hampered with debts, less embarrassed with financial difficulties, and possessing equal leisure with ourselves, commenced a course of rivalry, in which they have proved but too successful. Unless, therefore, Great Britain is prepared to sustain her power and influence with foreign nations abroad—unless she can meet her vast difficulties at home by her mere agricultural strength, (which she most assuredly cannot,) it becomes a sacred duty in our rulers, whilst legislating for the common weal, to see that the privileges of each are balanced with equal hand.

If France, Belgium, and the United States are rivalling us in the cheapness of their fabrics—when it is considered that these countries have their energies for producing their fabrics for the foreign market free and unfettered by a multitude of imposts—whose food is untaxed—who have no public burdens which a prodigious debt imposes to struggle against—such rivalry becomes doubly formidable. It has been proved from recent eye-witnesses, that of late unprecedented strides have been made in the Low Countries in the woollen manufactures, and our transatlantic competitors are equally enterprising and successful in their rivalry. With the skill and indomitable energy, therefore, so much vaunted as belonging to our working population, it is much to be feared that Great Britain will, unless some favourable juncture turn up, yield to the overwhelming advantages possessed by these rivals. But if Great Britain nursed up and duly cultivated those advantages with which she is undoubtedly gifted above other nations, and appropriated them to the reduction of her debts and mortgages, she might successfully compete with all other nations whatsoever.

The woollen manufacture of England received a very powerful stimulus in the reign of the third Edward ;—that enlightened though warlike prince, saw the advantages of commerce to this country, in order to constitute her a great and powerful nation.

The long succession of wars and intestine troubles which afterwards at various intervals occurred until the reign of Henry the 7th, was of course inauspicious to England's growth as a commercial nation. It was not until the days of Cromwell (who, whatever party politicians may say concerning him, enacted many enlightened measures for the protection of our foreign trade,) it was not until the days of Cromwell and the Second Charles, that our foreign trade expanded to any positive magnitude. But under the three Georges, and during the greater part of the last century, it assumed a shape and complexion which it at present bears, and which at its close, notwithstanding the decrees of the French usurper, laid the tribute of almost all nations at our feet. But with Napoleon's downfall, the affairs of Europe were changed. The continental nations began to manufacture their own fabrics. For a considerable period England has felt this rivalry in foreign markets ; her manufacturing population has often, in consequence, throughout the land, been reduced to deep distress—sometimes, in many districts, been brought to the verge of absolute starvation, were it not for elemosynary aid, and the provision which the laws have made for the destitute. This last-named has in many districts of our land been found to be of a very intolerable nature. These local taxes press very heavily upon the middle and manufacturing classes, and still further add to their inability to meet the foreign trader in the markets of Europe. Our great trading establishments in the manufacturing districts of England are calculated to strike upon the mind, and to impress it with an enlarged idea of our commerce, and the extent of our maritime intercourse with the other nations of the earth. But if these establishments, having a capacity of doing a vast business, are comparatively idle, — if they languish for lack of employment, turning their surplus hands over to parochial relief, and thus adding to the general onus of excessive taxation,—the revenue, so far from being assisted, is depressed and injured.

Say not that the emporiums of our maritime isle are on the grandest scale—say not that the London Docks, St. Catherine Docks, the East and West India Docks, with their vast warehouses, are on a very enlarged plan of magnitude. Venice had likewise magnificent emporiums filled with the wares of many nations. Two or three centuries back her " spoils" and her riches acquired from distant countries, were the envy of Europe. Now, shorn of the streams of wealth which supplied her storehouses, she is sunk as a maritime power immeasurably below the rank she held at the battle of Lepanto.

Look at Spain—her commerce, except in the article of wine, is all but annihilated. Prior to the discovery of the Mexican and Peruvian mines, her active and enterprising character was eminent, both on the side of war and of commerce. A very extensive barter with various countries of Europe in fine wools existed, during the whole of the last century; which is now lost, as Saxony supplies a better article, and the vast flocks of sheep which furnished clothing for the patrician ranks of Europe, are now dwindled to a faint shadow of what they were fifty years back.

In the face of these memorable examples must not England, though at the present time the mart of general commerce, exercise vigilance and foresight in order to preserve it? True, we possess among us energy, enterprize, and perseverance. Our skill in producing the wrought fabrics of human ingenuity, and our advantages of position, are alike conspicuous above almost all others. But while chained with such a grievous load of taxation, can it be expected that we should go on triumphantly?

While thirty-two millions sterling must be annually raised to discharge the interest of our debt, and the various other pecuniary liabilities which devolve upon us, we can scarcely hope to throw aside all foreign competitors. While restrictions, monopolies, and class-legislation continue to occupy so considerable a share in our fiscal code, we are cramped and trammelled in our commercial operations beyond any other existing power. While, again, the staple food which supports the mass of our manufacturing population is subject to heavy imposts, from which our rivals are comparatively free—while those rivals are actively engaged in cutting us out from every foreign market, a most unequal career is allotted us. Until, therefore, our revenue, legitimately derived from regular sources, shall bear some more adequate equivalent to our expenditure, our condition cannot be a prosperous one. We rather retrograde than advance, inasmuch as our liabilities are imposing upon us unnatural taxation. Our magnificent manufacturing establishments, our commercial docks and warehouses, will not, it is feared, long sustain their pre-eminence under all the disadvantages enumerated. Alas for England! when the period shall arrive which witnesses the rapid decline of her commercial ascendancy!

It has long been reiterated as an axiom in commerce, that a nation, in order to grow rich, should buy in the cheapest and sell in the dearest market. But the commerce of Great Britain is sometimes, so far as state enactments go, carried on upon principles the very reverse. Our colonies, for instance, might be rendered available for much more of the raw produce which supplies our manufactories than they generally have been. Australian wools might be made to supersede those of Saxony to a greater extent than has ever yet been done. The raw cotton, again, of our West Indian islands might supply our native looms, without purchasing of the French and the Dutch. We likewise may be said to buy our labour in the dearest market when we pay higher wages, in consequence of the artificial price of the staple subsistence of the workman, produced by the restrictive duties on foreign corn. Added to this, the ramified imposts which circle through our code of commercial intercourse with the different portions of our extended empire, throw oftentimes very serious obstacles in the way of our successful competition with foreigners.

The sentiment of Adam Smith, that "heavy taxes on necessaries become a curse on any community, equal to the barrenness of the soil, or the inclemency of the heavens," has been often reiterated; but, spite of the alleged impolicy of such taxes, and their tendency to utter ruin, will it be said that England, at the present moment, is not the victim of such taxes? No one surely, unless a wholesale dealer in paradoxes, will venture to assert it.

Is it, under these circumstances, a matter of wonder, that pauperism, with all its attendant evils, has, for the last twenty-five years, increased in a quadrupled ratio. The sums lavished in the French revolutionary wars, during the twenty preceding years, were frightfully large. Indeed, that one thousand seven hundred millions sterling should have been expended in that short space of time, in opposing the French usurpers, will, in a future age, surpass belief. Four hundred and fifty millions sterling were then added to our funded debt. The terms on which the vast loans constituting it were negociated, being by no means favourable to prosperity.

Without, however, looking back with amazement to the means by which the people of Great Britain sustained a weight of taxation so enormous and overwhelming, our views should be prospectively directed to our present condition, to the means we have of emancipating ourselves from our debts, mortgages, and embarrassments, with which we seem on every hand surrounded.

That our prospects are appalling, take the following picture, penned upwards of twenty years ago, as a specimen. Who will say, that in the present age our prospects are materially changed.

"On the hypothesis," says an Edinburgh reviewer, of the year 1826, "that the income of the United Kingdom is equal to three hundred and fifty millions, it is plain that very little less than one-third of the entire revenue of the industrious classes is swallowed up by taxation, and by the bounty of the growers of corn; or which is the same thing, every poor man is obliged to labour two days out of six, not for the benefit of himself or his master, but in order to satisfy the demands of the treasury; and this, in addition to one-third of the profits of all fixed capital, such as lands, machinery, and of the professional income devoted to the same purpose! Surely it is unnecessary to seek elsewhere for an explanation of the difficulties in which we are involved! No country was ever subjected to such a scourge; nor can there be the shadow of a doubt, that it is owing to the government claiming for themselves, and allowing, or rather forcing the growers of corn to claim, in exchange for their produce, too great a share of the earnings of the industrious classes, that the latter have not enough left to support themselves."

Away, then, with this one-sided legislative policy, which considers only a certain privileged class of the empire! Let the blessings, which Providence pours around us, be equally diffused, and the distress of the manufacturing portion of our empire will be greatly alleviated. Let cheap corn from Poland and America, the sugars of Brazil, the timber and iron from the neighbourhood of the Baltic, cambrics from France, and silks from Spain, be freely imported. Let our rulers renounce a selfish and monopolizing system, and the interest of the empire will visibly and manifestly improve. Want and destitution, which have so frequently raised their heads in our land, would no longer visit so many of our local districts, entailing upon those districts a load of parochial taxation.

If, notwithstanding, there were not, Sir, still resources, which *have not been sufficiently cultivated*, the expectation of paying off our last funded debt would be altogether hopeless. Why, for instance, should not her fisheries be made instrumental in assisting to liquidate it? If her colonies, through the influence of prejudice or party, are not always placed to the highest account in our fiscal laws; the ocean, which washes our sea-girt isle, offers exhaustless stores to our industry. As has been pertinently observed, "there is a continual harvest ripe for the gathering, without the labour of tillage, without the expense of seed and manure, without the payment of rent and taxes. Every acre of the sea is far more productive of wholesome, palatable, and nutritious food, than the same quantity of the richest land."

It is, Sir, supineness of no ordinary character which withholds us from grasping these bounties to a far greater extent than has been usual amongst us. A pamphlet has been lately put forth on this subject, in the shape of an appeal, by Admiral Sir J. Brenton, in which he observes :—

"The difficulty of procuring food for our rapidly increasing population has become a subject of most awful importance, and is well worthy of the most serious consideration. It does appear most extraordinary that with all the elements of the most entire national prosperity, and in the enjoyment of profound and long continued peace, we should find so numerous a portion of our population sunk in misery and degradation in a degree hitherto unknown in this country."

As he justly says again—

"There is no country in the world which possesses greater advantages for carrying on the most profitable and abundant fisheries than our own. Our rivers with their estuaries and bays, indeed the whole range of our coasts, abound with fish, offering safe and sheltered ports for our fishermen."

But the grand arena on which the stores of the ocean are poured forth with the greatest profusion, is that of the herring fishery. Nothing save our own supineness and negligence could prevent our securing almost a monopoly of this fishery. The stations or ports for the herring are chiefly Hastings, Folkestone, Cardigan, Swansea, Whitby, Scarborough, Great Yarmouth, and Lowestoft. Of these Great Yarmouth is by far the most considerable, although no mean share of activity prevails at the latter place.

The prodigious shoals which, prompted by their migratory and gregarious propensities, leave the Arctic seas in the month of June, bifurcate, as is very well known, into two grand divisions, one of which is precipitated unbroken into the German Ocean, and fills the bays and estuaries on the eastern shores of Britain with their teeming myriads.

In a former number of the Colonial Magazine, I suggested a plan for enlarging the scale of the herring fishery at Lowestoft—why could not the means be increasingly adopted at the Yarmouth fisheries? Other fishing boats or smacks are allowed to frequent the Yarmouth grounds, and to sell their cargoes at its Michaelmas mart. In the year 1784, fifty-five boats were fitted out from Yarmouth, forty from Lowestoft, fifty from Whitby and Scarborough, and sixty-two from Holland, thus allowing our rivals in this traffic to come upon our very shores. I am aware that the state of things is much altered since this period; but Yarmouth had then declined in its operations in this trade, compared to the position in which it previously was. It has been previously known to employ two hundred fishing vessels, each furnished with an abundance of nets of twenty-one yards long by eight and a half deep. The subsequent speculations of this fishery are conducted pretty much as at Lowestoft; but in point of magnitude, there is no question that the scale on which it is carried on might be very considerably enlarged. A large additional supply of boats might leave this port, provided with all the requisites for taking this fish to a far greater extent than is now practised.

In like manner, the herring station of the highlands and islands of Scotland might be correspondingly enlarged; thus leaving to our neighbours the Dutch, but scanty gleanings of the harvest they now enjoy. We might thus supply distant countries with this fish, to the exclusion of the Dutch; and contribute to enrich a branch of our national trade.

Why should not, then, a provision be hence made for reducing our debt? Certain portions of these extensive captures, in the various stations of our coasts, might be set aside for this purpose; and upon the assumption that our fisheries, both of the herring and other fish, which frequent our seas in vast multitudes, might be indefinitely enlarged.

"We abound," says Admiral Sir J. Brenton, "in all that can give encouragement and stimulus to enterprize and industry. We have capital, skill, energy, and patriotism, which—if duly brought into action, must be productive of everything which can contribute to national and individual prosperity—would give relief or employment to all our idle and starving multitudes."

Is there any reasonable cause why government should not place one thousand or two thousand boats at each of the greatest herring stations, from the Orkneys to the Thames, duly equipped and registered for the capture of these myriads of the deep, on a more extensive scale than has yet been practised. These boats, when freighted with their cargoes of from six to eight, ten, or twelve lasts, each might be taken to separate curing houses, also duly registered, from whence they might be shipped off by steamers to the distant markets of the world. A department might be created for the management of this new source of finance, under due supervision, and the proceeds might be fairly appropriated to the enlargement of these fisheries, partly re-invested in stock, which would make lucrative returns. These returns would continually accumulate under each re-investment, and would be placed under the management of a financial board, which would be responsible alone to the legislature for its proceedings.

In like manner, again, our invaluable cod fisheries, off Newfoundland, and on the great Sand Bank, might be equally rendered available to reduce our national liabilities. Ships duly equipped, and appointed by government, and framed for the seas and operations of those latitudes, might be stationed there. The vast arena which is opened in these seas for our piscatory operations, not one hundredth part of which has been adequately gleaned, offers to us a harvest far beyond what we have yet gathered. This harvest might be made principally our own. The French well know the value of these extensive grounds, and they will profit by our negligence. We have certainly a prior right, both in the Sand Banks and the Gulf of St. Lawrence. The different latitudes and localities in this gulf, present to those who will be at the trouble of taking them, shoals of fine fish, in all their variety of abundance; but the cod, which in incalculable myriads frequent these extensive shallows, which, for one hundred and fifty leagues and upwards, off the shores of Newfoundland, line the bottom of the Atlantic, form a rich harvest of piscatory wealth, which may be said to be yet ungleaned.

England's government might then here also station her fishing vessels, in numbers far exceeding what has ever yet been seen in those latitudes. The neighbouring coasts of Newfoundland offer ample dressing places for the immense captures which would then crown our increased endeavours, whence they might be shipped off, by our steamers, to the distant markets of Europe and Asia.

From a survey of the state and history of our cod fisheries, it is impossible not to perceive that they might be considerably enlarged, and that a corresponding increase of revenue might result from the judgment, and skill, and vigour, with which these fisheries are prosecuted. Instead of angling with a hook and line, strong nets, of a texture and size peculiarly adapted to the process, might be substituted; and facility in the mode of capturing this excellent and well-flavoured fish made more commensurate with the prodigious multitudes, which the amazing fecundity of nature has driven periodically to resort to these spots.

A provision, then, of the kind here suggested, might indubitably be made, towards forming a separate and reserved fund, which constantly accumulating might succeed at length in materially reducing the amount of our national liabilities. It is altogether visionary to dream of being on a fair footing of competition with other commercial and manufacturing nations. Nothing short of a fond and crazed imagination can look at the state of our financial system, and our trading prospects, and think otherwise.

These extensive sources of traffic in our colonial regions would be subject to the same supervision and registry as those of our native isle, and may be thought equally available in creating a national fund which may succour us in our extremity.

Thus might the stupendous provision which nature throws into our power, both in our native seas, and those of our colonies, be made instrumental in contributing a higher revenue to the state than it has ever yet done.

That something, then, on the part of the legislature, or on the part of those who administer the laws, both to relieve our drooping commerce from the shackles which oppress it, and to extend its field of operation, is demonstratively evident, if we are to sustain our ascendancy in the foreign market.

It was once said by the body of French merchants to Louis XIV., upon the occasion of carrying up some remonstrance on the subject of trade—"Laisse nous faire." But it is not enough that government "let us alone." Impolitic enactments, and a load of promiscuous taxation, have reduced us to those difficulties, and to that depression, at which we must be assisted.

It is, then, we reiterate, little to the purpose, to point to our magnificent establishments for commerce in the metropolis, and numerous corners of the land. When the stream which supplies them is cut off, they will only stand existing records of the decay of our national wealth, and the sphere of our national influence. The palaces of Venice long sustained the affluence and the commercial grandeur of that enterprising city. A continued series of bad policy, inflexibly persisted in, may reduce our influence as a commercial power, whilst other nations, profiting from our misadventures, will rise to affluence and ascendancy.

If England, in these days of general enterprise, is eclipsed in the great emporium of the world as a commercial power, her days of glory and of triumph are numbered.

E. P.

Avon House, Wilts.
Feb. 18th, 1844.

On the Use and the Practicability of the Construction of

A CANAL OR OTHER COMMUNICATION FROM THE ATLANTIC TO THE PACIFIC.*

One of the most remarkable and beneficial effects of commerce and manufactures is the stimulus which they give to works of art, by which easy and rapid communication may be extended through the various inland ramifications of countries. The carriage of heavy goods, by roads, is always tedious and expensive, and often impracticable from local impediments of mountain, swamp, or sandy desert; and, wherever good water-conveyance can be obtained, it has many advantages. Our oceanic water-communication is surprisingly convenient between the various parts of the earth which we inhabit; but it occasionally occurs that this also is made indebted to man's ingenuity, who cuts through the comparatively narrow barrier between seas, the natural access to which is only to be gained by a long and weary circuit, which too often damps the ardour of enterprising speculation in the pursuit of riches.

The first improvement of this kind of conveyance and transit, has probably been that of operating upon streams, to render them navigable; though we know that in Egypt, from its peculiar situation, and the circumstance of the periodical inundation of its great river (the Nile), canals, both for the conveyance of goods and for the distribution of the water on the higher grounds, for the purposes of irrigation, were adopted at a very early date. In China also, they have been in extensive use from a very remote period. In Holland they are identified with a low country, and are essential to the protection of the land from the water, while their facilities for traffic are immense. In England, the progress of the art of inland navigation is very distinctly marked. It was not till the middle of the last century, that it had proceeded further than the mere straightening, embanking, and deepening of rivers; but experience had shown that navigations of this sort were inconvenient, and liable to constant deterioration, and, too often, even destruction. The rivers which were thus subjected to the control of art, were found speedily to change the form of their beds. Gravel and sand were swept away by the rapids of the rivers, and deposited in banks and shoals in the ponds below. During floods, the works were overtopped by water, and frequently injured; and the crooked naviga-

---

* Continued from No. 1, page 13.

tion, with the trackage against the stream, was at all times laborious and dilatory. These difficulties suggested the advantage of leaving the natural bed of the river, and forming a separate cut, with pond-locks. Since the first work of this kind, canal-making in Great Britain has wonderfully succeeded and spread, and, in its execution, streams have been crossed, valleys embanked, and even mountains bored through, in the completion of works which were at first conceived to be impracticable. Nor have other parts of the world been still, in the advance of improvement. The United States of America, among others, may boast of most expensive triumphs of art in canal formation, assisted as she has been by her ample rivers and extensive lakes.

It is probable that the art of canal-making has now arrived at its climax, being about to be almost superseded by an improvement of vast importance—that of locomotive engines on railways; but their necessity in some cases will continue to exist, and we are perhaps, indeed in all probability, destined yet to see works in this kind of conveyance, which, in magnitude of design, and boldness and skill of execution, shall prove that the art is as yet but in its progress to perfection. The wonderful and unexpected advance which only a few years have made in the power of transit, both as regards extent and speed, prevents us from fixing any bounds to the imagination, in its speculations as to the events of the future. But let us not digress too far from the immediate subject of this article.

If appearances in the framework of the terrestrial universe were alone to be considered, as we have already said in a preceding number of the Magazine, the Isthmus of Panama would seem to be the exact spot pointed out by the great index of nature as being the most convenient place for a junction of the waters of the Atlantic and Pacific Oceans. The ligature of land which unites the two vast portions of the American continent, is here narrower by far than at any other of its points, namely, only thirty miles across at one place; while it is stated that here also the great chain of the Andes, in more than one place, subsides to an almost entire level with the land at its base, so that if the land itself do not rise to too great a height, or present too formidable obstacles of other characters, it is supposed that a canal is easily practicable. A Mr. Lloyd, who visited the isthmus, and examined it, with immediate reference to the making of a railroad over a tract of country extending between the mouth of the river Trinidad, on the Atlantic Ocean side, and the river Chorrera, on the Pacific Ocean side of Panama, has expressed his opinion in favour of the success of the measure; but, as his investigation was not directed to the merits of a canal, his information, however satisfactory and valuable it may be in relation to the immediate object and scope of his task, is quite inapplicable to a work, the fulfilment of which depends upon very different data. All the information which we are presented with by this gentleman is, to use his own words, "that the spot where the continent of America is reduced to nearly its narrowest limits, is also distinguished by a *break*, for a few miles, of the great chain of mountains (the Andes), which otherwise extends, with but few exceptions, to its extreme northern and southern limits, a combination of circumstances which points out the peculiar fitness of the Isthmus of Panama for the establishment of a communication across." It is to be regretted that Mr. Lloyd, as is the besetting sin of travellers in general, has omitted to be more explicit; whether by the term "break," he means an entire cessation of mountainous elevation, does not appear; we can, therefore, attach no stronger meaning to his statement than that which, coupled with the accounts of others, and the known characteristics of the vast mountain-range under consideration, we are warranted in allowing it, we see nothing to establish any more than the fact that at one or two points the chain is nearly unlinked by depression. It is very much to be deplored, that he has even omitted to give us the height of the cordillera in its passage through Panama, as well as that (above the level of the sea) of the occasional diminutions of altitude of the mountains. There is nothing whatever at all established by Mr. Lloyd to show the sufficiently easy admission of accomplishment of a canal such as should be large enough for all kinds of ship-navigation.

It is imagined by some persons, that a passage could be effected through the isthmus by joining the head-waters of the rivers of Panama, some of which flow to the Atlantic, and some to the Pacific; but we deem that such an attempt would be useless. The largest of those rivers, the Chagres, which falls into the Atlantic, after receiving the Trinidad and some other minor streams, has a bar and other obstacles which would preclude its being turned to any successfully sufficient use, as far as it is navigable into the interior, namely, up to the town of Cruces, which is about thirty-four miles from its mouth, in a south-westerly direction. On the opposite, or Pacific side, the largest river is the Rio Grande, the upper part of which is stated to approach to a distance of *about* four miles from the Mandingo or Obispo, a tributary of the Chagres; but, as these are even less practicable for ships than is the Chagres, any one venturing to trust to their help, would "take as little by his motion" on the one as on the other. Even supposing the intervening country to be, as reported, nearly a level, which we doubt, of what use could it be to join two almost worthless water-courses, for they are in truth, for all useful navigable purposes, little better. By doing so, a junction of the two oceans would no doubt be fulfilled to the letter, just as Sancho Panza's tailor culprit achieved from a shred of cloth nine Lilliputian coats; and, what is more, the course through that junction would be quite practicable for any one desirous, by way of variety, to paddle his hobby from one sea to the other, in the shape of a canoe, as did a certain priest, as we are told, who was curate of Novita, a place in the interior of the eastern extremity of the isthmus. The well-vouched story of the good curate goes thus: The river Atrato, which we have before alluded to as rising in the isthmus where it blends with the southern portion of the continent, flows into the Atlantic; and another river, most euphoniously hight the San Juan de Chirambira, rejoices in a course into the Pacific. The upper branches of these two rivers, approach, it is said, in the usual inexplicitness of Panama geographical language, to that most intangible approximation of *about* ten or twelve miles to each other, at the 6th degree of north latitude. A *quebrada*, or large rent or ravine, extends from one river to the other; across this space, a natural convenience which it seems was turned to good account by the priest, who made the Indians attached to his cure dig a channel at the bottom of it. The ravine being subject to periodical accumulations of water, proceeding from the heavy rains peculiar to the tropics, occasionally became sufficiently swollen to form a continuous water-communication between the two rivers in question; and, consequently, a passage, however impracticable it might have been, as it no doubt was, from one ocean to the other. One story goes so far as to relate that cacao has been frequently transmitted from ocean to ocean, a circumstance which to us appears to be quite absurd. It is altogether unlikely that there would be any profitable inducement for submitting that article of produce to an expensive coasting voyage on the Pacific, in the first place, and then to a troublesome shipment across the continent on its lengthy way in search of an European market; such an adventure could only be attended with loss. But, the fact is, that commodity is, generally speaking, in this part of America, the produce of the interior of the country, and, in the nature of things, there would not therefore be any necessity for so ridiculous and unnecessary a process as that would be of first of all conveying it into one sea, and then across the country again to the other; it would obviously be only requisite to take it to one or other ocean, wherever that step was practicable. Cacao is an article which, unlike Madeira wine, does not improve, but rather greatly deteriorates, by making long voyages.

There is, however, a fact of great importance in our present disquisition, which the publication of our priest's speculative enterprise makes us acquainted with, namely, that a quebrada exists at a point situated between the two rivers, which could not be the case were not the land there of considerable height, as all persons having any acquaintance with the character of Central-American geology must know: quebradas are formed on the sides of mountains and declivities by the action of vast periodical mountain-torrents forcing their way down to the lower land. It is quite possible, we admit, that during the rainy season of Panama, where it rather pours than rains, our frolicsome Spaniard may have found a welcome pastime and relief from the dull monotony of catholicizing Indians, in being inventive and ingenious enough to discover and put in practice a new amusement, in manipulating and pushing his canoe from one river to another, with the assistance most likely of an occasional uplifting on shoulders, where the other mode of navigation was stubborn. If, in believing that our bold ecclesiastic did not enact peregrinations of a more extended character than that which we conform to, we cannot help it, we must bear the consequences of our heresy.

Humboldt, whose authority we look upon as being in this, as on all other matters which he has favoured the world with, of great authenticity and weight, is by no means encouraging as to Panama affording any facilities as a point of transit by canal. He tells us in plain terms, that in his view of the matter, such a project has no foundation for its probable accomplishment. It is true, that he made no actual survey or personal observation of the locality during his residence in the neighbourhood; but, as he was not likely to express an opinion upon light grounds, but upon the best information that he was enabled to obtain from sources likely to be credible, we shall pay great regard to that opinion. He thinks that the project might admit of a trial at only one point, we mean Cupica Bay, the most southerly portion of Panama lying on the Pacific. At a distance of fifteen miles inland, over a country which he was informed is perfectly level, or having only a gentle rise, lies the river Naipi, a branch of the Atrato. The conjecture is simply that Cupica Bay might, by means of the Naipi, be made to communicate with the Atrato, (which is said to be a large river flowing into the Atlantic,) by forming a canal across the interval between Cupica Bay and the Naipi, an interval which it is said has been ascertained to be an almost perfect flat. But even here, Humboldt thinks that a canal of sufficient magnitude, such a one as would be easily and readily available for ships of the largest burden, would not be of practicable execution. Were it not large enough to allow vessels of the ordinary trading tonnage, to pass through it freely, safely, and expeditiously, it would be of no useful practical avail to any sufficient extent; for we see, in the examples already before us in the cases of the Eyder and Caledonian canals, the first of which forms a good communication from the North Sea to the Baltic, through Denmark, as does the latter from the North Sea across Scotland to the Atlantic Ocean and the Irish Channel; yet, notwithstanding their apparent eligibility, in consequence of some inconvenience attaching to both, a long and circuitous voyage is still preferred. Independently of the reluctance which mankind have in going out of the beaten track, under any circumstances, in an occupation which is so irksome as is navigation, every fresh deviation from the ordinary routine of its at best troublesome arrangements, is calculated to unsettle and harass. The apparently easy progress up the river Thames to the docks of London, is often pregnant with much more actual trouble and even danger, than the entire voyage from the East or the West Indies.

From a careful consideration of all the information of which we are in possession with respect to the features of Panama, both touching the geography and statistics of the Isthmus, we are forced to no other conclusion than that there is a comparatively considerable height in the land between the two oceans washing it. We have no authority for there being any greater depression in the country than what is termed an "almost perfect flat," and that evidently considered with reference to the immediate apparent base of the mountain-range, and not, as it should have been, with respect to the level of the sea; the base of the mountains is itself, in all probability, several hundred feet higher than the ocean. Regarding the fitness or the capacity of the rivers of Panama for useful navigable purposes, we are shown nothing in advancement of the question as to those streams being at all capable of being made subservient to useful ship-navigation. From their natural situation, they could not be any more than that which they are—that is to say, the drains for the off-pourings from a narrow portion of mountainous continent, and, as such, shallow, rapid, and broken in their descending progress, and almost invariably clogged at their embouchures with, we should apprehend, almost irremedial banks of mud or sand, while their margins are covered with vast thickets of the mangrove tree, difficult to be penetrated, and not to be removed without a vast amount of labour perseveringly applied in the slow eradication of the tenacious and fast reappearing forest. Circumstances such as we have stated, render these streams fit for nothing more than very indifferent and limited boat or canoe traffic, and that invariably interrupted either by the sudden floods of periodical tropical rain-storms, or by intense, all-absorbing droughts. After, we trust, an accurate investigation of the various points to be considered in giving an opinion as to the accomplishment of a channel across Panama, we perfectly agree with Humboldt in coming to the conclusion, that a canal such as would, from its size, be of any service to the general shipping world, is now quite impracticable there. It is not our province to look towards futurity and anticipate what the march of human improvement, ingenuity, and enterprize may hereafter bring about. When the Isthmus shall have become, as it is fair to presume it will with time become, a densely peopled and greatly civilized territory, such an undertaking would be, there can be no doubt, a comparatively easy one. On the judicious selection of two conveniently placed ports on the respective oceans, a sufficient canal might certainly, with the application of adequate labour and at a necessarily enormous expense, be formed from sea to sea, and that without reference to the rivers of the country, which we would put altogether out of the question, except as furnishing a supply of water for this artificial canal which it would be better to open quite independently of their courses; for any attempt to fashion their beds into a canal would be quite abortive, when it is considered that they are really little better than the offspring of periodical supplies, which are even now not uncapricious and uncertain, and would become infinitely more so, as the clearing the region from forest advanced, population became considerable, and improvement in agriculture extended, and induced modification and amelioration of climate. Such changes—and in countries such as Panama they always take place—would cause a great decrease of water in its largest rivers, while its smaller ones would dwindle into mere rivulets, if they were not altogether obliterated.

We look upon any project for the immediate cutting of a canal across the Isthmus of Panama as chimerical. No capital that the undertaking could command would at present suffice to carry it to completion, seeing its surpassing magnitude and the insurmountable obstacles opposed to its accomplishment by a now almost perfectly wild, most unhealthy and inhospitable country; a country having no government entitled to be called one, affording few labourers, and furnishing little, if anything, of the requisite towards the carrying out of so stupendous and mighty a work; one requiring the greatest abilities in its plan and for its direction, vast pecuniary means for its accomplishment, and the most liberal efficiency in all the complicated details of its most difficult, expensive, and protracted execution.

Having offered our sentiments on the conjectured projects for a passage through Panama, we will now address ourselves to a consideration of the remaining point which has attracted attention, and recommended itself as a place of communication between the two great oceans of the world, namely, the state of Nicaragua in Central America. It has found great favour with those conversant with its advantages, favour amounting to a predilection which we think it entitled to, for the reasons which we shall proceed to state.

Nicaragua is one of the five states which recently composed the federal government of Central America; we say composed, for, unfortunately, there has been an interruption of the good understanding which lately existed among the component states of the Republic, which has led to some of them having set up for themselves in the political arena. We hope, however, soon to see them all again in conjunction, harmoniously pursuing their common interests. The other four powers are Guatemala, Salvador, Honduras, and Costa-rica. Guatemala, as being the most extensive and populous, and therefore the most important, contained the seat of government in its city of the same name, which is a place of large extent, and situated in a delightful climate, free from the extremes of heat and cold, having little vicissitude of temperature, and in which the productions of Europe grow side by side, in some instances in the same field, to be gathered by the same reaper. The total amount of the population of the five states of Central America, which comprise an extent of territory of about 124,000 square miles, amounts to nearly 2,000,000 of souls, distributed in twelve cities, twenty-one towns, and more than seven hundred villages, without including some of those occupied by the less civilized aboriginal Indians. The government, before the late secession, consisted of a president, vice-president, and eleven senators, forming the upper branch; and of a chamber of representatives, consisting of forty-two, making up the other portion of the legislature. The executive power was confided to a president, elected to serve for three years, with liberty to name three ministers of his own choice; the legislature, however, being elected by the people. The Roman Catholic is the dominant religion of the state; not, however, with so strict an intolerance as entirely to prohibit other worships. Slavery here, as in Mexico and the South American republics, has been swept away as a pollution. Foreigners settling there, on becoming citizens, which they have every facility for doing, receive a portion of land, exempt from any tax or impost for a period of twenty years. Spaniards, natives of Old Spain, as well as other foreigners, enjoy the same rights with the other subjects; by a law, however, passed on the 7th of July, 1828, not only commercial intercourse with Spain, but even the admission into the country of Spanish merchandise, is prohibited. The English and the North Americans of the United States carry on a very lucrative trade here, where there are landed-proprietors having considerable capital in specie of gold and silver. Upon the whole, this government adopts, in its commercial relations, a much more liberal course than does any of the other young republics of the New World.

The republic dates its independence of Spain from the 21st of September, 1821, when it became a part of the Mexican confederation. It subsequently separated from Mexico, and finally made its declaration of independence, as a distinct government, on the 1st of July, 1823. Its territory extends from the 8° 46′ to the 17° 51′ of north latitude, having New Granada as its southern, and Mexico for its northern boundary. It is watered by twenty-three navigable rivers, twelve of which fall into the Atlantic, and eleven into the Pacific Ocean. A town has been lately formed on the Pacific, which has become the seaport of the city of Guatemala, on that side. Not long ago, the yearly revenue of the republic amounted to 240,000*l.*, and her public debt to 2,400,000*l.* The general character of the soil of Central America, in which there are numerous volcanic manifestations, is one of very great fertility. Besides its producing well both articles of inter and extra tropical growth, it furnishes the best indigo in the commercial market, of which it exports annually to the amount of 400,000*l.* Its cochineal is also greatly esteemed, and large quantities of this insect-dye are collected from its extensive plantations of the nopal plant, which is a species of cactus. Sugar, coffee, cacao (or chocolate), and cotton, are also staple commodities, as well as large herds of black cattle, horses, and swine; and, in the higher lands, wheat is grown, and extensive flocks of sheep are fed, whose wool is manufactured on the spot into various articles of clothing and necessity, which would bear a comparison with those made in Europe. The silkworm has already begun to repay the enterprise of some of the larger and more intelligent landed-proprietors of the neighbourhood of Guatemala, which is not surprising, when the fitness in point of range and equability of the temperature, and the adaptation of the soil to the growth of the *morus multicaulis*, are considered. In addition to the objects which we have enumerated, medicinal and other drugs and oils are plentiful in Central America, as well as a variety of fibrous plants, admirably calculated for cordage and ropes, and for being woven into articles for clothing, and other economical purposes. It abounds with valuable wood, embracing many varieties, some of the principal of which are mahogany, a kind of teak called Santa-Maria, and several descriptions of oak and fir.

[To be continued.]

DUTCH SETTLEMENTS IN ASIA.

ORGANIZATION OF THE COLONIAL GOVERNMENT—RELATIONS OF THE GOVERNOR-GENERAL WITH THE TRIBUTARY PRINCES—DUTCH-INDIAN ARMY—INDUSTRIOUS AND AGRICULTURAL PURSUITS OF THE JAVANESE—COMMERCIAL COMPANY, NAMED HANDEL-MAATSCHAPPY—INCOME OF THE ISLAND OF JAVA. *

THIS last system, which continued in vigour for some time, and of which the bad effects were aggravated by time, continued in Java up to 1830. However enormous this territorial impost, which demanded from the cultivator a third of his profits, might be, the Javanese are of too good composition to have revolted against similar extremes; but their very sluggishness made itself felt, by the inconveniences it occasioned government, more than all the rebellions possible. It is to the enlightened administration of General Vandenbruch that the substitution of a labour-tax for this totally unproductive impost is due. This tax would appear extremely oppressive, were it attempted to be introduced in an European country; we might say, in an actual state of civilization, to introduce it would be impossible; but at Java, it has been established without the least resistance, and it is to this is due that great extension of its productions, and rapid growth of its wealth, that has been remarkable for some years past. Let us trace its workings.

Since the new law, every native owes to government each year, as tribute, sixty-six days labour, that is to say, nearly one-fifth of his time, upon the requisition of the chiefs of his district. These chiefs receive the orders of the resident of the province as to the nature of the task to be undertaken, and upon the subdivision of the work, which is fixed after the periods of ploughing and the harvest. That portion of the time which is not consecrated to the cultivation of the land granted by

* Continued from No. 2, page 79.

the government to the colonists, is employed in the reparations of the roads, in the formation of canals, and in carrying on any works of public utility which proceed from the government, and the different jobs required by the public service. When once the Javanese peasant has completed his heavy task, he is at liberty to dispose of the rest of his time, and to work on his own account, without fear of any interference; and, to induce him to cultivate and improve his land, the government has established, near at hand, in every district the most remote and distant from towns, warehouses where he can carry his produce, and receive in exchange merchandise or money. This wise precaution has been taken by the government from the perfect knowledge of the Javanese character which it has doubtless acquired. It was necessary to give the peasant this facility for overcoming his indolence and satisfying the liveliness of his desires; whenever an object excites the envy of these natives, they would give all the world for instantaneous possession of it, but it loses all its value in their eyes if the necessity exists for seeking it afar; their wants are the necessities of children, and require to be promptly satisfied, for they have also the principle of mobility. The Dutch have felt the advantages of thus placing their manufactures within reach of the inhabitants of the interior; they calculate greatly on this as a means of increasing their wants, and thus forcing them to become industrious; and by these means they procure an immense quantity of coffee, pepper, and rice, that they pay for instantly at the prices fixed by the tariff.

In all their labours, whether it be the culture of the colonists' lands, or the completing some work of public utility, the Javanese are always guided by their chiefs, and obey their order most punctually. They are particularly distinguished for a remarkable intelligence in executing canals for irrigation, and that instinct common to people habituated to cultivate rice, supplies admirably the best instruments and the most scientific methods of levelling or surveying employed by European engineers. It is by pipes made of bamboo, and by the slight movements of earth, that with a rare precision they direct any stream of water whatever, which descends the mountains, in the most varied directions, and upon the most unequal ground, in such a manner as to water a hundred different fields of rice which it encounters in its passage. Their *coup-d'œil d'aigle* never deceives them, and these works are performed with the greatest rapidity.

The Javanese, apathetic by nature, is, by way of compensation, endowed with that docility which is proper to indolent characters: so much has he been accustomed to obey, that it actually becomes a necessity for him to be commanded; two men of the same class, and of the same rank, finding themselves engaged together upon some sort of labour, one will find himself immediately the superior, without the least contestation. Above all, they dislike being noticed in their work, and the Europeans only lose time in troubling them with their *surveillance*, especially if they attempt to induce the workmen to hasten their job with a speed which is totally foreign to their character, and which entirely takes away the use of their faculties. The Dutch respect these feelings and habits; it must be allowed that their character, naturally cold and patient, is better adapted than that of other nations to accommodate itself to these sluggards. However, their yoke, thanks to this, is by no means too heavy upon this people, despite its exigencies.

In the fear of clashing too much against the prejudices of the people, no attempt has yet been made to establish a civil state for the natives. The Javanese, like all Mahometans, are ignorant on the subject of their age, and the government thus finds itself deprived of the most exact method of obtaining a true statement of the population; yet, nevertheless, (thanks to the subdivision of this population in quarters, in cities, and in small villages, having each of them a chief, whose authority extends over a limited number of families, of whom he is perfectly acquainted with each member,) an estimate tolerably accurate has been made, and from which it appears the number of inhabitants may be stated at nearly nine millions, although the last official returns, some time since to be sure, did not elevate the figure above 7,500,000. The Dutch consider that the land as yet uncultivated in the island would abundantly furnish the means of support to a population of three times the amount; and they look with the utmost satisfaction upon the increase which has taken place since their regaining the island in 1815. Amongst this number are to be counted 200,000 Chinese, paying a tribute; they are located in all the sea-coast towns, for they, equally with Europeans from other countries, are not allowed to establish themselves in the interior. Although the Chinese, during the last war in Java, when Dippo-Hegero unfurled the standard of rebellion, performed great and signal services for the benefit of the Dutch, and having interests in common with them, formed an auxiliary aid powerful enough to balance the bulk of the native population in case of revolt, the government, fearful of the spirit of intrigue and of industry of these people, who prove themselves powerful rivals to European commerce, have loaded them with considerable taxation, subject them to every sort of petty vexations, and exact securities whenever one appears in the country, in order to stay, as much as possible, the crowd of emigrants from the Celestial Empire, that annually descend upon the coasts of Java.

The annual budget of the government of Java shows an expenditure of eight millions of florins, in which are comprised the expenses necessary to maintain the establishments of Sumatra and the Malayan Islands, whose revenues are not sufficient for their support; from these the Moluccas and Borneo may be excepted, who need only occasional aid, owing to the monopoly they enjoy in tin and spices, which is still profitable. The revenues arise from the custom-house dues, the poll-tax (commonly called "the Chinese pig-tail tax"), the management of the opium and the arrack trade, and that of all fermented liquors or drinks fabricated in the country.

The Dutch exchequer has not allowed any known means of raising revenue by the imposition of taxes to escape it, but the branch of income by far the most considerable, and which most contributes to supply the balance of the receipts and the expenditure, so favourable to the government, is that derived from the monopoly which it reserves to itself in the purchase of every species of colonial produce raised upon the land granted by them. These productions it resells to the agents of the commercial company, styled *Handel-Maatschappy*, and which, in its turn, exercises a complete monopoly over the whole of Dutch India. This society was started in 1819, under the immediate patronage of the king of the Netherlands, Frederick William, and who, to encourage the capitalists of the Low Countries to assist in its formation, purchased himself shares to the amount of 20,000,000 of florins, and guaranteed to those interested an interest of 4⅛ per cent.

When the Dutch government succeeded the Indian Company in the administration of its vast possessions, by taking its debts and burdens, commercial relations were entertained with all countries—a reserve alone of some advantages to the Dutch being made in the scale of duties. However honourable this to the government, in conceding to the state of affairs which no longer admitted despotic companies with exclusive characteristics, it was not long in perceiving that the advantages secured to their own country were totally inefficient; and the English, by their adventurous spirit of enterprise, their superiority in capital and navigation, were in possession of the markets of the Netherland possessions over-sea, and enjoyed an exclusive trade there. It was, therefore, to rival them that it was thought wise to form the society of *Handel-Maatschappy*. This society, whose character is purely commercial and subordinate, possesses a capital of 97,000,000 of florins. At Java it possesses simply a factory, governed by a president and two members; it would not be possible for it to hold lands here, for its functions are to govern the cultivation of all the lands. Compelled to make use only of vessels built in Holland, and commanded by Dutchmen, it is not allowable for them to own ships in their own right, it being necessary that the benefit of its freightages should be participated in by as large a number of vessels and of individuals as possible; and that its success may be felt in every part of the monarchy, it is expected to average the arrivals and departures from Europe of the vessels employed in its service, in such manner that Amsterdam shall have $\frac{21}{40}$, Rotterdam $\frac{15}{40}$, Dudrecht $\frac{2}{40}$, and Mildebourg the remainder, being $\frac{2}{40}$ likewise.

The government functionaries deliver at the factory the produce they have acquired in Java; and the society undertakes to transport it to Europe, at a certain freightage, which reached in 1839 to about 2¾d. per kilogramme, or 2 lbs. English, of coffee, and 2¼d. per 2 lbs. of sugar. The government would find but little difficulty in augmenting its revenue by the sale of the products in Java itself, but it would not thus have achieved its purpose, which was to employ the Dutch marine in the transport of these productions, and to make the great market of Holland in requiring their transmission there. In the present day it is beneath the Dutch flag that all the trade between the Indies and the metropolis of Holland are carried on, whilst before the formation of this society scarcely half the commerce was carried on by the Hollanders. The end then of this great institution has been on this point fulfilled. To encourage ship-building, premiums were originally given, but at the end of a short time these became totally unnecessary; but the impulse given by them became such, that in 1839, after their withdrawal, there were constructed in the docks of Holland 123 vessels, of 39,918 tons of burden, intended for the Indian trade, and the society at that time employed 150 large vessels, of 116,000 tons; from whence the number has not ceased increasing.

The charter of the *Handel-Maatschappy* expressly stipulates that the society shall make use of the products of the country for its commercial enterprises. King William, in causing this clause to be inserted, aimed at restoring the national manufactures, a task extremely difficult in a country like Holland; he met, on this subject, with determined opposition, but, owing to the engagements which he obliged the society to fulfil with the manufacturers, who had commenced producing upon the faith of this command, to the extent of his credit, and to the judicious custom-house dues, and the protection given by the politic authorities to these manufacturers, in the space of twenty years, Holland has arrived at the point of abstracting the providing of Java from the English; in proof of this, the following statistic details may be relied upon:—in 1824, the home manufacturers exported to Java cottons to the amount of 25,000*l.*, and the English manufacturers supplied the market to the extent of 220,000*l.*; but in 1839, the former had manufactured for Java, cottons to the amount of 620,000*l.*, whilst the industry of England had only produced 270,000*l.*

After this digression upon the Commercial Society of the Low Countries, I feel induced to speak of the revenues of the Island of Java. Upon authority of the highest respectability, I am assured, that in 1838, this colony, after defraying all expenses of administration, paid into the coffers of the home-government a net revenue of twenty-three millions of florins; if this account be true, this colony surpasses the others, not excepting Cuba, whilst, without ceasing to advance in prosperity, it pays the expenses of its government, and yet gives a large property to the mother-country. Nor can this state of things exist without furnishing a powerful argument to the partisans of colonization to make use of against their adversaries, who, supporting their position on the principles that it is impossible to show, from the balance of receipts and expenditure of these establishments, any direct source of revenue, regard them as ties upon the well-being of the parent state, entirely forgetting to take into account the amount collected for the treasury by the custom-house receipts, and the impulse they give to the maritime commerce of the state.

It is easily conceivable that a colony like Java, returning such an immense revenue to a country so insignificant as Holland in size, and which so much contributes to its prosperity, should be distrustful of strangers, and especially of its great commercial rival, Great Britain, who not unlikely envies it the possession of so fine a source of receipts; and consequently the policy of M. Vandenbruch is followed up, and all communications between the natives of the interior and strangers are, if possible, totally prevented, in order that no spirit of hostility may be manifested to their government.

Holland regards as false and untenable the doctrines of free trade, so much harped upon by English public men; if the truth of these doctrines condemns in theory the acts of the Dutch government, as founded on a bad basis, it is not less necessary to acknowledge that it is neither to the interest of Holland, or the people of Java, that its colonial rival should cause their return to a more liberal system. Experience has already shown, that if the Indian was not compelled to labour in order to pay his tax, a large portion of this fertile island would be yet uncultivated, and that, receding into the state of misery and serfage, they would retrograde towards that barbarism from which they have been partially delivered at immense cost. It is impossible to deny that the actual management, fiscal and oppressive as it may be, has ameliorated, and materially too, the condition of the country; were this the only good produced, the Dutch conquest would have been advantageous to the conquered, and would perfectly justify the government to a certain point. D.

COLONIAL STATISTICS.

[NEW SERIES.]

NO. II.—THE BAHAMAS.

Geography.—The Bahamas are a range of islands, 5,424 miles in the aggregate area (according to Porter's Tables); east-north-east, they are 360 miles from Havanna to New Providence; south-south-east, 460 miles from Savannah. They were discovered by Columbus on his first voyage in 1492; and were first settled by the English in 1629. The extent from south-east to north-west is between latitude 21° and 28°, and longitude 71° and 81°.* The Bahamas comprise Turks Islands, the Caicos, Inaqua, Mayaguana, Crooked Island, Long Island, Watling's Island, the Exumas, San Salvador, Eleuthera, New Providence, Andros, Lucaya, Bahama, and numerous smaller islands, islets, and keys, computed at upwards of five hundred. The principal island is that called New Providence; its capital is Nassau. Many of the Bahama Islands rise almost perpendicularly from an immense depth of water, and are generally of calcareous formation, presenting no great elevation or variety of configuration throughout the whole range. The surface is undulating, marshy, and sandy. The navigation is intricate and dangerous. Political and commercial influence is almost exclusively centered in New Providence, which is the seat of government, and most of the other islands have been consigned to neglect. The recommendations of New Providence are, its relative situation with the Florida Channel, and the excellence of its harbour; it is not, however, the

* The *Colonial Chart*, published in 1842, marks the latitude at 21° to 27° north, and the longitude at 71° 10′ to 79° 10′ west.

largest of the group. New Providence presents a flat surface, a double range of rocky hills running parallel with the northern and southern coasts, at a distance of about 2½ miles from each other. The Bahamas are not very valuable for production or trade, nor for commercial and military position; but, as containing a large proportion of cultivable land, beyond the requirements of their present population, they are a first-class colony to England, because suitable for immigration and settlement.

Geology.—The geologists state that the bases of these islands have been formed of coral reefs originating with moluscæ, which, unpossessed of locomotive powers, have organic functions destined for the secretion of the lime required for their calcareous coverings.

History.—In 1629, New Providence was colonized by the English (the natives were then totally extinct), who remained till 1641, when the Spaniards drove them from the island, murdered the governor, and committed many acts of cruelty. In 1666, the English again colonized in the Bahamas, and were again expelled from New Providence in 1703.* Pirates after this made a rendezvous of the islands, but these invaders were kept in check by Captain W. Rogers, R.N., who was, in consequence, appointed governor, and then reduced the outlaws to obedience. Captain Rogers, however, was expelled in his turn by another enemy, an American squadron, who, under Commodore Hopkins, attacked and plundered the settlement, and carried off the governor (1776). The Spaniards were in possession of the islands in 1781; and they were restored to the British crown, by treaty, in 1783. Indeed, they had been just previously captured for England by an enterprising American (Colonel Devaux).

Military.—The military force consists of the New Providence regiment of militia, and a marine corps; the regular troops amount to about 600 men.

Cities.—Nassau is the capital of the Bahamas, having a population computed at 7,000; the town, nearly facing the entrance of a capacious and well-defended harbour, situated on the north side of the island (New Providence), rises from the beach, and extends over the acclivities of the hills in the back ground. The streets are well laid out, regular, bustling, and remarkable for cleanliness, which latter qualification is uncommon to most West India towns; the public buildings are respectable specimens of colonial architecture.

Government.—A governor (Major-General Sir F. Cockburn); a council of 12 members; and an assembly of between 20 and 30 members, including delegates from the subsidiary settlements. The executive government is modelled after that of England, as in most of the West Indian settlements under the British flag. The expenses of the different establishments are as follow: Civil establishment (paid by Great Britain) 1836, 2,589*l.*; judicial establishment, 3,400*l.*; ecclesiastical establishment, 140*l.*—Civil establishment paid by the Colony, 2,775*l.*; judicial, 3,707*l.*; ecclesiastical, 1,915*l.*

Population.—5,500 Europeans, and 17,548 other races, making a total of 23,048 lives, according to an estimate drawn from the census of 1839. By way of comparison we add the population of the several islands in 1832: whites, 4,674; blacks, 4,069; slaves, 9,765—total, 18,508. The increase in the European population was therefore, in 1832, 826; and the total increase of population in 1832, 4,540. The proportion of compensation under the emancipation act to the Bahamas, was 128,340*l.* 7s. 5¾d., the relative value of slaves being 290*l.* 15s. 3¾d.

Language.—As in Jamaica, the languages spoken are the English and the African.

Religion.—The church establishment and numerous schools are liberally provided for. The Episcopalian, Wesleyan, Baptist, and Presbyterian forms of religion are tolerated. Christ Church and St. Matthew, in New Providence, are the principal churches. There are four public schools; that in the town of Nassau is capable of containing 200 pupils. The Wesleyans have two sabbath and two catechetical schools in New Providence. They have also ten Sunday schools in the various out-islands; nearly 1,000 white and coloured children are instructed gratuitously.

Commerce.—The chief articles of export are cotton, salt, dye and other woods. We quote from that usually correct *vade mecum*, the *West Indian Manual*, published so lately as 1842, the following necessary particulars of the description and quantity of produce raised in 1831:—

Indian corn	bushels	30,350	@ 4s. 4d.	market price.
Potatoes and yams	lbs.	74,250	" 6s.	per cwt.
Peas and beans	bushels	3,225	" 5s. 10d.	per bushel.
Pine apples	dozen	38,465	" 2s.	per dozen.
Cotton	tons	22	" 0s. 5d.	per lb.
Melons and pumpkins ...	dozen	30,500	" 3s. 0d.	per dozen.
Ochre	lbs.	31,300	" 0s. 2d.	per lb.
Cassada	tons	19	" 10s.	per cwt.

In the same year were exported—cotton, 69 bales; bark, 70,320 lbs.; brazilletto, 255 tons; fustic, 308 tons.

The quantity of salt exported in 1834 amounted to 442,031 bushels, valued at 16,291*l.*

Gross exports in 1834, 92,802*l.*; imports, 142,021*l.* The official statement of 1839 values the imports at 190,113*l*, and the exports at 106,840*l.* The tonnage inwards, 1834, was 34,150, employing 2,251 men; and outwards, 31,607 tons, employing 2,090 men. The revenue of the Bahamas in 1837 amounted to 25,165*l.*, and the expenditure to 27,193*l.* The average annual value of the productions of these islands is 269,806*l.*, as computed from Parliamentary documents.

A table of imports and sales of cotton wool at Liverpool for the years 1840-41-42, supplies us with a good comparative view of the value of Bahamas cotton for the years mentioned; but we are obliged to take Bahamas' in connexion with Peru, common West India, and Laguira descriptions of cotton. The imports at Liverpool of cotton wool from Bahamas, Laguira, &c., were—1840, 20,038 lbs.; 1841, 26,722 lbs; 1842, 11,750 lbs. The sales of same were—1840, 3,200 lbs; 1841, 6,560 lbs.; 1842, 240 lbs. The current prices were, in 1842, 4¾d. to 6½d. per lb.; in 1840, the current prices were 7d. to 8d. per lb.; and in 1841, 5½d. to 7d per lb.

The table above quoted is certainly an unfavourable index of the commercial prosperity of the Bahamas.

Climate, Productions, Agriculture.—The climate is decidedly salubrious. The highest mean temperature is 92°; mean, 78½°; lowest, 63° 1'. The Bahamas produce ship-timber of a superior quality; logwood, brazilletto, fustic, green ebony, satin-wood, cotton, tobacco, sponge, &c. A very limited quantity of rum, and 16,000 gallons of molasses are annually exported from New Providence.

The summer and winter (hot and cold) and wet and dry seasons are well marked; the cold season lasts from November to May, during which period the sky is remarkably clear and serene. The mortality of the island is less by comparison than that of England. The deaths in 1826 were only one in forty-five.

The grants of crown land in the Bahamas that had been made previous to 1827, according to an official return published in that year, amounted to 408,486 acres; the total of acres of these vacant lands was 2,434,000. There are numerous small islets not enumerated in the return whence we have drawn the above statement.

The agricultural stock in the Bahamas in 1831 consisted of horses, mules, and asses, 1,165; horned cattle, 3,250; sheep and goats, 5,975; swine, 3,755.

Provisions.—European and tropical vegetables and fruits thrive in abundance; there is an excellent supply of meat and poultry, and the coasts abound with fish.

Prices of Produce and Merchandise.—Horned cattle per head, 10*l.*; horses, 18*l.*; sheep, 1*l.*; goats, 16s.; swine, 1*l.* 17s. 6d. per cwt.; milk, 1s. per quart; fresh butter, 2s. per lb.; salt butter, 1s. 3d. per lb.; cheese, 1s. per lb.; wine, 2s. per dozen; brandy, 8s. per gallon; beer, 10s. per dozen; tobacco, 1*l.* 17s. 6d. per cwt.; Indian and Guiana corn, 4s. 4d. per bushel; oranges, 4s. 4d. per thousand; butchers' meat, London prices. Wages for labour—domestic, 1*l.* 4s. per month; predial, 1s. 6d. per day; trades, 3s. per day.

The Arms of the Bahamas.—The arms of the Bahamas are a British ship in full sail, canvass spread, and streamers flying, upon a rippled sea—other vessels sailing in the distance. The motto is "*Expulsis piratis restitutio Commercii.*"

THE CAYMANS.

THREE islands forming a dependency of Jamaica, called the Grand Cayman, Cayman Branque, and Little Cayman; the two latter within five miles of each other, and about thirty-four miles north of the former. Grand Cayman is about a mile and a half long, and a mile broad, and is the only one inhabited. It is very low, and has no harbour; anchorage on the south-west side. Soil very fertile, producing corn and vegetables, and plenty of provender for goats, dogs, &c. In 1827 the population was estimated at 1,600. Most of the inhabitants are reputed descendants of the English buccaneers, and excellent pilots and seamen. A chief, or governing officer, is elected among themselves, and they frame their own local laws, although justices of the peace are appointed from Jamaica.

THE HISTORY, CULTIVATION, AND CONSUMPTION OF SUGAR,

ACCORDING TO THE LATEST AUTHENTIC RETURNS.

THE sugar-cane appears to be of Oriental origin, although its western nativity has many advocates. It is, however, highly probable that it was transplanted from the interior of Asia into the Island of Cyprus, by the Saracens, and soon afterwards into the fertile fields of Sicily, where considerable quantities were produced about the year 1150. It appears that some time in the year 1166, William the Second, king of Sicily, gave to the convent of St. Benoit a mill for crushing sugar-canes, together with certain privileges, experienced millers, and various appurtenances. It is also more than probable that the *arundo saccharifera* must have been first imported into Europe at the period of the Crusades. Albertus Aquinas, who wrote a history of the events of the Levant when Saracen power was declining, and the Normans began to adventure in those waters, says, that sugar was extracted from the cane by a systematic process at Acre and Tripoli, and that on one occasion, when the Christian soldiers were short of rations, they had recourse to the sugar-cane, which they chewed for subsistence. From Sicily the cane travelled to Madeira, in the year 1420, when Don Henry was regent of Portugal, and there, as well as in the Canaries, its success was complete. Indeed, those islands enjoyed a monopoly, and supplied the whole of Europe with this agreeable commodity, until the discovery of America opened new fields for enterprise.

Some doubt exists as to the source whence the Brazilians obtained their first cane; the Portuguese had a sugar colony at Angola, on the African coast, contemporaneously with their plantations in the Canaries, and it must have been from either or both of these it was transported to Brazil. Columbus is believed to have brought the sugar-cane to Hispaniola on his first voyage, and so rapidly did its cultivation spread over that island, that on his return about 1494, he found it in general adoption, and giving a very entire occupation to the islanders. The Spaniards and Portuguese reserved the cultivation to themselves for a length of time, and it was not until the 17th century that the cane was imported into Barbadoes from Brazil, and thence into the other English West Indian islands and possessions. Mexico, Peru, and Chili were then admitted to a participation in its advantages, and to these succeeded the French, Danish, and Dutch colonies.

The species of cane cultivated at Madeira was the *Creole*, or common kind. It grows luxuriantly within the tropics, where a moist soil can be obtained, and sometimes at an elevation of 3,000 feet above sea-level; on the mountains of Caudina-Masca in Mexico, it is cultivated at an elevation of about 5,000 feet. The *Otaheitan* cane came into the West Indies later than the *Creole,* about the close of the 18th century; it is stronger, taller, of quicker growth, more productive, and will grow in grounds too poor to nourish the Creole. It weighs a third more, yields a sixth more of juice, a fourth more of sugar, than the old variety; and it gives four crops for every three of the Creole. Humboldt speaks of a third variety, which he calls the *Violet* cane, which had been transported into America from Java: it flowers earlier than the others, but its product is less.

Sugar can be produced from other vegetables besides the cane. In France and Prussia, it is extracted from the beet-root; in some parts of France, from grapes; in India, from the date; in America, from the maple of Canada and the United States (*acer saccharinum* of Linnæus), the stalk of the Indian corn, and the Mexican agave: none of these plants, however, yield nearly such a quantity of saccharine matter, or so freely, as the sugar-cane. None of their sugars can stand in competition with cane-sugar in a fair and free market; and attempts to substitute the other classes of sugar for that of the cane, by the aid of restrictive or prohibitive duties, which have been made in different countries of Europe, appear on the eve of being abandoned.

We have shown that the sugar-cane is, properly speaking, a tropical plant. In the north of India, and in Louisiana, it is cultivated as far north as the 30th degree of latitude; and it seems formerly to have flourished on the north shores of the Persian Gulf. In Louisiana, however, the canes are liable to suffer from early frosts, which materially diminish the produce; and the peculiar physical conformation of the regions adjoining the Persian Gulf, and lying in the nook enclosed by the Hymalaya and the mountains of Afghaunistan, raise their average temperature far above that which prevails in most countries on the same parallel of north latitude. In China, the cultivation of the cane does not seem to be attempted north of the Poyang lake, about 29° north. The principal plantations are between that and Canton, in Fokien, and in the islands of Hainan and Formosa. In the southern hemisphere, the cane does not appear to be cultivated with success south of 24°. The sugar plantations most remote from the equator are those in the vicinity of Rio Janeiro, and in the northern provinces of La Plata. The sugar countries, therefore, may be considered as limited to 30° north, and 24° south of the equator. They consist of two groups, the Western or American, which have been created by European skill and enterprise; the Eastern, where the manufacture and trade may have been carried on from a remote period, but where European energy is now beginning to give them a new impetus.

In the following view of the sugar-trade, we shall direct attention principally to cane-sugar; then speak of the *sugar-importing* countries, and any internal manufacture of sugar from other vegetables than the cane, from which its supplies may be derived; and thence pass to the *sugar-exporting* countries, which may be classified under two great groups—the countries west and east of the Cape of Good Hope.

I. Importing Countries. *Great Britain.*—The reports of revenue, &c., for 1840, presented to both houses of Parliament, contain two tables, which, as they serve to illustrate the sources whence Great Britain draws her supplies of sugar, and the countries to which the surplus not entered for consumption is re-exported, are given here :—

TABLE I.—SUGAR IMPORTED INTO THE UNITED KINGDOM IN 1840.

Places from which Imported.	Into Great Britain.	Into Ireland.	Total.
	Cwts.	Cwts.	Cwts.
British West Indies	2,019,934	194,830	2,214,764
British North America	2,917	...	2,917
Cape of Good Hope	11		11
Mauritius	545,007	...	545,007
British East Indies, viz.—			
East India Company's Territories	482,782	...	482,782
Singapore	15,875	...	15,875
Ceylon	73		73
Siam	9,250	...	9,250
Java	31,918	...	31,918
Philippine Islands	69,981	...	69,981
China	2	...	2
New South Wales and Van Diemen's Land			
Foreign West Indies, viz.—			
Cuba	304,063	...	304,063
Porto Rico	87,171	2,412	89,583
Cayenne	1,569	...	1,569
United States of North America ...	4		4
Columbia	1,625	...	1,625
Brazil	215,962	...	215,962
Peru	57	...	57
Europe	50,401	...	50,401
Total	3,838,603	197,242	,035,845

TABLE II.—SUGAR EXPORTED FROM THE UNITED KINGDOM IN 1840.

Countries to which Exported.	Raw Sugar.			Refined Sugar.		
	From British Possesns.	Foreign.	Total of raw Sugar.	Actual Weight.	The same stated as raw Sugar*	Total stated as raw Sug.
From Great Britain—	Cwts.	Cwts.	Cwts.	Cwts.	Cwts.	Cwts.
Russia	165	39,816	39,981	15,165	25,781	65,762
Sweden and Norway ...	......	1,806	1,806	769	1,307	3,113
Denmark	......	5,904	5,904	2	3	5,907
Prussia	......	50,570	50,570	142	241	50,811
Germany	56	4,392	4,448	2,549	4,333	8,781
Holland	......	24,398	24,398	145	247	24,645
Belgium	1	40,825	40,826	......	......	40,826
France	......	2,636	2,636	582	990	3,626
Portugal, the Azores, and Madeira	......	400	400	969	1,647	2,047
Spain and the Canaries ..	......	4,611	4,611	11,910	20,247	24,858
Gibraltar	......	6	6	5,840	9,928	9,934
Italy	......	17,034	17,034	70,066	119,112	136,146
Malta	......	9,700	9,700	6,794	11,550	21,250
Ionian Islands	......	1,737	1,737	7,688	13.070	14,807
Morea and Greek Islands	......	186	186	1,159	1,970	2,156
Turkey	......	4,653	4,653	33,376	56,739	61,392
Syria and Palestine ...	... ..	757	757	817	1,389	2,146
Egypt	......	223	223	1,052	1,788	2,011
Morocco	......	......	......	1,432	2,435	2,435
West Coast of Africa ...	15	605	620	339	576	1,196
Cape of Good Hope ...	......	3,266	3,266	932	1,584	4,850
St. Helena	......	42	42	13	22	64
Mauritius	......	......	......	3,305	5.619	5,619
East Indies and China...	13	50	63	2,449	4,163	4,226
Australia (including New Zealand)	151	617	768	12,311	20,929	21,697
British North America..	......	1,150	1,150	30,127	51,216	52,366
British West Indies ...	275	28	303	19,907	33,842	34,145
Foreign West Indies ...	......	1	1	21	36	37
United States of North America	......	5,485	5,485	56	95	5,580
Mexico and States of S. America	......	92	92	373	634	726
Guernsey, &c.	7,314	531	7,845	4,758	8,089	15,934
Total from Great Britain	7,990	221,521	229,511	235,048	399,582	629,093
From Ireland—						
France	......	1	1	......	......	1
British West Indies ...	......	......	......	131	223	223
Total from Ireland ...	......	1	1	131	223	224
Total from United Kingdom	7,990	221,522	229,512	235,179	399,805	629,317

These are the most recent tables that show the distribution of British sugar—the channels into which the British sugar-trade runs. It must be remarked, however, in order to prevent erroneous inferences, that

* 34 cwt. of raw to 20 cwt. of refined. This proportion, although still used in official calculations, is now known to be incorrect.

the importation of about 50,000 cwt. of sugar from "Europe," in 1840, was an exceptional case; and such an entry will not be found in any other year.

The supply of sugar in this country may be said to consist exclusively of cane-sugar. In 1838, we find 129 cwt. of beet-root sugar entered as having paid the excise duty; in 1839, 16 cwt.; and in 1840, 104 cwt. These quantities are too inconsiderable to admit of any other inference than that the manufacture of beet-root sugar is with us merely an amusement for amateurs. The total of sugar imimported into Great Britain in 1842, was 234,963 tons. Of this quantity, 193,823 tons were entered for home consumption, 20,094 tons exported in a raw state, and 21,966 refined.* The sugar entered for home consumption was exclusively the produce of the British West Indies, and the districts of British India, from which sugar is now allowed to be imported at the West Indian rates of duty. The differential duty on foreign sugar was in effect prohibitory. In the circular of a great mercantile house in the city, for the previous month, we read—"The first three months of the present year show a much greater consumption than the same period in former years, being 42,500 tons against 35,500 in 1842, and 38,000 in 1841; and there is every prospect of its extension."

France.†—A considerable proportion of the sugar consumed in France is manufactured in the country from beet-root. In 1837, 543 manufacturers of beet-root sugar produced about 35,000 tons. In 1838-9, 560 manufactories, all except five actively at work, produced nearly 40,000 tons. In 1840-41, 388 manufacturers produced about 26,000 tons. The annual average consumption of beet-root and colonial sugars together, for seven years, has amounted to about 93,600 tons. In 1840, about 78,000 tons of foreign and colonial sugar were imported into France. To this must be added nearly 26,000 tons of beet-root sugar manufactured in that year, giving an available total of 104,000 tons; and about 10,500 tons were exported, leaving for the consumption of the whole of France in that year, 93,500 tons. Sugar imported into France is, as in Great Britain, liable to heavy duties Even beet-root sugar is subjected to an excise duty of 6s. 10d. per cwt. These duties, the limitation of the number of ports into which sugar may be imported, and other vexatious restrictions, have all been im-

* Accounts relating to trade and navigation, ordered to be printed by the House of Commons, 17th February, 1843.

† Commercial Tariffs, Part IV.—France. Presented to both Houses of Parliament by command of her Majesty, April, 1842, and printed in former numbers of this Magazine.

posed with a view to promote the growth of beet-root sugar. They combine to augment the price of sugar in France, which, while it averaged in the Antilles, in 1840, 22s. per cwt., averaged at Havre 53s. 6d., (the average duty-paid price of sugar in the London market was in the same year 74s. 2½d.,) and at Paris considerably more.* The falling off in the production of beet-root sugar in France of late years is the consequence of inability to keep its ground in the market against cane-sugar, labouring under all the disadvantages mentioned. The complaints of the colonial merchants and the shipping interest, and the impatience of the consumer, are working a change in public opinion on the subject of beet-root sugar. Committees were appointed in 1840 and 1841, and their reports have led the government to entertain the proposal to *prohibit* the manufacture of beet-root sugar, and to indemnify the manufacturers.†

QUANTITIES OF SUGAR IMPORTED INTO AND EXPORTED FROM FRANCE, DISTINGUISHING THE COLONIAL SUGARS.

IMPORTED INTO FRANCE.

Years.	Colonial.		Foreign.		Total.	
	Quantity.	Value.	Quantity.	Value.	Quantity.	Value.
	Kilogrammes	Francs.	Kilogrammes.	Francs.	Kilogrammes	Francs.
1834	83,049,141	51,700,000	12,080,451	6,900,000	95,129,592	58,600,000
1835	84,249,890	52,600,000	10,434,289	6,200,000	94,684,179	58,800,000
1836	79,326,022	49,400,000	9,461,555	6,100,000	88,787,577	55,500,000
1837	66,535,563	41,700,000	10,618,467	6,200,000	77,174,030	47,900,000
1838	86,992,808	55,000,000	12,389,707	7,200,000	99,392,515	62,200,000
1839	87,664,893	54,800,000	6,396,818	4,100,000	94,461,711	58,900,000
1840	75,543,696	47,300,000	17,355,299	9,300,000	92,898,995	56,600,000
1841	85,850,823	54,400,000	21,511,816	11,900,000	107,362,639	66,300,000

* Comparative table of the duties leviable on the importation of sugar into the principal consuming countries, stated in shillings per hundred weight:—

	Raw. s. d.	Clayed. s. d.	Refined. s. d.
Great Britain—West India Colonies	24s. and 5 per ct.	....	168 0
— British India			
— Mauritius			
— Foreign India	32 0	....	....
— Foreign	63 0	63 0	....
France—French colonies, average	18 0	25 6	prohib.
— Foreign average	31 0	36 0	prohib.
Holland	16 6	....	82 0
German Customs Union, or Zoll-verein—for refining	16 0	....	...
" " " for sale	30 0	....	32 0
Lumps for refining, under special control	17 0	....	....
Austria—for refining	14 0	. ..	....
— for sale	27 0	....	33 0
United States of America	11 6	18 6	28 0

† Last return of the manufacture of sugar from beet-root in France, dated March, 1844:—There are 384 beet-root sugar manufactories in operation, or 59 less than in the same month of 1843. The quantity manufactured during the last season was 24,284,043 kilogrammes; and that sold for consumption, 20,447,120 kilogrammes. The duty levied on this produce amounted to 2,392,561 francs.

ENTERED FOR HOME CONSUMPTION.

Years	Colonial.		Foreign.		Total.	
	Quantity.	Value.	Quantity.	Value.	Quantity.	Value.
	Kilogrammes	Francs.	Kilogrammes	Francs.	Kilogrammes	Francs.
1834	66 475 430	43 700 000	4 366 804	2 000 000	70 842 234	43 900 000
1835	69 339 548	44 800 000	3 292 480	1 500 000	72 632 028	46 300 000
1836	66 188 958	41 800 000	1 012 833	500 000	67 201 791	42 300 000
1837	66 489 668	41 700 000	3 342 966	1 600 000	69 832 634	43 300 000
1838	68 146 685	43 300 000	3 309 480	1 500 000	71 456 165	44 800 000
1839	71 613 062	45 100 000	655 340	300 000	72 268 402	45 400 000
1840	78 445 086	49 200 000	6 666 360	3 100 000	85 111 446	52 300 000
1841	74 514 503	47 500 000	12 042 268	6 000 000	86 556 771	53 500 000

EXPORTS OF RAW SUGAR.

Years.	Colonial.	Foreign.	Total.	
	Quantity.	Quantity.	Quantity.	Value.
	Kilogrammes.	Kilogrammes.	Kilogrammes.	Francs.
1834	53,056	5,056,734	5,109,790	5,500,000
1835	4,350,876	8,146,527	12,497,403	11,600,000
1836	5,570,000	6,387,099	11,957,099	10,800,000
1837	652,361	7,326,072	7,978,433	8,200,000
1838	9,385,962	8,755,358	18,141,320	15,800,000
1839	8,511,135	6,260,442	14,771,577	12,600,000
1840	172,732	6,234,188	6,406,920	6,600,000
1841	357,607	5,953,299	6,310,906	6,500,000

EXPORTS OF REFINED SUGARS.

1834	53,351	2,692,799	2,746,150	5,700,000
1835	1,259,625	2,940,257	4,199,882	7,000,000
1836	6,538,732	884,844	7,423,576	11,100,000
1837	2,085,075	2,046,021	4,131,096	9,600,000
1838	2,779,177	2,808,499	5,587,676	10,200,000
1839	6,366,127	544,434	6,910,561	11,600,000
1840	466,107	3,203,136	3,669,243	10,600,000
1841	40,952	8,065,485	8,106,437	13,300,000

Holland.—In 1840, the value of sugar imported into Holland from all parts of the world, is said* to have been—

From Dutch Indies	£1,243,785	From England	£85,833
" Cuba & Porto Rico	656,333		
" Hanse Towns.......	227,708	Total	£2,432,749
" Brazil	219,000		

Of this total, sugar to the value of 2,014,183*l.* was imported into Amsterdam alone. We have no statement of the value of the sugar imported into Rotterdam in 1840; but in 1841, it was 259,720*l.*

* Commercial Tariffs and Regulations, Part VI.—Holland. Presented to both Houses of Parliament by command of her Majesty, 2d February, 1843, and printed in the previous numbers of this Magazine.

From this it may be inferred that the importation of sugar into Holland centres in these two ports. One-half of the sugar annually imported into Holland appears to be drawn from its own colonies. Of this portion, 15,000 tons are from Surinam,* the rest from Java. The quantity of sugar exported from Java in 1840 was 61,378 tons, two-thirds of which, being about 40,000 tons, added to the 15,000 from Surinam, gives 55,000 tons of sugar imported into Holland in 1840, from its own colonies. It appears from the table of values, that the quantity of sugar imported from other countries about equalled the quantity imported from the colonies. In 1840, therefore, there cannot have been less than 110,000 tons of sugar imported into Holland, about half the quantity imported into Great Britain in the same year. The population of Holland does not exceed 3,100,000; and the general high taxation of Holland, joined to the frugality of the people, limits the demand for sugar to far below what would, under more favourable circumstances, be consumed by the Dutch at home. Raw sugar to the value of 276,000*l.* is stated to have been re-exported in 1840. The refined sugar exported in the same year is estimated at 2,112,000*l.* The bulk of the sugar imported into Holland is intended to be re-exported as refined sugar. It is a forced trade.

A monopoly of the Java sugars is given to the Colonial Association of Holland (Neerlandische-Handel-Maatschappy). The inhabitants of Java are obliged to cover a fifth part of their estates with sugar, which is paid as rent. The sugar is prepared in private factories, to which money is advanced by government, who are repaid in raw sugar received at the rate of 15s. 3d. per cwt. This sugar is delivered by the government to the company's agents, at certain ports, and shipped for Holland by the company at fixed rates, free of duty, at the risk of government. The company dispose of it by public sales "as speedily as possible," and account to the government for the proceeds. The sugar thus obtained by forced labour is sold at a low price to the refiners, who act as if they were to receive for ever a bounty which would enable them to engross the home-market of continental Europe. The effect of forcing the cultivation of sugar for the Dutch refineries has been attended with great loss. Rnssia prohibits the importation of refined sugar; Germany imposes high differential duties on refined sugars, and admits raw sugars for refineries; France imposes high, and England prohibitory duties, both on raw and refined sugars. The loss of Belgium to Holland has reduced the home consumption one-half. The production of Java

* Surinam Almanac, and "Dutch Settlements in Asia," in our present and previous numbers.

has gone on increasing, and the Dutch have been obliged to go on refining beyond the demand of the market, to avoid greater loss. There have already been failures from this cause in Rotterdam and Amsterdam; but the chief revenue of Java is derived from sugar, and the Dutch navigation depends upon the sugar-trade. By the arrangement of 1839, the Dutch government is bound to persevere in this system till 1850.

Denmark.—The quantity of sugar imported into Copenhagen, in 1838, was—

	Cwts.
St. Croix sugar	52,187
Foreign plantation	40,803
Total	92,990

The German province of Holstein is supplied with sugar from Hamburg; but we have no means of ascertaining the quantity. The duties on sugar in Denmark are moderate, and the prices are low; but the whole supply does not exceed the demand.*

Hamburg, and other German States not included in the Zoll-verein.—Hamburg and Bremen are the emporiums of sugar for all the German states (except Austria) not included in the Zoll-verein. Hamburg, in addition to the supplies with which it furnishes those countries, exports largely to Prussia, and sends a considerable quantity of sugar to the north-western provinces of Austria. The customs-duties, both in Hamburg and Bremen, are little more than nominal. The quantity imported into Bremen, in 1838, was 6,200 tons. The importation of Hamburg, in 1840 and 1841, amounted to—1840, 45,300 tons; 1841, 30,200 tons. The stock remaining on hand, at the end of 1841, was 8,700 tons. The sugar transported from Hamburg, by the Elbe, in 1837 and 1838, to the Prussian dominions alone, amounted to—

	In 1837. Tons.	In 1838. Tons.		In 1837. Tons.	In 1338. Tons.
Raw	18,300	18,800	Refined	1,100	1,200

The German Zoll-verein.—The customs union of Germany resembles France in this respect, that a large portion of its sugar supply consists of home-manufactured beet-root sugar. It differs from France in this respect, that it has no colonies, and, we might almost say, no maritime trade. The following table† shows the amount of the colonial sugar-trade, in the states of the union, in the years 1837 to 1840, inclusive:

* Commercial Tariffs and Regulations, Part III., presented to both Houses of Parliament by command of her Majesty, 7th February, 1842.

† Commercial Tariffs and Regulations, Part V.

IMPORTS.			EXPORTS.		
Years.	Refined.	Raw and lump sugars for refiners.	Years.	Refined.	Raw and lump sugars for refiners.
	Centners.†	Centners.		Centners.	Centners.
1837 ...	213,740	1,140,168	1837 ...	30,788	56
1838‡ ...	....	....	1838 ...	21,936	25
1839 ...	....	....	1839 ...	21,227	199
1840 ...	269,964	1,414,148	1840 ...	42,808	310

Professor Dietrici (from whose official work on the commerce of Prussia and the Zoll-verein, in 1837-39, these tables are taken), states the quantity of beet-root sugar annually produced in the territories of the League, as far as it had been ascertained, as follows:—In Prussia, eighty-nine manufacturers produced annually 112,268 centners of best beet-root sugar; thirty-six in the other states of the union produced 32,942 centners; in all, 145,210 centners, or about 6,500 tons.

It appears, therefore, that in 1840, about 55,000 tons of colonial sugar were imported into the states of the union; at least about 6,500 tons of beet-root sugar manufactured in them, and nearly 2,000 tons exported. This leaves about 59,500 tons for internal consumption. The produce of the beet-root sugar manufactories would, according to this statement, amount to nearly a tenth part of the whole sugar consumed in the union. The production of this tenth is promoted, and perhaps rendered possible, by the duties imposed on imported sugar; which we have stated along with those of France and other countries.

The colonial raw sugar consumed or refined in the customs union, is derived almost exclusively from Holland and Hamburg; very little is imported from England in the eastern Baltic ports of Prussia.

The Austrian Dominions.—The sugar consumed in Austria is partly beet-root and partly cane sugar. Professor Dietrici estimates the quantity of beet-root sugar annually produced in Austria at nearly 3,200 tons; and, from the sickly state of the manufacture, there is good reason to believe that this is not an under-estimate. The great emporium of colonial sugar is Trieste. There is a growing sugar-trade from Hamburg to Bohemia and Galicia. In 1839, about 1,500 tons found their way through this channel into the Austrian dominions. Some sugar is imported into Venice, which does not come through Trieste; in 1836, it amounted to upwards of 1,096 hhds., valued at 101,031*l.* A recent official statement gives the quantity of sugar annually imported into Trieste from 1832 to 1841. As a good deal has been said about the increased consumption of sugar anticipated in Austria from

† The Berlin centner = 103.3 lbs. avoirdupois English.

‡ These years are left blank in the original tables of Professor Dietrici.

the reduced duties of the tariff of 1838, a table, showing the imports of 1838 (the year in which the new tariff came into operation), of the three years preceding that year, and the three following it, is here subjoined:—

IMPORTS OF SUGAR INTO TRIESTE.

Years.	Raw. Tons.*	Refined. Tons.	Total. Tons.	Years.	Raw. Tons.	Refined. Tons.	Total. Tons.
1835 ...	19,800	2,195	21,995	1839 ...	26,050	5,832	31,880
1836 ...	27,500	5,500	33,000	1840 ...	23,446	4,400	27,846
1837 ...	15,680	4,064	19,744	1841 ...	18,595	8,525	27,120
1838 ...	2,2154	8,000	30,154				

Belgium.—The total importation of sugar into Antwerp, in 1838, was 15,000 tons. Professor Dietrici estimates the annual average of beet-root sugar manufactured in Belgium at 15,000 tons. We have no means of estimating the quantity of sugar exported from Belgium.

Italy.—The sugar of Italy (the Austrian provinces excepted) is drawn principally from Holland, France, and England. The quantity we have found it difficult to ascertain: it appears to be about 35,000 tons.

Spain and Portugal.—The statistics of the sugar-trade of the Peninsula, like those of Naples, remain a blank. M. Montveran estimates the consumption in Spain at 41,000 tons.

Sweden.—The accounts of the sugar-trade of Sweden and Norway are somewhat antiquated, and not very minute. In 1829, 90,334 cwt. of sugar was imported into Sweden; in 1831, the importation amounted to 97,106 cwt. Norway and Finland are in part supplied with sugar from Sweden.

Russia.—Nearly 35,000 tons of sugar were imported into Russia in 1838, by way of Odessa and St. Petersburgh. According to the official journal of Berlin, there were, in 1841, 174 manufactories of beet-root sugar in Russia.† The amount of the produce of these establishments is not mentioned: Professor Dietrici estimates it at 156,600 Berlin centners—this, however, is mere conjecture.

United States of America.—The United States, notwithstanding the very considerable quantity of sugar produced in them, belong to the importing countries. In 1839, the import of sugars was 195,231,273 lbs. at a cost of 10,000,000 dollars. In 1840, about 120,000,000 lbs. were imported, valued at about 6,000,000 dollars. The greater part of this

* In the original table the quantities are stated in centners of Vienna (123¼ lbs. avoirdupois); in converting them into English weight, fractions have been disregarded.

† Preussische Staats-Zeitung, 1841, No. 117.

was retained for home-consumption. The quantity of sugar produced in the United States, 1841, appears from the following table:—

	lbs.		lbs.
Maine	263,592	Mississippi	127
New Hampshire ...	169,519	Louisiana...	88,189,315
Massachussets ...	496,341	Tennessee	275,557
Rhode Island... ...	55	Kentucky...	1,409,172
Connecticut	56,372	Ohio	7,109,423
Vermont...	5,119,264	Indiana	3,914,184
New York	11,102,070	Illinois	415,756
New Jersey	67	Missouri	327,165
Pennsylvania	2,894,016	Arkansas	2,147
Delaware...	......	Michigan	1,894,372
Maryland...	39,892	Florida	269,146
Virginia	1,557,206	Wisconsin	147,816
North Carolina ...	8,924	Iowa	51,425
South Carolina ...	31,461	District of Columbia	......
Georgia	357,611		
Alabama	10,650	Total	126,164,644

The quantity of sugar imported into the States, in 1841, was, of brown sugar, 163,276,309 lbs.; white, clayed, or powdered, 17,646,019 lbs.; loaf, 68,060 lbs. The value is stated in the treasury report to have been 8,804,700 dollars. This, added to the quantity produced, gives for the total consumption of the United States, in 1841, about 132,200 tons. In Louisiana, Mississippi, Alabama, and Florida, sugar is manufactured from the cane; and the produce of these countries amounts to within thirty-five millions of pounds of the whole produce of the States. According to a statement published by Mr. P. A. Degelos, of New Orleans, which enumerates every plantation in the state of Louisiana, with the number of hogsheads produced by each, we notice that the crop of 1842 reached the very large amount of 140,316 hhds., being about 5,000 hhds. more than the highest estimate. The product of molasses he computes at 52 gallons for each hogshead of sugar, which would give a total of 7,296,432 gallons. The whole number of plantations is found to be 668, of which 361 use steam, and 307 horse power. Louisiana, Alabama, and Mississippi are at the extreme verge of the cane-cultivation: almost every alternate year the canes suffer from the early frosts. The prospects of increased population and cultivation in Florida are rather remote. The remaining thirty-five million pounds of sugar is prepared from maple in the thinly-settled districts, and from beet-root in the rest. Some experiments were made by the French chemists, towards the close of the last century, on the yield of sugar from the maple, which clearly showed that the cultivation of this tree for the manufacture of sugar could not pay in an old settled country. The beet-root is not likely to compete any better with the cane in America than in Europe. There is every reason to believe, then, that the United States, with their rapidly increasing population, will continue to import sugar, and that to a greater extent than they have hitherto done.

From a table compiled from annual reports of the secretary of the treasury, it appears that the quantity of brown sugar imported into the United States in twenty-one years, from 1821 to 1841, amounted to 2,025,020,096 lbs., of which 1,778,996,140 lbs. were consumed in the United States. The quantity of foreign brown sugar exported during the same period (twenty-one years,) amounted to 296,004,776 lbs. The quantity of white sugar imported into the United States in the same twenty-one years was 214,464,415 lbs., while the consumption was 104,669,095, and the exports 109,813,330 lbs.

The following is the quantity, in pounds and value, of sugar imported into the United States for twelve years previous to 1833:—

Years.	Quantity.	Value. Dollars.	Years.	Quantity.	Value. Dollars.
1821	... 59,512,835	3,553,582	1827	... 76,701,629	4,577,361
1822	... 88,305,670	5,034,429	1828	... 56,935,251	3,546,736
1823	... 60,789,210	3,258,689	1829	... 63,307,294	3,622,406
1824	... 94,379,814	5,165,800	1830	... 86,483,046	4,630,342
1825	... 71,771,479	4,232,530	1831	... 109,014,654	4,910,877
1826	... 84,902,955	5,311,631	1832	... 66,452,288	2,933,688

QUANTITY IN POUNDS, AND VALUE OF SUGAR, IMPORTED INTO THE UNITED STATES IN EACH YEAR FROM 1833 TO 1841.*

Years.	Brown.	White clayed.	Loaf.	Total Quantity.	Total Value.
	lbs.	lbs.	lbs.	lbs.	Dollars.
1833	85,689,044	11,999,088	46,035	97,734,167	4,757,523
1834	107,483,841	7,906,014	1,670	115,391,525	5,538,044
1835	111,806,880	14,229,359	2,096	126,038,335	6,806,425
1836	181,243,537	10,182,578	926	191,429,041	12,514,647
1837	120,416,071	15,723,748	9,899	136,149,718	7,203,800
1838	139,200,905	14,678,238	2,948	153,882,091	7,586,629
1839	182,540,327	12,690,946	895	195,232,168	9,921,956
1840	107,955,033	12,984,552	1,035	120,940,620	5,581,012
1841	165,963,083	18,233,579	68,261	184,264,923	8,802,734

British Colonies.—The British colonies in which sugar is not produced are, British North America, the Cape of Good Hope, and the settlements in New Holland and New Zealand. The following is the state of the import of sugar into them in the year 1839:—

* In this sum, the import from India is included.

Colonies.	RAW SUGAR. British Plantation.	Foreign.	East Indian.	Refined British.
	lbs.	lbs.	lbs.	lbs.
British North America.........	1,629,560	16,667,323	164,257	3,086,184
New South Wales and Van Diemen's Land	6,636,050	9,318,590*	....	787,490
Cape of Good Hope............	2,839,115	816,061	109747	51,789
Total....................	11,104,725	26,801,974	274,004	3,945,463

Northern Asia.—Though the quantity cannot be ascertained, it is known that considerable quantities of sugar are imported into the northern provinces of China, and into Chinese and Independent Tartary.

South America.—There is also a growing demand, the exact quantity of which cannot be ascertained, in the southern provinces of La Plata and Chile.

It is but too apparent, from this review, that any estimate of the total annual consumption of sugar in the sugar-importing countries, founded on the collective amount of their importations, must be imperfect. The data are insufficient. And any other method of attempting to arrive at the quantity consumed, must evidently be fallacious. The great importing markets in Europe are Great Britain, France, Holland, Russia, Hamburg, and Trieste. Their imports are re-exported in part, to supply the demand of the rest of Europe, North Africa, and Western Asia. Each of them imports a portion of its sugar from some of the others; but the effect of this, in making the sum of their total exports too high, may be set off against the unknown quantity imported into Spain and Portugal, and small quantities imported direct into Italy, Russia, and Sweden. The total imports of the United States, and of the British colonies which do not produce sugar, are ascertained with tolerable accuracy. But our ignorance of the quantity consumed by the importing countries of eastern and northern Asia, and in Chile and the provinces of La Plata, renders it impossible to ascertain the whole annual consumption of sugar. The quantity actually passing through the market of the importing countries, in the course of a year, as far as can be shown in figures, is here given:—

	Tons.
Great Britain (1842) retained for consumption	198,823
France (1840) colonial retained for consumption, and beet-root	93,500
Holland (1840) imported	110,000

* In this sum the import from India is included.

		Tons.
Denmark (1838) imported		4,650
Hamburg (1840) imported		45,300
Prussia and Zoll-verein (1839) beet-root sugar		6,500
Belgium (1838) colonial and beet-root sugar		30,000
Russia (1840) imported	35,000	42,700
" (1841) beet-root sugar	7,700	
Austria (1841) imported at Trieste	25,120	28,320
" (1841) beet-root	3,200	
United States of North America (1841)		132,000
British colonies not producing sugar (1839)		18,800
Total		706,593

The quantity of sugar retained for consumption in France and Great Britain has been taken, because what is exported would have been repeated in other countries; the total imports of Holland and Hamburg are taken; but the colonial sugar imported into the Zoll-verein, and into Austria overland, and Switzerland, as drawn from these markets, is omitted; the sugar in Italy, Spain, and Portugal, cannot be ascertained.

Statement of the sugar stocks on hand in the leading importing markets of Europe, on the 1st of March for each of the years 1840, 1841, 1842, and 1843. They are sufficiently close to show that the annual consumption must pretty nearly equal the annual importation: it is obvious that in almost every country the use of sugar is on the increase; and hence it follows, that the actual produce of the exporting countries is no more than sufficient to supply the existing demand.

STOCKS OF SUGAR, IN TONS, ON THE 1st OF MARCH, 1840–1843.

	In 1840. Tons.	In 1841. Tons.	In 1842. Tons.	In 1843. Tons.
Holland	10,700	16,600	15,550	3,100
Hamburg	7,000	5,750	6,750	8,500
Trieste	5,600	8,400	2,900	3,950
Antwerp	1,000	2,800	4,150	2,000
Havre	500	2,500	2,600	7,000
	24,800	36,050	31,950	19,550
England	39,875	47,900	43,000	43,000
Total	64,675	83,950	74,950	63,050
British plantation in England ...	26,995	27,650	28,200	31,450
Foreign sugar	37,680	56,300	46,750	31,600

NEW ZEALAND.

An historical account of the colonization of the group of islands which bear this name was given in the December number of the former series of the Magazine, bringing it up to that date. In February, the story was continued and closed; when an account had been received that an affray had occurred in Cloudy Bay; but, with the hope that the next news which would arrive would gratify the connections of those who have emigrated, with more cheering prospects. So far from this being the case, the authentic details of the affray are amongst the most horrible and afflicting of any slaughter which has ever been recorded in English history, and the conduct of the local government not merely inexplicable, foolish, and impotent, but attended with a vindictiveness towards the settlers, which must be reprobated by their natural protector, the Colonial Minister, at home. All instructions by Lord John Russell, and some by Lord Stanley, have been unheeded, with a determination to treat them with contempt. It is due to our readers, it is necessary towards the character of the *Colonial Magazine*, not only to continue the history, but to explain the details of this lamentable affray, in which so many brave colonists have been inhumanly butchered.

Not the slightest blame attaches to the government in Downing-street for the appointment of Lieutenant Shortland, the acting-governor. The late Governor Hobson, with whom he had served at sea as a lieutenant, named him the Colonial Secretary, a most lucrative employment;* the death of his patron placed him in his late position; and, certainly, his acts, his proclamations, prove him to have been wholly unfitted for the situation.

Far be it from us to find fault with Lord Stanley; he is, we know, much occupied; there are but few of the documents which pass through his office which he can examine, that is a part of his business which he

* See page 56, House of Commons Papers, 11th of May, 1841—Table of fees "for filing any memorial with the Colonial Secretary, or opposition thereto, £5;" so that every opposed memorial for land claim, yields him £5 from the claimant, £5 from the opposer, and for the "final report, £5," independent of many other fees. It is impossible to examine the official list of claims already made (see Terry, page 124:—339 claims for 6,125,198 acres in the northern island; and 38 claims for 19,278,000 acres, in the middle island) without concluding that it is the interest of the Colonial Secretary to permit, if not encourage, claimants and delay. It is possible that much of the mischief which has occurred may be attributed to the circumstances here stated.

confides to secretaries and confidential clerks; but, by reading such articles as were printed in the December and February numbers of this Magazine, and as this will be, with authentic references to almost every sentence—in one quarter of an hour, his lordship will attain as much knowledge of facts as any one can acquire in a month's reading, and more than any clerk in his office is willing to lay before him. Again, it is a most wholesome check upon what they collect for him, and upon governors and colonial secretaries as to what they write home; and, if it be taken as it is meant, in a friendly manner, it must be of essential service.

The history of the colonization of New Zealand is a dark blot in the history of our country, but more particularly since the year 1839. It commenced with the visit of the Rev. Samuel Marsden, in 1814, who established the missionary stations with the purest motives; and we had little knowledge of the island or their inhabitants, but from the representations of the missionaries, until the year 1838, when a committee of the House of Lords, of which Lord Devon was chairman, was appointed to make an inquiry into their state. The missionaries were established in the north-eastern part of the northern island; they had been sent out by two missionary societies, the Church of England and Wesleyan Missionary Societies at home. These societies have committees for their management, and secretaries by whom they were represented before committees of both houses of parliament. As well as missionaries sent out by these societies, there were French Roman Catholic missionaries, under the direction of a French Bishop of Pompalier. The English societies agreed to divide the northern island, the Church of England missionaries taking the eastern, while the Wesleyan took the western; but neither extending their missions far to the southward. But there was this difference between them, the Church of England missionaries were allured by the committee of the society at home, to acquire a limited quantity of land;* the Wesleyan missionary committee do not permit their missionaries to acquire land;† the

* In July, 1830, the committee at home came to the following resolution: "That under the peculiar circumstances of the New Zealand mission, the committee are of opinion, that purchases of land from the natives, to a moderate extent, should be authorized, as a provision for their children after they are fifteen years of age; the nature and extent of the purchase to be, in each case, referred to the committee for their sanction, after having been considered and approved in a meeting of missionaries." (Page 165 of the Appendix to the House of Commons Report, 3d of August, 1840.)—We concur entirely in this opinion; and, if our advice was followed, some pains would be taken to carry it into effect.

† One of them (Mr. White) did so, but was dismissed from the mission.

Catholic missionaries are all single men, and never attempt to acquire land. There is no difficulty in tracing in many of these missionaries, and particularly those of the Church of England, a determination to possess themselves of as much land as possible, and to monopolize the government of the country. It is impossible to believe that the committees of these societies at home, which consist of many excellent noblemen and gentlemen, could have lent themselves to any such absurd endeavour, had they been acquainted with the real facts; and one of the objects of this paper is to enlighten them, since we perceive the same system of deceit going on, and contributions gathering from the public from statements which cannot be true.* In addition to the missionaries, there were some settlers, the number greatly exaggerated,† chiefly

* A public meeting was lately held in London of the Church of England Missionary Society, Mr. Labouchere in the chair, at which it was stated that there were 35,000 native communicants in New Zealand. If this be the case with the Church of England missionaries, what must be the number who follow the Methodist and Catholic missionaries? Upon reading the statement, we turned to the Report of the House of Lords, to ascertain who were the persons whom the Society termed "communicants," and at page 240, found them to be "persons who take the sacrament;" and, in making this examination, we happened to turn to page 185 of the same Report, and there is a table of the stations, "schools, scholars, congregations, and communicants, in the mission of the Church Missionary Society in New Zealand, 1st of May, 1838," and find the number of communicants to be 178; but this was a statement delivered in on oath to a Committee of the House of Lords, but when a statement was to be made to a public meeting, the chief object of which was to gather money, then the number, in the spring of 1844, was 35,000! Again, it is not long since that a statement was made at one of these public meetings, that 400 Testaments were sent to Cloudy Bay, and as soon as their arrival was known, there were 700 eager candidates for them. Cloudy Bay is one of the greatest extent, with very few inhabitants—the accurate Deiffenbach calculated them when there, men women, and children, at 400 (see his table, vol. i., p. 195).

† Lords' Report, page 264. Mr. Coates on the 11th of May, 1838, calculated the number at 500, believing that the greater number were in the neighbourhood of the Bay of Islands. Many circumstances have since come to light, which show that their number by no means amounted to so many. Mr. Coates is, we believe, correct, that the greater part were located at or in the neighbourhood of the Bay of Islands. Now, when Captain Hobson (30th of January, 1840), with all the military parade which a ship of war could give him, universally welcomed, went there, there were but forty-one signatures to an address of congratulation (see page 6 of House of Commons Papers, 11th May, 1841). The whites at Hokianga were very few, beyond those attached to the Wesleyan missionary stations; in Cook's Straits, there was Mr. Barrett at Port Nicholson married to a native woman; Mr. Guard and Mr. Thoms at Cloudy Bay; Mr. Evans, and one or two Americans, at Kapiti, or the adjoining islands—all having formed whaling-stations, and each having some English sailors in their employ, but their boats were chiefly

at the whaling-stations, one of whom, Mr. Thoms, has had so much to do with the late afflicting massacre, that it is some importance to mention them—but more of that in the sequel.

There was a native in the neighbourhood of the Bay of Islands, Shunghee, who appears to have borne much more of the character of a chieftain than any other of whom we have read, but neither he or any other individuals "had any right to the sovereignty of the country, and, consequently, possessed no authority to convey a right of sovereignty to another."* We are the last to fall out with this account of the power of the native chiefs, and, at any rate, in this respect, entirely coincide with the statement made by Mr. Coates. Shunghee however, went to England, was presented to our George IV., received presents from him, and whilst there, made some bargain with the French Baron de Thierry, clothing him with sovereign power over a certain district of country, and selling him the land. It was a speculative scheme on the part of the individual, who was without capital, surveyor, emigrants, or any means of founding a colony. An attempt was made in London by a foreigner to get up a company to support the Baron, but nothing came of it. Shunghee, instructed by his European visit, determined to become the Napoleon of New Zealand, made war on all his neighbours, his wife Kiri assisting him in battle; but, although victorious, he was wounded, and died of those wounds.† Thousands fell in the course of these wars.

The attempt of Baron de Thierry had no effect upon the Colonial Minister at home, but it was an interference with missionary power or possessions at the antipodes, which roused some of them, and the resident, Mr. Busby, into immediate action. It was determined to raise an apparent native sovereign power—chiefs, a mere rank, being those who were not slaves, were exalted into the position of chieftains, as if

worked by natives. Deiffenbach has given a minute account of these people, we may refer to vol. i., chap. iv. page 109, also to page 99—but this is a part of his work which should be consulted in much more than one or two pages. In the neighbourhood of Akaroo, or Port Cowper, there were one or two European settlers, we are speaking of white settlers. The coasts and bays were visited during the season by American, French, English, Danish, Bremen, &c. vessels engaged in the whaling business, who had considerable communication with the natives, but these cannot be called colonists.

* These are the words of Mr. Coates in his evidence before the Lords' Committee. See page 244 of the Report.

† The account was sent to England by the Church of England missionaries, and by the secretary of the Society laid before the Committee of the Lords. See the Report, page 220, and following.

they were the heads of distinct tribes.* A declaration of independence was signed; † a flag was selected, ‡ and hoisted as a signal of national independence. The whole was a manœuvre, concocted and prepared by Mr. Busby, § apparently to prevent the assumption of power or proprietorship by the French baron; but circumstances have since come to light which unveil its real object. Could it have been maintained, it would have clothed a few individuals with immense property, as well as the exercise of political power. Settlers in Australia and Van Diemen's Land, by themselves or their agents, and Americans, were making what they called purchases of land from the natives. This manœuvre was meant to stop all such transactions. The parties to it as witnesses or certifying to its authenticity, were—

1st. Mr. Busby, and he claims 50,000 acres, which he valued at 30,000*l.* ‖

2d. Henry Williams, missionary C.M.S. He claims 11,000 acres;¶ but we suspect that this is only a part of what he intended to have had, as it was stated by Mr. Blackett, after his visit there, that his property was as large as Mr. Fairburn's, of which we will speak by and by.**

3d. George Clark, C.M.S., who purchased land lest it should fall into the hands of unprincipled persons.††

4th. James C. Clendon. This witness was a great land-jobber; ‡‡ it was of him that Governor Hobson agreed to purchase land for the

---

* See the evidence of the Rev. F. Wilkinson in the Lords' Report, p. 96. He is asked, "Is every one called a chief who is not a slave?" Answer—"I fancy so." "The native inhabitants are divided into three classes—chiefs, freemen, and slaves."—Hodgskin's Narrative of Eight Months' Sojourn in New Zealand. p. 18.

† It will be found printed in two places in the Lords' Report, p. 179 and 244.

‡ See Sir George Gipps' account of this transaction, p. 75, House of Commons Papers, 11th May, 1841.

§ So stated by Sir George Gipps; but it is "a manœuvre," to use his words, from which great mischief has arisen, and which in England has duped ministers, members of the committees of missionary societies, and thousands who to this hour were unaware that such a trick had been practised.

‖ See this stated in Sir George Gipps' letter to Lord John Russell, dated 16th of August, 1840; p. 62, Parliamentary Papers, 11th of May, 1841.

¶ See the official table in Deiffenbach, vol. ii. p. 168.

** See questions and answers, No. 471 and 472, in Mr. Blackett's evidence, p. 64, Parliamentary Papers, 3d of August, 1840.

†† So stated by Mr. Coates and the Rev. Mr. Beecham, Lords' Report, p. 259.

‡‡ See question and answer in Mr. Blackett's evidence, No. 394, p. 61, Parliamentary Papers, 3d of August, 1840.

government, which Sir George Gipps refused to confirm,* and for which a composition was reluctantly sanctioned by Lord Stanley.† Mr. Clendon has been made a member of council at Aucland, and consequently is placed in a position to take part in proclamations and ordinances, which may serve that place, in the prosperity of which he is more interested than any one, at the expense of other settlements.

5th. Gilbert Moir, merchant. We have met with no trace of this gentleman having had a personal interest in this transaction.

It may be asked, how value was to be given to the lands acquired? an answer is readily given. Irregular colonization was making rapid progress; with its progress value attached to the land everywhere; and so long as the sovereignty of any civilized power was warded off, the firmer became these titles; besides, the missionaries applied to colonists in Australia to come and settle with them.‡

[To be continued.]

THE EMIGRANTS.

" Downward they move, a melancholy band,
Pass from the shore, and darken all the strand."—GOLDSMITH.

BY THE AUTHOR OF "HOURS OF THOUGHT, OR POETIC MUSINGS."

BORNE o'er the bosom of the trackless main,
Far from the shore they loved, and left with pain;
Compell'd, by hard necessity, to rove,
And quit those scenes of early bliss and love,
That close endeared them to their humble shed:
But those endearments now, alas! are fled:
The straw-thatched roof, whose curling smoke was seen;
The shady lane, and oft-frequented green,
Where many a gambol drew the village throng,
At eve, when old and young their sports prolong;
Graceful 'bove trees the ancient spire uprose,
In calm seclusion, emblem of repose;
The purling brook, that turned the cotter's mill;
The dark-robed wood, and softly swelling hill,

* See Hobson's despatch dated 4th of August, 1841; p. 144, Parliamentary Papers, 12th of August, 1842.

† See Lord Stanley's despatch to Governor Hobson, 10th of May, 1842; p. 148, Parliamentary Papers, 12th of August, 1842.

‡ See Mr. Montipire's evidence to this effect, Lords' Report, p. 59.

From whence low bleatings murmured thro' the vale,
And rustic's joy came o'er the passing gale.
Such mem'ry pictured in her loveliest dress;
How keen their anguish, words but faint express,
As wafted hence their sorrowing tears they flow,
Their trials real, and unfeigned their woe;
Lone wand'ring exiles, doomed in grief to part,
And leave their country with an aching heart,
To far Australia, or Van Diemen's shore,
A num'rous band, those regions wild explore;
Or wide dispersed, Canadia's woods they range,
The lonely settlers of the forest strange.
Before their gaze the swelling distance shows,
Mountains o'ermantled in eternal snows;
Far as the eye can stretch huge forests rise,
Or dreary moors, or plains of other skies;
A rugged soil, that claims enduring toil,
That oft the labourer doth resist and foil,—
The Emigrants thus feel the curse renewed,
Ere yields the stubborn earth, by toil subdued;
Perchance their little group of children round
Join in the task—young tillers of the ground;
A world before them spread,—a houseless band,
Such are the wand'rers of a foreign land;
And should their enterprise succeed, how blest,
The prospect 'homebound,' to return and rest;
Spend the sweet close of their remaining days,
Their setting sun descend in peaceful rays,
Once more revisit their own happier clime,
With feelings stronger felt by lapse of time;
Review the spot they sorrowing left behind,
When misery drove them outcasts to the wind:
The same delightful scenes engage the eye,
Their only wish is there at last to die;
The same engaging charms allure them still,
The sloping meadows and the rippling rill;
The cheerful woodland pipe of joyous swain,
The swinging sign-post and the stile remain,
That they so often climbed, when ruddy youth,
Happy and heedless of life's sober truth,
Enjoyed the present thro' the live-long day,
Nor gave a thought to-morrow in their play;
Such lovely scenes their influence sweet o'ercast,
Their wand'rings softened, and their hardships past,
Their fondest wish, their chequered troubles o'er,
To Albion's shore return, nor migrate more.

PECKHAM.

COLONIAL INTELLIGENCE.

India.—The news from China and India is of the following dates—China, December 28th; Gwalior, January 30th; and Bombay, February 4th.

On the 28th and 29th of December two severe battles were fought in the vicinity of the capital of Gwalior; one of Maharajpoor, the other of Punniar, in which our forces proved victorious.

The British army, under the commander-in-chief, was about 14,000 strong, of which 300 were cavalry, and 40 pieces of artillery. The forces opposed to them were composed of 15,000 infantry, 3,000 cavalry, and 100 guns. Our loss on these occasions has been very severe, the list amounting to 144 killed and 866 wounded.

Nine British officers have fallen in action or died of their wounds—viz., General Churchill, Colonel Sanders, Major Crommelin, Captains Stewart, Magrath, and Cobban, Lieutenants Newton and Leaths, and Ensign Bray. On the part of the enemy the casualties are estimated at 3,000 to 4,000 killed, and twice as many wounded. The fort of Gwalior was immediately after surrendered to our troops, and the leading chiefs at once tendered submission; our army retires within the Company's territories immediately, and we are not to occupy that country, nor in any way to intermeddle with its internal arrangements.

During the action his Excellency the Governor, Lady Gough, and her daughter, were frequently at the side of the commander-in-chief, exposed to great danger.

India is in general peaceful.

The commander-in-chief has appointed Major-General Valiant, to act as quartermaster-general of her Majesty's forces, vice Churchill, deceased, until her Majesty's pleasure be known.

Affairs in the Punjaub are by no means settled, and it was reported that the Affghans had taken possession of Peshawur.

In Scinde matters are much the same. Our troops are recovering a little from their sickness.

Letters from Gwalior to the 12th of January, quoted in the *Delhi Gazette*, describe matters there as gradually settling down. The regiments lately in the service of that state were being disbanded, and many of the men had consented to enter the contingent army, which was to consist of 20 field-pieces, 2 regiments of cavalry, and 7 of infantry.

The expenses of the campaign were to be paid down forthwith.

Lord Ellenborough was to leave Scindia's capital on the 17th of January on his return to Calcutta.

List of killed, wounded, and missing, in the right wing of the army of Gwalior, under the personal command of his Excellency the Commander-in-Chief, in the action of Maharajpoor, on the 29th of December, 1843:—

Camp, Chounda, January 1, 1844.

General staff, 2 officers and 6 horses killed, and 2 officers and 3 rank and file wounded.

Artillery Division. Horse—2d troop, 2d brigade, 1 rank and file, and 2 syces and grasscutters, and 6 horses killed, and 6 rank and file, 2 syces and grasscutters, and 2 horses wounded, and 3 horses missing.

3d ditto, ditto—1 syce and grasscutter, and 4 horses killed; and 3 rank and file, 6 syces and grasscutters, and 3 horses wounded, and 1 missing.

2d ditto, 3d ditto—1 trumpeter and drummer and 13 horses killed; and 1 sergeant and havildar, 12 rank and file, and 7 horses wounded; and 1 syce and grasscutter and 2 horses missing.

Foot—1st company, 1st battalion, and No. 10 L.F.B., 1 sergeant and havildar, and 4 horses killed; and 4 rank and file, and 1 syce and grasscutter wounded; and 1 horse missing.

1st company, 4th battalion, and No. 17 L.F.B. 1 ordnance driver wounded.

4th company, 4th battalion, 1 officer killed.

Cavalry Division. 3d brigade—her Majesty's 16th Lancers, 2 rank and file and 21 horses killed; and 1 sergeant and havildar, 6 rank and file, and 9 horses wounded.

1st regiment light cavalry, 1 officer, 1 rank and file, and 15 horses killed; and 2 rank and file and 6 horses wounded; and 1 rank and file, 1 syce and grasscutter, and 1 horse missing.

Governor-General's body guard, 6 horses killed; and 1 rank and file and 1 horse wounded.

4th irregular cavalry, 1 trumpeter and drummer, 1 rank and file, and 5 horses killed; 1 officer, 1 native officer, 1 sergeant and havildar, 2 rank and file, and 8 horses wounded.

4th brigade—4th light cavalry (lancers) 1 native officer, 1 rank and file, and 14 horses killed; and 1 officer, 2 native officers, 7 rank and file, and 10 horses wounded; and 2 horses missing.

13th light cavalry, 4 rank and file and 18 horses killed; 3 officers, 1 native officer, 3 sergeants and havildars, 3 trumpeters and drummers, 19 rank and file, and 14 horses wounded; and 2 syces and grasscutters and 7 horses missing.

2d Infantry Division. 3d brigade—Divisional staff, 1 officer wounded.

Her Majesty's 40th foot, 1 sergeant and havildar, 1 trumpeter and drummer, 21 rank and file, and 1 horse killed; and 8 officers, 11 sergeants and havildars, 2 trumpeters and drummers, 138 rank and file, and 1 horse wounded.

2d regiment (grenadiers), 1 trumpeter and drummer, and 3 rank and file killed; and 3 officers, 3 sergeants and havildars, and 31 rank and file wounded.

16th regiment (grenadiers), 1 officer, 1 native officer, and 18 rank and file killed; and 3 officers, 7 native officers, 17 sergeants and havildars 2 trumpeters and drummers, 130 rank and file, and 1 horse wounded; and 1 rank and file missing.

4th brigade—14th native infantry, 1 sergeant and havildar, and 1 rank and file wounded.

43d native infantry, 1 rank and file killed, and 4 rank and file wounded.

3d Infantry Division. Divisional staff, 1 horse killed, and 2 officers wounded.

Her Majesty's 39th foot, 1 officer, 2 sergeants and havildars, 1 trumpeter and drummer, 26 rank and file, and 2 horses killed; and 10 officers, 17 sergeants, and 157 rank and file wounded.

56th Native Infantry, 6 rank and file killed, and four sergeants and havildars, 1 trumpter and drummer, and 33 rank and file wounded, and 1 rank and file missing.

7th Company of Sappers and Miners, 2 rank and file wounded.

Khelat-i-Ghilzie Regiment, 1 rank and file killed, and 1 rank and file wounded.

Escort to Governor-General's Agent, 1 syce and grass-cutter, 1 horse killed, and 1 horse wounded.

Killed.—European officers, 6: native officers, 2; non-commissioned officers, drummers, and rank and file, 94; syces, 4.—Totals, 106.

Wounded.—European officers, 34; native officers, 11; non-commissioned officers, drummers, rank and file, 629; syces and ordnance drivers, 10—Total, 684.

Missing.—3 rank and file, syce, 4—Total 7.

Grand total of all ranks killed, wounded, and missing, 797.

Head-Quarters Staff. Major-Gen. Churchill, C. B., Quartermaster-General, Queen's troops, killed.

Lieutenant-Colonel E. Sanders, C B., Deputy Secretary to the Government Military Department, killed.

Captain G. Freid, arm amputated.

Captain Somerset, Military Secretary to the Governor-General, severely wounded.

Artillery Division. 4th Company of the 4th Battalion.—1st Lieut. Leaths, killed.

Cavalry Division, 1st. Light Cavalry.—Major G. R. Crommelin, C.B., killed.

4th Light Cavalry.—Cornet S. M. St. John, severely wounded.

10th Light Cavalry, Captain Mellish, slightly wounded.

Ditto Cornet R. G. Simeon, slightly do.

Do. Cornet J. Shaw, severely, leg amputated.

4th Irregular Cavalry, Lieutenant and Adjutant O. Cavanagh, leg amputated.

2d *Infantry Division.* Brigade Staff, 3d Brig. —Major-General Valiant, K.H., severe contusion on left breast, wounded.

Her Majesty's 40th Foot, Major Stopford, dangerously wounded.

Do. Captain Coddington, do.

Do. Lieutenant Eagar, slightly do.

Do. Lieutenant Thomas, severely do.

Do, Lieutenant Huey, do.

Do. Lieutenant Dawson, slightly do.

Do. Ensign O'Brien, do.

Do. Lieutenant and Adjutant Nelson, severely wounded.

2d Regiment (Grenadiers), Captain Maclean, slightly do.

Do. Lieutenant Mainwaring, do.

Do. Ensign Gilbert, do.

16th do.—Lieutenant Newton, killed.

Ditto—Lieutenant Colonel M'Laren, C. B., slightly wounded.

Ditto—Brevet-Captain Balderston, severely wounded.

Ditto—Lieut. Graydon, severely wounded.

3d *Infantry Division.* Divisional Staff—Major-General Littler, contusion.

Ditto — Captain H. M. Graves, severely wounded.

Her Majesty's 39th Foot—Major E. W. Bray, very severely wounded.

Do.—Captain R. N. Tinley, severy wounded.

Do.—Captain C. Campbell, slightly wounded.

Do.—Lieutenant and Adjutant Munro, severely wounded.

Ditto—Lieutenant J. S. Atkinson, severely wounded.

Ditto—Lieutenant H. Gray, very severely wounded.

Ditto—Lieutenant R. H. Currie, very slightly wounded.

Ditto—Lieutenant H. G. Colville, very severely wounded.

Ditto — Ensign S. G. Newport, slightly wounded.

Do.—Ensign T. Scarman, severely wounded.

Ditto—Ensign T. D. Bray, killed.

J. R. Lumley, Major General,
Adjutant-General of the Army.

Return of Ordnance captured from the enemy, by the right wing, army of Gwalior, on the 29th of December, 1843.

Camp, Chounda, Jan. 1, 1844.

Howitzers,	brass,	12-pounder	....	2
Ditto	ditto	18-pounder	....	1
Guns,	ditto	4-pounder	....	1
Ditto	ditto	4½-pounder	....	4
Ditto	ditto	4½ pounder	....	6
Ditto	ditto	5 pounder	....	3
Ditto	ditto	6-pounder	....	14
Ditto	ditto	6½-pounder	....	4
Ditto	ditto	6¾-pounder	....	2
Ditto	ditto	7-pounder	....	3
Ditto	ditto	8-pounder	....	2
Ditto	ditto	8½-pounder	....	1
Howitzers	iron	12-pounder	destroyed	2
Guns	ditto	3-pounder	ditto	3
Ditto	ditto	3½-pounder	ditto	3
Ditto	ditto	6-pounder	ditto	3
Ditto	ditto	12-pounder	ditto	2
		Total	....	56

Several tumbrils of ammunition have been destroyed; in one of them, cash to the amount of 3,141 rupees, Gwalior. was discovered, which will be paid into the military chest.

J. Tennant, Brigadier,
Commanding Foot Artillery, Army of Gwalior.
(True copy)
J. R. Lumley, Major-General,
Adjutant-General of the Army.

General Orders by the Right Hon. the Governor-General of India.

Camp, Gwalior Residency,
Jan. 4th, 1844.

The Governor-General directs the publication of the annexed despatch from his Excellency the Commander-in-Chief, reporting the operations of the corps under his Excellency's immediate command, and of that under the command of Major-General Grey, against the mutinous troops which overawed and controlled the Government of his Highness the Maharaja Jyajee Rao Scindiah, and attacked the

British forces on their advance to Gwalior to his Highness's support.

The Governor-General deeply laments the severe loss in killed and wounded which has been sustained in these operations; but it has been sustained in the execution of a great and necessary service, and the victories of Maharajpoor and Punniar, while they have shed new glory upon the British army, have restored the authority of the Maharaja, and have given new security to the British empire in India.

The Governor-General cordially congratulates his Excellency the Commander-in-Chief upon the success of his able combinations, by which two victories were obtained on the same day, and the two wings of the army, proceeding from distant points, have been now united under the walls of Gwalior.

To his Excellency, and to Major-General Grey, and to all the general and other officers, and to all the soldiers of the army, the Governor-General, in the name of the Government, and of all the people of India, offers his most grateful acknowledgments of the distinguished service they have performed; nor can he withhold the tribute of his admiration justly due to the devoted courage manifested by all ranks in actions with brave enemies, who yielded their numerous and well-served artillery only with their lives.

The Governor-General's especial thanks are due to Her Majesty's 39th and 40th Regiments, to the 2d and 16th Regiments of Native Grenadiers, and to the 56th Regiment of Native Infantry, which took with the bayonet the batteries in front of Maharajpoor.

Her Majesty's 39th Regiment had the peculiar fortune of adding to the honour of having won at Plassey, the first great battle which laid the foundation of the British empire in India, the further honour of thus nobly contributing to this, as it may be hoped, the last and crowning victory by which that empire has been secured.

Her Majesty's 40th Regiment, and the 2d and 16th Regiments of Native Grenadiers, again serving together, again displayed their pre-eminent qualities as soldiers, and well supported the character of the ever victorious army of Candahar.

The corps of Major-General Grey, suddenly attacked at Punniar, after a long march, carried the several strong positions of the enemy with a resolution no advantage of ground could enable him to withstand; and Her Majesty's 3d Buffs and 50th Regiment added new lustre to the reputation they gained in the Peninsular war.

Everywhere, at Maharajpoor and at Punniar, the British and the native troops, emulating each other, and animated by the same spirit of military devotion, proved that an army so composed, and united by the bonds of mutual esteem and confidence, must ever remain invincible in Asia.

The Government of India will, as a mark of its grateful sense of their distinguished merit, present to every general and other officer, and to every soldier engaged in the battles of Maharajpoor and Punniar, an Indian star of bronze, made out of the guns taken at those battles; and all officers and soldiers in the service of the Government of India will be permitted to wear the star with their uniforms.

His Excellency the Commander-in-Chief is requested to furnish the Governor-General with nominal rolls of all the officers and soldiers engaged in the two battles respectively, in order that the star presented to each may be inscribed with the name of the battle in which he was engaged.

A triumphal monument, commemorative of the campaign of Gwalior, will be erected at Calcutta, and inscribed with the names of all who fell in the two battles.

The Governor-General directs that the words "Maharajpoor" and "Punniar" shall be borne upon the colours or standards and appointments of the several regiments, troops, and companies, respectively engaged in those battles.

A royal salute and a *feu-de-joie* will be fired at all the stations of the army, on the receipt of this order.

By order of the Right Hon. the
Governor-General of India,
F. Currie,
Secretary to the Government of India
with the Governor-General.

China.—Business at Chusan and Canton is generally dull. Captain Brooke proceeds to England, as the bearer of the supplementary treaty and despatches from Sir Henry Pottinger. The port of Shanghaye was officially opened on the 17th of November, by Captain Balfour, the appointed Consul.

Colonel Butterworth, Governor of the Straits of Malacca, arrived at Penang on the 21st of November.

By private letters from Hong-kong the pleasing intelligence has been communicated that the fever had entirely ceased in the island, and the whole of the troops were convalescent and able to perform their duties. The fever had, however, greatly reduced the appearance of the men, as those attacked by it describe themselves as the remnants of men, being merely skin and bone, and more like skeletons than live members of the human race.

New South Wales.—Sydney papers to the 7th of November, bring the published accounts of the revenue of the colony for the three quarters of the year just closed, and according to these the net deficiency compared with the same period of 1842 was £29,049, a considerable falling off having occurred in the amount received for duties paid on spirits imported, on tobacco, and auction fees. The gross revenue is stated at £274,596, and upon the receipts of the year Sir George Gipps says he expects a decrease of £50,000 or £60,000 compared with 1842. This return is alluded to by the papers as showing more satisfactory results than were expected, and the decline in the spirit duties is considered a favourable feature in the present condition of the population. An act had been passed suppressing colonial distillation, which it was also thought would have the beneficial effect of diminishing the use of ardent spirits. A report had been made to the Legislative Council on the subject of the existing monetary depression, and a bill, suggesting remedies, founded on that report, was about being brought into the House for discussion. The usual official return of the four banks now carrying on business in the colony (viz., Union of Australia, Australasia, Commercial, and New South Wales) had appeared, the results of which, as respects their condition to pay their notes and provide for their deposits, are satisfactory, as the excess of coin and assets in general is much above their total liabilities. No improvement in trade is noticed in these accounts, but the merchants assert that as the wool season had scarcely commenced, it was not to be expected. It appears that the period for trade in Sydney is between the months of November and April, and hence it is said, that in the course of the next arrival or so, we may look for some favourable change in the aspect of affairs in Australia. As long as the import trade is kept within a proper limit with the export trade, Sydney, as a rising colony, will no doubt be able to pay her way, and eventually release herself from the present depression; but it will require much prudence on the part of shippers here, even when a change takes place, to allow affairs to assume a steady and healthful aspect, should they again attempt to increase their supplies to these markets.

Hobart Town.—Hobart Town papers of the 18th of October notice the arrival of a vessel, called the Sisters, from New Zealand, having on board several families who had left Nelson in consequence of the alarm created by the late massacre of the natives. The same ship brought a request from the local government to Sir Eardley Wilmot for the assistance of troops, and the promptitude with which that request was met is alluded to by the papers in the highest terms of praise, the Sisters having arrived on the Friday, and 100 soldiers being on their way to New Zealand the following Sunday. There is nothing else worth notice. Wheat was 3s. 6d. to 3s. 9d. per bushel, flour of first quality £10 per ton, and potatoes £5 to £6 per ton.

Tahiti.—Restoration of Otaheite to Queen Pomare.—The *Moniteur* of the 1st of March contained the following intelligence.

Government have received despatches from the Island of Tahiti, dated 1st and 9th of November, 1843.

Vice-Admiral Dupetit Thouars, who arrived in the Bay of Papeti on the 1st of November, to carry into execution the treaty of the 9th of September, 1842, which the King had ratified, deemed it his duty not to adhere to the stipulations of that treaty, but to take possession of the island.

Queen Pomare has written to the King to demand the fulfilment of the stipulations of the treaty which assured to her the internal sovereignty of her country, and to pray that she be maintained in her rights.

The King, by the advice of his council, not finding in the circumstances reported sufficient grounds for abandoning the treaty of the 9th of September, 1842, has ordered the pure and simple execution of that treaty, and the establishment of the French protectorate in that island.

West Indies.—Intelligence from the West India Islands has been received to the following dates—Jamaica, the 9th of February; Barbadoes, the 4th; Demerara, the 3d; and Trinidad, the 1st. This vessel brings 1,116,000 dollars, having the Mexican mail on board, but the principal of this sum is supposed to be on mining account, though it is said 75,000 are consigned to the Mexican agency as remittances towards the dividend due in April next.—The *Jamaica Despatch* of the latest date thus refers to matters in that island—

"There is little alteration in the political horizon of our island since the transmission of our mails per last packet Our legislative body as well as the Grand Court, have resumed their deliberations in Spanish Town; and we expect both the legislative and the executive branches of the government will take an early opportunity of contradicting some of the misrepresentations of the British press relative to their opinions on the necessity of an accession of free labourers for this colony. Bishop Spencer has been duly installed, and the church of St. Jago de la Vega created a cathedral. Religious instruction and general education are progressing rapidly, and everything but the panacea for all our evils—increased cultivation—is proceeding harmoniously. The weather is still dry and disagreeable, and the prevailing north breezes have caused some sickness. We have, however, escaped the alarming shocks of earthquake felt at Grenada, Barbadoes, and other of the neighbouring islands."

Private investigation connected with the late robbery at the Jamaica bank is alluded to as tending to a discovery of the culprit.

According to the Demerara papers, the weather, notwithstanding its variable character, was on the whole favourable for agricultural operations. At the meeting of the British Guiana bank a dividend of 2 per cent for the half-year had been declared. The business of the establishment appears to have improved under a vigorous inquiry adopted by a competent committee called in by the directors to satisfy the public of the stability of the establishment. Mercantile affairs showed symptoms of increased confidence, and though the improvement was slow, there was every hope that the steadiness observed would not readily again relapse into the depression from which they were now recovering. A slight shock of an earthquake was felt in Demerara on the 19th of January.

The Barbadoes accounts give very little interesting news. The weather continued changeable, and few of the overdue vessels from England had arrived.

From Trinidad, Dominica, and Antigua scarcely a fact comes worthy of record.

Cape of Good Hope.—Papers to the 30th of December have been received, and the latest intelligence they bring from Natal is to the 18th of the same month. The crops in this new settlement were abundant, and, notwithstanding the representations that the soil was too rich for the cultivation of grain, the "yield" of wheat was expected to exceed 2,000 muids. Mocke, it appears, had released the Loyalist farmers, and after copying the papers they had in their possession, they were quietly permitted to prosecute their journey.

The following extract of a letter from Pietermauritzburg gives a short narrative of the state of feeling in the Natal country:

"All is quiet here, and every hand employed to cultivate the ground. Oberholster and two other commandants from the other side of the Draakberg have come up with the signatures of all persons of their field-cornetcies to submit to the English government. Mocke, De Kock, and another (I think Vermeulen) are the only three who as yet refuse submission. Oberholster left yesterday this place again, and his influence amongst his fellow Boers will procure many deserters of the Republican faith."

The crops in the neighbourhood of the Cape presented a favourable appearance, and some of the farmers anticipated reaping double the quantity of grain they did last year. At Roggeveld, if locusts or blight did not injure the grain, it would be fit for the sickle within a couple of weeks. On the frontier complaints are still made of the ravages of the locusts, and in Tarka and Cradock they had done much mischief. In Graham's Town the wool was being brought down for shipment, and the quality is highly spoken of. Altogether, affairs, both social and political, are fast improving.

Mauritius.—Advices from this island to the 10th of December, but, politically speaking, they are devoid of interest. A *Price Current* of the 6th December gives a review of the sugar-market for the week ending the 5th of December, which states that about 10,000 bags had been put up at public sale, of which only 6,000 found purchasers; subsequently, however, a further quantity was taken by private contract. The average of prices was as follows:—white, 8 dollars 7 cents; fine yellow, 7 dollars 40 cents to 7 dollars 65 cents; good quality do. 7 dollars 18 cents to 7 dollars 35 cents; middling do. 6 dollars 25 cents to 7 dollars 85 cents; low do. 6 dollars. Fine gray, 7 dollars 25 cents; good do. 6 dollars 80 cents; middling do. 6 dollars 10 cents to 6 dollars 25 cents; low do. 5 dollars 50 cents; good brown, 6 dollars 15 cents to 6 dollars 20 cents; middling do. 5 dollars 60 cents. The quantity of sugar exported to London in September had been 774,218 lbs., in October it amounted to 4,722,491 lbs., and in the month of November to 8,883,893 lbs., making a total for the three months of 8,380,602 lbs. To Liverpool the exports in October amounted to only 535,298 lbs., but in November a further quantity of 3.087,728 lbs. was shipped to that port. The exports to Scotland during the quarter had been 2,110,206 lbs., and only 729,734 lbs. to Ireland; making a total of 16,731,831 lbs. exported to the several ports. The exports to foreign places amounted to 210,368 lbs., making a gross total of 16,962,199 lbs., against 17,451,592 lbs. in the corresponding period of 1842. Freights to London, Liverpool, and Bristol were £2. 15s. to £3 per ton of 20 cwt. net, and £2. 15s. to Glasgow and Leith. The rate of exchange on London for Treasury bills at 30 days' sight was from 7 to 8 per cent. premium, and private bills at 90 days from 1 to 3 per cent. discount. Sovereigns were quoted from 9 to 10 per cent. premium, and British silver 2 per cent. premium.

Canada.—The *Montreal Gazette* of the 1st of February, says:—It is understood, that despatches were received at Kingston on the 24th of January, conveying Her Majesty's approval of all the measures of his Excellency the Governor-General, and an assurance that in the pursuance of the same policy he may rely on the cordial support of the Ministers of the Crown. The attempt made by Mr. Buchanan to arrange the difficulties between the Cork and Connaught men on the Welland

Canal had proved a failure. It is said that there are 5,000 men, and as many women and children, on the line of the canal, and that by no possibility can employment be found for more than 3,000. The people were in great distress.

Addresses still continued to pour in to his Excellency Sir Charles Metcalfe. He had appointed Mr. James Macaulay Higginson to be his Civil Secretary.

The Oregon Negotiation.—We learn from Washington that the new British Minister has opened the negotiation for the settlement of the Oregon Territory with Mr. Upshur, the Secretary of State; but that some difficulties have occurred in the preliminaries, which may cause some delay, although not insuperable in their nature. It is also generally understood that the President and his Secretary are very solicitous of settling, on an honourable basis, this vexed question; perhaps somewhat arising from the fact that Mr. Webster monopolized all the honour in the Ashburton treaty. We apprehend no difficulty, however, on this question between the Executive and the British Government. The principal obstacle will be in the Senate. Mr. Benton and the extreme *gauche* of the "young democracie," are endeavouring to create, in advance, a party opposition to any treaty that settles the controversy by compromise—and from the position of the Presidential question in the western states, we do verily believe that he may succeed in rejecting such a treaty. Circumstances, however, may turn up to give a new direction to events. The war feeling, however, against England, is at its very lowest ebb at present among the "democracie," and it will be difficult to raise it from the "vasty deep." Whigs, northern Abolitionists, and southern Nullifiers, are all for peace, on fair and reasonable terms, and they, all together, outnumber in influence the Benton ultra section. The singular rise of a deep commercial excitement, caused by the recent rapid advance in stocks, cotton, and other staples, and the increase of the foreign trade, will all contribute to repress political agitation of a character injurious to peace and prosperity.—*New York Herald.*

Ordnance Estimates.—The estimates of the office of ordnance (including barracks, surveys of the United Kingdom, commissariat, and military and civil superannuations) for the year 1844–45, have just been printed by order of the House of Commons. The total sum to be voted for the current year amounts to 1,840,064*l.*, which is less by 9,078*l.* than the amount voted in the year 1843-44. There will be appropriated, for ordinary, 621,599*l.*; for extra-ordinaries, 1,020,991*l.*; superannuated, 163,680*l.*; and for commissariat supplies, 174,688*l.*; making altogether an amount of 1,980,958*l.* As, however, sums to the amount of 140,894*l.* remain to the credit of the ordnance-office, the estimates for the current year are of course reduced to 1,840,064*l.*

Admiralty.—The following is an account of the respective amounts voted and expended during eleven years (from 1832 to 1843 inclusive):—

Year.	Voted.	Expended.
1832	£114,460	£112,806
1833	104,070	107,854
1834	104,551	108,028
1835	108,844	107,935
1836	110 302	109,789
1837	111,683	117,588
1838	112,637	117,152
1839	113,924	118,816
1840	122,096	120,505
1841	121,844	122,662
1842	121,449	129,182

Navy Estimates for the Years 1844–45 have just been printed. As compared with the last vote for the financial years 1843–44, they result in an aggregate unusually approximate. The "grand total" to be voted for the current year is 6,250,120*l.*; the grand total for the last year was 6,382,990*l.*; so that there is a reduction in the present estimates for the navy, from their amount for 1843–44, of 132,870*l.* For the current year the total for the effective service is estimated at 4,004,758*l.*; for the non-effective, 1,398,651*l.*; total for the naval service, 5,403,409*l.* For the services of other departments, 846,711*l.*; together, 6,250,120*l.* The chief items of these estimates are—Wages, 1,170,476*l.* (Service afloat, 23,500 seamen, 2,000 boys, 4,500 royal marines; service on shore, 6.000 royal marines;) victuals, 544,960*l.*; admiralty-office, 126,826*l.*; registry of merchant seamen, 2,980*l.*; scientific branch, 38,076*l.*; her Majesty's establishments at home, 127,927*l.*, and abroad, 22,426*l.*; wages to artificers at home, 649,104*l.*; ditto abroad, 42,080*l.*; naval stores for building and repairs of ships, docks, &c., 1,053,965*l.*; new works, 298,866*l.*; medicines and medical stores, 20,165*l.*; miscellaneous services, 61,630*l.* Half-pay, namely, to officers of the navy and royal marines, 742,296.; military pensions and allowances, 495,626*l.*; civil pensions and allowances, 162,959*l.* The estimates for "services of other departments of the government" comprise, army and ordnance departments (per conveyance of troops), 160,890*l.*; home department (convict service), 96,527*l.*; and post-office department (contract packet service) 432,541*l.*

OBITUARY.

Biddle, Nicholas, Esq., the eminent American financier, Feb. 27th, at Andalusia, near Philadelphia. He was born in the city of Philadelphia, on the 8th of January, 1786. His paternal ancestors emigrated with William Penn. His father was Charles Biddle, a Revolutionary Whig, who was active in the American cause during the war of independence. At the period of the birth of Nicholas, he enjoyed the second office in the state, while Benjamin Franklin held the first. Other members of his father's family distinguished themselves by their intelligence, valour, and devotion to the cause of their country. His fortitude was conspicuous to the last. He leaves a widow, several children, and numerous relatives and friends, to mourn his loss, at an age when they might well have hoped to witness the exercise of his varied powers in their full vigour.

Carey, Major-General Sir Octavius, C. B., K. C. H., commanding the Cork district, Ireland, March 13th, at London, aged 58. The gallant general was of Norman descent, the family having come to England with William the Conqueror. Married, 1818, daughter of Mr. R. P. le Marchant, of Guernsey; entered the army in 1801, as cornet in the 29th Dragoons, and he attained the rank of Major-General on the 10th of January, 1837, created a Knight Commander of the Guelphic Order, 1835, and Knight Bachelor, 1830.

Halford, Sir Henry, Bart., March 9th, in the 78th year of his age. The deceased eminent physician was born on the 2d of October, 1766, and received his early education at Rugby School, and at Christchurch, Oxford. He afterwards studied medicine at Edinburgh, and commenced practice, in conjunction with his father, Dr. Vaughan, a physician of high reputation, at Leicester. In 1792 or 1793, he settled in London, and rose with wonderfully rapid steps to the very first practice. In 1820 he was elected President of the College of Physicians, and remained in that office until his death, having been re-elected every year for nearly a quarter of a century. Sir Henry Halford was physician to four successive sovereigns, three of whom he attended in their last illnesses, as well as many other branches of the Royal Family. So great was his celebrity, that it occurred to him, in the course of his practice, to be consulted by several sovereigns of other states, as well as by a great many foreigners of the very first distinction. As a physician Sir Henry Halford was a favourite with all classes, and enjoyed in a remarkable degree the confidence of his patients. In consultation he was much regarded by his professional brethren on account of the quickness of his perception, the soundness of his judgment, and the readiness and abundance of his resources. In society he was prized, for to strong natural sagacity and good sense he added the charm of a highly classical taste, and considerable literary attainments. Sir Henry Halford was created a baronet by George III., and changed his name from Vaughan to Halford in compliance with the will of his maternal great-uncle, the last Sir Charles Halford, of Wistow, in Leicestershire, whose estates he inherited. He was Knight Grand Cross of Hanover, a member of the Royal Society, and of several other literary and scientific bodies, trustee of Rugby school, &c. He married a daughter of John, eleventh Lord St. John, of Bletsoe, by whom he has left one son and one daughter.

Hall, Admiral, the much esteemed friend of the Emperor of Russia, in whose service he was employed, Feb. 18th, at St. Petersburgh, aged 60 years. He was formerly a lieutenant in the British service, and was afterwards made an admiral in the Russian navy. His death was very sudden, having taken place during divine service in the English church at St. Petersburgh.

Hill, Lord William; while following the staghounds in the neighbourhood of Whitton, near Ipswich, a fatal accident occurred to his lordship, March 18th. The horse which the unfortunate nobleman was riding, fell, and rolled over him, and before he could be removed to the barracks, he was dead. The accident threw a deep gloom over Ipswich and the regiment to which the deceased nobleman belonged. Lord William Hill was the third son of the present Marquis of Downshire, and was only in his 28th year. He had entered the Scotch Greys in 1834, and his commission as Lieutenant is dated October 21st, 1836. He was much esteemed in his regiment, as well as by a large circle of private friends.

Lonsdale, the Right Hon. William, earl of Lonsdale, viscount and baron Lowther, and a baronet, K.G., lieutenant-colonel in the army, and lord-lieutenant of the counties of Cumberland and Westmoreland, March 19th, in the 87th year of his age, at York house, Twickenham. He was the eldest son of the Rev. Sir W. Lowther, of Little Preston and of Swillington, by the daughter of the Rev. C. Zouch, vicar of Sandal, in the county of York. His lordship married on the 12th of July, 1781, the lady Augusta Fane, daughter of the earl of Westmoreland, by whom he had two sons and four daughters. The earldom devolves upon his eldest son, long known as Lord Lowther, who was raised to the Upper House during his father's lifetime, in September, 1841, when the present ministry was organized, and the office of Postmaster-General conferred on the heir of the house of Lowther. Lord Lowther is unmarried, and in the 57th year of his age. Should he die without issue, Colonel Lowther, the member for Westmoreland, will be his successor.

Sweden, his majesty Charles John XIV., king of, March 8th, at Stockholm, in the 81st year of his age, and in the 30th of his reign. His son and heir assumed forthwith the Royal authority, under the style of Oscar II., and announced his intention of continuing the government of Sweden and Norway in the footsteps of his late father.

LONDON . FISHER, SON, AND CO , PRINTERS.

FISHER'S

COLONIAL MAGAZINE.

COMMUNICATION BETWEEN LONDON AND PARIS IN FIFTEEN HOURS, *viâ* THE BRIGHTON RAILWAY, &c.

BY W. B. PRICHARD, ESQ., C.E., F.S.A., ETC.

THE determination of the best route between London and Paris has become a very interesting and a very important question to the public at large, and is not one of indifference to the Brighton Railway Company; neither party ought any longer to continue silent sufferers from the inaction or neglect manifested by those who have the care of their convenience in the one case, and their prosperity in the other. It is due not only to the shareholders, but likewise to the nation, that every available means should be employed for the immediate realization of those advantages which the London and Brighton Railway holds forth, for the attainment of a regular, safe, and expeditious communication between the capitals of these two great kingdoms.

To show distinctly the advantages derivable from an increased rapidity of conveyance, I may refer to the remarkable augmentation of traffic produced by railway communication. In almost every case where a railway has been constructed between places previously connected only by roads, the passenger-traffic has increased more than fourfold. A like effect has resulted from the establishment of steamers between various places on the coast, previously connected only by sailing vessels; for instance, the vast number of passengers conveyed daily by steamers to Gravesend, Margate, Ramsgate, Folkstone, Dover,* and other such ports, the South-Eastern and the South-Western Routes to France,

* Return of Passengers between Paris and London, from the 2d to the 9th of April, 1844, (one week): by Boulogne, 1,133; by Calais, 369. At the corresponding period of 1843, the numbers, by Boulogne, 754; by Calais, 346; from which it appears that the opening of the railroad has conferred great advantages on Folkestone and Boulogne.—*Times*, 18th April, 1844.

since the opening of their respective railways, and the establishment of steam-navigation, has increased fivefold.

Now, that the Brighton Railway is capable of drawing to itself a large portion of this trade, besides multiplying at the same time the total amount of intercourse, by affording a still more expeditious and economical route, will be readily shown by a comparison of the lengths of the three lines of communication.

The distance viâ Southampton stands thus: Vauxhall per railway to Southampton, 77 miles; Railway station to Royal Pier, and thence by sea to Havre-de-Grace, 122 miles; Havre to Rouen, 57 miles; and to Paris per railway, 85 miles—total distance, 341 miles. The time occupied is as follows: Railway to Southampton (average), 3 h. 15 m.; Railway station to the pier, and delay in removing baggage, 45 m.; passage to Havre, 12 h.; thence to Rouen per diligence, 8 h.; and to Paris per railway, 4 h.—total time, 28 h. The fare is made up of the annexed items: Railway to Southampton, 1*l.*; steamer to Havre, 1*l.* 1s.; diligence to Rouen, 12s.; and railway to Paris, 13s.—total charge, 3*l.* 6s.

The length by the South-Eastern Route stands thus: London Bridge to Folkestone, 82 miles; Folkestone to Boulogne, 27 miles; Boulogne to Abbeville and Amiens, 74 miles; and thence to Paris, 82 miles—total distance, 265 miles. Time occupied thus: London to Folkestone (average) 3 h. 15 m.; thence to the harbour and loading baggage, 45 m.; to Boulogne, 3 h.; from thence to Paris, 22 h.—total, 29 h. The fare thus: London per railway to Folkestone, 17s.; to Boulogne, 8s.; and thence to Paris, 1*l.* 16s.—or total charge, 3*l.* 1s. By the way of Dover the distance is increased by 26 miles; the time by 3 hours; and the fare by 4s.

The distance by the way of Brighton and Shoreham Harbour, stands thus: London Bridge by railway to Shoreham Harbour, 55 miles; Shoreham Harbour to Dieppe, 83 miles; Dieppe to Rouen, 35 miles; Rouen by railway to Paris, 85 miles—total distance, 258 miles (or if Havre de Grace be taken as the French port, the distance is greater by 34 miles). Time of transit at present is thus: Railway to Shoreham, 2 h. 15 m.; removing of baggage, &c., 45 m.; voyage to Dieppe, 8 h.; thence to Rouen, and loss of time at customs, 5 h.; and from thence to Paris per railway, 4 h.—or total, 20 h. The fare is made up as follows: London to Shoreham (average), 14s. 6d.; per steamer to Dieppe, 1*l.*; to Rouen, 7s. 6d.; and railway to Paris, 13s.—being a total charge of 2*l.* 15s.

It is perfectly evident, therefore, that the route through Brighton and Shoreham Harbour viâ Dieppe, has an advantage in distance over that by Southampton of 83 miles, and over that by Folkestone of

7 miles;—a saving in time over Southampton of 8 hours, over Folkestone of 9 hours; and in money, as now charged, over Southampton of 11s., and over Folkestone of 6s. Now, although the Brighton Railway has an advantage over all the other routes in *distance*, in *time*, and in *money*, still the average number of passengers is *far less* than that taken through Southampton, and hardly a tithe of that travelling by way of Folkestone. This extraordinary discrepancy cannot be accounted for on any other supposition than that there is something radically wrong. That such really is the case I have practical evidence, and I will at once proceed to show where the mismanagement exists.

The various evils which have given to the last route the worst character are in some measure produced by a division of the responsible bodies directing its interests; but principally owing to the bad condition of Shoreham Harbour. The austere and opulent Commissioners of that port care little about the amount of passenger-traffic, so long as the vessels continue to run, and hence one of the important links of communication, by the Brighton Railway, is left wholly uncared for. The Railway Directors have in consequence no control over the traffic; and the shareholders of the railway are consequently the sufferers.

It may be remarked, in passing, that the Directors of the South-Eastern (Dover) Railway have wisely avoided all such difficulties, by purchasing their own harbour, thus obtaining a direct command over the whole route; whilst they have, at the same time, obtained the hearty co-operation of the inhabitants and corporate body of Boulogne, and, by their extraordinary enterprise, have secured every desideratum. So important did the inhabitants of Folkestone and Boulogne consider the establishment of this route, in connection with their towns, that in July last a meeting was held to consider the necessary measures for affording a rapid and a regular communication from port to port, and 1,000*l.* was immediately subscribed to guarantee the navigation against loss. In consequence of this, the sleepy spirits of the inhabitants of Dover have been roused from their slumbers, and they have wisely determined on building a landing pier for the accommodation of the continental steamers.* A similar state of things exists on the South-Western Railway. Some of its Directors are the principal persons connected with the Southampton Harbour, piers, &c. The same indi-

* Owing to the very wretched condition of Dover Harbour, which is dry at low water, H. M. Mail Packets lie outside, and the moment they receive their mail bags depart; this circumstance, coupled with the exorbitant charges of the boatmen, is a great drawback on the Dover route.

viduals are Dock Directors, and the shareholders have subscribed their thousands for the purchase of steamers of speed and power, which are directly under the control and command of the railway company.

To return, however, to the defects existing in the arrangements of the Brighton Railway. The trains, on leaving London, arrive in Brighton generally in 2 h. 15 m.; 10 min. is lost at the station before the train proceeds to Kingston Wharf; here, very often, one hour is spent in getting baggage, &c. on board the steamers, which then proceed on their voyage, the Dieppe packet calling at the Chain Pier, where another hour is lost. The connection between the trains and the steamers is very defective; at times the first train brings passengers for France, at other times the middle-day train, and then the evening one; in fact, all times of the day are starting times, and no two days alike. The same defects are still more visible on the return of the steamers. The packets arrive very often either too soon on the flood, or too late on the ebb, and thence have to wait for want of water in the harbour. I have myself seen them thus delayed for two hours. Again, on the arrival of the steamers and passengers at the landing-wharf and search-house, their baggage, boxes, and trinkets are ransacked by the officers of customs, and in such a manner, that travellers are kept from one to four hours, as I have myself witnessed. If this detention happen late in the evening, the passengers are constrained to remain in Brighton during the night, or one batch is sent off, and the other detained. At other times, the passengers are landed at the Brighton station just after the train has started, and there they have to wait for the next. Other inconveniences there are, which, like those already mentioned, are eminently prejudicial to this railway; those that have been specified are, however, amply sufficient to prove my position.

We now come to the consideration of remedial measures. To secure that great desideratum, a more expeditious transit between the two capitals, and at the same time obtain the means of drawing to the Brighton Railway a larger proportion of traffic than it has ever yet enjoyed, it will be requisite to ensure to the public, *regularity*, *certainty*, *safety*, and the *lowest possible remunerative fare;* and to point out the modes by which these may be ensured is here my principal object.

1. *Regularity.*—That the communication is now irregular is notorious. The Continental passengers leave London by almost every train throughout the day, and on no two days alike. Take the table of departures for September, 1843, and you may find the starting-time on successive days stated thus:—8 30 A.M., 10 30 A.M., 12 0 A.M.,

2 0 P.M. It will be seen, too, on comparing the times of arrival of the trains, with the time of departure by the packets, that there is great irregularity here also. Take, for instance, the arrangements for the 20th of September, on which day the packet leaves Shoreham Harbour at 8 o'clock P.M., whilst the train which brings passengers to be conveyed by it reaches Brighton station at 6 h. 30 m., thus involving a detention, after deducting time to Shoreham, of 1 h. 15 m., which 1 h. 15 m. must be spent on board the steamer, for there is no hotel at the harbour. Again, on the 16th of September, the steam-packet departs at 4 o'clock P.M., the very moment the train is reported to arrive in Brighton station, which is distant 5 miles. The same thing happens on the return of the steamers, as may clearly be seen on comparing the railway time-bill with the hours at which the steamers are stated to arrive in the month of September:—5 0 A.M., 6 0 A.M., 7 0 A.M., 8 0 A.M., 9 0 A.M., 10 0 A.M., 11 0 A.M., 12 0 A.M., 2 0 P.M., 3 0 P.M., are the hours specified: only three of these, out of the ten (if you allow half an hour for searching) will catch the trains. Such is the confusion produced by these various mismanagements, that it is almost impossible for strangers to ascertain the necessary information respecting times of starting, unless they spend the day before in hunting for bills of departure at one office or another; no uniformity of time is aimed at, and the consequence is, that the passengers are, in actual fact, two days on their way between the two capitals. These evils arise in great measure, as I have already stated, from the route being under different interests. To get over the difficulties, and to bring the actual time of travelling within the compass of one day (or an uninterrupted 15 hours), I would propose, that all the Continental passengers should start from London Bridge at 7 0 A.M., arrive at Shoreham Harbour at 9 0 A.M., Dieppe at 2 30 P.M., Rouen at 6 0 P.M., and Paris at 10 0 P.M.; and the same system should be followed on the return trip. Establish this as an universal rule, start from London every morning through the week and year at 7 o'clock, arrive in Paris at 10 o'clock at night, and it may soon be proclaimed, and with a clear conscience, that "*this is the highway to Paris.*"

2. *Certainty and Safety.*—To establish the superiority of this line of communication, and to obtain the confidence and support of the public, it will be necessary to obtain a good character for punctuality. This will in a great measure be secured by judicious railway arrangements. As I before stated, it will be necessary to despatch the Continental trains (which should by all means be marked as such in the railway bills) at 7 o'clock precisely every morning, without exception, and all passengers' baggage, parcels, &c. intended to cross the Channel,

should be placed in a sufficient number of carriages at the end of the train. This train should perform its journey in 1 h. 30 m., or at the rate of 33 miles per hour, which speed is commonly performed on many other railways. On the arrival of the trains at the engine-shed of the Brighton terminus, where the tickets are generally collected, the carriages with the French passengers should be immediately detached, and an engine be kept in readiness to proceed with them direct to the harbour. This would entail no extra expense, because there is, at all times, a pilot engine with the steam up connected with the Kingston coke ovens. At present, there is no direct communication between the main line at the Brighton terminus and the Shoreham Branch. When a carriage is intended to proceed from London to Shoreham, it has to be taken into the Brighton station, there to undergo several operations on the turn-tables, and cross other lines of rails, before it can proceed. But to avoid loss of time, it will be necessary to construct a single line of rails of about 11 chains radius from the before-mentioned stopping-place to the east entrance of the tunnel on the Shoreham Branch. By this means time will be gained, and all interference with the regular traffic avoided. Allowing 5 minutes for the detachment of the train, 10 minutes for the transit to Kingston wharf, and 15 minutes for getting carriages, baggage, and passengers on board, we have a total time of 2 hours expended between London and the packets.*

The next requisite for securing certainty, safety, and despatch, will be, an efficient pier, or other equivalent works, at which steamers may land and embark their passengers at *all times and states of tide.* The want of this is the principal cause of derangement in the present system. The harbour of Shoreham being a tidal harbour, as I before stated, the steamers can neither land nor embark their passengers except at tide times. Hence the different hours of departure and arrival. To remove this great obstacle to the despatch of the steamers at 9 o'clock every morning, agreeably with the before-named arrangement, it is desirable so far to improve Shoreham Harbour, or rather the packet accommodation, as to be able to ship and unship passengers at all hours of the day or night. This end can be easily attained; indeed, there is no practical engineering difficulty about the matter. In reality, the Commissioners of the Harbour ought to afford this accommodation; but I have a practical proof that they will do nothing towards such improvement so long as they are able to divide (as they have done for years past) 12½ or 15 per cent. To do anything *effec-*

* A competent, active, experienced, and respectable person should be appointed at this wharf, to superintend all the operations connected therewith;—for the want of such person the trade and traffic have suffered.

tually, it must be done by the shareholders of the Brighton railway. The proposed works might be completed for the sum of 4,000*l.*

The third point will be the establishment of a line of *powerful, fast, and efficient first-class steamers*, directly under the management of the Brighton Railway Company. The steamers now employed are the property of the "General Steam Navigation Company," and the Brighton Railway Directors have no control whatever over them! No doubt the Packet Company would, as far as it was consistent with their own interest, act on any suggestion of the railway company; but, of course, they must have the selection of their own boats for the station, whether they are *really fit or not.* The vessels at present in use are the "Dart," a regular "Old Tub," that has many a time darted into the harbour piers, owing to her being utterly unmanageable. The other is the "Menai," a small river boat, having nothing about her fit for this station, except her experienced commander, Goodburn; and the one lately added to the list, the "Venezuela," is a small steamer that was originally built for the house of Messrs. Cavan, Brothers, and Co., to be employed in the cattle trade between the Spanish main and the West India ports, and was afterwards sold, and again re-sold to the "General Steam Navigation Company," and is altogether unfit for her present duties and station. As a practical engineer, I have no hesitation in stating, that none of the above boats are calculated for the work demanded by this important station. I am borne out in this assertion by the Deputy-Chairman of the Railway Company, who repeatedly expressed his opinion, at the commencement of this season, that they were inefficient; and he endeavoured to induce the "General Steam Navigation Company" to supply their places with others of sufficient power and speed.

I would, however, thoroughly impress upon the public the fact, that, to make this route "The Highway to Paris," the railway company must have steamers *of their own*, adequate to the wants of a great traffic, which should be placed under the *sole* command of the railway directors. These vessels* should be built of iron, and draw when loaded not more than from six to seven feet of water. Were such steamers despatched every morning at 9 o'clock, immediately after the arrival of the train, no difficulty whatever would be experienced in performing the voyage to Dieppe (83 miles) in 5 h. 30 m.†, and the journey to Paris in 15 hours.

* Their power, burden, and speed I shall detail in another paper.

† As great a rate is attained by several of H.M. mail packets, on different stations; and even by river boats on the Thames,—witness the "Prince of Wales," a new steamer on the Margate station.

Respecting the mode of raising the money, I propose that the shareholders of the London and Brighton Railway should subscribe 2*l.* per share, to be placed in trust with the Directors, who shall have the power of purchasing the iron steamers, and making the other arrangements necessary to carry the object into execution. £2 per share would give ample capital both for the purchase of steamers and the construction of landing works. The railway company would thus obtain entire control over the arrangements, and by so doing secure a vast increase of traffic, which would not only yield a handsome return for the outlay, but would likewise increase the dividend on the present capital. And even if profit does not immediately accrue to the shareholders from the money thus advanced, yet its employment in this manner, under the most unfavourable circumstances, must be productive of a *considerable benefit* to them as railway proprietors. I may remind the shareholders that establishing an Auxiliary Steam Packet department is nothing new,—other railroad companies have done the same thing; as, for instance, the South Western, South Eastern, Glasgow and Greenock, Preston and Wyre, and Blackwall railways.—Indeed, those companies consider it necessary for their prosperity to have such aids to their traffic. It is therefore unwise to allow the advantages that might in like manner be secured to the Brighton railway, to lie dormant.

To realize the full benefits to be derived from the proposed arrangements, it would of course be necessary to come to an amicable understanding with the Paris and Rouen Railway Company.* The Brighton Railway Company should by all means exert themselves, and that promptly, to obtain a railway from Dieppe to Rouen, the distance being only 35 miles; and they would be sure to obtain the cordial co-operation of the inhabitants of Dieppe, who would not be more backward than their respected neighbours at Havre, Rouen, and Boulogne in such an undertaking. Or if the French should not have sufficient spirit, an English company could be easily formed to carry this object into effect. This would be far more important to the Brighton Railway Company than a branch line to Lewes or Worthing. As a railway from Dieppe to Rouen could not be made in less than two years from this time, it would be necessary for the present to enter into proper arrangements with diligences to perform the journey at the rate of from 10 to 12 miles an hour. The time thus occupied, added to the 4 hours per railway to Paris, would make, in conjunction with the times

* The South Western Railway Company have exerted themselves to obtain a railway from Rouen to Havre, and to render their voice more effectual are taking shares in that company. Their influence is felt even at the Paris terminus.

already specified, 15 *hours for the entire journey;* and it might be done by the aid of the proposed railway in less than 14 hours. Having thus detailed the arrangements necessary for carrying out my proposition, I may proceed to consider,—

3. *The Lowest possible Remunerative Fare.*—So much has been said at railway meetings and written in railway papers upon the question of low fares, that it is almost unnecessary for me to enter upon it. For myself, I must confess, that I am a stanch advocate of low fares. I admit that a company is perfectly justified in obtaining as large a remuneration as they can obtain; but the question is, how may this best be done—by high profits and small traffic, or by low profits and great traffic? I, in company with many others, think the latter; 100 passengers at 3d. per mile may not pay so much as 200 at 2d., and if by low fares and greater expedition the 200 can be obtained, it must be clearly the most advantageous. Experience must, however, in all cases of this kind, determine the matter; and I therefore content myself with *appealing to the fact,* that wherever the low-fare system has been adopted, in connexion with increased facility of intercourse, additional profit has been realized.

The average fare from London to Brighton is 13s. 6d., and 1s. to Shoreham, and the steam packet charge to Dieppe is 1*l.*, making between London and Dieppe a total fare of 1*l.* 14*s.* 6*d.* I would propose, however, that all passengers for France should receive one ticket, freeing them from London to Dieppe, for 1*l.* 2*s.*, made up of packet fare 12s., and railway fare 10s.; such being the charge for the after cabin and first class; that for the fore cabin and second class would stand thus—packet 9s., railway 7s., or total 16s. Of course the reduction must only apply to the through-traffic. The regular fare of the railway would remain the same, and for those using the steamers only, the fare might be, fore cabin 11s., and after cabin 15s. A corresponding reduction in fare must be obtained between Dieppe and Rouen of 2s, leaving the French railway as at present, (if an understanding cannot be entered into with the directors of that railway, for the reduction of fare for the English passengers). The position, as respects this route being "*the highway*" between London and Paris, will then stand thus:—

Distance 258 miles.—Having an advantage over Southampton of 83 miles, over Folkestone 7 miles, and over Dover 30 miles.

Time 15 hours.—Being an advantage over Southampton of 13 hours, over Folkestone of 14 hours, and over Dover of 17 hours.

Expenses 2*l.* 0*s.* 6*d.*—An advantage over Southampton of 1*l.* 5*s.* 6*d.*, over Folkestone of 1*l.* 0*s.* 6*d.*, and over Dover of 1*l.* 4*s.* 6*d.*

To obtain all these advantages, it will be requisite to carry into effect all the improvements I have proposed. The steamers *must be the property of the railway company;* the landing works must be executed by them; and they must have a proper and an equitable understanding with the harbour commissioners for a reduction of harbour dues, which at present are most *exorbitant.* During the whole of last year, the average charge on each vessel per trip was 5*l.*, and many a time there were not five passengers. This being amended, and some other minor matters (which I shall be happy to detail) being rectified, the *foundation of prosperity* to the London and Brighton Railway will be laid. For the superstructure no apprehension need be entertained.

The irresistible voice of public opinion would soon force government to establish the post-office communication on this "Highway to Paris."

It should be remembered too that at present comparatively none of the commercial capabilities of this route have been developed. If the directors had steamers of their own, they could deliver goods, packages, parcels, &c., in London, from Rouen, Paris, Dieppe, Havre, and the coast of France, for half the price at which they could be conveyed by any other route; also excursion parties might be got up for the coast, leaving London in the morning, and returning in the evening; and others for Dieppe, Channel Islands, Isle of Wight, Beachy Head, Selsey Bill, Hastings, Arundel, Littlehampton, &c., which would prove very profitable, if not to the steamers, *certainly* to the railway proprietors.

In concluding this paper, I would earnestly impress upon the minds of all parties interested, the propriety and *necessity* of using every exertion for the attainment of a regular, expeditious, and safe communication by the Brighton railway, and for the establishment of a proper line of powerful first-class steamers, to ply between Shoreham, Dieppe, and Havre-de-Grace, by means of which the journey to Paris may be performed in the time proposed. Such an arrangement must be made *some time or other:* whenever it is made, it will bring a vast increase of profit to the proprietors of the Brighton railway; and they may as well begin to reap that profit *at once*, as leave it to be gathered by others.

William B. Prichard.

London, 30, Wilmington-square.

NEW ZEALAND.*

(OUR TITLE THERE.)

THE parent societies at home, the Colonial Minister in Downing-street, and many of the people of England, were gulled by it;—not so Sir George Gipps, he was nearer the spot, he knew what was going on, and it will soon be told how he saw through and treated it. It was soon after this, that the New Zealand Association was formed, as has been stated, with the names of its committee, at page 431 of the December number of this Magazine; it was then not doubted but that it would receive the cordial co-operation of the Church of England Missionary Society; a deputation consisting of the Hon. Captain Wellesly, R.N., the unfortunate Captain Arthur Wakefield, and Dr. Evans, LL.D., waited on the secretary, Mr. Coates, to propose to draw with its committee in colonizing the island; this was in June, 1837. The answer given by this gentleman was, that "*he would thwart them in every way in his power;*" the whole of this is minutely related at page 432 of our December number. At that time the manœuvre stated by Sir George Gipps was not known; the public were not aware of it; it was only known when the Parliamentary Papers were printed, 11th of May, 1841; nor were the landed acquirements of Mr. Busby and the missionaries known. This dreadfully promised "thwarting" can be now accounted for, but at that time it could not be explained. The New Zealand Association was assailed by pamphlets from Mr. Coates; the speech, however, of the Hon. Francis Baring, in the Commons, on the 19th of June, 1838, was an excellent exposition and answer to them, and cannot be referred to too often. A committee of the Lords was formed, as has been already stated, and before it Mr. Coates and the Rev. Mr. Beecham appeared, as the representatives of their respective societies. They offered the most determined opposition to the colonizing of New Zealand under any form, or by any person whatever, not even by the British crown. They gave the following reasons—

1st. That it was an independent state under its own government;† and to prove it, he delivered in the declaration to which reference already has been made; and, as farther proof, spoke of its flag.‡ The

* Continued from our April Number, page 184.

† Lords' Report, page 242—States this not merely as his own opinion, but as that of the committee.

‡ See Mr. Blackett's evidence, question 444—"Is there any portion of the natives who in any way use the flag themselves?" Answer—"Not any." Page 63

answer to this is, Sir George Gipps's statement, that the whole was a manœuvre concocted and prepared by Mr. Busby.*

2d. That the whole land of the island was appropriated, and the property of either tribes or individuals.†—The first authority which shall be given to contradict this audacious assertion is that of Governor Hobson: "the native chiefs have neither power over the soil, nor authority over those who reside on it;"‡ and then the numerous valleys and plains, never trodden by man, or claimed by a human being—a list of many of them will be found at page 455 of the December number of this Magazine—and since then others of immense extent have been discovered. The murdered Cotterel walked through one in the Nelson district, which he calculated at 200,000 acres. Deiffenbach, in pursuing the Valley of the Hutt, could meet with neither man nor beast.§ The fact is, that the country is most thinly populated,|| and the few there

Parliamentary Papers, 3d of August, 1840. And so also was it in the other matter, which has been so much insisted on, of the recognition of their flag, "the flag having in fact been granted to them rather than acknowledged. Various flags were sent to them, out of which they were permitted to choose, and they probably chose that which had the gaudiest colours. New South Wales has been permitted, in the same way, to use a distinguishing flag, and some of our coasters sail under it, but not on that account is New South Wales an independent power." Extract from Sir George Gipps's speech, printed at page 75 of House of Commons' Paper, 11th May, 1841.

* See paragraphs 2, 3, 4, and 6, of page 75 of Parliamentary Papers, 11th of May, 1841, in the latter—" Mr. Busby's declaration of independence, for it was his, was indeed, I think, a silly as well as unauthorized act, but it was no more; it was, in fact, only (as I have said before) a paper pellet fired off at the Baron de Thierry."

† Lords' Report, page 254, Mr. Coates says—" I apprehend, as far as I can draw an inference from what is incidentally stated, that the whole of the country is considered as the possession of one chief or other." Question—" That the country is parcelled into jurisdictions of particular chiefs?" Answer—" I believe so." Page 85, House of Commons' Report, 3d of August, 1840: Question 734—" But you consider the whole island as being portioned out among different tribes?" Answer—" No doubt the whole of the land is the property of one tribe or another; I think that has been clearly shown from the communications of the missionaries."

‡ In his despatch, 25th of May, 1840, printed at page 16 of Parliamentary Papers, 11th of May, 1841.

§ See Deiffenbach, vol. i., p. 86.

|| Lords' Report, page 8, Colonel Nicholas—" I think it a fair price for the land, considering the immense quantity of land which, from the scantiness of the population, is totally valueless." Page 199, Mr. George Clark, 29th of July, 1837, remarks, after a battle between the tribes, " The total loss of life on both sides did not exceed fifty souls; but, considering what a thin population we have, this loss to the country is equal to a thousand souls from one of our large manufacturing towns."

are living on the sea-coasts;* whilst the interior of the country is the undivided unappropriated domain of nature, and clearly the waste lands of the crown, over which the rights of sovereignty should be exercised when wanted.†

3d. A very undefined term is used, "The Rights of the Aborigines," that we are not justified in exercising the practice of sovereignty, there being inhabitants on the soil, in consequence of which it belongs to them exclusively; and even in treating with them to settle in the country, we are acting unjustly.

"That the acquisition of New Zealand would be a most inadequate compensation for the injury which must be inflicted on this kingdom itself, by embarking in a measure essentially unjust, and but too certainly fraught with calamity to a numerous and inoffensive people, whose title to the soil and to the sovereignty of New Zealand is indisputable, and has been solemnly recognized by the British Government."

These are a part of the instructions given by the Marquis of Normanby to Governor Hobson, in the year 1839.‡ These instructions must be a little divided:—

1st. That the colonization would "too certainly be fraught with calamity to a numerous and inoffensive people." Is this true? are the people numerous, inoffensive also? Lord Normanby never could have read the evidence, on oath, before a Committee of the House of Lords.

The Rev. J. Butler, on the 10th of October, 1821, says—

"The natives are covered with lice and filth to the last degree; and, withal, a proud, savage, obstinate, and cruel race of cannibals."§

The Rev. A. N. Brown, 19th of October, 1836—

"In about two hours afterward, Ngakuku arrived, accompanied by two other natives, bearing the mangled corpse of his only little girl, who had been murdered in the fight; they had taken away her heart and the top of her head, as an offering to the Evil Spirit."‖

---

* Lords' Report, page 335, Captain Fitzroy states, "that the natives live almost entirely on the sea coast."

† The Hon. Francis Baring, whose opinions as to New Zealand should receive attention from the Colonial Minister, whoever he may be, contemplated it in the following question and answer in the Lords' Committee (see Report, page 157)— "Is it not the intention of the association to introduce the exercise of their authority over those parts they do not themselves colonize?" "It is necessary we should have a right of that kind, in fact we could not do without it."

‡ The instructions will be found printed in Terry's New Zealand, page 10.

§ Lords' Report. It must be borne in mind that this is evidence submitted to the Committee by the Secretaries to the Church of England and Wesleyan Missionary Societies.

‖ Lords' Report, p. 203.

The Rev. Mr. Knight, 22d of September, 1836—

"I walked, almost petrified, past bodies, which here and there strewed the ground, until I came to a place where a number of bodies were laid out, previously to their being cut up for the oven."*

The Rev. A. N. Brown, 25th of August, 1836—

"We then went on to the spot where Waharoa's party lay encamped, and where for two days after the battle, they remained to gorge on sixty human bodies."†

The Rev. Mr. Leigh—

"After my arrival in New Zealand, I learned that Shunghee and his party slew 1,000 men, 300 of whom they roasted and ate before they left the field of battle."‡

This list might be continued page after page, but it is too afflicting and painful to continue, and is only brought forward to shew how completely Lord Normanby must have been duped by the clerkcraft of his office, to call these people either "numerous," or "inoffensive." But then they were "entitled to the soil." Upon this subject, the opinion of Sir George Gipps shall be given: he is a gentleman of striking good sense, and not only near the spot, but constantly seeing natives from New Zealand. Seven chiefs, as they were called, in August, 1840, went to Sydney, and sold to Mr. Wentworth the whole of the middle island, twenty millions of acres, for 200*l.*§ Sir George Gipps immediately erased Mr. Wentworth's name from his council, and in his speech gave the following opinions:—

"They are, first, whether uncivilized tribes, not having any settled form of government, and not having any individual property in the land, can confer valid titles to land on individuals not of their own tribes; and, secondly, whether the right of extinguishing the native title, or the right of pre-emption (as it is technically called), does or does not, exclusively exist in the government of the nation which may form a settlement in the country occupied by such uncivilized tribes. This is allowed to be American law; and Mr. Wentworth, as well as the other counsel heard against the bill, has confessed, that if it can be proved to be English law, the preamble of the bill will be vindicated, and all the enactments of it be conformable to justice. Now, gentlemen, to prove to you that this was English law before it was American law, I shall read to you some extracts from books of acknowledged authority in the United States; and, to prove to you that it is English law still, I shall produce to you the opinions of some of the most eminent of living English lawyers."‖

So much for Sir George Gipps; and then, that Governor Hobson, as has been already stated, that "the native chiefs have neither power

---

* Lords' Report, p. 204. † Ibid, p. 205. ‡ Ibid, p. 207.

§ See a despatch from Sir George Gipps to Lord John Russell, dated 16th of August, 1840, printed at page 63 of Parliamentary Papers, 11th of May, 1841.

‖ Ibid, page 65.

over the soil, nor authority over those who reside on it;" * but then Lord Normanby adds, they had a right to the sovereignty, which had been solemnly recognized by the British government. As far as the recognition goes, it was entirely in consequence of the unauthorised manœuvre, prepared and concocted by Mr. Busby; and had Lord Glenelg known the facts, neither he nor any other colonial minister could have recognized any manœuvre of the kind.† The truth is, that the natives never had a sovereignty, or knew how to exercise one, and Lord Normanby never could have stated this in his instructions to Governor Hobson; had he previously read the Report of the Lords' Committee, he would have there found that the manœuvre did not answer the purpose of those who prepared and concocted it: it was a mere "paper pellet fired off" at the Baron de Thierry. The natives themselves knew nothing about it; and that, the concocters themselves afterwards stated—

> "Your petitioners would observe, that it has been considered (alluding to the manœuvre) that the confederate tribes of New Zealand were competent to enact laws for the proper government of this land, whereby protection would be afforded in all cases of necessity; but experience evidently shows that in the infant state of the country, this cannot be accomplished or expected. It is acknowledged by the chiefs themselves to be impracticable." ‡

There wants no other answer to Mr. Coates and the Rev. Mr. Beecham's nonsensical "hypothesis" of a native government. But, then, says Mr. Coates, the petition for sovereignty, from which an extract has been made, although signed by most of the missionaries, was not signed as missionaries, but only as individuals; it has not C. M. S. attached to their names.§ So much for soil and sovereignty; but then another plea was urged, that missionary communication had answered every purpose, and civilized two-thirds of the larger island.‖ It may be gathered from the whole of the evidence of the secretaries of the missionary societies, that through the religious instruction of their missionaries, civilization was making rapid strides; so much so,

* In Governor Hobson's despatch to Lord Normanby, dated the 25th of May, 1840, and printed at p. 16 of Parliamentary Papers, 11th of May, 1841.

† This recognition will be found at p. 159 of the Lords' Report.

‡ This will be found in the Lords' Report, p. 399; the petition was signed by 36 of the principal missionaries and catechists.

§ Second Paragraph, at p. 267 of the Report of the House of Lords.

‖ So stated by Captain Fitzroy, in his evidence on the 21st of May, 1838. See Lords' Report, p. 338. This is a gentleman of undoubted integrity; he did not state this of his own knowledge, and it shows how much he must have been imposed on.

that on the 6th of June, 1837, the committee adopted resolutions which were submitted to a public meeting on the 1st of June, 1838, declaratory of their opinion, that "New Zealand with her native population may adorn the page of future history, as an industrious, well-ordered, and Christian nation;" * and the entire object of these gentlemen was to make statements to prevent the colonization of these islands. They have been in communication with but a small spot of country,† and they draw deductions from it for the whole group, extending 900 miles, of which they absolutely know nothing. The horrible account of wars, cruelties, and cannibalism attaches only to their own little circle. Similar circumstances can hardly be traced to the natives of Cook's Straits. They have suffered by the successful invasions of Raupero and Te-whero-whero; ‡ these barbarians came from the north; the former fixed himself at Kapiti, or one of the small islands in the mouth of Cook's Straits, sold (as he called it) these islands over and over again,§ and attained, from his reckless cruelties, the character of being one of the most savage barbarians in the world; but this does not appear to be the character of the natives in those parts.

There is no doubt but many of the missionaries have acted from the purest of motives, and their exertions merit the greatest praise. Their perseverance is admirable—their sufferings most painful; and it is to be lamented that the result has been so trifling. They have wanted the aid of civilization, for Captain Fitzroy has most truly stated, that "colonization and the settlement of the country is in no way at variance with a missionary establishment; they only require to be carried on in concert with it."‖ The objection is to those, who, under the cloak of being missionaries, are meddling politicians, or secret buyers of land for their own purposes; but the deceptions which were palmed upon the Committee of the Lords in 1838, and that of the Commons in 1840, are as disgraceful as they have been mischievous.

* These resolutions and declaration were delivered to the Committee of the Lords by Mr. Coates, on the 14th of May, 1838, and are printed at p. 243 of the Report.

† Sir George Gipps says "the declaration of independence was made moreover only by a few tribes in the Bay of Islands, not extending so far south as the Thames." p. 75, Par. Papers, 11th May, 1841; Lords' Report, p. 167, Captain Fitzroy speaks of the influence of the residents 20 or 30 miles round the Bay of Islands.

‡ Deiffenbach, vol. i., p. 162, gives a minute account of the barbarous excursion of this savage. § Ibid, vol. i., p. 110.

‖ See his evidence, Lords' Report, p. 177.

But for the representations of Mr. Flatt, made known to the world in Mr. Gibbon Wakefield's pamphlet, entitled a "Letter to Lord Glenelg," their immense landed speculations would have been concealed; these, however, were pretty well published by the Hon. Francis Baring's speech in the Commons, June 1838. It remained, however, for themselves to confirm the fact by claiming 96,219 acres.* Then the Rev. Wm. Williams stated the population in the neighbourhood of Kaputi, or Entry Island, to be about 18,000.† This was perfectly untrue—an expression which would have been softened into erroneous, if its object had not been discovered. The whole population from Taranaki to Port Nicholson, and on both shores of Cook's Straits, is only 6,490.‡ Now for the object of the false statement—it was to prevent emigration being directed to the Straits, and to give value to the landed purchases of the speculative missionaries of the north; for this purpose Mr. Williams forwarded a petition to the Queen, which, by order of the Committee of the Church of England Missionary Society, through their secretary, Mr. Coates, was forwarded to the then Colonial Minister Lord John Russell, § and transmitted by his secretary to Mr. Somes, the Governor of the New Zealand Company, and in his reply, that gentleman pointed out its object—"that if Mr. William's project were adopted, emigration could only be directed to the northern part of the island." || The representation as to Mr. Fairburn's land, comes from the committee at New Zealand, of which Mr. Henry Williams was the chairman, and to the purchase of which he was a party, is spoken of before the Committee of the Lords as a mere trifle—as a retreat for himself and wife, when his labours were past, and as a trifling provision for his three children; ¶ but when a commissioner arrives to settle these matters, he claims 40,000 acres.** Then as these matters are by degrees detected, the excusing it by saying that they were bought in trust for the natives, is a quibble unworthy of straightforward dealing. It was forbidden on the 2d March, 1836, by their employers the committee of the Church of England Missionary, Society.†† Sir

* The official table of these claims will be found in Deiffenbach, vol. ii., p. 168.

† Lords' Report, p. 180.

‡ See the table of their locations, names of tribes, families, and numbers, in Deiffenbach, vol. i., p. 195.

§ Mr. Coates' letter with its inclosure, is printed at p. 139, Par. Papers, 11th of May, 1841.

|| Ibid, p. 142.

¶ See the statement made by Mr. Coates, at p. 263 of the Lords' Report.

** See a copy of the official table at p. 168, vol. ii., of Deiffenbach.

†† See Lords' Report, p. 262.

George Gipps, with his usual acuteness, as soon as he knew it, refused to sanction it;* and yet the date of a large purchase of the Rev. Henry Williams is in the year 1839.† These purchases were all made in secret, and in a concealed manner.‡ Their employers have been by these means led very unintentionally to mislead the public in their annual reports, and it behoves their respective committees to examine into the truth of these statements; the writer of this article has no other knowledge of them, but that which he has traced in authentic documents, and on this account has taken no little trouble to afford a reference to every assertion made. A great deal of the representations in regard to the chiefs are very contrary to the evidence given by two respectable gentlemen, Mr. Blackett and the Rev. F. Wilkinson, who assert that they will say or sign anything for a blanket.§

As to the lamentable want of success of the missionary reign, it is proved by the worst population being in the neighbourhood of the missionary stations, and that from their own accounts, delivered to the committee of the Lords; and this was up to the year 1838; and a recent traveller, Mr. Bidwell, states, that he saw all the remnants of one of these horrid feasts in the neighbourhood of the best of the missionary stations; || and even since the arrival of Bishop Selwyn at Aucland, there has been a war between tribes, and roasting of prisoners.¶ The state of disease amongst the natives is afflicting,** two-thirds of the children born dying at an early age;†† just in those places where missionaries most abound—as in the Bay of Islands, Kaipura, and the River Thames, the wars have been the most sanguinary, and the number of natives diminished to a most frightful extent;"‡‡ and

* See Lords' Report, p. 261.

† See the copy of the official table of land claims, at p. 168, vol. ii., of Deiffenbach—H. Williams, May 1839, 2,000 acres.

‡ See the sensible statement of Mr. Somes, in his letter to Mr. Vernon Smith, dated 29th of March, 1841, and printed in the second paragraph of p. 142, Par. Papers, 11th May, 1841.

§ See p. 107 of Lords' Report, and p. 63 House of Commons Papers, 3rd of August, 1840.

|| P. 7 and 8 of "Rambles in New Zealand," by John Carne Bidwell.

¶ See the details p. 155, vol. iv., of "New Zealand Journal," being No. 90, of June 10th, 1843.

** See the evidence of Mr. J. Watkins, a surgeon, before the Lords' Committee in the Report, p. 30 and p. 21.

†† This was stated by Mr. George Clark, the lay agent of the Church of England Missionary Society: see Lords' Report, p. 197.

‡‡ Deiffenbach's Report to the New Zealand Company, printed at p. 63 of the "New Zealand Journal," vol ii., being No. 30, for March 13th, 1841.

to the extent that "the depopulation of the country has gone on until district after district has become void of its inhabitants; and the population is even now but a remnant of what it was in the memory of some European residents." *

The rapid depopulation of the country does not rest upon the single and respectable authority of Mr. Busby—it is the universal statement;† but it will be asked, Is war and cannibalism the fault of the missionaries? Certainly not; but then they should not state that they have put an end to them, and give it as a reason why the country should not be colonized, and the people civilized by amalgamation with a civilized race. Are the missionaries at all responsible for the prevailing diseases? It is to be feared they are, since Dr. Deiffenbach has traced a great deal of the diseases and shortening of life to the changed habits of the natives, in consequence of their advice.‡ Are the missionaries in any degree to be charged with the shortening of life through bad food,§ want of clothing, and sheltered houses? ‖ Inasmuch as they have prevented colonization by a civilized race, they are; for a change can only occur in consequence of amalgamation and imitation. A remarkable instance occurs in the Chief Apeko, at Nelson, building for himself a similar habitation to the cottage of the lamented Captain Arthur Wakefield.

---

* This is not the statement of any grumbling emigrant, but that of the government resident accredited to the missionaries, for which see Captain Fitzroy's evidence at p. 169 of the Lords' Report. "He was sent there in a high character, and was accredited to the missionaries." Now, what is stated in the text as to the depopulation in the missionary districts, is from Mr. Busby, and reported to the Lords' Committee, at p. 340 of the Report.

† So stated by Mr. Coates, Lords' Report, p. 180; again, p. 181—"The increasing depopulation is stated in our information;" "the population is diminishing there unquestionably." Again, p. 264.

‡ The reader is particularly recommended to examine the 2nd chapter on "Diseases of the Natives," in the 2nd vol. of Deiffenbach's work, p. 16.

§ See Mr. Coates's evidence as to this, Lords' Report, p. 180; Mr. Watkins's, surgeon, p. 13; and Mr. Clark's, p. 197.

‖ See the sensible statement of Mr. Davis, delivered by Mr. Coates to the Lords' Committee, in the Report, p. 249.

(To be continued.)

On the Use and the Practicability of the Construction of

A CANAL OR OTHER COMMUNICATION FROM THE ATLANTIC TO THE PACIFIC.*

Santiago de Guatemala, the metropolis of Central America, (for we hope ere long to see it again such in fact,) is situated in the western part of the country, about thirty miles from the shores of the Pacific Ocean, and in the midst of a large handsome plain, surrounded on all sides by well-cultivated hills of a moderate height; its elevation above the level of the sea is not less than 1,800 feet; it is supposed to contain 50,000 inhabitants. It has a well-organized British consulate, and there are in it several large English mercantile houses. It corresponds, in its business-transactions, principally with the English settlement of Belize, in Honduras.

The houses of Santiago de Guatemala are neatly built, but never exceed one story in height—a necessary precaution in a country liable to be visited by earthquakes. Many of the churches are large, and of fine architecture, having their interior richly adorned, and in some cases possessing altar-pieces by Murillo, in his first flights towards celebrity. The streets are spacious, well paved, and clean. The market-place is large, handsome, and convenient. The present city is the third capital of the same name which has existed within the last eighty years. The original, which was unfortunately erected on the declivity of a great volcano, in a valley fronting the Pacific, contained about 7,000 families, and was destroyed by an earthquake in the year 1751. Having been rebuilt a little farther to the northward, in a romantic spot now called the Antigua, or Old City, it wás again destroyed in 1775 by an earthquake of even a more terrific character than the first. Although the greater part of the inhabitants were buried in the ruins, and the city was removed by order of the government to the spot on which it now stands, which is twenty-five miles to the north of the Antigua, the latter is still a favourite place of resort; the congress of the states was held in it, and it has seldom a resident population of less than 19,000 inhabitants.

The exterior communications of the republic are chiefly carried on by the ports of Omoa, Ysabal, and Truxillo, on the Gulf of Mexico; and those of Iztapa, Acajutla, and Realejo, on the South Sea. Omoa is

* Continued from No. 3, page 153.

the most important of all these, not only on account of its strength, which causes it to be considered the key of the country on this side, but from its being the great point of communication between Europe and the federal states. It is situated on the shores of the Gulf of Honduras, about 160 miles to the north-east of the metropolis. Iztapa, the old port of the country, is now but little frequented, though it is the nearest to Santiago de Guatemala. The northern and eastern coasts of Guatemala have obtained the name of the Mosquito Shore, from their being chiefly inhabited by the tribe of the Mosquito Indians.

The population of the State of Nicaragua is not much inferior to that of the State of Guatemala. The town of Leon is the capital, and is situated about eight leagues from the western shore of the Lake of Leon, and four leagues from the shores of the Pacific Ocean—in latitude 12° 20′ north, and longitude 86° 16′ west. Four leagues to the uorth-west of Leon, and also on the Pacific, is the town of Realejo, inhabited entirely by *ladinos*, a mixed race, proceeding from the intercourse of the white and the aboriginal Indian, and who are chiefly employed in ship-building, in which they are very expert. The harbour formed by the large and beautiful river of the same name is excellent, and capable of containing 1,000 vessels commodiously. Here, the conveniences for ship-building are great, as timber, cordage, sail-cloths, pitch and tar, may be procured in abundance; spars for masts are also plentiful. In the year 1836, the population of Nicaragua was as much as 350,000—consisting of 110,000 whites, 120,000 ladinos, and 120,000 Indians.

It is interesting to know that Nicaragua was the first province subdued by the Spaniards in the New World; it was discovered and partially settled by Gil Gonzales Davila and his companions so early as 1522. It derives its name from a powerful cacique, who was one of the first to enter into amicable relations with the Spaniards, and submit to the rite of baptism.

We have given this rapid sketch of the States of Central America generally, and of Guatemala and Nicaragua in particular, as being essential to the exposition of the foundation upon which we build our views of the superior suitableness of Nicaragua for the admission through it of a communication from ocean to ocean. It is evidently, we have shown, an altogether superior country to Panama, whether we consider it with reference to its climate, productions, population, or the advanced civilization of that population. It is, from every indication, a region destined to increase in political importance, whenever it shall possess a well-organized, suitable government. It has, there can be no doubt, all the elements requisite for the foundation of a powerful state. We will observe here, that Nicaragua and the other provinces of Central America, from already containing a considerable population, could furnish a large number of labourers for carrying on an extensive work, and European labourers and artificers might be sent thither to assist in the work, without that periling of life, which would be certain if such were sent to Panama. Let us also see whether, along with these advantages, Nicaragua has any local superiority over other places, as a point of transit by canal.

In the first place, there can be no question that, in a line of communication through the State of Nicaragua, the lake of Nicaragua would in itself form an unexceptionable element for adaptation to navigable purposes. Its position near the middle of the neck of continent, is highly favourable to its resources as a powerful auxiliary in forming a channel from sea to sea. It is ninety-five miles in length, and thirty in breadth; it is in many parts of immense depth, and has one throughout of seldom less than sixty feet. The surface of its waters is not less than 128 feet above the level of the Pacific Ocean. This great basin receives many streams, and discharges its superfluous waters by the river San Juan, which, issuing from its south-eastern extremity, flows by a course seventy-nine miles long into the Atlantic Ocean, some distance below the castle of the same name, which is memorable as having been once attacked and destroyed by a British force under Lord Nelson, although not, however, without considerable comparative loss to us. Several small islands deck the bosom of the lake; the rich pastures on its borders abound with neat and other cattle; and its banks which are nearest to the Pacific afford a plentiful supply of wood, stone, and all other materials requisite for building-purposes. On its north-west side, it communicates with another sheet of water called Lake Leon, or Matiares, and which is upwards of thirty-five miles in length, and nearly fifteen in breadth, by means of a channel called the Rio Tapitapa, which is about twenty miles in length. The distance of the Pacific Ocean from the point of the lake of Nicaragua which is the nearest to it, is fifteen English miles, and from the lake of Leon the distance is still less. Here, then, we have a considerable river leading from the Atlantic Ocean into the lake of Nicaragua, and on passing through that lake, we arrive at a land-barrier of only fifteen miles, through which, if it did not vary in its character from ordinary cases, a passage by canal would enable us to reach the opposite ocean. Why can it not be done? There are obstacles; let us, therefore, see what those obstacles are, and whether they be surmountable.

As stated already, the lake of Nicaragua presents no difficulty; not so, however, with the river San Juan; and in the space between the lake and the Pacific, a most formidable impediment is presented by the intervention of the range of the Andes, low as they nevertheless there become. But we cannot do better than here refer to the account of the locality as given by Mr. Stephens,* an intelligent American traveller who visited the spot, and was assisted in his labour in collecting data by a Mr. Baily, an intelligent engineer, who had paid much attention to the investigation of the matter.

"Our encampment (says Mr. Stephens) was about in the centre of the harbour of San Juan, which was the first I had seen on the Pacific. It is not large, but beautifully protected, being almost in the form of the letter U. The arms are high and parallel, running nearly north and south, and terminating in high perpendicular bluffs. As I afterwards learned from Mr. Baily, the water is deep, and, under either bluff, according to the wind, vessels of the largest class can ride with perfect safety. Supposing this to be correct, there is but one objection to this harbour, which I derived from a Captain D'Yriarte, with whom I made a voyage from Sonsonate to Caldera. He told me that during the summer months, from November to May, the strong north winds which sweep over the lake of Nicaragua, pass with such violence through the Gulf of Papagayo, that during the prevalence of those winds it is almost impossible for a vessel to enter the port of San Juan. Whether this is true to the extent that Captain D'Yriarte supposes, and if true, how far steam-tugs would answer to bring vessels in against such a wind, is for others to determine. But at the moment there seemed more palpable difficulties. I walked along the shore down to the estuary of the river, which was here broad and deep. This was the proposed termination of the great canal to connect the Atlantic and Pacific Oceans. I had read and examined all that had been published on the subject in England and America; had conferred with individuals; and I had been sanguine, almost enthusiastic, in regard to this gigantic enterprise; but on the spot the scales fell from my eyes. The harbour was perfectly desolate—for many years not a vessel had entered it; primeval trees grew around it; for miles there was not a habitation. Since Mr. Baily's, not a visit had been paid to it; and probably the only thing that keeps it alive even in memory is the theorizing of scientific men, or the occasional visit of some Nicaragua fisherman, who, too lazy to work, seeks his food in the sea. It seemed preposterous to consider it the focus of a great commercial enterprize—to imagine that a city was to rise up out of the forest, the desolate harbour to be filled with ships, and become a great portal for the thoroughfare of nations.

"Looking back," says Mr. Stephens, in describing his sensations when he had crossed the mountain-range between the Pacific and the lake of Nicaragua, in exploring the route of the canal towards that lake, "I saw the two great mountain-ranges, standing like giant portals, and could but think what a magnificent spectacle it would be, to see a ship, with all its spars and rigging, cross the plain, pass

* Incidents of Travel in Central America, &c.

through the great door, and move on to the Pacific. Before reaching the lake, we heard the waves breaking upon the shore like the waves of the sea; and when we emerged from the woods, the view before us was grand. On one side no land was visible; a strong north wind was sweeping over the lake, and its' surface was violently agitated; the waves rolled and broke upon the shore with solemn majesty; and opposite, in the centre of the lake, were the islands of Isola and Madeira, with great volcanoes rising as if to scale the heavens."

After describing the scenery of the lake as being grand and beautiful, Mr. Stephens reaches the river Las Lajas, which, according to a survey made by Mr. Baily, is the terminating point of the proposed canal; and having now examined the route as well as he was enabled, he gives us the following data, which Mr. Baily furnished him with, as having been ascertained by the latter gentleman himself:—

"By measurements begun on the side of the Pacific Ocean, and which were carried over to the lake of Nicaragua, the length from the Pacific to the lake of Nicaragua was ascertained to be 28,365⅔ yards, or 15⅘ miles. The height to be surmounted was this: the sum of the ascents was found to be, in round numbers, 1,047 feet; and that of the descents 919 feet; the difference of 128 feet being the height of the surface of the lake above the Pacific Ocean at low water. We now come to the communication with the Atlantic, by means of the lake of Nicaragua and the river San Juan. The lake is 95 miles long; in its broadest part, 30; and averages, according to Mr. Baily's soundings, 15 fathoms of water. The length of the river, by measurement, with all its windings, from the mouth of the lake to the sea, is 79 miles. There are no cataracts or falls; all the obstructions are from rapids, and it is at all times navigable, both up and down, for piraguas (boats) drawing from 3 to 4 feet water. From the lake to the river of Las Savalas, about 18 miles, the depth of the San Juan is from 2 to 4 fathoms. Hence commence the rapids of Toros, which extend a mile, with water from 1½ to 2 fathoms. The river is then clear for 4 miles, with an average depth of from 2 to 4 fathoms. Then come the rapids of the Old Castle, but little more than half a mile in extent, with water from 2½ to 5 fathoms; when begin the rapids of Mico and Las Balas, connected and running into each other, and both together not more than a mile, with water from 1 to 3 fathoms. Then the river is clear 1½ mile to the rapids of Machuca, which extend 1 mile, and are the worst of all, the water being more broken, from running over a rugged rocky bottom. The river then runs clear, and without any obstruction, for 10 miles, with water from 2 to 7 fathoms, to the river San Carlos; and then 11 miles, with some islands interspersed, with water from 1 to 6 fathoms, to the river Serapequea, the measurements of 1 fathom being about the points or bends, where there is an accumulation of sand and mud. It then continues 7 miles clear, with water from 2 to 5 fathoms, to the Rio Colorado. The Rio Colorado runs out of the San Juan in another direction into the Atlantic. The loss of the latter, according to measurement taken in the month of May, 1839, was 28,178 cubic yards of water per minute; and in the month of July of the same year, during the rising of the waters, it was 85,840 yards per minute, which immense body might be saved to the San Juan by damming up the mouth of the river Colorado, or rather, its exit from the San Juan. From this point there are 13 miles, with soundings of from 3 to 8 fathoms. The bottom is of sand and mud, and there are many small islands and aggregations of sand, without trees, which could very easily be cleared away. The last 13 miles might be reduced to 10, by restoring the river to its old channel, which has been filled up by collections, at points, of drifted matter. An old master of a piragua told Mr. Baily, that within his memory trees grew half a mile back. The soundings were all taken with the plotting-scale when the river was low; and the port of San Juan at the mouth of this river, though small, Mr. Baily considers unexceptionable.

"According to the plan of Mr. Baily, the whole length of the canal, from the lake of Nicaragua to the Pacific, would be $15\frac{2}{3}$ miles. In the first 8 miles from the lake, but one lock is necessary. In the next mile, 64 feet of lockage are required. In the next 3 miles, there are about 2 of deep cutting, and 1 of tunnel, and then a descent of 200 feet in 3 miles, by lockage, to the Pacific. Thus far of the canal across the isthmus. The lake of Nicaragua is navigable for ships of the largest class, down to the mouth of the river San Juan. This river has an average fall of 1 6-7th feet per mile to the Atlantic. If the bed of the river cannot be cleared out, a communication can be made either by lock and dam, or by a canal along the bank of the river. The latter would be more expensive, but, on account of the heavy floods of the rainy season, it is preferable. I have good authority for stating that the physical obstructions of the country present no effectual impediment to the accomplishment of this work. A canal large enough for the passage of boats of the usual size could be made at a trifling expense. A tunnel of the length required is not considered a great work in the United States of America. The sole difficulty is the same which would exist in any route in any other region of country, viz., the great dimensions of the excavation required for a ship-canal. The data here given are of course insufficient for great accuracy; but I present a rough estimate of the cost of this work furnished me with the plan. It is predicated upon the usual contract-prices in the United States, and I think I am safe in saying, that the cheapness of labour in Nicaragua will equalize any advantages and facilities that exist there. The estimate is as follows:—

	Dollars.		Dollars.
From the lake to the east end of the tunnel............	8,000,000	to	10,000,000
Descent to the Pacific....................................	2,000,000	to	3,000,000
From the lake to the Atlantic, by canal along the bank of the river......................................	10,000,000	to	12,000,000
Total.................	20,000,000	to	25,000,000

Which is but about the sum contemplated as the cost of the enlarged Erie Canal."

Mr. Stephens speaks in raptures as to the accomplishment of this canal being at the present time quite within the reach of enterprise; yet, however considerable the advantages of this route over any presented by the Isthmus of Panama, and we consider them to be great, we think that a sufficient number of the objections attaching in that case, are inherent in the present, as hinderances to its present fulfilment. The cost—and we think he has much underrated it in the above estimate—in the present backward state of society in Central America, would be far too considerable to be met by any contrivance. The population of Nicaragua and the other Central-American States is, indeed, far more numerous, and society there infinitely more forward in advancing civilization, than in Panama; but such a work, for its successful accomplishment, requires the means, appliances, and influences of a country far more settled and improved than are those States.

With respect to the feasibility of a transit, partly by canal for small vessels, and partly by rail or other road, we consider that such an undertaking might at present, with much advantage to the country, be carried out at Panama; or that even an entire railroad for steam-carriages might there be found practicable. At all events, no time should be lost in tracing and consolidating a good practicable macadamized highway. In the case of Nicaragua, there does not seem to be any too great difficulty to encounter in clearing the river San Juan from some, if not all, of its obstructions, so as to admit of its being navigable for a larger class of vessels than those now proceeding up it into the lake of Nicaragua; and a good carriage-road ought not to be left unmade over the space between the lake of Nicaragua and the Pacific. Attention to even these comparatively little matters, when they are contrasted with the monster canal of which we have treated, would produce incalculable benefits;—greater works must be left to the gradual but certain effects of time. NICARAGUENSIS.

COLONIAL STATISTICS.

[NEW SERIES.]

NO. III.—THE ISLAND OF TRINIDAD.

Geography.—The island of Trinidad is one of our most valuable insular possessions in the West Indies, ranking next in dimensions and importance to Jamaica. In extent it is 50 miles by 32 miles; 2,020 miles in area. The latitude of Trinidad is 10° 38′ north per Espana; the longitude 61° 38′ west. The island is south by east 94 miles from Grenada, east 328 miles from La Guayra, and lies contiguous to the coast of South America, and to the confluence of the river Orinoco, forming with its western shores, and those of the opposite continent, the gulf of Paria. Two ridges of wooded mountains, extending nearly across the country, run parallel with the northern and southern coasts. The centre is diversified with many wooded hills, the highest of which attains an elevation of about 2,400 feet, producing mahogany, cedar, and several other kinds of cabinet woods; and the intermediate valleys are generally fertile.

Geology.—Trinidad is described as presenting an alluvial country in an active state of formation; it has been observed, that the land encroaching on the sea on the south-west coast is increasing the territory. Several craters exist in the island, some of which give occasional indications of not being extinct. The mineral Pitch Lake requires especial notice. The following account is given by a recent traveller, Mr. Anderson:—

"The bituminous lake, or rather plain, in the Island of Trinidad, is known by the name of Tar-lake; by the Spaniards called La-Brea, from its resemblance to, and answering the intention of, ship-pitch. It lies in the leeward side of the island, about half-way from the Bocas to the south end, where the mangrove swamps are interrupted by the sand-banks and the hills, and on a point of land which extends into the sea about two miles, and is exactly opposite to the high mountains of Paria, which are on the north-west side of the gulf of the same name, which separates the island from the Spanish Main.

"On a close examination, the lake is found to be a composition of bituminous scoriæ, vitrified sand and earth, cemented together, and, in some parts, beds of cinders only are found. In approaching the cape there is a strong sulphureous smell, sometimes disagreeable. The bituminous plain is only separated from the sea by a margin of wood, which surrounds and prevents a distant prospect of it. Its situation is like that of a savanna. It is liquid an inch deep in hot weather."

South of Cape Dela Brea is a submarine volcano; on the east part of the island there is another, which in March and June gives several detonations resembling thunder. There are also several mud volcanoes.

History.—This island was discovered by Columbus, on his third voyage, in 1498; was settled by the Spaniards in 1588, and surrendered to General Abercromby in 1797. According to some, the island was named Trinidad by Columbus, on account of the three mountain-tops seen in that position; according to others, in conformity to the holy Trinity. The island was first densely peopled by Caribs. Sir Walter Raleigh visited it in 1595, and states that the inhabitants then cultivated excellent tobacco and sugar-canes. Sir Walter took San Josef from the Spaniards, but the English government disowned this action of hostility.

Climate.—The dry season commences with December, and ends with May; the east, north-east, and north winds then become less cool, the heat is at its height by the end of June; storms commence, and augment in frequency and violence during August and September, and in October they occur almost daily. The hygrometer varies much in different seasons; in the rainy season it is usually between 85° and 90°; in the spring, between 36° and 38° in the day, and about 50° at night. During even the hot and stormy season the thermometer rarely stands at Port-of-Spain before sunrise so high as 74°, and in the country occasionally as low as 68°; from sunrise to sunset 84° to 86°, falling in the evening to 82° or 80°; in August or September, the mercury rises sometimes to 90.

Fruits.—January produces sappidilloes, pomegranates, sour-sops, plantains, bananas, papas, or papaws. The vegetables are, okros, capsicums, cocoa-nuts, angola pease, sweet potatoes, yams, tanias. April—Java plums, mangoes, pines, Otaheitan gooseberry, Jamaica plums, breadfruit, &c. May—water melons and cashew apples. July—the avocado pear, or alligator pear, or, as it is named, subaltern's butter, from its inside resembling very yellow fresh butter, both in consistence and colour. August—the yellow plum. September—sugar and custard apples, sea-side grapes, and Portuguese yams. December—guavas and sorrel; mountain cabbage always is in season.

Rivers.—The island is well watered by numerous rivers, the principal being the Caroni, on the west coast, which is navigable for several leagues; the Nariva on the east coast, and the Moruga on the south.

Harbours.—The Gulf of Paria, formed by the west shore of Trinidad and the opposite coast of Cumana, may be said to form one vast harbour for ships. The principal ports are Port Royal, Port of Spain, the Careenage, Gasper Grande, Maqueribe, Las Cuevas, (where Fort Abercrombie is situate,) Rio Grande, Boat Island, &c., &c.

Chief Towns.—Port-of-Spain, the capital, is described as one of the finest towns in the West Indies. The streets are wide and well laid out; the houses, which are built of stone, commodious, and the public buildings very superior, particularly the Protestant church, the barracks, market-place, &c. The climate is considered equal in salubrity to any other of the West India islands, and the town has the advantage of lying beyond the limits of the hurricanes. Port-of-Spain is well sheltered, situated within and on the north-eastern quarter of the gulf, on the northern entrance to which are three islands, forming four channels, called the Dragon's Mouth; the westernmost island of the group, *Chica-Chiccana*, affording, besides the gulf in general, (which has a good anchorage,) a port capable of receiving the largest fleet. The southern entrance from the Atlantic into the gulf called the Serpent's Mouth, is about eleven leagues wide; but vessels never attempt an *egress* in this direction, owing to the currents from the Orinoco setting through it so strong as to render it impracticable. The number of towns and quarters in Trinidad is forty, exclusive of Port-of-Spain. The towns Tagarigua, Arouca, St. Joseph, Savannah Grande, Santa Cruz, north and south Naparima, Diego Martin, and La Brea, have the largest populations.

Government.—The delegated government is composed of a governor, who is also styled commander-in-chief (Colonel Sir H. G. M'Leod); a council, consisting of 3 members, (Sir H. M'Leod, Lieutenant-Colonel Chichester, and Colonel Fuller); and a committee of 12 members. The following is a correct list of the present crown-officers: Colonial Secretary, A. White, Esq.; Chief Justice, G. Scotland, Esq.; First Puisne Judge, L. Johnston, Esq.; Second ditto, A. Gomez, Esq.; Registrar, J. J. Cadiz, Esq.; Advocate, S. Rotheray, Esq.; Marshal of the Admiralty Court, R. Palgrave, Esq.; Clerk of the Council, T. Johnston, Esq.; Treasurer, J. Walker, Esq.; Attorney-General, E. Jackson, Esq.; Solicitor-General, C. Warner, Esq.; Marshal, A. Clogstoun, Esq.; Registrar of Deeds, G. La Coste; Collector of Customs, C. Chipchace, Esq.; Harbour Master, R. Stewart, Esq.; Chaplain of the Forces, Rev. D. Evans; Botanist, Mr. Lockhart; Inspector of Health, T. Anderson, M.D.; Agent in London, G. Baillie, Esq.—In 1842, the legislature raised the governor's salary from 3,500*l.* to 4,000*l.* per annum. A change is about to be made in the constitution of the island, by assimilating its laws more strictly to those of England. The appointment of a government commission has been announced, for the suppression of squatting; and the functions of the persons named to compose this body seem to be the examination of the validity of the claims of any occupant of crown-lands who has not obtained his grant from government. All occupiers will have to give full information of title to such lands, and no claim will be received in cases where possession has been taken after August, 1838 (the date of abolition of apprenticeship in the West Indies).

Religion and Education.—The established religion is the Episcopal; there are Catholic and Wesleyan sects. Trinidad has been created an archdeaconry; the rector, Rev. Mr. Cummins, holds the appointment. From a parliamentary return of the number of schools in 1835, it appears that there are public and free schools at 11 of the towns; and there are likewise 23 private schools. On Sundays, Thursdays, and Saturdays, upwards of 400 children are instructed in the church, for want of school-rooms. The only Protestant place of worship is the church at Port-of-Spain. The value of this living was reckoned, in 1835, at 638*l.* There are two Roman Catholic chapels, one in Port-of-Spain, designated St. Mary's, congregation from 1,000 to 1,200 persons; and one in Carenage, St. Peter's, congregation about 1,200.

Language.—The Spanish, English, French, African, and American languages are spoken.

Currency.—As in Jamaica and in the other West India possessions, the currency of the United Kingdom has been recently adopted. Mr. M'Culloch, in his "Commercial Dictionary," explains the nature of West India currency in a few clear sentences: "West India currency is an imaginary money, and has a different value in different colonies. The value it bears, as compared with sterling money, was supposed to represent the corresponding value of the coins in circulation in the different islands at the time the proportion was fixed; these coins being for the most part mutilated, and otherwise worn and defaced, currency is in all cases less valuable than sterling. The following are the values of 100*l.* sterling, and of a dollar, in the currencies of the different islands:—

	Sterling.		Currency.		Dollar.		Currency.		
Jamaica	£100	=	£140	......	1	=	£0	6	8
Barbados	100	=	135	......	1	=	0	6	3
Windward Islands, (except Barbados)	100	=	175	......	1	=	0	8	3
Leeward Islands	100	=	200	.. ...	1	=	0	9	0

But these proportions are seldom acted upon, the exchange being generally from 10 to 20 per cent above the fixed par. British silver money is a legal tender through all the British colonial possessions.

Population.—From the period this island surrendered to the British flag (1797), the population has steadily increased, though other parts of the West Indies have been subject to considerable fluctuations. From tables that now lie before us, we shall be able to show the gradual increase of the population from 1797 down to the present time. In 1797, we find the census giving a total of 16,636, viz., 2,151 whites, 4,476 free colours, and 10,009 slaves; these numbers we find increasing in a small ratio every year, till 1834, when the numbers stood as follows: White, 4,201; free colour, 18,724; slaves, 22,359—total, 45,284. Thus in eight years the population was nearly trebled. Nothing has occurred, since 1834, in the colony, to obstruct the progress of the numbers of the population; and, in the absence of any official return for the last ten years, we may reasonably infer that at this date the population has increased at least 30,000, computing from the scale of increase presented by the tables we have examined. Dr. Meikleman, in his recent evidence before a parliamentary committee, states that the population has trebled since emancipation.

Commerce.—The chief products are sugar, rum, coffee, and cocoa. From the richness and extent of the sugar soil, it is capable of producing more than a sufficiency of sugar for the consumption of Great Britain, and as cheaply as in any other part of the world. The imports of Trinidad for the year ending September, 1841, were—from Great Britain (in value), 403,548*l.*; British West Indies, 23,055*l.*; North American colonies, 57,092*l.*; United States, 17,260*l.*; other flags, 5,844*l.*;—total, 506,799*l.* Some statistics in recent West India papers give the produce of Trinidad up to 1843: the sugar exported in the year 1843, amounted to 22,615 hhds., 1,327 tierces, and 4,836 barrels, against 19,176 hhds., 1,401 tierces, and 3,783 barrels in 1842. The coffee exported was 124,583 lbs., against 398,363 lbs. in 1842. That the above statement may not go without the means of a fair test, we extract from M'Culloch's "Commercial Dictionary" (1844) the subjoined official account of the quantities of sugar, &c. imported into the United Kingdom from Trinidad in 1841:—Sugar, 284,605 cwts.; molasses, 78,090 cwts.; rum, 2,297 cwts.; coffee, 38,622 lbs.; cocoa, 2,493,302 lbs. The sugar imports of 1841 show an improvement of some cwts. on the previous two years; but a falling off, as compared with the amounts of the eight previous years; in 1831, the importation of sugar from Trinidad was 327,167 cwts.; in 1834, 339,615 cwts.; this latter quotation being the highest in the official tables last published.

Agriculture.—The last agricultural report published under the authority of the chairman of the Trinidad Agricultural Society (Hon. W. H. Burnley), refers satisfactorily to the general healthy appearance of the land; the report notices a manifest improvement in every description of field-work; and it is said, that "should the planters succeed in enforcing good weeding, their cane-pieces will show highly favourable. The last sugar-crop exceeded, by about 3,000 hhds., that of the preceding year." As connected with the interests of agriculture, it may be noticed that, at the close of 1843, a vessel had arrived at Trinidad with 216 emigrants from Rio de Janeiro; they found, when landed, immediate employment. Another vessel with 300 more was promised. The quantity of unappropriated land is set down in the government returns at 1,378 square miles in area.

Revenue.—The annual revenue, according to the official estimate of 1835, is satisfactory, as compared with the expenditure: revenue, 1835, 41,754*l.* 19s. 7d.; expenditure, 1835, 35,779*l.* 17s. 7d. (See *Commerce.*) The expenditure for 1835 was as follows: civil government, 10,756*l.*; judicial establishment, 8,649*l.*; ecclesiastical ditto, 3,428*l.*; miscellaneous, 9,116*l.*

The Press.—"Port-of-Spain Gazette," "Trinidad Standard." [No account of the West India Press appears in any of the statistical works we have consulted; but, as the subject is appropriate, we have collected the necessary information, and shall therefore enumerate the newspapers published in the West India colonies, in this place.] The following are filed at the North and South American Coffee-House:—Jamaica: "Jamaica Times;" "Morning Journal;" Cordovo's "Price-Current, and Shipping List;" "Royal Agricultural Society Reporter." Demerara: "Times;" "Chronicle." Barbadoes: "Barbadian;" "Mercury." St. Kitts: "Times." St. Lucia: "Palladium;" "Independent." St. Vincent: "Gazette." Grenada: "Times." Dominica: "Colonist." Tobago: "Gazette." St. Domingo: "Herald;" "Chronicle." Antigua: "Register." Honduras: "Belise Gazette." Cuba: "St. Jago Gazette." Guiana: "Herald."

Troops.—92d Highlanders; the service companies of this regiment were removed from Barbados to Trinidad in May, 1843. This is the first Highland regiment that has ever been on the island.—Every freeman of Trinidad is enrolled in the militia, which is composed of artillery, cavalry, and infantry, with a very numerous staff; the muster is about 4,500; and an efficient state of discipline is kept up.

The Colonial Arms.—The arms of the colony are represented by a British man-of-war lying-to in the bay of Port-of-Spain, whilst a boat manned by a full boat's crew is making for her. The motto runs as follows: "*Miscerique probat populus, et fœdera jungi.*"

SONNET—THE NELSON MONUMENT.

HAIL, thou gaunt figure of hard-favour'd man,
That, like Stylites on his shaft of stone,
At once a martyr seem'st, and on a throne!
What depths that unquench'd eye doth search and scan!
What masterdom of war is in the span
Of that surviving hand! Hail, Britain's own,
Austere, inflexible, aloft, alone,—
Her patriot-hero of the oceän!
Is any knows not that intrepid brow?
Ask then of Trafalgar; ask of the Nile;
Ask of the waves ennobled by his prow;
Ask Fame, and ask the Frenchman. Yon tall pile,
That rears heav'n-high thy form, exalts not thee,
NELSON! thou name of glorious memory.

April, 1844. C. J. C.

EUROPEAN SPORTS AND PASTIMES IN INDIA.

BY E. H. MALCOLM.

Say, what abridgement have you for this evening?
What mask? What music? How shall we beguile
The lazy time, if not with some delight?

SHAKESPEARE.

PROBABLY a few pages of gossip respecting European life in India, under its recreative phases, may prove acceptable to those of our readers at all inclined to the unbending mood, or willing to relieve their craniums of the weight of statistic knowledge, and withdraw awhile from the dry study of political economy and colonial interests.

In those portions of Hindostan inhabited by Europeans—for instance, Calcutta, Agra, Madras, and Bombay—the society is of a mixed or hybrid character, constructed and regulated on principles, which latter partly obey Eastern manners and customs, whilst still evincing a strong penchant for the more congenial manners and customs of Old England; yet, from peculiarity of position, Anglo-Indian* society is neither like the one thing nor the other, but altogether *sui generis.* Its mixed nature produces about as disagreeable an effect as is certain to be produced on our grandmothers when the flavour of their Souchong has been destroyed by an admixture of sloe-leaves. The deleterious decoction is sure to sour the tempers of the old ladies, and so it is with society at the presidencies; everything they eat, drink, hear, see, or do, is so *mixed* as to prove decidedly unpalatable and unpleasant until they get used to it; and when, indeed, they do, they are themselves the cause of unpleasantness in others.

Measuring the *esprit de corps* of our Indian connexions by an instrument we must invent for the purpose, and call our *homometer,* it would seem to be but lukewarm in its nature; the instrument shows the vitality at Calcutta dull and depressed to a degree under which a Sheridan must be parboiled, and could not exist twenty minutes; nor could stupidity itself survive such an atmosphere a single day, deprived of the well-known restoratives, brandy-pawny and cheroots.

* We use the term "Anglo-Indian" for convenience, and apart from any consideration of its meaning as applied to Indian castes merely.

Let us see whether we are countenanced by other writers in the estimate we have drawn of English society in India. A resident * of many years in the East writes in the following strain of the said society : —

" A circumstance which prevents the tone of the Anglo-Indian's mind from becoming strengthened, or preserving its elasticity, is the humdrum nature of the only society he has. Dine where you will in Calcutta, you are sure to meet either the same people, or some of the same people, or, all in all, the same description of people ; so that your faculties have no new exercise—nothing to polish or to keep them keen ; no new range or species of intellect to encounter ; and thus they become either rusted, or stiffened, or worn, by one kind of constant use, into such unwhetstonable bluntness, that they are past all renewing by the time they come into collision with the better exercised minds of England, and are bewildered, or soured, or stupified, by the too late discovery."

Here is evidence of the society being but second-rate in regard to manners, customs, and even intellect, save in respect to local affairs. The adventurer on his arrival in India must, however, get used, and he will then find his English mind subsiding to the miserable level. So much for social dulness and uninstructiveness.

It will now be our duty to find all the excuses we can for such an existence, and therefore this article will dwell henceforward upon the "lights" of Anglo-Indian life, leaving the "shadows" to take care of themselves. To describe the places of public resort, amusements, pleasures, sports, and follies of our expatriated countrymen, will afford us plenty of occupation, and perhaps combine to produce a readable chapter.

A card of the amusements for the day, open, to be participated by the European and educated native community of Calcutta, is regularly published in each of the morning papers, and a similar programme is prepared for the public of the other presidencies, and published in the principal journals. Fashionable life at home is of coursé closely imitated. *Soiré* at the Hanover-square concerts is reflected at Calcutta by Mr. Linton or Mr. Osborne at the Town Hall ; Lady Bab Blazington's *soiré* in Bryanston-square finds a reflex in Mrs. C. S. Brown's *soiré* in Chowringhee. The July meetings of the Horticultural Society, in Waterloo Place, also have their counterpart at Calcutta in November ; and the eminently fashionable flower-show at Chiswick is in due season attempted to be rivalled by the Honourable Company's Botanical Gardens on the banks of the River Hooghly. The Chiswick gardens of London fashionables are, indeed, admirably daguerreotyped in these botanical gardens. The grounds are thrown

* *Asiatic Journal*, September, 1843.

open to the public from November to March twice a week, (Saturdays and Sundays). Scientifically considered, they must hold a high position; the Chiswick botanists would, indeed, be proud of possessing some of the rare tropical plants preserved and flourishing in a temperature for which they are, by nature, alone suited, and which temperature nor Chiswick, nor Chatsworth, nor any other place in exotic England, could produce, with the aid of all their dung, peat, tobacco-smoking, and similar hot-house artifices.

The Anglo-Indian lounger, like the idler of the West End, assumes the foppery of patronising scientific and literary societies, which daily meet and discuss science and literature with tea and sandwiches.

The Asiatic Society of Calcutta is the most useful of these institutions originated by fashionable humour. The Asiatic Society periodically publishes at Calcutta a journal of its proceedings, copies of which are sent home at convenience, to be forwarded by the London agents to numerous subscribers in the United Kingdom. The work is printed at the Bishop's College press, Calcutta, and is a respectable specimen of colonial typography.

The motto of the journal tersely explains its objects—it runs as follows: "*The bounds of our investigation will be the geographical limits of Asia, and within these limits the journal's inquiries will be extended to whatever is performed by man or produced by nature.*"

The Royal Asiatic Society of London acknowledges its Calcutta and Bombay branches as connexions of vital importance to its well-being; because these branches prosecute their researches in Asia, not merely by the intervention of books, but by more practical means; the celebrated scholars and travellers whose names are familiar as household words to the ear of the educated man of the 19th century—Princeps, Burnes, Gerrards, Chodzko, Atkinson, &c., &c., were pilgrims of the Calcutta and Bombay shrines. The first enthusiastic aspirations of these classic travellers were encouraged, fostered, and developed by the branch societies, which readily thought to employ the actual services of men imbued with the spirit of travel and the love of antiquity. The society's funds have ever been applied to the uses of enterprising agents in the pursuit of scientific knowledge; and as the mission of the traveller has become known and better understood, the example set by him has been respected and sometimes emulated—correspondence with the society has increased—new interest in the latter's views awakened, and the result has been, that by an acquisition of funds and an extension of utility, the society is now the more capable of infusing new life and fresh courage into the hearts of its wearied and drooping labourers, journeying upon the heights and in the valleys of the Himalayas; amidst the snow-clad mountains of Affghanistan; or in Hindostan, laboriously investigating the antiquities of the Indus and the sacred Ganges. A stream of Asiatic lore and knowledge has been constantly kept flowing onward from the depths and wilds of Asia, by the exertions and liberality of the Asiatic Society of Bengal, its Bombay branch, and the energies of enterprising volunteers, who have penetrated the country and communicated the results of their travels.

The meetings of the Asiatic Society at Calcutta are set down in their programme of the last season for 9 A.M. twice a week. Converzationes of the agricultural, the agri-horticultural, and other artistic and scientific institutions, as also lectures, educational examinations, political assemblages, &c., take place in due rotation at the presidencies, during the season, and materially tend to relieve the monotony of Indian life. The steam people are always at their vexed question, and thus keep up an excitement which at least answers the purpose of driving away ennui, though very little beneficial progress is made by the resolves of one day being invariably negatived the next, as is the fact. The human steam-engines of India exercising the greatest power, are those ever-noisy locomotive salamanders, Messrs. Greenland and Turton, Grant and Hume, and Messrs. Ouchterlony and Cowasfre Rustytomtowagy, or whatever may be the latter's real but unspellable patronymic. The latest notable thing done and performed by these worthies was to get up a steam-meeting at the Town Hall of Calcutta, when their speechifying led to nothing more than a vote of thanks in favour of some "illustrious obscure," who is an outsider of the London press; for that whereas the said penny-a-liner had wriggled his anatomy into the large room of the London Tavern, wherein a steam-meeting was held not long ago, and had informed the meeting that *his* sentiments were in favour of a steam communication direct with Calcutta instead of Bombay. But we return to our *moutons;* besides the intellectual, political, and steam engagements of the Anglo-Indian public, there are the commercial interests to allude to—the bank, fund, and company meetings; so that, gentle reader, you perceive that the European world of the East is not without incentives to activity, of a utilitarian as well as pleasurable kind. Nor ought we to forget to mention the public and private balls and reunions got up for the behest of the ladies, the more aristocratic being under the patronage of the vice-regal court, and the plebeian countenanced by the *ton* of the mercantile class. It is satisfactory to know that the pursuit of these gaieties has generally a philanthropic object. We might find room for some account of the merry-makings in India, especially of a Calcutta ball, but that Captain Bellew and Peregrine Poulteney are even now prominently before the world as delineators of acknowledged ability in this field of Anglo-Indian life.

At each of the presidencies and principal stations of India is perpetuated the most ancient and universal of all national customs; we allude to the establishment of rendezvous or malls, wherever a town of any consequence exists.

A road on the bank of the river Hooghly is the grand mall of the Calcutta denizens; it is there called "the drive;" and this Rotten Row of the "city of palaces" is crowded every evening, presenting a view of great variety of costumes and vehicles. *Peregrine Poulteney* describes "carriages and horsemen, barouches, britchzkas, landaulets, phaetons, poney-phaetons, curricles, coaches, buggies (cabs), of all sizes and descriptions, thronging and jostling along the road like a cavalcade from Epsom races." In the throng of Calcutta loungers, the same indications of fashion's vagaries are seen as in the drive of Hyde Park; the fop, the politician, the militaire, the civilian, and the clerk; the patrician beauty, the merchant's wife, and the *roués* mistress meet cheek-by-jowl to look and be looked at, and to find amusement and enjoyment in laughing and sneering at one another. In the Calcutta drive one may probably observe, side by side, the elegant beauty of the Governor-General's court, and the overdressed and vulgar citizens (the wife perhaps of a shroff or money-lender), turbaned and bedizened, and looking like—to institute a broad comparison—like a badly-dressed theatrical amateur of the Chowringhee theatre in the character of Othello. But the contrast is no more peculiar to the mall of the Indian capital than to that of fashionable London, since the latter exhibits oddities quite as remarkable.

In one thing especially, however, does the esplanade of the East differ from the well-known Rotten Row of the North. There is no such thing as a pedestrian lounger in the former. In the eyes of the Oriental, a respectable European degrades himself by walking. Persons of moderate means are compelled, *ex necessitate rei*, to hire a a conveyance of some sort immediately on their arrival at the presidencies; and, by the way, the inexperienced seldom escape being victimized at first by the thoroughly dishonest race of native jockeys and bearers or carriers of palanquins, who are adepts at cheating and robbery; fellows who will indubitably rob an Englishman of any luggage he may have, if he do not look confoundedly sharp, take especial cognizance of the number of the vehicle he hires, and keep a sharp eye upon the said number, so that no jugglery with it occurs. Another notorious cheat to which the griffin or tyro is subjected in his commerce with the natives, is being imposed upon with bad money. The Hindoos have a mood of perforating good rupees, and cleverly excavating the metal to the amount of three-fourths of their value, and then substituting baser metal. This piece of ingenuity is performed by native women in their sanctuaries, to which the coiners are well aware no police officer will so far violate the customs of the country as to penetrate.

We have now, we believe, gone over the routine of fashionable life in the East, except that we have hardly taken notice of an amusement exceedingly popular, viz. the theatre; but we are saved any further observations here upon that subject, by referring the reader to a previous article, which appeared in the *Colonial Magazine* of June last, under the heading of "Theatres in the British Colonies. We part, then, with concerts and reunions, balls and assemblies, literary and scientific institutions, public meetings and steam companies, to quote a few words from an amusing and useful work just published, regarding a favourite recreation, whose delights, pastoral and pasty-ral, we had well nigh overlooked—we mean the *pic-nic*.

"A day at Barrackpore Park, (says Mr. Stocqueler,*) which is a lovely piece of ground, and on which the government keep up a menagerie and aviary, allows the mind a holiday which it often stands in need of; and as the settledness of the weather between November and March is uniform enough to almost insure a party of this kind against the *contretems* of a ducking, the temperature so pleasant as to involve no other risk to health from the unusual exposure to the skyey influences, there is a great deal of cordial cockney enjoyment derivable from such excursions when the party is well assorted, and where it is understood that a spinster may be spoken to more than once by a bachelor without his being thereby involved in the inferential 'offer,' which on more formal occasions would be taken to be comprised, or at the very least intended, by such very deep familiarity. The party can go by land and return by water, or *vice versâ*, and thus obtain a variation of travel, which in returning, especially from these exciting excursions, is well adapted to keep the mind from flagging, or feeling jaded by its long and unusual state of joyous excitation. In the opposite direction, to wit, down the river Hooghly, the company's botanical gardens (already alluded to) are an equally delightful resort of a pic-nic character."

In defiance of the nature of a tropical climate, and the obstructions of country, Englishmen have shown themselves determined not to exile themselves so completely as to forget "their own country sports" and amusements, which, says Mr. Stocqueler in his Hand Book, "the

* Hand Book of India. Allen & Co. 1844.

English have been famous throughout the world for carrying with them, as the snail does his shell. Nor (continues the same writer) does the City of Palaces, despite all obstacles of climate, form an exception to the general rule. Accordingly, Calcutta can boast of its race-course and its hunt; cricket, archery, and rackets, also having their votaries. Regattas occasionally enliven the banks of the Hooghly, and four-in-hand, or tandem, varies the monotony of the evening drive. Of these sports, however, the turf is pre-eminent in popular estimation, and, as such, a short sketch of its origin and present state may not be unacceptable."

FORWARD, WESTERN AUSTRALIA!

In our February number, we gave some extracts from the *Swan River News, and Western Australian Chronicle*, to afford our readers an idea of the position of the colony of Western Australia, and the probabilities and indications of its advance; but we did not expect to be so soon called upon to refer to the subject (which we then promised to do), or to have such early occasion of laying before our readers a farther report of the rapid onward march of the colonists. The March and April numbers of the *Swan River News* contain notices of some interesting transactions in the colony, not the least important of which is the production of iron and steel:—

When (asks the editor) shall we have discovered all the resources of Western Australia? It is but two months since we made known the first attempt at manufacturing olive oil, and in the present number we record an experiment for the production of flax. The colonists are highly to be commended for not being content with the simple staple products of wool, oil, and bone; wine and currants were but lately added to the list, and now we have been startled at finding that iron and steel have been produced from ore abundant in the colony. A paper descriptive of certain experiments in the manufacture of these valuable metals was read by Mr. Nash at the last meeting of the Agricultural Society held in October. We have not yet seen the minutes of that meeting, but the following abstract from Mr. Nash's report has reached us.

It is stated that iron ore in strata, or raikes, is to be found in the colony to any extent, yielding a larger per centage of metal than the average of ores in England. On Mr. Nash's property, a mass of iron ore, embedded in limestone, 400 yards in length, and about 40 in breadth, was lately discovered. Its depth in the springs, which rise in the solid ore, was 6 feet; but it was apparently a much greater depth. The following experiments on a very contracted scale, and with a small portable forge, are reported—

"1st Experiment.—100 grains of raw iron ore, with 50 per cent of charcoal, luted up in a crucible of blue clay, one hour in the forge, twenty minutes of which in a white heat—50 per cent of cast iron. 100 grains of cast iron, smelted half an hour with 20 per cent of lime—9 per cent of wrought iron. 100 grains of wrought iron, smelted one hour, with 50 per cent of lime—cast steel.

"2d Experiment.—100 grains of raw iron ore, with borax and charcoal, produced a small quantity of pale-green glass, &c.—25 per cent of iron.

"3d Experiment.—100 grains of raw iron ore, with charcoal only—54 per cent of iron.

"4th Experiment.—10 lbs. of ore ran easily into a black lava, but for want of sufficient power only a few grains of iron were produced in white enamel.

"Memorandum.—The ore does not appear to contain either sulphur or arsenic, either of which would render it brittle."

The paper stated also, that, in the neighbourhood of Williams River, iron ore is found in small cubical and, in some instances, spherical masses, on the surface of the ground, yielding 2 or 3 per cent more metal than the above; it is described as being black and very hard, and brings sparks from steel. In several other parts of the colony, iron ore is found lying on the surface.

We are exclusively enabled to give the above outline of Mr. Nash's report, but shall enter more into the details of the subject, when we receive our file of the Perth papers. Mr. Nash deserves great credit for bringing so important a subject forward, and has added another instance of his indefatigable zeal in behalf of cultivation and production, to his former valuable services.

A short paragraph from the *Perth Gazette* tells us of the production of another article of commerce and exportation:—

Western Australian Flax.—Sufficient attention has not been paid to a plant that grows abundantly in this colony, and requires but little care; and we are only surprised that it has been so much neglected, especially as we are now endeavouring to form an export-trade: we allude to the *Phormium tenax*, from which flax of a very superior quality can be made by a simple and inexpensive process. Experiments have already been tried, but not on such a scale as we would wish to see.

The industry and ingenuity of the colonists in discovering these new products and future sources of wealth, deserve to be rewarded by the means of cultivating them to advantage. This they at present enjoy only to a very limited extent, for labour appears to be still sorely required. We find, in connection with this subject, and in No. IV. of the *News*, the Report of a Committee of the Legislative Council appointed to enquire into the amount of labour required, and the best means of introducing it. The Committee report thus:—

Your Committee, having collected the opinions of various individuals resident in several districts, and more particularly of the secretaries and members of the Agricultural Societies, are of opinion that the number of labourers and others of the working-classes required to be introduced for the year 1844, exclusive of married women and children, should be as follows—

Shepherds or youths to attend flocks	100
Farm servants	200
Domestic and other men servants	50
Female servants	50

forming a total of 400 adults and youths of both sexes, and that a number annually augmented in the progressive ratio of about one-third would be required for the ensuing years; which numbers they strongly recommend should be shipped in two or more divisions, and at intervals of from four to six months of each other. In this estimate, the Committee have taken into consideration the inconvenience to which the colony might be subjected by the sudden introduction of a greater number of hands than could be readily engaged within a short period after arrival, as well as the disappointment which might occur to the immigrants if, on their arrival, they should find the labour-market overstocked, and themselves cast upon the local government for support; with this view, the Committee have kept the estimate considerably below that of several persons whom they have consulted, and for whose opinions they entertain respect. They would suggest also, that it would be highly desirable if the persons selected for emigration were, with few exceptions, young and single, it being almost invariably the case that the unmarried are immediately taken into employ, whilst the married, especially those with families, remain unengaged for a considerable time, and constitute a serious burden to the local government.

In consulting the other branch of the inquiry referred to them, namely, that of providing for the expense attendant on the introduction of the above-mentioned number of immigrants, your Committee are of opinion, that it is doubtful whether a sufficient amount of funds for that purpose can be expected to arise from the sale of crown-lands, previous to the expiration of the year 1844; and therefore recommend that application should be made to the home-government for the money to meet the expenses, to be advanced from year to year, in the way of loan, to be repaid out of the proceeds of future sales of crown-lands, and that the Legislative Council should secure the payment of the interest upon such loans from the internal revenue of the colony, by passing a vote for the required amount to be included in the annual estimate of expenditure. Your Committee consider that the proposition of a loan for this purpose will appear to be both reasonable and just, when it is borne in mind that a large proportion of the expenses of the survey department, as well as a considerable amount of expenditure connected with the aborigines, and for the immediate benefit of that race, have been annually paid from the internal revenues of the colony, since the earliest date of the regulation of its expenditure by means of colonial legislative enactment.

Your Committee are of opinion that no measure would be more likely to assist the rapid advance of the colony, to expedite the sale of crown-lands, and consequently to ensure the rapid repayment of the loan or loans above alluded to, than the constant throwing into the mass of population, such additional numbers as may thus from year to year be required. Should the above proposition not be acceded to, your Committee would advise the adoption of some well-considered system of bounties to be offered, as an inducement for the introduction of labourers at the expense of private individuals. This, however, is a question which your Committee are not prepared to offer any definite opinion upon, until they shall be assured of the decision respecting a loan which may be come to by the government.

From the above Report, it will be seen that an increase of labour is much wanted, even *per se*; but if, by any means, an increase of *capital* were to be introduced, the demand for labour would be tenfold. The population of the colony is at present small, but the last return, compared with that of the former year, shows so considerable an addition, that we are almost induced to infer from it the commencement of a reaction in the public mind in favour of the colony, and certainly a more extended consciousness of its eligibilities among emigrants. The following census for 1843 is from the *Perth Gazette*:—

Districts.	Males.	Females.	Total.
Murray	98	35	133
Perth (County)	1288	1018	2306
Plantagenet	170	90	260
Rottenest	3	3	6*
Sussex	90	64	154
Toodyay	112	53	165
Wellington	302	177	479
Wicklow	5	—	5
York (County)	236	109	345
Total	2304	1559	3863

Population of Perth:—

Males, above 12 years	445
Males, under 12 years	171
Females, above 12 years	337
Females, under 12 years	200
Total	1153

The slow progression of the population, in a colony of such rare advantages, shows either that those advantages are not generally known, or that rival interests have been at work to depreciate and misrepresent it. Western Australia perhaps owes her former tardy accessions of numbers to both these causes combined; but there is now happily a party in England determined to disabuse the minds of the public, and to put the colony in her own fair position, by stating facts and putting forth plain unvarnished statements. They have indeed much to say in recommendation of it, and we cannot but think that if such reports as the following had been published before, we should not now have heard of any want of labour:—

Encouraging to Emigrants.—Four Scotch shepherds, no one of whom has yet been five years in the colony, are now about to hire land, and set-up as sheep-farmers on their own account. These men, who were all brought in by private individuals on the bounty-system, have long since paid up the whole of their passage-money, and are now possessed of a joint flock of 600 sheep, purchased entirely with money laid by out of their wages. We consider this a good example of the success that awaits the steady and industrious immigrant to this colony.—*Inquirer*, November 8th.

The following is a strong testimonial in favour of the *general* merits of the colony. It appears in No. III. of the *Swan River News*, and is, we understand, written by an extensive farmer on the Swan, whose name is in possession of the editor :—

Extract of a private letter, dated "Perth, 13th October."—"We find the natives of great use in clearing and burning; they are well satisfied with a good mess of rice after they have done work. My native boy goes on very well, and is getting to be useful to me; I should be sorry to part with him. My opinion is still the same, that any person who is steady and industrious may get on better here than in England, particularly those with small capitals to begin with. A gentleman who came out by the last ship, and is going on to Adelaide, where he has been before, told me he considers this a much finer country in every respect; and, had he not been under an engagement to go there, he should certainly have staid here. Another gentleman, supercargo to the *Velocity*, a sharp, clever man, who has been here twice, and has been in nearly every settlement belonging to England, said he had not seen one that he thought so well of as this, being so well situated for trade, with almost a tropical climate, and yet plenty of rain to grow everything in perfection."

These are statements, which we have not been accustomed to hear, as other colonies have hitherto been extolled at the expense and to the disparagement of Western Australia. She, however, now appears determined to come forward before the public; and, when she fairly shows herself in all her advantages, we consider her prosperity to be sealed. "To be admired, she needs but to be known."

LINLITHGOW VESPERS—A BALLAD,

(WRITTEN FOR THE COLONIAL MAGAZINE.)

Founded on the tradition, preserved by Buchanan, that shortly before the battle of Flodden, James IV. of Scotland, while at vespers in the Cathedral Church of Linlithgow, was visited by the supernatural appearance of an old and venerable man, who warned him against the war he then contemplated with England, assuring him that its issue would prove equally fatal to his country and himself.]

BY JOHN HOWDEN, B.A.

It was a gay and glittering train that to the temple stream'd,
And in the ray of golden eve their gorgeous vestments gleam'd,
The very flower of knight and dame were there, of Scottish land,
And well I ween that summer's sun ne'er beamed on nobler band.

It swept along, that gallant train,—and now eve's shadow falls
On yon cathedral's dreary pomp, and high and hoary walls,
Which now, 'mid footprints of the past, soar in sepulchral gloom,
A spectre of departed days, a blight on nature's bloom!

We wander now along its aisles, and tread, with awe profound,
Its marble floor now crusted o'er—its consecrated ground—
Where fading flowers on moss-grown tombs for those gentle hands do sigh,
That tended them in other years, in times long since gone by!

But then, old pile, the beauteous day was thine, as now it's ours—
The sun shone bright on thy stately walls, and on thy sculptur'd towers,
And beauty's rose, and music's strain, did bloom and breathe in thee,
Though now the boding voice of years speaks forth unceasingly!

It swept along, that gallant train,—and now the sun hath set,
And the rising moon is pouring down a track of silver light,
The deep-blue firmament above is broken by white clouds,
And the stars reflect themselves far down amid the lucid floods!

O! 'twas a glorious sight to see that noble train sweep by,
Their bright array, their costly gems, their robes of gorgeous dye,—
The soft breeze wav'd each snowy plume, and stirr'd each silken train,
And the moon's pale light from armour bright was mirror'd back again.

And there amidst that gallant band one stately form was seen,
You knew him by his lordly step, and by his princely mien,
And there, though now more staid his step, and calm his bearing high,
I ween the proudest of that band was proud to catch his eye!

And now they've gain'd the holy shrine, the solemn music thrills
Sweetly into the secret heart, and soothes its mightiest ills;
Most mournfully it swells above the foliage of the trees,
And tremulously dies away upon the hushing breeze.

The king hath knelt to prayer,—when, lo! full in the altar's light,
A venerable man is seen, his hair of lustre bright,
His robe of azure; smooth his brow; his smile so sad, so sweet;
His eye of gentlest blue, though now with mystic meaning lit.

He's laid his hand upon the king, he's whispered in his ear,
But what the words, or what the sense, no ear save his can hear;*
The king starts to his feet, but dim and death-like is his eye,
A long-protracted, silent gaze of 'wilder'd vacancy!

But where the aged man? no more he fills the sacred place,
But silence is on every tongue, and pale is every face;
Each heart beats quick, and every glance is one of doubt or fear,
But he—where is that mystic man? the echo answers "where?"

Enough to say, in few short days when in unequal strife,
Our good King James to southern hands resign'd this mortal life,
'Twas known that holy aged man had whisper'd in his ear,
Beware, beware, the coming field, beware the English spear!

---

* There is a slight departure here from the letter of tradition.

REVIEWS OF NEW BOOKS.

ART. I.—*Western Africa,—its Condition,—Christianity the Means of its Recovery.* By J. D. East. London: Houlston and Stoneman.

Certainly those unhappy descendants of Ham appear, by their sufferings, to have fulfilled the prophecy, for no part of the world has been so long overshadowed by ignorance and destitution as this ancient quarter. From Egypt to the Atlantic, along the northern border, the arts of peace have occasionally been cherished, and some few fortunate patches on the south and eastern latitudes; but, with these exceptions, all Africa is one great scene of ignorance and barbarism. It is time that the blessing, which has also been recorded, should visit this land of wailing, and Englishmen have not been backward in their efforts to regenerate these luckless beings. Climate has assuredly militated against their meritorious labours, but, from melancholy experience we have derived a lesson; and, in future, let us employ as agents of our bounty and our instruction, those whose constitutions have been peculiarly adapted, by the all-wise Ruler of the universe, to the scorching rays of a tropical sun. This, we believe, is amongst Mr. East's cautious plans for civilizing Central Africa, and few reflecting minds will feel disposed to question its prudence and propriety.

A vast treasury of knowledge relating to the habits, propensities, and diversions of the aborigines is collected in this very important volume, and some of the fundamental errors of many who meant well, but performed miserably, in their treatment of the slavery question, stated and exposed, in language calculated to command both attention and respect. It is our author's opinion and our own, that Christianity should be taught to the poor negro even before civilization, and for these, amongst other reasons—viz., that his very worst and most immoral habits are at once corrected by Christianity; whilst vices, still greater than his inheritance, are inculcated by civilization. Now, this is very clearly shown by the author in many ways—one must here suffice. The extent to which polygamy prevails in Africa may be imagined, when it is remembered that Islamism is the dominant religion, and our author writes—

3. What is the result? No small part of the present degradation of this unhappy country may fairly be traced to it. One inevitable consequence is to make one passion, and that the strongest of which human nature is the subject, sovereign and all-controlling. The gratification of this one passion is made almost the sole end of life. It hence becomes all-absorbing, and lays all else tributary to itself. That this is in truth the case, the condition and habits of African society bear too ample testimony. Major Denham, for example, speaks of Bornu as a country where "love and war are the chief occupations of the people, and where one of the greatest incitements to the latter is the desire of unbounded indulgence in the former."

This is one, but not the only effect of polygamy, as it prevails in Africa. Major Gray, speaking of it as the crying sin and main-spring of the pernicious tendency of Mohammedanism, remarks, "Polygamy is the fruitful source of jealousy and distrust; it contracts the parental and filial affections; it weakens and disjoints the ties of kindred; and, but for the unlimited influence of the Maraboos, and the fear of hell, must totally unhinge the frame of all society. The father has many wives; the wives have many children; favouritism, in its most odious forms, sets in; jealousy is soon aroused, and revenge unsheaths the sword which deals forth destruction.

"But it is not to the domestic circle—it is not to the family arrangements—it is not to the fearful mischiefs it leads to upon the social system," he adds, "that I look alone; but to its division of the soil, and to its mutilation of the different states, than which nothing can prove more destructive to a country. The jealousies of the mothers, while exciting to domestic hatred, lead to external civil war; and states rise and set with a sort of harlequin operation; and when they are sought for, vanish in the air, and 'leave not a wreck behind.' The consequence of these wars is, that during the precarious conquests of these chiefs, their whole employment is plunder; and where that cannot be procured, the forfeiture is life. All order and morality are upset, all right is unknown; and the effect must be the degradation of society, and the dismemberment of empire in that ill-fated portion of the world."

Now, all this anarchy and inhumanity—all these deplorable consequences—are anticipated and provided against by a single act, the establishment of the Christian religion, which forbids plurality of wives.

We now come to the minor premise of the grand syllogism,—"that civilization, if taught before or without religion, is the fruitful parent of vice." Hear Mr. East in support of it:—

Perhaps never more than one purely benevolent attempt was made to advance civilization in this way. This was in connexion with the Wesleyan society about forty years ago. The case was laid by the secretary of this institution before the Aborigines Committee. He says, "Dr. Coke, the founder of our missions, was induced to form a plan for the purpose of introducing civilization among the Fulahs of Western Africa. A number of well-disposed artisans of various descriptions were engaged to go and settle among the Fulahs; and it was calculated that, after some progress had been made in civilization, missionaries might then be sent to preach the gospel to those whom civilization should have thus prepared. However, the undertaking failed entirely; and it failed for this very reason, that the agents who were engaged to carry the scheme into execution did not find sufficient motives to induce them to persevere. They reached Sierra Leone, and there their courage failed them. The motives which had influenced them to embark in the undertaking, were not powerful enough to impel them to advance into the interior of the country, and settle among the Fulahs for the purpose of merely civilizing them." For similar reasons, any effort of this kind whatever would in all probability prove equally abortive.

But Europeans, influenced by the prospect of their own personal aggrandisement, have located themselves among the aboriginal inhabitants of heathen countries. What has been the result? Without entering into the merits of European colonization in general, which, it may be safely affirmed—in the foulness of its iniquities, the injustice of its oppressions, and the bloody cruelty of its systematic atrocities—equals all that can be related of human depravity in connexion with any other subject; without entering into this question generally, we may glance at that view of the effects of European intercourse upon barbarous tribes, which the evidence before the Aborigines Committee presents. An extract from the 20th page of the minutes of that evidence, published by the missionary secretaries examined by this committee, is itself a volume. In regard to the pernicious influence of the immoral conduct of Europeans upon the natives, it is said, "the evidence given under this head is of so very painful a nature as to be inadmissible in a volume intended for general perusal."

The concluding portion of the examination of D. Coates, Esq., and the Rev. Messrs. Beecham and Ellis, will show the nature of their evidence. The emphatic answers which they here return, are, be it remembered, abundantly justified by facts previously stated. For these the reader is referred to the volume which contains their evidence.

"4329. To Mr. Coates.—Is it your opinion that Europeans coming into contact with native inhabitants of our settlements, tends (with the exception of cases in which missions are established) to deteriorate the morals of the natives—to introduce European vices—to spread among them new and dangerous diseases—to accustom them to the use of ardent spirits—to the use of European arms and instruments of destruction—to the seduction of native females—to the decrease of the native population—and to prevent the spread of civilization, education, commerce, and Christianity; and that the effect of European intercourse has been, upon the whole, a calamity on heathen and savage nations?" To these inquiries, separately proposed to each of the above-named gentlemen, they returned an unhesitating, emphatic, and unqualified affirmative reply.

In this melancholy statement there is too much truth, and in the remedy which the author suggests we sincerely concur. He has not taken up a fanatical, partial, preconceived theory, resolved to sustain it at any hazard; he has stated the case of the dark men—dark indeed, with the address of a skilful writer, the knowledge of a diligent inquirer, and the familiarity of a right-minded philanthropist. Let those who sincerely contemplate the extinction of the traffic in human beings pause, before they dedicate their concentrated efforts to the punishment of the offence—neglecting totally the origin of the crime. Let them endeavour to stifle the monster, slavery, at its birth, rather than allow it to stalk abroad, and scatter wretchedness and sorrow to such excess. They should not be disheartened by the vast area which Africa occupies—the various tribes that occupy it—the different languages spoken—the numerous climes to be endured by missionaries; for *native* agents, who alone will prove serviceable, can be found competent to the glorious task. Until this is done, we but undertake to purify the water at the river's entrance to the sea, instead of ascending to the fountain, and correcting the cause of the impurity which has pervaded the whole current.

Africa (writes Mr. East) is under the dominion of the most savage despotism. Even its freemen are, in most cases, little more than the vassals of their rulers—and, in some, altogether at the disposal of their merciless tyranny. Africa is a land of slaves. Three individuals out of every four are slaves; and, in some places, not more than one in seventy are free. Africa trades, both within its own borders and with foreign nations, in the flesh and blood of its own population, and is hourly bleeding under the inflictions of this most inhuman traffic.

ART. II.—*Piety and Intellect, relatively Estimated.* By HENRY EDWARDS, Ph. D. London: Simpkin, Marshall, & Co.

The present age, notwithstanding the wide diffusion of information upon the common affairs of life, and the superiority and dominion which intellect has been able to establish, is happily less marked by the pressure of "minute philosophy," than the close of the last century. Still Mr. Edwards is a benefactor to his country and her dependencies, by cautioning them against ascribing the daily miracles of art and science to human reason solely; and, against mistaking revelations in many instances for discoveries of unaided intellect. The more learned, educated, informed, the mass of mankind, the greater the necessity to warn them against that pride which would impiously arrogate for reason, intellect, and human faculties alone, all those great discoveries in the laboratory of nature in which the civilized world almost literally revels. Our author does not, in avoiding Scylla, fall into Charybdis; he does not pass from dogmatism to scepticism; nor deal in any respect in widely-separated and contradictory extremes; he confesses boldly, and with that candour that pervades his pious and philosophic pages, that common sense is the common star by which we should steer through the arena of life, and, that to disclaim the best exercise of reason would be to abdicate that throne on which our kind is placed in the animal kingdom. But, he demonstrates with a brightness as intense as light itself, that until revelation beamed on the world, the resources of nature lay buried from the scrutinizing eye of reason only. That civilization, now spreading even amongst the luxurious, sensual Mohammedans, is the inseparable companion of Christianity;—that Christianity, its systems and institutions, never could have been known, but by the aid of revelation;—and hence, therefore, that this divine fountain of knowledge, although unseen by myriads, is contributing a large supply of the gross amount of human knowledge, discoveries, and happiness.

As a specimen of the author's powers of perspicuousness and systematic arrangement, we give the following extract, showing the inferiority of mere secular, to heavenly learning; the reader, however, is not to decide upon the meaning of the whole passage *per se*, it must be taken in conjunction with previous, as well as subsequent sections, to be distinctly understood:—

All knowledge considered apart from some definite object, application, and end, is void and useless; so that the richest heir of genius, and the most opulent man of learning, regarded solely and exclusively as active intellectual agents, only resemble a vain visionary, a dreaming man, or a mere automaton. Knowledge, then, whether regarded as literary or scientific, as scholastic or popular, as speculative, experimental, or practical, as ornamental, pleasing, or useful, must be estimated by the latter quality. In this we discover the superior excellency of heavenly wisdom, which invariably leads to and ends in the most peaceful, pleasurable, and profitable results, both in the present life and in the life to come, and thus infinitely outweighs mere secular learning, which has no such fair fruits to exhibit. There is a necessary and firmly-established connection subsisting between heavenly wisdom and real beatitude, which cannot be predicated of mere human learning. Were we sinless as angels, this connection would still exist; but as fallen beings, and as probationers for eternity, the workings, bearings, and effects of spiritual and saving wisdom, have an importance which must scorn competition with their apparent importance considered in reference to pure intelligences; for "they that be whole need not a physician, but they that are sick." How much superior then must this wisdom be, or at least appear to be, when considered in reference to secular learning. We all acknowledge that there is a vast amount of knowledge that passes through the human mind, such for instance as that possessed by children, by the vulgar, and by savages, which all truly enlightened and educated minds disregard and despise; but let us only calmly reflect, and we shall discover that the more refined mental accomplishments, and the higher branches of secular knowledge, are equally impertinent, uninteresting, and unprofitable, when contrasted with heavenly wisdom; and that the trifling and toyish knowledge possessed and prized by the illiterate and imbecile, is not more low and despicable, when compared with the higher and nobler branches of human science and learning, when contrasted with that knowledge which purifies, settles, and saves the soul.

We most heartily recommend this admirable Work not only to our numerous readers who now dwell amongst the aborigines of our colonies, and are daily employed in the blessed duty of imparting knowledge to them, but we join our wishes with those of the pious author, that men of all orders of intellect, grades in society, parties and peculiarities, may become acquainted with the irrefragable evidence here adduced, that reason without revelation is incompetent to the end at which all should aim.

ART. III.—*The Doctrine of Changes.* By the Author of "The Morning and Evening Sacrifice." London: Hamilton, Adams, & Co.

The low state of genuine literature has, for a quarter of a century past, excluded the entrance of ethics, metaphysics, and theology from all popular catalogues. Works of excitement, not of reflection, seem to engross the public wholly. If our author's theory of continual changes in all universal affairs shall happily prove applicable in literature, we then shall not despair of seeing a work embodying such deep and sound reflections adopted by parents as a fireside companion, without incurring the odium of being affected, pedantic, or unfashionable. It is one of the crying shames of English—we mean strictly, exclusively English—education, that so little can be taught by lecture, so little done by the tutor to induce, or to inculcate habits of attention or reflection. Yet in Scotland the case is far otherwise; there *vivâ voce* lectures are effective in every school; there attention is absolutely requisite; and, as reflection is the necessary offspring of that invaluable habit, the North Briton becomes, at an early age, a student in ethics, logic, political economy, and other abstract subjects, tributary in no mean degree to the formation of character, and fitting the man for the duties of social life.

The Work before us is of the ethical school, abounding in salutary views of thought upon the instability, we should rather say the mutations that keep pace with the flux of time. It is extraordinary how universal the doctrine of changes is in its application; all objects on earth are its prey; the heavens themselves afford an equally perfect illustration of its power; and, leaving material things, whose nature appears but transient, and subject to decay, if we enter on the consideration of the spiritual, intellectual, or immaterial world, we shall find the exertion of its dominion there also.

To treat of such subjects as the interesting contents of this volume, we should set no limits to our effusions; but, as circumstances have already raised strict boundaries, we must forbear. An extract or two, however, may be admitted, to illustrate the writer's application of his doctrine to both spirit and substance, or mind and matter. The following caution against rash reform, and discontent generally, may be read with advantage by modern politicians and ignorant emigrants:—

> Hence it is obvious, that changes such as human nature, or the human condition, has hitherto been subject to—unless they be considered as violent efforts of nature to shake off a previous malady—are to be regarded as things not in themselves to be desired but to be avoided, and when they have actually occurred, demanding the wisdom and caution of experienced and intelligent men, not assuredly to hasten them onward—but to modify and abate them—the tendency of the human mind in such times being obviously to rush into precipitate courses—and to move towards its purposes, with no measured or well-regulated pace—but, under the influence of passions of constantly augmenting force, and which are only increased in their energy and in the disorder which they occasion, by the multitudes who have partaken of, and communicated the common expression.
>
> It being thus made obvious that men are as subject to great deviations from the right course in their public as in their private transactions—and that in the former, as well as in the latter, they often involve themselves in augmented misery by their very attempts to improve their condition, it becomes one of the most imperious duties of moral wisdom to point out the various nature of the deviations into which men are thus apt to fall, and, as far as mere speculation can succeed, to guard their understandings, at least, against the admission of those vague or erroneous views by which such deviations are usually preceded and accompanied.

Our author's theory of material mutations is perfectly consistent with the Mosaic account of the formation of our globe, and may be read for instruction by those who are so weak as to tremble at the relation of recent geological discoveries. It is also a good specimen of his style:—

> We accordingly find, in corroboration of this idea, that it is but recently that mankind have attained any just idea either of the size and form of the world itself—of the different countries that constitute its surface—of the variety of tribes that make up the great family by which it is inhabited—or of the most remarkable of the other organised forms which also have a place among the things of this earth. Now such ignorance is surely an unequivocal symptom of a race but beginning to emerge from a state of infancy and error—just awakening to a perception of their real situation—commencing to form an acquaintance with each other and with the scenery around them—and apparently only entering upon that grand field of discovery and of knowledge, which the vast storehouse of treasures that the organized forms of the earth present, seems to offer to their research.
>
> And as the human race seems thus to have run but a small part of the course over which they are destined to proceed—and the very world which they inhabit to be but a comparatively recent production of Almighty power—in so far at least as its present form and peculiar arrangement are concerned—what idea are we naturally led to entertain respecting the boundless extent of the ages that must yet revolve before the plan of Providence respecting this world shall be concluded—and respecting those changes that must occur to diversify the almost infinite lapse of years that have been assigned to it. But vast as this anticipated range must be, there is nothing in the idea of time itself, or in the nature of the plan which is going on throughout the universe, as far as man can comprehend that plan, or in t[illegible] attributes of the Divine Being, as conceivable by man, that

can entitle us to limit that range by confines suited to the narrowness of our more usual modes of thought. On the contrary, there is scope for the fullest and most enduring career which imagination can assign as the destined portion of our world—and there thus seems to be everything in its appearances—in its relation to the vast scheme of universal nature—and in the attributes of the Being by whom its destiny has been marked out and determined, that should lead us to conclude that our world, and the race of beings by whom it is peopled, are but yet in the infancy of their existence—and that they have before them a career still to be accomplished which the understanding and fancy of man altogether fail in attempting to ascertain or to limit.

ART. IV.—*Buenos Ayres, Monte Video, and Affairs in the River Plate.* By ALFRED MALLALIEU. London: Blackwood & Sons.

With the piquant style of this very able *brochure* we have less to do than with the sterling nature of its information. While so large a portion of the civilized world is hourly closing the gates of commerce against us, does it not most seriously behove our rulers to watch narrowly, and improve judiciously, every opportunity, every open, however insignificant, through which a new channel for traffic may appear? Now, has this been done in the case which Mr. Mallalieu has so distinctly laid before the Foreign Secretary, which relates not to a trifling, but to a most promising prospect of extending trade; and we assert it boldly, that the Rio de la Plata is the principal channel in the New or Western World, through which British manufactures may hereafter hope to find their way to profitable and largely-consuming markets. Let our author himself be heard on the necessity for cultivating friendly relations with the people of the South American Republics:

Great Britain has a stake of precious import—material interests of large and ascending consequence involved—in the conversation and cultivation of good opinion and friendly alliance with the States of the New World. In most of the States of the Old World, and in one leading State of the New, the conflicts of interests, real or imaginary, bitter rivalries political or commercial, or all combined, are, as they have long been, gradually impairing the value, and circumscribing the sphere of our commercial relations. Fresh barriers of restriction or prohibition are raised against us every year, and on every side. From exclusion as competitors at home, these States have advanced, under favour of home protection, to meet and compete with us in foreign neutral markets,—even in those of Spanish and Portuguese-America amongst the rest. Conciliation, concession, corn-law abolition, customs laws' abolition, full and entire, on our part, would be now, as ever they would have been, powerless to stem this current of hostile feeling—this combination of exclusive tariffs—this concurrence of rival interests. It would require the faith, all the more implicit and enthusiastic because unreflecting, of the anti-corn law league leaders, to believe otherwise. Untaxed foreign corn might, perhaps, cheapen manufactured products at the cost of the wages of labour, and so far diminish the pressure of competition in neutral consuming countries, but it would not open one opposing market the more to British manufactures; hostile tariffs would only be surcharged the more to compensate the difference of price and ward off competition. And, after all, domestic industry has its rights everywhere, the defence and promotion of which are of the bounden interest, no less than of the obligation, of the governing power. With the Americas, west and south of the United States, we have no clash of industry or interests. There we have not to encounter rival power-looms, or self-acting mules, or steam-power in all its gigantic forms of force, still more depreciating human labour, deteriorating the standard of the human species, condemning and casting out an adult male population to the brute functions alone of propagation.* The traffic, with Spanish America at least, is one of almost simple barter.

* I beg to be understood as casting no imputation on the manufacturers. As a body, they are as commendably distinguished for humanity and all the charities of life, as they are unsurpassed for talent, energy, and the honourable industry which has enriched themselves and their country. They are themselves but the subjects of that iron necessity which Lord Brougham had in view, when he wrote that—"a nation which founds its greatness on manufactures sleeps on a volcano."

We exchange finished fabrics and wares against the raw products on which manufacturing ingenuity and industry are again expended and made reproductive.

I find, on reference to the Parliamentary returns, that the export of British and Irish produce and manufactures to the "States of the Rio de la Plata," (no separate account being kept under each head of Buenos Ayres and Monte Video), is declared for—1841, at £989,362; 1842, £969,791. These amounts are irrespective of foreign and colonial merchandise re-exported thither, value not stated. I have little doubt that these returns fall short of the real amount exported, in consequence of the custom which gains so much with merchants, of entering their ships for other parts, so as to conceal the nature and extent of their operations for the time.

The conjoint population of the Argentine federation, and the republic of the Uruguay, may be taken at about or not much in excess of one million. The consumption, therefore, of British wares, would be at the rate of £1 per head by these returns, and supposing the whole consumed in these two States. Some, although not a very considerable proportion, would, however, pass by the Parana into Paraguay. The exports of British and Irish produce and manufactures to the United States of North America, were, for 1841, £7,098,642; 1842, £3,528,807.

The average would give upwards of five millions and a quarter, or, say at the rate of 6s. 3d. per head of seventeen millions of population. I find, in the *Journal des Débats* of February 23d, last year, quoting from the returns of the Buenos Ayres Custom House, that the exports of products from that port alone, for the fourteen months running, from November 1840 to the end of December, 1841, were estimated or declared at sixty-six millions of francs, or say, in round numbers, £2,640,000 sterling: and the calculation of the imports in the same paper is carried to about the same amount, making the large total commercial movement for that State alone, of £5,280,000. The returns of value per foreign country are not given, but of 638 vessels, of 124,981 aggregate tonnage, in which the exports were shipped, 157 vessels of 37,807 total burthen were British; or not far short of one-third of the whole tonnage employed. It is more than probable that one-half, or nearly, of the imports, consisted of British wares and products. The trade is, moreover, an ascending trade; in 1837, the exports, by the custom-house returns of Buenos Ayres, were estimated at the value of 5,637,188 Spanish dollars only, or about £1,127,500 sterling; and the Board of Trade tables here render the declared values of produce and manufactures exported thither, at no more than £696,104. The commerce of Monte Video, by the latest returns received, employed:—

In 1840, Vessels inwards and outwards 1522, aggregate tonnage		270,269
Of which British.............271	do.	58,150
Total imports, value approximative	£1,125,000	
Of which from Great Britain................	440,000	
Total exports	1,380,000	
Of which British........................	373,000	
In 1837, the total imports were valued only at........	785,000	
Exports at..........................	740,000	

Here is sound reasoning, just conclusions deduced from incontrovertible facts. Here it is clearly demonstrated, that trade with Buenos Ayrean States is extremely valuable; it is also confessed on all hands that we, Britons, are groaning under taxation, which though not exactly tyranny, is scarcely tolerable, to shore up a sinking revenue; from which premises, the inference is, that we ought to have cherished, with a lover's fondness, the infant trade which arose on the broad bosom of the La Plata. That we have not done so, that we have not improved the prospect—but, on the contrary, have abused the confidence of the people; fomented their squabbles, and actually permitted the French to enter and possess themselves of the soil, and the trade, and the affections of the people. This most unfortunate result of British protection is shown most indisputably, by Mr. Mallalieu, to have followed from diplomatic incompetence, from *untoward* circumstances connected with our naval functionaries during the sanguinary conflict between the Monte Videans and Buenos Ayreans. The consummation of the bungling is to be deplored; but, at the same time, repetitions should be provided against in future. How this is to be done we have often pointed out in the pages of this

Magazine, and the reader will find the same arguments earnestly pressed upon the attention of the Secretary for Foreign Affairs, in the opening pages of the pamphlet now before us. We do not expect to find in every admiral of a fleet, a Collingwood in diplomacy, or a Nelson in decision, but we have a right to demand that delicate questions—or rather the stations where such are likely to arise—shall be entrusted to the direction of judicious, experienced, unbiassed men; or that the gallant commander shall himself be so placed in connection with the resident British consul of the ports, that no difference of sentiment between them shall in any case appear. But the system of government in other cases, in the Peninsular war, in the Affghan struggle, in the Chinese conquest, has been to give to a political agent, as speaking the language, and acquainted with the national character of the respective people, plenipotentiary authority. Had this been done in the case of Mr. Mandeville, an honourable, able, experienced servant of the crown, we should not have now to regret the protracted misery of our South American friends, and the consequent suspension of our trade with that part of the globe for upwards of five successive years.

Thrice and four times have we protested against the appointment of persons obviously, and notoriously, unqualified for positions of diplomacy, or government, in foreign countries and in our colonies, proceeding under the guidance of gentlemanly feeling to the utmost lengths in our candid exposure. Youth, corruption, stupidity, ignorance, inexperience, infirmity of body or mind, have each in turn been charged against individuals whom the chances of life, that is, personal influence with the powers that be, may have elevated to the responsible position of viceroyalty, or consular representation. But, having exceeded our just limits in noticing the startling statements of Mr. Mallalieu, we have only room for one more extract touching the qualifications of our commercial and political agents, and must refer the reader to the work itself, which will amply compensate him for trouble and time in its perusal:—

It should be worthy of deliberate verification, therefore, from whatever quarter the diplomatic and consular staff for service in Spanish America be drawn or refreshed, whether from the bureaux of Downing Street or from the general storehouse of national capacities, that the special requirements for such service be possessed for comprehending and dealing scientifically with the peculiar configurations and characteristics, morally, intellectually, industrially, or physically, of such nearly new peoples, if not new regions. Something more is wanting towards an acquaintance wi h that new world which Canning called into political existence, than historic readings and recollections of the contests of Cortes in imperial Anahuac, or the sanguinary subversion of the throne of Manco Capac by the Pizarros and Almagros. So far as practicable, or the personal *matériel* be at command, those should be selected for delegation conversant with the peculiar genius of comparatively new races, mixed of origin and qualities. For the profitable and efficient exercise of representation, it would be well that education and antecedents should be practically grounded, more or less, on personal experience, and profound study of the fitful career of countless revolutions, which in these later times have followed the first dawnings of emancipation from metropolitan thrall in the States of the New World, and of the eventful scenes and actions of memorable interest by which that emancipation was so triumphantly worked out, through the entire range of that vast World of the West extending from the Gulf of California, north, to Cape Horn, its southern extremity. Better still, if to that experience and that study of facts were joined personal acquaintanceship and appreciation of the chief characters and actors, who, at the point of the sword, or by the more subtle combinations of policy, had succeeded in carving out places among the nations of the earth for realms almost unknown, but in which the seeds of mighty empires are germinating, none the less vigorously perchance because sown amid the wild blasts of war, and their properties hardened, however their onward development retarded, by a long winter of internal distractions.

ART. V.—*Waverley Novels.* Abbotsford Edition. Vol. V. London: Houlston & Stoneman. Edinburgh: Cadell.

We encounter no little difficulty *solvendo grates dignas* to the publishers for the continuance of their splendid presents to us. Scott's labours to elevate the character of fiction, and render its admission to the family circle either profitable or safe, have precluded posthumous praise; and the magnificence with which this crowning edition is produced, renders editorial eulogies vain. Volume V. contains the whole of "The Monastery," and "The Abbot," illustrated by landscape and historic subjects, one copied after nature, and by masters of the graphic art, the other either from antique original portraits, or designs by the master-spirits of the age. From the nine beautiful engravings on steel which adorn the volume, the publishers have judiciously selected "Melrose from the Quarry," by Stanfield, for their frontispiece. It is a gem of art, displaying the sublime character of that romantic vicinity with the most unerring truth, and executed with an elaborateness and care which the greatest masters only ever seem capable of acquiring. This single subject would have been a sufficient illustration for "The Monastery," unaided by its three companions on steel, and no less than seventy-two highly-finished and pleasing woodcuts. Amongst the latter, we recognize a design by Wilkie, "Henry Wardour before the Sub-Prior," as correct, natural, and graceful as Columbus or any of his great and solemn works; and we rejoice to perceive, that Williams has not disturbed its inimitable repose in transferring it to his block. "Lochleven and its Castle," forms the frontispiece to "The Abbot;" and, although Stanfield here has got the waves to control, which he always does most happily, the scene is unequal in grandeur of effect to "Melrose from the Quarry." It is with himself, however, that we contrast him, and he is as nearly equal at all times as any painter of the age we live in. Upwards of seventy woodcuts are associated in "The Abbot" with five steel engravings, to complete the combination of talent which is devoted to honour the productions of Scott—all of considerable merit. "Roland Græme and Catharine Seton before Queen Mary," is from a sketch by Wilkie, and bears the impress of his head and hand; and there is a very agreeable view of the ruined "Hall of Old Seton," by M. A. Cadell, which is clearly and well engraved by Williams. Neither of these, however, are amongst the works of greatest attraction, but they are rich in that ability of design, excellence of drawing, and perfection of cutting, with which the volume absolutely teems.

ART. VI.—*The Young Composer, or Progressive Exercises in English Composition.* By JAMES CORNWELL. London: Simpkin, Marshall, & Co.

The repugnance which the schoolboy feels to composition arises altogether from the defective mode in which it is pretended to be taught in all our schools. Whenever we place in the hands of youth works on history, geography, or other definite branches of education, many apply themselves to the task with the most laudable industry, others with less labour and pains, but none wholly repudiate the study. Why is it then that in composition the case is so completely different? It is because the teacher does not place in the hands of the pupil a task to prepare—set systematically in a certain page of a regular class-book—but, on the contrary, throws him wholly on his own resources, to perform a duty which children of a greater growth would not be capable of performing. Disgusted by the impediments which an inconsiderate master has left in his way, the pupil despairs of success; and one out of one hundred, blessed with a genius for authorship from infancy, alone distinguishes himself and triumphs above his ill-used fellows. The pupil should be taught the rules, or some rule, for composition, before he is commanded, under a penalty, to write a theme on such bald unqualified words as on *Troy! Athens! Rome! Carthage!* &c., and, instead of leaving the youthful mind to turn the eye inward upon itself, and discover by reflection, the latest and more difficult operation, rules for guidance in the most abstruse branch of education, greater aid should be administered in this than in any other.

Mr. Cornwell has furnished an admirable primer in this description of literature, a very valuable addition to ordinary, or what should be ordinary, school-books. His process may be commenced when the pupil comprehends distinctly the different parts of speech, and is capable of analyzing a sentence. He has carefully avoided the adoption of technical terms of strange and deterring sound, employing common terms in usual meanings, so that the familiar phraseology of elementary works is made accessary to the introduction of a new but necessary branch of English education. Had we any hesitation in recommending the addition of "The Young Composer" to the regular contents of every satchel, its having rapidly reached to a sixth edition would dissipate our doubts at once.

ORIGINAL CORRESPONDENCE.

SHIP-MASTERS, SHIPS' ARTICLES, LOG-BOOKS, &c., &c.

To the Editor of the Colonial Magazine.

Since my several commentaries in reference to these matters, to which you have given publicity, a deputation of gentlemen, on the subject of remodelling the laws relating to our mercantile marine, having been favourably received at the Board of Trade, I am induced to recall attention to my late complaints and suggestions; and particularly on the present useless, incomprehensible chaotic document termed the ship's log, and to the existing form of ship's articles, equally controvertible and valueless to the owner, the interests of the ship, the discipline and character of the sailors, &c. I wish to be understood as referring more especially to the causes and effects thereof in the colonies, where the owner cannot interpose in person, and where the law has to be expounded for justice by inexperienced persons, and the agents set at defiance by parties whose objects and designs may be at variance with the truth and interests of the ship, and of the owner, who has nothing but the articles to create the slightest control on the men, who well know that pseudo-philanthropy is too often with them, and that if they can only obtain a ship here, come what come may, or do what they will, howsoever ruinous to their employer, they are sure to be better off by quitting in a colonial *port*, as I will show, and have heretofore demonstrated, more particularly in reference to salvage matters.

As it would be supererogatory to recite the many instances and ways, I will confine myself to the facts that ships' articles are not held efficiently sacred, nor sufficiently binding on the feelings, conduct, and future interests of the ship's company; neither are they generally dealt with as they should be in respect to the interests of the ship-owner, whose voyage and objects are so mainly at the mercy of the master and men he pays, feeds, &c., and whose ship and property are held *à priori* responsible to and for them.

I do not myself see why the owner in such position should not be equally a party binding the ship's articles, in which it is held that he has no power contrary to the will or caprice of the master. I refer to two cases only, of many within my knowledge, (irrespective of that above alluded to,) the one occurring in Jersey, the other in the Falkland Islands; in the first, after the ship's company was completed and the vessel ordered to sail, the owner was compelled to dismiss the master, who thereupon influenced the crew to strike, telling them that his dismissal vitiated the articles, and that they were no longer bound thereby; and they consequently adopted his advice, and the result was, that a fresh crew had to be procured, the owner losing his advances, &c. In the second, the vessel was fitted in London, the articles signed for the voyage from and back to London, specially binding the master and crew to the orders and powers of the agent in the Falklands, who, after many cautions and admonitions to the master for inebriety, neglect, and disobedience, whereby several losses and accidents to the vessel, &c., had occurred, was compelled to dismiss him from the ship, paying him nevertheless his wages; which attained, he urged the crew to strike, and to mutiny for full payment to the day, which the governor of the settlement, upon being applied to, ordered, notwithstanding that the articles specified otherwise. To this the agent was forced to submit, when the crew quitted, and refused to rejoin unless at colonial wages, and on their own terms; in this view of the case the governor concurred, alleging that the agent had not the right to enforce the articles after he had dismissed the master, and without much difficulty and insult from whom could the agent obtain the log-book, &c.

Now for the consequences: no seamen were to be obtained on the island, where the government was hiring all hands for shore-work, at wages varying from £60 to £80 per annum, with rations, &c., and of which several of the men availed themselves; and only by the agent shipping landsmen in his own employ, could he recomplete the vessel's crew.

By directing attention to these points of embarrassment to the owners and agents, and of disregard to mutual interests and discipline, the parties who have now associated, for the purpose of approximating our mercantile marine to that of our navy, will not of course object, in the highly important national objects they have in hand, to receive for their consideration any remarks made with the intentions instigating G. T. W.

COLONIAL INTELLIGENCE.

India.—The India mail of the 1st of March communicates some events of considerable importance. The great result of the late victories near Gwalior has been the tranquillization of India. Gwalior has been settled—a new treaty has been formed—the young sovereign has been placed on the throne—a contingent has been raised, and placed under the care of British officers—the old unruly troops of Scindiah have been disbanded.

The cause of the dissatisfied spirit exhibited by these soldiers has arisen from their unwillingness to go to Scinde, which is said by them to be a foreign country, and where an extraordinary sickness prevailed, which obliged them to provide for their families at home, instead of taking them in their company; and, as they cannot do so without extra allowances, which are not granted, they have in some regiments positively declared that they will not go to that sickly country. In the Madras regiments that were ordered to Scinde, similar feelings were found to prevail.

The Bombay troops, to whose bravery the conquest of Scinde is mainly owing, have not, notwithstanding their sufferings in the campaigns, and during the lately sickly season, shown the smallest unwillingness to go to Scinde; on the contrary, one of their regiments actually volunteered to go thither.

The great point of interest to the Indian politician is Lahore, where every prospect exists of another revolution breaking out in the course of a few months.

The news from the Affghan countries was, that Yar Mahomed had expelled the Suddozies, or sons of Schah Kamram, from Herat, that he had declared himself the ruler, and that under the protection of Persia, he was endeavouring to form an intimate junction between himself, the Sirdars of Candahar, and Dost Mahomed of Cabul, to whose notorious son Akhbar he had offered his daughter in marriage; the offer was accepted, and a sort of confederacy had been formed. The hatred between the Affghans of Cabul and the Sikhs is likely to produce a quarrel; for the former desire ardently to obtain Peshawur, and all the districts to the west of the Indus.

In Scinde there was no disturbance, for Sir Charles Napier continues to keep up the army of occupation to 15,000 men. The sickness is described as diminishing, and the prejudice against the occupation had abated, though the dissatisfaction of the Bengal and Madras soldiery on being ordered there was still very great. Sir Charles Napier continued in good health.

The settlement of the Mahratta Government at Gwalior appears to be complete; the soldiers who formerly served the Government, on being disbanded, immediately joined the contingent. Their Government has paid about a quarter of a million for the expenses of the late war, and ceded certain possessions lying between their territories and Bundelkund, which will have the effect of obliging the refractory chiefs in those districts to submit to the terms proposed by the Supreme Government. Arrangements were made to compensate the Ryots for any injury done to their crops and fields by the march of the British troops. This was a most unusual proceeding in that country, and had given great satisfaction; and the inhabitants, in expectation of a better rule hereafter, were highly pleased with the moderation of their British conquerors.

The important state called the Nizam's dominions is also growing every day more debilitated. The Nizam had amassed great wealth while his government was managed by Chundoo Lull, but his troops were not paid.

The outcry against Lord Ellenborough has in a great measure subsided. His Lordship was expected to arrive in Calcutta about the end of February. The only place within the confines of India which was likely for some months to occupy his Lordship's attention is Munipoor, a petty state near the Birman frontiers, where a petty revolution has taken place, in consequence of family disputes. Birmah was not disposed to enter into the dispute, which must be soon settled.

Lieutenant-Colonel Outram, who lately proceeded to India, has been appointed Political Resident at Nemaur, in Candeish.

Mr. Anderson, who two years ago governed the Presidency of Bombay, having relinquished his situation as member of the Council there, the Hon. L. R. Reid was sworn in a member on the 1st of March. Mr. Anderson left Bombay on that day to return to Europe.

One of the late objects of curiosity in Bombay was the Archbishop of Goa, who arrived there in January last, and who, in conformity with the treaties and conventions with Portugal, exercised his jurisdiction as the supreme ecclesiastic. There are three or four Italian friars there, who pretend to have a mission from the Pope, and who cause great confusion. The native Christians have petitioned for their removal by the Government, as being religious nuisances. Their great want is a British Roman Catholic Bishop, which is likely to be obtained as soon as these Italians withdraw, as there is an Irish Bishop, whom all are disposed to obey, when proper arrangements are made with the Archbishop.

Thus the British empire in the East may be described as in repose, for the trifling disputes about certain additional pay (batta) that exists in certain regiments, will produce no bad results, as an explanation with the Bengal and Madras Sepoys, and an augmentation of the Bombay army, will remove all the difficulties. It is possible that an attempt may be made to exaggerate the disaffection of the troops, as if productive of serious consequences; but these exaggerations deserve no credit whatever.

Bombay.—The continued existence of the causes as accounting for the dulness of trade, combined with the partial interruption of business occasioned at this season by the preparations of the natives for the celebration of the Hoolee Festival, has rendered the present month one of great inactivity in a commercial point of view. The inquiry for nearly all descriptions of imports has been extremely limited, and the sales, as will be perceived, are comparatively few and unimportant. The prices of copper exhibit scarcely any change. There have been no sales of spelter, and we retain last month's quotations for this article. Tin plates are in some request, and command rather higher rates.

Of the cotton manufactures, in which business has been done during the past month, low qualities of gray and bleached jaconets and gray Madapollams, appear to have been most in request, while for muslin, fancy cambrics, and Turkey red goods, there has also been a fair inquiry, and the whole of these, with the exception of the latter, the prices of which, notwithstanding the demand, have slightly given way, have fully maintained the rates current last month. There has been no improvement in gray longcloths, and bleached have declined 1a. to 2a. per piece; gray sheetings and domestics also continue greatly depressed. There have been few transactions in prints, but prices are without change. Zebras are still neglected, and unsaleable, save at rates that must leave a ruinous loss to shippers. The sales of yarns have been very limited, and few alterations in prices have taken place.

Money continues extremely plentiful, but does not appear to induce speculative operations. Bombay Bank Shares are at 42 to 43 per cent. premium, and those of the Bank of Western India at 28 to 30 per cent. Sovereigns each, 11r. to 11r. 3a.; Bank-notes per pound, 10r. 8a. to 11r.

China.—The accounts from China are down to the 24th of December, but there is scarcely anything worth noticing. Business in Canton had, however, considerably improved; but in the article of opium, both at Canton and other places, hardly any sales had been effected, but at considerable loss to the holders. The ratification of the supplementary treaty had been received from the emperor, and Captain Brooke, of the 55th regiment, was on his way with it, and other despatches for the home government.

New South Wales.—Advices from Sydney to the 3d of December have been received; and these accounts, alluding to the depression of late reigning in the colony, speak in terms justifying the expectation that a reaction will before long take place, since, through the medium of the Insolvent Court, the "adjusting process," as it is termed, is rapidly at work. To prove that the colony is neither ruined nor impoverished, figures are given, showing that its natural wealth, its live stock, its agricultural improvements, its buildings, and its capital, are much more abundant. Ten years ago it is stated that the number of acres under crop was 60,520, while last year they were 115,660. 15 years ago its sheep were 536,000, they are now estimated at 6,000,000. Seven years ago, when in its most palmy state, its coin was £420,720, last year £475,390; and in 1832, its exports amounted in official value to £384,344, while in 1842 they had risen to £1,067,411. The increase of population during this period is very fairly allowed and included in these estimates, and therefore no objection can be raised to the statement on that head; but it is nevertheless much to be doubted whether the temptation held out for emigrants to go and purchase at present prices is in reality so alluring as the notion evidently intended to be conveyed. An idea, however, may be formed of the sacrifice experienced in the realization of property under the present state of affairs, when it is asserted that land valued by the act of Parliament at a *minimum* of 20s. per acre, may be bought at a tenth or a twentieth of that price; fat cattle from 7s. to 20s. per head; horses, from £1 to £3; sheep, from 18d. to 2s.; and property of every other description at a corresponding discount.

These papers also notice the arrival of Captain Fitzroy, the Governor of New Zealand, in the ship Bangalore, on his way to Auckland. The report of the Thomas Lord, arrived there from New

Zealand, was highly favourable, and spoke of the success of the southern fisheries at New Zealand.

Papers from Hobart Town to the end of November, from Port Phillip to the 18th of November, and from Mauritius to the 30th of December, have also been received, but none of them contain interesting intelligence. The Hobart Town and Port Phillip advices notice some slight improvement in trade. The hope is expressed that with the reduction of interest and the progress of the wool season, an improvement in the general affairs of the colony will take place. The clip is expected to be abundant, and superior in quality, while already in a few cases 10d. per lb. had been obtained for good samples. Freight might range from 1¼ to 1¾ per lb. From Melbourne we learn that the fly had appeared in the potato grounds, and great damage was feared would result from their ravages. The Mauritius papers afford not the least news, being filled with extracts from the English journals just then arrived out.

Cape of Good Hope.—Papers to the 28th of February have come to hand to-day, which state that the product of the fisheries of the colony was increasing. A shipment had been recently made to the coast of South America, which it was hoped would be shortly followed by others. The banks of the Agulhas are found to be the most profitable source, and the idea is cherished that in time a barter trade between the Brazils and the Cape may be established through this medium. As yet the Mauritius has been found the best market for the article. To show that there is a steady increase in the trade, the value of the fish exported last year was £8,011, while in 1835 it only amounted to £495. The latest advices from Natal represent affairs there as proceeding quietly, and much is said in favour of the soil and its fitness for an extensive cultivation of cotton and tobacco. The singular fact is noticed in the Cape papers, of the receipt of later intelligence from England *via* Bombay than by the direct route. These papers give the particulars of revenue for the quarter ending the 5th of January. According to this table, it appears that the total value of imports entered at Table and Simon's Bays amounted to £169,996. 2s. 8d., while those entered at Port Elizabeth amounted to £40,943, making a gross return of £210,939. 2s. 8d. The items of export showed Table and Simon's Bays as contributing £56,935, and Port Elizabeth, £23,713, making a total of £80,648. The vast difference between these two returns, the imports so far exceeding exports, is accounted for by the fact of the Cape being a commissariat port, and in a considerable degree supported by the expenditure of troops, &c. Among the exports, wine figures for £14,717, and wool for £11,000.

An official statement, appearing in the frontier papers, of the losses of certain farmers resident in the eastern division of Albany, by Caffer depredations, since 1837, given under their own signatures, shews that the losses of horses, during that period of six years, are ascertained to be 441; of oxen, 736; and of cows, 347 (sheep and goats, which have been stolen, and must amount to a very great number, being omitted). Now, if we calculate the average value of horses at £10 each, we will find the value of horses stolen by the Caffers in six years—in only a part of a single district of this colony—to amount to £4,410, or 176,400 Cape Guilders; of oxen, at £4 each, to amount to £2,944, or 117,760 Cape Guilders; and of cows, at £2 each, to amount to £694, or 27,760 Cape Guilders, making the whole loss sustained during the above period to amount to £8,048, or 321,920 Cape Guilders.

West Indies.—The mails from the West Indies have arrived, and the papers reach to the 10th of March from Jamaica, and from the other islands to a corresponding date. The House of Assembly at Jamaica had closed, after a tedious sitting of three months, with an address from the Governor, the Earl of Elgin. The labours of the session appear to have included the passage of a bill for the purpose of obtaining a census of the colony, the appointment of commissioners to inquire into the island charities, the establishment of industrial schools, the erection of a lunatic asylum, grants of money to the sufferers by the fire at Kingston, and aid in encouragement of emigration. These matters are pointedly alluded to in the Governor's speech in terms of satisfaction. Stock is represented as suffering much from the want both of food and water; and some parts of St. Thomas's in the East and St. George's, with the opposite extremity of the island in Westmoreland, form almost the only exceptions to this prevailing calamity. No favourable change in commercial business is stated to have taken place. Sugar ranged from 20s. to 28s. 3d. for 100lb.; coffee, 50s. 7d. to 76s. per 100lb.; and rum, good descriptions of proof 21, at 4s. to 4s. 1d. There is no news in the other papers worth extract. Business was dull at Demerara and Barbadoes, and a scarcity of provisions is complained of in the former island.

Canada.—There is not any news of importance from Canada. On the 21st of Feb., the church of St. Paul in the western province was accidentally destroyed by fire. Its cost was £1,600, and raised by the English and Irish settlers.

We quote the following favourable notice from the *Montreal Herald*:—"We stated some time ago, that the hopes of good wheat crops were again giving life to the farmers in Lower Canada, and we are happy to say, that a great breadth of wheat land will be laid down next spring. The success of last year in different parts of the province has given them courage. We also observe by the Upper Canada papers, and the fact is confirmed by private intelligence, that great quantities of wheat are now stored in the lake towns, ready for shipment to Montreal. Last year, we trust, will turn out to be the first of a revival of the good old times, when Lower Canada, as well as Upper Canada, 'waved with yellow grain.' But bad as the times have been, we are not aware that any farmer in Lower Canada has ever considered ten bushels per acre a very good crop, 'and five not a bad one.' Our contemporary of the *Gazette* has fallen into a great mistake in making such an assertion, probably in consequence of the writer having but little experience in the country."

The Ionian Islands.—The opening of the fourth session of the seventh Parliament of these States took place on the 4th of March. His Excellency the Lord High Commissioner delivered on this occasion a long speech, in which he called the Assembly's attention to the necessity of seriously providing for the progressive improvement of the laws and legal institutions, confining himself to the laying before them a report, framed by some eminent lawyers, calculated to prevent protracted litigation, which might arise from intermediate jurisdiction. He recommended to the Assembly the acts adopted by the executive power with respect to the judicial district sessions. He announced that the regulations sanctioned by the Assembly for the separation of the municipal accounts from the general revenue and expenditure, and the law in force for the construction of roads, to accelerate agricultural improvement, will be brought before them for approval. He said that such a financial division would facilitate the extension of professorships and faculties in the University, and the project for improving the primary schools; and concluded by saying that the expenditure still exceeded the revenue, which he attributed to the reduced prices of the staple products, but hoped that financial alterations would enable him to meet the expenditure of the present year, and to complete the works now carrying on. The President made the following reply:—That the Legislative Assembly would take into consideration the important points wisely developed by the Lord High Commissioner — that it would conscientiously second in the most effectual manner every measure tending to improve the condition of the people it represents; and concluded with inviting his Excellency to honour the assembly with his presence, and thus give an opportunity of publicly expressing its sentiments.—*Government Gazette*.

The French Tariff.—The *Journal des Débats* states, that the Customs Bill introduced into the Chamber of Deputies by the Minister of Commerce, is composed of an aggravation of tariffs, with the exception of articles of hempen and linen cloth and thread, which are to continue to pay the same duties as at present, and an alteration made in the manner of collecting the duty on cattle entering France from Piedmont, which is to be collected hereafter by weight, instead of by the head. The duty on machinery of all kinds is to be raised. The duty on foreign produce imported into Algeria is to be raised, in violation of one of the best established principles of public administration, that countries which are growing into civilization have need to receive at the lowest possible price all the materials of labour. In fine, a war has been waged against two articles which have presented themselves at our ports in great quantities —hogslard from the United States, which our soap-boilers employ in large quantities; and seeds producing oil, which come from the Levant, to the great benefit of the soap manufacturers of Marseilles, for whom the oil of sesamé is a corrective for olive oil, and from which agriculturists derive the greater quantity of the oil cake used in the fattening of cattle, and in manuring land. The public in general found their advantage in the importation of this seed, as the oil of sesamé cold-drawn, is good for domestic use. In fine, the French navy, for whose interests the French Government is so j s solicitous, found in the transport of oil-seeds an unexpected occupation. In 1834, the oil-seeds of every description imported into Marseilles represented 1,306,000 kilogrammes, equal to the freight of seven or eight ships. In 1842, Marseilles imported 36,700,000 kilogrammes, which would supply freight for 200 ships. This was a fortunate chance, which is now about to be sacrificed by the imposition of an increased duty of 100 per cent. The 40 magnificent oil-mills, which were established at Marseilles, are menaced with destruction, and the 55,000 acres, which were supplied with oil-cake for manure, must remain uncultivated. And this is called protection. But such are the inconsistencies to which the Government exposes itself when it listens to the complaints of the partizans of prohibition.

Civil Contingencies.—An account of the sums expended under the head of "Civil Contingencies" in the year 1843, and an estimate of the amount required for the year 1844, have just been issued from the Treasury Chambers at Whitehall. It appears that the gross total amount of money disbursed in 1843 was £116,405, exhibiting a decrease, compared with the expenditure in 1841, of £13,730; and an increase, compared with 1842, of £1,023; the amounts in the two last-mentioned years having been respectively £130,135 and 115,382. These disbursements include the extraordinary expenses of the Ministers at foreign Courts; special missions, foreign and colonial; outfit and equipage of the Ministers at foreign Courts; the expenses of entertaining and conveying persons of distinction, such as ambassadors, governors, &c; the expenses defrayed by officers of the household (not being part of the civil list); and various public services. The expenditure in Ireland amounted to £2,791, which is included in the above-stated sum of £116,405. The estimate of the amount that may probably be required to defray the expenses under the head of "Civil Contingencies," for the year ending the March 31, 1845, gives a sum of £100,000.

Bank of England Notes.—A return of an account of notes of the Bank of England in circulation, the amount of deposits and securities, and amount of bullion in the Bank at the close of business, in every week, from the 7th of July, 1840, to the 2nd of March, 1844, has just made its appearance. It is a pity that the framers of this return have neglected to append an annual general abstract, by which the reader might be enabled, at a glance, to make himself acquainted with the policy of the Bank in regard to their assets and liabilities. Taking only the present year—for it would require considerable time and labour in order to afford a summary of the whole period—we find, that on the 6th of January, 1844, the bank-notes in circulation amounted to £19,528,000 (including those issued by the branches), and that at the same time bullion to the amount of £15,271,000 was lying in the Bank vaults; on the 13th of January the bank-notes in circulation amounted to £21,268,000, and the bullion to £15,299,000; on the 20th of January the bank-notes in circulation amounted to £21,954,000, and the bullion to £15,376,000; on the 27th of January, the bank-notes to £22,030,000, and the bullion to £15,555,000; on the 3rd of February, the bank-notes to £22,061,000, the bullion to £15,692,000; on the 10th of Feb., the bank-notes to £21,791,000, and the bullion to £15,803,000; on the 17th of February, the bank-notes to £21,578,000, the bullion to £15,974,000; on the 24th of February, the bank-notes to £21,307,000, and the bullion to £16,107,000; and on the 2nd of March instant, the amount of bank-notes in circulation was altogether £21,206,000, and the bullion in the coffers of the establishment, £16,162,000. It appears from a second return (moved for by Mr. C. Wood, M.P.), that the total number of country bankers who act with Bank of England notes exclusively, amounts to 43 (2 being in the metropolis, 7 at Liverpool, 7 at Newcastle, 7 at Portsmouth, 5 at Birmingham, and 4 at Manchester), and the total amount of their credit £2,429,000. The rate of discount charged to the country bankers who have fixed amounts is stated at £3 per cent. per ann.

Sugar.—The Secretary of the Treasury, Sir G. Clerk, Bart., has laid upon the table of the House of Commons a paper containing a statement of the total quantity of sugar entered for home consumption in the United Kingdom, and also of the quantity of British refined sugar exported on drawback, in each year from 1830 to 1843 inclusive. It appears from this return, that the net quantity of sugar actually retained for home consumption was, in 1830, 4,057,224 cwt.; in 1831, 4,076,251 cwt.; in 1832, 3,879,808 cwt.; in 1833, 3,766,405 cwt.; in 1834, 3,928,556 cwt.; in 1835, 4,022,841 cwt.; in 1836, 3,593,137 cwt.; in 1837, 4,048,663 cwt.; in 1838, 4,021,240 cwt.; in 1839, 3,830,390 cwt.; in 1840, 3,595,407 cwt.; in 1841, 4,057,879 cwt.; in 1842, 3,868,437 cwt.; and in 1843, 4,036,991 cwt. We may, therefore, state the average annual quantity in the United Kingdom, of this important necessary of life to be, in round numbers, about 4,000,000 cwt, The statement of the quantity of British refined sugar exported on drawback during the same period exhibits very unequal results. For instance, whereas as much as 320,846 cwt. of double refined sugar was exported from the United Kingdom in 1834, and as much as 260,096 cwt. in 1838, only 94 cwt. were so exported in 1843. The same with single refined sugar, of which 33,237 cwt. were exported in 1833, 52,510 cwt. in 1835, and only 61 cwt. in 1843. The total quantity of such sugar exported in 1838 amounted to 266,703 cwt.; whereas in 1843 only 155 cwt. were exported.

Commands in Chief.—The following commanders in chief will be relieved in the course of the present year, as their periods of service will have expired:—Of the Pacific station, Rear-Admiral Thomas, appointed 5th May, 1841; of the West India and North America station, Vice-Admiral Sir C. Adam, K.C.B., appointed 17th August, 1841; of the Mediterranean, Vice-Admiral Sir E. W.

C. R. Owen, K.C.B., G.C.H., appointed 14th October, 1841; and of the Brazils and Cape of Good Hope station, Rear-Admiral the Hon. Josceline Percy, C.B., appointed 17th December, 1841. Vice-Admiral Sir W. Parker, K.C.B., of the East India Station, appointed 12th May, 1841, is already succeeded in the command-in-chief by Rear-Admiral Sir T. Cochrane, K.C.B., who was second in command in the East Indies; Captain Chads, of the Cambrian, hoisting a commodore's broad pendant, as second in command to Sir T. Cochrane. The admirals and captains, superintendents of the dockyards, with the exception of Portsmouth and Malta, were appointed in 1841, but hold their commissions for five years.

The Cost of the Poor.—From returns just prepared for Parliament, respecting the amount expended for the relief and maintenance of the poor, &c., it appears that there are 590 unions in England and Wales, of which the population was 13,993,967. The average annual expenditure for the relief of the poor, three years prior to the union, was £5,608,934. In 1841, the expenditure was £4,288,520; in 1842, £4,438,660; and in 1843, £4,679,495. Under this head of expenditure are included the costs of maintenance, out-door relief, establishment charges with salaries, workhouse and emigration loans repaid, and other purposes immediately connected with the relief of the poor. The number of in-door and out-door paupers relieved in 1841, in England and Wales, was 1,116,523; in 1842, 1,235,437; and in 1843, 1,333,247. The number of illegitimate children (in-door and out-door) relieved during the quarters ending Lady-day, 1841, was 29,123; in 1842, 29,357; and in 1843, 29,699. Thus the proportion of illegitimate children, in 1843, to every 1,000 of the total number of paupers relieved in that year, was 22.3; and the proportion of illegitimate children in the same to every 1,000 of the population was 2.1. This return is exclusive of places not united under the Poor Law Amendment Act. The above will show that the expenditure has been yearly increasing at the rate of about £6,000 or £6,500, and the number of paupers from 100,000, to 120,000, while the number of illegitimate children increases annually at the ratio of 300.

Trade in Dublin.—The first quarter of the present financial year having arrived at maturity, the accounts present for this port an increase of £20,804 in the customs' receipts, and nearly 1,400 in the number of documents passed for warehouse goods over the corresponding quarter of last year. The sums received for the several quarters being, 1843, £218,162; 1844, £238,966. The month of March in this year has not produced any of the above increase; but, on the contrary, the receipts have diminished during it, as compared with the same time of 1843, some £440; March, 1843, giving £81,047 against £80,407 received in the month just ended. In the year, and also in the quarter, up to the 31st of March, a great diminution has taken place in the quantity of leaf tobacco relieved from the custody of the warehouses by payment of duty, the quantity released from April, 1842, to April, 1843, being 1,695,709lb.; from April, 1843, to 31st of March, 1844, 1,594,879lb., or a deficiency of 90,812lb. against the last year. For the quarters ended the same time the decrease is more obvious, being 37,230lb., equal to a duty of £5,864—the quantities relieved in the first three months of 1843 being 435,817lb.; in 1844, 399,587lb. The relative stocks in the bonded warehouse, on the 31st of March, 1843, and 31st of March, 1844, were for the former, 575,073lb.; for the latter, 397,139lb. The increased consumption of tea, sugar, and coffee is steadily progressing, and gives true indication of the confirmed good habits of the people, and of the happy effects of sobriety.

The Revenue.—The quarterly and yearly revenue tables are made up to the 5th of April. The increase in the quarter is—Customs, £384,910; Excise, £85,316; Stamps, £45,885; Taxes, £1,987; Property Tax, £107,627; Post-office, £30,000; Crown Lands, £30,000; making a total increase in the ordinary revenue for the quarter of £685,725. There is a decrease under the head "Miscellaneous" of £500,264, which, though balanced against them in the account, scarcely affects the sources of revenue derived from the industry of the people. The total increase in the quarter, both of ordinary and extraordinary revenue, is £825,298, from which, deducting the decrease, there is a sum of £325,034 more than in the corresponding quarter of 1843, to be applied to the service of the State. In the year there is a decrease on the amount of Stamps of £12,699, and in the amount of Taxes of £73,064, but on all the other branches of the ordinary revenue there is a considerable increase. The total increase, deducting the decrease of the revenue for the year, is £4,318,167, which is, however, less than the amount of the Property-tax, £5,356,887, by £1,038,720.

Lord Ellenborough.—The Court of Directors of the East India Company have recalled Lord Ellenborough from the Governor-Generalship of India.

New Zealand.—On the motion of Mr. Aglionby in the House of Commons, on the 27th April, a committee was appointed to inquire into the New Zealand tenure of land question.

NEW SOUTH WALES.

Abstract of the Estimated Expenditure of the Colonial Government for the Year 1844.

		£.	s.	d.
1.	Civil and Legislative Establishments	51,013	9	6
2.	Surveyor-General's Department	15,000	0	0
3.	Department of Public Works and Buildings	58,091	12	5
4.	Church Establishments	6,022	10	0
5.	School Establishments	14,050	12	0
6.	Medical Establishments	5,270	13	0
7.	Pensions	0	0	0
8.	Establishments for the Administration of Justice	10,517	14	6
9.	Police Establishments	60,549	3	0
10.	Gaol Establishments	11,185	3	0
11.	Miscellaneous Services	17,843	4	0
		250,343	1	5
	Proposed Expenditure under the Act of the Imperial Parliament, 5 and 6 Victoria, cap. 76	80,150	0	0
	Total Amount	£330,493	1	5

Statement of Proposed Expenditure under the Act of the Imperial Parliament 5th & 6th of Victoria, cap. 76.

For the services detailed in Schedule A.		£33,000
For the services detailed in Shedule B.:—		
Colonial Secretary	£6,486 13 6	
Colonial Treasurer	4,629 9 6	
Auditor-General	2,994 0 6	
Stationery for these Departments	600 0 0	
Additional clerical assistance, and to meet other unforseen expenses	289 16 6	
		15,000
Salary of Clerk, and miscellaneous expenses of Executive Council		600
Pensions		1,550
Public Worship, Schedule C.		30,000
Total Amount		£80,150

Colonial Secretary's Office,
Sydney, 1st August, 1843.

E. Deas Thompson,
Colonial Secretary.

Ways and Means, 1844.—Estimated Statement of the Ways and Means required to meet the Expenditure of the Year 1844, exclusively of that chargeable on the Revenue arising from Crown-Lands.

Head of Revenue.	Sydney.	Port Phillip.	Total.
Duties on Spirits	£100,800	£29,800	£130,600
Duties on Tobacco	41,500	9,400	50,900
Ad valorem duty on Foreign Goods imported	25,200	3,350	28,550
Miscellaneous	4,500	2,770	7,270
Post-office	18,000	3,000	21,000
Duties on Colonial Spirits	10,000	....	10,000
Publicans' Licences	17,000	3,000	20,000
Auction Duties	8,000	2,150	10,150
Tolls and Ferries	5,000	100	5,100
Fees and Fines of Public Offices	28,110	8,660	36,770
Collections by the Agent for the Clergy and School Estates	4,000	....	4,000
Interest on Public Moneys	1,500	500	2,000
Assessment on Stock, and Fees and Fines collected by Commissioners of Crown-lands	16,000	10,000	26,000
Quit-rents and Redemption of Quit-rents	25,000	...	25,000
Depasturing and other Crown-land Licences	10,000	9,660	19,660
Miscellaneous Receipts	2,000	1,000	3,000
	315,610	83,390	
Total			400,000
Gross Revenue for 1844, including Special Receipts—Sydney			351,435
" " Port Phillip			87,295
			£428,731

The collector of customs estimates the revanue under his collection at 190,000*l.*, but it is included in the foregoing estimate at the amount realized in 1842, or 172,000*l.*—making a difference of 18,000*l.*—The estimate of the revenue of Port Phillip, forwarded by his Honour Mr. La Trobe, has been adopted, being considered fair.—The other items are estimated on a reference to the revenue of 1842, and the half-year ended 30th June, 1843.

Compendious View of the Population, Agriculture, Trade, Commerce, Wealth, and Taxation of New South Wales (including the District of Port Phillip), during a course of Twenty-One Years, from 1822 to 1842, inclusive.

YEARS.	Population.	Acres under Cultivation.	Exports.	Imports.	Shipping Outwards.		Shipping Inwards.		Vessels Built.		Vessels Registered.		Value of Oil Exported.	Value of Timber Exported.	Value of Grain Exported.	Wool Exported.		Auction Duty.		Value of Land Sales.	Coin.	Ordinary Revenue.
					Number.	Tonnage.	Number.	Tonnage.	Number.	Tonnage.	Number.	Tonnage.				Quantity.	Value.	Sales.	Duty.			
			£	£									£	£	£	lbs.	£	£	£	£	£	£
1822	..	...	......	......	...	..	...	...	3	163	3	163	...	...	...	172880	...	...	...	...	...	40265
1823	...	...	......	......	...	...	...	...	3	182	3	182	...	...	...	189240	...	...	...	...	...	28388
1824	...	...	......	......	...	...	...	...	5	157	5	157	...	...	...	275560	...	21879	328	279	...	49191
1825	...	...	......	......	...	...	...	...	2	119	2	119	...	...	...	411604	...	37010	555	5548	...	65733
1826	...	...	106600	360000	60	17020	62	17178	12	654	19	1634	...	...	...	552960	48384	38423	567	2596	...	69478
1827	...	...	70314	362324	63	14501	103	26508	9	434	19	1732	...	...	...	407116	24306	45529	682	2274	...	75495
1828	...	...	90050	570000	69	24186	137	32559	6	162	13	478	26431	11428	54823	834343	40851	88368	1325	5004	...	91306
1829	...	...	161716	601004	168	37586	158	37342	7	462	5	428	54975	16293	42640	1005333	63555	81890	1228	2710	...	99478
1830	...	...	159459	420480	147	28822	157	31225	3	78	25	1777	59471	5218	23344	799750	34907	94927	1423	943	...	102743
1831	...	...	324168	490152	165	35252	155	34000	5	112	38	3224	95969	8401	27691	1401284	75979	90224	1353	2597	...	117447
1832	...	...	384344	604620	194	42857	189	41350	5	220	21	2143	147409	6132	13365	1515156	73559	94386	1415	12509	...	122163
1833	60794	60520	394801	713972	213	49702	210	50164	6	393	29	2655	146855	13153	14211	1734203	103692	102675	1540	24956	...	138469
1834	66212	74811	587640	991990	220	53373	245	58532	9	376	19	1852	157334	7941	15850	2246933	213628	155156	2327	41844	...	161960
1835	71592	79256	682193	1114805	269	66964	260	63019	7	303	21	2267	180349	10489	72920	3893927	299587	209353	3135	80784	...	184208
1836	77096	87432	748624	1237406	264	62834	269	65415	9	301	39	4560	840220	14611	146149	3693241	369324	313171	4697	126458	420720	193451
1837	85267	92125	760054	1297491	402	78020	400	80114	17	760	36	3602	183122	14463	61006	4448796	333166	321346	4820	120427	427432	226900
1838	97912	92912	802768	1579277	409	93004	428	91777	20	808	41	6229	197644	6382	64313	5749376	405977	409166	6137	116324	520127	202520
1839	114386	95312	948776	2236371	548	124776	563	135474	12	773	79	10862	172315	8815	285110	7213584	442504	513388	7700	152962	516069	244777
1840	129463	126116	1399692	3014189	665	163704	709	178958	18	1207	98	12426	224144	20971	217063	8610775	566112	1246742	18701	316626	397581	311748
1841	149669	115130	1023397	2527988	690	172118	714	183778	35	2074	100	11250	127470	7604	201632	8390449	517537	963696	14455	90387	462624	403592
1842	159889	115660	1067411	1455059	633	134970	628	143921	26	1357	89	9948	77012	5800	113070	9428036	595175	686088	10291	14574	475389	414156

OBITUARY.

Abinger, the Right Hon. James Scarlett, baron Abinger, chief baron of Her Majesty's Court of Exchequer, and a privy councillor, April 7th, at Bury St. Edmunds, aged 76 years. He was the descendant of a family which settled in Jamaica as long ago as the first establishment of the colony. At an early period of life he came to England, and after being for a short time at a public school, he was a fellow-commoner of Trinity College, Cambridge. He was called to the bar in 1791, and on the 22d of August, 1792, he married the third daughter of Mr. Campbell, of Kilmorey, in Argyleshire, by whom he had three sons and two daughters. In 1816, Mr. Scarlett was called within the bar, and vested with a silk gown. In 1820, he entered the House of Commons as member for Peterborough. In 1827, during the Canning administration, he was attorney-general, and received the honour of knighthood. In the Peel and Wellington ministry of 1834, Lord Lyndhurst removing from the Court of Exchequer to the Chancery, Sir James Scarlett was appointed chief baron, and at the same time was called to the House of Peers by the title of Baron Abinger. His first wife died in the year 1829, and after remaining a widower fourteen years, he married, in 1843, the daughter of the late Lee Steere Steere, Esq., of Jayes, in Surrey. He was for many years attorney-general for the county palatine of Lancaster. He is succeeded in his title and estates by his eldest son, Robert Campbell Scarlett, who was born, Sept. 5th, 1794.

Alock, Captain Chambré Brabazon Ponsonby, of the Bengal Engineers, April 5th, at Bath.

Bell, General Robert, of the Hon. East India Company's service, March 26th, at London, in his 86th year.

Browne, Colonel John Frederick, C.B., March 25th, at Langharne, Carmarthenshire, South Wales, in the 77th year of his age. The deceased colonel had seen considerable service during a period of upwards of 60 years. He served in Flanders during the campaigns of 1793-4, and 95, and ably distinguished himself at the siege of Nimeguen, and the sanguinary sortie thence. In 1796, he assisted at the reduction of St. Lucia, and rendered considerable service throughout the campaign of 1801 in Egypt, especially in the actions of the 8th, 13th, and 21st of March. In 1805, he accompanied the expedition to Hanover, and in 1807 went on active service to Zealand. In the following year he went with the expedition to Sweden, and the next year took part in the Walcheren expedition. Subsequently he was required for the operations in the Peninsula, and he gained considerable distinction at Barrosa, under Lord Lynedoch, commanding there the 28th Regiment. For his gallantry there he received a medal. His commissions were dated as follows:—Ensign, Sept. 15th, 1781; lieutenant, Jan. 31st, 1788; captain, Sept. 24th, 1795; major, July 9th, 1803; lieutenant-colonel, July 25th, 1810; and colonel, August 12th, 1819.

Brown, John George, Esq, Lieutenant 6th Regiment Madras Native Infantry, eldest son of the late Archibald Brown, Esq., of Glasgow, April 6th, at Hastings.

Chetham, Margaret Kezia, wife of Rear-Admiral Sir E. Chetham, April 11th, at Forton Lodge, Hants.

Denton, Captain Charles, of the Hon. East India Company's service, son of the late Rev. Isaac Denton, of Keswick, Cumberland, Feb. 22d, at Bombay.

Fane, Francis William, Esq., Rear-Admiral of the White, March 28th, at Bath.

Hodgson, Emilie Maria, wife of Major-General Henry Hodgson, of the Bengal army, April 12th, at Paris.

Hope, Lieutenant Charles William, Royal Engineers, youngest son of the late Lieutenant-General Sir John Hope, G.C.H., March 24th.

Lindsay, the Hon Hugh, brother to the late and uncle to the present earl of Belcarres, April 23d, aged 79 years. He served his country in early life in the Royal Navy, and was present in several actions under Lord Rodney and Lord St. Vincent, and among others that of the 1st of June. For many years he represented in Parliament the boroughs of Perth, Caspar, and Dundee.

Macqueen, Alexander, Esq., M. D., of Her Majesty's 3d Foot, son of the late Donald Macqueen, Esq., of Corrybrough, Invernesshire, Jan. 24th, in the camp at Gwalior.

Martineau, Henry, second son of the late Thomas Martineau, Esq., of Norwich, Oct. 20th, 1843, at Wellington, New Zealand, aged 47.

Nicolls, Anne, wife of Lieutenant-General Sir Jasper Nicolls, K.C.B., April 2d, at Rome, on her return from India, aged 61.

Salvin, Lieutenant-General Anthony, at Finchley, April 5th, aged 86 years.

Simson, Lieutenant-Colonel, K. H., town-major of Hull, April 12th, at his quarters in the citadel, in the 61st year of his age. The deceased gallant officer served through a considerable portion of the Peninsular campaign, was present at the battle of Vittoria, and at the last fight before Toulouse. On the preliminaries of peace being signed, the 43d, and other regiments of the light division, were ordered to America, where they took part in the war of reprisal for the outrages committed in Canada. At the attack on New Orleans, Captain Simson, leading the storming party against the principal redoubt of the enemy's position, was thrown into the trench by a round shot, causing the severe wound which resulted in the amputation of his left leg and thigh, and rendered him unfit for further active duties. He then retired with the rank of Major, but afterwards received his staff appointment, and the brevet of Lieutenant-Colonel, with the Hanoverian Guelphic Order, as an acknowledgment of his services.

Watson, Anne, wife of Major-General Archibald Watson, of the Bengal Light Cavalry, and daughter of the late Archibald Scott, Esq., of Dunninald and Usan, Forfarshire, March 31st, at Inchbrayock, near Montrose.

LONDON: FISHER, SON, AND CO., PRINTERS.

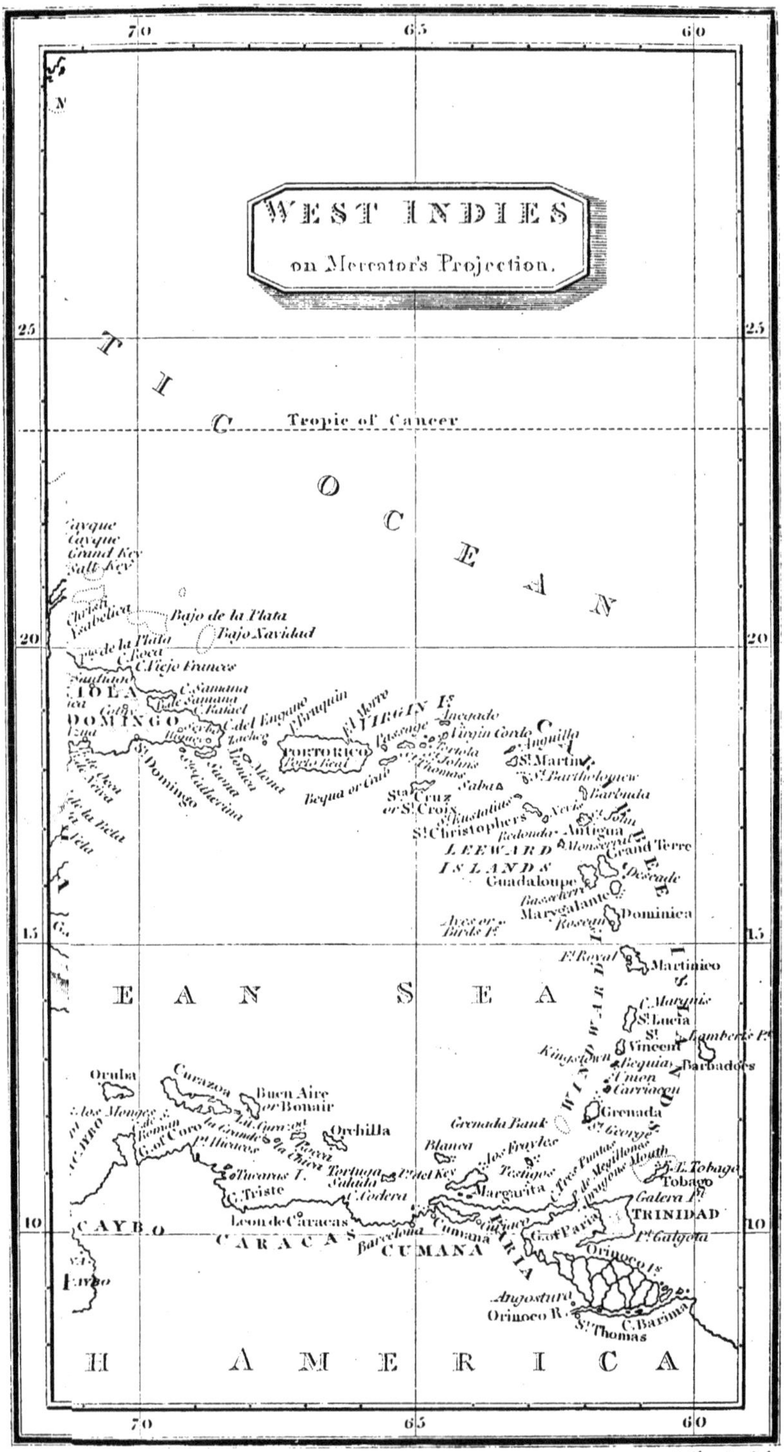

Cooper del.t et Sculp.t

FISHER'S

COLONIAL MAGAZINE.

RANDOM RECOLLECTIONS OF THE MOSQUITO SHORE IN CENTRAL AMERICA.

BY THOMAS YOUNG,

AUTHOR OF "NARRATIVE OF A RESIDENCE ON THE MOSQUITO SHORE."*

The Albino.

WHEN first I visited the Carib village of Sereboyer, situated about thirty miles to the westward of Black River, on the Mosquito Shore, the captain of the place, who rejoiced in the patronymic of John Bull, drew my attention to a child, apparently about three years old, and perfectly white. Carelessly glancing at it, I concluded that it belonged to some white man, but was astonished to hear it was not so.

Having read that a tribe of white negroes had been discovered in Central Africa, and that solitary cases of perfect whiteness amongst

* The author's interesting and truthful narrative has been previously noticed in favourable terms in our pages, as well as in those of the principal periodicals in the kingdom. We more readily give a present preference to his "Random Recollections," from a conviction that the Mosquito Shore, although in the eleventh hour of our commercial distress and over-population pressure, has attracted the grave consideration of the legislature, and is, therefore, from its facility of access, likely to become an important colony, or settlement, or both. Government have, after much nonsense and coquetry, at last taken possession of this central position in the Western World, and the Hon. Patrick Walker has received the appointment of Consul-General, &c. of our Mosquito acquisitions. That a canal, a railroad, a turnpike-road, or some scientific means of transport, will very shortly be employed to connect the Pacific and Atlantic Oceans, in this vicinity, no doubt now exists; in which case, who can foretell the advantages likely to attend British commerce by our secure tenure of a country at once beautiful, fertile, and susceptible of improvement?—ED.

other negroes had been reported, it struck me this was one of those anomalous instances. Calling the mother to me, who spoke English indifferently well, I examined the child, and saw at once that the blood of the white was not running in its veins; the thick lips, the formation of the nose, the curiously-shaped head, the woolly hair (which was white), all plainly indicating its Carib origin. The eyes appeared of a pinkish-blue, and had, in the daytime, a peculiarly vacant expression; and, it was manifest that, from the manner in which it peered about on hearing its mother's voice, that objects by the light of the sun were so confused in its vision, as to be undistinguishable; at night, however, the child can see as well as other children, and in some measure loses that idiotic expression which it has in the daytime. The eyebrows and eyelashes, like the hair on its head, were white; and, with the livid whiteness of the skin, the vacant stare, and its moanings and mutterings, rendered the poor creature anything but a pleasing object of contemplation.

I saw the child afterwards, and it apparently throve well; but the lividness of its complexion increased with its growth, and, as the features became more marked and distinct, they were also more forbidding.

The child's father was a coal-black Carib, who had died some time previous to my arrival at the village; the mother was copper-coloured. She had had three children before the Albino, by whose premature death the fondness of the mother became concentrated in the survivor. On several occasions, when at Sereboyer, Antonia would come to the house at which I took up my quarters, (Captain John Bull's), and appeared to have something heavy on her mind; several times she appeared on the point of speaking; at length, one evening after a long silence, pointing to her child, she said energetically: "This picaninny white; him fader black; him moder black (so she called herself); God send this picaninny white; you Englishman white; you take this picaninny; what for you no mind him? him no belong to Carib; God send him white, white man to take him."—Several Carib captains and others happening to be present, and hearing this harangue, said, "Oh yes! very good! this is Carib child, but him come white, for white man to mind him." I endeavoured to combat their (to them) conclusive reasoning, without avail, until I explained to them the injustice of taking the child from its mother, who so loved and cherished it; impressing upon them that God was good; that he sent to the world what he thought best; and that, if we did not love and protect our own children, we could not expect others to do so. All those present who understood English sufficiently well, applauded the little speech, while Captain Bull translated it into Carib, for the benefit of those whose acquaintance with the English language was but limited. All were delighted; Antonia particularly so; for she must have done violence to her feelings by offering her child to me, under a mistaken notion. She manifested this by running up to me, weeping bitterly, kissing my hand, and saying in Spanish, "Gracias, gracias, Senor." Intending to start early on the next day, I was glad when the scene was over.

On the following morning, just as I had turned out of my hammock, four women arrived, bringing their cartow-reears (wicker-baskets which they carry on their backs, suspended by a band round their forehead). These women belonged to Antonia's family, and they brought in plantains, eggs, and cassada-bread, which they presented to me with evident marks of pleasure. On my departure, they, with several others, accompanied me to the seabeach, severally shaking hands, and crying out, "Adios, adios, Senor, hasta la vista!"

On my after visits to Sereboyer, I was sure to receive presents from either Antonia or some member of her family, who in return would only receive some coloured-glass beads, a few sticks of negrohead tobacco, or some other trifle; thus evincing the natural kindness of this interesting people (the Caribs), of whom so little is known.

The Caribs—Their character—Their desire for a School Establishment —Anecdote.

The high character of the Caribs on the Mosquito Shore, for faith and probity, and their rapid strides towards civilization, show them to be well fitted for the great boon of education, from those devoted and generous individuals who spend their best days endeavouring to bring the besotted heathen, and the superstitious Indian, within the pale of Christianity. Among the many noble qualities which the Caribs possess in a pre-eminent degree, may be enumerated sagacity, ingenuity, intelligence, and cleanliness; and eagerly indeed would the white man be received by them, when coming with the gospel in his hand. Here is a field, in which their labours would soon meet with reward; here are eager and expansive minds quite alive to the blessings of religion; here are sheep, but there is no shepherd to gather them to the Redeemer.

It is melancholy to think of the very many good men who have, in their efforts to convert the heathen, fallen victims to the cruelty of the inhospitable savage, or lingered on in disease in an unhealthy climate, returning to their homes with ruined constitutions, and without having effected what they had so ardently striven and prayed for, and for which labour of love they had toiled through years of sufferings and privations, and for an object which, in the majority of cases, is absolutely unattainable. I have heard the Caribs on the Mosquito Shore bitterly lament that there was no good Englishman to teach them, as their brethren were taught at the large Carib town established at Stann Creek, near the British settlement of Belize, Honduras; at which place a church has been built some years since, and where sermons are regularly preached in English.

I have known Caribs strenuously apply themselves to acquire a knowledge of reading and writing, and I have often given them lessons in both. One man in particular, whom I took much notice of, by name Manuel Acostá, of Cape Town, used to walk to my house, a distance of seven miles, on a Sunday afternoon, to receive lessons in reading English; he was a frequent visiter, until, from a long and severe illness, I was reluctantly compelled to request him to discontinue his visits.

This man could read in Spanish, and was, to all intents, a good Catholic, as also were many of his countrymen; the whole of their religious opinions being obtained from the padré of the Spanish cathedral at Truxillo. This is not what they desire, and I am persuaded, that if a person were sent to them who could combine the duties of schoolmaster with that of pastor, he would be received with manifestations of delight and affection, and a short time only would elapse before numerous pupils, young and old, would attend regularly to receive the instruction which they so much covet.

A missionary there would have but little trouble, as nearly all the males above fourteen or fifteen, speak and understand English, many of them French and Spanish; and, as for provision, they would immediately, as the head people told me, build him a house, fell a large plantation, plant it with bread-kind, supply him with fish and game, and consider themselves under his guidance and control.

Happening one Saturday to be at the house of Manuel Acostá, and having given him a lesson in reading English, I stretched myself on one of the large and clean cotton hammocks, which are always slung in Carib houses for such a purpose; and, while thus reposing, and silently observing the graceful wreaths of smoke from my cigar, the light from the pitch-pine torches illumining all around, and the noise produced by innumerable chirping crickets and croaking tree-toads forming a most inharmonious concert, a gentle tap was heard at the door. Manuel arose from his recumbent position, saying in Spanish, "Enter, my children."

Immediately ten or twelve little boys and girls came in, making profound obeisances, and, putting their tiny hands together, they commenced, saying, in a low tone, their aves and paternosters. On ceasing, they advanced to me as being a white man, bowed their heads, and claimed my benediction. Touched by this little incident, I put my hands on each of their heads separately, and spoke kindly to them. The same ceremony was gone through by Manuel, who then arranged them in a class, and began teaching them prayers from a small Spanish book, printed at Madrid, which he had purchased at Truxillo. Their lesson being finished, they went their way, having first chanted a hymn to the Virgin Mary. Unprepared for such a scene, I sat astonished, listening with great attention, and admiring the good young man, who with the little, the very little he knew, was stimulating others by his example. This man thus employs himself; he never attends the assemblies and revelries of dancing and drumming, customary amongst the Caribs on Saturday evenings. Several Caribs have some small and rude paintings of the crucifixion of our Saviour, and at sunset lighted candles are invariably placed before them, which are permitted to burn till sunrise.

On the expulsion of the black Caribs from the island of St. Vincent by the British, many of them, after wandering in search of a home, settled on the Mosquito Shore, where they are now sojourners, increasing in numbers, and respected for the many noble qualities which they possess. Although so much good may be effected amongst this class of beings, who are so eager and so susceptible of improvement, it would be but labour lost to endeavour to convert the native possessors of the soil — the superstitious Mosquito Indians — from their wretched state of ignorance and Sookeeaism. Years and years must elapse before even the slightest benefit could be derived to them. The children, in order to the accomplishment of this object, must be separated from their families and friends, or all means would be useless. It has been tried on a small scale, but the attempt was soon abandoned, the projectors finding that the Mosquito Indians would not suffer their children to go to school unless the white men paid for their loss of time. Speaking on this subject with an old and intelligent chief, called Colonel Pablo, he gravely argued, "Ah, very good—spose me send my picaninny your school, you must pay me."—"What for?" I asked. "Because," said he, "when him at school he no work; he no fish; he no catch crabs; he no get fruit; he do nothing; him fader him moder work for him. When him at my wattler, him fish, him catch crabs, him get fruit, him work in the plantation, him fader sit down and smoke him pipe."

Who can wonder at this, when we find that in favoured England there are thousands of parents who refuse to allow their children to be educated gratuitously; and even when they do, they consider they are conferring a favour on those who are endeavouring to benefit them? What a stigma rests on moral England, which permits so many of its children to die without education, and without even a partial knowledge of the Redeemer; while the natives of far-off shores have such vast sums sent to them in the vain hope that they one day may become Christianized!

Amongst such a people as the Caribs a great harvest would soon be reaped; amongst our own countrymen the benefits arising from a more extended system of education would soon be felt; but it is as useless to endeavour to reclaim the inhabitants of Central Africa from their paganism, or the impetuous mountaineers of Affghanistan from their faith, as it would be to reclaim the Mosquito Indians from their superstition and Sookeeaism—so great is the difference between the Caribs and the Mosquitians respecting their religious ideas and opinions.

Wherever I have been, I have found bigotry, superstition, and despotism more or less: generous, good, and noble qualities I have also found in the human family everywhere, and often, indeed, where I least expected.

Bathing in Central America—Mode of washing clothes.

The visiters of Ramsgate and other seaport towns have often been heard to complain of the manner in which bathing is practised by many of those partial to that very agreeable pastime; and our newspapers have teemed with letters from their correspondents on the subject.

Some authors have spoken of the not particularly delicate mode of bathing as practised in Germany; and in a recent work (Lady Vavasour's, I think), there is a sad complaint respecting the French; thus, as we find that Europeans are not over scrupulous in such matters, we cannot wonder that the people of Central America see no impropriety in both sexes bathing together. The Spaniards, the Ladinoes, and the Caribs enjoy the delightful bath, and attach no importance to companionship.

One morning, when at the seaport town of Truxillo, being very warm, and not very willing to wend my way to the cooling waters of the Rio de Cristal, I resorted to a small nook of salt water near my residence, and in which I had previously bathed. Proceeding along a pass, on each side of which were numerous fragrant lime-trees, impregnating the morning air with sweetness, I arrived at the spot, and leisurely set about uncasing—amusing myself by idly picking up some flat stones, and casting them on the water to make ducks-and-drakes of them. Tired at length, I was on the point of entering into the water, when, on hearing some loud cries, I turned round and observed at a distance a tall Carib woman, who, by her gesticulations, invited me to bathe by her side. The sudden apparition took away all thoughts of bathing, so, speedily equipping myself, I went homewards, ungallantly leaving the good lady to imagine all manner of things of the buckra, who, coming to bathe, took off his clothes and then put them on again. On mentioning the circumstance, I was told that the place I had selected was very bad, there being many jagged stumps of trees and rough stones there, and that the Carib woman knowing me to be a stranger, by her cries invited me to bathe near her, and thus prevent me, perhaps, from being seriously hurt.

The inhabitants of the Mosquito Shore, with the exception of the Caribs, show great disinclination to indiscriminate bathing. I have known Mosquito men, when the English have been enjoying themselves in the refreshing water, go to some distant place where they could also bathe, but only amongst their own kin—indicating not only a delicacy of feeling, but an unobtrusiveness equally pleasing and commendable. At other times I have seen them bathe, but in such a manner that the most delicately framed mind would not have been shocked—contrasting strongly indeed with the custom adopted by many falsely calling themselves civilized. This trait of character, so admirable in every one, but particularly in rude uncultivated savages, would not be despised by the most refined European. I have seen on several occasions Mosquito girls in the water, who fled like frightened fawns on my nearer approach.

The Mosquitians have a curious idea of English women, and one man who had been working at Belise for a long period, said to me, when talking of the comparative merits and demerits of the English and Mosquito women—"Master, English girl fine too much—Sookooner ebery day no more, so so wash hands, so so wash face. Mosquito girls, ah! Yamnee Polly ebery day go in water one, two, tree times. Mosquito girl all face." This ingenious argument I in vain tried to combat, but so impressed was Mr. Lord John Russell, as he delighted to be called, with the force of his reasoning, that he left me in a kind of triumph at having so well advocated and convincingly shown the superiority of his countrywomen.

The Caribs, I have already observed, are not at all particular in bathing, and I have frequently seen them in the water, especially at Truxillo, and they were not the least disconcerted at my appearance, but talked on with the same ease as if in their habitations.

The mode of washing clothes adopted by the Caribs is primitive enough; they go to a running stream, being on those occasions but very slightly apparelled; they select a large flat stone, and after rubbing the clothes with soap, they pound them vigorously with sticks, now and then dipping them in the stream; or they rub them on the stone, a practice by which they most certainly contrive effectually to clean the clothes, but the diminished stock of your wardrobe plainly indicates that they are equally effectual in destroying them. A practice not unlike this prevails in Scotland and in Ireland, where it is called beetling.

Failure of a French settlement at Cape Gracias à Dios—A Frenchman—King Robert Charles Frederic—Murder of George Frederic—Attempt on King Robert's life—Affection of the Mosquito men for their mothers—The Mosquitian idea of freedom, and reason of.

About twelve years ago the French sent a vessel to Cape Gracias á Dios, on the Mosquito Shore, on board of which were a number of people who had quitted the gaieties of a Parisian life and the sunny skies of Southern France to settle there, and to establish themselves in such parts of the Mosquito territory as they should find most suitable to their respective purposes, anticipating that their adopted country would soon be under the protection of the eagle of France.

Consistently with French policy on such occasions, most of the immigrants were young and unmarried men, it being supposed that they, with their natural lightness of heart, would soon intermarry, or take under their protection the native women, by which the people would become attached to them as Frenchmen, and that a field would thus be opened for French enterprise. As it was calculated, so it commenced; several took native women for their wives, and all appeared prosperous. Dwellings were quickly erected, and the time passed merrily away—no thought for the present, or corroding care for the future. The place was healthy, the natives apparently friendly, and for a time all went on well. They had many implements of husbandry and tools with them, most of which, however, were ill adapted to an uncultivated country, or the wants of its inhabitants. Their merchandise was of that description as to be in little request by the natives, who soon discovered that the new-comers were not like their friends the English, and consequently became less frequent in their visits, the Indian women remaining faithful to their white husbands. The French had found that, before they could do anything with the Mosquitians, they must either learn the Mosquito dialect or English, as a medium by which they could converse, and many of them therefore applied themselves to the latter. The ship they expected came not—their provisions were scanty, and the natives felt no inclination to carry them supplies; firstly, as having nothing wherewithal to satisfy them for their productions, and secondly, because they were only Frenchmen. The then King George Frederic sent them some young bulls to kill, and with these they contented themselves for awhile; no further aid appearing, their unpopularity with the natives increasing, and all their brightly-cherished hopes fading rapidly, they separated. The surgeon was accidentally shot; some penetrated into the interior towards the Spanish towns, which a few succeeded in reaching; while others fell victims to the river fevers, exposure to the mid-day sun, and the heavy dews at night; others caught the debilitating intermittent fever, from the swampy nature of part of the country which they traversed, and from the too frequent use of cold-bathing, which they resorted to, to refresh their parched-up frames. Some reached the seaport towns of Truxillo, Omoa, Belize, &c., until at length but one solitary Frenchman remained at the Cape, out of the whole number brought from France, and he is still residing there, having everything around him that he can require, and having no wish to leave his adopted country for even his loved La Belle France.

This man being the only gunsmith in the kingdom, his services are considered so valuable, that he could with difficulty be dispensed with; but, in the event of any mushla (drink) or other rejoicings, he is often reminded of his unfortunate connection with France, for the drunken Mosquito Indians come to his door, swearing in good English, offering to fight, English fashion, and calling him all the opprobious names they can think of, which are not few—for they have been well schooled at the various mahogany works where they have been employed.

The King Robert Charles Frederic, who died about the commencement of the year 1843, leaving as his executors Colonel Macdonald, the late superintendent of Belize, and G. A. Brown, Esq., of London, like his countrymen, had a great dislike to Frenchmen, and whenever he was at the Cape, and became a little excited by liquor, used to repair to Monsieur B——t's house, and abuse him in unmeasured terms as he shook his fist—"You are a d—n Frenchman, sare. I could hang you if I like. How dare you come to my country? Hold your tongue, sare, or by goles I will fight you." Monsieur, however, took it all in very good part, and contrived to escape being either hung or shot; and so soon as the fumes of the liquor had gone off, the king became appeased, and he contritely made many ample apologies.

The king was very thin and very short, and his antics were often of a ludicrous nature when under the influence of liquor, of which he was immoderately fond. He received a part of his education in Jamaica, of which he invariably took care to inform his auditors, and had a particular penchant for talking of his knowledge of English grammar, or any other grammar that might by chance be mentioned. He was gravely asked one day if he understood gibberish grammar, to which he replied that he had learnt it in Jamaica, and that his very good friend, the superintendent of Belize, often practised it with him. He had an extraordinary attachment to the art and science of English boxing, in which he considered himself an adept, and he has often been heard to say emphatically, "I don't care tree damns for the finest Englishman as ever was—by goles I can fight him;" generally adding as a clincher, "My brother (King George Frederic, his predecessor, of whom it is mentioned that not a more powerful man existed in the kingdom) was a strong fine man, but I is a finerer." This was said in such apparent earnestness as to be irresistible.

These were but foibles—his good qualities were many; for generosity, faithfulness, hospitality, and friendship to the English, he was most conspicuous; and if he could have conquered his habit of intoxication, and had manifested an example of temperance to his people, he might have done much in effecting a change in their present debased condition; but while he and his chiefs indulged in the vitiated taste for strong liquors, we cannot marvel that the common people, not prevented by law, reason, or morality, should tread closely in their footsteps.

The king's second son Clarence, now about fourteen or fifteen years old, has been receiving his education at Belize for the last three years and upwards, under the auspices of the superintendent, Colonel Macdonald. He is very intelligent, and report speaks most favourably of him in every particular, and it is likely, from his having imbibed English habits so early in life, that he may be the means of greatly benefiting his countrymen—providing that he does not, as many have done before him, fall into the ways of his forefathers, and thus become a half-civilized savage; acquiring all the vices of the white men, and but few of their virtues. This is, however, not expected; yet it is to be hoped that he will be kept under the fostering care of the gallant colonel till his mind has been properly formed, and his education so directed that he can receive the crown as king, and prove, by his example to his subjects, how easy it is to abstain from intoxicating liquors, and other things which do hurt to the body; and he may then also be the means of introducing and encouraging many good men to come, who will teach them the way to salvation. I know not the reason why the eldest son of the king was not taken by the English to educate. I have heard that he was affected with a cutaneous disorder, common amongst the Indians on this shore; but surely there must be something else, or that would not be sufficient to render him unfit to be his father's successor.*

The king, George Frederic, brother of King Robert Charles Frederic (of whom mention has been made), always testified the greatest friendship for Englishmen, who could traverse from one end of his kingdom to the other without expense, for the natives, by his positive commands, attended to all their wants without payment; and, if by chance this order was violated in any one instance, and the king heard of it, the culprit would be sent for, and severely flogged, with straps made from the dried hide of the manatee, or sea-cow.

This king, whose love for the English was so unbounded, had no regard whatever for his own countrymen, forcibly possessing himself of their wives and daughters; and, to such a degree did he carry his excesses, as to warrant the saying of Bryan Edwards, when speaking of the infamous Governor Park, "that he spared no man in his anger, nor woman in his lust."

The king at length fell a victim to the terror to which he had driven one of his wives. This woman, during his temporary absence, became acquainted with a man named Cuffee; and, on the king's return, being informed of some suspicious circumstances, he swore a bitter oath, that if she proved *enceinté*, he would assuredly slay her. He had frequently before this amused himself by slashing her with his cutlass when in his drunken freaks. The threat operated so intensely on the mind of the woman, who feared she was likely to become a mother, that she secretly enlisted in her cause the man Cuffee and a slave of the kings. These three, one night when the king was in a heavy stupor, from the effects of the enormous quantity of mushla (an intoxicating beverage made from the bitter cassada-root), came to the hammock in which he was lying, and strangled him.

* Since these notices were written, their prophetic spirit has operated upon our government. Clarence has been adopted by the nation; Colonel Macdonald, resolved upon a valuable consummation of his project, has brought him to this country, and he is now receiving, in London, an education for good or evil—ED.

The woman and Cuffee were afterwards hanged, the slave escaped their doom, and was very lately in the service of Robert Charles Frederic. To show how reckless these people are of life, and to prove that with them death is divested of its terrors, I shall relate one instance among many which came under my notice. Cuffee, who was a very tall and powerful man, on arriving at the tree to which the fatal cord was suspended, scornfully smiled, and coolly tried its strength, saying, "This rope not strong enough;" adjusting it round his neck, he told his numerous relatives and friends near him, who were filling the air with their dismal wailings, that his sentence was a just one; then saying "Good-by, some day we shall meet again," he jumped from the place on which he was standing, but the cord (as he had prognosticated) broke in twain, casting him heavily on the earth; recovering from the shock, and gasping painfully, he, unassisted, arose, for the bystanders were too much horror-stricken to render him any aid; at length, low murmurs arose amongst the multitude, the wails of the women, as they threw themselves at the feet of the king, suing for mercy, were heart-rending; the piercing shrieks which occasionally burst out from some agonized mind; the menacing gestures and cries of the Indians, plainly indicated how much this sad scene had worked upon them. The king remained inflexible; Cuffee was a notorious character, and he was anxious that the earth should no longer be polluted by his presence; a strong rope, procured from an English trader in the bay, was carried to the king, who examined it, and signified his wish that the execution should proceed; Cuffee said to them, as they adjusted the rope, "Ah! Massa King, me too much sorry; me poor feller; you kill me now; you no kill my moder"—. Cuffee could say no more, for he was cast off into eternity.

Two or three attempts were also made upon the life of Robert Charles Frederic, the last one being when he was staying at Monsieur B——t's house at the Cape. A native got into his sleeping-apartment, and would have strangled him, had not his struggles and the cries of his wife alarmed the Frenchman, who rushed to the spot just in time to save the king's life, and to secure the criminal. He was confined in the stocks in Monsieur's yard for a time, but, being some distant relation of the king's chief wife, some thirtieth cousin, he was pardoned, and set at liberty; to so great a degree do they respect the ties of consanguinity.

It is related by Mungo Park, that the Africans invariably say to each other when quarrelling, "Strike me, but do not curse my mother;" and so it is with the Mosquito Indians. I have heard them abuse each other in the most virulent manner, which they endured with perfect stoicism, but the moment anything was said about their mothers or their sisters, especially about the former, their eyes would flash fire, and mischief would ensue. I once saw an old Mosquitoman so moved, that the tears trickled down his furrowed cheeks, while the young men gazed on him with pity, and their violent gestures indicated what was raging in their minds. Had it not been an Englishman that spoke the heedless words, I would not have answered for the consequences; as it was, knowing the power of the English, and considering themselves under subjection, they were afraid to resent it. Understanding their tongue, I advanced to the old man, patted his cheek, and said, "Friend, the Englishman is not cross; he only wants you to do what you have promised; the English are your good friends; they give you physic, bring you cloth, beads, guns, macheets, and everything else. Go; go, and when you come back we will talk together." The old man caressed my hand while I spoke, and went off with a light heart.

With this people little is to be done by harsh measures; they are very sensitive, and I have known them run away, after having worked some time, because they had been reprimanded, perhaps in a harsher tone than they thought was right. Their idea of freedom is very strong, and once, when General Lowry came to see the English at Black River, he stayed some hours; and, on wishing to return to his residence at Plantain River, he found that his dorey's crew had not come in from the bush, where they had been sent hunting. Seeing three or four men idling about, who had arrived that day from the neighbourhood of Croata, he commanded them to jump into his dorey and paddle him home, a distance of 16 or 18 miles. They one and all refused. Lowry, who possesses more influence than any other Mosquito chief, stormed and blustered, all to no purpose; they steadily persisted in their refusal, one of them (their spokesman) saying in English, "General, me free man; me no want to work for you; me no your picaninny; me no your soldier; me no go; me stop here; to-morrow me work for white man." This sort of independence must not be considered singular, as it is easily accounted for, by the fact that numbers of Mosquitomen annually quit their native shore for Belize, and other places, where mahogany-works are carried on, and where they are sure to find employment, being dexterous hunters and fishers, and remaining employed for one, two, or even three years, they adopt the opinions of the Caribs and negroes whom they fall in with at such places, and return to their homes laden with cloth, powder, shot, muskets, &c.; having a good knowledge of the English language, and being imbued with that sort of independence and love of liberty, for which the English are distinguished, but fonder than ever of swearing and drinking; they return home rollicking blades, and their curious accounts of the English at Belize, their manners and customs, of the quantities of grog to be had, and many other inducements, inflame the blood of the youth of the country, who, already predisposed to regard Englishmen with favour, no sooner arrive at a proper age, than away they sail for Belize, as their fathers did before them.

[To be continued.]

THE CAPE OF GOOD HOPE—ITS FUTURE GOVERNMENT.

In the excellent little work, "The Cape of Good Hope," &c. by John Centlivres Chase, Esq., noticed in this Magazine, we find the letter of the Colonial Secretary, containing the answer of Lord Stanley to the petition to the Queen in council, which had been transmitted and recommended by the governor of that colony, Sir George Napier, from the inhabitants, praying for a "representative form of government, assimilated in principle and form to that of Great Britain, composed of a governor, appointed by the crown; an executive council, also appointed by the crown; and a legislative assembly, composed of representatives freely selected by the people."

The inconsistency of the several parts of the prayer of this petition, demonstrating the little consideration which had been given by those who drew it up, to the details of the important changes they demanded, induced Lord Stanley to refer a series of questions to the colonists, for the further explanation of their views and desires. These queries, as detailed in Secretary Craig's letter, dated "Colonial Office, Cape Town, July 25th, 1842," were as follow:—

"1. Do the petitioners contemplate that the legislative assembly to be elected by the people, should be the only legislative power in the colony? or, is the council, called executive in the petition, also to possess legislative functions? And what, if any, are to be the legislative functions of the governor?

"2. If, as the language of the petition would seem to import, the legislative assembly is to be the only legislative power in the colony, how can the change suggested be considered as an assimilation in principle and form to the government of Great Britain, or to that established in any other British colony?

"3. This query is, in substance, how are the representatives to be proportioned throughout the colony?

"4. As to how the representatives are to be selected, whether from among the inhabitants of the electoral districts, or residents in Cape Town?

"5. Where are the votes of the electors to be taken?

"6. On the bestowal of the right of representation, coloured classes and mixed race, &c.?

"7. Is there to be a property-qualification for the electors? If so, of what nature, and to what amount?

"8. Is there to be a property-qualification for the elected? If so, of what nature, and to what amount?

"9. On the limits and details of the property-qualification?

"10. Is the division into the two districts, eastern and western, to affect the constitution of the assembly?

"11. By what machinery do the petitioners propose that voters should be registered, and the business of the election managed?"

The author, in the appendix, answers these queries in a paper headed "A Representative Government: the question considered, as proposed by Lord Stanley; or, a plain and succinct plan for forming a Representative House of Assembly, and an Executive Legislative Council, in the colony of the Cape of Good Hope."

First, in some "general considerations," he recommends that the number of representatives shall depend on the electoral population of the district, in the ratio of 1 to 5,000; that the members should be paid, on account of the difficulty of finding men of independent fortune who could afford to give their services gratuitously; that the limitation of the franchise be strictly confined to the European population, the English and Dutch; and the selection of a central spot for the meeting of the assembly:—

"The house of assembly to be distinct in itself, and independent of the government, or executive legislative council; to have the power of originating bills, of presiding over the revenues of the country, voting the supplies, authorizing the necessary public works and improvements, to possess the power of appointing committees of its own members to inquire into all public questions, and the power of calling all persons before them for examination, &c.; in a word, the possession of those privileges generally conceded to popular assemblies in all countries. These would be undoubtedly great powers to delegate to an independent body of men; and, as such, would require some counterpoise or check, and this would be found in the composition of an executive legislative council, to bear the same relation to the house of assembly that the house of lords does to the commons of England; to be composed of the governor, principal official members of the government, and two or three of the senior merchants of Cape Town, appointed by the crown. . . . .

"There is another principle that I should be inclined to include within the legislative council, that of constituting it a court of appeal from the lower courts. . . . The governor of course would have the care of *all* on his shoulders, directing and attending to the details (as at present) of the civil and judicial departments throughout the colony, presiding in the executive legislative council, opening and closing the house of assembly, issuing proclamations; in a word, attending to those details which devolve on the executive government of every civilized country."

The author then proceeds to take the queries of Lord Stanley in order; his answers to the first and second may be inferred from what has been already quoted; in his reply to the third query he suggests that the representatives be distributed as follow:—

Western Province, 14.		Eastern Province, 11.	
Cape Town and District	5	Graham's Town and Albany	3
Stillinbosch and District	2	Grafreinet and District	2
Worcester and District	2	Utenhay and District	2
Swillendam and District	2	Cradock, 1—Colesberg, 1	2
George, 1—Beaufort, 1	2	Somerset	1
Clanwilliam	1	Port Elizabeth	1

He suggests, that the payment of members might be confined to those from remote districts. The substance of his answers to the other queries, may be generally inferred from the foregoing. The qualification of an elector he fixes, of strict European birth or descent, a rent-payer of 10*l.* in town, or 20*l.* in the country; for the representatives he proposes no qualification but abilities, as best suited to the circumstances of the country.

This is but a mere sketch of Mr. Chase's answer to the queries, but it is sufficiently in detail; for no person interested in Cape affairs will omit to peruse his most useful little book.

Mr. Chase evidently has a loyal and truly English leaning towards that form of government under which our country has risen to the high and glorious position she holds among the nations of the globe; it is strange that the great feature which distinguishes it from the new *quasi* imitations which have sprung up since the beginning of the century, in the present limited monarchies of Europe, namely, the hereditary upper house of parliament, did not suggest to him the possibility of further assimilating his proposed form of colonial government to that of the mother-country, by the admission of hereditary councillors to his upper house, who would constitute a provincial nobility, and would help to tie the colony still closer to its parent.

In the words of the petition above quoted, that the new government should be "assimilated in principle and form to that of Great Britain," it would be a grand step to adopt the intention evidently indicated by the government when the first constitution was granted to the Canadas, by the clause reserving to the crown the right of nominating to hereditary seats in the council—In other words, the formation of a colonial peerage. Why that idea was never carried out has not been explained; most probably it fell into oblivion, owing to the culpable want of attention to colonial affairs, of which all the colonies had too much reason to complain, and in many points have still. It should be the object of Great Britain to give to her colonies a form of government in every respect assimilated to her own—all her institutions should be transplanted with the settlers. The more perfectly identical the institutions of the colonies are with those of the mother-country the more indissoluble will be the bonds of their affection, the more perfect their attachment.

In all the colonies there are to be found men who, comparatively with the system of the mother-country, should look to the honours of the peerage; some from their status in the province, as extensive and influential landowners — some from eminent public services. The colonists seem to be cut off from the fountain of honour; the stream flowing from it is exhausted upon those nearer the fountain-head; even the lowest honour conferred by the crown, knighthood, has been but rarely granted to a colonist, and there is but one instance within memory of a baronetcy.

The colonial parliaments, as the assemblies should invariably be called, are of course subordinate to the imperial parliament, and so should the colonial nobility be to that of the empire. The title given might be baron, with the style honourable—his honour—the honourable baron. Why should not the proprietor of the Talbot county, in Upper Canada, have a seat in the legislative council of Canada as the Honourable the Baron Talbot? Sir Andries Stockenstrom, of the Cape of Good Hope, was made a baronet for his services; such proportionate services in the mother-country, with his property and position, would have advanced him to the peerage. If, instead of making him a baronet of Great Britain as Sir Andries Stockenstrom of Maasstrom, would he and his family and friends not have been more gratified by his having been made the Honourable the Baron Maasstrom, or, had he preferred to retain his family name, the Baron Stockenstrom of Maasstrom?

The object of conferring dignities as the reward for public services, is not only to recompense the recipient, but to excite emulation in others. By granting a title which may tempt the rewarded person to quit the colony, in order that he may enjoy the dignity conferred upon him nearer the metropolis of the empire, and among men holding like honours, the public benefit accruing from the sovereign's grace is in a great measure destroyed; he is no longer a present example of what merit may attain. An honour which would fix the individual upon the spot, would conduce to make others of his fellow-colonists endeavour to earn the like. (Vide p. 282 of this volume.)

It appears strange that a nation having a monarchical government like Great Britain, should continue to rear broods of young republics in her colonies, which, when they reach maturity, are to degenerate into the democratic tyrannies of the States of the North American union, who disgrace their parentage by acts of swindling which would drive a private individual from the society of honest men. Had those colonial legislatures been composed of two houses, formed on the model of the mother-country, they would at least have separated from her as respectable monarchies, with fixed and stable governments, incapable of refusing to pay their just debts.

The new government of the Cape would assimilate more nearly in principle and form to that of Great Britain, if constituted as follows: A governor appointed by the crown, with an executive council formed as at present; a legislative council, consisting of the members of the executive council, and a president and members nominated to it by the crown; some hereditarily, with the title of baron, and some as suggested by Mr. Chase—say two or three, for life, or residence in the colony, selected from the leading merchants of Cape Town, in order that the mercantile community shall be represented in the council; and lastly, of a representative chamber, elected by the people, consisting of members from the towns and counties. The whole to be called the Provincial or Colonial Parliament.

Mr. Chase appears to have been too limited in his number of representatives, and indeed, we think that he would himself admit that, to give a fair representation, some new counties should be formed; two members are certainly too few for Graf Reinet, and there are populous spots in some of the other districts, as worthy of being represented as even some of the county towns. About thirty would be a sufficient number of members for the lower house. Mr. Chase recommends the use of the English word county for the colonial districts, in which we fully coincide; and we would further recommend, should new counties be formed, that the Dutch system of giving them names depending upon local peculiarities, or after eminent individuals, should be adopted, rather than the very objectionable English method of repeating the names of places in the United Kingdom.

Perhaps the payment of members may be necessary in a young country, especially those called from a long distance, but it would be a better system to pay a fixed sum for the session or year, than a daily rate. The session would probably rarely last three months, but say four—sixty pounds would cover the expenses of travelling and extra-expense in Cape Town, and would be something near what Mr. Chase proposes in the aggregate. The electors may chuse to name some resident of Cape Town as their representative, and so save the expense of paying their member; but the sum is so small that it would not be felt by the district, and it is desirable that the members of districts should be persons having local knowledge and interest.

A word on Natal. It seems that the government still hesitates about the final settlement of that new colony. It is most desirable that there be an end put to all uncertainty there. The missionary party at Cape Town, who, in their zeal for the blacks, have done much towards creating a war of races among the whites, putting the Dutch against the English, have put forward the name of Sir Andries Stockenstrom as the fit person to govern that settlement. Sir Andries Stockenstrom would be placed entirely in a false position, in being sent to Natal. No good could possibly result from his presence there, and his talents and zeal would be quite thrown away. He was removed (*vide* Lord Normanby's speech in the House of Lords, when he was secretary for the colonies), from the post of lieutenant-governor at Graham's Town, solely on the ground of his exceeding unpopularity. By his officially expressed opinion, speaking as the lieutenant-governor, that there was no law against the farmers quitting the colony if they did not chuse to remain, he was the immediate cause of the emigration of the boors; and, that it was utterly impossible that the reclaimed farmers, now settling at Natal, can ever place confidence in Sir Andries Stockenstrom, it is only necessary to read the famous letter of the unfortunate Retiff, their leader, which may be taken as the manifesto of the boors on their crossing the border.

VAN DE KAAP.

Gibraltar, May, 1844.

SYNOPSIS OF THE MODIFIED TARIFF PROPOSED IN THE UNITED STATES OF AMERICA, FOR 1844, *et seq.*

On the 8th of March, 1844, a bill was introduced in the United States' House of Representatives, by the Committee of Ways and Means, recommending many important alterations in the tariff of duties as then levied. Its leading feature is a reduction of the general average from the present rate of 35 per cent to 30, until September, 1844, after which date 25 per cent shall be the maximum. It suggests ad valorem rates for several of the specific charges now imposed, and makes the foreign cost and charges the basis of valuation; it also extends the time for goods to be entitled to drawback. The following is a synopsis of the bill, as taken into consideration, (having been previously printed,) by the Committee on the State of the Union, and which modification, there is reason to believe, will become the law of the Republic:—

Sec. I.—Enacts that, from and after the 1st of September, 1844, the duties imposed by the act of 30th August, 1842, shall be changed, modified, and reduced, in manner following:—

1st. On all coarse unmanufactured wool, the value whereof, at the last port or place whence exported to the United States, shall be 7 cents, or under, per lb., the duty shall be 15 per cent ad valorem, instead of 5 per cent,* as per act of 1842. On all other unmanufactured wool, 30 per cent ad valorem, instead of 3 cents per lb., and 30 per cent ad valorem.

2d. On all manufactures of wool, or of which wool shall be a component part, except milled or fulled cloth, known as plains, kerseys, Kendal cottons, carpetings, flannels, bockings, baizes, blankets, worsted, stuff goods, ready-made clothing, hosiery, mitts, gloves, caps, and bindings, 30 per cent ad valorem, instead of 40 per cent, as per act of 1842.

3d. On all milled or fulled cloth, known as plains, kerseys, or Kendal cottons, of which wool shall be the only material, the value whereof shall not exceed 35 cents the square yard at the last port or place whence exported, 20 per cent ad valorem, instead of the duties imposed per act of 1842.*

4th. On all carpets and carpeting, of wool, hemp, flax, or cotton, or parts of either, or other material not specified, 30 per cent ad valorem, instead of duties imposed per act of 1842.*

5th. On all woollen blankets, the actual value of which, at the place whence exported, shall not exceed 75 cents each, there shall be levied a duty of 10 per cent ad valorem, instead of 15 per cent, as per act of 1842.

6th. On all hearth-rugs, 30 per cent ad valorem, instead of 40 per cent, as per act of 1842.

---

* Reduced to a scale, ad valorem, by the treasury department, they range from 40 to 87 per cent.

7th. On woollen yarn, 25 per cent ad valorem, instead of 30 per cent as per act of 1842. On worsted yarn, 20 per cent ad valorem, instead of 30 per cent, as per act of 1842.

8th. On woollen and worsted mitts, gloves, caps, and bindings, and woollen or worsted hosiery made on frames, 20 per cent ad valorem, instead of 30 per cent, as per act of 1842.

9th. On flannels, of whatever materials except cotton, and on bockings and baizes, 30 per cent ad valorem, instead of 14 cents per square yard, as per act of 1842. On coach laces, 30 per cent ad valorem, instead of 35 per cent, as per act of 1842.

10th. On ready-made clothing, of whatever materials, worn by men, women, or children (except gloves and hosiery, and similar manufactures made on frames), hats, bonnets, shoes, boots, and bootees, imported in a state ready to be used as clothing, 30 per cent ad valorem, instead of 50 per cent, as per act of 1842. On all articles worn by men, women, or children, other than as above specified, made up wholly or in part by hand, 30 per cent ad valorem, instead of 40 per cent. On clothing finished in whole or in part, embroidered in gold or silver, 30 per cent ad valorem, instead of 50 per cent, as per act of 1842.

Sec. II.—1st. On all manufactures of cotton, or of which cotton shall be a component part, not otherwise specified, and excepting cotton-twist, yarn, and thread, and such other articles as herein otherwise provided for, 25 per cent ad valorem—proviso of second section of act of 1842 repealed.*

2d. On cotton-twist, yarn, and thread, bleached or unbleached, coloured or uncoloured, and on spools or otherwise, 25 per cent ad valorem, instead of various duties. as per act of 1842.*

Sec. III.—1st. On all manufactures of silk not otherwise specified, except bolting-cloths, 20 per cent ad valorem, instead of 2 dollars per lb., as per act of 1842.† On silk bolting-cloths, 15 per cent ad valorem, instead of 20 per cent, as per act of 1842.

2d. On silk twist, or twist composed of silk and mohair, and on sewing silk, 1 dollar per lb., instead of 2 dollars per lb., as per act of 1842. On pongees, and plain white silks, for printing or colouring, 20 per cent ad valorem, instead of 1 dollar 50 cents per lb. On floss, and other similar silks purified from the gum, dyed and prepared for manufacture, 15 per cent ad valorem, instead of 25 per cent. On all raw silks, comprehending all silks in the gum, whether in hanks, reeled, or otherwise, 12½ per cent ad valorem, instead of 50 cents per lb. On silk umbrellas, parasols, sun-shades, silk or satin shoes for men, women, or children, silk or satin laced boots or bootees for ditto, men's silk hats, silk or satin bonnets for women, silk shirts and drawers, made up wholly or in part; silk caps for women, turbans, ornaments for head-dresses, aprons, collars, caps, cuffs, braids, curls or frisettes, chemisettes, mantillas, pelerines, and all other articles of silk made up by hand, in whole or in part, and not otherwise provided for, 25 per cent ad valorem, instead of the various duties imposed by the act of 1842.‡

3d. On unmanufactured hemp, Manila, Lunn, and other hemps of India, jute,

* Reduced to ad valorem by treasury department, ranging from 49 to 63 per cent, some being 150; such as handkerchiefs.

† 40 to 65 per cent.

‡ Per Treasury Document, ad valorem, ranging from 50 to 75 per cent.

Sisal grass, coir, and other vegetable substances not enumerated, used for cordage, 30 per cent ad valorem, instead of the various duties imposed by act of 1842.* On codilla, or tow of hemp and flax, 25 per cent ad valorem, instead of 20 dollars per ton. On tarred and untarred cables, and cordage and cables, yarns, twine, pack-thread, cotton bagging, of whatever material composed, and on any other manufacture not otherwise specified, suitable to the uses to which cotton-bagging is applied, whether imported under the designation of gunny cloth, or other appellation, 30 per cent ad valorem, instead of the various duties imposed by act of 1842.†

4th. On stamped, printed, or painted floor oil-cloth, furniture oil-cloth, made on Canton or cotton flannel, other furniture oil-cloth, oil-cloth of linen, silk, or other materials, used for hat-covers, aprons, coach-curtains, or similar purposes, and on medicated oil-cloths, 30 per cent ad valorem, instead of the various duties imposed by act of 1842.‡

Sec. IV.—1st. On iron, in bars or bolts, not manufactured, in whole or in part, by rolling, 15 dollars per ton, instead of 17 dollars per ton, as per act of 1842. On bar or bolt iron, made wholly or in part by rolling, 20 dollars per ton, instead of 25 dollars per ton. On all iron imported in bars, for railroads or inclined planes, made to patterns, and fitted to be laid down as rails, upon such roads or planes, without further manufacture, 10 dollars per ton, instead of 25 dollars per ton: *Provided* security be given that, if not permanently so laid down within the prescribed time arranged by the secretary of the treasury, in one year, the full duty of 20 dollars per ton, shall be paid.

2d. On iron in pigs, 7 dollars per ton, instead of 9 dollars per ton, as per act of 1842. On vessels of cast-iron, not otherwise specified; glazed or tin hollow ware and castings, sad irons or smoothing-irons, hatters' and tailors' pressing-irons, cast-iron butts or hinges; iron or steel wire, described in said act as not exceeding No. 14, over that, and not exceeding No. 25, and over No. 25, silver or plated wire; round or square iron or braziers' rods, of 3-16ths to 10-16ths of an inch in diameter, inclusive; iron in nail or spike rods or nail plates; slit, rolled, and hammered iron, in sheets, except —— iron, hoop iron, iron slit, rolled or hammered for band iron scroll iron or casement rods; iron cables or chains, or parts thereof, manufactured in whole or in part, of whatever diameter, the links being of the form peculiar to chains for cables; all other chains of iron, not otherwise specified, the links being either twisted or straight, and when straight, of greater length than those used for cables; anchors or parts of anchors, manufactured in whole or in part; anvils, blacksmiths' hammers and sledges; cut or wrought iron spikes; cut iron nails; wrought iron nails; axletrees, or parts thereof; mill irons and mill cranks of wrought iron; wrought iron for ships, locomotives, and steam-engines; iron chains, other than chain cables; steam, gas, or water tubes, or pipes made of band or rolled iron; and tacks, brads, or sprigs,—30 per cent ad valorem, instead of the various duties imposed by act of 1842; and the last clause of the 2d proviso of the 2d subdivision of the 4th section of the said act, which imposes a duty of 15 per cent ad valorem upon the cost of the articles embraced therein, repealed.§

3d. On all old or scrap iron, 6 dollars per ton, instead of 10 dollars per ton, as per act of 1842.

---

* Per Treasury Document, ad valorem, 40 per cent.

† Per same, from 71 to 188 per cent. ‡ 67 per cent.

§ Reduced to ad valorem, ranging from 45 to 235 per cent.

4th. On screws made of iron, called wood screws, brass screws, and brass battery or hammered kettles, 30 per cent ad valorem, instead of the various duties of act of 1842.*

5th. On all steel in bars, except cast, shear, and German steel, 1 dollar 50 cents per cwt., instead of 2 dollars 50 cents per cwt., as per act of 1842. On solid-headed pins, and all other package-pins, and on pound pins, 30 per cent ad valorem, instead of duties as per act of 1842.

6th. On japanned-ware of all kinds, or papier maché, and plated and gilt wares of all kinds, cutlery of all kinds, and all other manufactures not otherwise specified, made of brass, iron, steel, copper, pewter, lead, or tin, or of which either of these metals is a component material, 25 per cent ad valorem, instead of 30 per cent, as per act of 1842.

7th. On lead in pigs and bars, old and scrap lead, leaden pipes, leaden shot, and lead in sheets, or in any other form not herein specified, 25 per cent ad valorem, instead of the various duties of act of 1842.

8th. On silver-plated metal in sheets, argentine, alabata, or German silver, in sheets, or otherwise unmanufactured, and on manufactures of German silver, bell-metal, zinc, or bronze, 20 per cent ad valorem, instead of 30 per cent, as per act of 1842.

9th. On coal, 1 dollar per ton, instead of 1 dollar 75 cents per ton, as per act of 1842. On coke or culm of coal, 30 per cent ad valorem, instead of 5 cents per bushel, as per act of 1842.

Sec. V.—1st. On all vessels or wares, articles and manufactures of cut-glass, cut-glass chandeliers, candlesticks, lustres, lenses, lamps, prisms, and parts of the same; and all drops, icicles, spangles, and ornaments used for mountings; and on all articles or manufactures of plain, moulded, or pressed glass, whether stappened, or the bottoms ground or punticed, or not, 30 per cent ad valorem, instead of the various duties imposed by act of 1842.†

2d. On all apothecaries' vials and bottles, not exceeding the capacity of 16 ozs. each, and all perfumery, and fancy vials and bottles, not exceeding the capacity of 16 ozs. each, 30 per cent ad valorem, instead of the various duties imposed, as per act of 1842.†

3d. On all black and green glass bottles, and jars, and on all demijohns and carboys, 30 per cent ad valorem, instead of the various duties imposed, as per act of 1842.†

4th. On all cylinder or broad window glass, and on all crown window glass, 30 per cent ad valorem, instead of the various duties imposed, as per act of 1842.† On all polished plate glass, whether imported as window glass, or however otherwise specified, not silvered, 20 per cent ad valorem, instead of the various duties imposed, as per act of 1842.† And if silvered, 25 per cent ad valorem, and if silvered and framed, 30 per cent ad valorem, instead of the various duties imposed, as per act of 1842, 2d proviso to 4th subdivision of 5th section, repealed.† And on all porcelain, glass, glass coloured, or paintings on glass, and on all articles or manufactures of glass, or of which glass shall be the component material of chief value, and not otherwise specified, 20 per cent ad valorem, instead of the various duties imposed, as per act of 1842.†

* Reduced to ad valorem, ranging from 45 to 235 per cent.

† Ad valorem duty, ranging from 186 to 243 per cent—average 180, computed by merchants.

5th. On chinaware, porcelainware, earthenware, stoneware, and all other ware, composed of earth or mineral substances, and not otherwise specified, whether gilt, printed, plain, or glazed, 20 per cent ad valorem, instead of 30 per cent, as per act of 1842.

6th. On tanned, sole, or bend leather, all upper leather not otherwise specified, calf and seal skins tanned and dressed, sheep skins tanned and dressed, or skivers, goat skins, or morocco tanned or dressed, kid skins, or morocco, tanned or dressed, goat or sheep skins tanned and not dressed, and all kid and lamb skins tanned and not dressed, skins tanned and dressed, otherwise than in colour, to wit: fawn, kid, and lamb, usually known as chamois, 25 per cent ad valorem, instead of the various duties imposed, as per act of 1842.† On men's boots or bootees of leather, wholly or partially manufactured; on men's shoes or pumps, wholly or partially manufactured; women's boots or bootees, wholly or partially manufactured; children's boots, bootees, or shoes, wholly or partially manufactured; women's double-soled pumps or welts, shoes or slippers, wholly or partially manufactured, whether of leather, prunella, or other material, except silk, 30 per cent ad valorem, instead of the various duties imposed, as per act of 1842.‡

7th. On men's leather gloves, women's and children's leather habit gloves, and extra and demi-length leather gloves, 25 per cent ad valorem, instead of the various duties imposed, as per act of 1842.‡ On leather caps or hats, leather braces or suspenders, and all other braces or suspenders, of whatever materials composed, except India-rubber, and on leather bottles, patent leather, and on all other manufactures of leather, or of which leather is a component material of chief value, not otherwise specified, 30 per cent ad valorem, instead of 35 per cent, as per act of 1842.

8th. On fur hats, caps, muffs, tippets, and other manufactures of fur, not specified, 30 per cent ad valorem, instead of 35 per cent, as per act of 1842. On hats of wool, and hat bodies or felts, made in whole or in part of wool, 30 per cent ad valorem, instead of 18 cents each, as per act of 1842.

9th. On hats and bonnets for men, women, and children, from Panama, Manila, Leghorn, Naples, or elsewhere, composed of satin, straw, chip, grass, palm-leaf, rattan, willow, or any other vegetable substance, or of hair, whalebone, or any other material, not otherwise specified, 25 per cent ad valorem, instead of 35 per cent, as per act of 1842.

10th. On feathers for beds, and on down of all kinds, on India-rubber oil-cloth, webbing, shoes, braces, suspenders, or other fabrics, or manufactured articles, composed wholly or in part of India-rubber; on all clocks, and on crystals of glass for watches, and on glass or pebbles for spectacles, or eye-glasses, when not set, 20 per cent ad valorem, instead of the various duties imposed, as per act of 1842; and so much of the proviso to 10th subdivision of 5th section, as directs the valuation of India-rubber braces or suspenders, at two dollars per dozen, repealed.

11th. On paving tiles and bricks, 15 per cent ad valorem, instead of 25 per cent, as per act of 1842. On metal buttons, 25 per cent ad valorem, instead of 30 per cent, as per act of 1842. On all other buttons and button moulds, 20 per cent ad valorem, instead of 25 per cent, as per act of 1842; and the first proviso to the 12th subdivision of 5th section, repealed.

---

† Treasury Document, ad valorem, 53 per cent.

‡ 50 to 75 per cent ad valorem.

SEC. VI.—On white or red leads, litherage, acetate, or chromate of lead, dry or ground in oil; on whiting or Paris white; and all ochres or ochry earths, used in the composition of painters' colours, dry or ground in oil; on sulphate of barytes; on linseed, rapeseed, and hempseed oil; and on putty, 30 per cent ad valorem, instead of the various duties imposed, as per act of 1842.*

SEC. VII.—On bank, folio, quarto-post of all kinds, and letter and bank note paper; on antiquarian, demy, drawing, &c., (all kinds of paper and pasteboard included and specified,) 30 per cent ad valorem, instead of the various duties imposed, as per act of 1842.† On all paper hangings, paper for screens or fire-boards, 30 per cent ad valorem, instead of 35 per cent, as per act of 1842. On all blank books, bound, 30 per cent ad valorem, instead of 20 cents per pound, as per act of 1842. On all other paper, not enumerated herein, 30 per cent ad valorem, instead of 15 cents per pound, as per act of 1842.

SEC. VIII.—1st. On raw sugar, (commonly called brown sugar,) not advanced beyond its raw state, by claying, boiling, clarifying, or other process, and on brown clayed sugar, 2 cents per pound instead of 2½ cents per pound as per act of 1842. On syrup of sugar or of sugar-cane, 1½ cents per pound instead of 2½ cents per pound, as per act of 1842. On all other sugars when advanced beyond the raw state, by boiling, clarifying, or other process, and not yet refined, 3 cents per pound instead of 4 cents per pound, as per act of 1842. On refined sugars, (whether loaf, lumped, crushed, or pulverized, and where, after being refined, they have been tinctured, coloured, or in any way adulterated,) and on sugar candy, 4 cents per pound instead of 6 cents per pound, as per act of 1842. On molasses, 3 mills per pound instead of 4½ mills per pound, as per act of 1842.

2d. On cocoa, chocolate, cinnamon, oil of cloves, crude camphor, indigo, ivory or bone black, oil of vitriol, and sulphuric acid, 15 per cent ad valorem, instead of the various duties imposed, as per act of 1842. On ginger ground, and ginger in the root, when not preserved, woad or pastil, alum, and coperas, and green vitriol, 20 per cent ad valorem, instead of the various duties imposed, as per act of 1842. On mace, nutmegs, cloves, Chinese-cassia, pimento, black pepper, camphor refined, opium, glue, gunpowder, blue or Roman vitriol, or sulphate of copper, almonds, prunes, sweet oil of almonds, dates, currants, figs, all nuts not specified, except those used for dying, Muscatel and bloom raisins, either in boxes or jars, and on all other raisins, 30 per cent ad valorem, instead of the various duties imposed, as per act of 1842.‡

3d. On olive oil in casks, spermaceti oil of foreign fisheries, whale or other fish oil, not sperm, of foreign fisheries, spermaceti or wax candles, and candles of spermaceti or wax combined, tallow candles, all hard soap except Windsor shaving, and all other perfumed or fancy soaps, and wash-balls and Castile soap, on starch, and pearl or hulled barley, 30 per cent ad valorem, instead of the various duties imposed, as per act of 1842.

4th. On salt, 20 per cent ad valorem, instead of 8 cents per bushel, as per act

* 100 to 146 per cent ad valorem.

† From 35 per cent ad valorem, per Treasury Document, to 97 per cent, computed by merchants.

‡ Spices from 50 to 90 per cent ad valorem; black pepper, 130 per cent.

of 1842. On vinegar, beef, pork, hams, bacon, cheese, butter, lard, wheat, barley, rye, oats, Indian corn or maize, wheat flour, Indian meal, and potatoes; on foreign fish, namely, dried or smoked, on mackerel and herrings, pickled or salted, on pickled salmon, and all other fish pickled in barrels, 25 per cent ad valorem, instead of the various duties imposed, as per act of 1842.

SEC. IX.—1st. On spirits from grain of first proof, 42 cents per gallon; on spirits from grain of second proof, 45 cents per gallon; on spirits from grain of third proof, 48 cents per gallon; on spirits from grain of fourth proof, 52 cents per gallon; on spirits from grain of fifth proof, 60 cents per gallon; on spirits from grain of above fifth proof, 75 cents per gallon, instead of the various duties imposed, as per act of 1842. On spirits from other material than grain, first and second proof, 38 cents per gallon; on spirits from other material than grain, third proof, 42 cents per gallon; on spirits from other material* than grain, fourth proof, 48 cents per gallon; on spirits from other material than grain, fifth proof, 57 cents per gallon; on spirits from other material than grain, above fifth proof, 70 cents per gallon, instead of the various duties imposed, as per act of 1842.

2d. On wines of all sorts, 30 per cent ad valorem, instead of the various duties, as per act of 1842.

SEC. X.—Unmanufactured cotton, guano, and sulphate of quinine, shall all be exempt from duty, instead of the various duties imposed, as per act of 1842.

SEC. XI.—So much of the act of 1842, as directs the manner in which the market value or wholesale price of goods, wares, and merchandise, imported into the United States, and subject to ad valorem duties, or duties based upon the value of the square yard, or any specified quantity or parcel of such goods, shall be ascertained, be and the same is hereby so modified, that to said value or price to be ascertained as provided for in said section, shall be added only the costs and charges, which shall have been incurred to and at the place of exportation.

SEC. XII.—All ad valorem duties under this act or the act of 1842, of which it is amendatory, which exceed 25 per cent ad valorem, shall be reduced to that rate on the 1st September, 1845.

SEC. XIII—Such parts of the act of 1842, as are not touched by this act, to remain in as full force as if re-enacted.

SEC. XIV.—The 12th section of the act of 1842, so modified, that all goods imported from within, or this side of the Cape of Good Hope, may remain in the public stores 120 instead of 60 days; and those from beyond the Cape of Good Hope, 150 instead of 90 days: provided 6 per cent interest be paid from time of entry to time of payment, on the duties, as part of the duties chargeable on said goods.

---

* 80 per cent ad valorem—Turk's island, 144.

COLONIAL STATISTICS.

[NEW SERIES.]

NO. IV.—THE ISLAND OF BARBADOES.

The exact period when and by whom Barbadoes was discovered, remains in doubt. It is supposed that the Portuguese christened the island with the name *Los Barbaros*, in reference to its rude state when first visited by them. Barbadoes was first settled by the English in 1605. Another authority says, that Sir William Curteen, an enterprising London merchant, was the first to effect a settlement on Barbadoes, in 1625; he acted on behalf of the Earl of Marlborough, who had obtained from James I. a patent for the island to him and his heirs for ever. Sir William Tufton was the first governor and commander-in-chief, and was appointed in 1629. For twenty years the encroachments of private interests, and especially the cupidity of the usurper, Cromwell, caused Barbadoes to become the prey of dissension and military aggression; but after the restoration, the attention of the British government was called to the state of Barbadoes, (1652,) and it immediately reformed its condition, and reduced it to a useful dependeney of the crown. Charles II. conferred the dignity of knighthood upon twelve gentlemen of Barbadoes, in testimony of their attachment to the royal cause, shown in their opposition to the aggression of Cromwell. Vide p. 274 of this volume.

Geography.—Barbadoes, situated in latitude 13° 5′ north, longitude 59° 41′ west, being at the extremity of the great American archipelago, is the most easterly of the Caribbean Islands. Its extreme length is 25 miles; extreme breadth, 14 miles; extreme altitude, 1,147 feet; the area covers a space of 166 square miles, or 106,470 acres. (Mr. M'Culloch computes the number of acres at 105,000 only.) The aspect of Barbadoes from the sea presents a monotonous outline of low undulating country, cultivation covering nearly the whole surface; for productiveness and extent of population, the island is remarkable; during the early periods of its colonial history, its prosperity was the envy of every other colony in the West Indies. The soil is generally good, varying from a rich deep mould to a light sand, with occasional tracts of red clay of considerable depth. It is indifferently supplied with water; but there are several springs, one of which is of a mineral nature, emitting a stream of sulphuretted hydrogen gas. In 1780, Barbadoes was ravaged by a terrific hurricane, which lasted for forty-eight hours, and devastated the island; of 11 churches, and 3 chapels, only 3 were left standing, and not more than 30 houses at Bridgetown, the capital; the mole-head, which cost the colonists 20,000*l.*, was destroyed, and the castle, battery, forts, &c., demolished; the loss of lives amounted to 3,000, and of property to 1,018,928*l.*

Climate.—Mean highest temperature in the shade, 89°; mean, 81°; lowest, 73°. Range of thermometer, on an average of five years, maximum, 87°; medium, 81°; minimum, 75°. The average quantity of rain has been calculated to be 58 inches. Owing to the flatness of the island leaving it open to the sea-breeze, and its extensive cultivation, it is peculiarly healthy.

Commerce: Productions.—The trade of Barbadoes has fluctuated very much at various periods, owing to hurricanes, &c. The average exports now: are sugar, 49,619,584 lbs.; rum, 1,320 gallons; molasses, 656,890 gallons. The other staples are arrowroot, cotton, ginger, and aloes. Formerly, indigo, tobacco, and fustic were cultivated. The average value of exports has been calculated from official returns to be 787,344*l.*; imports 627,047*l.* The following details will serve to prove the accuracy of the above statements: the total value of exports for the year ending January, 1838, was 897,990*l.*; of which 773,077*l.* was to Great Britain and Ireland; the imports for the same period amounted to 606,586*l.* The exports of 1838 exceeded those of 1834, by 273,305*l.*; and those of 1832, by 489,627*l.* The following is the official account of the quantity of sugar produced in Barbadoes during the five years preceding 1838: 1833, 384,971 cwts.; 1834, 394,527 cwts.; 1835, 344,689 cwts.; 1836, 373,428 cwts.; 1837, 405,713 cwts. From this table, it will be seen that sugar production has slowly but steadily increased, up to the last quotation. M'Culloch, in the last edition of his "Dictionary of Commerce," states that Barbadoes exports about 21,000 hhds. of sugar, of 16 cwts. each (336,000 cwts.), annually; which is a fair deduction from the tables above copied. But the imports of sugar into the United Kingdom from Barbadoes, in 1841, were only 257,108 cwts.; and this was some improvement upon the imports of the previous year.*

We now proceed to the articles rum, molasses, and coffee. The quantities imported into the United Kingdom from Barbadoes, were,—

	Rum.	Molasses.	Coffee.
1834	2,170 gallons.	55,553 cwts.	77,868 lbs.
1835	1,798 "	58,125 "	57,825 "

* The equalization of the East and West India sugar-duties, judiciously effected by the act 6 and 7 Wm. IV, cap. 26, has, by occasioning a considerably-increased exportation of sugar from India, contributed in so far to countervail the decreasing exports from the West Indies.—*M'Culloch.*

From a table of the import and sales of Barbadoes cotton wool at Liverpool, for the years 1840-41-42, we arrive at the following particulars :—

Imports...1840 ... 370	1841 ... 412	1842 ... 225
Stock.....1840 ... 320	1841 ... 910	1842 ... 900

Showing that the sales have been but trifling. The aggregate annual value of the productions of Barbadoes is 1,270,863*l.*

The revenue in 1835 was 27,580*l.* 4s. 6d., and the expenditure 27,580*l.* 4s. 6d. Barbadoes ranks in the first class amongst British colonies valuable for their productions and trade. A colonial bank has been established on the island. By the last report of the directors it appeared, that the balance in favour of the bank was 22,052 dollars, from which amount a dividend of 3 per cent. had been declared.

Colonial Expenditure.—[From 1828 to 1836.] 1828, 18,566*l.* ; 1829, 19,943*l.*; 1830, 18,566*l.*; 1831, 18,354*l.*; 1832, 18,354*l.*; 1833, 16,536*l.*; 1834, 17,841*l.*; 1835, 27,580*l.*; 1836, 29,373*l.*—*Blue Book.*

Cost of civil establishment in 1834, 7,268*l.*; ecclesiastical establishment, 3,910*l.*

Population. — Barbadoes, according to the latest returns, has a population of about 16,000 whites, 2,700 free people of colour, and 68,000 slaves — total, 86,700. In the year 1670, the population amounted to 50,000 whites, and 100,000 coloured and negroes. The proportion of compensation awarded under the Emancipation Act, was 1,721,345*l.* 19s. 7d.; the average value of a slave from 1822 to 1830 being 47*l.* 1s. 3½d.

Crime. — A statement of the number of prisoners in the gaols throughout each year, from 1829 to 1836, shows a gradual increase of crime in the colony, but not a greater increase than may be fairly allowed to a growing population, and the character of the offences is seldom serious.

Government.—A governor; council of 12 members; assembly of 22 members; Governor and Commander-in-chief of Barbadoes, Tobago, Grenada, St. Vincent, and St. Lucia, Right Honourable Sir Charles Edward Grey, Kt.; Commander of the Forces in the Windward Islands, Lieutenant-General J. Maister; Bishop of Barbadoes and the Windward Islands, William H. Coleridge, D.D.; Archdeacon, Venerable Thomas Parry, M.A.; Clerk of the Crown and Prothonotary of the Common Pleas, P. J. D. Lynch, Esq.; Secretary and Clerk of the Council, and Remembrancer of the Court of Exchequer, G. White,

Esq.; Provost Marshal, B. Wolrand, Esq.; Deputy, J. Walton, Esq.; Registrar in Chancery, Chief Justice Sir R. B. Clarke; Attorney-General, H. E. Sharpe, Esq.; Solicitor-General, J. Sealy, Esq.; Judge of the Vice-Admiralty Court, Registrar of ditto, T. H. Byde, Esq.; Collector of Customs, A. Stewart, Esq.; Agent in London, J. P. Mayers, Esq., 60, St. James's-street.

Religion.—Established religion, the Episcopal: there are sects of Wesleyans and Moravians.

Education.—From a statement of the number and description of the schools in Barbadoes in 1834, it appears that there were 28 establishments, and nearly 2,000 scholars. The students of Codrington House receive their board and education for 35*l.* per annum, and are examined and ordained by the bishop, if intended for the church. At the cathedral school about 160 white children are educated, precisely upon the plan of the national school in England.

Cities.—Bridgetown, on the shores of Carlisle Bay, south-west, having a population of 25,000. The other towns are, Spikes or Speights Town, west; Hole or James Town, west; Austin's Town, south. There are upwards of 20,000 houses in Bridgetown. The handsome and spacious barracks of St. Ann's, with their fine parade, are at the southern extremity of the town. The square, with Nelson's statue, is well laid out, and many of the houses are handsome. The government house, called *Pilgrim*, is about half a mile from Bridgetown. The fort of St. Ann's is small, but strong, and is well stored with arms and ammunition. It contains many thousand stand of arms in perfect order.

Military.—Service companies of the 2d battalion of her Majesty's foot, 23d, 46th, 71st, and 92d foot, are located here; the militia force is six regiments strong. The windward position of this island has, from an early date, caused it to be regarded as an important military post and rendezvous, whence a descent might with greater readiness be made upon the other insular possessions on these seas. The mean ratio of mortality among the troops for 33 years has been calculated at 13.4. March is the healthiest and October the most unhealthy month of the year in the Windward and Leeward Islands.

The Colonial Arms.—The device on the shield is partly of a mythological character, and represents a figure (the British monarch) holding the trident in his right hand, and standing erect in a triumphal car or chariot, which is drawn by fiery steeds, and seen dashing through the waves of the ocean. The design appears to be typical of the dominion of the seas which Great Britain holds in right of her naval conquests.

ON THE RIGHTS OF THE ABORIGINES IN CASES OF COLONIAL SETTLEMENT.

BY JOSEPH STAMMERS, ESQ.

THE history of colonial settlements is so fraught with cruelty, deception, and injustice, that it cannot be read by any person of sensibility, and still less by the true Christian, without frequently calling up to his cheek the blush of honest indignation.

Without giving entire credence to those stories of imaginary innocence and happiness with which the narratives of some voyagers have invested the natives of the islands of the Pacific, or the more inland dwellers of the newly-discovered continents of ancient travel, it is impossible to deny, that wherever the European foot has trod, not only has it conveyed diseases previously unknown to the aboriginal race, and manners at variance with every correct and social principle, but a system of pillage and usurpation has been pursued, which, after depriving the natives of their homes and their hunting-grounds, has ended in leaving the miserable remnant of a once populous and noble race to the lingering process of absolute extermination.

It may be well, therefore, to consider this great and interesting subject with the attention to which it is entitled. What right has the civilized European thus to intrude upon the simple and untaught native of the distant shore?

Let us suppose that we are listening to the naked savage so beautifully described by Erskine, "in the indignant character of a prince surrounded by his subjects, and addressing the governor of a British colony, holding a bundle of sticks in his hand as the notes of his unlettered eloquence":—

> "Who is it," said the jealous ruler over the desert encroached upon by the restless foot of English adventure, "who is it that causes this river to rise in the high mountains, and to empty itself into the ocean? Who is it that causes to blow the loud winds of winter, and that calms them again in summer? Who is it that rears up the shade of these lofty forests, and blasts them with the quick lightning at his pleasure? The same Being who gave to you a country on the other side of the waters, and gave ours to us."

The terms which are generally used to designate the right of the European to intrude upon the shores of the savage are "the right of conquest;" but, to say that any European power became possessed of certain colonial territories by "the right of conquest," is a mere begging of the question; for, after all, the difficulty recurs in its entire original force. What is the right of conquest? Does the human mind in its integrity, and apart from the teachings of man, recognize any such right? Has the great Giver of every good and perfect gift, who appointed the habitations of all the dwellers on the earth, bestowed upon this nation, or upon that, the right of intrusion upon the possessions of its weaker neighbour, the right of thrusting out, by gradual usurpation, or of destroying by the power of the sword, the simple and untaught race whom they find in the full and peaceful possession and enjoyment of the wide-spreading lands, the fertilizing rivers, the untainted atmosphere, and all those rich and splendid gifts of nature which are so evidently *not* of man?

Now, let us try the question by the *argumentum ad hominem*, and let us see how it looks, when the usual course of things is reversed. *We* will become, for the sake of the argument, the persons intruded upon, and some other great and warlike nation shall be the intruders; and this is no very violent supposition, for, after all, the right, as at present claimed and exercised, can only be put upon the ground of the right of the stronger against the weaker. If, therefore, we can imagine a nation infinitely mightier than our own in the mechanical powers of aggression, with what feelings should we perceive them pouring down upon our coasts, taking possession of our ports, establishing themselves upon our native soil, building fortresses for their protection, and eventually lording it over the oppressed inhabitants of the land.

Our minds are unwilling to take this view of the subject. We are apt to look upon it as a moral impossibility. It is *not* a moral impossibility. The adventure would no doubt be full of peril to the aggressors; the spirit of our countrymen would rise, I trust, to the height of the emergency, and in my heart I should hope and desire that every foot that touched the sacred soil of Britain, with the view of conquest, would be repelled with indignation; and such, no doubt, would be the universal feeling of the nation. But are *we* the only persons who have a right to such feelings? Would not the Peruvians, had they been aware of the designs of their invaders; the inhabitants of Bengal and Bombay, in more recent times; and the New Zealanders, of our own day—be entitled to maintain the same reverential love for their fatherland, and ought they not to be expected to burn with the same indignation at the very idea of intrusion?

It is very singular that this subject does not appear to have been much considered by the writers upon natural law. As far as I have been able to discover, neither Grotius, nor Puffendorff, nor Burlamaqui at all touch upon it. Mr. Justice Blackstone rather intimates than expresses an opinion upon the question, in the following passage from the second volume of his Commentaries:—

"Upon the same principle was founded the right of migration, or sending colonies to find out new habitations, when the mother-country was overcharged with inhabitants, which was practised as well by the Phœnicians and Greeks as the Germans, Scythians, and other northern people. And, so long as it was confined to the stocking and cultivation of desert uninhabited countries, it kept strictly within the limits of the law of nature. But how far the seizing on countries already peopled, and driving out or massacring the innocent and defenceless natives, merely because they differed from their invaders in language, in religion, customs, in government, or in colour; how far such a conduct was consonant to nature, to reason, or to Christianity, deserved well to be considered by those who have rendered their names immortal by thus civilizing mankind."

Vattel, however, has touched the question in another manner; in the 18th chapter of his first book, he says:—

"There is another celebrated question to which the discovery of the New World has principally given rise. It is asked if a nation may lawfully take possession of a part of a vast country in which there are found none but erratic nations, incapable, by the smallness of their numbers, to people the whole? We have already observed, in establishing the obligation to cultivate the earth, that these nations cannot exclusively appropriate to themselves more land than they have occasion for, and which they are unable to settle and to cultivate. Their removing their habitations through these immense regions, cannot be taken for a true and legal possession; and the people of Europe, too closely pent up, finding land of which these nations are in no particular want, and of which they make no actual and constant use, may lawfully possess it, and establish colonies there. We have already said that the earth belongs to the human race in general, and was designed to furnish it with subsistence; if each nation had resolved from the beginning to appropriate to itself a vast country, that the people might live only by hunting, fishing, and wildfowls, our globe would not be sufficient to maintain a tenth part of its present inhabitants. People have not, then, deviated from the views of nature, in confining the Indians within narrower limits. However, we cannot help praising the moderation of the English Puritans who first settled in New England, who, notwithstanding their being furnished with a charter from their sovereign, purchased from the Indians the lands they resolved to cultivate. This laudable example was followed by Mr. William Penn, who planted the colony of Quakers in Pennsylvania."

Now, if Mons. Vattel is right in his general proposition that "nations cannot exclusively appropriate to themselves more land than they have occasion for, and which they are unable to settle and to cultivate," some very curious consequences will follow. It will be found that there are countries in the world, and civilized countries too, in which there are vast tracts of uninhabited territory; according to Mons. Vattel's proposition, these (wherever they are to be found), if the inhabitants of the country are unable to settle and to cultivate them, are the common property of mankind; but what would the Czar of all the Russias say to a settlement of the unemployed artisans of our large manufacturing towns upon the uncultivated parts of his dominions? Would it be enough to state, that we could prove, distinctly, from Mons. Vattel, that according to the law of nature we had as good a right to be there as the emperor himself, or any of his subjects? And, although Vattel confines his proposition to erratic nations, what better right have we to intrude upon the erratic than the settled tribes? The Tartars, for instance, are found roving over the immense plains of their country, and seeking, in the luxuriance of natural productions, what is obtained by others from the laborious process of agriculture. Who is to say to them, If you settle, the land is yours; but, according to Mons. Vattel, because you are erratic, you have no sort of proprietary in it? The Indians want large tracts of country for hunting-grounds, immense streams for fisheries, entire forests for dwelling-places; their habits and manners must be completely altered before they could dispense with them; whole generations must pass away before you could bring them near to the customs of civilization; you would say, "Live in a town;" but the answer of the Indian would be, "I cannot live in a town; I hate a town; the manners of its inhabitants disgust me; there is no air, no light, no wide beauty of the landscape to please my eye; I must hunt, and shoot, and fish, or I cannot live. Besides, you, who call yourselves our white brethren, what do you get by living in towns?—are you any better for it than we poor red Indians? You buy, you sell, you cheat each other, you say of each other what is not true: no, no, I *cannot* live in a town."

Now where is the answer to this truthful and unlettered eloquence? Certainly not in Mons. Vattel; and, if the practice of some of the best men that ever peopled the earth, I mean the Puritans and Quakers of the seventeenth century, be any authority upon this question, the "*moderation*" (as it is called) of such men as the Pilgrim Fathers, and William Penn, the founder of Pennsylvania, is of more weight in establishing the reverse of the proposition, than all that Vattel has alleged in its favour.

Even the American government, though not quite so celebrated as some others for a strict and accurate attention to the deep-seated principles of justice and humanity, have, in their treaties with the miserable remnants of those once numerous tribes of Indians which are daily dwindling out of existence before the rapid advance of what is called civilization, and falling as quickly as the mighty trees which once overshadowed their dwelling-place, hushed their children to sleep with their gentle murmurs, or bending for a moment beneath the storm, taught the rude and untutored minds of these sons of nature that there was One riding upon the wings of the wind, before whose power even the primeval oak of the forest must bow down from his lofty aspirings; even the American government has acknowledged the native rights of the Indians to the soil upon which they dwell.

The supreme court of the United States has expressly declared, that the person who purchases land from the Indians, within their territory, incorporates himself with them, and, so far as respects the property purchased, holds his title under their protection, subject to their laws. If (say they) they annul the grant, we know of no tribunal which can revise and set aside the proceeding.

Mr. Wirt, the late attorney-general of the United States, has recorded his opinion—

"That the territory of the Cherokees is not within the jurisdiction of the State of Georgia; but within the sole and exclusive jurisdiction of the Cherokee nation, and that, consequently, the State of Georgia has no right to extend her laws over that territory."

General Washington, in a speech to one of the tribes of Indians, in 1790, not only recognizes the same national independence, but adds—

"Your great object seems to be, the security of your remaining lands; and I have, therefore, upon this point meant to be sufficiently strong and clear. In future, you cannot be defrauded of your lands; you possess the right to sell, and the right of refusing to sell your lands; the sale of your lands in future will depend entirely on yourselves."

Reluctantly as this declaration appears to have been made, and guarded as it is in its terms against *future* encroachment, who does not perceive that it, in effect, lays open the whole question, admits the right of the Indian to exist where God had planted him, and is a tacit and implied disclaimer of those rights which have been so erroneously supposed to exist in all civilized nations by Mons. Vattel?

Let us now see how far the history of colonization agrees with the views of justice propounded by these authorities.

When Columbus launched forth upon the mighty and untraversed waters which were to carry him to the yet undiscovered shores of the western hemisphere, what a multitude of blessings might have been expected to accompany him with reference to the simple people upon whose coasts he was about to land! How may the bright and sparkling minds of the close of the fifteenth century have followed the departing sails of the Spanish expedition, with hopes of many nations listening for the first time to the pure and simple truths of the Christian religion, casting the miserable objects of a depraved idolatry to the moles and to the bats, and partaking not only of all that civilization could confer in the shape of knowledge and refinement, but of hopes and prospects which are as far above the value of human science as the heavens are above the earth.

He sailed upon his expedition, the vessels faded from sight upon the verge of the horizon; the invincible patience of the noble commander was proved to the uttermost; and, having surmounted every difficulty and impediment of the voyage, the mariners descend upon the long-wished-for shore, a Te Deum is sung, and a crucifix is planted upon the soil: but did any of the proper blessings of civilization follow? Hear the reply, in the language of a native chief called Hatuey:—

"He stood (says Las Casas) upon the defensive at their first landing, and endeavoured to drive them back to their ships. His feeble troops, however, were soon broken and dispersed; and he himself being taken prisoner, Velasquez, according to the barbarous maxim of the Spaniards, considered him as a slave who had taken arms against his master, and condemned him to the flames.

"When Hatuey was fastened to the stake, a Franciscan friar, labouring to *convert* him, promised him immediate admission into the joys of heaven if he would embrace the Christian faith. 'Are there any Spaniards (says he, after some pause), in that region of bliss which you describe?'—'Yes,' replied the monk, 'but such only as are worthy and good.' 'The best of them (returned the indignant Cazique) have neither worth nor goodness. *I will not* go to a place where I may meet with that accursed race!'"

The mode in which the Dutch have conducted themselves in their attempts at colonization, have almost made them the *opprobrium humani generis.*" In India, at the Cape of Good Hope, and in Japan, they have brought such a stigma upon the very name and symbols of Christianity, that their expulsion from the latter country has been followed by a sort of commemorative indignity which is done to the cross by the Japanese.

Their manner of first gaining a footing in Batavia is thus recorded by the historians of Java:—

"In the first place they wished to ascertain the strength of Iakatra, the native town, on the ruins of which Batavia was built. They therefore landed like peons, or messengers, the captain of the ship disguising himself with a turban, and accompanying several natives of the Coromandel coast. When he had made his observations, he entered upon trade, offering, however, much better terms than were just, and making more presents than were necessary. A friendship thus took place between him and the prince; when this was established, the captain said that his ship was in want of repairs, and the prince allowed the vessel to come up the river. There the captain knocked out the planks of the bottom, and sunk the vessel to obtain a pretence for further delay, and then begged a very small piece of ground on which to build a shed for the protection of the sails, and other property, during the repair of the vessel. This being granted, the captain raised a wall of mud, so that nobody could know what he was doing, and continued to court the favour of the prince. He soon requested as much more land as could be covered by a buffalo's hide, on which to build a small poudok. This being complied with, he cut the hide into strips, and claimed all the land he could enclose with them. He went on with his buildings, engaging to pay all the expenses of raising them. When the fort was finished, he threw down his mud wall, planted his cannon, and refused to pay a doit."

Without describing, however, the oppressions of the Portuguese, when establishing colonial settlements in various parts of the world, or the treatment of the Hottentots at the Cape of Good Hope, by the Dutch and by the English, let us turn to one splendid instance of justice and humanity in the person of William Penn, whose treatment of the natives when establishing the colony of Pennsylvania, stands out in remarkable and refreshing contrast to the customs of the world around him, and furnishes the rule by which all attempts at colonization should be guided.

It is well known that William Penn received a grant of the territory, to which he gave the name of Pennsylvania, as payment from the government for money due to his father, Admiral Penn; but the principles of William Penn did not allow him to look upon that gift as a warrant to dispossess the first inhabitants of the land. He had accordingly appointed his commissioners the preceding year, to treat with them for the fair purchase of part of their lands, and for their joint possession of the remainder; and the terms of the settlement being now nearly agreed upon, he proceeded very soon after his arrival to conclude the settlement, and solemnly to pledge his faith, and to ratify and confirm the treaty, in right both of the Indians and the planters. For this purpose, a grand convocation of the tribes had been appointed near the spot where Philadelphia now stands; and it was agreed that he and the presiding Sachems should meet and exchange faith under the spreading branches of a prodigious elm tree that grew on the banks of the river. On the day appointed, accordingly, an innumerable company of the Indians assembled in that neighbourhood and were seen, with their dark faces and brandished arms, moving in vast swarms in the depth of the woods that then overshaded that now cultivated region. On the other hand, William Penn, with a moderate attendance of friends, advanced to meet them. He came unarmed, in his usual plain dress, without banners, or mace, or guards, or carriages, and only distinguished from his companions by wearing a blue sash of silk network, and by having in his hand a roll of parchment, on which was engrossed the confirmation of the treaty of purchase and amity. As soon as he drew near the spot where the Sachems were assembled, the whole multitude of the Indians threw down their weapons, and seated themselves on the ground in groups, each under his own chieftain, and the presiding chief intimated to William Penn that the natives were ready to hear him. Having been thus called upon, he began :—

"The great Spirit (he said) who made him and them, who ruled the heaven and the earth, and who knew the innermost thoughts of man, knew that he and his friends had a hearty desire to live in peace and friendship with them, and to serve them to the uttermost of their power. It was not their custom to use hostile weapons against their fellow-creatures; for which reason they had come unarmed. Their object was not to do injury, and thus provoke the great Spirit, but to do good. They were then met on the broad pathway of good faith and good will, so that no advantage was to be taken on either side; but all was to be openness, brotherhood, and love!' After these and other words he unrolled the parchment, and by means of the same interpreter conveyed to them, article by article, the conditions of the purchase, and the words of the compact then made for their eternal union. Among other things, they were not to be molested, even in the territory they had alienated, for it was to be common to them and the English. They were to have the same liberty to do all things therein relating to the improvement of their grounds, and providing sustenance for their families, which the English had. If disputes should arise between the two, they should be settled by twelve persons, half of whom should be English and half Indians. He then paid them for the land, and made them many presents besides from the merchandise which had been open before them. Having done this, he laid the roll of parchment on the ground, observing again that the ground should be common to both people. He then added, that he would not do as the Marylanders did, that is, call them children, or brothers only; for often parents were apt to whip their children too severely, and brothers sometimes would differ; neither would he compare the friendship between him and them to a chain, for the rain might sometimes rust it, or a tree might fall and break it; but he should consider them as the same flesh and blood as the Christians, and the same as if one man's body was to be divided into two parts. He then took up the parchment, and presented it to the Sachem who wore the horn in the chaplet, and desired him and the other Sachems to preserve it carefully for three generations, that their children might know what had passed between them, just as if he himself had remained with them to repeat it.

"The Indians in return made long and stately harangues, of which, however, no more seems to have been remembered, but that they pledged themselves to live in love with William Penn and his children so long as the sun and moon shall endure. Thus ended this famous treaty, of which it has been remarked with much truth and severity, 'that it was the only one ever concluded which was not ratified by an oath, and the only one that never was broken.'"

In this treaty we see the proper mode of effecting a colonial settlement. It is a noble example to the whole world of the policy of truth and justice; and although it might have been sneered at, when it occurred, as an affectation of singularity, and an absurd deviation from the custom of the nations of the earth, it stands to this day a monument of virtue to which many of those who are accustomed to the base and tortuous conduct of mankind, look up with veneration.

Nor should the great lesson which William Penn, the persecuted Quaker of the seventeenth century, taught to nations and kingdoms, be lost upon us as individuals. We should learn from it to pay no regard to long and inveterate usage, when it comes in contact with settled principles of truth and virtue,—we should be instructed by it to remember, that the customs of the world are not worth a thought in comparison with the higher dictates of religion, and that the name which has been the subject of a thousand derisions upon earth, is often that which will deserve to be established in the affections of heavenly dominations and hierarchies for ever.

REFORM IN THE COLONIAL OFFICE.

MR. JAMES STEPHEN.—*SUUM CUIQUE.*

THE rumour is probably well founded, that Mr. Stephen is knocked up at last.

Whether he is dismissed in declared disgrace, as he deserves to be,—or whether he is to be pensioned and baronetted, or sinecured, as is likely,—it is said that in some way or other he is to be got rid of.

The form of the thing is of no very great consequence to the colonies, or to the colonial interests of the country, or to the interests of the aborigines of the colonies and to humanity; but in all these respects his removal will be a great, substantial gain.

In point of principle, indeed, he ought to be tried for the many malversations charged upon him—but colonial history will afford a compensation for the loss on this head, which our extremely imperfect colonial administration exposes us to.

If, too, Mr. Stephen live long, he will be punished by seeing the horrible things which have befallen us in the colonies in his time, gradually disappear after his departure from office.

Seeing, however, that as yet rumour is our only security for the fact of this happy change being really in progress, it is fitting that every means be taken to hasten it by showing Mr. Stephen in his true colours. For this purpose, the following illustrations of his character are republished from very various sources.

The first is in the nature of sharp-shooting, from the *tirailleurs* of the columns of the *John Bull*; of which we will only say, that with great ability, the writer has shown far too much tenderness to his unhappy victim.

The experience of the last ten years irresistibly proves that changes of Colonial Secretaries of State make no material change in the measures, and worse than none in the manners, of the Colonial Office. Lord Glenelg succeeds Lord Ripon; Lord Glenelg is pitchforked out, whilst sound asleep, to make way for Lord Normanby; Lord John Russell undertakes to put all right; Lord Stanley steps into "the office," on a change of ministry, as if born to govern dependencies as well as to inherit Knowsley. But to what purpose? Is there a colony a straw the better for all these successions? Has a single colonial grievance been remedied? Is there one dependency, beginning with Heligoland and ending with Canada, that is satisfied with the treatment it has received or is receiving? There is no man bold enough to reply affirmatively to one or all of these questions.

Inquire in the City, at the West-end, in any of the provincial ports connected with the colonies, or of persons acquainted, by correspondence or studies, with our transmarine possessions—ask in the colonies themselves—interrogate ex-governors, retired functionaries, or dismissed *employés*, wherefore this is so? Why change of minister brings no change of policy—no alteration of treatment? You will receive but one answer; varied perhaps in form, but in substance the same. "The Colonial Secretary of the day," this man will tell you, "is a mere puppet in the hands of Mr. James Stephen." That will exclaim, "Stephen is the curse of the office." "Mr. Stephen prevented the importation of Sierra Leone coffee," allege the African merchants. "Mr. Stephen caused the rebellion in Upper Canada," years ago wrote Sir F. Head. "Mr. Stephen has ruined us," protest the New Zealand Company. "Mr. Stephen is the bitterest enemy of systematic colonization," declare the Wakefieldites. "Mr. Stephen stands between us and free labour," complain the West Indians. "Mr. Stephen intercepted my despatches, and never submitted them to his superior," told ex-Governor Campbell to a Committee of the House of Commons. "Mr. Stephen maintained the export duty on cinnamon to our injury," interpose the planters of Ceylon. "Mr. Stephen hinders our obtaining a constitution," roar out the colonists of the Cape of Good Hope: "he caused the Caffre war and the Natal question," they add *sotto voce*. "Mr. Stephen is our evil genius," join the Australians in one general chorus.

In these charges there is, doubtless, some exaggeration, and, may be, not a little injustice; but if there were not a shadow of foundation for any one of them, the universal odium in which Mr. James Stephen is held by every colony, colonist, colonial merchant, and person connected with the colonies, is a most serious obstruction to the good government of these dependencies. There is, however, too much foundation for many of these accusations; Mr. Stephen *is* the blight—the bane—the evil genius of the Colonial Office; and until he be removed thence, public confidence in that department of the state never *can* be restored. No one complains of Mr. Phillipps, of the Home-office; not a murmur can be heard against Mr. Addington, of the Foreign-office; and yet, from north and south, east and west, there is one general exclamation against Mr. James Stephen, of the Colonial Office. It is no political outcry; for Whigs as well as Tories join in it.

It is no temporary clamour; for louder and louder it has been growing for the last eight years. It is no *clique* prejudice; for men that have no confidence in each other unite to declaim against him. It has no single origin; its sources are as numerous as the transactions of the Colonial Office are varied.

Who is this so potent Mr. James Stephen? By birth, the son of the late Mr. Stephen, Master of Chancery; by profession, a lawyer; in habits, industrious; in intellect, acute and cunning, but narrow and contracted; in disposition, cool and malignant; in temper, unforgiving; in appearance, unpleasantly sanctimonious; in associations, "saintly;" to his superiors, obsequious and useful, leading them by appearing to follow; to his inferiors, full of the "pride that apes humility;" careful to avoid coming into collision with strangers; and studiously shunning the smallest appearance of power. Formerly he was the law adviser of the Colonial Office; but on the retirement of Mr. Hay, by suggesting the economy of having a law adviser and an under-secretary in one and the same person, he secured his own appointment to the vacant post, and left "the office" without the control and supervision of a consulting counsel, which it had always previously enjoyed. As a lawyer, Mr. Stephen never rose to mediocrity; as an administrator, he rose to the head of the red-tape school; as a statesman, he is pitiable; as a public man, he has not gained one admirer, not even a single defender; though powerful, he is universally disliked; though in a position to have achieved permanent fame, he is pursued by general condemnation.

We repeat it, if public confidence is to be restored to the colonial department, the primary, the indispensable condition of the restoration is the retirement or dismissal of Mr. James Stephen. Whilst he remains there, no one can, no one will confide in it. He has become so universally unpopular, that, were he as pure as snow, his removal would be necessary, in deference to the general feeling. But more of Mr. James Stephen.

The second illustration of Mr. Stephen's character is of a graver character, and proceeds from weighter parties. It comes out for the good of us all, from the miserable and dangerous imbroglio into which the abuses of the Colonial Office have thrown New Zealand affairs; it consists of as strong a declaration as was ever made by men of business, except old Lord Ellenborough's, in the House of Lords, that a direct falsehood has been told, and that Mr. J—s S——n is the teller of it.

The New Zealand Company is beginning to redeem its character for common sense. After doing enormous mischief by a system of acquiescence in evil, of which a just portion of the punishment has fallen on themselves, they seem to be recovering their senses. Hence the following exposure :—

"When publishing the correspondence, (say they, in the 12th report,) we owe it to ourselves to state, that its suppression hitherto, so far as we are concerned, arose from no engagement or understanding with the Colonial Office, but was determined on spontaneously by ourselves as being required by the amicable sequel of the controversy. We trust, however, that under no circumstances should we have been tempted to publish one side of any part of the controversy without the other. A different view of the obligations of honour seems to have actuated the Colonial Office. In answer to two long letters from your governor to Lord Stanley, dated the 24th and 25th of January, 1843, his lordship, in Mr. Hope's letter of the subsequent 1st February, gave a summary of what he understood to be the conclusions of the New Zealand Company with respect to native rights to property in land. *This summary represents the Company as an unprincipled rapacious body, utterly regardless of the rights and welfare of the natives. This summary, we find, was made public in New Zealand by the local government on the* 19th *September,* 1843, *but unaccompanied by any portion of the two letters whose conclusions it purports to express.* We refer you to those two letters, and especially to that of the 25th of January, which relates exclusively to the natives. When you shall have read those letters,—when you shall have seen how contrary to the truth is the accusation founded on them,—you will perceive all the unfairness of publishing that accusation without a word of the letters. The impolicy of thus, in the name of her Majesty's government, proclaiming the company as foes to the natives, is another matter, of which we take no notice here : our present business is with the unfairness of the proceeding. Viewed in this light, we cannot help connecting it with the unfounded reproaches addressed to us by Mr. Hope on the 4th instant,—with the alterations of the Agreement of May last without our knowledge,—and with a portion of the suppressed correspondence of 1843, to which we must now direct your attention.

" We here allude, in the first place, to a quotation of certain words from Lord John Russell's agreement, in Mr. Hope's letter to your governor, of the 10th of January, 1843; which words, as quoted by Mr. Hope, have a meaning totally different from that which they bear in the sentence from which he extracts them, and of which they form an essential part. You will find this extreme unfairness exposed in your governor's letter to Lord Stanley, of the 24th January, 1843. We allude also to the manner in which the Colonial Department treated a letter from your governor to Lord Stanley, bearing date 24th November, 1841, which we withdrew on the 10th of January, 1842, and sent in again on the 30th January, 1843. You will obtain a knowledge of the whole matter by reading Mr. Hope's letter of the 15th February, 1843, and your governor's reply of the 22d February. And, finally, we allude to a letter from Mr. Stephen, one of the Under-Secretaries of State for the Colonies, to Lord Stanley, dated 1st March, 1843, which his lordship transmitted to us on the 15th of the same month. That letter closes the correspondence in Appendix C., and appears unanswered. In fact, it never was answered. It did not reach us till the correspondence preceding it had resulted in amicable negotiation between Lord Stanley and ourselves; and we then deemed it imprudent, on account of those interests of which wewere bound to take care, without regard to our personal feelings, to send an answer, *which must have been so very painful to Mr. Stephen, as a positive re-assertion of the statements which he deliberately contradicts, together with ample proof that some of the minutely circumstantial evidence which he brings in support of the contradiction, cannot be founded in fact.*"

[The letter of Mr. Stephen, thus plainly dealt with by the New Zealand Company, is published in the Appendix to their Report. It is an elaborate refutation of "an " assertion that would represent him, as he says, first as having betrayed his duty, and " then as having endeavoured to shelter himself against this reproach by an unfounded "contradiction of it;"—and it closes by a sentence not very likely to increase the equanimity of the learned member of the House of Commons named in it. Three individuals are asserted by the Company, to have met Mr. Stephen on this occasion; and in denying that he ever met *two* of them at all, he admits treating with the third, Mr. C. Buller,—adding, that *whether* "*Mr. Buller's recollection, or his, be the more entitled* " *to credit, is a point respecting which he has no solicitude.*"]

Our third illustration of Mr. Stephen's character is taken from a pamphlet, just published, on the right of being heard at the Privy Council. It is a portion of a case stated in the pamphlet, and with other parts of which our readers are not unacquainted, namely, the appeal of Mr. Bannister, formerly attorney-general of New South Wales. This portion is new; and it does nothing more, and nothing less, than charge "somebody" with having forged a judgment of the Privy Council. It gives the ground of this heavy charge; and it will leave little doubt on the minds of most readers of the pamphlet, who know any thing of the business of the Colonial Office these many years, as to the individual who must come point-blank within its range. We give the whole paper, *verbatim*:—

Some years ago, the case of Mr. Bannister was actually sent to the Privy Council; but admission to that board was refused to him pending the discussion!

The circumstances, however, of an alleged decision in the Privy Council, are remarkable, as set forth in a petition to the House of Commons against it, printed in the Appendix to the 44th Report on Public Petitions, 1834, p. 1693.

In July, 1832, the king referred to the Privy Council a petition from Mr. Bannister.

In August, 1832, the Secretary of State answered it from documents in the Colonial Office.

In August, also, Mr. Bannister applied at the Council Office to see the said documents, in order to be prepared with his proofs in the case, and in order to go to a hearing of it with knowledge of what had been alleged against him.

He was informed at the Council Office, that a memorial must be presented to the Lords of the Council for leave to inspect the documents, and he presented such memorial accordingly.

He went, day after day, to the Council Office on the matter, and on the last day of August, 1832, he was informed that the lords and proper officers were out of town, that much time would be required for examining the said documents, and that nothing could be done in the case for several months.

Mr. Bannister waited several months, expecting leave to see the documents to be granted, and at length he presented another memorial to the Lords of the Council, stating that he had evidence to produce in the case.

In 1833, his agent was told, that so early as the 15th day of September, 1832, a letter was written, to inform him that there was nothing in the petition to induce the lords to recommend his Majesty to revoke his former decisions; and the agent was also told, that with the minute of this report on the council-books, access could not be allowed to the documents.

Mr. Bannister then presented a memorial to the Lords of the Council, stating, that he had not received the letter of the 15th day of September, 1832, and that their lordships could not justly report upon the said petition without hearing him, and that he could not go to a hearing safely, without evidence, nor without seeing the documents produced against him, and praying that the error made by their lordships on the 15th day of September, 1832, should be corrected.

But he was unable to get attention paid to the said memorial; on the contrary, his agent was told at the Council Office, that the case was considered to be settled.

In vain has Mr. Bannister endeavoured to get the injustice done on this occasion rectified, and he has reason to believe, that the Council was as much abused on this occasion, as he was himself wronged.

The president of the Council, in 1832, the Marquis of Lansdowne has stated to Mr. Bannister, and expressly authorized him, "to make any use he might think proper of the communication," that he was not heard at the Privy Council on this occasion; which, to the best of his lordship's recollection, "arose from this case not having been considered as one of those which the Privy Council was justified, in conformity to its usual practice, *to come to any decision upon*, not being in the nature of a judicial appeal, without its being recommended to their consideration by the Colonial Department."

And yet, a judgment is asserted to have been delivered against Mr. Bannister in September, 1832, although he had been told at the office that nothing *could* be done in the case for many months. The probability clearly is, that the Marquis of Lansdowne's recollection is not in fault.

If it be probable that the Privy Council was abused in this case, it is quite certain that the House of Commons was equally abused, and the present Lord Monteagle *most unworthily* made an instrument in the misrepresentation of the party. The petition, in 1834, stated the case somewhat as set forth above, and prayer, "That the House would intervene with the king, in order that the Privy Council might be directed to examine the case, and hear petitioner, as justice required." But Lord Monteagle stated the matter thus:—Mr. Secretary Rice, "The case of this gentleman may be stated in two words. He voluntarily resigned his office; another gentleman was appointed to it; and then, Mr. B. repenting of the step he had taken, applied, by petition to the Privy Council, to be restored. *This case was fully enquired into*, and it being said that Mr. B. had voluntarily resigned his situation, *the Privy Council was of opinion that he had no claim to be restored.* Failing in his petition to the Privy Council, Mr. B. now seeks for the interference of the House. I think the House will agree with me, that the case is one in which it can take no steps.*

It is needless to add, that not one word of what the Secretary of State said in parliament was correct; in other words, the instructions put into his hands in his office, to meet the petition, were false instructions; and the Under-Secretary of State or whoever gave Mr. Spring Rice (the present Lord Monteagle) those instructions, must have known they were false. The chapter and verse of all this is too specific to admit of any doubt; and must not Mr. Stephen have had a prime share in the business?

The pamphlet suggests one motive for his malice against Mr. Bannister: the case, it says, originated in an intrigue in Sydney, which was fostered in Downing-street:—

It is beyond doubt, that the Secretaries of State themselves have been little acquainted with the facts, having refused to hear Mr. Bannister, and having left

* *Mirror of Parliament*, June 30, 1834, p. 3106.

the case mainly to one or more subordinate members of the Colonial Office, the principal of whom, Mr. Stephen, had connections in New South Wales involved in the case, who *probably* influenced him.

This part of the pamphlet concludes by showing Mr. Stephen as the official instrument in the rejection of specific measures approved by all parties, and even thought well of by Lord Stanley, as asserted, and calculated to save thousands of lives, and millions of money, in the colonies. On this point, the implication is plain, that as such good measures, and the proposer of them (Mr. Bannister), do not suit Mr. Stephen, they are rejected together.

With such *recent* accusations, added to a world of old ones, on his back, if Mr. James Stephen be not already removed from the Colonial Office, he will soon go. Things are bad enough in this office; but it is morally impossible for any public man to stand all this. We therefore congratulate our fellow-countrymen all the world over, on the prospect of their being at length relieved from a rougher rider than Sinbad's old man of the island; and we add a congratulation to Joseph Sturge, on the coloured man being also likely to be relieved from Mr. James Stephen. "There is no safety for the coloured man," said Joseph Sturge, at the Anti-Slavery Convention of 1840, "so long as James Stephen is at the Colonial Office." We heard him say this, and the shout of applause yet rings in our ears.

But pursuant to our motto, we are bound to be just. Give the devil his due. *John Bull* errs in saying Mr. Stephen is "saintly" in his associations. Mr. S. hates those philanthropists, and they know it. Love of *self*, not of philanthropy, rules him. He is no saint! but one of the large family of By-Ends, of John Bunyan. *John Bull* errs also in saying that Mr. S. has not a single defender, nor one admirer. When Joseph Sturge burst out as above stated, the late Sir J. Jeremie, and another really good man, did vindicate him, and a poor business they made of it. A clerk in the Colonial office, too, who is much esteemed in the literary world, Mr. Taylor, has dedicated a book, called the *Statesman* (lucus a non lucendo) to "James Stephen, as the man, *within the author's knowledge*, in whom the active and contemplative faculties most strongly meet." (The *Statesman*, 12mo. Longman & Co, 1836.)

Although Mr. Taylor's *knowledge* has been acquired in a place, the Colonial office, unpropitious to forming an elevated, or a correct view of character; and although the particular book thus dedicated in homage to Mr. Stephen's character, was with reason declared, at the time, to abound in principles (drawn from the author's *experience* in that office, as he asserts) which make the teeth chatter, and the blood run cold, it is nevertheless true that this respectable gentleman, so spoiled by bad company, is an "admirer" of Mr. Stephen—as the two respectable members of the Anti-Slavery Convention of 1840, were his "defenders."

Still, if Mr. Stephen is not already dismissed, or provided for, it is clear he must go. His *incapacity* is at length matter of demonstration. At Hong-kong, his mere want of foresight and care, drove Sir H. Pottinger to the desperate expedient of an illegal proclamation, and to trust to parliament for his indemnity. In South Africa, a fearful loss of life, on the part of British subjects, and on the part of the negroes at their hands, attest the same incapacity. In New Zealand and in Australia, every species of ill has already happened, and worse must come, under the same influence. In North-western America it is the same. And Mr. Stephen is a lucky man indeed, if what is done, and doing, of the same character, in the South Sea islands, be not laid at his door.

Bayswater, 29th May, 1844

LINES ON THE PURSUITS OF GENIUS AND LEARNING,

ADDRESSED TO THE 'LITERATI' IN ALL COUNTRIES.

BY J. S. HARDY.

" I can make lords of you every day, but I cannot create a Titian," said the Emperor Charles V. to his courtiers, who had become jealous of the hours and the half hours which the monarch stole from them that he might converse with the man of genius at his work.

[D'ISRAELI'S LITERARY CHARACTER.]

Ye! wakeful spirits, o'er the midnight oil,
Who ply your task, in one unceasing toil;
Your books, the sweet companions of the hour,
That have a silent and all-winning power,
The world scarce knows of, in your brooding cell,
Whose mental alchemy hath powerful spell,
The crucible that brings forth purest gold,
Is yours, ye sons obscure, of genius mould;
Yet little heeded, in your great employ,
Who labour still with soul-ennobling joy;
The same divine, immortal spirit reigns,
As moved Apelles, or a Titian's pains;
As drew the spark, that flash'd from Milton's breast,
Or fired a Pindar, and was Goethe's guest;
That bade our own immortal Shakespear soar,
On roaming Fancy's wing, new worlds explore.
Sons of seclusion, why should ye repine?
Your toil is noble, and the work divine:
A true nobility awaits his name,
Who presses on th' ascent that leads to fame;
And tireless tracks, the eagle flights of mind,—
Arts, science teach, a blessing to mankind.
How poor the heraldry of noble birth,
Compared with yours, ye great ones of the earth;
Undying honours, that ennoble man,—
A regal splendour, that makes theirs but wan;
Mind is the gem, that hath the truest worth,
This the rich diamond—theirs the dross of earth.
What ardour kindles in the studious soul,
Borne, on the car of knowledge, to the goal,
In emulation, 'midst the gifted throng,
Is soul-rapt poesy, divine in song;
Music, all-thrilling, as the airs of heav'n;
Painting and Sculpture, like to Phidias giv'n;

And there deep sage Philosophy in sight,
With bright Urania, soars the stars of night,
Castalia's nymphs, a fair celestial band,
That in the mazy dance, join hand in hand,
Yours gifted race, the Athenian's sacred hours,
The fount whence flows the stream from Learning's bowers;
Nurtured in climes, tho' wide as zone from zone,
Congenial spirits vibrate to one tone;
As mountain's spring flows murm'ring underground,
Its goal, vast ocean, in its depths profound,
So ye, your sinuous course, unruffled sped,
And pour your tribute's store, by Science led.

PECKHAM.

REVIEWS OF NEW BOOKS.

ART. I.—*Our Indian Empire: its History and Present State.* By CHARLES MAC FARLANE. London: C. Knight, Ludgate-street. Parts I. and II.

At all times *apropos*, Mr. Knight's publications were never more so than in this instance. We have just added two vast sections of Asia to our Anglo-Indian empire,—just exercised powers, through the *imperium in imperio* of Leadenhall-street, in recalling our governor-general with less notice than we give to our domestics,—we have closed, in what way we need not observe, a sanguinary conflict on this side the Indus,—and subdued the oldest empire in the world far beyond the Ganges. What period, therefore, could possibly demand, with more real necessity, a popular history of our possessions in India, and our Asiatic relations generally? The two parts of Mac Farlane's interesting work already published, are acceptable securities for those yet to appear; and should the author forget neither himself nor his readers in the future progress of his labours, his volumes will unquestionably become the most valuable and readable epitome of our Indian history that has yet appeared. Others, and those pondrous tomes, have professed to supply the public with the information which they should possess to qualify them for distant legislation, but their labours are too recondite and voluminous in some instances, and without all authorities, references, or evidencial documents in others. This condensation, besides being perspicuous in style and free from factious bias, unites the qualities of popularity and authenticity—by giving the sources of information in foot-notes. Commencing with our early Oriental conquests in 1612, the parts published extend to the memorable trial of Warren Hastings, including decidedly the most stirring period of our intrusion, spoliation, and misgovernment of Anglo-India. What romantic narrations are the conquests and depredations of Clive, the victories of Coote, and the government of Hastings! yet the pomp of Wellesley and the early life of Wellington remain to be told. To those connected with India, these pages abound with exciting intelligence; to the ordinary inquirer into history, they present a romantic and chivalrous narrative of events.

Both for the sake of illustration, and from peculiar applicability to passing and to present circumstances, we shall quote a passage relative to former opinions upon our mode of governing our Indian possessions, and the Regulating Act of 1774, all which, notwithstanding dates, deserves the best attention of our readers:—

This "Regulating Act," as they called it, was to come into operation in England on the 1st of October, 1773, and in India on the 1st of August, 1774.

The court of directors, the court of proprietors, and nearly all men interested in the affairs of the East Indies, raised a storm ten times louder than before; and they courted and obtained the influence of the corporation of the city of London, which was then in the most determined opposition to government, and to everything done or proposed by Lord North. Remonstrances and petitions poured in upon parliament, but did not affect the votes of the large ministerial majority. It was curious to hear that anomalous body, the company, which assumed to exercise an absolute authority over fifteen millions of men, and which certainly had not yet learned the slow and difficult task of exercising that authority with moderation and wisdom, and for the greater happiness of the natives, resting one of their greatest complaints on the injury that would be done by the ministerial alterations to constitutional liberty, the rights of election, &c. The raising of the qualification of the voters, by which about 1,200 proprietors were disfranchised, was held up as a political enormity then, and it appears to have been considered in the same light many years after the struggle, the excitement, and the violence were over. Mr. Mill seems to deplore it as a blow struck at the power of the democracy. "In one respect," says he, "the present experiment fulfilled the purpose very completely for which it was intended. It followed the current of that policy which for many reasons has run with perfect regularity and considerable strength, diminishing the influence of numbers in affairs of government, and reducing things as much as possible to the oligarchical state." * To this lamentation may be opposed the unruly, blundering, selfish, and corrupt conduct of the court of proprietors, and the very serious facts that they, from the immediate and incessant control they exercised over the directors, were almost as much an executive as an elective body: that such a numerous executive had never been known to go right and straight; that they were as far as possible from promising to be an exception to this unchanged and unchangeable rule; and that their mistakes and faults directly affected the prosperity of thousands of individuals at home and of millions abroad. Complaints were also made that, by rendering the situation of director of four years' duration instead of one, and free for that time from the control of the court of proprietors, the influence and operation of the ministry would be great and certain: but then, on the other hand, the annual elections had been proved most mischievous; they had, as Clive affirmed, swallowed up nearly all the time and attention of the directors, and new members of that body were liable to be outvoted and turned out of office just as they were beginning to learn its duties, or to know something of the complicated machine which was to be superintended. There were defects, and of a serious nature, in the measure proposed by ministers, who do not appear to have considered it as final, but rather in the light of an experiment which might be modified and altered as time and experience should point out. Such as they were, their proposals were embodied in two acts, which were carried through both Houses by immense majorities, and received the royal ascent forthwith. The company continued their complaints and lamentations, but, except among the Wilkites in the city, they found very little sympathy. They had, in fact, grown unpopular as a body, and, whatever doubts may have been entertained in some quarters as to the wisdom of the new measures, or the propriety of augmenting the authority of parliament, which then signified little more than the influence of the court and ministry, the universal feeling appears to have been that some interference was indispensable, and that what was no longer a group of factories, but an empire, ought not to be trusted to the sole management of a trading company, who bought and sold fractions of principalities and powers in 'Change Alley.

Although an admirable impartiality prevails in every page of Mr. Mac Farlane's books, we regret to perceive that the character of Clive has so far won upon his affections, that he has dealt too favourably with that able soldier and politician,

* Hist. Brit. Ind.

but cruel, unjust, and irreligious man. His services to his country are not questioned,—on the contrary, they have been rewarded; but his iniquities and barbarities are too glaring to be pardoned. How would the Romans have treated a general who reserved the spoils of a conquered city for his private purposes! What wealth might now accompany the dukedom of Wellington, had the hero who bears it seized the plunder of the Peninsula, and appropriated it to his use! Would the Leadenhall Street parliament have voted £25,000 to the Marquis Wellesley with the same unanimity, had he accepted presents of diamonds from the Indian people! Yet Clive plundered indiscriminately to enrich himself, and had no hesitation in accepting the richest presents from any whom terror or meanness had induced to make them. Lastly, as to the impious close of his turbulent career, none deny the act of self-destruction, and few will coincide with our author in his charitable defence of the suicide—the belief that he sought to escape the tortures of a guilty mind, is widely spread, and sufficiently founded to secure its continued currency.

We look with some interest to the future parts of this valuable little history, particularly to the share in the government of India, which the author shall ascribe to *Colonel Wellesley* during his brother's dazzling administration.

ART. II.—*The People's Gallery*. Part VIII., containing Four Engravings, after Original Pictures, &c.; with Descriptive Letter-press, by the Rev. G. N. WRIGHT, M. A. London: Fisher, Son, & Co., Newgate-street.

If the cheapness of this amazingly popular work of art astonish us, its excellence is not less calculated to create surprise. We can understand the practicability of cheap letter-press printing, the aid of steam being lent to effect the object; but here, where manual labour, or rather dexterity—for steel-plate printing is a delicate operation—can alone be employed, the enterprise that has produced a work of such superior excellence is truly astonishing. Four highly-finished engravings decorate each *Shilling Part*, accompanied with letter-press, by the editor, or some other popular writer. With a due, and we hope profitable vigilance, the publishers contrive to keep up with passing events; and a melancholy announcement, the destruction of the ancient border-castle of Naworth, one of the seats of the Howard family, has presented an opportunity of displaying their laudable activity. The fate of this ancient and interesting pile must occasion very wide-spread regret, from the associations of poetry, and history, and romance, that are connected with it. The view in "The People's Gallery" is from an original drawing, taken on the spot, by Mr. Allom, the illustrator of "China" and "Constantinople," engraved by Le Petit with his best abilities; and the description of what Naworth was, is more full than could have been expected, where space is necessarily so limited. The other subjects are, "An Only Son," "The Lady of the Palace," and the "Falls of Niagara;" the last very eloquently described by Dr. Greenwood, of Boston.

ART. III—*Sacred Architecture: Its Rise, Progress, and Present State.* By R. BROWN, Esq. Part V. London: Fisher, Son, & Co.

Where literature or taste exists, there also will a love of architecture prevail. It is the boast of this age, that knowledge is diffused, and the fine arts cultivated, with greater spirit and energy than in those that have preceded; this then is the period most happily suited to the publication of such a work as Mr. Brown's.

His mode of treating the solemn subject is remarkably judicious; and his arrangement and description open to the uninitiated the mysteries of the art, while the student will perceive that his improvement constitutes one of the leading features of the design. The previous Parts have treated of Egyptian, Grecian, Roman, Lombard, Saxon, and Norman styles; in the present Part, the author has arrived at the most interesting to English readers, the Gothic. We felt deeply interested in Mr. Brown's lucid views of more ancient styles, and in his distinct and perspicuous descriptions of some of the greatest architectural monuments of past ages, but our interest seems to rise as he proceeds, and perhaps it is for this reason we consider his account of our ecclesiastical style the very best part of his work. His origin of the Gothic manner is unquestionably the true one, although high authorities are contradicted by his proofs; but we are indebted to him more sincerely for his courage in adducing his arguments in the front of such an array of learned men. The plates are executed with the utmost care and address.

If we were asked, For what class of readers is this very elegant production intended? our answer would be, for none especially, for several beneficially. The bishop and his suffragans will do well to supply themselves with a copy, before they either disfigure an old church, or raise a deformed new one; the man of education may here practise his knowledge of the manners of classic kingdoms; and the votary of art may take useful lessons in his profession from the drawings and directions which the author, himself eminent as an architect, has laboriously concentrated in his rich and scientific pages.

ART. IV.—*Order of the Daily Services of the United Church of England and Ireland, arranged for use in Choirs and Places where they Sing.* By THOMAS TALLIS, Newly Edited by JOHN BISHOP, of Cheltenham. London: Cocks & Co., Princes-street, Hanover-square.

At a period when the glorious and beautiful service of our church is menaced with innovations, it is particularly gratifying to receive such an evidence of its original, genuine, unimprovable form, in this admirable and ably-edited reprint. Familiar with the works of Causton, Johnson, Oakland, Shepherd, and Turner, the editor has given the public the benefit of his experience, profound knowledge of church music, and distinguished abilities, in his edition of the labours of one of the greatest musicians of the sixteenth century. However pure in taste, and rational in conception, the cold formula of our sublime service seems to require some auxiliary to dispel the apathy that displays itself too often and too extensively in our churches. Music, harmony, was wisely employed by our ancestors, for the acquirement of this most desirable end, and it is solely from the proneness of mankind to run from darkness into light, and *vice versâ*, that Reformers have so completely neglected this beautiful, national, and impressive accompaniment of worship. Perhaps we have fallen upon better times; possibly our recent Continental connection may have improved our taste for the works of Handel and Hayden, and persuaded us to become sensible of the benefits we enjoy in their possession. Mr. Bishop's improved reprint presents, at a moderate price, in an encouraging limit, and most easily-intelligible arrangement, the whole choral formula for Morning and Evening Service, the Litany, and Holy Communion, with the rubrical directions belonging to them. Here then we are enabled, without risk of falling into any of the lately-opened pits of controversy, touching the celebration of divine worship, to return to the usage of former ages. Mr. Bishop's little manual of the choral mode should be a text-book in every Protestant family; and parochial clergy should make themselves so familiar with its contents, that those of their flock who need advice in understanding its rules, may know where to apply for information. We anticipate, therefore, an extensive sale for the "Order of the Daily Service," which, although a small volume, is a great work. The editor has prefixed a very interesting account of all publications connected with the choral service that appeared during the progress of the Reformation and subsequently, besides a biographical notice of Thomas Tallis, to whom so much praise is due for his valuable labours in methodising the Service.

ART. V.—*Scripture Prints, from the Frescoes of Raphael in the Vatican.* Edited by J. R. HOPE, D.C.L. London: Houlston & Stoneman.

Our native artists complain that painting, as well as music, has been rejected by the church, in its rage for reformation. There may be both truth and justice in their lament; but, surely, the Wilkie or Landseer schools, though perfect in their path, would not be adapted to the lofty dome or the overarching vault of the lady-chapel, or the upper division of a richly-traced screen? No; there is a style of painting suited to the church, as there is a character of music; and, when our artists produce suitable subjects, treated also in a suitable style, and still find churchmen inexorable, then, and not before, will they be at liberty to protest against bigotry and discouragement. We have always maintained the theory of the facility with which scripture truths are communicated by prints and paintings and sensible representations, restricted within due bounds: when angels, with or without wings, shall be jealously admitted. and no impious efforts made to materialize Jehovah; and we hail with pleasure the production of a work such as Mr. Hope's, which, although not free from one of our objections, teems so abundantly with redeeming qualities. Here are the unapproachable works of the first of all designers in the graphic art—unapproachable from the distance over sea and land —but more especially unapproachable in the lofty genius which they exhibit. It is a benefit to the artists, to the community, to make them familiar with works which possess that greatness of manner that alone can hope to conquer the repugnance of the Church of England to the re-admission of painting and statuary into their temples of worship. The First Part of Mr. Hope's Scripture Prints contains six oblong folio designs from the Old Testament, equal in drawing and composition to anything that has ever been published of the memorable master. The manly figure in the foreground of "The Deluge," the first of the series, supporting the dead and dripping female, is a most noble conception, and expressed with correspondent powers; and the horse on the left is living, and conscious of its perilous position. But our criticism, for praise or censure upon Raphael's labours, must be vain. The grouping in all the subjects, the landscapes, as accessories introduced to complete the design, and the drawing of the respective figures, are all the production of a master-mind, and expressed with an ability that never will be excelled. Consoni, an eminent Italian draughtsman, is engaged to make drawings from the original frescoes, to illustrate the Old Testament; but it appears to be the editor's intention to copy from other masters for the illustaration of the New. The other subjects in this part, besides "The Deluge," are, "Abraham and the Angels;" "Jacob and Rachel;" "Joseph's Dreams;" "Pharaoh's Dreams;" and "The Finding of Moses."

THE EXHIBITIONS.

AMONGST the collectæ of the "Pandora's Box" of attractions thrown open to London sight-seers, the idler — particularly the travelled idler — finds in the better sort of day-exhibitions, his amusement consulted in an intellectual spirit, altogether superior to vulgar taste, which by the bye is generally frivolous and vicious. The old Indian and the sexagenarian colonist, retired, both, from active life, and desirous of "living at home at ease" for the short remainder of their days—a class composing a large proportion of town *habitués*—have a never-failing means of exorcising their familiar devil, gaunt *ennui*, by calling to memory the talismanic names of Panoramas and Dioramas, Polytechnic Institutions, Egyptian Halls, National Galleries, Zoological Gardens, and the like, with which establishments the metropolis abounds; indeed, the recreative resources of London, confining ourselves to those that are purely intellectual in character, present a rich field for the indulgence of pleasurable anticipations and realizations, to all who can find time to pursue their fancies unrestrictedly. With proper deference and due respect be it spoken, that to those who possess affluence, and *nothing to do* but to *reduce* what they have *multiplied*, the exhibitions of London are so *necessary*, that the term *luxuries* as applied to them seems a misnomer; they are only luxuries to the people who turn from the toils of existence to seek in such amusements a delightful relief.

The grand source of attraction at the exhibitions now is China; the "*arcana imperii*" of the Celestial Empire having by British conquest been laid bare, the costumes, habits, manners, science, arts, trades, agriculture, and genius of this wonderful people have naturally engaged the peculiar attention of Englishmen, and particularly of speculative persons, who, with an eye to lucre, have formed museums and picture-galleries, in propitiating public patronage.

"China here! China there! China everywhere!" Our countrymen are prying in at the gates of Pekin; some of them have written books about what they saw when in China; artists, fresh from the Canton River, are calling attention to sketches which were taken on the spot; antiquarians are displaying the antiquities they have collected; painters are painting what they never saw except on paper; engravers are engraving from thrice second-hand copies; at the exhibitions, theatres, picture-galleries—in the legislature, in the church, in the coffee-room, China has been of late the engrossing theme. The question is not now, "Where is China?" but, "Where is *not* China?" We must be in the fashion, and give to China the preference in this page.

Permit us, then, friendly reader, to offer you our arm; we pick you up at *Grindlay's* Club-room; it is noonday, the sun just past the meridian—and broiling weather; so we will e'en find the shady side of the street, and wend our steps to Leicester-square; whither arrived, an expressive nod addressed to the trim little lady at the end of the long passage is our passport to the Panorama. We are soon at the top of the broad staircase, and *voila!* here is Hong-Kong; the view is misty and undefinable for the minute, but the charm of the painting gradually breaks upon you. Is it not magnificent? the more so, because the sun is shining without with eastern splendour; this then is the island and bay of Hong-

Kong. What bold and sublime scenery surrounds! We must linger for awhile, and new charms will please the eye; that zig-zag foot-path up the steep mountain, we can trace from one of the streets of the little Anglo-Chinese town below; in its course there are various delightfully situated gentlemen's seats. From these we revert to the town (Victoria) and the Happy Valley, (happy indeed!) and the islands and mainland adjacent. Stupendous appears the scene, as it is in reality. Now, turn we to the bay, and gaze on the extraordinary variety of Chinese craft, lying upon its broad and peaceful bosom. These craft, indeed, contrast uncouthly enough with the elegant architecture and complicated rigging of the British flag-ships lying in the harbour. Whatever be the advance of civilization in China, its navy must not be mentioned as any indication of it. Such things as Chinese ships have never been seen out of the Yellow Sea; certes, the best of them could not live a storm in the Mediterranean. You have carefully observed the figures in the painting, good Sir Reader; these have been done by another artist than Burford—by his *collaborateur* in fact, *Sellous.* Sellous is the gentleman who was recently a successful cartoon exhibitor—these figures, you will agree with me, have much of character about them; they have been cleverly hit off and carefully painted; only you are liable to fall into an error that similarity of costume may betray you to—we allude to the people who are tending the different boats and barges. That rough weather-beaten personage in the red smock, who is steering the boat to the pleasure-barge at hand, is not of the gender masculine; it is a woman, to the best of our belief, and the guide, here, confirms our opinion beyond dispute; yes, the Chinese women make very useful marines, and are far more numerous than the class of canal bargemen we are acquainted with in England.

Before leaving the Panorama, we will give a good hard look at the outlets of the bay, east and west of us; now, can anything be more natural? we feel the sensation of a passenger on board a ship which has just got clear of the Channel, and is entering upon the broad waters of the ocean; a feeling of freedom, dashed by a stronger feeling of loneliness. But the chops of the Channel present a raw and gloomy aspect, not the blue waters and the bright burnished sky of the Eastern clime.

Will you ascend the hundred steps to the top of the building, for the sake of viewing the gay picture of the Royal Landing at Treport?—it is a subject *passé* enough. We may save our legs, and no harm done to our loyalty either, for Queen Victoria is villanously libelled in the portraiture of this panorama; albeit, every other principal portrait, and the painting is crowded with figures, is a likeness.

A few minutes' drive in a cab, and we are at the doors of the red pagoda, through which we must pass, ere we can enter the Hall of Lanterns. The Chinese Collection has been enriched, since we last visited it; it has, we perceive, been also much improved in arrangement, and, what is of more consequence to the public, is now more accessible than heretofore, by reason of a reduction in the price of admission. Has not this magnificent salon, we are promenading, an air of the chastest elegance? Though so spacious, and so profusely decorated and furnished, yet how light and roomy! We have heard complaints of disappointment by some visitors of this Museum; they saw a great many things like what they had seen before, at Madame Tussaud's; as for the fishes in the bottles, and the stuffed birds and beasts, they had had a surfeit of such matters; there was nothing extraordinary about the paintings, nor about the screen-work; they supposed that such matters could be better ordered at home, and so forth. The only objects of real attraction to these persons were the colossal idols, the "three precious Buddhas," that are sure to catch the eyes of the *profanum vulgus* on entering the room. There was no mistake about the idols; they were the biggest men of ochre ever exhibited in this country! This is the *summum bonum* of vulgar criticism.

Why were not the dissentients of whom we speak, not pleased with the Chinese Collection? Because, in short, they did not understand it: they could not *think*, as well as *look;* they had no imagination, no powers of reflection, or of association and contrast; no information, beyond what was merely local; had they been educated, they would have viewed the Collection with deeply-seated pleasure, with infinite gratification; and would have gone to the pagoda again and again, to return again and again, enlightened, delighted! For one shilling, to be on visiting terms with China and all grades of its people; to know them, never to forget them! An omnibus-ride to entirely effect what a six months' voyage by sea could *not!*—for, though you actually go out to China, and arrive at Canton, and proceed to Hong-Kong and Chusan, and thread all the streets of the different places, nevertheless you would not dare to break down the barriers of exclusiveness, and intrude upon the privacy of mandarins, and literati, and fashionable ladies, (even at their toilets!) as these same are shown to you in the Hall of Lanterns. Verily, the hours passed in the examination of the Chinese Museum are not ill spent! If this be your first visit, it is but initiatory; we must come again; we have lounged two hours away, and you seem already tired. Likely enough! the mind is bewildered, rather than satisfied, gazing on so much! If you are partial to French dishes, good soups, or lamb-chops breaded, we crave your company to dinner, at Bertholini's, which done, we will leave you to decide, whether we shall renew our sight-seeing: a few steps from the *restaurant*, will take us to the *Adelaide Gallery*, a very kaleidoscope of curious sights, a babel of sayings and doings; besides being musical as Orpheus, and perhaps a little too theatrical in every respect. Should not this be to your taste, we can trundle over one of the bridges, and visit the *Surrey Zoological Gardens.* Here the *Caves of Ellora* were pictured with a truthful effect last season, and the *Fire of London* is to be the allurement of the present. Or, capricious reader, shall we return to the Chinese Pavilion, and witness the evening display called the "Feast of Lanterns?" The hall is then "girt about with piles of light," diffused from magnificent porcelain Pagodas, of 9 stories high, built at Nankin, at a cost of four years' labour, and 10,000 dollars! Soft lustre, sweet perfume, 'celestial' music—enchantments, such as Orientals only have hitherto been permitted to enjoy, are at our command. Allons! To Hyde Park Corner again

COLONIAL INTELLIGENCE.

India. — By the overland mail, which left Bombay on the 1st of April, we learn that tranquillity prevailed in all parts of our Eastern empire.

The chief intelligence relates to the conduct of a part of certain native regiments on the north-west frontier, which refused to march to Scinde, in consequence of some allowances granted to the troops on the banks of the Indus, during the time of war, being withdrawn when that province was declared to be in peace, and annexed to the British Empire in India. Much more alarm had been created than it deserved, but the value of the exaggerations had become known before the mail left Bombay.

The Governor-General arrived in Calcutta on the 28th of February, and was well received. He was met by an address of welcome on his return from the successful campaign of Gwalior, and in the reply stated his desire to remain in that city, unless his presence should be required elsewhere. This had been interpreted as if he contemplated a journey to the north-western provinces, where the disputes between the Affghans and Sikhs will, in all probability, require him to take some effective steps before the end of this year. Considerable discussion has taken place concerning some recent acts of patronage by Lord Ellenborough.

In Gwalior all has progressed quietly and satisfactorily; the old forces have been completely disbanded and broken, and their cantonments are to be levelled with the ground. The young Rajah has been married with all due ceremony to two young ladies, and all disaffected persons have been summarily ejected. The new contingent was arranged, and the people appeared satisfied. It is worthy of remark, that the neighbouring district of Bundelkund has been thoroughly pacified by the subjugation of Gwalior; and so far was that pacification effective, that the whole of the Bundelkund contingent had volunteered to proceed for three years to Scinde, thereby demonstrating that the late disaffection relative to money matters in the four regiments of Bengal had not any extensive ramifications.

The news from Scinde represents that district as tranquil and comparatively healthful. The Bombay troops there were satisfied to retain it, and an augmentation in that army was expected. Sir C. Napier still continued to be an object of undeserved censure to some of the newspapers, but the public opinion in India was decidedly favourable to the gallant old warrior.

A Government notification was issued on the 12th of March, regulating the compensation to be given to the Sepoys in Scinde, where the prices of different articles were too high, and granting to the troops in cantonments there the field allowances of Hindostan, which allowances are to begin from the time the troops reach the frontiers. The cost of this grant is variously estimated; it has been calculated at £50,000 per annum, but the improvements going on in the districts on the borders of the Indus will soon repay it. Fortunately for India, the flourishing state of the revenue will not cause any pressure from the grant of the batta to the Scinde and Gwalior armies. Such is its prosperity, that the Governor-General has issued a notification abolishing the transit duties in the Presidency of Madras. This is considered as a most useful measure, as introducing uniformity into the various provinces of India.

From Lahore the news is of great importance. There a civil war is raging; a chief called Cashmeera Singh, a bastard of Runjeet, is opposed to the new Prime Minister, Heer Singh, and, as the Sikhs support him, it is probable there will be another revolution within a few months in the Punjaub. The notorious Affghan leader, Akhbar Khan, has led his troops to invade Peshawur, and he will, in all probability, force the Lahore Government into an application to the Governor-General for assistance. It is not improbable that there will be another conflict with the Affghans on the plains of the Punjaub, where the Indians, when not aided by the English, have almost always been routed by the hardy mountaineers. It seems that these northern mountaineers think they have an established right to overcome the people to the east of the Indus; and when they lately invaded Peshawur, they were surprised at being beaten back by the Sikhs under foreign generals. The conquest of their country by the British army had surprised them; yet now again they are to be seen moving to the Indus, and there the British army must again meet and defeat them. The Sikhs have lost their weight in the scale of India since the death of old Runjeet, and it is therefore imperative on the British Government to be prepared to conflict with the Sikhs against the Affghans, and not to allow them to make a junction, which might lead to numberless invasions on the fertile north-western provinces of the Company's territories. The late rumours of a mutiny amongst the native troops, had encouraged both the Sikhs and Affghans to exhibit an hostile spirit towards the British. The antipathy between the Affghans and the Sikhs is proverbial; they are continually quarrelling, and as the Sikhs have latterly, by means of foreign generals and British aid, been successful, the former now seek an opportunity of having another conflict, for they are anxious to become masters of Peshawur and of Cashmere.

Great anxiety prevailed in India respecting Colonel Stoddart and Captain Conolly, as the rumours on the subject were conflicting.

Lord Ellenborough had ordered an addition of ten men to each company of the Bengal and Bombay armies. The 1st Bombay European Regiment was raised to the rank of Fusileers, and a great wish was expressed, that a company of Fusileers should be selected in each of the other regiments, as the Sepoys have a taste for such practice, and it would infuse a daring spirit of enterprise and bravery throughout the whole army. The propriety of an increase of the Bombay army had been admitted by the Governor-General, and lists had been prepared of the officers to be appointed to four new corps, from which it appeared that the colonels had served 40 years, the lieutenant-colonels upwards of 30 years, the majors more than 25, and the majority of the captains 19 and 20 years, while it would leave the average of two brevet-captains to each regiment after 15 years' service. There was a great wish expressed in Bengal and Madras that Scinde should be made over to the Bombay Presidency as an appanage, and that its army should be augmented to meet the demand on its services. In such circumstances, the augmentation of 10 regiments would be necessary; but the Bombay army has never yet been stained with mutiny on any occasion whatever.

That most worthy knight, Sir Jamsetjee Jeejeebhoy, of Bombay, whose purse and charitable intents appear alike unbounded, has come forward with an offer to Government of investing £36,000 in Government securities on behalf of the poor Parsees of Bombay, Surat, &c., and this was backed by the Parsee Punchazet of Bombay with another gift of £25,000 more. Verily, this is true nobility, and needs no comment. Besides this, Sir Jamsetjee proposes to expend another £18,000 in supplying the city of Poonah with water, to be raised from the river which runs by it, and distributed by pipes everywhere. Be it remembered, also, that Sir Jamsetjee's private charities do not stop, and that his tens, fifties, and hundreds go to every needful subscription which is set on foot, as well as those plentiful ministerings to the wants of the poor which all who know him are well aware of. Honour to such a man! May more in India emulate his example, and give in lasting institutions what now is wasted in idle shows, and upon more idle and worthless Brahmins.

It is very satisfactory to observe, that the Governor-General's plans for the extension of trade have been so successful as they have proved in the direction of Bahawulpoor, Bikaneer, and generally among the western states. Roads have been constructed by the local rulers across the deserts, wells dug, duties defined and reduced, and trade protected. All this cannot fail to be of advantage to our interests, and though the rivers of Scinde as yet show no signs of increased trade, yet British manufactures may pass by land-carriage from Hindostan to the west, freed from vexatious exactions and oppression. We have seen no peaceful results from supremacy like this for many years —may more follow it elsewhere! There is no point upon which native rulers prove more intractable in general than in that of transit duties, all that passes through their territory being considered fair spoil. The present negotiations, therefore, prove to have been conducted with great tact and skill, and will, no doubt, benefit them in the end, from the extended traffic on the new lines from Hurriana, &c., westward to Mooltan, Bahawulpoor, and Scinde.

China.—The news from China comes down to the 27th of February, but presents nothing remarkable. Sir H. Pottinger was at Hong-kong, which island was healthy. He was, while waiting for his successor, engaged in regulating some of the buildings at Victoria, and also in making proper arrangements for the trade at the new ports. The Chinese were robbing houses and plundering the foreigners as well at Macao as at Hong-kong.

New South Wales.—Papers from Sydney to the 5th, and from Hobart Town to the 20th, of January, have arrived, but they bring very little intelligence. The opening of the new year was regarded as favourable to business, and the expectation is entertained that the bad effects of last year will now gradually wear off.

Adelaide papers to the 3rd of January have also come to hand. More steadiness is noticed in trade, and the colonists appear in better spirits now a revival seems likely to take place. Captain Grey, the governor, was indisposed, but his illness was not considered dangerous. The late cattle-fair had been well attended, and the stock offered brought tolerably good prices.

MAURITIUS.—Private advices received from the Mauritius to the 26th day of February, state that a hurricane had been experienced there on the 21st of that month, which had done some damage. Grand Port and Savannah appear to have been the chief scenes of the destruction. Only two vessels were loading for London, and these but slowly, owing to the late incessant rains having prevented the sugar coming down from the interior. A country vessel from Calcutta, with Coolies and a cargo of rice, was on the reefs outside the harbour.

CAPE OF GOOD HOPE.—Papers to the 16th of March have been received, but there is little of news worth extract, on the state of matters either political or commercial, at Cape Town on the frontier. The latest intelligence from Natal is that a large party of Boers residing in the Bechuana country has tendered their adhesion to the British Government, and everything is reported as tranquil. Commissioner Cloete, it is stated, was about to cross the Draakberg, and examine for himself the condition of affairs in that extensive country. Several rumours had been spread relative to the hostile intentions of the emigrants; none of which, however, have been realized.

At Port Elizabeth another gale had been experienced, but, fortunately, unattended by serious damage.

A curious correspondence is published in the Cape papers, showing the purpose for which the Brazilian visited Natal last year. This, it will be remembered, was the vessel ordered off by the English authorities at that port, the supposition being, at the time of her appearance, that it was connected with political intrigue between the Boers and the Dutch. It now turns out, that communication having taken place between the authorities at Amsterdam and the emigrant farmers of Natal, on the subject of the want of religious instruction in that colony, the Ministry of the Dutch Reformed Church sent out the Rev. Mr. Ham, with his family and assistants, with the view of encouraging the proper observance of religious duties ; and this vessel was freighted to convey them to their destination. As no one was allowed to land, no explanation could be made, and Mr. Ham, after shifting about from Mozambique to Madagascar, and thence to Delagoa Bay, has been obliged at last to remain at the latter place till he could inform the emigrants of his arrival, and obtain the necessary means of reaching them. The rev. gentleman has suffered much distress, and, to add to his calamities, his wife and child have died in the course of his wanderings. The papers say, that if the Brazilian had touched at the Cape, and the nature of the mission been fully explained, not the least difficulty would have interposed ; and all the pain and distress which Mr. Ham has experienced could have been avoided.

WEST INDIES. — The papers received from the West Indies reach to the 9th of April, from Jamaica ; from Bermuda, April 22; Demerara, April 6; Barbadoes, April 8; and Trinidad, April 4. The most important intelligence conveyed by this opportunity is the rising of the blacks in Hayti, and the sacrifice of life and property following the revolt. The Jamaica journals, referring to the condition of the weather, state that no satisfactory change had taken place. A few partial showers had fallen, but generally speaking the drought continued in the majority of the parishes. No improvement deserving notice could be reported in the trade of the island, nor was any, it appears, expected till agricultural operations had taken a brisker turn than had been the case for some months past. The bad weather, it is stated, leaves the labouring population without employment, and consequently they were without the means which they would otherwise have of making purchases. St. Thomas's in the East, to which Lord Elgin had recently paid a visit, was one of the few parishes that had been favoured with genial weather, and where good crops were to be seen. With respect to politics, it is observed that the next general election is looked forward to with much interest and even alarm by some persons, who imagine, but from what cause is not apparent, that the constitution of the House of Assembly will undergo considerable change. The curious fact is recorded, that the Grand Jury of the Surrey (Jamaica) Assizes had reported in the matter of a trial before them, that the present post-office was an uncertain and unsafe medium of conveyance, especially for the transmission of money. The loss of money is attributed to improper and irresponsible persons being intrusted with the care of the mails.

Business continues flat, and small prospect of improvement appears to present itself. Mr. Thomas, the manager of the Bank in Barbadoes, had been found guilty of robbery, and sentenced to a term of imprisonment with hard labour. The weather in some localities had been rather more favourable for the crops.

The accounts from the other islands afford little news of interest. The weather at Barbadoes had been seasonable, and the plantations showed the benefit of the late rains. At Trinidad the Council were occupied with the promulgation of ordinances for the internal improvement of the island, but labour, it was feared, would be insufficient to carry the necessary works for execution. The Demerara papers allude to the absence of Mr. Bagot, the chief registrar, and the serious charge of fraud is made against him; but such appears to be the vindictive spirit of the public writers in this colony, that all they advance should be received with much caution, and therefore it is only proper to mention the allegation, without entering into details at present. There appears to be no change in business-affairs in this quarter of the West Indies; and, generally speaking, matters seem to bear a smooth and quiet aspect throughout the several islands.

CANADA.—We learn that the public offices connected with the seat of government at Kingston, would close on the 15th of April, and would be opened in the city of Montreal about the 20th of May. It is rumoured that Colonel Bullock, adjutant-general of militia, as well as Colonel Jarvis, chief superintendent of Indian affairs, will remove to Toronto, and that Mr Anthony B. Hawke, chief emigrant agent, will remain in Kingston.

On the second day of the election at Montreal, the scenes of the preceding day were renewed with an increase of violence. Partisans of the different candidates cut and destroyed each other's clothes, and resorted to every species of annoyance calculated to prevent their opponents from exercising the right of suffrage. The number of persons suffering from contusions, or more serious injuries, is said to be very great. The majority for Drummond (Liberal) over Molson (Conservative) was 920. Mr. Molson, the Government candidate, having entered a protest, resigned any further contest. He intends petitioning against the return of Mr. Drummond.

AMERICAN MINISTERS.—The following list of all the foreign ministers plenipotentiary, times of their appointment, salaries, &c., of the United States, is given by a New York paper:—Edward Everett, of Massachusetts, appointed 1841, to Great Britain; residence, London. William R. King, of Alabama, appointed 1844, to France; residence, Paris. Charles S. Todd, of Kentucky, appointed 1841, to Russia; residence, St. Petersburgh. Henry Wheaton, of Rhode Island, appointed 1837, to Prussia, residence, Berlin. Daniel Jenifer, of Maryland, appointed 1841, to Austria; residence, Vienna. Wilson Shannon, of Ohio, appointed 1844, to Mexico; residence, Mexico. Henry A. Wise, of Virginia, appointed 1844, to Brazil; residence, Rio Janeiro. Washington Irving, of New York, appointed 1842, to Spain; residence, Madrid. Caleb Cushing, of Massachusetts, appointed 1843, to China; residence, Pekin. The salary of each of the above ministers is 9,000 dollars per annum, with an outfit of 9,000 dollars.

HOME INTELLIGENCE.

GOVERNOR-GENERAL OF INDIA.—At a Court of Directors held at the East India House, on Monday, May 6th, Lieutenant-General the Right Hon. Sir Henry Hardinge, K.C.B., was appointed unanimously Governor-General of India. It is expected that his Excellency will leave England early in the month of June, and that he will proceed by way of Marseilles, Suez, &c., so as to leave no time in entering upon the important functions of his high office.

LORD ELLENBOROUGH.—The subject of Lord Ellenborough's recall, and the production of papers relative thereto between the Government and the Board of Directors of the East India Company, was brought before both Houses of Parliament on Tuesday, the 7th of May. In both cases the application was refused. The Earl of Ripon's reply to the Marquis of Normanby was quite a specimen of the official curtain, and really did not let out the smallest glimpse of the secret, which for the present is doomed to remain in obscurity. Mr. Hume's motion in the Commons was met by Sir Robert Peel, who, with his usual dexterity, glided from the troublesome past into the golden regions of the future. When put to the vote, there appeared against Mr. Hume's motion, 197; for it, 21; majority, 176.

GRAND ENTERTAINMENT BY THE EAST INDIA DIRECTORS TO SIR HENRY HARDINGE.—On Wednesday evening, May 12th, the Directors of the East India Company entertained Sir Henry Hardinge, the Governor-General of India, and other distinguished guests, at the London Tavern. The preparations were on a very splendid scale. The Coldstream band was in attendance.

The number of guests were about 150, including the chairman (Mr. Shepherd), and the deputy-chairman (Sir H. Willett):—Sir Henry Hardinge, the Duke of Wellington, the Duke of Buckingham, the Duke of Buccleuch, the Earl of Jersey, Sir R. Peel, the Earl of Haddington, Lord Stanley, the Marquis Camden, the Earl of Lincoln, Earl Delawarr, the Earl of Liverpool, the Earl of Dalhousie, Lord G. Somerset, Lord Combermere, the Lord Mayor, Mr. Astell, Mr. Goulburn, Sir James Graham, Sir George Murray, Sir Edward Knatchbull, Mr. Gladstone, Sir

Frederic Pollock, the Solicitor-General, Sir T. Fremantle, and other distinguished persons.

As soon as dinner was over, and grace had been said, the health of Her Majesty the Queen, the Queen Dowager, His Royal Highness Prince Albert, the Prince of Wales, and the rest of the Royal Family, having been duly responded to, the Chairman said he now rose to propose the health of a distingushed guest, whose appointment to the Governor-Generalship of India they were met there to celebrate. The toast was received with loud applause, and drank with three times three.

Sir H. Hardinge rose and said:—

"Mr. Chairman, my Lord Duke, and Gentlemen,—In acknowledging the compliment you have just paid me, I will at once say that I am deeply impressed with the importance of the trust that has been confided to me, and I beg to offer to you, Sir, as the Chairman of the Court of Directors, and to the other members of that Court, my most grateful acknowledgments for your having considered me worthy of so high a trust as that of the Governor-Generalship of India. The assurance which we have just heard from the Chairman, that my appointment was unanimously approved of by the Court, and that I should receive the cordial support of the Directors, is most gratifying to me; not on account of any private feeling merely of personal satisfaction, but because it will enable me to perform my public duty in India with more weight and authority, when it is known that I carry with me the support of the Court of Directors, men well versed in Indian affairs, and the confidence of my late colleagues, and, above all, that my appointment has received the confirmation and sanction of Her Majesty's high authority. Gentlemen, the greater portion of my public life has been passed under the eye and instruction of my illustrious commander, the Duke of Wellington. I had the honour, as the chairman has stated, of passing under him through the whole Peninsular war, and on the termination of the peace I had the honour to be selected to conduct the civil department of the Ordnance in the House of Commons, of being appointed Secretary at War, and after that Chief Secretary for Ireland. I only mention these things to show, that I am well aware of the value of such an instructor, and how much I owe to such a master. Under his counsel and advice, I hope to be able to carry out any arrangements that may be necessary for the support of our great and gallant Indian army. I hope also to be able to promote the advantage of my own country, and to ameliorate the condition of the Indian population. I may, perhaps, venture to say, that I have known the miseries and the risks of war. I cannot say I have known its vicissitudes, because under that illustrious commander our armies never knew what vicissitudes were. In everything that regards the Indian army I shall always take the deepest interest; but let its efficiency be what it may, and however brilliant its recent successes may have been, I hope that the result of those successes will be that which should always be the legitimate consequence of war,—a long, lasting, and durable peace; and that the people of India will derive from those wars all the blessings of peace, in the amelioration of their condition, their improvement, their education, in short, in all those advantages which constitute the happiness and secure the prosperity of a nation. Peace and commerce are already restored with China, and a long continued tranquillity prevails in almost every part of India, except in the case of those internal dissensions in the Punjaub, with regard to which every possible precaution has been taken. I go out, therefore, with the most unbounded confidence in the Indian army, that it will maintain the national honour, and also with a full belief that the sway of Great Britain will be maintained over the intelligent, cheerful, and industrious people of India. In conclusion, I can only say, that I go out with the most sincere desire to exert my best efforts to serve the public, and, if Providence bless my efforts, as long as those principles shall guide them, I may hope in some respect to be able to contribute to the advancement of the mighty and the mutual interests of England and India."

The Right Hon. Baronet sat down amidst loud cheering.

The meeting was afterwards addressed by the Earl of Haddington, the Duke of Wellington, Sir Robert Peel, the Duke of Buccleuch, and Sir R. Houston, when the company separated.

Meeting of West India Proprietors. — On Tuesday May 21, a very numerous meeting of noblemen and gentlemen connected with the West India interest was held at Willis's Rooms, King-street, St. James's, to petition Parliament against any reduction of the duties on sugar, coffee, and cocoa, which shall not embrace a similar reduction on articles imported from British possessions. Viscount Combermere was called to the chair, and in a short speech opened the proceedings of the meeting; which was afterwards addressed by the Earl of Harewood; Sir E. Hyde East; Lord Saltoun; Mr. Carrington; Lord Reay; Mr. W. A. Mackinnon; Viscount St. Vincent; Sir. A. Grant, Sir W. Coddrington; Sir A. L. Hay; Sir R. C. Dallas; Mr. Hibbert; Sir J. Stewart; Sir J. R. Reid; Mr. P. M. Stewart; Sir. J. K. James; Mr. Arcedeckne; Mr. Burge, Colonel Lindsay, and other gentlemen, when a number of resolutions were passed and seconded; and it was agreed, that petitions embodying the resolutions be presented to the House of Lords by Viscount St. Vincent, and to the House of Commons by Mr. P. Miles.

Thanks were voted to Lord Combermere for his conduct in the chair, and the meeting separated.

"The North-American Colonial Association of Ireland."—In consequence of an article which appeared in *the Times*, commenting upon the position of the affairs of this society, the directors of the association determined on calling an "extraordinary meeting," which was done by the following advertisement:—

"North-American Colonial Association of Ireland:—The directors of this association hereby give special notice, that an extraordinary meeting of the shareholders will be held at No. 7, Broad-street-buildings, in the city of London, on Thursday, the 23d inst., at 12 o'clock at noon precisely, for the purpose of taking into consideration the allegations and insinuations contained in an article relative to the affairs of the association, which appeared in *The Times*, paper of Tuesday, the 7th instant.

"By order of the Board,
"James Dewar, Secretary.
"7 Broad-street-buildings, London, May, 9."

The meeting took place at the time and place appointed. So extraordinary a proceeding as a meeting of the unfortunate shareholders of this company appeared to have created considerable excitement in the office, though, from the paucity of persons present, it would seem to have occasioned very little out of doors. On entering the room, our reporter, although specially invited, was subjected to a very North-American cross-examination as to uninteresting particulars about his individuality, and from all that passed it seemed as if the presence of unrecognized shareholders would be deemed exceedingly annoying, if not intrusive.

Earl Fitzwilliam, the governor of the company, took the chair shortly after 12 o'clock, at which hour 20 or 21 persons were present, the majority being directors. The meeting was addressed by nearly all the gentlemen present, whose speeches were more of a recriminatory than explanatory nature; and after a sitting of upwards of four hours' duration, a vote of confidence was passed in *The Times* directors, and the meeting broke up.

Mr. Edward Ellice addressed a letter to the *Times*, on the 27th May, explanatory of his connection with the above association, in which he claims to assert that the annual value of the *settled* part alone of the Beauharnois estate is £5,000; whereas at the meeting he had estimated the whole only at £3,000; and that out of the £150,000 purchase-money, *only* £25,000 was paid in cash; that the sum of £28,000, the remainder of the deposit, was paid in shares; and that from the whole sum there was deducted an agency of £5 per cent, for Mr. Gibbon Wakefield.

Colonial Church Society.—The annual meeting of this society was held Wednesday evening, May 1, in the great room, Exeter-hall. Captain Sir. E. Parry, R. N., presided. The Hon. W. Cowper, M.P., Mr. J. P. Plumptre, M.P., Mr. G. Finch, Mr. J. Labouchere, the Rev. A. Thelwal, and a great number of the lay and clerical friends of the society, were on the platform.

The gallant Chairman said that the object of the society was to provide church accommodation for the various colonies and other dependencies of the British Crown. He considered that a society which steadily followed out that design was eminently calculated to promote the glory of God, and the best interests of mankind. It was satisfactory to know, that at the close of the year they could look without repining to the society's operations, nor were its future prospects less gratifying. The spiritual destitution which a very few years back had prevailed in some of the British colonies, more especially in the Cape of Good Hope, in the Bahama Islands, and Western Australia, had attracted the society's attention. In proportion as England extended her territorial dominion, she was bound to extend the blessings of Christianity to her newly-acquired possessions.

The secretary read the report, which gave a detailed account of the society's operations in Nova Scotia, Western Australia, the Cape of Good Hope, the Bahama Islands, and various other parts of the world. The subscriptions and donations received during the past year amounted to £3,775, exclusive of collections in the colonies.

The report was adopted; and several resolutions having been proposed, and spoken to by Mr. G. Finch, the Rev. J. Yorke, Mr. J. Labouchere, the Hon. and Rev. B. Noel, &c., the meeting separated.

Corn-laden Ships and Corn Statistics.—A return of the number of ships laden with foreign corn entered inwards at the various ports of the United Kingdom during the period between the 5th of January, 1843, and the 5th of January, 1844, (in continuation of Parliamentary paper, No. 150, of the session of 1843.) It appears that the total number of British ships which imported foreign corn in the past year amounted to 655, and the total number of foreign corn-laden ships to 1,220; exhibiting the decisive difference in favour of foreign, and against British shipping, of 565. The total quantity of foreign wheat so imported in British vessels, amounted to 314,322 quarters; and the total quantity carried by foreign vessels, to 622,301 quarters, or just double the quantity carried by English ships. The quantities of barley, oats, beans and pease, and flour, brought by British ships, were respectively, 22,585 quarters, 50,198 quarters, 58,664 quarters, and 284,896 quarters. The corresponding quantities of those grains carried by foreign vessels amounted, respectively, to 158,006 quarters, 34,859 quarters, 34,849 quarters, and 80,530 quarters.

NEW SOUTH WALES.

EXPORT OF OIL.—Return of the Quantity and Value of Oil, &c., Exported from the Colony from the Year 1828 to 1842, inclusive.

Year.	Sperm Whale.	Black Whale.	Whalebone.	Seal Skins.	Value, as entered in the Return of Exports.
	Tuns.	Tuns.	Tons. Cwt.	No.	£
1828	311	28	0 17	8,723	26,431
1829	871	45	1 0	11,362	54,975
1830	983	98	9 16	9,720	59,471
1831	1,571	505	28 5	4,424	95,969
1832	2,491	695	43 6	1,415	147,409
1833	3,048	418	0 0	1,890	146,855
1834	2,760	975	43 15	890	157,334
1835	2,898	1,159	112 0	641	180,349
1836	1,682	1,149	79 0	386	140,220
1837	2,559	1,565	77 8	107	183,122
1838	1,891	3,055	174 0	3 cases	197,644
1839	1,578	1,229	134 14	7 cases	172,315
1840	1,854	4,297	250 0	474	224,144
1841	1,545	1,018	84 13	41	127,470
1842	957	1,171	60 5	162	77,012

EXPORT OF TIMBER.—Return of the Quantity and Value of Timber Exported from the Colony from the Year 1828 to 1842, inclusive.

Year.	Cedar.	Blue Gum, Pine, and other Timber.	Treenails.	Value, as entered in the Return of Exports.
	Superficial Feet.	Superficial Feet.	Number.	£
1828	847,805	285,541	65,837	11,428
1829	940,486	608,647	181,817	16,293
1830	368,830	179,403	23,959	5,218
1831	580,393	416,857	24,316	8,401
1832	418,930	233,653	186,831	6,132
1833	1,086,437	147,170	328,503	13,153
1834	899,492	30,065	212,467	7,941
1835	907,921	145,628	178,969	10,489
1836	1,409,467	{ 3,778 feet and 106 logs }	35,094	14,611
1837	116,828	18,828	62,989	14,463
1838	699,066	9,000	73,450	6,382
1839	729,001	{ 823 deals 15 logs }	40,588	8,815
1840	1,250,786	151,500	4,350	20,971
1841	513,139	1,000	26,890	7,004
1842	522,882	27,404	55,644	5,800

IMPORT OF LIVE STOCK.—Return of Live Stock Imported into the Colony (including the District of Port Phillip) from 1828 to 1842, inclusive.

Year.	DESCRIPTION OF STOCK.				
	Horses.	Horses, Mules, and Asses.	Horned Cattle.	Sheep.	Sheep and Hogs.
1828	......	132	......	3,443	......
1829	......	16	......	2,215	......
1830	......	12	......	10	......
1831	......	Not stated	......	66	......
1832	......	......	......	36	......
1833	......	......	......	......	......
1834	6	......	......	......	62
1835	11	......	......	......	137
1836	8	......	4	.....	449
1837	92	......	97	55,208	307
1838	185	......	74	9,822	192
1839	652	......	135	17,567	359
1840	1,008	......	244	19,598	252
1841	863	12	156	530	50 hogs
1842	113	......	89	638	65 ditto

N.B.—The sheep have principally been imported from Van Diemen's Land to the District of Port Phillip. The horses have chiefly come from South America.

NEW SOUTH WALES.

RETURN of the Number of NOTES in Circulation of the several BANKS during the undermentioned Periods.

BANKS.	From 1st January to 30th June, 1836.	From 1st July to 31st Dec. 1836.	From 1st January to 30th June, 1837.	From 1st July to 31st Dec., 1837.	From 1st Jan. uary to 30th June, 1838.	From 1st July to 31st Dec., 1838.	From 1st January to 30th June, 1839.	From 1st July to 31st Dec., 1839.	From 1st January to 30th June, 1840.	From 1st July to 31st Dec., 1840.
	£. s. d.	£. s. d.	£. s. d.	£. s. d.	£. s. d.	£. s. d.	£. s. d.	£. s. d.	£. s. d.	£. s. d.
New South Wales	32138 0 0	27665 0 0	28875 0 0	26209 0 0	25486 0 0	24909 0 0	26771 0 0	28498 0 0	34222 0 0	31712 0 0
Australia	35939 0 0	33632 0 0	30113 0 0	26424 0 0	27437 0 0	27764 0 0	30319 0 0	30436 0 0	32146 0 0	25724 0 0
Commercial	28160 0 0	32049 0 0	40522 0 0	45946 0 0	47229 0 0	50130 0 0	59855 0 0	62190 0 0	74193 0 0	70381 0 0
Australasia	11894 18 4	12780 17 0	14771 3 10	16751 5 7	17148 16 2	18799 6 7	25763 10 5	30820 0 0	42542 17 8	48529 18 5
Union of Australia	......	......	......	......	.....	......	......	18261 0 0	34506 0 0	39382 5 2
Totals	108131 18 4	106126 17 0	114281 3 10	115330 5 7	117300 16 2	121602 6 7	142713 10 5	170205 0 0	217609 17 8	215729 3 7

BANKS.	From 1st January to 31st March, 1841.	From 1st April to 30th June, 1841.	From 1st July to 30th Sept. 1841.	From 1st Oct. to 31st Dec., 1841.	From 1st January to 31st March, 1842.	From 1st April to 30th June, 1842.	From 1st July to 30th Sept., 1842.	From 1st Oct. to 31st Dec., 1842.	From 1st January to 31st March, 1843.	From 1st April to 30th June, 1843.
	£. s. d.	£. s. d.	£. s. d.	£. s. d.	£. s. d.	£. s. d.	£. s. d.	£. s. d.	£. s. d.	£. s. d.
New South Wales	31637 0 0	29467 0 0	27925 0 0	28694 0 0	27015 0 0	26885 0 0	26898 0 0	26213 0 0	25126 0 0	25256 0 0
Australia	25162 0 0	24244 0 0	20782 0 0	19021 0 0	18533 0 0	18058 0 0	17118 0 0	16622 0 0	......	......
Commercial	63543 16 11	62057 9 2	58392 13 10	53592 3 0	52482 3 10	52723 3 0¾	47758 13 10	45444 4 7	44681 16 11	44388 13 10
Australasia	53369 17 0	54313 12 5	50595 15 5	47538 9 2	52033 16 11	49233 6 1	46789 0 0	44539 19 11	49780 17 0	49671 9 2
Union of Australia	27706 7 9	29684 11 5	30230 12 3	27783 6 0	27258 12 10	29107 2 5	27964 0 0	26667 15 2	30852 0 0	33589 2 11
Sydney	17591 0 0	19730 0 0	20155 0 0	19037 0 0	18955 0 0	19409 0 0	19052 0 0	19669 0 0	19605 0 0	16744 0 0
Port Phillip	3792 0 0	4111 9 3	4980 10 9	4662 10 9	3969 3 1	3710 4 7	3526 13 4	2496 7 8	1005 1 6	392 10 9
Totals	222802 1 8	223608 2 3	213061 12 3	200328 8 11	200246 16 8	199125 16 1¾	189106 7 2	181652 7 4	171050 15 5	170041 16 8

RETURN of COIN in the Colonial Treasury, the Military Chest, and the several Banks, on the 31st December, in each Year, from 1836 to 1842.

YEAR	Colonial Treasury.	Military Chest.	Banks.	Totals.	Increase on Previous Year.	Decrease on Previous Year.
	£. s. d.	£. s. d.	£. s. d.	£. s. d.	£. s. d.	£. s. d.
1836	218,630 0 0	....	202,090 2 11	420,720 2 11	....	....
1837	245,250 0 0	....	182,182 11 6	427,432 11 6	6,712 8 7	....
1838	163,000 0 0	....	520,127 11 5	520,127 11 5	92,694 19 11	....
1839	124,100 0 0	....	391,969 16 7	516,069 16 7	....	4,057 14 10
1840	38,900 0 0	49,151 18 9	309,529 15 0	397,581 13 9	....	118,488 2 10
1841	25,000 0 0	10,000 0 0	427,624 17 9	462,624 17 9	65,043 4 0	....
1842	Nil.	32,409 14 5	442,980 4 3	475,389 18 8	12,765 0 11	....

FRENCH AND SPANISH TRADE.

From the report of Senor Mateo Durou, recently removed from the Spanish consulate at Bordeaux, we gather the following statistics of the commerce between France and Spain, during the year 1842. It appears, from this report, that the imports into France from Spain, by sea, amounted to 29,740,267 francs; and by land, to 9,263,335 francs. Total import into France from Spain, during the year 1842, 39,003,602 francs. The articles of highest amount were—wools, 8,743,364 f.; lead, 5,365,474 f.; oil, 4,837,828 f.; fruits of all sorts, 3,928,326 f.; cork-wood, 3,359,802 f., (estevas); mats, 2,167,839 f., (esparto); raw material of do., 1,474,969 f.; wines of all sorts, 809,166 f.; woollen-stuffs, 764,813. The French exports amounted to 34,161, 622 f. by sea, and 37,330,699 f. by land. Total, 71,492,321 f.; showing a balance in favour of France, according to Senor Durou's report, of 32,488,719 f. The principal articles of French export to Spain were—cotton-stuffs, 21,768,450 f.; woollen do., 11,177,387 f.; silk do., 8,190,636 f.; mules, 3,519,600 f.; linen-stuffs, 3,393,932 f.; merceries, 2,230,926 f.; machinery, 1,449,661 f.; furniture, 1,163,180 f.; paper, books, and prints, &c., 1,290,582 f.; wood of all kinds, 1,035,392 f.; porcelain and glass, 946,726 f.; iron and steel, 850,842 f.; nails, 807,819 f. The total importations into France, from Spain, were—1839, 37,351,914 f.; 1840, 42,684,761 f.; 1841, 37,162,689 f.; 1842, 39,008,602. The total exportations from France into Spain, were—1839, 82,656,086 f.; 1840, 104,679,141 f.; 1841, 100,893,906; 1842, 71,492,321. In the same year there entered French ports, proceeding from Spain, 901 vessels, of which 492 were Spanish, 374 French, and 35 of other nations; and there left French ports, for Spain, 590 vessels, of which 446 were Spanish, 94 French, and 50 of other nations. How far this statement is to be relied upon, we are unable to say. The greater part of the French trade being a smuggling trade, must be taken into account; but Senor Durou may have had sources of information that enabled him to make a tolerably accurate calculation. It is published, at all events, with his signature as Spanish consul, and dated Bordeaux, December 30, 1843; and must, therefore, be viewed as official.

EXPORTS OF PORT WINE FROM OPORTO.

The official list of the exportation of wine from Oporto during the year 1843, shows that while the export to Great Britain alone has been 21,244 pipes, that to all other countries, including British colonies, has been only 5,156 pipes. In 1842, the exportation was 21,728; so that the fall off last year was 500 pipes. We must, however, look to the years 1839 and 1840 to see the real extent of the decline, the exportation to Great Britain being 26,159 pipes in the former year, and 25,678 in the latter. The decline in the wine trade is naturally accompanied by an increase of agricultural distress in Portugal; and accordingly the official statement of emigration, which is published in the government journal, gives some melancholy facts. In the first half of 1842, the number of poor persons emigrating to Brazil was 459 from Oporto, and 47 from Lisbon. In the last half, the number from Oporto was 775, and from Lisbon 218; and in the first half of 1843, the respective numbers were 715 and 291. The hardships which these poor people have to undergo, are of the most fearful description; and some of them, on their arrival in Brazil, are obliged to sell themselves for a term into slavery. And this distress is brought about solely by bad management, for Portugal is but thinly populated, and contains provinces which are yet but imperfectly developed, and which only require cultivation to become most abundantly productive.

DEBTS OF INSOLVENT HONG MERCHANTS.

By a late letter from Canton, we are informed that the Hong merchants have made arrangements to pay off all the old debts of the insolvent Hongs, which has been insisted on by the mandarin, preparatory to the commencement of the new system. Of the 1,560,000 dollars required, it is believed that How-qua will pay 1,000,000 dollars; Poon-ke-qua, 130,000 dollars; Gow-qua and Sam-qua, each 100,000 dollars; Mow-qua, King-qua, and Sao-qua, 50,000 dollars each; Foo-tae and Pun-hoy-qua, each 30,000 dollars; and Ming-qua, 20,000 dollars.

OBITUARY.

Allen, Henry Archer, Esq., lieutenant in the 4th regiment of Royal Irish Dragoon Guards, May 23, at the vicarage, Northop, Flintshire, aged 20.

Anderson, Lieutenant-Colonel Robert, R.H., late of the 21st regiment of foot, April 30, at Winterfield House, near Dunbar.

Bannerman, Edward, Esq., late of the East India Company's Madras Civil Service, April 20, at Cairo, on the overland-route from India.

Beckford, William, Esq., late of Fonthill Abbey, May 2, at Bath, in the 84th year of his age.

Biddulph, Ann, widow of the late Simon Biddulph, Esq., formerly of Tamworth, in the county of Stafford, February 10, at Bathurst, Cape of Good Hope, aged 79 years. She was only daughter of Thomas Burnet, Esq., captain and commander in the Royal Navy, and great granddaughter of the celebrated Gilbert Burnet, bishop of Salisbury, and (upon the death of her brother, the late Major-General John Burnet), became sole legal personal representative of that learned prelate. She was a good type of the English gentlewoman; studiously decorous in her deportment, and incessantly active in the discharge of her domestic duties.

Boaden, H. F., Esq., at sea, suddenly, on board the Thomas Coutts, March 14, aged 40. His remains were committed to the deep on the following morning with all due solemnity, and every possible indication of respect, by the passengers, ship's company, and military on board. The deceased was youngest son of the late James Boaden, Esq., well known in the literary and dramatic world. United to his mercantile pursuits in Bombay, Mr. Boaden for a long period filled the responsible situation of agent to her Majesty's navy, to the entire satisfaction of the crown. He was also for a series of years the confidential adviser of Sir Jamsetjee Jejeebhoy, whom he regarded as his best friend and patron, and to whom he was to have returned in two years' time. By this painful affliction, a widow and only son (aged 9 years) are left to deplore the irreparable loss of a most excellent husband and affectionate father.

Capper, Captain Cawthorne, third son of Jasper Capper, Esq., of Stoke Newington, Middlesex, January 14, at Macao, aged 31.

Carpenter, Eliza, wife of Admiral Carpenter, May 23, at London, in the 76th year of her age.

Clark, Richard, Esq., formerly of the East India House, May 9, in the 85th year of his age, at London.

Garnett, Rev. William, late of the island of Barbadoes, May 13, at St. Heliers, Jersey, aged 85 years.

Geary, Captain Henry, of the Royal Artillery, January 13, at sea, on board her Majesty's ship Rattlesnake, on her voyage from Hong-Kong to Portsmouth.

Gentle, William, Esq., formerly of Honduras, May 17, at London, aged 65.

Grieve, Mr. Andrew, late of the Hon. East India Company's Service, April 29, at Islington, aged 88 years.

Griffiths, Henrietta, widow of the late Colonel Griffiths, of the Bombay army, April 29, at Castle Heddingham, Essex, aged 64.

Hutchinson, Captain Marley, late of the 53rd regiment, third son of the late G. P. Hutchinson, Esq., of Egglestone, in the county of Durham, May 13, at Bilting, Godmersham, Kent, aged 81.

Irvine, John, assistant commissary-general, February 1, at Hong-Kong.

Jackson, Ensign Outram Montague, 26th regiment Native Infantry, youngest son of Rear-Admiral Jackson, C.B., March 17, at Malligaum, Bombay Presidency, aged 17.

Lethbridge, Lieutenant Thomas Christopher Mytton, of the 85th regiment of Light Infantry, eldest son of John Hesketh Lethbridge, Esq., and grandson of Sir Thomas Buckler Lethbridge, Bart., of Sandhill Park, Somerset, March 31, at St. Kitts.

Lowther, Sir John, Bart., May 13, at Swillington House, Yorkshire, aged 85; and on the 17th of the same month, Lady Elizabeth Lowther, his wife, in her 74th year.

Malcolmson, John Grant, Esq., M.D., F.R.S., formerly of the Madras Medical Establishment, and latterly of the firm of Forbes & Co., of Bombay, March 23, at Dhoolier, while on a tour through Guzerat and Candeish, aged 41.

Morrell, Thomas Palmer, Esq., son of the late Lieutenant-Colonel Robert Morrell, of the Bengal army, March 2, at Calcutta, aged 37.

Nicholas, John Edward, Esq., volunteer of the first class, only son of the late Captain John Nicholas, R.N., on board her Majesty's ship Albatross, in the West Indies.

Price, Major-General William Phillips, Hon. East India Company's Civil Service, May 7, at Abergavenny, aged 68.

Stedman, William, Esq., M.D., Knight, of Dannebrog, April 7, at the Danish island of St. Croix, West Indies, aged 80.

Stubbs, General Sir Thomas William, April 27, at Lisbon.

Trafford, Thomas William, Esq., second son of Sir Thomas Joseph Trafford, Bart., of Trafford Park, Lancashire, and late Captain in the Royal Scotch Greys, May 7, at Trafford Park.

Vowell, Catharine, relict of Major Vowell, of the 88th regiment, May 10, at Exeter, aged 72.

Walton, Jacob, Esq., rear admiral of the white, April 11, at New York.

Wells, Lady, relict of the late Sir John Wells, G.C.B., April 30, at Worthing, aged 75.

Wilbraham, Mr. William, mate of her Majesty's ship Illustrious, only son of the late Captain Wilbraham, R. N., and nephew of George Wilbraham, Esq., of Delamere House, Cheshire, March 15.

LONDON: FISHER, SON, AND CO., PRINTERS.

FISHER'S

COLONIAL MAGAZINE.

NEW ZEALAND.

AN IMPARTIAL EXAMINATION OF THE APPENDICES TO THE COMPANY'S TWELFTH REPORT.

We have given, since the month of December in the past year, to the Anglo-New-Zealand public, so much information as to the colonization of the islands which collectively bear the name, that anything material on the subject will of course not be expected in our pages. Our readers must be aware that "there was something rotten in the state of Denmark," but neither they nor ourselves could have ever dreamt of the extent of the mischief, or that any office in our government could have been so cruelly conducted towards those whom it was its duty to have protected, as is shown by the development lately made by the Directors of the New Zealand Company in their 12th report.

It is no longer a question between a joint-stock company and a Colonial Minister; an appeal by the directors is made from that minister to his colleagues, that is, to the whole administration, to parliament, and lastly, to the public opinion of the reflective world—which, no doubt, will be re-echoed in the faithful page of history: still, however dark and disgraceful the past may have been, until all is finally wrecked, hope will cling even to the drowning mariner, and why should it not exist amongst the wantonly and wickedly ruined settlers in Cook's Straits—the relatives of the murdered—the loyal supporters of the Queen's authority—the connexions at home of 10,000 settlers at the antipodes—the insulted British public, unused to a solemn compact between the government of England and a portion of its subjects being treated by any office as waste-paper, are indeed matters of grave consideration.

We began these papers strongly prejudiced in favour of Lord Stanley; we had entire confidence in the manly independence of his acknowledged talents, and believed it impossible that it ever should be our duty to relate the melancholy tale which the twelfth Report of the New Zealand Company and its appendices exhibit. We have examined its pages with grief—it contains the heaviest charges ever made in modern times against a British Minister. In one respect Lord Stanley has acted well; he has made no objection, he has assented, almost courted an inquiry, by a committee of the House of Commons, into his conduct; in his lordship there was no quibbling—no reference to precedents, for the purpose of creating delay. It was Mr. Labouchere and Mr. Vernon Smith, both having served the office of Under-secretaries in the colonial department, who, like the sensitive plant, seemed to shrink from any examination as to the past conduct of the office. Mr. Roebuck, who appeared as ignorant as man could be of anything connected with the subject as to which he so rashly talked, ventured to rather more than hint that the conduct of the Company had been "fraudulent," and had ended in "folly." He has now the opportunity of making good the charge. If he had not been named a member of the committee, after what he said in the house—if he meant to retain his character as a public man—he was bound to have laid before the committee the circumstances which had justified him in making so broad a charge; and no doubt it was to enable him to make it good, or to retract what he had so rashly uttered, that he was placed on the committee—thus clothing him with the power of calling for documentary or personal evidence to establish his assertion.

It seems to be agreed that all party-feeling should be sunk—the majority of the committee are ministerialists; so far from there being any objection to it, we feel satisfied, that all connected with the afflicting state in which so many British colonists have been abandoned to slaughter, would have gladly referred their charge to the other members of the cabinet. The committee has the responsibility of a jury, bound in honour and common honesty to examine into the truth of the accusations brought against the Colonial Minister, and report the verdict to parliament for the benefit of her Majesty's Ministers.

The members of the committee are:—

Lord Howick—Chairman.
Mr. Aglionby.
Mr. Cardwell.
Mr. Chartaris.
Mr. Robert Clive.
Viscount Ebrington.
Lord Francis Egerton.
Sir John Hanmer.
Mr. Hawes.
Mr. George William Hope.
Sir Robert Harry Inglis.
Viscount Jocelyn.
Mr. Milnes.
Mr. Wilson Patten.
Mr. Roebuck.

Having said thus much of the committee, we will proceed to analyze the principal objects of inquiry which will be brought before it. There was in the December number of the old series of the magazine a very fair history of the colonization of the islands, and for a knowledge of it we refer our readers to p. 426 and 427, with some confidence. We must premise what we have to say by stating that the idea of a joint-stock company for colonizing New Zealand originated with a Colonial Minister, Lord Glenelg; for this we beg to refer to the speech of the Hon. Francis Baring, in the House of Commons, on the 19th of June,

1838. Do not let the date deter any one from examining the statement; the complaints then made by that well-instructed and honourable gentleman, the Deputy-Governor of the ill-treated New Zealand Company—what he then said has not yet become mere matter of history; all of which he then complained is still in practice, and has been practised for some years, in the most wanton manner, to the ruin of thousands—to the slaughter of our valuable countrymen, to the dishonour of the British name.

The New Zealand association * refused to merge into a joint-stock company, but, finding it the only means by which these favoured islands could be colonized, or even saved from becoming a dependency of France, a number of its members formed themselves into one, for the purpose of treating with the resident native inhabitants for a territory—being an attempt to carry into execution the principle of systematic colonization, by combining land, labour, and capital together, not alone to the benefit of the emigrant settler, but also to improve the position of the aboriginal inhabitants, by reserving for them a tenth part of the land, to which, in time, value would be given through the means of planting civilization in their neighbourhood. This was putting into practice the following observation from the leader in the *Times* of March 29th, 1843:—

"We have more men and money than we know what to do with—we have starving workmen, anxious to be employed, who serve no other purpose here than to keep down each others wages—we have countless wealth lying barren in the hands of its possessors—and, finally, our colonies present us with tracts upon tracts of rich land, palpably capable of furnishing food to the one and profitable investment to the other, honestly and wisely administered. Each of these materials for increase of wealth, power, and happiness, we possess in startling abundance; but they stand apart, and threaten our ruin, instead of confirming our greatness. Certainly no object could be devised more worthy of a master-mind, than to bring together the elements of good."

What says the editor of a periodical devoted to social interests in every land—

"The discovery of that principle we regard as amongst the most important improvements which have hitherto been effected in the science of human society."

This, too, was the opinion of nearly all the capitalists, bankers, merchants, ship-owners, &c, who signed the City Memorial to the Prime Minister in April, 1843, previous to Mr. Buller's motion for a committee to enquire as to the benefits of systematic colonization. A deputation from the memorialists waited on Sir Robert Peel to present it, and urge its adoption; it consisted of Mr. Masterman, Sir Matthew Wood, Mr. Lyall, and Lord John Russell, Mr. Thos. Baring, Alderman Thompson, Mr. J. Melville, and Mr. Samuel Gurney. The opinions of these gentlemen, and the great mass of city names whom they represented, might be supposed to have carried some weight; but neither their opinions nor the principle itself had any effect with

* The names of the associators will be found at p. 431 of the December number of the magazine, consisting at first of ten members, subsequently of seventeen of the most honourable public men in the kingdom.

the Prince Rupert of the House of Commons. Like a jib-horse, he dashed off without control—knocked down Mr. Buckingham, the ex-member for Sheffield, who was no party to the principle or the memorial. The sessions of parliament was near its close, and thus the matter has rested for a while; still, "on this all-important subject, Charles Buller has raised a warning voice, which has vibrated through the land; and deep and awful would be the responsibility of those by whom that warning voice should be disregarded."*

Unfortunately, Lord Stanley is only a debater—it is the Alpha and Omega of his character—he is nothing beyond it. A Colonial Minister has an immense area under his care; he has to watch the well-being of millions of British subjects, inhabiting parts of the empire so distant from each other, that it is a common saying, that on it the sun never sets. As an off-hand ready debater he perhaps may be compared to Peel, but he wants that Fabian policy, for which the premier is so conspicuous. Peel's speeches are astonishing from their profound erudition. If he has to talk upon renewing the bank charter, he soon proves himself to have examined all writers upon currency and political economy; if a ten-hours' labour-bill is to be discussed, his knowledge of the powers of a state are exemplified from a store-house of information, drawn from facts in all countries as well as his own.

Loud are the complaints from various quarters of our colonial empire against Lord Stanley, but never was ignorance of the circumtances under his guidance so completely exposed, as by this book, the twelfth Report and its appendices. It proves him to be a most inferior man; he has turned his back upon himself. His incapacity is most striking; he appears to have had but one object in view; he has chosen to fancy the directors and the brave settlers as his enemies — as poachers on his manor—and he rushes into a supposed hostile camp with a gallant bearing, reckless of the consequences. His own loss of reputation never strikes him. The Fabian policy of Sir Robert Peel is despised by him; but the sufferers by his rash decisions, who prayed for his protection, are not paralyzed; if they can do nothing else, they can tell their tale, and they have now ample materials—materials which will show to the descendants of their slaughtered countrymen the true causes of one of the most dreadful massacres upon record.

Lord Stanley opposes himself without reason, but with unexampled temerity, to—

Joseph Somes, Esqr., Governor.
The Hon. Francis Baring, Deputy-Governor.
Henry A. Aglionby, Esq., M.P.
John Ellerker Boulcott, Esq.
John William Buckle, Esq.
Charles Buller, Esq., M.P.
Viscount Courtenay, M.P.
Sir Isaac Lyon Goldsmid, Bart.
James Robert Gowen, Esq.
Archibald Hastie, Esq., M.P.
Sir Ralph Howard, Bart., M.P.
William Hutt, Esq., M.P.
Viscount Ingestrie, M.P.
William King, Esq.
Ross Donnelly Mangles, Esq., M.P.
Steward Majoribanks, Esq., M.P.
Alexander Nairne, Esq.
The Lord Petre.
Jeremiah Pilcher, Esq.
Sir John Pirie, Bart, Alderman.
John Abel Smith, Esq., M.P.

* Vide Mr. Buckingham's reply, prefixed to a former No. of this Magazine.

William Thompson, Esq., Alderman M.P.
Edward Gibbon Wakefield, Esq.
George Frederick Young, Esq.
Thomas Cudbert Harrington, Esq., Secretary.

The Report states the complaints which the Company has to make of the conduct of the Colonial Minister, and his secretaries, Mr. Hope and Mr. Stephen; and, however respectable the names of the Directors who have unanimously agreed to it, credit could not be given even to their assertions, was not every fact stated by them followed up by reference to authentic documents.

It seems that a deputation of the Directors have had at times personal interviews with Lord Stanley; but, that nothing should rest upon conversation, the pith of what passed at these meetings was reduced to writing, and appears as a correspondence—the whole of which is printed, in an alarmingly voluminous book, divided into eleven chapters, of which it is proposed to give a succinct account; the size of the work prevents its being read; it is not a continuous story; its want of chronological order distracts the mind, but it will ever remain as a land-mark of reference, exhibiting the barbarous manner in which the constituents (the settlers in Cook's Straits) of the New Zealand Company have been treated by the Colonial Minister and his subordinates. The monument now erecting to the memory of the slain will be a lasting memorial of that treatment. These appendices want a copious index; this may be easily supplied, and would greatly add to their use. Before beginning to analyze the huge volume before us, it will be necessary to draw the reader's attention to some facts chronologically arranged, and out of which the whole matter in dispute has arisen.

1769.—The illustrious Cook, agreeable to the law of nations, proclaimed British sovereignty over the group of islands called New Zealand.* Infinite pains seem to have been taken by several Colonial Ministers to do away with the right established by Cook, and thus to throw the islands to other powers.†

1787.—A royal proclamation appointed Captain Philip "Captain-General and Governor-in-Chief, in and over the territory of New South Wales and its dependencies;" extending from Cape York, latitude 11° 37′ south, to the South Cape, latitude 43° 30′ south; and, inland, to the westward, as far as 135° east longitude, comprehending all the islands adjacent in the Pacific Ocean, within the latitudes of the above-named Capes.

1814.—The Governor of New South Wales and its dependencies declared New Zealand to be a dependency of his government; and, by regular commission of *dedimus potestatem*, appointed justices of the peace to act there, some of whom were natives, thus treating them as British subjects.

* This and the subsequent circumstances connected with it, has been traced with singular accuracy, in a letter from Mr. Somes to Lord Palmerston, dated 7th of November, 1839, and printed in these Appendices, i., 22.

† This will be found in a memorandum transmitted from the Colonial Office to Lord Palmerston, as a sort of reply to Mr. Somes' statement, and is printed at i. 28.

1819.—Governor Macquarrie appointed an English magistrate in New Zealand.

1822.—A French nobleman, the Baron de Thierry, formed a scheme for planting a colony in New Zealand; he made a contract with the natives for a considerable district of country, and was assisted in it by Mr. Thomas Kendal, one of the early Church of England missionaries. He went to England, got his deed confirmed by Shungee, a native chief, lodged attested copies of it in our Foreign Office, also in the Office for Foreign Affairs in France, and in that of the United States in Anglo-America. He endeavoured to form a company in London, and after years of perseverance went to Sydney, to enlist emigrants to populate the land, and to support the sovereignty which Shungee and others had ceded to him.* The Baron, in the deed, described himself as of Barhampton, in the county of Somerset, and of Queen's College, Cambridge; his purchase, as he called it, was made in the same manner, perhaps in a more legal form, than those which had been made by the English missionaries. At that time, our Colonial Ministers took some pains to repudiate the sovereignty which had been proclaimed by our illustrious countryman; still it is evident that Mr. Dandeson Coates was right, in asserting, "that neither Shungee, or any other chief, had any right to the sovereignty of the country."† Shungee in England might have learnt what "sovereignty" meant, but previously to his arrival on our shores, neither he nor any other native had an idea of the signification of the word.

1823.—A British act of parliament, 4th of George IV., cap. 97, extended the jurisdiction of the courts of New South Wales to New Zealand, by name.‡

1825.—Lord Durham, the Right Hon. Edward Ellice, and others, formed a joint-stock company, for the purpose of colonizing the islands of New Zealand, which was approved by the then Colonial Minister, the Right Hon. W. Huskisson, who promised them a charter for the purpose.

1830.—Captain la Place, a French naval officer, visited the Bay of Islands, and officially reported to the French government that the English missionaries there not only refused him refreshment for his sick, but set the natives upon him.§

In this year, a series of the most barbarous murders ever related,

---

* A copy of the deed will be found at page 299 of the Lords' Report, reprinted by the Commons, 8th of August, 1838; and the account in the text is condensed from that given by the Rev. Mr. Beecham to the committee, and the papers delivered by him to the committee.

† See this statement in the evidence of Mr. Dundeson Coates, at page 244 of the above Report

‡ 57 Geo. III., cap. 53; 4 Geo. IV., cap. 96, sec. 3; and 9 Geo. IV., cap. 83, sec. 4—are very contradictory, and were no doubt acts passed for different purposes; they evince not only gross carelessness in legislation, but yet greater ignorance in the Colonial Department, to have suffered them to pass; one asserting one thing, and the next a contrary.

§ Voyage de la Favorite, tome iv. p. 35.

was committed by Raupero, in which he was assisted by an Englishman, Captain Stewart, for which he was afterwards tried at Sydney, and acquitted, for want of evidence. It became a subject of correspondence between General Darling and the Colonial Minister, Lord Ripon, and no doubt the records belonging to it are in the archives of the Colonial Office.*

1831.—November 16th, a letter to King William IV., from thirteen New Zealand chiefs, was transmitted to Lord Ripon, praying the protection of the British crown, from the neighbouring tribes.

1832.—June 14th, Lord Ripon despatched Mr. Busby as British Resident, with an answer to the chiefs, reminding them of the benefits which they would derive from the friendship and alliance of Great Britain.†

This British Resident, Mr. Busby, was accredited to the missionaries,‡ as if they had been the power exercising sovereignty; but his instructions, as to how he was to conduct himself towards the natives, were given to him by Sir Richard Bourke, the Governor of New South Wales.§

1835.—In the course of the previous three years, that is, between 1832 and 1835, Mr. Busby, the Resident, and some of the missionaries, had, like the Baron de Thierry, entered into agreement with the natives for vast districts of country.‖ These were transactions concealed from

---

* The details of these horrid murders will be found related on oath by Mr. Montefiore before a Committee of the House of Lords, on the 6th of April, 1838, and printed at page 55 of the Report of that year. See also further atrocities committed by this horrid wretch, in Mr. Halswell's letter to Colonel Wakefield, 23 H, of the Appendices.

† The construction put on this letter by Mr. Stephen, the Under-Secretary of the Colonial Office, will be found printed at I 29, paragraph 5. This letter shows vast cunning; its object, no doubt, was to put aside British sovereignty, and may do great mischief, as between France and England, as evinced by the speeches of M. Berryer and other deputies in the French Chamber, on the 28th and 29th of May, in endeavouring to monopolize the government of New Zealand for the missionaries. The Under-Secretary of State for the Colonies was throwing open the question of the French flag floating there; and it seems by these debates, that the ownership of land by Frenchmen is still a subject under discussion between M. Guizot and Lord Aberdeen. Mr. Stephen must not imagine that his object has been hidden.

‡ "He was sent there in a high character, and was accredited to the missionaries;"—these are the words of Captain Fitzroy, in his evidence, printed at page 169 of the Lords' Report.

§ They will be found at page 8 of Parliamentary Papers, 3rd August, 1840.

‖ Mr. Busby has claimed, before the commissioners, 8,105 acres at one spot, and 40,000 acres at another. (See a copy in the official table in Terry's "New Zealand," page 122-3.)—The Rev. Henry Williams, December, 1833, claimed 1,000 acres; William White, a Wesleyan missionary, January, 1835, 1,153 acres; Rev. Wm. Fairburn, January, 1821, 400 acres; Rev. James Kemp, 1835, 6,000 acres; Rev. John King, 1835, 3,000 acres. (See a copy of the official table of claims, in Deiffenbach, vol. ii. p. 168.) But this is a small part of the vast districts claimed by fifteen missionaries, the greater part of which they date as having attained about the time of the landing of the emigrants at Port Nicholson, in the year 1839. (See the copy of the official table, in Deiffenbach, as above.)

their employers,* and hardly known to the British public. The Baron de Thierry had also arrived at Sydney, and was enlisting emigrants to go to New Zealand;† it was necessary to do something to prevent colonization by him or others; Mr. Busby therefore "prepared and concocted a manœuvre," to deter the Baron from continuing his plan; and, whether intended as such by him at the time, or was only adopted since, by the secretaries to the missionary societies in London, it has been used as an instrument to prevent all European colonization, to thwart the benevolent and noble attempt by the New Zealand Company, and has deceived and gulled Colonial Ministers, committees of parliament, committees of missionary societies, and the British public; but, thanks to the straightforward character of Sir George Gipps, he completely exposed the trick, in a speech to his council;‡ and, thanks to Lord John Russell, he sent it, with other papers, to be printed by the House of Commons. The "manœuvre" was this: to establish an apparent native sovereign power, which had no existence; and the argument used was this: that in attempting to establish British sovereignty, England was unjustly attacking an independent state. The witnesses to Mr. Busby's "manœuvre" were, the Rev. Henry Williams, chairman of the Church of England missionaries in New Zealand; George Clark, the lay-agent of the Church of England Missionary Society in London; Mr. Clendon, who has since played a conspicuous and most interested part in endeavouring to establish Aucland; and Gilbert Muir, a merchant.§

1836.—August 1st, a Committee of the House of Commons, in consequence of the orders of the House, made a Report as to the waste-lands in the colonies of the British empire.

It was in this year, that most of the missionaries in New Zealand (knowing that "the manœuvre" already described by Sir George Gipps was a mere burlesque), signed a petition to King William IV., praying for the colonization of New Zealand.‖

---

* See Mr. Coates's solemn oath, before the Committee of the Lords, that the respective committees of the missionary societies had never heard of it, until it was made known by a pamphlet, being a letter from Mr. Gibbon Wakefield to Lord Glenelg.—See also page 142 of Parliamentary Papers, 11th of May, 1841, being a letter from Mr. Somes to Mr. Vernon Smith, dated 29th of March, 1841, paragraph 4, describing the public manner in which the treaty between the Company and the natives was conducted by their agent, and the concealed manner in which these transactions were carried on between the missionaries and the natives.

† All this is stated in the evidence of the Rev. Mr Beecham before the Lords' Committee, printed at pp. 299—306.

‡ Sir George Gipps's speech, exposing the "manœuvre," was made on the 9th of July, 1840; and that part of it in which this exposure is made, is printed at page 75 of Parliamentary Papers, 11th of May, 1841.

§ The papers stating this, will be found at page 178 of the Lords' Report, 1838.

‖ This petition, with the names of the parties, amongst which were thirty-six missionaries, will be found in vol. ii. p. 141, of Polack's "New Zealand;" at the end of which the following remarkable passage will be found, in allusion to the previous manufactured declaration of a native independent government: "Your petitioners would observe, that it has been considered that the confederate tribes of New Zealand were competent to enact laws for the proper government of this

1837.—May 22d, the New Zealand Association was formed, a history of which will be found at page 431 of the December (1843) number of this Magazine.

June 6th —This raised the anger of the Committee of the Church of England Missionary Society, who determined that the islands should not be colonized; they immediately came to resolutions in support of the manœuvred trick, since exposed by Sir George Gipps, and finished by resolving—

"That for the reasons assigned in the preceding resolutions, the committee are of opinion that all suitable means should be employed to prevent the plan of the New Zealand Association being carried into execution."*

July 6th.—They wrote to the missionaries in New Zealand that "the committee have therefore determined to give the scheme all the opposition in their power."†

December 20th.—The Wesleyan Missionary Society came to a resolution to oppose the colonization of the island; a deputation of their committee waited on the Colonial Minister, Lord Glenelg. to urge their opposition.‡ The Rev. Dr. Hinds could not believe that it was the opposition of the societies, but merely that of the secretaries.§ To a certain degree, it is evident that the reverend gentleman was correct; but it is almost evident that the committees, when they came to these resolutions, were deceived, through the false manœuvre, and believed that they were speaking of a country, the inhabitants of which were living under the control of a native independent sovereign government, and that the many excellent noblemen and gentlemen of whom these committees were composed were ignorant of the petition, showing the contrary which had been forwarded to the Colonial Office. Some of them, however, cannot plead this excuse, since Lord Glenelg, Mr. Stephen, and Mr. Labouchere, were secretaries in the Colonial Office.

---

land, whereby protection would be afforded in all cases of necessity; but experience evidently shows, that in the infant state of the colony, this cannot be accomplished or expected. It is acknowledged by the chiefs themselves to be impracticable."—Again, there is another passage: "Your humble petitioners express with much concern their conviction, that unless your Majesty's fostering care be extended towards them, they can only anticipate that both your Majesty's subjects, and also the aborigines of the land, will be liable to an increased degree of murders, robberies, and every kind of evil." (House of Lords' Report of 1838, page 340.) —This petition being mentioned to Mr. Coates and the Rev. Mr. Beecham, on the 11th of May, 1838, they objected to it, because the signatures had not "C. M. S." attached to them, said they were unofficial signatures, and were only the names of individuals. (See their evidence, at page 267 of the above Report.) Such a quibble is unworthy of notice, and is only stated to show their knowledge that there was no native government in existence; although they endeavoured to impress the contrary on the Committee of the Lords, and delivered in "the prepared," "concocted," and "manœuvred" paper, to prove it. (See House of Lords' Report of 1838, page 244.)

* For the whole of these resolutions, &c., see page 244 of the House of Lords' Report.

† See the evidence of Mr. Coates and the Rev. J. Beecham, at page 251 of the above Report.

‡ See the evidence of the Rev. J. Beecham, at page 294 of the above Report.

§ "I cannot say that the Church Missionary Society object to it, but the Secretary of the Church Missionary Society has, individually, written against the plan."—Dr. Hind's evidence, at page 131 of Lords' Report, 1838.

It is presumed that none of them were present at the meeting of the Church of England Missionary Committee, when a resolution affirming the truth of the manœuvre was come to, or any one of them would have said, "You cannot pass such a resolution; a petition, signed by most of the missionaries, has arrived at the Colonial Office, asserting just the contrary."

It is important to state the object of the missionaries in New Zealand praying for colonization, the secretaries to the societies at home opposing it with extraordinary pertinacity.

The missionaries in New Zealand, as has been already stated, in the year 1835 fancied that they had acquired great tracts of land, to which value would have attached, could they have prevented the establishment of any governing European power; and for this "the manœuvre" was put into practice, with the hope of effecting it, and an endeavour was made to attract immigrants to settle on their land;* in this they did not succeed. Their plan failing, it became their interest to have the country colonized; they joined in a petition, telling the truth, although directly contrary to "the manœuvre," but wished emigration to be directed to the north of the northern island, where they had acquired land;† and thus their opposition to a settlement in Cook's Straits, which did not answer their purpose.

---

* See Mr. Montefiore's evidence to this point—"It is a notorious fact, that the missionaries do hold very large quantities of land in New Zealand. I have seen letters from them to their friends, inviting them to come there; that they would find their most sanguine expectations realized, describing climate, &c."—Page 59, Lords' Report.

† This was pointed out by Mr. Somes, in his letter of the 29th of March, 1841, to Mr Vernon Smith, printed at page 142, paragraph 4, in Parliamentary Papers, 11th of May, 1841.—See also a petition of the Rev. William Williams, dated 1st of February, 1840, transmitted by order of the Church of England Missionary Society, in a letter from Mr. Coates to Lord John Russell, printed at page 140 of Parliamentary Papers, 11th of May, 1841, in which the following paragraph appears: "That, proceeding upon the reasonable supposition that the natives in the southern part of this island will advance in the arts of civilization, and particularly in agriculture and the rearing of cattle, as is the case with those in the northern part, the limited portion of pasture-land, which is confined exclusively to the coast, will soon be wholly occupied by the natives." The settlement since made at Port Nicholson, proves the entire of this statement to be untrue, and leads to the belief, that the object in making it was to direct emigration to the north.—Again, Mr. Coates delivered to the Lords' Committee, on the 11th of May, 1838, a statement received from the Rev. William Williams, in which he gave reasons for thinking, 'approximated to truth,' "there are no other inhabitants in the southern part of the island, except in the neighbourhood of Entrey (Kapiti) Island, where the number is about 18,000." (See Lords' Report, page 180.)—Here then, is Mr. Williams's own statement, completely contradictory of that in his petition above; or is there any truth in his statement of a native population of 18,000 in the neighbourhood of Entrey or Kapiti Island? From Taranaki to Port Nicholson, and both sides of Cook's Straits, an extent of many hundred miles, there were only 6,490 inhabitants. (See Deiffenbach, vol. i., p. 195.) Mr. Clark reduces the 18,000 to 2,000. (See page 173, Parliamentary Papers, 12th August, 1842.) And Mr. Halswell has counted them at Port Nicholson, and found them only 541. (See G, No 52, in the Appendices.) What, then, was the object of Mr. Williams's statements? Obviously to deter emigrants being sent to Cook's Straits, of which Entrey Island is the entrance, and hoping that it would be the means of sending them to the north, where Mr. Williams and his friends had acquired property.

The direct object of the secretaries of the Church of England Missionary and Wesleyan Missionary Societies, in their persevering opposition to the colonization of New Zealand, is so inexplicable, that it is impossible to trace it. It was developed by the Hon. Francis Baring in the House of Commons, on the 19th of July, 1838; and every member of the committee now examining the affairs of New Zealand would do well to read over the report of the speech of that respectable and highly-informed gentleman; and, to show the committees of the two societies the opinion entertained of their secretaries by the religious world, a quotation shall be made from an article in the April number of the *Christian Remembrancer*, being vol. viii., No. 40, p. 397—

"So lawless was the state of society at that time, that the missionaries themselves united in soliciting such a government as would secure peace and tranquillity, even at the expense of their own power; *not so, however, the home-societies, the project suited neither Mr. Dandeson Coates nor his Wesleyan coadjutors The one was determined to resist any interposition of British sovereignty, the others 'steadily to maintain those principles by which they had been actuated in resisting the proposed scheme for the colonization of New Zealand.'** Three years after this petition (from the resident missionaries and others), praying for colonization, which was, thanks to manœuvring, ineffectual; the New Zealand Society arose," &c.†

It was in this year, that the Hon. Captain Wellesley, R.N., the unfortunate Captain Arthur Wakefield, R.N., and Dr. Evans, LL.D., waited, as a deputation from the New Zealand Association, upon Mr. Dandeson Coates, to request the co-operation of the Church of England Missionary Society in colonizing New Zealand; his reply was, "*that he would thwart it, in every way in his power.*"‡ The horrid threat has not been confined to words; the lay correspondent of the society, Mr. George Clark, was appointed chief protector of the aborigines, and he appointed his son, a beardless youth of eighteen years old, his sub-protector, and their interference between the natives and the settlers have had the most mischievous and thwarting effects ever since, until it ended in the massacre of the 17th of June, 1843. The horrid threat, the warning, the promised thwarting, has rung in the ears of the relatives of the murdered men ever since. We are ignorant whether any or what correspondence has taken place between Mr. Coates and Mr. Clark; this afflicting opinion has been formed by the direct and public written instructions, quoted by the *Christian Remembrancer*, and those laid by Mr. Coates himself before the Lords' Committee, in 1838.§

1838.—The colonial minister, Lord Glenelg, proposed that the association should merge into a joint-stock company, the history of which will be found at p. 435 of our December number of the magazine.

It was in this year that a committee of the Lords was appointed to inquire into the then state of the islands of New Zealand: Earl Devon

---

* This sentence is taken from the written instructions from the Committee of the Wesleyan Society to their missionaries, printed at page 183 of Parliamentary Papers, 3rd of August, 1840.

† There is much due to the *Christian Remembrancer*, for this honest exposure; the editor of that respectable publication will find a warm coadjutor in the writer of this article in the spread of Christianity at the antipodes.

‡ See page 4 of Parliamentary Papers, of the 3rd of August, 1840.

§ See the reference already made, page 251 of the Lords' Report.

was the president. The secretaries of the two missionary societies were allured to give what evidence they pleased, to lay whatever papers they chose before this committee; the state of the inhabitants was summed up by Mr. Coates, and the Rev. Mr. Beecham, in the following words:—"I may venture to affirm, there is no crime of which they are capable, of which they are not guilty. Reason is completely dethroned, and the reins of government given up to the passions altogether; and by these they are carried to the greatest extremes. Their temporal condition is equally bad; they are filthy in the extreme; never wash themselves, but as often as they can besmear themselves with red ochre and oil, which in hot weather makes them offensive—many of them literally swarm with vermin; their huts in general are nothing better than poor people's hogsties in England; are much the same height and size, and into them they creep, through a little hole at one end; they have neither furniture nor cooking-utensils; and the poor filthy mats that serve them for clothes by day, serve them for bedding by night."* Farther missionary authority for the wretched state of the aborigines will be found detailed at p. 204 and following, of the May number of the magazine—their condition should be compared with the plans of amelioration described by the excellent Mr Halswell, not only in his report to the company, but in his whole correspondence, printed in the appendices,† a real philanthropist must rejoice in the consequences of their improved condition, by amalgamation with British settlers; no such benevolent plans as the reserves of the company, has been before attempted for their amelioration; and when it is opposed by the whine of interference with "the rights of the aborigines," it is a mere ignorant howl, which has less reason in it than "the rights of man" or "the rights of women," much run after just now, as if the kind protection of the stronger sex was not the sweetest right which had been allotted to them by nature—so it is with the rights of the aborigines, who, left alone, seek the protection of civilized man.

1839, 2d of May.—The New Zealand Company was formed, reckless of the threatened thwartings of the committees of the Missionary societies—a history of this will be found at p. 436 of the December number of the magazine. A paid-up capital of £100,000 was immediately raised—land was sold to the amount of £100,000—a ship, the Tory, under the command of Captain Chaffers, carrying out Colonel Wakefield, the principal agent of the company. Dr. Deiffenbach, a naturalist Mr. Heaphy, a draughtsman, Dr. Dorset, a surgeon, Nayli, an interpreter, left Plymouth within ten days after the formation of the com-

---

* This was the account given to the Committee of the House of Lords, and printed at p. 212 of their Report, 1838.

† This Report will be found printed at p. 111 of vol. iii. of New Zealand Journal, being No. 61, of May 14, 1842. It will be found also at G No. 46 in the Appendices, being p. 79 G. Every line from Mr. Halswell is most valuable, and will be found at G 47, G 50, G 51, G 52, G. 53, G 54, G 58, G 59, G 60. This letter announces the reserves being taken from his management, and placed with gentlemen at distant Aucland—H No. 18, H 19, H 20, H 21, H 22, H 24. That such a man should be superseded by an ignorant presumptuous boy, certainly was carrying the promised thwarting into practice.

pany, reached Cook's Straits in ninety-six days, and an agreement to form the settlement in Port Nicholson was made publicly with the natives, much after the manner of the celebrated treaty between the illustrious Penn and the red Indians of North America.* This was followed by the Cuba carrying out Captain Smith, R.A., and a staff of surveyors; and in

September, 1839, by five ships, carrying out 1,500 emigrants, determined to prove, that the combination of capital and labour might be effected without the expense of a single shilling of public money.

No sooner had the company been formed, and the preliminary expedition under Colonel Wakefield sailed, than the then colonial minister, Lord Normanby, thought it necessary to so far yield to public opinion, as to appoint "some British authority" in New Zealand;† and this was

* The interesting account of this treaty will be found in Ward's Supplementary Information as to New Zealand, published by Parker in 1840—at p. 143 to 145 of Parliamentary Papers, 11th of May, 1841—the treaty itself at p. 159 of Parliamentary Papers, 3d of August, 1840, and under the letter F of the Appendices from pages 1 to 150, a minute account of all relating to the Company's purchases from 1839 to 1842, consisting of—

1. Despatches from Colonel Wakefield, Captain Chaffers, and Dr. Deiffenbach.
2. Instructions from the Court of Directors to their Officers.
3. Copies of the several Deeds entered into between the Company and the Natives, and signed by the latter after their contents had been fully and publicly explained. This should be printed as a distinct volume; it is a most entertaining and interesting narrative and faithful record of one of the most interesting circumstances in modern history.

† The letter of Mr. Stephen, a copy of the Treasury minute of the 19th of July, 1839—the Marquis of Normanby's instructions to Captain Hobson before departure, and his reply, will be found in the Appendix I., from p. 4 to p. 20; they are all written upon the assumption that the manœuvre described by Sir George Gipps was a fact; but even Captain Hobson pointed out to the Marquis of Normanby, as Sir George Gipps had before him, (p. 75 Par. Papers, 11th of May, 1841,) that "the declaration of the independence of New Zealand was signed by the united chiefs of the northern island only—in fact, only of the northern part of that island; and it was to them alone that his late majesty's letter was addressed on the presentation of their flag; and neither of these instruments had any application whatsoever to the southern islands."—p. 17, I. It will, however, be well at this place to make some extracts from Sir George Gipps's speech to his council on the 16th of August, 1840, when New Zealand was a dependence to his government; as it will show how completely false the statements of the committees of the missionary societies were, that New Zealand was an independent state, and that to colonise or civilise its savage inhabitants, was an unjust interference with their rights. The following extracts are taken from p. 75 Par. Papers, 11th of May, 1841.

"The declaration of independence was made, moreover, only by a few tribes in the Bay of Islands, not extending even so far south as the Thames. Mr. Busby has told you that it was entirely a measure of his own concoction, and that he acted in it without any authority from either the Secretary of State or the Governor (Sir George Gipps) of this colony, who was his immediate superior. . . It is not even pretended, that the natives could understand the meaning of it; still less could they assemble yearly in congress and pass laws, as Mr. Busby, in his declaration, has made them to say that they would do. . . But supposing the declaration to have been a genuine and a valid one, the only effect of it would have been to prevent Captain Hobson from taking possession of the island in which it was made, by virtue of the right derived from the discovery of Captain Cook. . . But again I say that New Zealand never has been, in point of fact, independent; it was done under the title of "consul," in the person of Captain Hobson. The instructions of the noble marquis are a tissue of misrepresentations: this shall be shown.

The Marquis of Normanby states—

"There is no part of the earth in which colonization could be effected with a greater or surer prospect of national advantage," but "embarking in a measure essentially unjust," because it would be "too certainly fraught with calamity to a a numerous and inoffensive people."

[What can there be "unjust" in colonizing islands nearly uninhabited?
The people are not "numerous"—the islands are as large as Great Britain—900 miles long.

Deiffenbach, vol. ii. p. 83, makes them			114,800
Terry	,,	176,	,, 105,400
Halswell	,,		,, still less

"Inoffensive."—Had Lord Normanby read Mr. Montefiore's Account, in Lords' Report of 1838, p.56—Did he not know that the account of the barbarous murderer, Raupero, was amongst the records in his own office, in the correspondence of General Darling with Lord Ripon?

Let Lord Normanby turn to vol. i. p. 162, for an account of the inoffensiveness of Te Whero Whero, to whom Governor Hobson awarded a payment of £250—(see his own authority for it at p 171 and 188 of Par. Papers, 12th of August, 1842)—for the butchery committed ten years before, as related by Deiffenbach.

Let him turn to vol. i. p. 98, for an account of Raupero's slaying a whole tribe.

Let him examine a trifling list of horrible murders in our own pages, 205 and following, in the May number—all reported from missionary authority in the Reports of the Lords in 1838. "Fraught with calamity"—Lord Normanby, read Mr. Halswell's account, printed at 99 G in the Appendices—

---

included in the commission of Governor Philip, and of every one of my predecessors, down to the time of Sir Thomas Brisbane, when, in consequence of Van Diemen's Land being separated from New South Wales, new boundaries were assigned to the government, and New Zealand, probably by accident, was omitted." This statement of Sir George Gipps entirely refutes the ignorant memorandum of the Colonial Office, enclosed to Lord Palmerston, 18th of March, 1840, by Mr. Stephen, which will be found printed at I, No 7, page 28, I. Mr. Stephen, on account of the omission pointed out by Sir George Gipps, was only exposing his want of knowledge of the history of the Colonial empire; but the secretaries of the missionary societies were worse than ignorant, they were availing themselves cf the omission, and, by its means, their employers, the members of the committees, were deceived, and were made the instruments of misleading the public. If any member of these committees reads these extracts from Sir George Gipps's speech, he is requested to examine the evidence of Mr. Coates and the Rev. Mr. Beecham, at pp. 243, 244, of the Lords' Report, of 1838 But Sir George Gipps proceeds—" But again, Gentlemen, it is not independence which confers on any people the right of so disposing of the soil they occupy, as to give to individuals, not of their own tribes, a property in it; it is civilization which does this, and the establishment of a government capable at once of protecting the rights of individuals, and of entering into relations with foreign powers; above all, it is the establishment of law, of which property is justly said to be the creature."

Again, in another part of his speech, p. 65, Par. Papers, 11th of May, 1841, Sir George Gipps anticipates and disposes of the question now at issue between the Colonial Minister and the Directors of the New Zealand Company. Sir George Gipps's opinion must have great weight with Her Majesty's Ministers and with Parliament; his great talents, his integrity, his experience, were the reasons which no doubt led Lord John Russell to send this speech to the House of Commons to be printed amongst its records—" *Uncivilized tribes, not having any settled form of government, and not having any individual property in the land, cannot confer valid titles to land. . . Whether the right of extinguishing the native title, or the right of pre-emption, as it is technically called, does, or does not, exclusively exist in the government of the nation which may form a settlement in the country occupied by such uncivilized tribes.*" When, therefore, Colonel Wakefield, as will be found in the whole course of his correspondence, called upon the local government in New Zealand to extinguish the native title, he was only putting into practice the speech of the highest authority in the Pacific Ocean.

"The anxiety of the natives for the introduction of the arts of civilized life amongst them, continues to increase, and they gladly avail themselves of the few facilities I have had it in my power to afford them from my private means. They now look back with abhorrence on the barbarous custom of burying the dead bodies of their people within their Pahs; and yet it is only a very short time back that I succeeded in breaking through this practice, notwithstanding efforts were made to counteract my endeavours. Their funerals are now conducted with great decency, and present an appearance which would not disgrace a better community. I intend, if possible, to take up the bodies of twelve natives, buried at Te-Aro Pah by the Wesleyan minister during the former year, and have them interred in the cemetery; the natives, if not interfered with, would be much gratified by such a proceeding."]

Want of space prevents our taking the instructions of Lord Normanby line by line, sentence by sentence, and placing a contradiction opposite the whole. We attribute these instructions to his having been gulled by the clerk-craft of the office. But what is to be said of his successors, at least of Lord Stanley, who has gone out of his way to confirm Lord Normanby's follies. But these instructions are by no means limited to positive follies: something must be said of the negative omissions. They contain no practical directions for protecting the settlers who had emigrated and gone to Cook's Straits—no scheme for colonization. Still this extraordinary man, Governor Hobson, went, as if he was infirm of mind, to the Bay of Islands,* entered into a bargain with a man of the name of Clenden to purchase a piece of land for the site of a capital for a country which he had no means of colonizing. Sir George Gipps refused his drafts—his purchase was converted into a private debt from himself to the seller, to get rid of which was probably one of his reasons for founding Aucland,† as distant in point of communication with the settlers in Cook's Straits, as if he had been at Sydney;‡ but he satisfied his creditor by granting him 10,000 acres of land; then had he gone to Wellington, where the settlers were, it afforded no opportunity for his officials to job and speculate in town allotments.§ Then again, fixing the seat of government at Aucland, in the vicinity of Fairburn, the missionaries' land,‖ was giving value to the property of these gentlemen, as foreseen by Mr. Somes on the 29th of March, 1841.¶ In addition to these reasons, the company appears to have ascertained that the selection of Aucland might be partly attributed to a power exercised over the Governor by individuals connected with a Scotch company;** and all but direct proof that Lieutenant Shortland, the Colonial Secretary, the now acting Governor,

---

* Captain Nias, who took him from Sydney to New Zealand, intimates as much, in his letter of the 28th of March, 1840, to Sir George Gipps, printed at p. 14 of Parliamentary Papers, 11th of May, 1841.

† An account of this unauthorized and silly transaction will be found in a correspondence at pp. 143—149 in the Parliamentary Papers, 12th of August, 1842; but the remarkable circumstance is, that contrary to Sir George Gipps's opinion, Lord Stanley, although finding fault, confirmed it, and suffered Governor Hobson to remain, to pursue his ridiculous career.

‡ See Dr. Selwyn, the bishop of New Zealand, at p. 6, in his letter to the Society for the Propagation of the Gospel.

§ This they all did, as will be found in a correspondence at pp. 129—142 of Parliamentary Papers, 12th of August, 1842. Twice Lord Stanley refused to recognize them,—see his despatch, 24th of September, 1841, printed at p. 130 of Parliamentary Papers, 12th of August, 1842; again, 28th of January, 1842, p. 141 of the same Papers. Captain Fitzroy, however, has been instructed to let them either retain the land, or compensate,—see p. 20 of the General Report of the Colonial Land and Emigration Commissioners, printed by order of parliament, 24th of August, 1843. It now, therefore, will be the interest of all these officials to recommend Aucland, and run down the settlements in Cook's Straits.

‖ See Lords' Report, p. 263; and Mr. Fairburn's claim, in the official table, Deiffenbach, vol. i., p. 186.

¶ See Mr. Somes's letter to Mr Vernon Smith, for a paragraph in it, printed at p. 142 of Parliamentary Papers, 11th May, 1841.

** A descriptive account of the maladministration of Governor Hobson will be found in a remarkable paper, being a letter from Mr. Somes to Lord Stanley, of the 24th of November, 1841, and, as far as Governor Hobson is concerned, will be found at pp. 54—69 C., and again in another, February 15th, 1843, printed at

was or meant to be a partner in that company.* At any rate, this letter and its date is most important; that of the 24th of November, 1841, acquits the Directors from the slightest charge of tardiness or supineness—proves them the faithful, able, untiring representatives of those whom they had been the means of sending to the antipodes—and throws the whole responsibility on Lord Stanley. Reader, remark its date—the massacre did not occur until the 17th of June, 1843; Lord Stanley, in November, 1841, was told what it was probable would occur—he treated it with heartless indifference: his lordship desired his secretary, Mr. Hope, to tell the Company that he was "not responsible to them."†—Who said he was?—but he is responsible to a yet higher tribunal, when his neglect, or his asperity of temper, prevented his giving the necessary orders to the local government to protect the settlers, whom Her Majesty, in entrusting him with the official seals of office, placed under his care. What answer can he give to the afflicted parents and relatives of the twenty-two slaughtered victims abandoned by the local government to the safeguard of one police magistrate and one constable, both of whom have been murdered in supporting their sovereign's authority? Mr. Somes' letter of November 24, 1841, 42 C, is one of the kindest, most sensible, and useful accounts of the state of affairs (by it, then brought under the review of the Colonial Office) which could be penned—whatever hostility Lord Stanley might choose to exercise towards the Company—the settlers were his wards, entrusted to his care by the highest authority; and in gratifying his asperity towards individuals, 10,000 helpless settlers have been abandoned to the musket and the tomahawk of savage barbarians. He has adopted the senseless vagaries of the Marquis of Normanby, which were superseded on the

25th of May, 1841, by Hobson's proclamation of British sovereignty‡—a proclamation productive of anything but good-will, but arising out of a vindictive feeling towards the settlers at Port Nicholson, who, until that proclamation, were, according to his previous declarations, on foreign land; but by this proclamation

---

pp. 211-12, C. These papers expose the conduct of the Colonial Office in an extraordinary manner; they were written with the unanimous approval of the twenty-four members of the direction, and, however afflicting the consideration, none who reads them can doubt that their truth has been tested by the horrid massacre of June last.

* See the statement in Mr. Some's letter to Lord Stanley, of 24th of November, 1841, at p. 65 C.

† The 4th paragraph of Mr. Hope's letter to Mr. Somes, of February 15th, 1843, printed at p. 199 C of Appendix C. The settlers landed in September, 1839, made an agreement to establish themselves with the resident natives, were put into possession by them. (See a letter from George Samuel Evans, R. Davies Hanson, Henry Morcuy, to Sir George Gipps, dated Sydney, 23rd of October, 1840, and printed at p. 78. Parliamentary Papers, 12th of August, 1842.) Governor Hobson went to Port Nicholson in August, 1841, appointed Mr. George Clark the correspondent of one who had promised to thwart the settlement in every way in his power, (an office which enabled him not only to break the treaty between the natives and the settlers, but to call in savages, to be paid for butcheries committed years before.) Of this conduct of the governor, the directors complain to his superior, the Colonial Minister: the following is the heartless reply of that minister, through the directors, to the suffering emigrants—"Lord Stanley thinks it enough to say, that he must decline to vindicate to the directors of the New Zealand Company the conduct of an officer enjoying her Majesty's confidence, in the administration of the government of one of the colonial dependencies of the British crown; of his responsibility to the Queen and to parliament on this subject, Lord Stanley is fully prepared to acquit himself—to yourself and your colleagues, in the direction of the New Zealand Company, his lordship acknowledges no such responsibility." This was February 15th, 1843; the slaughter occurred June 17th. Had Lord Stanley then listened to the application of the directors, it never would have occurred.

‡ See Hobson's despatch, May 25th, 1840, printed at p. 15, Parliamentary Papers, 11th of May, 1841; and his proclamation, dated 23rd of May, 1840, previous to the proclamation of British sovereignty, being D, No. 22, and printed at 27 D.

he meant to encircle them within the net of high treason; and he sent soldiers and mounted police, and fetters,* to put down as loyal a body of men to their father-land as ever existed.†

The proclamation of British sovereignty by a governor, annihilated the blanket cession to a consul ‡—a consul, according to his own account, accredited only to a few chiefs in the northern part of the northern island,§ who, when he arrived in the country, he found "had neither power over the soil, nor authority over those who reside on it."‖ From the paucity of the population, the greater part of the country was uninhabited, unoccupied, and without an owner; all such parts, from the hour that the proclamation of British sovereignty occurred, became the waste-lands of the crown; this is a material point; the reader is requested to turn to page 204 of the May number of our Magazine, in reference to the deceit practised upon the Lords' Committee, and which, in all probability, was the origin of Lord Normanby's instructions. These instructions were, in point of fact, the treaty of Waitangi. The natives were got together to sign it, in the same manner as their former signature of independence; the falsity of which has been so completely exposed by Sir George Gipps. The having exercised one trick, to prevent the colonization of the country, leads to the belief that the independent character given of those who signed at Waitangi was anything but true; but, at any rate, it was confined to those who assembled there. Members of the mission running to other parts of the island, exchanging blankets for signatures, is a farce too ridiculous to attain for them the slightest respect. Their chairman, the Rev. Henry Williams, had but a short time before been taking active steps in Cook's Straits and their neighbourhood to prevent colonization; ¶ and no sooner was the treaty of Waitangi signed than he was sent by Governor Hobson to Cook's Straits to obtain the signature of the savage Raupero to it **—a visit which sowed the seeds of the dreadful massacre by that barbarian in June, 1843, and enabled Governor Hobson to throw a doubt upon the company's treaty with the natives.†† This

§ See Heaphy's Narrative, p. 9.

† See the correspondence between Lieutenant Shortland, Colonel Wakefield, Governor Hobson, and Sir George Gipps, p. 79-80, Parliamentary Papers, 11th of May, 1841; also printed in Appendix D, pp. 29—32.

‡ This burlesque upon all treaties, in return for the blanket-cession of sovereignty, will be found at p. 9 of Parliamentary Papers, May 11th, 1841, drawn up with all the technicality of a lawyer, as if the subscribing parties knew what they were doing, or who had any other object but attaining a blanket.

§ See Captain Hobson's letter, previous to sailing, to the Marquis of Normanby, dated August, 1839, and printed 17 I, in which he states this,—his expression is, "to them alone."

‖ In Governor Hobson's despatch of the 25th of May, 1840, printed at p. 15; but this observation occurs at p. 16 of Parliamentary Papers, 11th of May, 1841.

¶ See an account of his conduct by Colonel Wakefield, dated Port Nicholson, 25th of May, 1840, printed in Parliamentary Papers, p. 142, of 11th May, 1841, who came to a compromise by allowing him a "slice for himself"—an acre of land in the site of what was to become the town of Wellington, which has been since confirmed by a deed of conveyance; for which see the colonel's letter to Mr. Wilson of the 24th of January, 1842, being E, No. 17, printed at p. 18 E. He went to Wanguani, and there, on the 17th of November, 1839, left the following paper:—"This is to give notice, that this part of New Zealand has been purchased of the native chiefs residing here, for the benefit of the native tribes, extending from Rangati-kei to Patea towards Taranaki.—Henry Williams." The natives denied the truth of the paper. See this statement in a letter from Mr. Somes to Lord John Russell, April 19th, 1841, being D, No. 37; but this circumstance will be found at p. 47 D.

** See this in Governor Hobson's letter to Major Bunbury, dated Patrea, 25th of April, 1840, at p. 18 of Parliamentary Papers, 11th of May, 1841. Also the Rev. H. Williams's letter, giving an account of this secular mission, dated Pahia, June 11th, 1840, being D, No. 24, and printed at p. 28 D.

†† Governor Hobson, November 10th, 1840. "The title to the land is disputed by the Church Missionary Society, who have bought extensive tracts of land in

conduct of Mr. Williams was contrary to the directions of the committee of the society in London,* who paid him for the performance of his Christian missionary duties, and had nothing to do with his mischievous secular interference.

The examination of New Zealand affairs must not be a superficial or skin-deep one—it must not be confined to the facts laid before the committee, but the causes and motives whence the facts have arisen must be examined. The terms of the treaty of Waitangi never would have been submitted to the natives, but from a belief in the scandalous falsehood that all the land was appropriated, and the property of some tribe or other.† The taking advantage of these misrepresentations, and arguing that the treaty of Wanguani is a just one, is something akin to an individual availing himself of an advantage by making use of stolen goods.

Something has been said of the mischievous interference of the Rev. Henry Williams, and of the influence which he exercised over the governor. Colonel Wakefield describes the conduct of other gentlemen of the mission to have been very different.‡

---

trust for the natives." See D, No. 35, printed at p. 42 D. Colonel Wakefield's letter to Mr. Wilson, dated January 24th, 1842, being E 17, printed at p. 18 E, shows the general interference of Mr. Williams, it would seem contrary to the opinion of the Church Missionary Committee at Pahia, as it appears that the committee refused to pay the expenses which he had incurred.

* The committee of the Church of England Missionary Society in London, on the 6th of April, 1836, came to the following resolution:—"That it should be recommended that the missionaries should not accept any trusteeship for the natives, nor interfere in any of their secular matters." p 262 of House of Lords' Report, 1838. Again New Zealand was a dependency to the government of New South Wales, until the proclamation of British sovereignty May 25th, 1840. Mr. Williams' conduct in these purchases, 17th of November, 1839, was in contravention of the orders of Sir George Gipps. See House of Lords' Report, p. 261, 1838. These circumstances go a great way to show by whom Governor Hobson was influenced, and coupled with the petition of the Rev. Wm. Williams, printed at p. 140 of Parliamentary Papers, 11th of May, 1841, and sanctioned by the committee of the Church of England Missionary Society in "directing" their secretary to send it to Lord John Russell to be laid before her Majesty. P. 139 Parliamentary Papers, 11th of May, 1841, prove how correct Mr. Somes was in thinking that some of the missionaries in New Zealand had a personal interest in directing emigration to the north. It is evident that the gentlemen of the committee were not only ignorant of what was going on, but, like Lord Normanby, were acting from the misrepresentations which were laid before them.

† At p. 204 of the May number of this Magazine there will be found, from authentic documents—first, the statements made; secondly, facts which prove their falsity. This a subject which merits the close attention of the Colonial Minister, since it is from these gross and scandalous misrepresentations that a great deal of his reasoning has been formed.

‡ In a letter from Colonel Wakefield, February 8th, 1842, he describes the great good effected by the Rev. Octavius Hatfield—calls him "a single-minded and sincere minister of the gospel." Instead of jealously asserting the rights of the church mission to land, or intermeddling respecting purchases from the natives, he has confined himself strictly to the duties of his calling as missionary. "He has always refrained from, and, it is understood, declined interference in, the secular matters of the natives, other than recommending a peaceable intercourse with their white neighbours on all occasions." Again—"The principal, Mr. Bumby, a liberal-minded, sensible, and legitimate missionary, receives his countrymen visiting the river with great hospitality."

The account which the colonel has given of the missionaries in many of his letters must prove interesting to the religious world, and particularly useful to the committees of the Church of England and Wesleyan Missionary Societies at home, as it will enable them to discriminate between those who are following their sacred calling, and those who only use it as a cloak to serve their interested purposes.

April, 15th, 1840.—There was a great city meeting in the Guildhall, the Lord Mayor in the chair, to petition the government to colonize New Zealand; and at it Mr. Young, the member for Teignmouth, denounced Mr. Stephen, one of the Under-Secretaries at the Colonial Office, as being the person who prevented it.*

Lord Elliot moved for a committee to report on New Zealand—the report was made 3d of August, 1840.

May 16th 1840.—A great meeting at Glasgow, in the unavoidable absence of the Lord Provost, Baillie Mitchel in the chair, for the same purpose; and at it Lieutenant Macdonnell, R.N., who was in New Zealand at the time, described the recognition of the independence of New Zealand, as set forth by the secretaries of the Church of England and Wesleyan Missionary Societies, before a committee of the House of Lords in 1838, as a farce; and yet this is the farce upon which Lord Stanley assumes that the treaty of Wanguani should be respected.†

October 40th, 1840.—A great meeting at Plymouth, Earl Devon in the chair, in favour of colonizing New Zealand.‡

November 18th, 1840.—Lord John Russell and the company came to an agreement, out of which the charter was formed for colonizing New Zealand.§

February 12th, 1841.—The Queen incorporated the New Zealand Company by a charter.||

February 13th.—The following day the company invited the minister, Lord John Russell, to a public dinner in the city, by whose advice it had been granted, where he met upwards of 200 of the most influential and reflecting men in England, of various political parties and religious opinions—uniting in their admiration of the policy of the government, using the company as an instrument for colonizing New Zealand.¶

Lord John Russell was soon after elected member for the city. The company met the minister in the most straightforward manner. No one doubted but Wellington was to be the residence of the governor, and the seat of government.—The directors wrote to their agent, directing him to welcome Governor Hobson in every possible way—to render him every assistance.** A fast-sailing vessel was despatched purposely by the company to carry the news.†† The company sent out the government house by one of their vessels, the Platina, to Wellington.‡‡—Colonel Wakefield was directed not to lose a moment in conveying these despatches to Governor Hobson, wherever he might be §§ All this occurred—but Hobson suffered four months to elapse before he took any notice of them. The company could send out nothing but copies; it is now doubtful, although a vessel was chartered purposely, whether the originals were sent from the Colonial Office at that time.|||| Captain Arthur Wakefield was one of the guests at that

* The report of this meeting will be found at p. 61, vol. i., of the *New Zealand Journal*, being No. 6 of April 18th, 1840.

† What passed at this meeting was well reported at the time in the *Glasgow Argus*; it was condensed, and printed at p. 118, vol. i., of the *New Zealand Journal*, being No. 9, of May 23d, 1840.

‡ A report of what passed at this meeting will be found at p. 263, vol. i., of the *New Zealand Journal*, being No. 21, of Nov. 7, 1840.

§ This agreement is printed at p. 5 C, being C No. 4, and is the solemn compact between the Colonial Minister and the Company.

|| This important document needs no comment; it will be found, as it ought to be, in front of the appendices.

¶ A report of what passed at this meeting will be found in a second edition of the *New Zealand Journal*, No. 28, of February 15th, 1841, being p. 45, vol. ii.

** See No. 162 D, printed at 216 D, for the instructions forwarded to Colonel Wakefield from the company, with the inclosures.

†† See this at p. 221 D. in a letter dated 18th December, 1840.

‡‡ See p. 219 D. §§ Ibid.

|||| Governor Hobson on the 11th September, 1841, wrote to Colonel Wakefield, "With the exception of the information derived from you, I am not yet in possession of any instructions on the subject of the second colony, but being desirous

dinner, and previous to it all the plans for founding the second colony had been arranged and agreed upon with the minister; the dinner was on the 12th of February, the arrangements for the second colony having been made on the 3d.* Lord John Russell remarking—that so soon as Governor Hobson knew of "the friendly relations," &c., which had occurred at the close of the year 1840.†

No one ever thought that Governor Hobson was sent to New Zealand for the mere purpose of a blanket cession of sovereignty, which he cut short by proclaiming a real one; no one supposed that he was attempting to found a colony without any means or any authority, and that at an immense distance from where the settlers had established themselves; but such was the case, and because he could not succeed, he turned on the settlements in Cook's Straits with most vindictive hostility, and was determined to remove everybody to where he was building his palace. This he attempted in four different ways:—

1st. By seducing the labourers to leave Wellington and to go to Aucland.‡

2nd. By refusing Captain Arthur Wakefield the liberty of founding the second colony where he pleased, agreeable to Lord John Russell's letter.§

3rd. By endeavouring to remove the French from Akaroo to Aucland.||

4th. By giving all the land to the company, in Cook's Straits, and proposing compensation in land at Aucland to previous purchasers to the company.¶

Of all the badly contrived schemes for founding a colony, that of Governor Hobson at Aucland was the very worst.**

Until Hobson's visit to Port Nicholson all was peace between the settlers and the natives; †† and the latter were rapidly mixing with the whites, learning the English language, and seeking employment from the strangers whom they had invited to settle on their land ‡‡ But Governor Hobson brought with him the lay agent of the Church of England Missionary Society, Mr. George Clark and his boy-son, and appointed them to the most important and delicate situations possible, that of protector and sub-protector of the aborigines, who have been set against the settlers; and it was from Mr. Spain's court, where these men were, *that the barbarian Raupero broke away, and committed that horrid slaughter on the 17th of June*, 1843, which Clark has since, in a public proclamation, justified.

We have now done with our chronological account of events connected with the colonization of New Zealand.

---

to promote the object of the company, I hesitate not a moment to act on the authority of the *copy of Lord John Russell's, which you were good enough to place in my hands.*" Now, delay was ruin, and this holding back of the original was most likely the clerk-craft of the Colonial Office. P. 158, Parliamentary Papers, 12th of August, 1842.

* They will be found at p. 132 of the Parliamentary Papers, 11th May, 1841.

† See Mr Vernon Smith's letter to Mr. Somes, 19th of August, 1841, at p. 15, Parliamentary Papers, 11th of May, 1841.

‡ See his government notice for this purpose, printed at p. 28 of Parliamentary Papers, 12th of August, 1842.

§ See the correspondence between Governor Hobson, Colonel and Captain Wakefield, from p. 156 to p. 161, of Parliamentary Papers, 12th of August, 1842, and Lord John Russell's letter.

|| See his letter and correspondence for this purpose, printed from p. 164 to p. 170, of Parliamentary Papers, 12th of August, 1842.

¶ See Governor Hobson's crown-grant to the company, p. 174. Parliamentary Papers, 12th of August, 1842, and Lord Stanley's confirmation of it, 12th of May, 1842, at p. 175; and in a letter to Captain Arthur Wakefield, dated 27th Sept., 1841, printed at p. 159 of Parliamentary Papers, 12th of August, 1842.

** See the account of it by Mr. Terry, one of Hobson's partisans, chap. 2, p. 135 to 146. See Deiffenbach's remarks from observations made on the spot, vol. i., p. 10 and 11, and the following chapter.

†† See Deiffenbach, vol. i., p. 94—hundreds of such testimonies may be found.

‡‡ See Mr. Halswell's Report, p. 111, *New Zealand Journal*, vol. iii., being No. 61 of 14th of May, 1842.

Previous to making a short analysis of the twelfth Report and its appendices, it will be well to state some conclusions which have been come to in consequence of not only having read the thick volume before us, but from having studied the parliamentary papers upon New Zealand, and read the evidence contained in the truthful volumes of persons who have either been in or written from the settlements; we allude to the volumes of the Hon. Henry Petre, Bidwell, Heaphy, the letters from emigrants—being very much those of labouring emigrants, published by Smith, Elder, & Co, in 1843; the letter of Dr. Selwyn to the society for the propagation of the gospel; the two remarkable volumes of the honest German Deiffenbach, and the single one of Terry; then we have examined with care the newspapers printed at Wellington, Nelson, and Auckland, and the *New Zealand Journal* printed in London, now in its fifth volume, and containing original letters and reports from all ranks and classes of persons; thus a judgment has been formed from information derived from the spot.

1st, then, we consider a treaty publicly made between assembled resident tribes —the object of it being explained to them by competent interpreters, having no object to attain—a binding instrument. It is because Penn made a treaty in this manner that it has been lauded ever since, and drawn forth the praises of Montesquieu, Burke, and Vattel; and such was the treaty between Colonel Wakefield on the part of the company and the aborigines of Port Nicholson, having for interpreters Nayti, a native who had been in England; and Barrett, an Englishman, who had married a native woman.*

2nd. Papers, the signatures to which were attained in exchange for a blanket, was a gratuitous piece of folly, to gratify some theorist at home, who was ignorant of the real state of the people. Such a paper is invalid. Let an examination be made how it has been attained; it was as follows:—

512 signatures for blankets at one place.—Page 99 Parliamentary Papers, 11th of May, 1841.

"Intelligence having reached them (the chiefs) that they were entitled to a blanket on signing."—Ibid, from the letter of the Rev. R. Maunsel.

"The blankets have been given at the rate of one to each leading chief, and it will require at least sixty more to complete the bounty throughout."—Ibid, p. 101, from the letter of the Rev. W. Williams.

"Notice of presents given by the governor to those who signed at Waitangi and Shouraki had preceded me, and may have reached Kawia; every one, therefore, who has any pretension to being a chief will flock to sign his name for the sake of obtaining a blanket."—Ibid, p. 102, letter of the late Captain W. C. Symonds.

"I have distributed eight blankets left by Major Bunbury; I have added four others of our society's stock. Several more blankets may yet be wanting."—Ibid, p. 104, letter from the Rev. James Stack.

"The chief would say anything that he wished for a blanket."—Evidence of the Rev. T. Wilkinson before the Lords' committee, 10th of April 1838, at p. 107 of their report.

"You can buy any chief over for a blanket in New Zealand to any opinion you think proper, for they are all to be bought over."—Evidence of Mr. Blacket, a naval officer, brother to the member for Northumberland, before a Committee of the House of Commons, p. 63, Par. Papers, 3d of August, 1840.

3d. All treaties made with resident natives should be binding on both parties, and respected by the local government and the colonial minister at home, and everything should depend upon residence; the payment for former butcheries,

---

* The manner in which this treaty was made will be found related at p. 143, Parliamentary Papers, 11th of May, 1841; and more in detail in the interesting and amusing journal of Colonel Wakefield, printed in appendix F of the twelfth Report, from p. 32 F to p. 59 F; again, from F 97 to 135 F; again, to F 140, at which the deed, dated 27th of September, 1839, will be found; it is also printed at p. 159, Parliamentary Papers, 3d of August, 1840.

such as those of Te-whero-whero * and Raupero,† is worse than follies—absolute wickedness—introduced for the sake of destroying the settlers,‡ although meant only to be "thwarting."§

4th. Cook's Straits should have a distinct government. Aucland may or may not flourish; it has nothing to do with the Straits.||

5th. The obligation to colonize Aucland, imposed upon the company contrary to the judgment of the directors, should be immediately annulled.

6th. Captain Fitzroy's advice should be adopted. of having one or two large frigates in the New Zealand seas.¶

7th. The Maori language should be allowed to drop, and the English substituted in its place. It will prove the chief means of amalgamating the races. All who heard or read Mr. Macauley's speech upon the difference of race in Ireland, in the early part of the session, will be convinced of the necessity of at once meeting this evil while it can be overcome.**

8th. The clergy, particularly the bishop and his coadjutors, should assist in forming infant-schools. Everything is to be done with the young, and little with adults.††

---

* See Deiffenbach, vol. i., p. 162, for an account of the slaughters of this wretch, which Hobson calls "rights of conquest." See p. 188. 12th of August, 1842.

† See Deiffenbach, vol. i, p. 98—" Raupero, at the head of the latter people, earned here inglorious laurels by shutting up his opponents on a narrow tongue of land, and then exterminating them." This is the only claim which he has to proprietorship in the southern islands.

‡ Governor Hobson awarded £250 to Te-whero-whero for his slaughter ten years before. See p. 171 and 188 of Parliamentary Papers, 12th of August,1842. Governor Hobson with Mr. Clark brought this barbarian from the north to Port Nicholson in August, 1841, until which time the settlers and the natives, contented with the treaty which they had made with the company, had lived in perfect peace. Te-whero-whero, after Governor Hobson's award in his favour, passed to Raupero, in the small island of Kapiti. This was one of the chief causes of the late massacre. See Mr. Halswell's Report at 81 G. Indeed, Mr. Clark's jealousy of the settlers was not concealed: "The natives, however, have but little chance of living long in the vicinity of such an interested and powerful party as the New Zealand Company; nor is it at all likely that they can escape the disadvantageous inducements which may be held out to them to alienate their present possessions, unless the protecting arm of her Majesty's government be continually thrown around them by a vigilant and well-timed interference."—Extract from G. Clark's Report to Governor Hobson, printed at p. 173 of Parliamentary Papers, 12th of August, 1842. This man's report, like the Marquis of Normanby's instructions, may be taken sentence by sentence, paragraph by paragraph, and contradicted by facts set opposite to them. Such reports, however, were carrying into practice the promised "thwarting" of colonizing the islands. Every one will say that it was the duty of the Colonial Minister to have known what was going on, and stopped, and not wait until death and ruin tested the wickedness of the scheme.

§ See the report of Mr. Clark, printed at p. 171 Parliamentary Papers, 12th of August 1842.

|| Extract from a despatch from Colonel Wakefield, dated 22d July, 1842:—"Nearly four months have elapsed since we received tidings from Aucland, except in the public papers of Sydney." *New Zealand Journal*, p. 18, vol. iv. Well may the bishop say that he finds Sydney easier of communication with Cook's Straits than Aucland.

¶ See Captain Fitzroy's evidence, p. 165, House of Lords' Report, 1838; again, p 175 and 176.

** See a paper in the *Colonial Magazine*, at p. 455 of the April number, and another at p. 77 of the 4th volume of the *New Zealand Journal*, being No. 84, of April 1st, 1843. This paper has attracted considerable attention at Wellington: it is a subject which merits the greatest attention.

†† The best authority for this are the missionaries themselves. Captain Fitzroy

9th. A memorial to be presented to his Excellency Governor Fitzroy, on his arrival at Wellington, has been drawn up and printed at p. 476 of the *New Zealand Journal*, being No. 115, for the 25th of May, 1844. This is a document which should receive the particular attention of the members of the committee deputed by parliament to examine the affairs of New Zealand.

10th. The evidence of Tarinki-kuri * before the court of claims should be examined, and, if found to confirm the treaty made between the company and the resident natives, it is a great cruelty to the aborigines as well as the settlers, not to cut the question of title short in one moment, and send out orders immediately to withdraw Clark, and Clark the younger, and Spain, and plant a sufficient military force to enable the settlers to retain possession of the land upon which they were invited to settle by the residents, as a defence against Raupero.

11th. It is difficult to explain why it is that the bishop is not resident in the Straits. The New Zealand Company have given a large sum of money for the sake of establishing the Church of England hierarchy in their settlements. A New Zealand Church Society was formed for the purpose of his residence being at Wellington; the plan of that society was submitted to and approved by the Archbishop of Canterbury. The people of England pay £600 a year, and it is not right that he and the governor should both be absent from where the people are.† He then is made a trustee for the reserves; this is a duty which he can never exercise at a distance. His present residence in the Bay of Islands is something like that of a late Bishop of Landaff's (Watson) at Windermere, his see being in South Wales.

12th. Lord Stanley's continued reference to the governor has become perfect nonsense; he has referred several matters to him which exclusively belong to London.

1st. The governor at Aucland is much more difficult of communication with the settler than if he was at Sydney. Ships have been forty-three days coming round. If a chart of the islands be examined, it will be perceived that from Aucland to Wellington it is the sail of a perfect circle.

1d. There is an absence of common sense in referring to the governor for notorious facts. In this respect the light-house affair is very striking. The foolish reference of Lord Stanley has cost at least thirty lives. An examination of the Wellington newspapers will show the wrecks which have occurred, and the lives lost in each wreck ‡

---

says, "*The missionaries seemed to think it was useless to try to effect any change among those who were old, and that they must begin with the children.*" See p. 166 House of Lords' Report, 1838. This is an opinion which ought to have great weight with the Colonial Minister, the Directors of the New Zealand Company, the members of the Church of England and Wesleyan Missionary Committees, and with the New Zealand Church Society. It is the true and probably the only means of amalgamation between the races. That excellent man, James Backhouse, an unsophisticated preacher of the gospel, in his narrative of a visit to the Australian Colonies, states that the missionaries there related to him the same thing. There are few more interesting accounts of how much the aboriginal inhabitants of a country are improved by civilization than will be found in this work. Mr. Backhouse saw man in his natural state, governed by instinct rather than reason, in the woods of Van Diemen's Land; he saw him removed to Flinder's Island—clothed, housed, and fed—reason dawning in many of his habits. Every real philanthropist should read this account at pages 79, 84, 165, 170, and 174. Every member of the aborigines' society should examine it previous to giving a rash opinion upon a subject as to which he is probably ignorant.

* This will be found in the *New Zealand Journal*, p. 472, vol. iv., being No 115, 25th of May, 1844.

† Appendix G contains all documents, letters, &c., connected with establishing the Church of England hierarchy in the company's settlements; a very interesting correspondence between Dr. Selwyn and Captain Arthur Wakefield, upon the subject of establishing infant schools and amalgamating the two races. See page 49 G.

‡ See Mr. Somes's letter to Lord Stanley, 2d Nov. 1841, offering to send a

Then when communications of the greatest importance are made through the governor, they may sometimes be hurled into a parliamentary report with the hope of their being buried there—and this is the only notice taken of them. The celebrated remonstrance of the six magistrates of Wellington, carried by Colonel Wakefield himself to Aucland, is a striking proof of this observation.* Had Lord Stanley paid attention to it, the massacre in Cloudy Bay would never have occurred, or the subsequent ruin of the settlers in Cook's Straits.

Having said thus much, the analysis of the Report and its Appendices shall be proceeded with.

1st. The Twelfth Report consists of 38 pages, and contains a melancholy account of not only the ruin of the New Zealand Company, but of the vindictive hostility of the local government, the confirmation of it by Lord Stanley, with reference to authentic documents to prove the facts. These documents are contained in 12 Appendices, and of these a short account will be given.

2nd. The charter of incorporation, dated 12th of February, 1841. A supplemental charter, dated 4th of August, 1843. These charters were granted after Sir George Gipps had exposed the manœuvre that had been practised by interested individuals after the treaty between Colonel Wakefield, on the part of the company, with the natives at Port Nicholson, had been made known to the Colonial Minister, Lord John Russell, after the falsehood of every part of the islands belonging to some resident tribe or individual had been proved, and, lastly, after the proclamation of British sovereignty had been proclaimed. So much for the time when the charters were granted; and, consequently, the terms of them are very different to the nonsensical authority appointed by Lord John Russell's predecessor, Lord Normanby; granted also after Governor Hobson had been to the spot, and detected the falsehood sent forth in England, and he officially reported, that "*the native chiefs had neither power over the soil, nor authority over those who resided on it.*" It was this knowledge, no doubt, which led Sir George Gipps to state the true and legitimate means of English settlers gaining a title; and this, the opinion of that important person, must have been known to Lord John Russell, when he agreed with the New Zealand Company for the charter.†

The Appendix marked A contains 35 pages.

1st. A letter from Mr. Somes to Lord Stanley, dated 29th of February, 1844, written very much in consequence of the account which had been received of the cruel massacre in Cloudy Bay, in June, 1843. It brought no answer.

2nd. A letter from Mr. Hope to Mr. Somes, dated 27th of March, 1844, proposing that the government should lend the company £40,000.

3rd. A letter from Mr. Somes to Lord Stanley, dated 2nd of April, 1844, in which was enclosed the Eleventh Report of the Company. This brings forth an answer.

4th. From Mr. Hope to Mr. Somes, dated 4th of April, in which, after acknowledging the receipt of the two mild and excellent letters of the 29th of February and 2nd of April, he says—" It is not Lord Stanley's intention to enter into or discuss the allegations made by you, on behalf of the New Zealand Company, in

---

lighthouse out, and Mr. Hope's reply of the 17th of November, promising to apply to the governor, p. 31, Parliamentary Papers, 12th of August, 1842.

* This remonstrance is printed at p. 108 of Parliamentary Papers, 12th August. It will ever remain as a memorial of the wisdom of those who signed it, and as a proof of the heartless, cruel neglect of the local government in New Zealand, and of the Colonial Minister at home; he never noticed it—to him it was a solemn warning of what might happen. All it foresaw has occurred. This neglect is thus placed in the records of parliament, and reference has so frequently been made to it in reviews, magazines, and newspapers, that it is anything but hidden within those records. It was printed at length at p. 14 of the May number of this magazine.

† Notwithstanding such frequent reference has been made to it, it is of so much importance, that it is impossible not to say, that it will be found in the 3rd paragraph, p. 65, of Parliamentary Papers, 11th of May, 1841.

these letters, as to past transactions between her Majesty's government and the Company." Still, it is a letter full of imputations against individual directors, accusing them of breach of confidence. This is replied to by

5th. Mr. Somes to Lord Stanley, in a letter 18th of April, 1841, in which Mr. Somes not only repels the insinuation, but corrects Lord Stanley's memory upon the testimony of himself, Mr. Alderman Thompson, and Mr. Aglionby; of course the misrepresentation could not have been wilful—still misrepresentation it was, and it would have been much kinder in Mr. Hope and Lord Stanley, to have concerted measures with the Company, by which the afflicting suspense in which the relatives of 10,000 settlers might have been allayed.*

6th. "A statement of receipts and expenditure by the New Zealand Company. from the period of its establishment in 1839, to the 14th of February, 1844, Audited by Mr. George Bailey."

Appendix B is termed "Agreement with Lord Stanley, 1843." It contains 16 pages.

1st. A letter from Mr. Somes to Lord Stanley, dated 8th of May, 1843. Many of these letters are the result of personal meetings between the Colonial Minister and a deputation of the directors. What has occurred is reduced to writing, submitted to a court of directors, and, if approved, printed and forwarded to every one of the twenty-four directors; thus they are clothed with the authority of a body of as respectable gentlemen as any in London. The letter in question was written in consequence of a compromise, after several meetings. It seems that Lord Stanley chose to construe the agreement which had been made between the Company and Lord John Russell, differently to what not only the Company believed to be its sense, but in a way which rendered it impossible for the directors to carry on their colonization operation. This is fully explained in the correspondence in the Appendix A, which was thought by the Colonial Minister worth noticing. Still, the chance of a new governor going out, and changing the silly, if not wicked system pursued by the local government; the directors therefore came to a fresh agreement with Lord Stanley, upon his promising to give directions to have the land-title settled in their settlement; that they would endeavour to prop the falling artificial colony at Aucland, by purchasing 50,000 acres of land in its neighbourhood;—and this is the substance of Mr. Somes's letter of the 8th of May, and to this agreement of attempting to colonize Aucland against the judgment of the directors arose, because they "felt that the interests of the settlers and proprietors were so completely at the mercy of the Colonial Office and the local government, with respect to the vital question of land-titles in the Company's settlements; that the proceedings of the local government in that respect, were leading to such fearful results; that the total ruin of their settlements, and terrible collisions between the settlers and natives, seemed so likely to grow out of the then state of the land-title question;—on all these grounds, they deemed it their duty to obtain some determination of that question by means of almost any sacrifice."† But still there is a third party to this arrangement, before it can succeed, viz, willing emigrants. Now, after Mr. Clark's report,‡ none but a fool will be persuaded to go to Aucland.

---

* The directors (p. 8 in the Report) have most manfully stated their opinion of these offensive insinuations. We can offer some excuse for his lordship, the letter is most probably drafted by some clerk in his office, evidently a lawyer; Mr. Hope greatly occupied, signed it perhaps without reading. The misrepresentation and subsequent insinuation are justly offensive to the directors, but that of which the public will complain is, that the Colonial Minister, occupied with his contemptible controversy, never thinks or says one word of the dangerous position of the settlers in Cook's Straits.

† Report, p. 13.

‡ See the report of Mr. Clark's visit to the Thames and Waikato, printed at p. 93 of Parliamentary Papers, 12th of August, 1842, and it will be perceived that it is the worst place to which emigration can be directed. The Mr. Clendon has had the first choice of 10,000 acres near the town.—See also Mr. Felton Mathews' report, printed in Terry, p. 145—"I need scarcely observe, that it is a

2nd. A letter from Mr. Hope to Mr. Somes, dated 12th of May, 1843, in which the following paragraph will be found—" Lord Stanley directs me to state his assent to these proposals, and to intimate further, that he will be prepared to issue to the Governor of New Zealand, instructions to the effect proposed in your letter, for effectually settling the question of the Company's titles to land in that colony."*

On the 19th of May, only seven days after this solemn agreement, he writes to Mr. Shortland, the acting-governor—

1. The agreement as to the Company's colonizing Aucland.

2. The adoption of certain arrangements for the settlement of the Company's titles to land in New Zealand.

3. The appointment of a judge, with independent jurisdiction, at Wellington.

4. The proposed appointment of some person to represent the head of the government at Wellington; but adds, " Although I have thought it best to communicate to you this correspondence entire, it is not necessary that you should adopt measures with reference to any except the first point to which I have adverted."† Thus, when the directors fancied, and were told by Mr. Hope's letter, that " Lord Stanley was prepared to issue," &c., and of course supposed it was done, he secretly directed the acting-governor not to carry his promise to the directors into execution. Governor Fitzroy did not sail until the latter end of June, went to Bahia, the Cape of Good Hope, and Sydney, thus leaving the settlers in Cook's Straits to perish, through the delay; the friends of the settlers fondly hoping that their friends at the antipodes had been relieved as quickly as it was in the power of the legal appointed protector, the Colonial Minister, to have done so;—and then the instructions to Governor Fitzroy concealed from the Company from the 26th of June, 1843, until the 1st of February 1844.‡

Appendix C is a special correspondence with the Colonial Department, 1840 to 1843; this consists of 219 pages.

C No. 4, at p. 5 C, is the agreement between Lord John Russell and the Company, which has been treated almost as waste-paper by the local government, and almost held in contempt by the Colonial Minister at home.

The correspondence as to the charter transmitted to Governor Hobson, March 10th, 1841, p. 18 C.

Lord John Russell, April 16th, 1841, in his letter to Governor Hobson, says—" The arrangements which I have made with the New Zealand Company will forbid the application of the act, in its present form, to the case of the lands granted to them."—p. 19 C.§

May 3rd, 1841, Lord John Russell says—" In consideration, however, of the benefits to be derived from the sale of land by the Company."‖

A remarkable letter from Mr. Somes to Lord Stanley, dated November 24th, 1841, 42 C, detailing the state of the Company's affairs, and the injury which the settlers were receiving from the vindictive hostility of the local government.¶ The

---

country so remarkably deficient in natural pasture, as to present, in its primitive state, the most scanty supply for the food of animals, even in the most favoured situations; and, over many extensive tracts of country, not a blade of vegetation on which sheep or cattle could subsist."

* Page 6 B.

† This will be found in Mr. Somes's letter to Lord Stanley, dated December 21st, 1842,—being C 52, printed at p. 132 C.

‡ See the last paragraph in Mr. Hope's letter to Mr. Somes, February 15th, 1843,—C. No. 68, at p. 199 C.

§ The reader is requested to look at the account of Governor Hobson's conduct, at pp. 54—70 C.

‖ See Mr. Labouchere's letter to Mr. Motte, March 11th, 1839,—D. No. 5, printed at p. 12 D.

¶ See Mr. Labouchere's letter to Mr. Hutt, May 1st, 1839,—D. No. 6, printed at 13 D.

following passage in this letter is everybody's business—"The settlers at Port Nicholson have, in the most formal manner, offered to defray all the general as well as local expenses of their own government, if only invested with a legal power of taxing themselves for the purpose. The expenditure of the government has not been incurred among them, or for them; on the contrary, they have repudiated it, and protested against the partial objects for which the governor has thought proper to incur it."—68 C.*

We cannot understand, after this, the Colonial Minister, in the course of two budgets, asking parliament for £100,000. Then, the warning in this letter of what might happen, if Hobson was allowed to pursue his mad career, and what has happened. Lord Stanley's feelings are not to be envied, now that it appears in print;—it is printed at pp. 42—79 C, and it is recommended to be read attentively by all who wish to understand the affairs of New Zealand.

Pages 87—99 C, another able letter from Mr. Somes to Lord Stanley, dated April the 29th, 1842.—These are followed by a long correspondence, powerfully sustained on the part of the Company, and as flippantly replied to by Mr. Hope. Mr. Somes to Lord Stanley, 21st of December, 1842, C. No. 52, printed at p. 130 C, is a protest against the mischievous interference of either Mr. Spain or any other commissioner, asserting and relying upon the early proclamation of the crown, by Sir George Gipps, printed at p. 2 of Parliamentary Papers, 11th of May, 1841—"That it shall be announced to all her Majesty's subjects in New Zealand, that her Majesty will not acknowledge as valid any title to land, which either has been or shall be hereafter acquired in that country, which is not confirmed by a grant to be made in her Majesty's name, and on her behalf."†

After this, Mr. Somes was only speaking the truth, when he said—"*The crown, in taking possession of New Zealand, set aside all European titles founded on purchases from the natives, and gave the Company, by the agreement, the first title which it ever gave to any lands in New Zealand.*"‡

The attentive perusal of Mr. Somes's letters,§ C, Nos. 51 and 52, is particularly recommended. Mr. Hope's answer to them, C, No. 53, printed at p. 135 C, is an assumption of authority which will surprise those who read it;|| but it draws forth an answer, in C, 54 and 55, printed at pp. 139—168 C, which will ever attract those who respect truth and powerful reasoning.¶ Again, C, 57, at p. 173 C,

* See Mr. Hutt's answer to Mr. Labouchere, May 1st, 1839,—D. No. 7, printed at p. 15 D.

† In a letter from Lord John Russell to Governor Sir George Gipps, dated December 4th, 1839,—being D. No. 17, printed at p. 20 D; although nominally addressed to Sir George Gipps, it was, in fact, to Governor Hobson, and in it will be found the objection of Lord Hill to sending troops to a spot where British sovereignty had not been proclaimed.

‡ We have ever thought the withholding of this letter should be a matter of special inquiry by a committee of parliament; it is a part of the deception practised in the Colonial Office to deceive the public. Lord John Russell, we are confident, knew nothing about it; whatever we may wish, we hardly know how to say as much of Mr. Vernon Smith. See his letter to Mr. Hutt, 2nd of May, 1840,—being D. No. 20, printed in the Appendix K, p. 6; it accounts for the sensitiveness which he exhibited when the committee was proposed; but we suspect, after all, that his conduct has arisen from an amiable desire to protect some subordinate in the office. It is one of the many proofs of what *The Times* calls "clerk-craft."

§ See these letters, D. No. 36 and 37, printed at pp. 43—50 D. Mr. Somes's letter is extremely important, since it is by no means limited to contradicting the falsehoods stated by Hobson, but it exposes his vindictive feelings towards the settlements in Cook's Straits, and relates the meddling interference of the Rev. Henry Williams, who, assuming the cloak of a missionary, was acting contrary to the direction of his employers, and, in fact, doing immense injury to both races.

|| D. No. 40, printed at 51 D; Mr. Vernon Smith's reply, D. No. 41; and Lord John Russell's letter to Governor Hobson, April 22nd, 1841, D. No. 42;—printed at pp. 51—56 D.

¶ See this letter, at 13 H.

Mr. Somes asserts, that "*the native title by occupation, has always been held by our law paramount to every other;*" and went on to say, that the Company "never urged any claim to the dispossession of the natives from any lands in their own occupation." What then is the whole correspondence about? Do Lord Stanley and Mr. Hope mean to maintain that natives coming from a distance, like Te-whero-whero and Raupero, ought to be paid for their former bloody butcheries? The vindictive hostility of Hobson determined that it should be so at the antipodes; but this was hardly to be expected in Downing-street. The truth is, that the secret contrivers of anti-colonization well knew that delay would answer the purpose; if the colonists were not slaughtered, they would inevitably be ruined; there was nothing to do but to mystify the subject; hurl it into a lengthened correspondence, and their aim was attained. It was early avowed; the Colonial Minister has glided, perhaps insensibly to himself, into their trap; and, unfortunately for his fame, and possibly future comfort of mind, will be reproached as the cause of the ruin of thousands, who were unfortunately placed under his care. Lord Stanley never met the case, in the course of this correspondence, of the ruin which was occurring in consequence of the corrupt placing the seat of government so distant from the people as Aucland. So far from it, Mr. Hope justifies it;* and the greater part of that justification is untrue. Ruin and slaughter have ensued in consequence of that officer's visit to Wellington; instead of being the protector, he was the oppressor of his countrymen in Cook's Straits,† and remained so to the hour of his death. His death never relieved the settlers from his oppression; his successor has been infinitely worse.

Appendix D is the general correspondence with the Colonial Department, from 1837 to 1843, in 224 pages.

It commences with a letter from Lord Glenelg to the late Lord Durham, dated December 29th, 1837, in which the former states that it had become "an indispensable duty, in reference both to the natives and British interests," to colonize New Zealand; and for this purpose, Lord Glenelg proposed a chartered company with infinitely greater powers than the directors wished. However, it will be well now to examine what was then offered. Mr. Labouchere and the Marquis of Normanby refused to carry it into execution. No one will read Mr. Labouchere's letter to Mr. Hutt, May 1st, 1839, and Mr. Hutt's answer, the same day,‡ without thinking that Mr. Labouchere made an incorrect statement of Lord Normanby's "ignorance of the course which the Company had adopted,"§ when Lord Normanby had assured Mr. Somes, Mr. Halswell, Mr. G. Ward, and Mr. Hutt, that "he would undoubtedly introduce a measure for the purpose, during the session."‖

So far back as December 4th, 1839, Lord John Russell chalked out a plan of defence which, had his wise plan been pursued by Governor Hobson, the slaughter in June, 1843, would never have occurred.¶ Evidently, Lord John Russell felt that he, as Colonial Minister, was the natural, as well as the legal protector of the emigrants.

Mr. Hutt's letter of the 23rd of April, complains of his letter having been withheld from parliament.**

Letter D 36, from Mr. Vernon Smith, and the reply to it from Mr. Somes, exposes the false statements which Governor Hobson had the hardihood to make against the Company.†† Mr. Somes, on the 3rd of April, 1841, brought before the Colonial Office the plan of the Company for founding Nelson, in consequence of which Lord John Russell wrote to Governor Hobson, April 22nd, 1841, to allow

* The instructions to Captain Fitzroy, varying from the agreement in Mr. Hope's letter, of the 12th of May, p. 6 B, were given to that officer before leaving England, on the 26th of June, 1843, and never made known to the Company until the 1st of February, 1844,—13 B.

† Mr. Labouchere to Mr. Hutt, May 1st, 1839,—printed at 13 D.

‡ Mr. Hutt to Mr. Labouchere, May 1st, 1839,—printed at 15 D.

§ Ibid. ‖ Ibid.

¶ Page 23, Parliamentary Papers, 11th of May, 1841.

** This has been referred to before. †† Printed at 44 D.

that settlement to be founded, beyond the limits which the natives by treaty had made over to the Company;* this, however, Hobson, in the plenitude of his tyranny and jealous spite, would not permit;† and, notwithstanding the letter of the Colonial Minister, and the arrival of the emigrants, and the spot finally fixed upon the waste-lands of the British crown, the local governor at distant Aucland never attempted to give the Company a crown-title, or to protect them; the consequence was the dreadful massacre which took place in June, 1843.

It is impossible to examine the Report, with its Appendices, without coming to the conclusion that the local government abandoned the settlers to the attacks of some of the most savage barbarians in the world, and that, in this abandonment, all the parties fancied they were serving their own properties in the north, by ruining the settlements in Cook's Straits. In doing this, they have, for many years, stopped the progress of colonization in New Zealand; a greater blight could not have been thrown over Aucland. Lord Stanley cannot plead ignorance of the mischief which was occurring; he was apprised of it by Mr. Somes, 27th of August, 1841; but it seems that Lord Stanley has drawn a line for himself, never to listen to anything, unless through a report from the governor.

A few extracts shall be made. Mr. Hope says—"In reply, I am directed to acquaint you that Lord Stanley postpones any observations until he shall have received the petition through Captain Hobson, and the explanations with which he will probably accompany it."‡ Hobson writes—"It is highly repugnant to my feelings to offer any defence against charges so unjust and so unfounded."§ A call for a lighthouse was universal and notorious. Mr. Somes, on the part of the Company, in a letter, November 5th, 1841, proposes on the part of the Company, to send the lights out, at a considerable expense,‖ but none to the public. Mr. Hope replies, on the 17th—"Lord Stanley desires me to acquaint you, in reply, that he can form no opinion on the subject, in the absence of any report upon it from the Governor of New Zealand, for which his lordship will immediately apply."¶ Meanwhile, ships were wrecked, their crews drowned; the governor as far off Cook's Straits as if he were at Sydney.

At page 96 D, the celebrated remonstrance of the following six magistrates to Governor Hobson, of the consequences likely to occur from his determining to found Aucland, without means of his making it the seat of government, is printed. It was signed by W. Wakefield, R. Davis Hanson, George Samuel Evans, Henry St. Hill, George Hunter, and Ed. Daniel.**

May 26th, 1841, is a despatch from Governor Hobson, in which the following paragraph appears:—"We find, for instance, a large portion of the press engaged in circulating the most exaggerated statements of its merits, (Port Nicholson); and a bird's-eye view of the settlement is exhibited in the windows of every print shop, to delude the unwary into a belief that it commands a plain surface; but the perspective, which would show it, as it is, broken and precipitous, is carefully

---

* This letter is D. No. 42,—printed at 55 D.

† Hobson's refusal will be found in a correspondence, D 42, with the letters of Colonel and Captain Wakefield, D 43, D 46,—printed at pp. 56—65 D in the Appendix D.

‡ Extracts from Mr. Hope's letter to Mr. Somes, September 28th, 1841,—printed at 83 D.

§ Governor Hobson, August 5th, 1841, in answer to the petition for his recall; but this petition, like Mr. Hutt's letter, is omitted in the Parliamentary Papers. It will, however, be found in the *New Zealand Journal*, vol. ii., p. 208, being No. 42, August 21st, 1841. The clerkcraft of the Colonial Office may hide such a paper for a time, but the concealment produces the effect of increased publicity being given to it.

‖ Mr. Somes's letter to Lord Stanley is D. No. 67,—printed at p. 86 D.

¶ Mr. Hope's reply, twelve days afterwards, is D 68,—printed at p. 87 D.

** This remonstrance was printed at length at p. 15 (of No. 1), of the February Number of the new series of this Magazine. It is not surprising that it attracts attention; Governor Hobson pointed out its importance to Lord Stanley,—see p. 124 D,—but wanted its wise principles applied to Aucland.

kept out of sight."* There is not a word of truth in all this, but such an account must have been written to him—possibly it was only a part of the promised thwarting.

Governor Hobson's account of his reception at Wellington is given on the 20th of October, 1841 † Lord Stanley believed it all, acknowledged it on the 24th of June, 1842; ending his letter by directing that "neither Colonel Wakefield, or any one connected with the company, should be appointed a member of the council." ‡ Hobson's speech at opening the legislative council, 14th December, 1841; § but it is followed by a letter dated 26th of March, 1842, in which he charges the settlers in Cook's Straits with a bitter hostility to Aucland, and proposes, as a remedy, that the company should colonize that settlement.|| It is evident that these were his own feelings towards the settlers in Cook's Straits. We happen to know that he wrote to Captain Arthur Wakefield, for whom he, in common with the whole public, entertained the highest respect, lamenting his own total failure at Aucland, and asking for the company's assistance; and, in order to procure it, Mr. Hope says, that the subject was alluded to in a personal conversation with the directors.¶ Mr. Somes replies by showing that no such allusion had been made.** The object, no doubt, of Mr. Hope's letter was to lead the company to propose colonizing Aucland. Mr. Somes replied, "but even if the New Zealand Company had any desire to aid in repairing the errors of a mistaken system, it would be in vain for them to attempt the task, without a full confidence in the support of the public." ††

Mr. Hope's scheme has failed, but Lord Stanley was determined to try it; he forced the company, contrary to the judgment of the directors, to adopt it; ‡‡ induced them to enter into a new agreement,§§ altered the instructions to Governor Fitzroy, without their knowledge or consent,|||| on the 26th of June, 1843; ¶¶ and never informed the company of it until the 1st of February, 1844.*** The object is too obvious—the settlements in Cook's Straits might go to ruin—the settlers might be slaughtered or starved; but Aucland was to be colonized. This might be the opinion in Downing-street, but the prejudice is far too great now generally against New Zealand, but particularly against Aucland, to reinvigorate it by any such subtlety.

January 21st, 1843.—A letter from Mr. Somes to Lord Stanley, informing him by an inclosure from Colonel Wakefield, of the serious consequence likely to arise from the commissioner coming to no decision as to the title, and that there had not been a communication from distant Aucland for four months: ††† upon which Mr. Somes made the following observations:—

---

* Page 103 D.

† Being D No. 83, printed at 105 D. This is a most disclosed account. Mr. Eurp is now in London, and he should be examined as to the contents of this letter.

‡ This letter is D 84, printed at 107 D, finished at 110 D. It would seem as if the Colonial Minister had been inoculated by the vindictive hostility of the local governor, towards the company.

§ D No. 97 printed at p. 121 D. In this speech he lauds the company, their settlers, and their settlements, but it ill accords with his conduct towards them.

|| D No. 98, printed at 122 D.

¶ D No. 98, printed at 123. This letter must not be lost sight of; it is full evidence that Governor Hobson was feeling the error which he had committed, and the failure which he was experiencing; but it is evidence also that Lord Stanley was convinced of it also.

** D No. 100, printed at 126 D. Mr. Somes's letter to Lord Stanley, January 13th, 1843. It has been done in polite words, but the pith of the letter was the governor telling Mr. Hope and Lord Stanley that they had made a statement which was not true.

†† Paragraph third of the above letter.

‡‡ See 12th Report, p. 13.

§§ B No. 1 and 2, printed at B 3 to 7.

|||| 12th Report, p. 11.

¶¶ In a letter from Lord Stanley to Governor Fitzroy, being B No. 8, printed at B 14.

***In a letter from Mr. Hope to Mr. Somes.

††† D No. 104, and D No. 105, printed at 134 and 135 D.

"We do not trouble your lordship with the endless complaints on this subject, which come to us from individual settlers, and which occupy the columns of the three newspapers published at Wellington and Nelson; but it is our duty to state, that the discontent and the hinderance to improvement thus occasioned are very much aggravated by the fact, that these neglected settlements furnish, by the taxes raised there, a revenue sufficient for defraying the cost of governing them efficiently." *

Had Lord Stanley done his duty, he would have immediately sent a governor to Cook's Straits, and not have attempted to prop up Auckland; all that Lord Stanley did was to remit these important letters to Governor Hobson for his report. † The correspondence has been continued, the directors making complaints to the Colonial Minister, and receiving a reply that they were forwarded to the governor. Voluminous as the Company's Report is, it is most interesting, but, from beginning to end, condemnatory of Lord Stanley. It is out of his power to refute it; it rests upon no story told; it consists of facts elucidated letter by letter, proving how completely he was made aware of the wicked conduct of the local government over which he had complete control. No warning has had any effect upon him; his lordship has chosen, contrary to common sense, to continue a hostile governor to the settlers. In all the correspondence, Lord Stanley has never met the distance of the seat of government—the folly of the governor of having formed it—the obstinacy with which he maintained it—or the ruin which has ensued from it.

Appendix E consists of 129 pages, entirely as to the company's land-titles. Want of space renders it necessary to bring this article to a close. We can only therefore call attention to this appendix, as clearly showing the justice of the company's claims, and the mischiefs which the governor's determination has entailed upon the natives as well as the settlers. The directors appear to justly appreciate the services of their agent, and the more this appendix is examined, the more will the reader lament such a reward as he has received for his strenuous exertions in favour of the aborigines as well as his companions in founding these settlements. His bravery was well known in leading the regiment which he commanded into action in Spain; and if ever man turned the sword into the ploughshare, he is that man. The feelings of those who have checked his noble career, are not to be envied; posterity will do both him and his murdered brother that justice which the authorities in Downing-street have denied him; but such is the state in which Lord Stanley has placed these settlements, that no one knows what he and the brave settlers have yet suffered.

Appendix F, G, and H form a volume of 147 pages, as we have already said, the interesting narrative of founding the settlements in Cook's Straits, and worthy of being placed by the side of the illustrious navigator who first discovered them. Cook's work was the seed, and these three appendices the fruit.

Appendix I consists of public documents relating to the colony of New Zealand, between 1838 and 1842.

Appendix K are accidental omissions and errors in the preceding appendices, in 16 pages.

We have now brought our melancholy task nearly to a close. The insignificant tools, Shortland, Clark, Clark the younger, and Spain, may be left to themselves; but how such gentlemen as Lord Stanley and Mr. Hope have been led into such errors is so unaccountable, inexplicable, that however much we lament it, we will not attempt to offer even a conjecture—their conduct in the Colonial Office in the affairs of New Zealand has not merely been that of wanton destruction, but there is every reason to fear that their wilful hostility to twenty-four of the first gentlemen in England, will have caused the loss of more life and property than we dare to contemplate. It may be all the clerk-craft of the office, but they have adopted it; and this deeply-stained page in English history will henceforth be ever attached to their names.

* Mr. Somes's letter to Lord Stanley, January 21st, 1843, printed at 134 D.

† See Mr. Hope's letter to Mr. Somes, February 1843, being D No. 107, printed at 137 D.

COLONIAL STATISTICS.

[NEW SERIES.]

NO. V.—THE ISLAND OF TOBAGO.

History.—Tobago, or *Tobacco*, so named after the pipe used by the islanders in smoking the herb now so extensively used, is one of the islands discovered by Columbus on his third voyage, 1498; it has been in turns possessed by the Dutch, French and English. The army-list issued by authority states, under the head "colonies," that Tobago was ceded to us by France in 1763. To enter a little into detail, it appears that so far back as 1580, the British flag was planted on the island; and in 1608 James the First claimed its sovereignty, no effectual colonization, however, taking place.

Tobago has been named the "Melancholy Isle," from its gloomy aspect as seen from the north, presenting a mass of lofty mountains, with black precipices, descending abruptly to the sea. A description of the island is said to have suggested the scenery of Crusoe's island to Defoe.

The physical structure of this island indicates a primitive or more ancient rock formation, analogous to that of the neighbouring continent; it has been noticed that there existed a striking dissimilarity between the Indians inhabiting Tobago when it was first visited by Europeans, and those of the insular Caribs, who have given their name to the group of islands, the Caribbees.

Geography.—Tobago is situated in latitude 11° 10′ north, longitude 60° 45′ west. It is only distant about six miles from Trinidad to the north-east, and south-west from Barbadoes 130 miles. The island is thirty-two miles in length, and twelve in breadth, covering an area of 319 square miles. Its extreme altitude is about 2,000 feet. The surface of the country, though rocky and precipitous, is very fertile. It presents an irregular mass of conical hills and ridges, with numerous valleys, which, in the southern quarter, are less abrupt in their acclivities; possessing, generally, a good soil, and through which a number of small streams make their way from the mountains to the sea.

Climate.—So recent as 1841, the accounts received represented great mortality, rather through climaterial sickness than from contagion or epidemic. Though moist, by being impregnated with saline particles, Tobago is not considered confirmedly unhealthy, "particularly, (says the historian of the 'British Colonies,') if proper attention were paid to preventing the exits of the mountain streams." But the island is certainly declining, notwithstanding it has borne a high reputation for fertility. The rainy season begins in June, and gradually becomes heavy until September. Dr. Lloyd reported to Sir James M'Gregor in 1827, that on some of the estates in the interior of Tobago no European resident had been buried for upwards of ten years. The ratio of mortality among the slave population was, from 1819 to 1832, one in twenty-four. Nautical men are interested in the fact of the currents round the island being very uncertain.

Towns.—Scarborough, the principal town, (population 1,550,) is situated on the south and west side of Tobago, along the sea-shore, (at the base of Fort George Hill,) and extends, with little uniformity, easterly, towards the fort. Fort George Hill rises to the height of 422 feet, of a conical shape, and crowned by Fort King George, the chief military station in the island. The other towns are St. Paul, Plymouth, and Goldsboro'.

Harbours.—On the windward side are numerous excellent bays, and on the northward is situate "Man-of-war Bay," capacious, safe, and adapted to the largest ships. Courland Bay is on the north side, six miles from the fort. The Richmond, a large river, passes through the leeward district. Sandy Point and King's Bays, like the above, are adapted for large ships; Tyrrell's, Bloody, Mangrove, Englishman's, Castaras, and Halifax Bays, have also good anchorage for small vessels. Halifax Bay requires a pilot, in consequence of a shoal at the entrance.

Population.—The last official return is that of 1839, which gives a population of 250 Europeans only; of other races, 11,498; total, 11,748. Proportion of compensation awarded under the Emancipation Act, 20*l.* 3*s.* 7¼*d.* The number of slaves registered was 11,621.

Religion—Education.—In the town of Scarborough there is a Protestant church, with a congregation of 300 persons at the best season; but service is not performed oftener than on two Sabbaths of the month, from climaterial causes. At St. Paul's town there is also a church, the living of which is valued at 400*l.* Here are two chapels, capable of holding 500 persons together, in the town of Plymouth and Goldsboro'. Tobago has likewise five dissenting places of worship, and four private schools. The St. David's public school had, in 1836, 140 scholars, and received a small grant from government in its support. St. Patrick's school, Montgomery, 200 scholars; a Wesleyan mission school was similarly supported.

Government.—Tobago is ruled by a lieutenant-governor, by a council of 9, and by a house of assembly, of 16 members, whose power and authority are similar to those of Jamaica. List of officials in 1841: Lieutenant-Governor, Major-General Sir H. C. Darling; President of the Council, W. Nicholson, Esq.; Chief-Justice, E. Sanderson, Esq.; Attorney-General, ———; Solicitor-General, J. Wattley, Esq.; Judge of the Vice-Admiralty Court, A. M'Pherson, Esq.; Registrar of ditto, C. Greville, Esq.; Advocate of ditto, R. Wimberley, Esq.; Master in Chancery, J. Keens, Esq.; Secretary, Registrar, and Clerk of the Council, J. Thornton, Esq.; Provost-Marshall, J. Le Plastrie, Esq.; Speaker of Assembly, H. Hamilton, Esq.; Clerk of the Assembly, W. S. Foster, Esq.; Treasurer, Lieutenant J. N. Jerves; Collector of Customs, T. Marten, Esq.; Harbour-Master, J. Duncan, Esq.; Agent in London, P. M. Stewart, Esq., 11, Upper Brook Street.

Military.—A fort-adjutant (Lieutenant O. Mackie, R.A.). The militia has a superior staff, and supports a troop of cavalry. 100 European regulars, and 750 militia constitute the whole military force.

Productions.—Staples: sugar, rum, molasses, cotton. Almost every kind that grows on the Antilles, or on Trinidad, flourishes at Tobago.

The orange, lemon, and guava, pomegranate, fig, and grape, in perfection. The cinnamon and pimento trees grow wild. The island produced, of sugar, 9,859,248 lbs.; of rum, 386,592 gallons; and of molasses, 94,520 lbs., in 1839. The importation of sugar in 1841, amounted to 48,164 cwts. The imports of all West India colonies were at their maximum in 1831. The valuable table to be found in M'Culloch's "Commercial Dictionary," (supplement), shows that the total imports from the West Indies, from 1831 to 1841, fell from 4,103,800 cwts., or about 205,000 tons, to 2,151,217 cwts., or 107,560 tons. An account of the quantities of sugar, rum, and molasses, imported into the United Kingdom from the West Indies, &c., in 1834 and 1835 (Parliamentary Paper, 1836), gives the following results as regards Tobago—

	Sugar unrefined.	Rum.	Molasses.
1834 ...	79,018 cwts.	272,787 galls.	11,646 cwts.
1835 ...	77,260 "	299,705 "	5,986 "

The above table is useful, as showing at a glance the averages of importations of Tobago produce.

Trade.—Products: sugar, rum, coffee, indigo, arrowroot, &c. In 1770, when the island belonged to England, the value of exports was, to the United Kingdom, 451,650*l.*; to America, 54,061*l.*; to other islands, 671*l.*;—total, 506,382*l.* In the years 1777-78, when the French had possession, the productions, consisting of sugar, cotton, coffee, indigo, &c., realized in the first year, 2,096,000 fr., or 87,332*l.* 6s. 8d.; in the second year, 3,691,000 fr., or 153,791*l.* 13s. 4d. In 1829, the value of its exports was, to the United Kingdom, 158,385*l.*; the imports being, 51,368*l.*—The crops of sugar have, as we have already shown, decreased considerably during the last few years. Tobago was appointed a free warehousing port, by order in council, 18th of May, 1841. From its shipping statistics, we learn that 20 vessels, of 4,814 tons collectively, were entered inwards, in 1834; and 22 ships, of 5,289 tons, entered outwards.

Revenue.—The official returns of 1836, supply the following items of revenue: poll-tax, 7,771*l.*; house-tax, 528*l.*; tonnage duties, 1,119*l.*; merchants'-tax, 324*l.*; tippling act, 100*l.*; police bill, 21*l.*; militia fines, 62*l.*; transient-traders tax, 41*l.*; miscellaneous, 1,734*l.*;—total, 11,708*l.*

Expenditure.—Total, 4,905*l.* The estimated value of the island before slave-emancipation, was 2,682,920.* The present estimated value of its productions is 516,530*l.*

Prices of Produce and Merchandise.—Horned cattle, 13*l.* each; horses, 30*l.*; sheep, 24s.; goats 1*l.*; swine, 1*l.* 5s.; milk, 8d. per quart; butter, 2s. 6d. to 4s. per lb.; cheese, 1s. per lb.; wheat bread, 4d. per lb.; beef, 9d.; mutton, 1s.; pork, 8d.; rice, 32s. per cwt.; coffee, 1s. per lb.; tea, 7s. per lb.; sugar, 25s. per cwt.; salt, 6s. per bushel; tobacco, 2*l.* 8s. per cwt.

The Colonial Arms.—The seal of Tobago represents three ships-of-war abreast, and apparently at anchor, in its largest bay.

* "History of the British Colonies," 1841.

A WELCOME TO PAPA;

ON HIS RETURN FROM CANTON, AFTER AN ABSENCE OF NINE MONTHS.

[SPOKEN BY HIS THREE CHILDREN.]

GIRL.

HAPPY children that we are,
Once again with dear Papa:
Sister—brother—one, two, three,
Standing smiling round his knee;
Each our little hand in his,
Waiting for a loving kiss;
And we'd rather lose our play,
Though it *is* a holiday;
For our kisses, like pet dove's,
Best can tell our childish loves.
Now we look up in his face,
As to coax a kind embrace;
Now we listen to his voice
Till our very hearts rejoice:
Haven't we good reason why—
Both our darling parents by?
Oh, how heavy hung the day,
While Papa did bide away!
Home seem'd only half itself,
All its fun upon the shelf;
Maids did mope, and chicks look wan,
And Mamma put mourning on.
But we mope and fret no more
Since Papa's inside the door;
Half a sight of his kind face,
In its old familiar place,
Brings good humour back amain,—
Home is once more home again,
Beaten dog would not look glum
Now our dear Papa is come;
Pretty Vic, she wagg'd her tail,
Barking loud to bid him hail;
You may call me silly child,
But, methought, e'en dolly smil'd;
Parlour, kitchen, nurs'ry, all
Flock'd to meet him in the hall.
How we laugh'd, and cried 'hurrah!'
Welcome, welcome, dear Papa!

ALL.

Happy children! Come, Mamma;
One cheer more for 'dear Papa':—
Hip hip hip—hurrah!

ELDER BOY.

Happy children that we are,
Clasping thus our dear Papa,
All his toils and hardships o'er
Upon sea and upon shore;

From the winds and stormy main
Safe and sound at home again.
Let us hope he will not roam
Any more so far from home;
Let us hope he will not stay
Any more so long away;
But for fear he ever should,
Let us try and all be good.
Then, when after-dinner comes,
And the pears and sugar-plums,
It will be so nice to hear
Where he's been this almost year;
How the ship we saw them tow
All across the sea did go;
How the boat shot o'er the sand,
How she brought him safe to land;
All about the caravan,
And the Turk and Chinaman.
Then, to sit upon his lap,
While he shows us on the map
With his finger all the track
Going out and coming back
There will be a treat! hurrah!
Welcome, welcome, dear Papa!

ALL.

Happy children! Come, Mamma;
One cheer more for 'dear Papa!'
Hip hip hip—hurrah!

YOUNGER BOY.

Happy children that we are,—
Dearly let us love Papa;
But be gentle in our joys,
Merry girl and not rude boys.
I remember we did cry,
When he wish'd us last good bye;
And to kiss him though so glad,
Then his kisses made us sad;
For we thought with childish pain
We might never kiss again;
How our dear Papa might be
Shipwreck'd far away at sea;
Drown'd perhaps, or forced to roam,
With no ship to bring him home.
But we drank his health down-stairs;
Night and morning in our prayers
Prayed to God, Papa to keep
From the dangers of the deep.
Now our hearts with pleasure burn
At his wish'd-for safe return.
Stoop, and let me kiss you, sir;
Kiss your little Highlander.
Here's the clan McQ***n—hurrah!
Here's a health to dear Papa!

ALL.

Happy children! Come, Mamma;
One cheer more for 'dear Papa!'
Hip hip hip—Hurrah!

C. J. C.

RANDOM RECOLLECTIONS OF THE MOSQUITO SHORE IN CENTRAL AMERICA.

BY THOMAS YOUNG,

AUTHOR OF "NARRATIVE OF A RESIDENCE ON THE MOSQUITO SHORE."*

Disinclination of the English to intermarry with Indian women—Anglo-Mosquito children—An Anglo-Mosquito woman—Peter Wallin, the Savanna King—Occurrences respecting.

THE English, as a body, are less inclined to intermarry with the natives of the country in which they are sojourning, than any other people; their love for their own country is too ardent; they are too prone to think of the comforts which they have been used to, and generally cannot give up all they suppose most desirable, merely for an Indian wife, whom they have to teach everything. And well it is, that it is so, for such ill-assorted alliances seldom produce anything but misery and degradation; if the children springing from such a union are permitted to exist in the superstition and wretched ignorance of the mother, a stigma must for ever rest upon the father. The children of white men by Mosquito women, after the father's death, are looked upon with but little respect; they seem to have lost caste, and drag on a miserable existence. I have seen several of these Anglo-Mosquito children, the mothers of whom testified the fondest affection for them —but the mothers alone.

One day, while at Cape Gracias á Dios, I proceeded to pay King Robert Charles Frederick a morning visit, and found, on my arrival, that a number of mahogany-cutters had come down the Wauks River to pass the Christmas week, and that the king had kindly offered to permit them to arrange their sleeping-places in his house, it being very large, and well adapted for such a purpose; the men had accordingly erected crickeries, and had hung up their mosquito-curtains or pavilions, so that the place had a most singular appearance.

The king's disinterested offer may be very easily accounted for, the mahogany-cutters, being Caribs and Belize creoles, could dance, sing, play the fife and drums; such being the case, and the king being immoderately fond of such enjoyment, thoughts of midnight revelry and rejoicing flashed through his brain. The mahogany-cutters, however, nothing loth, entered into the spirit of the thing, with that hilarity and excessive vigour and delight for which they are so characterized, and for some days, the ear-piercing fifes, the noisy drums, accompanied his royal Majesty, wherever his royal Majesty's will led them, and "Over the water to Charlie," "Bonnie Laddie," "God save the Queen," and two or three other tunes, were alternately played; added to which, the most grotesque dancing, and loud cries, called singing, sufficiently

* Continued from No. 5, page 270.

amused us during the Christmas holidays, when no work whatever is done by either Caribs, negroes, or Mosquitomen, on any pretence whatever.

Calling upon the king one afternoon, I observed, with something akin to surprise, a very fair and finely-shaped girl, with beautiful hair hanging round her head in clustering ringlets, simply fastened by a band of dyed native cotton, employed in mechanically stringing small and variously-coloured beads. Round her ankles and wrists were tied bands, composed of curiously-strung beads. There appeared such an air of simplicity and gentleness about her, that my curiosity was excited. On inquiry, I ascertained that she was the daughter of an Irishman by an Indian woman, and that the father had left her from her infancy to the care of her mother, and that she was then living in concubinage with one of the mahogany-cutters. I advanced, and addressed her in English, which, although she understood, no persuasion could induce her to speak; once only, in her gratitude, after I had given her some medicine, which restored her from a bad fever, I asked if she liked the English, to which she timidly replied, "Oh, yes, too much!" Finding I could not persuade her to continue the conversation in English, I mustered up as much of the Mosquito dialect as I then knew, and soon discovered what a void was there, so lost, so completely shut out from civilization; her ideas centered in stringing beads, and not having been used to work in the plantations, like the other Indian women, she could do comparatively nothing. Often have I noticed, when things were talked of, to her incomprehensible, how her large dark full eyes would inquiringly look; and sorrowed that one who might, under proper tuition, have been an ornament to her sex, was even less informed than the swarthy beings around her—and yet with the blood of the white man running in her veins!

Others I have noticed, that, with their light-blue eyes, hair—and, in two or three instances, blue eyes—plainly evinced their Saxon origin, contrasting strongly with those with whom they were mingling.

Another was the child of a woman called Keekee-tarrer, the sister of the chief, Mr. Peter Wallin, who delights in calling himself King of the Savanna, in contradistinction to the King of the Mosquito Shore, at which the latter, Robert Charles Frederick, when alive, felt excessively indignant. This child's father is reported to have been an officer in the British navy.

Peter Wallin, the self-constituted savanna king, has, from some unexplained cause, conceived a great dislike to the English; his prudence, however, prevents him from showing any malignity, for he well knows their power; and fear, if no other motive, keeps him quiet. He is very intelligent, speaks English well, but it is rarely he converses except in his native tongue. Residing in the savanna, some distance from Cape Gracias á Dios, he lives a happy life of indolence; his hunters supply him with game, and his wives with the products of the plantation; he possesses cattle, horses, pigs, and poultry; and can there, surrounded by his own immediate followers and partizans, assume the character, and maintain the position, of a savanna king; but, however strongly his people may support him in that character, there are few indeed who would render him any assistance, if he attempted anything against the English; although, as in all other parts of the world, men are to be found to commit crimes at the instigation of others. Two or three instances have come to my knowledge, which prove that Mr. Peter Wallin had the will to attempt wrong, but had not the courage to execute it.

On one occasion, two Englishmen visited him, and were received by him and his sister, Keekee, with incomparable hospitality; but, from some suspicious circumstances, they feared that these marks of friendship were but assumed. Having heard nothing particularly favourable about Mr. Wallin, they determined, on an opportunity occurring of consulting with each other, to keep up a good fire, and not to retire to rest. Notwithstanding all Wallin's entreaties, he could not induce them to sleep; they passed the night in great trepidation, as the Indians were at times very troublesome, swearing, quarrelling, and fighting amongst themselves. Grey morning at length dawned on the weary watchers, and gladly they returned homewards, unscathed, vowing never again to venture in the savanna king's district. At one time, they were much astonished, for, on provisions being placed before them, they were presented with silver spoons, on which were engraven crests. How they could have got there, was to them perfectly inexplicable; but, not considering themselves in safe quarters, they very prudently refrained from asking any impertinent questions, although their curiosity was so much excited.

Two young men, Mr. C. and Mr. H., on another occasion proceeded to Mr. Peter's house, and were received with so much friendliness, that their suspicions were totally disarmed. The evening passed merrily away, till at length it was time to retire to the sleeping-places which had been prepared for their reception, with pavilions to protect them from the worrying mosquitoes. Mr. C. was armed with pistols and a sword, but, deceived into security, he left his sword standing up against a post in the hut.

Many other sleeping-places were in the same apartment, occupied by men, women, and children; some of the Indians stretched themselves in their rope hammocks, others lay coiled up in their polpooras, while some few squatted down by the fire, to receive its warmth, and to smoke their short black pipes. Mr. C. had slept some time, when he was awakened by hearing a whispering; he slowly lifted up one end of his mosquito-curtain, and saw, by the dim light cast in the apartment by two or three pitch-pine torches, that his sword had been taken out of the scabbard; his pistols were not to be depended upon, being small, and Birmingham make; at the extremity of the hut he saw two or three Indians in earnest conversation; thoroughly alarmed, and knowing there was nothing like surprising an enemy, he jumped on the ground, seized hold of the sheath of his sword, and with a loud cry ran towards the men, and commenced beating them violently about their heads and faces, swearing at them for having stolen his sword; when one man, to escape the blows which were falling thick and fast upon him, pulled the sword out of part of the thatch where it had been hidden, threw it on the ground, calling out loudly for mercy. Mr. H. hearing the noise, arose, and seeing his companion so busily engaged, assisted him, till they saw no attempt would be made at that time upon them. On their seating themselves close to the fire, and adding more wood, Mr. Peter Wallin came in from a distant hut, to know the reason of the disturbance, and on being informed, appeared much exasperated, saying, "that the thief who had stolen the sword should be flogged at once, as no white man, when under his roof and protection, should be molested." This did not allay the misgivings of the two young men, who were pretty sure that Wallin was the proposer of an attempt to be made upon them. Little more was said on the subject, but from what afterwards transpired, there does not appear any reason to suppose that Wallin meant mischief, but that the glittering handle of the sword, and the good quality of the blade, excited the cupidity of the Indian who took it.

Mr. U——n, a resident at the Cape, had a number of cattle on the savanna, and some time ago he purchased a cow from a Mosquito man (Captain John Williams), living at Croata. During a temporary absence of Mr. U——n, the cow was seized by Peter Wallin for a debt which he alleged the man at Croata owed him. Mr. U——n, when informed of the occurrence, (he himself being invested with full powers as a magistrate, and with the consent of another magistrate,) sent word to the king, and despatched several Belize creoles, headed by Mr. C. just named, to recover possession from Wallin. They were eight in number, and well armed. On reaching Mr. Peter's house, the news spread around of the white men's arrival, and many Indians came. Wallin, when told of the object of their visit, swore no white man—no, nor the king himself, should take any beeve belonging to him. Fearing that his obstinacy might perhaps lead to a disturbance, Mr. C. very decidedly pulled a pistol out of his pocket, cocked it, and, holding it to Wallin's head, swore he would shoot him dead if the cow he had taken was not immediately restored. Mr. Peter sullenly gave an order for its capture. An old bull was at length brought in; it would not do; again the chase was renewed, and a cow brought in. This was kept as a recompense for the loss of time and the expense of hiring the Belize creoles, while, to the intense mortification of Wallin, he was perforce obliged to give positive orders for the cow that had caused the quarrel to be captured, which it speedily was.

With the two cows they returned to the Cape, their arrival being greeted with pleasure by the Indians residing there. An order came from the king that three times the value of the cow should be taken from Wallin, but this was not exacted; at the same time the king sent a quarter-master to Mr. Peter to tell him to take care—or, "by goles he would hang him."

Since then no further attempt has been made by Wallin, who keeps aloof, for he well knows the uselessness of contending against superior force, while the whole body of natives, seeing that justice is equally administered to all, are satisfied, and no aggressions of any moment take place; and there is less fear of personal violence or midnight robberies on the Mosquito Shore, than in the civilized city of London, protected by its numerous and well-organized body of police.

Cape Gracias á Dios abounds with hideous croaking toads, and, as soon as the sun sets, a stranger would be startled at the noise which immediately commences. Some of the toads are of a monstrous size, and on my return home one evening with a companion and my favourite dog Jack, an immense one was seen by us in the pass, as if to impede our progress. Jack waited not for encouragement, but at once attacked the loathsome creature, and in an instant we heard its bones crunching in his mouth. In vain we called—Jack would not quit his delicious *bonne bouche* till we were out of sight. In about a quarter of an hour we were alarmed by hearing the most dismal howls; rushing out *en masse*, we discovered that the sounds issued from my poor dog. Well indeed might he howl, for his head was swollen to a shocking size; his breath became short—his limbs quivered. We bled him in the feet, in the tongue, in the ears, all to no purpose—in less than ten minutes after we heard the first yell of pain, he died a shapeless mass, unquestionably poisoned—poor Jack's penchant for toads having given him a *coup de grace*.

During the autumnal rains in 1839, at the village on Black River bank, a Mosquito man named Roberts, at the entreaties of his *cara sposa*, determined to set off hunting. He tried to induce some or one of the Indians to accompany him, but in vain, for most of these people have an invincible dislike to rain; so preferred lazily to swing in their hammocks, chanting some monotonous song, or squatting near their wood fires, smoking, and existing upon a few roasted plantains or bananas, than to run the chance of not only being unsuccessful in the chase, but also to endure the "peltings of the pitiless storm." Mr. Roberts, however, being ravenously inclined, and urged on by his wife, at length set off, his little dog trotting by his side; and it was imagined that, by his superior skill and dexterity in hunting, and great knowledge of the various passes and resorts for game, that he would speedily return with a good supply, although in the rainy seasons the hunters generally have to go far away into the bush.

Two—three—four days elapsed—no Roberts appeared; and misgivings ran through the tribe that some accident had happened, or that the Oulasser (the devil) had carried him away. After a grand talk, several Indians proceeded in search of him, for some time without success; at length they came to a narrow but deep creek of water, on crossing which they fell upon the trail, and soon reached the spot where the body of poor Roberts lay much mangled, and with the loss of one of his legs. Myriads of large ants were crawling over the body, which emitted a horrible effluvium. Poor Mr. Roberts, on crossing the piece of water just mentioned, must have had his leg taken off by an alligator; contriving to reach the shore, he crawled to his death-bed, where, alone and unassisted, he died a miserable death. The mutilations on his body were made by numerous small animals, and in a short time, if it had not been found, there would have been nothing left but a heap of bones. No trace was found of the little dog.

Robert's body was carried to his native village, and buried with rather more than usual demonstrations of grief, comprised in sundry more vollies being fired over his grave, and in two or three extra casks of mushla being made, to drink in his commemoration.

Public attention has been for some time past attracted to Central America, and to the riches with which it abounds, yet it is very little known, and the Mosquito shore cannot be pointed out on the map by one person in a thousand; and why should all this ignorance remain? One of the finest countries in the world is, with all its great advantages, absolutely less thought of than a little nook, or a desert island, ten or fifteen thousand miles off. Central America has within itself every variety of climate; it teems with mines producing valuable metals in wonderful abundance, and tropical productions of the most important kinds. In the waters of the sea-coast, in the bays, inlets, and lagoons, fish in infinite varieties and numbers swarm to an astonishing degree. The woods abound with game of the rarest and choicest sorts in incredible quantities, while the valuable woods and the fruits of the earth are lavished on the natives of this favoured country in profusion; so that it would appear that it has been more bountifully supplied with everything for man's sustenance than any other country in the world; and from what I have myself seen and heard, I should say that the Mosquito Shore is as highly, if not more highly favoured than any other part of Central America, as it lacks nothing but the mines, which are more frequently the causes of misery and wretchedness, than of happiness or prosperity.

Mr. Stephens, the celebrated American writer, has published two separate volumes of his researches and discoveries in Central America, more especially at the ruins of Copan and in Yucatan; the drawings in the two volumes are considered very valuable, and were taken by an Englishman, Mr. Catherwood.* I was told when at New York, in March, 1842, that Mr. Stephens had cleared 20,000 dollars by his first volume, in America alone. This proves the interest the Americans take in that part of the globe, which he so well describes.

Mr. Stephens is, however, somewhat straitlaced, for when he arrived at the British settlement of Belize, he was entertained, by an English merchant resident there, to second breakfast. On seating himself at table he found himself placed between Dr. Y. and Mr. A., both men of colour. He of course expressed no displeasure at it, and a man of sense would have considered them as his equals, which they were in every respect as to rank, character, and education; but, no, on his return to New York, he published his first volume on Central America, and mentioned the incident of being at second breakfast at Belize, and of having a man of colour on either side of him. On my arrival at Belize this was discussed there—how much to the disadvantage of our over-nice American may easily be calculated.

The inhabitants in the interior towns of Central America are willing

* This gentleman has since brought a more extensive and valuable collection of architectural drawings from the same regions, to London, where they are now being lithographed.

to exchange their valuable productions for British manufactured goods, how much to the interest of the British adventurer requires but little discernment to discover. That it can be done, and that effectually, can be proved ; and the Mosquito Shore, therefore, possesses superior advantages to the English for the establishment of trading speculations. It has a line of sea-coast of 500 miles, uninterrupted by any Central American or Spanish settlement. Its central position, and the affection the inhabitants entertain for the English, warrant the assertion that our merchants, with proper management, would find an opening for the disposal of vast quantities of the goods which have been so rapidly accumulating in their overcrowded warehouses.

If ever the grand canal between the Atlantic and the Pacific oceans be completed, which, from its importance, must sooner or later occur, immense advantages will inevitably accrue to the adjacent countries and islands; but no place will receive so much benefit as the Mosquito Shore, to the southward of Cape Gracias á Dios ; more particularly, as through that kingdom the Spaniards would send their goods for shipment, and vast herds of cattle could be raised on the fertile savannas ; besides numerous other results which would be developed in the course of time. The Mosquito Shore has attracted much notice, and that it will ultimately be considered a prize worth having, there can be but little doubt. The English established themselves at Black River and other places previous to the year 1778, but in that year the then existing government entered into a treaty, under a mistaken idea, with Spain, in which they consented to give up all their forts on the Mosquito Shore, which they did ; and the residents at Black River, wanting English protection, and not being willing to settle under another flag, quitted their homes, and wandered forth in search of others. The English, discovering their mistake, re-established their forts, and sent a few troops there, but ultimately the forts were demolished and the troops withdrawn.

The Spaniards afterwards settled at Black River, built many houses, erected a fort and a large church, and all was apparent prosperity ; but the deep-seated hatred of the Mosquito Indians to the Spaniards at length burst forth, and, in their vengeance, they stormed the Spanish fort and town in the dead of the night, and slew many of the inhabitants—the rest made their escape. This happened about thirty or forty years ago, and from that period the Spaniards have had no footing in the country.

In the year 1820, Macgregor, so notorious for his Poyais Bonds, attempted to form a settlement at Black River, and so many of his countrymen were deceived and duped by his heartless scheme, that it failed almost before it was commenced. Of those who were sent to act as pioneers in this Utopia, as it was described, many fell victims to exposure and insufficient supplies of food, while the few remaining, finding that they were not supported by the concocters of this precious scheme, contrived to make their sad condition known to the merchants at Belize, two of whom—the late Marshall Bennet, and another gentleman whose name I have forgotten*—despatched a schooner to their

* J. W. Wright.

relief, which safely carried the miserable survivors to Belize, where, amongst the warm-hearted and compassionate inhabitants, they received that assistance which they so much needed.

In the year 1839, an enterprising English company again attempted the settlement of Black River; the account of its failure and the disastrous occurrences with which its officers had to contend, is fully set forth in the "Narrative of a Residence on the Mosquito Shore."

The Belgians have been for some time past turning their attention to the formation of a colony about the neighbourhood of Blewfields, to the southward of Cape Gracias á Dios; thinking, perhaps, that if they could establish themselves on a firm footing there, possession of the most important points of the Mosquito Shore might be finally obtained, so that in the event of the canal being opened at the Isthmus of Panama, to connect the Atlantic with the Pacific Ocean, they may derive some great national benefit by their increase of commerce. If the Belgians should establish themselves, and make friends with the natives, all will be well, but they have the same difficulties to contend with at first as the French had before them. The Americans have had for a considerable period many traders on the coast, and several of that enterprising people have settled on the shore. The main products of the country, and even much from the very interior, find their way to the American markets of Boston and New York. The sarsaparilla, the hides, the skins, the tortoise-shell, &c., of the Indians; and much cochineal, indigo, silver, hides, &c., from the Central American towns in the interior, are either bartered with the traders on the coast, or are conveyed to the sea ports, from whence the Yankee ships sail. The Yankees, in exchange for the numerous productions which they find ready for shipment on their arrival, bring cottons, linens, hardware, crockeryware, and miscellaneous articles of provision.

The people from the Caymans Islands, near Jamaica, build small schooners, and send them to fish for turtle at the Mosquito Keys, to the southward of the Cape Gracias á Dios; these turtle, when caught, are sold either at Belize or Jamaica, from which latter place they are shipped for England. The turtle caught on the Keys, off the Mosquito Shore, are considered the finest of all their species.

Altogether, from the very numerous productions of the country—from its admirable situation for trade—from the many parts on the coast and interior which are noted for healthfulness—from the great notice which has been taken of it by the European and other powers—from the immense gains to be reaped in an agricultural point of view—from the success which must accrue to those occupied in breeding cattle—from its proximity to the Isthmus of Panama, it may be fairly presumed that ere long some power will step in and possess itself of this valuable territory; but to no nation will it be so important, or produce such great results, as to the English, for the inhabitants are essentially English in their ideas, and have been so from the time of the Old English Buccaneers till now—loving and respecting the English, adopting their names, and believing themselves under their subjection. The Americans would also have no difficulties on this head to encounter, for, being the same in everything as the English—in features, form, and language—their occupation of the country would not, I am fully persuaded, meet with any opposition from the natives. Should the Americans at any time possess themselves of this shore, the English nation will see with regret what a valuable spot has been taken, and will reflect with sorrow upon the facilities that were offered them to settle thereon, and which in their supineness they suffered to be wrested from their grasp.

The French have now possession of Tahiti,* and the communication by the canal at Panama will bring that country six weeks, or so, nearer to them. The French, against the will of the inhabitants, and notwithstanding their fierce opposition, have possession of Algiers and the surrounding country. The English in India are continually striving to increase their territories, possessing themselves of cities and nations under some pretext or the other—deposing the reigning chiefs or sovereigns, to place creatures of their own in their stead. The thousands annually slain in India may be accounted for by the insatiable thirst which the English have for conquest; aggrandizing themselves at the expense of the native kings and inhabitants, and enriching themselves with the spoils of the dead—the despatches teeming with the glorious achievements of the British troops, who, with their accustomed gallantry, perform every duty, however hazardous or arduous, at the command of their leaders. Who can wonder that sometimes they fall victims to the rage of the infuriated savages? Witness the melancholy fate of the 44th regiment of foot in the defiles of Affghanistan, so ably described by Lieut. Vincent Eyrie, and so vividly portrayed by Lady Sale. No one can blame the officers and men, who are but as moving machines, who are only considered as "ciphers in the great account;" they do their duty, and pity it is that so many should fall by the rifles of the natives, and the malignity of the climate in which they are suffering such hardships and privations. Who can refrain from blaming any government which endeavours forcibly to possess itself of that to which it has no right, and against the will of the whole population, and without any pretext whatever for quarrelling. The death of the resident, Sir W. Macnaughten, by the fierce Abba Shah Khan, is lamentable, but why should a whole nation be destroyed for the insane fury of one man? Sir William, it is said, tried to overreach Abba Shah Khan, but was deceived, and on meeting was pistolled; and the war-cry raised, the destruction of the 44th quickly followed, and the Affghanistans rejoiced; eventually, however, our brave fellows became victorious, sacked and destroyed the city of Cabul, and were withdrawn. Thus ended the project of conquering Affghanistan.

The English, who are so willing to run every risk at such an immense distance from home, are forsooth very tender about taking possession of a most important country near at hand, which is in a measure offered for their acceptance, because they are fearful of exciting any jealousy amongst the other powers. France or America, when the time arrives, will not consult John Bull about the propriety of taking possession of this shore; and when a cry is made of illegality,

* Doubtful.

they can reply, "Ah, my very good friend, you take what you like—I take what I like."

In the year 1839, the Columbians falsely laid claim to part of the Mosquito Shore, as far north as Cape Gracias á Dios, and the commandant of San Andres issued a proclamation, commanding the inhabitants of Corn Islands and other places to pay no more taxes to the Imposter, as he was called, Robert Charles Frederick. This affair, however, was settled, I believe, by the late superintendant of Belize; but it is evident that the Columbians consider it a prize worth trying for. The noble and capacious harbour of Bocca del Toro is now in their possession; and, by ancient records, there is every reason to suppose that it was formerly annexed to the Mosquito Shore.

The Central American States some short time back endeavoured to open negotiations, to the effect that Cape Gracias á Dios might, to all intents and purposes, be considered a Central American port, except in the name, and they proposed to erect at each a fort and other buildings, and to make the Cape a regular depôt, that they might the more readily carry on their trade with Havanna, which at present they can only do at much loss of time and expense. This scheme was mooted in the various chambers of Leon, Segovia, Guatemala, &c., and was unanimously agreed to; but, notwithstanding the golden pill offered to King Robert Charles Frederick, in the shape of harbour-dues and customs, he refused the offer unconditionally. By the advice of his private secretary, Mr. Haly, a translation of the document sent by the chambers to him was sent to Belize, and another to England.

The name of the "Mosquito Shore" has, from a variety of causes, an unpleasant sound to English minds; in their vision, myriads of insects, snakes, alligators, and the other frightful objects generated in a tropical climate, present a picture of a total want of comfort; and, although many have said, "What's in a name?" I contend that the name of the Mosquito Shore conveys to the generality of readers nothing but extreme wretchedness and endless misery. It is not my intention to combat all the erroneous ideas entertained of this part of the world; suffice, it to say, that there are many better informed, who know that the horrid accounts of that coast, of its climate, and the multitude of its diságremens, are in the main untrue.

Some reviewers lately, when speaking of that place, have, indeed, broadly asserted, that it is nothing but a mass of howling wildernesses, dismal swamps, and putrid savannas; thus conveying a most disgusting picture of a land which deserves so much better. To rescue it, therefore, from some portion of unmerited opprobrium, I will commence by stating, that the term Mosquito (by some called Musquito, by others Moscheto) Shore, was first used by its discoverers not on account of the numbers of that troublesome little insect—although they are numerous enough, as in all other tropical countries—but by reason of the many shoals, sandbanks, keys, islets, &c., by which their approach to the mainland was interrupted; conveying an idea, as they were troubled by these impediments, of myriads of mosquitoes tormenting one; and it has ever since been denominated the Mosquito Shore.

From the southernmost part of the kingdom to Main Cape, beyond Cape Gracias á Dios, to the northward, the coast is generally flat, and the whole face of the country appears one evergreen mass of bush; on examination, however, many noble pine ridges, and dry and extensive savannas are found, on which tens of thousands of cattle could find subsistence; these, if tended by Spanish herdsmen, from the interior Central American towns, would increase wonderfully; feeding on the luxuriant herbage, they would give plenty of milk, but not near in the same proportion as English cows; this the Spaniards make into cheese (gueso), first abstracting the cream, to make what is called mantiquilla, butter.

Instead of exporting the cattle to the islands of Jamaica, &c., and to the ports of Belize, Omoa, &c., they could be slaughtered, the fat cut off, and the animal juices expressed, and made into cakes, after the method in vogue with the Germans. This will keep sweet and wholesome for years. By packing the cakes into small casks, a ready sale could be found in any quarter of the globe, at a much less price than others could supply it; for, the first price of a beeve not being more than from 3 to 5 dollars (12s. to 20s. sterling), and payable in goods, it may easily be conceived, that after the first outlay, what important results might be obtained from the savannas being public property, from the rapid increase of stock after the third year, and from the ready sale which the solid cakes of expressed animal juices, the hides, and the fat, would meet with.

From Main Cape, proceeding to the westward, the sea-coast, and the country inland for some distance, is of the same appearance as described to the southward. High land is observable about Caratasca; again, the Patook Hills, and then the high mountains of Black River (another inappropriate name), and high land can be seen in the interior from thence, and on some parts of the sea-coast, until the lofty and verdure-clad mountains of Truxillo are arrived at. In this space of country, at least 500 miles of sea-coast, there are many eligible situations for the enjoyment of health, as far as can reasonably be expected within the tropics, and free from those malignant fevers which cause such fearful havoc amongst the human race; there are, certainly, river fevers, and the country intermittent fever; the latter, although very debilitating in its effects, may be soon cured by change of air, attention to diet, and proper medicine.*

In this extent of country there are high lands and low lands, rich soil and poor soil, some places more fitted for agricultural purposes than others, some better adapted for trade, others again in which only cattle could be reared with success—as in all other countries, some

* I have known, and have heard from good authority, of numerous instances of Europeans having lived in the Mosquito Shore to a good old age. In Roberts' Narrative, published in 1826, a Mr. Boggs is mentioned, as being then an old man, and in 1841 he died, his only companion at the time being a young man of the name of Stonehewer, who, unassisted, dug a grave and buried him, and remained alone, a weary watcher, until some Poyais Indians came to the hut, and removed him from his loneliness.

situations are more eligible than others. In England, the marshes of Essex, the fenny parts of Lincolnshire, the hop-grounds of the low parts of Kent, are alike noted for agues and fevers; so again are many towns approximating to London, for instance Chalk, Milton, &c. If strangers locate in such places, and are exposed to the continual miasmata arising from moist lands, how soon they become attacked with fever and ague is well known. Then in Central America, if a man pitches his tent on the borders of a swamp, or in its vicinity, even if on high and dry land, the consequences of such an act of imprudence will soon be perceptible, and nothing but speedy flight to a more healthy locality will prevent him from being attacked with the chilling ague-fit and the hot fever-blast. In the Mosquito Shore, where, for ages, vegetable matter has been decomposing, and the sun prevented in many parts, by the interminable bush and tangled thickets, from drying-up the dankness of the earth, it behoves a man well to consider on the best means of preserving his health. If it be madness in England wilfully to run into danger, by any person predisposed to intermittent fever, to reside in agueish districts, so it would be worse madness for a man in the Mosquito Shore to erect his dwelling "where danger lurks in every blast;" a man's reason ought to prompt him to select a spot for his habitation on poor soil, such as sand, stone, or rock, not on the rich alluvial soil which, when disturbed, causes such debilitating effects upon the constitutions of Europeans. Plantations should be made on such ground, at some considerable distance from the habitation of man, and health would by these means be preserved.

The situations that are considered to be more healthy than others on the Mosquito Shore are, Blewfields, Branckman's Bluff, Cape Gracias á Dios, the island of Turgin, in Caratasca lagoon, Patook pine-ridge, Black River pine-ridge, and all the other dry pine-ridges throughout the country; the Poyais Mountains, at the top of Black River; the Carib settlements, on the sea-beach, to the westward of Black River, especially those at Little Rock, Sereboyer, and others adjacent thereto. The island of Turgin is considered one of the finest spots in the Mosquito Territory; standing, as it does, in the centre of the noble lagoon of Caratasca, and directly facing the points from whence comes the sweet sea-breeze, it must unquestionably be healthy. The island stands high, and is alternately savanna, and pine-ridge, and woodland. It is well suited for breeding cattle, and for raising provisions and such staples as might be thought best.

The island was granted by King Robert Charles Frederick, by a regular deed, to which I and several other Englishmen were witnesses, to an Englishwoman, for certain considerations—which were, washing, mending, and making the clothes for his children, and for his favourite wife.

Having reserved the island as a *bonne bouche,* and knowing its value, he generously gave it to the only Englishwoman at the time on the coast, for the kindness which she had shown to his children.

SPEECH OF SIR ROBERT PEEL ON THE BANK OF ENGLAND CHARTER.

Delivered in the House of Commons at Westminster, on Monday, May 6, 1844.

Mr. Speaker,—There are occasionally some questions of such vast and manifest importance, and which prefer such a claim, I should rather say such a demand on the attention of the house, that all rhetorical prefaces, dilating on the magnitude or enjoining the duty of patient consideration, are entirely superfluous and impertinent; I shall, therefore, proceed at once to call the attention of this committee to a matter which enters into every transaction of which money forms a part. There is no contract, public or private,—no engagement, national or individual, which is unaffected by it. The enterprises of commerce, the profits of trade, the arrangements to be made in all the domestic relations of society,—the wages of labour, the transactions of the highest amount and of the lowest, the payment of the national debt, the provision for the national expenditure on the one hand, and the command which the coin of the smallest denomination has over the necessaries of life on the other, are all affected by the decision to which we may come on that great question which I am about to submit to the consideration of the committee. Sir, the circumstances under which the duty imposed on me arises are shortly these:—In the year 1833, an act of parliament passed which continued to the Bank of England certain privileges until the year 1855, and after the year 1855 until parliament should determine to give one year's notice to the Bank of its determination to revise the charter. Before, however, the expiration of the full period of twenty-one years, before the arrival of that term of 1855, there was reserved to parliament the power, after the lapse of ten years, by notice to be given to the Bank, of revising the charter and reconsidering this whole subject. That period will arrive in August next. After August next it will be competent to this house, by notice given through the Speaker, to intimate to the Bank that within six months next following, this house will reconsider the charter of the Bank of England; but, that opportunity permitted to go by, the charter of the Bank, and all the privileges it confers, will endure necessarily until the year 1855. In the present state of this country—in the present state of the currency—after the inquiries which have been instituted, after the degree to which public attention has been called to this subject, the members of her Majesty's government feel it to be their duty to avail themselves of the opportunity thus given to them by law, and to submit their views to parliament on the subject. They are of opinion, that inquiry having been so extended that all the information which is essential to the formation of a satisfactory judgment has been collected, they should have been abandoning their duty if they had not undertaken maturely to consider this subject, and if they did not now come forward on their responsibility to submit to the consideration of parliament at once and without protracted inquiry, the measures which in their view it is desirable should be adopted.

Sir, I am perfectly satisfied that the members of this house, rising superior to all party considerations, and to all private interests, will consider it their duty to apply their deliberate and impartial consideration to this great subject. I have that confidence in the House of Commons, from past experience of their superiority to mere party views and personal interests where matters of such paramount importance come under consideration, that such will be the course they will pursue on this occasion. I ask you to-night for no decision. If I can, I would deprecate the delivery of any positive opinion. I ask you to listen to the proposals I shall make—to hear the evidence and arguments by which they shall be supported—to read and consider the resolutions which I shall move, only *pro formâ*; and, after having so deliberated maturely on the subject, to come to the discussion, and then pronounce your cool and impartial judgment upon it Sir, I am not shaken in the confidence I repose in the house by publications I have seen, inviting the attendance of members on this subject. I hold in my hand the resolutions adopted at a meeting of the general committee of private country bankers on the 17th of April last. I find that they resolved,—

"That the refusal of government to give information on the subject of their measure concerning banks and issue, naturally leads to the conclusion that it is their intention to propose some measure affecting country banks generally, and this meeting considers it most probable that it relates to the local circulation of the country."

They then resolved,—

"That under these circumstances it is most desirable that the banks of issue, whether private or joint-stock banks, should unite to oppose any alteration in the local circulation of the country, or in the conditions on which it is now allowed by law; and that the several joint-stock banks and banks of issue throughout the United Kingdom, be invited to co-operate with the private bankers in such opposition."

The third resolution is,—

"That all bankers be requested, as far as possible, to bring the question fully under the consideration of all members of parliament with whom they may be acquainted or connected, and endeavour to induce them to oppose any such alterations in the local circulation of the country."

Sir, I complain not of these resolutions. I complain not, at least, of the bankers inviting members of parliament to attend and consider this subject; but I do hope that members of parliament will resist the subsequent appeal, and that they will not come down here determined beforehand to oppose any alteration in the existing law, which may be proposed for their consideration. I ask you, after having maturely considered the great principles on which any alteration of the currency must proceed, are you so satisfied with the existing state of things—are you so convinced that it is utterly impossible in any particular to suggest any alteration, that you will come down here prepared, before hearing the discussion on the subject, to oppose an insuperable obstacle, by previous concert and understanding, to any alteration in the existing law? I know that to be impossible. I hold in my hand the evidence which should make it impossible that any such previous compact and understanding, if entered into, could be fulfilled.

ISSUE OF PROMISSORY NOTES.

My immediate proposition appears to relate to banking concerns, and in particular to the issue of promissory notes; but, considering that ten years have now elapsed since this subject was brought under consideration, I hope I shall be excused if I do not merely limit myself to the consideration of those principles which on a superficial view appear to determine the issue of promissory notes. I hope I shall be allowed to go deeper into the principles which govern this great question. I cannot discuss here the principles on which we should establish the engagement to pay a certain definite value unless we are agreed on the principle as to what constitutes the measure of value in this country. That is the foundation of the whole of this subject. It is impossible to raise any superstructure merely regarding paper credit and paper currency, unless we first consider the principles which determine the value of that of which paper is merely the representative; and it is impossible that we should come to a common agreement as to the issue of paper, unless we are agreed as to certain great principles relating to the measure of value and the medium of exchange. Now, sir, I very much fear that there is not that common agreement as to these other and greater principles to which I am alluding. I am afraid there is not an universal agreement as to what in this country is the standard and what actually constitutes the measure of value. Sir, I invite discussion on that first and preliminary question, the foundation of all others. What, I ask, is by the law and practice of this country the measure of value? What is that which determines all contracts? I will strip the question of all merely technical phrases. I want to consider it in a popular point of view. The denomination of value is a "pound." I won't talk of "measures of value;" I speak only of that with which you are in the every-day concerns of life perfectly familiar; and my first question is this,—What is a "pound?" and what is the engagement to pay a "pound?" Unless we are agreed on that, it is in vain you attempt to legislate on the subject. If a "pound" is a merely visionary theory, a fiction which does not exist either in law or in practice, in that case one class of measures relating to paper currency may be adopted; but if the word "pound," your common denomination of value, signifies something more than a mere visionary fiction—if a "pound" means a quantity of the precious metals of certain weight and certain fineness—if that be the definition of a pound," in that case another class of measures relating to paper currency will be requisite. Now, the whole foundation of my measure rests upon the assumption that according to practice, according to law, according to the ancient monetary policy of this country, the meaning of a "pound" is neither more nor less than a certain definite quantity of gold with a mark upon it to determine its weight and fineness, and that the engagement to pay a pound means nothing, and can mean nothing else, than the promise to pay to the holder on demand, when he demands it, a definite quantity of the precious metals. What is the meaning of the "pound" according to the ancient monetary policy of this country? The origin of the term was this: In the reign of William the Conqueror a pound of silver was the pound of account. The "pound" represented both the weight of metal and the denomination of money.* By subsequent debasements of the currency a great alteration was made, not in the name, but in the intrinsic value of the pound sterling, and it was not until a late period of the reign of Queen Elizabeth that silver, being then the standard of value, received that determinate weight which it retained without variation, with constant refusals to alter it, until the year 1716, when gold was practically substituted for silver, as the exclusive standard of value. The standard of silver, up to 1716, was fixed about 1567; but in 1717, the value of the guinea was determined to be 21s., and, for a certain period, both gold and silver constituted the standard of value. But in the year 1774 it was enacted that no legal contract should be discharged in silver for any sum of more than £25. That, therefore, made gold substantially the measure of value in the country, and it continued to be the measure of value legally and practically until 1797, when that fatal measure for restricting cash payments by the bank was passed, enabling parties to issue paper money at their discretion without being convertible into coin, which disturbed not only the speculations, but the theories and notions of men with respect to the standard of value.† From 1797 to 1810 public attention was not much directed to this important subject; but in 1810 men of sagacity observed that the exchanges had been for a considerable period unfavourable to this country—more unfavourable than could be accounted for by anything that could be called balance of trade or the monetary transactions of the country. A committee was appointed to inquire into the subject, and opinions then novel were stated—namely, that the "pound" meant, in fact, nothing else than a definite quantity of the precious metals, and that those who promised to pay a pound ought to pay that quantity. That theory was very much contested at the time. The House of Commons was not convinced by the arguments used in favour of it. The opinion of the public mind, that had prevailed since 1797 up to that period, (1810,) was, that this was a mere delusion, a visionary speculation; and that something else was signified by a "pound" other than a definite weight of the precious metals.

Those who contested the doctrines maintained by Mr. Horner, and others who agreed with him, were asked to specify what in their opinion was a "pound"—what the denomination of a pound sterling was; and I must say that they had the fairness to give their definition in sentences which, at least, enabled you to comprehend their meaning, although you could not comprehend the meaning of the thing signified. To show how men's minds had been confused and perverted from the truth, on which the light of demonstration has been shed, one has only to look to the definitions there given of a "pound sterling." I admire the gentlemen for having given their definitions — they adopted a more honest and straightforward course than those who in our day write interminable pamphlets on the currency, but never allow us to guess at their meaning. One writer said, that a "pound might be defined to be a sense of value in reference to currency as compared with commodity." Another writer, who pretended that he had exhausted his faculties in considering this subject, was dissatisfied with that definition, thinking the public had a right to something more definite and tangible, and that "a reference to currency as compared with commodity" was not very

* It was the ancient money integer in most parts of Europe, and was at first a pound-weight of silver, from which 20 shillings were coined, or 240 pence. Of Roman origin, it was introduced into Middle-Ages Europe by Charlemagne, who divided the *livre* (libra) into 20 sous, each sou again into 12 deniers. William the Conqueror brought the livre, or pound, to England, where it has ever since continued, although in some other countries a decimal monetary system is established.

† Upon the report of Sir Isaac Newton, "that gold was considerably over-rated in the mint with regard to silver."

obvious to enlightened minds. He said, "there is a standard and there is an unit which is the measure of value, and that unit is the interest of 33*l.* 6s. 8d. at 3 per cent, that being 1*l.*, and that being paid in a bank-note as money of account." The last definition which I shall quote from these three parties, writing without concert, and coming to their own determinations with respect to the standard of value, is this, "The standard is neither gold nor silver, but it is something set up in the imagination, to be regulated by public opinion."

REPORT OF THE BULLION COMMITTEE.

It was supposed at that time that the doctrines propounded by the Bullion Committee were the visionary speculations of theorists, and were unknown in the former monetary history of this country. But that is not the case. Refer to every writer of eminence before 1797—to Mr. Locke, to Sir W. Petty, to any one who wrote before 1797, and who had not been familiar with inconvertible paper currency, and you will find they arrive at precisely the same conclusions with the Bullion Committee. Take the opinion of Mr. Harris, an officer of the Mint, and a most eminent writer on the subject long before the Bank Restriction Act He said, "In all countries there is established a certain standard both as to weight and fineness of the several species of coins. In England a certain quantity of fine silver is appointed by law for a standard,"—he wrote when silver was the standard,—"all payments abroad are regulated by the course of exchange, and it is founded upon the intrinsic value, not on the mere names of the coin." Anticipating the discussions now going on in the world, this writer 150 years since laid down the true principle with respect to the measure of value, and he said, "Alter it if you please in your own dominions; you may break the public faith and curtail the long-established measure of property, but foreigners will make ample allowance for whatever you do, and that, however we may rob and cheat one another, they will secure themselves, and take advantage of our discredit by bringing the exchange against us."

In that simple statement, written 100 years since, lies, as I contend, the only true theory of the measure of value and the circumstances which govern it; and I wish I might now consider this as the elementary truth of established value; but it has been my duty, feeling the importance of this subject, to read as far as I can the different publications upon it, and I am perfectly convinced that there is not in the universal public mind of this country any general prevailing opinion what that is which constitutes the measure of value. I suppose that men give proof of their sincerity when they publish an octavo volume, and this (holding up a large volume) is a good specimen of the truth of what I say, as it is a most complete proof that with respect to those great truths which, as I said before, to many of us appear established upon some species of evidence as clearly as a proposition of Euclid, there is no general opinion, and that upon the subject of value there is no general concurrence. This book was published in Birmingham on the 25th of January, 1844, and more than one person, I presume, contributed to the publication of it. I wish to do justice to all parties, and I will say at once that I do not believe that in any other town than Birmingham this publication could have been produced; and I do not believe that it is in the power of any one man to write so much nonsense as is contained in it. It is the production of "Gemini," and I must state precisely as it is stated in the preface, that it is right to mention, that although some of the great principles brought forward are stated to be the principles of the Birmingham economists, yet they are by no means desirous that Birmingham alone should claim the honour of drawing public attention to our unjust monetary system; for the real fact is, that the same principles have been advanced in various parts of the United Kingdom. Well, then, what are the principles contended for by these gentlemen? First, they laugh at the notion of using as a standard now that which was used 300 years since. They say that the property of this country has increased—that the mercantile transactions of this country have increased—and to have that as a standard now which was used in the reign of Queen Elizabeth, although it has been adhered to ever since, shows a want of knowledge and illumination that is almost culpable. Now, there would be just as much sense in saying that we have increased in population, we have established railways, we have increased in wealth, and therefore, with all the advantages of our new position, we ought now to have sixteen inches to a foot. There is no more reason why a pound should not be bound by all transactions notwithstanding our increase in wealth,—there is, I say, no more reason why you should change a pound than to say a foot shall be a foot and a half. Then it is said—and this is repeated over and over again—and is one conclusive proof I have that he who says these things has no more conception of the truth with respect to the measure of value, than he has of any speculations in the most distant parts of the globe with which he is wholly unacquainted;—it is said, what a monstrous injustice and folly it is to tie down the Bank to issue gold at the old price of 3*l*. 17s. 10½d. an ounce. Now, what is the meaning of this? The only meaning of an ounce of gold for 3*l*. 17s. 10½d. is simply this—that it is the relation which silver bears to gold with respect to value. When you had a double standard, you said that a pound of gold should be coined, I think, into 44 guineas, and that a pound of silver should be coined into 62 shillings, and you made them each a legal tender; and if you will make the calculation, you will find that a pound of gold being coined into 44 guineas, and a pound of silver being coined into 62 shillings, the relation of gold to silver is about 152.13 to 1. What then is the meaning of now asking that the Bank should issue gold at the rate of 5*l*. an ounce? I perfectly understand you if you say that all those who have contracted debts or engagements shall be allowed to pay their debts in that way,—that is, 5*l*. being, in the payment of a debt, an equivalent to what 3*l*. 17s. 10½d. used to be; and if you mean to enact that, enact it simply—make that the discount from the debt. But, depend upon it, that if you attempt to say that one ounce of gold shall not represent 3*l*. 17s. 10½d. in silver, but 5*l*., silver and gold will be more powerful in your legislature, and you will find it utterly impossible to alter the relative value of silver and gold. As Mr. Harris said, make what regulations you will about the payment of your own debts, cheat and rob yourselves if you will, but you will still have the foreigner to contend with—he will not be bound by your legislature, nor will you yourselves. The alteration will only affect past contracts—it will not affect future contracts. The quantity of gold, the real value of coin, will determine all future contracts; they will be entirely governed by it. Raise the sovereign to 22s. or 23s., if you will, but it will not have any corresponding effect abroad. But, observe, I do not deny that that may produce matter for consideration. All contracts during the inconvertibility of paper having been made through a different medium of exchange, when you restore that convertibility, that subject may demand consideration. But I only want to convince you of what is now the complete measure of value. What are the prices in the bullion-market now? Silver is not a measure of value. You will find that in the bullion-market the ratio of gold to silver differs very little from that established in the reign of George I. I believe that new silver is about 5s. an ounce—and not 5s. 2d.; but that is the relation of gold to silver, and varies very little from what it has been.*

Those who contend that there ought to be a relaxation of the currency, think, and rightly, that an abundance of the precious metals, although it would not alter the ounce of silver with reference to gold, yet, by making gold more abundant, it would influence prices, and act in favour of the debtor. But I very much doubt, looking to the increased supply of gold from Russia and other places, whether or no, if it were desirable to attempt an alteration of the standard,—I very much doubt, I say, whether you would procure a relaxation of contracts by now adopting silver instead of gold.

THE BEST STANDARD.

The third objection is, that it is most unwise to take as your standard an article which serves not only for the purpose of coin, but which is also an article of

* In William the Third's reign, an extensive silver coinage was executed at several country mints, as well as at the London one. The principle on which it was based became a subject of controversy between Mr. Locke and Mr. Lowndes. The latter proposed to regulate the new coinage by the existing market-price of silver, although that price (exceeding its mint-price) arose from the deficiency in the weight of those coins by which silver and all other commodities were bought and sold. Mr. Locke perceived the error, and contended that if the coinage were executed at a higher rate than the standard of the 46th Elizabeth, or 5s. 2d. per ounce, it would be done at the expense of justice and integrity between the government and the people, and his honourable reasoning was adopted.

commerce.* Wise men write pamphlets to show that you have taken gold as coin, and to serve as a measure of value, but that that same gold is also as bullion an article of commerce, and likely therefore to be taken out of the country. Now, I maintain it is just because it is an article of commerce, and subject to the same laws as other articles of commerce, that it becomes fit to be taken as the standard, and our security as a measure of value—because precisely the same laws which regulate the import and possession of all other articles of commerce, regulate the import and possession by this country of bullion. Bullion is distributed according to certain laws which we cannot understand, and which we cannot control. The supply of bullion is regulated amongst the different countries of the world according to their several necessities. Each country, for reasons we cannot dive into, commands a sufficient supply; and I go further than most men on this subject—I say that coin and bullion, as articles of commerce, are regulated by precisely the same principles as those which regulate other articles of commerce. Some say, that when there is a deficient harvest and a demand for corn, all the coin will be sent out of the country, because there is no other article which at the time we can send in exchange for it. I say, there is no distinction now whatever between coin and bullion; but there is a preference, perhaps, for coin, and wisely, in my opinion, because there is a certain guarantee that it is of a certain weight and fineness; but, depend upon it, coin will never be sent out of the country for corn, unless it is more profitable to send out coin than anything else.

There is no reason why, because coin is of the usual value, that it should be sent out, unless it is sent out when it is dearer in all other countries than in this. The law that governs it is exactly the same as that which governs other articles of commerce, and it is proved by this—when there is a sudden demand for coin, if it is more profitable to send out woollen or cotton manufactures than to send out coin, then depend upon it they will be sent out; and if they are unprofitable, then coin and bullion, which are identically the same, will be sent out; but there is no reason why coin should be exported in exchange for foreign corn, other than such as regulates the export of any other article, namely, that it is profitable. These are in my opinion the great elementary truths which apply to the measure of value. If they can be contradicted, I want them to be contradicted in some clear and definite statement on the other side.

I have not bewildered you with talking about measures of value. I have taken a pound, and if you contest my description of a pound, and of the objection to pay a pound, if a man engages so to do, let me know what your defiinition of a pound is, and what you think a man who contracts to pay a pound contracts to pay. But I object to the obligation, which hon. gentlemen might impose upon me, of reading a pamphlet, or perhaps an octavo, stating what the definition of a pound is; but the real fact is, that although there are great elementary truths, yet occasionally there are small occurrences which appear to be contradictions of them—circumstances which, not well explained, will affect them; and ingenious writers take hold of these little circumstances, and say—"These do not conform to your great principles, and therefore your great principles are not true." Why, when Sir Isaac Newton deduced the truth of the planetary system, from the great principle of gravitation, there were some slight phenomena and disturbances which appeared to contradict his theory, and which he could not reconcile. But subsequent philosophers, on the ground which he had acquired from error, carrying their researches further still, reconciled all these phenomena and disturbances to the original great principle; and that which at first appeared to be a contradiction, turned out to be a confirmation of the elementary truths which Sir Isaac had discovered. And so it will be here. If you had every circumstance, everything tending to some apparent deviation, fully explained to you, depend upon it, you would find it possible to reconcile all with the great truths originally propounded. Now, if these principles are correct, it would be quite consistent with them, to establish some other measure of value than that which you have taken. You have taken a pound, and a certain quantity of gold; but you might, consistently with these principles, if you were now at liberty to decide for a new state of society, adopt

* It is, therefore, fluctuating in its value, and offers irresistible inducements to the melter, forger, clipper, and sweater.

silver instead of gold. You might, if you thought it desirable, adopt a standard of a new metal; you might abolish coin altogether, and adopt the principle contended for by Mr. Ricardo, viz., allow no bullion to be exchanged for notes, except in large quantities; that small notes should be issued for guineas and sovereigns, and when a man commanded £50 in notes, he might then, if he liked to take the trouble, demand bullion from the Bank. I say it is consistent with all of these great principles, to adopt the whole of these alterations; but, in my opinion, in our present position, nothing could be more unwise than to depart from the great principles which regulate the coinage of this country. I am not speaking of any particular measures; and I assume that seven-eighths of the gentlemen I now address, concur with me. I admit that you might select some other mode of establishing the same principle; but, before you depart from the present mode, I would entreat you to recollect the measure of value which you have—viz., gold, and that is the measure you have had practically for nearly one hundred years, always excepting the period of the *Bank restriction*.*

You should bear in mind, that all the great writers on the subject—Sir William Petty, Mr. Locke, Mr. Harris, and, last of all, the the Earl of Liverpool—were all decidedly in favour of a single standard of value. Mr. Locke was of opinion that silver ought to be the metal selected for the standard of the country. He said it was the money of account in the world, and had assigned reasons which, with all deference to that great authority, appear to me erroneous, why silver, instead of gold, should be taken as the standard of value; and, if you had a free choice between them, there is nothing which would not leave it perfectly open to you to select it. But, as your transactions for so long a period of time have been founded upon a single metal, and that metal gold, and you determined to have coin performing the functions of the lower orders of society throughout England and Wales, I do hope that nothing will induce this house to disturb the monetary arrangements in this respect. That which you have used, is in exact conformity with the opinions and views of the ablest writers on the subject, not prejudiced by exciting circumstances, but writing under a different state of things, and in conformity with the opinion of the greatest recent authority upon the regulation of coinage—I mean the first Earl of Liverpool, who, in his letter to the king, which, I think, contains as much truth and sound sense upon the subject as any publication that emanated from the press, strongly recommends that we should adopt as the principle of our coinage, the very principle which is now established. Lord Liverpool says—"After full consideration of this extensive, abstruse, and intricate subject, I humbly offer to your Majesty, as the result of my opinion,"—now this was in 1804, that is before silver had been made a merely representative coin—"first, that the coin of this realm, which is to be a principal measure of property, and the instrument of commerce, should be made of one metal; secondly, that in this kingdom, gold coin only has been for many years past, and is now, in the opinion of the people, the principal measure of property, and the instrument of commerce. It has been observed, that in a country like Great Britain, so distinguished for affluence and the extent of its commercial connections, gold coin is the best adapted to be the principal measure of property in this kingdom; and, accordingly, gold coin is now the standard coin, or, as it were, the sovereign archetype by which the value of all other coins is regulated, and by which the prices of all commodities bought and sold are adjusted. For these reasons, gold coins should be made as perfect, and kept as perfect as possible. And, thirdly, where the functions of the gold coin cease, there the functions of the silver coin should begin; and where the functions of the silver coin cease, there the functions of the copper coin should begin; and so far gold, silver, and copper, should be made a legal tender. But silver and copper should be subordinate and subservient, and merely representative coin, taking their value from the gold coin, according to the rate which the Sovereign sets upon it."

[To be continued.]

* A return to peace, unfavourable state of exchanges, bad harvest, and dread of invasion, caused so great a run upon the Bank, that, on the 25th of February, 1797, only £1,270,000 of treasure remained in its money-chests. An order in Council prohibited the directors from further payments in specie; and soon after was passed the Bank Restriction Act, exempting the directors from paying in cash, and authorizing an issue of £1 and £2 notes, in lieu of gold.

COLONIAL INTELLIGENCE.

India.—The Indian mail of the 1st of May does not contain any very remarkable intelligence. The dissatisfaction which prevailed, at the departure of the April mail, amongst the native troops, had ceased. The Supreme Government had, by the adoption of judicious, and at the same time severe measures, brought the Sepoys to a full sense of duty.

The Bengal regiments that have gone to Northern Scinde are likely to find employment, in consequence of a revolt brought about to the north of Shikarpore, by a chief named Bejee Khan, who, having placed himself at the head of some cavalry, attempted to plunder the country. There was to be a general assembly in May of the Beloochee chiefs at Hydrabad, when a conference was to take place between them and the Governor of Scinde. This measure is calculated to remove any dissatisfaction which may still have existed in that country.

The heats had set in there with great force, but the health of the troops did not appear to suffer. Kurrachee was improving fast, and buildings were rising around it. Regulations were adopted for levying 3½ per cent. duty on goods landed there.

Every effort is made by certain parties to irritate Sir C. Napier by criticism and censure. He is allowed to be a gallant soldier, but his acts as Governor and administrator are commented on by his opponents with acrimony. It is necessary to explain that fact, in order to place his character in a fair light before England. He has taken the command as Colonel of the 22d Regiment, and his address to the regiment on that occasion is worthy of both.

The news from the Punjaub represents that country in as disturbed a state as ever. Another member of the Dogra family has fallen the victim of his own nephew.

Lord Ellenborough had remained for some months at Calcutta, where he had organized various improvements. Among them may be specified, besides the abolition of the Madras transit duties, the organization of a military police, from which great benefit was expected.

Heera Singh is master at Lahore as long as the troops, who receive from him double the pay they used to receive from old Runjeet, will allow him. He is possessed of talents, but he is not a favourite with the old Siekh families, many of whom are intriguing against him. The only support he possesses is in the army, which is like the Prætorian band in other times.

The death of Sir William Casement, after nearly 50 years uninterrupted service in India, had produced a vacancy in the Council at Calcutta, which was filled up by the appointment of Mr. Millett. The cholera was ravaging the three Presidencies, but not to any great extent. The 11th and 42d Madras regiments had suffered severely.

Calcutta.—The most important item of intelligence from Calcutta is the account of the third opium sale of the season, which took place at Calcutta on the 15th of April. The total proceeds of the sale amount to 5,268,275 rupees, or over £500,000, leaving a clear profit to the Hon. Company of about £400,000 sterling.

Bombay.—From the 1st of January to the 31st of March, the imports of copper into Bombay have been 8,373 cwt; of iron, 52,970 cwt; lead, 2,361 cwt; steel, 2,988 cwt; spelter, 6,139 cwt; quicksilver, 16,200lb; tin plates, 1,156 boxes; coloured and printed goods, 61,185 pieces; gray and bleached cotton, 626,735 pieces; twist and thread, 914,735lb.; woollens, 7,225 pieces; beer, 1,364½ hhds; cochineal, 26,931lb; saffron, 1,140½lb; cotton, 32,727,705lb; coffee, 536,549lb; indigo, 70,079lb; pepper, 12,248 cwt; silk, 449,276lb; wool, 673,385lb; ivory, 215 cwt. The exports of copper from the 1st of January to the 31st of March were 8,287 cwt; iron, 52,179 cwt; lead, 2,756 cwt; steel, 3,162 cwt; spelter, 6,007 cwt; quicksilver, 9,386lb; tin plates, 363 boxes; coloured and printed goods, 369,650 pieces; gray and bleached cottons, 391,537 pieces; twist and thread, 802,937lb; woollens, 5,155 pieces; beer, 393 hhds., and 21,961 dozen; cochineal, 18,842lb; saffron, 604lb; coffee, 1,093,810 lb; indigo, 58,784lb; pepper, 11,325 cwt; silk, 275,675lb; wool, 910,432lb; and ivory, 2,089 cwt. The export of cotton from Bombay, from the 1st of January to the 31st of March, 1844, was, to China, 31,842 bales, and to Great Britain, 98,242 bales — together 130,084 bales. In the corresponding period of last year, the exports amounted to 103,857 bales — namely, to China, 26,699 bales, and to Great Britain, 77,188 bales.

China.—The news from China extends to the 10th of March, but contains nothing worth notice. A ship was seized with opium on board in the port of Shanghai, and sent down to Victoria, where she was subsequently liberated on payment of a fine of 500 dollars. This seizure appears to have been brought about by a British merchant, who compelled both the Chinese authorities and the British Consul to take official notice of the opium being on board. Several chests were thrown into the sea, and others injured. This step has brought the question of the treaty and of the opium smuggling into discussion. Commerce continued in a most depressed state in Canton, and raw cotton was particularly dull. There was an unusually large stock of cotton yarn, and a total absence of demand, with very large stocks on hand. The opium-market was dull. Excepting for Bengal qualities, the market was well supplied. The estimated total value of goods imported into China is stated at 25,000,000 dollars. The exports of tea to Great Britain in the month of February was, of black, 5,330,406lb., and of green, 2,423,629lb. Total in February, 7,775,042lb. The exports to Great Britain in eight months, from the 1st of July, 1843, to the 29th of February, 1844, in 66 vessels, was of black, 29,480,326lb., and of green, 5,766,453 lb. Total in eight months, 35,246,779. Robberies by night and by day are still of frequent occurrence, particularly in Hong-kong, where it is in contemplation to establish an efficient harbour police establishment. On the authority of private correspondents, it is said that two opium clippers had been seized by the Chinese officers. We observe, from a statement of the foreign trade with China, in respect to imports recently received from Canton, that the total estimated amount of legal trade averages annually 11,205,370 dollars; and the opium trade, at a rough estimate, 13,794,630 dollars, giving a total value of goods imported yearly into China, 25,000,000 dollars—yielding an estimated amount of duties under the new tariff of 456,275 taels.

His Excellency the Hon. C. Cushing, Envoy Extraordinary and Minister Plenipotentiary from the United States of America to the Court of Pekin, with his suite, arrived in Macao roads on Saturday last, the 24th inst., on board the United States' flagship Brandywine, Commodore Parker, His Excellency's suite consists of six gentlemen, Mr. F. Webster, Secretary of Legation, Mr. O'Donnel, Mr. M'Intosh, Dr. Kane, Mr. West, and Mr. Hernisz. And we understand that the Rev. E. C. Bridgman, D. D., and the Rev. P. Parker, have been appointed joint Chinese Secretaries to the Legation.

NEW SOUTH WALES. — From Sydney we have accounts to the 16th of February, and from Launceston to the 12th of December. There is nothing from either place of a commercial character worth communicating. The general statistics of New South Wales denote a rapid rate of advancement. Ten years ago the number of acres under crop was 60,520; last year it was 115,660; and this is stated to be only one-fifth of what is required for the present population. The number of sheep in the colony 15 years ago was 536,600; it is now 6,000,000, and Great Britain alone could take the produce of 20 times as many in common seasons. Of horned cattle, at the same period, the colony possessed 263,000; it has now 800,000. Seven years since, when its affairs were most flourishing, the coin in circulation amounted to 420,720*l.*; last year it was 475,390*l.* In 1832 its exports amounted to 384,344*l.* in official value; and in 1842 to 1,067,411*l.* The sheep now in New South Wales, it is estimated, according to the ratio of Great Britain, would supply food to about 3,200,000 inhabitants, and its cattle to 2,500,000. The proportion of imports per head, indicative of the substantial prosperity and comfort of the inhabitants in general, as compared with those of some other countries, is given as follows:—Russia, 8½*d.*; Prussia, 32*d.*; France, 11*d.*; United States of America, 17*s.*; British North America, 1*l.* 11*s.* 7*d.*; British West Indies, 3*l.* 12*s.*; New South Wales, 11*l.* 15*s.*! In contemplating these statements, we cannot but concur in the remark of the Sydney journalist, that the present embarrassments of the colony are "nothing but the natural and proper punishment of an extreme infatuation."

Extract of a letter, from Van Diemen's Land, dated Feb. 13th, 1844.—"Such is the fearful aspect of the Australian colonies, such the universality of bankruptcy, and such the prevailing panic, that confidence is at an end. Pressure is generally applied, and ruin entailed. Hundreds of men of high standing have gone, and hundreds more are sure to follow. A great portion of those who have their lands mortgaged must succumb. Highly improved land, which 18 months since would have realized 40*s.* per acre, now sells at 20*s.* Horses now sell at 15*l.* each, for which a year ago from 40 to 80 guineas were paid; sheep, 5*s.* per head; cows, some of which were imported into the colony, 50*s.* per head. There is a horrible fashion in the colony to push every unfortunate debtor through the Insolvent Court, which sacrifices the property, and causes much loss and expense to the creditors. A dividend of 5*s.* to 10*s.* in the pound might often be realized by time and forbearance, when by the process of the Insolvent Court, the result is from 1*s.* to 2*s.* 6*d.* in the pound; and yet I should think, that 49 out of every 50 are thrust through this court. The prosperity of this colony is destroyed for many years to come. Since the ridiculous convict probation system has been in force, its character is entirely changed. Armed ruffians traverse its length and breadth. The bond far out-number the free; life and property are daily becoming more insecure; and from being a quiet, tranquil home for industrious man, it is becoming the plague-spot of the south. Now, indeed, with great truth and honesty, may a virtuous people at home be warned against contact with the felon-deluged shores. The hopeless colonists begin to entertain the opinion that the British Government intend, by the large monthly importations of pollution, to drive them to despair. If things go on as they lately have done, I do not think that two years hence any one will be safe in the interior at noon-day. The felons are allowed to choose their own masters, bargain for their own wages, and quit their service in a month, the Crown maintaining them when their caprice leads them to quit a master.

New Zealand.—The latest intelligence from New Zealand advised the safe landing of the new Governor, Captain Fitzroy, who had gone a tour of inspection through the Bay of Islands.

Africa.—Cape of Good Hope papers to the 16th of April have come to hand. Sir P. Maitland, the new Governor, contemplated some revisions in the laws of the colony, which appeared to give very general satisfaction. News from Natal to the 5th had been received at Graham's-town; according to which the Boers seem not altogether to relish English supremacy, and it was rumoured that several intended again to retire beyond the bounds of our sovereignty.

The following statistics relative to the wool-trade of the Cape of Good Hope, from the year 1836 to 1843, show the improvement that has been made in the cultivation of the staple, and the rapid increase in exports during the last two years:—

	lb.	lb.
1836.		
Table-bay, from January 5th, 1836, to January 5th, 1837	256,625	
Algoa-bay	116,674	
1837		373,299
Table-bay	227,833	
Algoa-bay	123,990	
1838		351,823
Table-bay	276,246	
Algoa-bay	204,481	
1839		580,727
Table-bay	378,839	
Algoa-bay	208,338	
		587,177
1840		
Table-bay	509,597	
Algoa-bay	401,521	
1841		911,118
Table-bay	536,979	
Algoa-bay	479,828	
1842		1,016,807
Table-bay	522,262	
Algoa bay	811,986	
Port Beaufort	101,901	
		1,436,149
1843		
Table-bay	352,767	
Algoa-bay	1,220,380	
Port Beaufort	181,610	
		1,754,757

West Indies.—Papers from Jamaica to the 9th of May, and from the other islands to corresponding dates, bring intelligence that plenteous rains had fallen, and though for a while stopping the manufacture of sugar, the young canes had greatly revived, and the aspect of the plantations was much improved. After so long a draught, the abundance of water was hailed as seasonable; and notwithstanding in Trinidad and Tobago regret is expressed that it has impeded the progress of the mills, there appears to be in all other places no fear that this delay will be of serious importance. The rains had been very general. The exports of sugar from Trinidad for the first four months of the present year had increased 2,000 hhds., compared with the same period last year. Cocoa had doubled, and coffee trebled, previous exports—a satisfactory symptom of the improvement of the affairs of this island. From Barbadoes the shipment of sugar for the first four months of the year had decreased by 2,400 hhds., but nevertheless a full average crop was expected, the estimate being that it would reach 25,000 hhds.

The advices from Demerara state that a loan act for immigration purposes had been hurried through the Legislature, the sum sought to be raised being £500,000, at the rate of 5 per cent. interest. However, as the sanction of Her Majesty must be obtained before it can become law, the *Guiana Times* says, "it is not too late for representation to be made on the subject to the Home Government."—The rate of 5 per cent. in the present plethora of capital in the London markets is urged by the opponents of the measure as an extravagant remuneration for the employment of the money, especially when the loan will, should it receive the sanction of the British Parliament, be, to a certain extent, under the guarantee of this Government. The plan is to raise £100,000 a year for five successive years; and a commission, if the measure is carried out, will be sent to London to administer the affairs connected with it. Emigration from Sierra Leone had proved a perfect failure, which is said to be the cause of the speedy passage of this loan act.

The following returns exhibit the income, expenditure, and debt, for the years 1841 and 1842, for each of the British West India colonies:—Of Jamaica, the incomes in 1841 and 1842 amounted respectively to 261,183*l.* and 321,945*l.*, whilst the expenditure was respectively 276,053*l.* and 303,195*l.* The debts due by the island at Michaelmas, 1841 and 1842, amounted respectively to 546,267*l.* and 613,297*l.* Of Barbadoes, the incomes of 1841 and 1842 were respectively 68,743*l.* and 73,023*l.*; and the concurrent expenditure 58,419*l.* and 55,503*l.*; the debt of 25,000*l.* due to Great Britain has been all paid off. Of Tobago, the revenue in 1842 amounted to 6,720*l.*, and the expenditure to 6,703*l.*; there were no debts due. Of Grenada, the incomes in 1841 and 1842 amounted respectively to 17,417*l.* and 15,933*l.*, and the expenditure to 12,656*l.* and 12,643*l.* Of St. Lucia, the revenue in 1842 amounted to 11,694*l.*, and the expenditure to 11,409*l.* Of St. Vincent, the revenue in 1842 amounted to 13,892*l.*, and the expenditure to 12,236*l.* Of Antigua, the revenue of 1842 was 17,083*l.*, and the expenditure 15,880*l.* Of Montserrat, the net revenue in 1842 was 1,871*l.*, and the total expenditure 2,244*l.* Of St. Christopher, the income in 1842 was 6,933*l.*, and the expenditure about 6,974*l.* Of Nevis, the income amounted to 8,834*l.*, and the expenditure 8,678*l.* Of the Virgin Islands, the income in 1842 was 2,332*l.*, and the expenditure 2,440*l.* Of Dominica, the income in 1842 was 8.504*l.*, and the expenditure 7,880*l.* Of British Guiana, the income of 1842 amounted to 243,895*l.*, against 163,579*l.* in 1841, whilst the expenditure amounted to 237,759*l.*, against 198,233*l.* in 1841. Of Trinidad, the income in 1842 was 109,545*l.*, and the expenditure 171,674*l.* Of the Bahamas, the income in 1842 was 21,943*l.*, and the expenditure 23,570*l.* It further appears, with respect to other colonies in other parts of the globe, that the income of the Mauritius in 1842 amounted to 255,209*l.*, and expenditure to 188,848*l.*

Canada.—The *Quebec Mercury*, without mentioning upon what authority, states it has learned that the Governor-General has formed a new Cabinet, and that the nominations shall be made public before his Excellency's departure from Kingston. The *Mercury* adds, that it is reported the Hon. Mr. Morris is to be Receiver-General, the Hon. H. Sherwood Solicitor-General, and that the Hon. S. B. Harrison is not to be Inspector-General.

The Provincial Parliament is convoked to meet in Montreal on the 24th of June.

Serious disturbances have recently taken place on the Lachine Canal, in Canada East. Mr. Secar, foreman, was shot at by a man who had been discharged from the works, and his left arm so shattered by a ball that amputation was performed.

An official paper announces, that at the instance of the American Minister in Great Britain, the British Government has pardoned ten of the American citizens sent to Van Diemen's Land for sharing in the Canadian rebellion in 1838, and that orders have been despatched accordingly. Their names are—Hiram Sharp, John Gillman, Ira Polly, Orrin W. Smith, Bemis Woodbury, George T. Brown, Daniel Liskum, Robert Q. Collins, John Thomas, and Edward A. Wilson.

Newfoundland.—According to advices received, the Newfoundland seal fishery this spring is considered a failure, the take reported being but 370,000, against that of last year, which was 700,000. The report from Peterhead contains nothing later from the Greenland Seas than was given last week, but adds the remark, that in 1842—the greatest year for success at the seal fishery ever known—30 foreigners arrived with 111,970 seals, and 14 English with 20,570. This season the number of vessels is much increased, but the quantity of seals already known to be got by the British ships up to the latter end of April, when the run was over, may be estimated to be about 44,000, and the foreign vessels 26,400.

Nova Scotia.—From a letter which has appeared in *The Times*, we find that Lord Falkland, the Lieutenant-Governor, is combating, although in a more limited sphere, for the same principles as Sir C. Metcalfe, the governor-general of Canada. It appears, that until last December his Lordship's Executive Council was composed partly of responsible-government men, and partly of Conservatives, when he appointed a Mr. Allmon a member of it. The responsible-government men immediately withdrew from it, avowedly in consequence of this gentleman's appointment; at the same time explicitly admitting, that until then Lord Falkland had conducted the government to their entire satisfaction. Since that period they have steadily refused to return unless Mr. Allmon retires, and in this they are supported in a house consisting of 51 members by a minority which, counting themselves, number 23.

It requires, therefore, a change of two or three members only, to place the Executive in a minority, and then the Home Government will be compelled to interpose its authority.

To those who are even but slightly acquainted with the political institutions and party interests of that colony, it will be apparent that Sir C. Metcalfe and Lord Falkland are embarked in the same contest. Lafontaine and Co. demand that the Governor-General shall make no appointment without their advice, or inconsistent with their interest; Howe and Co. insist that the highest offices in the gift of the Sovereign shall be such as they shall not disapprove, *i. e.* their nominees. To effect the object in Canada, Lafontaine and Co. resign, and refuse to return except on their own terms; Howe and Co. in like manner in Nova Scotia seek to coerce the Queen's representative in the free exercise of Her Majesty's prerogative, by a determined and factious opposition, and by a similar refusal. These worthies actually protracted the reply to the Lieutenant-Governor's speech at the opening of the last session, a business which had never before occupied more than 24 hours, until 14 days had elapsed, and this by interminable harangues.

HOME INTELLIGENCE.

Sir Henry Hardinge.—On Friday, May 31st, a Court of Directors was held at the East India House, when Lieutenant-General the Right Hon. Sir Henry Hardinge, K.C.B., Governor-General of India, was unanimously appointed to succeed to the office of Commander-in-Chief of the Company's Forces in India, in the event of the death, resignation, or coming away from India, of General Sir Hugh Gough, G.C.B. His Excellency left London on the 5th of June, to assume the functions of his high and important office.

The Chinese Ransom.—On Wednesday morning, June 19th, Her Majesty's ship Wanderer, Commander G. H. Seymour, arrived at Portsmouth from the East Indies. She has brought home another instalment of the Chinese ransom, consisting of 1,000,000 dollars in sycee silver, which is contained in 250 boxes, each box containing 2,800 taels. It was received on board the Wanderer at Penang, on the 19th of February last, from Her Majesty's ship Dido, the Hon. Captain Keppel commander. On Thursday the Wanderer went into port to be paid off, and the money was immediately transferred to the Royal Mint, London.

Isle of Man.—From a return just printed, we find that in the year 1843, there were imported into the Isle of Man from Great Britain and Ireland alone, 2,984 quarters of wheat, 12,658 cwt. of flour, 1,672 cwt. of meal, 434 quarters of oats, 227 cwt. of potatoes, 16 head of cattle, 1,120 sheep, and 6 pigs. Nothing was imported from foreign countries, as far as the above-mentioned articles were concerned. During the same year there were exported from the Isle of Man to the United Kingdom, 7,582 quarters of wheat, 22 cwt. of flour, 127 cwt. of meal, 5,015 quarters of barley, 1,370 quarters of oats, 117,779 cwt. of potatoes, 307 cattle, 180 sheep, and 308 pigs. The average prices of the several species of corn, in 1843, were as follows, viz., wheat, 50s. 1d.; barley, 29s. 6d.; and oats, 18s. 4d; the average rate of duty paid on foreign wheat in the United Kingdom having been simultaneously, on wheat, 14s. 3d.; on barley, 6s. 11d.; and on oats, 6s. 2d.

Shipping.—Some valuable statistical returns of sailing-vessels registered at each port of the United Kingdom (including the Isle of Man, &c.) in the year 1843; of vessels entered and cleared coastwise in 1843; of the number and tonnage of vessels registered at each of the ports of the colonies; and of vessels built, registered, sold, wrecked, and broken up, during the same period, have been laid before the House of Commons, and from which we quote the following:—In England alone, the gross total number of sailing-vessels under 50 tons registered at various ports on the 31st of December, 1843, amounted to 6,155, measuring altogether 185,832 tons. The number of sailing-vessels above 50 tons so registered on the 31st of December last amounted to 10,672, measuring altogether 2,019,414 tons. The total number of steam-vessels registered under 50 tons was 337—tonnage, 8,119; and the total number registered above 50 tons amounted to 309—tonnage, 63,923. In Scotland, the gross total number of sailing-vessels registered amounted to 3,549 (of which 1,215 were above 50 tons), and the total number of steam-vessels 138, of which 97 were above 50 tons' measurement. The gross total tonnage (including vessels of all sorts) amounted to 481,670. In Ireland, the number of sailing-vessels registered amounted altogether to 1,921 (of which more than half were above 50 tons); and the number of steamers, 81 (of which 76 were above 50 tons). The gross total amount of tonnage was 198,469. The gross total number of sailing-vessels that entered inwards coastwise in 1843, amounted, in England, to 98,295; in Scotland, to 19,053; and in Ireland, to 16,476. The total number cleared outwards during the same period being, respectively, 108,105, 19,788, and 9,979. The total number of steam-vessels entered inwards, coastwise, amounted, in England, to 9,294; in Scotland, to 2,688; and in Ireland, to 2,651. The number of steamers cleared outwards was, in England, 8,992; in Scotland, 2,311; and in Ireland, 2,989. The gross total tonnage of all the vessels so entered inwards, coastwise, in 1843, at the various ports throughout the United Kingdom amounted to 12,532,307; and the gross total tonnage of all the vessels cleared outwards, coastwise, during the same period, to 12,571,031, exhibiting the very slight difference between the measurement of the inward and outward sailing-vessels, of only 38,724 tons. Respecting the colonial, it appears that the total number of British sailing-vessels which entered inwards for the colonies at various ports of the United Kingdom during the year 1843 (including the repeated voyages) amounted to 6,404, whose tonnage was altogether 1,405,054; and that the total number cleared outwards was 6,264, whose tonnage amounted to 1,427,233. The total number of foreign vessels entered inwards, and cleared outwards, only amounted to 45 and 36, respectively. The total number of steamers entered inwards from our colonies in 1843 was 344; tonnage, 72,477; and the total number cleared outwards for the colonies, 357; tonnage, 80,185. The total number of British sailing-vessels entered inwards from foreign ports at all the ports of the United Kingdom and the Channel islands, (including their repeated voyages) amounted to 11,263, tonnage, 1,737,210; and the total number of British vessels cleared outwards for foreign ports during the same period amounted to 11,228, tonnage, 1,791,755; the total number of foreign vessels simultaneously entered inwards and cleared outwards having been respectively 8,259 and 7,375. The uumber of British steamers so entered inwards and cleared outwards was respectively 2,439 and 2,314; and the number of foreign steamers respectively, 533 and 548. The number of sailing-vessels built and registered in 1843 in the ports of the United Kingdom amounted to 653, tonnage, 77,034; and the number of steamers, 45, tonnage 83,097. The total number of vessels wrecked, sold, and broken up in the same year, amounted to 778, tonnage 132,732.

The Exchequer.—An account has been published, by order of the House of Commons, of all monies received during the year ended April 5th, 1844, to the account of Her Majesty's Exchequer at the Bank of England and of Ireland; the amount of all Royal orders and Treasury warrants received; and of the credits and transfers made by the Controller-General of the Exchequer, the payments by the Bank of England, and the balance remaining to the account of the Exchequer at each bank on the 5th day of April, 844 (Good Friday), per act of 4th William IV., cap. 15. It appears, from the paper thus prepared by the clerks of the Exchequer offices, that the total receipfs during the past year, 1843, amounted to the sum of 77,024,004*l.*; that there remained a balance of income in the Bank of England on Good Friday last amounting to 1,679,578*l.*, and one in the Bank of Ireland amounting to 633,671*l.*; making altogether a gross sum total amounting to 79,337,254*l.* The balance of credits at the Bank of England on the 5th of April, 1843, amounted to 656,878*l.*, and on the 5th of April, 1844, to 601,264*l.* The total payments made by the Bank of England during the past year amounted altogether to the sum of 73,279,673*l.*

Customs' Duties.—An account of the gross and net receipts of the Customs' duties collected at each custom-house of the United Kingdom during the year ending the 5th of January, 1844, as compared with similar receipts during the previous year, has been printed in the shape of a Parliamentary paper. We find that the total amount of the gross receipts collected in the port of London was, in 1843, 11,354,702*l.*, against 11,422,251*l.*, collected in 1842. The total amount of the net receipts of the same port was in 1843, 10,784,959*l.*, and in the preceding year, 10,836,025*l.* No grand total is given of the receipts throughout the kingdom, but only the total amount collected at each port; and hence it would require several long and toilsome additions in order to arrive at a general result. It is known, however, that the gross total receipts arising from our customs' duties amount to between 22,000,000*l.* and 23,000,000*l.* annually, of which London alone contributes a proportion of 50 per cent.

Promissory Notes and Bullion.—From a return respecting promissory notes and bullion, it appears that the gross total amount of the promissory notes in circulation throughout the United Kingdom was, during the month ending the 6th of January, 1844, altogether 35,774,259*l.*; the bullion in the coffers of the Bank of England being at that period 14,638,000*l.* During the month ending the 3d of February, 1844, the amount of promissory notes in circulation was 39,056,539*l.*, and the amount of bullion in the Bank vaults, 15,480,000*l.* During the month ending the 2d of March, 1844, the promissory notes amounted to 38,612,587*l.*, and the bullion in the Bank to 16,011,000*l.*; and during the month ended the 30th of March last, the total amount of promissory notes in circulation throughout Great Britain and Ireland was 37,935,893*l.*, there remaining at that period 16,322,000*l.* in the form of bullion in the coffers of the Bank of England.

STATISTICS OF NEW SOUTH WALES.

AGRICULTURE—POPULATION.

Return showing the Quantity of Land in Cultivation, (exclusive of Gardens and Orchards,) and the Population of the Colony of New South Wales (including the district of Port Phillip), from the year 1833 to 1842 inclusive.

YEAR,	AGRICULTURE.																			POPULATION.			
	CROPS.										PRODUCE.									ADULTS.			
	Acres Wheat.	Acres Maize.	Acres Barley.	Acres Oats.	Acres Rye.	Acres Millet.	Acres Potatoes.	Acres Tobacco.	Acres Sown Grasses and Oats.	Total Number of Acres in Crop.	Bushels Wheat.	Bushels Maize.	Bushels Barley.	Bushels Oats.	Bushels Rye.	Bushels Millet.	Tons Potatoes.	Cwt. Tobacco.	Tons Hay.	Male.	Female.	Children.	TOTAL.
1833	36679	14125	3603	2078	668	40	907	396	2024	60520	559225	338375	48738	12667	9599	..	1440	2733	1981	39387	11220	10187	60794
1834	48667	16482	3195	2719	700	51	960	182	1855	74811	780700	357601	59731	37182	10840	760	1050	1599	4481	42008	12065	12139	66212
1835	47051	20831	2903	2278	599	59	1081	331	4133	79256	526266	503314	47249	13155	7461	727	1336	2146	2315	45259	12647	13686	71592
1836	51616	17503	3062	4276	720	14	977	461	8803	87432	884244	390132	62057	23412	10818	18	1870	4145	14853	48375	14550	14171	77096
1837	59975	18381	2551	3893	493	80	1165	533	5054	92125	692620	632155	51447	17119	6753	695	2102	2034	5627	52099	15918	17250	85267
1838	48060	25043	2922	3767	429	39	1783	925	9939	92912	469140	556268	32103	13416	4878	353	3496	4952	6960	57485	18000	22427	97912
1839	48401	22026	3490	6793	483	46	1115	424	12534	95312	805140	525507	66033	27788	7008	283	2601	2509	25923	63784	21998	28604	114386
1840	74133	24966	5144	5453	609	115	2594	381	12721	126116	1116814	777947	105389	66020	8863	3338	11050	4300	21329	70021	25476	33966	129463
1841	58605	25004	5423	5892	495	47	4027	380	15257	115130	832776	503803	90172	62704	5507	1072	11141	2642	17175	75474	33546	40649	149669
1842	57533	26192	4817	4235	473	99	4768	223	17320	115660	746228	559719	82624	81311	4402	1201	11676	2010	16676	76528	35762	47599	159889

Colonial Secretary's Office,
Sydney, 1st June, 1843.

E. DEAS THOMSON,
Colonial Secretary.

Note.—This Return does not include the Crops and Produce beyond the boundaries of location.

NEW SOUTH WALES.

EXPORTS.

RETURN of the VALUE of EXPORTS from the Colony of New South Wales, (including the District of Port Phillip,) from the Year 1826 to 1842, inclusive.

Year.	To Great Britain.	To British Colonies.		To South Sea Islands.	To Fisheries	To United States.	To Foreign States.	TOTAL.
		New Zealand.	Elsewhere.					
	£	£	£	£	£	£	£	£
1826	101,314	......	1,735	.....	......	....	3,551	106,600
1827	70,507	......	4,926	......	......	....	881	76,314
1828	84,008	......	4,845	......	......	....	1,197	90,050
1829	146,283	......	12,692	......	......	....	2,741	161,716
1830	120,559	......	15,597	......	......	....	23,503	159,659
1831	211,138	......	60,354	......	......	....	52,676	324,168
1832	252,106	......	63,934	......	......	....	68,304	384,344
1833	269,508	......	67,344	......	......	....	57,949	394,801
1834	400,738	.....	128,211	......	......	....	58,691	587,640
1835	496,345	39,984	83,108	2,696	38,445	18,594	3,011	682,193
1836	513,976	36,184	136,596	9,628	35,918	13,697	2,625	748,624
1837	518,951	39,528	118,447	485	54,434	10,617	17,592	760,054
1838	583,151	46,924	113,716	7,137	33,988	11,324	6,525	802,768
1839	597,100	95,173	194,684	1,347	34,729	18,568	7,175	948,776
1840	792 494	215,486	304,724	6,621	27,864	27,885	24,618	1,399,692
1841	706,336	114,980	123,968	13,144	18,417	4,837	41,715	1,023,397
1842	685,705	131,784	166,239	3,005	22,862	17,101	40,715	1,067,411

NOTE.—From 1826 to 1834, the value of exports to South Sea Islands, New Zealand, &c., is included with that of "Foreign States."

IMPORTS.

RETURN of the VALUE of IMPORTS into the Colony of New South Wales (including the District of Port Phillip), from the Year 1826 to 1842, inclusive.

Year.	From Great Britain.	From British Colonies		From South Sea Islands.	From Fisheries.	From United States.	From Foreign States.	TOTAL.
		New Zealand.	Elsewhere					
	£	£	£	£	£	£	£	£
1826	280,000	......	30,000	......	......	......	50,000	360,000
1827	253,975	......	63,220	......	......	......	45,129	362,324
1828	399,892	......	125,862	......	......	......	44,246	570,000
1829	423,463	......	135,486	......	......	......	42,055	601,004
1830	268,935	......	60,356	......	......	......	91,189	420,480
1831	241,989	......	68,804	......	......	......	179,359	490,152
1832	409,344	......	47,895	......	......	......	147,381	604,620
1833	434,220	......	61,662	......	......	......	218,090	713,972
1834	669,663	......	124,570	.....	......	......	197,757	991,990
1835	707,133	35,542	144,824	1,420	141,823	13,902	70,161	1,114,805
1836	794,422	32,155	220,254	1,972	103,575	22,739	62,289	1,237,406
1837	807,264	42,886	257,427	1,764	80,441	9,777	97,932	1,297,491
1838	1,102,127	53,943	255,975	5,548	71,506	8,066	82,112	1,579,277
1839	1,251,969	71,709	504,828	3,863	186,212	23,093	194,697	2,236,371
1840	2,200,305	54,192	376,954	1,348	104,895	24,164	252,331	3,014,189
1841	1,837,369	45,659	286,637	24,361	87,809	35,282	200,871	2,527,988
1842	854,774	37,246	260,955	10,020	64,999	20,117	206,948	1,455,059

NOTE.—From 1826 to 1834, the value of imports from the South Sea Islands, New Zealand, &c., is included with that of "Foreign States,"

Colonial Secretary's Office,
Sydney, 1st June, 1843.

E. DEAS THOMPSON,
Colonial Secretary.

OBITUARY.

Baker, Mary Anne, the beloved wife of W. F. Baker, Esq., Royal Navy, January 29, at Bronti Bungonia, New South Wales.

Barclay, Rev. Patrick, late minister of the parish of Sandsling, Shetland, on 12th June, at Maida-cottage, Elgin, North Britain, aged 86.

Barron, Lieutenant-Colonel Thomas, of the Hon. East India Company's service, Bengal establishment, May 25, at Cheltenham.

Bernard, Lady Catherine, relict of the late Col. Bernard, of Castle Bernard, in the King's county, Ireland, in London, in the 51st year of her age,

Berwick, Captain T., 3d West India Regiment, June 4, at Portsmouth, on his return from the river Gambia.

Brown, Lieutenant-Colonel Joseph, late of the Bombay army, June 4, at Kensington Gore, London.

Campbell, Thomas, Esq., author of "The Pleasures of Hope," and other poems, June.

Campbell, James Drummond, Esq., Assistant-Surgeon in the Hon. East India Company's Service, April 29, at Bombay, aged 27.

Casement, the Hon. Major-General Sir William, K.C.B., Member in Council, April 16, at Cossipore, East Indies. In the field he was a brave and gallant soldier, in council patient, dispassionate, and sagacious, and in private life his many virtues secured him the esteem and affection of all who knew him. For 47 years he served his country with fidelity, and at length fell a victim to his honourable zeal and strong sense of duty. At the request of Lord Ellenborough and the Council he continued to discharge the duties of his office in a time of difficulty and danger (though he had previously taken his passage, and was about to return home), and in the arduous labours of office fell a victim to cholera, in his 64th year. In thus yielding up his life he made a sacrifice to duty, which, while it deprives his family of a protector and friend, affords to the service a bright example to admire and imitate.

Codd, Captain Augustus Frederick, of Her Majesty's 63d Regiment, March 24, at Madras, in his 29th year.

Collard, Captain Thomas, late of the 81st Regiment, and Adjutant of the South Hants Militia, May 29.

Cooke, Francis, Esq., late of the Hon. East India Company's Service, June 18, London.

Delafosse, Robert, M.D., ensign of the 26th Bombay Native Infantry, third son of the Rev. D. C. Delafosse, rector of Shere Surrey, April 29, at Bombay.

Drayner, Captain James, of the ship Carnatic, of London, April 22, at Madras.

Flintoft, George, Esq., Paymaster and Purser in the Royal Navy, June, 15, in Helmsley Blackmoor, Yorkshire.

Franks, Mr. Robert Hugh, March 28, at the Cape of Good Hope, aged 48.

Frederick, Lieutenant-Colonel Thomas, May 28, at Holybourne Alton, aged 80.

Foster, Ann, the widow of Charles William Hyatt Foster, Esq., late of the Admiralty-office, Somerset-house, on 22d June, at her residence, Bayham Cottage, Camden-town, aged 64.

Frederick, Lieutenant-Colonel, of Corsham, Wilts, June 4, at Dalston, aged 70.

Glenlyon, the Dowager Lady, on 21st June, at Dunkeld.

Hodgkinson, George Foley, Esq., late of Calcutta, on the 23rd June, at Aberdeen-place, Maida hill, aged 36.

Manley, Barbara, Baroness de, June 5, at London. Her Ladyship was the only child of Anthony, fifth Earl of Shaftesbury, by Barbara, only daughter of Sir John Webb, of Canford, in the county of Dorset, and married, in 1814, the Hon. William F. S. Ponsonby, third son of Frederick, Earl of Besborough, created a Peer at the coronation of Her Majesty.

Mead, George, Esq., late Superintending Surgeon in the Hon. East India Company's Service, at the island of St. Helena, on 31st of May, in the Borough of Southwark, London, aged 78.

Ostle, Captain William, on 2d June, at Commercial road, Stepney.

Outlaw, Lieutenant T. F. V., of the Madras Sappers and Miners, on the 26th March, at Bombay.

Pemberton, Caroline, the wife of the Rev. Dr. Pemberton, vicar of Wandsworth, Surrey, and niece of the late Randle Jackson, Esq., of Fir-grove, Brixton, on 21st June.

Presgrave, Susanna, widow of the late Colonel Duncan Presgrave, of the Hon. East India Company's Service, on 9th June, at the hotel de France, Brussels.

Tait, John Fleming, Esq., one of the Government Surveyors for the Island of Ceylon, on the 8th May, at Malta, on his returning to England.

Tattersall, Sibylla Jane, the beloved and lamented wife of G B. Tattersall, Esq., of her Majesty's Ceylon Rifle Regiment; on 19th of June, at 18 Chester-terrace, Eaton-square.

Thompson, Vice-Admiral Norbone, on the 28th at London, in his 75th year.

Thornhill, John Bensley, Esq., of the East India Company's Civil Service, on 15th April, at Calcutta, in his 36th year.

Turner, Captain Jellicoe, Royal Navy, fourth son of the late Charles Turner, Esq., of Rochester, Kent, on 4th June, at Stevenage, aged 59.

Ward, Rev. James, M A., late Fellow of New College, Oxford, in May last, at Malta, aged 30.

Weir, Louisa Catherine, wife of Captain J. G. Weir, late 29th regiment, and only daughter of Frederick Price, Esq., on the 2d June, at Southampton.

LONDON: FISHER, SON AND CO., PRINTERS.

FISHER'S

COLONIAL MAGAZINE.

SIR CHARLES METCALFE IN CANADA.

"It is not in the terrors of the law, or in the might of our armies, that the secure and honourable bond of connexion is to be found. It exists in the beneficial operation of those British Institutions which link the utmost development of freedom and civilization with the stable authority of an hereditary monarchy, and which, if rightly organized and fairly administered in the Colonies, as in Great Britain, would render a change of institutions only an additional evil to the loss of the protection and commerce of the British Empire."

REPORT OF THE EARL OF DURHAM.

"SAVE me from my friends!"—When will one cease to have occasion to repeat the saying of the wise Spaniard, who first told men that he ever dreaded a foe's wisdom less than a friend's folly? But the other day the advocate of Colonization and Colonial rights seemed likely soon to have no one to oppose him in the beaten way of argument. The old fear that Colonies must always be lost as soon as they should begin to be worth having, was fast dying away; and with it that feeling of almost indifference to Colonies and Colonization to which it had mainly given rise. The long threatening precedent of 1776 had at length just been set aside by one of happier omen. Though neglected grievances had ripened, in all our North American Provinces, into general discontent; and though, in two of them, ill-managed and tardy concessions had even forced the discontent into premature rebellion; yet for the other Provinces the concessions had been made in time; in Canada, the miniature civil war which broke out, had been successfully put down; the danger, for the moment imminent, of a war with the United States, had been averted; and, last and best, the Union of the two Canadas had restored them a free constitution, their House of Assembly had tried its powers, the Executive had placed itself in harmony with the public voice, and the Colony, so long the most troublesome of our dependencies, for the first time boasted a Provincial Government as strong as it was possible for popularity to make it. The experiment had been made, and was successful. Colonies, all but lost by the old system, had been won back by the new. What then, in spite of 1776, was to prevent their being kept? Thinking men of all parties were gladly yielding themselves to the belief that they could be kept; and well aware before of the vast importance of Colonization as a social and economical relief to the overburdened masses of our population, rejoiced that the last objection to it was removed. The politician was ready to admit that Colonies could not be founded too fast, nor too great facilities be afforded for their rapid growth, nor too liberal securities be given, in the shape of decidedly popular institutions, for their good government.

What a time for our friend's folly to choose for mischief! No sooner are things thus beginning to look settled, than we hear that in Canada and Nova Scotia, almost at the same instant, they have managed to unsettle them. In both Provinces, popular men brought into power by the new system have abandoned office; in both, the old war-cries of the popular party are raised, as of old, against the Provincial Executive. Whatever the difference between the two cases, (and I hold and mean to prove that in reality there is the most essential difference between them,) the Provincial papers, almost without exception, speak of them as part and parcel of one struggle, as springing from the same causes, and involving the same principles. To all but those who are well acquainted with the details of the political controversies of the Colonies in question, or have some special means of information to rely upon,—that is to say, to almost every one, the news comes as of a mere quarrel, in two Provinces at once, between the popular party and the Governors,—a quarrel just like the old quarrels that a few years ago threatened the loss of a great part of our Colonial Empire; but far more threatening, because seeming to show the utter inefficiency of the new system on which we were beginning to rely for its preservation.

Responsible Government for Colonies, say some, its opponents from the outset, has proved itself the folly we always said it was. It has been tried, and is a failure. The having conceded it to our North American Colonies is hurrying on their last struggle for independence—has absolutely sealed their fate as dependencies of the Empire—has rendered it next to impossible to refuse its early concession to our other Colonies, and has thus made the danger of our soon losing them also more imminent than ever. Others again, of old its lukewarm or less zealous friends, without quite believing in, still cannot wholly disbelieve these prophesyings of evil. The confidence that is not based on full information and settled views, is always over apt to give place to apprehension. They more than admit the case to be a doubtful one, and rather wish than think its dangers overstated. A third class, still advocates of Colonial Responsible Government, admit to themselves with regret that perhaps the event may prove the system to have been given in British North America too late or too grudgingly to prevent evils which previous mismanagement had made inevitable; and lament the possibility there is that a failure so occasioned may now be set down to the wrong cause, may not only carry back the public mind to its old habit of indifference to Colonies, but impress upon it a settled aversion to Colonial free government, and thus most seriously prejudice Colonial interests, by preventing or long postponing that consummation so devoutly to be wished for—the establishment by the national voice of an enterprising, enlightened, and comprehensive system of Colonial policy.

For my own part, all the observation and thought I have been able to give the subject, leads me to rank myself with those who least of all incline to these misgivings. It may be rash to say too confidently that it is impossible for the experiment of Responsible Government to fail in any of our Colonies. It was not tried in Canada till after the case had been proclaimed desperate without it; and even then its failure is not as yet so much as probable. Neither there nor any where else can it be the cause of failure. In every Colony, without exception, we must try it, sooner or later, unless we mean to throw away all chance of success.

It may be worth the while of such as would willingly form right conclusions on a subject of national importance, to bestow a little thought on this. Colonies, to be sure, do not yet regularly figure in Queen's speeches, nor usually make much noise in Parliament; but the subject of colonization has, for all that, begun to take a deeper hold on the public mind than this silence would imply, and is in reality one of more importance in a national point of view than nine-tenths of those even who call themselves its advocates have any idea of. And this question of the true principles of Colonial Government is one, of which not only every public man, but every man among us having any pretensions whatever to political information or discernment, ought to be thoroughly master. It is not too much to say, that upon our Colonial Empire depends, and from henceforth must more and more depend, our national greatness. If the public mind is to be uninformed and careless as to the policy which alone can keep that Empire, what likelihood is there that the Government will be so enlightened as, of its own accord, to mark out for itself that policy, so persevering in its watch over itself as steadily to adhere to it?

There are those, I am well aware, who will incline to think it a useless labour, this attempt to preserve a Colonial Empire at all. It was long held that Colonies must necessarily separate from the Mother Country, whenever they arrive at that stage of improvement which may enable them to assert their independence; and many yet take it for granted that they always will. But upon what sort of ground, I feel bound to ask, does this notion rest? All depends upon the temper of mind in which they may be when they reach this stage. Will they wish for separation, or will they not, is the question? What right have we to presume, as a matter of course, that they will seek so great a change, whether they have or have not any real reason to be dissatisfied with their actual condition? It is nothing to say that in this or that instance, ancient or modern, Colonies have in fact desired and gained for themselves independent nationality. In every one of these cases there has been an obvious cause for their having done so, in the injustice or folly with which they have been treated. Colonists carry with them from home just as strong a feeling of attachment to that home as those who stay there cherish; nay, the very leave-taking tends to make the feeling, for their after-life, the deeper. The memory of the heart deals always far more with its sunshine than with its clouds. To their dying day, the old country is emphatically "home." They seldom or never fail to teach the lesson to their children; and their children and their children's children are seldom or never slow to learn it. The instinct of country of the natives of a Colony must point to the land of their birth, the only country they have personally known; but the old-country remains the home of their traditions, the father-land whose institutions and glories they love to dwell upon as still their own. Why is it that this lesson of attachment has so often been unlearned? Why, indeed, but because powerful influences have been wantonly called into play, to counteract the otherwise natural tendency of things? The colonial tie has been made irksome to Colonists, in spite of all that education and habit have done to make them cling to it. They have been treated as an inferior class in the distribution of the honours and emoluments of the state; almost any man of metropolitan birth being preferred in practice to almost any man of provincial origin. They have been thwarted as regards the conduct of their own affairs,—their local government systematically carried on, under the auspices of the parent state, just as they would not have had it carried on if they could have helped it. Metropolitan law-makers have sacrificed their interests to some imagined interest of the mother-country, or sought (for sometimes, as in 1776, the folly was even carried to this last extravagance) to deprive them arbitrarily of rights, which they valued too highly to endure to see taken from them. Causes like these there have always been, to account for colonial disaffection, wherever it has existed. Is it in the nature of things, that they must always be in operation wherever colonies are to be found? If so, then indeed we may hold that colonies cannot possibly be retained in their connexion with the parent state; but surely, not otherwise.

And what, after all, is this concession of Responsible Government, as it is called, that the most mouselike politician can by possibility picture it to himself as likely to endanger the connection of a Colony with the parent-state? What is it but the practical recognition of the Colonist class as equally entitled with the Metropolitan to the enjoyment of the inherent political and civil rights of the British subject; the treatment of the Colony, not as a mere appendage, but as an integral portion of the Empire? It gives the Colony so favoured, free institutions as nearly as may be resembling those of the Mother-Country; the political institutions which we have a right to take it for granted they will prefer before any others that could be offered them. It leaves them to manage their internal affairs with no more interference than is in the nature of things inevitable. And it implies the regulation by the Imperial authority, of those great general questions of public policy which must not be left to any other control than its own, in that spirit of fairness and consideration which it is as much the interest of the Parent-State to manifest, as of the Provinces to require.

Hasten the loss of Colonies, indeed, by a policy like this! Yes, when the taking away of all excuse for discontent shall become the means of driving men from loyalty into disaffection.

But a Province left thus to itself, says a certain class of objectors, might just as well be declared an independent state as not, for anything the Parent-State is to gain from the connection. To call it still "a Colony" is an absurdity in terms. I am well aware that from the fact that colonies have so constantly been governed on the opposite principle, the word has acquired what may be called a historical sense, and means with many a territory governed from abroad for interests foreign to its own. In this sense of the term, Provinces governed as they ought to be would doubtless cease to be Colonies; but not in any other. Ask the political economist. He must reply, that a well-governed Province—and no country inhabited by freemen can be well governed unless it is popularly governed—that a well-governed Province not only is as much a Colony as a Province unpopularly and badly governed, but that it is by far the better kind of Colony of the two. The stream of colonization pours in upon it from the Mother-Country, and its commercial value increases in consequence, all the faster and more steadily for the increased prosperity which good government necessarily ensures it.

Or ask the statesman. Must not his answer be, that to every useful intent, a country thus circumstanced remains a Colony so long as the government of the Parent-State presides over the administration of its affairs, and regulates the general interests and foreign policy of the Empire? What can it matter to the Mother-Country which of two sets of Colonists hold office within their own Province, and see to the making of its roads and bridges, and to the administration of its other local affairs, provided always the Province recognizes her supreme authority, and does not seek to contravene the general laws and rules of policy by which the Empire as a whole is bound together? The one danger the statesman apprehends is, that this political tie may be severed, that the Province may some day or other come to have a foreign policy of its own; that it may then cease to welcome our surplus population, to invite our trade, to swell our national resources for peace or war; that it may even join in the war of tariffs against our manufactures, transfer its alliance to a hostile state, or adopt a directly hostile policy of its own. Can he fancy that to avert this danger, to prevent the Colonist from losing all his love for the Mother-Country, and resolving not to submit to her authority in the few cases where she has an interest in his so doing, and where too she has strong inducements to study his interests as well as her own, it is necessary for her interference to vex him at every turn, in matters about which he feels and knows that no one but himself is either tolerably well informed or ever so slightly intrusted? One is forced to think that there are men whose profound acquaintance with human nature has led them to this sage conclusion; but in very truth, no one can pretend that such reasoners are not far enough from being statesmen.

It may be said, perhaps, that however well all this may look on paper, the scheme is utterly Utopian and impracticable. The essentially dependent position of a Colony, and the very different state of society that must prevail there, where all is new, from that which exists here, where everything is old, make it impossible to carry out the project.

Unquestionably, it is impossible to establish in a dependency the literal and exact transcript of the political institutions of an independent state. Unquestionably, also, the social condition of a colony, however founded, must differ materially from that of the parent-state; and more especially where the aristocratic element prevails in the latter as it does with us. The privileged classes are much less apt to leave their country than are the unprivileged. Poor men emigrate in crowds, peers, almost never. Arrived, too, in a colony, the poor man and the rich are thrown on their personal resources, as they never could have been at home. The rich man quickly sinks, unless his industry and enterprise sustain him; and the poor man as surely rises, unless his follies or vices keep him down. There is thus everywhere a strong natural tendency towards equality of condition, which at once makes hereditary aristocracy impossible, and admits neither of the immense wealth, nor yet of the extreme destitution, which are to be found side by side in the Old World. Nor is the state of things much more favourable to church-establishments than to aristocracy. A large proportion, perhaps more than half of all who emigrate from the United Kingdom, are Irish Roman Catholics; and a very considerable proportion of the remainder belong to neither of the established churches. The general colonial tendency, besides, is as decidedly towards independence of thought and the recognition of an entire equality of religious rights, as it is towards social and political equality.

It is clear enough, then, that in attempting to give to our Colonies political institutions essentially modelled upon our own, it is idle to think of their adopting all our aristocratic peculiarities, be they ever so cherished or venerable, whether in Church or State. In the one or two of our most recently-planted settlements, where pains have been taken in the first instance to transplant an organized society of rich and poor, landholders, merchants, tradesmen, artisans, and labourers, all together, and to have them carry at once with them from home into the wilderness their church and school-house, a state of things promises to grow up more like our own than is to be found in our older colonial possessions. But no such marked inequalities of rank as prevail at home can by any chance be made a lasting feature of the social state, even in colonies so founded. As to hereditary rank, with here and there perhaps a solitary exception, it is a thing not to be thought of. The political franchise, too, must be more extended, and representation more nearly apportioned to population, than with us. And as regards privileged church-establishments, every Colony had need be allowed altogether its own way. If it want them, they are easily to be had. If not, it will be worse than folly to try to force it to put up with them.

Does it follow that the British Constitution cannot in its essential features be given to a Colony,—so much of it, that is to say, as the Colony can ever want or make useful? No doubt there are politicians who would draw this inference from the premises I have laid down; whose delight is so especially in the church and aristocracy, and who regard with so little partiality the more popular features of the Constitution, that while they would fain impose the former on every Colony, at whatever cost, they had a little rather not be obliged to see the latter prevail in any.

The true question to be answered is this, Which of all that host of usages and institutions to which we give the collective name of the British Constitution, is in reality to be called its essential characteristic? Very vague notions naturally enough prevail on this point. The Constitution being unwritten, the cry is perpetually raised whenever any political change of magnitude is under discussion, that it threatens the Constitution; and with many the cry avails to create the impression that almost every existing institution is somehow or other an essential part of it. But, for the purposes of the present inquiry, this question must be looked into more closely. It is the more important to do this, from the fact, which I shall establish presently, that the want of clear and correct ideas upon this very point is not only the primary cause of whatever vague apprehension prevails in this country about the concession of Colonial Responsible Government, but has also occasioned those blunders of some of our colonial friends which have lately contributed to increase that apprehension. One and the same lesson is wanted, to teach us confidence, and them caution.

It is not then the existence of a hereditary aristocracy, with extensive privileges and vast wealth, that is the essential characteristic we are looking for. Other countries in abundance have such an aristocracy, without possessing anything in the shape of political institutions ever so remotely resembling the British Constitution. This country, too, had its hereditary peerage for centuries before what we now recognize as the Constitution was in existence. Nor yet is it to be found in the generally aristocratic character of our institutions, the gradations numberless of rank and degradation, of wealth and poverty, the wide contrasts of the privileged and unprivileged classes, and the unequal distribution between them of political power. These also are found to co-exist with all sorts of forms of government besides our own. So too, are established Churches and Lords Spiritual, of every kind and creed. All these a nation may have, and know nothing of the British Constitution. Our Colonies may have it, and know nothing of them.

The really essential features of the British Constitution, to which everything else in it is altogether secondary, are two in number. The first consists in its mode of reducing to practice, by means of a strictly-defined and jealously-maintained system of ministerial responsibility, the old maxim that "the King can do no wrong," that his acts and intentions must always be right, and may not, under any circumstances, be so much as imagined to be otherwise. The maxim itself is one of very ancient date, and of universal currency wherever monarchy exists; indeed, it may be said to be the first instinct of that unreflecting loyalty which invites, and, in the history of the world, has so often produced, despotism. So, too, is the notion of ministerial accountability an old one, perpetually acted upon in fact in all countries, wherever, under the pressure of real or fancied injury, people's loyalty or cowardice have not been strong enough to keep them true to the faith of non-resistance. Popular movements for redress of grievances are sure to strike first at the Crown's servants, at obnoxious agents of its power, who are supposed to have gone beyond its instructions, or at some unpopular favourite, who is thought by his influence over the Sovereign to have perverted them. It is only after vainly avenging itself on the petty instruments and more prominent abettors of mis-government, that discontent strikes at the Sovereign himself, tries to force him by express stipulations to respect the public rights, or, failing that means to secure the end desired, aims its blows directly at his throne or life. All this, however, in the earlier stages of the struggle for good government, it is sure before long to do; for the Sovereign never fails to take such steps in behalf of his servants and favourites as in the end identify his cause with theirs, and leave the mal-contents no other alternative. In this country, as in every other where authority has ever been resisted, these rude means have been tried again and again, but with very indifferent success. Our history for several centuries is the record of their perpetually proven insufficiency; of Great and Forest Charters given and renewed times without number, yet never adhered to; of popular vengeance repeatedly visited upon the ministers of oppression, yet no less richly deserved by their successors; of civil wars more than once changing the succession to the throne, and ending at last in the temporary overthrow of the throne itself, and the public trial and execution of a King for alleged treason; of conflicts with the Prerogative still needing to be renewed under his successors, and resulting again in a dethronement, though happily not in the experiment of a second Commonwealth, or the canonization of a second Royal Martyr. From that last revolution, however, dates the wiser practice which has since prevailed, the system now never for a moment departed from, of ascribing every public act of the Sovereign, without exception, to the agency or advice of certain of his servants, functionaries of State named by him and holding office during his pleasure, but who stand before the country as the Responsible Ministers of the Crown for the time being, must defend all its acts in Parliament so long as they are in office, and must yield their places to other men the instant they are no longer able to do so with success.

The second grand characteristic of the Constitution, is to be found in the admitted practical ascendancy of the House of Commons. At first summoned at long and varying intervals, a mere adjunct to the Upper House of Parliament, simply to assent to such new imposts as the Sovereign's necessities or extravagance might demand, it has by slow degrees risen to the real, though carefully veiled mastery of every interest in the State. Once humbly praying for redress of grievances, apologising for the very necessity as it did so, and quietly submitting to royal rebuke for its presumption; then demurring, though with bated breath, to increased taxation, while old complaints remained unattended to; rehearsing presently, in new tones of tempered menace, their catalogue of popular rights and wrongs, and refusing point-blank to talk of the King's wants, till he should have said something to the purpose about the urgent wants of his most faithful but by this time rather refractory Commons; it is at length seen making war upon its Sovereign, dethroning and beheading him, suppressing by its vote the House of Lords, and for a time converting the very Kingdom into a Commonwealth under its own sole rule. The victim of its triumph, and for the time rendered ultra-loyal by the lesson, we find it again driven, in spite of itself, into its old course of reluctant money-votes, discussions of all manner of state questions and remonstrances against all manner of grievances, till, by the Revolution of 1688, fairly established in an ascendancy more lasting than that which Cromwell's victories had before given it,—an ascendancy the safer, and yet not a whit the less real, for being so masked and guarded as to be compatible with the safety of the Throne and the preservation of the House of Lords. To all practical intents, the House of Commons, though in theory but the third estate of the realm, has become the representative embodiment of the nation as a whole. The Upper House is the especial representative of the aristocracy, a grand council of revision less amenable than the Lower House to popular control, with higher rank and more show of privilege, but having far less of the reality of power. The Sovereign, as the supreme head of the nation, secure in the responsibility of his Ministers, retains unquestioned every Prerogative required for the administration of its affairs. If his Ministers cannot so shape their course, as to carry with them the House of Commons, they either must induce him to dissolve the House, or must resign; for the powers of the House are such, that without assailing the Prerogative, or so much as threatening a single Minister with impeachment, it can make the government of the country impossible, in the extreme case of a determined refusal of the Ministry to meet its wishes. It can stop the supplies, and refuse to pass the yearly Mutiny Bill. The Sovereign may still choose and command his servants as before; but, except so far as the Civil List goes, he can no longer pay, and ceasing to pay, can besides no longer punish them. His very army and navy on a given day would stand released from every obligation of discipline. From the extent of this power, it necessarily follows, that its exercise is really never thought of. Long before things come to this pass, a Ministry not having the confidence of the House, always finds itself under the practical necessity of retiring, or trying what it can do with a new House. Should the new House too prove adverse, the struggle is at an end. No Ministers so outvoted would dare cling to office; and the Sovereign has therefore to find others to take their places, and do for him what they have failed to do.—The House of Lords has no such power as this. It may modify the policy of Ministers, or may greatly embarrass them (provided they are not overwhelmingly strong in the support of the House of Commons), by placing its veto on their measures; but it cannot turn them out, so long as the Commons are their friends, or are even willing to let them stay in office. Against the determined will of the Commons, backed by the public voice, it cannot for any length of time make a successful stand, even in its veto of a legislative measure; for, as the Commons virtually control the Ministry, and the Crown can always create Peers, there is ever a quiet influence at work tending to assimilate the Upper to the Lower House. And in any crisis of peculiar urgency, such for instance as occurred in the days of the Reform Bill, it is always within the power of the latter to insist upon the exertion of that influence to any extent that may be necessary to secure the end in view.

Such, I repeat, are the two cardinal principles of the Constitution, the strict adherence to which is absolutely essential to its existence; the first, that Ministers must assume the entire responsibility of every act of the Crown while they remain in office; the second, that the popular branch of the Legislature must have that ascendancy in the State which will enable it to force them out of office, if the acts and principles they appear before it to defend, are such as it is disposed deliberately to condemn. These conceded, the rest is matter of necessary inference. The check upon the powers of the Sovereign is so perfect, that it ceases to be felt. His Prerogative and his person at once become absolutely unassailable; for both are identified at every instant with the most obvious interests of the statesmen who lead the party or parties that constitute for the time being the effective majority of the nation. Nor does this safety of the Prerogative rest merely on the interest which the Ins, with their majority, have in maintaining for themselves the powers they need for the due administration of the Government. The Outs have the same interest in it; as their leaders may soon in turn occupy the Treasury Benches, and the prerogatives of the Crown be wanted to shield and strengthen them. In like manner, the Ministers of to-day may be the Opposition of to-morrow, and must have an eye to the chances of future popularity, independent of the mere possession of executive power. The system is thus a constant check on the otherwise inevitable tendency of party to rush into extremes. By consent of all, the highest prize, the Crown, is placed hopelessly out of reach; so that the incentive is wanting to that turbulent atrocity of party-warfare which is natural to the Elective Monarchy or Republic, where the opposite policy is adopted. And the prizes that may be gained, brilliant enough for the most aspiring ambition, can seldom be won, and never kept, except by men who display a reasonable degree of moderation in their pursuit or exercise of power. Every possible security is given for the perpetuity of the system, the constant maintenance of the same essential principles of government, be the party of the majority what it may. And the Government must always be a real and effective one; since, whatever the other checks interposed by the Constitution, it must always rest upon, and be the impersonation of, the working majority of the House of Commons. There can be no uncertainty as to its character and policy. The temper of that one legislative body determines them.

In fact, from the era of the establishment of these great principles, discontent has been driven to an entire change of tactics. Instead of uselessly assailing the Crown, it at once lays its charges before the People against the People's House; sets itself to work with the constituencies, to carry future elections against the ruling majority; or, if its projects be too vast for a mere appeal to the constituencies to suffice to bring them about, enlists the unrepresented masses in its agitation, to force alike electors and elected to give their earnest heed to popular distresses, to demands for cheaper bread, reform in the apportionment of the representation, universal or household suffrage, and the protection for the poor voter of the vote by ballot.

It is strange that so many people seem to take it for granted, that Colonial Liberalism, however it may affect admiration of the British Constitution, must secretly be aiming at republican institutions. The suspicion implies a compliment to the latter, which I own I am not disposed to join in paying them. The one cause of those results in the United States which *some* Liberals here have ascribed to an imagined superiority of their institutions over ours, is really to be found in the social condition of their people; in that sparceness of population and abundance of land and food, which make it impossible they should as yet have any "uneasy classes," like those which with us form a large proportion of the constituencies, and beneath them make up the threatening aggregate of the unrepresented masses. Visit upon as large a portion of their people the fearful wretchedness of our pauper millions, or give those millions the comfort which theirs enjoy, and the extended suffrage which it would naturally bring after it; and what would the comparison then be? Our Colonies, it should be remembered, enjoy this vast social advantage in as high a degree, to say the least, as the United States. Why should the *bona fide* working out of the principles of the British Constitution leave them anything to hope or wish for, from the establishment in its stead of a proclaimed Democracy?

In point of fact, it is easy to show that the Democratic system not only is not better than the one we have to offer them as a model, but that in a variety of most important particulars it contrasts with it most unfavourably.

The greatest, and no doubt the best constituted Democracy the world has ever known, is that of the United States. It may well be doubted whether any much better machinery could be contrived for the carrying out of the Democratic principle of government. Its founders were men of extraordinary energy, discretion, and ability; brought up in the best school of politics, and forced by great events to make themselves great men. It will be long before another occasion can arise, so favourable in every way for the successful establishment of a great, well-organized Republic.

These great men copied largely from the model the Old Country set before them, but from the necessity of their position were unable to copy its really essential principles. Some of the ablest among them were most anxious to have made the copy more like the original; in fact, to have retained Monarchy, and not utterly renounced Aristocracy. But the task would have been hard, perhaps impossible; even though the people had given them, what it actually refused, the permission to make the experiment. The founder of a dynasty can surround his throne by no illusion save one, the illusion of military glory. Without it, his throne has no security. With it, the liberties of his people have none. The people of the thirteen States could hardly have chosen but as they did. Yet so choosing, their whole framework of government, copy elsewhere as they might, became a new experiment. Their Presidential election must be a direct choice, by the people, of a citizen to take rank with reigning Sovereigns. The more frequent such election, the more constant the excitement it must keep up throughout the nation; the less frequent, the more terrible, so often as the time for it should come round. Elected by the people, it was impossible he should fail to think himself their representative, as much entitled to claim to speak their voice on any given question, as any body of men chosen by them to be their delegates in Congress. Known, too, by his past life, as the politician of a certain party, the advocate of certain views and measures, he must of course insist, throughout his term of Office, on maintaining those views, no matter what may be the views of the other branches of the Legislature. His powers, therefore, must be so defined, as neither to allow him to overbear them, nor them to overbear him. His *veto* upon legislative acts is to avail only when the acts in question are not sustained by a vote of two-thirds in both branches; but, with this limitation, it is a personal power which he may exercise, and actually does exercise, as often as it suits him. He appoints to office, but only with the "advice and consent" of an independent body, the Senate, often hostile to himself and his policy. Yet through this ordeal his very Cabinet Ministers must pass. Of course, they must have a political existence apart from his, and from each other, as well as he from theirs. He is not answerable for their acts, nor they for his. He may dismiss, but can scarcely ever be said to command them; they may advise him, but certainly cannot be said to have any means at their command of making him follow their advice. If they resign, he can soon find others; for it is not the confidence of the country in an entire Cabinet, but the mere assent of the Senate to the appointment of this and that individual, that is needed to enable him to fill their places. This assent he can always get, sooner or later, for some one who will do well enough to serve his turn; and till he does get it, *ad interim* appointments are an easy expedient. A Cabinet of this sort could be no Ministry, in our sense of the word, even though its Members were not expressly excluded from the Legislative Bodies, by that feeling of jealousy with which an Executive organized under an elected head must always be regarded by the people. From this exclusion, the Legislature and Executive can correspond only by addresses or requisitions on the one side, and messages and returns on the other. To get on at all with business, each House is driven into an organization of Standing Committees, each with its Chairman of the politics that suit the majority, who has duties to perform in the House considerably like those of a Minister in Parliament; and, provided the majority is of the President's party, the arrangement answers tolerably well. But both Houses may be at feud with the President and his Cabinet, and yet the latter hold their ground; or again, the Houses themselves may be at feud with one another, in which case, as both are equally chosen by the people, neither can be in a position to make the other yield. The Representative majority may thus be of one party, the Senate of a second, and the President of a third; and all three able to insist on their respective preferences, let the dead-lock cost the country what it may.

Such capacities for obstruction would be unendurable, but for the device of pretty frequent elections. The contending powers appeal perpetually to their one master, the People. The intervention of the People can alone decide between them; and in proportion to the frequency or infrequency of that intervention must be the obstinacy of their contests, whenever they are brought into collision. The framers of the Constitution of the United States displayed great ingenuity in their contrivance for making it as constant as possible, without resorting to that extravagance of yearly elections which characterises the more rudely democratic Constitutions of nearly all the individual States. The House of Representatives is directly elected by the people, for the term of two years, each State sending a delegation nearly proportioned to its population. The Senators are chosen for a term of six years, two from each State, and by the votes of their respective Legislatures; one-third of the whole body retiring every second year. Vacancies, however, by resignation and death (for very few Senators are young men, and they are a class of men in great request for Governorships, Foreign Missions, and other high Offices) make the process of renewal considerably more rapid than the Constitutional rule prescribes. The President is elected for a term of four years, by the vote of the people given in their several States, each State throwing a number of votes equal to the number of its Senators and Representatives together; or, if no candidate succeed in gaining a majority of all these votes, by the House of Representatives, in which case the vote of the delegation of each State counts alike. With such rapid changes of the leading actors, it is easy to see that no obstruction any of them can offer is ever likely to last long. Their perpetual collision must have the one merit of perpetual variety.

At the same time, however, there can be no doubt that the resort to these different modes of electing increases the risks of collision between the three elected powers, and makes indeed the chance of their all pulling one way at any given time a very slight one. It is nineteen years since the younger Adams became President; and as he was the man of a minority, chosen only by the House of Representatives, after failing of his election by the people, it was not strange that his administration never commanded the support of the two Houses. Andrew Jackson, his successor, twice chosen by the people, and personally popular from first to last, was still hardly any better off. At first it was the Senate that was hostile; more than once in the course of his war with the United States' Bank, both Houses thwarted his favourite schemes, and left him no revenge but to veto theirs; and at the close of his eight years of office, when the Senate had at last become what he wished, the other House, moved by a newer tide of popular feeling, was in any thing but a reliable temper. He left office without ever having had his own way in legislation. What he did, he did by dint of executive boldness—by stretches of prerogative in sheer defiance of his fellow-lawmakers, such as no Sovereign would think of trying with an English Parliament. When Van Buren succeeded to the Presidency, the Senate was with him, and the House hostile. Four years after, when he left it, his party commanded neither. The great revulsion of public feeling caused by the general distresses of the time, for a wonder, gave the country a President, Senate, and House, all of one party; but the wonder was too great to last. Harrison's death devolved the Presidency on the Vice-President, a politician of the party in the ascendant, but one who happened to have some notions of his own not altogether identical with those of most of its other leaders. In a few weeks' time, accordingly, he had committed himself one way, and they another. The President, for the last three years, has been at variance with the two Houses; more bitterly so, if possible, than any of his Predecessors ever was before him.—At no time in the whole nineteen years, do we find the Executive strong in the confidence of the Legislature; the makers and administrators of the laws not at variance; the machinery of government and legislation working smoothly.

Another peculiarity of the system requires a passing notice. The Constitution, in place of being, as with us, a mere affair of law and usage, its authority paramount simply because it is never questioned, is a written Instrument enacted with peculiar formalities, not open to amendment except in a certain prescribed manner, admitting of authoritative interpretation only by the Courts of Law, and, as the paramount law of the land, having such effect as to make null and void all other laws not strictly conformable with its provisions. The Courts of Law consequently have to sit in revision of the proceedings of the Legislature, not merely to interpret, but positively to allow or disallow them; and in the discharge of this duty no other power in the State can rightfully interfere with them. They rule a law to be unconstitutional; and it has become inoperative. The Executive has no longer the means of enforcing its observance. Congress may re-enact it; but the new law is worth no more than the old.—Here again is a power absolutely foreign to our system, absolutely essential to theirs; a power, too, that is still further obstructive; an absolute Judicial *veto* upon acts passed by all three branches of the Legislature. I am far from saying that on the whole the existence of this power is an evil. Its non-existence would be fatal to the system; and it therefore does much more good than harm. But it is impossible not to see that it must tend to two results, among others. By constituting the Bench a political power, it drags the Judges of the land continually into politics; makes it an object with contending parties to have it occupied by men of their own school; exposes the Judges to the influence of political alliances and hostilities, and the Judiciary itself to inevitable danger from the democratic spirit against which it is thus specially set to guard, and which in turn is driven to assail it as the one anti-democratic Institution of the State. It is hard to imagine that the Judiciary can very long maintain its independence against such assaults. Indeed, indications are not wanting that they have already proved only too successful in undermining it.—The worse result of the two, but not the only one that calls for remark. This judicial *veto* has the further bad effect of adding to the confusion of the grand *melée*, of making it still harder to ascertain where the real governing power of the country resides,—more impossible, if the expression may be pardoned, for any party assuming to conduct the government ever to obtain that ascendancy which is in fact necessary to the existence of a real Government.

To the instinct of jealousy that presided over the contrivance of the whole system, all this multiplying of checks and balancing of powers appeared, no doubt, the constitutional "one thing needful." The people's servants were to be prevented from abusing power. What rule so simple as that of trusting them with no power to abuse?

A simple rule enough. But the question is as to its efficiency. What sort of a Government does it result in? Trust a public servant with no power, and you impose on him no responsibility. Mischief is done; but he declares it was not done by him. He could not help it; you must call to account those who would not let him have his own way in the matter. You do so, and they one and all make the same excuse; each accuses others, and protests he was forced to do whatever you blame, prevented from doing what you would have wished. The more evenly balanced their powers of mutual embarrassment, and the shorter the term of their appointments, the less their responsibility. The public, eternally busy electing them, or others instead of them, cannot have time to make itself master of these endless controversies, and must decide for or against each upon all sorts of grounds, foreign to the true question of his own real merits. Hence arise, on the one hand, a license of partisan-attack upon all political opponents, and on the other, an audacity of conduct on the part of those liable to such attacks, both alike inconceivable in their recklessness, except by those who have themselves witnessed the actual results of the system. The one safeguard men seek is that of party. They must speak and act *en masse*, each as his political friends wish or will let him; and the one aim of each party is by all means to damage its opponents. This caution observed, no one need trouble himself to look much further. There is little fear that anything he can say or do for his party will ever rise up in judgment against himself. All hangs on its defeat or triumph. With every alternation of party ascendancy follows the instant seizure, by the victors, of the utmost possible amount of official spoil; removeable incumbents, high and low, all turned adrift to make the more room for the new-comers. The triumph is always too short-lived and too partial for either side to have time to stick at trifles.—Ample security in such a state of things that the country shall never want for political excitement; but what chance of its ever having any thing that can be dignified with the name of a *bona fide* Government,—a body of public men really conducting its affairs upon fixed views of public policy?

That this is no fancy-sketch will be readily admitted by every one at all conversant with such matters, who has ever visited the United States and given any measure of attention to the subject of their politics. Indeed, even of their own people—those of them, that is to say, who allow themselves to observe and reflect—there are few, I venture to think, who are not aware that the case is as I have stated it. The despotism of public opinion forces every professed politician to call the institutions of the Great Republic perfect, and the voice of the Majority infallible; and few dare openly raise their voice against the received formula. But by their mutual recriminations all parties more than admit the contrary; and, dosed as the Sovereign People are with flattery, they are not so wholly its dupes as one might fancy. Flatterers and flattered, all who think in their hearts, know better, however they may shrink from saying so.

Nor are the evils I have been describing the fault of the people of the United States, rather than of their political institutions. They are not accidents, but necessary results. The quasi-sovereignty of the individual States, each with its own Constitution, Executive, Legislature, and Judiciary, aggravates them, but is not their cause. They follow inevitably from the first principles of the system, the absolute sovereignty of the people, the abrogation of the forms of hereditary monarchy, the refinement of precaution necessary where limits are to be set to the powers of elected rulers. The wonder is, that the American people have made the system work as well as they have. Their social and economical advantages, as a people without paupers, have done much for them. But the people themselves are, besides, a most extraordinary people; their natural genius for self-government such as perhaps no other whole nation ever had before. They came into existence as a nation, with established laws and usages admirably calculated to secure them the advantages of good government, be their form of government what it might. To the South and South-West, the existence of Slavery has interfered with the operation of this influence; and throughout the far West, population hurries back into the wilderness too fast for civilisation by any chance to keep pace with it. But these influences have as yet by no means finally prevailed. The general high character of their criminal and civil codes remains; and the administrative machinery of their municipal systems is everywhere good, and in many States hardly admits of improvement. By superficial observers these advantages have sometimes been spoken of as a result of their form of government; but nothing can be further from the fact. They are the result of a state of things that existed while the States were still Colonies; before their present republican Constitutions were thought of. And, but for their conservative tendencies, the radical defects of those Constitutions would have made themselves vastly more manifest, long enough ago.

What is it, then, that is to make any large class of the people of any of our Colonies secretly desirous to exchange the political institutions of Great Britain for those of the United States? Of course it is possible to imbue them with this feeling. The old system of colonial misrule is an infallible specific for the purpose. Deny them the political institutions of the parent state, and they are no British Colonists if they do not seek any other form of political freedom they may have any chance of getting instead. Offer them, on the other hand, freely what they want; and rely on it, their hearty choice will be the system they have been used to and understand. What miracle is to render the foreign novelty of Republicanism the more attractive system of the two?

As regards the North American Colonies, where this spirit has been most apprehended, the truth is, that all the mismanagement of the old *regime* has by no means brought about any such result. It produced universal discontent and some disaffection. But the Great Republic was too near for even discontented men altogether to admire the prospect its institutions held out to them. In its worst days Canadian Liberalism never sought Democracy but as a *pis aller*, and most reluctantly. At the present moment it would puzzle one to find a single man in public life in all British North America who would not indignantly repel the charge of harbouring any, the very slightest, inclination towards it. As to the practical results of the democratic institutions of the United States, few give the subject such close attention as to form any very clear notion of the *rationale* of what they see and hear. But see and hear they must; and the jarring of the machine startles them none the less for their not knowing precisely how and where it is out of order. Besides, the whole country is a Border country, and its people regard the States with only too much of the Border feeling. The Lower Provinces settled by loyalist refugees from the old Colonies; the bulk of the population of Lower Canada, French Canadian; and Upper Canada, first colonized by refugees, and then fought for by their sons; tradition everywhere ministers to the feeling. Republicanism is little likely to have so much as justice at their hands.

Can the British Constitution, then, in its essentials, be granted to our Colonies? If it can, we may make ourselves quite easy about Republicanism.

We have seen that for this purpose it is not necessary they should have a hereditary Aristocracy, nor yet those other wide distinctions of class which prevail among us, nor yet any churches "by law established." These peculiarities of our social condition are not easy of naturalisation in colonies; and to try to force them into existence would be sheer folly. But is there any thing to prevent the successful introduction into our colonies of all that is necessary? Cannot each have a House of Assembly, occupying within its limits a position of qualified ascendancy analogous to that of the House of Commons? Cannot such House of Assembly be allowed to regard the Representative of the Crown in the same light as that in which the House of Commons regards the Sovereign; to fasten upon those Provincial Office-holders through whose Ministerial aid he carries on the Government, the same kind of responsibility to itself, which the House of Commons attaches to the Ministers of the Crown at home? And is not the recognition of these principles just as much the true keystone of the system in a Colony, as in Great Britain?

To what cause is it owing, that misgovernment and discontent have so long been the constant accompaniments of our Colonial rule? We have never meant to tyrannise; yet it seems as if in every one of our colonies we had done so notwithstanding. Whose doing has it been? If it can be shown, that in every instance the mischief is clearly traceable to the non-recognition of these principles; that in all our Colonies where the existence of slavery has not interfered with the otherwise necessary tendencies of the colonial system, we must refer it wholly to the influence of an irresponsible oligarchy of Provincial Office-holders, a sort of natural formation of the earlier æra of all colonial history, everywhere moulding to its own fashion alike the Governors whom it surrounds and the Metropolitan authority that sends them; that though this has not been altogether the state of the case in those Colonies where slavery has till lately prevailed, there has at least been in them as in the others (though from another cause) a refusal to allow the representatives of the free class, who alone could speak as for their Colony, the substantial control of its affairs, and that now slavery is at an end the like social tendencies are steadily at work in them as in the other Colonies; if all this can be shown, as I am well assured it can, the inference is inevitable, that the only way to put an end to the mischief is at once to admit and act upon the principles, to give each Colony in good faith a voice in its own affairs, to make its resident Officials responsible to its Representatives, and so force them to make and keep its local government popular, instead of odious to the great body of their fellow-colonists.

First, then, for the rise and progress of discontent in Colonies where slavery has not existed.

The principal Officials of a new colony are necessarily men who bring their commissions or letters of appointment with them from the old country; and even for some time after a colony has passed through its first stage of progress, as no great number of Colonists can advance any strong pretensions to its higher official employments, the practice, so agreeable to the tastes of Downing Street, of still sending out from home some of its better paid functionaries, is extremely apt to be kept up, and all the Office-holders of that grade to be tacitly regarded as holding their offices by a pretty secure tenure, in fact as incumbents for life, with a sort of right, besides, to certain comfortable facilities in the way of official provision for their families after them. Residing together at the seat of government, and forming among themselves the privileged society of Government House, their families associate on terms of intimacy, and intermarry. A common interest and common feelings array them into a Court caste, assuming to itself, from the very anti-aristocratic tendencies of the Colonial state, which admit of no other aristocracy to eclipse or rival that of Office, a kind and degree of consequence within its little sphere, such as no mere Office-holder class could any where else venture on, and parading an extravagance of courtier-notions, such as none but courtiers so singularly tempted by their position could well venture on imagining.

Colonial Governors, on the other hand, seldom or never stay long in a government. Accident aside, their appointment is limited by a rule of the Colonial Office to a term of a few years; and in practice, the limit thus set is often not reached and very seldom indeed exceeded. Nor are they generally selected with any sort of care. Now and then, when the affairs of a particular Colony may happen to have forced themselves upon public attention, as for instance Jamaica did in 1839, and Canada in 1838, '39, and

1843, a Governor may be specially chosen for the sake of his qualifications. But otherwise, the selection is a mere affair of patronage; and the influence of a man's friends a much weightier recommendation of his claims than any reputation for ability he can possibly bring to back them. And further, as very few Colonial Governments hold out any sufficient inducement for civilians of the required mark, Parliamentary men, Diplomatists, men known at the Bar, or high in any branch of the Civil Service, to seek them, the great majority of the candidates for such posts are military and naval men, Captains, Colonels, and Generals, men who have had to serve more or less in the Colonies, and may pretend therefore, with some show of reason, to understand colonial subjects better than other people can, accustomed to the parade of authority and fond of it, and condemned besides to an alternative of poor pay and sheer want of occupation. The consequence is, that with the exception of a few of the more important Colonies, which have lately for particular reasons had Civil Governors sent to them, Colonial Governorships have been regarded not merely as a branch of the ordinary patronage of the Administration for the time being, but as a branch specially devoted to the benefit of middle-aged and elderly gentlemen, members of one or other of the United Service Clubs, and lucky enough to have a little more interest with the powers that be, than their fellows who may chance to be their rivals.

That Governors sent out in this way are more likely to be controlled by the Officials of their respective Provinces, than to control them, is a proposition that hardly needs proof. The first Governor of a Colony may have some chance of being master of the people he brings out with him; but every one who comes after him comes as a stranger, and finds the Official gentry in quiet possession of the ground and perfectly at home. They form his Council of advice. He must ask them for information upon all matters of business; must hear all they have to say, and if they are half as clever as their position is tolerably sure to make them, stands little chance of hearing much else to any purpose. They tell His Excellency precisely what His Excellency is sure to like best to hear; are wonderful admirers of Prerogative, especially the Vice-regal article; affect aristocracy, and are complaisant enough to make their Aristocracy the emanation and ornament of His Excellency's Court; are sticklers for Church and State, and without requiring him to be ever so little sanctimonious, are quite ready, if he is the least in the world that way inclined, to exalt His Excellency into a Deputy "Defender of the Faith." The privileged leaders of the fashionable society of the Capital, their professional and commercial neighbours must follow suit or be nobodies, people "not in society," beyond the Court pale, and shut out from all hope of Court favour. In a small community, where everybody aspires to vie with everybody else, (and this is the nature of the levelling tendency that prevails in every Colony,) this sort of exclusion is not to be thought of. The received gentlemen,—government officials, officers of the garrison, merchants, lawyers, doctors, men of any standing,—all respond to the Court creed. What can the apers of gentility do but gabble it after them? The gentry, professional and mercantile, of the seat of Government thus gained, that of the other towns can but side the same way; and the Oligarchy of the Bureau, master of these town interests, and having besides no small amount of government advertising and other patronage at its own disposal, secures a pretty firm hold upon the pocket-conscience of the Provincial Press. Jealous enough of all who come out from home to seek any of the offices it regards as its own *appanage*, it takes good care to enlist the sympathies of every new-comer of mark, not suspected of such felonious motives. He is welcome to rank as of the Aristocracy of the Province, to figure as a Justice of Peace, or hold any other minor office of mere honour anywhere out of the Capital, provided only he will keep himself from being troublesome about places that give money, or the money-making privilege of a Governor's ear. To be sure, it may be unpalateable to the natives and older residents of the country, this seeming preference of new-comers; but even this result has its advantages. It makes a capital excuse for not letting them run off with any of the richer prizes, and yet helps the party to a class of supporters that can be made very useful though so cheaply gained. The old residents of the rural districts are precisely the people it can least count upon. The whole order of things must disgust them, at any rate; for it is impossible they should not soon find out how completely it postpones themselves, their feelings and their interests, to the interests and vanity of a mock aristocracy with which they can have absolutely nothing in common. Our Office-holders have therefore nothing to lose in this quarter. It is part of their court creed to profess peculiar attachment to the connexion of the Province with the Parent State; and no wonder, as by their reading their own ascendancy and the connexion are synonymous terms. If, by such professions and a few places of no value, they can secure the aid of the new-comer class, the more plainly the dissatisfied show their annoyance the better. Dissatisfaction with the system is in Court cant disaffection to Great Britain. The Officials have gained their hearts' desire, when they have forced their adversaries into opposition to everything that ninety-nine Governors out of every hundred are certain to affect; when Church and State notions, aristocracy, loyalty to the Crown, and devotion to the Mother Country, are all identified with themselves and their ascendancy, when the sweets of office are monopolized by adherents of this sound doctrine; when townsfolk, gentry, and old-country people are their allies; when the press is at their disposal, and the feelings of the hostile mass of the people of the Province are branded by it as revolutionary, democratic, and disloyal.

Set down, now, in the midst of such a state of things, Governor after Governor, picked up as Governors are; give each a term of service too short for any but a thoroughly clever man to be able to make out the peculiar features of the local politics, and the real character of the people he has to deal with, before it shall be time for him to come away; and to what sort of position are they doomed? What chance have they of seeing with other eyes, or hearing with other ears, than those they find so complaisantly ready to their use the instant they arrive? As they see and hear, so must they act, and so report their acts. The people of the Province must weary over the endless repetition of the old game—new Governors, one following another, all meaning well, perhaps, yet all in turn befooled by the same flatteries of the same men, into the same career of unpopularity. And the books and shelves of Downing Street must be loaded with ever-new versions of the old account of it, variously enough signed, but most suspiciously alike in their estimate of Public Officers' services and claims, of the priceless merits of the loyal party, and the deeply dangerous temper of the disaffected.

With Colonies of inconsiderable extent or population, this state of things may go on almost indefinitely, without ever making noise enough to attract attention beyond their own limits. If they have not charters securing them the form of representative institutions, all they can send home will be a few ill-advised Memorials for redress, from folks angry and simple enough to waste their time in writing to Her Majesty's Principal Secretary of State for the Colonies; grumbling letters to other people; and newspapers, with perhaps now and then, on occasions of more than usual provocation, a pamphlet or two of complaint, to no one in particular; and when arrived, memorials, letters, papers, and pamphlets, hardly any body sees them, and of the few who do, almost no one cares about their contents. Where there are representative institutions, the case is rather better, but not much. Protests from the popular branch of the Legislature will find their way periodically to Downing Street, but will give no one much trouble after they get there. A Member of Parliament may occasionally put a question to the Minister, or move for a return; but no one else hears the answer, and perhaps he does not himself read the return when he has it. People, Parliament-men, and Ministers, all are too busy to be listening to trifles. And what can the grievances of the people of a little colony be but trifles—that is to say, to any judgment save their own?

In a Colony, on the other hand, which has once passed its day of small things, and become the home of a community of some importance, enjoying the right, as the people of such a colony must, of being represented in a legislative body that can claim the character and privileges of a Provincial House of Commons, matters must soon go further. Whatever advantages of position its office-holder party may at first have, (and for some time they will continue to be great,) the popular branch of the Legislature must sooner or later reflect the popular feeling. In apportioning the representation they may favour their seat of government and its sister towns and villages where their strength lies, and everywhere their party may be the earlier and the better organized; but the Colony is country, not town, and the bulk of its people not poor tenants, but a thriving landowner yeomanry—the last class of people in the world to let themselves be long led by the nose by a set of townspeople and make-believe squires, of whom they know little, and whose notions and manners they must like less. The counties must send most Members, and the farmer population poll most votes. As to his Excellency, we have seen how he must stand. His Executive Council, the legacy of his predecessors, is of the true official colour; not an organized Cabinet of Heads of Departments, charged or chargeable with the conduct of the public business, for that might involve a responsibility not at all to official taste; but simply a few gentlemen styled "Honourables," some of them rejoicing in the enjoyment of other and more lucrative offices, others merely Councillors, but all of the fraternity; a body with hardly any functions assigned to it—consulted on state matters as much or as little as the Governor may please, not bound to defend his acts, its members sworn to secrecy, and their oath interpreted by themselves so as practically to shield them from accountability even for what they may have counselled. Sometimes this body has itself been the Upper House of the Provincial Parliament; but, generally, there is a Legislative Council besides, made up of much the same material, but its Members sitting in Parliament as Provincial Peers for life, and, like those of the other House, with open doors. What chance the Lower House, under such circumstances, has of being treated by Councils or Governor as a House of Commons, may be readily guessed. If in their interest, it is welcome to vote supplies and pass Bills which they will suffer to become law; if only not hostile, it may vote as it likes, with an assurance that no vote not pleasing to them will ever come to much if hostile, it may count on seeing them do pretty nearly all they choose in spite of it, and on getting its own way in nothing. It is a Commons' House of the Tudors' or first Stuart's day, not of these better times of the House of Brunswick.

But the times are not those of the Tudors or first Stuart. The Members of the Lower House know too well what a Member of Parliament is at home, for this abatement of their own consequence to suit them. They know, too, that the provincial Honourables who put the slight upon them are not Lords and Privy Councillors after all, and pay them back their full measure of contempt—perhaps with interest.

The quarrel begins, like the earlier quarrels of our own House of Commons, about money; not that Colonial Parliaments are apt to grudge supplies, or object to a well-stocked Treasury, as our old Parliaments used to do. They are seldom or never niggardly in this respect; but then every Member wants from the full purse as good a share as he can get of grants for the advantage of his own constituents. Roads, bridges, canals, river-improvements, harbours, public buildings, schools, agricultural societies, charitable institutions, and the like, are the objects for which they expect that he will take care there shall be funds forthcoming. They have economical notions, too, as to the rate of pay that ought to content the public servants. In the midst of their rude plenty they see so little money, that a small money-income seems to them a fortune. On every account, therefore, their representatives must fight down salaries, and bring all manner of revenues and fees to swell the surplus available for the more popular branch of the public expenditure. The grandees, on the other hand, share neither feeling. They have no objection to a surplus, because it is a convenient thing to have Members' mouths well stopped with local grants. But they have no notion of making such grants the first object, and the welfare of their own pockets the second. Their style of living and notions of emolument date from the happy time when they had no House to quarrel with. They cling to salaries and office-fees as personal property, and to crown revenues and funds raised under certain special Acts, as properties of the Crown, with which the House has nothing to do, but which the Crown, through its Representative, is to spend as it pleases, or rather (for that is what the thing must be in practice) as they please. And their pleasure is to help their friends and themselves from the fund as largely as they can. Every question about the proceeds of an obnoxious fee, every allusion to the extravagance of a salary, every call for clearer statements of accounts, or offer to provide by vote for services paid out of Crown funds, or hint at the principle that all the public funds ought to form one revenue, is a fresh blow for them to chafe at, and such blows must begin soon and last long—must last, in fact, till they shall have gained their end.

Though the first, this money-struggle is not the only one. The people, and therefore their representatives, want to have their business with Government promptly and carefully attended to; and they want to be treated with personal civility and consideration into the bargain. But it by no means suits our little great men to work harder than they can help, or to take the trouble to be more civil than they need be to a set of annoying country people whom they never see but to be bored with their importunities. In a new country, where the rapid spread of the population calls for perpetual changes of Executive and Judicial machinery to meet the wants of new districts; where lists of Magistrates, Militia-Officers, and other local functionaries of all sorts, must be constantly under revision; where every kind of public improvement, ever so little out of the common way, demands the intervention of Government in aid of local or private enterprise; where without its help people cannot keep up schools or charities, and where, therefore, it must give money for all these objects, and ought, besides, to take some oversight of the spending of such money; where, above all, every man is a land-owner or land-buyer, and Government the great land-seller and authority for title-deeds; people of all classes are brought into constant personal relations with its chief officers, to an extent that can hardly be imagined by those who have always lived in an old country, where the functions of government are so much less extensive. A very slight indulgence by an "Honourable" in the habit of indolent *hauteur* into which, from his position, he is so apt to fall, is a source of such annoyance and wrong to thousands as they must deeply and abidingly resent. And this popular resentment must find voice on the floor of the people's house.

Again, the great body of the people and their representatives demand the selection of popular men, men of their own class and feelings, to be their Magistrates, petty Judges, Officers of Militia, local Land Agents, Post Masters, Collectors of Customs, Clerks of the Peace, Sheriffs, and so forth. With the oligarchy, the one recommendation required for all these employments is subserviency to itself; and its protégés are therefore precisely the class of men who cannot possibly discharge their duties to the public satisfaction. The discontent caused by the personal shortcomings of the Chiefs, is as nothing to the heart-burnings that the arrogance, indiscretion, and sometimes iniquitous misconduct of all this army of their hangers-on, give rise to. Appeal, people soon learn to think almost a waste of time—for they want confidence alike in all to whom they can appeal—the higher Officers of the Executive, the Judges of the higher Courts, and even the Juries that may be brought together by their Sheriff-enemies.

In fact, from first to last, unpopularity is the characteristic of the entire system. The office-holder party, in all its political doctrines no less than in its official habits, is absolutely alien to the prevailing opinions and feelings of the country. The opposition is everywhere a contradiction.

Left to itself, the contradiction would soon be at an end, and the prevailing popular feeling (as at home) make itself that of the Administration. But the official party in a colony is entrenched in a position of peculiar strength, and commands, besides, the aid of a powerful ally. All they do is done in another name than their own. It is always his Excellency that commands. They, good people, are merely his Excellency's faithful servants, loyal subjects of her Majesty, whose zeal for the connexion with the parent state and her Majesty's crown and dignity makes them heartily welcome her Representative, be he who he may, and serve him do what he may, though by so doing they earn the hostility of the separatist faction that vilifies them. An exaggeration of monarchical forms marks their style of official correspondence. Decisions of all sorts, even to the details of the land-granting department, are put in writing as the Governor's own; letters are answered and acknowledged as if always laid before the Governor, and the answer or acknowledgment in each case specially commanded by his Excellency. There is an almost total absence of departmental organization and responsibility. The Secretary's Office is the central chaos, where all business meets, and whence all orders issue. And very generally, as if the better to keep up the pretence of the Governor's personal agency as the originator of its decrees, the Officer in charge of it is his Private Secretary, a gentleman who came out and is to go away with him. Other public officers get the Governor's authority at every step, of course in the precise terms they themselves suggest, either through this Secretary, or else in the shape of orders in Council; for which, however, no individual Councillor can be held specially responsible, as the orders are still the Governor's, and the advising or consenting Councillors are personally shielded by their oath of secrecy.

A consequence of this system is, that almost every complaint against a public Officer becomes in some sort a complaint against a Governor. The Official, in answer, points to his authority for the act complained against—perhaps the Governor's own order—perhaps that of one or more than one of his predecessors. In either case, the Governor is bound to acquit the man, and almost bound to sustain the act. The complaint is carried in appeal to the Colonial Office. But it has now become doubly a charge against the Representative of Majesty; and as such, the Colonial Office, the patron-general of all the Viceroys, is doubly bound to dismiss it, if excuse of any sort can be furnished or found for its so doing. This done, the poor complainant, if obstinate enough still to think he has been ill used, may persist in it that the Mother-Country, the Crown itself, has denied him justice—the very thing it best suits the plans of those who really wronged him, that he should be driven to think and say.

Sometimes, however, a case is so bad or so strongly pressed, (supposing, for instance, the House of Assembly the complainant,) that the Colonial Office cannot summarily dismiss it, and the Governor has to maintain his ground in a series of despatches, with a chance of finding himself at last not victorious. His decision is half set aside; and if the matters in dispute are more than usually grave, it may be necessary to send out the redress instructions by a new hand, and the old Governor is accordingly recalled—as courteously as possible, perhaps to be sent to repeat his blunders somewhere else, but, at any rate, sorely to his own mortification, and, for the moment, somewhat to that of his provincial prompters. But the new man is as the old; it is hard, but they can contrive some way of practically nullifying the concessions he comes out to make; and he, with the fear of humiliation and removal now before his eyes, cannot but take a lesson from their mode of operation, and make their position and his own stronger by refining a little upon his predecessor's practice. Before authorising them, he takes the precaution of getting authority himself from Downing Street; so that, in case of further appeal, he may have all the advantage there that they enjoy when the first appeal is made to him. The Office is as easily led into the habit of precise instructions to himself, as he is into the self-same habit with them; for the same vanity of fancied power is flattered equally in either case. Nor does he, in point of fact, find himself more fettered by it in the one case than they in the other; for the Office is, if possible, more dependent on him for information, than he is on his own prompters. He at least is on the ground, though a stranger. The Office is thousands of miles off, and the people in it, through whose hands his despatches pass—never were on the ground, and never will be.

The officers of the Provincial Government tell him what they please, and he gives them back their wishes as instructions from himself; but wherever he sees a glimmering of risk, he first writes home the statements that have satisfied himself, and the Office is then kind enough to direct him to act upon them. There is delay, to be sure, but generally not much, if the matter so interests the powers behind the Vice-regal throne as to make them urgent. Where, as will often happen, delay is in fact their object, the machine is perfect to their hand. Changes are demanded that they do not relish, and dare not or cannot bring the Governor to venture on peremptorily refusing. He must wait orders, then. When it suits him he will write for them, and in the terms that suit him. The Colonial Secretary has not information enough to enable him to decide; as how should he have, when the despatch before him does not give it? Further particulars are called for—to get them more time can be taken, and when they are got, they can easily be made the pretext for fresh doubts and postponements, till at last, it does not matter what the decision is. Sometimes, indeed, when disputes have run to such a length that the Colonial Office begins to grow suspicious, and in its turn shrinks from responsibility, it interposes delays of its own, that alarm and harass its now visibly powerless Governor, as much as they irritate his complaining Third Estate. When things have come to this pass, the Government of the unlucky Province has become what Lord Durham, after personal experience of it, happily enough termed a "Constituted Anarchy;" irresolution, discontent, disorder, alone are everywhere. But at every stage, be it borne in mind, of the weary progress of the system to this result, it has been first on Royalty through its Governors, and then on the Parent State through its Colonial Office, that the petty Provincial clique, for whom alone the system has existed, have contrived to throw the grand burden of the disgrace and odium of their own paltry policy.

Not that I mean to say that in these provincial quarrels either party is wholly right or wholly wrong. Of those who side with the faction of the Officials, many (of the more independent of the townspeople, for example, and in most cases the majority of the new-comers,) do so with the best motives, and in the full belief that its opponents are all it styles them. In a party so formed, there must be many honest men, attached to it from opinion, and not from interest; and even as regards those whose interests are bound up in the course they take, it is hard to say precisely where the influence of opinion ceases and that of interest begins. The party, as a whole, is by no means without principles of action higher than the mere instinct of the place-man. And for a time at least, the nature of its materials is likely to give it rather the superiority than otherwise, in respect of information and that kind of intelligence which depends more on education than on mere native shrewdness and capacity. The popular party, again, on the other hand, cannot but number in its ranks some mere office-seekers, whom disappointment alone has driven to them, and who have no higher object than to force themselves into place, and punish the dispensers of the loaves and fishes for having disappointed them; and the general unaptness of countrypeople for active leadership in politics, will put such men more forward as leaders of the party, than its interests, or indeed its feelings, otherwise would let them be. It would be strange, too, if the party itself made no mistakes—if its prejudices and passions did not sometimes lead it wrong, and give its more politic antagonists advantages of which they are too happy to avail themselves.

In many matters, for example, the public opinion of a Colony is apt to settle down upon a scale of remuneration for its public Officers, as decidedly too low, as their own price for themselves is too high. Country-farmers are bad judges at all times of a town-gentleman's expenses; and when, above all, they set themselves to fix how much, of what they regard as their own money, and want for uses of their own, they should allow to a set of gentlemen, between whom and themselves there is anything but a friendly feeling, their judgment is not likely to be better than usual. The proclaimed anxiety, too, of their representatives to get all the surplus they can save from the ordinary expenses of government, for grants in which their constituents have an interest, and their hostility to the men at whose expense they would economise, are calculated to cast a suspicion upon the demands they make; even when, as often is the case, their real moderation and fairness of purpose are far from justifying it.

Again, this economy of theirs where the Crown and its servants are in question, admits of being placed in most disadvantageous contrast with the profusion that marks their money-votes for their favourite uses; and, still more, with certain practices on their part inevitably growing out of it, which are very near of kin to the jobbing tastes they so loudly condemn in their opponents. To get the most he can for his own section, every Member is in a manner forced to try his hand at what is technically styled "log-rolling." As there is no one in the House who is accredited to speak and act for Government, the rule of the Imperial Parliament, which requires that the Crown should authorise every proposal for a money-vote before the House can entertain it, is altogther impracticable, and every Member may urge his own pet claims in the House as he best can, when and in whatever way he chooses. A, B, and C, therefore, lay their heads together, and fix on some supposed grant or grants for which they are disposed to make common cause. D. E, F, and G have done the same for some other project. Each party gladly buys the other's help by promising its own in payment; and any one who annoys either by opposition may look out for their jointly returning him the compliment whenever his own job, whatever it may be, that he must get done on pain of ruin with his friends who sent him to the House, comes up for discussion. No very sufficient guaranty for fairness, judgment, or economy, in the outlay of the large sums of the public money so distributed! Nor is this all, or even the worst. The spending of this public money must be entrusted to some one. But the House has learned distrust of the Governor and those about him, and dare not swell the corruption fund already at their disposal by letting them have the choosing of the parties. It names its own commissioners (sometimes Members of the House, sometimes only their friends) in the Appropriation Bills; and the public grants now assume the appearance of a corruption fund of its own. As to any sufficient oversight and control of such Commissioners, it is out of the question; and there must therefore, in the nature of things, be much waste, and some downright peculation; of all which the House and the popular party must bear the odium. Indeed, the system so invites abuse, from the unchecked spending power it gives to the body which should be the check on all expenditure, that suspicion must attach to it at every turn. The most honest, no less than the most corrupt of its agents, must be liable to find himself suspected.

Another result of the state of things I have been describing, follows from the irritation and sense of irresponsibility which it tends to produce in the minds of the popular leaders. Here, where unpopularity once clearly ascertained is enough to drive a Government out of office, we can hardly realise the effect on the public mind of the system of keeping men in place, in spite of unpopularity, and perhaps even of proveable misconduct. Disliked, despised, defeated on the hustings, powerless in the House, they still enjoy their emoluments and honours. Votes of want of confidence are a farce. The opposition, able to thwart them in everything else, cannot make them yield. They can thwart its purposes quite as much as it can theirs. Court of impeachment for it to resort to, there is none; for the Upper House and the Judges are theirs. It is driven into a mode of warfare suited only to the peculiar position it is placed in—a warfare of personal vengeance, of charges against individual public officers, the embodiment of its hostile feelings, preferred before the House, investigated there by itself, and forced upon the Governor and the Colonial Office as verdicts on which they must pronounce sentence of dismissal on the asserted culprits. The accused complain that they have had no hearing; and the prosecutors cannot well say they have. But, in truth, the proceeding has no real judicial character about it; it is a faulty course, but one into which the false position of those who take it has forced them. On all sorts of subjects the same cause compels them into similar extravagances. Hopeless of office, and fearless therefore of its responsibilities, they may deal in complaints and claims of every kind, just as it suits them. Whatever happens to strike a popular fancy, they can engage to fight for. Every notion that involves a shadow of unpopularity, they can renounce. If after long enough training in this school they be found to have learned something of its lessons, who can wonder at it, or blame for it aught but the school itself?

More mischiefs follow, from the use that is made of the Governor's name and the Colonial Office to authorize and sanction whatever is unpopular. Without abating an iota of the odium that attaches to the resident Officials, it gradually brings people to regard all Governors and Colonial Secretaries as their willing accomplices. It becomes a common thing to attack the Head of the Provincial Executive in much the same style of unceremonious personality as is used to those who surround him. Members of the House freely arraign his acts, and charge them, not on presumed advisers, but upon himself. His recall is demanded, instead of merely their dismissal. His successor, whatever his instructions or first intentions, the instant of his arrival, finds himself and the authority he represents distrusted, and begins to distrust in turn. Before long he too is attacked, and becomes hostile. The Colonial Office finds its Governors one after another all served alike, and justifies itself by at last firmly believing that concessions merely make things worse, that the popular clamour cannot be satisfied, and must simply be put down, or else the Colony abandoned. Public opinion says much the same; and on both sides most people begin to think, and a great many openly to say, that early separation is inevitable. And all for matters of dispute that involve no Imperial interest whatever—for the sake of quarrels between two classes, the large class and the small, of the Colonists themselves!

It is obvious to remark how greatly such errors, wherever fallen into, must strengthen the position of the official party, as well within the Colony as in its influence with the Metropolitan Authorities. Yet, be their consequences what they may, I ask again, whose fault they are? What are they but natural results of a system from first to last absolutely anti-British? Who but the authors and abettors of the system are to blame for them?

Colonists and persons conversant with Colonial affairs, cannot fail to recognize the outline I have been giving of their natural history, imperfect as it is. In particular cases there are of course peculiar features, to which I have purposely avoided allusion, that I might the more clearly establish the essential character, and thereby the general first cause, of the whole mischief. In a conquered Colony, for example, where the majority of the people are of another origin, and speak another language from our own, the official party, so soon as it begins to feel its weakness, sets itself up as the patron of the British race; encourages dissension (no hard task) between it and the race of the majority; finds it for a time extremely pleasant to keep down opposition by such means; but at last discovers that the feud it has fostered is not so easy to manage as to excite—that its allies have other objects and passions than its own, and, in fact, as heartily despise as its enemies detest it—that it is a powerless third party in a "war of races," which, end how it will, cannot fail to prove fatal to itself. Such has been the course of events in Lower Canada; but the "war of race" ending of the Lower Canadian troubles, much as it differed in some of its appearances from the common Bureaucrat quarrel, was yet merely its result. But for the earlier stage, the later had never been. The jealousies of the two races would have signified very little, if an execrable system of mis-government had not aggravated them, as for a time it did, into hostility. Again, where, as in Upper Canada, the newly-arrived colonist-class is peculiarly strong in numbers, and consists, in great part, of a gentry of half-pay officers—the men of all others best fitted to lead it into habits of subserviency to the powers that are, and where also, the Orange Institution has naturalized itself and become their ally, an official party so favoured may alternate with the popular party in the control of an Assembly, to which Villages as well as Counties send Members, and which is returned under old-fashioned election-laws, well qualified to make intimidation easy, and a fair polling of the full strength of any County hard. Yet is it not therefore a whit the less truly the unpopular party, though a distant or careless observer may fail to become aware of the fact. The very circumstances that mislead him are really making the popular discontents and animosities only so much the deeper and more dangerous. Or, again, as in Nova Scotia and New Brunswick, some timely modifications of the system may stay its otherwise downward tendency, and things may begin to mend before all the later stages of misrule shall have been passed through. But the tendencies are all there, notwithstanding; and unless so checked, would infallibly have run their full course.

In those of our Colonies which till lately have been slave-colonies, a state of things has hitherto existed in some respects considerably different. Where slavery exists, there can be no yeomanry class, which elsewhere forms the mass of the Anti-Bureaucratic party. The entire free population is an Aristocratic party, between which and the Officials there are few causes of dispute, and many sympathies. They are besides held together in presence of the slave population within the Colony; and the relations in which they both stand to it are threatened by a common enemy, the anti-slavery movement in the Mother-Country. Their most obvious interests, no less than their feelings, must lead them to maintain a good understanding with each other.

It was from this quarter, in fact, that their chief causes of discontent arose. Public opinion at home first menaced and then resolved on overthrowing the institution of slavery. Then public opinion, the slaves having nothing to do with it, was quite the other way. Officials, planters, agents, merchants, white men of all ranks and classes, save and except a few despised missionaries, with here and there a stray adherent of the free colour, as heartily despised as themselves, all shared the same feeling. The close union and collective strength of the West India interest at home, enabled the Colonies to make their struggle a pretty obstinate one; but the great measure once fairly determined on in spite of them, the smaller and Crown Colonies had no alternative but submission on the best terms they could beg. Wherever the legislatures had any considerable power of independent action, they could interpose difficulties. And Jamaica, as the most important of the group, could venture on being absolutely refractory. We had made a certain class of the inhabitants of certain colonies to all intents "the people" of those colonies; and had given them in that character certain chartered rights, under which they claimed to be allowed to conduct their own affairs their own way. So long as we let them have their own way, they gave us no trouble with any complaints on that score. But after a time we insisted on raising another class to their level; they protested loudly against the interference, as an invasion of their rights; the Colonies, as we had constituted them, were become discontented.

The great social revolution is, however, now effected. A free moral population, in many respects unlike that of our other colonies, but, if possible, still more alien than theirs in feeling to the heretofore ruling party, and, at the same time, far outnumbering it, has been called into existence. For some time to come, it is likely to have much less weight than its numbers, but for its old habits of dependence, would give it. But its influence must be continually increasing, as those habits shall by degrees give place to the habits of free-men. Other changes besides have taken place. The do-nothing policy of the old system is passed away. Planter-rule at an end, the government of each colony must henceforth busy itself with undertakings that, under planter-rule, would never have been thought of as forming any part of its duties. Every detail of rural administration must be looked after. Wherever there is Crown land unimproved, active steps must be taken to bring it into cultivation. Improvements of every description must be encouraged; and a sufficient supply of immigrants, of a race capable of out-door labour, somehow or other secured; or the breaking up of the industrial arrangements of the slave system, and the impending changes in the sugar-duties, must between them absolutely destroy the productive resources of the colonies. They must consequently economise their revenues, that the money may be forthcoming for these uses of necessity. The white population has a new interest in the merging of all fees and Crown revenues in the one common fund of the colony, the reduction of salaries, the enforcement on the public servants of activity and zeal in the performance of their functions. Failing readily to take the lead of public opinion in respect of these its new demands upon them, the Official class, supposing them to be sustained in office after the old fashion, will fast make itself just as odious, to white and black alike, as the Bureaucracy of the Colonies where slavery has been unknown has ever been.

"That something must be done to correct this omnipresent vice of the official system in our Colonies, if we mean to keep them or have them worth the keeping, must, I think, be clear to every one. What that something must be, is no less clear, I believe, to every one at all correctly informed, who has given any measure of consideration to the subject. Most people, unfortunately, know so little and think so little about it, that several quack remedies, absolutely unsuited to the case, have found considerable favour. I propose, therefore, first to dispose of these, before showing the applicability of the very simple remedy which, fairly tried, cannot prove other than effectual.

"It is of no use, then, to fall back upon the jealous policy of trying to keep Colonies small, and making them do without popular constitutions. Petty Colonies, it is true, always supposing them too remote from each other to be able to band together for common objects, cannot force us by their clamour to give them that potential voice in their internal government which all Colonies, whether they can get it or not, must long for. And so long as they can be kept without representative institutions, so long a set of petted officials may annoy and misgovern them, without their being able to offer any effectual resistance, or our being troubled with any loud expression of their discontent. But what then? You have shut up your patient in the dark, well gagged and strait-waistcoated; but because you no longer hear and see that he is suffering, is he therefore cured? The misgovernment of your agents becomes all the worse, and the discontent it causes all the more inveterate, for the precautions you have taken that neither shall force itself to notice, and be remedied in time. And, besides, of what earthly value could Colonies be, so insignificant, so scattered, and so few, as to be retainable under such a rule?

Not less unavailing for every useful purpose is the newer half-and-half recipe of Colonial-Office jealousy,—the plan of giving Colonies a semi-popular Constitution, with no House of Commons in it, but a mongrel legislative body, neither Commons nor Lords—part chosen by the People, and part by the Executive. Suppose the Executive chooses to the satisfaction of the People; we have much such a House as they would have chosen themselves, and may rely on its taking much the same course as a *bona fide* House of Assembly would have taken. To what end, then, the refusal to let them choose the whole body at once? We have simply shown distrust, and thrown away an integral part of the machinery of British legislation—the institution of an Upper House of revision—at the best, for nothing. Or suppose, what is much more probable, that the Executive names men whom the People never would have named; and what have we then, but the old quarrel between those they do send, and the local Government—with this difference, that the people are likely to begin it all the sooner, and to carry it on all the more pertinaciously, for the distrust with which they have been treated at the outset, and that the local Government, beginning the struggle with greater advantages of position, and therefore under more temptation to an abuse of its powers, is likely to give them all the graver occasion of complaint.

Great importance, again, has been attached by Provincial Officials generally, and, in consequence, by the Colonial Office, to the securing of "an adequate Civil List," in exchange for the Crown Revenues, so as to place the Governor, the Judges, and as many as possible of the Executive Officers of the Government, beyond the risks of the yearly money-vote of the Assembly. The revenue and salary struggle has constantly taken the form of a struggle for or against some such *project*, demanded as the condition on which alone the required surrender of the Crown Revenues could be assented to by the Colonial Office. And, provided always that the authoritative establishing of such a Civil List is the act of the Provincial Legislature, and that the bargain driven with it is not too hard a one, the object is a desirable one to effect. The Governor and Judges should not be dependent on yearly votes, which may vary in amount, if it can possibly be helped; and it may be well that some of the most indispensable Officers of the Executive should be placed, in respect of the amount of their emoluments while in office, on a like footing of security. A Colonial Assembly is certain not to assent to this, until first tolerably well assured of its own powers and the disposition of the Government it is dealing with; and this point gained, a moderate Civil List is every way likely to work well. But after all, at the best it is little more than a symptom of improvement in the political condition of a Province, and can never be its producing cause. And as to the favourite official notion of a Civil List to cover all the more pressing items of expenditure, and enable the Provincial Executive to get on in spite of a stopping of the supplies, the idea is utterly preposterous. No House of Assembly ever can, or indeed ever should, assent to so monstrous a proposal; for it would just be a throwing away of one of its chief means of exerting a popular influence on the Executive, a mere tempting of the official power to courses which would bring it into collision with the people. Add the further and graver error of making such a Civil List the work of the Imperial Parliament; and instead of allaying contentions, it becomes almost inevitably their cause. It is the grand grievance, against which the House must protest without ceasing, till such time as it shall have been remedied; and, what is worst of all, it is a grievance of the Mother-Country's own proclaimed creation, one which it alone can remove, and that by an act of the same highest authority that imposed it. This great mistake was made at the instance of the Colonial Office, on the occasion of the Union of the Canadas. Thanks to the declared concession in other respects, of the great principles of popular government, it has happily as yet done no apparent mischief. But few people out of Canada are probably aware how completely this result is owing to the popular course the Provincial Government has been wise enough to take in this respect. No Canadian Official has ventured, in his place on the Treasury Benches, to defend the Civil List of the Union Act, or to propose to the House of Assembly to recognise the fact of its existence. Lord Sydenham himself set the example of allowing his Ministers to speak of it as a matter which it was merely not expedient to draw into immediate discussion, and in the meantime *to ask of the House a vote for the year, of the amount it granted, on account of the services which it professed to place beyond the dangers of such yearly vote.* The same course has been taken ever since. The House has voted the sum yearly, and always under express protest against all recognition of other authority for the grant besides its own. At its last session it went further, and addressed the Crown, by a vote all but unanimous, for the repeal of the obnoxious clauses of the Union Act, engaging itself in that case to vote an adequate Civil List, though not to so large an amount. As the case stands, paradoxical though it may sound to say so, the Provincial Government has *practically* no Civil List at all to rely upon. Sir Charles Metcalfe, like a prudent man, is doing his utmost to cut down the actual expenditure for the services the Union Act professes to provide for, so as to bring it within an amount likely to meet the approval of the House hereafter. The House voted the supplies, after the resignation of his late Ministers, Civil List amount and all, as in former years. Had it refused them, it may well be doubted whether he could have found any public men or man in all Canada bold enough to be party to the making a single payment out of the Provincial Chest under the authority of the Union Act. Most assuredly the men who have stood by him, and on whose support he has to rely for the success of his administration, would have been slow to run the risk; and no man who should ever do so, unless under most peculiar circumstances, would be likely to show himself to much effect on the hustings, or in the House, after; for hearty opposition to the principle of a Civil List, imposed by the Imperial Parliament, is a pledge that public opinion forces on all its servants, without exception or reserve.

It is impossible upon any sound principle of political reasoning to deny, that on this point the Canadians are right, and those who imposed or would now maintain this constitutional anomaly, utterly wrong. It galls without checking; and if it checked, the kind of check it would impose would be one that on general principles ought not to be imposed—one that could not be imposed without tending to serious mischief by disturbing the true balance of the system, by taking from the House a means of control which it ought to have, by giving the Officials a substantive power they ought not to have.

Still, the fact is, that by both parties this Civil-List controversy is apt to be made more of, in the Colonies, than its real importance merits. It is not the mere right to refuse supplies that gives the House of Commons its actual power; for an Executive, with an army at command, and an unresisting people, would make short work of *taking* what supplies it might want. It is to the virtual command the House has of the army, through the mutiny Bill, and still more to the tried resisting temper of its constituents, that it owes its ascendancy, and that ascendancy enables it wholly to dispense in practice with its theoretical power of stopping the supplies. Precisely so with a Colony. If weak, and unsustained by public opinion in the Mother-Country, it has not and cannot have the real power to control its Executive, through the supplies, or in any other way. If strong, either in its own resources or in the support of the public voice at home, it has this power; and no mere Civil List can prevent its being exercised. It is our true policy to give our Colonies both these sources of strength, to an extent that may enable them to secure their own good government. Deny them this necessary power, and misgovernment follows from their want of it, and discontent and at last disaffection from their misgovernment.

Never so little conducive, however, to the desired end would it be, to suffer to be acted out the policy of encroachment on the Prerogative, into which the Colonial Assembly, in a state of permanent collision with the Executive, is naturally led. An Assembly so circumstanced may not be able to help acting on the system—may feel it necessary itself to name its friends to do the work it wishes done, as otherwise it would merely be leaving the work for its enemies to mar. But it is one thing to have the Executive, as it ought to be, in harmony with the representative body, and quite another thing for the representative body to set up as a counterpoise and rival to an Executive with which it is in collision—a quasi-Executive of its own creation—a class of public functionaries directly amenable to itself—Commissioners specially named in its appropriation bills — Members and standing Committees of the House charged by its vote with duties properly Executive. All this is merely so much machinery of collision—part and parcel of the "constituted anarchy" which it is the great object to get rid of.

A plan which has found favour with some Colonists is that of making the Legislative Council, or Upper House of the Provincial Parliament, an elective body. At a certain stage of the controversy between the Assembly and the Officials, when the latter are beginning to apprehend the consequences of too much direct Executive interference, and the Legislative Council is composed not so much of themselves as of their friends, and has ceased therefore to have altogether the look of an official body, they are very apt to make great use of its intervention to destroy the measures of the Assembly. People's attention is drawn more to the instrument than to the cause of the annoyance; and the doctrine finds supporters, that what is wanted is such a reform of the Legislative Council as can only be attained by having it elected by the people. Those who thus argue, however, are quite mistaken. The principle once admitted, that the temper of the Executive must, as at home, be kept in harmony with that of the elected House, there is nothing to fear from the non-elected. Here, the House of Commons rules, though checked by a House of Lords so infinitely more powerful and independent than the Legislative Council they are thus afraid of. Society is here beyond comparison more aristocratic in its constitution and tendencies than with them. Their Peers can never form a class like ours, in respect either of rank or wealth; and the influence the Executive can exert over them must be proportionally greater. And as none of them sit by hereditary right, the Executive has besides the naming of every individual—a power our executive has never had, and the want of which has still not prevented the House of Commons from making itself, by its hold on the Executive, the paramount Estate of the Realm.

But the objection to this proposal is not merely that it is the wrong one, that the change it seeks may be done without. It not only will do no good, but must do harm. It is essentially a republican expedient, and alien to the British system of government; though some doubtless have advocated it who would disclaim republican intentions. If elected by the same constituencies, at the same times, and in the same way, the two Houses will be (accident aside) mere echoes of each other, and might as well sit and debate in one room as in two. If elected by different processes, the Members of the Upper House, for example, representing larger constituencies, or chosen by a class of voters having a higher franchise, or by electoral colleges or municipal bodies, (and these are the projects which, to avoid the obvious absurdity of two merely echoing Houses, have been most in vogue,) disagreement would be probable. And of two elected Houses, supposing them to disagree, neither can have the means of overcoming the resistance of the other. The Executive may side with either, as it pleases, or may even appeal from both to the people. And when it has so appealed, the Houses may still differ, and the Executive be free as before to treat either or both as in the wrong.

A less sweeping change has been advocated by some who do not favour the elective

Legislative Council project. It has been said that it would be better to have the Councillors named for a term of years, than for life. Such an alteration might do some harm, and could at any rate do very little good. Legislative Councils, as they are, are more to be complained of for undue subserviency to the Executive, than for undue independence. Appoint to them for a term of years, and every Councillor is directly the obedient, humble servant of the Executive. If he offends, he will be disgraced by not having his appointment renewed. With the number of Councillors, as it ought to be, unlimited, the influence of the House through the Executive over the whole body will always be quite sufficient. To bring it to bear directly upon every individual member, would be to make the body merely contemptible.

No party in any Colony, that I am aware of, has ever thought much good could be done by a more rigorous and minute superintendence of the details of government in the various Colonies, by the Colonial Office; but the Office has repeatedly tried its hand at the experiment, though with no encouraging measure of success. Its orders go to the Colonial Officials, and by them are first interpreted, and then acted on according to such interpretation, or neglected, as they think best. Nine times out of ten, the Office never hears how they have seen fit to understand its instructions, what they have done under them, or whether they have done any thing. They make their own reports (for on such matters the despatches are theirs in reality, not the Governor's who puts his name to them) when and how they please. If the suspicions of the Office make it impossible for them to get quietly rid of the orders by just not minding them and saying nothing about it, it is easy to get up a correspondence about their meaning, and give more information and raise difficulties, till they are suitably amended or fairly given up. How should it be otherwise? The Colonial Office has no means of keeping them in check. They know their ground of old, and are perfectly familiar with the subjects they have to correspond about. The Governors sent out by the Office as its agents must write as they dictate, or cannot know how to write at all. As for the Colonial Minister, the supposed author of its decrees, he has his seat in the Cabinet and in Parliament to look after. It is ten to one he never visited a Colony in his life, and knows no more about Colonial affairs when he kisses hands as Colonial Minister than every public man within the four seas must know; and that, unluckily, is little enough in all conscience. Busy always with the home politics he understands so much better and must care so much more for, how is he in the course of a short incumbency to master a thousandth part of the detail it is necessary he should be familiar with, to comprehend the mass of manuscript that he has to sign, and the yet more frightful mass of manuscript which it purports to answer? His Parliamentary Under-Secretary cannot help him overmuch. Be his industry and ability what they may, his chief reliance must be on the other Under-Secretary, whose position in the Department, unlike his own, has no reference to the changes of home politics. This functionary can seldom fail to be a man of first-rate capacity for business, and is likely to have other qualifications besides; and the same thing may be said, probably, of a great many of his official subordinates. But the information they can command on Colonial subjects must be mere Office information. Hardly any of them can know any thing about the Colonies beyond what the despatches tell them; and the few who do must soon find themselves so spell-bound by the red-tape *genius loci*, so tied down to the task of making themselves walking indexes of the state-papers they live by, as to be able to put such further knowledge to little practical use. But the Secretary may look beyond the Office. To be sure he may; and may find, ever ready to give him as much counsel as he may wish, plenty of ex-Governors, and military men returned from other Colonial commands, a smaller number of Colonial officials, who have retired, or been removed, or are in England on leave of absence, and, if need be, the City representatives of the merchant-friends of the Colonial Officials who are at their posts. They are quite right, the Colonists, to put no great faith in the Office as a machine for the prevention or reform of abuses, by the mere means of its powers of meddlement and correction in detail.

Yet, inadequate as it may be for such a purpose, the maintenance of its general superintendence over Colonial affairs is an indispensable necessity. Governors must be named by the Crown, and instructed by the Crown; or else the republican elective system must be resorted to, and that on every account is an impossibility so long as the Colonies shall retain their connexion with the Crown of Great Britain. The idea has sometimes been entertained, that it would be well to adopt the policy of forming our several groups of Colonies into so many Federations, and devolving on each Federal Government the general oversight of its subordinate Provincial administrations, so as to relieve the Colonial Office of the greater part, at least, of its duties in this respect. To this plan, however, supposing always the character of the union in question to be such as the use of the term "Federal Union" properly implies, there are serious objections.

By a Federal Union I understand a machinery of government modelled on that of the

United States; so far, that is to say, as to give to each of the confederated Provinces an Executive, Legislature and Judiciary of its own, and to the Confederation a General Executive, Legislature and Judiciary, with certain strictly limited powers, besides. It may be taken for granted, that even for the several Provinces of such a Confederation the republican balance-machinery of an elected Governor, Council and House, is not to be thought of; and the Federal Government can scarcely be allowed to name the Provincial Governors, for that would be to make it their sovereign authority, and the Union any thing but a Federal one. If, then, the Crown is to name the subordinate as well as the chief Governors, the duties of its Colonial Minister are not a whit lessened, but on the contrary are made more arduous and complex, by the arrangement; for the power that appoints must command, and having to command on this system Governors of different ranks in close official connexion with each other, must assign exact limits to their respective powers, and decide between them in the thousand cases of doubt or difference that must be perpetually arising between them. And how is it to decide? The Federal Legislature pulls one way; this Province and that pull in other ways; the Governor-General is perhaps in difficulty with his House of Commons, and half or more than half the Lieutenant-Governors (though acting all together and under the same instructions) are getting on admirably with theirs; or he may stand right with his Assembly, and the majority of them be at feud with theirs. Can he and they, representatives of one and the same authority, be suffered to counteract each other's policy, for the sake of the local popularity each may thereby gain for himself?—The cure would be worse than the disease; the clashing of the wheels within wheels harder far to deal with than the jarring of the simpler machinery they are meant to replace.

That the principle of collision, as reduced to practice in the federal system of the United States, is any thing but the sound principle of good government, I think I have already shown. They, however, could not do otherwise than as they did in acting on it. They were thirteen Sovereign States, so united geographically that their several Sovereignties, independently exercised, were incompatible with one another. The powers they delegated to their Federal Government were all powers of *Sovereignty*,—those which they were physically unable to exercise to any advantage apart,—the treaty and war-making power, the supreme control of the army, navy, post-office, currency and commercial taxation, of the Union. Our Colonies need no other bond of union with each other than they have already in their common union with the whole British Empire. They have no powers of Sovereignty to be incompatible; and none can be delegated to any confederations into which they can be formed, unless at the expense of the existing Sovereignty of the Empire. We cannot let them coin money, make tariffs, keep up armies and navies, treat with foreign States, and make peace or war; and yet keep them a portion of the Empire. The parallel, little as it would promise were it ever so perfect, does not hold at all.

It may be very desirable sometimes to unite two or more Colonies, I readily admit. Little Colonies hold out such temptation to misgovernment, that wherever a group of them can be formed into a single Province without great difficulty, there would be material advantage in their Union. But the union ought not to be Federal; the new Province, to be kept, should have but one Executive and Legislature; every other administrative or law-making power within it, should be subject to its laws and government—in a word, merely Municipal.

In some Colonies a good deal has been thought of the advantages to be derived from the employment of accredited agents in England, to keep the Colonial Office, the Houses of Parliament and the public better informed as to their views and interests. At one time or another, several Colonies have employed such agents; and now and then, when they have been specially sent to effect certain objects and go back again, their services have been of value. But the question is not of special missions in rare cases of emergency, but of the system of having permanent agents residing at the seat of the Imperial Government. The mere employing of some one in London, perhaps a Member of Parliament or perhaps not, to ask interviews, make speeches and write letters, to order, for a particular Colony, can never do it much service. Agents of this class are seldom Colonists; for few Colonists are to be found living in London for their own pleasure, and few Colonies would pay their representative enough to induce a capable man to leave his adopted or native country and live in London for the mere sake of that appointment. Besides, a settled residence in London may be said to de-colonize such a man, be he ever so thoroughly a Colonist at first. In a few years' time, the country he represents will have outgrown his recollections, whatever he may do to keep them up. The information he is to deal in he must then obtain from newspapers and letters, just as every one else does. And every one else who cares enough about the Colony to get newspapers and letters from it, and read and talk about them, will put himself and be put by others on a level with him. As for the Colonial Office, with its despatches coming fresh to it by every mail, it will soon learn to laugh at his pretensions to instruct it, and will class him as an authority far below the smoother-tongued advisers whom he is commissioned to discredit. In plain truth, no agent but one can be of real use to a Colony for any length of time, in that quarter. Let a Province have a Governor surrounded by popular servants, and his agency in Downing Street will be worth something indeed. With it, no other will be wanted. Without it, no other worth having can be had.

The project has been entertained, not, it is true, by any political party either here or in the Colonies, but by some speculative writers, of a representation of the Colonies on the floor of the House of Commons, by way of making that body, and thereby the Colonial Office, better able to discharge its Imperial functions. At first sight, the plan may seem to have much to recommend it, but it by no means bears looking into. The House of Commons is generally admitted to have too many Members, as it is; and were it not so, there would still remain the strongest objections to the number being increased in this particular way. The Colonies could seldom or never be content to return others than Colonists as their representatives; indeed, if they were, their Members would be of as little value as so many mere resident agents, for any information they could render on colonial subjects. Delegates coming from the colonies would be just as incompetent to take part in the local politics of the three kingdoms, as the representatives of England, Scotland, and Ireland to manage the internal affairs of the Colonies.

No one can suppose that by giving the Colonies representation in one of our Houses of Parliament, the necessity of allowing them subordinate local legislatures will be done away; and as to drawing a line between the local legislation of the three kingdoms and the imperial legislation in which alone the Colonies have an interest, and letting the Colonial Members vote only on the latter, that also would be practically impossible. How then could Members from Canada or Van Diemen's Land be suffered to have a voice on English and Irish affairs, while those for Middlesex and Dublin are to have none on Canadian and Australian questions? Were their number ever so trifling, this difficulty could not fail to make itself felt; for their true policy would be to band together to further their own ends, and their vote on English, Scotch, and Irish questions would then immediately become formidable. But this is far from all. The truth is, that whatever their number, the fact of their presence in the House would be more likely to operate unfavourably on Colonial interests than otherwise. At present, the Imperial Parliament, while it claims full power to legislate on all matters affecting the Colonies, shows itself in practice extremely reluctant to meddle at all in their concerns. Place ever so few Colonists on the floor of St. Stephen's Chapel, and the chief cause of this salutary reluctance were instantly removed. Legislation for the Colonies, there is too much reason to presume, would quickly become the rule, instead of being, as it is now, the rare exception. It is ridiculous to imagine that the Colonies can ever have as many Members allowed them as they would require for the fair representation of their views and interests, in the face of the 658 representatives of the United Kingdom. Overpowered by numbers, their representation must be. And, what with the difficulty in the Colonies of finding the required number of men to undertake such a mission for any rate of pay that could be afforded them, the distance they would be removed from their constituents, the strong temptations they would be under to postpone their constituents' interests to their own, and the power they would always have of throwing at least the larger share of the odium of their acts, whatever they might be, upon their 658 metropolitan fellow-members, their practical responsibility to their constituents must be extremely slight. Under such circumstances, I repeat, their having seats in St. Stephen's Chapel would do the Colonies more harm than good.

What is it the Colonies want of Parliament? That it should legislate for them as much as it can,—or as little? Most certainly, the less Parliament meddles with their affairs, the better they are pleased, and the better their affairs prosper. They want to be let well alone, to have no one, not even Parliament, standing in their sunshine. On those large questions of general policy, on which the Imperial Government and Parliament must decide, they desire to have their views known, and their interests thought of. Make their Governors, then, represent them. A Ministry can always secure the favourable attention of Parliament to its plans; and a Governor, as a thing of course, commands always the fair, not to say favourable, hearing of the Ministers whose servant he is. The Cabinet gained, all is gained.

View the matter in what light we may, we are forced to the conclusion, that the one remedy, without which everything else will be a mockery, is the simple one of making our Governors distinctly understand that it is their business to govern popularly; that they are to ascertain the state of the public mind as the Sovereign does at home, and to treat it, when ascertained, with the same sort of consideration. To enable them to do this, we must give each his House of Commons; and make all parties, Governor, Commons, and public servants, clearly aware that the chief Officials of the Province, instead of being suffered to keep their tenure of office, as heretofore, secure by sheltering themselves behind the orders they put into the Governor's mouth for their own guidance, are to be treated as answerable to the Province for all his public acts to which, either by direct ministerial agency, or indirectly by remaining in office, they shall at any time render themselves parties; and are not to be kept in office in defiance of the public voice, should the House of Commons of the Province deliberately condemn those acts, and declare its want of confidence in them as their abettors and presumed advisers; in a word, that in place of the Governor's being the scape-goat for ever sacrificed for their sins, they are to keep their places, as his Ministers responsible to the Province, so long only as they can defend his acts and their own with success.

Such is the sum total of what is required to constitute the true system of Provincial Administration; the so much controverted principle of Colonial "Responsible Government;" after all, nothing new, no theoretical innovation threatening one knows not what practical results; but a mere extension to our Colonies of an old rule or two of Government long ago reduced to every-day practice by ourselves at home, so easily and constantly kept in practice among us, that in all our political controversies nobody ever now-a-days alludes to them otherwise than as postulates of our Constitutional system, which one would as little think of questioning or proving as he would the postulates that grace the first page of the introduction to the six books of Euclid.

In Colonies differently circumstanced, the system admits of being developed under widely differing forms. Wherever, as we have seen is still the case in some of our Colonies, the Officials have not as yet been brought into collision with the popular feeling, it may for some time involve no proclaimed or apparent change in their position. A Governor merely announcing and acting on the general principle that the wishes of the Colonists are to have all the weight that can be given them, may make the old machinery of office, though very imperfect, work on smoothly enough for years; the Officials around him undismissed and unthreatened, so long as their good sense or good fortune shall keep them from getting into disfavour with the representative body. If, on the other hand, they have not been sensible and lucky enough to keep clear of this disfavour, they may expect very quickly to feel some of its effects. Individual Executive Councillors will have to make way for more popular men. At first, probably, the retiring men will not be of the number of the well-paid Officials; or if they are, they may manage to retreat adroitly from their unpaid responsibility as Councillors without losing their other offices. And perhaps at the very first, the new Councillors may not all have seats in Parliament. Before long, however, this must become an essential requisite; and then again, at no distant day, must follow the demand that Executive Councillors shall not be called on to render their arduous and responsible services for nothing, while the old officials, retaining their old births, are well paid for the easier, subordinate sort of work they have to do under the Councillors' direction. Where, as in Canada on the occasion of the Union, the opportunity happens to offer for an entire re-modelling of the official corps, the Executive Council will naturally be made up at once of leading Officials, all having seats in one or other branch of the Legislature, after the fashion of Cabinet Ministers at home; and the line of political responsibility will be so drawn as to make them the parties specially answerable for the Governor's acts. To this state, with the further probable addition, before long, of a class of secondary Officials, recognized as Members of the Government, though not of the Executive Council or Cabinet, the system must everywhere tend more or less rapidly. It is scarcely to be supposed that in any of our Colonies the peculiarities of the organization of our Cabinet Council will be exactly copied. The Executive Council is likely in all to be both Cabinet and Privy Council; its Members few in number, and ceasing to have anything to do with it, whenever they cease to be Members of the Provincial Administration for the time being.

Be the precise form, however, in each case what it may, the principle is in all the same. The one general rule to be laid down is simply that the wishes of the people are to be as far as possible acted upon by the Executive. The practice in each Colony, as at home, will come of itself. A House of Assembly will take care not to attack a Governor personally, when it has once fairly learned that it can gain such changes of Provincial men and measures as it may desire, in any other way. And a Governor who understands that a quarrel with the Assembly on any mere question of Provincial men or measures may be expected to lead to his recall, will seldom bring things to that extremity. He will incline rather to choose new Councillors himself, than to put the Crown to the trouble of choosing a new Governor.

Is it said, as by some it has been, that under such a system the Governor is stripped of all power, and reduced to a mere puppet in the hands of a Provincial Junta? The assumption is singularly gratuitous. Who does not see that in this respect the Governor of a Province stands in a far stronger position than the Sovereign of an independent state? Should his Councillors seek unduly to enlarge the sphere of their influence at the expense of his own, he has a power to fall back upon, which his Sovereign in a like case has not. He may appeal, not merely to their political antagonists within the Province, but to the Imperial Government; and if his cause of quarrel be good, he is not likely to appeal in vain. He is the party in direct communication with it. The representative within the Colony, not merely of royalty in the abstract, but of the British nation and power generally, it must be very much his own fault indeed, if he have not influence enough, if his position under the new *regime*, with a Cabinet and Parliament to deal with and govern by, be not far higher and more honourable than under the old,—when every mail brought him precise instructions on the most trifling details of his administration, emanating almost every one of them from no higher source than the brain of some perhaps clever but always unknowing and unknown subordinate of an Assistant Under-Secretary in the Colonial Office.

Unquestionably, in the supposable case of the selection of a weak, incompetent man as a Governor, his Ministers would have a larger share of power than would fall to their lot under an abler man. But this fact, so far from forming an objection to the system, is in reality one of its recommendations. It would give the Colonial Office a new motive to pick out proper men. Heretofore, except in extraordinary cases, one man has been pretty much the same as another. Downing-Street on the one hand, and a knot of irresponsible Colonial politicians on the other, have (either or both of them) played "Captain's Captain" with all Governors; neither having much fancy for Captains of inconvenient ability; and men of real talent, no strong motive for fancying the Captain's place. The new order of things is calculated to reverse all this. Downing-Street, if it means to preserve for itself any power, must benefit the Colonies by sending them out able men, to govern popularly. And failing to do this, it at least cannot injure them by handing over the management of their affairs to a lot of interested local oligarchies of its own creation; but will have to place the power it surrenders in the hands of those men in each colony who, on the score of personal popularity and influence, have the best right to hold it, and are the most likely to use it well.

It has been asserted, I am well aware,—and if often asserting could prove, it were well proven,—that all this is irreconcileable with the essential distinction there is between an independent country and a dependent Province. The position of a Governor bound to obey the orders of a higher authority, it is said, is altogether different from that of a King. This plan makes it in effect the same; and cannot be put into operation without at once rendering his Province a virtually independent state, without in a very short time making it an independent state in all respects. A little closer examination will show that it does no such thing.

The distinction between the two cases is admitted. A Colonial Governor cannot be held incapable of doing wrong, as a King can and should be. The Sovereign of the realm has to do only with his own people; the Governor of a colony stands in relation not merely to the people he is sent out to govern, but also to the Sovereign who deputes and can recall him, to the Parliament which has an unlimited power of legislation in matters affecting his government, to the people whose will the Parliament embodies. We all know, that for a long time past, our fathers and ourselves have acted on the principle that we will not hold the Sovereign answerable for his acts, but will throw the blame of them, if any there be, on his Ministers, as men who are loyally presumed to have advised him into every blunder or wrong that any one may charge against his government, as men whose business it was at any rate to have advised him better, to have resigned office rather than be parties to the acts we censure. Now what is there to prevent the people of a Colony from pursuing a like course with their Governor? Will it not in fact be the wisest thing they can do, provided always they have the substantial power that we have, of making any Ministers they find fault with retire from office?

What has this to do with the relations between their Governor on the one hand, and the Crown, Parliament, and People of the Mother Country on the other? It is true enough that *they* cannot agree to regard his Provincial Ministers as the parties responsible for his acts, and so suffer him to disobey orders on the ground that this or that Council or Cabinet of highly influential gentlemen of the colony he is governing advised him so to do? On such a system the Imperial authority would have no one responsible to it at all; for were it to command the Governor to change his advisers by way of punishing them for their bad advice, those gentlemen would merely have to counsel him again to do no such thing, and the second instructions would be quietly shelved beside the first. The only functionary in a colony whose responsibility to the Parent State is worth any thing, is the Governor. His Provincial servants are not of the Parent State, but of the Province. The authorities at home, therefore, cannot release him from his accountability for every action of his government. Strictly speaking, it will not even do to say that the responsibility is to be divided between him and his Ministers; he answering to Great Britain for his conduct in cases where Metropolitan or Imperial interests are involved, and they for him to the Province in all others. Who is to determine the character of each case as it occurs? The higher authority, it is self-evident, must always define its own sphere of action; just as a Superior Court of Law does, wherever a question arises between itself and an Inferior Court. Resting as it always must with the Imperial authorities to decide what questions are imperial and what provincial, it must always be in their power, if they choose, to control the action of the Governor. In other words, he cannot be otherwise than responsible for every act of his administration, *to them*.

But this seeming difficulty is after all one of mere theory. Responsible Government is not conceded unless the Governor's instructions enjoin on him as a rule, that he is so to conduct his administration as to carry with him, in matters affecting the Province, the vote of the House of Assembly. Now what is the effect of such an instruction? The Colonial Office may still give him whatever orders it may please; but to be consistent, these orders will require to be all interpreted with a constant reference to this, its first and chief command. On questions of purely imperial policy they may be peremptory, and he must then execute them to the letter—that is to say always, provided such execution be a thing possible. On questions of provincial concern they must be held to be conditional; and he will have to try to carry them out,—but if the temper of the Province be such that he cannot act on them without thereby setting it against him, the general command laid upon him to govern through the Assembly will be his warrant for deferring to its wishes, and reporting home the difficulty he has met with as an insurmountable obstacle. It will be for the home Government simply to judge of the sufficiency or insufficiency of his endeavours to bring his Ministers and House to their views. Satisfied of his fidelity and judgment, they must be content. He has disobeyed no order. He would have disobeyed their most positive order, had he risked a collision for the sake of a conditional instruction. It may happen some day, for it is hard to say what may not happen, that Downing Street may insist on his literal obedience to some such instruction, and he find it absolutely impossible to bring together a set of Provincial Ministers who will take the responsibility of helping him under it. In such a case, there is a collision between the Parent State and the colony, and the question is whether either, and which, of the two will give way. Unless, after due explanations, one or other shall see fit to yield, the Parent State has before her the alternative of governing the Colony by force or abandoning it to independence. But it is no peculiar result of Responsible Government, this state of things. On the contrary, I shall show presently how very much it lessens the risks of its being even brought about. We must look first, however, to its practical results with regard to the relations which it establishes between the different authorities of the Colony itself. These ascertained, it will be easy to show its operation as between them and the authorities of the Empire.

The tendency of the system, as I have shown, is to establish in each colony a council of resident Colonists responsible to its legislature for the Governor's acts, and more or less closely resembling our Cabinet Council, according to circumstances. The closer this resemblance, the more perfectly has the system been introduced. Wherever it is in any thing like full operation, the members of this responsible Cabinet must act together in the conduct of the administration, except in those comparatively few cases where they may avow the "open question" policy; must all be answerable, (except as may regard any open question) for the public acts and declarations of each of their number, as well as for the public acts and declarations of the Governor whom they serve. Whatever the Governor says or does is said or done by them, unless to escape such responsibility they at the time retire from office. Whatever any one of them says or does is in like manner the word or deed of all of them, unless at the time they unequivocally repudiate it by either making him leave the Ministry or leaving it themselves.

As a matter of course, a Provincial Ministry, once organized on any thing like this footing, must undertake and be answerable for the satisfactory conduct of the Parliamentary business of the country. It must speak on all occasions for the Crown, in both Houses, conduct Government measures, and especially move and carry the supply votes required for the public service. It is important the Crown should resume, wherever it can be done, its right (abandoned in most colonies) of initiating all money-votes; so that its Provincial Ministers may be made directly and obviously accountable for the whole expenditure of the public funds. There will be little difficulty about this, when once the people and their representatives shall have become habituated to the usages to which the presence of Ministers of the Crown in Parliament must lead; but till then, the innovation will be viewed with distrust, and ought not therefore to be prematurely urged.

Well organized, however, or ill, the *sine quâ non* of their position is the necessity under which they are placed of carrying with them the sense of the House of Assembly. The Crown having declared that it will not regard its higher ministerial servants in a Colony as holding office otherwise than on what may be termed a political tenure, that it will consider reasons of state policy at all times sufficient cause for their removal or resignation, they stand before the country bound to defend the whole course of the Representative of the Crown. If condemned by the public voice in so doing, they must resign; or the Crown, to act out the declarations of its Imperial Ministers, must remove them. A single defeat on a legislative measure, of course, need not unseat them, any more than it need unseat Ministers here; but a vote of want of confidence, a defeat on a motion for necessary supplies, or on any other motion of importance upon which they may have taken a special stand, or a series of minor defeats showing them not to possess the confidence of the popular body, must force them to the alternative of a dissolution of Parliament or loss of place.

So far, all we find is a tendency to the closest approximation possible, towards long-established British usages. But as regards the relations between them and the Governor, it becomes requisite to note an essential distinction between what is the British and what must be the Colonial usage. The Governor of a colony, we have seen, is not the mere representative of the Crown, but its servant also; as much its Minister as they, though of another and higher grade than theirs, responsible for every act to which he is a party, not indeed to the Colonial Legislature as they are, but to the Crown, and to the Parliament and people of Great Britain who suffer no Minister of the Crown to be otherwise than accountable to themselves for the discharge of his trust. On the shoulders of a Governor's Provincial Ministers this accountability to Imperial authority sits lightly; for they are far off, and it knows little or nothing of them. But on the Governor its weight falls quite otherwise. His orders come to him direct from home; he must explain or defend all he does to the Ministers of the Crown at home, whenever they require it, and his acts may be disavowed, and he censured or recalled, if they should think his reasons insufficient. Unable to devolve this responsibility on any Provincial advisers, or even to share it with them, his position calls on him to take a far more active part in public affairs than the Sovereign is under any necessity of taking. The Queen is always safe in following her Ministers' Counsel, and may follow it therefore just as implicitly as she chooses. He is no such thing. They may advise him to do what may cost him his Commission; and it will seldom be enough for him, when his acts may be questioned, to say merely that they were advised. A weak man, to be sure, or a man whose habits or health may not admit of close attention to business, may in point of fact give his Council as free scope, and himself as little trouble, as he pleases; but he does so on his own risk. A man of mind and character, equal to the fatigue of his duties, will not leave other men to do them. Before acting as his Ministers propose, he must want to hear their reasons, and to be satisfied besides in his own mind that they are sound. The general type of the Colonial Governor, under the system of Responsible Government in its best estate, ought not to be and must not be the "King Log."

"The Governor of a Colony greater than his Sovereign!" cries some astonished provincial Liberal who has not yet thought quite as deeply as he has felt upon the subject, "the Queen's Representative take upon himself personally, within his Province, a larger share of the duties and therefore of the powers of government than the Queen his mistress does at home! Her Majesty's Provincial ministers held more in check by a mere Viceroy—their fellow-minister, as you style him—than her Imperial ministers are by Royalty in person!"—Brave words, doubtless, and hard to answer, were it not sense more than sound that one fears in argument. Who does not know that the Premier's views are a ten times greater check on the freedom of the majority of a Cabinet, than the Queen's are? Yet who complains, therefore, that the constitution recognizes the Premier as greater than the Queen? Every body is aware that the Premier has to look so closely after his colleagues, because, being the Queen's chief minister and nothing more, he is specially held accountable for his associates in the ministerial trust. The Governor of a Colony is *so far*, in the position of a Premier as this, that he too has to answer for his Cabinet; to be their sponsor to the Empire just as much as they are his to the Province. It is not that he is greater than the Crown, but on the contrary because he is merely the Crown's servant, that he must personally have more to do within his Province than his mistress need do at home. The question is not of any prerogative to be enjoyed by him, which the Queen has not, and therefore cannot delegate. The Queen has the undoubted *right* to attend as closely as she pleases to all manner of State affairs. The inconceivable amount and multiplicity of the public business simply set limits to her physical power of attending to it. And as a Sovereign, having ministers who must assume the entire responsibility of it, her prerogative in this respect is not her duty. With her Representative it is; and the amount of business which it brings under his charge, though great, is yet so much less, that he can in effect exercise a kind and degree of oversight of it, as a whole, such as it would be ridiculous to suppose that any Sovereign of an immense Empire could possibly exercise over its world-wide machinery of imperial government.

But there is more to be said. Whatever a Governor may be to the Crown, and to the Imperial Parliament, he is nothing less within his colony than the Crown's Representative; and the Colony is after all nothing more than a powerful municipality of the Empire, its local laws made valid, nay, its very corporate existence given it, by Imperial authority. To the Empire the Queen is simply a Constitutional Sovereign, the limit the Constitution sets to her authority being in effect the will and pleasure of her subjects. To the Province, the Governor is as much the Representative of the Empire as of the Sovereign. The virtual responsibility, so to speak, of a Sovereign to his people consists in the risk he would run of being dethroned by them, if he were to excite the nation by mis-government into rebellion. That of a Governor to his Province is in his danger of recall by the Imperial power, if the complaints of the Province should induce it to think he is doing wrong. A nation has a direct hold on its Sovereign, which the people of a Province have not on their Governor. He is not greater than a King, but they are less than a nation.

That a Colony has no good reason, constitutionally speaking, let its people be ever so devoted to the more strictly popular characteristics of the Constitution, to complain of this necessary practical result of its position as a Colony, is easily shown. The British Constitution here in Great Britain, where the purely monarchical check is no doubt rather less than it tends to be with them, is any thing but a contrivance for giving to a popularly elected body, the representative of the national will, an immediate, absolute, unchecked control of the whole power of the state. It is the power that rules, because it is the strongest power; but its rule is no despotism. The Upper House is strong, too; and the Crown, surrounded by Aristocracy and sustained, besides, by the confirmed aristocratic and monarchical habits of thought of the entire nation, is no mere passive agent of the ruling Third Estate. The checks interposed by the Constitution yield before the deliberate will of the Third Estate, but not to its caprices. No form of government can ever work well, unless it provides checks upon the ruling power sufficient for this purpose. The caprices of unchecked power—of despotism, in other words, whether centred in a single ruler or in an oligarchy or in an elected body, —— by the mischiefs they inflict, create disturbing forces that convulse society in their effort to throw off the incubus. The over-balanced machinery of Transatlantic Republicanism forms no Government at all; but caprice-rule, be it of a Grand Turk, or of a Venetian Senate or of a National Constitution, is a Government if possible worse than none. We have seen that in a Colony the aristocratic check upon the popular impulses is greatly weaker than it is at home. Its Legislative Council is not of itself a power in the State, as the House of Lords is. The Province absolutely requires, for the very security of its popular government, that the Crown be within it more a power of itself than it either need be or can be to the Empire.

Be it remembered, moreover, that this greater check is after all one of very slight disturbing power. It consists merely in the necessity under which it places the leaders of the ascendant party in a Province, of securing for their proposed measures the assent of the representative of the Imperial power, an assent which he can have no motive to withhold lightly. It is not a supposable thing, that he will be instructed, or that without instructions he will be inclined wantonly to thwart the wishes of the party that sustains him with its friendly majority. The inevitable tendency of the system, as I have shown, is to make the home Government choose capable men as its representatives, and trust its interests to their discretion when so chosen. If, then, the proposed measures of a Provincial Cabinet are such as to make the Governor demur to their propriety, the chances are that it will eventually shape its course in regard to them all the more prudently for the delay and discussion which his demur will have occasioned. Indeed, without his often or perhaps ever demuring seriously to any project, the knowledge on their part that they have got so to frame and so to state their projects as to satisfy him that he may safely lend them the weight of the approbation of the power he represents, must always be a most salutary restraining influence. It is the thing most wanted in all political controversy, — an ever acting inducement to party moderation in the exercise of power.

Peculiar, however, as the relation of a Governor to his Cabinet is in this respect, there is nothing in it to warrant them, or the Parliament or people they represent, in treating the Governor personally, otherwise than as the Cabinet, Parliament, and people of Great Britain always treat the Sovereign. It is one thing for the Governor to feel that with reference to Great Britain he is a mere minister of the Crown; and a very different thing for them to regard him in that light with reference to their Colony. They strike at the first principle of the Responsible Government system, if they do so.

They force him, be his inclinations what they may, into the false position of one who is a party to their political struggles. They compel the Imperial Government, whose servant he is, to be continually taking part with or against him in those struggles,—in a word, to be always exercising in their internal affairs an interfering influence which the Colony must dislike as amounting to a perpetual and most harassing control. They will bring back upon themselves, to the best of their power, all the evils and annoyances of the old system which it is the very object of the new to get rid of.

No feature in the British Constitution is more obvious to remark, than the exceeding jealousy with which it provides against the possibility of the Crown's being drawn into collision with the People, and so losing any of those constitutional prerogatives without which it would cease to have the power to conduct the government of the country with effect. *A multo fortiori* should the people of a Province take care to observe all the conservative usages which for this end the good sense of parties at home has established. Here, the one danger to be apprehended is an undue weakening of the Executive authority, which after all is but what the nation chooses to have it, and might therefore in case of need easily be strengthened again by the nation, if it chose. There, there is the further danger of collision in the mean time with the Parent State, of a government at once inefficient and unpopular, and withal by no means admitting of the same easy restoration to its normal integrity of power.

The Sovereign himself, for instance, except in his Coronation Oath, never gives, and is never asked to give, any pledges or assurances whatever as to his future course of action, either to his subjects collectively or to any individuals or public bodies. Whoever gives a pledge or promise of any sort makes himself by that act responsible to the party to whom he gives it. The promises of Royalty are made, therefore, through its ministers, and are constitutionally regarded as theirs and theirs only. The King himself must be unbound, free always to act or refuse to act on any and every occasion when his ministers may offer him their advice. Were he not so, ministers would have an indefinite power of fettering, through the Sovereign, their successors; and he would besides become so completely a party to their acts that a change of Ministry could hardly take place without a change of Sovereign too. The only case of seeming exception to the rule is really no exception at all. Ministers taking office do so of course on such terms, that is to say, with such Colleagues and on such avowed principles, as they see fit. And the species of negociation that takes place on such occasions may at first sight seem to be a requirement on their part of an engagement to themselves from the Sovereign. But it is no such thing. The Sovereign gives no promise, and they ask none. They state their views and wishes, not for an indefinite or contingent future, but for the certain present. He determines how far he can then and there act upon these views. Determine as he may, his decision is for the present, and binds him in no sense for the time to come. To take a recent case, and one that presents more of the semblance of a pledge from Royalty than perhaps any other that could be named, Sir Robert Peel's famous stipulation for the removal of the Ladies of the Bedchamber. The proposal to the Queen was limited to a single act, and contemplated no engagement, expressed or understood, from herself to the expectant Premier. He could not take office but with a Cabinet of his friends and a Royal Household not made up of his enemies. Of what the Queen was to do or not to do after he should have taken office, there was not a word. The Minister can always retire from office, if he should not like what the Sovereign may do or mean to do. That one check is all he can either have or ask for. And it is and must be just as truly the one sufficient check in a Colony as in a Kingdom.

Again, as a necessary consequence of the same general principle, no public man or set of men may constitutionally assume an attitude of antagonism towards the Crown. If any one chooses to violate the rule by any act or word discourteous to the Sovereign, he has disqualified himself for the public service; no man so offending being ever forced on Royalty. And with good reason; for the offence is one that argues a want of sense and temper, for which no popularity or talent could ever make amends. Nor may a Cabinet place itself in unnecessary collision with the Crown, any more than an individual. No Minister or Ministers either while in office or after leaving it, may charge upon the Sovereign any general personal intentions or opinions from which he or they dissent. Those intentions and opinions every one is bound to presume right; and be they what they may, Ministers at any rate are not answerable for them, but simply for the advice they tender, or may be presumed to tender him, and for his acts as the evidence of what that advice was. To draw the personal opinions of the Sovereign into controversy, is to put the question to the country, of his fitness or unfitness for the throne, instead of the true constitutional question of their own fitness or unfitness for office; to set about a revolution, not a change of Ministry. Besides, the knowledge they have of those opinions must be derived mainly from their communications with him at the Council Board and in the transaction of their other official business. For the business of the country to be carried on satisfactorily, the most perfect confidence should mark the intercourse, at once of the Sovereign and his Ministers, and of the Ministers with each other. How is this to be, if any information obtained through such means be liable ever to be divulged, unless with the unequivocally expressed mutual consent of the parties? Once let men regard confidential transactions as not strictly secret, and all confidence is at an end.

Hence the absoluteness of the rule, that in case of a resignation, no retiring Minister may enter into any explanation whatever as to the cause of his resigning office, until expressly permitted by the Crown to do so; that there must always be Ministers responsible for such permission; and that the extent and tenor of the explanations may in no way go beyond or contravene any limitation, express or implied, of the permission given. As to a permission to bring into debate the personal views of the Sovereign, that is a sheer impossibility. No retiring Minister could dare ask it, nor any Minister in office be a party to the granting of it. The resignation must always turn on *some one or more special facts*, and in defending and discussing it nothing confidentially known may be disclosed beyond what strictly relates to such fact or facts. The fact or facts on which a resignation turns must, further, always be *of the present time*. No past transactions can be brought up, except in so far as they may be clearly necessary to the right understanding of the present; and then there must be absolutely no charge of malfeasance founded on them, even against a colleague. What is done is done. Every Minister has made himself accountable for every public act, whether of the Crown or of his Colleagues, which he has suffered to pass without instant resignation. Could he relieve himself from that accountability by asserting afterwards that he protested, or objected, or was not advised with, he were no responsible Minister at all; he might stay in Office half a life-time, and to the last disclaim all personal agency in every transaction that any one should find fault with. Nay, with such a rule, a Ministry might even purposely mislead the Sovereign, by bad advice or criminal remissness, into errors grave enough to compromise his Crown, and then slip out of the trap themselves, by declaring to the Country, that they remonstrated, and remonstrated in vain, and were at last forced to retire from his counsels by his determined persistance in mis-government. Such a case, doubtless, were an extreme case; but it might occur, were the rule other or less absolute than it is. Ambitious politicians behave none the worse for having strict rules to go by.

In this country, by long usage, all these rules have become so much a thing of course that one hardly ever has to state them. But in a Colony, where the old system has been long in operation, and where people have consequently learned to regard the recall of a Governor in a light so very different from that in which every one would look upon the deposing of a King, it may be necessary to argue them out at length and dwell upon them, till men's minds shall have become thoroughly habituated to them in their practical application to colonial politics.

There is really equal if not even greater need in a Colony, for the requirement of a strict observance of every one of these fixed rules of the Constitution. The choice in either case is between two systems; the one, the plan by which the people hold the head of their Government answerable, and for any change of policy have to seek his removal; the other, the plan of holding his Ministers to account, and trying merely to change them. As an independent nation, if we resolve on revolution, we can have it. No one else has anything to do or say in the case. But a Colony, seeking even redress of grievances by clamouring for the recall of its Governor, brings itself into controversy with the Parent State, whose Minister the Governor is; and may or may not be able to gain its immediate end, according as the Parent State may be more or less decided in its opposition, and more or less powerful. Gain it or not, the struggle must at any rate be far more tedious and exasperating, and its results therefore far more to be feared, for the fact of this inevitable intervention in it of a strong third party. Time out of mind, that system of getting rid of Governors has been in full operation. With what results? The conversion of thirteen Colonies—after a long war, in which they were more than once nearly beaten, and could not have succeeded after all, but for a degree of folly and mismanagement on the part of the then Imperial Government such as it is little likely to be soon guilty of again,—into a foreign state; a steady progression towards an unavailing anarchy of excitement and discontent in every other.

The Colonial Office has in fact promulgated the new system; late in the day, it is very true, perhaps more hesitatingly and in terms more nearly bordering on the ambiguous, than it should have done. But, nevertheless, by its repeated abjurations of all wish to govern colonies otherwise than in the interest, and in accordance with the well understood wishes, of their people; and by the Russell rule, that declared the tenure of the higher offices in the colonies henceforth political, it has said all it was essential for it to say, to put the new system into operation. It has but to be wise enough to keep its practice to the rule it has laid down. The Colonies themselves have to do the rest; and the success of the experiment, supposing always the Office not suddenly smitten with insanity, will depend on the way they set about it. Let their public men adhere strictly to the safe usages of the Mother Country; let the same wise moderation mark their course which here has consecrated those usages, and without which even here the political machinery of which those usages form an essential part never could have been made to work, and could not now be kept at work a twelvemonth; and there is nothing to prevent them from entirely succeeding in the attainment of their ends. Let them, on the other hand, show any other temper; let them seek to overleap or force down barriers which possibly some of them, unused to the practice of constitutional rule, may mistake either for mere matters of form, or for restrictions on the popular principle of government; and, however indisposed the people of Great Britain may be to meddle ever so little in their affairs, they will soon find out to their cost that the age of miracles is gone by, and that upon their principles the maintenance of the constitutional system is an impossibility. If the Governors to whom Great Britain delegates the authority of her Crown, are to be treated in their several Provinces, not as the Crown is treated at home, but as objects of political hostility and attack, Great Britain will be forced to stand by and see fair play, to support them whenever she may think fair play is not given them. There is but one kind of popular rule that she can extend to her colonies; the kind she keeps for herself. A signing and sealing automaton, fettered by engagements for the future—the tongue-tied, thought-tied agent of a set of Colonial Councillors, who if they see occasion may release themselves from all responsibility by asserting that all or any of his past acts were not theirs—a mere salaried state-puppet—is not the Representative the British Crown must have in its several colonies, to maintain unimpaired the relations that must subsist between them and the Empire.

A question of fact, remains, and must be answered before we can proceed further. The late Nova Scotia and Canadian resignations, how came they to happen as they did, if Colonial Responsible Government is the safe system I have stated it to be?

An answer that seems to have satisfied the gullibility of some people's suspicion in Canada, throws all the blame on Downing Street and its two Governors Lord Stanley, they say, must have given orders, or Sir Charles Metcalfe and Lord Falkland must have laid their heads together, with or without Lord Stanley's privity to the plot, for the recall of the fatal concession of Responsible Government. The charge is gravely made in Canada, though I am not aware that any one has thought it could be of much use to make it any where else. Lord Stanley has said in Parliament that he had given no such orders. Mr. Viger, Sir Charles Metcalfe's leading Minister, a veteran Responsible-Government man, and an honest man above suspicion, has declared in Sir Charles's behalf that he had had no such previous communication either with Lord Stanley or Lord Falkland. The authors of the charge treat these disclaimers as a mere pleading of "not guilty." Counter-evidence of its truth they cannot have. Let us see whether the facts are such as to warrant us in attributing to it any, the very faintest shadow of credibility.

The Nova Scotian case it is easy enough to understand. There had been there, from the time of Lord Falkland's arrival in 1840, a sort of coalition Cabinet, framed upon terms to which Lord Sydenham, when he visited Halifax in the summer of that year, had brought several leading Liberals to agree, and which he had recommended for adoption as embodying the smallest amount of concession that could be made available. Sir Colin Campbell's Executive Council had been defeated in the House in the month of February previous, on the vote of want of confidence, by a majority of 30 to 12; and one Member of it, Mr. J. B. Uniacke, had resigned in consequence, stating that he understood the Russell tenure-of-office Despatch then just published to be a concession of Responsible Government, and should act on it accordingly, however much till then he had opposed those who had contended for it. Sir Colin had told the House they were quite mistaken, and in a very short time had pushed the quarrel to the point of forcing it to call upon the Crown to recall him. By Lord Sydenham's advice he was recalled, though with all imaginable courtesy of manner, and with the substantial *douceur* of another colonial government to console him. Lord Falkland on his arrival found five Members of the Executive Council who had seats in neither House. To four of them he intimated that the Queen had no further occasion for their services; and he desired the fifth, Mr. M'Nab, a gentleman who had been appointed after the vote of want of confidence and was the only Liberal in the whole body, to obtain a seat in the Assembly. This done, he called to his Cabinet either three or four other gentlemen who had or could get seats in Parliament, Mr. J. B Uniacke being one, and Mr. Howe (the only man of the three or four who could be said to be of the popular party) another. The House stood more than two to one against the old Official party. In this coalition Cabinet the majority of the House numbered just two votes; a third member, long a minority leader, was a recent convert to its views of Responsible Government; while five Members were of the minority party! Most of its Members had to serve without pay, the two Liberals among the number; most of the better paid Officials kept their offices free from the troubles and risks of the Executive Councillor's position.

However, the Liberals generally assented to the terms, though not a few grumbled at better not being given. Parliament was dissolved, a new House of the same political complexion was returned, and the coalition Ministry received its support and sanction. At one time, for a few months, a third Liberal had a seat in it; and for about a twelvemonth before it was broken up, Mr. Howe held an office of emolument, that of collector of Provincial Customs for the Port of Halifax; but beyond this there was no approach towards a fairer distribution of the honors and rewards of office. The minority, though thwarted by their Colleagues at the Council Board, were all the while the real leaders of the Goverment, because they sustained it by their majority in the House. On two several occasions, first in the session of 1841 and then during that of 1842, two of the old-school Councillors (Messrs. Johnston and Stewart) who had seats in the Upper House, spoke there of the principles on which the Administration was founded, in a manner that implied its non-admission of the Responsible-Government principle. On the former occasion, Mr. Howe was content to contradict them in his place in the Lower House, but on the second, his friends and he had to insist on the distinct embodiment of the views of the Cabinet upon the point at issue, in a written document to be read as their joint confession of faith in Parliament. For the time, the difficulty was got over. The House recorded its confidence in the Ministry by a vote of 40 to 8; the political friends of the two Councillors giving 27 votes for and 3 against the motion; and those of the six, voting 13 for and 5 against it.

Such a state of things was not likely to last for ever. The dissensions in the Cabinet became more threatening; the Liberals in the House, less complaisant and yielding. The balance of parties, they insisted, was all one way, and that not theirs. They were damaging themselves with their friends by the support they gave it. Their leaders must have more voice in the Cabinet, or they would very shortly have less in the House. The party of the old officials, on the other hand, elated with the accession of the Conservatives to power at home, thought of nothing less than getting entirely rid of their antagonists and reverting to a Government of their own framing. At this juncture, some leading men of the Baptist persuasion (a very numerous religious body in Nova Scotia—a full fifth, it is said, of the entire population of the Province) got into a quarrel, on matters foreign to politics, with Mr. Howe. His Colleague, Mr. Attorney-General Johnston, himself a Baptist, took part in the dispute; and the two Ministers, long rivals and jealous of each other, became open personal enemies. Among other promising openings for political collision between them, was an application for a Provincial grant for a Baptist college. Howe and his friends generally had made up their minds that the old practice of frittering away the public grants in aid of half-a-dozen little sectarian make-believe Colleges, was a bad one; and that the Province ought instead to found and endow handsomely a single University in which the existing institutions might all be merged. The House was for carrying out this view; and the grant to Acadia College was refused. Johnston made himself the champion of its claims; and directly after the session of 1843 was over, set out on a tour of agitation through the Counties where the Baptist body was most numerous, to hold meetings and make speeches against the University project. Howe, in return made a like tour in another direction to agitate in its favour. The alienation of the Baptists was too tempting an opportunity to be lost. What with the divisions in the Cabinet and the temper of the House, it was clear that change of some sort was impending; and the Council majority carried their point that the change should begin with a dissolution of the latter. The step was resolved upon and taken, while Howe was still out of town. The two parties in the Cabinet and their respective friends went to the Hustings in open hostility, each party charging the other with intrigue. The Elections took the Liberals every way at disadvantage, and though they claimed a majority of the new House, their opponents insisted upon it that the majority was theirs. Mr. Howe, it seems, expressed to Lord Falkland his conviction that by somewhat re-modelling the Cabinet, so as to make sure of all the Liberals, a good working Government could be formed; and offered either to remain in office with that view, without Mr. Johnston, or (if his Lordship wished) to retire and leave Mr. Johnston and his friends to any other policy they might prefer. Lord Falkland was desirous he should continue in the Council, and Mr. Johnston too; and with some reluctance and after consultation with his friends, he consented, and Mr. M'Nab with him, to meet the new house with the Council as it stood, though adhering to his former opinion that the Coalition on its then terms could by no possibility last long after the House should have come together. A few days after, the Johnston section of the Cabinet took their next move. Lord Falkland acquainted Messrs. Howe, M'Nab and Uniacke with his determination to make their five opponents six, by calling to the Council Mr. M. B. Almon, Mr. Johnston's son-in-law, a Halifax banker, generally respected as a gentleman and man of reputed integrity and wealth, but who had never sat in Parliament, was not then a Member of either House, and was all but unknown as a politician except from his having been active in opposing Mr. Howe's return for the County of Halifax at the election that was just ended. That the three gentlemen at once tendered their resignations was no great wonder. The one marvel is, that such cause for instant resignation could possibly have been given them. Neither Downing Street diplomacy, nor Lieutenant-Governor's unaided brain, could ever have hit upon the notion. It bears the true stamp of Provincial Bureaucratic genius.

The meeting of the Legislature has given neither party the triumph to which they both seem to have looked forward. Mr. Johnston and his five Colleagues did not dare contest the re-election of the former Speaker, though one of the most openly decided of their opponents in the House. But upon the question of an amendment to the Address, implying a declaration of want of confidence, the Opposition failed, after a fortnight of debate, by a vote of 26 to 24, (or rather 26 to 25, for one of their number, the Speaker, could not vote,) no member being absent. The same majority of one was the utmost they could muster on a second test-question a few days after. On the Civil List Bill, their great and apparently their only Government measure, they avoided the show of defeat by leaving all the amounts named in it to the mercy of the House; moving the actual salaries of the incumbents merely *pro forma* and letting the Opposition cut them all down as it chose. In one case only, where Mr. Uniacke thought a proposed reduction too low, and was for having an amount fixed between theirs and that of his Opposition friends, they ventured on a division, and were defeated by a vote of 27 to 20.

No Government can stand long with so little strength as this. Overtures, accordingly, are said to have been already made to the retiring Members, to induce them to resume their seats; but as yet to no purpose. The offered terms, as report states them, gave little promise of success. The six gentlemen, Almon among them, were all to stay in, on the one side; the three ex-Councillers might come back on the other, and a tenth seat at the Board might be given to a Catholic with whom they should be willing to act. Considering the experience they had just had of a coalition of this one-sided kind, the circumstances of Mr. Almon's appointment, his relationship to Mr. Johnston, the fact that those who made the offer could barely, even with all the use they could make of Lord Falkland's name, whip up a majority of one to stave off the necessity of resigning, while those to whom it was made were strong enough to beat them hollow on their money votes, it would have been a strange thing had the proposal been closed with. The precise terms of the refusal are not distinctly stated; but the amount of the counter-demand appears to have been an equal representation of the two parties in the Cabinet.

Let well alone by the Colonial Office, all this will soon right itself. The Nova Scotian ex-Ministers merely resigned when they could not help it, adhered exactly, in resigning, and have continued to adhere since, to all the constitutional observances which are considered binding on ex-Ministers of the Crown at home. There is no theoretical demand preferred; no voluntary quarrel on their part with the representative of the Crown. Their opponents have tried hard to play the old game of making him their scape-goat, and with some measure of success; but for this the ex-Ministers are not answerable. Responsible Government, in a word, has done no harm in the world, and is doing none. On the contrary, it has been keeping the Nova Scotian Liberals for several years in a temper of singular moderation, and at this moment is still keeping them, (though in opposition, and with a great deal to exasperate them) from all extravagance of demand. Parties happen to be nearly balanced; but it does not matter a straw to any Imperial interest which of the two may gain the upper hand, or what terms of truce they may hit upon to serve while their present balance of power shall last.

But now for Canada. The Union made Lord Sydenham give the Canadians a much nearer approach to an English Cabinet than he had seen fit to let the Nova Scotians have. The first Executive Council of Canada consisted of nine of its principal Officials, a Presiding Councillor, two Provincial Secretaries—one for Lower and one for Upper Canada—four Law Officers, two for either division of the Province, the Receiver-General, and the Chairman of the Board of Works. Unfortunately, the whole French race in Lower Canada were in uncompromising opposition; and in the broken and disjointed state of every other party in the Province, the Governor's personal influence and tact were the main reliance of his Cabinet—a coalition, besides, in itself, of a somewhat heterogeneous character. Just as Parliament met, Mr. Baldwin, his Solicitor-General for Upper Canada, without any previous consultation with his colleagues, advised his

Lordship, in writing, of the necessity there was in his opinion of immediately obtaining the support of the French Canadians, and tendered his own resignation in the event of the advice not being directly acted upon. Lord Sydenham accepted the resignation, and Mr. Baldwin, a Minister the day before, took his seat to debate the answer to the speech from the throne, as a leader of the Opposition. He carried with him, however, in this move, some three or four only of his friends. Lord Sydenham's dexterous management kept the great body of the Upper Canadian Liberals on the Treasury side of the House; and the Cabinet, though again and again in the greatest possible danger, lasted out the session, carried an immense mass of important measures—some, it is true, miserably enough put together—and seemed stronger in the House when Lord Sydenham died than it had ever done before.

The real strength, however, had not been theirs, but his. At the opening of the Session they had, of course, been obliged to promise that they would resign in case of their failing to receive the support of the House; and, shortly before it ended, to make themselves active parties to the passing of a string of Resolutions that affirmed, with tolerable distinctness, the determination of the House that the principal Officers under the Governor were thenceforth to be regarded by it as a Provincial Administration. But, in fact, till Lord Sydenham's death, their ministerial position had rather been a form than a reality. They had constantly relied on him far more than he on them. With Sir Richard Jackson as Administrator, and afterwards with Sir Charles Bagot as Governor-General, the state of things became widely different; and every one soon felt the Executive Council to be a Provincial Ministry in more than name. Before his death, Lord Sydenham's consciousness of the weak points of his position had led him to make some overtures to the French Canadians, but their deep sense of the wrongs he had done them made reconciliation impossible. His Cabinet, feeling still more its weakness when deprived of his personal influence and fertility of political resource, from time to time kept up the effort; but isolated at Kingston from everything Lower Canadian, and suspected as predominantly Upper Canadian in its composition, and still more as the creation of Lord Sydenham, its attempts availed little. Several elections caused by casual vacancies, replaced friends by enemies; and by the time Sir Charles Bagot had been in Canada a few months, it was a perfectly clear case that the Council as it stood could never get through another Session. Two plans for strengthening it offered, and both were tried. The one was that of recruiting from both the Upper Canadian parties, to gain at any rate the utmost possible *quantum* of Upper Canadian support; the other, the larger policy of still trying to win over the great hostile party of Lower Canada. In pursuance of the former, the appointment of Inspector-General of Public Accounts, with a seat in the Executive Council, was offered to Mr. Hincks, an Upper Canadian Member, who for a short time had been the most zealous of the three or four special adherents of Mr. Baldwin when he went into opposition, but who had voted against them soon after for some of Lord Sydenham's measures, and had quarrelled with them desperately in consequence; and the post of Solicitor-General for Upper Canada, vacant since Mr. Baldwin's resignation, was tendered at the same time to a leading and very decided partisan of the defunct official party, Mr. Cartwright. That gentleman, however, after some time had been spent in the negociations for this double accession to the Cabinet, positively refused to come in with Mr. Hincks. Mr. Hincks therefore came in alone, and a few weeks after, the Solicitor-Generalship was given to another gentleman of Mr. Cartwright's politics, who had not then, but was at an early day to get, a seat in Parliament. Meanwhile, to carry out the other plan, a vacant Chief Justiceship in Lower Canada was given to the ablest and most popular of the French Canadian Judges, the Commissions of the Peace were revised, and most of the Magistrates restored, who had been dismissed, from political considerations, in 1837 and 1838; the Solicitor-General for Lower Canada was made a Judge, and his former office and seat at the Council offered to more than one of the popular French Canadian leaders. But the offer should have been larger. No one man dared take office alone; and the place was still unfilled when Parliament met.

In September, 1842, Sir Charles Bagot opened the second session of the Canadian Parliament, with an Executive Council that could not possibly work through it. Both the plans had failed. The new Inspector-General had not made the Government a bit stronger with the Upper Canada Liberals than it was before, though his appointment had given great umbrage to their opponents. The new Solicitor-General (not yet in Parliament) had equally damaged it with the Liberals, and had done it as little good with his own friends. Lower Canadian support it had none to trust to; for the advances it had made to the French, though not sufficient to gain them, had fully sufficed to alienate their antagonists. Defeat thus imminent, the negociation with the French Canadian leaders was resumed. They refused to take office with the then Attorney-General for Lower Canada, Mr. Ogden, or without Mr Baldwin, in consideration of his having gone out for their sake the year before; and Mr. Baldwin would not come in with the lately-appointed Solicitor-General for Upper Canada, nor yet without some one of the small section of his own party, who had at that time thoroughly adhered to him. Mr. Draper, the Attorney-General for Upper Canada, one of the most capable men in the Council, and who had been one of the most decided in urging upon Sir Charles Bagot the policy of justice to the French Canadians, was upon such terms, political and personal, with Mr. Baldwin, as prevented their possibly acting in concert; and had, therefore, backed his advice for the reconstruction of the Cabinet, with the unconditional offer of his own resignation. Mr. Ogden was expected in a week or two from England, but there was not time to wait his return. The Cabinet was reconstructed, by the admission, in their room, of five new Members, two of them French Canadians, one a Lower Canadian of British origin, sitting in Parliament on their interest, and two Upper Canadians brought in as their allies. Of the six Members who had kept their places, five had been in office under Lord Sydenham; but only one, Mr. Sullivan, the *ci-devant* Presiding Councillor of Sir Francis Head and Sir George Arthur, had ever been politically implicated in the acts of preceding Provincial Governments. The rest were all recognised political Liberals; and Mr. Sullivan had by that time made as much profession of Liberalism as of any thing else. The strength of the new Administration was in a few days shown by a vote of the House, of 55 to 5, to thank Sir Charles Bagot for having formed it. No Council could possibly have been stronger; none could have more entirely commanded the support of the whole popular party in both sections of the Province.

Immediately before the opening of the third session of Parliament by Sir Charles Metcalfe, one of the Provincial Secretaries, Mr. Harrison, was under the necessity of resigning; the Council having determined to make the removal of the seat of Government from Kingston to Montreal a Cabinet measure, and his seat in the House being for Kingston. Except, however, on that one question, he did not go into opposition; and upon that question, though of course opposed by many of their Upper Canadian friends, the Administration succeeded in obtaining a decided majority. The Session had lasted about two months; most of their measures (and their number and magnitude were beyond all precedent) were in progress, a few had passed the two Houses, and some were still only promised; when, without note of preparation, it was suddenly announced in the Assembly one Monday morning, that nine of the ten Councillors were out of office. They had sent two of their number on the Friday to lay certain views of theirs before Sir Charles Metcalfe; had discussed them with him in full Council the next day; had tendered their resignations on the Sunday; and on Monday morning came down to Parliament no longer Ministers.

Two days after, followed the formality of the explanations in Parliament; of the peculiar manner and style of which, more hereafter. Then came a motion for a vote of confidence in the ex-Ministers, modelled on the Ebrington motion of 1832; and then a two-days' debate upon it, full of further explanations of all sorts, all offered, by the way, in the absence, from an illness which confined him to his room, of the one Executive Councillor who had remained in office. The debate ended in an Address to Sir Charles, of a most happily ambiguous tenor, first in few words assuring him that the House thought his ex-Ministers quite right, and then, by a long-winded awkward disclaimer, indirectly censuring the course which everybody knew they had taken. Sir Charles made answer that he was sorry to find from the beginning of the Address that the House had been led into a total misconception of his views; repeated his declaration of what those views were, as opposed to what others had asserted them to be; and finished by entirely concurring with the House in the concluding part of its Address. More debating after the old fashion followed, and a desperate scramble to save a little of the wrecked legislation of the Session. But Sir Charles warily keeps out of the trap laid for him by his late Ministers, and persists in not calling the Minority to take the Treasury Benches, and throw on him the odium of an anti-popular dissolution. In a fortnight from the resignation, the Treasury Bench still unfilled, the Session ends; Sir Charles telling the two Houses how entirely against his inclination had been the interruption of their labours, and hoping they should meet again to renew their efforts for the public good with more success. A new Executive Council is sworn in, of three Members, to serve till such time as the arrangements for a full and lasting Cabinet can be completed; Mr. D. B. Viger, one of the most popular and trusted of the French Canadian leaders, and Mr. Draper, the gentleman who a year before had resigned office to further the carrying out of the popular policy, taking office with Mr. Daly, the Provincial Secretary who had not gone out with his former colleagues. The questions in dispute have since been matter of discussion for the public. With what results, the next Session, or—failing that—the next Parliament, will show.

A striking feature of the ex-Councillors' explanations, and one about which there can be no mistake, consists in the marked stress which they laid on *bygone transactions*. In place of simply stating, as English ex-Ministers always do, the one or two pending matters which immediately occasioned the resignation, they opened up the whole course of Sir Charles's past administration, charging upon him, in the vaguest manner imaginable, the general delinquency of having habitually acted in certain matters against or without their advice. Mr. La Fontaine's note to Sir Charles, stating to him the tenor of the explanations they were going to make, complains that a certain alleged difference between him and them "has led not merely to appointments to office against their advice, but to appointments and proposals to make appointments, of which they were not informed in any manner, until all opportunity of offering advice respecting them had passed by." Their speeches in the House abundantly made good the promise of this text. Past appointments and offers of appointments were talked of as fluently as though Sir Charles had dealt in nothing else ever since he came to Canada, and had been dealing in them all the time without ever deigning to take their advice about them. When pressed with the home question, why, after staying in office so long with such grave cause of complaint, they had at last resigned just when and as they did, there were allusions to a petty appointment or two of quite recent date, but no distinct statement of the exact circumstances of any particular case whatever. The general complaint was what they dwelt upon; the evidence that was to prove it, a mere general disclaimer on their part, of no one could tell how many of the acts for which, as Ministers of the Crown at the time and after it, they were themselves to all intents and purposes accountable to the country!

Particulars doubtless there were given, unsparingly enough, such as they were, about several of these past transactions; but it was in the heat of discussion that they came out,—in that partial, fragmentary style which marks *ex tempore* debate, and in the absence, besides, of any one able to speak to facts in behalf of the Governor, the party whom this procedure of theirs virtually put upon his trial. How easily, and how far from fairly, any case whatever so gone into is sure to be made out, no one can require to be told. Were it not matter of notoriety, one would scarcely believe it possible that public men who had borne Her Majesty's Commission as Provincial Privy Councillors, and who seem to have persuaded themselves and others that their only ambition was to be in Canada what Cabinet Ministers are in England, could ever have fallen into so prodigious a misconception of the first requirements of constitutional usage as between the Crown and its Ministers, and of common fair dealing as between man and man.

Great stress was laid, for example, upon the somewhat recent appointment of a Speaker of the Legislative Council. Lord Sydenham had named to this Office, Mr. Jameson, the Vice-Chancellor of Upper Canada; the Assembly, during the first session, desirous that the incumbent should be a person holding no other office of emolument under the Crown, had refused to attach a salary to the office, except upon that condition; and at the opening of the third session he was in consequence serving without pay. As an Upper Canadian Member, Mr. Jameson took an active part against the Administration on the seat-of-Government question, and about a fortnight after the beginning of the session voted for an Address to the Crown, by which the Council, in the absence of most of its Lower Canadian Members, and before the House had approached the discussion of the subject, prayed that the seat of Government might be permanently fixed within Upper Canada. Directly after, he waited in person on Sir Charles Metcalfe to tender his resignation of the Speakership. But the fact was, that the Councillors from Upper Canada were so generally adverse to the Government on that question, that there was only one of those not in opposition, who could by any possibility have been placed in the Speaker's chair; and that one gentleman was the Presiding Executive Councillor,

Mr. Sullivan, a salaried officer of the Crown, *the one Member of the Cabinet who had a seat in the Upper House.* To have named him its Speaker would have been a most extraordinary step, to say the least. To have named an opposition Member would have been to make a resignation of the Cabinet next to inevitable. And to have named a Lower Canadian (the Speaker of the other House being from Lower Canada and of French origin) would have been to exasperate the sectional feelings that were at the time so strongly excited against the Cabinet as to be endangering its stability. Sir Charles, rightly enough impressed with a sense of the almost impossibility of finding a new Speaker just at that juncture, appears to have at once told Mr. Jameson that his resignation could not be accepted, and that he must therefore continue to hold the office for some time longer. About three weeks after, the House of Assembly sustained the Government policy of removal to Montreal; and the Legislative Council (its Lower Canadian Members by that time present) was called upon to rescind its former vote by concurring in the Address to that effect. Mr. Jameson stated that in the event of its so doing, he could and would not retain his seat as Speaker. The majority, however, this time was against him; the minority protested and seceded; and the Speaker's chair, *coûte qu'il coûte*, had to be filled. In a day or two it was filled, by the appointment of Mr. Caron, a French Canadian gentleman, well qualified for the appointment, and a decided supporter of the Ministry.

It was nearly three weeks after this appointment had been made, that the communications took place between the resigning Ministers and Sir Charles, which led to their abandonment of office. Yet in Mr. Baldwin's explanations as offered in the House, and still more strongly in Mr. Sullivan's in the Council, Sir Charles's whole course in reference to it was inveighed against. He had not chosen to take their advice before refusing to let Mr. Jameson embarrass the Government by persisting in his first tender of resignation; and when afterwards the resignation was persisted in, he had still chosen to act without their counsel or knowledge in his offers of the appointment to one and another of the Legislative Councillors. Again and again was this sweeping assertion echoed in different debates; till at last, in answer to some random hit of a speaker he was answering, another ex-Minister, Mr. Hincks, admitted that the Council *had* given Sir Charles their advice upon the subject, and had recommended the appointment of Mr. Sullivan—making it fresh matter of assertion and complaint as he did so, that Sir Charles surely must have been disclosing the secrets of the late Cabinet to their enemies! This over, a little more disclosure followed. Mr. La Fontaine felt called upon to state, what before neither he nor any of his colleagues had so much as hinted at, that directly after Mr. Jameson's resignation he had waited, in behalf of his colleagues, upon Sir Charles, and had made him acquainted with their views as to the relative eligibility of the several persons to whom the appointment might possibly be offered. The gentleman who accepted it was admitted to have been one of those whose nomination they had thus approved beforehand. The two or three gentlemen who were known to have declined the honour, were also of this number of the approved. But it was understood that a note had been addressed to a gentleman who was not of the number, desiring him to call on Sir Charles, of course, to receive the offer of the appointment. The note was not said to have been delivered; indeed, the story went that the Councillor addressed (one of the Upper Canadian minority) had left town before it was written. The ex-Minister had not seen fit to resign at the time, either for this presumed *intention* on Sir Charles's part, (for, on their own showing, it went no further,) of acting in opposition to their counsel; or because, in offering the place to one and another Councillor whom they had recommended to him, he did not follow the order they would have wished, and therefore did not at last light upon the man they wished most; or because, three weeks previously, he had given Mr. Jameson a verbal answer without the formality of first asking them what the answer ought to be. When other circumstances afterwards led them to resign, what business had they with these transactions? Above all, what business had they to speak of them, as, on their own confession, they did, otherwise than truly? To this hour, Sir Charles has never had it in his power to give his version of the tale they have told so strangely.

Another illustration. As far back as the summer of 1842, before the formation of the La Fontaine-Baldwin Cabinet Sir Charles Bagot is said to have been on the point of giving an office of considerable emolument to a gentleman who had been strongly recommended to him from England, and to have been deterred from doing so by the remonstrances of his then Executive Councillors, who wished that an appointment of a more popular character should be made. The place remained undisposed of till after the re-construction of the Cabinet; and Sir Charles Bagot's understood personal wishes in the matter were not acted on. Will it be believed, that on the occasion of this resignation, more than a twelvemonth afterwards, and under another Governor, a gentleman who had been of the Executive Council, both before and after the re-construction, Mr. Hincks, told the whole story in the House—of the letters sent to the late Governor by his friends in England, the way the disappointed applicant had come to get them, the intentions of the deceased Governor, and the successful opposition to them of his Councillors—with the significant addition, that the poor man had since received an appointment of profit from Sir Charles Metcalfe! Whether the appointment was conferred on him by the advice or merely with the consent of himself and his colleagues, he did not go on to say; nor yet did he add, that it was one of very trifling emolument, a mere nothing in comparison with that which Sir Charles Bagot had been on the point of giving him.*

---

* NOTE.—A pamphlet, well known to be Mr. Hincks's, written in answer to Mr. Viger's pamphlet in defence of his own course in taking office, gives Mr. Hincks's excuse, such as it is, for this terrible *faux pas*—in the words following:—

"The simple question is—had these statements anything to do with the subject under consideration? Now, one cause of the difference between the Governor and the Ex-Ministers was, that appointments had been made without or against the advice of the latter. This fact was undisputed. What possible objection then could be made to the furnishing of instances in which it had been done? Mr. Viger is entirely astray in his charge that one of the Ministry made disclosures with regard to what took place in Sir Charles Bagot's time. The case to which he refers, and which was simply an illustration of the manner in which strangers were fastened on the country by means of letters from English friends, was not given in any way on information obtained by the gentleman who alluded to it, as a Member of the Council, but on private information open to any other individual as well as to him."—*Page 12 of "The Ministerial Crisis, Mr. D. B. Viger and his Position."*

Open, he should have said, to any individual to whom either Sir Charles Bagot, or the gentleman in whose favour the letters were written, might have seen reason to communicate it in confidence; for no one else could possibly have known it but through a breach of confidence on the part of some such person. An Ex-Minister of the Crown, to offer such a plea in justification of his having told on the floor of the House a tale of this sort—a tale which *he* must at any rate have heard in his late official capacity, whatever any one or two other persons might possibly have done,—of his having sought, by indirection, to fasten the odium of the transaction on a Governor who had, in fact, been less a party to it than he, the whilome Councillor of the deceased Governor, had been himself.

Having mentioned this pamphlet, it is impossible to help giving two more short extracts, to show the style of assertion of this ex-Cabinet Councillor. They are chosen simply as the shortest out of many that equally call for comment.

On the subject of Mr. Viger's statement of the rule as to Ministerial explanations, it words are,

"He [Mr. Viger] says, 'ils peuvent obtenir de lui (the Governor) la permission de faire connaitre aux Chambres Législatives les points sur lesquels leurs vues se sont trouvées différentes.' 'They may obtain permission from him (the Governor) to make known to both Houses of the Legislature the points on which their views are found to be different.' Mr. Viger goes on to add that they can give no explanations with regard to facts of public notoriety; and refers to past history for examples. We shall have something more to say to Mr. Viger about 'precedents,' but we deny altogether his position that the Ministers are precluded from giving such explanations as may be required for the public good."—Page 7.

Mr. Viger in his pamphlet never added anything so nonsensical. The words immediately following Mr. Hincks's extract, and which he thus paraphrases instead of quoting or translating, are these—"ils ne peuvent AUTREMENT donner d'explications que sur des faits connus d'avance et d'une notoriété publique, comme l'histoire des quarante années dernières en fournit quelques examples."—"They cannot OTHERWISE offer explanations unless as to facts known beforehand and of public notoriety, as the history of the last forty years shows" The use of making Mr. Viger talk nonsense may readily be guessed. The pamphlets appeared in different languages, and the same people would not generally read both. But one does not look for this sort of political pettifogging in the known writings of a public man.

Again, speaking of a particular appointment to an office of trifling emolument, the Clerkship of the Peace for the Bathurst District in Upper Canada, one of the very few places lately given to a new-comer from England:—

"Acting on this principle, the judicial office of Clerk of the Peace was given to a stranger from Britain, utterly ignorant of its duties, in preference to a Canadian Lawyer of respectable character and talents!!! Such is the Responsible Government of Messrs. Viger, Draper, and Daly."

Of Messrs. Viger, Draper, and Daly! The appointment having been made before those gentlemen constituted the Cabinet, when the writer and his colleagues were themselves in office, *and not having occasioned their resignation!* One almost fears to state the fact, lest it should be thought a thing incredible. But so the fact is, notwithstanding.

One specimen more. A vacancy had occurred in the Collectorship of the Port of Toronto, nearly four months before the resignation, and had been filled by the appointment of a Mr. Stanton, a gentleman who formerly held the commission of Queen's Printer for Upper Canada, and had been a heavy loser by the arrangements consequent upon the union; the Queen's printership for Canada having been conferred on other parties. 'As Mr. Stanton was understood not to be a political friend of the Executive Councillors, and the place (though its emoluments by no means equalled his losses) was one of the best that had fallen vacant since they had held office, there had prevailed a general impression that the appointment must have been more Sir Charles's act than theirs. Early in the course of the debates on their resignation, Sir Allan Mac Nab threw it in their teeth—asking them how it was they had come to put up so long with the treatment they were then complaining of, and why, in particular, they had not resigned, as he maintained they ought, when Sir Charles required them to become parties to that special act. Another speaker or two said the same thing after him. The previous statements of the ex-Ministers had been more than general enough to cover it as one of the acts they were disclaiming; and for the sake of their popularity among their friends, it was well it should be understood to be disclaimed. So far, accordingly, as silence through the rest of a long debate could go, disclaimed it was. But on the next day, the question was put to them point-blank as to the share they had or had not taken in it; and when Mr. Hincks admitted that they had advised it, but accounted for their having done so by actually explaining to the House that they had been led to the step by their knowledge of Sir Charles's personal opinion as to the weight of Mr. Stanton's claims for past losses, and not by their own opinion either of those claims or of the peculiar propriety on any other ground of his appointment. They had, proposed it, and yet threw the weight of it all on him. Fancy an ex-Chancellor of the Exchequer trying to get through such an answer across the floor of the House of Commons!

The measure of the injustice dealt out to Sir Charles Metcalfe in these debates may be inferred from these illustrations, but they can by no means tell it all. They are merely so many instances in which the Ministerial disclosures bore on their face the evidence of their own unfairness. Sir Charles has as yet had no opportunity of offering, through Ministers sitting in the House, his version of the whole case. When he has, more will probably be known. But even then, all is not likely to be brought out; and as to the effect on the public mind which has been produced by the *ex parte* pleadings of his late Ministers, there is no chance of its ever being entirely done away. Follow what may, there are many from whose minds nothing whatever can remove the fixed impression they were calculated to make, and in fact have made.

There was one act, and one only, of all that the ex-Ministers directly and indirectly called in question, which was of a character to justify them, according to English rule, in citing it as the cause of their resignation; that is to say, provided always they had cited nothing else of all they did cite. Sir Charles Metcalfe had determined on reserving for the expression of the Queen's pleasure the Secret Societies' Bill, a measure which had been brought into the Lower House. and passed as a Government measure. Supposing, however, that instead of taking the course they did, they had made this act their reason for resigning, and had adhered in so doing ever so closely to the constitutional rules of time and style, it would still have been no proper ground on which to rest a step of so grave an import.

What were the facts of the case? The Orange Institution had been in full operation in Upper Canada for a number of years, and had allied itself politically with the anti-popular party. The semi-suppression it met in Ireland in 1835 did not reach it in Upper Canada; Sir Francis Head and his Provincial Government not choosing to follow William the Fourth's example in regard to it. Since then, it had been frowned upon by the Executive, though to no great apparent purpose, as the number of its lodges was understood to be increasing, and it continued to be, from its organization, a political power of some importance. This importance, however, it owed more to the exaggerated apprehensions of those whom it assailed, than to any resources of its own; for, with all its organization, its adherents generally were far from being an influential class in the community, and leaders of mark they had none. Their name was a sort of synonym for violence and intimidation—a bug-bear to frighten electors and public meetings with; and in it their great strength lay. The mere votes they could give were quite a secondary matter. It was naturally part of the policy of the Upper Canada Liberals to endeavour to strike down this hostile and mischievous association; and three of their Government measures in the last session of the Canadian Legislature were framed with this declared design. One of these was a Bill to provide for the orderly holding of public meetings, by which special and somewhat arbitrary powers were given, for the preservation of the public peace, to the Chairmen of any public meetings called with certain formalities. A second was a Bill of a similar character for the prevention of public processions. And the third was the Secret Societies' Bill itself. All were passed by the two Houses, the third with more opposition than the other two, more than one shrewd supporter of their general object maintaining that the two would be likely to do more to effect it than the three. Sir Charles Metcalfe was perfectly ready to give the Royal sanction to the first and second, but decided to reserve the third for the Queen's sanction or disallowance at home.

Mr. La Fontaine's note does not in so many words complain of this determination as involving a breach of faith on the part of the Governor-General, though it implies as much. The speeches in Parliament went further, and the newspaper articles of the ex-Ministerialist party have since gone further still. The charge of bad faith is unequivocally the charge preferred before the country. Here, such an accusation against the Sovereign would be unequivocally disclaimed; and yet a Sovereign, acting in a similar manner, would in point of fact have laid himself far more open to it. A King must do one or other of two things with every Bill that is laid before him, must approve or else veto it; and if he has agreed to let his Ministers bring in a Bill, they have a right to take it for granted that when it shall have passed the two Houses, it will certainly receive his sanction. But a Governor is not in this position. Three courses are open to him—approval, the veto, or reservation; and this last course is positively enjoined on him by his general instructions in a variety of cases, and may be specially enjoined upon him in others. If he lets his Ministers introduce a measure, they have a right to understand that he neither means to veto, nor unnecessarily to reserve it. But there the parallel ceases. While a Bill is pending, he may receive orders from home to reserve it, and, in that case, he must obey them, let his Ministers say what they please. Or, again, his general instructions may require him to do so; in which case, as they can have no right to suppose that he has any idea of not obeying, they ought to understand from his permission to introduce the measure, nothing more than this—that he does not mean himself to veto it, that he will send it home as he is ordered, and will send with it their reasons in its favour.

That this was precisely Sir Charles Metcalfe's position in regard to this Bill, is undeniable. Every Governor's instructions require him to reserve all Bills which by law ought to be laid before the Imperial Parliament; and also "*every other Bill which you shall consider to be of an extraordinary or unusual nature*, or requiring our especial consideration and decision thereupon." Now, what was the tenor of this Bill? It absolutely disqualified, not only for service on Juries, but for all office or employment "of what nature or kind soever," under the Provincial Government, or under any of its officers, or under any Municipal or other corporate body within the Province, every person whatever who might be or should become a Member of, or "in any way associate himself with," any Society however designated (the Masonic Association alone excepted) having any required or customary oath, declaration, or obligation, either of fidelity to the Society or its individual members,—or of obedience to its orders or those of any committee, officers, or other members of such Society,—or of secrecy as to any proceedings of the society, or of any committee, officers, or other members of it,—or having any secret signs or methods of communication between its members or officers, or any of them. It required of all persons holding any such office or employment at the time the act should become law, to file, on or before a given day, a written declaration in a prescribed form, setting forth that they were not members of any such society within the meaning of the Act, on pain of immediate loss of office in case of failure. It imposed the same test-declaration on all persons who should in future be elected or appointed to any such office or employment. Certain public officers were to take and record these declarations, and their registers of them were to be open to public inspection. For any and every act of office that might be done by any person who should have neglected to comply with the act, there was imposed a fine of five, twenty-five, or a hundred pounds, according to the nature of his office or employment; recoverable within six months by any private suitor, or within twelve at the suit of the Crown. For any false declaration, there was fine and imprisonment "at the discretion of the Court." And any licensed tavern-keeper or other seller of beer or spirituous liquor, allowing any meeting of any such Society or Committee, "or select portion of such Society," anywhere about his premises, was to forfeit his license, and be rendered incapable of taking out another for twelve months after, upon summary conviction before two or more Justices of the Peace. Was not such a Bill "an extraordinary and unusual" one? On what Statute-Book, Provincial or Imperial, is there anything like it to be found? If the Royal Instructions did not apply to it, to what description of Bill could they apply?

But they mean nothing at all, says a high Canadian authority,—no other than Mr. Ex-Attorney-General Baldwin; not, indeed, (so far as the world knows,) in any official report, nor yet from his place in the House, but in a set speech at a public dinner given to himself and his resigning colleagues at Toronto, on the 28th of last December. To avoid all suspicion of inaccuracy, I quote the words of the report given by authority in the *Examiner*, the newspaper *par excellence* of his party:—

"It was true, it was said that the Royal Instructions required the reservation of the Bill in question. In his opinion, the Royal Instructions required nothing of the kind. From the manner in which these instructions were spoken of in the document referred to, one might be led to suppose they were some new and special instructions growing out of the present real or supposed state of public affairs; but it was no such thing. They were the same old stereotyped instructions which had been on record in the Colonial Office for generations, which had been framed with a view to an entirely different state of things from that which now existed, and a copy of which had been enclosed in the same envelope with every Governor-General, [so stand the words in the report,] he was going to say from time immemorial, but certainly for at least upwards of a century or more; and yet these instructions were not deemed to require the reservation either of the 41th Geo. 3, (the Act under which Mr. Gomlay was banished,) nor the more recent Acts for attainting people of treason, and depriving them of their legal remedies for wrongs done them under colour of authority, which were certainly as deserving of the designation 'unusual and extraordinary,' as the Bill to which he referred. In fact, colonial history would show that these same Royal Instructions had seldom been invoked, except for the purpose of defeating or delaying measures earnestly desired by the great body of the people; and how far the present application of of them was entitled to be otherwise considered, might be judged of by what he had said of the manner in which the measure had been dealt with by the representatives of the people."—*Speech of the Hon. Robert Baldwin, from the Toronto Examiner of the 3d January*, 1844.

Strange language, truly, to come from a gentleman who has three several times served as an Executive Councillor, and twice borne her Majesty's Commission as a Law-Officer of the Crown!* The Statute-Book of Upper Canada has been

* NOTE.—Not the strangest, though, that can be quoted. The following is from a later speech by the same gentleman, and the words are those of the report given in the same paper:—

"A hope appears to be entertained that by a constant repetition of the assertion [of the Governor-General's concurrence in the Responsible-Government Resolutions of 1841] in the shape of answers to addresses, the people of Canada have so little of intelligence and so crude a notion of their rights, that they will at last be persuaded to believe it. (Hear.) He (Mr. Baldwin) doubted not that the Head of the Government had practised Responsible Government, as the Governor-General was pleased to interpret it,—and of course, being in his estimation a '*yet undefined question*,' we cannot wonder if in preparing a definition for his own particular convenience, he left a large margin for the benefit of that Constitution which favoured the exercise of a practically irresponsible and despotic power. But he (Mr. Baldwin) felt convinced that the people of this country were not such a set of children as to be satisfied with a mere bauble because it was called '*Responsible Government*'—they had been contending for a substance, not for a shadow. And the question for the country to decide was, whether they were in effect to go back to the old system under the new name, or whether they were to have Responsible Government in reality, as practically acted upon in the Mother-Country. (Loud Cheers.) 'A rose,' it was said, 'by any other name would smell as sweet,' and he would venture to say that the poppy would be equally disagreeable to the sense, and equally deleterious in its effect, though dignified with the name of the Queen of flowers. (Enthusiastic cheering.) If they were to have the old system, let them have it under its new name—'the Irresponsible System,' 'the Compact System,' or any other adapted to its hideous deformities; but let us not be imposed upon by a mere name. We were adjured with reference to this new-fangled Responsible Government, in a style and manner borrowed with no small degree of care from that eccentric Baronet who once represented the Sovereign in this part of her Majesty's Dominions, (Sir F. B. Head,) to 'keep it,' 'cling to it,' and not to 'throw it away!!' [Words quoted from Sir Charles Metcalfe's reply to the address of the Warden and disgraced by more than one blot which never would have been upon it, in all probability, had these Royal Instructions not been set at naught by his official predecessors. And he is entitled, therefore, to make their example his rule; to regard the Royal Instructions as revoked by the fact of their occasional disregard of them. One is led to wonder how far, as a lawyer, he would be prepared to carry out this doctrine of tacit revocation. The same Instructions require a Governor to *refuse* his assent in certain cases. Is he bound to obey them in this respect? Or how many instances of past disobedience—his own, or his predecessors'—would suffice to warrant him in considering that order also as thereby revoked?

But, say the ex-Ministers, the Governor did not let us know his intentions soon enough. We were allowed to carry the Bill through both Houses, and only learned his determination afterwards, when it was too late for us to intimate it to our friends without discrediting our own sincerity. We should have had the opportunity of stating, while the Bill was under discussion, that it probably would be reserved. And had not they? The tenor of the Royal Instructions was as well known to them as to Sir Charles; and it was as much their business to tell him that he ought to reserve the Bill, as his to tell them that he meant to do so. From their style of complaint one might suppose, that, till the last moment, they were left in real ignorance of Sir Charles's views about the Bill. *But the fact is not so.* It is only one more specimen of the special-pleading style of their explanations.* Sir Charles's note of protest in answer to Mr. La Fontaine's *précis* of their intended statement, emphatically declares the fact that his consent went only to the sanction of "Legislation on the subject, as a substitute for Executive measures which he refused to adopt on account of their proscriptive character;" and further, that he had told them plainly he regarded their Bill as "an arbitrary and unwise measure, and not even calculated to effect the object it had in view." There was no saying how the Bill might be amended before it should be brought up for the Royal assent; and it would therefore have been rather out of place for him to say, when its form was not yet finally determined, what he would do with it in case it should be. Knowing all they did, if they supposed it was going to be sanctioned, without previous reservation, in the shape in which they suc-

---

Councillors of the Gore District.] (Hear, hear.) They all, no doubt, remembered the story of the little Red Ridinghood, and the poor child's astonishment and alarm, as she began to trace the features of the wolf instead of those of her venerable grandmother; and let the people of Canada beware, lest when they begin to trace the real outlines of this new-fangled Responsible Government, and are calling out, in the simplicity of their hearts, Oh, grandmother, what great big eyes you have! Oh, grandmother, what a great big nose you have! it may not, as in the case of poor little Red Ridinghood, be too late, and the reply to the exclamation, Oh, grandmother, what a great big mouth you have! be, "that's to gobble you up the better, my child." (Cheers and much laughter.)"—*Speech of the Hon. R. Baldwin; at the General Meeting of the Reform Association of Canada, held at Toronto on the 25th of March,* 1844; *from the Examiner of the 10th of April.*

What if the *Morning Chronicle* were some fine day to give us a laugh over a like piece of eloquence from some last great speech of "plain John Campbell" to some great non-dining assemblage of the laughing lieges of Auld Reekie!

Everybody remembers with what indignation Mr. O'Connell felt it incumbent on him to disavow all thought of reference to the Queen, when he the other day travestied part of a Queen's speech. Yet here is a gentleman who, unlike Mr. O'Connell, has been an Attorney-General and Cabinet Minister, who professes all imaginable zeal for the closest possible assimilation of Canadian to British usages, and nevertheless talks in public speeches of Governors and their Instructions as sent out "in the same envelope;" accuses the Representative of the Crown whose Minister he has been, of personally aiming at "irresponsible and despotic power," and trying to impose upon the people by false professions; and, for a laugh's sake, soberly lends him the likeness of our old nursery friend Grandmamma Wolf.

All who know Mr. Baldwin speak of him as in private life a person of amiable character, an honourable man, and a gentleman. The habits of anti-Governor warfare, for which the old colonial system has to answer, must be inveterate indeed, to have misled such a man into hostilities of this sort against a Governor like Sir Charles Metcalfe!

* Note.—It is a little singular that the inconsistency of this part of their statement with another, of which I shall have to say more hereafter, seems never to occur to them. With one breath they represent the reservation of this Bill as having taken them by surprise, and in the next they describe Sir Charles's whole policy as one of settled "antagonism" to their views. Their principal newspaper, the *Montreal Pilot* edited by one of themselves (Mr. Hincks) rings the changes on Sir Charles Metcalfe and Orangeism, to the very point of making the encouragement of the Orange Institution seem the great object of Sir Charles's government. Where Sir Charles is known, such nonsense can only raise a smile; where he is not, it may well enough for a time answer the end it is meant to serve. But no one can envy those who resort to it their choice of means.

ceeded in carrying it through the two Houses, they must not only have held Mr. Baldwin's monstrous doctrine of the virtual revocation of the Instructions, but must have taken it for granted that Sir Charles had not the honesty and courage to venture on holding out against it. He may well be pardoned if he did not beforehand suspect them of either the one notion or the other.

Other and (if possible) yet graver objections to the tenor of these explanations remain still to be stated. All this train of unwarrantable half-disclosures was gone into to prove a general proposition which they laid down as the ground of their resignation. In the words of Mr. La Fontaine's note, this proposition was neither more nor less than this—"That his Excellency took a widely different view of the position, duties, and responsibilities of the Executive Council, from that under which they accepted office, and through which they had been enabled to conduct the Parliamentary business of the government, sustained by a large majority of the popular branch of the Legislature;" that is to say, that his Excellency was irreconcileably at variance with them and the country, as to the principle of Responsible or (to use another word) Constitutional Government! All they said about appointments and the Secret Societies' Bill, was said to establish two points; the one, that this opposition of views existed; the other, that it made their continuance in office impossible. They went even further than to cite this sort of evidence. They declared, that on their lately remonstrating with him on this condition of public affairs, "his Excellency not only frankly explained the difference of opinion existing between him and the Council, but stated that from the time of his arrival in the country, he had observed an antagonism between him and them on the subject." So says Mr. La Fontaine's note. Now, let his Excellency have explained or stated what he may, all passed in the confidence of the Executive Council Room, by word of mouth, and in the course of an argumentative discussion that is known to have lasted several hours,—no fewer than eleven persons taking part in it, nine against two, and no one's words taken down to ensure their being faithfully reported. A Governor's opinions proved in this style! Were but the like experiment ever tried by any ex-frequenter of the model Council Board where the Queen's most excellent Majesty presides in person, people would know what to say of it.

Out of Canada, one scarcely knows how to state the fact, all notorious as it is, that at the time Mr. Baldwin announced to the House all this, and more to the same effect, he had in his pocket Sir Charles Metcalfe's written answer to Mr. La Fontaine's note, in which he complained, that the proposed statement omitted all mention of the transaction, which he regarded as that upon which the resignation really took place,—the demand, namely, which Messrs. La Fontaine and Baldwin had made upon him the Friday previous, "that he should agree to make no appointment, and no offer of an appointment, without previously taking the advice of the Council; that the list of candidates should in every instance be laid before the Council; that they should recommend any others at discretion, and that the Governor-General in deciding should not make any appointment prejudicial to their influence,"—the fact, that this demand was accompanied by an intimation that in case of its not being complied with, their Colleagues who agreed with them, and themselves, would immediately resign; that the subject was discussed at great length in Council the next day; and that their resignation the day after was the direct consequence of his persisting in his refusal to tie his hands by any such engagement. Yet thus it was; and this reply said more, too. It declared positively, that so far from holding the opinions about to be ascribed to him, he "subscribed entirely to the resolutions of the Legislative Assembly of the 3rd of September, 1841," and considered any other system of Government impracticable; it showed the necessity under which he was acting in the matter of the Secret Societies' Bill; and ended by protesting in terms against the proposed explanations, "as omitting entirely the actual and prominent circumstances of their resignation, and as conveying to Parliament a misapprehension of his sentiments and intentions, which had no foundation in any part of his conduct." In the face of all this, did Mr. Baldwin give the House the whole of the explanations thus protested against, saying no word of the existence of the protest, letting fall no hint of the possibility of the Governor's not admitting their literal correctness,—nay, indignantly asserting, when the question was put to him, that he had his entire permission to make them!* Sir Charles, it would appear, had been asked verbally for the usual permission to explain. What the words of his answer were, no one has stated, but it is certain he required to be put in possession of a written outline of the explanations contemplated; a fact not easily reconcileable with an intention on his part that his words should be understood as an unconditional leave to his ex-Ministers to say anything they might choose. Against Mr. La Fontaine's note, when he saw it, he certainly protested in strong terms, and in writing. But it never seems to have occurred to the gentlemen that that mattered anything. They ask no question, offer no reply, take no step to come to a decent understanding with the Head of the Government, as to the matters of fact at issue; but forthwith say precisely what he has objected to their saying, and maintain that he gave them leave.

Is it said, as possibly it may be, that the fact of such gross blunders having been fallen into is a proof that Responsible Government for Colonies is impracticable? To what cause, let me repeat, are they to be set down? Not to the fact that in Canada, Responsible Government has been lately conceded, but to the fact that it had been before so long withheld. Certain Canadian public men, we find, have been too thoroughly trained by the long prevalence of the old system, into habits of thought and feeling at variance with the new, to be able all at once to throw them off. Give them time, then; the Responsible-Government principle is not to be condemned for not having wrought a miracle.

The disadvantages with which the system has had to contend in Canada have, in truth, been most peculiar. The trial of it was not begun till after the old system had led to civil war, and an entire suspension of free government. When at length it was tried, the first experimenter, Lord Sydenham, introduced it so partially, that his successor, with little or no semblance of free will, had to undo no small proportion of all that he had done; and the *bonâ fide* carrying out of the principle was thus made to look much more like a popular triumph, than a willing concession. Add to this the fact, that on Lord Sydenham's death, the Executive Councillors, to whom he had allowed so small a share of political power, found themselves suddenly in possession of the whole power of the Executive; that for several months they had only to deal with an Administrator of the Government, who, as a military man in the *ad interim* discharge of a duty not properly his own, was of course well pleased to incur as little responsibility as possible, and therefore did everything exactly when and as they advised him; that Sir Charles Bagot, a diplomatist who had been for some years retired from the fatigues of public life, was still new alike to the duties of Governorship, and to the affairs of Canada, when the great re-construction took effect; that almost from that time, with an Executive Council naturally rather more disposed than before to regard *itself* as "the Government," he was a martyr to an illness so distressing, that for months he was scarcely able to sign the papers which absolutely required his signature, and quite unable to bear the fatigue of reading them; it will readily be perceived in how difficult a position Sir Charles Metcalfe must have found himself placed, on his entering upon his duties as Governor-General. A hard-working man of business all his life, and a veteran Governor withal, it was impossible he could think of not personally attending to the duties of his high office, of signing papers blindfold, without knowing what was in them, or saying for ever yes, without first understanding why. No Councillors ought to have mistaken this for an evidence of distrust; but men in their position are apt to make that kind of mistake, and it is certain that some of them did. Confidence is not, the instant suspicion is suspected. Had the Canadian Councillors, indeed, been what their after course shows they were not, clear-headed, cool, far-seeing politicians, they would soon have put everything right, by meeting what they must then have seen was not mistrust, with a courteous frankness that could not have failed to win for them

---

* Mr. Baldwin's answer to Mr. Viger's question on this point, is reported in a Canadian Pamphlet ("Responsible Government for Canada"), the work, evidently, of one who was a witness of the scene, and the statements of which seem to have met no contradiction,—in the following words—"I have; and if I had been refused it, I would have come down to this House, would have stated at once the fact, and would have fearlessly called upon the House to believe of myself and my colleagues everything good and nothing evil." "British precedent again!" adds the writer; and no wonder.

the entire confidence of the honest, sensible man they had to deal with. But unfortunately, it was not so to be. Sir Charles Metcalfe was clearly made to feel, at a very early stage of his administration, that he was not regarded by them with confidence; and the "antagonism," about which so much has since been said, soon became an established fact. People in Canada have not yet unlearned the old fashion of besieging Governors and their Private Secretaries with applications that ought rather to pass through the Secretary of the Province, or some other Provincial Officer of the Government. No Governor can prevent this, let him wish it ever so. Those who think the Ministers unfriendly to themselves, will try the experiment of applying to Government-House direct; and a large proportion of such applicants will make it part of their business to complain that they have received, or expect to receive, injustice at their hands. Sometimes a Governor may be pardonably indisposed to hand over these communications, in the usual course, to the Minister or Ministers whom they may concern, from the feeling that to do so would merely be to damage a perhaps well-meaning though indiscreet man. But whether he takes this course or not, it will be impossible for him, if he be a man of business, to help looking closely to the dispositions that are afterwards made in regard to the particular matters to which such communications may have related. In most cases, they are likely to have more or less reference to the exercise of patronage; and on this subject, the Canadian ex-Ministers had a fancy for talking rather indiscreetly. All Ministers take sufficient care of their political supporters; but these gentlemen were fond of everywhere announcing this preference of party friends as their settled principle of action, and so gave an air of probability to every charge that could possibly be trumped up against them on this account. What but "antagonism" on the subject of patronage could grow out of such a state of things, between a man like Sir Charles Metcalfe and themselves?

I am far, however, from believing their account of the state of things in this respect to be the fair one. They never could have remained so long in office, had it been his *practice* to make appointments, and offers of appointments, not merely against their advice, but even without their knowledge. Their mode of dealing with special facts, we have seen, is infinitely too suspicious to warrant one in believing, on such poor evidence, anything so incredible. In fact, as to the *making* of appointments, it was absolutely impossible for him to act unknown to them, except in reference to some dozen petty employments, the official nomination to which happens to have been left to pass through the hands of the Civil or Private Secretary. The Provincial Secretary, an Executive Councillor, is the officer who has the charge of the engrossing, sealing, and countersigning of all Commissions whatever; and an Attorney-General, another Councillor, either drafts the Instrument, or countersigns it with the Secretary. Appointments not made by Commission, with the very few exceptions already noticed, take effect by an official letter of some Executive Councillor, generally the Provincial Secretary. As regards *offers* of appointment, the custom has been for the Governor to act personally in cases of high trust, such for instance, as an Executive Councillorship, or as the Speakership of the Legislative Council. But in other cases, it is always the Secretary of the Province, or other Executive Councillor within whose Department the appointment lies, who has to make the official offer. The Governor is under no formally-admitted obligation to consult all his Counsellors about all appointments; but he is under the practical necessity, more than ninety-nine times out of the hundred, of acting through some one or more of them; and they, therefore, can make sure of knowing what he is about, in time to be able to remonstrate, if they see fit so to do, before the act is done. Their position in this respect is as nearly as possible that which English Ministers of the Crown are perfectly content to occupy. The demand they made upon Sir Charles for an assurance beforehand, that he would always consult them collectively before making any appointment, or offer of appointment, great or small, and that, after thus consulting them, he never would appoint, or offer to appoint, any one whose nomination might prejudice their interests,—or, in other words, who might not be of their party,—apart from its being unconstitutional, was neither more nor less than an impracticable absurdity. Their *rôle* as Ministers was to secure good appointments, and prevent bad, if they could, by the tender from time to time of their advice and counsel; or failing that means, to resign upon some adequate occasion of a refusal on the Governor's part to defer to their advice.

That Sir Charles's "antagonism" was not what they represented it, a feeling of hostility on his part to the principle of Responsible Government, or even to the general policy of their legislative or other measures, is tolerably clear, independent of his own repeated declarations, from two facts; the first, that to the day of the resignation, he had taken no step which even their ingenuity has been able to point out, indicative of a disposition on his part to call to his counsels Anti-Responsible-Government men, or even any other men than themselves; the second, that when they resigned on a ground that left him no sort of option about accepting their resignations, he still called on none but known Responsible-Government men to take their places. His present Councillors adhere unequivocally to the principle. For some six months he has carried on the government with an incomplete Council, and hardly any but acting Heads of Departments. And yet, not one offer of one of the vacant places to any but Responsible-Government men has been laid to his charge.

There was an antagonism of personal feeling, and it had doubtless led to some collisions. Sir Charles had not acted readily on all their suggestions, and they had not been wise enough to take his in good part. Some few appointments which they had wished, he had perhaps refused to make; and some few others that they did not like, he had probably insisted on. Possibly, he may have once or twice directed that his own view should be acted upon, without first hearing what theirs was; but if so, they had thought it their best course to give way at the time, and had thereby barred their own right to complain afterwards. In the matter of the Secret Societies' Bill they had, as they thought, borne down his remonstrances; had brought in and carried through their measure, confident that he would not dare act on his own sense of right, in the face of their majority; and did not find out their error till it was too late for them easily to repair it, for in their confidence they had not thought of intimating the possibility of a reservation for the Royal sanction, when alone the intimation might have been given without damaging them. There may have been some other embarrassments springing from the same general source, of which none but the few behind the scenes as yet know anything. And there were unquestionably some of another kind, that went to aggravate them. The business of the session was in a most unsatisfactory state; more work had been undertaken than could possibly be got through with; one question was immediately pending, on which many of the best informed observers were confident they must have yielded ground, or met a defeat that would have been most mortifying, though of itself probably not fatal; a quorum of the Upper House could hardly be kept together, and every one was feeling that the fate of a session, which which had need last two months or more, hung by a thread, almost from day to day. It is pretty well known, too, that some of their least discreet supporters (from Upper Canada, principally) had been galling them more or less with distrustful reproaches, for not carrying out more thoroughly the patronage-views of the *extrême gauche*. The measures of the session, if carried, were to create a great amount of patronage; and they were threateningly told, that this at all events *must* be dispensed in a manner to meet the views of that section of their friends. Irritated and pressed upon from these different quarters, exaggerating no doubt, in consequence, in their own minds the character of the antagonism that seemed most of all to thwart their wishes, and not-yet familiar, from Constitutional practice, either with the necessary embarrassments or with the true resources of their position, they made a dead set for the attainment of the full powers they had enjoyed under the dying Sir Charles Bagot; trusting, probably, that Sir Charles Metcalfe would not stand out against their threat of resignation, or that, if he should, they could soon force themselves back on him with renewed popularity, and on their own terms, or else drive him home to make way for a new Governor who should be as yielding as they could desire.

They mistook their man, and still more their ground of quarrel. Sir Charles had no course but to meet their demand with a steady negative; for the practical abdication it invited from him, to a strong mind and high heart could be no alternative at all. When they tendered their resignation, his coolness and courage were equal to taking them at their word. Committed to the struggle, they thought only of taking every lawyer-like advantage of position, and forgot all constitutional rule in their eagerness to identify the country with themselves, and hurry him and the country into the direct collision which was to bring about their desired triumph.

Of the many strange pretensions which the ingenuity of politicians at one time and another has managed to advance, not the least singular is the claim these ex-Ministers have insisted on urging, to the virtues of forbearance and moderation in all their proceedings. It is asserted that, but for these amiable qualities, they would have resigned much sooner, and not waited, as they maintain they did, till they could wait no longer. Far be it from me to say that Ministers of the Crown ought to resort to the *ultima ratio* of resignation on light occasions: so grave a step is not to be taken if it can be helped. But what sort of forbearance and moderation is it, that puts off the resignation merely that a longer string of counts may swell the indictment at last, when the day of resignation comes? Fair practice enough perhaps for a lawyer bent on securing an Old Bailey conviction; but the Crown and its Representatives are not prisoners in the dock, and ex-Ministers, of all men, may not treat them as if they were. They may wait their time, and resign when they see fit. Their right to choose the time, and the act or acts that make most for their cause, is unquestionable. But their forbearance and moderation are not then to range at will over all time and all acts, in search of evidence on which they may beg a judgment from the country in their favour, and against the Crown.

I repeat, then, that the anomalous state of things to which this unhappy blundering has led in Canada, is in no way a consequence of the concession of Responsible Government. On the contrary, the fact that Responsible Government has been conceded, is at this moment the one rational ground of hope for an eventual favourable issue of the controversy. The Ex-ministers' cry has been, that the concession is not yet a reality; and were this the fact, resistance to them, so far as Colonial public opinion goes, would be hopeless. But as the case is, it is far otherwise. The ground they stand upon trembles under them. When their resignation was announced, the majority of their Parliamentary friends made little secret of regretting it as a false step. The whole movement of the House upon the matter was one of singular reluctance. With all the bold assertions that were hazarded to prejudice the House against the Governor, all the shade thrown over the demanded pledge, and all the appeals freely made to personal and party feelings, it was up-hill work to muster the majority of two to one for the vote of confidence in the ex-Ministers; and the vote was bought at the price of their consent to a second clause, expressly disavowing the notion of any such demand as it was notorious they had just preferred and backed by the tender of their resignations. A complete Cabinet has not yet been formed; but the three gentlemen who form the present provisional Council, men long ago committed to the Responsible-Government principle, and to a liberal, popular policy of administration, avow themselves accountable Provincial Ministers, and are so avowed by Sir Charles Metcalfe. Those of the ex-Ministers who have been appearing in public since Parliament was prorogued, and the more active of their supporters, have latterly been more violent in their language than they were at first; unaware, one would think, of the universal rule, that what party-leaders gain by this course in one way, they more than lose in another,—that, however violence may please the zealous friends of whose support they are sure at all events, it must estrange from them the class of friends they are less sure of, and should therefore take most pains to keep. In Upper Canada, were it not for some counter-indiscretions, of a like character, of the party calling itself "Conservative," the operation of this one cause would make their defeat at the next general election certain; and, as it is, it makes it probable. In Lower Canada, the French-Canadian party sees its most trusted leaders at variance, Viger, the Governor's chief adviser, La Fontaine and Morin, ex-Ministers. And, much as its old habits tend to throw it into support of the latter, nothing has yet appeared to show that they will succeed in doing so.*

* The Montreal City Election, to the seeming contrary notwithstanding. The ex-Ministers' Candidate, Mr. Drummond, was proclaimed elected, but how? The Constituency numbers 4,000 votes, and more; some say 5,000. And at the close of the time allowed by law, the poll stood 1,383 to 463, more than half the votes unpolled. His friends claim for him 984 French votes; the number of voters of the French race being as many as 2,000, and most likely more. It is known, too, that all the first day, the polls were so disgracefully blockaded by Irish canal-labourers in the Drummond interest, that it was next to impossible for Molson men to get up to vote, and that at the opening of the poll on the second day, Molson withdrew in consequence, under protest, and took away his agents from the polling-booths; so that all that day there was no show of objection to anybody who came to offer a Drummond vote, and of course scarcely any polling but for Drum-

Leaders and led, the French-Canadian race are essentially a monarchical, innovation-dreading people. The appeal to their habitual distrust is for the time a formidable weapon; but, met by the defence of a careful avoidance of the old policy that gave rise to the feeling, it must by degrees lose its efficacy. Indeed, it has lost much of it already. The course for the Government to adhere to is that which Sir Charles and his advisers have entered on; the persevering offer of Responsible Government on the nearest possible approach to English practice, the determined refusal of anything beyond. Suppose the Parliament dissolved, either after trying another session, and finding the present House in the humour to insist on the return *en bloc* of the late men to power, or without first calling it together at all; the new House, however many of the old Members may have seats in it, will come together a Body uncompromised by the indiscretions of the past, and the question will be put anew, whether or not Canada has public men reasonable enough not to quarrel for shadowy impossibilities. Should the new House, on its meeting, and the country, by its after-expression of opinion, show that it has not, the collision will have taken place, which must end in the alternative of government by the Mother-Country, till such time as the Province shall have learned wisdom, or of separation before that time shall come. The Imperial Authority has no other to fall back upon. Will the Canadians in cool blood persist in driving it to make the choice? Not yet believing them all beside themselves, I am slow to think they can. There is passion enough, and misconception enough, to make the case one of serious import; to call for all the temper, and at the same time for all the plain-spoken decision, that the Home-Government can oppose to it. But, so treated, there is no reason yet for presuming the case hopeless. Facts as little prove the charge of deliberate disloyalty of intention against any political party, or any number of leading men in Canada, as the fact that the charge is harped upon as it is, proves the statesmanship and good sense of those who are fondest of dealing in it.

But it is time to pass to the consideration of the results of the principle of Responsible Government in another point of view, the only one remaining to be taken to establish its correctness and sufficiency. I have shown, I trust, that if any thing will succeed in placing the government of our Colonies on a satisfactory footing as regards the administration of their internal affairs, it is the thorough fearless adoption of this principle. It remains to show that it promises to maintain the relations of the Empire and the Colonies on a footing equally satisfactory. On this point, after the explanations already given incidentally, it will not be necessary to dwell at any great length.

One consequence of the adoption of the system seems not to have been yet very clearly perceived—at any rate, it has not, that I am aware of, been very clearly stated—either here or in the Colonies. It is this. The Governor of a Colony once placed in his true constitutional position, as Representative, to his Province, of the Crown and Empire; and surrounded accordingly by Provincial, as the Crown here is by Imperial, Ministers; it follows necessarily that he ought to be trusted by the Crown and Empire as the *sole* Representative of their authority, at least so far as Civil affairs are in the case. Between the Civil and Military business of a Colonial Government, the distinction is so obvious and marked, that there is no necessity for a Civil Governor's having immediate command of the Forces, or for their Commander's having to correspond with his official superiors only through the Governor's intervention. Indeed, such a regulation would merely embarrass

---

mond. Of his 1,383 votes, 960 were thus tendered—how many of them good and how many bad, the skilled in elections may be left to guess.

But Molson polled hardly any French votes. What then? There was nothing to hinder French voters from coming up against him, but everything to deter any from showing their faces in his favour. Of all the nuisances in the world, a French-Canadian perhaps shrinks most from that of collision with an Irish mob. Most of the French Canadians siding with Mr. Viger, it was well known, were not likely to have voted for Molson, owing to gross mismanagement on the part of some of his active electioneerers. But a very fair number of them had promised him their votes. The unscrupulous tactic of the anti-Viger party succeeded in making it impossible for them to redeem their promise; on purpose that it might look as though there was no Viger party at all. In this they have overshot their mark, and proved (if anything) too much. But they have *not* by any means succeeded in proving that they had themselves the support of half the French population even of the City of Montreal; where it is well known there has always been more of the excitable, anti-Government feeling than is to be found anywhere else in the whole Province.

all parties to no purpose. But even as regards Military affairs, in Colonies where the Governor is not a Military man, and where therefore the troops are under the direct control of another Commander than himself, it should be distinctly understood by all parties that his is within the Colony the higher authority of the two; that it is his right (if he see occasion) to direct, and the duty of the Military Commander to obey, subject always to after-appeal to the decision of the authority that commissions both. A Civil Governor would very seldom have occasion to interfere, in point of fact. What is wanted is merely that he should be placed by the Crown as nearly as possible in its own position of recognized supremacy within the Province. It is an object to dispose the Colonists readily to extend to him, as the delegate of the Sovereign, the immunities and respect which all accord to the Sovereign himself. And to this end, the authority of no other servant of the Crown whatever ought to be placed before them as in any sense a concurrent authority with his. Military Commanding Officers, however, provided there is this distinct understanding that they are to obey his orders if he gives any, may well enough correspond direct with the Horse-Guards, Ordnance, and Treasury.

But what is to be said of the practice, not yet done away with, of suffering some of the Civil Officers of a Province to stand in the position of semi-independence so degrading to the authority of the Governor, which the right of direct correspondence with the authorities at home gives them? *If*, for instance, to secure the great imperial object of uniformity in Post Office arrangements, it be necessary to vest the appointment of Colonial Deputy Post-Masters General or Post Office Surveyors in the authorities of St. Martin's Le Grand, so be it; but not otherwise, for unless for some such end, the principle of Responsible Government requires the vesting of Provincial patronage in the Provincial Crown, so to speak, not in the Imperial. It *is* necessary, no doubt, to that unity of action of the Department which it is a proper object of Imperial policy to maintain, that the general authority for Post Office proceedings in a Colony should originate in Imperial legislation, that Deputy Post Masters General should receive their orders from, and that their acts should be reported to, my Lord the Post Master General. But why not through the intervention of the Governor? What Department of a Provincial Government involves a greater number of details of purely Provincial administration, for which his advisers ought to be responsible to the Province? The people of one part of a Township want a village Post Office here; those of another corner want it there: a Deputy Post Master General may put it in a third place, or perhaps say that the Post Office of the adjoining Township will do very well, and put it nowhere. A village Post Master is disliked, charged with incivility or neglect of duty, suspected perhaps of mal-practices as regards the secrecy of the correspondence that passes through his hands; the Deputy Post Master General, rightly perhaps, keeps him in his place. The people who think themselves in any such case aggrieved address the Governor; but the head of the Post Office acts under orders from home of which the Governor knows nothing. His answer to the Provincial Government, if it takes up the matter, is likely enough to be, that he has reported the case home, and got my Lord's approval of his decision, or that he is waiting my Lord's confirmation or reversal of it, or that he will immediately submit the question for my Lord to determine how far his instructions admit of this or that decision being come to. This is no position for the Governor of a Province, nor yet for his Provincial advisers. The people look to them to make the administration of their local affairs satisfactory. How can the General Post Office, thousands of miles off, keep an eye to details of this sort, to such purpose as to prevent its Officer from making mistakes calculated (perhaps without a shadow of blame on his part) to render the Department most unpopular? Nay, must not its uninformed interference, if active and extending to details, often lead him into mistakes which he would not otherwise think of making? The Secretary of the Post Office, or some one for him, takes a notion into his head, and makes it a rule of action in some class of cases. The Deputy Post-Master General may feel that it is wrong; but it comes to him from his official Chief, and how is he to get it set aside? Make such rules pass through the Governor, and the Colonial view of things may be represented as it ought to be; but never otherwise.*

* A well-known illustration of this truth, and one in which the principle involved was of the last

The Post Office Department is not the only branch of the Civil Service that is at present in this anomalous position. The collection of the Customs, at least at such ports as have been directly recognized or erected by Imperial authority, and for such duties as rest on Imperial enactment, is effected under the authority of the Commissioners of Customs; and their Collectors receive their orders and make their reports direct. But in many Colonies there are Ports of entry besides, which rest on Provincial enactments, and in all there are Provincial duties levied. Sometimes, as in Nova Scotia, there are in consequence two distinct establishments for the two services; an Imperial and a Provincial Collector side by side at the same port. In other cases, the Collector for the Board of Customs, where there is one, is placed in the strange situation of discharging both duties, and taking his instructions from both authorities, though neither has the means of knowing what the orders of the other are! Here, too, and wherever else in the usages of any particular Colony there may be any other like anomaly to be found, the principle must be carried out, to make the machine work as it ought. Let the Imperial authority exercise whatever amount of control may be really necessary for the general interest; but let the Governor of the Province be its one controlling agent. To have more, can never lead to anything but confusion, complaint, and mischief.

The correspondence of every Governor with Downing Street should of course remain as it is, in his own hands; the Officer whom he may specially charge with its superintendence, his own Secretary,—not any settled resident of the Province, nor even one of his responsible Provincial advisers. In this there is nothing whatever to prevent their views from being made known, as they ought to be, to the Home Government. A Governor will act most unwisely, if he either fails to communicate their views with his own, or keeps them otherwise than well-informed as to the tenor of his communications. It may, perhaps, not be amiss to have it understood that a particular class of dispatches is always open for their consideration and advice. But every Governor must feel that he is free to communicate his own personal impressions in the most perfect confidence, as well as theirs, and the Colonial Secretary must, besides, know that he is so; or the Official correspondence will soon become a mere form, and its real business be done by unrecorded private letters, instead of by dispatches.

Another consequence of the system has been oftener dwelt upon, and from its exceedingly obvious character, need here be little more than mentioned. It is this; that as regards matters of a purely Provincial character, the rule of the Colonial Office ought to be that of absolute non-interference; and as regards matters which are half Provincial, or affect Imperial interests to no great degree, that of decided unwillingness to interfere. It should choose its Governors with

---

Importance, may be taken from a date not very remote, the time of the introduction of the Steam Ship mail communications with British North America. The General Post Office, for some fancied convenience of its Accountant Branch, laid down the rule that all letters passing either way must be prepaid to Halifax and should not be prepayable beyond. So that upon every letter both the sender and the receiver were to be required to make a money payment. To have enforced such a rule would have been to deprive the Colonists, in particular, of half the advantages the new system held out to them; for there is nothing that new settlers (the class most of all dependent on old-country letters) find so embarrassing as these money payments. The per-centage of letters which the rule must have stopped both ways, would have been enormous.—The first orders given on the subject had been vague, and the Deputy Post-Master General for Canada had put a common-sense interpretation on them, by announcing that prepayment might be made for the whole postage, and need not be made for any. This announcement he was ordered to revoke; and he must have done so, but for the lucky accident that Lord Sydenham, the then Governor, was a man of interference, who did not mind stretching a point when he saw fit Thanks to his energetic way of taking up the matter, the Provincial view for once prevailed; but the point was not gained easily even by him, and never could have been carried by the Deputy Post-Master General alone.

At this moment the Colonial papers state that the greatest possible difficulty is experienced in Canada, in finding Post-Masters to serve the Country Offices; and it is apprehended that a large proportion of all the Offices will have to be shortly abandoned in consequence. The Department at home has just deprived the Post-Masters of the franking privilege, which was their principal remuneration: and without making any compensatory addition whatever to their other almost nominal emoluments. The privilege may have been a bad thing: but this summary way of dealing with it may prove a worse. No one knows what the Deputy Post-Master General may or may not be reporting to his Principal on the subject, nor what chance there is of any thing that he may report about it being attended to.—Such representations ought to be the business, not of a Post-Master General's dependent Deputy, but of the Provincial Government.

care, and having chosen should trust them. As long as a Governor retains enough of the confidence of his Sovereign's Ministers to be kept in Office, he should be sustained. If not in their perfect confidence, he had better by half be recalled at once, than kept in place to be watched and doubted. No Colony respects or trusts a Governor who is not thought to be respected and trusted by the power that sends him. The true guardian for each Colony, of Imperial interests, is the Governor; the Officer sent out to the Colony, surrounded there by its leading public men as his advisers, and charged with the care of its administration, and no more; not the Colonial Minister, the Officer who can know little or nothing of the Colonies but through his several Governors, and has besides the affairs of all of them equally in his charge at once. Where his Governors go with the Provincial wish, the strong presumption is, that he may safely follow. When they feel it incumbent on them to hold back, (and I have shown that it is by no means their business to play the part of ciphers,) he too may well pause to make sure whether they are right or wrong. If ever he comes to think them wrong, let him put them right, or if need be, recall them as promptly as he will; but till he does, let him sustain them thoroughly; let him set the Colonists the good example of always treating them as if he had a confident reliance in their being right.

These principles admitted, one more, in every respect equally important, follows. The policy of the Empire in reference to its Colonies, on matters involving decidedly Imperial interests, should be thoroughly Colonial. I do not mean by this, that Colonies should be favoured, right and left, with protecting duties at the cost of the British consumer, to build up new pet Colonial class-monopolies. The policy I advocate is perfectly compatible even with the *cautious* abolition of those that are already in existence. Create every facility for a steady well-ordered emigration, of the right kind, at once to swell their population and augment their capital and industrial resources generally. Confirm them in the priceless advantage of the financial security of British public credit; not simply by a guarantied public loan for one or another, on some occasion of rare emergency, but by aiding at all times their efforts in these respects, to an extent short perhaps of the downright guaranty, but still calculated to advance their interests, and yet more, by requiring them in their public financial projects and the character of their monetary institutions and bankrupt laws, to adhere to those sound principles of commercial honour which alone have made British credit what it is, and can make and keep theirs what it should be. Give them ungrudgingly as near an apprach to the privilege of free trade with foreign countries as the nature of our commercial relations with those contries will allow. And maintain for them the very nearest possible approach to an absolutely free trade with the Mother Country and with one another; relaxing in their favour the protective regulations of our Tariff, as speedily as may be, whether we have or have not occasion to relax them in favour of foreign states; and insisting on it, that the duties which they may levy on our productions and each other's shall never be of a protective, but always of a strictly fiscal description. In a word, treat them in all these respects, as Sir Robert Peel has most wisely said they ought to be treated, as so many British Counties—so many integral portions of a vast Empire "one and indivisible." As far as possible give their professional men the "open sesame" to professional life in the Mother Country, in exchange for like advantages to be enjoyed by our own in the Colonies. Few or no Provincials would ever avail themselves of the right; but the mere right all would value highly. Recruit for the Army and Navy in the Colonies as well as at home; and let the Horse-Guards and Admiralty put some measure, even though it be not a large one, of their patronage to Colonial use. No great number of Colonists would be likely to sigh for musket, sword, or cutlass; but all would be proud to be in these respects on the full footing of the Metropolitan class. Make them, in one word, by the whole character of our policy, feel themselves to be less Colonists than British subjects. It is this large boon they want; not any of the mere petty, doubtful boons that the old policy, miscalled Colonial, doled out to them to be over-balanced tenfold by the restrictions which it put upon them. This policy announced and persevered in can leave them nothing to demand; must make them feel that they can but lose by change, instead of gaining. About our foreign policy, in the common acceptation of the term, they at present none of them care any thing; and so long as it shall continue to maintain the essentially pacific and commercial character which it has now so thoroughly established for itself, they are none of them likely to be in any hurry to concern themselves much about it.

Suppose now these great principles of action to be in good faith reduced to practice, where is the danger in it of the sacrifice of any Imperial interest on the one hand, or of Provincial disaffection or the loss of any of our Colonies, on the other? Take even the extreme case of a Colony where long perseverance in the opposite policy may have led to an unreasonable state of the public mind that is not at once satisfied with such an offer, what better course can be taken than to make it in all sincerity, and abide by its results? In any other case how can the policy fail of producing and maintaining the most entire satisfaction? Admit that questions may come up from time to time between the Imperial Government and those who represent the views of particular Colonies. Their discussion, carried on confidentially, as in each case it would have to be, between the Colonial Secretary, the Governor, and his Provincial advisers, all of them parties interested in preventing it from making mischief, would be a vastly different affair from the angry collisions of the old system. And at the worst, there would be the threat of separation as a last weapon—no longer in the hands of a complaining Colony, to be used with doubtful effect, but in those of the Parent State, where the power to use it could not possibly be questioned.

The conclusion I have, I trust, established may be summed up in few words. It is not by unworthy distrust, by hesitating as to the loyalty or looking with an eye of suspicion on the rapid growth of Colonies, that the term of their colonial existence is to be prolonged. To keep their people loyal, they must be confided in, their interests advanced, their feelings consulted, their judgment convinced of the fact that their political position is so advantageous to themselves that all change must be for the worse. The jealous policy against which I have protested tends, besides, as little to make Colonies valuable for the time being to the Parent State, as it does to make their connexion lasting. Colonies are of value simply because they enlarge the productive territory of the nation that plants them; thus adding directly to the means of support at its command, and opening a wider field for its energies, as well by the advantages they hold out to the settlers who resort to them, as by the markets they create for the various industrial products which the manufacturing and commercial capacities of the old country furnish. In no other way can any colony add to the resources of a State. The barren right to rule it is worth nothing. Keep it in what one may call its infant state, and just so long is it kept a drain on the resources of the country that maintains it. It is when it has passed the stage of mere dependence, and begins to grow rich and populous, that it begins to be worth having. Its worth is in strict proportion to its means of contributing to the general weal; and he who, to lessen as he may think the chances of its being soon lost, would in any way check its progress, has hit upon the one sure way of making its early loss likely and perhaps desirable.

If these views are not wholly wrong, it is no less obvious that a country in the peculiar condition of Great Britain should not only extend her colonial possessions as widely as she can in new directions, but should look well to her old settlements, doing all she may to increase their resources, and at the same time to attach them to herself. The small extent of her proper territory, her redundant population and her overflowing wealth, all point to colonization as the means by which alone she can do anything really effectual to increase her present power, or even to escape the threatened alternative of national decline, and eventual downfall. The millions clamor for cheaper bread and higher wages. The wealthier few (those alone excepted, whose wealth is enormous) sigh for higher profits. How are they all to have their wish? Do we become apostles of free trade? Other nations do not become its disciples fast enough to meet, or make show of meeting, our pressing necessities. For the relief we need, we must look to what we can do for ourselves, not to anything we can preach them into doing for us. The wants of our poor and of our rich resolve themselves at last into one and the same thing—*more land*,—land, which in the first place may furnish them directly or indirectly with more food, or in other words cheaper food, than they can get now, and with a more abundant or cheaper supply of raw material for their manufactories,—and which in the second place, from the abundant return it shall yield to the industry of those who till it, may become the home of new millions to be purchasers of the goods they have to exchange for that food and raw material which they cannot raise fast enough at home. Supply this want, and all else must follow. The profits of the rich man and the wages of the labourer must rise together, under the influence of a cause that would meanwhile be bringing raw material in greater plenty to the one and bread in greater plenty to the other. The population of the country must increase and its aggregate wealth multiply, so much the faster for the process of dispersion which would be carrying off men and money, useless at home, or worse, to new scenes of productive employment. We are doing much to this end. In every quarter of the world we have colonies, already; and the inherent enterprise of our people, the world over, is busy founding new ones. So be it. We run no risk of having too many. Some risk there may be of our perhaps acting as though we thought new Colonies all we want; of the great truth being practically overlooked, that new Colonies before they can be of any essential use must have become old, in resources if not in years; that old Colonies have acquired a value, and should be prized and dealt with accordingly; that the oldest, *cæteris paribus*, must ever be the best worth keeping carefully.

True it is, that the wide Continents we are colonizing promise at some distant day to maintain communities too powerful for the precise colonial relation, even as I have been describing it, to continue for ever to subsist between them and the people of these Islands. But that period is distant, though inevitable. All we can certainly know is that it will come; that at some future time our Colonies, powerful as the Parent State or more so, must either, thanks to mismanagement, have become independent states more likely to be its enemies than its hearty friends, or else, through a wise foresight, have been kept closely bound to it,—confederacy, in some shape, by degrees taking the place of the old bond of union,—the British nation continuing still united, so far as perpetual peace, mutual good understanding, freedom of commerce, and identity of foreign policy, can unite it,—these Islands still its Metropolis, though their people be no longer the admitted holders of its whole Imperial power. All we can do is to take care of the present and near future. The future that is far off will take good care of itself. For this age and the next it is enough to know that Colonies, built up by our own people, and gifted with our own free institutions, must be bound, alike by the natural feelings and the commercial wants of their people, to ourselves and our policy, no less than to our trade; that neither the one tie nor the other need we, nor yet if we are wise shall we, ever let go or loosen.

SONNET—KENSINGTON GARDENS.

FOR "FISHER'S COLONIAL MAGAZINE."

A franchis'd prisoner's carol by the way,
  Tun'd in a green spot of a weary place;
  A joy-bell, swelling for a sonnet's space
  To a heart's descant, in Petrarcan lay;
A song of gratitude, to breathe the day
  Unclogg'd with stifling fume, my limbs to brace
  With exercise not irksome, and to trace
  Something of God's creation as I stray.
For, under shade of chesnut, oak, and lime,
  With lawn and mirroring wave on either hand,
  Flocks feeding round, birds singing merry chime—
Smiled on by flowers, and by heav'n's breezes fann'd;
  He must be child of some far happier clime,
  My hymn of thanks who should not understand.

C. J. C.

COMMUNICATION BETWEEN LONDON AND DUBLIN.

COMMERCE and communication have made such accelerated movements between the most remote and opposite parts of our globe, that we now very naturally express surprise at neglect of proportionate and simultaneous improvements at home. The utmost activity prevails and is likely to prevail in drawing Paris and London closer by several hours, while the public have too long rested content with the length or distance in time that still exists between London and Dublin. It is probable that steam power at sea has attained its maximum velocity—say twelve miles an hour; so that the voyage between Liverpool and Kingston must continue to average thirteen hours, and, in unequal weather partake of that character. But, even an increase of speed would not affect the point—that is, the propriety of taking the shorter and more certain line of communication.

For some few years back, since Liverpool has caused the abandonment of Holyhead, and the desertion of that magnificent line of turnpike road through North Wales, suggested by Sir Henry Parnell, and executed by Telford, many attempts have been made to bring the question of the eligibility of Holyhead and Dyn-llaen Harbours to a satisfactory and true conclusion. Suspicion of preference naturally attached to those ancient Britons who desired to carry the railroad through the county of Glandwr, and this feeling threw their best efforts into the cold shade of ministerial indifference. But the actual *bonâ fide* construction of a railroad from Chester to Menai Bridge, of which no doubt need now exist, has revived the whole question *de novo.*

Passing over the reports hitherto made upon the Harbours of Holyhead and Dyn-llaen, as trifling in quantity of information, and directly wrong, we shall invite attention to the full and elaborate statement of Mr. Page, which leaves nothing further to be desired :—

The requisites of a Harbour of Refuge, says the Report, are—

That it should afford shelter and security for vessels which otherwise must be driven on a lee-shore.

That, with depth of water for large ships, the holding-ground should be sufficiently good to bring a ship up, which may enter it in a gale of wind.

That the nature of the shore should be such as to allow of vessels saving themselves, or at least the crews and cargo, by beaching upon it; and where the formation of a breakwater may be required, it should be so disposed that no injurious effects should result in decreasing the depth of water, &c.

That it should possess an easy access for a disabled ship, during the most violent gales, and that its position, if determined solely with regard to saving life and property, should be such as to afford a refuge on that coast, where, from the direction of the winds and tides, wrecks are most prevalent.

If to these requirements it affords room for working out of the harbour during contrary winds, it will comprehend almost all the requisites for a perfect harbour of refuge.

Now, taking the sailing directions of the Admiralty for a guide, it appears that Holyhead is deficient in every one of these requisites.

Besides, the inner harbour is dry at low water,—the race of the tide here is highly dangerous,—the coast is perilous owing to sunken rocks, —and experience warns our navigators of its insecurity.* *Contra*, take the following account of Dyn-llaen and Neffyn Harbours from the same authority :—

"These are very sure and excellent harbours for ships that may be driven by stress of weather into Caernarvon bay. The pier at Porth-dyn-llaen, which was begun to be raised by a gift of £600 from King George the First, but never finished, is now almost in ruins, and, if not looked after, this excellent harbour will be greatly destroyed.

"There is a small pier at Neffyn, which is found very useful for the herring-fishery and coasting vessels. This pier is falling to decay."

In the Admiralty "Sailing Directions for North Wales" (1843), before quoted, the bay of Porth-dyn-llaen is described as "clean throughout, with the exception of the rock called Carreg-y-Chwislen, which may be approached within fifty yards on all sides, is two cables in length from Porth-dyn-llaen Point, leaving a clear sound with five fathoms. The bottom is sand over clay, and the depth decreases gradually to the beach. In its present state the bay affords no shelter with the wind from N.N.W. to North,† but from all other points of the compass it may be adopted as a convenient and safe anchorage."

In the bay of Porth-dyn-llaen, as also in the adjoining bay of Neffyn, there is an extent of coast of 5,000 yards in length, in which a vessel may beach; the holding-ground is sand over clay, the latter appearing in many parts through the sand, between high and low water marks. Protected by its own promontory, and the high lands behind it, from the prevailing gales, and shut in by the Rivels from the east, it is open to few points of the compass.

The character of the coast generally in the vicinity of the Rivel Mountains is highly favourable to mariners, as well as are the set and strength of the tides. And the comparison instituted by the reporting engineer, reduces the issue to a moral certainty.

Comparing, from this accurate description of the two localities and my own observations and inquiries, their natural capabilities in the most important features which may fit them for harbours of refuge, viz. *the holding-ground*, which in one is a natural formation, clay to the surface, and which has enabled vessels to ride out tremendous gales, and in the other the probable result of drift, *the facility of beaching* so extensive at Porth-dyn-llaen, and so limited, if any can be assigned to it, at Holyhead, *the shelter afforded* to vessels by the natural protection in each place, *and the strength and set of tides*, which are regular and gentle at Porth-dyn-llaen, and amount to a race in the neighbourhood of Holyhead, I am decidedly of opinion, that for a harbour of refuge the bay of Porth-dyn-llaen is preferable to the bay of Holyhead.

It may be further remarked, that there is space at Dyn-llaen for the construction of shipping stores,—no apprehension of drift,—a tenacious clay bottom,—a fitting site for a light-house, and on which site, as it projects 3,500 ft. into the sea, a light ought in any case to be shown; from these considerations we say, it is obvious that Dyn-llaen is incontestably adapted for a harbour of refuge for vessels navigating the Channel, in preference to the rock-bottomed basin of Holyhead. Indeed, the area of the latter at low water is only four acres—its depth daily diminishes; and if Mr. Walker's plan of extending the pier were adopted, further deposit would rapidly take place. It is sug-

* Thirty-nine wrecks were seen on shore in *Holyhead Bay* at one time.
† Seven points.

gested, therefore, to construct at Dyn-llaen a breakwater of 5,600 ft. to protect 400 acres, or of 8,650, to protect 960 acres,—for which work materials are already provided by nature. The expense of the former would be 400,000*l*,—of the latter, double that amount.

The preceding statements refer to those ports as places of refuge—safe asylums for the mercantile marine of the world, or of our own empire, at all events; the following observations apply to them as packet-stations, whereby communication between the capitals of the sister-islands may be accelerated, and the seat of government brought more immediately within the reach of the Irish people. With respect to winds, the most prevalent in the channel is the south-west, which would be a side-wind both ways between Dyn-llaen and Dublin, the most advantageous to steamers, as it enables them to steady themselves by canvass; so also are the tides favourable to this port, whence it is calculated that regularity in the transmission of the mail would be ensured by adopting the Dyn-llaen station, an advantage that must be forfeited by retaining Holyhead.

Having said so much upon the eligibility of a station for packets, it remains to add some few remarks upon the lines of railroad proposed. Mr. Brunell's by Tremadoc, is, for various commercial reasons, little better than visionary. Commercial arguments have decided upon the Conway line from Chester; but, the most feasible of all, (if government could be induced to act,) was Mr Prichard's, which accompanied Telford's road, q. p. into the Vale of Llanrwst to Conway, and thence along the shore to Bangor. This admirable project was too late in the field, but, one day it will be executed.

Having reached the Menai Bridge, a new difficulty presents itself, in the additional strain which a train would occasion, besides its being borne by half the chains and rods only. This fearful experiment is strenuously discouraged by Mr. Page, so that a break in the line to Holyhead occurs, or a new bridge must be built. As the latter would incur immense cost, and require probably the removal of the Swelly Rocks, at an expense of about 20,000*l*. additional, and, as Holyhead Harbour might, after all that expenditure, prove inefficient, and be abandoned by government, a company will hardly venture upon the speculation. The question then is narrowed into the information conveyed by the accompanying table. Since Dyn-llaen is the eligible port—since the Menai Bridge is an insurmountable difficulty—since a few miles of rail from Bangor will reach Dyn-llaen—and since a bill is passed for carrying a line from Chester to that city, let the inhabitants of Bangor, Caernarvon, and the adjoining district, form a line from Bangor to Dyn-llaen of their own, and take on the Irish passengers. If they never go to Dyn-llaen there is remunerating traffic between these towns, and the carrying of the Straits would be transferred to them. If Dyn-llaen were, and it must be, made the packet-station, they would have ten per cent. for their money, and a general improvement of their properties would attend the enterprise.

TABLE SHOWING THE THREE PROJECTED LINES OF RAILROAD BETWEEN LONDON AND MENAI BRIDGE.

CASES.	Distance in Miles.		Speed by Locomotive Power, in Miles per hour.	Speed by Atmospheric Power, in Miles per hour.	Time by Locomotive Power, for the whole distance.		Time by Locomotive Power to Didcot in the 1st Case, to Chester in the 2d and 3d Cases.		Time by Atmospheric Power from Didcot to Porth-dyn-llaen in the 1st Case, from Chester to Porth-dyn-llaen in the 2d Case, and from Chester to Holyhead in the 3d Case.		Stoppages by the way, including in the 3d Case 15 minutes for crossing the Menai Bridge.		Total Time by Locomotive and Atmospheric Power to Porth-dyn-llaen in the 1st Case, *viâ* Worcester; in the 2d, *viâ* Chester; and to Holyhead in the 3d Case.		Time by Steamer to Kingston from Porth-dyn-llaen or Holyhead.		Time lost Embarking and Landing Mails, and conveyance to the Dublin Post-Office.		Total Time performing Journey between London and the Dublin Post-Office—Atmospheric and Locomotive Power, and Steamers.		Total Time performing Journey between London and the Dublin Post-Office, using Locomotive Power for the whole distance from London to the Port of Embarkation.	
	M.	CH.	M.	M.	H.	M.	H.	M.	H.	M.	H.	M.	H.	M.	H.	M.	H.	M.	H.	M.	H.	M.
I. From London to Porth-dyn-llaen by Mr. Brunell's broad-gauge line, *viâ* Worcester, thence by Dolgelly and Tremadock, according to the Report of Sir Frederick Smith and Professor Barlow	260½	0	40*	50	6	30¾	1	19	4	10	0	40	6	9	5	0	0	44	11	53	12	55
II. From London to Porth-dyn-llaen, *viâ* Chester, according to the Report of Sir Frederick Smith and Professor Barlow, deducting 5 miles, which Mr. Walker has suggested may be saved by deviations of existing lines	269	76	36†	50	7	30	5	2	1	46	0	40	7	28	5	0	0	44	13	12	13	54
III. From London to Holyhead, *viâ* Chester and the Menai Bridge, according to the Report of Sir Frederick Smith and Professor Barlow, deducting 5 miles, which Mr. Walker has suggested may be saved by deviations of existing lines	267	0	36†	50	7	25	5	2	1	41	0	55	7	38	5	0	0	44	13	22	14	4

* Deduced from performance of Great Western engines. † Deduced from performance of engines on narrow-gauge lines.

SPEECH OF SIR ROBERT PEEL ON THE BANK OF ENGLAND CHARTER.*

DELIVERED IN THE HOUSE OF COMMONS AT WESTMINSTER, ON MONDAY, MAY 6, 1844.

THESE are exactly the principles which now regulate the measure of value. You have one measure of value—the gold coin. You have abolished silver as a legal tender for any sum beyond £25. You have coined the ounce into 66s., instead of 62s., the extra 4s. being for seignorage; and you have made silver subordinate and subservient, to use the words of Lord Liverpool, to the other, viz., the gold coin. You have, therefore, a single standard—you have that standard which has been for the last hundred years the standard of value. You have silver and copper coin as ancillary and subordinate coin, and that is the best arrangement which can be made for the security of the monetary system. At any rate, that has been the system which has permitted a man of the humblest classes in society to obtain £5 in gold, for five pounds worth of produce or value. You have now allowed the lower classes the use of gold in their transactions, and by so doing you have taken a more perfect security for perfect convertibility, than by saying that he who should produce £100 in notes should be able to exchange it for gold coin. I know that it is said, that by some change, you might diminish the chance of panic, and confirm the security of the farmer; but I doubt very much whether any legislation to guard against panics, would have any beneficial effect. I believe you might adopt certain regulations which would give you greater security against that evil —against which it is impossible directly to guard yourself—by preventing the depreciation of gold. I believe that it would be a greater security against even that evil, by having gold coin circulated throughout the country, by manifesting a confidence against such panics, than by any regulations of law to protect against its effects. I have now done with the principles which I think determined the measure of value, and which I think in this country ought to regulate, as far as coin is concerned, the medium of exchange. I hope I have not exceeded the limits I ought to take in declaring my opinion upon so important a subject. But, when a great question comes under our review, there is a great advantage in reviewing the elementary principles relating to it.

I now come to that which is a most important part of the subject; and here, again, I must be allowed to state what appears to me to be the principles which should regulate our paper circulation—I mean the circulation of promissory notes payable to the bearer on demand. I speak of those, and those only. When I speak of money, I mean by money the coin of the realm, or I mean promissory notes payable to the bearer on demand—payable in the coin of the realm. Now, I will not trouble myself, or retard the house, by any refined speculation about a variety of other kinds of paper currency. I shall say little or nothing on the great question which was discussed in the Bank Committee, as to whether deposits, or checks on bankers, or bills of exchange, partake of the nature of a currency.† I say

---

* Continued from No. 6, page 375.

† "The currency I consider to be, in strictness of language, according to the apparent derivation of the term, that part of the circulating medium, such as the coin of the realm, and Bank of England and country bank-notes (although not a legal tender), which pass current from hand to hand, without individual signature, such as appears on drafts or endorsements. I am doubtful whether cheques upon bankers might not be included, from their perfect similarity to bank-notes, in many of the purposes for which they are employed; at the same time, there is the feature of distinction I have mentioned, viz., that cheques require the signature of the party passing the draft, and that they do not pass from hand to hand. Bills of exchange I consider as a part of the general means of distributing the productions and revenues of the country, and therefore as constituting a part of the circulating medium. I consider also, that the simple credits by which goods are in many instances bought and sold, come likewise under the general description of the circulating medium, in as far as the prices of com-

that in some respects they do, or for aught I know may, partake of the nature of a paper currency; but, looking at it with reference to that particular point with which, and with which alone, I have to deal, namely, the effect which a paper currency has on prices, the effect it has on exchanges, the effect it has in disturbing the measure of value and banishing gold,—I say that a promissory note payable to bearer on demand, is of a totally different character from all those other descriptions of currency, and that it has a totally different effect. In the first place, the nature of the instrument is different. It performs the office of a currency; it passes from hand to hand; no personal guarantee is required; it acts as a substitute for coin; it is not like a bill of exchange, which requires an endorsement at every transfer; it is a substitute for money; it performs the functions of money; and it acts on prices as money does. Observe, I do not say that those various transactions connected with paper credit, and the circulation of paper, have not an effect on the supply of the precious metals, or in determining the economy of the issue of the precious metals; but the fact is, that they disperse instead of keeping up the amount of the precious metals, and thus afford a guide to the keeping up of the amount of those precious metals. They resort to the general market of the world, and if you can save the five or six millions that go to other quarters, to that extent, and to that only, is the bearing of that paper circulation on the intrinsic value of gold—one hardly perceptible in this country. It alters the value of gold as to other commodities, in a slight degree, because one country requires rather a less supply than others. I think all experience shows that these promissory notes, payable on demand, have a different effect on prices and exchange from that of those kinds of paper currency on account of which the attempt is made to induce us not to interfere to regulate the issue of promissory notes. Now, at an early period in the history of the Bank, when there was an entire confidence in its stability—I speak of more than a century ago, when the shares that had been issued at 60 were at 112—at that time the Bank paper was so depreciated, that a guinea in gold was worth 30s. in paper—the same being the case as regarded silver; and the exchange was greatly against this country. What did the Bank do? They had lent large sums to the government, they had lent money on mortgages and in other ways, and they had sent out large issues of paper, until they lowered the value of their paper until the price of a guinea was 30s. What, I say, did the Bank do? They took the advice of eminent men, and they determined to limit the number of the promissory notes they issued; and the consequence was, that the exchanges became in our favour, and the value of their notes was restored.

In the history of the Scotch banks you will find that the same things occurred. You will find that the exchanges were most unfavourable to Scotland. They adopted the same measure which was adopted by the Bank of England at a former period—they diminished the number of their notes, and the exchanges were restored again. Now, those who have attended to the subject, are aware that a very able report was made in the year 1804, upon the exchanges between Ireland and this country. In Ireland, the bank-notes of the Bank of Ireland had become very much depreciated in value, so that 118 bank-notes of the Bank of Ireland were required in order to purchase 100 of the Bank of England, and the guinea was of great value as compared with the Irish bank-notes. A committee was appointed to consider the subject. The directors of the Bank of Ireland positively denied that there was any over-issue of their notes. They said that they never issued any more than what the people demanded in the legitimate course of things. But the committee told them that they would never restore the exchanges to par unless they diminished the issue of their notes. They were still incredulous; but the exchanges became still more unfavourable, and at last they said, "Let us try the remedy of the committee, and reduce our £3,000,000 of issue to £2,400,000." They did so; and the consequence was, that the Irish bank-notes soon afterwards regained their proper value. Is not this a reason and proof that promissory notes

---

modities are in question; however, a simple contract of sale, whether any payment passes eventually or not, is commonly entered in the price-currents without distinction from those for which any actual payment is made. I cannot consider that transferable debts (such as deposits in the hands of bankers, against which the depositors are entitled to pass their drafts), constitute circulating medium, but only the actual transfers."—*Evidence of J. Tooke, Esq.*, 1840—*Report on Banks of Issue*, p. 297.

exercise an influence on the exchanges which bills of exchange and checks on bankers do not exercise? But it is said, "If there are £300,000,000 of promissory notes, and they were all presented at the same time, the Bank could not pay them; and, therefore, it is no use adopting any regulations as to promissory notes, unless you extend them to bills of exchange and all other paper circulation that is founded on your metallic currency." I hope, however, that the house will be prepared to admit this principle – that a promissory note payable on demand, is a different thing, and involves a different principle, from the other forms of the circulating medium. The attempt to place them all on the same footing was made at the time of the Bank restriction. Then, also, it was said, "Do not apply your principle to the promissory notes, unless you are prepared to extend it to the other descriptions of paper currency." Lord Liverpool, however, touches principally on that point, in the treatise to which I have already referred. He says—"It is a very common artifice" (I scarcely like to use so strong a term as the noble earl applied) "practised by those who have written on the subject of a paper currency, to confound paper credit with paper currency;" this applies to what has been written between 1800 and 1815;) "and even to confound the higher sorts with the inferior sorts, such as immediately to interfere with the use of the coin of the realm. Paper credit, is not only highly convenient and beneficial, but is even absolutely necessary in carrying on the trade of a great commercial kingdom. Paper currency is a very undefined term as used by speculative writers. To find arguments in its support, at least to the extent to which it is at present carried, they have been obliged to connect it with paper credit, so that the principles on which the use of paper credit is truly founded may be brought in support of a great remission of paper currency." Now, is not the case the same at the present moment? Are there not those who are attempting to deter us from regulating a paper currency (by which I mean a currency of promissory notes, payable on demand), because they tell us that we ought to contemplate something more extensive? "No," says Lord Liverpool, "a paper currency, strictly speaking, consists of notes or bills, payable and convertible into cash on demand by the persons who issued them, at the will of the owner."

Yes, Sir, I assume a paper currency to be a different one—in the essential character to which I refer and which induces us to deal with it—from those other kinds of paper credit, which, depend upon it, will regulate themselves, if you will only adhere to the measure of value, insist on immediate convertibility, and don't be afraid of any mass of bills of exchange that may be in circulation. The foundation of those valuable instruments of commerce is that metallic standard which you ought to guard against depreciation, direct or indirect. But it has been contended by very eminent men, that the only security you need take against an excessive issue of paper currency is immediate convertibility. This doctrine indeed appears to have the sanction of authorities no less eminent than Adam Smith and Ricardo. They assume that the paper engagement should always be literally fulfilled—that there should be no postponement by means of paper; but they say also, that if you secure practical immediate convertibility, then there will be no immediate apprehension of conversion. If that opinion be not well-founded, it would be no reflection on those eminent men. We are in a constant state of transition, and we are constantly making new discoveries as to the rules which regulate our paper currency. At the same time, the house would, no doubt, be disposed to abandon an opinion sanctioned even by such men as Adam Smith and Ricardo, if, from subsequent lights that have been thrown on the subject, they should become convinced that they were in error. Now, I shall contend, both upon reason, and also upon the admissions of advocates of free competition—and this will be a most difficult and important part of the subject—that convertibility into gold, together with unlimited competition as to issue, does not give sufficient security.

First, to look at the argument as derived from reason alone,—I admit that in free competition there is a great advantage as regards the supply of most articles. Free competition, taken generally, is calculated to give you the articles you require at the cheapest rate. But, in commenting on that principle, as attempted to be applied to a paper currency, I say that a paper currency is governed entirely on principles different from those which govern almost every other article. Of currency, I do not want the greatest quantity at the cheapest price. What I want is this—that I shall be able to command a supply of that paper currency whose value shall be exactly conformable to gold, and that that supply shall be given to me by parties in whose honour, integrity, and solvency I shall have the greatest confidence. I don't want, therefore, the cheapest article; I want the best. And the quality of that article is to be governed by quite other principles than those of competition, because it is definite and fixed, not variable,—fixed in this way, that the amount of paper currency must be determined by the relation it bears to the gold currency. If it exceeds that, then it is in excess. Therefore, all that the country, as I think, requires, is, that it shall have the greatest supply of paper having its value determined by a corresponding amount of gold, and that that paper shall be issued in quarters entitled to the highest credit. A very different doctrine, however, is supported by those who contend for unlimited competition; and I beg to call the attention of the house to some of the admissions which they make in the course of their argument in favour of unlimited issue. Those who hold the same opinions as I do, contend, that were unlimited competition allowed, although it might be very possible that the issue of notes must ultimately conform, yet that a considerable interval might elapse before that conformity was established, and that the means of establishing it, though certain in their operation, yet would produce great embarrassment and inconvenience, before they were entirely successful; that there is not that immediate and close sympathy between the issues of paper and its professed value in gold, that there ought to be; that the country is not immediately alive to the depreciation that is going on, until ultimately reminded of it by that silent monitor—gold; and that by neglecting its early warnings, you force on the Bank the necessity of precipitate contractions. That doctrine was referred to by several of the country bankers who gave evidence before the committee, in support of their views; but that evidence is, in my opinion, a complete confirmation of the opposite doctrine to that which they maintain. One gentleman was examined—Mr. Hobhouse, a banker in the south-west of England, and a brother, I believe, of the right hon. baronet the member for Nottingham, who spoke with some authority, from his having been chairman of the Committee of Private Bankers, and their selected organ. What account did he give of the issues of private bankers? He was asked—" With a rise of prices, would there be an increased paper issue by country bankers?" He answered—" Yes, there will be an increase in the local circulation when prices rise.* Gold is a commodity, of which there may be a glut, as well as a scarcity; and I could never see any reason to be frightened at an export or drain of gold." He was then asked—" Ought not there to be a contraction of the circulation, under such circumstances?" He answers—" Whether there ought, or ought not, I cannot tell; but I am sure that, in fact, there could not be. I am perfectly satisfied that it is quite impossible for these local currencies to be influenced by the price of gold or the foreign exchanges?" He is then asked—" Does it not often happen that your circulation is increased in the beginning of a drain of gold?" He answers—" Yes; we do not pretend that our circulation is at all governed by what I have stated already."

Another witness who was examined was Mr. Stuckey. He was asked this question—" Supposing, for instance, it should be ultimately thought that it is desirable that the country circulation should have a general conformity to the state of the foreign exchanges; do you conceive that this could, in any way, be effected by the country bankers?" He answers—" I do not at present see how it could be accomplished; and I may take the liberty of going further, in answer to that question, and saying, that it appears to me, that the country issues, as conducted in the west of England, have very little, or nothing, to do with foreign exchanges."

Now, the effect of this evidence is, that country banks do not control their

---

* The following truths are elementary, and have been received as axiomatic. "The value of money is in the inverse ratio of its quantity; the supply of commodities remaining the same. Increase the quantity of money, prices rise; decrease the quantity of money, prices fall. On the other hand, the quantity of money remaining the same, increase the quantity of commodities, prices fall; decrease the quantity of commodities, prices rise. So that, a decrease of the quantity of money produces the same effect on the price of a commodity, as an increase of the quantity of the commodity itself."

issues according to the state of the foreign exchanges. The amount of their issues depends upon prices. When speculation flows, and prices rise, that is the time at which a check is required on the increased issues of the country banks. Yet that is the very time at which you stimulate their activity. What I now seek to establish is, that unless there is some kind of a controlling check, there is a danger that just at the period when the warning is given, so far from that warning being attended to, it acts in an opposite direction. Prices are rising. The country bankers tell you they have no control over their currency. The increase of price determines their increase of issue, and there is going on at the same time this double operation of an increased speculation, and an additional stimulus given to that speculation. And this arises because the country banks have no control over their own issues. There is a total abnegation of the effect of the foreign exchanges. The first witness from whose evidence I quoted, when asked whether the circulation of country banks was governed, as that of the Bank of England was, by the state of exchanges, fairly admitted that it was not the fact.* He was asked—"Does it not mean that when a drain of gold was beginning, that was the time when frequently the circulation of the country banks was increased?"—that is to say, at the very time when there ought to be a simultaneous gradual contraction. The answer of Mr. Hobhouse is—"Yes; there is an increase at the beginning of a drain of gold, and the circulation is not governed by it." So that the competition amongst the country issuers is stimulated by that feeling so natural to man, which prompts a banker to say—"It's of no use for me, individually, to contract my issues, when others won't do the same. I shall suffer by doing so. My individual efforts will produce no effect on the aggregate, while some competitor will take my share." And thus, each refusing to make that individual sacrifice, which, indeed, 'is useless, where only made individually, the crisis comes†—there is a demand for gold which cannot be satisfied, and the end of all is, much individual suffering, and fortunes ruined; until at last it becomes necessary to establish that equilibrium between and paper which nothing can establish, where there is a tendency to depreciation, but prudent and firm measures. I deduce, therefore, as well from the experience of those who know the practical working of the subject, as from the reason of the case, that you will not, without such measures, be able to secure yourself against great fluctuations in the value of paper, and great vicissitudes in your mercantile transactions. If we call in the aid of experience as well as of reason, and also the admissions of opponents, I think the case is almost conclusive; for what has been the condition of the United States? Let us take warning by the misfortunes of our neighbours. There you had no private banks, but only joint-stock banks, nominally and theoretically on good principles. You had excellent arrangements for immediate convertibility, based upon the infinite liability of shareholders. But you had also the unlimited purchase and increase of issues to meet increased prices, and the consequence was a sudden crash, a total suspension or check to payment, individual fortunes ruined, public credit destroyed, and the commerce of the whole United States paralyzed. If immediate convertibility is a check, why has it not operated as such in the United States? But in the United States, so long as the power of, in some measure, controlling the issues was confided to a central bank with extensive privileges, its influence, though not suffi-

* The state of foreign exchanges is not perceptible in the respective localities, nor are prices or the state of trade immediately affected by them.

† The following is a return to an order of the honourable the House of Commons, dated 16th of May, for an account of the number of Private Banks which became bankrupt in the years 1839, 1840, 1841, 1842, and 1843, with the amount of dividends paid, so far as the same can be ascertained:—

Year.	Number of Bankruptcies.	Of which were Banks of Issue.	Number that paid Dividends, and Amount of Dividends.
1839	9	—	1 under 5s.; 1 under 10s.; 7 no dividend.
1840	24	8	2 under 5s.; 4 under 10s.; 1 under 15s.; 17 no dividend.
1841	26	11	5 under 5s.; 6 under 10s.; 1 under 15s.; 1 under 20s.; 13 no dividend.
1842	12	4	2 under 5s.; 9 no dividend; 1 dividend not ascertained
1843	11	6	2 under 5s.; 1 under 10s.; 1 under 15s.; 1 under 20s.; 6 div. not ascertained.

The injury sustained by the public from country banks is not to be estimated from failures solely, but also from the over-issues of the surviving banks, at periods of excessive speculation and over-trading.

cient to prevent occasional failure, did keep their issues within some bounds. Their conduct was regulated by rules, and the other banks were compelled, in some degree, to conform to the principles of the ruling bank of the United States. But, the ruling principle destroyed, individual competition went on, and the result was much individual suffering and something very like a national bankruptcy. The example, then, of the United States, is a strong proof in favour of that proposition for which I contend, viz., that perfect, unlimited competition and convertibility into gold, is not a complete security against over-issue.

EXTENT TO WHICH IT IS PROPOSED TO CARRY THESE PRINCIPLES.

I have now stated with respect to the measure of value,—with respect to the coinage and currency,—and with respect to promissory notes payable on demand, the broad and general principles which I think ought to regulate these three great elements of our monetary system. I have done on this occasion what I have done on others. I have stated, without the slightest compromise or concealment, the leading principles which, in my opinion, ought to regulate those matters; and I now have to state the extent to which I propose to carry out those principles. If I do not carry out those principles immediately to their full and entire extent, I may be told, as I have been told before, that these are very good principles laid down in the abstract, but that, practically, I shrink from their application. Nevertheless, the opinion which I have formerly expressed, I still entertain—that it is of great importance in public men to lay down the great principles by which important measures should be regulated; and, in discussing a question of such magnitude as the present, I had rather it were said—"You fall short in the application of your principles," than that "You have concealed or perverted those principles, for the purpose of covering your limited application of them." In addressing the house on this important subject, I have, in the first instance, stated principles which I deem to be correct, and which ought to be the rule and guide of our future legislation, and I now have to consider, with the same unreservedness, how far attention to circumstances, to existing interests, to the usages and habits of the community, demands a modification or limitation in the immediate application of those principles. All I can promise is, that I will propose no practical measure which is inconsistent with the principles which I have laid down, and which I should think did not tend to lead to their ultimate and complete fulfilment. It is, however, most important that the men who are responsible for the management of the affairs of a great country like this—seeing how easy it is, by immediate legislation, so to affect private interests, as to create panic, or introduce confusion, into the monetary transactions of the country—it is most important that they should take care, first, that they did as little of practical evil as possible by the application of sound principles; and, next, that for the sake of effecting an extensive and comprehensive reform, they did not raise prejudices against the progress of that reform, by pushing forward the application of their principles in a manner incompatible with the due consideration of private and personal interests. In what mode—admitting the principles I have announced to be correct,—in what mode should we proceed to provide for the present establishment of them, and their ultimate adoption, taking care at the same time that, in the interval, there should be as little risk of the occurrence of the evils against which we wish to guard, as possible? Some have contended, and I am not prepared to deny the force of their statements, that we have a new state of society to deal with, and that by far the wisest plan would be, to claim for the state the exclusive privilege of the issue of money, as we have claimed for it the exclusive privilege of coinage. These parties argued, and I think justly, that the state is entitled to the whole profits to be derived from that which is the representative in the state for money; and, that if the state had the power of issuing money on sound principles, there would then be established a controlling power over all issues, which would prevent the possibility of fluctuation, and insure, as far as possible, an equilibrium for the currency. At the same time, there have been men, whose judgment was also entitled to weight, and who have expressed a different opinion on this subject. This question was under the consideration of the house when Lord Althorp brought forward the Bank Charter Bill, in 1833. It had also been the subject of consideration in the committee; and Lord Althorp, in moving the extension of the Bank Charter, expressly discussed this very question of a single bank of issue, to be constituted by and responsible to the government. Having mentioned the name of Lord Althorp, I must, though I differ from that noble lord in respect to politics, bear testimony to his integrity and soundness of judgment in all such financial matters as I am now referring to. No man who ever filled the office which the noble lord then held, is entitled to stand higher in public estimation, as respects a character for honour and integrity. On the occasion to which I have just referred, Lord Althorp said:—

"Another point for consideration is, whether the profits, which must necessarily be derived from the circulating medium of the country, should be possessed by government, or should be allowed to remain in private hands? Now, sir, the advantages, the only advantages, which I have been enabled to discover in a government bank, as compared with a private company, are those which result from having responsible persons to manage the concern, the public deriving the benefit of it; but then, on the other hand, I think these advantages are much more than counterbalanced by the political evils which would inevitably result from placing this bank under the control of the government. I think that the effect of the state having the complete control of the circulating medium in its own hands, would be most mischievous. Under these circumstances, sir, I certainly am prepared to propose the continuation of a single bank of issue in the metropolis, subject to the control of the publicity of their accounts. If we were now, for the first time, establishing a system of banking on which the country should proceed, I think this would be the most advisable mode of establishing a bank in the metropolis; but, sir, this proposition has the additional advantage—and it is no mean one—that it will occasion the least change; because I certainly am of opinion that, unless some great advantages could be derived from a change in the monetary system of this country, nothing could be more ill-advised—nothing could be more useless, than to depart from it."

In the latter part of Lord Althorp's observations, so far as they apply to the Bank of England as compared with the establishment of a government bank, I entirely agree. The true policy in this country was to work with the instruments you have, as far as you can, and if you can carry into effect your great principles without the disturbance of private interests, I am of opinion that you would gain a double advantage by so acting, provided always that the course you adopt is perfectly consistent with the establishment of your principles. This brings me to an explanation of the practical measures which I propose for the regulation of the matters I have submitted to the consideration of the house. I will explain them almost without comment, in order that the house may be in full possession of the plan recommended by the government. We think it of great importance to increase the controlling power of a single bank of issue. We think it the wisest mode to work with the instruments which exist, and to select the Bank of England as that controlling and central body, rather than to appoint commissioners, acting under the authority of parliament, for the purpose of the issue of a paper currency. I therefore propose, with respect to the Bank of England, that it should continue in possession of its present privileges of issue—but that there should be a complete separation of departments in the Bank—and that the banking business should be administered on principles perfectly different from those on which the department of issue should act. I propose that there should be an actual separation of these two departments of issue and banking—that there should be different officers to each, and a different system of account. I likewise propose that to the issue department should be transferred the whole amount of bullion now in the possession of the Bank, and that the issue of bank-notes should hereafter take place on two foundations, and two foundations only:—first, on a definite amount of securities; and after that, exclusively upon bullion; so that the action of the public would, in this latter respect, govern the amount of the circulation. There will be no power in the Bank to issue notes on deposits and discount of bills, and the issue department will have to place to the credit of the banking department the amount of notes which the issue department by law will be entitled to issue. With respect to the banking business of the Bank, I propose that it should be governed on precisely the same principles as would regulate any other body dealing with Bank of England notes.* The fixed amount of securities on which I propose that the Bank of England should issue notes is £14,000,000, and the whole of the remainder of the circulation is to be issued exclusively on the foundation of bullion. I propose that there should be a complete and periodical publication of the accounts of the Bank of England, both of the banking and issue department. Objections have been urged, in 1833, to frequent publications of these accounts, but my opinion is, that these objections are without foundation. I have the strongest opinion that nothing would better conduce to the credit of the Bank itself, and to the prevention of panic and needless alarm, than the complete and immediate disclosure of its transactions. I would, therefore, propose to enact by law, that there should be returned to the government a weekly account of the issue of notes by the Bank of England—of the amount of bullion—of the fluctuations of the bullion—of the amount of deposits—in short, an account of every transaction both in the issue department and the banking department of the Bank

* Separation must inevitably produce weakness. How is the bank of issue to pay off the ultimate £11,000 of notes, whose security is the government debt? and how is the banking department, in cases of mercantile difficulties, to increase their loans on discounts, without having recourse to imaginary or unavailable securities? However, as both banks are to remain under one and the same body of proprietors, extreme cases may be anticipated.

of England; and that the government should forthwith publish unreservedly and weekly a full account of the circulation of the Bank.*

PRIVATE AND JOINT-STOCK BANKS.

I think it desirable, in order to make the whole plan more clearly understood, that I should now state the regulations we propose to establish with respect to other banking establishments, and afterwards, that I should revert to the subject of the Bank of England, and state the terms which we have made with the Bank, subject to the ratification of parliament. Our general rule is to draw a distinction between the privilege of issue and the conduct of the banking business. We think they stand on an entirely different footing. We think that the privilege of issue is one which may be fairly and justly controlled by the state; and that the banking business is a matter in respect to which there cannot be too unlimited and unrestricted a competition. In this latter respect, we think that the Bank of England ought not to be subject to greater restrictions than other banking establishments, but that it should be put on an equal footing with them, as the principle of competition, which ought not to govern in case of issue, ought to operate in respect to the banking business; and that after the issue has once taken place, it is then important that the public should be enabled to get the use of that issue on as favourable terms as possible. With regard to banks in England and Wales, other than the Bank of England, we propose, therefore, from this time, that no new bank of issue should be constituted. We limit on this matter, and for the present at least, that which I think an evil in the case of issue—unlimited competition. As I have stated, our object is to effect this great change with as little detriment as possible to individual interests. We therefore do not propose to deprive existing banking establishments, which are now actually banks of issue, of the privilege they possess. We do not wish to raise that alarm which we fear would be excited, if there should be any sudden or immediate extinction of the power of issue in respect to these banking establishments. We therefore propose to leave the existing banks, which are actually banks of issue, this privilege of issue, subject to the condition that they should not exceed the existing amount of their issue,—this amount to be determined on an average of a definite period. This is necessary, in order to enable the Bank of England to be acquainted with the extent of the issue it would have to compete with.

The amount of the issues of these banks might be determined on the average of the last two or three years. I know I am liable to be told that the issues of these banks may be much larger, under particular circumstances and at particular periods, than at others; but I have obtained returns, of a confidential nature, from ten of the best conducted banks in the country,—six of them being in agricultural and four in manufacturing districts, and the amount of their variation of issue is much less than might be imagined. If, however, there should at any time be a demand for an increased issue, there would always be the means of supplying it; as the banks would have nothing else to do but to sell securities and demand bank-notes from the Bank of England, and to deal in notes of the Bank of England. While we thus restrain the issue in private establishments, we intend to facilitate the banking business. The joint-stock banking companies have not at present the privilege of suing and being sued. There are two descriptions of joint-stock banks—those constituted under the act of 1826, and those established under the act of 1833. The time has come when you should determine whether you would permit and encourage the system of joint-stock banks, or extinguish it. If you determine to retain the system, then you ought to give the banks every facility for the transaction of their business. The joint-stock banks ask for the privilege of suing and being sued; but this privilege, if granted, is a privilege not only to them, but to the public, who would then have pointed out some defined authority against whom they might seek redress for any wrong done. We therefore proceed on the principle of facilitating banking operations by the amendment of the law, distinguishing those operations from the privilege of issue.

[To be continued.]

---

* Being modelled after the banks of Venice and Amsterdam, our great national Bank observed the strictest secrecy with respect to its accounts, until the year 1797; after that date, reports of the amount of notes began to be made to the government, and occasionally to be published in the newspapers. In 1832, the Parliamentary Committee on Banking exposed so much of the private management of the Bank, that less secrecy has been practised ever since. In the *monthly* returns now made by the directors, there is an omission of the private deposits in the monthly averages, and in many other respects they are unsatisfactory. Since 1834, returns are made upon the average of the preceding quarter, the amounts of thirteen successive weeks are added together, and the sum divided by thirteen. The defect of this plan is, that it does not show the *progress* during the quarter, but, on the contrary, tends to conceal it.

REVIEWS OF NEW BOOKS.

ART. I.—*Narrative of a Visit to the Mauritius and South Africa.* By JAMES BACKHOUSE. London: Hamilton, Adams, & Co.

The readers of the *Colonial Magazine* are already acquainted with the name of Backhouse, through our favourable notice of his visit to the Australian Colonies. The present volume is in the same Christian, and we may add also, utilitarian spirit; for, while the primary duties of humanity are kept steadily in the fore-ground, the most useful information connected with the aborigines, natural productions, and climate, of every region visited by the traveller, are supplied in perspicuous and intelligible language. Were we disposed to emigrate, we should prefer the south of Africa to any of our colonies. Its half-way position between England and the Indies, its varieties of climate, its numerous productions, and the spotless character of the original colonists—superiorities over penal settlements, are distinctly shown in the "Visit to South Africa," which should be placed in the hands of every voluntary emigrant by a General Public Board, for the direction and protection of all who feel a desire to seek their fortunes in another clime. Perhaps there is less known of the Mauritius than of any of our eastern insular possessions, from obstinate perseverance in the use of the French tongue by the islanders, and, on this account, although many other reasons might be urged, we shall extract a few lines to enlighten the reader's darkness upon the subject:—

"The town of Port Louis," (the capital of the island), writes the traveller, "is beautifully situated on the west side of the Mauritius, in a cove formed by a series of basaltic hills, portions of which are woody; they vary in height from 1,058 to 2,639 feet. The Pouce, *Thumb*, which lies directly behind the town, is the highest point. The lower portion of many of the houses is of hewn basalt, and the upper portion of wood; others are entirely of wood, painted. The streets are rather narrow; they are laid out at right angles, have footpaths with basaltic curbstones, and are macadamized. Many of the houses have little courts in front, well stocked with fine trees and shrubs, and beautiful date and cocoa-nut palms. There are magnificent acacias, with large yellow flowers, as well as tamarinds and other trees, in some of the streets; and bananas, caladiums, marvels of Peru, and many other striking plants, on the border of a stream from the mountains, that runs through the town. An open space, like a race-course, lies behind the town: it is called le Champ de Mars, and is bordered by several large villas, built in a style of neatness and elegance, like those in the neighbourhood of cities on the continent of Europe.

"The population of Port Louis in 1836, was 27,645, of whom 6,679 males and 6,664 females were free, and 8,247 males and 6,055 females were apprentices. Most of the latter, and some of the former, were persons of colour.—French is the language universally spoken.

"We took up our abode at Massey's Hotel, the only decent inn in Port Louis. It is three stories high, and has the hall and lower rooms floored with marble. The walls are covered with paper exhibiting large landscapes. The stairs and floors of the upper rooms are painted red, as is common here, and rubbed bright. The beds are covered with muslin curtains, to keep off moschettos these insects being numerous, and the heat rendering it necessary to have the windows open at night. Here, for four dollars *(twelve shillings)* a-day each, we had small bed-rooms, with breakfast at nine o'clock, and dinner at half-past five, at the table d'hôte. The latter was in French style, consisting of a great variety of small dishes, and succeeded immediately by coffee. Burgundy wine diluted with water was the common beverage at dinner; but though considered as adapted to the climate, and probably it is the most so of any fermented liquor, yet persons who, for the purpose of discouraging drinking customs, have taken water only, have found themselves better rather than worse for discontinuing the use of the Burgundy wine."

His visit to the prisons is deserving of a careful perusal. His feelings are not of the same morbid character on such occasions as those of our sorry sentimentalists at home. He looks upon the infirmities of his species with mercy, but with firmness; whence the essential value of his opinions:—

"In the Bagne Prison, slave apprentices, sentenced by special justices, as well as Indian labourers, were confined. Of the former, there were in the prison 139 at the end of 1836, and 172 at that of 1837. The deaths in this prison amounted to 20 in 1836; in 1837 to scarcely half that number. The building consists of several large rooms, in which the prisoners sleep on wooden platforms. In some respects it may be considered more as a depôt than as a prison, as parties preferring complaints against their masters are confined here, till their masters shall be summoned to answer to the complaints. Among the complainants were companies of Indian labourers, who had quitted the plantations on which they were engaged, considering themselves hardly used or deceived. Many of these, on entering the prison, are found to be affected with the itch. The period for which prisoners are sentenced to this place, varies from a few days to a few weeks. The food of prisoners in these prisons, which consists chiefly of rice, costs 3d. a-day each, and their clothing £1 a-year, making a total annual average cost for each prisoner of £5. 11s. 3d.

"While the labouring population were in slavery, their masters, or overseers, executed summary punishment in many cases, such as, during their apprenticeship, required to be examined by a magistrate. This brought rather a larger proportion of the coloured class, for a time, into the prisons.—At the period of our visit to the Mauritius, we often heard strong fears expressed, that after the period of emancipation, there would be no safety in living in the island; but on enquiring the result, of a gentleman of our acquaintance, with whom we met after the emancipation had taken place, we did not find that the anticipations of outrage from the emancipated slaves had been fulfilled. The only complaint seemed to be, that many of the women, instead of going to the field to labour as formerly, chose to stay at home to take care of their huts and families!"

The adventures of the author in the "great Karroo," afford an invaluable lesson to all future travellers, whether we estimate his narrative by his patience under privations, or his unclouded observation of natural objects. His picture of heat is admirable and affecting, and his notice of the phenomenon of mirage very instructive:—

"The mirage in this country often causes the mountains to appear as if they were cut off by the base, and raised into the air. It also presents the appearance of water in the most arid parts of the karroo. To-day we crossed the dry beds of several rivulets; and in one of them, the stones looked as if they were standing out of water. Often as we had been deceived by such appearances, we now made ourselves sure of water, but on coming to the place there was not a drop. The illusion vanished, and left us to feel more keenly the thirst which the great heat had occasioned. The mirage is probably occasioned by the contact of two strata of air of different degrees of density; the surface of the lower stratum may, in some measure reflect light in a similar manner to that in which water reflects it, when in contact with air. The heat now became so great in the middle of the day, that the dogs, in trying to shelter themselves, would often lie down under such bushes as they could find; but these were generally too small to defend them effectually from the scorching sun. After the wagon had passed to some distance, the poor animals would howl through fear of setting their feet on the heated ground; but at length they would spring up and gallop to a bush or stone beyond the wagon, under which they would again lie down.—After passing a deserted house, we came at a bushy valley, in which there was a beautiful spring of clear water, under a cliff of purple, shivered slate, surmounted by clayey sandstone, and resting on firm argillaceous rock. The water flowed a few hundred paces, filled some rocky pools, and then sunk again into the earth. The cattle and horses enjoyed the freshness of this clear spring, and the latter browsed greedily upon a short bulrush, *eleocharis*, which clothed the moistened earth, in the bed of the river, with a lovely green, a colour rarely occurring in the dreary Karroo."

For the present, our duty to Mr. Backhouse is discharged; but his volume will long continue to hold an honoured place in our colonial library, for reference as to customs, climate, natural resources, social condition, and other important topics, valuable to those who would honestly direct, or be honestly directed. Three maps of South Africa have at so many different periods appeared in England, the original basis of each being the researches of Mr. Centlivres Chase; on these Arrowsmith formed an excellent map. Mr. Chase subsequently published his own labours, in his volume on Algoa Bay, an improvement of course on his imitators; and Mr. Backhouse has engaged the able coadjutorship of Mr. Wyld in producing the fullest map of our South African Colonies which has yet been published; it is worth more than the publishers demand for the volume and map inclusive. In this age of illustration, it would be unpardonable to omit mentioning, that nearly fifty woodcuts give interest to the work, and contribute to the formation of clearer notions of the regions described by the writer.

Art. II.—*Knight's Library for the Times—Our Indian Empire.* London: Knight & Co.

This useful and able compilation has reached a third part without any abatement of interest or defalcation in style or spirit. The period which it embraces is fraught with stirring incidents in the camp and the cabinet, and the great names that occur in these pages should be as familiar as household words to every subject of the empire. Although Clive laid the foundation of our Indian conquests, it was reserved for the Wellesleys, undoubtedly, to show how those conquests could be retained—a task more difficult than the acquisition. Surprise, treachery, power, may at any time effect a people's subjection; wisdom only can keep them in submission. Here, for the first time since a history of India has been attempted, is the fair share which the Duke of Wellington had, in the reduction and government of the Peninsular portion of Hindostan, candidly acknowledged and clearly proved. We looked with some feeling of interest to this part of Mr. Knight's history, because all his predecessors have ascribed the *sole* administration of the Anglo-Indian government to the Marquis Wellesley—*the sole error* of promoting Colonel Wellesley so rapidly, to that eloquent but pompous statesman—omitting all mention of the *de facto* participation which the future conqueror of Napoleon had in every principal operation of the field and the cabinet, during that very eventful period of history. This is partly owing to the publication of the Marquis Wellesley's despatches—partly to the silence of the illustrious Duke,—a silence imposed by fraternal affection,—and partly to the want of those documents, the Wellington Despatches, without which no Indian history could have been completed, and of which Mr. MacFarlane has prudently availed himself. This epitome, therefore, is necessarily the best Indian history our press presents, because it is the first that has chosen its information from the most authentic sources. The system of quoting authorities cannot be sufficiently applauded; indeed, without this addition the pages of Scott's historic novels are as authentic as those of all such histories. The mode here adopted, of referring to the Wellington Despatches, the most extraordinary production of the age, is not very happy; it rather leads the youthful reader to imagine that Colonel Gurwood was the author, than the amanuensis or transcriber. Indeed, however honourable the position, and high the character of the Colonel, for bravery and principle, the Despatches do not derive any additional value in the estimation of his countrymen, or of foreigners, from having been edited by an officer of the Duke's own army,—a personal friend of the hero,—and one who has received from him distinction and substantial benefit. For instance, will not a Frenchman complain that the reply of his Grace to Marshal Ney, when the latter asked him to intercede for his life with the iniquitous tribunal that murdered him, has not been given amongst the despatches; but, instead of it, we find an explanatory note accounting for its omission. The Wellington Despatches are good, excellent, invaluable as far as they go, and Mr. MacFarlane has done well and wisely in building his narration of events in our Indian empire upon their contents,—but *all* the Wellington Despatches are not yet published.

ART. III.—*Hints on the Establishment of Schools, &c.*, published by the Committee of the Home and Colonial Infant-School Society. London: Ridgway, Gray's-Inn Road.

The first, the best, step towards the permanent prosperity of our infant Colonies, is to educate their infant population, and the purest source to draw hints from on the subject is the parent country. Here wealth, experience, talent, and true Christian principles combine in bringing plans for mental cultivation to the most rapid and real maturity, and the little work before us, which to quote would be to supersede, is one of the most efficient instruments that can be employed by the charitable in our Colonies, in laying a solid substructure of happiness and piety amongst the juvenile portion of these growing countries. Minutely detailing the arrangements of schoolroom, discipline of scholars, duties of teachers, description of books, character of recreations, salaries of teachers, and defining the duties of Committee and of Visitors—few essential points would here seem to have been forgotten. As teachers and paid officers, from fear of removal, will probably be attentive to their various avocations, it is hardly necessary to recommend to their most careful perusal the Hints on Schools; but, those amiable, disinterested, and exemplary persons, who so cheerfully and diligently act as Visitors, will find much assistance from the suggestions addressed to them in the concluding section of the Committee's instructions, to which we earnestly point their attention.

NOTICE.—The first volume of the Wycliffe Society's Publications, containing select writings of Wycliffe, under the editorship of the Rev. Dr. Vaughan, of Lancashire College, is in the press, and will be ready for delivery to Subscribers in the ensuing Autumn.

COLONIAL INTELLIGENCE.

India.—By the Overland Mail we have papers from Bombay to the 20th and from Calcutta to the 11th of May. The principal intelligence contained in them relates to the state of the Punjab, which appears now to be more distracted than ever. A bloody fight is stated to have taken place on the 7th of May, between Heera Singh, the present Prime Minister, and the party of the sons of Runjeet Singh, who are opposed to him, led on by Ittur Singh, a chief of considerable influence.

It was reported that the governor-general was on the eve of going from Calcutta to the north-western provinces, and would be attended either by Sir Hugh Gough or Sir Charles Napier, with two large corps of troops.

The disturbed state of the Punjab is calculated to hasten the movements of the British Indian armies in that direction. The attempts lately made to corrupt the fidelity of the British sepoys, and the large sums sent to Ferozepore and its vicinity, (170 000*l.*) have excited a strong wish for punishing the unprincipled chiefs of Lahore. The large force of 80,000 men was therefore ordered, and it was thought Lord Ellenborough and Sir C. Napier would undertake the conquest of the Punjab, the former as a diplomatist and a politician, and the latter as a general.

In Bombay there was a discussion going forward respecting the conduct of the native justices, who had not exerted themselves to procure the arrest of a man named Aloo Paroo, against whom evidence had been discovered to prove his being implicated in the burning of the five ships from that harbour during the last two years, and also of his being connected with the gang of pirates, smugglers, &c., discovered in 1843.

The threatened movement of the notorious Ackbar Khan on Peshawur had not taken place. The position of his father, Dhost Mahomed, was by no means satisfactory; his age, his infirmities, and the complicated state of the affairs of Cabul, would, it was thought, induce him to resign his sovereignty into the hands of Ackbar.

The news from Scinde extends to the 16th of May. Sir Charles Napier was busy in making preparations for the meeting of the Beloochee chiefs, which was to take place on the 24th of May, when it is said that upwards of 17,000 of them would attend, each having an unarmed attendant. Thirty thousand men assembled to deliberate would present an odd appearance. It was supposed that Sir Charles had some important measures to propose to their attention. In Upper Scinde, where General Simpson, (who was to be succeeded by General Hunter,) commanded, nothing remarkable had occurred.

In Gwalior there were several intrigues fomented by the Queen Dowager against the British and the Regent established there; but a caution and a threat had been given her on the part of the Supreme Government. Tranquillity prevailed in the capital, and the people were satisfied, for an excellent police had been arranged there by the British officers.

One of the freebooting chiefs of Boghilkund has had his castle levelled to the earth, and is himself a prisoner, in consequence of his refusal to obey the orders of the Supreme Government, and to restore some plunder which he had taken from some merchants, British subjects, who were travelling through the country. This decided act of the British authorities is highly acceptable to the ryots and tradesmen, who are delighted when those petty tyrants are punished for their robberies and insolence.

The other parts of India were tranquil, and expected to be so during the rainy season.

China.—The dates are from Macao to the 10th, and Hong-Kong to the 8th, of April, but the intelligence is still destitute of political news. Malwa opium was said to have declined very materially in price in consequence of its inferior quality.

Admiral Sir W. Parker was at Madras on the 11th of May, when he was fêted by the inhabitants.

With regard to commercial intelligence, the money-market at Calcutta remains without alteration — capital continuing abundant for all commercial purposes.

Government securities preserve their buoyancy, and several weighty transactions have taken place in them.

Exchange is rather more lively.

At Bombay, the near approach of the rains has caused the buyers for the interior to suspend their purchases, and the sales of imports during the month are, in consequence, very limited. Those that have been made were chiefly for local consumption or on speculation.

New South Wales. — Papers from Sydney to the 30th of March have been received, but they give no news of an important character. Business, it is stated, was reviving in the colony, and the prospect of a better condition of trade is pointedly adverted to. The demand for manufactured goods had increased, and prices were advancing; while, in reference to the general state of the markets, it is said, the tendency was decidedly in favour of improvement.

Hobart-town and Launceston papers have also come to hand. Fine flour at the mills was 10*l.* per ton, and wheat 3*s.* 6*d.* to 3*s.* 9*d.* per bushel. The grain markets altogether appear to be looking up.

Cape of Good Hope.—The political news from the Cape of Good Hope is of little or no interest. The municipal elections were the only matters of such nature that occupied attention, and these were passing over quietly compared with previous contests. A notice had appeared from the Governor calling in the notes, which are to be exchanged for Treasury bills at the same rate of British silver, and as the amount of this part of the debt of the colony is about £20,000, there will remain after it is paid off £20,950 debentures bearing interest to be liquidated. It is stated that no further issues of notes will take place, the resources of the Treasury being said to be now quite sufficient to meet such demands. All the banks and public companies are called upon forthwith to take these notes in for exchange, the desire of the Executive being that they shall be paid off as speedily as possible.

From a document published in the Cape papers, it appears that the total exports for the year ending the 5th of January, 1844, were valued at £349,438, against £354,095 for the year 1843. Wine, flour, skins, and unenumerated articles show a decrease, while on the other hand, wool, horns, and hides show an increase. The table of imports for the same period shows an excess of £45,477 against 1843, the gross value for each respective year being £807,270, and £761,793. The amount entered for consumption in 1844 was £730,220; and the amount warehoused £77,050. Of this amount, £135,914 were entered at Port Elizabeth. With respect to exports, it appears that the increase in wool has been 178,692lb., Table Bay having shipped 169,495lb. less than in the former year, while the shipments from Port Elizabeth have increased to 268,479lb.

The first of the Sydney mail-packets (the Mary Sharp) arrived in Table Bay on the 20th of April, having left the Downs on the 6th of February, being 2 months and 14 days on the passage.

West Indies.—The whole of the papers are filled with articles against the government measure for the reduction of the duty on foreign coffee and free-labour sugar; and in all the islands meetings were being held to memorialize the Queen on the subject. Upon the calculation that the alteration in the duty of sugar will cause a reduction of 5*s.* per cwt. on the produce of the West Indies, the planters of Demerara alone, it is said, will annually lose £140,000.

The *Jamaica Morning Journal* thus sums up the general affairs in the island—"The Grand Court is sitting, but there is nothing in its proceedings which demand any particular notice at our hand. The rains have been pretty general, but there are some localities which still require more moisture, and where they have not been as heavy as could be wished. The weather in and out of doors is exceedingly close and oppressive, and June promises to be remarkable for a scorching sun and strong sea-breezes. A serious riot recently occurred at Taylor's Caymanas Estate, in St. Catherine's, between the Creole or native negroes, and some African emigrants located here. The cause of the dispute is the circumstance of the Africans labouring at a lower rate of hire than the Creoles have been in the habit of receiving or are disposed to receive. One of the Africans had his arm broken, and others received cuts and were severely beaten. The ringleaders have been arrested, and will be brought to justice. The Creoles have not succeeded in their object, which was to drive the Africans off their property, and the result will be that the former will have to leave or consent to accept the same rates as the latter are doing. Dry weather continues in the parish of St. Dorothy. In Hanover delightful rains have fallen, and the face of the country presents a most cheering appearance. Westmoreland has concluded with large crops, and a promise (if the seasons continue favourable) of a rich and abundant harvest next year. The ex-president Herard of Hayti has arrived in this city, having been compelled to leave that island to avoid the danger which threatened him. Our island remains healthy, buttrade is dull. Money has never been known to be more scarce or difficult of collection than it is at the present moment. The movements in the mother-country, it is apprehended, will make things worse than they are."

Lord Elgin is becoming more and more popular, and has the esteem and respect of all classes.

Dominica.—We learn from the report of the mail-agent the extraordinary fact, that the island of Dominica is in a state of open insurrection, and is under martial law, the cause being an attempt to take the census. If this information had not been confirmed by private letters received by the steamer, we should not have credited the existence of such a feeling amongst any British colonial population.—*St. Lucia Independent Press.*

CANADA.—All accounts, both public and private, represent the condition of Canada as highly prosperous, and as requiring nothing but internal peace to secure a long continuance of prosperity.—An announcement is made in the official gazette, that the provincial parliament stands again prorogued till the 3d day of August, but not for the despatch of business.—The papers speak of the reception of Sir Charles Metcalfe on his arrival at his new seat of government, Montreal, as very warm and highly flattering to him. He arrived on the 22d, and made his public entry on the 24th, amid great splendour and enthusiasm.—The nomination of J. S. Green as Secretary of the Treasury had been unanimously rejected.

From the opening of the canals to the 15th of June, 304,624 barrels of Canadian and 46,408 barrels of American flour, and 111,021 bushels of Canadian and 95,227 of American wheat, had been received at Montreal. This is more than three times the quantity received in that port to the same date of the previous year, when it was not more than 111,801 barrels of flour and 48,211 bushels of wheat; and this extraordinary increase furnishes a striking proof of the impulse given to the Canada corn-trade by the Government Bill of the session before last. The quantity of flour shipped to this country up to the same date from Montreal and Quebec was 140,600 barrels of flour and 136,248 bushels of wheat. With regard to the prospect of the present year's harvest, a Montreal paper of the 27th ult. says—"All the accounts represent the breadth of land laid down in both provinces with wheat as unprecedented, and the crops as looking remarkably healthy. Strong hopes are entertained that the ravages of the fly will be very much circumscribed; and from the formation of agricultural societies, and the increased attention devoted by the journals, in both languages, to agricultural topics, we think a reasonable hope may be entertained of a permanent improvement of the culture of the soil." With regard to the Canada timber trade, which was said to have been ruined by the reduction of the duties on Baltic timber, we learn that it is in a healthy and prosperous state, means having been found of bringing the timber down from the interior at more moderate rates.

The Halifax papers contain accounts of a great fire at Harbour Grace, Newfoundland, which commenced on the evening of the 5th ult., and was not subdued until half-past 2 o'clock on the following day. The loss on this occasion is stated to be 30,000*l*., and but little of the property destroyed was insured.

Orders were received by the last mail from England, directing the fortification of several important points of defence in Newfoundland. The works on Partridge Island, at the entrance of St. John's harbour, which are to be on an extensive scale, will be commenced the coming week, as will also those at the Grand Falls, on the route to Canada.

LORD LIEUTENANCY OF IRELAND.—At the Court at Buckingham Palace, the 10th day of July; present, the Queen's Most Excellent Majesty in Council. Her Majesty in Council was pleased to declare the Right Hon. William Lord Heytesbury, Lieutenant-General and General Governor of that part of the United Kingdom called Ireland.—*London Gazette*, July 12.—His Excellency has since arrived at Dublin.

SIR HENRY HARDINGE.—The Queen has been pleased to nominate and appoint Lieutenant-General the Right Hon. Sir Henry Hardinge, Knight Commander of the Most Hon. Military Order of the Bath, to be a Knight Grand Cross of the said most Hon. Order.—*Downing Street*, July 1.

THE REVENUE.—The quarterly return of the revenue presents the same favourable results which have distinguished the returns of several quarters past. The four important items of Customs, Excise, Stamps, and Taxes, present an aggregate increase over the corresponding items of the quarter ending July 5, 1843, of 448,574*l*., distributed with some inequality between these four several heads, the Customs' department alone appropriating no less than 312,029*l*. out of that entire increase; and the department next in importance as an index of the monied prosperity of the country, viz., the Excise, appropriating 85,479*l*. out of the remainder. The increase respectively on these heads on the entire year ending July 5, 1844, is the somewhat startling sum of 835,349*l*. for the Customs, and 420,073*l*. for the Excise.

With these elements of increase, our readers will not be surprised to learn that the total income of the year just ended exceeds that of the year previous by a sum of no less than 2,440,336*l*.

LONDON: FISHER, SON AND CO., PRINTERS.

FISHER'S

COLONIAL MAGAZINE.

ON LABOUR IN OUR WEST INDIAN AND SOUTH AMERICAN POSSESSIONS.

In the number of this magazine for the first of December, 1842, we stated our sentiments on the then high price paid for the obtainment of labour in our West Indian and South American colonies, and as to how far there, at that time, seemed to be any remedy for the evil. We shewed how the change from a state of slavery to one of freedom, while it cleansed from the filth of man-dealing our until then polluted hands, had, yet, in doing so, inflicted upon us a weight of punishment, which, however justly retributive, pressed too heavily to be borne; from a sufficient and certain provision, our colonists had been reduced to a precarious pittance, and a prospect of destitution but too apparent and too certain of realization, if not averted by proper means. We had, certainly, compromised ourselves by engaging in a guilty traffic, which the spirit of Christianity recoils at as abhorrent and detestable, and as morally ruinous to all concerned in; but, while we, as colonists, were the immediate agents, our countrymen at home, in the mother-country, were not less implicated in the foul abomination: "*Quid non mortalia pectora cogis, auri sacra fames.*" They forged the chains, and taught us to rivet them; we, in an evil hour, were too apt in obeying and carrying out the instruction. The whole country were either actually or constructively participators in the crime. Sensible of this, in the hour of need, when the propriety of wiping away a public stain was seen, a liberal compensation for present pecuniary losses, was allotted by the State to those who were more immediately affected by the step; and there is no reason, we feel certain, to apprehend from Government aught but a continuance of the liveliest solicitude for, and attention to, every amelioration that our further wants, consequent upon the great change, may render just and expedient.

In the paper alluded to, we showed that the transition from a state of slavery to one of freedom, from various causes, some of which we then mentioned, placed our labouring negro population in a condition to be enabled to dictate to their employers, wages which could not be profitably given; noticed some plausible but erroneous plans, which several writers had recommended, in relation to an amelioration of the then mode of obtaining and applying labour; and then ventured to offer our own humble views of the subject, as the fruit of long residence in the places concerned, views not biassed by that long sojourn, we hope, because an instructive one in this our enlightened country, while it made us little susceptible of bigotry, before we went abroad, has, since our return to Britain, been sufficiently established and confirmed, we trust, to render us proof against any of its assaults. But, to return; we recommended that, in the first place and above all things, the white colonists in the West Indies should if such still unhappily existed, cast off every remnant of the prejudices which were pointed at a man's complexion during the existence of slavery, and endeavour to obliterate even the remembrance of the black having been in subjection to them; to omit no attention to the moral and social improvement of all classes, without regard to colour or complexion, attending not only specially to the improvement of the black and brown portions of their communities, but also to their own general educational enlightenment, as being calculated to have a powerfully beneficial influence, by the operation of good example, on the lower orders.

The internal improvement also of the various colonies, we spoke of as being of the greatest consequence. The towns should be better regulated than they are now, as to plan, buildings, police, and other matters, and villages should be formed at convenient places. Land in general should be better defined, enclosed, and fenced in, and that belonging to the crown correctly ascertained, and then put under the surveillance of proper and sufficient officers; but care should be taken not to put unnecessary or odious restrictions upon the means for its obtainment by purchasers at moderate prices; such as are obviously resorted to for the purpose of preventing the labourer from acquiring it, in order the more effectually to compel him to work for hire on the land of others, should be by no means put in practice. On the contrary, facilities for bringing about the entire occupation of all the uncultivated or waste land, would be the most, if not the only, effectual means of preventing vagrancy and squatting, and inducing the peasantry to seek manual employment on the property of others. Wholesome legislation bearing equally on all, without distinction, and embracing as few restrictions upon the labouring classes as might be advisable, should be carefully provided; we need not say that there are enactments of the colonial legislatures which are very far from being imbued with the spirit of this our recommendation. A straightforward, upright, and manly consideration for the just interests of their peasantry, as it is the duty, so also would it be for the undoubted benefit and advantage of our West Indian planters. It is of very great importance, that those in particular, of our colonies, should be made by proper attention, more inviting places of residence to settlers than they have hitherto very correctly been considered; and it would not be very difficult to work the change. If the foregoing points suggested by us, and many other obvious ones, were carefully attended to, rapid improvement would follow, and, from becoming infinitely more desirable than they now are, these possessions would receive their fair share of settlers of all descriptions, including artisans and field-labourers of all kinds, the great good effects of which would soon be incalculable.

The West Indian colonies being made desirable places of residence, no pains should be then spared in publishing, as much as possible, by means of fit agents, the advantages offered by them. Besides the coast of Africa, this could be done on the continent of South America, in the United States of North America, and in the island of Madeira, and the Azore, and Cape de Verde islands. The various places in the Mediterranean would also be important parts to communicate with; Malta has a dense and poor population, many of whom might better themselves by leaving their home. Persons from all these places would answer well as agricultural labourers; it would be requisite, however, to pay great attention, on their first arrival, to emigrants from the Mediterranean, Madeira, and the Azores and Cape de Verdes. Their introduction should not at first be in large numbers, and their comforts in the beginning should be very closely attended to. They should have very light work to perform, at the outset, and that as much in the shade as practicable, having a long respite from labour, in the middle and hottest part of the day, as practised by the *peons* of South America, who find their account in doing so. These latter are a hardy race of mulattoes proceeding from the intercourse of the white European and the aboriginal Indian: in their own country, and also in the island of Trinidad, which is much frequented by them, they are considered quite equal to the black for all labouring purposes; indeed, for some special occupations, such as felling timber, for example, they are unquestionably superior to him. Perhaps, however, it would be found a good general rule, that whites should, rather than undertake manual labour in the fields, employ themselves as artisans, manufacturers of produce, or tenders of cattle. The great bane of the humbler description of whites, in warm climates, is the addiction to excess, and their want of due care of their persons, as it respects their often remaining in wet clothes, and also exposing themselves unnecessarily to the hot sun, or to sudden chills from draughts. If our observations on all these points were attended to by them; if they took great care of themselves, lived comfortably and well, but, abstemiously avoiding, above all, spirituous liquors, their success would follow, and thus, thousands and hundreds of thousands, who would otherwise drag out a miserable, wretched, and half-starved existence in their native countries, might obtain ease, competence, and comfort, and sometimes even affluence. There are, we need hardly say, numerous instances of persons, from the humblest grades in their own native places, who, having settled in the West Indies, have amassed ample fortunes: not only the capitals of Great Britain and Ireland, but also many of those of the rest of Europe, attest this.

A large white population from Spain, and from other countries, which are similar in climate to those which we have mentioned, succeeds perfectly well at Porto Rico, and there is no apparent reason for our not doing so in our West Indian colonies, if the same care and temperance should be consulted by it, as is no doubt practised by the other. After the trials that have on several occasions been made, we speak with great diffidence in regard to the employment, in the West Indies, of person from the colder parts of Europe. They have been tried from England, Scotland, and Ireland, and from France and Germany, and with almost entire failure, we mean for agricultural purposes; but we, nevertheless, think that, even from those places, many persons might proceed thither and settle, as trades-people and artisans, in the towns, or as head-men on the plantations, to perform the most important offices in conducting the process of sugar or other manufacture; or, they might undertake various employments in the middle class of society, which will now every day, since the establishment of freedom, go on increasing. Many might profitably carry on farms for raising cattle and provisions, for both of which there is now considerable demand in the colonies. For the latter, in particular, there is great request; and a larger supply might reduce its present high price, and have some effect, perhaps, on the general high rate of wages.

We have now placed before the reader, the exact state of our colonies in the West Indies at the period when we last addressed him, and we are sorry to say that little, if any relief, has since then been found, although increased facilities have been devised by the government of the mother-country, for carrying on an emigration from the coast of Africa on a more extended scale than that hitherto permitted. The natural question, therefore, now is: Have we any remedy for the present suffering; can we find out any means for effecting great immediate improvement, or must we look for a much better state of things, in the slow, but certain, operation of time, which eats down all difficulties and obstacles? We are of the latter opinion, time only can bring much relief. In our former article, to which we have referred, we purposely, as we therein stated, refrained from any remarks on expected competition, by introduction into our colonies of fresh supplies of labourers, and any contemplated reduction of wages that might be supposed consequent thereon; and we did so, because we feared that it was not calculated to have any immediate effect of the kind; an opinion which has been proved to have been correct, as at British Guiana and Trinidad, a large influx of labourers has tended rather to raise than depress the amount of wages. We shall proceed to show that such a competition as will reduce the price of labour much below the present one, is comparatively remote, and that other economical agents must therefore be brought into play. But, before we give our opinion on the points which are involved in the consideration of the matter, it is essential to settle that upon which the whole question hinges and turns. Without doing this, we should be writing to no purpose, and, having accomplished it, the whole matter will then clearly lie in the small compass of a nutshell.

The whole question turns, obviously, upon competition, as all questions, having for their object an inquiry into the causes affecting the price of labour, must turn. Let us, therefore, see how necessitous labour, which is the parent of competition, is to be brought about, by the ordinary workings of circumstances, in the tropical communities of the West Indies and South America. We say, tropical communities, using a wide term; for, we must not consider the West Indies alone, but along with all places, whether insular or continental, which from their vicinity and their similarity of productions, are calculated to affect at all, in any way, the demand for labour, by holding out pecuniary inducement or local enticement. If such a consideration be, as it no doubt is, to a certain modified extent, applicable to an investigation of the laws which govern the price of labour in Europe, it will also be so in respect of those which affect it in South America, and the vicinal islands. If, in the first, where removal from one country to another does not very often take place, for reasons which are inherent in a highly civilized state of society, there is, yet, a tendency to an equilibrium of the price of wages in the general labour-market; how much more must a similar doctrine apply to regions with a scanty population, and offering keen incentives and enticements to, and great facilities for, adventure and change of abode? A short statement of some of the rules which govern the supply of labour, will be essential here.

The proper way of regarding labour is, as a commodity in the market: it, therefore, has, as well as everything else, its market price and its natural price. The market price of labour is regulated by the proportion which, at any time, and any place, may exist between the demand and the supply: its natural price is governed by other laws, and consists in such a quantity of the necessaries and comforts of life, as, from the nature of the climate and the habits of the country, are necessary to support the labourer, and to enable him to rear such a family as may preserve in the market an undiminished supply of labour. That the labourer must usually obtain for his work a sufficient quantity of those things which the climate may render necessary to preserve himself, and such a family as may keep up the supply of labour to the demand, in healthful existence, is self-evident; and when we consider that things not originally necessary to healthful existence, often become so from use, and that men will be deterred from marriage, unless they have a prospect of rearing their families in the mode of living to which they have been accustomed, it is obvious that the labourer must obtain for his work, not only what the climate may render necessary, but what the habits of the country, operating as a second nature, may require. From this account of the natural price of labour, it is evident that it may be liable to very considerable variations, according to local and other circumstances.

The natural price of labour, though it varies under different climates, and with the different stages of national improvement, may, in any given time and place, be regarded as very nearly stationary. While the natural price of labour is thus steady, its market price, as has been already observed, fluctuates perpetually, according to the proportion of its supply to the market. The price which labour fetches in the market may often be considerably more, and often considerably less, than that which, from the climate and habits of living, is necessary to maintain the labourer and his family. But notwithstanding those occasional variations, the natural and the market price of labour, have a mutual influence on each other, and cannot long be separated.*

If these principles, so clearly laid down, be admitted to be sound and unanswerable, how will they apply, for instance, to our South American colony of British Guiana, under the circumstances of the undeniably extraordinary fertility of that country, when an exceedingly small part of the most fertile land in the country is occupied; when a population at least one hundred times as great as the actual one could be sustained from the products of the soil, without inconvenience? It necessarily follows, that the natural wages of labour must be low in such a country; and so far, it might appear that the planter was not prejudiced by the change from slavery to freedom, inasmuch as he would be required to give only low wages. But can he induce his former slave, now made free, to work for those wages? If not, he must raise them, in order to induce him to work. But it must be remembered, that there is a limitation in the extent to which he could raise them; any rate of wages, given to a slave made free, which would materially exceed the expense that was incurred under the slave system, for the average entire support of an individual working-slave, could not now be afforded by the master. To this expense would be superadded the interest of the money paid by way of compensation for his manumission; but, beyond that limit, he could not go, without a palpable diminution of his profits. Nor could he proceed with his cultivation of the soil at all, if the rate of wages materially exceeded the amount gained by the price of the manumission, and by his exemption from future expense in having to support the slave. Other countries, when the slave system was in force, or when density of population, diminishing the means of subsistence, compelled the labourer to work, as the only means of acquiring a subsistence, would undersell him in the market of the world. Very slight consideration of the circumstances in which the black labourer is now placed in Guiana, and in Trinidad, and some of the other islands, will leave little doubt as to the causes of the present high price of labour, and will convince us that, unless he be stimulated by large wages, he will not work. Indeed it may be doubted whether any considerable increase would be certain to accomplish that purpose so effectually as to secure his constant and continuous labour; and it could easily be shown that the master could not afford to offer that temptation, that is to say, to pay such wages, in his character of a producer of sugar.

A man has only to settle himself where he pleases within the colony of Guiana; he has only to retire up the river, a few miles back from the extreme margin of the very small portion of occupied ground, when he will find space enough, as we have before said, for a vast population, who could spread themselves and their descendants without any serious obstacle being opposed to them by the diminished and scattered aborigines of the country. On this new location, he would be able to obtain, by the strenuous exertion of one single day, enough to satisfy all his natural and artificial wants for the space of a week. In addition, he would have the resources of the river and the woods, for the supply of fish and game; and

* See Ricardo's "Principles of Political Economy," p. 91, 3rd edition.

he would enjoy that state which all men are disposed to agree is the state most congenial to the human being in tropical climates, that of repose. The same causes which it is here shown are operating, and will continue to operate in an increased ratio, upon the present black population of Guiana, will work in a ten-fold degree upon emigrants from Africa. It may be said that all these anticipated consequences might be prevented by the passing of a law declaratory of the appropriation of all the ungranted land of the colony, to the use of the crown, and thereby effectually preventing the self-location of any one in the manner detailed. Undoubtedly such a law could be passed; but, could it be enforced? It could not; and if it could, it would be highly impolitic to make such an enactment, when it is considered that a settler, by crossing a creek not wider than a street, would find himself in the territory of Venezuela, where there is every facility, from the gratuitous occupation of land in a region quite as desirable as, and in many parts far superior to Guiana. The same observations which apply to Guiana, do so in a great measure to the island of Trinidad, a very small portion of which has been reduced into a state of cultivation. The large extent of the island, and the very great excess of waste land over that reclaimed from the forest, would render it quite impracticable to adopt an effectual preventive watch over it, even if such were desirable, which we think is not, for the same reasons which apply to Guiana: the coast of Venezuela is so near to Trinidad, and the intervening sea so placid, that it can be easily reached by the smallest canoe in two or three hours. In Jamaica and the other islands there is, comparatively with the above-mentioned places, little unreclaimed land, so that prudent and proper restrictions are there quite susceptible of being put in practice, and would not be regarded in so odious a light as in them. In the two first-named places, we feel assured that any stringent measures to prevent the easy occupation of land, would be looked upon as being quite of a dog-in-the-manger character, and would have the effect of disgusting and driving away valuable settlers, to the great injury of the best interests of those valuable and important colonies. We fear it is too much the practice in West Indian legislation to look more to immediate and fleeting advantage, than to gradual, steady, and permanent benefit. This was natural enough when the West Indies were only *used* for the purpose of enabling one to acquire fortunes to spend in the mother-country; but, as matters have now there changed, and the inhabitants, to do any good for themselves, must make them their home, it is their duty and interest to take a more enlightened, liberal, and comprehensive view of things, as they are calculated to tend to general advancement and prosperity, than they were formerly accustomed to adopt.

It may be proper here to make some observations with reference to the circumstances of India and the West Indies, as illustrative of the relative prices of labour in those places. It is difficult to conceive at first how so great a disparity in price can exist in the two places, but the causes are easily found. India has a population dense in the extreme; she has little or no unoccupied land of the first class of fertility, and her capital, however large in the aggregate, is extremely small in proportion to the extent of space, and to the density of population upon which it is employed. Taking Guiana, for instance; it, on the contrary, has a population fearing no proportion to her territory; she has vast quantities of unoccupied land of very great fertility; and she has a large capital employed upon a very small space, a fact which arises from the extraordinary fertility of her soil. And yet, notwithstanding these clear distinctions between the two countries, marked by the hand of Providence, the same reasoning is sometimes made to apply to both; from which it is erroneously supposed, that because a Hindoo is constrained to work at agricultural labour for wages, an inhabitant of Guiana and the West Indies will necessarily do the same. The Hindoo labourer receives no more than three-halfpence per day; and why are his wages not higher? Because his employer knows, that if the labourer does not work for that sum, he has no alternative but that of comparative starvation. There is no waste land that he can cultivate with profit; no waste land, from the cultivation of which he himself can derive greater advantage than he would obtain as a labourer receiving wages; and so cheap are his food and his clothes, that the sum of three-halfpence per day suffices for providing them. If it could be supposed possible that the climate of India should become colder, and the soil less genial than it now is to the production of the staple of the country, rice, the money-price of labour, namely wages, must increase, or the people would most certainly perish: the explanation of those desolating famines which have been recorded in Indian and in Chinese history, as of such frequent occurrence, is no doubt to be found in a failure of the rice-crop. This too great density of population in the East Indies, as compared with their inadequate life-supporting capabilities, points to a remedy, in emigration thence to the West Indies and South America, which, while it would ease the discomforts and alleviate the wants of the population in the former, would better the condition of the two latter countries.* Such an emigration would now be greatly aided by steam navigation. But there are great political difficulties, it seems to us—however Machiavellian those obstacles may be in its being encouraged to any extent by a circumspect government. The same hinderances do not apply to Africa, nor to those parts of Europe which we have endeavoured to direct more active attention to, as affording large emigration swarms, than has hitherto been turned toward them.

We may take it for granted, without the fear of contradiction, that, generally speaking, no competition whatever for work exists amongst our West Indian and South American labourers; on the contrary, we may as safely assert, that there is great active competition used amongst employers, for the purpose of obtaining their very precarious services, at even greater wages than can possibly allow any remuneration to remain for the master after payment of the servant. The planters must uphold their plantations, or abandon them to destruction, which a very trifling neglect is calculated to occasion. Rather than allow this to take place, and encouraged by the expectation of better times, they prefer submitting to what they consider to be only a temporary loss, and, accordingly pay the labourer his own price. This is a state of things which, it may be imagined, has not been quietly submitted to by the planters. For some time, by combination and various other efforts, they strove to regulate wages, and keep them within a reasonable compass; but, the impolicy,

* The experiment is now partially proceeding.—Vide Colonial Intelligence, *seq.*

mischievous tendency, and utter uselessness of such a course, were soon so apparent as to convince all, that such measures were fraught with the most disastrous consequences, and if persevered in, could end no otherwise than in ruin to the planter, when it was considered, as we before pointed out, that the labourer had little or no inducement to undertake the trouble of labour, and could not be coerced in countries where man's wants are few, and nature's unappropriated gifts are still scattered about in profusion, to be used by the first possessor.

On the neighbouring continent of South America, namely, taking that part which extends from the mouths and banks of the river Orinoco, as far as Mexico, labour is dear, and far from being plentiful; it is, generally speaking, thinly scattered, except in and about the large towns, where there is sufficient competition to make its price somewhat more moderate than it is in the country places; but that competition is yet by no means strong enough to prevent work from being of a very desultory and capricious character, even in the largest cities. But, whatever the nominal price given for the labourer's services in those places, may be in amount, it is obvious that it must be a high one in proportion to the means of the employer, when it is seen that the employed can afford to be idle. There is no reciprocity between the desire to employ and that of obtaining employment, for when the labourer is applied to for his work, the invitation is accepted by him with indifference for the most part, and often even with refusal. In India, as we have before stated, the labouring class must work or starve, for there, there is no waste land to fall back upon. In South America,however, the easy occupation of land, and its amazing fruitfulness, together with the great abundance of cattle, which have there run wild, its plentiful supply of game and fish, and its other great natural resources, render the support of life so easy, that the inhabitants are only incited to work for hire by the desire of earning wherewithal to enable them to purchase a few of the plainer and coarser necessaries and luxuries of life. Since the independence of Venezuela, however, from Old Spain, a great part of it has ceased, almost entirely, to be an exporter of agricultural produce; and why? Because labour is too dear to allow of any profit to the grower. In this we discover the reason why, during a part of the year, the Venezuelan peon, of the opposite coast of Paria, seeks for work in the island of Trinidad, to enable him to buy a few necessaries to take back with him to his plot of ground in his native country: he cannot procure any labour in his own neighbourhood, because there is none; it has been put out of demand by the declaration of general freedom in the State, and the consequent abandonment of the sugar and cacao plantations, which, with free labour, would not be able to compete with that of slaves, as it existed in Brazil, and in Cuba, and the British, French, Danish and Dutch West Indies, and as it still exists in all of those places not belonging to Great Britian. There is a doctrine of Dr. Adam Smith's, which lays it down, that free is far cheaper than slave labour; and we quite subscribe to it, as an abstract proposition; but, practically, it is incorrect in its application to the systems of slavery which now exist, and have lately existed. Dr. Smith's conclusion rested, in its practical point of view, upon the assumption that the law restricted, in a just and accurate way, the exactions of the master from the thews and sinews of the slave. Any one, however, who has been at all impartially conversant with slavery, as it lately existed in our own colonies, and now is tolerated and carried on in the possessions of Spain, and in the Brazils, &c., must feel convinced, that if the laws intended for its due regulation were or are sufficient in their wording to protect the bondsman, and we unhesitatingly doubt that they are, or were, yet, no vigilance of any body of officers, however zealous in their endeavours to discharge correctly their disagreeable and sickening duties they might be, could be sufficient to insure the slave from being overworked, and otherwise oppressed. Not that we mean to say that there were no good and just, as far as they could be considered in such a case, as good and just masters in our colonies, whose conduct in regard to their slaves was conscientious, for we know that there were many good ones; but such persons were those who constituted the exception, not the rule; a rule which applies not to any particular set of men, but which is universal, when man takes upon himself an illimitable and unnatural control over the body and actions of his fellow man, and places him in a situation analogous to that of his beast of burden in many points, and in some respects, even more hard than that of that animal would be considered, if we could fancy it conscious of its life of drudgery, under the capricious and changeable tasking of a master, not the less likely to apply the spur and the whip, when he was himself smarting under the goad of want, or other misfortune, or influenced by passion in its thousand forms of whim or recklessness.

The demand for labour, which already exists in most parts of a new and fertile country like South America, together with the allurements to settlers which are offered by so magnificent a region, exert now, and must increase in having a powerful influence on the price of labour in the neighbouring islands. It is a country which, from its great advantages, cannot long remain in its present comparative state of backwardness. Enjoying, as it does, exuberant fertility, and a diversity of climate capable of favouring the successful cultivation of most of the productions of Europe, and all those of our West Indian possessions, besides many valuable ones peculiar to itself, it must in due time become of political importance. Its young republics are already beginning to settle down in some order, after their recent successful struggle for emancipation from Old Spain. It is true that their progress in national advancement, even in the short time of their independence, has not been so good as might have been expected from their great natural resources; but some allowance must be made for the force of habitual supineness, acquired by them under long-continued misrule, which has had the seeming effect of almost palsying their energies. The contracted policy of their late parent-state has had its benumbing influence upon them, an influence which long endurance has, as it were, burnt in; but, now that the baneful incubus has been cast off, the cause having ceased, the effect must soon also disappear, and allow them to rise speedily in the scale of nations. When this rise begins, and it cannot be remote, it is clear that it must create a vast demand for labour, and consequently a competition with other places in which a like demand shall exist. There is no doubt that the West Indies will, ere long, have a powerful antagonist, in those parts of South America which are sufficiently near to affect them; and when that takes place, the success of either party must of course depend upon its respective advantages; let us see what they are.

In South America, there are vast tracts of country, which are undeniably far superior, in point of fertility, climate, and natural productions, to any of the adjacent islands of the West Indian archipelago, and more eligible than they are for the growth of the principal staple tropical commodities of sugar, coffee, and cacao, and well adapted also for producing cotton. Let us take, for an instance, our own colony of British Guiana, on that continent. How immeasurably superior is it to our insular possessions in general fertility! Hardly one of them ventures into even a comparison with it. If South America, with her great fertility, enjoyed also advantages which she is now without; if she had a good, secure, and stable government, there would be no question of the superiority of her very great producing capabilities, when sufficient capital was employed, as it certainly would be employed, in eliciting her vast natural resources. In short, let us figure to our imaginations what would be the certain and speedy results of the application of British capital and British enterprize, in that splendid region, were it part and parcel of our own excellent government; we need not say, that were such the case, our West Indies would sink into comparative insignificance. As long, however, as our islands continue to be so far, as they now are, before the South American republics, in the advantages of good government, so long will it be well with them; but when those advantages are more nearly equalized, a more contracted lot will assuredly attach to nearly, if not all, of them; they will then, with perhaps one or two exceptions, such as Jamaica and Trinidad, as produce-islands, fall into a secondary position, and must be content to confine themselves to the growth of cotton, for which they are well adapted, and the cultivation of the now considered minor articles of produce, such as arrow-root, cassada-flour, and tapioca, ginger, and the pepper commonly known by the name of Cayenne pepper; and also the fruits and vegetables used in the various comfits, preserves, and pickles, which are so excellent, and which can be prepared so well there. Pine-apples, oranges, and lemons, limes and citrons, might be exported by them to the mother-country, now that steam ensures a short voyage, and their preservation. In most of the islands, along their extensive and beautiful sea-beaches, vast quantities of cocoa-nuts might be most easily raised, for obtaining oil, cordage, and the various other important articles which its valuable fibre can be manufactured into. Not only could the growth of the indigenous spice, pimento, be greatly extended in the West Indies, but many of the spices of the East might be most advantageously grown. In the islands of St. Vincent and Trinidad, the nutmeg-tree has thriven admirably, particularly in the latter colony, where it succeeded so well, under the able superintendence of the government-botanist, Mr. Lockhart, as to enable him to send to London a parcel, which, on being inspected by the best judges, did not suffer in a comparison with the best samples from the East and, in consequence a most favourable report, obtained for him the gold medal from the society for the encouragement of arts, &c. The tree, since Mr. Lockhart's success, has become common in the island; but its more powerful competitor the sugar-cane, has hitherto kept it from being turned to much account. Speaking of Trinidad puts us in mind of there being already there an extensive line of cocoa-nut trees, extending a distance of sixteen miles along the eastern shore of the island, from Manzanilla point, to the mouth of the river Orotava or Orotoire. They were accidentally planted there more than a century ago, in the following manner: a vessel laden with cocoa-nuts, and bound for some place in the river Orinoco, was on her way wrecked near the spot on which the cocoa-nut forest now stands, when the nuts being washed on shore, they, in process of time, in a highly favourable situation, multiplied to their present large extent. Before Trinidad came into the possession of Great Britain, these cocoa-nuts were very acceptable to the French fleets of men-of-war, whose crews often regaled themselves upon them. Besides the articles of commerce which we have enumerated, as being likely to be one day more attended to than they now are in the West Indies, the turtle fishery there might be made much more valuable than it is at the present time; and it may not be generally known, that a whale fishery of some extent might be carried on there. Such a fishery does already exist at Trinidad, and would certainly be profitable, if properly conducted, which hitherto has not been the case, either as to sufficient capital for, or experience and expertness in the undertaking. Whales are, indeed, so plentiful at that island, as to have attracted the enterprise of vessels belonging to the United States of America; but which we presume were not permitted to fish so near the shore as to bring them within the British limits.*

We abstain, on the present occasion, from making any remarks on the "colonial policy," to use the term of a celebrated writer, which may be involved in the foregoing observations, in reference to a contingent modification of the present exportable products of the West Indies, as such is foreign to the scope of our immediate purpose, which is merely to show, that the expectation of any great reduction in wages, in our South American and West Indian colonies, is not to be looked for, before that cause shall have come into action, which alone can have the effect of moderating them in such countries, namely, the comparatively remote circumstance of a dense population exhausting the natural means of subsistence, now so abundantly afforded by them, and thereby compelling man to compete with man for the obtainment of his daily bread. If any of our colonists expect any early material cheapening of labour to take place, they grossly deceive themselves. We have endeavoured to point out to them their true situation; for, it is better that they should avoid vain and deceitful hopes, and bring themselves to consider and see their correct position, whereby they may be enabled to found just expectations upon sure ground, than that they should set their anchor in the loose sand of fallacy and disappointment. Their clear and obvious course is, to make the most of present circumstances; as they cannot cheapen

* The Gulf of Paria, between Venezuela and Trinidad, was named by Columbus, on his discovery of the island, *Golfo de Balena*, or Whale-gulf, from the great number of whales seen in it.

labour, let them endeavour to lessen it, in short; let them critically pass in review before their minds, every point in which they are interested in their colonies, and ascertain whether such points be not susceptible of improvement, and the saving of expense. If this be done, certain benefit must be derived from it. We will close this paper, by offering a few suggestions on some of the more prominent topics which offer themselves for consideration, with a view to improvement, in the colonies of which we now treat.

The most crying evil in our sugar growing colonies, has proceeded from too frequent laxity and want of caution in the appointment of Governors and other official persons in them. It is too obvious to need much stress, in calling particular attention to it, that colonies can never thrive under the baneful influence of men, who, often, idependently of their absolute unfitness for any charge in the direction of others, are any thing but respectable in their reputation, or examplary in their private conduct and bearing. What respect can colonists entertain for worn-out political intriguers, or for men of broken fortunes, fortunes, not accidentally affected by mischance, but often by practices, which most persons find it difficult to distinguish from acts having very hard names. Scrupulous attention should always be bestowed on the selection of all officers for public situations in the colonies; and, more particularly, the posts of governor, judges, attorney-general, and treasurer, &c., should, as the principal ones, be most narrowly sifted. What must have been the moral effect in one of our colonies, when a governor, on being sued at law for the plate which he had used, or, it is probable, was actually using on his table, had the adamantine face to set up as a plea to the action brought against him in the courts of the island, that he, as governor, was not liable to be sued; and his government was thus set up by him as a cloak to protect him in evading the just right of an honest creditor, and that by one receiving a salary of £3,000 sterling per annum, out of which he could, as far as his personal comforts were concerned, with comparative ease have settled the demand, which amounted to only a few hundreds. But, the man had been steeped in the brazen pool of iniquitous assurance, before he found his way to the West Indies as a governor, where his only qualification was his consistency in proceeding onward in his crooked career, until death, happily for those under him, terminated his pitiable existence. We might cite even more glaring instances of the reprehensible conduct of judges, attorneys-general, treasurers, &c., but we refrain from doing so, as it is both unpleasant, and beside our present purpose, to observe on the subject more emphatically than we have done. An unfit appointment does incalculable harm to a colony. In the case of a bad governor, it is kept down, and all its efforts to rise are paralyzed. Let our colonists, therefore, when bad men are sent to them, legitimately point out the evil, that it may be redressed.

In the next place, our colonists must make the best use in their power of their present available means for carrying on the cultivation of their soil. We would not, however, in anything which we have said, be understood as not recommending them to use their most active and strenuous exertions to forward, by all possible means, immigration into our islands and other possessions,* from all parts of the world whence desirable settlers may be obtained, of every description, more particularly artisans and agricultural labourers; for it is a course which would be most beneficial in other respects, even if it had little effect for the present in reducing wages. But, above all, let our sugar, and other planters, bring out more the resources which they have within their own immediate command and grasp, and which have hitherto been so little drawn upon by them. They must determine, in future, to apply their own shoulder to the wheel, and that practically and energetically; they must cast off the supineness of which they have been, hitherto, accused with too much justice, as they must in candour admit. They should strive most assiduously to improve the culture of their land, which they could the more effectually do, did they study a little of the theoretical and more of the practical part of the science of agriculture. A more general introduction than has yet taken place, of the plough and other labour-saving implements, for tilling the soil and planting and reaping its produce, the planter would find to be of vast use and profit. From our own experience, we know that agriculture in the West Indies is little advanced from infancy, while the sugar-growers in the East have made great progress in acquiring a correct knowledge of it, however deficient they may be in preparing and manufacturing the juice of the cane. From the almost general lack of the information required for doing it, there are few persons in our colonies capable of conceiving, much less of carrying into successful operation, improvements in their present crude, and comparatively hap-hazard, modes of tillage and manufacture. Many of those things which are at present performed by manual labour, could easily be infinitely better and cheaper done by means of machinery.

Great benefit would accrue to our planters, if they induced, by proper encouragement, men of science and experience to settle among them, such as agricultural chemists and civil engineers, of undoubted attainments. Were such persons within reach, their services would prevent great actual loss, and be the means of increasing the returns of property. A liberal fee to such gentlemen would be repaid ten-fold by the correction of injudicious or mistaken management, and the increased scope which it would open in a multitude of ways, for profitable exertion. We conjure the planter to consider well the hints which we have offered as to the present posture of affairs in our western colonies; if he do so, we feel assured he will agree with us, that his present relief is to be found as much in the points which we have suggested for his immediate adoption, as in any system of immigration that could be brought about. We say again, that as labour cannot be sufficiently cheapened, let the necessity for it be considerably diminished.

R. A.

---

* An immigration of Coolies is just now taking place.

A JOURNEY OF ONE THOUSAND MILES ACROSS THE PENINSULA OF HINDOSTAN,

FROM MADRAS TO BOMBAY.

BY CAPTAIN F. B. DOVETON.

A LAND journey of a thousand miles through such a country as India, ought not to be absolutely unproductive of interesting matter, however monotonous in character Oriental scenery may be. In the hope therefore of occasionally stumbling upon something that may excite attention, I shall proceed to give some details, in connection with my own experience in such a case:—

After a delightful sojourn at the Cape, for the benefit of my health, I once more disembarked from a Masoolah boat, at Madras, in December, 18—, having safely encountered the watery ordeal of its perilous surf. It was a sore thing to exchange the soft air, the fruits and flowers, of Southern Africa, for the scorching sun of India, and the sands of Choultry plain, the sweets of ease and independence, for the restraints of *duty*, and the occasional *wigs* of official superiors. A salve there was, it is true, for this sore, in an increased scale of pay and allowances. I was not long permitted to enjoy the luxuries of the presidency, scarcely a week having elapsed when I received orders to be off to Jaulnah, a Madras frontier-station, nearly 700 miles distant, and in the direction of Bombay, the road lying through Nellore, Ongole, Hyderabad, and Beder. The prospect of such a march (for every journey in India is called a march, travel as you will) staggered me not a little, after the comparative quiescence of the Cape; for know, reader, I was encumbered, or rather blessed with the encumbrance of a family, which necessarily obliges every man in the East to travel *en prince*, however humble his disposition and resources.

On the 16th of January, our three palankeens were packed, courie baskets stored with provisions, medicine-chest replenished, and a tattoo pony purchased, to carry the cook and the tea-kettle; whilst he bore the spit in his hand, like another Don Quixote. When darkness had set in we bid farewell to our hospitable relative, with whom we had been sojourning, and, composing ourselves in that most luxurious of all conveyance, a palankeen, our noisy train (for we numbered forty-seven) threaded its way through the extensive suburbs of Madras, by the light of flambeaux. A sensation of loneliness passed over me, as we left behind us, for many a day, gaiety and civilization; besides, one often fancies in the East, that the further we recede from the sea-coast, the further we recede from England; as an unbroken, however lengthy sea-voyage, contrasts favourably with the toil and trouble of a land journey, especially in India, when gloomy visions of cholera, dysentery, "*et hoc genus omne*," will occasionally intrude themselves upon the most unreflecting. In the present instance, the motion of the palankeen and the monotonous song of the bearers soon lulled me to sleep, from which, a couple of hours after, I was roused by the bumping of the palankeens one against the other, and a splashing noise, as we forded a piece of water which happened to lie en route. At midnight we reached Pulava-Chultram, thirteen miles from Madras, and the light of the moon showed us a group of tents, which proved to be the encampment of a brother officer and his wife, who had left Madras that morning, and was now on the road to join his regiment at Naghore, a distance of seven hundred miles, by easy journeys. Unseasonable as the hour was, he came out to greet me *en deshabille*, and we made an arrangement to meet on the following morning at the next stage, and pass the day together. Our mode of travelling differed materially. He moved leisurely at the rate of twelve miles a day or thereabouts, having his tents and all his baggage with him, as if marching with troops. I, on the contrary, being anxious to get over the ground, had sent my baggage on a week before, and now, with a full set of bearers to each palankeen, we traversed twenty-five or thirty miles during the night, resting during the heat of the day at one of the traveller's bungalows. This mode of travelling is expensive, and of course less comfortable, as it is necessary to condense one's wants; but then the ground is got over faster, a great object in India, where women and children are concerned, who cannot share in the delights of knocking over the snipe and floriken, which render a march across the plains of Hindostan so attractive to a sportsman. Though obliged by my mode of travelling to be equipped in "light marching order," I still contrived to stow away my double-barrel and a good supply of ammunition in the pulkee, and seldom failed during a halt to pick up something or other in the shape of game, without straying far from the bungalow.

Our first halt was at Goomdepoondy, nearly thirty miles from Madras, where, according to agreement, we passed a pleasant day with my old friend and his wife. The character of the country varied but little till we arrived at Nellore, a civil station and a place of importance, one hundred and eleven miles from the presidency. Through the whole route the scenery was flat and uninteresting; but there was no lack of fertility, and, owing to the heavy rains, there was a freshness and verdure in the vegetation, which to a traveller in the East is most grateful. It was on the fifth day after leaving Madras that we reached Nellore, where we were hospitably entertained by the medical officer of the station, Dr. C——, a kind and good man. So much frequented was his house by travellers like ourselves, whose introduction to him had only preceded us by a day or two in the shape of a letter from a mutual friend, that his house went by the old English name of the "Red Lion." Nellore is due north of Madras, and close to the sea-coast. It enjoys a fine climate, and is celebrated for the fertility of its soil, and a superior breed of cattle; a Nellore cow being highly prized by all such as are particular about the quality of their milk; that fluid in India being usually a very watery affair. Whilst at Dr. C.'s, the double-barrel came into play, for I discovered that snipe and partridges were to be found in his garden, and I was not long in bagging some of them. A garden in India, be it understood, is not quite so *bien soignée* as a kitchen-garden at home: ground in that vast country is of far less value, and the enclosure round the house of a European often enjoys the advantage of a snug brake, or bit of jungle (a more orthodox word in treating of India,) which may shelter a hare or a partridge, and a tempting patch of swamp for a snipe,—no trifling recommendation to a sporting occupier.

On the 21st, at eight in the evening, we pursued our journey, and on the following morning pulled up at the traveller's bungalow, twenty miles distant, having during the night passed through the camp of the 4th Light Cavalry, and a strong detachment of European Infantry, the latter under the command of another friend and brother officer, Captain H. On the 24th we were at Ongole, somewhere about two hundred miles north of Madras. This is a large native town with a stone fort, which is garrisoned by a company of invalids under a European officer, no very enviable position for a man sociably disposed. The character of the country from Nellore highly uninteresting, being flat, dry, and apparently not over fruitful. The road, the whole distance from Madras, was within a short distance of the sea-shore, from which it is separated by a ridge of sandbanks. The noise of the distant surf during the night had a pleasing effect, and helped to lull us asleep as we jolted along in our palkees.

Upon quitting Ongole, which we did on the same evening, the road took a more westerly direction, leading us inland and towards Hyderabad, from which we were now distant two hundred miles. The first stage was a long pull for the bearers, being twenty-four miles, the name of the place Ardingha, a fine grain-country, but then suffering cruelly from drought, consequently no game was to be found, though I beat perseveringly for it, leaving not a tuft of grass untried. Here we found the sub-collector of the district encamped administering justice and collecting the revenue. His tents and turbaned officials formed a striking scene beneath the shade of a noble clump of trees, and carried one back to the patriarchal ages. This gentleman was very civil to us palankeen-travellers, and sent us over the half of a fat lamb; no bad thing on such an occasion, when good eating was scarce. Our next march was to Rompechurlah, twenty-nine miles, and the following to Peddagoorul, twenty-two miles, each day being passed in the traveller's bungalow. The character of the country as we moved in a westernly direction was now undergoing a change; its face was much covered with long grass or stunted bushes; whilst the surface was broken by low stony hills, shooting up abruptly from a monotonous flat; this is very much the character of the Deccan, which we were approaching, and to which there is a gradual though almost imperceptible ascent from the eastern coast of India, till the traveller looks down with wonder from the western Ghauts upon the Concan and the ocean.

At Peddagoorul, I fell in with a natural peculiarity which deserves a special notice, though I am not geologist enough to do the subject justice. Whilst out shooting in the immediate neighbourhood of the bungalow, amongst some low underwood, where hares abound, I was much struck with the stony nature of the ground. An uneven bed of rock covered a surface of many acres, which were evidently formed of prostrate trees of a gigantic size, in a state of petrifaction. The origin of the rock was too clear to be mistaken; and what renders the case more remarkable is, that the country is quite devoid of trees to a considerable extent. Should this cursory notice ever catch the eye of any geologist travelling by that route, I hope his attention may be drawn to the spot, for I am satisfied if these petrifactions were subjected to a scientific investigation, they would prove to be one of the most remarkable objects of interest in Southern India.

On the morning of the 29th, we reached Pondigul, on the celebrated river Kistnah, which empties itself into the bay of Bengal, a little to the southward of Masulipatam, and at this point is the boundary between the Company's territory and that of the Nizam. Here we came up with our baggage, which had hitherto preceded us, but; "*miserabile dictu*," one of the carts had during its progress upset in some water, and irreparable was the damage done to my wife's wardrobe and bandboxes. At this place, close to the bungalow, was a large white tomb, erected over the remains of an officer, who was here overtaken by that never-tiring traveller Death. Such melancholy memorials are not uncommon in India, in similar localities. Upon this occasion it did not fail to give us a qualm, for, a night or two before, our darling child, a girl of five years old, had been attacked with severe illness which was fortunately overcome by the timely administration of a dose of calomel. The sudden stoppage of your train of palankeens, in the dead of night, to attend to a sick child, on a bare and barren tract, perhaps hundreds of miles from medical advice, is a gloomy and anxious affair. At such times we of course were obliged to have recourse to a box of lucifers to obtain a light, as, when the moon was up, we used no torches; and this process puzzled our dusky followers not a little, clusters of turbaned heads peering over our shoulders at the time. I fear they suspected us of dealing in magic.

Having crossed the Kistnah in a *basket* boat, we were now in the Deccan; and in the territory of the Nizam, of which Hyderabad is the capital. This basket-boat is a queer thing to look at, but it is well adapted for its purpose. It is made of wicker-work, and is covered with leather, whilst its form is circular. A circular motion is I believe the most natural one, and it was in this way we made the transit of the sacred stream. Four more runs brought us into the large military cantonment of Secunderabad, (close to Hyderabad) a distance of about four hundred miles from Madras, and this we had achieved in a fortnight without any serious drawback. As our dusty train neared the place, we fell in with a European soldier here and there, which in addition to the civilised dwellings in the distance, have ever a very cheering effect on the Indian traveller. To this place, as at Nellore, an introduction had preceded us, there being no inns in the East, and we were soon luxuriously established in the hospitable house of Captain

B——, with whom, though strangers at first meeting, we soon struck up quite a friendship, for unceasing was the kindness he showed to us wayfarers. Under his auspices we were introduced to everything worthy of note at Hyderabad and its vicinity, taking an airing every evening in his carriage, during the week we halted. Amongst other places, we visited Bolarum, an attractive spot, a few miles distant, and the head-quarters of the Nizam's troops. Here we spent an agreeable day with Captain M——, the paymaster.

Hyderabad is too well known from its central position and the important part it has ever played in the political history of British India, to require that much should be said of it here. It is the residence of the Nizam, by whom the country is governed *nominally*, for being one, and the most important of the subsidized states, the administration is much controlled by the British resident, who has moreover the entire superintendence of the Nizam's troops, which are a highly disciplined and efficient force, officered, with a few exceptions, from the Company's army. There is also a powerful subsidiary force of British troops stationed at Secunderabad, amounting to scarcely less than seven thousand men of all arms. The Nizam, of course, is bound by treaty to maintain and pay these troops.

After a stay of eight days at Hyderabad, we were once more on the road, but our mode of travelling was altered. We had previously only moved at night, and then twenty-five or thirty miles at a time, halting by day at a bungalow; but these grateful shelters are not erected on the road we were now to tread, consequently it was requisite to take tents with us, and to march leisurely in the cool of the morning, halting at the usual stages, which are selected according to their facility in supplying the traveller's wants. We arranged therefore accordingly, and we hoped to get to our destination, distant two hundred and sixty or two hundred and seventy miles, in about fifteen days. Through the kindness of our host, who had the power of assisting us with bearers, we made a capital start, having got over forty-eight miles the first night. During the night we passed through the remains of the celebrated Golcondah, and next morning at nine we reached Moonoopilly, and found the tents pitched and breakfast comfortably prepared for us, the baggage having preceded us by some days. But all was not long to be *couleur de rose*; for my dear wife was taken very unwell, and threatened with a severe attack of fever. Still we pushed on after having halted one day, having despatched an express to Secunderabad for some leeches and other remedies, to relieve my wife's throbbing temples. In two marches we encamped on a plain close to the splendid remains of Beder; here we halted for a clear day, and the leeches having speedily been forwarded, their application had a most favourable effect, and my patient rapidly mended; and the weather, which was delightfully cool, was not without its influence.

Beder is a remarkable place; and our first view of the ruined city, and the splendid Moorish relics in its vicinity, peeping out from amidst the dusk and dense foliage that surrounded them, was fine and striking in the extreme. A low turreted wall ran round the city, which was further protected by a deep and wide dry ditch, that must have been excavated by extraordinary labour, many parts appearing to have been hewn out of the solid rock; the formation of which I now forget, but I am disposed to think it was granitic. Beder stands on a noble elevation, and commands a very distant prospect. The attractive features of the place, however, are the extensive and numerous mosques and tombs in the neighbourhood. Some of these are still very perfect, whilst the architecture is most rich and graceful. The mangoe tree is the most common, and maize the principal grain in cultivation. I narrowly missed having some good sport here in the shooting way. About nine at night, when sitting in my tent, a native ran in telling me that a *cheetah* was close by, having a design apparently upon one of my bullocks that was pitched hard by. As ill luck would have it, my own trusty double-gun had been sent on in advance with the other things, I therefore snatched up a sepoy's musket to shoot the brute, which I saw plainly at a very short distance; but to my great annoyance the lock snapped, and away went the *cheetah* into the jungle, and I was thus cheated out of the trophy I had calculated upon, in his beautiful skin.

On the 16th of February we were at Hulburgah, fourteen miles. On the 17th at Daneecooperah, twelve miles. This place is noted, I see in my journal, as a *vile* spot; hot, dusty, stony, parched, and poverty-struck. It was made up of a small dirty village and a ruined fort. The country, however, though unattractive in appearance, produced grain of all kinds in abundance, and flocks of shy antelopes frequently crossed our path. There was little now to vary the monotony of our route till we reached Jaulnah. The character of the country was much the same. It was undulating and stony, but apparently very productive, though the habitations of the natives were wretched and comfortless. On the 23rd we crossed the famed river Godavery, which falls into the sea within a short distance of the Kistnah's mouth; and without incurring any very marvellous adventures we reached the military cantonment at Jaulnah, on the morning of the 28th, after a tedious and anxious march of seven hundred miles, which occupied us six weeks. European travellers in these parts are of course rare, once or twice I believe we fell in with one, but it was like two ships meeting at sea, or two camels in the desart. One little incident there was, however; one of our female servants was attacked with fever, and was apparently in a bad way. It occurred to me that bleeding would relieve her, I therefore with the consent of her husband bled her in the arm with my penknife! and I flattered myself I performed the operation "*secundum artem.*" Unhappily, however, it was of no avail, as the disease had gone too far, and she died a day or two afterwards.

Jaulnah is one of the most distant of the stations occupied by Madras troops. It is situated in the Deccan, and belongs to the Nizam; and the troops, now reduced to one regiment of cavalry, one of infantry, and a troop of horse-artillery, form a part of the Hyderabad subsidiary force. There is nothing particularly attractive about the place, but the climate is deemed healthy, especially in the cool season, which is of longer duration than to the southward. There is, nevertheless, a good deal of fever at Jaulnah, and the land-winds blow here with indescribable fury, scorching up and blasting every thing. This neighbourhood has witnessed many a tough encounter during our wars with the Mahrattas. Not many miles distant is the famed field of Assaye, where the star of Wellington first rose; when, with four thousand five hundred men, he defeated ten thousand of Scindiah's regular infantry, and twenty thousand cavalry, supported by one hundred pieces of cannon. These were all captured by us; but our loss was fearful, nearly two thousand men having been put *hors de combat*.

Having been a wanderer many times in search of health, I looked forward to a long period of repose at my new station, where I filled a desirable post on the staff, but my hopes were deceived—once more I was overpowered by climate, and after only one year's residence, I found myself again in a palankeen en route to Bombay, whence I was to embark with my family for England. On the evening of the 10th of January, 1838, we started, and reached Aurungabad on the following morning, distant forty miles, having had fresh bearers posted for us half way.—We were hospitably received by Colonel Roberts, who was then commanding the division of the Nizam's troops stationed at Aurungabad. These troops are not inferior to the Company's in dress and discipline, whilst the men are remarkably fine. Their main or only defect is a paucity of European officers. Aurungabad, formerly the capital of the Mogul empire, was built by Aurungzebe, and its relics are still very beautiful, particularly the marble tomb erected over Aurungzebe's favourite daughter. The country here is more undulating than about Jaulnah, and better clothed with trees. Within sight of the place is the renowned fortress of Dowlatabad, famed for its grapes in times of peace, and in war-time for its security from assault. Hard by, the caves of Ellora are to be seen by the curious.

Our next move was to Toka, on the Bombay side of the Godavery, thirty miles; where we passed the day in tents, despatched expressly from Jaulnah, there being here no bungalow to shelter the traveller, though one was building. This morning is noted in my journal as *bitter cold*, a circumstance not unworthy of note in India. Toka is a large place, surrounded, as is customary in these parts, with a high stone wall. The houses are lofty, with flat roofs and small windows. The country is uninteresting and level, but productive in grain, especially maize and jonnuloo. We quitted Toka at seven P. M. on the same day, and reached the traveller's bungalow at Imaumpoor (thirty miles) on the following morning. The approach to this place was unusually interesting for this part of the country, being by the Jour Ghaut, which is very abrupt and picturesque, though the road is good. The table-land is very park-like and beautiful, being thickly studded with noble trees. The bungalow which sheltered us was very cool and comfortable, it had formerly been a mosque, but was now converted to the more legitimate purpose of a refuge for Christian travellers. On the afternoon of the same day we moved on to Ahmednuggur, where we passed the following day (Sunday) in peace and quietness, under the hospital roof of Captain H——.

Ahmednuggur is a place of note. It has a small square stone-fort, with semicircular bastions and ditch. The native town, or Pettah, is populous, well built, and encircled by a strong wall; this latter was taken by assault, formerly by the troops under Sir A. Wellesley, and cost us the lives of many officers and men. Ahmednuggur is the head-quarters of the Bombay artillery, and at the period of my visit was occupied by one battalion of European, one ditto of native artillery, and one regiment of native infantry. Off again at seven in the evening, and on the following morning found ourselves at Seroor (thirty miles.) It is a large place, and was formerly an extensive cantonment. Now it is of little note, being occupied only by one hundred irregular horse, but, a few Europeans' bungalows, belonging to the civil officers of the district, give it an air of civilization. Forward was again the word, at half-past five in the evening, when, after a pleasant run of forty-two miles, over a capital road, we were established in a friend's bungalow at Poonah, by six in the following morning. Poonah is a large military station, being the head-quarters of a division, and there being a grand review in progress on the morning of our arrival, we were regaled upon entering the cantonment with the rattling of musketry and the roar of artillery. An incident occurred during the previous night, which I shall now relate:—

About two A.M. I was awoke by the noise of running water; when, putting my head out of the palankeen, I perceived we were crossing the Beemar river, the town of Corygaum being visible on its northern bank. This place is celebrated for the successful resistance of a handful of British troops against the Peishwah's army, on the 1st of January, 1818, Our only troops were a detachment of Madras European artillery, and a Bombay native battalion, but they displayed the most devoted gallantry, and a large number fell. This proud achievement has been properly commemorated by the erection of a handsome obelisk enclosed with iron railing on an elevated spot hard by. On one face of the column, in English is an appropriate inscription; and on the reverse one, the names of all who were killed and wounded in the action. On the other two faces the same is inscribed in Mahratta, the language of the country. There was not much moon upon this occasion, and I had already forded the river and ascended its steep bank, taking in as good a view as the dubious light would allow of so memorable a spot, (such sites have great charms for a soldier!) when up shot the obelisk to my left at the distance of sixty or seventy yards, the existence of which I was unprepared for. I instantly halted the cavalcade of Palkees, and in spite of the keen night-air, and with my head only protected with a night-cap, off I went at a run to the interesting spot, followed by a Masulchee, (torch-bearer.) The gate was very properly locked, so I escaladed the iron railing, and read the inscription on the obelisk by torchlight. Though a trivial incident, the circumstance attending it clothed the matter, in my professional eyes, with considerable interest. All is interesting that relates and does honour to the gallant dead; and on this spot their deeds will long live: "*Dulce et decorum est pro patriâ mori.*"

I left Poonah on the same evening, and, by a road practicable for gentlemen's carriages, reached Kandallah on the summit of the western Ghaut on the following morning. The traveller's bungalow here afforded superior accommodation, and, as we drew near the termination of our pilgrimage, comforts began to multiply. Let me, however, honestly record that we experienced a slight drawback during the preceding night, my palankeen having broke down soon after leaving Poonah, we patched it up with rope after a fashion, and managed to scramble on to Kandallah, where it was properly repaired, but I caught a violent cold from imprudent exposure to the night-air.

On the afternoon of the 17th of January, we were again on the move, but for the last time. During our descent of the western Ghauts into the Concan, the scenery was magnificent, and the prospect most extensive. Descriptions of scenery are always failures, whatever may be the capacity of the describer, and I fear readers generally skip them. I shall only say, therefore, regarding the present instance, that there was abundance of rock, wood, and water, tumbled together in the most admired and picturesque disorder, through which meandered a very steep, but good road, a lasting monument of Sir John Malcolm's administration of the Bombay government. Early on the morning of the 18th, we reached Pauwell, where we, palankeens and all, were embarked in a Bunder boat, and, after a comfortless transit of a few hours, safely landed at Bombay on the Mazagong Bunder, and half an hour after we were lodged at a friend's house, having traversed nearly one thousand miles from the period we left Madras.

EMIGRATION, AND THE NEW ZEALAND COMPANY.*

While emigration is calculated to improve the circumstances of those who embrace it, and to bring into cultivation the vast colonial possessions of the British empire, it requires judicious management, and should be voluntary on the part of the emigrant; no false colouring should be put forth in order to induce the inexperienced or unwary to leave this country for any of the colonies, to suit the views of speculators or jobbers in such transactions, and which has too frequently led to greater privations than those experienced by the want of employment at home.

Again, it is necessary, in order to carry out colonization successfully, that those who emigrate are not only capable of labour, but that they are of industrious habits, and tractable dispositions; it will be of no

---

[* Although these remarks upon the relative position of the New Zealand Company, both to the natives and to the colonial office, are contrary to our often-expressed opinion, we have consented to admit them, on the principle of "*audi alteram partem.*" We must not, however, omit to refer the reader to our June number for the most full and explicit replies to every argument here put forward. In that number he will find the objections of *Vidi* anticipated and disposed of; nor should we now have been guilty of this *husteron proteron*—this putting of the car before the horse—this publication of the answer before the question, were it not that we personally esteem the writer of this article, respect his principles and his talents; and from the opportunities he has had of making himself acquainted with the subject, he is eminently entitled to a patient hearing.—Ed.]

advantage to a colony, but the contrary, if the idle and the profligate be sent from this country; it would hinder its advancement, and become a serious burden, where industrious habits and regular conduct are of so much importance, both for the improvement of the lands, and the example necessary in countries where so much depends on the conduct of the labourers for the establishment of order, and the advancement of the interests of those places where they are located. And to these sources may be frequently traced the well-being and prosperity of colonial lands under cultivation, or the contrary; while the requisite qualifications of those placed to direct the works carrying on for the improvement of colonial possessions is equally indispensable, both as to experience, sound judgment, and the ability to rule with discretion, firmness, and perseverance; as the post of such is not dissimilar to the commander of a merchant-ship, the good management and requisite discipline, both for the interest and safety of all, largely depends on the intelligence, self-command, and temperate conduct of the commander; and which would seem to demand the strictest scrutiny by those empowered to select individuals from among the candidates for such appointments.

Emigration may be fairly viewed, when rightly conducted, as the means permanently to establish the interest of the settlers, the colonies, and the mother-country, in all its connexions with these colonies, both commercial, political, moral, and religious, which, although last-named, not least in forwarding the best interests of the colonial possessions. Colonial improvements, which cannot be carried on but by the introduction of capital and labour, may be viewed as a means of removing that commercial lassitude so frequently experienced in this country—of insuring colonial fertility being made available, which, if combined with every desirable arrangement, anticipation will be scarcely capable of measuring the future cultivation and population of our colonial possessions; they, like America, whose young beginnings were, by means of emigration, under much greater difficulties than those which now present themselves, as it will be found, that in those days there were no provisions made for the protection and assistance of the emigrant beyond what his own means enabled him to secure: these colonies may grow up into states and kingdoms; and what, it may be fairly asked, is in the way of such advancements when New South Wales, Van Diemen's Land, and New Zealand, have made their respective advancement in civilization, commerce, and cultivation, (when the present generation shall have passed away,) under the protection and guardianship of England, whose colonial possessions, notwithstanding the narrow compass of her own sea-girt isle, constitutes her one of the largest empires throughout the five great divisions of the globe.

But in order to insure such advancements, the soundest judgment, combined with extensive experience, entirely apart from speculative motives, must be called into action; and in which that department of the government on which these matters devolve, should take a leading and an active part, by taking care they employ none for governors and lieutenant-governors, downwards, in the management of colonial affairs, but men in every way qualified for the performance of the important duties of their offices, who should thoroughly understand their deep responsibility; and thus selected, when so far removed from the seat of government, they may with confidence be allowed the utmost latitude for the exercise of their own judgment, without being clogged by restrictions, which might prevent them, in the absence of the necessary instructions, from carrying out measures of the deepest interest, and which delay of a few months might render abortive.

As well might the commander of a fleet or an army, in the face of an enemy, wait for instructions for making an attack when their respective positions were most favourable, as individuals, at some 16,000 or 18,000 miles' remove, wait for instructions respecting every movement. Let the appointments be given to men of discretion, experience, firmness, self-command, temperate, ardent, and persevering, with full authority to carry out the spirit of their instructions, and the result need not be feared. Much difficulty would be prevented, a foundation of success would be laid in all colonial undertakings, which would prevent the many mistakes; and these consequences, which have occurred in every instance of settlement for a succession of years—beginning at Algoa Bay, then Swan River, then South Australia, and now New Zealand, in all of which mistakes have taken place in the first attempt at settlement, which have not only militated against their advancement, but have occasioned considerable difficulties, in all of which either the governors and other executives have been recalled, shortly after their arrival, or the tenor of their instructions so altered from time to time, that the greatest difficulties have been created, and in none more so than the last-named place, which has led to the most serious results, from causes which if but due discretion had been exercised, might, to a considerable extent, have been prevented—evidence the admission of the directors of this undertaking, while they attach the failure of the undertaking to the opposition met with by the governor and his executives, and the non-fulfilment of the arrangements entered into with the Secretary of State for the Colonies.*

That numerous failures have taken place, much suffering endured, many lives sacrificed, and the most fearful dissensions have arisen, occasioned by injudicious attempts at colonization, must be admitted on all hands.

The New Zealand Company's attempting to colonize New Zealand, before any government existed in an extensive degree, involved the company in difficulties, and when an attempt was made to establish a government, and a governor sent out with this object in view, the company's agent and the executive differed in every material point, such as the method pursued in obtaining possession of the lands from the natives, the most eligible site for the seat of government, &c., and which differences unfortunately increased to the widest extent the difficulties the company's agents had to encounter, not only with the native tribes, but with their own people, and those who had gone out from England in expectation of having their respective acres cleared for them, and ready for their occupation immediately on their arrival.

---

* Vide Article "New Zealand," by W., in p. 179 of this volume.

But how contrary was the result—many waited for from one to two years, and left again in disgust.

Colonel Wakefield's position was anything but enviable under such circumstances; discontented settlers and labourers, with the governor, the missionaries, the protectors of the aborigines, opposed to him, and taking part with the natives against the method he pursued in obtaining possession of the land, which, before an attempt at settlement, was literally of no value, as the natives had neither the means nor inclination of bringing it into a state of cultivation, and but for their former intercourse with New South Wales, Van Diemen's land, and the whalers, they might, and would gladly have been contented with; but the experience they had gained in traffic, aided by the favour shown them by the executive, the missionaries, and the gentlemen appointed their protectors, the company could hardly expect to secure to themselves these large tracts of land by mere barter; and in reasoning fairly, and without prejudice, it may be asked, how could the company expect faith to be kept by those, who their agent in his report designates "lawless and heedless savages?" It is true the bartering system was on a liberal scale, but when these "savages" discovered the improvements the land was capable of, what they had disposed of for a few bales of clothing, boxes of muskets, and the like, was it not reasonable to conclude they would feel dissatisfied, and prevent, as they have done, the progress of the company's works, and the distribution of the lands?*

This mode of barter might do very well for their pigs, their fowls, their potatoes, their eggs, their vegetables, and the like; but to suppose the New Zealanders would rest satisfied with such for giving up the best portions of the land, river-frontages, &c., is a folly hardly to be entertained, unless compelled by force. Hence the melancholy affair at Wairoa, when probably the very muskets they had received in barter were used in taking away the lives of those who endeavoured to expel them, evidently setting forth the impracticability of securing quiet possession by such means.†

The New Zealanders, long before the formation of the company, had extensive communications with our colonies and settlements in the southern hemisphere, and were considered in their transactions shrewd and calculating; and if the agents sent from England by the company were not aware of this, they undoubtedly were not suited for the arduous task they had undertaken. Hence is to be traced the failure and disasters which have frequently followed attempts at colonization in new settlements.

Even the New Zealand youths, who were engaged as cabin-boys in vessels trading between New South Wales and those islands, were observed to display a shrewdness and cunning, seldom met with in

* The natives had no title to these lands; they had never before occupied them, any more than we occupy the wastes of every part of America, North and South.—Ed.

† The acquisitions of Pennsylvania and of the Cape of Good Hope, the latter by the Dutch, contradict the writer's opinion.

boys similarly situated of countries in a civilized state; and it would be but reasonable to conclude that their parents partook of the same intellect, or propensities, or instinct, or whatever other term may be applicable in such cases.

Is it therefore to be wondered, that these "savages," as the agent reports them to be, possessing these propensities, should have acted as they have done, in reference to the bartering system employed by the company to obtain possession of the lands, particularly as they appear to have been aware that both the executive, the missionaries, and their protectors, did not consider the means employed for obtaining their lands either fair or sufficient?

I should be among the number of those who would gladly join in casting the smoothening oil over the disturbed waters, considering that the introduction of capital and labour, such as the New Zealand Company had the means of doing, into countries or colonies capable of vast improvements, to be the best means of employing, with advantage, the redundant capital and superabundant population of England.

But it must be proceeded with judiciously. The exercise of sound judgment, coupled with deep-rooted experience, must be employed to ensure success in undertakings of such importance. The tracing of maps or charts by a body of men seated at home and at ease, without the above requisites, is not calculated to insure success, more than colonial secretaries or under-secretaries are for their office, unless they have obtained, by practical experience, a knowledge of the method of managing the possessions for which they are called on to legislate.

In every part of the globe, where the British flag is unfurled, and has gained an ascendancy, justice must be administered, the aborigines must not be dispossessed without proper consideration, nor treated with inhumanity, or driven into the interior of a country to perish as heretofore, to make place for speculators whose object is aggrandisement. Such might suit the days when Columbus first discovered the new world, when the aborigines were sacrificed by thousands,* and their lands, their houses, their silver and their gold, divided between the most abandoned of the invading Spaniards, who, in all their expeditions against the mild and inoffensive natives,† caused the cross and crucifix to be borne before them, their only crime being that they were natives of a land in which the precious metals abounded, the discovery of which, however, has proved the greatest curse that could befall a nation. The introduction of the wealth thus obtained annihilated the industry of that unhappy country, while judgment, such as ought to be a warning to others, has befallen the Spaniards for their inhumanity to the natives of South America, far beyond the third and fourth generation.

But to proceed. It was the duty of the governor, on his arrival in New Zealand, however detrimental to the interest of the company, to

* The New Zealand Company never occasioned the loss of a single life.

† Vide article already referred to for a complete reply as to the missionaries.

protect the interest of the natives, and to inquire into every particular in reference to the transfer of their lands, &c , and to see that those of the natives, who had bartered lands to the company, had a just right to do so.

That the agents of the company had an arduous task to perform will be readily admitted, both in their dealings with the natives, their own people, and with the executive, and which the existing differences with the missionaries and protectors of the aborigines tended to increase, contending, as they were, for two separate interests, and which deprived them of the assistance and advice of these parties in the very difficult position we find them placed in, both with the natives and their own labourers, who appear to have been disorderly and impertinent on all occasions.

It certainly would have been as judicious in the first promoters of the New Zealand project, as it is astounding that so many men of business-like habits are connected with it, if they had waited until government had taken possession of New Zealand as a British settlement, by consent of the native chiefs, and prepared the way with them for systematic colonization, arranging, at the same time, all matters relative to the transfer of lands, native reserves, remuneration, &c. Such a course would have avoided all the difficulties in which the company find themselves involved, and which was the more necessary, as the coast was infested with deserters from the ships employed in the whaling trade, and escaped convicts, and others of equally depraved habits from the surrounding colonies and settlements, who set an example of insubordination, both among the native tribes with whom they had associated themselves, and the johnny-raws from this country, aware, as they were, that the establishment of an orderly government would be detrimental to their views and interests, and interrupt them in their refractory habits.

Again, the New Zealanders, who frequented the coast, were too well acquainted with traffic, to remain satisfied with the means employed by the company's agent to obtain possession of the best of the lands; nay, more, it was worse than folly to suppose they would remain content, by receiving a new coat or any other article of dress, which in a month or two would be either worn out or tired of, and which system of barter, by the bye, Messrs. Cooper and Levi, or any other of the good folks at Sydney, might have more readily engaged in, than a company formed in London. The warehouses and stores in Sydney were bearing down with British manufactures, and which might have been obtained at a much less cost, (instance the failures in that colony,) without the expense of freight from England to New Zealand—with this advantage, that the above-named gentlemen were more familiar with the manners, customs, habits, propensities, &c., of those with whom they would have to make their bargains, as also accustomed to the climate, from having been resident there for some seven, fourteen, or twenty-one years, than any individual sent out by the New Zealand Company possibly could be.

That the disputes which have existed between the executives, the missionaries, the protectors of the aborigines, and the company's agents, have militated against the company's interest, must be admitted. But each had a duty to perform with probably self-interest predominating, which always produces the seeds of dissension in such undertakings, and which renders it more necessary for an executive to prepare the way for such extensive operations as the New Zealand Company had in view in establishing themselves in New Zealand, and which would have prevented the very serious affairs which have occurred, as well as the charges and complaints both to the colonial authorities and the directors of the company.

In conclusion, it may be observed, that the undertaking was too gigantic, and that it would hardly be expected to be successful under the many disadvantages with which it was surrounded. At the commencement there was no acknowledged government in New Zealand, and the native tribes who had possession of tracts of land one day, might be overpowered by another tribe and dispossessed on the following, under such circumstances it would appear impracticable to obtain quiet possession unless every tribe was satisfied.

And the company could hardly have expected the natives would have been satisfied with the means employed to obtain possession of lands by their agent. Now, the Marquis of Normanby, with his wonted shrewdness and foresight, felt, that by simply sending out a captain of the navy as lieutenant-governor, without an attendant or an adviser, (what jack would call a " man-of-war without force,") if even he had been wise as an oracle, could not have set matters to rights, that were in a state of confusion and disorder when he got there.

I write advisedly. I had the pleasure of being a messmate of the late lieutenant-governor, of whom the company's agent so largely complains in all his reports, and I am persuaded it would be foreign to his disposition, to have placed difficulties in the way of the company's advancement and interest, unless they ran contrary to the instructions he was acting under, and the duty he had to perform; and hence I would repudiate those charges, and say it was the difficulties in which the company and their agent involved themselves by premature measures, and not the acts of the governor, further than in the strict performance of his duty, that has occasioned the jeopardy of their affairs.

Indeed no company, labouring under so many disadvantages, thus slightly glanced at, could have looked forward with any prospect of success, without protection. "Lawless and heedless savages" to contract with, contaminated by the example of escaped convicts and deserters from ships, of the vilest description of character—profligate and abandoned.

VIDI.

COLONIAL STATISTICS.

[NEW SERIES.]

NO. VI.—BRITISH GRENADA.

British Grenada, or as it is otherwise spelt Granada, is situated in latitude 12° 3′ north, longitude 61° 50′ west. The island is 78 miles from St. Vincent south-south-west. In extent covers an area of 125 miles, or 80,000 acres, about five-eighths cultivated. Its extreme length is 25 miles, and extreme breadth 15 miles; extreme altitude 3,000 feet. The capital is George-town, with a population of 2,213 individuals; the other towns are Goreyave, L'Abaye, Charlotte Town, and Granville Town.

Climate.—Like that of the adjoining island, St. Vincent, the climate is equable; the highest temperature is 85°, the mean 80°, and the lowest 74° 1′, as ascertained by the tables of Major Tulloch, an established authority.

History.—The island is one of those discovered by Columbus on his third voyage, in August, 1498; it was first settled by the French in 1650, and ceded to Britain in 1763. In 1650, the French governor of Martinique, Du Parquet, collected 200 hardy adventurers, for the purpose of seizing on the island. Du Parquet thus established a colony in Grenada, and built a fort for its protection.

Government.—The government consists of a Lieutenant-Governor, a council of 9 members, and an assembly of 27 members. The first British governor was Brigadier-General R. Melville, he held the appointment in 1764. The following is a list of the officers of the present government:—Lieutenant-Governor, Colonel C. J. Doyle; Chief Justice, J. Sanderson, Esq.; Attorney-General, W. S. Davis, Esq; Solicitor-General, W. Snagg, Esq.; Secretary, P. O. Rowley, Esq.; Treasurer, J. B. Gaff, Esq.; Speaker of the Assembly, J. Hoyes, Esq.; Clerk of the Assembly, W. C. Ker, Esq.; Provost-Master-General, F. Jackson, Esq.; Collector of the Customs, T. Holmes, Esq.; Harbour-Master, A. Martin, Esq.; Agent in London, J. Marryatt, Esq.

Country.—One of the most prominent features in the wild romantic scenery of Grenada, is Mount St. Catherine, (Morne Michel), an altitude of 3,200 feet above the ocean level.

Rivers.—The rivers are numerous, 26 in number, but not large; the principal are those of Great Bucolet, Duguisne, and Antoine, on the windward; and St. John's, and Beau Sejour on the leeward.

Lakes.—Near the centre of the island, at an elevation of 1,740 feet, amidst the mountain scenery, is situated the Grand Étang, an almost perfectly circular fresh-water lake, two miles and a half in circumference, and fourteen feet deep; another lake, Antoine, of nearly similar size and form, is situated on the east coast, only half a mile from the sea, and but 43 feet above its level; it has been increasing in size for the last 60 years, and is supposed to be the crater of an exhausted volcano; quantities of scoriæ have been repeatedly found near its brink. On the south shore, near Point Saline, there are extensive salt ponds.

Subsidiary Islands.—A group of small islands called the Grenadines lies between Grenada and St. Vincent, a portion of which are subsidiary to this island; viz., Cariaçoa, about 21 miles in circumference, and forming one parish, in which a small town called Hillsborough is situated, and Round Island, and Levora.

Geology.—The mountains and different parts of the low lands consist of strata of red and grey sandstone, greywacke, alternations of horneblend, hard argillaceous schist, and a variety of gneiss. An imperfect species of granite is common, a very coarse porphyry is also sometimes seen; limestone, basaltic rock, fuller's earth, sulphur, and specimens of the natural magnet, are found. Some of the warm sulphurous springs in the hilly parishes of St. Mark and St. John's are hot enough to boil an egg. Of the several hot chalybeate and sulphurous springs that exist, the former are the most numerous; and one of these, at Annandale, in St. George's parish, is very remarkable for its heat and strong metallic impregnation; the mercury rises to 86, and, since the earthquake of 1825, both the temperature and impregnation have been very sensibly increased. A hot spring in St. Andrew's parish emits considerable quantities of carbonic acid gas; it contains iron and lime, and possesses a strong petrifactive quality.

Towns.—The island is divided into six parishes or districts, Sts. Patrick, Andrew, John, Mark, David, and George. The three first-named are productive in sugar, coffee, and cocoa. St. George contains the capital of that name, and the fortifications and military posts of Richmond Hill, Fort King George, Hospital Hill, and Cardigan Heights. It is also the chief seaport, the residence of the Governor, the station of the Courts of Judicature, &c. This district has 28 sugar estates, 20 coffee settlements, and 8 coffee plantations.

Roads.—From the structure of the island the roads are necessarily indifferent, and consist chiefly of bridle paths, the most ordinary means of conveyance from one point to another near to the coast being by canoes.

Water-Works.—Water-works for supplying the town with water were commenced in 1836.

Population.—In 1753 the population consisted of—whites, 1,263; coloured, 175; negroes, 11,991; in 1834 there were—whites, 801; coloured, 3,786; negroes, 23,536; total, 28,123. Proportion of compensation under the Emancipation Act being about 26*l.* 4s. per head. An Act has passed the Legislature of Grenada, has been approved of, assented to by the Lieutenant-Governor, and proclaimed; it authorises the Lieutenant-Governor to appoint eight paid commissioners to divide the town and parishes into several districts, and to employ enumerators to take the population on Monday, the 3rd of June (last.)

Religion.—The Episcopal is the Established Religion; there are also Catholic, Wesleyan, and Presbyterian denominations. The number of the established church, livings, &c., in Grenada, in 1836, was as follows:—St. George, value of living, 277*l.*; United Parishes, 264*l.*; St. Patrick, 200*l.*; St. Andrew's and St. David's, 264*l.*; Cariaçoa, 290*l.*

Education.—Grenada supported 12 schools in 1838; the number of scholars to each ranged from 68 to 164, male and female; the mode of instruction is Bell's. The five principal schools are supported by Government. The Colonial Government contributes an annual grant of 200*l.* to what is called the Central school.

By an official account of the appropriation of the respective sums of 25,000*l.* each, voted by Parliament in the sessions of 1835, 1836, for the promotion of negro education, it appears that in St. George's Town a school of 130 scholars is supported at a cost of 225*l.*; at Cariaçoa 200 scholars, 210*l.*; at Charlotte Town 160 scholars, 250*l.* District Committees are established under the Society for Promoting Christian Knowledge, and the branch association in aid of the incorporated society for the conversion and religious instruction and education of the negroes. There is also a society for the education of the poor.

Productions.—Commerce.—Quantity of sugar, rum, coffee, and cotton exported to the United Kingdom at different periods:—

	Sugar.	*Rum.*	*Coffee.*	*Cotton.*	*Cocoa.*
	cwts.	gals.	lbs.	lbs.	lbs.
1827	214,721	1,052,576	41,888	296,618	224,934
1830	213,160	298,933	28,541	—	—
1838	156,798	234,919	21,647	109,945	426,626

The sugar crops in 1763, amounted to 11,000 hhds.; they increased up to the year 1776, and fell off subsequently until 1805, when the crops produced 14,000 hhds. The imports of sugar in 1841 were 84,270 cwts.

The aggregate annual value of the productions of Grenada from parliamentary documents is 935,782*l.* The official value of exports and imports to and from the United Kingdom, in 1829, was exports, 359,813*l.*; imports, 93,015*l.* The exports from the United Kingdom to Grenada, in 1834, were in value, 68,908. Forty vessels inward of 10,876 tonnage, and thirty-six outward of 9,809 tonnage, were at the island in the same year.

Income and Expenditure.—A return of the income, expenditure, and debt of Grenada for the years 1841 and 1842, has just been printed by order of the House of Commons. The income of Grenada in 1841 and 1842 amounted respectively to 17,417*l.* and 15,933*l.*, and the expenditure to 12,656*l.* and 12,643*l.*

Military.—The military force consists of a numerous and well-constituted militia, seven regiments strong.

The Colonial Arms.—The machine used for extracting the sugar from the cane is represented, together with slaves occupied in carrying bundles of the cane and submitting the same to the operations of the machine. The motto beneath the device is "*Hæ tibi errent artis.*"

MEXICO, ITS COMMERCIAL RESOURCES, &c.

(FROM "MEXICO AS IT WAS AND IS," BY BRANTZ MAYER, ESQ.)

THE territory of the Mexican republic contains an area of 1,650,000 square miles, and allowing that the square mile will maintain, under ordinary careful cultivation, a population of 200 persons, we shall have the sum of 330,000,000 for the total ultimate capability of the Mexican soil.

In 1793, according to the report made to the King of Spain by Conde de Revellagigedo, the population of New Spain, exclusive of the Intendencies of Vera Cruz and Guadalaxara, was as follows:—

Indians	2,319,741
Europeans	7,904
White creoles	677,458
Different castes	1,478,426
	4,483,529
To which add the population of Vera Cruz and Guadalaxara, according to the estimate of 1803	786,500
Total population in 1793	5,270,029

Baron Humboldt estimates it to have been, in the year 1803, 5,837,100; and Mr. Poinsett, in 1824, 6,500,000.

In 1830, Burckhardt, the German traveller, rated the several classes of Mexicans thus:—

Indians	4,500,000	Mestizos, and other castes	2,490,000
Whites	1,000,000		
Negroes	6,000	Total	7,996,000

Another estimate, in 1839, reduces the sum to 7,065,000, and gives *eight inhabitants to the square mile;* but the most complete and accurate of the recent calculations, is that which was made by the government itself (without special enumeration), and served as a basis for the call of a Congress to form a new constitution, under the plan of Tacubaya, in 1842:—

Departments.	Population.	Departments.	Population.
Mexico	1,389,520	Chiapas	141,206
Jalisco	679,311	Sonora	124,000
Puebla	661,902	Queretaro	120,560
Yucatan	580,948	Nuevo Leon	101,108
Guanajuato	512,606	Tamaulipas	100,068
Oajaca	500,278	Coahuila	75,340
Michoacan	497,906	Aguas Calientes	69,698
San Luis Potosi	321,840	Tabasco	63,580
Zacatecas	273,575	Nuevo Mexico	57,026
Vera Cruz	254,380	Californias	33,439
Durango	162,618		
Chihuahua	147,600	Total, in 1842	7,015,509
Sinaloa	147,000		

Since the year 1830, the population of the republic has been diminished by the ravages of small-pox, measles, and cholera. In the capital alone, it is estimated that about 5,000 died of the first-named of these diseases, 2,000 of the second, and from 15,000 to 20,000 of the third.

Although the estimates of both Poinsett and Burckhardt may be too high, yet, assuming the statements of 1842 and of 1793 to be nearly accurate, we find in forty-nine years an increase of only 1,774,111 in the entire population. Again, if we assume the population to have been 6,000,000 in 1824 (the year, in fact, of the establishment of the republic), we find that, in the course of eighteen years of liberty and independence, the increase has not been greater than 1,044,140.

The several castes and classes of Mexicans may be rated in the following manner :—

Indians	4,000,000
Whites	1,000,000
Negroes	6,000
All other castes, such as zambos, mestizos, mulattoes, &c.	2,009,509
Total	7,015,509

It appears, therefore, that the Indians and negroes amount to 4,006,000, and the whites, and all other castes, to 3,009,509. A resident of Mexico, remarkable for the extent and accuracy of his observations, estimates, that of the former (or negroes and Indians), but 2 per cent. can read and write; while of the latter, at a liberal estimate, but about 20 per cent.

Taking this computation to be correct, and using the estimate of the decree of 1842 for the basis of the population, we shall have :—

Of Indians and Negroes who can read	80,120
Whites and all others . , ...	607,628
Total able to read and write out of a population of 7,000,000	687,748

This would appear to be a startling fact in a republic the basis of whose safety is the capacity of the people for an intellectual self-government. Let us, however, carry this calculation a little farther. If we suppose that out of the 1,000,000 of *whites*, 500,000, or the half only, are *males*, and of that 500,000, but 20 per cent., or but 100,000, can read and write, we will no longer be surprised that a population of more than 7,000,000 has been hitherto controlled by a handful of men; or that, with the small means of improvement afforded to the few who can read, the superior classes, who wield the physical and intellectual forces of the nation, have forced the masses to become little more than the slaves of those who possess the talent of control.

Commerce and Manufactures of Mexico.

The commerce of Mexico has been sensibly diminishing for the last ten years. This is attributable to the continual revolutionary disturbances of the country, the decrease of the wealth of the people, and the pecuniary embarrassments to which most of the inhabitants have been subjected by the non-payment of government loans and unfortunate investments.

In 1832 and 1833, the products of the custom-house amounted to about 12,000,000 dollars per annum. In 1839, on account of the French blockade, they fell to near 3,000,000 dollars; in 1840, they rose again to 7,000,000 dollars; and, in the following year, fell to little more than 5,000,000 dollars, which sum may be divided among the different ports as follows :—

	Dollars.		Dollars.
Vera Cruz . . .	3,329,802	Monterey	96,853
Tampico . . .	883.039	Acapulco	17,182
Matamoras . . .	312,403	San Blas	208,845
Marattan . . .	383,159		
Guyamas . . .	55,814	Total . .	5,287,097

This corresponds to about 12,300,000 dollars of importation annually, divided (according to an estimate) in the following manner:—

	Dollars.		Dollars.
From England	4,500,000	From Spain	500,000
" France	3,000,000	" Genoa, & other ports	1,000,000
" Hamburgh	1,500,000		
" China	1,000,000	Total	12,300,000
" United States	800,000		

The expense to the government, for the collection of this revenue, was 348,290 dollars.

The exports from the republic (chiefly, of course, of its own productions) may be rated at—

	Dollars.
Precious metals—Specie, through Vera Cruz	4,000,000
" " " Mazatlan and San Blas	2,500,000
" Silver and gold, through other ports	5,000,000
" " through Tampico	7,000,000
Cochineal, jalap, vanilla, sarsaparilla, and hides	1,000,000
Sundries	500,000
Total	20,000,000

From this estimate it will be seen that about 18,500,000 dollars, *in the precious metals*, are exported annually from Mexico. The mines produce near 22,000,000 dollars of silver, of which it is calculated that 12,000,000 dollars are coined in the seven mints of the republic, *per annum*.

From the above calculations, it will be observed that there is a difference of about 8,000,000 dollars between the *imports and exports*, a large portion of which is estimated to be covered by *smuggling*.

The following table will afford an idea of Mexican commerce more in detail (so far as the eastern coast is concerned). In regard to the western coast, it is impossible to state anything with certainty. The chief contraband trade of the republic has been carried on there with the most unblushing audacity, until very recently; so that statistical returns would only tend to deceive.

Commerce of the Port of Vera Cruz.

	ONE YEAR. From 1st Jan. to 31st Dec. 1841.		SIX MONTHS. From 1st Jan. 1842, to 1st July.	
	Entries.	*Departures.*	*Entries.*	*Departures.*
English	45	42	26	21
French	31	33	13	17
American	39	37	19	19
Spanish	36	35	12	15
Hamburgh	5	5	3	4
Danish	5	4	1	1
Belgian	3	3	1	0
Bremen	4	4	1	1
Prussian	2	2	2	0
Sardinian	4	5	2	2
Colombian	5	5	2	3
Mexican	37	43	20	26
Total	216	218	102	109

Passengers in 1841	1,109
Immigrants	459
Increase of population	614

Foreign Trade with Tampico, from 1st Jan. to 31st Dec. 1841.

Nation.	ARRIVALS. No. of vess.	Tons.	No of crew.	Value of invoice in £'s sterling.	DEPARTURES. No. of vess.	Tons.	No. of crew.	Value of invoice in £'s sterling.
				£				£
British men-of-war and packets	19	......	...	66,735	19	......	...	1,120,397
Br. merchantmen...	9	1,041	70	215,900	8	951	62	4,800
United States	24	2,572	108	49,025 8-2	24	2,437	155	119,840 5-2
Mexican	18	864	120	14,800	18	885	123	3,960
Hanseatic	4	592	42	83,000	3	462	32	35,000
French	6	690	65	64,000	10	1,290	110	40,000
Spanish	9	1,004	89	26,000	7	786	70	2,000
Sardinian	1	110	9	6,000	1	110	9	600
Danish	1	62	5	1,200	1	62	5	......
Total	91	6,935	568	£526,960 8-2	91	6,983	567	£1,326,597 5-2

N.B. The pound sterling is valued at five dollars United States currency.

Foreign Trade with Tampico, from 1st Jan. to 31st June, 1842.

Nation.	ARRIVALS. No. of vess.	Tons.	No. of crew.	Invoice value of cargo.	DEPARTURES. No. of vess.	Tons.	No. of crew.	Invoice value of cargo.
				dolls.				dolls.
British men-of-war and packets	14	......	...	269,953	14	......	...	2,845,240
Br. merchantmen...	8	1,270	62	310.000	5	687	39	7,125
American	15	1,277	91	43,320	13	1,092	83	171,980
Mexican	20	976	142	58,000	17	983	119	8,250
Hanseatic	2	260	19	105.000	2	260	19	5,000
French	4	497	35	200,000	5	541	44	175,000
Spanish	2	194	22	45.000	4	402	37	4.000
Sardinian	1	136	77	25.000	1	136	7	3,000
Colombian	1	57	10	6,000	1	57	10	4,000
Total	67	4,667	338	1,062,245	62	4,158	358	3,223,505

N.B.—The importation in British vessels and royal mail steamers, is entirely quicksilver.

Trade with Matamroas—1841.

The whole trade of 1841 was carried on in vessels from the United States of North America—vessels, 32; tonnage, 2,345.

EXPORTS TO THE UNITED STATES.

	Dollars.		Dollars.
Specie.....................	352,766 87	Horses and mules	800 00
Hides	117,334 00		
Wool	15,943 00	Total	486,834 87

IMPORTS FROM THE UNITED STATES.

Countries where manufactured.	Silks. dolls.	Woollens. dolls.	Cottons. dolls.	Linens. dolls.	Ironware & machinery. dolls.	Paper. dolls.	Jewelry. dolls.	Sundries. dolls.	Total. dolls.
England...	1,040	25,046	146,280	23,768	3,921	......	......	3,140	203.195
Germany ...	......	......	2,051	40,947	......	......	......	246	43,244
Spain	......	......	......	......	......	......	......	8,060	8.060
U. States...	......	......	25,640	......	15,120	......	......	66.140	106.900
France......	2,340	4,148	31,480	......	270	1,680	452	5.334	52.301
Havana ...	......	......	......	6,597	......	......	......	13,245	13,245
Total value	3,380	29,194	205,451	71,312	19,311	1,680	452	96,165	426,945

From having a trade worth upwards of 9,000,000 dollars in 1835, the Americans have been reduced to a comparatively insignificant commerce of 1,000,000, at the extreme, in 1843!

This complete decay of trade with the United States of North America is easily accounted for on the ground of jealousy, dislike, and the desire to encroach, which the States have exhibited in the Texan affair; to which, however, should be added the estimate which the Mexicans have been taught to make of their own geographical position and resources by the English. We have reminded them of their numerical strength, of their climate and productions, the probability of the trade of the old world passing across their territories, and the certainty, therefore, of their independence being preserved by the first-rate powers of Europe, in opposition to traitors at home, or violence from neighbouring countries. The feelings of the majority in Mexico are republican, solely from a hatred of Spanish tyranny, but she has looked to England steadily for pecuniary aid, for protection as consequential to such loan, and, for trade and commerce as the natural result of both. From which it is plain that they do not repose more confidence in republics than in monarchies, but the contrary, and that their form of government was forced upon them by the necessity of the case, and by the disposition of mankind to fly from one extreme to the opposite. Horror of a tyrannical monarchy drove them into love of republicanism.

A favourite mode of raising loans in Mexico, hitherto, has been that of granting permits to merchants (chiefly Englishmen) to introduce *cotton twist* into the republic. This is a prohibited article; prohibited for the purpose of cherishing the manufacturing establishments of the country. That these have progressed to a very considerable extent, ***and have entirely outstripped the production of the cotton planters of Mexico***, will be seen by the annexed table, which has been obtained from the most authentic sources:—

STATISTICS OF MEXICAN MANUFACTURE.

	No. of Factories each Department.	Spindles established.	Spindles in erection.	Total.
In Mexico	12	30,156	......	30,156
Puebla	21	35,672	12,240	47,912
Vera Cruz......	7	17,860	5,200	23,060
Guadalaxara..	5	11,312	6,500	17,812
Queretaro......	2	7,620	......	7,620
Durango	4	2,520	......	2,520
Guanajuato ...	1	1,200	......	1,200
Sonora	1	1,000	......	1,000
Total	53	107,340	23,940	131,280

There are *three* manufacturing establishments in the department of Durango, that may be calculated at about 4,000, which, added to the 131,280, will give a grand total of 135,000, *at least*. The number of *looms* in the republic is not presented, because *data* have been furnished only in relation to those moved by machinery. An immense number of *hand-looms* is in constant occupation.

1.

	Pounds.	Dollars.
The cotton factories of the republic consume, *daily*, with the 107,340 spindles in actual operation	39,755	
Which produce, in spun thread, at the rate of one-third of a pound for each spindle	35,780	
Which, converted into *mantas* and *rebosos*, have a value of...		39,358

2.

	Pounds.	Dollars.
The same factories, after the 23,940 spindles in erection are in operation, will consume, *daily*	48,622	

	Pounds.	Dollars.
Each spindle will produce of thread	43,760	
Which, converted as aforesaid, will amount in value to		73,804
3.		
The consumption of cotton in the year, of three hundred working days, with 131,280 spindles, will be	14,586,666	
The produce in thread	13,138,000	
The produce in manufactured value, as above		14,440,800
4.		
The 131,280 spindles, working day and night, will consume	24,797,332	
Produce in thread	22,317,600	
Produce in manufactured value as above		24,549,360
5.		
The 131,280 spindles will occupy (working only by day) ...	8,753 looms.	
" " " (working by day and night)	14,880 "	
Number of operatives employed by day	17,000	
" " " day and night	29,000	
6.		
It will require for the 131,280 spindles working *by day*	145,666⅔ qtls. cotton.	
The produce of the country, at the utmost, is not more than	50,000 "	
Leaving a deficit of	95,666⅔ "	
* But if the spindles work *day and night*, they will require	247,973½ "	
Produce of the country, as above..	50,000 "	
Leaving a deficit of	197,973½ quintals.	

The value of the Mexican manufacturing establishments may be stated, in round numbers, at 10,000,000.

Hitherto the cotton crop of the republic has not greatly exceeded 50,000 quintals; which, calculated at a mean of 35 dollars the quintal, will give a total valuation of the produce at 1,750,000 dollars. The estimate we have presented in the foregoing tables shows, however, that the spindles, *working day and night*, will require 247,937½ quintals, or, in other words, that there is a deficit of 197,973½, which, valued at the same rate, will amount to 6,929,072 dollars.

Many persons have been induced by this condition of the market, and the prohibition of importing the raw material, to commence plantations of cotton; but we doubt whether the habits of the agricultural population will permit their prosperity. They dislike to adventure in new branches of industry. If their ancestors wrought on cotton plantations, they are content to continue in the same employment; but it will be difficult to train the new labourer to the newer cultivation.

The cotton crop of Mexico has been very variable in value. At Tepic, on the west coast, it has been as low as 15 dollars the quintal; at Vera, Cruz, on the east coast, 22 dollars and 34 dollars; while at Puebla and in the capital, it has risen to 40 dollars, and even 48 dollars.

The average price of *mantas* (cotton cloth) of one *vara* width, in 1842, was about 25 cents. the *vara*; and of *twist*, No. 12 to 22, about 75 cents the pound. It was estimated that, if cotton fell in consequence of im-

* At the town of Lowell, alone, they make nearly a *million and a quarter* yards of cotton cloth per week, employ about 9,000 operatives, (6,375 females,) and use 433,000 lbs. of raw cotton per week. The annual amount of raw cotton used is 22.568,000 lbs., enough to load 50 ships of 350 tons each; and of cotton manufactured, 70,275,910 yards. 100 lbs. of cotton will produce 89 yards of cloth.—*Hunt's Magazine.*

portations being allowed, or a large crop, to 25 dollars the quintal, these articles would be reduced to 18¾ cents the *vara* for the first, and to 50 cents the pound for the second. This condition of the market would prevent all importations from abroad, even aided by smuggling.

There are about 5,000 hand-looms throughout the departments, which will work up all the spun yarn into *mantas* and *rebosos* as fast as it can be made. Many of these looms are entirely employed in the manufacture of the common rebosos, the consumption of which is so great among the poorer classes. The value of these looms is estimated at between 6,000,000 and 7,000,000 dollars. The number of persons employed, in every way, in manufactures, cannot be much short of 30,000.

The power made use of for the movement of the factories is water; which is abundant, for that purpose, all over the country, proceeding from small streams falling from the mountains into the neighbouring plains or barrancas. Owing to the scarcity of wood, and the costliness of its transportation, steam cannot be advantageously applied. There are several manufactories of cotton balls, or thread, in Mexico, but they are not of very great importance. Paper factories are working with considerable success. There are two near the capital, one at Puebla, and one in Guadalaxara. Their productions are good, but inadequate to the consumption. The quantity of this article used for *cigarritos*, or paper cigars, is inconceivable. The best coarse wrapping or envelope paper is made in Mexico from the leaves of the Agave Americana, the plant which yields "pulque." It has almost the toughness and tenacity of iron.

Both at Puebla and Mexico there are several glass factories, making large quantities of the material for windows and common tumblers. Their produce is, nevertheless, insufficient for the wants of the country.

Woollen blankets, and some very coarse woollen clothes or *baizes*, are also manufactured in the republic. The blankets are often of a beautiful texture, and woven, with the gayest colours and patterns, into a garment that frequently costs a fashionable cavalier from two to five hundred dollars. As this is as indispensable an article for the comfort of a lépero as of a gentleman, and as necessary for a man as a reboso is for a woman, the consumption may be readily imagined.

The Revenue and Resources of Mexico.

The income of the Mexican government is derived from revenues on foreign commerce, imposts on internal trade, imposts on pulque, export duty on the precious metals, lotteries, post-office, stamped paper, taxes, tobacco, powder, salt-works, and several other sources of trifling importance.

In 1840, these revenues are stated in the report of the minister of the treasury as follows:—

NETT PROCEEDS, AFTER DEDUCTING EXPENSES OF COLLECTION.

	Dollars.		Dollars.
Imposts on foreign commerce	7,115,849	Extraordinary subsidy.........	103
" interior "	4,306,585	Arbitrio extraordinario	78,177
" property, income, &c.	466,061	Capitacion	483
Exchanges, &c.	307,427	Donations	13,662
Creditos Activós	3,309		
Balances of Accounts	355	Total	12,744,157
Enteros de productos liquidos	452,146		

In 1839, the revenues amounted to 11,215,848 dollars. The income from the post-office department (which is not included in the statement for 1840) was 178,738 dollars, in 1839. In 1840, the lotteries produced the gross sum of 215,437 dollars; but, as the expenses connected with their management amounted to 158,485 dollars, it left a balance of but 56,952 dollars for the government. The "*sealed paper*," or stamp tax, produced 110,863 dollars, but as this impost has been nearly doubled during 1842, the revenue must at present be proportionally greater.

It was impossible to obtain any of the official documents of 1841 and 1842 (in consequence of the disturbed condition of the country), with the exception of the custom-house returns for the former year:—

Custom-houses.	Tonnage duty. Dollars.	Net proceeds after deducting cost of collection. Dollars.
EAST COAST—Vera Cruz	31,032	3,374,528
" Tampico	7,363	1,019,046
" Matamoras	3,525	279,627
WEST COAST—Mazatlan	6,245	397,213
" Guyamas	2,092	46,189
" Monterey........	810	85,982
" Acapulco	573	7,193
" San Blas	2,719	190,270
Total	55,259	5,399,948

It will be perceived that the custom-houses of Tabasco, Campeche, Sisal, Isla del Carmen, and Bacalar, are not included in the preceding statement, in consequence of the separation of the first (during the period) from her allegiance to the republic, and on account of the rebellious condition of the rest. At the date of the statement, reports from Goatzacoalco, Alvarado, Tuxpan, Huatulco, Manzanillo, La Paz, Pueblo Viejo, Altata, Loreto, San Diego, San Francisco, Soto la Marina, and from the frontier posts of Paso del Norte, Comitan, Tonala, Santa Fè de N. Mexico, y Presidio del Norte, had not been yet received at the treasury office in the capital. The costs of the collection of this revenue amounted to 52,886, and the salaries of officers to 295,404 dollars.

No one who has resided any length of time in Mexico, either connected or unconnected with commerce, can fail to have heard of the extent to which smuggling has been and still is carried on in the republic. This infamous system, alike destructive of private morals and public integrity, has become a regular business in portions of the country; and, after having been, to a great extent, suppressed on the eastern coast, has for several years occupied the attention of numbers on the west. Mr. Mc Clure calculated that the republic possesses "a frontier of five thousand miles, including the sinuosities, windings, and turnings of bays, gulfs, and rivers on the Pacific; 3,000 miles on the United States of America and Texas; and above 2,500 on the Gulf of Mexico; making, in all, 10,500 miles of frontier to guard against illicit trade, ***without an individual on the one thousand two hundredth part of the space, to give notice of any depredations that may happen.***"

Now, although the estimate of this philanthropist may appear rather fanciful, when we remember that, wherever there are smugglers to ***introduce,*** it is probable that there are individuals to ***receive,*** and consequently that the government *might* be protected; still it is undeniable that the territory is vast, the population scattered, and the corruption of government agents has been as shameful as it was notorious.

National Debt.

The national debt of Mexico is one of very considerable importance, and may be divided into the two great classes of Foreign and Internal debt.

The internal debt amounts to 18,550,000; and in 1841 the customs were mortgaged to pay this sum, in the following subdivisions :—

		Dollars.
17	per cent. of the customs devoted to a debt of	2,040,000
15	" " " " "	,410,000
12	" " " " "	2,100.000
10	" " " " "	3,100,000
8	" " " " "	1,200,000
10	" " " " tobacco fund debt	9,700,000
16⅔	" " " " interest on English debt ...	....
10	" " " " garrison fund	....
98⅔		18,550.000
1⅓	balance, clear of lien, for the government.	
100		

The foreign debt is still larger than this; and (including the above) the entire national responsibility, as it existed at the end of last year, stands

	Dollars.		Dollars.
Internal debt	18,550.000	Claims for Hilazo	700.000
Debt to English creditors ...	60,000,000	Bustamante loan	500,000
U. S. claims and interest, say	2,400.000		
Copper to be redeemed	2,000,000	Total	84,150,000

Until 1841, the whole of the revenue, except 11⅓ per cent., was appropriated to the payment of 18,550,000, while the remaining claims were entirely unprotected by securities. Shortly after the accession of Santa Anna to power, he *suspended* (by a decree of the 16th of February) the payment of the first five funds charged upon the customs, as stated in a preceding table, but reserved the *active appropriation* for the tobacco and *English interest debts*. This, as may well be imagined, created great dissatisfaction among the mercantile classes, and among numbers of persons who had invested their capital in government loans, with a reliance upon the *revenues* as a solemn pledge for their redemption. Santa Anna, however, withstood the torrent manfully. He was assailed by legations, newspapers, and individuals, but nothing could induce him to yield the pressing wants of the government to their importunities. He was, in fact, forced to the measure. The national credit was irremediably impaired, and he found it impossible to obtain loans. The consequence was, the seizure of the customs, by the *suspension* of their prior appropriation, until he was enabled to relieve his treasury.

Independently of the English debt, the claims upon the Mexican government have usually been created by means of loans of the most usurious character.

On the 20th of September, fifteen days before the treaty of Estansuela, the administration of President Bustamante offered the following terms for a loan of 1,200,000 dollars. It proposed to receive the sum of 200,000 dollars in *cash,* and 1,000,000 dollars represented in the *paper or credits* of the government. These credits or paper were worth, in the market, nine per cent. About one-half of the loan was taken, and the parties obtained orders on the several maritime custom-houses, receivable in payment of duties.

The revenues of the custom-house of Matamoras have been always hitherto appropriated to pay the army on the northern frontier of the republic. During the administration of General Bustamante, the commandant of Matamoras issued bonds or drafts against the custom-house for 150,000 dollars, receivable for all kinds of duties as cash. He disposed of these bonds to the merchants of that port for 100,000 dollars; and, in addition to the *bonus* of 50,000 dollars, allowed them interest on the 100,000 dollars at the rate of 3 per cent. per month, until they had duties to pay, which they could extinguish by the drafts.

Another transaction, of a similar nature, developes the character of the government's negotiations, and can only be accounted for by the receipt of some advantages which the act itself does not disclose to the public.

The mint at Guanajuato, or the right to coin at that place, was contracted for, in 1742, by a most respectable foreign house in Mexico, for 71,000 dollars *cash,* for the term of *fourteen years,* at the same time that another offer was before the government, stipulating for the payment of 400,000 dollars for the same period, payable in annual instalments of 25,000 dollars each. The 71,000 dollars in hand, were, however, deemed of more value than the prospective 400,000! This mint leaves a nett annual income of 60,000 dollars!

With such a spendthrift abandonment of the resources of the country, continued, for a series of years, in the midst of the pressure of foreign claims and domestic warfare, it is, indeed, wonderful that Mexico has so long survived the ruin which must inevitably overtake her with a debt of 84,000,000 dollars, and an annual expenditure (as will be seen from the succeeding statement) of 13,000,000 dollars, independent of payment of interest, balances, and loans. Yet with all these incumbrances, created under the most usurious exactions, it is greatly to her honour that she has not *repudiated* the claims of her creditors; a moral and political firmness in which she may well be emulated by many other states.

The minister of the treasury of Mexico has just published a decree, by which the president directs 25 per cent. of all the receipts of the custom-houses of the republic to be set apart as a "*sinking fund,*" to pay the public debt. This fund is to be inviolable. The decree provides for the *consolidation and funding* of the debt at the rate of a 6 per cent. stock, for which it will be exchanged by such as choose. Those who do not embrace this arrangement with the government are to have their claims liquidated, only, *when out of the sinking fund now created, those who accede to the exchange of stock shall have been first of all paid!*

The debt of Mexico may be fairly estimated at 82,000,000 dollars, which at 6 per cent., bears an annual interest of 4,920,000. The actual income from customs *and all resources* may be set down at 13,000,000, 25 per cent. on which will produce a fund of 3,250,000 dollars, or 1,670,000 *less than the interest on the whole debt!* It may well be asked, whence is to proceed the "*sinking fund,*" so long as such a deficiency exists?

The entire expenses of the Mexican government for 1840, including the supreme powers, diplomacy, treasury, judiciary, political, ecclesiastical, instruction, benevolence, punishment, salaries of various officers of palace, rents, pensions, &c., war-office, dividends on foreign debt, amounted to 13,155,922 dollars.

Mines and Coinage of Mexico.

In treating of the resources of men and money of Mexico, it will not be uninteresting (after knowing that the production of the mines amounts in value annually to about twenty-two millions, of which twelve find their way to the mints) to present a statement of the total coinage of the country, derived from the records of the earliest periods to which access could be had:—

TABLE OF THE COINAGE OF MEXICO, FROM THE EARLIEST PERIODS TO THE PRESENT DAY.

	Dollars.
The mint of the city of Mexico was established in the year 1535, but there are no returns for the first 155 years, that is, until 1690. If we take the average of the coinage of these years to have been 1,000,000 dollars, we shall have	155,000,000
From 1690 to 1803, inclusive	1,355,452,020
1803 to 1821, inclusive	261,354,022
1822	5,543,254
1823	3,567,821
1824	3,503,880
1825	6,036,878
1825 to 1831 (on an average, three millions per annum)	15,000,000
1831	13,000,000
1832	12,500,000
1833	12,500,000
1834	12.040,000
1835	12,080,000
1836	12,050,000
1837	11,610,000
1838 to 1843 (averaging twelve millions)	60,000,000
To this must be added the coinage of state mints, not included in above:—	
Guanajuato from 1812 to 1826	3,024,194
Zacatecas " 1810 to 1826	32,108,185
Guadalaxara " 1812 to 1826	5,659,159
Durango " 1811 to 1826	7,483,626
Chihuahua " 1811 to 1814	3,603,660
Sombrerete " 1810 to 1811	1,561,249
All of these for the five years (after 1826), since which they have been calculated in the general coinage	60,000,000
Total	2,068,597,948

This amount is less than it has been made by several other writers.

SPEECH OF SIR ROBERT PEEL ON THE BANK OF ENGLAND CHARTER.*

DELIVERED IN THE HOUSE OF COMMONS AT WESTMINSTER, ON MONDAY, MAY 6, 1844.

It is said that the law with respect to joint-stock banks is defective in other respects and that difficulties are thrown in their way. We mean to put a stop to these. The place where notice was to be served or to issue is not sufficiently defined; but this doubt will, of course, be removed by giving to joint-stock banks the privilege of suing and being sued. The joint-stock banking companies are bound by the acts of an unauthorized partner, for it is the principle of partnership that the acts of one bind the rest of the partners. But if you choose to have joint-stock banks, with 1,000 partners—there being no means on the part of the controlling power by which they could exercise discretion as to the admission of a partner—it appears to me unjust to make the acts of any one partner bind the whole. We propose, therefore, to alter the law so as to make the acts of an individual director bind the whole concern, for the appointment of an individual to the station of director implies, or ought to imply, confidence in him; but it is not fair to subject the joint-stock banking companies to responsibility on account of the acts of an unauthorized partner.

The great complaint of the joint-stock banks in London is this,—that they cannot accept bills for a less date than six months. Other private banking establishments in London had an unlimited power of acceptance, but joint-stock banks in London labour under the prohibition I have mentioned. This had been insisted on by the Bank of England, when the last charter was discussed, in order that the joint-stock banks should not come into competition with that establishment and the private banks, by being allowed the power of acceptance for a less date than six months. We propose to place the joint-stock banks in London on a perfect equality in this respect, and to give them the power of accepting bills of any amount and for any period. It is thought by some that this privilege might be perverted, so as to give rise to something like the substitution of a bank-note of a certain kind, and of a circulating nature. The power has been held by private banks from time immemorial, and it has not hitherto been accompanied by any abuse; and why should it be anticipated that joint-stock banks would abuse such a power, by using it contrary to the intentions of the legislature? But I give public notice, on this opportunity, that if the power should be abused—if it should be attempted to circulate small bills, so accepted, within the limits reserved to the Bank, I shall not hesitate to appeal to parliament on the instant, for the purpose of correcting that evil. We do not mean to establish a small note currency, but to facilitate the operations of banking, by putting joint-stock banks on an equal footing with others. These, then, are the facilities we propose to extend to the joint-stock banks.

Now, as to the conditions or restrictions we propose to apply to all existing joint-stock banks. In the first place, we require of all such banks—I do not know if it need be confined to banks of issue—the condition to which I now allude—viz., that there be a full and complete periodical publication of the names of all partners and directors. This is what the London and Westminster Bank voluntarily publishes. See what the security is which we are told the public possess in the case of these banks—that each partner is liable to the extent of his whole fortune for the debts of the bank to which he belongs. Very well. Let the public then know who the partners are. Let us know the transfers that take place; let us determine how long the responsibility for the possession of shares will attach to a party; as we have the comfort of unlimited responsibility, give me the names of those who so guarantee us.

There is another condition we have a right to insist upon. We are to continue to existing banks the privilege of issues. Let us know the amount of the issues. We are going to demand from the Bank a weekly account of issues, the privilege of which stands on distinct and separate grounds, and no bank exercising or permitted to exercise it, ought to object to the weekly publication of the amount of its resources. Let the Bank have the opportunity of knowing how far its operations in controlling the currency are promoted or obstructed by the concurrent issues of other banks. I know what the objection to this is. It is that rivals may take advantage of a "weak place." Well, that knowledge is just what I wish to secure. I want to get the information for the public. You have an easy mode of getting rid of the obligation: I would say to the joint-stock banks, "Go and deal with the Bank, and accept bank-notes in lieu of your own, and the publication insisted upon cannot be necessary;" but, if the privilege of issues be to be continued, let the public and the Bank subject to the same rules the fluctuations in the amount. We know it will do no harm. It cannot injure a well-

---

* Concluded from No. 7, page 450.

conducted bank. It will be of public advantage. As to the public drawing erroneous inferences from the accounts, why I believe the public will very soon grow sagacious upon the subject. And when they are in the habit of seeing 200 or 300 banking accounts they will not draw conclusions unfavourable to a bank on account of some alteration, either increase or decrease, in the amount of issues in any particular week. It is the complete and thorough publicity of such matters which is not less a guarantee against abuse, than a protection to all honest dealers. Now, as to the existing Bank, I do not intend to pry into their affairs. Above all, I do not desire to take any securities which the public may find delusive. I think the attempt at interference in the carrying legislation, so far as the attempt to control the action of these banking bodies with reference to any other concerns than those connected with the privilege of issuing, is not advantageous. I have had my attention drawn to the subject, and I have been invited to inspect certain forms of accounts, proposed to be prescribed, drawn up in various ways—"deposits," "issues," "bullion," "overdrawn;" but the more I looked at them, the more dissatisfied, or unsatisfied, I have been. I deprecate, I repeat, the taking of delusive securities above all things. Tell the public they must rely upon their own vigilance—that they must deal with those they know—(we are to enable them to do that)—and that they will watch their own business. But if I say, "here is a form of balance-sheet, to be published periodically—rely upon that;" I am afraid I shall lead to delusion, instead of conferring a benefit. I apply this test to the proposed form of prescribed balance-sheet. Here is the one approved (let me take it) of the Manchester or some other great bank that has failed. I have generally found that the establishment must have adopted the form without giving the least insight into their affairs. "Overdrawn accounts," for instance—one of the heads of these proposed forms —where the banking is on the principle of the Scotch banks, having a current account, paying interest upon deposits, but charging none on advances, there is always an "overdrawn account," and (applying this test) the balance-sheet, with its head of "overdrawn accounts," would mislead with reference to those banks conducted on the Scotch principle; and, therefore, though if the security were available, we should have a right to demand it, as we cannot devise any form which the fraudulent might not evade, I am inclined to abandon the attempt, and not to require from existing joint-stock banks any particular form of balance-sheet. So as to the limitation of the nominal amount of shares, many have proposed that joint-stock banks should be prohibited from having shares of amounts less than £100 or £50, or some fixed amount. But as, under the encouragement of the legislature, banks have been established with £20 and £10 shares, and now exist—and, I believe, in many cases, have conducted their business satisfactorily—it would be harsh now to insist on an alteration of amounts of shares in the case of existing banks, and we, therefore, propose no measure of that kind.

Then, again, as to calling on all existing banks to invest a portion of their capital in government securities, I have considered this maturely; but, again, I fear the consequences of interfering upon the point. I doubt the wisdom of insisting that paid-up capital should be invested in government securities—it is affecting public interests; and, unless we introduce government interference into all these concerns, I am afraid not any good would be accomplished by attempting to control the banks now existing through legislation, and I deprecate it as inconsistent with the true principles upon which banking ought to be conducted. But then as to future companies, I have a right to make what regulations I please, and to adopt as to them what I deem a better principle for their establishment. We propose, then, that no new joint-stock bank of deposit (of course it cannot be one of issue) shall be constituted except upon application to a department of the government for this purpose; that there shall be a registration of all prospectuses—and probably a certain amount of paid-up capital, and a limitation as to the amount of shares—and one uniform deed of settlement, the deeds at present being drawn up with no fixed form; surely, they had better be drawn from one model, which should be strictly adhered to by all future establishments of this sort, enabling the public to look under certain heads for certain subjects, ("regulation of the appointment of directors," or any other head, for instance)—above all, regulating the mode of insuring audits, insisting upon plain and simple accounts; not descending into minute details, we may thus establish banks conforming in their regulations to certain leading principles, not interfering with the Bank of England, taking the issue of the Bank as theirs; we may thus establish banks which will attract public confidence and carry on a proper and profitable business; and this we think a legitimate extent and object of intervention on the part of Parliament—directed to the purification of the system of banking; and we will not exclude from the participation in these advantages any of those banks, now existing, ready to conform to the proposed regulations. Having stated the general regulations as to other banks, I now (in order to lay my whole scheme before the house) revert to the position of the Bank and the relation in which it is to stand to the Government. I interrupted my statement as to the Bank, because I could make our future relations more intelligible by describing the regulations we meant to apply to these joint-stock establishments. I have, however, stated issues are to be allowed the Bank on a fixed amount of securities—that amount £14,000,000. We propose to continue (seeing no advantage in a change) upon the present terms the existing loan of £11,000,000 made to the Government, at 3 per cent. We might pay it off; but, seeing the stable character of the Bank now to be a great central bank of issue, controlling the issues of all others by the action of its own, I see no advantage that could arise to the Government from paying off its debt to the Bank, which debt is to be assigned as part of the security on which the issues of the Bank are to take place. There will then remain £3,000,000, to be upon Exchequer-bills and other securities, on which the Bank are to have entire control. We propose that the Bank should have a limited right in certain cases of necessity to limit its issues upon that portion of the amount of £14,000,000 of securities, viz., £3,000,000. Circumstances might arise in which the Bank* (it is not beyond the limits of possibility) might find it necessary to restrict its issue (to restore the exchanges, &c.) within that amount of £14,000,000. In that case we propose to give to the Bank the power of diminishing the £3,000,000 of securities deposited in addition to the £11,000,000 of debt assigned. I do not know if I have made myself entirely intelligible. The Bank has £3,000,000 in addition to the £11,000,000, fairly within its control. I can hardly conceive a case in which the issues could safely be limited to less than £11,000,000. But then, we propose this—we propose that of every issue taking place beyond the £14,000,000, the profit shall belong exclusively to the Government. The Bank shall not be allowed to issue notes beyond £14,000,000 without transferring the entire net profit of the additional portion to the Government. But here it is necessary to interpose a check, in case issues should be ever unwisely denied; and we propose that the Bank shall be restrained from making any issue on an additional amount of securities excepting after reporting the circumstances to the Government, and having the assent of three of its members to the step. Let me illustrate what I mean, by a particular case. The ordinary issue is £14,000,000. Supposing the Bank to negotiate with some of the issuing banking bodies, and that the latter should agree to annihilate £2,000,000 of their issues, and to substitute for those issues the same amount of Bank paper, there would, in that case, be a gap in the circulation of the country to that extent, and it would be open to the Bank (as there existed that void) to increase the issues to that amount. You ought not, though the profits belong to Government (it may be said,) you ought not to prevent the issue of the £2,000,000, because you have not to that amount bullion, as the foundation of the equality of that amount corresponding with the total; but you may increase the securities by £1,200,000. We propose, then, that such increase shall not take place without the sanction of three members of the Government. The only circumstance I can foresee justifying the increase of issues (beyond the ordinary amounts) is the necessity for filling up a void. I propose this, not for the purpose of intermeddling in the affairs of the Bank, but to introduce some additional guarantee for the public. The amount of securities having been fixed by Parliament, we will not allow them to be increased at the discretion of the Bank, and without the concurrence of the Government. I wish to explain myself as fully as possible. Let me here advert to the "legal tender." A clause in the charter enables country bankers to exchange their notes for the notes of the Bank. I opposed the insertion of that clause. I thought it inconsistent with the great principle of immediate convertibility. The argument was that it had a tendency to diminish panic, and prevent a "run" for gold. In my view, the less Parliament interferes in such subjects, the better. But still I found established this power, and I thought it my duty to facilitate the extension of the Bank currency by continuing that clause, tending in its operation to familiarize the public with Bank paper. I see no advantage in the clause; but, making great changes, thought it advisable to avoid making more than necessary. Now I come to the pecuniary engagements made with the Bank upon the part of Government. The Bank is to retain the privilege of issuing notes on the securities to the amount of £14,000,000, on an interest of 3 per cent. The gross gains of the Bank upon this total of issue would be £420,000. Let us see, in estimating the net profits, what will be the deductions to be made. First, we estimated the cost of the

---

* The issues are regulated on the principle that the circulation is to be kept always up to a certain level without redundancy: and the adjustment is made by the state of the foreign exchanges:—(emergencies excepted.) When the exchanges seem declining, and a contraction of issues consequently advisable, the directors await the actual demand for gold; they still rest tranquil, forbearing only from issuing notes instead of those that have been returned and paid in gold. These precautions are necessary, that trade may be affected the less by a contraction of the currency. A contraction or diminution in the circulation is affected either by raising the rate of discount for bills, or by the sale of securities, or both: an expansion, by reversing these operations.

issue. The Bank, for the sake of the public, conducts its issue on a liberal principle. It does not re-issue notes; it provides the means of keeping every note issued within 10 years; it gives therefore great facilities to the public in the detection of fraud or the tracing of transactions within that period. The total cost to the Bank, on an issue of £20,000,000, has been estimated (by the committee of 1833) at £117,000, but I am inclined to take it at about £113,000, which, taken from £420,000, leaves £303,000. There is then to be deducted about £60,000, composition with the Stamp-office for the privilege of issuing notes. Then there is about £24,000, paid by the Bank to those bankers who undertake to issue Bank of England notes (taking 1 per cent. received on a payment of 3 per cent.) The result, after substracting these items, is £220,000 derived from the issuing of notes. We are going to affect the privileges of the Bank in this respect—by permitting joint-stock banks to enter into competition with the town banking business. What is the sum we are to claim from the Bank for continued privileges? The Bank think we ought to make a material deduction from the sum they have hitherto paid—£120,000. Our answer is, that though is some respects we affect their peculiar privileges, we give increased stability to their banking business. We, must, therefore, insist on an equal payment in future. We have, of course, had negotiations on the subject; and I must, in justice to the gentlemen who have conducted it on the part of the Bank (the Governor aud Deputy-Governor), declare that I never saw men influenced by more disinterested or more public-spirited motives than they have evinced throughout the affair. They have, so far as was consistent with their more direct duties, endeavoured to perform their public obligations to the utmost. They have united the performance of their parts as managers of a great institution, bound to consult the interests of the proprietors, with the discharge of their duties as the heads of a central National Bank. They have shown every disposition to promote the public interests without stipulating for exclusive privileges, and their conduct all along has been marked by the greatest liberality. I hope the house will feel that in the resolutions which I intend to propose there is nothing to which the Bank and the country ought not to accede with readiness. Hitherto the Bank of England have been accustomed to pay to the Government a sum of £120,000, and now that which I propose is that they should in addition to that sum pay once for all £60,000, being the amount of composition for the issue of their notes, which will bring the entire amount to a sum fo £180,000, and thus we shall arrive at the amount payable during the existence of the Bank charter. I do not believe that the net profit which it will be in the power of the Bank of England to obtain by means of its operations as a bank of issue will exceed £100,000. Now, before I go further, I should wish to remind the house that the sum which the Government pays the Bank for the management of the public debt is £248,000. From that the sum of £120,000, will have to be deducted, together with the sum for composition on account of stamps, which raises that, as I before stated, to £180,000. The difference between that sum and the £248,000, which the management of the public debt costs, will form the balance that the Bank of England is to receive from the Government. I hope I have so far succeeded in making clear to the house the statements and reasonings which I have endeavoured to lay before them; and I now, therefore, proceed to another part of the subject, namely the duration of those privileges which it is intended the Bank should continue to enjoy. Ten years ago the Bank received a renewal of its charter nominally for 21 years, giving to Parliament the power of revising that grant when we reached the end of that period at which we have now arrived. That which we at present propose is that there should be a power of revision at the end of 10 years; in this respect, however, differing from the previous plan, that whereas formerly there existed the same power of revision at the end of 10 years, which we now propose to reserve, but there existed at the same time a liability to lose that power if Parliament did not take advantage of it precisely at the end of the 10 years, and by such omission on their part they conferred upon the charter a continued existence for the remaining portion of the term of 21 years. But it is our intention that Parliament should possess the power of revision at any time within the latter 11 years, of those 21 years which are to constitute the whole period. Thus the revision may be at the end of 10 or at the end of 12 years. I conceive it will be much better for the public that the Government should not be exposed to the loss of any opportunity which, after the first ten years, may render a revision of the charter necessary. Of course it is only fair that the Bank should have a year's notice of any such intended revision as that which I am now contemplating. I hope and trust that the Bank will consider this a just arrangement; and I think they ought to regard a year's notice as a long notice; but I have no wish in any respect to curtail or diminish it, though I am sure the public will feel that Parliament should be as much as possible unfettered in its right of revision. In all other respects I propose to leave other banks on the same footing with the Bank of England. There can be no sort of doubt that Parliament do possess the right, whenever they choose to exercise it, of regulating banks of issue in whatever manner the public interests may seem to require; but I do not propose to interfere with them to any greater extent than that which I have already stated; and the house will also not have forgotten that the measure which I intend to submit to their consideration is one clearly limited in its operation to England and Wales. Of Ireland and Scotland I have said nothing; for I have thought that the task of dealing with this country was sufficiently extensive, and I did not wish that it should be complicated by the arrangements which the condition and necessities of other parts of the United Kingdom might render necessary. Let us in the first place, establish our system of banking and of issue upon sound principles in England, and let us reserve the affairs of Scotland and of Ireland as matters of separate consideration. We ought not to permit anything to complicate those interests; they should be dealt with by separate means, and I have therefore excluded them from the operation of the present measure. Allow me in this place to remind the house that I have not proposed to legalize any new banks of issue, nor to permit the formation of any new joint-stock banks, except after registration, and after subscription to such regulations as the Government may see necessary to impose upon them and upon joint-stock banks generally, for the improvement of the system of joint-stock banking. These regulations, I repeat it, are to be confined to England and Wales. I believe that in Scotland the circulation is rather diminishing than increasing; but with that we have at present nothing to do: we have to deal only with two great principles—one is that there shall be no new banks of issue, and the other is to subject joint-stock banks to the approval of Government. With respect to banking, the case with Ireland is one of a peculiar kind. The Bank of Ireland is in a different position from that in which the Bank of England stands, and there is no change which can be made in the Irish banking system which will not require the most mature consideration. Whenever the house thinks proper to go into that question, or whenever the Government find it necessary to call upon the house to go into it, we should be prepared to give it a full and unbiassed consideration; but for the present we are to bear in mind that it is not now before us. I have said nothing on the subject of small notes, and I do not suppose that the house expected that I should. Let me establish first the great leading principles which I have been laying before you, and do not require that they should be mixed up with any extraneous matter. I have avoided those topics, because I felt that if I introduced them I should raise a storm about me which no efforts of mine could allay. One of my objects has been to make the propositions, statements, and observations which it became necessary to address to the house in such a manner as not to create any alarm; and, as I now approach the close of this prolonged discourse, I might, perhaps, under other circumstances, have thought it necessary to offer some apology for the length at which it has been necessary for me to trespass upon the patience and attention of the house. Upon such an occasion as this, however, it is, I presume, not requisite that I should make any apology for having taken up so much time; nay, I venture to hope that the house will indulge me with a few minutes longer, while I briefly recapitulate that to which you have given so much and such attentive consideration. I propose to give to the Bank a continuance of its present privileges, restricting it as a bank of issue to a circle round London, of which 65 miles shall be the radius. I likewise propose that it should consist of two departments, one being for the purposes of banking, the other for those of issue; because, as the house well knows, those branches of business ought to be carried on upon totally different principles, I then propose that the issue of the Bank of England should be restricted to £14,000,000 upon a fixed amount of security, and that when they went beyond that, there should be a power of determining and regulating the excess of issue. It is further intended that there should be a weekly publication of accounts by the Bank; so that every merchant should be able to regulate his dealings by means of the information which those accounts would present. Next, there are to be no new banks of issue nor any joint-stock banks excepting such as register themselves, and subscribe to the regulations which the Government think it expedient to propose; thus giving all the assurance which circumstances permit that those establishments will work as advantageously for the public as the nature of their constitution permits. The existing banks shall continue to enjoy their privileges, provided that they do not exceed certain definite limits as set forth in documents to which Parliament will have access, and portions of which will consist of calculations founded upon the average of the two preceding years. Banks which are at present banks of issue shall continue to enjoy that privilege; but, if they should at any time discontinue their issues, they shall then lose that privilege. With this check, and with the frequent publication of the names of the partners, there will, I venture to hope, be sufficient checks imposed upon that class of banks. Besides that, if the Bank of England publishes weekly accounts, all other bankers will from thence know how to regulate their operations; and I doubt whether it may not be expedient to state the *maximum* amount of issue during the week so that bankers and the public may exercise their discretion in applying for further issues of notes or for an exchange of their securities into gold. I have now, I trust, given a full outline of the measure which her Majesty's Government intend to introduce, and the principles upon which that measure is founded. I will not interfere with existing interests, and I do not this evening intend to call upon the house to come to any vote or to express any opinion, and I venture to hope that individual members will consider the whole of the subjects brought forward before they pronounce any opinion upon a question so extensive and important, either for or against the proposition now laid before them. In the course of to-morrow I intend to put the house in possession of the correspondence which has taken place beween the Government and the Bank of England on this subject. Hon. members will there see more minutely detailed the principles on which this measure has been prepared; and they will likewise see in that correspondence a full justification of the terms which we have made with the Bank of England. This information is, I maintain it, necessary to a formation of sound opinions respecting the important measure which the Government have felt it their duty to submit to the consideration of Parliament. I do not deny that if these principles be assented to, that assent will be to me a great personal gratification. A quarter of a century has passed away since I first brought forward that great measure which for ever abolished the system, according to which the issue of bank-notes was then conducted. To me it will, therefore be a source of great personal gratification if I now succeed in inducing the house to agree to a measure calculated to give additional stability to that which Parliament adopted in the year 1819, and to prevent those fluctuations so dangerous to commercial enterprise. But my gratification will be of a much higher and purer description than any satisfaction of a merely personal kind if I should be fortunate enough to have contributed in any material degree to prevent a recurrence of those calamities which at different intervals have marked the last 20 years, such as the panics which occurred in 1826, 1834, and 1839. When I see the danger arising from the Bank of England having recourse to foreign establishments; when I look at the fluctuations which have taken place in our currency, defeating all the calculations upon which commercial enterprise could rest; when I look at the details of the failure of joint-stock banks; when I remember the amount of the dividends paid; and when I know that that amount is no test of the suffering and anxieties of the humbler classes who have been connected with them; when I see joint-stock banks paying their dividends after long and tedious processes; when I remember the number of £10 and £20 original shareholders; when I recollect the ruin which they have occasioned—into the details of which I will not now enter—my gratification will be at the highest and purest kind, if I prevail on the house to adopt a measure that will give steadiness to the character of our resources, which will inspire confidence in the circulating medium, which will diminish all inducements to fraudulent speculation and gambling, and shall ensure its just reward to commercial enterprise, conducted with honesty, and secured by prudence.

ODE.

"Is it peace?"—2 KINGS, ix.

"That is the question."—SHAKSPEARE.

[FOR THE COLONIAL MAGAZINE.]

Upon my ear from far
Strange sounds confus'dly jar,
Which of some unshap'd ill inform;
Like a weird woman's wail,
Or mutterings of the gale
Before the storm:
An angry swell, it comes anear;
And now I hear
Its accents—"War! war! war!"

A little island of the southern sea
(Aye may that wave Pacific be!)
A gentle queen did sway,
Whom Albion's sons had taught the better way
Of Christ, and his true faith:
And she, (such bias hath

On simple minds the sense of benefit)
Were it for soul or kingdom that she car'd,
To her good teachers still repair'd;
Still sought their counsel, and still follow'd it.

But other strangers there were brought;
And they with force and wile
Stirr'd her weak ire,—then on her wrought
To cede her ocean isle:
They seiz'd it in the French king's name,
And spread the Frenchman's oriflamme.
A fugitive on her own ground,
To British refuge straight she hied
And where a British bark did ride,
Pomare asylum found.

Say, did a British subject wrong
To harbour the distrest?
The weak to shelter 'gainst the strong,
And bid in hope to rest?
Or was it in Pomare a crime
To cheer her chiefs, and bide her time?
Such conquest soldiers sham'd:
The victors for their meed were blam'd,
And France the plunder'd crown disclaim'd:
Yet her vain officers, the while,
Would lord it o'er the vanquish'd isle;
And seized, their ardour high to fan,
A consul and an Englishman;
Proclaiming that, if Frenchman fell in fray,
His English blood should pay.

Britain the lion-heart! Britain the free!
Oak-ribb'd Britannia, queen of the sea!
Dost thou sleep? dost thou sleep?
No; buckler'd and helmeted, lance in hand,
She sits on her rock on the ocean's strand,
The watcher of the deep;
And a tranquil eye doth keep,
Altho' the buccanier's rude stroke
Might fretful spleen provoke.
The lion, if a fly his mane hath skaken,
Doth not in wrath awaken;
Though if the tiger's striped might assail,
His grim crest will not quail.
Albion hath a nobler heart
Than to play the blust'rer's part
And gentler course hath taken.
Her valiant neighbour, courteous as strong,
Will sure atone the wrong:
Too just one act of rapine to allow,
Trust to her justice now:
Nor jealous honour will deny,
That noblest pledge of amity.

Frenchmen! We hold your right hand still.
Frenchmen! We bear you all good-will.
We know you brave of old;
Our valour too is told;
Think us not then less bold—
We would embrace you, not your red blood spill.
First of the world, we would in league advance—
England with France:
We treasure her good-will:
Her friendship prize—yet still
To keep our friend, we must be circumspect
Our honour to respect:
But oh! be banish'd far
Honour's last champion—War.

Hark to those sounds again !
But now in softer strain
The menace of their tone subsides,
And music's voice alone abides,
In sweet and slow decrease
And like the diapason of the blast
That hath o'er harp-strings pass'd,
It gently dies away.
Yet, as in words, those parting whispers say,
"Peace ! Peace !"

August, 16, 1844. C J C.

REVIEWS OF NEW BOOKS.

ART. I.—*Rambles in Germany and Italy, in* 1840-42-43. By Mrs. SHELLEY. London: Moxon, Dover Street. 2 vols. 8vo.

This is not a tour in search of the picturesque by a devotee of art, or a copyist of nature's most playful smiles—it is an inspection of the social, literary, and moral condition, of ancient and celebrated kingdoms of Europe, *now* moss-grown and ivy-clad, and decayed at the core, in which the writer passed some three or four entire years. Sufficient time has, therefore, been appropriated to the project, and very sufficient talents, accompanied besides by a liberality of sentiment calculated to render her volumes politically useful, especially as it is connected by a style of composition feeling, finished, and forcible. Mrs. Shelley's work possesses more than a passing interest; the pleasantness of her narrative will ensure popularity; her philosophical and political strictures will fix public attention, both here and on the continent. So soon as her sentiments shall have become diffused amongst the enslaved descendants of the Bruti and the Gracchi, conscience will be released from bondage. The descriptive passages or chapters are full of charms, both of composition and observation; but they excite admiration of the author herself, rather than of her subject, the field she rambles over having been the scene of so many agreeable rambles before her time. These, therefore, although some of the most delightful reading, we pass over, for what is more solid and serviceable to the improvement of commerce, and to the political condition of the Italians, on which alone the extension of commerce necessarily depends. And on these considerations Mrs. Shelley has thrown much light, indulged freely in observations of the utmost value, and evinced a discrimination and judgment, which some had dared to doubt whether her sex possessed.

Alluding to the prospect of amelioration in the Austrian States, she writes—

I wish I could see a few Carbonari; but I have no opening for making acquaintance—I should like to know how the Milanese feel towards their present government. Since the death of one of the most treacherous and wicked tyrants that ever disgraced humanity—the Emperor Francis *—the Austrian government has made show of greater moderation. As the price of the restoration of Ancona by the French, the exiles were permitted to return. While we were at Como, we had seen the honoured and noble Gonfalonieri, returned from Spielberg, the shadow of a man; his wife no more—his life withered, as a glorious exotic transported to the North, nipped by frosts it was never born to feel. In commerce, also, the Austrian is trying to improve. A railroad is projected to Venice—a portion of it is already constructed They are endeavouring to revive trade, as much as it can be revived in a country where two-thirds of the produce of taxation is sent out of it; and it may be guessed what a drooping, inert revival it is. But the curious thing about the policy of present arbitrary goverments is the encouragement they give to the education of the poor. Even the Emperor Nicholas, we are told, desires to educate the serfs. From whatever motive this springs, we must cling to it as a real blessing, for the most extensive advantages must result to the cause of civilization from the enlightenment, however partial and slight, of the multitude. Knowledge must, from its nature, grow, and rooting it out can alone prevent its tendency to spread.

We ought, however, to consider one thing in the establishment of the normal schools by Austria.

---

* It is enough to refer to M. Andryane's account of his imprisonment in the fortress of Spielburg to justify these words. The barbarities of fabled tyrants fall far short of the cold-blooded tortures imagined and inflicted by this despot.

To our shame be it spoken, the education of the poor is far more attended to in Germany than with us. In Prussia, Wurtemberg, and, above all, in Saxony, the normal schools are admirable. Austria was forced to appear to do the like; and they do so in a way which they hope will increase and consolidate their power. Government allows no schools but its own; and selects teachers, not as being qualified for the task, but as servile tools in their hands. The books they allow can scarcely be guessed at in this country, so totally void are they of instruction or true religion. The Austrian hopes to bring up the new generation in the lights he gives, and to know no more than he teaches. He has succeeded, and will probably long continue to succeed in Austria, but in Italy he will not. If the physical state of the poor in Lombardy is ameliorated, they will be tranquil; but hatred of the stranger must ever be a portion of the air he breathes.

It is against the rich and high-born, however, that the Austrian wages war. A hatred of the German is rooted in the nobility of Milan; they are watched with unsleeping vigilance: above all, the greatest care is taken that their youth should not receive an enlightened education. From the moment a young man is known to hold himself free from the prevalent vices of the times, to be studious and high-minded, he becomes marked; he is not allowed to travel; he is jealously watched; no career is open to him; he is hemmed in to a narrow and still narrower circle; till at last the moss of years and hopelessness gathers over and deadens his mind For the present governments of Italy know that there is a spirit abroad in that country, which forces every Italian that thinks and feels, to hate them and rebel in his heart.

Again, as to the adoption of free trade, and its apparent effects on the quondam queen of Eastern commerce—

When I was here last, the duties on all imports to Venice were high, living became expensive, and the city languished;—it is now a free port; everything enters without paying the slightest toll, with the exception of tobacco. The Emperor of Austria grows a wretched plant, to which he gives this name, on his paternal acres, and will not allow his subjects to smoke anything else. If that were the only misdeed of his government, I should not quarrel with him, but only with the people, who do not thereon forego the idle habit of cigars altogether.

The free port gives a far greater appearance of life and activity to the city than it formerly had; and some luxuries—such as Turkish coffee, and, indeed, all things from the East, are much better and cheaper than with us. To the Venetians, coffee stands in lieu of wine, beer, spirits, every exciting drink, and they obtain it in perfection at a very low price. The Austrian is doing what he can to revive trade, so to increase his store; for two thirds of the taxes of the Regno Lombardo-Veneto go to Vienna. He desires that railroads should be made, and one is being constructed from Milan to Venice. Nay, they are in the act of building a bridge for the railroad carriages from Mestre to the centre of the city; however convenient, it is impossible not to repine at this innovation; the power, the commerce, the arts of Venice are gone, the bridge will rob it of its romance.

For one other extract we must find space—its prophetic character entitles it to notice; and, coinciding in the sentiments it conveys, we desire to see them recorded for reference at the day of fulfilment, as well as for the purpose of marking our respect for them unequivocally. The author thinks, rightly enough, that the doom of the triple crown is sealed, that the rays of liberty have pierced the mists under which the anomalous papal rule has contrived to escape unscathed amidst partitioning of kingdoms, and she has briefly, yet fully, described the grounds of these her Just conclusions,—

"The Pope and his prelates, alone, are invested with political, legislative, and administrative authority, and constitute the state. From education and from system they are despotic, and repel every liberal notion, every social progress. The people pay and obey: all the offices, all the employments, great and small, are in the hands of the clergy. From the Pope to the lowest priestly magistrate, all live on the public revenues, whence springs a system of clients, which existing principally in Rome, yet extends over the whole of the papal dominions, and creates a crowd of dependants devoted to the clergy. Corruption is the mainspring of the State, which rests on the cupidity which the absence of all incentive to, or compensation for, honest labour inspires: yet nearly all are poor, and poorest is the Head of the whole; who, shrinking from all improvement, fearful if the closed valves were opened, he should admit in one rushing stream, with industry and knowledge, rebellion, yet finds that the fresh burdens which his necessities cause him to impose on the people fail to increase his revenue.

The Romans, themselves, submit without repining, their state has existed, such as it is, for centuries; the abode of the Pope and concourse of strangers enrich—the church ceremonies amuse them. But out of Rome the cry has been loud, and will be repeated again and again. The Marches bordering the Adriatic, Romagna, and the four legations, (four cities, each governed by a Cardinal legate,) suffer evils comparatively new to them; and the memory of better days incites them to endeavour to recover their former independence These states formed, it is true, a portion of the pontifical dominions before the French revolution; but they existed then on a different footing, and enjoyed privileges of which they are now deprived. Bologna in especial considers herself aggrieved.

ART. II.—*Our Indian Empire.* By CHARLES MACFARLANE, Esq. Vol. I. Part II. London: Charles Knight.

The more we read of this readable work, the better we like it; "increase of appetite grows by what it feeds on." Without the least abatement from the pleasant, popular, style in which the author commenced his useful history, he has become even more diligent in searching after the best authorities, and equally cautious in following them. The Part before us opens with the government of Lord Moira, afterwards Marquis of Hastings, a man who inherited a princely fortune from his accomplished mother, acquired a second by marriage, succeeded to a third in India, and was always professing to economise, yet somehow or other, like the respected old lady in Goldsmith's memorable story, he never grew richer. We do not quarrel with the author, for his admiration of Lord Moira's character, for he was certainly passing honest as a statesman; but how can he call a man "*high-minded*," who truckled with the Nabob of Oude for the musnud, a fact which Mr. MacFarlane himself condemns, as below the dignity of the position he occupied. Still, and notwithstanding his squeezing of the nabob, a decidedly Chinese practice, and some other exceedingly painful facts that detract from his character, Lord Moira's government was creditable to himself, decidedly humane, and beneficial to the Company's interests.

In the midst of seriousness, mirth occasionally intrudes; nor does the contrast prove unwelcome—the transition relieves, if it does not always gratify—and gives a *locus* to look back from, and arrange our chronology. Of this character is the somewhat romantic story of Trimbukjee's escape from captivity, through the courage and fidelity of a follower. It reminds us of the discovery of Richard the Third's place of confinement on the banks of the Danube:—

As soon as these horrible circumstances came to the knowledge of the Hon. Mountstuart Elphhinstone, our resident at Poonah, he insisted that Trimbukjee should be given up; and as the general voice of the Mahratta people backed the demand, the Peishwa, Bajee Rao, found himself under the necessity of yielding. Trimbukjee was arrested, and thrown into the strong fortress of Tanna, on the island of Salsette, not far from Bombay. But his imprisonment was not of long duration. A common-looking Mahratta groom, with a good character in his hand, came to offer his services to the English commandant of the fort. He was accepted. The stable where he had to attend his horse was close under the window of Trimbukjee's prison. He was observed to pay more than usual attention to his steed, and to have a habit, while currying and cleaning him, of singing snatches of Mahratta songs. At length, in December, 1816, Trimbukjee disappeared from his dungeon, and both horse and groom from the stable. And now it was recollected that the groom's singing had been made up of verses something like the following—

"Behind the bush the bowmen hide,
  The horse beneath the tree;
Where shall I find a knight will ride
  The jungle paths with me?

There are five-and-fifty coursers there,
  And four and-fifty men;
When the fifty-fifth shall mount his steed,
  The Deccan thrives again!"*

The history proceeds to detail, with conspicuous regard to truth, and with a laudable impartiality, the sanguinary conflicts called the Mahratta and Pindarree wars; the desperate onslaughts that occurred in reducing Apa Saheb; and the inhuman, almost incredible barbarities of the Cingalese campaign. Crushed by the powerful arm of Britain, obliged to yield a reluctant assent to her humane and prudent laws, and terror-stricken by the example of those who dared to persevere in checking our ambition, the seiks, and nabobs, and kings of the Hindooland, laid their robes and their sceptres at Lord Hastings' feet, and he had the honour and happiness of seeing Central India in the enjoyment of comparative repose, before he resumed the rank of a private man, and embarked for that land which he was never to see again:—

The reputation of the British in India has never stood higher than at the conclusion of the Pindarree and Mahratta war; and during the four remaining years of Lord Hastings' government the face of Central India was changed to an extent which would have appeared almost incredible to any one who had not contemplated upon the spot the rapid progress of the change, and studied the causes by which it was produced. No war had begun in a higher motive, or had ended in a more positive good to mankind. "The campaign which had just terminated," says Malcolm, "was not an attack upon a state, or upon a body of men, but upon a system. It was order contending against anarchy; and the first triumph was so complete, that there ceased, almost from the moment, to be any who cherished hopes of the contest being either prolonged or revived; the victory gained was slight, comparatively speaking, over armies, to what it was over mind. The universal distress, which a series of revolutions must ever generate, had gone its circle, and reached all ranks and classes. The most barbarous of those who subsisted on plunder had found that a condition of continued uncertainty and alarm could not be one of enjoyment.

* Bishop Heber, Indian Journal. "This," adds the Bishop, "might have been a stratagem of the Scottish border,—so complete a similarity of character and incident does a resemblance of habit and circumstance produce among mankind."

The princes, chiefs, and inhabitants of the country had neither national feelings, confidence in each other, nor any one principle of union. When, therefore, the English Government, too strong to be resisted, proclaimed every district to be the right of its proprietor, on condition of his proving himself the friend of peace and good order; and when men found that the choice between such a course, and that of contin ing the promoters of anarchy, was an option between its friendship or hostility, all concurred in submission. There appeared in a few a difficulty to conquer habits, but in none a spirit of opposition The desolated state of the country was favourable to the change, for it presented an ample field for the revival of industry in peaceful occupations; but the paramount influence which the results of the war gave to the British Government over several of the native states, was the principal cause of that peace and prosperity which ensued. Our officers were enabled to give shape and direction to the efforts of these states, which became an example to others; and a tone of improvement was given to every province of Central India."*

ART. III.—*A Grammatical and Etymological Spelling-Book.* By J. HEARD. Houlston and Stoneman, Paternoster-Row.

The elementary mode of instruction suggested by Mr. Heard, in this little work, is deserving of attention from every teacher, and as every parent is *ex officio* a member of that profession, its interest is extended in proportion. It is quite certain—an acknowledged fact—that Spelling-Books in general are employed as an exercise for the memory, the *mind* being left out of consideration; and therefore it is that parrots and monkeys, and other grades of the creation, inferior to man, but possessing memory and a peculiar formation of the organs of voice, may be also taught through the medium of such treatises. There can be no objection to the education of such animals, but surely a system suited to them must be unequal in applicability, in extent of usefulness, in real character, to one worthy of the powers of the human intellect. This appears to have been the author's conviction, and in these few pages before us, he has adopted a system in which, from the first moment of the development of the infant mind, its faculties will be exercised, insensibly, and with facility, in learning our native language analytically. Spelling-books are generally arranged according to the number of syllables in each word—in 'Heard's,' the *roots* (monosyllables) are collected into one division; this section of substantives is followed by another of adjectives—a third, of primitive verbs; all with simple definitions.—The pupil who has been taught on this system, becomes gradually, instructed in the primitive, radical, essential terms of the language, from which all others are formed,—of which they are only modifications,—and, consequently, having learned the meaning of the root, he can guess, or say certainly, how to spell and what is the explanation of the compound.

We shall be glad to see the plan universally adopted, and, while Mr. Heard strongly recommends its introduction in schools of mutual instruction, (the worst in the world, and only justified by necessity,) we hope to see it used wherever languages are taught.

ART. IV.—*The Sequential System of Musical Notation.* By ARTHUR WALRIDGE. London: Simpkin, Marshall, & Co.

We refer the reader to our former notice of this new method of notation, for an explanation of its professions—in the publication now before us will be found its practice. Influenced by the theories of Rousseau, the author has boldly attempted to root out old prejudices, to subdue our bigotry to long-established systems, and induce us to adopt a "more universal language in this art of music." The sequential system avoids the complicated part of the present notation, parts which not one in a thousand knows anything about, and extending his views much beyond Rousseau, whose system only applied to the performance of simple airs, presents a perfect mode by which the most difficult pieces may be written, understood, and executed. Those who have ambition and adventure enough to make themselves masters of this invention, will find the undertaking less difficult than the Arabic appearance of the symbols might induce them to suspect; and the combination of letter-press directions and of illustrative plates, in the last edition of the author's work, discloses all the mysteries of the mode in a clear and intelligible manner. Although prejudice, bigotry, and personal interest, will struggle strenuously and in co-operation, to exclude the Sequential system from immediate popularity, they will not be powerful enough to interrupt the favour of the discerning and the educated classes of society.

* Memoir of Central India.

COLONIAL INTELLIGENCE.

India.—The dates from India and China by the overland mail are from Calcutta, June 7th; Ceylon, May 31st. China:—Macao, April 21st; Chusan, April 8th; Hong-Kong, April 24th; Delhi, June 8th; Lahore, May 29th; Madras, June 8th; Manilla, March 20th; Scinde, May 31st and June 4th; Singapore, May 19th. The London mail of May 6th reached Bombay, per *Victoria* steamer, the 6th of June

The news brought from India by the Bombay mail of the 19th of June is of considerable interest.

The intelligence from the Punjaub represents that country in as disturbed a state as ever. Dhulop Singh, the boy-king, has been dangerously ill of the small-pox; and his prime minister and his mother, yet a young woman, are said to have been discovered intriguing, to the great dissatisfaction of the Sikh troops, who rule in that country, and wait but an occasion to create another revolution to their own profit. The defeat and death of Ittur Singh, and Cashmeera Singh, who attempted to upset the power of Heera Singh, has for a time consolidated the power of the prime minister. Peshora Singh, who fled from the battle, and surrendered himself a prisoner, was said to have been killed; this report excited the Sikh soldiers, who were not pacified until the prisoner was shown to them. The utmost care was taken on the British frontiers to prevent any collision with the Sikhs; but as yet no satisfaction has been given for their invasion of the British territories after the defeat of Uttur Singh. The report respecting the assembling of a large army on the Sutlej had died away, although some warlike preparations were making, such as the collection of camels in Scinde, and of military stores at Ferozepore. It is well to be prepared, for if the popular stories are to be believed, the Sikhs are anxious for an opportunity of invading India, and plundering its wealthy towns, and of course measuring arms with the British troops.

The state of Scinde is satisfactory, and promises to become much more so. One of the chief sources of curiosity subsequent to the departure of the last mail from Bombay for Europe, was the meeting of the Beloochee chiefs at Hydrabad. The meeting was convoked by the orders of Lord Ellenborough, and, under the careful arrangements of Sir Charles Napier, passed over quietly. There is no doubt that the inhabitants of Scinde have begun to feel the benefit of a good and regular government. Their property is secured to them, "if they are peaceable and do not intrigue against the British Government." The cultivators of the soil are not subject to the former cruel exactions, and they are allowed a full scope for their industry. The population of the banks of the Indus does not now amount to a tithe of those who in ancient times cultivated its soil. The system of the Ameers depopulated the country, and rank vegetation is consequently luxuriating there, and causing a malaria destructive of life. Some time must be required to accustom the inhabitants to the present government, and then they will increase and multiply the products which a most fertile soil can bear, and the country will become healthful, as it formerly was.

The great assembly of Beloochees at Hydrabad, on the 24th of May, had several objects:—To cause all these wild chiefs to make their allegiance personally. To try the fealty of the chiefs, and see if they really felt confidence in the Government, and would obey orders. To show them that the Government had confidence in them, and had no fear or distrust of them. To hear all complaints or represeutations that existed. All these points enabled the Governor to form a general guess at the temper of the Beloochee population. About 20,000 people were supposed to have been collected. All were orderly in the extreme. They were kept divided, as caution was necessary. There was some sickness in Scinde, arising from the heats, but not more than in other well-known parts of India. Exposure to the sun had produced the deaths of fourteen men of the 86th regiment, and of some women and children.

Sir Charles Napier was at Kurrachee in the beginning of June—a strong proof that nothing of striking importance was dreaded which could demand his presence in any part of that province.

There was some excitement in the Cabinet of Gwalior in consequence of the orders of the Supreme Government to take possession of the flourishing Mahratta town of Boorhanpore, and to imprison the father of the young Queen Dowager of Gwalior, Tara Baee, as he was supposed to be involved in certain intrigues; but those orders were countermanded after an explanation, and all was peace and tranquillity there.

The abrupt recall of Lord Ellenborough had produced a great sensation at Bombay, from which place alone intelligence has reached us. It was not known there what course Lord Ellenborough intended to adopt. The news of the recall is supposed to have reached him on the 14th or 15th, and he might desire the *Bentinck*, then on the point of starting for Suez, to wait a few hours for him. It was supposed by others that his Lordship would await the arrival of Sir Henry Hardinge.

There was a severe storm in Calcutta on the 18th of May, and a slight one at Madras on the 3d of June. The rainy season had set in at different places, but without strong gales or heavy fall. An expectation prevailed amongst the natives of the rains being late but abundant.

At Calcutta exchange has fluctuated very little, 1*s*. 11⅝*d*. to 1*s*. 11½*d*. being the rate, at which a large amount has been sold. Freights without any material alteration.

At Bombay trade is dull. Freights have slightly given way, and may be quoted for London and Liverpool at 2*l*. 15*s*., at 3*l*. for first-class ships, and 2*l*. 10*s*. second class; China at rs. 14 per candy.

Government securities have slightly advanced. Exchange on England firm. Six months' bills at 1*s*. 10½*d*. to 1*s*. 10¾*d*. per rupee; bills at 30 days' sight at 1*s*. 10*d*. On Calcutta, at 30 days' sight, rs. 100¼. On Madras, at sight, rs. 100½. On China, at 60 days', rs. 214 per 100 dollars.

CHINA.—The *Canton Press*, of the 16th of March, says, "On Monday last some Manilla seamen, belonging to a Swedish ship at anchor at Whampoa, had a quarrel with the Chinese, who began to pelt them with stones, upon which the Manilla men charged the mob, and, it is said, stabbed a Chinese. The mob, however, after having been dispersed in the first instance, soon returned, and threw stones at the seamen in the company's garden, and the latter had to take to their boat. As usual in such cases, the mob then assembled in front of the factories in formidable numbers, and some apprehensions were entertained that they might proceed to violence, but a detachment of police and soldiers was sent by the authorities from the city, and the mob was dispersed soon after dark without having done any damage. Her Majesty's consul had meanwhile, we understand, sent to Whampoa for assistance, and in consequence about 200 men from the ships arrived in boats early next morning, at which time, however, we are happy to say, everything had returned to its wonted quiet.

The China authorities were disposed to act with perfect good faith towards the British, and it was even said that the Emperor was about to make arrangements whereby the trade in opium would be legalised.

The accounts of the state of the markets differ but little from those last received. For opium there was a better demand at Macao. The drug at Shanghae was declining rapidly. The bills on London at six months' sight, under credit from Baring, Brothers, and Co., have been negotiated at 4*s*. 4*d*. to 4*s*. 4½*d*., but the rate is soon likely to be at 4*s*. 3*d*., perhaps 4*s*. 2*d*. On Calcutta; Sir H. Pottinger is still drawing at 30 days' sight, at 222 rs. for 100 Mexican dollars, which rate continues during the present month, after which the rate, it is supposed, will again be fixed for another month.

Freight to London continues as before, 3*l*. per 50 cubic feet, and tonnage abundant.

An amended translation of the Chinese treaty has been published, which shows that we have stipulated for something more or something less than we intended; and great blame has been cast upon Sir Henry Pottinger for so great an oversight. The upshot is, that we find the island of Hong-kong, as our main commercial depôt, considerably less valuable and important than we conceived it to be.

THE FALKLAND ISLANDS.—The following has been received at Lloyd's:—"Downing-street, August 9th.—Sir, I am directed by Lord Stanley to inform you, that in consequence of the superior advantages of Port William, in the Falkland Islands, over Port Louis, the Governor has been authorized to remove the site of the principal town, which had been originally fixed at the latter, to Port William. By a despatch recently received, it appears that the removal has been effected, and that the Governor expected to be able to transfer his residence to Port William before the 30th of June last. (Signed) G. W. Hope.—Mr. W. Dobson, Secretary, Lloyd's."

NEW SOUTH WALES.—The first session of the first legislative assembly of New South Wales closed its sittings on the 28th of December last. The famous Pfandbrief bill, which, after having undergone the fullest discussion by the council and the press, was, in the face of the most solid and unanswerable objections, read a third time and passed.

From official returns laid before the Legislative Council of New South Wales, we gather that the population on the 30th September, 1843, amounted to 164,026 souls, of whom 102,447 were males, and

61,579 females. The proportion of females to males since the discontinuance of transportation has made rapid advances, which progressive correction of "the great moral blot" on the social constitution of New South Wales, should alone be considered equivalent to any pecuniary loss caused by the discontinuance of the importation of convict labour.

The export of horses to India from Sydney may now be considered a safe speculation, if the data be correct, and which there seems to be no reason to question. A return laid before the Legislative Council of Sydney shows that there are 56,000 horses in that colony, and in consequence of the excess of supply beyond any existing demand, really good horses can be obtained at 10*l.* a head, which would probably realise in India 60*l.* a head.

It appears that the quantity of coals exported from Sydney, New South Wales, during the year ending 6th of January, 1844, to the United States and British North America, amounted to 47,926 chaldrons; the total imports during that period amounted to 53,360*l.*, and the exports to 75,182*l.*

The Sydney wheat market for the week ending January 13th, was fully supplied from the interior. Prices ranged from 3*s.* 6*d.* to 4*s.* for prime samples.

For flour there has of late been no demand except for immediate consumption. Fine flour is selling at 20*s.* per 200 lbs. cash. Seconds at 16*s.*

The 2lb fine loaf is still at 3d. Recent copious rains have removed all uncertainty as to the forthcoming crops of maize, and the holders of last year's growth are pushing it into the market at 1*s.* 6*d.* to 1*s.* 9*d.* per bushel, whilst the retailers are asking 2*s.* to 2*s.* 6*d.* only, and there is no prospect of any advance. Of barley there is a good supply, but the inquiry is languid, although the quality good. The wholesale prices quoted are 1*s.* 6*d.* to 1*s.* 10*d.*, and the retail 2*s.* to 2*s.* 6*d.*

Oats, which are plentiful but small and light, sell at 1*s.* 4*d.* to 1*s.* 8*d.* wholesale, and 2*s.* to 2*s.* 3*d.* retail.

The carcase butchers' prices for well-conditioned beasts are 25*s.* to 35*s.* each, and 45*s.* or upwards for large prime bullocks. The supply within a few miles of the city was fully equal to the demand. —*Sydney Herald.*

We are glad to find it stated in the Sydney papers that, "whatever may be the present position of New South Wales, the time must shortly come when, as a field of investment, it will present numberless and renewed attractions, and as a seat of commerce, operations the most extensive and extraordinary."

Hobart Town.—Hobart Town papers of the 8th of April have come to hand, but they contain no news of importance. The bushrangers were troublesome to the sheep-farmers, though a good look-out was kept upon them. The wheat markets were well supplied with grain, and prices ruled from 3*s.* 6*d.* to 4*s.* per bushel. The figure accepted for the commissariat supplies had not transpired.

South Australia. — The following statistics of the colony are taken from the *Royal South Australian Almanac*, published February, 1844, and consists of 300 printed pages of matter, which must have been procured at great labour and expense.

To begin with the population, the general results are as follows:—

Male adults in the Colony	5516
Female adults	3991
Male children	3636
Female children	3373
Total	16516

Of these 4,820 are resident in Adelaide, and 1,314 in the villages within the Municipality, leaving for the country districts 11,382.

The land under cultivation in the province is divided into districts, and the name of every cultivator or proprietor is given, but the general results are as follows:—

	Acres.
Wheat	23286
Barley	3272
Oats	667
Garden	615
Other crops	1080
Fallow	513
Total	29433

In these returns, the coincidence with the government ones is very striking, there being but a difference of 743 acres, and of which 513 acres in our returns are land lying fallow.

The return of the Commissioner of Crown Lands up to Sept. 5th, 1843, was as follows:—

Sheep, including weaned lambs	249732
Cattle, above six months old	18945
Horses, above six months	788

To this the commissioner appends a note, stating that "this does not approximate to the whole number," either of horses or cattle in the Province; but allowing 30 per cent. as the average annual increase of sheep, he estimates "the probable number of sheep in the Province in November last at 331,000."

The results as exhibited in the returns and tables compiled for the Almanac, however, are as follows:—

Sheep of every description	402187
Cattle	30018
Horses	1693
Pigs	6354
Goats	2680

The following statement, showing the amount of the Ordinary Revenue, and of the Expenditure of South Australia, for each Quarter, from October 17th, 1838, to December 31st, 1843, has been published by his Excellency, for general information:—

	Revenue exclusive of Land Fund.			Expenditure.		
1838.	£	s.	d.	£	s.	d
From 17th Oct. to 31st Dec.	1448	1	7	2058	14	2
1839.						
QUARTER ENDING						
31st March	4118	0	1	8954	6	8
30th June	4375	6	7	16204	7	10
30th September	5637	16	2	33461	17	3
31st December	5694	19	4	34291	15	9
	19826	2	2	92912	17	6
1840.						
31st March	7371	5	4	30114	6	0
30th June	8142	10	3	36557	4	7
30th September	7272	18	6	43139	14	6
31st December	7413	0	10	60155	14	4
	30199	14	11	169966	19	5
1841						
31st March	8195	15	11	51638	12	6
30th June	7748	6	2	20985	19	1
30th September	5402	9	5	16243	2	9
31st December	5374	4	5	15603	18	4
	26720	15	11	104471	12	8
1842.						
31st March	6320	5	8	17021	10	5
30th June	5727	14	8	14869	4	3
30th September	5449	16	3	11058	10	9
31st December	4576	7	11	11495	1	10
	22074	4	6	54444	7	3
1843.						
31st March	7786	6	11	8974	5	7
30th June	4749	19	4	7232	8	5
30th September	6734	10	4	6926	19	8
31st December	4871	18	7	6659	2	10
	24142	15	2	29842	16	6

WESTERN AUSTRALIA.—Amongst all the discussions of the political economists of Western Australia the subject of labour and immigration seems to be best understood; it is here they descend from their lofty imaginings and grapple with unsophisticated facts. The committee of the Legislative Council, after a very careful consideration of the disadvantages under which the settlers and cultivators are painfully progressing for want of willing and satisfied labourers (of whom there is evidently a lamentable scarcity amongst them), have published a report, from which the other Colonists might borrow perspicuity and other useful qualities in the compilation of future declarations having reference to any want of labour in the market;—

We copy the following "progress of invention in Western Australia" from the *Swan River News and Western Australian Chronicle* of July 1st.—"We are glad to find that, while a spirit of persevering industry is pushing on in the beaten track, a companion-spirit of enterprise and ingenuity is exploring the by-paths of science, and rendering them accessible to the colonists of Western Australia, and available to their purposes. There are clear heads as well as strong arms in the colony, and they are busy in mechanical exploration, giving additional combinations of strength and power to facilitate its progress. A Mr. Alfred Carson, not many months since, exhibited a plough of his invention, which combined many advantages. by which the prize was gained in the ploughing match of 29th Sep., and for which a silver medal was awarded to the inventor by the Agricultural Society. Mr. Carson's prolific invention next produced what he designated an Eolian wheel, or forge-blower, which Mr. Samuel Moore has described as throwing Clark's patent blower completely into the shade. In three months after this, we again heard of Mr. Carson as the inventor of a new steam engine, which combined immense power in small space, with simplicity of construction and of operation, and economy of fuel, friction, and expense. While the necessary steps were being taken for securing a patent in England for this invention, Mr. Carson, in conjunction with another settler, has invented a reaping machine which was to be brought out—and probably has been—ere this. This rapid train of discoveries, succeeding each other in the brief space of three months, augurs well for the colony: while it counts among its population inventive genius so prolific as this, it possesses a powerful auxiliary of its own vast resources, and a valuable alleviater of the evils entailed by scarcity of labour and capital."

CAPE OF GOOD HOPE.—Papers which extend to the 2d of June have been received, but bring very little intelligence. The missionaries are said to have exercised much influence upon the natives from the Namacqualand district to the interior, and it seems to be believed that, if properly carried out, commercial intercourse could be established with them, and the soil made profitable and productive. Among the recent improvements introduced at the Cape was the establishment of a weekly mail with the frontier; and for the protection of the coast the long-talked-of light was to be erected on the Agulhas Point, and a breakwater built in Table Bay. The news from Port Natal is that everything is proceeding quietly in that quarter, and the markets are reported to be well and abundantly supplied with provisions. According to a statistical account which appears in these papers, the number of vessels entered inwards during the quarter ending the 5th of April last, was 29, with 5,626 tonnage, while the number entered outwards was 27, with 5,571 tonnage. The imports for the same period were valued at 38,730*l.*, and the exports at 35,654*l.*, the wool shipments representing of the latter item 20,246*l.* The accounts from the frontier by this arrival are less unfavourable as respects the catalogue of depredations by the Caffres.

The return of the trade of Port Elizabeth for the quarter ending the 5th April, shows the value of the goods imported at 38,730*l.*, and the exports at 35,654*l.* The ships inwards amounted to 29, of 5626 tons, and outwards to 27, of 5571 tons. Everything indicates steady improvement, and although it has been slower in its progress than some of our other colonies, it has been subject to no reaction ruinous to individuals, as has been the case in the Australian group. Midshipman Radcliff, and two men of Her Majesty's ship Bittern, had been drowned at Natal, by the cutter upsetting in the act of going ashore at Natal.

West Indies.—The dates by the last arrival from the West Indies are:—Jamaica, 24th; Demerara, 20th; Trinidad, 21st; Barbadoes, 24th; Grenada, 26th; St. Thomas, 31st; and Fayal, August 13th.

In most of the places, the sugar duties bill was a topic of bitter complaint. The Jamaica papers, however, say that one cheering feature in the aspect of colonial affairs was the zeal and energy with which the resident planters had been pushing forward improvements in agriculture. The preparation and manuring of the land, the planting and clearing of canes, and a variety of other matters, were now performed much more economically and effectually on the most extensive plantations. Nor were these improvements confined to the sugar estates. On the coffee properties guano manure was being tried, and as far as the appearance of the trees enabled one to judge, with every chance of success. The advices from the country generally were to the effect that the rains have been abundant. In some districts near the coast, a want of rain has been experienced, but appearances led to the conclusion that there would soon be a fall of water in those places, for it was close and cloudy weather, with little or no wind. A fire had occurred on St. Toolie's estate, in Clarendon. The estate had just finished crop, and the sugar on the premises was destroyed. The reduction of postage throughout the island had taken place, and the working of the altered plan gave considerable satisfaction. The House of Assembly had been further prorogued to the 20th of August next. The yellow fever, accompanied by the black vomit, had made its appearance in the island, and the cases already occurring were fatal.

The first railway ever formed in the British Colonies is about to be constructed in the island of Jamaica, between Kingstown and Spanish Town. The length is twelve miles, though powers have been obtained from the House of Assembly to carry the line some miles further, if the projectors should think it desirable; and from the extraordinary facilities presented by the form of the land on the rich plain which extends from the sea eight or ten miles into the interior, round the greater part of the island, it is not unlikely that it will ultimately be carried much further.

Sugar was scarce at Jamaica, and commanded better prices in consequence of the near approach of the 1st of August, the time of departure for the homeward-bound vessels. The transactions between the 8th and 18th of the month had been at prices varying from 23*s.* 3*d.* to 26*s.* per 100lb.

In the Trinidad Legislative Assembly, the estimates of revenue and expenditure showed a deficiency of 43,109*l.*, the latter being reckoned at 82,236*l.*, and the former at 39,126*l.* To meet the difficulty it had been determined to increase the import duty on specified and unspecified articles to such an extent as to leave no greater sum than 1,064*l.* to be provided for, which it was considered would be amply made up by increased exportation, the present estimates being based on the returns of 1843. The new tariff would not come into operation before the beginning of October next, and it is stated that, notwithstanding the increase alluded to, the scale of duties at Trinidad is much lower than those of the other colonies. The announcement of the consent of Her Majesty's Government to the immediate introduction of English criminal law and trial by jury had been received with much satisfaction by the colonists.

The weather in Demerara, Barbadoes, and the other principal islands, is described as favourable for the crops, though in certain districts there are the usual complaints of the effects of the dry or the wet, as the case may be. In Demerara it was expected the heat would produce sickness. The Roman Catholic squabble is magnified by the editor of the *Guiana Times*, and dilated upon at much length.

Antigua and St. Kitt's.—At eleven o'clock on the night of Wednesday, the 17th of July, the island of Antigua was visited by another severe shock of earthquake. By those who were in Antigua when the earthquake took place in February, 1843, it is considered that this last shock was equally severe, though of much shorter duration, and, from its uniformly undulating motion, it did not cause such devastating effects. At the southern extremity of the island, this shock was felt with great violence, and being considered as the forerunner of one more destructive in its consequences, the inhabitants of English Harbour left their houses, the soldiers at Block-house-hill rushed from their barracks, and the sick got out of the hospital: but the confusion and terror thus occasioned, and which were increased by the darkness of the night, soon subsided, and daylight restored English Harbour and the Ridge to their wonted appearance, bustle, and occupation.—Very unfavourable accounts of health at St. Kitt's have been received.

CANADA.—No approach has been yet made to the formation of a properly organised administration by the Governor, but rumours are rife, and anxiety great on the subject. There still continue to be marked indications of the growth of party feeling and religious animosity in Canada. A serious riot had nearly occurred in Montreal, on the occasion of laying the foundation stone of a new church, at which the presence of the Governor was expected. An attempt was made to parade Orange lilies and flags, at which the Roman Catholics took offence. A scuffle ensued, and part of the scafolding giving way, a lady had her leg broken, and several others more or less injured. In addition to this, a desperate affray took place on July 12th, at Drummonsville, Canada West. The report states, that a great concourse of Orangemen had met there, intending to hang the effigy of O'Connell; upon learning which, the Roman Catholic Irish from the Welland Canal became incensed, armed themselves, and went to the scene of the Orange celebration, giving out that they were going "to shoot at a mark."

We received an account of the trial and conviction of the pirates of the Saladin, and we now learn since, that Carr and Galloway, the two men indicted for the murder of Captain Fielding on board the same vessel, were acquitted, though directly against the charge of the court. This Fielding, it will be recollected, was a passenger in the Saladin, and was the instigator of the murder of Captain M'Kenzie, and a principal actor in that tragedy. He himself, with his little son, was afterwards put to death by the crew, and for this act Carr and Galloway were tried and acquitted. The enormity of Fielding's conduct seems to have caused the jury to overlook that of his murderers. The four men convicted, named Anderson, Travasgurs, alias Johnston, George Jones, and Wm. Haselton, were publicly executed at Halifax on the 30th of July.

NEW BRUNSWICK.—We are sorry to have to record an awful conflagration at Harbour Grace, New Brunswick, which destroyed property estimated at more than £30,000. The following is taken from the *St. John's Morning Post.*

"HALIFAX, JUNE 29.—About the hour of nine o'clock, on the night of Wednesday last, the 5th instant, a fire broke out suddenly in the premises adjoining those of Messrs. Thorne, Hooper, and Co., at Harbour Grace, and the wind blowing freshly from the westward, the fearful element, aroused as a giant from his slumber, gathered all its strength for an awful display of its devastating powers. Amongst the heaviest sufferers, and the earliest, were Messrs. Thorne, Hooper, and Co., and Peter Brown, Esq., whose properties were swept entirely away. Houses, stores, oil vats, all fell alike before the march of the insatiable conqueror.

"About half-past two o'clock on Thursday morning the glad tidings were announced that the work of destruction was at an end, and the fire would spread no further, though it continued burning throughout the day, and was far from being extinguished in the afternoon when we left Harbour Grace."

HOME INTELLIGENCE.

THE EAST INDIA TRADE.—A parliamentary return has just been printed showing the amount of our import and export trade with several of the principal colonies of the Crown, with the possessions of the East India Company, the United States of America, and with Mexico and South America, in the year ending January, 1844. The following are some of the principal facts which it exhibits:—The value of the British and Irish goods exported in the year 1843, to the British West Indies, was £2,882,441; to the United States of America, £5,013,504; to the East India Company's Territories and the Island of Ceylon, £6,404,519; to the Mauritius, £258,014; to China, £1,456,180; to the British North American Colonies, £1,751,211; to the Island of Cuba, £624,871; and to Mexico and South America (exclusive of the Brazils), £3,286,327. The most remarkable fact shown in the above list is, the wonderful increase in the India and China trades, which, though both of them still comparatively in their infancy (the former having sprung up since 1815, and the latter since 1832), now surpass the trade with the United States, and supply a vent for goods of the value of nearly eight millions sterling a year. For this increased trade the cuuntry is chiefly indebted to the East India Committees of Liverpool and Glasgow, which spent years in battling against the commercial monoply of the East India Company before they could open the vast regions of India and China to the British Empire. Of the exports to India, in 1843, £3,937,414 worth consisted of cotton goods and yarn, and of those to China, £871,939 worth. Amongst the imports from the latter country, were 42,779,265 pounds of tea, and from the former, 1,099,562 cwts. of sugar.

Dinner to Sir R. Sale and Sir W. Nott.—On Wednesday evening Aug. 14. the Court of Directors of the India Company gave an entertainment in their characteristic style of magnificence and sumptuous hospitality, to celebrate the return to their native land of those two distinguished officers, whose achievements have stood so proudly prominent during the late Affghan war—the former distinguished for his gallant and masterly defence of Jellalabad, and his association with one whose name will live amongst the noblest recollections of female heroism; the other equally conspicuous for great services, and the fortitude, skill and valour which he displayed under the most trying circumstances. Unfortunately, indisposition, the consequence of severe and harassing campaigning, prevented Sir W. Nott from attending, to receive personally the high and flattering compliment which it was intended he should share. Amongst the ladies in the gallery were Ladies Sale and Nott, the former being accompanied by her daughter, Mrs. Sturt. Their presence was hailed with loud and repeated bursts of acclamation; indeed the least allusion to the heroic conduct of the former lady was, during the evening, the signal for renewed plaudits. The dinner took place at the London Tavern.

The chairman of the East India Company presided. — Amongst the distinguished guests we noticed:—the Earl of Ripon, the Earl of Dalhousie, the Earl of Lincoln, Lord G. Somerset, Lord Eliot, Sir R. Peel, Sir G. Murray, Sir E. Knatchbull, the Chancellor of the Exchequer, Sir T. Fremantle, the Lord Mayor, Sir J. Macdonald, Sir R. Campbell, Sir J. Pelley, Lieutenant Peel, R.N., &c.

Arrival of Mr. Pritchard from Tahiti.—We have to announce the unexpected arrival in London of Mr. Pritchard, the British consul at Tahiti, who having been, in flagrant violation of the law of nations, arrested and imprisoned by the French authorities, has obtained his personal liberty, only on condition of immediately quitting the island, not having time allowed him to secure his official papers, or even to bring away his wife and children. By stratagem, and with the assistance of friends, he succeeded in getting off three of his children, who were on another island, and these he has brought home; and his wife and other children he has been compelled to leave at Tahiti under French *protection* and surveillance. The Protectorate grew more and more persecuting and oppressive; many of the chiefs and others of the best people favourable to the Queen were imprisoned, Queen Pomare was herself proscribed, and the English missionaries were marked out as the objects of peculiar hatred and vindictive annoyance. Providentially some British men-of-war arrived and the Queen has now taken refuge on board of one of them, instead of remaining cooped up in a little cutter. Official intelligence of these transactions has been brought by the Vindictive, Captain Nicolas, C.B., which arrived from Valparaiso.

Ocean Steam Navigation.—A paper has been printed and circulated in the city, showing the progress of private enterprise in Ocean Steam Navigation, the facts in which, being presented to the eye at one glance, are interesting, though in an isolated form they have always been accessible. The line of steam communication between England and America was established in 1838 by the "Great Western steam-ship," and maintained by that vessel, the "British Queen," and the unfortunate "President" till 1842, without the support of Government, or any contract for conveying the mails. The line to Halifax and Boston was established by Mr. Cunard, on obtaining a Government contract of 57,000*l.* per annum to convey the mails 186,300 miles. The line to the West Indies was established in 1482 by parties who, in 1840, took a contract for 240,000*l.* per annum to convey the mails 684,816 miles. The line to Malta and Alexandria was established in 1840-1 by the Peninsula Company, who took a contract for 31,000*l.* per annum to convey the mails 72,000 miles. The lines between Calcutta and Suez was established in 1842 by the India Steam Company of Calcutta, but no assistance has been granted by Government for the mails. The line between Calcutta and Suez in 1843 and 1844 was (and is now) occupied by the Peninsula Company's vessels, with a grant of 20,000*l.* per annum for five years from the Indian Government, on condition of their performing 38,080 miles in the first year, 57,120 miles in the second, and 114,200 in the third.

Abdication of Mehemet Ali.—The following important intelligence reached Paris by telegraphic despatch on Tuesday:

"Alexandria, July 27.—His Highness the Viceroy has just suddenly left Alexandria, declaring that he renounces for ever Egypt and public affairs, and that he retires to Mecca. Ibrahim is at Alexandria. The city is quiet."—

Mehemet Ali, one of the most remarkable men of his time—is now an old man, and his retirement from active public life was an event naturally to be expected. Although, as announced, he may retire to "the Holy City," it is likely that he will watch with attention the progress of his son, Ibrahim Pacha, to whom the succession of the Pachalick of Egypt had been secured by the Treaty of 1841. It is worthy of note that this abdication should have occurred so soon after the announcement of the Treaty between Egypt and Great Britain, arranged by Sir Henry Hardinge, on his way to India.

Under present circumstances—the right of the Porte to name a new Pacha having been cut off—the abdication is an event comparatively unimportant. But in a country like Egypt, commanding the overland route to India, and with a ruler of such turbulent dispositions as Ibrahim, it would be hazardous to calculate upon the permanence of that good understanding that now exists, especially in the event of any rupture between France and England.

By the latest intelligence it was stated that Mehemet Ali had returned to Egypt, but his future movements were not known.

Coolie Labourers.—It is understood that her majesty's government have finally resolved to convey a considerable number of Coolie labourers from the ports of Calcutta and Madras, to the colonies of Guiana, Trinidad, and Jamaica. The agents to conduct this emigration have already been appointed, and it is to commence after the first of October next. The ships are to be chartered in India by public tender, in conformity with the provisions of the Passengers' Act, and they will arrive in the colonies at a favourable period for obtaining cargoes for this country, while they will have besides the whole seaboard of America open to them. It is arranged that the emigration of Coolies shall, in the first instance, be limited to 15,000, and of these, 5,000 are allotted to Jamaica.

Pauperism.—The following is an abstract of returns presented to Parliament respecting paupers in Union workhouses in England and Wales. Returns have been received from 486 unions in England, and from 24 in Wales. The number of married paupers in the workhouses of England, on the 30th of March, 1843, "who have been there above five years," was 671, and one in Wales. The number of such paupers in English union workhouses above 50, was 555, and one in Wales. The number of such paupers under 50 years of age was 116 in England, and none in Wales. 58 of such paupers in England (and none in Wales) may be considered able-bodied. There were 5,697 married paupers in the workhouses of England, and 145 in those of Wales, who had been therein less than five years. In England, 2,160 of such paupers had been admitted more than once, 1514 twice, 750 thrice, 361 four times, 161 five times, 87 six times, 69 seven times, 52 eight times, 33 nine times, 21 ten times, 9 eleven times, 22 twelve times, 23 thirteen times, 6 fourteen times, 3 fifteen times, 3 sixteen times, 15 seventeen times, 5 eighteen times, and 12 twenty times and upwards. The numbers for Wales under the same heads, are 53, 37, 11, 2, 3 (five times, and none oftener.) There were 4,799 married male paupers in England, who had "died in the workhouse since the passing of the Poor Law Amendment Act," and 43 in Wales; while there have died 3,271 females in England, and 22 in Wales. The next return relates to absconders. In 332 unions that have sent returns in England and Wales, in 1839, 298 persons were charged with having absconded from within the workhouse, and 2,326 from without the workhouse, leaving their wives and families chargeable to the union; in 1840, the number was 299 from within, and 2,535 from without the workhouse; in 1841, 324 from within, and 2,494 from without the workhouse; in 1842, it had increased to 2451 from within, and 3,709 from without the workhouse; and lastly, in 1843, the number was 447 from within, and 3,600 from without the workhouse (exclusive of the returns from unions and single parishes under local and Gilbert acts.) From those numbers, 4,255 have been apprehended, and 3,864 became re-united to their families without being previously apprehended. Such is an abstract of returns that occupy nearly fifty folio pages of figures.

Foreign Shipping, &c.—A return, containing an account of payments out of the consolidated duties of Customs for the difference of rates and charges due on foreign vessels, &c., has just been printed, having been ordered on the motion of Mr. J. T. Wawn, the member for Tynemouth. It hence appears, that the total amount of monies issued out of the consolidated Customs for the above purposes, (under the act 59th George III., cap. 54) was—in 1820, 9,204*l.*; in 1821, 10,899*l.*; in 1822, 11,583*l.*; in 1823, 9,044*l.*; in 1824, 8,402*l.*; in 1825, 18,729*l.*; in 1826, 30,068*l.*; in 1827, 25,481*l.*; in 1828, 20,450*l.*; in 1829, 25,386*l.*; in 1830, 19,482*l.*; in 1831, 29,792*l.*; in 1832, 23,859*l.*; in 1833, 24,709*l.*; in 1834, 23,701*l.*; in 1835, 25,827*l.*; in 1836, 29,156*l.*; in 1837, 24,288*l.*; in 1838, 25,777*l.*; in 1839, 32,572*l.*; in 1840, 34,313*l.*; in 1841, 31,041*l.*; in 1842, 24,998*l.*; and in 1843, 25,754*l.*

PUBLIC INCOME AND EXPENDITURE.—THE BALANCE SHEET.

An Account of the Net Public Income and Expenditure of the United Kingdom of Great Britain and Ireland in the year ended 5th July, 1844.

Income or Expenditure.	Applicable to Consolid. Fund. £.	s.	d.	Applicable to Other Pub. Ser. £.	s.	d.	Total. £.	s.	d.
Ordinary Revenue									
Customs	18781676	14	2	3000000	0	0	21781676	14	2
Excise	13033467	9	1	....			13033467	9	1
Stamps	7046501	10	10	....			7046501	10	10
Taxes (Land and Assessed)	4197515	19	7	....			4197515	19	7
Property Tax	5247663	19	10	....			5247663	19	10
Post-office	638000	0	0	....			638000	0	0
Crown Lands	145000	0	0	....			145000	0	0
1s. 6d. and 4s. in the £. on Pensions and Salaries	5216	19	3	....			5216	19	3
Small Branches of the Hereditary Revenues of the Crown	33759	7	10	....			33759	7	10
Surplus Fees of Regulated Public Offices	53865	16	8	....			53865	16	8
	49182667	17	3	3000000	0	0	52182667	17	3
Other Receipts.									
Money from China under the Treaty of August, 1842	184802	7	8				184802	7	8
Imprest and other Monies	105402	0	3	....			105402	0	3
Money received from the E. I. C.	60000	0	0	....			60000	0	0
Unclaimed Dividends (more than paid)	14635	16	9	....			14635	16	9
	49547508	1	11	....			52547508	1	11
							52547508	1	11

Expenditure.	£.	s.	d.	£.	s.	d.
Funded Debt.—Interest and management of the Permanent Debt	24648421	2	11			
Terminable Annuities	3888513	3	7			
Total charge of the Funded Debt, exclusive of £8,884. 3s., the interest on Donations and Bequests	28536934	6	6			
Unfunded Debt.—Interest on Exchequer-Bills	511812	3	2			
				29048746	9	
Civil List	390545	15	2			
Annuities and Pensions for Civil, Naval, Military, and Judicial Services, &c., charged by various Acts of Parliament on the Consolidated Fund	564653	12	3			
Salaries and Allowances	238632	1	5			
Diplomatic Salaries and Pensions	180752	10	2			
Courts of Justice	736378	18	10			
Miscellaneous Charges on the Consolidated Fund	242063	12	10			
				2353026	10	8
Army	6086394	5	1			
Navy	6358219	0	3			
Ordnance	1977267	12	2			
Miscellaneous, chargeable on the annual grants of Parliament	2849837	3	2			
Opium Compensation	1257616	11	3			
China Expedition	821020	0	0			
Insurrection in Canada	25300	0	0			
				19375654	11	11
				50777427	12	3
Excess of Income over Expenditure				1770080	9	8
				52547508	1	11

OBITUARY.

Anderson, Major J. J., late of the 10th Foot, one of the Military Knights of Windsor, August 7th. The veteran knight had seen much service in the East and West Indies, and was a Knight of the Royal Hanovarian Guelphic Order. He was buried at St George's Chapel, Windsor, with military honours.

Beighton, the Rev. Thomas, formerly of Derby, April 14, at Pulo Penang, in the 54th year of his age, for 25 years a devoted and faithful missionary.

Campbell, Lieut. James Robert, 42nd Madras Native Infantry, second son of the late Sir Duncan Campbell, Bart, of Barcaldine, Argylshire, May 15th, on his march from Secunderabad to Kemptee, in his 22d year.

Colonna, Princess Donna Maria Pignatelli di Monte Leone, wife of Prince Don Prospero Sciarra Colonna, August 8, at Rome, suddenly, in her 42nd year. This distinguished lady was the last branch of the celebrated Cortes family, to which Ferdinand Cortes, the conqueror of Mexico, belonged.

Colley, Lieut. A. F., of the Ceylon Rifle Regiment, only son of the late Major Augustus Keppell Colley, Royal Marines, May 26, at Jaffnapatam, East Indies.

Crichton, Mr. James, colonial surgeon, Perth, Swan River, Western Australia, August 11, in London.

Daniel, Captain Cyrus, paymaster of her Majesty's 55th regiment of Foot, April 19, at sea, on board the Fairlie, on his passage to England from China.

Drummond, Samuel, Esq., member of the Royal Academy, August 6, at Soho Square, London, aged 79 years.

Fullerton, Lieut. William Robert, 46th regiment Madras Native Infantry, eldest son of the late Charles Fullerton, Esq, Madras Civil service, May 19, at Kemptee, East Indies, aged 28 years.

Galway, Rear-Admiral, August 9, at an advanced age. This gallant admiral entered the navy on the 19th of February, 1786, and had seen considerable service in his profession. At the battle of the Nile he ably distinguished himself under the eye of the immortal Nelson, being senior lieutenant of the Vanguard, that hero's ship. At Walcheren he commanded the Dryad; and in 1811 was actively employed on the north coast of Spain, in co-operation with the patriots, or national party. He captured the Clorinde French frigate in 1814, that vessel of war having previously had a severe action with the Eurotas. His commissions were dated as follow—Lieutenant, 24th of June, 1793; Commander, 3d of October, 1798; Captain, 29th of April, 1802; and Rear-Admiral, 10th of January, 1837.

Goate, Captain, C B., August 17, at Bury St. Edmonds, in his 76th year. He was appointed Lieutenant in 1790, Commander in 1799, and Captain in 1809, and was 21st on the list of Captains. He was Lieutenant of the Orpheus at the capture of La Duguay Trouin, French frigate, in 1794; assisted in the capture of Malacca in 1795; and in the Mosquito was actively employed in the rivers Elbe and Weser in 1809.

Huntingfield, Lord, August 10, at Heveningham Hall, Suffolk, in the 66th year of his age.

Keane, the Right Hon. Lord, G.C.B., K.C.H., the gallant captor of Ghuznee, died of dropsy, August 26th. He was a Lieutenant-General in the army, and Colonel of the 43rd Regiment of Foot. [*A Biographical Notice in our next.*]

Lemon, J., Esq, late of St. Ann's, Jamaica, August 7, at Camden Town.

Matcham, Charles Horatio Nelson, Esq., sixth son of the late George Matcham, Esq., of Ashfold Lodge, Sussex, at Bookham, near Yap, New South Wales, aged 38.

Newport, Major Christopher, late of the Bombay army. August 15. He commanded his regiment for nearly three years in Scinde, after the occupation of that country, the climate of which so affected his health as to oblige him to retire from the service.

Powerscourt, Richard Viscount, August 11, at Rochester, where he had arrived with his family from Rome. His lordship was born in 1815; succeeded to the title 9th August, 1823; and was married on the 20th January, 1836, to Lady Elizabeth Frances Charlotte Jocelyn, eldest daughter of the Earl of Roden, born on the 13th December, 1813, and has issue three children.

Parsons, the Rev. John, of the island of Barbadoes, 28 years vicar of Marden, Wilts, and late Fellow of Oriel College, Oxford, July 31, at Bath.

Petit, Mr James Orfeur, late of her Majesty's Customs, London, July 28, in the 74th year of his age.

Shaw, Henry Thomas, fourth son of Lees Shaw, Esq., and nephew of Sir Robert Shaw, Bart., of Bushy Park, near Dublin, was accidentally drowned near Kingston, Jamaica, in June last, aged 21.

Smith, John Davidson, Esq., the much-esteemed projector of the Beulah Spa, Norwood, August 8, at Ealing, aged 57.

Sewell, Lucinda Marianna, wife of Henry Sewell, Esq., and eldest daughter of the late Major-General Nedham, July 28, in the Isle of Wight, aged 32.

Scott, Major-General Edward, July 26, at Bath, aged 82 years. The deceased had served with distinction at St. Domingo, in 1794 and 1725; and in Ireland during the rebellion of '98. He accompanied the expedition to the Ferrol and Cadiz, under Sir James Pulteney; and afterwards repaired to Egypt for the campaign of 1801. For his services in Egypt he was rewarded with a medal and the Order of the Crescent. His commissions were dated as follow—Ensign, June 29, 1780; Lieutenant, August 4, 1781; Captain, June 30, 1790; Major, September 1, 1795; Lieut.-Colonel, January 1, 1801; Colonel, July 25, 1810; and Major-General, June 4, 1813. General Scott had retired from the service for several years.

Thomson, William, Esq, late merchant of Tobago, in the West Indies, August 10, at Islington, in his 63rd year.

Vizard, Arthur, Esq., cornet in her Majesty's 15th Hussars, May 23, at Bangalore, East Indies, consequent on a fall from his horse.

LONDON: FISHER, SON AND CO, PRINTERS.

FISHER'S

COLONIAL MAGAZINE.

LABOUR IN THE COLONIES.

"Here let us rest, and lay out seed-fields; *here let us learn to dwell.* Here, even here, *the gardens that we plant will yield us fruit;* the acorns will be wood and pleasant umbrage, if we wait. How much grows everywhere if we do but wait! Through the swamps we will shape causeways, force purifying drains; we will learn to thread the rocky impossibilities; and beaten tracks, worn smooth by mere travelling of human feet, will form themselves. Not a difficulty but can transfigure itself into a triumph; not even a deformity but, if our own soul have imprinted worth on it, will grow dear to us."—THOMAS CARLYLE.

CONSIDERABLE alarm has been created in our Asiatic colonies, and allowed to endure for a considerable period, at the prospect of a decrease in the supply of labour; nor has the apprehension been diminished by the uncompromising hostility of government to systematic emigration. Habituated to ill-usage from successive colonial functionaries, the Australasians are now looking inwards upon themselves for counsel and relief, and it is especially requisite, *in limine*, that the poorer classes, the apparently weaker but virtually stronger parties to the covenant, shall be made fully sensible of their real position. If, as unquestionably has been the case, poverty, decay of trade, increased taxation, depression in every member of commercial existence, have occurred of late years in our South-Asiatic colonies, what parts of our empire have been spared similar visitations? If wages were low when the emigrant quitted his native land, how could he expect that they enjoyed an unnatural height in the colony to which he was sailing—or, if they did, that such height would remain stationary until his arrival? As much might he expect the tide to suspend its return to low water, in order that his ship might ride successfully into every tidal harbour. When the artificial state of things, to which we shall presently refer, produced a temporary plethora in Australia, the labourer partook of the full flow; and if he neglected to avail himself of the harvest, and providently to lay up for the winter from his labour's produce, let him not now complain of fortune's fickleness, or the inhumanity of an employer, whose own profits have fallen in the same or even a greater ratio,—in some cases ending in his bankruptcy, ruin, and death from a broken heart.

Upon the lamentable decline of trade which occurred towards the close of the year just past, when thousands became insolvents publicly, and privately many men were in no better condition, the labouring population, shaded under the attractive but usurped title of "Working Men," declaimed against low wages, inhuman masters, and the distributions of Providence. This most serious subject, serious in its effects in calming the feelings of the poor and the suffering,—serious to the interests of the colony, and lastly, most important to the ends of humanity, has been very ably handled by the editor of the *Sydney Herald*.*

The question, who *are* 'working men?' might be answered by another: 'In young colonies, who are *not* working men?' Look throughout New South Wales, from the cobbler's stall to the governor's writing-desk, from the tenant of a cabbage-garden to the lord of broad acres, and you will see nothing but varied species of the genus Working Man. All, without class-exception, are toiling hard, some with their hands only, some with their hands and heads both. The judges are working men; and anxious and laborious is their task. The governor is a working man; and we should like to know where, in the whole colony, there is a man who works harder. Tinkers, tailors, mechanics, ploughmen, bullock-drivers, stockmen, shepherds, farmers, graziers, clerks, shopkeepers, merchants, lawyers, government officers, and even *editors*, are all obliged to earn their bread by "the sweat of their faces." The man who, in New South Wales, gets bread and cheese without work, is a living phenomenon—*rara avis in terris.*

Correctly speaking, therefore, these announcements to working men apply to the whole community; for we are a community of working men. We have no class to which the epithet is not strictly applicable; we have no class to which it is applicable in any special sense. But by the words "Working Men" they mean only *some* of the working men, as by the word "People," they mean only *some* of the people. They mean the *receivers* of wages in contradistinction from the *payers* of wages; journeymen in contradistinction from masters; the reputed poor in contradistinction from the reputed rich. They make the distinction, and lay emphasis upon it, because they think it their interest to do so. In mere numbers, the employed far exceed the employers; they constitute the masses of society: it is therefore an important object with these scavengers of the press to generate amongst the multitudinous majority a strong feeling of prejudices and interests peculiar to *the class;* and then, by pandering to these class prejudices, and professing to stand forward as the bold champions of these class interests, to build up for themselves a still more important class—a class of customers. The scribblers are neither fools nor dunces. They know well what they are about. They are perfectly aware that in this country the words "Working Men," and "People," designate all ranks and conditions amongst us. We have no peerage, no aristocracy: we are all working men; we are all, as the *Register* says of Sir James Dowling, "emphatically of the people." But though the demagogues know this as well as we do, they are too wise in their generation to admit it. The admission would be dangerous to the profits of their craft. It would never do to place our little society upon the broad level of popular equality: for then they would have no peculiar ground to tread upon—no imaginary grievances to bewail,—no imaginary rights to vindicate. Their ends are better answered by stickling

* 21st March, 1844.

for social subordination; by insisting upon it that the receivers of wages are the only working men, the only people, in the colony; all the rest being wealthy drones, or haughty aristocrats.

They live by setting the class "*working* men" against the class *paying* men—the class "*people*" against the class *employers* of people—the class *journeymen* against the class *masters*. The inconsistency is glaring enough to be laughed at, were it not full of pernicious consequences. The interests of employers and employed are in this country so closely identified with each other, so firmly bound together by mutual dependence, that any attempt to separate them must be injurious to both. Upon what does the prosperity of the *working* classes depend, but upon the prosperity of the *employing* classes? And why is it that of late work has been so scarce, and wages so low, but because landowners and capitalists have been depressed in their circumstances? Injure the capitalist, and you injure the labourer; injure the master, and you injure the servant; injure the woolgrower, whose avocations are the well-spring of all our profits, and you injure the whole population. The classes must rise or fall together. Neither can do without the other. The flockowner depends for the safety and productiveness of his flocks upon the faithful services of his shepherd; the shepherd depends for the permanence of his employment, and the sufficiency of his wages, upon the profits which his master derives from the fleece.

To instil into the minds of what are called the working men, a feeling of class separation, or of class independency, or of class antagonism and rivalry, towards the classes from which alone they can obtain employment, and with whose welfare their own is necessarily interwoven, is, therefore, a cruel wrong to society at all times; but in the present enfeebled state of the colony, when hearty co-operation amongst all classes is essential to the recovery of health and vigour, it is cruelty and wickedness of the most aggravated kind.

Now, to every sentence in the preceding extract we heartily subscribe, because we think it a fundamental principle in the establishment of reciprocal kindness, and of a just understanding between employer and employed, and we recommend its thoughtful perusal to home as well as to colonial readers. But, *fiat justitia*, hear also some of the plaints of the labouring man, which are not to be unheeded, which are not unknown in this *laughing* land, and which are amongst the very worst commodities imported by capitalists into the Australian colonies,—we allude to the truck system,—or system of rations, as it is called in the colonies. The following complaint of "one of the working classes," addressed to the same impartial editor, is a full and fair *exposé* of the way in which the system is capable of being worked, and of the pressure which may be readily applied by a griping employer in districts so circumstanced as newly settled lands, remote from large towns:—

"As there are often letters written to you, by settlers, stating the great demand for labour, and the remunerating rate of wages which is received, I beg you will insert the following contradiction of those statements.

"That there is a demand in this the Yass district at present, I totally deny; the roads are thronged with persons looking for employment, and who are encouraged here by such reports; and which, perhaps, were circulated for the express purpose of getting a superabundance of labour, so as to have it in their power to dictate the rate of wages they would employ them at. That this is at present the case, there is not the slightest doubt of, occasioned by such a competition for employment, to the injury of those whose engagements have expired, or are about to expire, as well as to those who are unengaged. That too many of the settlers have taken advantage of such a state of things, by reducing the ration and wages to low-water mark, I am sorry to say has been the fact; but it would be unfair was I not to add, that there are others, who scorn to take advantage of their present distress by giving such a rate of wages as would deprive them of even the common necessaries, not to speak of the comforts, of life; but who give as high a rate of wages as is consistent with their present low rate of profits. It is rather strange, that in any communications from settlers in the interior, although the high rate of wages, and the demand for men, is blazoned forth, they omit to mention the enormous and *extortionate prices they charge for their goods!*

"We often hear that even £20 was refused by men in such and such places, but we never hear the reason of such refusal. They did not tell us that they charged such prices for their goods that the greater part of that £20 would find its way back to them again; nor did they tell us that very likely these men were well aware that the party offering that £20 would pay with orders which were then, and most likely would be, 'no good.' These things are kept profound secrets. If they would be so obliging as to mention, for general information, the rates they charge for clothing, &c., &c., the persons who were about to proceed to such a district would then know how much he would have *to deduct from the rate of wages* mentioned, to find what he would have at the end of his term of engagement. But I am afraid they will be backward in doing so, as it would expose their extortion, and have the effect of forcing them to reduce their charges when it became generally known; but as they will not do so, it must only be done for them. It is really scandalous the rate they charge for goods which cost them little or nothing. They seem determined, if they give a remunerating rate of wages, (as they call it,) to have a remunerating profit from their goods. In this district, and I believe in every other, the prices charged are as high as they were four years ago, when wages were double what they are at present, and when goods and their carriage cost them double, if not triple, what they now do. But as a few facts are worth a bushel of assertions, I will produce a few figures to elucidate my statement. As £15 is about the average rate of wages here, and the following weekly ration—10 lbs. flour, 10 lbs. meat, 3 oz. tea, 1½ lb. sugar—I will take this as a foundation to work on; and take what a man will actually require, and the prices charged. When the settlers and your correspondents tell us that £15 per annum is the average rate of wages, (and which they consider very liberal these times,) let them also tell us that the person engaging will require, during the twelve months, three pair slop moleskin trousers, for which he will be charged 14s per pair, which will amount to £2 2s.; that he knows he will be obliged to draw three pairs of slop boots, for which he will charge him 14s. per pair, which will amount to £2. 2s.; that he is aware that he must get, at least, six striped shirts, for which he will charge him 4s. per shirt, which will amount to £1. 4s.; that he will require a moleskin slop jacket, for which he will charge him 15s.; that he will require two cabbage-tree hats, for which he will charge him 6s. per hat, which will amount to 12s.; that he is well aware he cannot do without a great coat for winter, for which he will charge him £2. 10s.; that as a matter of course, except a man was deranged, he would never think of doing without bedding &c., for which he will charge him—a pair of blankets, £1. 10s., rug 10s., bed-ticking 10s.; that he is particularly wide awake to the fact, that the man will require on an average three ounces per week of colonial negrohead tobacco, for which he will charge him 7s. per pound, which will amount in the year to £3. 4s. 9d.; that he knows he will be obliged to get at least four pounds extra tea per year, to accommodate the distressed and weary traveller invited here, with settlers' remunerating wages, for which he will charge 6s. per pound, which will amount to £1. 4s.; that he is aware that tea without sugar is a very insipid beverage, and that he will require at least half a pound per week for the same purpose, for which he will charge him 9d. per pound, which will amount in twelve months to 19s. 6d.; that he is aware he will require one pound of soap per month, for which he will charge him 1s. per pound, which will amount in twelve months to 12s.

"And, he is also well qualified to tell him, on coming to get his remunerating wages, at the end of his twelve months, that the sum total drawn amounts to £17. 15s. 3d.! that his wages amounts to £15; consequently, that he is actually £2. 15s. 3d. in debt; although the man did not get anything but what was absolutely necessary! And thus the poor fellow is left without a farthing to pay the shepherd for the sheep-dogs he bought of him. If any person will take the trouble of comparing these prices with the cost prices, and allow a fair business profit, say 25 per cent., also allow for carriage what is charged, 8s. per cent., they will find that the settler pockets one-half of the poor man's wages in clear profits!—that he pockets more than the manufacturer, shipper, merchant, &c., all of whom have a profit. He actually pockets more than them all! more profits than the articles originally cost in Sydney after passing through so many hands!! If their business in that way was extensive, it ought to pay better than wool-growing; were they to sell at a reasonable rate, the man, in place of being in debt, would have between £4 and £5 due him; but that would not be so convenient or agreeable to the settler. Thus, at a moderate calculation as to what a man would require, and the prices charged within fifty miles of Yass, he would be in debt at the end of his twelve months. This is what some of the settlers call remunerating wages! These prices they cannot deny they charge, and I appeal to the settlers themselves, to their account-books, if men on an average do not draw more than is here stated. As to the prices charged, I could name not one, but fifty establishments, were it requisite, where even in some things more is charged. But the question is, will the settler allow him to be in debt at the year's end? Decidedly not. What is he then to do? Why, he must want some of the common necessaries of life; do without a great coat in winter—without a bed to lie on. If he has lost any sheep (he will be fortunate if not), he is charged double market-price for them; and must of course give up still further the necessaries of life. He must give up exercising hospitality to the poor weary traveller, who perhaps has travelled hundreds of miles, looking for employment, and may have to travel hundreds more before he finds it. He must give up the luxury of smoking, otherwise deprive himself of some other necessary to gratify that appetite, and he must give up the partnership that had existed for the purpose of subscribing to a newspaper. How are those who are now engaging at from £10 to £12 per year to manage at these prices of stores? I am unable to answer the question otherwise than by saying, that they must be completely miserable. I really pity those who are engaged at such rates; the poor deluded immigrant, who perhaps has left a home where they were comfortably and decently clothed, to come to a colony where all the remuneration they will receive for their services will be an uncomfortable life, and a deprival of even its common necessaries. Supposing even that they get employment, they will only be supplying the place of so many others, who will lose theirs, by refusing to take as low wages, and that at a time of the year when everything is slack; the lambs are all weaned now, so there will not be any extra men required until sheep-shearing. I hope this will have the effect it is intended it should have—to excite public attention to the extortion of the settlers, and to show them the necessity of reducing their charges, so as to make their stores *more as a convenience to their men than as a source of profit and extortion.* To expose the fallacy of the term 'remunerating wages,' when coupled with their charges, it is useless for them to say that they do not want men to buy out of their stores, when perhaps there may not be any other place within fifty or one hundred miles where they could buy cheaper. If there was, would the settler give the cash to buy with? Or would the orders, in the most of instances, be cashable? Would he allow the man to go to a place where he could buy cheaper? These are questions which they must answer before they talk of not forcing to buy. The fact is, there is no compulsion, only they are so circumstanced that they *must.* I would again bring it under the notice of the settlers, and servants registry-office keepers, always when stating the rates of wages in certain districts, also to name the rates of clothing and provisions. If this was done, £12 might be better than £18, where that £18 was accompanied with extortion. Perhaps you, or some of your correspondents, would inform me if men are bound to pay unfair charges."

In long-settled districts, public opinion may carry sufficient punishment along with it, and tend to correct or repress the crime, but, in lone localities, other means should be employed. Stipendiary, and therefore responsible, magistrates, constabulary, protective societies, should be authorized to fix, beforehand, the cost of the necessaries of life to the labourer, so that his wages shall not be wrung from him by extortion, nor every hope of laying up a few shillings for his earnings be heartlessly dissipated. We dwell emphatically on this necessity for surveillanceship, from the belief, that labour in the colonies, to be productive of mutual benefit, a fair proportion of happiness, and the ends of its being spared by the mother-country, must and ought to be equally distributed. This has not been the case, whatever may happen, as the evidence of a Sydney-man well acquainted with the question assures us." Thus writes Veritas, of Sydney.

"Emigration to this colony was intended more particularly to support the country interest, but the colonial government has in this, as in sundry other instances, been criminally indifferent in all which pertains and may promote the advantage of the settler. The deep cogitation of the executive conclave, when directed to the class, appears ever to manifest itself in devising schemes for extorting taxation. The struggling settler, in many parts, is unconscious of the existence of a government, from any assistance which it confers: his associations and cognisance of delegated supreme authority have had relation only to assessments, licenses, and other exactious calamities, which he is unable to meet. The prosperity, nay, the existence of the colony, is absolutely dependent on the success of the settler, his good fortune being the true basis of that of every class. A consideration of his interest should therefore be paramount to that of every other. The settlers may with great reasonableness complain of the injustice with which they have been treated,—the labour imported for their benefit never having been distributed over the colony, and latterly being diverted from its legitimate purpose to be expended upon unnecessary works in this overgrown and comparatively useless city. The folly of this latter proceeding must be now indisputably clear to all, and not a word was uttered in the Council in its furtherance. It is, however, to be hoped the Council will not attempt precipitately to locate families permanently, but confine its operation to the transmission of the unemployed, principally to the more remote districts, rather than to Illawarra or other places moderately contiguous to Sydney, from which place such parties may, without exertion, and but little cost, supply themselves. The sum voted may, if economically used, be serviceable to the distant settlers, but if expended upon supplying those who reside within sixty or eighty miles of Sydney, the distant places, where the insufficiency of labour is most destructively experienced, will be but little better off than if the grant had never been voted. It should be borne in mind, that the unfortunate settlers on the Clarence River, or at Moreton Bay, and the country westward of those districts, have not only to pay higher wages and give larger rations, the latter being, from freight, storage, and other incidental charges, very expensive; but they have hitherto had to pay £2 for the passage of each adult, and it not unfrequently happens, that after landing they proceed to hire themselves to other parties. There is little doubt of there being an abundant field for labour, as the flockmasters know to their cost; in fact, they are in a process of being ruined, inasmuch as they have been compelled to give their servants high wages, as, if dismissed, they could not possibly be replaced. Many settlers aver with great truth, that the excessive price of labour, which the Government might, at all events, to a great degree have obviated, has been the most potent agent in their ruin. Mechanics, failing to procure employment in their trades, must engage themselves in such other work as the colony presents until the times improve. The rations, which some members of Council undervalue, forms, I maintain, a most important item of expense, and no master can afford to ration a man with three or four children, for the man's services only; the ration, however, needs reformation, the superfluities of tea and sugar should be discontinued; in some districts they never have been generally allowed, a practice worthy of imitation in all. The neglect of the Executive in omitting, so many years, to distribute the labour in the colony, has been most oppressively felt by that most enterprising class who have made their home in the far interior. The colony generally can boast but very moderately of the patronage of His Excellency. Surely the negation of every project, suggested for the advancement of the country, is not the duty of a Governor: for instance, as was lately the case, an expedition to Port Essington, an experiment, it is true, with which all parties were interested, and respecting the propriety of which there was an entire harmony of opinion, was thwarted: to some minds the rejection might appear wanton,—to others, petulant. Such denials are intimations not to be disregarded. that if we desire to progress we must bestir ourselves. I am no financier, but the Governor of New South Wales should be one; I would recommend parties to read the evidence published by the Monetary-Confusion Committee, and afterwards decide to what extent the miseries from which we are at present suffering, are traceable to the mis-government of the colony."

This querele—the partial distribution of able-bodied men—is reiterated in New Zealand; idlers are permitted to lounge about the streets of Auckland, while employment with remunerating wages is offered to them, or, at all events, might be had by seeking for it in the country. But the question was fairly tested last winter by the inhabitants of the city of Sydney, who felt the weight of the evil, witnessed the growing malady, and resolved, in consequence, to ascertain publicly, what was the true cause why so many *Tibure ament Romam*, and cannot be persuaded to seek for occupation in the rural districts. Although we could state perhaps more briefly the circumstances in which this effect originated, the reasons assigned by the committee will necessarily find that respect from the reader, and be entitled to that authenticity, with which we desire that they should be invested.

NEW SOUTH WALES.—*Report from the Select Committee on the petition from distressed Mechanics and Labourers.*—" The select committee of the legislative council, appointed 8th November, 1843, to take into consideration a petition from upwards of 4000 of the inhabitants of Sydney, soliciting the attention of the council to the distressed condition of the numerous unemployed artisans and labourers in the city of Sydney, having accordingly taken the same into consideration, and examined various witnesses, both as to the actual condition of the unemployed in Sydney, and the demand for labour of various kinds in the interior, have agreed to the following report:

" Your committee have ascertained, beyond the possibility of doubt, that there is at present a very large number of persons, of the industrious classes, totally unemployed, and without the slightest prospect of employment in the *city of Sydney*; since the appointment of your committee, an inquiry has been instituted, at their particular desire, by a few intelligent and benevolent persons (themselves of the working classes) of whose integrity, as well as of their general fitness for such an office, your committee have reason to think favourably, to ascertain the number, conditoin, and circumstances of the unemployed, in the various branches of business pursued by the industrious classes, in the different wards of the city, exclusive of those who have recently obtained temporary employment, either from the government or the corporation, and the following is the general result of this inquiry:

Total number of persons, of the industrious classes, whether mechanics or labourers, at present unemployed in the city 1243
Total number of adult females (the wives of the married) dependent on these persons for their subsistence 804
Total number of children dependent on these persons . . 1701

List of the occupation of these persons—

Labourers of all descriptions	474
Carpenters	119
Stonemasons	57
Blacksmiths	31
Cabinet makers	48
Coopers	3
Shoemakers	36

Tailors	47
Painters	37
Plasterers	14
Shipwright	15
Compositors	30
Bricklayers	9
Upholsterers	5
Engineers	7
Coachmakers	1
Combmakers	2
Other handicrafts not included under any of the above heads	348

"Although it was no part of the duty of your committee to inquire into the cause or origin of a state of things so utterly unprecedented in the history of this colony, they deem it incumbent upon them to state, that for several years previous to the commencement of the present pecuniary crisis, the colony had been enjoying a season of unexampled but unreal prosperity—prosperity based on the illusive anticipation of extraordinary returns from the investment of funds borrowed, chiefly from English capitalists, at an exorbitant rate of interest, and expended in what has ultimately proved ruinous speculation in land and stock; in accordance with the uniform course of human affairs, this period of unnatural excitement has been succeeded by a corresponding period of deep and general depression—the state of extraordinary inflation has been followed at length by a state of collapse. In passing through this trying process, the whole framework of society throughout the colony has fallen into a state of extreme derangement, from which there is little prospect of its recovery for some time to come; the *employers* of labour have for the most part been reduced from supposed wealth to actual embarrassment; while many, both in town and country, have actually become insolvent, either from their own imprudent speculations, or from the bankruptcy of others. A check has thus, in the mean time, been suddenly given to improvement of every kind throughout the territory, and the industrious classes have, in comparatively large numbers, been altogether deprived of their usual means of subsistence.

"In regard to what may appear an extraordinary accumulation of persons of the industrious classes of Sydney, your committee would observe that it has arisen from various causes.

First—"From the extraordinary demand for *medical labour*, as well as of unskilled labour of all kinds *in the capital* during the years of imaginary prosperity. The numerous *buildings* that were then erected in Sydney, and the extensive commerce of a large seaport town, afforded employment, at *high wages*, not only to a large number of mechanics, but also to numerous labourers—of both of which classes, however, the greater number are now suffering from want of employment.

Second—"From the fact that a large proportion of *bounty immigrants*, introduced into the colony at the public expence during the years 1839, 1840, and 1841, consisted, not of agricultural labourers and shepherds, but of individuals and families *from the cities and towns of the mother country*, who accordingly brought with them to the colony the habits and feelings of a town population, and are *naturally averse to go into the interior on any terms.*

Third—"From the circumstance that very many of these immigrants were persons having *large families*, who, although willing to have gone to the country as farm-servants on reasonable terms, were precluded from every opportunity of doing so, from the inability of the settlers to maintain a large family of immigrants for the labour of a single individual.

"The first measure of relief that suggested itself to your committee, as one of urgent necessity, was that of providing immediate subsistence for families in actual destitution; and they are happy to state that from twenty to thirty families, in extremely destitute circumstances, have already been relieved, and that such relief will continue to be afforded in cases of a similar kind, as they may occur; there can therefore be no apprehension of actual want in any instances in which the parties take the proper means of letting their situation be known.

"The second measure of relief that suggested itself to your committee, was that of draughting off as many of the unemployed of the class of mere labourers, to those *localities in the interior*, or along the coast, in which there was a fair prospect of their obtaining employment at reasonable wages; and your honourable house having been pleased to approve of the resolution which your committee took the liberty to transmit to the Executive at their first meeting, viz., to appropriate £500 for providing the means of conveyance to the interior, with rations until they should be offered employment, for such families as can be disposed of in this way, the immigration department will, of course, have means of relief for this important purpose immediately available, to the extent mentioned, under the supervision of the Executive; and, small as this appropriation may appear in comparison with the number of families at present out of employment, your committee are of opinion that, if judiciously expended, in connection with such efforts as may be practicable, with a view to the disposal of families, in the capacity of hired servants in different parts of *the interior*, a very considerable amount of relief will be afforded to the city; in the hope, however, that a sufficient number of families will be found willing to proceed to the interior, in various directions, to render the expenditure of a still larger amount for conveyance and rations absolutely necessary, your committee would beg to recommend that a further amount of £500 should be appropriated for that purpose, subject to the contingency of its actual expenditure.

"Mrs. Chisholm, whose name is so well known in the colony for her disinterested and untiring benevolence, has succeeded in making conditional arrangements for locating not fewer than thirty families of the unemployed, on an eligible tract of unimproved land in the district of Illawarra, and it is not improbable that, in the event of the practicability of the plan being demonstrated, it will be adopted in other instances with great benefit to all concerned. For it cannot be denied, that while the settlers, generally, are unable to maintain large families, and to give remunerating wages besides for the labour of a single individual, such families would be much better situated, as well for their own comfort and the future welfare of their children, as for the general benefits of the community—especially in raising grain, to obviate the necessity for future importations of that article from beyond the seas—if they could any way be *located as small farmers on their own account*. The formation of such a tenantry as these families would prospectively form, is decidedly a great desideratum in the social system of this colony.

"John Dunmore Lang, D.D.,—Chairman."

"Sydney, November 24th, 1843."

This dispassionate document is rather compromising; its authors were perfectly familiar with the real name and nature of the disease, but wanted the moral courage to declare it to the patient.—Why not declare openly what they knew to be the case,—that, although commerce had declined, demand and prices for every kind of exports had fallen, sheep and black cattle lowered extravagantly in value, and misery existing in many shapes—still, *labour* never could be dispensed with; it was the origin of all property; employers, whether small or large capitalists, could not exist without it; capital unemployed is so much dross, there was no property without labour: *labor omnia vincit*—why not declare candidly, that a large share of the Sydney suffering was attributable to love of a city life, where pleasure seemed more within the reach of the sensualist,—a portion also to disinclination to work, even *pro tempore*, for fair remuneration, a portion also to confessed idleness and irregularity? why not tell the patient honestly, "part of your complaint is produced by yourself, the other part we shall assuredly attempt to remedy." Where was the Agent for Emigration, whose duty should have been to keep an office open for the registry of unemployed hands, to which masters might apply, and, where the wages they could afford to pay should also be duly entered; the magistrates could then, with certainty, determine whether an individual refused fair compensation for his services, and what his real motives were for lingering in the city, and increasing the amount of distress.—We do not mean to ascribe a desire to act dishonestly, or a passion for pleasure and idleness, to the poor fellows who cross the ocean in search of a mere viaticum on their pilgrimage through life; but, improper characters must be guarded against; and, besides, the honest and industrious will feel no reluctance in giving their names, residences, and references, when out of work.

We felt much satisfaction in the perusal of an article in the *Australian* of the 8th February, upon the condition of the labouring classes during the panic period, the close of 1843, in which the discontented in that land of promise, deprecated immigration, and bade the farmers repent, and disgorge their treasures.

" The amount at the credit of depositors in the Savings Bank, and the amount of Revenue derived from those two popular luxuries, spirits and tobacco, are comprehensive indices of the circumstances, comforts, and habits of the humbler ranks: and, although the said amounts for the past year show a large decrease as compared with 1842, we must, nevertheless, draw from them the positive conclusion, that, while the representatives of property have been involved in embarrassment and monetary difficulties, the social plague of poverty and distress has not spread widely among the labouring classes. From the summary of the Savings Bank and its branches, we find that there were on the 31st of last December, 2781 depositors, at whose credit an amount appeared of £123,213 6s. 5d., the average of each deposit being about £44. This statement certainly shows a large decrease on the year—the total on the 31st December 1842, being as follows, namely: depositors 3710; amount £169,357. 17s. 10d.; average amount of each deposit £45. 12s. But, in tracing the causes of this falling-off, we must not forget the serious run on this establishment which continued for two whole days in May last; and we have no hesitation in declaring our belief, that but for the panic which then frighted the infatuated depositors, the balance-sheet of the Bank for the last year would have exhibited almost as large a total as in 1842. As it is, the summary presents a result both congratulatory and honourable to the Colony. It has been alleged, and justly too, as a reproach to New South Wales, that, while the consumption of spirits in Great Britain is not above the rate of one gallon and five-eighths for each adult, it should average in the Colony two gallons and a half per head. But in juxta-position with this indefensible fact, we may state with pride, that a comparison of the statistics of the British and New South Wales Savings Bank will show, that in the comparative number and amount of the deposits, the proportion is about 17 to 11 in favour of the colonists; and that while the average amount of each of our deposits is, as we have already shown, about £44, in Great Britain it is not above £33. To this we must add, as a forcible commentary on the favourable comparison we can boast, that the magnitude of our Savings' Bank deposits is a gratifying proof of the frugality and industry of that portion of our community, who, to a certain degree, are sufferers from the circumstance of the Colony not possessing those advantages of fixed capital, which the languor and apathy of the large proprietors have failed to create. The total annual value of real property in England alone, which is assessed to the poor rates, may be estimated at sixty millions sterling, and we do maintain that the proof of the economy and foresight of a large portion of the humbler classes of this Colony, exhibited in the foregoing statements, is the more significant by reason of the particular comparisons it awakens."

To this evidence of labour or employment having been found in the last year, we now proceed to show that a demand still existed for that origin of property, that essence of commerce, that tributary to healthful, happy existence, when the latest advices came away from

Sydney. Scarcely had the denunciations of the political charlatans of Sydney gone forth, when two vessels arrived with immigrants, and, upon the fortunes of the new-comers, hear the evidence of eye-witnesses.

"Upwards of *six hundred new arrivals, per* Herald *and* Elizabeth, *have readily obtained comfortable situations, at rates of wages with which they have declared themselves content.* We visited both these ships almost daily pending the engagements of the people, and entered into minute inquiries as to their views and expectations, and particularly as to the hopes under which they had been induced to emigrate. It is true that they had been led to indulge in notions of rates of wages as extravagant as they were incompatible with probability; but every individual we conversed with confessed very candidly that *he had incomparably improved the condition of himself and family by obtaining the situation he found offered to him on his arrival here.*

"Whence comes it, then, that, while six hundred new-comers readily find profitable employment, two thousand persons, with families dependent upon them, persons who have been some time in the colony, should be unable to avail themselves of similar good fortune? The answer is to be found in the letters lately received by the immigration agent, from the magistrates in the several country districts of the colony, respecting the demand for labour, and the rates of wages in their respective neighbourhoods; and in the evidence given before the select committee on immigration, of the late session of the legislative council. The magistrates are consentient in declaring that in their districts considerable demand will exist for some time to come for farm labourers, shepherds, and hutkeepers; and the evidence proved that, notwithstanding the '*limitation of the means, and enterprise of the employers of labour*,' it was difficult to procure men in Sydney at the rate of wages which the proprietors could afford to give. Mr. George M'Leay had been endeavouring, for the last month, to obtain men, but could not; he had advertised for labourers, at £12 a year, but only had *two applicants*, and that he had subsequently offered £15, at the immigration barracks, in vain. Dr. Thompson declared that he had no doubt *any industrious man*, going to Port Philip, and living frugally, might earn a comfortable independence. He, himself, had nine instances of his own men, who had sums in the savings' bank, varying from £30 to £80 and £120 each. Many gentlemen have informed us that the unemployed labourers in Sydney refuse any rate of wages under £20 a year, and that the mechanics decline any occupation save that to which they have been trained. Now, as the immigrants per *Herald* and *Elizabeth* gladly accepted wages varying from £12 to £15, and as the artisans among them cheerfully betook themselves to rural occupations, when they were apprised of the depression in mechanical pursuits, the difference between their comfortable prospects, and the misery of the unemployed 'old hands,' is easily accounted for."

A supply of labour is also requisite in Van Diemen's Land, but the circumstances under which it is to be furnished are somewhat different from those that existed before it was made a penal colony.

From the *Hobart Town Advertiser* March, 1844:—

"We must assert that the number of prisoners sent into the colony—the absolute insufficiency of control—and the regulations which are orderd from home—must tend to increase crime, immorality, and disorder. But we do this, not to depreciate the colony, but to produce a change in the system. So far from wishing to prevent immigration of capital and capitalists, we have always insisted that the only remedy for the evils consequent on the deluge of crime which is poured in upon us, is the importation of both—the one to neutralize numbers by numbers, the other to employ and reform.

"But this is not to be done by concealing the disease until it becomes fixed in the system, nor by denying or making light of the symptoms to the physician. Such a course may result in the destruction of the patient, but will scarcely tend to his cure. To make the cure a radical one, or even to alleviate the disease, all must be told, and truly, and effective measures must be taken to eradicate the disorders.

"With us the evils are, the want of *free immigration* to countervail the tide of convictism—sufficient capital to employ—and, as a corollary, sufficient power to control, and sufficient inducement to reclaim the prisoners. The remedy has been tried, and has been successful. Once before we were in a similar state as regarded the relative position of the free and convict population. It was found impossible to continue so. Grants of land and other inducements were given to induce the immigration of capital and capitalist—spite of gross abuses these measures were successful. The government were relieved of heavy expenses—the colonists prospered—the prisoners became better and more comfortable—and the balance between, preponderated in favour of the free population—the colony flourished. Then came the absurdities of the land regulations—the determination to turn this country into a gaol—the concurrent, if not consequent distress and ruin—and the evils which are now only 'the beginning of an end.' Let the iteration be tiresome as it may—we again and again repeat that similar effects will spring from similar causes; and that to render the colony prosperous, we must again have recourse to the remedy which in an identical state of things was before successful."

From our colonies at the Cape of Good Hope the same appeal comes, accompanied by loud complaints against the local authorities, for not suppressing insubordination amongst candidates, or rather pseudo-candidates for labour. In these remonstrances, which are given below, somewhat startling and very unexpected statements are made, of refractory conduct on the part of the Coolies imported from India by the Mauritius. This is a point of moment just now, when these Anglo-Indians are so far preferred to the starving part of our domestic population, by being carried to the West India islands, there furnished with houses, occupation, wages, and lands, while little short of resistance to the tide of emigration from the British isles, is offered by the home-government. We give the extract, however, rather to show the lack of labourers at the Cape, than to reproach the authors of the Coolie deportation now in progress, which will probably be the preservation of our sugar islands in the new world.

From the *Graham's Town Journal*, May, 1144:—

"Facts are continually coming under our notice, showing the great *dearth of labour* which prevails throughout this part of the colony, and the idleness and insubordination of many of those who are actually in employment. It would be a most useful and important undertaking, would the government but set to work in good earnest to ascertain the cause of this, with a view to the application of a suitable remedy. That it does not arise from a paucity of hands, is evident—hence we must look for the origin of the evil in some defect either in the laws, or remissness in those who administer them. At the present moment we do not purpose to do more than advert to the subject, and to which we are led from finding in a Mauritius paper before us, that the same complaint is equally as rife there as amongst us, and that the mischief is attributed in the same manner, either to inefficient power in the law or in the executive to suppress vagrancy. A large proportion of the Coolies obtained from India had deserted from their masters, and were wandering about the country—to the great detriment of property and subversion of that order, which it is so desirable to maintain in every community, and especially a mixed one. The following extract from the *Cerneen* of the 22d March, will show the difficulties the inhabitants of the Mauritius are contending with, while at the same time it points to the causes from whence they spring:—

'The pretensions of our labourers are becoming more exaggerated every day, and the reason of this is obvious; to such as propose to them five rupees, a very proper rate of wages, the only one indeed that the interest of both master and servant will admit of at present, they reply that the course of Cooly immigration has been arrested by government; on the other hand, the police are either unwilling or unable to do anything against the desertion of the labouring population, and the streets and highways are swarming with Cooly venders, as if the country had spent fifteen thousand dollars solely for the purpose of having a few thousand more cake-sellers. —The unofficial members of council, justly alarmed at the increasing desertion of labourers, at their extortionate demands of wages, and the reports we reproduced in our paper on the subject of the interruption of the Cooly immigration, have just addressed to his excellency the governor a letter, in which they call his attention to each of these points, request him to be graciously pleased to give explanations on the matter, and suggest to him the means of remedying the evil. They reckon at eight thousand, the number of labourers absent from work, express their astonishment at our not having received any labourers from India since the putting in force of the new system which was to ensure to the colony five hundred men per month, give it as their opinion that the quantity of EFFECTIVE labour our agriculture enjoys at present is not in proportion with its wants, and urgently request him to increase the number of immigrants to twelve thousand men per annum, a number which would compensate for desertion, departure, and mortality.'

We have now endeavoured to show, that the supply of labour is insufficient in Van Diemen's Land, in South Australia, in New Zealand, and at the Cape of Good Hope, upon evidence that must carry conviction along with it, and therefore be sufficient to direct those who meditate emigration, in the formation of a sound conclusion. All false alarms, as to the actual impossibility of finding employment by the well-disposed and really industrious seem wholly to be dismissed, and, if only a better system of settlement for the labouring immigrants were adopted, one which, by granting them cottages and gardens, would identify them with the soil, we should feel fewer compunctious visitings at recommending those who could find no vacancy at home, to seek one in our colonies. It is undoubtedly an inconsistency, if not a hardship, that the poor English, Irish, and Scotch, who decline parochial relief, and prefer even lingering death to the horrors of a modern workhouse, cannot avail themselves of the free transport now bestowed upon the Indian Coolie, nor obtain, in the wastes of our colonial possessions, a space as large as the emancipated African enjoys in Jamaica and Trinidad. We shall conclude this evidence of the actual want of a fresh supply of hands to cultivate freshly-settled lands, with an extract of more than common length, but pardonable from its contents, showing, that while immigration must inevitably relieve Great Britain of her surplus labour, the harbours of the colonies are open to receive the adventurers, and capitalists are ready to welcome and employ them.

From the *Sydney Herald*, 10th February, 1844:—

"That there is great distress amongst the employers of labour, is admitted by the labourers themselves, who, however, judging from the proceedings of their meeting on Monday last, have formed very erroneous notions of the causes whence that distress has sprung, and of the means whereby it may be alleviated. They have recorded it as their opinion, that 'much of the present alarming distress is attributable to the late extensive and injudicious system of immigration;' and that 'until some change for the better be brought about, the renewal of emigration to this colony would only aggravate the distress, without benefiting the immigrants themselves.' A more matured acquaintance with the recent history of the colony would have taught them, that but for the copious immigration of the last three years, the distress would have been much deeper; and that without a steady continuance of immigration, the distress cannot be effectually relieved, but may, on the contrary, become worse and worse.

"In so far as the distress has consisted of the low state of profits from agriculture and sheep-farming, its cause must evidently be traced, as we noticed on Thursday, to the undue cost of production; and as the wages of labour form a chief element of that cost, it is clear that whatever has had the effect of adapting wages to the circumstances of the times, must have operated, immediately and actively, in diminishing the distress. Immigration has had that effect; immigration, therefore, instead of a *bane*, as the labourers allege, has been a substantial *blessing*. Four years ago, the settlers were deprived of their olden supplies of assigned convict labour, and were thrown entirely upon the resources of free labour. The natural effect of such a transition, supposing the labour-market to have received no fresh recruits, would have been an immediate rise of wages. A rise of wages at *that juncture*, occurring simultaneously with a fall in the price of wool, and a monstrous rise in the price of land, would have been one of the heaviest calamities that could have befallen the country. It would, in fact, have been absolute ruin. Neither the farmer nor the grazier could have stood up against it. Flocks and herds must have been turned adrift in the wilderness; our arable lands must have been abandoned; and the whole colony have become one wide scene of devastation and despair.

"Most fortunate it was that at this perilous crisis the tide of immigration rolled in upon our shores in unexampled fulness. Just as we had been deprived of convict assignment, and were threatened with an overwhelming scarcity and dearness of labour, thousands upon thousands of free labourers began to arrive in the market. The sudden demand was thus met with as sudden a supply. The impending calamity was warded off by the only human interposition that could possibly have availed. The gap in our ranks was filled up; the deficiency in the number of our labourers was made good; the exorbitancy of wages was checked; the grazier was enabled to retain his flocks and herds, the agriculturist to go on with his farm, the colony, as by a timely miracle, was saved.

"All this is matter, not of speculation, but of incontestable fact. And yet our labouring classes have been persuaded to believe, that to these most seasonable supplies of free workmen, 'much of the present distress is attributable!'

"Equally erroneous are the conclusions they have been taught to form, as to the expedients by which the distress may be assuaged. They would put a stop to immigration 'until some change for the better shall be brought about.' There can be no change for the better *but one*—an increase in the profits of our great colonial investment. We have shown that there can be no considerable augmentation of profits, without a decided abatement in the cost of production; that of one of the two chief elements of cost, the price of land, there is no prospect of abatement for many years to come; and that therefore the only expedient to which we can turn with any hope in its practicability, is a reduction in the wages of labour. To this purpose spoke all the witnesses before the select committees of the last session of council. At the present prices of wool, and under the subsisting land regulations, nothing can make the fleece remunerative but CHEAP LABOUR—cheap, that is, with reference to the actual returns of its produce. There was a time when flockmasters might regard the question of wages as one of liberality or parsimony; when they could well afford to be liberal, and when parsimony would have been a just ground of reproach. That time has gone by. The question is now one of *mere possibility*. As regards the prosecution of their pursuits, it is one of *life* or *death*. It is not what they are *expected* to give, or what they could *wish* to give—but, simply and sternly, what they CAN give. Whatever may be the promptings of their humanity—however anxious they may be to escape those imputations of niggardliness which the working classes are but too ready to cast upon them—they are forced now to this strait alternative, EITHER TO GIVE LOW WAGES, OR TO GIVE UP WOOLGROWING. These are the horns of their dilemma; and, say what demagogues will in their speeches *ad captandum vulgum*, and send what petitions they choose to parliament, from these horns there is no escape.

"Nor does this dilemma involve the settlers only; it involves all orders and degrees of the people; it involves the well-being, if not the very existence, of the colony. Upon the question, shall rural labour be sufficient and cheap, or insufficient and dear? depends the ulterior question, shall Australia flourish or decay—march onward in the progress of civilized nations, or relapse into her primitive poverty and barbarism?

"Now, even were we to admit for a moment that the colony is *at present* supplied with adequate and cheap labour, what would the anti-immigrationists gain by the concession? The movements of the country are not circumscribed like those of a mill-horse. They are in their very nature progressive and diffusive.

Flocks and herds are increasing and multiplying all the year round. Hundreds are perpetually swelling into thousands, and thousands into tens of thousands, and tens of thousands into hundreds of thousands, and these into millions, by a law of creation which it would be foolish and sinful to resist, and which it is both our duty and our interest to carry out. With this increase of live stock, the necessity for shepherds and herdsmen of course keeps pace. The sufficiency of yesterday is an insufficiency to-day; and hence even the cautious Sir George Gipps deemed it his duty to report to the Secretary of State, that an accession of ten thousand people per annum would be requisite to meet the ever-growing demand for rural industry.

"For what earthly reason, then, can the continuance of immigration have been thus selected by the working classes as an object of virulent opposition? We know of none—we can conceive none—but the mistaken love of monopoly. The people who have been instigated to this opposition are taught to believe, that more immigration would do harm to their class, and its stoppage do them good. Nothing could be more contrary to the truth. If immigration stop, employers will wax poorer and poorer, and employment of course become scarcer and scarcer. If immigration go on, in judicious adaptation to the wants of the country, employers will be able to extend their operations, new capital will be invested in the soil, profits will revive, and work and wages be within the reach of all. In trying to stop immigration, therefore, the labouring classes, to use a vulgar metaphor, are 'cutting their own throats.'"

SPORTS AND PASTIMES IN INDIA.*

BY E. H. MALCOLM.

So far back as 1808, a jockey-club was formed at Calcutta, from which time annual races took place until the year 1832, when a commercial panic put a stop to the amusement; and for four years it was neglected, and even discountenanced by government; but in 1836 the races were again renewed with great spirit and success, the Governor-General, Sir C. Metcalfe, giving a piece of plate to be run for. The supporters of the Indian turf are composed exclusively of gentlemen, either members of the civil or military services, or wealthy individuals, whose pleasure it is to encourage sport. There are no gamblers or blacklegs who speculate as a means of livelihood.

"The race-course itself forms part of the esplanade surrounding the glacis of Fort William, and is adorned with a handsome stand; where, on a cold and fine morning in January, the beauty and fashion of Calcutta delight to congregate, and around which the motley groups may vie, in point of singularity, though not in number, with Epsom on a Derby day. The wealthy Hindoos in their carriages, and the stately, sedate-looking Mussulmans, are alike present to view the *tumosha*, as it is called." †

The races, as do most of the amusements of India, commence at sunrise, and terminate by ten o'clock; this is a necessity, which is borne the better from the convenience which it consults. The business of the day is not trenched upon in the pursuit of the pleasures of the field.

* Continued from page 225. † Stocqueler.

The example liberally set by Sir Charles Metcalfe, of patronizing the races in purse and person, was annually followed by his successor, Lord Auckland, who, with his family, made a point of attending them, and, during the rule of the subsequent governors-general they have been favourably regarded; Lord Ellenborough proved himself a munificent patron of the sport, during the recent season. Even on the frontier station of Ferozepore racing has lately taken place under the auspices of the Governor-General, who was himself present at them.

A few of the details of turf management in India may not be unacceptable. We have before us at this moment a card of the December meeting of the Anglo-Indian Epsom, which we beg to present to the ordinary reader as a curiosity, and to the sporting man as "something more," because its perusal may probably extend his sporting knowledge, and at the same time introduce him to some of the more prominent names connected with the Bengal Jockey Club:—

December Meeting, 1843-44.

Nominations to the Stakes closed on the 1st *December,* 1843.

Purse of 50 *G. M.* (*Gold Mohurs*), *Auckland Cup, Weights and Distance.*

Mr. Maclean's b. a. h. *Glenmore.*
Mr. Jones's b. a. h . . *Chusan.*
Do. gr. a. h. . . . *The Friar.*
The Squire's " . . . *Walmer.*
" b. a. h. . . . *Rochester.*
" " . . . *Gauntlet.*
Mr. Allan's gr. a. h. . . *Glendower.*
Mr. West's gr. a. h. . . *Commissioner.*
" b. a. h. . . *Mistake*
" gr. a. h. . . *Cruiskeen.*

This race was followed by one on the succeeding day for the *Bengal Club Cup,* and another for a purse of fifty gold mohurs. We need not repeat the list of running-horses, but the names of other sporting men occur as competitors in the various heats.

The best Arab ever brought on the Bengal turf is described by the *Calcutta Idler,* in his latest contribution to the *Calcutta Star,* to be *Elepoo,* "an Arab that has won every Derby on the Indian turf. Barring accidents, (continues the *Idler,*) *Elepoo* is fully certain to prove himself as great as a *plate* horse as a *maiden.*"

The horses employed for Indian racing are galloways, Cape country breeds, New South Wales horses, and Arabs. There are race-courses, in addition to Calcutta, at the other presidencies, and at Agra, Mhow, Patna, Ferozepore, Dacca, &c., &c. (The Madras races were given up from want of encouragement, last season.) The names of the gentlemen who mainly support the Bengal turf (1843-4) will be found completed in the following short enumeration: Messrs. Lovell, White, Cloud, Fuller, Lisle, Black, Captain Pattinson, Messrs. Felix, Roberts, Fitzpatrick, Major Parsons, Captain Lovatt, Colonel Reynolds, Mr. Millison, Captain Mersham, Messrs. Henry, George, Wilbraham, North, Douglas. In former years, when racing was discountenanced by the authorities, any servant of the government engaged on the turf was compelled to adopt a *nom de guerre* to prevent his being a marked man, and so it remained until Sir Charles Metcalfe took off the ban; the odium removed, sporting men in India had no occasion to, and do not, assume an *alias*. At this time a government stud is kept up.

The jockeys of the Indian turf are occasionally picked from the light weights of the native community; but, generally speaking, the riders are the owners.

A correspondent of the *Englishman*, reporting the Patna races, which came off on the 31st of last December, gives some insight into the mode of betting adopted. It was a galloway sweepstakes, gentlemen riders, catch weights, half a mile:—

> "Betting now began to run high, several *pots of jam* were staked on the event; six to five in *pints of Gamble's oysters* was offered on the field, against *Paddey*, and a *real York ham* to a *Berkley cheese* on *Paddey*, against *Miss Wicket*, the favourites. The scene became most exciting. The start for the second heat was beautiful, and for the first quarter you might have covered the whole lot with a sheet of the *Englishman!*"

The Patna "*Vates*" alludes to one of the matches as having been won easily, the horse (maiden Arab) doing the last half mile in one minute and one second; the two miles, in four minutes fifteen seconds. He then tells us that in a quarter-mile heat an 11 st. 11 lb. horse won easy in 29 seconds. These particulars are only cited here as showing what sort of running is performed in India. The racers, for weight, are selected from animals of seven and eight stone to eleven and twelve stone. The *Favourite* fetches an equally extraordinary price in India with that given in England. We have already named *Elepo* oas the *Little Wonder* of the season. The chief races at Calcutta are held in December, and denominated "the *Great Weller Stakes* of 10 gold mohurs each, with 50 gold mohurs from the funds, for maiden Arabs;" also "the purse of 50 gold mohurs added to a sweepstakes of 25 gold mohurs, seven and eight-stone horses."

"The chief characteristic of the Arab as a race-horse, (says Mr. Stocqueler,) is its bottom and power of endurance, rather than actual speed, rendering them peculiarly adapted for the description of races in vogue in Calcutta, which are seldom less than two-mile, and often extend to three-mile heats."

Hunting has been introduced in India much upon the same footing that the Italian Opera has obtained in England. Anglo-Indians do not hunt and enjoy the sport with the *gusto* of a Warwickshire squire, but with the same sort of feeling that affects the majority of Englishmen when they resort to no less a place than the Opera House. Fashion has her slaves everywhere, and we accommodate ourselves to her "fantastic tricks," though it may pain us to perform the homage. Fox and hare hunting, and all similar British sports, are as decidedly out of place in India, as elephant catching in England, Ireland, or Scotland. One of the Calcutta papers, in examining this subject, remarks, that an Anglo-Indian "runs into his fox in thirty minutes, without a check, instead of hunting him four times as long. The story is told in three words: a find—a burst—a kill. Where—exclaims the

Calcutta Editor, with the enthusiasm of the huntsman, and writing with a vigour and feeling reminding us of the way Knowles has dealt with the same theme in his comedy of the *Love Chase*—" where is your field dotted with striving dogs? Where are the select few, apart from the rest, with most sweet voices and persuasive action, trying a cast? Where the expectant eyes and ears that wait upon each motion and each sound? and where is the burst of music that broke upon the ear as the scent was again picked up?" Hunting with the hounds, though by no means of a first-rate description, is still a diversion considerably supported by the bloods of the City of Palaces.

Some good hunting of its kind is obtained in Ghazeepore, Allahabad, and the Neilgherry Hills, (in the Bombay presidency). An animal called jungle-sheep supplies good sport on the hills; it lives in pairs, is nimble, wary, and shy, and is accordingly difficult to slay, though, from the delicious flavour of its flesh, sought after with much anxiety.

To the Calcutta hunt (says the "Hand-Book of India") the palm of superiority has been awarded, both from the better adaptation of the country about Calcutta for the diversion, and from the style in which the club is maintained. The hunt itself has existed since the year 1820; the kennels, situate at Alipore, the southern suburb of Calcutta, in convenience, extent, and appearance, might vie with the best in the mother-country. Thirty couples of hounds, selected from the draughts of the best kennels in England, are annually imported at a cost of 200 to 250 rupees (20*l.* to 25*l.*) per couple. The season commences in November, and ends in April; the pack meets also in the first month of the rainy season, June. The sport is commenced very early in the morning, and is concluded before the sun gains power. "The chase-loving Anglo-Indian rises by candle-light, drives himself to cover either at Dum-Dum or Gowripore, a distance of eight or nine miles, where the hounds having also performed their journey on a spring-van, throw off at sun-rise (half-past five), and probably finish their second jackal by nine o'clock, returning home to breakfast by ten." The same writer affords his readers the following insight of the game hunted in India:—

"The substitute for the English fox is the jackal, somewhat larger in size, and, when fairly put to the stretch, nowise inferior in speed; his nature, too, is similar, as he partakes of the love for poultry so strongly displayed in his English prototype." The country is next described: "The country, technically so called, consists of plains, or generally cultivated gardens, raised, to avoid the inundation consequent on the rainy season; jungles of bamboos densely planted, on which the Indian village is situated, and which requires no small skill on the part of the rider and hounds to thread when going the pace." Large ditches form the boundaries of the different gardens, or bamboo-rails, about the height of an English sheep-hurdle.

It appears that the breeding of hounds is impracticable in India, from the character of the climate; even out of the importations, few of the couples of one season survive the next.

The Neilgherry Hills, (of which we have before spoken,) by the Malabar route, 133 miles from Bombay, are a favourite resort of the Bombay and Madras officers on furlough, and who delight in shooting. The Neilgherries are described, rather extravagantly perhaps, as "breathing an atmosphere such as our first parents inhaled in Eden—so inviting is the open air, so gentle the heat of the sun." It is a fine sporting country, and the elk, hog, and deer afford excellent hunting. For the dog and gun, woodcocks are the great attraction. The bagging of the first bird of the season is an epoch held in jubilee by the natives, and great is the pride felt by the European who has shot more than a hundred birds in a season. It is incredible the avidity with which the sport is followed, and the high reward paid for intelligence of their appearance. The officer on leave on the Neilgherries who has communicated the foregoing information, states that the game was very scarce in the last (1843) season; neither, he says, is the elk now common.

In the winter season Europeans are wont to resort for amusement to the athletic exercise of cricket; for which the indolent natives, by the bye, look upon them as absolute maniacs. The latter specially abominate this sport, as being the acmé of drudgery; and, egad, so it must be in the tropics! It was capricious fashion who introduced cricket into the country, and not the *bonâ fide* inclinations of his silly votaries. Whilst we are alluding to cricket-playing, it may be mentioned, *en passant*, that a Hindoo has seldom or ever been known to catch a cricket-ball; when desired to stop one and deliver it, he usually runs alongside the ball till its volant power is spent, and then as warily avoids contact with it, as any one would avoid a red-hot poker. There was, however, a few years back, known to Calcutta cricket-players, a native enjoying the soubriquet of "Mutton," who, though not much of a dabster at "catching," "bowling," or "batting," would intercept the flying ball with rare courage, interposing his person in a very grotesque position, rather than the ball should enjoy its mid-air career. "Mutton" was consequently considered a *rara avis*. Cricket associations abound; that at Calcutta being the principal, and giving tone to all others. Wickets are pitched on the Calcutta ground, and matches of consequence frequently played, throughout the months of November and December. Some idea of the facility with which cricket is played in the tropics may be formed by reading the descriptions of the sport written by resident writers in the Indian papers.

Golf is played at every station of any importance in Hindostan, the close of the year being the favourable season. The Bombay Golf Club forms the *point d'appui* of the sport. Some of the first gentlemen of the country are enrolled as members. The club annually presents valuable prizes of plate and medals to successful golf players, who are also members, and is in systematic communication with the golf clubs at home; with one at Blackheath especially, to which club a gold medal was lately despatched through Colonel Cannan. The compliment is awarded by one club to the other, in return for privileges mutually conferred. In the Bombay presidency golf is played more frequently than in any other portion of India; it is spiritedly kept up at Colabah, Kurrachee, Mangalore, and Poonah; at the latter place the ground is considered peculiarly excellent.

But many readers who are not acquainted with the customs of Scotland, will infallibly ask, what kind of game, after all, is this golf? and we shall not be causing tedium by explaining:

"It is a game played with clubs of a peculiar form, and balls.* Holes of a size fit to receive an ordinary-sized tumbler are made in the ground in a series, at the distance of from 300 to 400 yards from each other. The player is furnished with a ball of about an inch and a half in diameter, formed of leather, stuffed as hard as possible with feathers; and this he plays from hole to hole with his club, he and his opponent contending which shall get it holed by the smallest number of strokes. The first thing to be done in playing is to don the costume of the club, a bright-coloured jacket, a cap, and a pair of strongly-nailed shoes, the last being always considered necessary, in Scotland at least, to give a firm footing while playing the long strokes. Much of the effect of the game is of course due to the nature of the ball, which, felt in the hand, seems as hard as a stone, but rebounds tremendously under a powerful appulsion; and under the hands of a good player, the ball is only touched, to be quickly lost in the distance."

But we return to our more immediate theme. With a necessarily brief notice of the aquatic sports of India we must close this chapter. "Trips on the water and over the water, up the river and down the river—jellies, jousts, junketing, and jaunts—skipping, sailing, shooting, and champaign;" these things (as a sprightly Calcutta writer informs us) take precedence of all others during the *Doorjah Poojah* holidays throughout October.

Boat-racing of a very superior order affords the Europeans of India plenty of amusement, when the season for it arrives—the season of elasticity and pleasure, when people "neither crawl nor drawl, but speak with emphasis; when cloth coats are being taken to, and cashmere waistcoats are embracing the more vital parts; so that the eternal *whites* are ceasing to be an opprobrium to new arrivals, who imagine they have got into a community of waiters and barbers."

The Calcutta Regatta Club has for some years flourished under the highest patronage. Prizes for good rowing (on the river Hooghly) are given out of ample funds. An annual subscription of sixteen rupees is required to constitute a resident member, and ten rupees a non-resident. The committee of the regatta club consists of the following gentlemen, residents at Calcutta. (We give this list, as we have given other collections of names in this article, because we believe there are many persons at home who will recognize with pleasure the nomencla-

* A full and interesting account of this Scottish game appeared in one of the numbers of *Chambers' Edinburgh Journal*. We have taken our explanation of the mode of playing golf from that accurate source.

tures of friends and connections long alienated from them.) Captain Onslow, Secretary; Captain Bowman, Captain Nisbett, Capt. Richards, Captain Mackenzie, and Mr. A. Thompson. Three six-oared and one four-oared boat are now the property of the club, in which some excellent matches have been tried, proving that the quality of the boat-builder, and the stamina of the rowers, were deserving of each other. The regattas, like other European sports which take place during the cold season, are productive of much vivacity and amusement. They are always well attended, particularly by the temporary visitors, whose new faces, in fact, serve to allure the listless residents of pseudo *ton* to the same haunts. "In this way only are the latter indemnified for the lethargic in-door lives they have led during the previous months of caloric, and are re-energized to again sustain the same infliction during the dull and insipid season which is approaching."

What a dirge is this over the tropical miseries of human life! The pleasures of our Indian friends would seem to greet them only in the language of Milton—

> "To make death in them live."

In conclusion, we have to beg our readers to accept what chit-chat we have supplied them with in the foregoing, merely as *facon de parler*, intended to amuse for its lightness and novelty. It has not been our intention to opinionate; neither have we wished to deal seriously with anything or anybody in the course of these observations. If, as it is likely, there be *pragmatists*, or *quidnuncs*, to answer to, for errors of omission and commission in this article, or its humble predecessors, our only mode of apology will be by requesting them to excuse us from taking the trouble of going out to Calcutta, where,

> "In cotton vest the people throng,
> With brazen noise of horn and gong,"

merely for the purpose of qualifying ourselves for writing more correctly on Anglo-Indian society.

ANOTHER GLANCE AT WESTERN AUSTRALIA.

If it be not a contradiction in terms, we may designate our magazine a "general class periodical," for it is so much a class publication, that it devotes itself to the interests of the colonies, shipping, and trade—while it is so far general, that it does not confine itself to any particular branch of those interests, but is the organ alike of foreign and home trade, and particularly of the whole of that vast colonial empire, on which the sun never ceases to shine, from the time when it rises upon the verdant plains of Eastern Australia, till its setting upon the western prairies of British North America. Confining ourselves to no particular colony, it is our duty to note the progress of each and all; and in doing so, we may occasionally receive great assistance from those distinct advocates which have recently sprung up, giving from time to time the progress of the particular colonies to which they devote themselves. South Australia and New Zealand have each had a separate organ for some years, but it is only lately that Western Australia has been represented among the metropolitan press. The consquence has been, that we have been long in the dark as to the movements of the settlers, but now we are enabled to glean accurate information of their progress; on two previous occasions we have availed ourselves of it, and we now propose to take another glance into the affairs of the colony. From it we gather, that Western Australia is not without her troubles, nor exempted from the depression which has been felt so severely by her neighbours. The embarrassment in her monetary affairs is by some ascribed to the recent commencement of a system of credit upon bills, while others contend that it arises from the extensive importations of goods and grain from the sister colonies, which are so ruinously overstocked. But, whatever may be the difference as to the cause, both parties seem to agree in one point—that the embarrassment is but temporary. If it arise from the bill system, we have the assurance of the governor that it is now being checked—if from excessive importation, we have confidence and consolation in the following facts:—

"Our own private correspondence informs us that business is slack, prices low, and goods too plentiful; but other letters, which we have seen, go farther than this, and infer from these indications of depression—*temporary* depression—some dismal injury to trade. Now we ourselves are not in the slightest degree surprised to hear that the market is overstocked, and prices consequently reduced below their remunerative rate; on the contrary, it is what we have long been prepared to hear, and is but the natural consequence of the depression in the sister colonies. But it is not necessary to devise a cure, for the evil is one which will provide its own remedy; the market being reduced so low by these inundations of imports from Sydney and South Australia, will become an unprofitable one to the exporter, and, being unable any longer to realise a profit on his goods, he will cease to send them, but seek a higher market, and thus will prices be restored to their *equilibrium.* In fact, this is not mere prediction; the *Water Witch* has been wholly employed for five or six months in carrying these imports into Western Australia from Adelaide, but in the last files of the *Cerneen*); Isle of France paper), we find her arrival reported at the Mauritius, "from Adelaide and Swan River with a cargo of sundries for this port." These "sundries" are part of her original cargo from Adelaide which could not be disposed of at Swan River without a sacrifice, and are consequently carried to the higher market of the Mauritius. The result of this will be that the Adelaide merchants will now ship to the latter place direct, and the market at Swan River, freed from these sudden inundations of their supplies, will recover its just rate, while a wholesome fear of the repetition of such importations will prevent the recurrence of exorbitant prices.

"But even allowing South Australia to be in such a wretched condition, that her merchants and producers are glad to dispose of their surplus stores at any price, it only requires a little exertion on the part of the Western Australian agriculturists to produce such a supply of grain at home, that the government can put a prohibitory duty upon the imported flour of Adelaide (the principal article of her export to her Western neighbour), and thus regulate the supply by the demand.

"To the new emigrant, the scarcity of money and low price of goods is rather an encouragement than an impediment. The capitalist can obtain a higher interest or his capital, and will require less of it for his own use, while the labourer will be enabled to live at a cheap rate, without any corresponding reduction of his wages, labour still being scarce and high."

These arguments are conclusive, and if they were not sufficiently supported by reasonable and common probability, they have already been proved correct by what has since actually occurred.

We were not aware of the existence of limestone in the colony, until we read the following:—

"In the 'Report of the Western Australian Agricultural Society,' (vol. i. p 43,) we find an interesting paper on the lime of the colony, communicated by Mr. J. G Austin, the architect, from which we extract the following particulars:—

"'There are three varieties of material suitable for lime, namely—the common stratified limestone, abounding in great masses throughout the numerous ridges and mounds in the neighbourhood of Perth and Fremantle, as likewise in sandy, detached (apparently) positions, between the neighbouring settlements, and which, in many cases, could be profitably worked, where locality to a seaport is convenient. The lime made from some of these appears to possess the greatest merit. Next in order comes the stone which is collected from the banks of the Swan, some of which produces tolerably good lime, but, from what I can learn, is not so good as that prepared from the above-mentioned stone. This difference is, perhaps, to be chiefly attributed to the deterioration of the natural qualities by atmospheric agency, consequent upon its exposed position, or from partial admixture of fossil and diluvium deposits, or it may be also partly owing to a different mode of conversion into lime. The other material alluded to is the shells of oysters, cockles, &c. which have been raised from the beds of rivers, &c. in the colony. These, if well purged from saline impregnation and carefully calcined, would produce a very excellent cement; but I am apprehensive that the very limited quantity that could be conveniently found, added to the cost of labour in raising them, for the present, would be a great barrier to its adoption.'"

We have also the statistics of the state of agriculture.

"The following statement of agricultural affairs for 1843, is from the Annual Report of the Western Australian Agricultural Society:—

LIVE STOCK.

Counties, &c.	*Horses.*	*Cattle.*	*Sheep.*	*Goats.*	*Swine.*
Perth	440	900	6,132	1,962	373
York	286	879	38,821	633	533
Toodyay	195	1,215	21,375	410	311
Murray	51	606	146	17	378
Leschenault	58	534	3,023	556	143
Sussex	56	406	604	135	170
Plantagenet	113	321	6,090	10	43
Williams	3	—	—	—	—
Totals	1,202	4,861	76,191	3,733	1,951

ACRES UNDER CROP.

Counties, &c.	*Wheat.*	*Grain.*	*Potatoes.*	*Gardens.*
Perth	1,163	181	45	209
York	652	247	—	—
Toodyay	417	102	—	20
Murray	304	2	11	16
Leschenault	110	9	17	9
Sussex	189	27	18	5
Plantagenet	48	30	9	15
Williams	—	—	—	—
Totals	2,883	598	99	274

Showing an increase on last year of 133 horses, 625 head of cattle, 15,811 sheep, and 238 swine; and of 844 acres of wheat; 45 of other grain; 20 of potatoes, and 5 of gardens; and a decrease of 1890 goats."

Some such authentic information as this for the guidance of emigrants has long been wanted; it is here given on the authority of the Agricultural Society:

Rate of Wages.—Agricultural labourers, from 3s. 6d to 4s. per day, without, or 30s. to 50s. per month, with, board and lodging. Journeymen artizans, from 6s. to 10s. per day. Gardeners, 5s. per day. Ploughmen and carters, from 4s. to 4s. 6d. per day. Head shepherds, from £30 to £40 a year, with board and lodging. Female servants, from £10 to £20 a year; and male servants, from £15 to £24 a year, with board and lodging. Herd boys, £1 per month, with board and lodging.

Prices of Agricultural Produce.—Wheat from 6s. to 7s. a bushel; barley and oats the same. Potatoes, from £10 to £12 per ton (higher than usual this season). Hay, £6 to £8.

Prices of Live Stock—A good cart-horse, from £25 to £40; a riding-horse, from £20 to £30. A pair of oxen, broken into work, £30 to £40. A good milch cow, with calf at foot, £12. Sheep, ewe and lamb, £1. A breeding sow, £2 to £4; pigs, two months old, 8s. each. Cape goats, per head, 5s.

Prices of Implements, &c.—A colonial-made farmer's cart, £20 to £25. A wagon of the same description, £50. Carson's plough, £7. A pair of harrows, from £4 to £5.

Prices of Provisions.—Salt pork, £5 per cask; fresh pork, 9d. per lb. Mutton, 7d. or 8d; Veal, 8d. to 10d.; Beef, 6d. to 8d. per lb. A pair of fowls, from 4s. to 5s. Bacon, 1s. per lb. Salt butter, 1s. 6d.; fresh butter, 2s. 6d. a pound; Milk, 6d. a quart, in the towns. Eggs, 2s. a dozen. The four-pound loaf, 1s. Flour, £22 a ton. Cheese—English, 2s.; Dutch, 1s.; Colonial, 10d. per lb. Tea, 2s. to 3s.; Coffee, 8d. per lb. Rice, 1½d. per lb. Brown sugar, 2½d. to 4d.; loaf sugar, 10d. per lb. English salt, 3d per lb.; colonial salt, £4 per ton. Pepper, 1s. 3d. per lb. Dried fish, £1 per cwt. Vegetables, about 2d. per lb. English beer, 2s. 6d.; colonial beer, 2s. a gallon. Rum, 15s.; brandy, £1; gin, 17s. 6d. a gallon. Cape wine, 4s. a gallon.

Prices of Domestic Articles.—Tallow candles, 1s.; sperm candles, 2s. 3d. per lb. Firewood, 10s. per cord. Common soap, 5d. per lb. Lamp oil, 4s. a gallon. Tobacco, 3s. per lb.

Prices of Clothing.—Coloured Shirts 4s. to 4s. 6d.; baize shirts, 6s. to 7s. each. Plush trousers, 6s. to 10s.; canvas ditto, 4s. 6d.; duck ditto, 4s. 6d.; moleskin ditto, 10s. to 13s. Moleskin coat and trousers, £1 10s. Moleskin jacket, 5s. to 8s. Manilla hats, 8s.; straw hats, 2s. to 5s. Laced boots, 17s; nailed boots, £1. Shoes, 10s. to 12s.; children's shoes, 2s. to 3s. Socks, 1s. 6d.; worsted stockings, 2s. Duck frocks, 4s. Gown prints, 8s. to 9s. Common shawls, 6s. Stays, 5s. Blankets, £1 per pair. Sheets, 8s. Rugs 4s.

Price of Land.—Good sheep-farms, of known good quality, may generally be purchased at from 3s. to 6s. per acre.

The following are the latest prices of stock that we find quoted:—

Prices of Stock—Guildford market, 23rd February.—A cow, £9 to £11—for a very fine one, £13 13s. was offered and refused; store pigs, weighing 40 lbs, 16s. a head; wethers, weighing 43 lbs., 18s. a head, (delivered at Perth); ewes, weighing 37 lbs., 16s. a head; steers, £11; an unbroken filly, £30. Fine wheat, 5s. 6d. per bushel; oats, same price.

The Legislative Council opened for the session of 1844 on the 8th of March, on which occasion the Governor delivered the following important address:—

"*Gentlemen of the Legislative Council*—I have been induced to call you together at this period, in consequence of a memorial which has been presented to me, signed by several respectable and influential agriculturists, respecting the deranged state of our monetary affairs, arising, it is stated, out of excessive importations; and requesting that this council might as early as possible take into consideration the actual condition of the colony, with a view to the adoption of such measures as may be deemed requisite to avert the impending evils. The official year not being yet concluded, I am prevented from laying before you documentary statements, of that period, of the revenue and expenditure; of the progress of the surveys; of the amount of the exports and imports; with other statistical details, all of which will be prepared so soon as the requisite information is in the hands of the government.

"I am not at all inclined to shut my eyes to the positive fact, that embarrassment to a certain extent does prevail in the country, and the wisest plan to adopt to overcome difficulties is at once to meet them. I shall be most happy, therefore, if we can attain to some general concurrence as to the real causes of this distress, and the proper course to be taken to alleviate it. But, at the same time, it does appear to me, that, looking over the whole face of the colony, and not confining our attention to any one particular portion of it, decided marks of gradual improvement are discernible. I think it would be impossible for any one to pass through the country, and compare what he may see now with what he may remember of it twelve months or two years ago, and not to be struck with observing the large quantity of new land that has been broken up; the much greater amount of every species of cultivation; the establishment of fresh farming locations; the increased facilities given to travellers by the opening of new lines of road; and the regular communication which is now maintained, by means of the post, with each separate station. But one and a principal advance which has been made towards a better order of things, is the much greater number than formerly of small farms, held by tenantry. It is well known in every country that the owners of estates, who may themselves attempt to cultivate them, and can only do so through the means of paid labourers, are not those who derive the most profit from the land; but by giving to those very labourers an interest beyond their daily or monthly hire, in the good working of a farm, a change is immediately effected; and the more widely a system of tenantry can be carried out, the more completely will the agricultural resources of this, and of every other country, be developed.

"One of the subjects to which your attention will, I expect, be first and most particularly turned, is the depression of the farming interest in the colony, and you will be called upon to decide whether any, and what, relief can be afforded. Connect with this, the question of the policy of a Corn Law will doubtless be made a matter of discussion. My own opinion on this point remains unchanged, though I still recognise it as one of the bounden duties of the Legislature to inquire again and again into the representations which may be made to them, of the injury under which any individual or class of the community is suffering, and which it is in the power of a legislative enactment, having regard to the good of all, to rectify. Before you enter upon this most important deliberation, I would request you to remember the difficulties which may press most hardly upon a people can never be traced up, or assigned, to any one separate or isolated source;—that the wages of labour, which enter so largely into the cost of production, still maintain themselves at a height much beyond what is warranted by the profits which stock and capital yield to the employers, or by the present cost to the labourer of the comforts and necessaries of life; that the fixed interest of money borrowed on mortgage by the landholders for the improvement of their properties, at a time when farm produce bears a fair value, must act as a serious burden and drawback to their exertions, now that the prices have fallen; and that there is scarcely a possibility of effecting any sales at all, even for those articles which do not come into competition with imports.

"The vicious system of credit upon bills, to which I have adverted on a former occasion, and which is now only beginning to be checked, has encouraged a ruinous expenditure, forestalled income, and created a vast accumulation of debt. I have endeavoured, from the best sources I had access to, to make a calculation of the amount of this paper now in circulation, and I believe I am under the mark when I state it at £35,000; whilst I am led to believe, that the books of the merchants and tradesmen of Perth alone, show debts amounting to fully £20,000 more; and you will still further bear in mind, that the monetary system of any country must necessarily be liable to derangement when there are so few exports, and when, consequently, almost every article imported—that is to say, every comfort or necessary not produced or manufactured here—must be paid for in ready money."

His Excellency then announced his intention of introducing the following bills during the Session:—1st, to amend the Act for the Building of Churches and Chapels, and the maintenance of ministers of religion in the colony; 2nd, to provide for the apprenticeship, guardianship, and control of the government juvenile immigrants; 3rd, to allow the aborigines to give evidence without oath; 4th, to prevent the unauthorised occupation of Crown Lands; 5th, for the regulation of streets in towns; 6th, to amend the "Improvement of Towns" Act; and, 7th, to regulate the summary proceedings of magistrates."

We think the following calls urgently for the attention of the Colonial Church Society, and the bench of bishops, as it is essential that our colonies should be Protestant countries:—

THE ESTABLISHED CHURCH IN WESTERN AUSTRALIA.—It behoves all friends of the Church of England to look to her supremacy in Western Australia; we will not say it is now threatened, but it may be as well to remind them that several Roman Catholic priests have lately arrived in the colony, and are raising a chapel at Perth for the celebration of their religion. We do not quarrel with their zeal and energy; on the contrary, they do them credit—we only wish the Church of England exhibited as much activity, and that one of the colonial bishoprics so long talked of, was erected in this colony. It is now some time since the colonists were so destitute of spiritual instruction, as to send a most pressing request to England for the aid of a minister of the Church, which was readily responded to by the formation of a "Western Australian Missionary Society," and the despatch of two clergymen to the colony, the Reverend Messrs. King and Postlethwaite. Besides these gentlemen, there are now, we believe, four others; but are six clergymen sufficient for a community of 4000 souls, scattered over an expanse of country 1,200 miles by 800, in extent? We should be indeed sorry to think that the society in question, when it changed its denomination to the more general one of the "Colonial Church Society," ceased to be reminded of the wants of that colony for whose benefit it was particularly formed; but when we see Western Australia placed far down in the list of projected bishoprics we naturally ask ourselves, why is this?

The colony is under the diocese of the Bishop of Australia, but he is located at Sydney, nearly 3000 miles beyond its limits, and it is therefore left to the care of six clergymen; the Rev. J. B. Wittenoom, M.A., the colonial chaplain, takes charge of Perth and its environs, and the Rev. George King, of Fremantle: the Rev. Mr. Woolaston officiates at Australind, the Rev. W. Mitchell, at the Middle Swan, the Rev. W. Mears, in the York district, and the Rev. Mr. Postlethwaite, at the Upper Swan; but as the district of each of these gentlemen is most extensive, and his congregation widely distributed, it is no light duty to attend to all, and notwithstanding their utmost exertions, it must be impossible even to perform it to their own satisfaction. It is true that there is also a Wesleyan minister at Perth, the Rev. Mr. Smithies, but the clergymen of the Church of England are totally inadequate in number to the wants of that church. Why then is the promised bishopric withheld? We had understood that, when Mr. George Fletcher Moore was in England, every arrangement was made, under the Bishop of London's sanction, and really we are at a loss to know what is the cause of farther delay. It cannot be the want of funds on the part of the Colonial Church Society, for no funds were asked for. Mr. Moore's suggestion was, that the colony should pay the expenses, and the following plans were under consideration:—1st., that the colonists should subscribe land to the amount of 12,000 to 15,000 acres, for which the Government should exchange one unbroken grant of the same extent, and transfer it to the Society, who should then pay the stipend of the bishop, proposed to be £600 per annum, (which would have been sufficient to support his rank, in proportion to the salary of the Governor, £800); 2nd., that the Government and the Society should divide the charge between them, the colonists still subscribing the value in land; or, 3rd., that the Government should at once make the requisite grant of land, to be sold for the maintenance of the bishopric. These several plans were placed under the consideration of the Bishop of London by Mr. Moore, and it was understood that one of them had been agreed to; but, although nearly two years have now elapsed since Mr. Moore's return to the colony, no farther steps have been taken.

We have given particular mention to these details that the subject may not be forgotten, and in the hope that they may have the effect of attracting the attention of the Colonial Church Society to it.

We find, among other indications of the colony's advancement at home, that an order has been sent by the Lords of the Admiralty, for a large quantity of the naval timber of the colony for the use of Portsmouth dockyard, and that a party of juvenile emigrants was despatched by the Government in the last vessel.

We look upon the depression which is admitted to prevail in Western Australia, in the same light as the editor of the *Swan River News*—as merely temporary, and capable of being relieved by a little exertion on the part of the settlers. There is nothing inherently bad—nothing radically wrong—to cause it: it arises from extrinsic circumstances, and the colony possesses such remarkable qualifications, that it is capable of triumphing over difficulties far more threatening than the transient one which has, no doubt, ere now, passed over it.

COLONIAL STATISTICS.

[NEW SERIES.]

NO. VII.—ST. VINCENT.

Geography and History.—This, the most lovely of the Caribbee Islands, is situate in 13° 10′ 15″ north latitude; 60° 37′ 57″ west longitude; N. N. E. 78 miles from Grenada, and nearly equidistant from Grenada and Barbadoes.

The extreme length of the island north to south is 24 miles, and the extreme breadth 18 miles; the area covers 131¼ square miles of land, or 84,000 acres, which are divided into five parishes, named St. George's, Charlotte, St. Andrew, St. David, and St. Patrick.

The island was discovered by Columbus in 1498, according to the authority of the historian of the British Colonies, but other writers aver that the precise date of the discovery remains in doubt. The first settlement was attempted by the French in 1655, in which they failed. It was subsequently taken from them by the English, in 1762, and finally ceded to Britain in 1763. (Vide *British Colonies* in the Army List.)

Scenery, Geology, &c.—In its configuration and general aspect, this island has been compared with its neighbour Grenada; the scenery of both has certainly the greatest claims to admiration.

"The series of mountains which occupy the central and southern districts of this island, beautiful in their forms and combinations, and rich in the variety of their vegetation, assume a more compact and uniform character in the northern quarter, where the loftiest mountain in the chain, the *Souffrière*, occupies the chief portion of the area, presenting towards the eastern or windward coast an extensive inclined plane, which possesses the finest soil in the island. The *Souffrière*, an active volcano, first threw out lava in 1818, but its most tremendous eruption occurred in 1812, when there issued from the mountain so dreadful a torrent of lava, and such clouds of ashes, as nearly covered the island. The crater is estimated at three miles in circumference, and 500 feet in depth. The valleys are the most beautiful imaginable; water is everywhere abundant, and the climate is reputed healthy."

The delicious valley of Beaumont is five miles long and one wide, entirely open to the sea, with lofty mountains at the upper part and sides, and throughout the vale a clear and rapid river.

The famed botanic garden about a mile from Kingston, occupies 30 acres of ground, in the form of an oblong square, the lower part level, but soon becoming a gradual ascent, until it terminates in a steep bill, a beautiful mountain-stream forming its northern boundary. Near the upper part of the garden, and in the centre, stands the governor's house, commanding a splendid view, immediately below the capital of the island, in front of the deep blue sea, in the distance a magnificent vista, bounded on each side by a long and spacious avenue of lofty forest-trees.

Soil.—The soil in the valleys is a rich tenacious loam, and occasionally a fine black mould; on the higher regions it assumes a more sandy character, and is less fertile.

Productions.—The staple productions are sugar and rum. The following enumeration of the fruits, esculents, &c., produced, will show the great variety of vegetable food afforded: sappadilloes, pomegranates, papaws, soursops, plantains, okros, peppers, cocoa-nuts, pigeon or angola peas, sweet potatoes, yams, taneas, cotton, chicori, granadillos, custard apples, guavas, cerasees, Java plums, mangoes, pineapples, Otaheite gooseberries, Jamaica and Ceylon plums, bread-fruit, silk, cotton, cloves, avocado pears, pompions, coffee, &c., &c.; nearly the whole of these fruits are in season throughout the year.

Climate.—The island is stated to stand high in reputation as a healthy station; hills and valleys, wood and water in abundance, are so disposed as to contribute to salubrity. Hurricanes have been severely felt in this island; that which occurred on the 11th August, 1831, destroyed property to the amount of 163,420*l.* The mean temperature at Kingston averages during the year between 68. and 86.

Towns.—These are Kingston, (S.W.,) chief town, Valliaqua (S.), Layon (W.), Barrowaille (W.), Chatteaubelair (W.) Kingston is on the shore of a deep and beautiful bay, protected by a battery (Cane-garden Point) on the south, and by Fort Charlotte on the north-west. Kingston consists of three streets, intersected by six others. There are about 300 of the larger-sized houses, the lower stories of which are in general built with stone or brick, and the upper of wood, with shingled roofs. The public buildings are plain, but substantial. The church is a large inelegant brick building, capable of containing 2,000 persons; it has an organ, a splendid chandelier, and a very handsome pulpit. This church was first opened for divine service in 1820, having cost the island and the home-governmentn early 50,000*l.* in its erection.

Roads.—The roads on the windward coast are tolerably good for thirty miles; their track in general is near to the sea-side. The highways are kept in repair by the proprietors of the estates, who have adjoining portions allotted to them by an act of the legislature, on which they are required to expend an estimated quantity of labour, and for which they are allowed a certain sum from the treasury.

Government.—The government of St. Vincent includes several small islands which lie between it and Grenada, and, as stated in the statistics of the latter colony, bear the name of the Grenadines. The first British governor appointed was Brig.-General R. Melville, in 1763. The following are the present governmental authorities:—Lieutenant-Governor, Lieutenant-Colonel Doherty; Chief Justice and Judge of the Vice-Admiralty Court, J. Peterson, Esq.; Attorney-General, P. Hobson, Esq.; Solicitor-General, J. R. Ross, Esq.; Colonial Secretary and Clerk of the Council, J. Beresford, Esq.; President of the Council, J. Peterson, Esq.; Speaker of the Assembly, H. N. Streeth, Esq.; Clerk of Patents, J. Drake, Esq.; Treasurer, G. Grant, Esq; Provost Marshal, A. Hobson, Esq.; Collector of the Customs, G. Huskisson, Esq.; Agent in London, J. Colquhoun, Esq.

Population.—In 1830 the population was computed as follows:—whites, 1,301; coloured, 2,824; negroes, 23,589: total, 27,714.

Religion—Education.—By a return of the number of churches, &c., of St. Vincent in 1836, we find that there are three livings, the whole annual value of which exceeds 1,000*l.*; there are three parsonage houses. Three dissenting places of worship exist in the parishes of St. George and St. Andrew. By the act 6 Geo. IV. (amended), the West Indian islands were divided into two sees. The salaries of the bishops, paid out of the 4½ per cent duties, are 4,000*l.* sterling each, with a provision for a retiring pension of 1,000*l.* after a service of ten years; and the sum of 4,300*l.* is at the disposal of the Bishop of Barbadoes for the maintenance of ministers, catechists, and schoolmasters in the diocese, with a limitation that no minister's salary is to exceed 300*l.* sterling.

Seven free schools are maintained mutually by the colony and the government; eight schoolmasters and schoolmistresses are appointed, receiving small salaries, ranging between 10*l.* and 80*l.* per annum. Total number of scholars, 161.

Commerce.—The commerce of St. Vincent is regulated by the officers of her Majesty's customs; a collector, comptroller, and three waiters constitute the establishment. The regulations of trade have been much simplified of late years, by the repeal of several hundred acts, and a consolidation of their provisions. The fees on shipping are now abolished.

The value of exports and imports in 1829, was—exports, 414,548*l.*; imports, 99,891*l.* There were exported in 1830—sugar, 261,551 cwt.;

rum, 173,262 gallons; coffee, 124 lbs. The imports of sugar into the United Kingdom in 1841 amounted to 110,205 cwts., about one-half the amount imported in 1831. The exports from the United Kingdom were for the year 1834, in value, 81,167*l.* For the same period, the number and tonnage of vessels inward amounted to 36 vessels, and 10,509 tons: outward, 40 vessels, 11,523 tonnage.

Currency.—Current value of coins in circulation: *silver coins*—Spanish dollar, 10s.; ½ dollar, 5s.; carolus, 2s.; pistareen, 1s. 6d.; quarter colonial coin, 4 dwts 9 grains, 2s. 6d.; English shilling, 2s. 3½d *Gold coins*—from the doubloon to the English sovereign. *Copper coins*—English penny-piece and stampee, 2½d. each.

Revenue.—Aggregate annual value of the productions of St. Vincent (parliamentary paper) 812,081*l.* The last published table, or comparative yearly statement of the revenue and expenditure of St. Vincent, shows that the revenue in 1836 amounted to 122,82*l.*, and expenditure for the same year to 115,54*l.* The local revenues amounted to 634*l.* in 1836.

Military Force.—The military force consists of a garrison of British regulars, composed of one wing of a regiment, with a few artillerymen, and a numerous militia, a full regiment strong. Fort Charlotte, Kingston, which fortification, placed on a rock above the level of the sea, contains barracks for 600 men, and has thirty-four pieces of artillery. There is another fort or battery on the island.

Colonial Arms.—The subject represented in the shield, is a slave making an offering upon an altar, which is guarded by the genius of peace. The motto inscribed beneath is, "*Pax et Justitia.*"

THE TREATY OF COMMERCE WITH CHINA.

To the Editor of the Colonial Magazine.

SIR, Ning-po, China, 19th April, 1844.

Observing in the *Canton Press* of the 10th February, 1844, extracts from the *London Mail* of November 4th, 1843, I read one from the *Examiner*—it will serve admirably for my text at present. I disagree from it almost entirely. I should say that its writer is not a merchant, and has never been in China; indeed, I may add, in the East at all.

If I recollect, the *Examiner* was a paper I read and liked much when in Europe, and if I remember its tone, spirit, and standing, likes the truth, and can well afford to be put right.

The *Examiner* says, "we have looked with some care into this document, (the Treaty of Commerce,) and are satisfied that it errs greatly on the score of over-legislation and meddling."

I reply, that you cannot *over*-legislate with China; you may ***badly*** legislate. Shirking and ignorant, would you wish quiet, comfort, stability, and that progress which stability ensures—that extension of commercial, of national benefits, the natural offspring of confidence—then *over-legislate* with them, i. e., have black and white for every casualty.

In the constant touching and revolution of affairs with *this* people, it is, as with two wheels which interlock and work within each other, there must not be a single tooth wanting. Thus, and thus only, is a system of perpetual jolting to be obviated.

I say the Chinese are shirking. Read public documents—consult private accounts. Does any one, indeed, doubt it? Therefore let us descend to the minutest particulars with them; leave no loop-holes, by which in any case they may establish a position against us. With *them* "over-legislate;" bind them with bonds to honesty.

I say they are ignorant. How could it be otherwise? for the first time since the world began have their eyes been opened to their true position. The blind man restored to sight notoriously sees inaccurately. Yes, they are ignorant; it would be "meddling" to put a learned man to his A B C, but this is the process for a child. The Treaty of Commerce is China's A B C, and Sir Henry Pottinger the schoolmaster who is abroad.

Thus have I met or attempted to meet—thus have I disproven or attempted to disprove, the *Examiner's* BROAD charge.

But what are the *positions* upon which that paper grounds it? Concisely then—

1. That Sir Henry Pottinger makes "government and its agents custom-house and police officers for the Emperor of China."

2. That "to carry the treaty into effect," Sir Henry Pottinger "contemplates the exercise of powers beyond the law."

3. That Sir Henry Pottinger makes "government the bondsman to the Chinese for the English merchant."

4. That the "costliness and complication of all this machinery is (are) but too obvious."

5. That Sir Henry Pottinger has involved "the British government in the responsibility of clearing the five ports of opium-smugglers."

6. That "it multiplies the points of *collision*" (connexion).

Now, seriously, I declare, respecting these objections in gross, that I do not believe there is a *single* individual (with the exception perhaps of opium-smugglers) *in China,* who has observed the working of the various items, who does not give each of them his approbation—*seriatim.*

1. "Government and its agents are made custom-house and police officers;" true, to a certain extent, and proper to that extent. The plan that Sir Henry Pottinger has adopted is simple. A British merchant vessel arrives, and delivers her papers, (register, manifest, &c.,) to the consul, who thereupon acquaints the superintendent of customs, and permission is given to discharge. A note is handed into the consular office daily of the day's work, certified by the custom-house officers, by means of which he (the consul) can ascertain the amount of duties when all is discharged. The merchant then pays the same over to a banker appointed for the purpose, and on the production of his receipt, a permit to depart is granted by the superin-

tendent of customs, which is shown to the consul, who immediately delivers back the ship's papers.

This arrangement gives great confidence to the Chinese; it facilitates business; it secures an impartial because disinterested arbitrator in the person of the consul; prevents on the one hand exaction—on the other smuggling; thus maintaining the honour of the British name, and securing peace to the two countries; and, finally, it puts the government of Great Britain in possession of the exact statistics of our trade with China, while the machinery to carry it into effect costs at each consulate about £20 per month.

In short, "the government of Great Britain" *sees* that the *Chinese* "custom-house officers" do no more than their duty, and that the English merchant does no less.

As to converting government and its agents into "police officers," the matter stands thus: if English sailors are riotous, the consul, who is also a magistrate, requests from the man-of-war, and sends, a file of marines for the guilty parties, tries and punishes them; thus preventing the spread of dissatisfaction and disturbance.

Had there been any consul with powers like these—had justice such as this been exhibited, for six months even, previous to the last Canton riots, it is probable that those fields of ruins there, would have yet been the palace stores and dwellings of the Dutch and East India Companies.

2. "That to carry the treaty into effect, Sir Henry Pottinger contemplates powers beyond the law"—"an announcement," the *Examiner* goes on to state, "sufficiently pointing out the difficulties which he himself anticipates."

When the *style* of "Butler's Analogy" was objected to, he remarked, that the question rested with the style *per se;* but, was the thing *wanted* to be said *better*, or otherwise expressed?

The reply is pertinent; it is not, are these difficulties but it is, are these necessary and inherent in the matter? It is not that powers beyond the law are *called* for, but are they *requisite?* Every generation requires powers beyond the former law, and every crisis demands them.

That was a crisis—a great crisis; it introduced a generation of 360,000,000 souls into the pale of civilization.

The work of Sir Henry Pottinger stands or falls by its merits—not by its departure from usage and its necessity of extended authority. Already, however, this at least has been granted, and I have no doubt the treaty itself thankfully recognized by government.

3. "That Sir Henry Pottinger makes the British government the bondsman." Answer: Yes, and government's security is the register of the vessel, which is worth generally more than ten times the amount of duty. The *vessel* is responsible both for her *own* dues and the duty on *the goods.* Those who charter their ships should mark this well. The answer to objection No. 1, in many places applies to No. 3,

showing that "the costliness and complication of the machinery" is anything but "obvious;" which is proposition—

4. To those on the spot it is well known that there is no "complication" at all; and, as to the "costliness," it would be better had the writer given particulars.

There must be some expense; but, from what I can understand, not for one moment to be compared to the resulting good; and while no injudicious expenditure is contemplated, it is well known to the authorities here, that appearance has a great effect on the Chinese mind, and that it will be best for the interests of England to give her consular establishments that position, in the eyes of this people, which her own dignity demands.

A moral influence is the cheapest government. The *esprit* of our name in war is best maintained by the respectability of our offices in peace.

5. That "Sir Henry Pottinger has involved the British government in the responsibility of clearing the five ports of opium-smugglers." *Negatively*, the treaty does this, for no opium-clipper would report herself, or give up her register, as no mandarin would give her a permit to depart, and hence the consul could not return her papers.

Nor, indeed, could any British officer accept such charge; he owes it to the country he represents to reject it, not to let the taint of smuggling "pass between the wind and its nobility."

But, further, if outside the ports, a smuggler fires on mandarin boats attempting to seize her; then, indeed, she is considered a pirate, and as such to be pursued and treated. Is this wrong? What! shall we send fleets to guard the shores of Africa from flesh-hucksters, and shall we endure an act of *piracy* within sound of our guns and within sight of our flag?

Again, if the consul is credibly informed of smuggling within the port, it becomes his duty to report the same to the local authorities:

1. To prevent suspicion of connivance. 2. To protect the interests of the honest trader, whose guardian he is.

6. "That it multiplies the points of collision." I might have imagined that *connection* was intended, but for what follows: "From the old-established market of Canton, (the *Examiner* continues,) it would have been neither prudent nor practicable to divert the course of trade; but when an additional island or two might have been easily obtained, there was no call for multiplying our difficulties five-fold by the opening of four new ports."

This is by far the most extraordinary statement in the article; and, first of all, I will endeavour to do away with the islands it has conjured from the vasty deep which we have not, and then take a look at the cities which we have.

1st, then, the Chinese won't seek us—we must seek them: *vide* their history. Therefore, islands won't do for trade.

2. If only a few inhabitants lived on the island, they would in a

short time be the victims of Ladrones and robbers. The island certainly would be left for our satisfaction or dissatisfaction; but the people, and the property? why, in Hong Kong, where there are perhaps 500 Europeans, independently of a regiment or two, four or five men-of-war, and an organized police; in the teeth of the governor, and notwithstanding that, five or six months ago the worst portion of the town was burnt down by order, and every man packed off to Kooloon who could not give a good account of himself. In the neighbourhood of Hong-kong, I say, the flag of piracy still waves, and in Victoria itself the hand of the robber is never quiet. Vide the *Canton Press* and the *Hong-kong Register*, passim. How far did the daring of the Ladrones carry them not long ago, to steal off a wharf there, where a watchman was on guard, two heavy pieces of ordnance?

No, no; islands won't do; if unprotected, they would be a prey—if guarded, far more expensive than the present system; and in any case, though very pretty no doubt in their own place, of no use to us.

Hong-kong is serviceable certainly; IT is the depôt of our trade, placed in the very position best adapted for vessels from Europe to call at for orders. We wanted one island as a depôt; we have it—we want no more.

"It would," says the *Examiner*, "have been neither prudent nor practicable to divert the course of trade from the old-established port of Canton."

I reply, It *was* "prudent," and *is* carried into effect; prudent, because cities of 300,000 to 600,000, situated as the keys of vast tracts of rich country, inhabited by peaceable and industrious men, and possessing an *immense coasting* and *foreign trade* to the Straits, &c., have been opened to the reception of goods of ours, which they wanted to buy and do buy, and for which it was becoming necessary to our very existence that we should find new markets. It would have been IM*prudent* with a vengeance, had we neglected such an opportunity. "Practicable"—why, we wished it, and they wished it, and we have done it, and it works as if it was oiled. What do men call that, if they don't call it "practicable?" ay, and operative too.

The grand error of the writer is, supposing that Canton can supply China. It can do no such thing, China is not England. The Hong merchants are not accustomed to pay bag-men.

Long before, if they ever went, that the Canton cotton goods found their way into the northern consumers' hand, they would have incurred so much expense, that the native manufacture would be the cheapest, this I fully showed in another letter elsewhere.

Let it be remembered, that we can now carry our goods upwards of 1000 miles farther into this country than formerly, (stopping at four points of the way, each of them rich in native shipping, before arriving at the fifth, Shanghai,) for the same or less expense than we formerly could land them at Canton; that thus landing their own to the consumer direct, our productions are burdened with one profit only, and that the silks and teas of the north stand in a similar position, that the only locality in which disturbance might be at all apprehended, even by the most timorous, is Canton, where hitherto we had been treated as an inferior race, with contumely, with exactions, with hardships, with confinement, from which, if we escaped for a moment, it was to be insulted by the opprobrious epithet of Fanqui, foreign devils, where a bad spirit still lives, which long ere this would have been crushed, had Elliot permitted our troops to occupy it; elsewhere our merchants are on the best terms with the Chinese, and every where our government with theirs.

In fact, Sir Henry Pottinger, with a reach of sagacity and an assiduity of detail which the *Examiner* calls "over-legislating," has rendered "collision" almost impossible. *Collision* indeed!—why, we visit with them, and they with us; we dine with them; we smoke with them; we drink with them; their wives and their daughters come to see us—that's the way we translate collision. And farther, a medical officer at four of the consulates tells me that he is *frequently* applied to by natives for advice, which I should think is not unusual in other stations. We live as neighbours should live. We go in and go out among this people, and none to do us hurt.

They are a very easy and quiet race, peaceful, and peace-loving—peace, peace in our time, I believe is their heart's desire.

Having, I think, satisfactorily rebutted the charge of commission, as laid by the *Examiner* against Sir Henry Pottinger, I beg to direct the attention of your readers to those remarks in that paper which accuse him of omission; and, first, as to warehouse room. The *Examiner* says, "One serious omission, however, has been made in the treaty—the absence of all provision for warehousing-room." I reply by giving an abstract of Article VII. of the Treaty, which "provides for British subjects and their families residing agreeably to the treaty of perpetual peace and friendship at the five ports, and for their being allowed to buy or rent ground, and houses, at fair and equitable rates, such as prevail among the people, without exaction on either side. The ground and houses so to be sold, or rented, to be set apart by the local authorities in communication with the consuls."

I have heard of no accusation of "exorbitant" rents since the peace, as alluded to by the *Examiner*, or any want of accommodation; but, as far as I understand, the Government is satisfied with the terms they have made for the site of the late East India Company's and Dutch Hongs, and I have very little doubt that it will accommodate all our people in Canton; while in the north, immense stores, capable of holding 2 to 4000 tons, with dwelling-house, garden-ground, and good, ay, and pleasant localities, are to be had from £130 *to* £150 per annum. This is the *literal fact* in the only two instances in which the *exact* sum is known to me.

I have at the same time no doubt but that, "*cæteris paribus*," in all cases, it is similar. So that not only has the treaty *provided* for our accommodation, but we are *actually* accommodated *well* at this present moment.

2. The *Examiner* proceeds to charge Sir Henry Pottinger thus:

"As to the duty on Tea, we cannot discover that the tariff makes any reduction, and the principle on which it is levied is just the same as before. In fact it is a duty on the weight, and consequently the same for tea worth eight taels, and for tea worth eight times eight taels; now Sir H. Pottinger ought not to have done this. He has made a distinction of duty for the different qualities of ivory, of nutmeg, of ginseng, and of sharks' fins, and might surely have done the same for tea." No—not at all—there is no parallel; he certainly could not do the same. Let us see; there are two duties, on ivory; one for *whole* teeth, one for *broken*. There is no whole tea and broken tea; nutmeg, 2 duties—one for *cleaned*, and one for *uncleaned*; there is no cleaned tea, and uncleaned tea. I need not, however, pursue this farther, as it is simply necessary to state that a very great deal of our trade with China will be carried on by barter, in which the parties mutually will put too high a money-value on their goods, and of course in any graduated scale of duty, the English merchant would always be paying the higher, if not the very highest duties, while purchasing the lower, perhaps the very lowest qualities of tea, thus paying an enormous per centage on first cost on an article that can ill bear it; or, on the other hand, if the duty was not to be fixed ad valorem, but by some arbitrary standard, as, for instance, the will of the Custom-house chief, continued quarrelling and continual delay would daily interfere with the transactions of our merchants. It is very difficult to fix a line of distinction. It may be said there is green tea and black tea, but in each class there is as much difference of quality within itself as exists between the two kinds. In fine, the whole duty amounts to but 1⅛d. (one penny and and a fraction) per pound, and it is scarcely worth while to split halves, especially when one may cut his own finger instead. I may add, that while in 1842 the charges on tea were T. 8. per pecul of 133⅓ and in the beginning of 1843 T. 6,0.0 0. The *whole* duty by the tariff is now 2,5.0.0, that is in the year 1842 to 1843 the charges on tea amounted to £2 13s. 4d., in the beginning of 1843 to 1844 to £2 5s. and now by the tariff to 16s. 8d. per 133⅓ lbs.

Third.—The *Examiner* says, "In one matter, Sir Henry Pottinger seems to have given way foolishly, and rather mischievously, to the Chinese; nor are the specifications of the tariff very honest on the subject. The precious metals, in any form, may be freely admitted into China, without any duty; but in the shape of coin only can they be exported. Now, the Chinese have no coinage; and, consequently, the export of gold and silver is still contraband in China, and this contraband trade will consequently be carried, as it has been some years back, to the yearly amount of a million and a half sterling."

I reply, It is more than surmised, that the severity of the Celestial Emperor's edicts against opium, arises partially from the dread of his Sycee being exhausted; and that, as, from a statement which I shall shortly exhibit, it will be manifest that in any lawful trade—in any transactions over which the superintendent or consul can exercise any control—the balance of trade is greatly against us; stands, in short, thus: that we owe China 2,600,000 dollars, in round numbers, annually, instead of her paying us £1,500,000, as their yearly deficit. An allusion to this tender subject, at present practically unimportant, might have caused vexatious delay, and excited suspicions not easily allayed.

There lies at this moment before me, a printed table, formed from the basis on which the tariff has been arranged, by a distinguished Chinese scholar, who, united to extensive mercantile experience in this country the ability and opportunity to digest the native customhouse-books, by which it appears, that China exports 14,000,000 dollars worth of goods per annum, and imports of legal articles 11,500,000 dollars worth.

Thus the recognized trade of the two countries leaves us a debtor; in short, a *payer* of dollars, instead of a *receiver* of smuggled Sycee; but independently of all this, China has plenty of coin of the Republics and of Spain, to meet for some time any increased sale of our manufactures. She annually imports, I see by the same authority just quoted, 1,000,000 dollars in coin.

I am aware that there is £2,250,000—not £1,500,000, as the *Examiner* incorrectly states—£2,250,000 of bullion annually extracted by the opium-smuggler, but his Excellency Sir H. Pottinger can scarcely be taxed with his tariff being dishonest, because it leaves men smugglers whom it was out of his power to reclaim.

I would, however, say that, *prima facie*, I should have liked treasure to have been free, principally because I dislike all temptation being left to smuggling; but, I repeat, that at present it is, and will be for years, a purely theoretic question; and, I would add, that I *hope* it may remain so. Our great object is to *extend* China's capacity, not to exhaust its resources—to get goods, not cash. Reciprocity will last, when the mines of Peru would be exhausted. The emperor may have insisted on this point too, and we could neither have, nor justly bring, the gains *all* on our side. While, as I have said, I prefer a declaration of free trade in bullion, I have given the facts, that the public may judge accurately. Like many other matters, I have no doubt that much may be said on both sides.

In conclusion, I should not have entered so fully into this subject, had I not feared that a paper usually so correct, and which, owing to the ability of its editor, commands so great a share of public attention, might stamp with its high authority a number of involuntary, yet serious errors, on a subject *second to none in importance;* for I believe that, even as the sun that now shines so brightly above me is just *rising* over England, so, shortly, shall the day-dawn of prosperity, from *this* far country, beam into the cabins and cottage-homes of my native land, bringing there joy and gladness of heart; shall light up our manufactories once more, greet our merchants, cheer our bustling quays and busy dockyards, and expand over all our prospects a bright heaven of blessings! V R.

COLONIAL LEGISLATION;

OR, PLANTERS AND LABOURERS.*

SIR,

DOUBTLESS ere this, yourself and readers will have perused the files of West India papers lately arrived therefrom, and having done so, will by no means feel astonished at the numerous acts of barbarity of which the Island of Dominica has been the scene—acts worthy barbarians of the darker ages, and yet apparently committed under the considerate paternal sway of a *planter* governor.

Your Magazine, sir, since its commencement under the title of "Fisher's Colonial," has ever pursued a straightforward and honest course in reference to the existing abuses of colonial legislation. I herein allude not to the authorities in Downing-street, but will confine myself solely to what occurs in the colonies. Efforts have been made in some of them to get rid of the crown-magistrates, which efforts, emanating from *base and corrupt motives*, have been, unfortunately, too successful in the Island of Trinidad in particular; and here, undoubtedly, the authorities of the Colonial Office alone are to blame; in the accomplishment of this they have so far succeeded, as to gain an ascendancy in their own hands, and thereby assume an irresponsible and arbitrary authority over the labouring population.

In looking to the Dominica files, in these days of Christianity and civilization, the circumstances therein narrated make one shudder with horror, and we are inclined to ask, Can such a colony belong to a British government?

In the absence of the governor, Major Mc Phail, his place is most unfortunately, and we may add, *iniquitously* filled up by a Mr. Laidlaw, "owner of two estates, part proprietor of a third, *and attorney for*

---

* *We copy, the following little comment from the* TIMES *of 20th September.*—" In reference to a letter which appeared in our impression of Tuesday'a date, upon the late insurrection in Dominica, which commented somewhat severely upon the conduct of Mr. President Laidlaw, it is but fair to state that his exertions have been viewed in a very different light by the Colonial Secretary, as will be seen by the following extract from a despatch, dated July 10th, and addressed by Lord Stanley to Sir Charles Fitzroy:—

"I have to acknowledge the receipt of your despatch, No. 21, of the 11th ult., with its enclosures, reporting the occurrence of disturbances among the labouring classes in Dominica, consequent on the attempt to take the census on the 3d of June, and the measures resorted to by the authorities, both civil and military, for quelling those disturbances. With whatever regret her Majesty's government have received this intelligence, it is gratifying to them to have to acknowledge the wisdom and decision which characterized the proceedings adopted by Mr. President Laidlaw on the occasion. The course pursued by yourself on your arrival at Dominica, has appeared to her Majesty's government to have been judicious and proper; and I have to signify to you her Majesty's approval of the prompt issue of a special commission to try, by the ordinary course of law, the insurgents who were in custody. I have not failed to bring under the notice of his Grace the Commander-in-Chief, the favourable mention which is made of the conduct of Major Hill and of her Majesty's troops. I request that you will convey to Captain M'Coy, of the militia force, her Majesty's satisfaction with the activity and judgment evinced by him on this occasion; and I am also to state the favourable impressions which her Majesty has received of the general conduct of that force."

sixteen or eighteen others, and one holding the same position and appointments during the reign of slavery! Such is the individual selected as an impartial, fit, and proper person to govern a population of negro labourers lately emancipated from his iron despotism! A school-boy frolic or disturbance occurs in some such locality as Point Michelle, which with a little decision and energy might have been quelled by half a dozen constables; instead of this proceeding, however, this heroic representative of majesty places the whole country under martial law! calls out the militia, principally consisting of managers, overseers of estates, and their myrmidons, who as heroically set to, a la Don Quixote, *vi et armis*—cutting down the innocent—wantonly and in cold blood shooting unfortunate and defenceless negroes—cutting off their heads, and, like those bloodthirsty wretches of Robespierre's days, carrying those heads about on poles. Fearing my indignation should lead me beyond the truth, I herewith subjoin a letter written on the spot, and by an eye-witness:—

"St. Christopher, 30th July, 1844.

"Sir,—By the last advices from Dominica, it appears that affairs are still carried on with the same violent and vindictive spirit on the part of the authorities of that island. Happily, the five unfortunate persons under sentence of death have been almost providentially reprieved. Their execution had been resolved on, and the day fixed for its taking place, by Mr. Laidlaw, when the Governor-general, Sir Charles Fitzroy, awaking at the eleventh hour from his strange lethargy, on reading, no doubt, the case of the unhappy John Philip Motard, judicially murdered for scratching Mr. Bremner's face with a stone, without even the shadow of a shade of proof of his throwing it, according to his indictment, with intent to kill, despatched an express to Mr. President Laidlaw, directing him to commute the sentences of these five unhappy persons. But will his Excellency ever forgive himself for leaving the prisoners, and the unfortunate Motard, to the tender mercies of Mr. Laidlaw and the planters of Dominica; Every one here is at a loss to imagine what were the grounds for the misplaced confidence of the governor in Mr. Laidlaw, that, visiting an island under his government, said to be in a state of rebellion, and certainly in a state of disturbance, he should, after a brief stay of forty-eight hours, have taken his departure, leaving everything in confusion and disorder, and hundreds of prisoners in the hands of their irritated employers, who were all in one, judges, juries, masters, and militiamen, whilst the heads of those who had already fallen were still exhibited on poles in the country. Sir Charles is a person of known humanity; but why did he not leave express orders with Mr. Laidlaw not to carry any capital sentence into execution without a reference to him, if the business on his hands was of so urgent a nature as to render his departure from the scene of the disturbance indispensable? The remarks of 'Pro bono Publico' and others, that he was influenced by his being a guest of Mr. Laidlaw, and his consort a connexion of that gentleman's lady, are certainly unworthy of any consideration. His Excellency's honour and humanity are beyond question, but he has committed two great mistakes: first, in having placed Mr. Laidlaw at the head of affairs; and, secondly, by trusting to that gentleman's discretion, instead of remaining himself in Dominica to see equal justice done. It is to be recollected that this was not the first disturbance in Dominica under Mr. Laidlaw. Soon after the departure of Major M'Phail, last year, and Mr. Laidlaw's assumption of the government, a general strike took place, which on some estates lasted till October. So much for the confidence that ought to have been placed in Mr. Laidlaw.

"The whole course of the law-proceedings in these cases has been disgraceful in the extreme. All parties seem to have been equally panic-struck and equally vindictive, and to have combined together to perpetrate injustice. Mark the difference of the two cases—of Motard, for scratching Mr. Bremner's face, and of Pierre and Toussaint for *murdering* (for the poor man is since dead) C. P. Marseille—the former hanged, the two latter sentenced to five years' imprisonment. Why this unaccountable difference? Simply because Bremner is a white man, a member of council, and a planter; whilst poor Marseille was nothing more than a black man and a labourer. This is equal justice to black and white in Dominica!

"The coloured people have not, I lament to say, behaved well throughout these unfortunate disturbances, but have combined with the whites to oppress their black brethren. The conduct of Mr. C. G. Falconer, the editor of the *Dominican*, the paper I refer you to, deserves the severest reprehension. He is a coloured man, and his paper is the organ of the coloured party. Yet mark the manner—the approving manner, almost—at least, not condemnatory—in which he speaks of the cruelties exercised by the militia on the unfortunate rioters; such as mutilating them, striking off their heads, and carrying them affixed on poles about the country. One thing regarding this gentleman would be incredible, were it not that his own words avouch it. He, Sir, you will recollect, was the foreman of the jury who condemned Motard, because *his* stone unluckily struck Mr. Bremner on the face, inflicting a wound now no longer visible, after—not *he*, but *Zavier*, and others, threatened to have Mr. Bremner's and Mr. Laidlaw's heads. Now, Sir, this very Mr. Falconer says, in his editorial article of the 17th July, speaking of the rioters, "and *talking (whether they meant it, or not, does not matter) about the heads of the gentlemen appointed by the Home Government to govern the island.*" What, Sir, did he, as the foreman of the jury who found Motard guilty for being present when others talked of having the heads of the gentlemen alluded to—did he, I repeat, (for such conduct is almost beyond the bounds of credibility,) consent to and deliver that disgraceful verdict, being, according to his own words, of opinion, that, whether the poor people *meant* what they said or *not* was *no matter?* After this, let not Mr. Falconer claim to be ranked amongst liberal men. He is, however, it appears, printer to the Legislature: let that be his consolation.

"I have said enough for the present, and shall not fail to let you know anything of importance that may yet take place. Allow me to say—and it is of the highest importance to the Secretary of State for the Colonies, that he should be made aware of it, for it is a fact—that the quiet, perhaps the existence, of all these colonies is, in a great degree, dependent on their not being, during the absence or on the demise of their Governors sent from home, placed under the administration of their respective Presidents of the Council, who are almost invariably planters, or mercantile persons in strict connection with the planting interest, and actuated with the same views. The Governors of not less than four of these islands are at present on leave of absence, and the administration in the hands of planters, who have been all their lives, at least until 1834, holders of slaves. These islands are, St. Vincent, Dominica, St. Lucia, and this island. St. Lucia is in a feverish state; nor would it be a matter of surprise, if like symptoms should manifest themselves in St. Vincent and St. Kitts. Whenever a planter is left at the head of affairs, there the labouring population are in imminent danger of being goaded into discontent. It should never be permitted for a moment longer than is necessary to send a substitute that can be depended on.

"I am, Mr. Editor, yours, &c., "N."

In a postscript, dated August 6th, he adds—

"I open my letter to refer you to the extraordinary address of His Excellency Sir Charles Fitzroy to the militia, before his departure from Dominica, in which he *praises that sanguinary body* for their FORBEARANCE! The *Dominican* of the 12th of June, in an article headed 'Proceedings of the Militia,' states, 'these bloodthirsty beings, so praised for their forbearance, wantonly shot some negroes who had surrendered, and struck off their heads! while Mr. Cochrane tied people (who were afterwards discharged by the Privy Council as innocent) so cruelly as to endanger their lives; yet these are the people whom His Excellency praises for their forbearance!'"

Thus much for the impropriety of allowing planter-governors full sway over their own but-lately emancipated slaves. It would appear that this is not the only colony suffering under such a grievance, as at present, the islands of St. Vincent, St. Lucia, and another, are similarly situated, and, to use the words of the above correspondent, "are in a similar predicament, and becoming very feverish." We recommend the Home Government to look to this, and remedy the evil, ere it become too late.

Leaving this matter to the serious consideration of Lord Stanley, we will proceed to another of no less moment—I mean the unjust, arbitrary, and imprudent attempt to reduce the wages of the agricultural labourer in the colonies. On this subject we will confine ourselves to the island of Trinidad, or, as it has been facetiously called, the "Island of Experiment." In selecting this colony, we do so from a sense of justice towards the neighbouring colonies—for, to our certain knowledge, it was this colony that impoverished the others, by clandestinely and most dishonourably enticing away their labouring population, by offering exorbitant premiums, far beyond what they well knew could be paid by their already-impoverished brethren in the islands of Tobago, Grenada, St. Vincent, &c., &c.

A proprietor of the colony of Trinidad thus gave me his candid opinion of this wanton act of selfishness:—

"I find," said he, "by the late papers, that a meeting of planters has been held, with the object of reducing the wages of the labourer—this *I consider a most imprudent step*—for to themselves and not to the labourers is due the merit of having raised those wages to their present (I admit) exorbitant rate. Three months previous to the Emancipation, I proposed that a scale of remuneration for labour performed should be made out, of a fair and adequate value; this it was proposed should be presented to the Governor, through whom it should be submitted to Her Majesty's Secretary of State for the Colonies, for his lordship's approval. Had this measure been adopted, *all would have gone well*. This was the opinion of several gentlemen, particularly the late lamented Mr. Thomas St. Hill, a highly honourable and eminent practical proprietor and planter of the Quarter of Chaguna, in that colony. Unfortunately, however, for the planters in general, a few *selfish* individuals (for I must in justice state that it was confined to the few—particularly a certain pseudo-M.D., well known as having been one of the most tyrannical of slavemasters) commenced a wholesale crusade among the estates adjoining their own, with the object of seducing the negroes away by the offer of a higher rate of remuneration than they then received—hence a system of rivalry commenced, which could only be attended with ruinous consequences to the home proprietor. In proof of this, a gentleman now with me assures me that to such an extent had their dishonourable practice arrived, in the Quarter of Cedros, that to save his estates from being totally deserted, he gave orders to his manager to offer an equivalent to his neighbour, who had been discovered on the beach in the act of enticing away those in his own employ."

Now, Sir, after such a statement—made from no other motive but pure disinterestedness—is it not an insult to common sense, on the part of these gentlemen, to accuse the labourers of *demanding* more wages than they can afford to pay? Such conduct is not only highly reprehensible, but might ultimately lead to serious dissatisfaction among the hitherto well-conducted and industrious peasantry. The island of Trinidad has received at least 20,000 emigrants since the Emancipation; the island is increasing in prosperity and importance; let the planters fulfil the promises held out to the labourers, whom they have won by "golden inducements" from the neighbouring colonies. The negroes had sealed what they considered a fair and honest compact with them, and none but the selfish ex-slaveholder need complain. It appears, by the last file of Trinidad papers, that the Governor, Sir Henry McLeod, has most unwisely allowed his council to give a vote for some 200,000 dollars, to be expended in the construction of a new Court-House, Government-House, &c. The Trinidad people have already establishments of this description, quite good enough for their present purposes, while I am afraid that the generality of the colonists would feel much better satisfied, were that sum, or one-half thereof, applied to the formation of bridges, roads, &c. This would also be an inducement for tourists and agriculturists to visit that *truly magnificent colony;* while, under its present state of woeful mismanagement, we have been confidently informed, by "an old inhabitant," that, throughout the whole of the four years the present Governor, Sir Henry McLeod, has been in the colony (with the exception of a steamboat trip to the port of San Fernandez), he knows no more about the island, than if he had remained quietly studying his military tactics—whereas, on the other hand, during the days of the "glorious and good Sir Ralph," as they called Sir Ralph Woodford, there was not a nook or corner which that excellent Governor did not visit, with the object of improvement and information. Times, however, have changed, and Trinidad is again in the hands of a plantocracy.* HOMO.

MUSCAT AND MATARAH.

THEIR COMMERCIAL RELATIONS WITH EUROPE.†

MATARAH is a creek in the port of Muscat, and, on its borders, is situated a wretched but somewhat extensive village, inhabited by mariners solely: it is also a place for building, refitting, and calking ships. During a night's lodging there, one is almost stunned by the noise of the tam-tam, and the cries of the sailors "larking" on shore. A crowd of idle women, of jugglers, and innkeepers reside here, in preference to Mucat, or Muskat, where merchants and private gentry dwell. The port there is not very safe, for when the wind blows from sea the waves beat with great violence upon the southern rampart, and, as the entrance is very narrow, it is difficult to manage a safe entrée; however, small vessels, *batila,* run little risk when they are properly moored. Much inconvenience, when the wind blows strongly, attends the immediate approach to Muscat by water, so that many foreigners, on disembarking, prefer the land-route to the capital. This experiment, however, is not always safe, but may be rendered suffi-

* By a system—which was indignantly condemned by Lord John Russell—the labouring population of Trinidad is again under the pernicious influence of a planter magistracy, with the direct sanction of the Governor.

† From the French of M. Fontanier, who twice visited this part of Arabia.

ciently so by an Arab dress, some knowledge of the country and of the language. A walk from Matarah to Muscat occupies a full hour, and demands much exertion, as it lies through a very rough district, and crosses over elevated basaltic hills.

It is difficult to give a sufficiently clear idea of the dark barrenness of the country: from station to station you may discern solitary houses and remains of castles, but not the least appearance of vegetation. Arrived at the town, a very extensive view is presented, but no vegetation is to be seen, save a few date-trees on the eastern border of the sea. Muscat itself also is surrounded by perpendicular cliffs, which reflect the heat so powerfully, that even in the month of January Europeans would be oppressed by its influence.

I proceeded to the house of our agent, Ben-Calfaun, (writes M. Fontanier,) who was then in his harem, and was shown into the outward apartment. Four or five handsome slaves from Nubia or Abyssinia, who were attending their master, hastened to offer me some water, and, taking me for a naval officer of rank, appeared very desirous to execute my commission. So soon as the agent had entered, and my arrival was made known, I was welcomed most graciously. Many persons of distinction in the town came to visit Ben-Calfaun, and, the son of the Imaum, who was regent during his father's absence at Zanzibar, sent to present his compliments. Amongst the Arabs of Muscat, who belong to a particular sect, it is not the custom to present pipes and coffee, as in some other Oriental countries; they seem rather to have borrowed their customs from the Hindoos, because they have not that brotherly familiarity with other sects of the creed which distinguishes Mahomedans. During my stay there, I never ate in company with any of the inhabitants, and my host who sent me my meals never divided them, although he acted differently towards the mariners, who were unprovided with native servants, or were unacquainted with the habits of the country. It was certainly not from scruple that he acted so, because he was acquainted with many Europeans, and he would not willingly have renounced the social habits contracted in his youth. In fact, the interior of his house, that is, the portion not accessible to strangers, was furnished in the same manner as those of the English in India. There were beautiful carpets, tables, chairs, clocks, and toys. Lamps were suspended around the saloons, and he ordered them all to be lighted, one evening that he invited me to witness the wonders of his palace.

There was also a private apartment which the owner kept most religiously sealed up, and another reserved for his own particular use, arranged something like the cabin of a ship, here he had his hammock slung. He assured me, that he had but one female in his family, and a few slaves; but as he had during my visit, kept them all shut up in a closet, I was not able to test his veracity on this point. I was, as I had anticipated, overwhelmed with politeness by Abdullah Jemal, whose property I had restored, at Bassora; and my travelling campanion, the old Youssouf. took advantage of the credit which that act of justice obtained for me at Muscat. A merchant in the town owed him five hundred francs, and, according to custom, did not care much about paying them. I interfered in his favour, and, upon threatening to complain to the governor, the money was immediately produced. The son of the Imaum, whom I visited, treated me with much politeness; he lived in a spacious house, upon the sea-side, and underneath it was a large vault, used as an audience-chamber. As it was impenetrable to the rays of the sun, and open to the sea-breezes, it was a most refreshing apartment.

The Imaum's son was a young man of an agreeable exterior, but his intellects did not appear to have been sharpened by education or intercourse: he seemed embarrassed, either from timidity or pride, sentiments which amongst the Arabs are manifested much in the same way. He offered me some sherbet, but did not take any himself; and as to the pipe, the second idol of a Turk, it is not known at Muscat. Our conversation, in addition to an exchange of compliments, related chiefly to the expected arrival of the Artemise frigate. I endeavoured to recall to his memory that France had held friendly intercourse with his forefathers; but his knowledge of history was so imperfect, that he did not appear to have any idea of such a fact.

Muscat is a prosperous place, because its commerce enjoys great liberty; there is no monopoly, the duty imposed is moderate, and the port capacious and safe. It was once conquered by the Portuguese, who were themselves driven out by the Arabs, whose chief, Assaf Ben-Ali then assumed the title of Imaum or Pontiff, and his descendants now govern this independent little state. At the farther extremity of the harbour are several batteries, and at the entrance several strong forts, built on the slope of steep mountains. The Imaum built a few ships of large burden as a naval force, but he has since thought better of this subject, and converted them into merchant-men: their number is now considerable, but they are all of the Arabian build. The population in the port has been estimated at 60,000, but this seems exaggerated, nor is it probable that there are so many in Muscat and Matarah united, although the latter place is as considerable as the former. The streets, as in all Asiatic places, are very narrow; and the houses, although vast and well-built, have that gloomy appearance which belongs to Oriental cities. None of the houses, not even the Imaum's palace, have gardens, or courts, or fountains, appendages so usual in Turkey and Persia. But this is attributable to the barrenness of the soil, and scarcity of springs: outside the town may be seen a few gardens and date-trees Their plan of irrigation is singular; when a well is discovered, it is opened, and enlarged in diameter, and a supply of leathern buckets provided; these buckets being suspended by ropes passed through pulleys, are raised to the surface by oxen. In order to save the animals from the excessive heat, they are not permitted to walk or draw on the open horizontal plain, but a deep hole, entered by an inclined plane, is sunk in the ground, in which the oxen are placed to work. To raise the water-bucket, the team descends the slope to the bottom;—to lower it again, they ascend to the surface, giving the advantage of their weight to their power in both cases. When the water has been emptied into the reservoir, the oxen and their guide descend, and re-appear again, as if they had come out of the bowels of the earth, and so on, repeating the process; the excavation is carefully covered, in order to guard the men and cattle from the exhaustion of heat. Few and inaccurate accounts only exist of the relations between the Imaum of Muscat and foreign countries,—indeed, none of an authentic character, until the commencement of the present century, when the English, after having consolidated their dominions upon the western coasts of India, entered the Persian Gulf, to rid that water of pirates. It may be said to have been little known, until Napoleon endeavoured to negociate with its sovereign, for the purpose of obtaining a key to India. He sent several emissaries, one of whom was taken at Bouchir by the English, who fortunately had intelligence of his mission. Codja-Mallah assumed the merit of having discovered the French agent, and ascertaining the secret of his journey.

The English considered the Imaum as an ally of France, and if they were not desirous to overthrow him, they thought proper to watch him closely. They kept cruisers near the Persian Gulf, and took precautions which puzzled their enemies. An event which happened to an Armenian at Bassora, named Codja-Avet, shows the extent of these precautions. This Avet was brother to the drogoman at the residence of Bassora, and had gone to trade in India and China. As he spoke a little English, and wished to pass for an European, he changed his costume. The merchantman that brought him over, touching at Calcutta, the collector detained him on account of his strange accent, suspecting him to be French; but he proved his innocence, and was permitted to continue his journey, after having resumed his Oriental costume. At length the same vessel dropped anchor at Muscat, when an English boat came on board, and, as no one understood the officer, they went in search of Avet, who was making preparations for an overland journey. Guilty, this time, at least, of speaking an European language, and of shaving himself, he was made prisoner, taken away from his vessel, and detained on board the pirate, which was fortunately starting for Bassora. With a safe escort he now re-entered his native town, and was conducted safely to his home. However, being anxious to see his family, and having the means, he opened a concealed door, and embraced them. The officer who had him under his charge, and the resident, were not a little surprised at his disappearance, and the latter threatened the governor of the city with punishment, if he did not instantly find and restore the fugitive.

The influence of the English in Muscat began to preponderate in 1819, when they attacked the pirates of the gulf, and destroyed the vessels in the harbour of Baz-el-Kaima. The fall of Napoleon had been understood there, as elsewhere. In 1821 they made an expedition under pretext of aiding the Imaum against the Wahabites, which had the effect also of watching the conquests of Ibrahim Pacha in Arabia. Their popularity could not but increase still more, after the intercession of the government of Bombay, in all the discussions which had arisen between the Imaum and his neighbours. This prince had the wisdom to understand that he had better abstain from hostile acts against his powerful allies; and his respect for them was advantageous to himself, since they scarcely ever opposed his projects. He had established a very lucrative commerce in his dominions, more by negociation than power, and his devotedness would find perhaps its legitimate reward, whenever he might be attacked by foreign enemies, or by his own subjects. It must not be supposed that he was better sheltered from the reverses of fortune, than other Oriental potentates. He did not ascend the throne until he had slain one of his uncles with his own hand, and his authority over the various tribes of the country of Oman was nothing less than absolute. It is difficult to say what mode of government appears legitimate to these people. They complain that Seyd-Saïd, the Imaum, had assumed sovereign authority—levying taxes, extending commerce, and doing every thing he ought not to have done. They pretended that such conduct vitiated his title to the Imaumship, but concealed the fact, that his subjects affected to call him by his name, not his title. He had himself no higher opinion of his rank, and he was always distinguished by his modesty. On a letter which I received from him, says M. Fontanier, I remarked a very simple seal, nor did he make any pompous display of his royalty. His son, also, was only dressed in the costume of distinguished Arabs generally. From the casual observations of his subjects, then, it appears that they conclude their government should be directed by an Imaum, or Pontiff, whose duty it is to advise in religious matters, for which the people are to pay him, whilst all the other tribes remain under the control of their Sheiks.

The freedom with which they speak of the illegal power of the Imaum, and of his arbitrary conduct, are evidences of the sincerity of their reproaches. Far from being able to reduce the chiefs of the neighbouring tribes to obedience, or even obtain their co-operation, he is obliged to purchase their honesty and subordination. Under the least pretence, the Sheiks come down to Muscat to pay homage, but will not retire until they have received presents. The great encouragement and security given to commerce, the moderate duties, the perfect liberty given to the inhabitants, and, finally, the situation of the port itself, were amongst the causes of the prosperity of Muscat, and the Imaum derived accordingly a rich revenue from the city. These, however, were insufficient for his ambition, and he derived some further profit from farming the principal ports of the coast of Mekran and Belouchistan. There his government was not so comfortable as in his hereditary dominions, and he extorted much more than £20,000 sterling, which he was obliged to pay annually to the king of Persia. His commerce was particularly lucrative, but, as the sale of the slaves was a principal branch, it was necessary to find an establishment on the coast of Africa, and accordingly he took possession of the island of Zanzibar. Visiting this new possession, and finding the climate more salubrious than that of Muscat, avoiding also by his absence the importunities of the Sheiks, he formed the resolution of remaining there, and this decision he executed in 1837. He assigned the government of Muscat to his son, seldom making his appearance there, and then only for very short periods.

The origin of his new establishment is rather remarkable. When France meddled in the affairs of Spain, in 1823, the British government, not thinking proper to intercede, by force, in Spanish colonial affairs, however, took into consideration the remonstrances of the humane, which had then reached England, against the treatment of the blacks, and sent a commission to the coast of Africa to prevent it. Captain Owen presented himself at the court of the Imaum of Muscat, and offered him a subsidy of 100,000 francs, on condition that he would prevent all Europeans (Spanish and Portuguese included) from purchasing slaves upon his territory. Nothing could be more acceptable to this prince than such a convention, because, exclusive of its enhancing the price of merchandise, he viewed with pleasure the probability of retaining so many negroes in the Mohamedan religion, who otherwise would be converted to Christianity. Consequently he accepted the proposition, nor would he receive any indemnity. But the treaty of the north-east coast of Africa was neutralized in a great measure by Arabian Sheiks, who, settled upon the coast, make excursions into the interior, purchase and carry away negroes, and embark them for Muscat and the Persian Gulf. Many of them are established at Bambaz and Zanzibar, and at other places. Seyd Saïd, more powerful than the Sheiks, and possessing more vessels, was not backward in supplanting them. The number of his negroes from Zanzibar amounted to 8,000 when M. Fontanier was at Muscat; he treated them as they do in the Antilles, and not according to the Eastern fashion. He had, through their assistance, established plantations of sugar, coffee, and cloves. It was about this period, that the Royal Asiatic Society of London elected him an honorary member, on account of the disinterested part he took in the abolition of slavery. The Society acted with the most amiable intentions, but the result only shows how an immoral act may be committed under an agreeable delusion that the contrary is the case.

Ideas of glory and power now perhaps inflamed the imagination of the Imaum, or, he might perhaps have feared attack from without, for he again collected a naval force. He had too much good sense to entertain any idea of struggling with the English, but he might have dreaded Absoul-Bassoul, Sheik of Bouchir, and, more particularly, Mohamed Ali. His aversion to the first was openly confessed; and one day, when he was on his pilgrimage to Mecca, he seized his person, and made him pay a ransom. The death of this Sheik soon after removed the Imaum's uneasiness; but, as to Mohamed Ali,—the success of his armies in Arabia, his ostentation, the confidence with which he presented himself as a powerful sovereign, so alarmed Seyd-Said, that he employed cunning and courtesy, maintaining with him a regular correspondence. Agents of these potentates were then continually passing between Muscat and Suez, bearing compliments and offers of service. Mohamed Ali told the Arabs that he was coming "as a storm to sweep from one extremity of the peninsula to the other, and that he depended upon the aid of his brother, the Imaum, whose enemies he would scatter." The latter declared that he possessed a powerful fleet, that his brother the Pacha wanted such a force alone in the Red Sea, and that he left it solely at his service. All these Oriental palavers, expenses of couriers, and robes of honour given to the envoys, ended, on the part of Mohamed Ali, in a threat to invade the Imaum's dominions, whilst the Imaum led him to understand that, with his fleet, he set all Egypt at defiance. We must render Seyd-Saïd the justice to say, that he was the first to tire of these useless boastings: he soon learned that he had nothing to fear from the Pasha, and in consequence reduced his fleet to what necessity suggested. Having built a three-deck vessel in the Arab fashion, he calculated that it would be advantageously disposed of as a present to the Governor-General, or the commander-in-chief in India: but finding that honourable sentiments must necessarily prevent those functionaries from accepting it, in 1835 he sent it, at his own expense, as a gift to the King of England. King William sent him in return a magnificent yacht, finished and furnished in the European style, with every luxury: it had been employed in the service of the Prince Regent.

So soon as any chance of a speculation appears in any part of the globe, the Americans are always sure to be seen in view. Muscat was now that speck, and attracted the attention of the New World. A ship of war, in 1835, touched on the Isle of Mazerah, and was obliged to enter the port for urgent repairs. This vessel, the "Peacock," had visited the coast of Africa and Muscat, and returned thence to Bombay. Two years afterwards, when M. Fontanier arrived at Muscat, the United States had already concluded a treaty with the Imaum, and appointed consuls at Zanzibar and Muscat, and these consuls had even time to arrive in India. The clerks of a commercial house hearing the narrative of the Peacock's voyage, wished to try their fortunes amongst those Arabs, and obtained for the purpose a formal nomination as consuls. Affairs turned out unfortunately, and these consular agents disappeared after a few years. This fact will be noticed again in speaking of the strange ideas which prevailed for some time as to the functions of consular agents; but the French are now beginning to imitate the Americans, and to establish consuls for the private use of certain merchants.

After 1835, French vessels appeared occasionally at Muscat, and the supplies required by the isles of Bourbon and Mauritius rendered communications with that port frequent. The government of the French colony endeavoured to methodize the connections by a convention with the Imaum, made in 1822 and in 1829: they wished to perfect the treaty in 1834, but the death of the commander of the "Madagascar," to whom negociations were entrusted, prevented their execution, so that so far from imitating the impatience of the Americans, the French remained sixteen years without being able to arrange an insignificant affair. Their agent only occupied the precarious situation which an officer in the navy had thought proper to confer upon him. Such were the relations in 1838 between the Imaum, his subjects, and foreign countries. He exercised but a very precarious authority in his own country, yet his government was so able, that his subjects were attached to him; he could reside at a distance without risking the public peace. The trade of his dominions attracted foreigners to his capital, and he was acknowledged by first-rate powers. Fortunately for himself, he is too remotely situated to become an object of speculation, or to think of transforming himself into a great character, although he possesses a better claim to such than others that enjoy it. From the limit of Muscat alone he has extended his authority over the greatest portion of the eastern coast of the Persian Gulf, and over several distant islands; he is the ruler of a considerable part of Arabia, and he has ports on the coast of Belouchistan, near to those of the English, he conquered Zanzibar, and Baubayo, and established his title to several of the Comoro Islands. The English and the Americans pay at Muscat 5 per cent duty, and the French 4 per cent. The treaty of the French was only applicable to the Bourbon Islands, where the Imaum's vessels were treated as French.

This prosperity did not proceed from the territorial riches of Muscat, for, notwithstanding the sobriety of the inhabitants, they are obliged to obtain many things from foreigners. Their rice is brought from India —corn and fruit from Persia. It is from thence also they procure salt. Fishing is the principal trade, and dried fish is in great demand in the interior. It is on the coast of this part of Arabia, as well as upon that of Persia, that the nourishment, not only of man, but also of animals, is so opposite. In the interior they grow dates, and many valleys are highly cultivated, and produce some banyan and mango trees of inferior quality; but these productions are far from being sufficient for consumption, and industry is much restricted. Muscat makes a sweetmeat for exportation of marshmallows, a mixture of gum-arabic and sugar, which is much esteemed, and is sold in earthen vessels. Bazaars here are busily occupied—everywhere well-furnished shops are to be seen, and every step one takes they come in contact with bales of merchandise. It is because the port is admirably situated: a merchant coming from India or the Red Sea dare not settle in the southern provinces without ascertaining if all is tranquil, but, he touches at Muscat, and often deposits his merchandise there. The changes of the monsoon, which do not pass over this city, is another reason for sojourning there. Secure against plunder, and being well treated, the merchant and the traveller willingly stop, and even brave the heat, as well as the dreadful fever called the "houmaï-gebi," which they say deprives the sick of all sensation.

Muscat is the most famous market for the products of India, the coasts of the Red Sea, and of the Persian Gulf. Its chief commerce consists in slaves, for it is useless to name the preserves which have been described. The inhabitants of Bourbon and Mauritius get asses from thence. Notwithstanding the activity which exists in this town, and although the inhabitants do not appear less noisy than in other parts, quarrels are not more frequent than in Persia or in Turkey. The population is, however, very much mixed; there are a great number of Banians of India, Turks, Persians, and also negroes; naked mountaineers from Adramont, armed with a gun, or with a two-handed sword, such as camel-drivers use, carrying sometimes a steel javelin, and remarkable for their long hair, which falls on their shoulders, constitute the only police of the place. They are stationed in various parts of the great bazaar, and patrole their rounds. There is a Cadi to administer justice; and the tranquillity here, where are so many means of disorder, is truly admirable.

Besides the transit trade, of which Muscat is the entrepôt, this town has a special commerce by sea, depending partly on European shipping, but principally on the Imaum, who possesses a great number of baglo. These ships, as well as those of the Gulf, frequent the port of Bombay, but do not limit their voyages to that port. Many bring slaves to Scinde; others traverse the coast of Malabar, to procure pepper, timber for building, besides cardamom and rice, and some go as far as Ceylon for cinnamon; in short, many, who are not afraid of entering the Bay of Bengal, carry dates and horses to Calcutta, from whence they bring rice, indigo, and sugar. The sailors of Muscat possess almost exclusively the trade of that town, and of the places on the south-east coast of Africa, whither they carry dates, and whence they bring Caffres, gold-powder, ivory, mother-of-pearl, shells, and a variety of drugs and copal.

BRITISH GUIANA.

A Statistical Statement of the Sugar Crops, as returned for Taxation for 1842 and 1843.

Crop of 1842.	Pounds of Sugar.	Rum—Gallons, Proof.							Gallons of Molasses
		24.	23.	22.	21.	20.	19.	18.	
Demerary ...	26349663	168584	487	7549	1452	9475	381201	220163	844886
Essequebo ..	17664411	156042	9647	18333	4349	39632	168932	40466	762833
Berbice.....	10659935	181740	10932	12079	....	16103	23664	....	412635
Brit.Guiana.	54674009	506366	21066	37961	5801	65210	573797	260629	2020354
Crop of 1843.									
Demerary...	26856544	221698	1956	1048	1748	4086	342331	178144	932817
Essequebo ..	18480822	200508	1616	11938	805	15862	83759	34565	882799
Berbice.....	10139698	155069	....	....	....	1080	12868	....	506990
Brit.Guiana.	*55477064	577275	3572	12986	2553	21028	438958	212709	2322606

* The return for one estate, which made 495,000 lbs. of sugar in the year 1842, has not yet been tendered for 1843.

The last year's crop presents, as may be seen, a slight improvement on that of the preceding year. The returns for 1841 were 52,043,897 lbs. of sugar, 1,543,652 gallons of rum, and 1,584,806 gallons of molasses.

PORTLAND, NEW SOUTH WALES.

A Statement of the IMPORTS, EXPORTS, and REVENUE of Portland, New South Wales, drawn up by a Committee appointed at a Public Meeting of the said Colony.

DATE. From	DATE. To	WOOL. Bales.	WOOL. Value. £	OIL. Tuns	OIL. Value. £	BONE. Tons.	BONE. Value. £	CATTLE. No.	CATTLE. Value. £	SHEEP. No.	SHEEP. Value. £	HIDES. No.	HIDES. Value. £	TALLOW. Tons.	TALLOW. Value. £	BEEF. Trcs.	BEEF. Value. £	WHEAT. Bushl.	WHEAT. Value £
Nov. 13, 1840 ..	Jan. 5, 1841 ..																		
Jan. 6, 1841 ..	April 5, — ..	814	8242	89	1600			120	720										
April 6, — ..	July 5, — ..																		
July 6, — .	Oct. 10, — ..																		
Oct. 11, — ..	Jan. 5, 1842 ..	306	1922					60	480	260	195							200	50
Jan. 6, 1842 ..	April 5, — ..	945	11044					27	270	600	320								
April 6, — ..	July 5, — ..	140	1523					80	800	826	482							114	39
July 6, — ..	Oct. 10, — ..	18	205	28½	565	2	150	220	2460	2975	1769								
Oct. 11, — ..	Jan. 5, 1843 ..	462	6939	20	600	4	320	70	750	2965	1302								
Jan. 6, 1843 ..	April 5, — ..	1277	13824					66	303	6341	3043								
April 6, — ..	July 5, — ..	157	1668	25½	765			59	290	1982	650								
July 6, — ..	Oct. 10, — ..	37	498	264	6540	9¾	1488	42	306	1926	808	270	100	6	128	242	950	100	15
Oct. 11, — ..	Jan. 5, 1844 ..	361	4244		5			100	566	6962	3221			7	191	134	516		
		4537	50109	427	10075	15¾	1958	844	6950	24837	11790	270	100	13	319	376	1466	414	104

DATE. From	DATE. To	POTATOES. Tons.	POTATOES. Value. £	BUTTER. Cwt.	BUTTER. Value. £	SEAL SKINS. Hhds.	SEAL SKINS. Value. £	SUNDRIES £. s. d.	No. of Vessels Inwards	Tonnage Inwards	Total Wharfage. £. s. d.	Total Duties. £. s. d.	Total Imports. £. s. d.	Total Exports. £
Nov. 13, 1840 ..	Jan. 5, 1841										28 19 4	37 10 9	294 12 5	
Jan. 5, 1841 ..	April 5, — ..										79 2 10	467 19 10	593 13 0	10562
April 6, — ..	July 5, — ..										56 0 6	784 12 6	157 12 0	
July 6, — ..	Oct. 10, — ..										42 5 0	398 19 6	2904 4 0	
Oct. 11, — ..	Jan. 5, 1842 ..								9	1000	38 4 6	666 7 5	3798 19 6	2647
Jan. 6, 1842 ..	April 5, — ..								13	1009	29 7 0	870 12 11	4631 0 8	11634
April 6, — ..	July 5, — ..	1½	18	2	10				10	928	11 4 0	249 3 6	5591 2 9	2872
July 6, — ..	Oct. 10, — ..								14	1394	8 9 2	173 16 3	6224 9 1	5149
Oct. 11, — ..	Jan. 5, 1843 ..					1	40	84 0 0	17	1857	9 7 2	93 3 2	6784 2 5	10035
Jan. 6, 1843 ..	April 5, — ..							148 0 0	23	2606	35 0 2	651 2 7	6657 10 10	17323
April 6, — ..	July 5, — ..					1	57	80 0 0	17	1412	20 6 7	454 15 9	2654 2 11	3510
July 6, — ..	Oct. 10, — ..			20	100			30 0 0	31	3674	39 12 7	545 9 11	5558 18 2	10963
Oct. 11, — ..	Jan. 5, 1844 ..			5	25			86 0 0	31	3799	33 13 9	382 3 11	4513 0 0	8854
		1½	18	27	135	2	97	428 0 0	165	17679	431 12 7	5845 18 0	50863 7 9	83549

NEW SOUTH WALES.

SALE OF CROWN LANDS.

To the Editor of the Colonial Magazine.

SIR,—Although the following resolutions may have appeared in some of our newspapers, I think that they ought to have a more permanent place in your valuable miscellany:—

"The great meeting of the landowners, flock-holders, and other residents of the cow-pasture and adjacent districts, which was held at Camden on Tuesday last, May 7, will form, or we are much mistaken, the era from which the colonists of New South Wales will reckon the disavowal, by all classes of the British public, of the erroneous system of colonization which now unfortunately enjoys the recognition of the Colonial Office. It will also add a brilliant page to the history of an interesting struggle which, end as it may, will furnish a valuable lesson to every colony where capital and labour are scarce, because land is dear, and whilst it signally illustrates the principles of the difficult art of colonizing, will afford a prominent case of instruction to the whole colonial empire."

The resolutions are as follows:—

"1. That this meeting having maturely considered the Government-regulations for the depasturage of Crown lands, which it is proposed should take effect from the 1st of July, 1845, is of opinion that they are calculated to create a feeling of insecurity, there being no certainty that a further increase of the impost then to be demanded may not be attempted at some future time; and that in practice they would be found vexatious to the occupants of Crown lands, as well as most injurious in their general tendency.

"2. That, from a concurrence of adverse circumstances, over which they could exercise no control, the pastoral interests of this colony have been suffering during the last four years under an alarming and unprecedented depression, from the effects of which they are only now beginning to recover; and that to impose additional burdens upon them at such a time is impolitic, not only with reference to this colony, but as regards important interests in England, which must inevitably suffer from any serious diminution in the production of Australian wool.

"3. That this meeting is of opinion, that it should be the policy of the Government to diminish, rather than increase, the amount of direct impost upon the pastoral interests; and that as the license was originally intended more as a certificate of character than for any other purpose, the fee for the same might with advantage be reduced to a nominal charge of 5s.

"4. That this meeting, whilst it recognizes the principle that the public lands of the colony are vested in Her Majesty in trust for the benefit of all her subjects, and more especially for the advancement of the interests of this colony, cannot but feel apprehensive of the consequences which may result from the local administration of those lands being committed to the authority of the Governor only.

"5. That such a power would, as this meeting conceives, enable the Executive at any time to set aside the exercise by the representatives of the people of their legitimate control over taxation, and may lead to serious collisions and troubles; that with a view to the prevention of these probable, although perhaps remote, evils, and to the converting to the utmost possible advantage, the vast resources derivable from the Crown lands of this colony, this meeting would suggest that the regulation and control of the administration of the Crown lands, under a judicious, well-defined, and comprehensive national system, should be confided to the Colonial Legislature.

"6. *That the whole system of administering the Crown lands of this colony requires to be remodelled, and placed upon a different footing*; that the minimum price of £1 per acre, affixed upon the Crown lands of Australia, by the act of the Imperial Parliament, 5th and 6th Victoria, c. 36, is so far beyond their general value, as to amount to a prohibition of their sale; *that the effect of this excessive price is to divert the stream of British emigration from this colony, and to obstruct the developement of its natural resources.*

"7. That this system compels dispersion of our population in lieu of encouraging concentration, and by preventing the acquirement of a secure and beneficial tenure, not only impedes the cultivation and improvement of the waste lands, but leads to a course of life in the remote districts of the colony, which is greatly to be deplored, and pregnant with the most alarming social evils.

"8. That looking upon the new depasturing regulations, already referred to, as indicative of an intention, on the part of the local government, to recommend a perseverance in the system of attaching a price to the Crown lands of this colony altogether beyond their value,—this meeting feels itself called upon to deprecate, in the most earnest manner, the further continuance of that system; and humbly to entreat Her Majesty the Queen, and the Imperial Parliament, to be pleased to sanction the alienation of the Crown lands of this colony, under the direction and control of his Excellency the Governor and the Legislative Council, upon such terms and conditions as may again attract a beneficial emigration to our shores—thereby sustaining and promoting the best interests of this colony, and the welfare of the empire at large." T.

COLONIAL INTELLIGENCE.

India.—The advices by the overland mail are from Bombay to the 31st of July; Calcutta, 14th of July; Madras to the 20th of July; and from China to the 21st of June. The news from India is not of great importance, although not destitute of interest. From Calcutta we learn that the recall of Lord Ellenborough had excited a strong sensation. Two hours after the arrival of the dispatch which brought it, and which reached Calcutta on the 15th of July, his lordship resigned his government into the hands of Mr. Wilberforce Bird. He was expected to leave Calcutta on his return to Europe early in August. Sir Henry Hardinge, who left Aden on the 6th of July, in the Hindostan, touched at Madras on the 20th, where he received a letter from Lord Ellenborough; and was expected at Calcutta about the 24th. Parties in India were much divided on the subject of his lordship's recall; the civil servants, among whom he attempted some not very welcome reforms, were almost to a man against him, whilst the military universally regretted the loss of so liberal a chief, and had arranged to give his lordship a parting banquet four days before the arrival of his successor. The great majority of the Indian newspapers express themselves highly indignant at Lord Ellenborough's recall.

The Indian papers mention a large increase in the trade of Bengal. In the year ending the 1st of May last, imports have increased to the extent of 76,21,283 rupees, and exports to the extent of 2,46,50,105 rupees. The increase in imports is chiefly attributed to British cotton goods. The shipments of indigo have increased to the extent of 63,160½ maunds. The large steamers seem to have opened a new route for commerce; and indigo, raw silk, silk piece-goods, and precious stones, to the amount of 1,76,261 rupees, have been shipped by way of Suez. The number of British ships had increased from 823 (in the preceding year) to 990, while foreign vessels had diminished from 96 to 94. The total imports to Bengal, including treasure, are set down at 6,47,66,562 rupees, and the total exports at 10,11,71,270 rupees.

The monsoon was exceedingly favourable. Forty inches of rain had fallen at Bombay within three weeks. The fall had been general in the country.

In Bombay public attention was drawn to a plan for making a railway to the Thull and Bhore ghauts, two great passes in the mountains of the neighbouring Concan country, by which all the trade comes to that port. The cost is estimated at £350,000, and a large number of shares were taken there.

In Bombay there was a trial going on of 18 Parsees for a murder committed at 2 o'clock in the day in one of the most public streets in the town, on the principle of the gang-murders which degrade India. Great excitement prevailed on the subject; the murdered man was one of their own tribe, and yet much money was expended in the hope of preventing the conviction of any of the parties. The ship Cameo, from Liverpool to Calcutta, with a cargo valued at £60,000, was lost off Kedgeree. The Candahar, from China, was totally wrecked near Bombay. The half-yearly abstract of the affairs of the bank of Madras has, we observe, been published in the papers, and which appears to be very satisfactory. The investments and profits of the bank have considerably advanced since December last. The advices from Singapore come down to June 12, but they are quite unimportant. Nothing of consequence doing in either Cotton or Opium. We learn from Hyderabad that Sir Charles Napier has just issued a very beneficial order, permitting white cotton to be worn, instead of scarlet cloth, by the officers and soldiers throughout Scinde; the jackets are to have regimental buttons, and to be of a regulation pattern. This, we should hope, is an introductory step to the more judicious clothing of our troops throughout India. Sickness prevailed amongst the men of her Majesty's 86th regiment; the other troops were tolerably healthy. From Upper Scinde our news is unsatisfactory. The court of inquiry assembled to investigate the causes of the reverse at Poolajee had scarcely closed its proceedings when another mishap, which occasioned the loss of 80 men, befell us. The grass-cutters of the 6th Irregular Cavalry having been employed in procuring forage, under an escort near Khanghur, were surrounded and set upon by a party of Belloochee horsemen, when about 80 men, including 30 of the cavalry party, were cut to pieces, and 50 were wounded severely. Sir C. Napier has recorded a most indignant general order in reference to the affair, highly blaming the conduct of Captain M'Kenzie, the Commander of the Irregulars. This is exactly the style of annoyance that may constantly be looked for, on a frontier so exposed and indefensible as that to which we have now advanced. Shere Mahomed is said still to be hovering about at the head of about 1,500 horsemen, but is reported willing to come in. We have at present little to apprehend from any chief or army of note; much to fear from irregular bands of plundering Belloochees, always on the wateh, and encouraged by the remembrance of past success, as well as by the examples now once more presented them of the means of successfully assailing us.

The excitement which prevailed at Lahore up to the end of the month of May regarding the affairs of this state has to a great degree subsided, and it is very possible that in consequence of the ascendancy which Rajah Heera Singh has, to a certain extent, secured, a war between his government and that of British India may for a time be averted, though the provocation which he gave in his assertion to the troops that we had afforded assistance to Sirdar Ittur Singh, was of a very grave nature, and has, we believe, led to remonstrances of a very serious kind on the part of the British authorities. It is impossible to say what, or whether any, change will take place in the policy of the Indian government consequent on the recall of Lord Ellenborough, and the appointment of General Hardinge, but rumours already prevail that the most positive injunctions have been received from home against any hostile demonstrations unless actually forced upon us by the attitudes of the Seikhs.

We learn from Affghanistan that Dost Mahommed appears to have beat down the opposition which his government experienced on his return to Cabool; and has now begun to relax in the severities at first probably found necessary for the establishment of his authority amongst the fierce and lawless races over whom he rules. Mahomed Ukhbar had been foiled at Bajor, but had been successful at Kooner: he had returned from Jellalabad, and been received in triumph at Cabool. His troops had reached the capital in detachments before him. All idea of making an attack on Peshawur, if any such in reality was entertained, appears to have been abandoned for the present. Commerce at Cabool was improving rapidly. The Chief of Koondooz was still said to threaten Bameean—a matter probably consideied of no great importance at Cabool—while the Bokhara baibarian was in terror of an attack from Persia. The chiefs of Candahar are said to be apprehensive of another attack of the British—a very groundless apprehension, we should think — and are cultivating the friendship of the Cabool ruler. The news from Herat is so conflicting that we can scarcely venture to attempt to reconcile the statements of the opposite authorities with each other.

China.—The news from China, which comes down to the 21st of June, is of little interest. Sir Henry Pottinger left Hong-kong on that day for Bombay, *en route* to England. He was to leave Bombay by the September steamer. Hong-kong continued healthy. The new governor, Mr. J. F. Davies, with his suite, landed there on the 8th of May. He was immediately sworn into office. Some disturbances had occurred at Canton between the Chinese and the Americans, but they were of trifling import. Piracy prevailed on the Chinese coasts, especially of small boats. Turkey opium had advanced in price, owing to the inferiority of the last crop of that of Malwa. The heavy rains which had fallen during the last month were likely to prevent all further military operations of any importance between June and October.

A letter from Bombay of the 31st of July states that an Envoy from the Celestial Empire, named Keysing, empowered to treat with the French and American Ambassadors, arrived at Macao on the 21st of June. In Canton and the neighbourhood of Hong-kong business generally is dull, owing in a great degree to the unwillingness of foreign merchants to take teas on barter for their goods, and the equal reluctance of the Chinese dealers to forgo the advantages of the old system. At Shanghae, where the trade is confined chiefly to British manufactures, little is doing; some parties, in order to effect sales, have been compelled to receive teas in barter at higher prices than those prevailing at Canton. At Ningpo there is scarcely any market. At Foo-choo-foo no consul has yet been appointed, and no business has consequently been done there. At Amoy, though trade is on a trifling scale compared to Canton, matters seem in a more healthy state than at any other of the new ports, and the place is gradually rising in importance. That China will, in the course of time, be an outlet for a very large quantity of the staples of British manufacture, is undoubted. But the question now is, how is she to pay for them? With the enormous drain upon her in the shape of compensation money, and the heavy annual burden of some 20,000,000 of dollars for opium, all paid in specie—unless there are mines in the interior of which Europeans are in ignorance—a few years will drain the greater part of the silver out of the country, and raise what remains to a factitious value. Even now, in Canton, the sales are, in many instances made in exchange for inferior teas; the price of the article sold being merely nominal, as it is impossible to calculate upon what these teas may realize in the English market.

The revenue derived from *opium and salt* is a subject which is dwelt upon at considerable length in the Indian papers, and the matter appears to have been brought prominently under review in consequence of the last sale of opium for the season having realized prices above those of any previous sale of the year. It is said the result of the sale could not have excited special wonder among those who are acquainted with the character of the trade carried on with the Chinese in the drug, though to parties at a distance it may appear somewhat singular that so profitable a traffic can be continued after England has entered into war with the Celestial Empire, the opium trade being considered in more than one respect the foundation of the hostility. The efforts of the Chinese to eradicate the traffic, and the military operations which grew out of the struggle, on the contrary, have apparently given it a firmer character. The question appears to have been raised whether it would not be as well to throw open the cultivation to public competition; but looking at the degraded position of the inhabitants of Assam, who are allowed the privilege, the Indian journals in several instances express the opinion, that looking at the question both in a physical and moral point of view, not only as respects China, but also as respects India, it would be better to limit the production by sanctioning the continuance of the monopoly. By the returns published from the Salt Board it is considered that the net profit of that article is rather more than a million and a half sterling. The revenue from these two sources, therefore, exceeds three millions and a half sterling, and is equal to that of the whole of the land-revenue of the Bengal presidency. The salt revenue of the year is raised it seems partly from the monopoly-prices fixed on the article manufactured in Lower Bengal, and partly from the import-duty on salt brought from other parts of India. It has been assumed, that of the quantity of 50 lacs of maunds of salt furnished for the consumption of the province, 46 lacs are native manufacture, and 9 lacs imported.

On the arrival of Messrs. Jardine, Mathison, & Co.'s opium clipper, *Magpie*, from the west coast, a case of treasure was missing valued at about £1,000 sterling. A few days afterwards, as the crew were heaving up the kedge, being about to start for another cruise on the coast, they brought with it the missing coin. It had been dropped overboard with a line made fast to an oar, to keep it from sinking too deep into the mud. No doubt, had the *Magpie* proceeded to sea, there would have been parties to fish up the bullion.—*Friend of China.*

New South Wales.—Sydney papers to the 12th of May have been received, but they add little to the information before made public. A general complaint is made of the recent regulations enforced for the sale of Crown lands. The *minimum* upset-price is said to be too high, especially in the present depressed condition of affairs, and little allowance is made for any honest intention the home-government may have had to suppress the ruinous speculation which took place two or three years ago, and at last resulted in much of the misery now experienced by the colonists. The new regulations have the effect of excluding from the market the needy adventurer, and place the land at the purchase of those who have really the means of paying for it when they have purchased. Some points may be objectionable and open to revision, but it is generally the fate of any useful measure, stringently enforced, to encounter opposition, till a steady and persevering trial has proved its efficacy. The statements published in these papers with respect to trade show that the improvement in business has not reached the anticipated height, though it is at the same time certain that more steadiness and firmness in the character of commercial transactions is perceptible. The export of horses to India, is said to be a profitable business; and hopes are expressed, in the recorded opinions of brokers in the London market, that Australian tallow will, before long, stand as a formidable rival with the produce of Russia and South America. Business transactions continued exceedingly limited, and there was no actual improvement in prices to notice. Wool in grease was fetching 7d. per lb., and choice flocks 1s. 1d. to 1s. 2d. per lb.; flour, according to quality, was £9 to £11 per ton; sperm oil was quoted £22 to £24 per ton.

Tahiti.—The news of French agression in Tahiti, and the expulsion of Mr. Prichard, had reached Sydney through the usual intercolonial channel, and had created much excitement. French domination in that locality is regarded with considerable jealousy by the Australian traders, who have established a rather profitable intercourse with the natives of the several groups of islands in the Pacific. Further accounts from Tahiti to the 24th of April, about one month later than those previously received. These state that the French had been cruelly murdering the natives by broadsides of canister and grape from their two heavy frigates. The unhappy Queen had been living upward of twelve weeks with her family on board the Basilisk, and during that long period had not dared to put her foot out of the vessel. The French are said to have carried out their confiscation of the Queen's property to so great an extremity that they had even seized upon the little presents of poultry, fish, and fruit which her subjects had from time to time provided. These trifles the French had appropriated to their own personal uses. During the year 1843, the arrivals and departures of commercial vessels at and from the island of Tahiti amounted to 98, viz., 67 whalers, measuring 22,517 tons, with 1,968 men, 11,820 casks of oil, valued at 8,545,200f.; 12 other trading vessels, measuring 3,906 tons, and crews amounting to 234 men; and 12 coasting vessels, measuring 302 tons, and navigated by 61 men.

New Zealand.—Accounts from New Zealand state that on the 12th of February an interview took place between his Excellency Governor Fitzroy, and the New Zealand chiefs concerned in the massacre at Wairau. After a request to hear from them their own account of the affair, which was complied with by Rauparaha, his Excellency having deliberated for some time, addressed the natives to the effect that, as the English had in the first instance been in the wrong, and the New Zealanders had been betrayed into unlawful acts both by their ignorance of English law, and by the great provocation they had received, no punishment should follow their offences. He concluded by assuring them that he would punish all attempts on the part of the English to wrong the natives, and exhorted the chiefs in their turn to exercise their influence to prevent the natives from any similar infringement of their mutual rights.

His Excellency was accompanied by Sir Everard Home, Captain of Her Majesty's ship North Star, Major Richmond, Mr. Commissioner Spain, Mr. Hamilton, Mr. Forsaith, and several officers belonging to the North Star, landed at Waikanae.

His Excellency and suite were received on shore by the Rev. Octavius Hadfield, Messrs Symonds and Clarke, and a large body of natives, who, to the number 400 and upwards, soon assembled in a large open enclosure within the pah. The governor addressed the assembly in a strain that cannot be too highly commended, and which is honourable to the English name; and we trust that the principle which it comprised will in future preside over our transactions with uncivilized nations. But, however we may strongly approve of Sir Charles Fitzroy's address, we still think, that before any act of leniency was shown, reparation for the past ought to have been given by the natives, nor ought we to treat with armed rebels with the blood of Englishmen scarcely dry upon their land.

Cape of Good Hope.—The chief feature of news in the papers of the 11th of July, is the statement of Customs' returns, which show an improvement; but it is remarked, that notwithstanding the public revenue increases so rapidly as to enable the Government to pay off its old debts, there never was a period before in which the colonists felt so extreme a monetary pressure, or when there were so many unexpected failures. The exports of wool for the quarter ending March, 1844, was as follows:—

	lb.	Value.
Table Bay	248,702	£11,862
Port Beaufort	324,491	16,038
Port Elizabeth	274,351	15,336
	847.544	£43,236

In the corresponding quarter of 1834 the quantity was not more than 51,792lb., valued at 3,498*l.* thus showing the progress of 10 years had increased the production of the staple about 16-fold. It appears by these same returns, that the gross amount of imports was valued at 226,117*l.*, and the exports at 114,399*l.* The increase in revenue does not arise from additional taxation, but is the result of improving commerce and a reduction of the expenses of the service. Mr. Woods, the collector of Customs, had been found shot in his house, and it was generally supposed that his death resulted from the accidental discharge of his fowling-piece, which he always kept loaded in his sleeping room.

The consideration of the estimate of revenue and expenditure for 1845 had been concluded, authorizing an outlay for the year, of 172,179*l.* 10s. 3d. Of this sum, 10,000*l.* had been allowed, to provide for emigration from the mother-country, and a sum of 10,658*l.* 18s. for miscellaneous services. A grant of 1,000*l.* towards the erection of a lighthouse at Cape Agulhas, and 4,000*l.* for the same purpose at Cape Receif, were understood to be included in this latter item. The consideration of the estimate had been preceded by a communication from the secretary to the Government of the state, of the public debt, according to which, it appeared that from the 1st of June, 1843, to the 17th of May last, a sum of 131,086*l.* had been paid towards the redemption of the Government promissory notes. Of the balance of 10,000*l.* still unredeemed, 1,800*l.* were in the Treasury, and 8,200*l.* still outstanding. In the course of the year it was expected that the whole of the public debt would be liquidated without in the least trenching upon ordinary colonial revenue. Late accounts had been received from Port Natal at the Cape, but they possess not the least feature of interest. Affairs in the new settlement appear to be progressing prosperously under British superintendence. Caffre squabbles on the frontier are dilated upon at much length by the Graham Town journalists, who record with minuteness every depredation communicated by the farmers. At Fort Beaufort the detention of the Caffre chief Botman as hostage for one of his followers, who had been detected thieving, had occasioned some excitement among the aborigines. They crossed the boundary, and threatened vengeance, but ultimately they were quieted by the appearance of the military, who, fully accoutred, were soon upon the ground, ready to meet their supposed assailants.

Mauritius.—Our latest intelligence is to the 26th of May. Murrain had attacked the cattle in the island, and under such a visitation, which from the journals seems to have proved destructive, every endeavour was being made to procure effective remedies. The other news is not worth extract. Exchange on England was 7 to 8 per cent. premium for treasury bills, and 3 per cent. discount for private bills.

West Indies.—The papers and letters from Jamaica reach to the 24th of August, and from the other islands to corresponding dates. The weather at Jamaica was favourable for the crops, but lightning had been experienced in several of the parishes, which had done minor damage to property. In the export markets, not much business had been transacted. The coffee crop being quite over, there was none on sale. Dark and middling qualities of sugar scarcely sustained previous prices, but fair was scarce, and commanded 31s. A sale of 100 puncheons of rum had taken place for export at 2s. 7d., equal to 4s. 1d. for home consumption. Business had also been done at 2s. 9d. for export, or 4s. 3d. for consumption. One lot at the latest date was held at 4s. 6d. per gallon, considered to be a long price. In the Jamaica papers the death of Mr. J. Simons, of Royal Vale estate, while out on a shooting excursion, is alluded to in terms of great sympathy. The unfortunate gentleman fell into one of the deep pits which are not uncommon in the mountainous districts of that island, the mouth of which was concealed from view by overgrown heath and furze bushes. At Jamaica there was a good export demand for rum, and prices had an upward tendency. Little remained on the north side, large quantities having been exported thence. The latest sales were made at 4s. 1d to 4s. 3d. and the finer quality had fetched 4s. 6d. all proof 21.

The Trinidad papers notice the dissatisfaction of the labourers at the late reduction of wages made by the planters, in consequence of the alteration of the sugar duties at home, and on some estates they had left work, refusing to accept the rates fixed by their masters. A bold attempt had been made by an hon. member of Her Majesty's Council of Government, Mr. Losh, a planter, to raise a loan, on Government security, of £200,000 sterling, for immigration purposes. The introduction of this ordinance, the manner in which it was hurried through the Council, and the apparent disregard manifested by that hon. Board to the views and feelings of the community generally on that question, have created a degree of excitement which has not been witnessed before in Trinidad. A combination, it was feared, would take place among them to resist the contemplated change. The planters have, it is said, been obliged to adopt this measure, in order to protect themselves, and stand in a position to compete in the London market with foreign free-labour production. A memorial from the most influential firms of the island had been presented to the Legislature against the proposed increase of duties on imports.

The weather in Demerara and Barbadoes had been favourable for agricultural purposes; and the promise of next year's crops was good. The estate of Maryville, in Demerara, upon which 380 hhds. of sugar had been manufactured, sold for 18,000 dollars, before the departure of the packet. Peace in Dominica was quite restored. The ringleaders in the late census-disturbance had been tried, aud five found guilty and sentenced to death. One had already undergone the extreme penalty of the law.

A society, entitled the Agricultural and Commercial Society of British Guiana, has been established at Georgetown for the purpose of promoting the industry and commerce of the colony by the establishment of a reading-room, and exchange and sample-room, for the daily meeting of commercial men, planters, and members of the society, and also by the offer of certain premiums for the improvement of the agriculture of the colony and other purposes. The society has been in existence since the 18th of March last, and at the date of the last report on the 25th of July numbered 274 members and associates. A list of premiums has been drawn up, which it is proposed to offer as soon as the funds of the society shall prove adequate. It was resolved that the list of the premiums should be submitted to the Governor and the Court of Policy, with a request that they might be paid out of the fund voted for agricultural improvements by the Combined Court.

Canada.—The intelligence from Canada announce the following list of a new ministry.—

President of the Council—Mr. Viger.
Secretary—Mr. Daly.
Attorney-General for U. C.—Mr. Draper.
Attorney-General for L. C.—Mr. Smith.
Solicitor-General for U. C.—Mr. Sherwood.
Solicitor-General for L. C.—Mr. Chabot.
Commissioner of Crown Lands—Mr. D. B. Papineau.
Receiver-General—Mr. W. Morris.
Inspector-General—Mr. Merritt.

It is also given out, that the ministry do not deem it advisable that the existing Parliament should be again assembled. If this be true, and it is countenanced very confidently by the *Montreal Courier*, a dissolution and general election throughout the province may speedily be expected to ensue. The above appointments are said to be good ones, comprising most of the moderate men of the colony whose talents and influence entitle them to public confidence.

Another *on dit* is, that the celebrated Papineau is on his way to Canada, to oppose the ex-ministry.

The great public works of the province are proceeding rapidly, but unfortunately are the cause of repeated outrages and breaches of the peace from the turbulence and ungovernable character of the Irish labourers employed on them, most of whom are, however, itinerants, going about every where in search of employment on canals, railroads, &c.

The prospects of agriculture this year are stated to be very good. The wheat-raising in the Lower Province had been particularly successful; the crops having suffered but little from the fly, the usual curse of the Canadian farmer, and hardly at all from the rust. The accounts from Upper Canada are also very flattering.

Trade was very dull in every branch, and unless very different accounts of the weather and the harvest in this country were received by the next steamer, they could not anticipate a very extensive and profitable "fall" business.

Arrivals of Produce at the Port of Montreal, to August 9, inclusive—(by Canal and River.

Canada.—10,341 brls. of ashes, 384,618 barrels of flour, 214,893 bushels of wheat, 6,832 barrels of pork, 1,581 barrels of beef, 514 kegs of lard, 1,944 kegs of butter, 420 barrels of tallow, 2,200 bushels of peas, 3,584 bushels of barley. United States.—800 barrels of ashes, 77,032 barrels of flour, 34,878 bushels of wheat, 13,305 barrels of pork, 173 kegs of lard, 143 barrels of tallow.

Total—11,141 barrels of ashes, 461,650 barrels of flour, 249,771 bushels of wheat, 20,137 barrels of pork, 1,585 barrels of beef, 687 kegs of lard, 1,944 kegs of butter, 563 barrels of tallow, 2,200 bushels of peas, 3,584 bushels of barley.

Same time 1843—9,943 barrels of ashes, 166,522 barrels of flour, 60,712 bushels of wheat, 6,400 barrels of pork, 617 barrels of beef, 440 kegs of lard, 950 kegs of butter.

Exports from Montreal and Quebec to August 9, 1844.

Montreal.—16,525 barrels of ashes, 154,604 barrels of flour, 210,212 bushels of wheat, 1,368 barrels of pork, 1,409 barrels of beef, 371 kegs of butter, 1,195 barrels of oatmeal, 48,887 bushels of peas, 53,553 bushels of barley, 20,388 bushels of oats, £40,225 specie.

Quebec.—1,862 barrels of ashes, 153,365 barrels of flour, 26,886 bushels of wheat, 2,262 barrels of pork, 648 barrels of beef, 557 kegs of butter, 1,225 barrels of oatmeal, 20,205 bushels of peas, 7,062 bushels of barley.

Total—18,387 barrels of ashes, 307,961 barrels of flour, 237,098 bushels of wheat, 3,630 barrels of pork, 2,057 barrels of beef, 928 kegs of butter, 2,420 barrels of oatmeal, 78,092 bushels of peas, 60,615 bushels of barley, 20,388 bushels of oats, £40,225 specie.

Same time 1843—17,487 barrels of ashes, 50,130 barrels of flour, 15,417 bushels of wheat, 4,849 barrels of pork, 689 barrels of beef, 779 kegs of butter, 1,048 barrels of oatmeal, 31,726 bushels of peas, 300 bushels of barley, 200 bushels of oats.

HOME INTELLIGENCE.

The Royal Christening.—The baptism of his royal highness the infant prince, second son of Her Majesty and Prince Albert, took place on Friday the 6th of September, in the private chapel at Windsor, in the presence of Her Majesty and other royal and distinguished personages. The Archbishop of Canterbury solemnized the rite of baptism, and the Duke of Cambridge named his Royal Highness "Alfred Earnest Albert." A state banquet was afterwards given by Her Majesty in St. George's Hall.

Visit of the Court to Scotland—Her Majesty and his Royal Highness Prince Albert, accompanied by the Princess Royal, the Earl of Aberdeen, and a select suite, embarked at Woolwich, on Monday the 9th of September, and sailed to Dundee, from thence to Blair Athol Castle, Perthshire, the seat of Lord Glenlyon, where they intend to remain until the early part of October, and then return to Windsor, where great preparations are making to receive Louis Philippe, the king of the French, who intends honouring our gracious sovereign with a short visit.

East India House.—On Wednesday, September 18th., a special General Court of Proprietors of East India Stock was held at the Company's House, in Leadenhall-street, for the purpose of considering a resolution, passed on the 21st ultimo by the Court of Directors, the object of which was to grant an annuity of £1,000 per annum to Major-General Sir William Nott, G.C.B., for his long services in India.

The chair was taken by Capt. Sheppard, who assured the meeting that it would not be necessary for him to occupy a large portion of the time of the Court of Proprietors in recommending the resolution of the Court of Directors for their adoption. Her Majesty has been pleased to confer the highest honour she could on General Nott, that of a G.C.B., and it was now the duty of the East India Company to offer him such acknowledgment as their means permitted. After paying a high compliment to General Pollock and Sir Robert Sale, and stating that the Court of Directors were ever ready to acknowledge and do honour to the services of their army, from the general to the sepoy drummer, the worthy chairman emphatically called upon the Court unanimously to confirm the vote of the annuity which the Court of Directors had sent for their approval. (Loud cheers.)

Sir Henry Willock, the Deputy Chairman of the Company, in warm language seconded the motion, which being supported by Mr. Weedin, was carried by acclamation, and the Court adjourned.

New Zealand Colonization.—The following are the resolutions at which the Select Committee of the House of Commons have arrived, as containing a summary of their opinions upon the whole subject;—

"1. That the conduct of the New Zealand Company, in sending out settlers to New Zealand, not only without the sanction, but in direct defiance of the authority of the Crown, was highly irregular and improper.

"2. That the conclusion of the treaty of Waitangi by Captain Hobson with certain natives of New Zealand, was a part of a series of injudicious proceedings, which had commenced several years previous to his assumption of the local government.

"3. That the acknowledgment by the local authorities of a right of property on the part of the natives of New Zealand, in all wild lands in those islands, after the sovereignty had been assumed by her Majesty, was not essential to the true construction of the treaty of Waitangi, and was an error which has been productive of very injurious consequences.

"4. That the New Zealand Company has a right to expect to be put in possession by the Government, with the least possible delay, of the number of acres awarded to it by Mr. Pennington; that the Company has this right as against the estate of the Crown, without reference to the validity or otherwise of its supposed purchases from the natives, all claims derived from which have been surrendered.

"5. That the Company, in selecting the land to be granted by the Crown within the defined limits, cannot claim the grant of any land not vested in the Crown.

"6. That means ought to be forthwith adopted for establishing the exclusive title of the Crown to all land not actually occupied and enjoyed by natives, or held under grants from the Crown; such land to be considered as vested in the Crown for the purpose of being employed in the manner most conducive to the welfare of the inhabitants, whether natives or Europeans.

"7. That in order to prevent land from being held by parties not intending to make use of the same, a land-tax, not exceeding 2d. an acre, ought to be imposed; that all parties claiming land should be required to put in their claims, and pay one year's tax in advance, within twelve months.

"8. That such tax ought not to be considered as applying to the whole estate of the New Zealand Company, so long as they shall continue to sell not less than one twenty fifth of the land granted to them annually, and to expend a fixed proportion of the proceeds in emigration.

"9. That such tax ought also not to be considered as applying to lands now actually occupied and enjoyed by the natives, or to reserves set apart and held for their benefit.

"10. That reserves ought to be made for the natives, interspersed with the lands assigned to settlers, with suitable provision for regulating their alienation, and preserving the use of them for the natives as long as may be necessary; and that these reserves ought not to be included in calculating the amount of land due to that Company.

"11. That as it appears by evidence, that the non settlement of the land-claims has been productive of great confusion and mischief in the colony, it is expedient to adopt measures for granting legal titles with the least possible delay to the actual occupants of land, unless under special circumstances of abuse.

"12. That the prohibition of all private persons to purchase land from the natives ought to be strictly enforced, except that land which may have been purchased by natives, they should be at liberty to sell again, provided the transaction be sanctioned by the protector.

"13. That it is highly important that the Governor should have more effectual means of enforcing obedience to his authority, and also greater facility for visiting frequently the different settlements; and that with this view it is expedient that an armed steamer, of moderate size, be placed at his disposal.

"14. That it is expedient that the settlers should be organized as a militia, under the orders and control of the Governor: natives, under proper precautions, being allowed to serve in it.

"15. That it is expedient that an attempt should also be made to raise and discipline a native force of a more permanent character, officered in general by Europeans, but in which any of the natives who may be found trustworthy may hold commands.

"16. That the employment of natives in the civil service of the Government, in any situations in which they can be useful, is highly desirable.

"17. That efforts should be made gradually to wean the natives from their ancient customs, and to induce them to adopt those of civilized life, upon the principle recommended by Captain Grey, in his report on the mode of introducing civilization amongst the natives of Australia.

[See papers respecting New Zealand, ordered by the House of Commons to be printed, May 11, 1841, p. 43.]

"18. That the principles in which the New Zealand Company have acted in making the reserves for the natives, with a view to their ultimate as well as present welfare, and in making suitable provision for spiritual and educational purposes, are sound and judicious, tending to the benefit of all classes.

"19. That the committee, upon a review of the documentary evidence relating to the loss of life at Wairau (without offering any opinion upon the law of the case), deem it an act of justice to the memory of those who fell there, to state, that it appears that the expedition in question was undertaken for a purpose believed by the parties to be lawful and desirable, and which also example in analogous cases had unfortunately led them to expect might be effected without resistance from the natives. The committee cannot withhold the expression of their regret at the loss of life which occurred, especially the loss of Captain Arthur Wakefield, whose long and distinguished services in the British navy are recorded in the papers before the committee, and of Mr. Thompson, the stipendiary magistrate, Mr. Richardson, the Crown prosecutor, Captain England, Mr. Cotterell, Mr. Patchett, and Mr. Howard.

THE COLONIAL SECRETARY.—Lord Stanley retires from the Commons, to become a Peer in his father's lifetime; and everybody asks what it means? As a young man, with all the confident if not the dignified bearing of aristocratic birth, proud in its own consciousness — with a ready tongue, and a vehement will, if not an earnest purpose—Lord Stanley acquired a renown for prowess in the Parliamentary lists; and it was assumed that the generous ardour of youth prognosticated a powerful but wiser maturity. The promise has failed. For two sessions, especially the last, he has shown premature signs of wearing out. He seems to be exhausted with the perpetual warfare that he provokes. Recklessly striking the friends behind him as well the foe in front, his own leaders were obliged to check him: he is tamed, but his subsiding passion displays no mature wisdom. His reckless assertion is slighted; his bitterness has lost its power through its triteness; and he sat uneasy-looking—often silent—neglected. In some important questions of his office, he exposed himself to proof of prevaricating and of mischievously sacrificing important interests to gratify some pique or spleen. He was convicted as a minister of evil. The Cabinet, they say, want speakers in the House of Lords; perhaps it is more, that Lord Stanley wants to be out of the House of Commons. The need in the upper house is obvious; but his colleagues never could have exercised a free choice in supplying it thus. Lord Stanley is not the kind of speaker wanted for the purpose. There are orators among the Peers, strong-spoken enough; there is Lyndhurst's trenchant, though polished irony, Brougham's ornate hyperbole and vituperation, Wellington's utter plain speaking—privilege of his high standing and his age; but in all these there is either an intellectual or a moral loftiness, and either real dignity or tact; the gladiatorial displays with which a Stanley once amused the Commons would be out of place—would not answer. Lord Stanley has never exhibited that strength and ability which are best seen in calm council. Some minor conveniences may be hoped from the arrangement. The Premier may have felt his gagged but impulsive colleague to be in the way where he was, and may have preferred, in dealing with many questions—Ireland for instance—to be without that sinister presence. Many colonial subjects would be more advantageously discussed in the absence of the Colonial Minister. Shelved in the Commons, the restless orator may still fancy that he is a statesman by being busied with real work, the explanation of measures in the Lords; the want of which was so damagingly exposed by Lord Normanby: he spoke of the lack of time, but it was partly owing also to the lack of workmen. Busied in that showy drudgery of debate, Lord Stanley might be made harmless. But can he be trusted not to break his tether? Whatever was his motive for backing out of the prize-ring to which he belonged in the Commons, Ministers can scarcely expect to profit much by the change. At first people hoped that there was going to be a new Colonial Minister: it would have been better for the Government.—*Spectator.*

ALGERIA.—A letter from Algiers of Aug. 13th, contains some statistical information respecting that country and the French force employed to keep it in subjection, which is well worthy of being referred to at this time, when all are anxious to ascertain the disposable means of France for extending the war into other parts of Africa.

In determining the present available force furnished by the population of Algeria, our informant starts from the estimate of the number of inhabitants at the occupation of the country by the French—namely, 1,030,000. From this gross amount is deducted 560,000 for the female population, the women being always in excess in Mohamedan countries. The number of 100,000 is then deducted for the male children, 70,000 for old men and slaves, leaving 300,000. Of these, 120,000 living in towns and cities under the surveillance of the French are unavailable, except in case of an insurrection. This makes 260,000, the number of male inhabitants capable of bearing arms against the French; and these, by the exterminating process which has been carried on for the last 14 years, as well as by flight and emigration, must now be reduced to 200,000.

On the other hand, the force which France possesses in Algeria is estimated, including the Zouaves, the *Legions Etrangeres*, and the National Guard, at 77,000, leaving scarcely more than two Algerians to one Frenchman. Taking into consideration, however, the number of Arabs who will not fight, those that are the allies of France, and the divisions caused by their internal feuds, the numerical advantage may really be said to lie with the French.

In all Algeria the number of Europeans is about 60,000, of whom more than half are not French, but consist of all European nations; principally, however, of Spaniards. In Oran, out of 8,000 or 9,000, there are 6,000 Spaniards. The 30,000 French civilians furnish only 6,000 colonists, the rest being employed for the army, traders, and hotel-keepers. The principal villages or colonizing settlements are enumerated as follows:—Drariah containing 57 families; El Achour, 60 families; Cheraga, 50 families; Hussein Dey (no account); Kouba (no account); Staouel (no account); Ouled, 50 families; Pressia, now beginning; St. Ferdinand, 30 houses; Sta. Amelie, 50 families; Orleansville, 5,000 or 6,000 persons; Baba Nosser, 60 families.

Many of the 6,000 French colonists are veterans who have been rewarded, after the old Roman fashion, by the gift of lands, very few Frenchmen having emigrated into Algeria. Many indeed are continually returning. With regard to the colonization of Oran, there are lands at a distance of six miles, and nothing beyond. It is said by old inhabitants, that it is unsafe to go alone three miles from the city. The Arabs of Oran have, however, been in constant war with the French, and it is from among them that Abd-el-Kader draws nearly all his resources.

In conclusion, then, the result of these statements is, that an army of 75,000 men is maintained by France at a cost of 80,000,000f. per annum for the protection of about 6,000 French colonists in Algeria, who do not return one franc back into the Treasury; and for these 6,000 colonists, already 50,000 soldiers have perished since the occupation.

Quarantine Regulations. — The following regulations with respect to the quarantine to be performed at the port of Marseilles, were established by order of the French Government, on the 14th of August last:—

With unclean bill of health.

Art. 1. French Post-office Packets, 19 days after debarking effects and passengers.—Passengers by these boats and their baggage, 17 days after landing at the Lazaret; 14 days only when the baggage shall have been *plombé* at the consulate of France at the port of embarking, and that this operation be legally certified.

Art. 2. French or Foreign Men-of-war, 17 days after the landing of passengers and their baggage.—Passengers on board these vessels, 17 days without *spoglio*, 14 days with *spoglio*.

Art. 3. Vessels with Pilgrims, 25 days.—Pilgrims, 25 days after landing.

Art. 4. Every other description of sailing-vessel or steam-boat, 21 days after landing suspected articles.—Passengers by these vessels, 17 days without *spoglio*, 14 days with *spoglio*. Merchandise, 21 days after landing at the Lazaret.

With doubtful bills of health.

Art. 1. French Post-office packets, 15 days after debarking effects and passengers.—Passengers by these boats and their baggage, 14 days after landing; 12 days only when the baggage shall have been *plombé* at the consulate of France at the point of embarking, and that this operation be legally certified.

Art. 2. French or Foreign men-of-war, 14 days after the landing of passengers and their baggage. Without passengers 12 days.—Passengers on board these vessels, 14 days after landing without *spoglio*, and 12 days with *spoglio*.

Art. 3. Vessels with pilgrims, 20 days. Pilgrims, 20 days after landing at the Lazaret.

Art. 4. Every other description of sailing vessel or steam boat, 15 days after landing suspected articles.—Passengers by these vessels, 14 days without *spoglio* after landing at the Lazaret; 12 days with *spoglio*. Suspected goods, 15 days after landing at the Lazaret.

With clean bills of health.

Art. 1.—French Post-office Packets, 12 days after debarking effects at the Laz ret.—Passengers by these boats and their baggage, 9 days after landing, and their baggage exposed to the air.

Art. 2.—French or Foreign men-of-war, 9 days, with or without passengers.—Passengers on board these vessels, 9 days after landing, and their baggage exposed to the air.

Art. 3.—Every other description of vessel or steam-boat, 12 days after landing suspected goods.—Passengers by these vessels, 9 days. Suspected merchandise, 12 days after landing at the Lozaret.

Belgium and the Zollverein. — "The treaty of navigation and commerce between these powers, has been signed by General Giblet, and Baron Arnim, bearing date the 1st of September, thus the difference has been terminated in the most prompt, and doubtless the most satisfactory way, for all parties."—*Courier Belge.*

PROROGATION OF PARLIAMENT.

House of Lords, *Thursday, Sept. 5.*

The session, protracted beyond the usual term by the proceedings of this House in its judicial capacity, was closed this day.

Their Lordships sate at ten o'clock, and were occupied in delivering judgment in various cases of appeal till one o'clock, the hour appointed for the prorogation, when the Lord Chancellor took his seat with the other Lords Commissioners at the foot of the throne; they were, the Lord President of the Council (Lord Warncliffe), the Lord Privy Seal (the Duke of Buccleuch), the Duke of Wellington, Earl Delawarr, and the Earl of Dalhousie.

The Gentleman Usher of the Black Rod (Sir A. Clifford) was then directed by the Lord Chancellor to require the attendance of the Commons.

In a few minutes the Speaker of the House of Commons, followed by members of that house, appeared at the bar.

The Lord Chancellor said—My Lords and Gentlemen, her Majesty, not having thought it fit to be personally present at this time, has commanded a commission to issue under the Great Seal for giving her royal assent to several acts which have been agreed to by both houses of Parliament, which commission you shall hear read.

The commission was then read in the usual manner by the junior clerk of the house.

The Lord Chancellor—In obedience to her Majesty's commands, and by virtue of the commission just read, we do declare that her Majesty has given her royal assent to the bills named therein, and the clerk is required to pass them in the usual form of this house.

The Lord Chancellor then, on behalf of the Lords Commissioners, delivered the following speech:—

"*My Lords and Gentlemen,*

"We are commanded by her Majesty, in relieving you from further attendance in Parliament, to express to you the warm acknowledgments of her Majesty for the zeal and assiduity with which you have applied yourselves to the discharge of your public duties during a laborious and protracted session.

"The result has been the completion of many legislative measures calculated to improve the administration of the law, and to promote the public welfare

"Her Majesty has given her cordial assent to the bill which you presented to her Majesty, for regulating the issue of bank notes, and for conferring certain privileges upon the Bank of England for a limited period.

"Her Majesty trusts that these measures will tend to place the pecuniary transactions of the country upon a sounder basis, without imposing any inconvenient restrictions on commercial credit or enterprise.

"We are directed to inform you that her Majesty continues to receive from her allies, and from all foreign powers, assurances of their friendly disposition.

"Her Majesty has recently been engaged in discussions with the government of the King of the French, on events calculated to interrupt the good understanding and friendly relations between this country and France; you will rejoice to learn that, by the spirit of justice and moderation which has animated the two governments, this danger has been happily averted.

"*Gentlemen of the House of Commons,*

"We are commanded by Her Majesty to thank you for the readiness with which you voted the supplies for the service of the year.

"Her Majesty has observed with the utmost satisfaction that by the course to which you have steadily adhered in maintaining inviolate the public faith, and inspiring a just confidence in the stability of the national resources, you have been enabled to make a considerable reduction in the annual charge on account of the interest of the public debt.

"*My Lords and Gentlemen,*

"Her Majesty desires us to congratulate you on the improvement which has taken place in the condition of our manufactures and commerce, and on the prospect that, through the bounty of Divine Providence, we shall enjoy the blessing of an abundant harvest.

"Her Majesty rejoices in the belief, that on your return to your several districts you will find, generally prevailing throughout the country, a spirit of loyalty and cheerful obedience to the law.

"Her Majesty is confident that these dispositions, so important to the peaceful development of our resources, and to our national strength, will be confirmed and encouraged by your presence and example.

"We are commanded by her Majesty to assure you, that when you shall be called upon to resume the discharge of your parliamentary functions, you may place entire reliance on the cordial co-operation of Her Majesty in your endeavours to improve the social condition, and to promote the happiness and contentment, of her people."

Then a commission for proroguing the Parliament was read.

After which the Lord Chancellor said—

"*My Lords and Gentlemen,*

"By virtue of her Majesty's commission, under the great seal, to us and other Lords directed, and now read, we do in her Majesty's name, and in obedience to her commands, prorogue this parliament to Thursday, the 10th day of October next, to be then here holden: and this parliament is accordingly prorogued to Thursday, the 10th day of October next."

The Commons then withdrew, and their Lordships separated.

THE RIGHT HON. JOHN, BARON KEANE,

G.C.B., K.C.H., &c. &c.

This highly distinguished and gallant officer, whose decease we noticed in our last month's number, was born in the year 1781, being the second son of Sir John Keane, Bart., of Belmont, in the county of Waterford, Ireland, by Sarah, daughter of John Keiley, Esq., of Belgrove. Being destined for the army, he received his first commission as ensign in Ward's regiment on the 11th of October, 1794; was lieutenant on the 30th of the same month; and captain in the 112th regiment November 12th, in the same year. He obtained his majority in the 60th regiment, May 27, 1802, and lieut.-colonel in the 13th foot August 20, 1803. While serving with his regiment in the West Indies he received the distinction of a cross-and-two-clasps for his gallantry at Martinique. Colonel Keane shared in all the honours of the Peninsula, and commanded brigades at the battles of the Pyrenees, Nivelle, Orthes, and Toulouse, for which he was rewarded with the Knighthood of the Bath, and the rank of major-general. On the 19th of January, 1818, Sir John Keane was appointed Governor of St. Lucia; and afterwards, in November, 1822, to the lieutenant-governorship and command of the forces at Jamaica.

On the 22d of July, 1830, Sir John Keane was raised to the rank of lieut.-general; and in the year 1833 he succeeded Sir Colin Halket, as commander-in-chief of the army in Bombay; and, after nearly six years' service in that presidency, on the 29th of October, 1838, Sir John Keane received authority from the government of India to organize and lead into Scinde a force intended to co-operate with the army then on the north-west frontier of India under the command of Sir Henry Fane. In the month of December following, however, Sir Henry forwarded his resignation to head-quarters, and the command of the combined forces devolved upon General Keane: He was now called upon to lead a considerable army, and to conduct operations requiring much discretion, delicacy, and tact in dealing with those half-friendly powers, whose existence is one of the greatest difficulties in the government of a semi-civilized land. With the open co-operation, and often in opposition to the secret intrigues of these wavering friends, the British commander in India has much to do, but his acknowledged gallantry and sound judgment overcame the difficulties with which he was surrounded; and, as a reward for his distinguished military services in Affghanistan, and especially for the storming and capture of the formidable fortress of Ghuznee, he was created Baron Keane of the United Kingdom, with a pension of £2000 a year for his own life, and that of his two immediate successors in the peerage; to which were added the thanks of both Houses of Parliament, as also those of the Court of Directors of the East India Company. In July, 1838, Lord Keane lost his first wife, and in August, 1840, he married the youngest daughter of the late Lieutenant-Colonel Boland, who survives him. After a long and painful illness, the mortal career of his lordship was ended in peaceful and domestic privacy at his seat, Barton Lodge, in Hampshire, August 26th, 1844, in the 64th year of his age.

It is but justice to the deceased nobleman to record, that he was one of the most distinguished officers in the British army. In Egypt, in our West Indian and American colonies, in India, and in the Peninsula, he fought manfully for the honour of his country, and has quitted the world with a reputation for professional skill and intrepidity which will not speedily be out-rivalled.

He is succeeded by his fifth child and eldest son, the Honourable Richard Arthur Wellington Keane, now Lord Keane, who was aid-de-camp to his lordship when he was in command of the army of the Indus, and shared in the honours of that campaign. He is a captain in the 37th regiment of foot, and a major in the army.

OBITUARY.

Baily, Francis, Esq., F.R.S., president of the Royal Astronomical Society, August 30, at London, in his 71st year. His scientific attainments were of the highest order; he was a doctor of civil law, member of the Royal Irish Academy, a fellow of the Linnean and Geological Societies, and a fellow of the Royal Society, having been elected of that body in 1821. He was correspondent for several learned and scientific societies abroad, amongst others, the Royal Institute of Paris, and the Academy Royal at Berlin.

Bathurst, the Venerable Archdeacon, September 10, at Cheltenham.

Cheeseman, Mr. Edward S F., purser and paymaster of her Majesty's brig "Star," July 8, at Ascension.

Courtney, Samuel, September 19, very suddenly, aged 45 years. The deceased was a compositor in the employ of Messrs. Fisher, Son, & Co. for the last ten years, and had so conducted himself as to merit the confidence of his employers, and the respect and esteem of his fellow-workmen.

Dales, Lieutenant-Colonel Samuel, K.H., August 28, at Greenhithe, Kent, in his 84th year. This gallant officer had seen much service in the army previous to 1807, when he retired on half-pay. He assisted at the taking of the French islands of St. Pierre and Miguelon, near Newfoundland, in 1793, and served under his Royal Highness the Duke of York, in Holland, in 1797, including the taking of Hoven, and the actions of the 2nd and 6th of October.

Dunlop, Andrew M'Queen, Esq., of the Bank of Western India, June 30, at Calcutta, aged 30, deeply regretted.

Durbin, Captain, of the 29th Regiment of Foot, second son of J. J. Durbin, Esq., of Cheltenham, June 25, at Hyderabad.

Eden, Sir Robert, Bart., of Windlestone and Beamish Park, both in the county of Durham, September 3.

Elliott, Robert, Esq., late of the East India Company's Service, September 7, at Much Hadham, Herts, aged 58.

Fisher, Captain Peter, Royal Navy, superintendent of her Majesty's dockyard, Sheerness, August 28, aged 63.

Fitzgibbon, Lieutenant-General, half-pay, 23rd Royal Fusiliers, September 7, at Plymouth.

Fryer, the Very Rev. William Victor, D D., chaplain to the Portuguese Embassy, and for many years principal chaplain of the late Portuguese Chapel, in South Street, London, September 6, at London, in his 79th year.

Hall, Captain Basil, Royal Navy, September 11, at Hasler Hospital, in his 56th year.

Hawks, Lieutenant John Shafto, adjutant of the 7th Regiment of Native Infantry, third son of the late John Hawks, Esq., of Gateshead and London, June 13, at Delhi, aged 34 years. By his demise the service has lost a highly intelligent a d efficient officer, and his brother officers a member of their society, whose uniformly upright conduct and abilities justly secured for him their esteem and respect: by the men who volunteered and carried his remains to the grave, his loss is much felt.

Hellard, Commander Joseph, R N., at Portsmouth, September 16, aged 74.

Heygate, Sir William, Bart., Chamberlain of the city of London, August 30, at Roecliffe, Leicestershire, in the 63d year of his age. He is succeeded in the important and lucrative office of Chamberlain by Alderman A. Brown.

Maule, Retired Commander George, at Lancaster, aged 56.

Murray, the Hon. James Erskine, a younger son of the late Lord Elibank, was killed, February 16, by a grape-shot, during an action of 37 hours' duration with the native pirates of the river Coli, in the island of Borneo. He was shot whilst pointing a gun on board his schooner, Yonge Quene, with which vessel and a brig he had left Hong-Kong the previous November, with all requisites for forming a settlement on that island.

Neville, Captain C. H., Royal Navy, September 7, at Thorney, Notts, aged 75. He fought under Lord Howe, on the memorable 1st of June, 1794; and served the office of Sheriff for the county of Nottingham.

Palmer, Henry Robinson, Esq., civil engineer, September 12, at Westminster. He was the favourite pupil, and for many years principal assistant, of the late Mr. Telford, civil engineer, and was one of the founders of the Institution of Civil Engineers, of which he was one of the vice-presidents.

Raigersfeld, Jeffrey Baron de, Rear-Admiral of the Red, September 7, at Weavering, Kent, aged 74. He entered the navy in April, 1783. His commissions bear date as follow—Lieutenant, 21st August, 1793; Commander, 21st September, 1797; Captain, 29th April, 1802; and Rear-Admiral, 17th August, 1840.

Ross, David, Esq, of Demerara, September 9, at Edinburgh.

Stirling, Sibella, wife of Major William Stirling, of the Hon. East India Company's Civil Service, August 30, at Guernsey. In the year 1836, she was shipwrecked on the uninhabited island of Astorva, where, during a period of 68 days, she maintained the dignity of her station, as well as that of her husband, by whose good example and great exertions under the influence of religious feeling the comforts of the crew of the shipwrecked vessel were attended to, and discipline preserved.—On the following day, Ellen Mary, youngest child of the above, aged 6 years; both of scarlet fever.

Whatley, Lieutenant-Colonel Sir Joseph, K.C.H. for twenty years Groom of the Bedchamber to their late Majesties George IV. and William IV., September 8, at Egham, Surrey, in the 80th year of his age.

Wright, Lieutenant Joseph, R.N., of the Coast Guard Service, Ireland, August 27, aged 50.

LONDON: FISHER, SON, AND CO., PRINTERS.

FISHER'S

COLONIAL MAGAZINE.

THE SYSTEM OF COLONIAL-CROWN-LAND GRANTING,

THE TRUE SOURCE OF THE DIFFICULTIES WHICH BESET EMIGRATION.

BY A SIXTEEN-YEARS RESIDENT IN CANADA.

WITHIN the last few years many persons have endeavoured to enlighten the public upon the subject of emigration; folios have been written in proof of this or that point, and the weight of talent thrown into the scale in the most specious arguments—glossing over, and, in fact, giving a character of sound sense to the most unheard-of propositions; propounding theories, which, in some instances, would entitle those from whom they emanated to the distinction of a cap-and-bells, and setting forth, in at least the opinion of the writer, the true panacea for the evils complained of, namely, a want of emigration both *from* the mother-country and *to* the colonies.

It would appear evident to me, that the public mind as yet has had nothing presented to it as a scheme of emigration which was thought worthy of action, or indeed consideration; for, of the numerous publications upon that subject, few, if any, have been the subject of more than a passing remark, and have then sought that oblivion to which their merits would naturally consign them. With the proper fear of such a fate as theirs before my eyes, and without stopping to inquire into the causes which led thereto, I shall attempt to put on paper the opinions which a sixteen-years' residence in Canada has enabled me to form upon the subject. My remarks will, in a great measure, consist of statements of facts drawn from the history of the country, with opinions thereon; and I shall endeavour to be as clear as possible, so that the natural inferences may be as obvious to the reader in this country, where the circumstances I detail are but little known, as they would be to the colonist; and this, I must say, is an object of great importance, for subjects are discussed and acted upon in this country—opinions mooted and debated with great ability upon colonial matters—which, while they receive the applause of people here, unacquainted with the subject in its various ramifications, very often contain in the eyes of the colonist, the most absurd propositions. A melancholy instance of the truth of this statement exists in a matter of much greater importance than a discussion in a magazine or newspaper, to wit, in the enactments of what I may call that child of ignorant parents, the Union Bill. In fine, I would remark, that though many of my observations may be applicable to other colonies of the empire, and in the main first principle are decidedly so in my opinion, yet I propose confining myself particularly to that part of the province of Canada formerly called Upper Canada; as being a place presenting greater facilities for settlement than any other part of the North American colonies, and also the one in which I have spent so many years of my life.

I shall in the first place run over, as succinctly as possible, the various settlements effected in the country, with the general motive-power which operated in any particular case. This plan I deem absolutely necessary, as by such means only can I proceed to show the effect the several systems of land-granting adopted has had upon emigration and settlement in the province.

In commencement, then, let me endeavour to draw the attention of the reader to the early history of Upper Canada, namely, the close of the revolutionary war in 1783. The first class of persons we find entering the province, were United-Empire loyalists — that is, men who had adhered to the British government during the revolutionary struggle. These men, in consideration of their attachment, got *free* grants of land for themselves *and their children*; and we find that at this period most liberal encouragement was held out to settlers of all kinds, by means of similar free grants to the heads of families. It is evident that the government of those days was anxious to foster and encourage settlement in the colony, freely giving, what indeed could be of no earthly use to them, the waste-lands of the crown, to every and any person who chose to ask for them; and though they may have acted improvidently—though they may have given, and undoubtedly did give, lands to many persons who should not have got them—yet I fancy they were not such blockheads as not to know *that what they gave only became of value to them from the fact of its being given and brought into use—that to make the province a subject of interest to the nation, or the possession of it of any possible consequence, it must be settled.* There was also in the commencement of the century a trifling influx of immigrants from the mother-country, chiefly Scotch, who established themselves, forming what has since gone by the name of the Glengary Settlement; and upon this principle, that is, free grants to settlers, the province continued increasing, till, in 1812, at the outbreak of the last American war, there were fifty thousand souls within its limits. And here it is worthy of remark, that the provincials, amounting to, according to the general proportion, ten thousand adults, or, say eight thousand effective men, together with the 49th regiment, and a few companies of the 8th, kept this province, with an open frontier of seven hundred miles, against all the attempts of the great, glorious, free, and enlightened republic which borders them; a great many liberty-capped heads marched into the country, and marched through it, but, in the latter case, as prisoners to their gallant opponents.

Right nobly did this handful of men deserve the title they brought to the country with them, namely, United-Empire Loyalists; right nobly did they deserve the title of Britons, for right nobly had they earned it, discharging the duties their country demanded of them. Through weal, through woe—through good report and evil report—through the frosts and snows of winters, and almost unheard-of hardships "in desert lands and lone," they clung to the British standard with a faith like that which clings to the Rock of ages. Theirs was that bond which should unite the people to a good government—the deep love of child to parent. With them there was no change; their regard for the institutions of their father-land admitted of no question; they were, in fact, up to this period, a little pet-colony of noble souls, whose nature was simplicity itself. With but few exceptions, they are gone; the car of time has rolled over them: peace to their ashes.

But to proceed. The war brought notoriety; the country which had hitherto lain comparatively unnoticed, began now to attract attention; numbers of old country-people flocked in, allured by the accounts of the fertility of the soil, *and the gift of it*; and this was not confined to people from the British islands only. Many Americans had been in Canada—compared with the *down-cast* states from which they came, it was a garden; their mouth watered to possess it, as a nation and as individuals. They sighed for a location; in fact, getting good land, and for little or nothing, was too much in the scale, even against freedom and republican institutions; and the consequence was, that from the close of the war till 1824 and 1825, numbers even of Americans came into the country as settlers.

From these times we have to deal with restrictions, which shut the door against Americans, and, finally, have well nigh done so against all other people. From these times Americans laboured, very properly, under disabilities from legislative enactment; and on the other hand, when it was seen that people were coming in great numbers, and probably would continue to come, to the province, it was conceived that something might be made out of them, whilst they made the country; and in consequence it was discovered, almost miraculously, that wild crown-land was, to use a legal phrase, of great value—to wit, of the value which the labour of the settler was likely to put upon it. It was determined to reverse the order of things, and, instead of allowing a man pay for his work, he was to pay in order to be allowed to work.

I will here make a few particular observations upon the last act of the drama of free grants to settlers, namely, the Robinson immigration; leaving to a later period of this article the more general consideration of the effect and utility of that measure, considered on the principle of what I may call foreign immigration.

In the year 1824 and 1825 the Honourable Peter Robinson, as government agent, brought from the south of Ireland several hundred heads of families, consisting in the aggregate of several thousand souls; they were brought to Quebec in ships chartered by government, were removed five hundred miles inland at the government expense, and located in some parts of the country in masses, and in others distributed amongst previous settlers. They got, in every instance, one hundred acres of land—free—each, and one hundred acres to each of their sons; they were provisioned for a year, and received implements of husbandry and assistance to build their houses and establish themselves on their land. One would have imagined that in such a country as Canada, where nature is ready to do so much, men thus favoured would have leaped into wealth and consideration in a short period, and, no doubt, such was the idea of the government; but what was the sequel? In those places where they were located in masses, the ideas, habits of indolence, want of energy, in fact, the debasing qualities which pervade the lowest orders of the Irish people, of which in a great measure they consisted, accompanied them, remained with them, and became inseparable from them, bound up as they were in a society of their own; and from their position and feelings, in a great degree shut out from communication with their neighbours of opposite creeds and sentiments. The great and general feature in their character seemed to be, that they were not suited for independence; they could and would work for another, but not for themselves. Thus, year after year found them decreasing in numbers, from the fact of their being compelled, in self-preservation, to seek employment from others. Thus has it been common to find them at work as day-labourers, with men who came to the country about the same time with themselves, without a fraction of capital, other than as their hands and health might be so considered. The little improvement which the government in the first instance urged and assisted them to make, stands, in many cases, after the lapse of eighteen or nineteen years, in its pristine state, and suggests to the mind of the passer-by something of a monumental character—whether it be of wisdóm or folly, we leave to the imagination.

The case was somewhat different with those who were intermixed with previous settlers from different countries, and of no fixed character. Their old habits found no companionship here; the force of example, and the operation and strength of the natural faculty of imitation, soon wrought a change in them; and though the circumstances under which they commenced operated for some time to their disadvantage, yet they, in the end, surmounted their difficulties in many cases, and made good settlers, exerting their energies profitably alike to themselves and to the country.

Although Mr. Robinson's emigration, as it is called, brought a great many people to the country—(and though the bulk of those people have eventually settled in the country—and though the natural advancement looked for by the government, and wanting in a great many instances in the present generation, or herds of families originally located, will be supplied by their children, who have acquired very different ideas, and understand the application of them)—yet, as a measure of immigration, it was a decided failure; it was an attempt to force a matter which cannot be forced, and was attended with an enormous expense; so great, indeed, that I have little doubt all the money or means which has been contributed to the resources of the country, by the entire mass who composed it, from their landing to the present day, would not pay the principal and interest: and I have as little doubt that the money expended in the passage and location of any one family of the party, if placed in equal moieties in the hands of three heads of families of either England, Scotland, or Ireland, not as a gift, but as the product of their own industry, joined to the wish to emigrate, and the gift of land on their arrival, would be sufficient to enable them to reach their destination; and with the industry so common to people of the class to which I allude, I should have no fear for the result; in fact, when land was attainable, to find men come to the country and become settlers without a fraction, was a case of every-day occurrence; and in looking now amongst our ablest farmers, not a few will be found who have worked their way from the seaport at which they landed, with a large family of helpless children, yet in ninety-nine cases out of a hundred these men have succeeded.

But to return. From these times, as I have stated, restrictions began to be thrown in the way of free grants to settlers. At first there was a patent fee on taking out a deed from the crown—six pounds six shillings and ninepence upon one hundred acres, and nine pounds some odd on two hundred acres; it was also incumbent, under these regulations, to perform what was termed settlement duty—this was to clear a certain portion of road in front of the located lot, a certain portion of land on the lot, (I believe an acre,) and build a house; upon affidavit of the performance of which, and the payment of the patent-fee, a deed would issue. Immense numbers of actual settlers entered the country and took up lands under these regulations, and the patent-fee only operating in case the party took out his deed. Numbers never, for many years, troubled themselves about it, but settled and improved their lands, content that they were entered on the government map as located. These regulations evidently aimed at compelling a settlement, but they failed in their object in many instances, and were the means of injuring the country very considerably, and, in some measure, returding instead of advancing its interests.

At the period of this patent-fee and settlement-duty regulation, lands were still given out with great freedom by the government, and numbers of people, already resident in the country, drew lands as settlers, who had not the most distant intention of becoming so on the lands so drawn. In immense numbers of these cases, the original locatee or nominee sold his right for a trifling consideration—say from ten to fifty dollars—in money, or goods, or cattle, or trade of any sort that he most stood in need of; and thus these location-tickets were bandied about from hand to hand, and, first or last, came into the hand of speculators or land-jobbers, who drove a regular trade in such things, together with the unlocated rights before mentioned, of the children of United-Empire loyalists, and of persons entitled to land for militia services during the last war. Upon those lands on which the regulations rendered it necessary, settlement-duty was done and sworn to in a manner peculiarly American; indeed, in such a wholesale business as was then done in the province in this department, people could not descend to particulars. I have no doubt many persons dreamt of the performance of the regulations, and awoke with the fact so strongly impressed upon their mind, that they swore to it. Some persons have been known to fulfil the conditions as to clearing the exact quantity of land, but, from their ignorance of surveying, (and surely that could not be imputed to them as a crime,) they made use of a squirrel's *foot* and the *link* of a watch-*chain* to represent those terms in the surveyor's calendar. Nevertheless, though a large quantity of land, intended by the government for general and individual settlement, through these means, fell into the hands of large holders—thus establishing wild-land monopoly to the injury of general settlement—the country received an immense accession of sound and healthy settlement under these regulations; the stream of emigration continued to flow steadily and with increasing energy to the colony; every year brought an increase in arrivals, and a prospect of still greater numbers in the next.

From recollection, I should say, that it was about the year 1827 that wild land, in unsettled townships, first had a price put upon it to the settler; that price was, in the first place, four shillings the acre, but it was a credit, and poor people did not fear the course as a creditor; so still the settlement of the country went on. The people went to work on the land, and, of course, took their own time to pay the price which it was put at to them; but still to those who paid even in six or eight years, it was during that period a dead weight, depressing their energies, abridging their comforts, and rendering them comparatively non-contributors to the revenue of the country, and thus curtailing their usefulness as members of the community.

The list published by the commissioner of crown-lands, at a late date, contains the names of many individuals who have not paid, and whose debt of twenty pounds is now doubled by interest. These poor people may have been unfortunate in the selection of a lot of land; they may have met with sickness—the stay of the family may have been laid low; and in any of these cases, if the twenty pounds could not be paid, how can the forty? Government might turn them out of possession—this it could not have the face to do; government might release them from the debt—this it wouldn't have the grace to do, besides, it would be a hardship to those who had paid. The present course seems to be the one most likely to be followed in these cases. It is quite likely the land, with their seventeen or eighteen years' improvement, together with the labour of their neighbours, may be of sufficient value to induce some monied man to advance the money on mortgage, and take out the deed from the crown; and in this case, the closing scene will not be distant. The family will find themselves some fine morning on the road, with perhaps fifty or a hundred dollars, or perhaps not so many pence, as the balance between the amount of their mortgage with law-costs, and the price of their house. This is a sorrowful picture, and when it occurs, as no doubt it does often, we can merely say, it is the effect which naturally would spring from such a cause as crown-sales to settlers.

In a colony, no matter in what quarter of the world, the relations between the crown and the subject are, as a natural consequence of the peculiar situation of both, more closely drawn than the circumstances of a general government would admit. In the colony, the government is placed, as regards the settler, in the light of parent to child—a good kind landlord and tenant, or an indulgent master and servant; every man is brought in contact with the crown—every man deals with the crown; the word of the crown is received by him as his safegard, his assurance—he places every reliance upon it, and trusts his all upon its faith. In this manner the crown may be said to be, and actually is, the guardian of every settler; his interest, his welfare, his all, as I have said, is at stake, embarked as he is, in what I may with propriety call the service of his country—that is, if the making of a market in the wilderness for the manufactures of the parent-state, relieving it of its superabundant population, and adding to its wealth and importance, can be called service. It becomes the duty of the government, then, to watch over the interest of the settler—to counsel him, to assist him, and not in any instance to relax that care and attention till he is firmly on his legs, and capable of struggling by himself. If this argument be admitted, how does it agree with fettering the settler with debt and keeping his nose to the stone with interest, and this, for what? For leaving the land of his fathers, with all its associations—enduring hardships and privations in a wilderness, in order to give the shadow of a value to the soil, and render service to his country. The capitation-tax passed by the assembly of Lower Canada was more honest, for it was scarcely concealed that the intention was (and certainly it was the wish) to prevent immigrants from landing in the country; but the government do more than this—they induce them to come, and then exact a heavy fine for having to earn their living and make themselves useful.

It required more stringent measures than any yet adopted to stop emigration; paying what appeared a small sum of money, with an almost unlimited credit, did not deter even poor people from locating land; and up to this period, namely, 1829-30, the emigration was great, and the settlement commensurate with it; in fact, the emigration-movement, instead of declining, seemed to be on the increase; and we now come to the consideration of that period, say from 1830 to 1835, when it was at its height, being also the period when wild land rose to its greatest price, ten shillings the acre at the upset; we come also to the consideration of a class of settlers of a different character to any that heretofore appeared in the Canadas, at least to the same extent.

For many years a bounty had been held out in the shape of a grant of the waste-lands of the crown to officers of the army and navy, as an inducement for them to proceed to and settle in the colonies. Up to 1830 but few persons of this description, comparatively speaking, availed themselves of this offer as regarded the Canadas, but at and about this time immigration had made and was making such rapid strides, that it would seem the subject was agitated through the length and breadth of these kingdoms; hence, numbers of officers of the army and navy, and very many civilians of a respectable class, embarked their all in the Canadian immigration-scheme, and during the period I mention, they crowded to our shores. Nor was it to be wondered at; statements of the yearly, nay, daily and hourly, increase of the country abounded; so fast was it filling up, so wonderfully pressing was the cry for land, so astonishing was the demand for locations in this so-lately-discovered El Dorado, that it was believed the government would soon have no land left: and now was the period to make a fortune by investing every disposable penny in wild-land; in fact, many people went land-mad, if I may so express myself; but one thing is certain, after the first attack, they never suffered a relapse, that I have heard of.

Under the original regulations in this case, a lieutenant was entitled to a grant of five hundred acres of land, and other officers in proportion; and it was suggested to the gentleman on half-pay, that it was much better for him to commute his admitted right, and receive instead of the five hundred acres an order on the colonial government for 150*l.* sterling, which he could apply in purchase of lands of much greater value than he could possibly procure as a free grant. He was impressed with the idea that he was most nobly acted by—most generously dealt with.

Now the commutation of his allowance would not have made much difference, if he had received land, as far as the crown was concerned, on which his grant was valued, (that is, free) and had only paid, or allowed the crown for lands, which they might have given him in good situations, the price or value which labour had put upon it: but herein lay the striking dishonesty of the transaction—he went to Canada, and found that sales of land were advertised to take place monthly, at the various agencies through the country; he was drawn to some particular part, simply by his travelling companions, or by prior reputation; he called upon the agent, and stated his desire to become a purchaser; the lists were shown him, and he there beheld columns of lots to be sold *by auction*, at the upset price of ten shillings an acre; to those who had no commutation money, the terms were one-fifth of the money down, and the remainder in four equal annual instalments; the agent of course directed him to the most eligible situation in which to invest his means, and of course he had confidence in him, as the officer of our honourable government; he was advised to go and look at the land, and make a selection; accordingly he inquires for the locality, and best means of becoming acquainted with it, and finds that it is necessary to hire a canoe and a couple of hunters, as they alone amongst white men are sufficiently acquainted with the woody tract as guides: it is probable he makes one of a party who set off on their exploring expedition, and travel up lakes and rivers from twenty to sixty miles, where the sound of an axe never was heard. If he has a spark of romance in his composition, he is delighted with his trip—the disagreeable appearance of a newly cleared country; stumps and ragged fences, has faded from his sight, he is in nature's own dominion; the cloudless sky of a summer's day, the beautiful lake, surrounded by, and reflecting in its clear waters, the dark green mantle of forest foliage, or shining like a polished mirror beneath the glorious noontide sun, or stretching away far in the distance, and presenting to view that beautifully indistinct outline of its shores, where the trees in groups appear like magic islands, floating on the vault of heaven; softly stealing the imagination away in dreams of fairy-land, entrancing the mind of the spectator with the powers of nature and her varied charms. Yes, if he has a spark of romance in his composition, he is delighted—he sees many spots that he would like, he must have this point, or that island: such a beautiful prospect! no matter what the price, that shall be mine, he says, (perhaps half a dozen others have said the same thing;) he returns to the agency office or establishment, singing, "A life in the woods for me;" he waits with all the patience he is master of for the day of sale; it comes at last, and never did man enter into a contest with greater spirit than he does into that which now takes place. A lot which he fancies is put up, it is stated at ten shillings an acre; when it's up to fifteen shillings immediately, and finally it is knocked down to our hero at sixteen and three-pence, seventeen and sixpence, or I have known a pound; he is delighted, in fact he's a made man. During this exhibition, the bystanders, the already initiated into the mysteries of colonization and wild-land valuation, are highly amused; they are well aware that the purchasers are making their fortunes, but it is on the principle of the man who is going headlong to destruction in point of circumstances, or who is about to complete his fortune by breaking his back, or blowing his brains out.

Well, away go the purchasers, civil as well as military, to commence their settlements: at enormous cost a house is prepared; and in the course of a little time, the family (if such there should be) transported alike, to and with the wilderness; then comes the enjoyment of life, which only the backwoodsman can appreciate. Such shooting, such hunting, such fishing, such glorious sport; and for the ladies, such boating excursions, such pic-nics, such parties, such real fun—oh! 'twas delightful, the place was a paradise—"a valley of Eden;" with the reverse of the picture kept quite out of view by fun and frolic: but the realities of life—curse those realities, they are continually pulling us down a peg, and interfering in a most especial manner with our enjoyments—yes, those damned realities found their way even into this home of happiness; and people began to find that procuring the necessaries of life from a distance of from twenty to sixty miles, was no joke; and though they after a time raised grain and other crops, yet as this was the product of hired labour at an enormous expense, there was nothing to bring to market to supply the wants of the family in the luxuries to which they had always been accustomed; these people could not live like the poor in similar situations, to whom potatoes, milk, bread, and a piece of pork, would fulfil every notion of abundance: they must have, but why enumerate,—the wants of the one were hundreds of things which the ground did not afford him; the other, wanted nothing more than the soil gave him direct or immediate means of procuring. The scene soon changed in other respects too; emigration slackened, the system of crown-land grantings had at length had its effect, and fell away; there were no new arrivals, to keep up the excitement, it would seem as if something unpleasant appertained to their neighbourhood, and "warhawk" was the word; our friends were left alone, and they were lonely indeed; their amusements and pleasant meetings were not of such frequent recurrence; in many cases a successful emigration began on their part, and numbers who possessed the means took wing, leaving the pleasant pursuits of a backwoodsman's life, with the fair chance of starvation, to seek a home and subsistence in some other portion of the world. Those who were left went battling on, but theirs was now a life of realities—the men did not hunt, shoot, or feast so much, but they in many instances worked a little, and their excursions were, frequently for a length of time, confined to the next clearance, probably a mile or two, to talk over the news, namely, that a canoe or boat had been seen coming up the lake some day or week ago, and then the mutual wonder who it was, and where could they be going—or when, shut out from the rest of mankind by the snows of winter, the propriety of the breakfast-table would be disturbed by an exclamation from some young female of the party—Oh, look! look!—there's a man! and the window would be filled with peering faces, and the spy-glass brought into requisition, to discover if the being, at the distance of three or four miles on the frozen glassy surface of the lake, was an Indian or a white man; if the latter, conjectures innumerable as to who it could be, where going, and would he come this way; yes, poor souls, they were in a fix, as Jonathan would say; and though many of them, through the aid of foreign income, have been enabled to outstrip the disadvantages incident to early settlements, and many others have acquired at least contentment with their lot, and a better understanding and application of their energies—many, too many—have suffered privations and miseries appalling to the feeling mind, and, for persons in their former station of life, doubly so. I willingly draw a veil over the sufferings of men, and delicate devoted women, and the fate of some driven to the indulgence of desperate habits by their blighted prospects.

In conclusion, as regards this class of settlers, when they came to the country without the wish to make their fortunes as land-speculators, and, acting on that principle, kept clear of the government shaving-shops, and, possessing a desire to seek society for themselves and their families, they laid out their money in the purchase of a cleared farm in the neighbourhood of some town or village; and when they escaped lightly through the hands of sharks and sharpers, who at first, with the most pleasing hospitality, dined and feasted them, then drove them in their carriage to look at this or that cleared farm, which they said they owned, and when one was met with which struck the fancy of the newcomer, it was sold to him, say for fifteen hundred pounds cash; and the same evening, pending the necessary arrangements, bought from the real owner, probably for one thousand pounds on credit! When, I say, he escaped being handled too roughly by these gentry, he generally found himself in a little time in the enjoyment of every comfort, joined to respectable society.

Let us now take a view of what I have called, the dishonesty of the treatment, which these men experienced at the hands of a paternal government. No man can deny, that there were inducements held out to them to emigrate; their intelligence and well-tried attachment to the crown, would strengthen the colony; it was natural that the government should wish to see them there, and promote that end by every means in their power. The commutation of his land-claim, by the officer, was in itself a matter of no importance, provided that he had received land at the same rate at which he surrendered it, and that it had not been made a means eventually of cheating him out of nearly the whole of what the government acknowleged he had a right to, as well as, in many instances, the contents of his purse besides. I do not say whether the home-goverment were the deceived or the deceivers, it is not my present purpose to draw a distinction between the home-government and the colonial, nor do I think that in this case a distinction would be admissible; the grant was the grant of this imperial government, and as such had a right to be borne out by them; but why induce the man to go to Canada under false pretences? why, I say, in a country where he is a total stranger, unused to its manners and its people, amongst whom there is a perpetual war of interest, amongst whom he could not look for advice—why turn traitor to him in his need, and withhold the honest counsel from the only quarter he could trust, that power upon whose good faith he had trusted, for whose honour he had probably bled? why misdirect him, I say, for the government must have known as well then, as one of their victims does now, that he was not suited for the place of a pioneer in the forest; and, that his attempts as a settler on wild land must be attended with expense which would crush him. And was this all? Did the matter end with misrepresentation only? Alas, no, he was deceived into pitting himself against others as ignorant as he was, at a public auction, to bid for valueless land; so that the miscalled government-bounty might dwindle to the lowest possible state, and his money follow it: and well did the crown succeed in curtailing its own gift, for in no case did these men receive more than half, and in numbers not a third or fourth, of the bounty which had induced them to leave home, friends, and feelings; they bought land from the crown at from ten to twenty shillings, which they could not now sell for two and sixpence. The bounty held out was so many acres of the waste lands of the crown; it was totally devoid of intrinsic value either from labour or situation; their labour alone could give it value; and the settlement of the country and labour of those settlers would alone give it the advantages of situation, the crown could confer no value upon it, for, without the same principle of labour, they could not make it yield a penny—yet, knowing all this, the crown, taking advantage of the ignorance of these men, most shamefully defrauded them out of what they openly appeared to accord them the right to; and not only defrauded them out of the bounty, but placed them in such situations, that they very frequently lost a portion, and sometimes their whole capital along with it. The Americans would call the whole transaction "a clean shave," the English of which is something connected with roguery.

The next class of the emigration of this period, which draws our attention, is that composed of pensioners, or "Government-scheme, No 2."

It would be needless to attempt a description of these persons, their habits, and propensities, the offspring of the peculiar mode of life in which their youth was passed: the indulgence of their passions, intemperance, an almost utter disregard for the morrow, together with long-seated habits of indolence, or at least a strong disinclination for hard labour, were poor qualifications for a Bushwatcher; but at the time of which I speak, the rage for immigration was at its height, the nation at large may be said to have made a movement towards the colonies, to which if a man got, no matter by what means, or how qualified, his fortune was made. Government threw its weight into the scale, and urged it forward by every means; their eyes were directed *most prudently* to procuring a class of settlers of sterling loyalty and tried attachment to the crown—this was right; and to the benefit of the nation at large, by relieving it of its superabundant population, and making a market for its manufactures—this was right also; add to which, the notion, that, in Yankee phrase, considerable of a rise might be made out of it, in the sale of lands and other trifles, amongst which the commutation of pensions held a conspicuous place. Whether this was right or not, no doubt it produced a pleasing sensation in the breasts of those from whom the idea emanated.

To the pensioners, then, a bounty was held out to emigrate. Now was the time when they could exchange a life of comparative privation for one of ease and plenty; they should receive one hundred acres of (valueless) land, a free gift, and about a hundred pounds in money, which in such a country as they were going to would render them at once independent; putting the land out of the question, fancy the bait which a hundred pounds would be to a man who had never seen so much money at a time in his life, in fact had no conception of such a mass; he would leap at the offer!—and what did government ask from him in return?—a mere nothing—only that he should surrender that paltry pension, that he never could make any thing of, that only came in time just to be spent, that merely put the bit in their mouths and nothing more; what was it to him that was to get a hundred pounds in cash, besides a whole hundred acres of land? why, that was more than big farmers had in this country. The old veteran entered with zest into the idea of changing his quarters; the spirit of his young days got hold of him, and he fearlessly entered into the contract with the honourable government of his country: had he faith in it? who dare talk of faith to him? he had that confidence in his country that knew no bounds, he was the peculiar child of his country; when disabled by his wounds, or services, he had a grateful country to fall back upon, which received him with affection, and made a provision for his wants, which would preserve his old age and debility, from poverty and distress,—who could doubt the faith of such a country? had not its every act towards him been kindness, and consideration? had it not taught him to look up to it as a parent, as the guardian of his privileges, the source of his maintenance, the staff and support of his declining years, of his barked and war-worn frame? he had earned it in the bloody breach, or the bayonet charge, midst the wild hurrah of the battle-field; his blood was the consideration; who dare doubt the gratitude of the nation ?—could any proposition come from such a source calculated to injure him ? or would his grateful country throw up its guardianship of him, and leave him to be the prey of circumstances ?—no, no, he had not such a thought, he firmly believed the proposal now made to him was for his benefit; in fact, he looked upon it as another proof of the gratitude of his country, and he accepted it without a misgiving as to consequences, without a thought that he was entering upon the fierce contést of interest with the stranger, deprived of the guiding hand that had watched over and directed his steps for years; alone and unfriended, he was how to embark on the world's troubled ocean, not with the buoyant spirits of youth, with which to combat adversity, not with strength of limb and muscle, with which to draw forth nature's treasures, but in the sear and yellow leaf, with the white head and palsied hand, the mutilated form and broken constitution, and with all the simplicity of a child in worldly matters. Yes, such were the circumstances under which these poor people determined to leave home, and friends, and country, feeling the most perfect confidence in the government, and with unbounded hopes of success. Let us proceed with them on their journey. They received their money, and made preparations for their departure; these preparations, and the parting glass with friends, made slight inroads on the purse; they travelled in company, took ship for Quebec, and laid in a stock of provisions for a five or six weeks' voyage;—but, alas! their name, their character of commuted pensioners, travelled with them—they had money—the six weeks was spent in getting to the banks of Newfoundland, or the gulf of St. Lawrence, and in some cases it took six more to get to Quebec; the ship was sure to be well provisioned, and in truth was merely on a cruise, in order to enable the captain to dispose of his stock, and that it was disposed of to advantage there is little doubt; as I have heard some of these people say, that something like half their money was gone when they arrived. Here was a highly creditable circumstance, which attended their immediate launch out of the hands of the government!

From Quebec they proceeded westward to their destination; and when arrived, and their eyes opened to the true state of the case, they found that the sum of money which they had received from the parental hands of the government, was expended, or nearly so, and that the land which they were to receive as a gift, and which some of them had set such store by, was not quite what they had conceived in their ignorance. Canada was not like any country they had seen, for, in their travels on the continent, or in their native country, they could always see the land; there were no fields, no meadows, no quickset hedges, no gardens, no orchards, no ditches even, no houses, no barns; and when their conductor or guide brought them unto the particular lot which they sought, and which he knew by certain cabalistic marks on the trees, and said, here's your land—the exclamation, where! was often returned, for in reality he could not see any; his prospect is bounded on all sides, at the distance at most of one hundred yards, by the stout stems of trees; he could not walk five paces in any one direction, without making the detour of some tree, perhaps a giant of the forest, such as he had never set eyes on before; round which he would probably march with mind fixed in wonder, and then strain his neck in the endeavour to bring his eyes to the position necessary to view the enormous pillar-like trunk, to the spot where, at an hundred feet above his head, it is lost in the dark and apparently impenetrable foliage:—where was he to plough, where was he to harrow, where to plant, where to sow, where to dig?—the trees must come down first, and how was that to be effected? had he muscle, had he nerve, had he strength of heart or constitution, did he know how to set about it, had he money to pay those who did? alas! alas, his strength was worn down in defence of his country, his money had been committed to his improvident hands, and was melted away—here was the moment of his disenchantment; up to this all had been expectation, all had been hope, his eyes were now opened to the full sense of his situation; he saw at a glance the magnitude of what he had forfeited, the utter insignificance of what he had obtained; he was alone in the world, he whose education had taught him to rely solely on others—alone, in the sharp contest of cunning with his fellow-men, a contest which, in the short period he had been a comparative free-agent, had proved so disastrous to him; he turned his eyes to his country, whose glory his blood had nourished, whose honour was established by his wounds, but he had nothing to expect from her, she had honourably fulfilled the conditions of the agreement which she had induced him to enter into, she had discharged her obligations to him; he turned to the future—misery, and privations, and hardships were there, and his spirit sunk within him as he bitterly cursed the bounty that had made him a beggar!

I have spoken of these men, as persons who had fought for their country, and it is as well that I should draw the reader's attention to the fact, that they were not, in hardly one instance, the soldiers of the present day; they were not the men who had served perhaps twenty-one years of an easy, happy life, and who then, with the health and strength of middle life, were discharged with a pension of a shilling a day; no, no, many of these men had not served more than five years, some seven, and some ten; but it was in the field, and five years of such service ought to weigh against a long life in a barrack; they were most of them discharged at the reduction of the army in 1816. I know one of them who had served seven years; he was shot through the body by the belt, on the heights of Pampeluna; he had the muscle of his left hip shot away in the lines at St. Sebastian; he was shot through the wrist at Vittoria, and had a bayonet-wound in his foot, received at the storming of Badajos: he was discharged in 1816 as unfit for service, with a pension of sixpence a day; yet such men were thought fit to make settlers of, in a country where the difficulties to be encountered are enormous.

First and last, this was a shameful transaction. What a glorious thing, what a great relief to the nation, the despatching several hundred poor with their families into a wilderness, to live or die as God would direct, and liquidating their claims upon their country with one dash of the pen—what a humane action! I should think old Mr. Bull must have been considerably tickled by the prospect of gain in the business; but a 'cute observer, I dare say, would have seen, that though he winked and looked sly with one eye, there was a tear of sympathy in the other; and it is now quite clear that the old gentleman has become convinced that it was a dirty disgraceful trick, to which he should never have lent himself. A tardy measure of justice has at length been meted out to the survivors, for many sunk, and they have again been placed on the pension-list, and allowed fourpence-halfpenny a day; and still one cannot help feeling for them, when you see an old man with an empty sleeve, a seared face, and perhaps a Waterloo medal, and contrast him with the dapper gentleman who receives a shilling a day.

As a scheme of emigration, this could not be considered a good one; at least, it is a question whether its benefits were not much more than counterbalanced by its evils, and the misery and suffering it occasioned to numbers; though many of these men surmounted their difficulties, and have, either by themselves or their families, become good settlers, I should think nearly, if not quite, an equal number were plunged in distress which they never overcame; their money was spent, and their land soon went into the hands of the first speculator who offered them a means of procuring the necessaries of life, and in this respect they became the agents of an injury to the country, instead of a benefit; thus, this second emigration-scheme, taken in hand by the government, was a decided failure, most clearly demonstrating the fact, both as regards the emigration of 1824 or 1825, called the Robinson emigration, or half-pay officer, or commuted pensioner scheme, of which I have last written—that colonists, to be successful, must embark in the matter of their own free will and accord, not influenced or coerced in the slightest degree, but with the most perfect knowledge of the responsibilities which they take upon them, and a firm determination to fulfil them by their own unassisted efforts, for never was there a more mistaken idea than that by assisting a man in the way these were assisted, or holding out a bounty for immigration in the manner that was thereby done, you forward his interests in a new country like Canada; on the contrary, you clog them: industry and poverty I have ever held to be the best capital that a settler can start with; and there is not a question but it has produced the greatest number of independent farmers and thoroughly valuable settlers in our country. The great error on both these occasions was the acting on the principle that every or any man would make a colonist, no matter what his character, habits of life or feelings, might be, only get him into a colony, he must do well; his fitness or unfitness, either in a moral or physical sense, was not considered of the slightest consequence; he was a human being, with perhaps half a dozen other human beings dependent upon his exertions, and he must make a valuable settler. This was, I say, the error; it brought hundreds of people to her colonies, who never could be of any use either to themselves or the country; from moral or physical inability, they were induced to go: they were not left to the unbiassed exercise of their own judgment, there was a bounty held out in the one case, an hundred pounds in money in the other; as the Irishman would say, *the run of the house for eating and drinking*, in fact, *the height of good living!* and what more tempting offer to the starving multitude of which it consisted? In both cases, the land which they were to receive as a gift, held either no value at all, and never troubled their thoughts, or it was estimated at the rate of value of a gentleman's park, according to the fanciful ignorance of the individual; in both cases were hundreds of people, who had never given the subject of emigration or the difficulties attending it a thought, and who, in the idea of a year's subsistence on government rations, or government bounty, reckoned on a life of ease and plenty; these emigrations did not consist of such men as those who, from the close of the war in 1816 to 1830, got together their little all in the land of their fathers, and, with sorrowful feelings but stout hearts, arrived with every information their anxious inquiries could afford, resolved to expatriate themselves, and make a home for their children in the woods; taking ship for a strange country where they knew they must land, in many cases, without the means of maintaining their families a month, or even less; working their way by little and little, hundreds of miles to their destination, acquiring a thorough knowledge of the country in their progress; and then acepting the government bounty of land with feelings of gratitude, and using it as so much capital, which the knowledge already acquired enabled them to apply with unbounded success to their advancement.—Yes, these men had industry, they had poverty, they were not placed in a false position as regarded themselves or the country, they well knew the responsibilities of their situation upon making up their minds to emigrate, they took every means to acquire information upon the circumstances of the country they intended to make a home of: they had no gift of a hundred pounds, or government rations, to depend on; their judgments were not warped by the prospect of a full pocket or a full belly; and what a wide difference between their present circumstances, or the circumstances of such settlers, and those of government protegés of the same period or standing—the one with houses, lands, cattle, comforts, in a word, worth from five hundred to two and three thousand pounds; the other, if even independent, but moderately so. I say then, and I defy contradiction—that in both these cases the government, in the main, failed; and the second instance is a further confirmation of the statement which I have elsewhere advanced, namely, that emigration cannot be forced, with advantage either to the emigrant or the colony.

I have already, in connection with the period of which I now write, namely, from 1830 to 1835 detailed and discussed the fortunes, mishaps, and merits of two classes of settlers, who, though of different circumstances in life, may yet be considered one body, actuated by one motive-power, the government; I shall now say a few words relating to the other classes of the emigration of this period.

The number of persons of the farming class, who came to the country during this period ('30 to '35) with means either small or large, was much greater than at any former time since the settlement of the province; they were a valuable class of settlers, inasmuch as they changed the face of things a good deal, by purchasing, in many instances, from private land-owners instead of the government, (just as should have been done by the half-pay officers, if they must have wild lands,) and as such lands were almost always situated in the heart of settlements, and had long continued an eyesore to the neighbourhood, and a drawback to its interests, lying, comparatively speaking, a dead weight upon the exertions of the people, obliging them to make roads, and fulfil all other duties which it would have been incumbent on a settler to have done; as well as compelling them to forego the advantages of a neighbour, for even that is of no small moment to a Bushenhacker, as there are reciprocal duties of a settler, which every settler feels himself bound to perform, by means of exchange-work, and without which the endeavours of any one individual would be almost hopeless: the settlement of such lands was of almost incalculable service to the neighbourhood in which they lay, as well as a benefit to the country. This class of settlers having money, which was the product of their labour and industry, did not care to throw it away, if they could help it, or part with it without having some apparent advantage or return for it; and, instead of going into the wilderness in search of the beauties of nature, like the gentlemen on half-pay, or being shoved off into some spot a little behind elbow, like the commuted pensioners, he purchased in a settlement, where he had well-established neighbours—where he had something like proximity to a market, as well as numerous other advantages, not to be thought lightly of; such as, a chance of hearing and joining in divine worship, the instruction of his children, and the numerous enjoyments arising from neighbourly admixture or communion with the well-established farmers of his vicinity. He benefited the colony by bringing into use and exercise a portion of its natural capital, that had long lain a blot on the page of its progress. He benefited the neighbourhood in which he purchased, by redeeming it of the dead weight of absentee land, and bringing to its aid the reciprocal assistance, which as a settler he must give, in order that he may receive; and he benefited himself by making a selection which secured him the advantages I have before enumerated, and which, as I have said cannot be thought lightly of; indeed the full value of which, to a beginner in the woods, a voluntary immigrant or exile from the associations of the home of his early years, cannot well be estimated. Numerous instances also occurred amongst this class of people, of their being possessed of capital sufficient to purchase cleared farms, and when they did so, they invariably introduced a better system of farming, making the land much more productive than it was under its former occupant, and still adding a settler to the country, in as much as the person from whom they purchased generally moved off with his family to wild land, and commenced anew a life which he was no stranger to; and in process of which he had a thousand advantages over the newly arrived immigrant, to whom he also was a great benefit, by affording him an opportunity of acquiring practical knowledge upon many subjects of great importance to him; teaching him ways and means of overcoming the various obstacles which are to be surmounted in clearing land, and which otherwise he would have to attain by his own personal experience.

This class of the immigration of 1830 to 1835, was decidedly of great advantage to the settlement of the country; they brought wealth to it as well as industry, and were particularly calculated for the course they adopted, namely, purchasing wild land in settlements, or cleared farms.

In these situations, their money was of use to them, it enabled them to make an advantageous purchase, and having located themselves in a good and old-established neighbourhood, they immediately made friends, or perhaps had connections previously settled there, who well knew the necessity, and how to direct them in making bargains for such articles of stock as they found it necessary to purchase—these men, generally speaking, escaped being *shaved* to any great extent, though I have known instances in which, through improvident conduct, they have been turned adrift upon the world penniless, after an eighteen-months' or two years' run.

It might be argued, that if the settler had money, he could locate himself as well in one place as another, and that he might make a settlement in the backwoods or interior, as well as he could in the old-settled country. At first view, it would indeed appear preposterous to say that he could not—it would be preposterous to assert it; if we could make human nature of a certain standard, if we could give to every man the knowledge necessary to enable him to make a good and proper use of his money; if we could open his eyes and his mind, on the moment of his coming to the country, to the perception and true estimation of facts and circumstances which were never dreamt of in his philosophy at any former period; if we could do this, the circumstance of a man's having money qualifying him for a backwood settler, would of course be admissible; but, as far as my observation and experience have gone, the general rule of success is on the other side, and I speak confidently when I say, that the chances of success as pioneer-settlers, of persons with means such as immigrants of the farming class may be supposed to possess, and the total absence of means on the part of others, supposing them both to get free grants of land, are as ten to one in favour of the latter. This, as an assertion, would have little weight—the few following passages may seem to exemplify it, however. The difference between the immigrant with means, and the one without, may be traced from the first moment of their entertaining thoughts of leaving their country: the one says—I'll immigrate; the little means that I have will be of service to me, it will make me independent: the other says—I'll immigrate, judging by what I hear of Canada, it's a good place for an industrious man, and, with the help of God, I'll try it; while we have health to work, we won't starve. Now, though these men are perhaps equally industrious, yet there is no question the one who has money will build upon it, and thus we may say, the one trusts in his money, the other in his hands:—from the moment of their landing in the country, the difference becomes more marked, the one is understood to be a man with means; he pays his way, and is caressed and taken by the hand most kindly by numbers, in such a way as to lead him to suppose he is a person of consequence; he starts for his destination, and arrives there, in his own estimation at least, an important man; and, as yet quite ignorant of the fact, that attentions have been lavished upon him, merely for the sake of his money, in order to take advantage of him, he pushes off into the wilderness, and settles on a lot of wild land. The other is comparatively a poor man, perhaps a pauper immigrant; he has at once to seek employment to support his family and enable him to reach his destination, which he may not be able to do for six, perhaps twelve months, according to the weight of family he may have to support; but his time has not been lost, he has been working for a living, and with it gaining capital—that capital that consists of knowledge, and without which all other is useless: thus circumstanced, he arrives at the long-sought goal, and settles on a lot of land, the adjoining one to which has been occupied, say for a year, by the monied man. This gentleman, in the year, has cut down from ten to twenty acres of wood, or rather paid for the cutting of it, and also for the logging of it; perhaps twice,—having first employed a man, who, before he had done two months' work, had probably managed to procure pay for the whole job, and levanted—and then employed another, who has not the work done in time, and thus throws him over the sowing season. He is a respectable man, and his family have been reared with certain feelings; he has money, in fact, he could not think of putting them into a shanty; Oh, no! that is what the poor people of the country make use of, he must have a house, and consequently a house is put up, which costs money; it looks well, and has a great air of comfort about it. He sets off into the settled township, to purchase a yoke of oxen; he is of course known to be a perfect *stranger*, and his fame as a monied man has also gone before him; and under those circumstances it is the bounden duty of every man *to take him in*—he can afford it, and money is such an object; he inquires for working oxen; an apparently respectable man, a farmer, tells him that he knows a first-rate yoke of oxen in his neighbourhood, the owner of which was talking of selling them some time since, but he could not say whether he was of the same mind now; however, he would recommend him to try, as they were the best working cattle he knew of in all that country. The farmer is just going home, and most kindly offers our gentleman a seat in his waggon—they arrive at the house of the owner of the oxen, where our friend is left, his companion hoping that he would suit himself, and saying, in Yankee phrase, that "the cattle was horrid good to draw, and plaguy smart—our friend finds the cattle in yoke, and working away admirably; they are certainly splendid working animals, and he at once expresses his determination to buy, if the owner will sell; but the owner says he does not know how he could do without, does not think he could part with them, could not get anything would answer him so well; at length, however, he is induced, though apparently much against his will, to part with them at a high price in cash; the bargain is conducted, the money paid, and our friend starts on his way homeward, driving his cattle, and rejoicing. Let us look at him a month after; the cattle work well—they are good, but, alas! they'd pick a lock, he has come to fisty-cuffs already with two of his neighbours on their account, and has had them put in pound repeatedly; in fact, they are so plaguy smart, there is no standing them; for if he and his family left the house for a short time, they would be into it, no matter how secured: sold they must be; but to whom—who will buy? he can't put them off on any one, they are well known; if he drove them about the country till doomsday, the fact, of his being anxious to sell, would be sure to prevent him; and, though his neighbours might be equally anxious to assist him, as his waggon-acquaintance was, the former owner, in order to rid the neighbourhood of them, yet no chance occurs, there is no person in his vicinity as great a fool, and possessed of money, as himself, and he is obliged to part with them for what, with their character, they will bring, say, one half of what they cost. It is the same with most other things the monied man wants; he may buy a pair of horses at a high price, one of which may be blind as a bat, and the other would think it disgraceful to draw anything but the empty waggon, and would beg to be excused from carrying even the harness up a hill: what is to be done with them? he can't sell them again for anything like his own money, for, like the oxen, every body knows them; they must go for half or fourth of what they cost; he does not know the country or people sufficiently, to enable him to trade them off successfully; nor, if he did, is he quite willing to swear them good, and sound, and in fact do everything but warrant them; he must lose; he'd never think of doing as I have known a Yankee do in a case where he got taken in; in a horse-trade, he gave a horse that wouldn't draw, but was a good roadster, for a horse that wouldn't draw, nor would he carry a stranger on his back; in case one got on, he was immoveable, and whip or spur only had the effect of making him lie down; the Yankee concluded his trade, and mounted to start for home, but found it was no go; so walked off with the halter in his hand, and, as he had five and twenty miles to go, it was no joke; but mark the national character, mark the eminent mental qualifications of the Anglo-Saxon race, mark the display of that faculty of which necessity is said to be the mother; who but the pure Anglo-Saxon, as he is found, and only found, in the land of liberty, the home of the free, would have thought of it? he actually made twelve dollars (three pounds) on the journey home, by betting with the loungers in the way-side taverns, that they would not ride the horse fifty or a hundred yards, or across the road, as the case might be. But to return to our friend, the monied man. In this way he goes on, till he finds he is out of cash, and left upon his own resources, which upon an examination of the catalogue, turn out *nil;* he gets into debt and difficulty, mortgages his land, and eventually sells it, or has it sold for him, by the sheriff, and moves into the woods again, commencing the world pretty much like a pauper emigrant, except that he is strongly wrinkled in the horn, *anglicè*, has a great deal of cunning. Sometime back we left our poor acquaintance on the next farm, let us see what becomes of him—he builds a shanty, (a house would be beyond his ideas,) he works hard, his wife works hard, his children also, even at the age of nine and ten; he goes to the old settlements for work, he takes cattle for pay, or rather works to pay for cattle; he has an acquaintance with the article he is in treaty for; he is probably trusted for a year or eighteen months for a portion of the price, and that still taken in work, when suitable to both parties; he is known to be poor, and has a character for honesty in his dealings, no one could gain by cheating him, but, on the contrary, it is the interest of those persons with whom he is in connection, and who trust him with their property, to forward his interests; by little and little he gets on, and at length he can confine himself to his own farm, and is not obliged to go out to labour; he still lives in a shanty, but you will see a fine barn, and good sheds and out-houses, about his place; and these will be filled in the season with grain and stock—grain, the produce of his labour, and stock, the natural increase of his first cow and sheep, with horses of his own rearing too; he still lives in a shanty, but his family are growing up, and they want room; and now that he has barns and out-houses sufficient, he thinks he ought to put up a house, and accordingly he builds a substantial one of wood, or brick, or stone; about these days also we may find that he is the purchaser at sheriffs' sale, or otherwise of the adjoining lot of land, which our monied friend had occupied: and about these days, all comparison between them is at an end. The emigrant, with means but without income, who plants himself on wild land in remote settlements, in nine cases out of ten retrogrades for the first ten years.

The remaining class of the immigration, of 1830 to 1835; namely, the pauper emigrants, or persons who had a little money, but still not sufficient to enable them to purchase land, I have now to consider. I place them last in the catalogue of the immigration of the period, because they had no claim upon my attention as settlers; they possess the character simply of immigrants or sojourners amongst us; and though Canada, west, has risen to its present state mainly from the exertions of such people—though more than one-half of its present population is composed of such people and their descendants—though in industry and devotion to their country they have ever stood foremost when established as colonists—though they are as a general rule successful colonists, and better adapted, mentally and physically, to encounter the difficulties of settlement than any other class of persons; yet the day when such people could immigrate with a prospect of success, is gone; notwithstanding all the proofs that the history of the province affords of their almost universal success, they are debarred from entering it as settlers; and thus, during the period of which I speak, and from thence to the present day, they have merely appeared amongst us as immigrants, who would remain in the province if they could get work, and, if they could not, their necessities of course forced them elsewhere; in this way the tens of thousands who landed in Quebec during this period, when immigration was at its height, and who from their landing in a British colony might be considered by their settlement likely to increase its population, passed off, and were dissipated like water, leaving hardly a sediment, not a tithe of their number, remaining. They travelled through the length and breadth of the land, they sought the liberty to cultivate the desert, to enrich the country by their labour, to convert the time-enduring forest into smiling fields, and by their industry and enterprise to build towns, and villages, the homes of artisans, mechanics, and merchants, by these means preparing the way for their countrymen yet in their father-land, and extending the market for the products of the industry of the nation; they sought to make for themselves a home under the guardian influence of British laws; actuated by British feelings, they asked for what was of no use, of no value, to the possessors, but what, in their hands and through their exertion, would become of great value and importance to themselves and their country—and they were refused! why, there was no land to give, the country we must suppose was filled up, the *nation* was large enough, there were about five hundred thousand inhabitants in it, (Upper Canada,) and there was no room for any more in the two thousand miles of forest which stretches away to the western ocean. No, England is determined, quite decided, that the continent may be colonized or peopled by immigrants from her shores, through the exertions or influence of a government, her enemy in principle and practice; in other words, that the American republic may stretch its arms from ocean to ocean, and eventually from pole to pole; she had rather keep her possessions in nature's pristine purity, reign mistress of the wilderness, till the revolutions of time, brought about by her own folly, wrests out of her hands, what, from the power of the giant she had given birth to, she has no longer strength to keep. So strange is the policy of Britain in America!

These thousands asked for land; they could not get it without a portion of money down, or, in latter years, the full price in cash; they had it not, they were driven to work to support their families, and, except as they might be able to get higher wages from a temporary scarcity of hands, their situation was in no wise different from what it had been in the land they left: there they had been serfs, and such they must remain; the object in promoting immigration, one would think, would be, or at least ought to be, settlement; but there was no settlement for these people, it was out of the frying-pan into the fire, with them; the fate of the Ishmaelites was theirs, they were to be wanderers. Did Canada offer them a subsistence in any way?—No! there was no public work, and for any others, the country began to be glutted with labourers, and consequently; wages so low, as to render it a tough business to support a family on unsteady work. What could they do? they could not go home again, for they had not the means; they must stand or fall by the step they had taken. And thus, after trying in vain for a home in any capacity under the government of their forefathers, they were compelled to seek refuge in the United States; and thus were they mere sojourners among us. Surely it is not too much to say, that it is a painful subject of regret, to think of the thousands of people who have been compelled to throw up British connections, and seek for that home amongst aliens which their own natural protector denies them; and this when we are aware of the fact that their expatriation and offer of service as settlers was for their country's good. They asked for what no possible value could appertain to, without them; they were repulsed in such terms as to make them feel that the stain of servitude was upon them. Far-seeing statesmen may think it wise to keep up land in this way; perhaps they mean, that in future ages, when population outgrows the earth, it may be sold by the foot, and the proceeds will pay the national debt. With my weak intellect, I must confess I am quite mystified; I must confess I should be inclined to turn the woods into green fields as soon as possible; I think they would produce more money or value that way. Ideas, like every thing else, seem to fluctuate a good deal. In 1824, the notion that any man would make a settler, was acted on: no matter how low he stood in the scale of humanity, both morally and physically, his prospects were considered by the wise of that day as sure. The philosophy of the present day seems to be, as regards a certain class of the human family, that they are only fitted for one station in life; and it has been determined by the wise men and rulers, at least of the British nation, to keep them there; it is this principle that sends the industrious children by thousands into foreign lands, in search of a home denied them by their country, alike at home or abroad, in the kingdom or the colony; it is this principle that renders it necessary to raise subscriptions, as I have seen talked of, to bring home the destitute immigrants from New Zealand, candidates for the workhouse; to bring them from a country where nature is surpassingly bountiful with the least possible outlay of labour, and where the government-constituted feudal lord rolls in wealth, while the poor man must eat the crumbs which fall from his table. Twenty shillings, an acre is a great price for land intrinsically worth nothing; it is a long price, to ask a poor man for leave to put a value on it; but doubtless the government are right even on other grounds, for if they allowed unrestrained settlement, there would be no land for future generations; New Holland is only said to be as large as Europe! It might be considered a great privilege by some poor man to be allowed to reside in the same neighbourhood with the Dutch boors at the Cape of Good Hope; perhaps the government would not ask him more than ten or fifteen shillings an acre for the land he might occupy; they would no doubt encourage him, if he had money.

The people of this class who remained in the country with us, became for the most part cotters, building shanties on the farms in the neighbourhood of which they could get work, and at the present day the country abounds with them—they exist in a sort of semi-poor state, many of the luxuries of life are denied, and consequently they are no revenue payers; and even their comforts may often be very much abridged. They seldom see more money than is absolutely necessary to purchase some articles which could not be procured without, and are paid chiefly in provisions and articles necessary for their family, which they procure by an order in their favour from the farmer with whom they work, on the merchant or store-keeper; so that for a man with a family to procure enough of money to pay for land, is a thing not to be hoped for—as Shakspeare says, their "cake is dough on both sides;" and they have no means of altering its character; they cannot well sink lower than they are, for common industry, with the acre of land or garden which some considerate soul gives them the use of, would always procure them a living in a country where nature is bountiful; and they cannot well rise higher, for they want the assistance of that capital, which for every purpose of life in that country is equal, and in many cases superior, to money—namely, land.

[To be concluded in our next.]

REMARKS ON THE GOVERNMENT, ETC., OF THE FALKLAND ISLANDS.

WHILST I am preparing for publicity, through the medium of your Magazine, the history of these islands, from the year 1500 to the present, with illustrations of the political and administrative principles, their unjust bearings, with their injurious workings, results, and prospects, I have been furnished with a variety of remarks and information from several observers, being official as well as non-official, who, thinking highly of the importance and capabilities of these islands, are desirous that I would send forth to the public their observations and opinions; from which it will be seen that the official mismanagement, tyranny, and injustice, which have from first to last prevailed there, and in connexion therewith, creating hostility, jealousy, treachery, loss, and disaster, have established for the place the detractive and injurious designation of the "Isles of Misfortune;" whilst their position and resources should and might entitle them to the better cognomen of the "Isles of Relief."

For these reasons I conceive, that by simply setting forth their own remarks, I shall have done all that is needful for the present; and as no doubt whatever exists that ere long the entire question in reference to those islands must become the subject of parliamentary investigation, with the *vivâ voce* evidence of witnesses, I deem it inexpedient to volunteer here the names of the parties referred to.

Although I have presumed to modify here the asperity of some of the words which have been applied in the delineations, still the style in which the asseverations are set forth may appear needlessly offensive, yet not otherwise censurable or questionable; for the proofs in my possession are so irrefragable, as to justify and urge me to say, that any legal disputation thereof would be hailed with delight; not in an individual or personal sense, nor in respect of private worth or private character, but upon the broad and admitted principle, that public men become public property, and though not to be calumniated without cause, nevertheless when they receive pay of the public to do their business in an efficient and constitutional manner, they must expect not only to be dealt with publicly on the merits and results thereof, but to be held equally amenable for injuries to individuals: and here I may observe, that assuredly as the chief functionary returns from his government, he will be made a personal defendant in a court of law for illegalities and injuries, whether designedly or erroneously inflicted, anterior as well as posterior to the British legislature passing the act for proposed legal interference or enactments of any kind whatsoever: and should the noble secretary even bring in and pass a retrospective indemnification bill—which he might feel disposed to do for the youth he has raised from the respectable rank of engineer and surveyor, to the dignity of a colonial governor—I am nevertheless warranted in saying that he could not thereby be absolved from the pecuniary responsibilities he has incurred to individuals, who ought, and who will doubtlessly be indemnified by the crown, if their worthy representative do not possess the requisite means to pay, or can justify himself as having acted according to orders, or from secret instigations; and which latter, I have strong reasons for stating, are likely to be elicited by other means than the voluntary confession of his Excellency, who may feel indisposed to adopt such course condemnatory of the Colonial Office, whence most of the evils so animadverted on may possibly have had their origin.

I content myself on this occasion with simply stating, in reference to one of the complaints hereinafter set forth, that I will, in my promised future exposition, clearly prove Mr. James Stephen to have acted therein with as much of malice and injustice as he has of illegality; and whilst he has used the name of the Colonial Secretary as his authority for such proceeding and instruction, I do not hesitate, in this instance, to dispute the proof thereof, notwithstanding that his lordship has declared to the house (in refutation of Mr. P. M. Stewart's remarks on the secret sinister influence and irresponsible agency of Mr. James Stephen) his personal supervision of all Colonial-Office orders, &c., &c.; for as his lordship could not legally, he would not otherwise than from the effect of gross misrepresentation to him, have sanctioned so flagrant and palpable an act of *ex-parte* injustice and injury, as could not be countenanced by the veriest tyro of a magistrate, and which any attorney's clerk would condemn and denounce!

To this and many similar wrongs have the aggrieved colonists submitted, and much property has been actually sunk, whilst hoping, if not for liberality, at least for impartiality, justice, and constitutional law to predominate in the colonial departments of the state, so materially under the influence and machinative management of Mr. James Stephen, who is now without the co-operation of any legal or practised colonial adjutors.

The rapid extension of our colonies, their commerce and population, with their prostrate condition and dissatisfaction, calling for national interference and legislative improvement, presented to the noble secretary the fine opportunity for trying his hand at popularity and pre-eminence as a colonial statesman; and with which view did he displace his noble well-intentioned predecessor—for his tardiness and consequently conceived inability to work out the required reforms, with the necessary measures for more systematic and extended emigration, as well as for better and more popular management both in the colonies and at home? All of which designs are now doubtless organized, but their promulgation delayed only for completion of those arrangements deemed essential to their reception generally with satisfaction and confidence — the first whereof being the exclusion *in toto* of the worthy and esteemed Mr. Mother-country, which every one must regret, unless he be shelved with a pension, and to such alternative none can object, whilst the white slaves of the colonies, and their friends in England, will, *nem. diss.*, greet his lordship as the minister of justice and benefits to the white as well as to the black. "Mais revenir à mes moutons:" I find the information and evidence so similar, that I may here save time and space by embodying them so as to make a more continuous and less tautologous commentary.

"It is really laughable the way they manage business here, at the same time it is sadly annoying to those having the misfortune to transact business with them, and certainly very detrimental to the interests and objects of the place as a naval and commercial station, or a colony. The way in which owners and masters, and all shipping matters, are treated at government-house, is monstrous. Don't fail to see Captain Baily coming home with copper ore, for if you desire further proofs of folly and undue interference, than those of the Princess Royal,* he will give you a pretty picture, and of the way in which he has been used by those jacks-in-office, from whom he sailed without his papers.

"Affair of the Hannah.—As this vessel has not yet arrived, and as proceedings will doubtlessly be instituted thereon, I should advise your waiting the owner's presence and proofs.

"Surely Captains Ross and Crozier will give the government such information as will cause the nautical transactions at least to be placed on a better footing. Talk of attractions for shipping—why, they are certainly such as will prevent any vessel putting on shore a second time.

"I was told that Captain Lock, disgusted with the authorities, set off to the Cape of Good Hope, to refresh and refit there; and many of the settlers have left from the same cause.

"His Excellency, as he is most improperly designated, is shortly to remove himself and sappers to Port William, where he has been making some preparation. I have paid the place an overland visit; and of all the miserable bog-holes in the Falklands, I believe Mr. M——y has selected one of the worst for the site of the town; and on riding past the government carpenter's shop, in the heart of the prospective town, in went my horse up to the girths in peat-bog; and myself, in springing off, stuck fast in the like predicament. I believe that five yards of dry land cannot be found on the spot laid out for the town.

"The compulsory removal hither is very disastrous; we were assured that Port Louis was to be the seat of government, &c., and we were compelled to pay there, in cash down, 100*l.* per acre for our town-land, on which we erected our dwellings, &c.; we are now informed that no compensation will be made us, nor can we be permitted to retain the land at country or suburban price, but must repurchase at Port Jackson, thirty miles distant, at 100*l.* per acre, (where ten acres are not worth so much as one here,) pull down and re-erect there our residences, &c., at our own cost, besides the loss from abandoning our gardens and improvements. It must further be borne in mind, that no assistance or allowance of any kind has been made to us, who have purchased lands and brought out settlers; nor have the government supplied us with any immigrants from the sums voted by parliament, or from the amounts paid to them for lands, duties, licenses, beef, &c. Now, I much doubt, if any private individuals had thus acted, whether they would not have been committed and tried for obtaining money under false representations.

"Some time since, the barque Venture was brought here in distress

---

* These were partially commented on in the letter which appears at page 246 of your Magazine, No. 4.

&c.; she was eventually condemned: I was employed to act as auctioneer to sell her, which the governor would not permit without taking out a license; and upon going to pay for the same, I was refused it by reason of some connection with Mr. Whitington, who was at variance with the governor.

"Things are getting from bad to worse here. Talk of justice! it is a mockery of the name at present. Mr. M——y is so capricious and despotic a man—his despotism amounting even to tyrannical interference with and ruling the affairs of the settlers as he does his sappers and miners; and he deems it rank treason in them to think even on their own private business contrary to his wishes. Such rules, laws, and regulations were never before heard of. Doubtless Mr. C—— will have told you about the 20s. spirit-duty, and Mr. Melville's appointment to a moiety thereof; this, incredible though it may appear, is nevertheless true.

"Many settlers have left the islands recently—thirteen at one time; and I think likewise of returning to England, for I am sick of this. We are limited as to where we may walk, even—taxation, fines, and forfeitures being the order of the day. There is no chance of your doing anything to advantage or satisfaction, unless you be such a disgusting toad eater as our government doctor is. Do the home-authorities intend to send out any people here? for presently we shall have none but officials left: we have paid plenty of money for lands, licenses, duties, taxes, beef, &c. By the way, Mr. J. B. W—— has paid the government a deal of money one way and another; and what becomes of it I don't know, for we are treated with government paper, of which I send you a specimen:

'No. 159. Anson, Falkland Islands.

'I promise to pay the Bearer the sum of Two Shillings and Two Pence on the part of the Colonial Government.

(Signed) 'R. C. MOODY,
'Lieutenant-Governor.'

"Now, as it is here legal tender, and *only redeemable at will, and not on demand*, we *must* take it, and keep it.

"As to the management of the cattle, it is so wretched and foolish that the Guachos have left; it is a shame also towards the settlers and shipping, the system being a monopoly by the government, who only retail, and at 2½d. per lb., always cutting off and reserving the fat for government-house. Much of the beef is such stuff, as, if exhibited in Newgate-market, would be burned, and the vender fined.

"Mr. J. B. W——'s account is 20*l.* a month for this trash; and for the heads of the animals only, the same price is extorted. This gentleman, who is really a most excellent man, and would be the making of the place if only fairly treated, has been most shamefully dealt with, and annoyed in different ways that you have no idea of; but he has the ability, and I expect the intention, to speak and to write for himself, and it is impossible that he can fail to obtain redress. Mr. M——y is jealous of his talents and position here, whence emanates his unjust and oppressive conduct towards him. You will recollect, that two years now passed,

I think, I wrote you a private letter, communicating to you what had been told me in confidence by Mr. A——, as to Mr. M——y's intentions, and, as he then inferred, instructions in respect of Mr. J. B. W——. I did not then believe in it, but it appears now as being too true; for, beyond all doubt, there is the clear combination of secret influence unfairly at work to thwart and to crush him, and which I deeply deplore, because, in truth, I can say, that I believe he has never, whilst here at least, wronged a soul, whilst he has been the sincere friend of the people and of the place, both in word and deed; and because I have dared privately to take his part, M——y has refused to do any business with me, and will, I expect, serve me out when he can. His pounding of Mr. J. B. W——'s sheep, and lastly, sending a party of his sappers to pull down the buildings, destroy the improvements, and turn everything out of the kraal forming part of Mr. W——'s premises, and which he had at and from the time of his arrival there in 1840. The place is not now even used in any way by the excellent governor.

"I send some further correspondence, &c., of the youthful Falkland government, by which, coupled with that previously transmitted, you will readily judge how fit a person has been deputed to govern a young colony, and will perceive that we are rapidly progressing in the depopulation of the islands. There are fewer persons now here than there were three years since; and the same statistic will presently apply to the shipping—the absence of both arising solely from the disgust felt by captains of ships and settlers at Mr. M——y's treatment and management, with the notoriety thereof. To speak of Tyssen as a colonial governor, he was a king both in word and deed, as regards the colony, compared to Mr. M——y, and I firmly believe that the errors of the former were of the head only. Mr. F. has truly depicted Mr. M——y's character, and Mr. M——y has verified the faithfulness of the portrait to a shade, in his late transactions with me and others. Amongst those who have left with their wives and families, are the Scotch people, but gone to the river Plate only. The latter have asked me to let them know when Mr. M——y has left, for they will all return, and I have promised to advise them; and I sincerely hope Mr. M——y's voice here will soon be turned into moody silence, or this place, instead of proving a national benefit and a blessing, will prove but a loss and a general disappointment. There is scarcely a soul, either man, woman, or child, that does not hate the despotic manner in which the government exercises its authority, and I believe there are but two of the whole detachment of sappers and miners who do not plainly say so. I do not write now from malice or from passion, ... I speak only as he has latterly proved himself, and in doing so, I feel I am only fulfilling that obligation which is imposed on me by my position here, and the great objects which such was intended to lead to; whilst delusive suppression or misrepresentation, on this or on other points, will tend only to further injury and disaster to this place.

"I was surprised by the perusal of the commissioners' reports and the papers published for parliament, and still more so by Mr. Jas. Stephen's ex-parte conduct. Now I am sincerely of opinion, that the less a settler has to do with government or government people, the better for his mind, body, and estate. A French vessel from Bordeaux put in here the other day, stated to be for water, but, from the manner and remarks of the commander, I think for other latent purposes. The American captain, Smyllie, of whom you have heard, (the daring independent Falkland cattle-hunter, and purveyor to the whalers and sealers of his station,) is now occupied with his American schooner in bringing horses and sheep from the Rio Negro for the governor and Mr. Robinson, who are become sheep-farmers, but who cannot, of course, even for their private ends, be guilty of any acts mean, paltry, or disgraceful, though their sheep can run at large over the government and other person's lands with perfect impunity; whereas settlers must pay one dollar for every sheep, goat, or pig which may happen to stray on the crown-lands.

"This brings me, with deep regret, to an account of the loss of all my English rams and ewes, which were doing so well. You will have heard of the military operations which were carried on against my kraal, &c., the depository of my live-stock, &c. Well, how or in what way all my bullock-dogs broke loose, I can't say; but, unprecedently as unaccountably, so it was, and one fine morning all *my English sheep only* were found dead; of course it was from their being South American dogs, and their being as discriminating as inimical to English blood, and success in the Falklands.

"I see it proposed officially in print that we are to have a government fishery, in addition to the government butchery, government cattle-farm, government model-farm, government sheep-farm, government stud and breeding-farm.

"Amongst other delusions in print (by order?) is one of fortune-making by the rifle. I think you are bound to undeceive people about the freedom of sporting here; we no more dare look at a wild animal than you dare to steal a horse in England; nor shoot geese, &c., without a license, and then only in certain places.

"And in respect of bringing over servants or labourers at immigrant settlers' cost; make it known, that unless the terms be made on a 35s. bond stamp, and properly settled and certified before a magistrate, they are deemed here illegal and invalid; and so also if the terms of remuneration therein specified do not fully equal what her Majesty's representative here deems adequate, colonial pay, &c., which is about 5*l.* per month, with rations and lodging. It was on the above Falkland law-premises that all Mr. J. B W——'s labourers, servants, and others, having written and mutual engagements for passage, with clothing, boarding, and lodging there, all at Mr. W——'s cost, were freed by his Excellency and then hired by himself; but as he makes the law, so he breaks it for himself, and from the will of this absolute monarch there is no other being to appeal to for redress. The Scotchmen before alluded to state, they quitted solely from his thus wronging them, and under violation of agreement."

On this subject Mr. J. B. W—— says,

"Mr. M——y has, by seductive and illegal means, deprived me of all my mechanics and labourers, and nearly all my servants, both male and female, by telling them their agreements were not binding, &c., which acted instantly so as to make them discontented, and to compel me, in order to reserve some, to submit to fresh and high terms, dictated to me even by those who had first gone out with me, and who were, till Mr. M——y's arrival, &c., quite satisfied and serviceable. Out of thirty persons thus expensively conveyed, &c., but few have withstood the temptations thus held out; and for these few faithful domestics he, Mr. M——y, has expressed to Mr. C—— and others a strong desire of obtaining them. It is now evident that it was contemplated by the governor to get labour and mechanics for himself, and at my expense, but I did not see it at the time so palpably; perhaps I was in some measure blinded by the exorbitant nature of the demands some of them proposed.

"Captain Onslow, R. N., has put in here on his way round the Horn, to Valparaiso, in his fine new frigate the 'Daphne;' himself and officers seemed to emulate each other in showing me every courtesy and consideration, which I reciprocated, being so different to the conduct of Captain Sullivan of H. M. brig 'Philomel,' who is on terms of close intimacy with Mr. M——y, with whom, after a few days, Captain Onslow was very distant, as, indeed, have been the captains of every vessel, whether government or merchant, with the exception of Captain Sullivan, from whom, as well as from Mr. M——y, I have received treatment as unjust as unmerited. Captain Onslow repeatedly condoled with me for my losses and difficulties here: he also expressed his extreme regret to find such little progress made since he planted here the British flag, as commander of H. M. S. 'Clio.' He says the place looks far more sad and miserable than it did then, and fewer persons resident; indeed, there will not shortly be a civil labourer left, for every ship putting in takes away two or three.

"Mr. M——y is just beginning to meet his deserts; as regards his personal comforts, he has not now one servant who came with him from England —all have left him and the islands, and he is now doing with two boys only, whom he got from ships. This is as it should be; it is a just retribution for him to feel the inconvenience and discomfort which his shameful conduct respecting my servants inflicted on me.

"I perceive that government positively refused to allow the nomination of emigrants, on account of the land-purchases we have paid for here. The governor is determined to get labour *coute qui coute,* as it does not come out of his pocket, whilst it most seriously affects us. The peat here, which is so abundant, is dearer firing, from the high price of labour and license-duty, than coals brought from England at 5*l*. per ton.

"Mr. M——y does not attach the necessary importance to conciliation and pleasing of the shipping-interest, which I conceive it requires, for without it no colony can possibly thrive; but what can you expect from a young person brought out of a military college, and placed as governor over the interests of business and business-men, whereof he is completely ignorant, and to conceal which he is continually committing acts of folly, injustice, and wrong?

"This is and will be ostensibly a port of refuge and refit for merchant vessels, and, as such, requiring a man conversant with those matters and shipping business: a military man is not adapted for that purpose; he confounds and disgusts masters of vessels, which cannot last long; for, assuredly as I am now writing to you, no vessel will put in here, except from necessity. My opinion may be considered biassed, nevertheless I affirm, that this place will never become a colony, so long as Mr. M——y is governor. I believe that Captains Onslow and Sullivan feel and know this, and that Mr. M——y cannot long remain. From what I have seen and know of Captain Onslow, I think he would make a most desirable governor for this place.

"The orders issued here by his Excellency are more arbitrary and impolitic than an ukase of the Russian Emperor. I will state a simple fact: a short time since, a dozen fin-backed whales were driven ashore on Long Island in Berkeley Sound. I went across the bay in my pleasure-boat with my two boys, to see them; we did not touch the shore. I gratified my curiosity of inspecting the fish, and returned home to dinner at five o'clock; about six o'clock I received a letter from his Excellency, demanding to know by whose authority I had dared to land upon Long Island, after having received notice to confine myself exclusively to those lands in my own occupation. So disgusted was I, that I made no reply.

"I hope you will receive my despatches per the Triton,* and the copied orders therein enclosed, which his Excellency Governor M——y has thought fit and expedient to put in force at the Falklands. Surely he would not dare to commit such egregious acts of absurdity in a larger community, or one nearer home.

I will for the present close this commentary with an extract from a letter from an official gentleman, now in England, who takes much interest in the Falklands, viz.:

"I hope you will not fail to let me know when my vessel is going out to the Falklands. I should have thought, with the further 10,000*l.* voted in the last session, that the government would have sent out persons, stores, &c., so long provided for by parliament. I much regret to hear the complaints and causes for dissatisfaction in the islands. I hope and trust such ere long will be removed. I am quite sure you will do no good by seeing Lord Stanley; on the other hand, you may do Mr. J. B. W—— more harm, for, depend upon it, those in authority here always hang to those in office abroad; and it must be a very powerful interest indeed that can make any impression. If the powerful New Zealand Company could with difficulty obtain a hearing, and then nothing satisfactory, what can one or two individuals expect? It reminds me forcibly of throwing your hat at the moon!"

* These despatches with enclosures have never come into my possession, neither can I obtain satisfactory proof where they are, although I have used considerable exertions to that end, and have satisfied myself such were placed in the bag of the ship which brought them from the islands, and that they were duly posted at Liverpool in the month of February last; yet the London post-office have not satisfied me by whom and to whom they were delivered!

I reserve for future numbers my further promised expositions, but I here remark, that if this continuous, desperate, spell hanging over the place, and so sadly influencing every exertion and action of ourselves and predecessors for the weal of the isles and their friends, be not supernatural, then there must have been much more than mismanagement at work, sustained by injustice with high and with low, which I will develop politically and practically; and in so conclusive a manner, as not only to enlighten the public, but to command the attention of the legislature.

G. T. W.

COLONIAL STATISTICS.

(NEW SERIES.)

NO. VIII.—ST. LUCIA.

History.—The Island was discovered by Columbus on his fourth voyage on 15th June, 1502; St. Lucia's day. The first settlement attempted by the English is put down, by the *West India Manual*, as having taken place in 1639; the same authority states that this attempt failed, and that the French effected a precarious settlement in 1650. In 1664, the English, it is stated, purchased the island of the Caribs, and dislodged the French; but in 1666 it was abandoned by the English, and was declared neutral in 1713. In 1762, it was taken by the English from the French, who had occupied it, in contravention of the treaty; but it was ceded to France in 1763, and again taken by the English in 1778. In 1783 it was restored to France, again to surrender to British arms in 1794. It was ceded to France in 1803, and finally taken by the English in the following year. On the authority of the table published monthly in the Army-List, the date of the final capitulation was, as stated, viz. 1803. "St. Lucia is now," (observes Mr. Osborne, in his Guide, published in the beginning of the present year) "a British colony in little more than the name. Property is chiefly in the hands of French settlers, who compose the principal portion of the society."

Geography.—St. Lucia, the citadel of our West Indian empire, is situated between 13° and 14° N. latitude, and 59½° and 60½° W. longitude; it is 90 miles N.W. by W. from Barbadoes. Lying more to windward than any of the other islands in the West Indies, (Barbadoes excepted,) it is asserted, that a fleet stationed at St. Lucia holds the most commanding position in the Archipelago; and to this circumstance is ascribed the pertinacity with which, it is notorious, England and France have contested the possession of the island. Its extreme length from north to south is 32 miles; extreme breadth, 12 miles. The area covers 317 square miles of space, or 203,000 acres, which are divided into nine parishes, the capital being Castries.

Scenery.—The structure of the island presents a singular contrast as regards its eastern (or central) and its western divisions. The former,

Capisterre, possesses scenery of a character mountainous to immensity, and picturesque beyond description. The deep and unwholesome ravines present an appearance of terrible wildness, and many of the mountains are so steep that no animal can ascend them The western part of the island, called Basseterre, on the contrary, exhibits scenery of a less elevated and irregular nature, but abounds in dangerous and pestilential swamps. The finest part of the country is the S.W. quarter, which is well cultivated and thickly inhabited.

Geology, Soil, Agriculture.—The earth is here of volcanic formation, containing a very active solfatara, or sulphur hill, from 1,200 to 1,400 feet in height. This volcano is of a kind that has no metal or lava. From the crevices of the earth issue condensations of sulphur, and jets of hot water are likewise produced. But, generally, the soil of St. Lucia is distinguished both for depth and richness: about 9,500 acres are now under cultivation. The lands under crop in 1842 were to the extent of 5,619 acres; 2,600 acres, in addition, were devoted to pasture; 9,486 acres remained until lately uncultivated. In 1841, however, double the amount of acres were lying waste, but in one year the agriculturists have made such great efforts as to lead to the belief that very soon the whole of the land yet remaining uncultivated will be applied to useful purposes. This is a favourable sign of the advance of the colony from its primitive state. Excellent timber is found in plenty. The following is an account of the live stock in 1842: horses, 744; horned cattle, 2,165; sheep, 1,794; goats, 712. The natural resources of St. Lucia, however, (says Mr. Edwards, in his History of the West Indies,) have not been fairly developed, owing in a great measure to the frequent international changes to which it has been subject.* Frequent earthquakes have occurred at different periods.

Climate.—Both of the districts of St. Lucia (Capisterre, E., and Basseterre, W.) are subject in an eminent degree to the operation of those agencies which are supposed to exert a baneful influence on the health of Europeans in tropical climates; and it has been estimated, at an average of twenty years, ending in 1836, that the annual deaths amounted to upwards of 122 in each thousand of the whites, and 42 in the same proportion of the black troops. The unhealthy state of St. Lucia may principally be ascribed to the primeval character of the island. Crowded with forest trees and dense underwood, intersected with deep ravines, which, being too narrow to admit of free ventilation, are at all times replete with moisture, and choked up with decayed vegetation in every stage of decomposition, abounding too in swamps, it is not surprising that malaria and disease are productive of excessive mortality. It rains nine months out of the twelve at St. Lucia. It is noticed, however, by Mr. Breen, that of late years the swamps have been partially filled up.

Government.—The laws in force here (the ancient laws of France,) at the time preceding the last cession to France, still prevail to a con-

* Mr. Breen, who was twelve years resident in St. Lucia, has written a valuable book on the colony, (just published, 1 vol, 8vo., Longman,) from which it appears that great agricultural improvement has taken place within the last four years.

siderable extent. All the papers, registers, and archives of the colony were burnt at the fire that destroyed Castries in 1790. The Supreme Court is constituted according to the provisions of the English order in council of the 20th June, 1831. The officials who now direct the government business are as follows:—Lieutenant-Governor, Colonel Graydon, the officer commanding the troops; Secretary and Treasurer, W. Hanley, Esq.; Chief Justice, J. Reddie, Esq.; Attorney-General, G. Agostini, Esq.; Provost-Marshal, H. McLeod, Esq.; Collector of Customs, C. H. Cox, Esq.; Agent in London, G. Baillie, Esq.

Chief Towns.—Castries, the capital, is on the western side; it lies at the bottom of a deep irregularly-formed harbour. It is one of the best harbours (says Mr. Coleridge, a recent traveller,) in the Windward Islands, having deep water and good anchorage ground. The steamer's boat will land you. The town appears almost deserted; the buildings are detached; they are chiefly composed of wood that had been warped and disfigured by the climate. The Government-House in Castries stands on a high hill above the town.

Wages for Labour.—Domestics, per month, (1844) 1*l.* 4*s.*

Prices of Provisions.—Wheaten bread, per lb., 4d.; beef, pork, mutton, 10d.; rice, 3d. to 7d.; coffee, 9½d. to 1s.

Currency.—Notes of Colonial Bank estimated at 40,000 dollars in 1840; 50,000 in 1841; 45,000 in 1842.

The Press.—The *Independent Press*, weekly newspaper, was established in 1838-9.

Harbours.—There are several good harbours at its northern extremity, and within the short distance of three miles from each other, are four large bays—Cul-de-Sac, Castries, Choc, and Gros-Islet,—all situated within view of Fort Royal, the chief naval dépôt of the French, and all admirably protected by the batteries of Mont Fortune, Vigi, and Pigeon Island.*

Population.—In 1834 there were 881 whites, 3,919 coloured races, and 13,438 negroes, comprising a total of 18,148 inhabitants. In 1842, the population consisted of 1,741 whites, and the remainder coloured races; total 26,830 souls. The white population is considerably on the increase.

Religion.—The inhabitants are chiefly Catholics. In 1842 there were seven schools, having 313 male and 58 female scholars. The cost of supporting these educational establishments was, for 1842, £1,181. 15s. 2½d., (charged to the Mico Charity). Private schools do not exist here.

Commerce.—The staple products are sugar, rum, and coffee. The total value of the exports in 1836, was 69,040*l.*, and in the same year the imports amounted in value to 60,344*l.* A Parliamentary return (1836) gives the aggregate annual value of the products of St. Lucia at 595,610*l.* The revenue of St. Lucia in 1842 amounted to 11,694*l.*, and the expenditure to 11,409*l.* (*Vide* Return of Income, Expenditure, &c., of British

* It was omitted to be stated in the account of St. Vincent, (last number,) that a detachment of H. M's 46th Foot is now stationed on that Island.

Colonies for the year 1841-42.) The quantities of the principal articles exported to the United Kingdom in 1838 and 1839 were:

	1838.	1839.
Sugar	61,691 cwt.	50,215 cwt.
Rum	7,493 gal.	14,051 gal.
Molasses	4,786 cwt.	11,029 cwt.
Coffee	143,266 lbs.	84,000 lbs.
Cocoa	16,225 lbs.	35 lbs.

A Parliamentary document, of date 1841, states that the imports of sugar from St. Lucia into the United Kingdom, that year, amounted to 51,115 cwts.; showing that the annual supply has been pretty regular since 1838.

Number and tonnage of vessels to and from the United Kingdom and St. Lucia: vessels inward, 14, of 3,003 tons aggregate; outward, 12, of 2,747 tons. In 1842, 253 ships, of 13,848 tonnage, were entered inwards, and 257 ships, of 13,883 tonnage, entered outward. (*Osborne's Guide*, 1844.)

Colonial Arms.—A series of fortifications, facing the sea, is represented as seen from the harbour at sunrise. The motto is "*Statio haud malefida carinis.*"

NOTICES OF THE HARBOURS OF THE BRITISH CHANNEL ON THE NORTH SHORE OF FRANCE, ETC.

BY WALTER B. PRICHARD, ESQ., C.E. F.S.A., ETC.

To the Editor of the Colonial Magazine.

SIR,—I presume it would be agreeable to many of your readers, at this juncture, just after a government commission has been sitting, on one side of the Channel, and examining for sites of refuge-harbours—and a royal prince writing on the other, to place before your readers some brief notices of the principal cities, towns, ports, and harbours, &c., on both coasts, but the French more especially. I shall commence with

DUNKIRK.—East Longitude 2° 20′, Latitude 51°. A port-town of the French Netherlands, in the province of Flanders, situated on the English Channel, at the mouth of the river Coln, 20 miles E. of Calais, 24 S.W. of Ostend, and 50 E. of Dover. The fortification of this port cost France more money than those of any other fortress in that kingdom. Dunkirk was taken from the Spaniards by the united force of England and France, and put into the hands of the English in the year 1658. It was sold to France in the reign of King Charles II., soon after which the fortifications were greatly improved; it was the rendezvous of the French privateers during subsequent wars, and many of these desperadoes grew rich with the spoils of the English. This in consequence offended England so much, that she insisted on the harbours being closed and the fortifications demolished at the treaty of Utrecht, in 1713, which was done accordingly. The harbour would never admit of large men-of-war; all the mischief arose from light frigates and privateers; but notwithstanding that by virtue of the treaty the fortifications were demolished, the French kings fortified it again, and repaired the harbour, so that it is now a very strong place. Although an immense sum of money has been expended in the restoration of the harbour, yet the French have found it impracticable to make it admit large ships of war, or vessels of considerable burden, but ships of 20 guns can go in at high tides. The inhabitants are numerous, and carry on an active and profitable trade in spirituous liquors, tea, plush, &c., &c.

CALAIS.—East Longitude 2°, Latitude 51°. The capital of the Pays Reconquis, in the province of Picardy, on the English Channel, opposite Dover, or 22 miles S.E. of that port, 140 N. of Paris, taken by Edward III., king of England, A.D. 1347, and lost in the reign of Queen Mary, 1557. It was formerly a good harbour, but is now so choked up, that it does not admit of large vessels. It is of immense value as a packet-station, being the nearest point of land to the coast of Great Britain. The town is well fortified, and a citadel commands both town and country; but its greatest strength lies in its situation among the marshes. It may be overflowed at the approach of an enemy. There is a canal running from it to St. Omer's, Graveline, Dunkirk, Bergues, and Ypres.

BOULOGNE-SUR-MER,—East Longitude 1° 30′, Latitude 50° 40′—is another port in the province of Picardy, the capital of the districts of Bolonois. It stands at the mouth of the little river Liane, which forms its harbour, and is divided into upper and lower town. It is 16 miles S.W. of Calais, and 130 N. of Paris. The upper town is well fortified, and adorned with a handsome square, where there was a Town-House, remarkable for its clock. The lower town being inhabited chiefly by merchants, &c., lies along the harbour, which was formerly very considerable. The harbour is defended towards the river originally by a mole, which shelters it from winds, in addition to recent improvements. It is much frequented by the Flemish and English, and has lately been made famous as the pet port (jointly with Folkestone) of the South-Eastern Railway Company, on account of the shortness and convenience of the passage from England to France. Near the harbour are some ancient ruins, and among the rest an octagon tower, said to have been raised by Julius Cæsar, besides some old fortifications built by the English, when they were masters, and possessed this city and port. The Emperor Maximilian raised a bank before the harbour, which affected its trade to an alarming degree. King Henry VIII. took it in 1544, and fortified the lower town, but finding it would cost him more to keep than it was worth, by a treaty in 1546, quitted it for 800,000 crowns. Of late it has undergone considerable improvement.

DIEPPE,—East Longitude 1° 15', Latitude 49° 55',—is 30 miles N. of Rouen, midway between the ports of Rye and Shoreham, and the point of communication with Brighton, and commonly called the "high-way" to Paris from London. It is on the N.E. coast of Normandy, at the mouth of the little river Arques. In the year 1694, it was almost destroyed by a bombardment from the English; but since that time it has been rebuilt with great beauty, after the model of the town of Versailles. It is of a triangular figure, and strongly fortified, though the works, it is true, are very irregular, occasioned by the unevenness of the ground. The streets are wide and level, and the houses for the most part well built with bricks. The town is separated from the sea by a long wall and deep ditch. The harbour, a century ago, was one of the most considerable on the coast, but will not now admit of ships of great burden. The castle, where the governor resided, is an ancient building. The town is adorned with a number of handsome fountains, and has twenty gates, twelve of which are situated along the quay. The inhabitants are, however, principally mariners, and a great trade is carried on in tobacco, lace, and different kinds of fancy ivory work, &c.

DESCRIPTION OF ADEN, IN ARABIA,

BY THE HON. CALEB CUSHING, AMERICAN MINISTER TO CHINA.

Aden, November 3, 1843.

IT is generally understood that, in taking possession of Aden, the English government has recently acquired a very important military post on the southern shores of Arabia, near to the Straits of Babel Mandeb, which commands the Red Sea and the Sea of Arabia, as Gibraltar does the Mediterranean and a portion of the Atlantic. But there are few persons, I presume, in the United States, who have any very distinct idea of the extraordinary natural features of this new stronghold of the Island Queen.

Aden is, even more than Gibraltar, a castle of nature's own construction. At Gibraltar, England has excavated for herself a citadel in the heart of a limestone mountain; at Aden, she has planted herself in an ancient crater, and sits secure within the primeval fortress formed by the lofty sides of an extinct volcano.

At some remote period, anterior probably to the creation of the human race, certainly anterior to all history, the southerly parts of Arabia, on the Red Sea and the Indian Ocean, appear to have been the theatre of stupendous volcanic revolutions on the surface of the earth. The whole coast abounds with enormous mountains of naked rocks, over which fire having once passed, their blackened surface frequently looks now as if proof against the action of sea and air, and in that arid climate they remain for ever comparatively destitute of vegetation. Their high peaks rise over the sea, seeming, in their rugged outline, and their dark sides and tops, to frown defiance against man and against time.

Certainly there never entered into my mind the imagination of anything so desolate in its general aspect as this whole coast of Yemen, which, if we did not know that the ancients acted in good faith in the matter, and from ignorance, we might suppose to have been called Arabia Felix in irony and derision. The Arabs stuck nearer to the mark themselves when they gave its name of tears and sorrow to the Strait of Bàb-el-Mandeb. Wherever you look, you see nothing but volcanic mountains, as if the whole substance of the earth had been on fire, and had bubbled up into every capricious form, covered always with the same blackened cinders and scoriæ. From Cape Bab-el-Mandeb eastward, you pass by a succession of these ancient volcanoes, separated from one another only by wastes of naked land, until you come to what is probably the most remarkable of all, namely, the confused mass of mountains marked in the old maps Cape Aden.

To obtain a clear perception of the general configuration of Aden, it is necessary to view it from several points.

On approaching Aden from the Red Sea, the voyager rounds Ras Sulhel, which is the extremity of a mountain-promontory extending far out from the mainland, and called Jebel Hassan; and he then passes through a narrow opening between this and another cape, called Ras Torshein, and thus enters a spacious bay, eight miles in length by four in width, called by the English, Black Bay. Here is ample and convenient anchorage for ships-of-war and other vessels. The bay is formed by Jebel Hassan and the low sandy shore of Arabia on the one side, and on the other by the promontory of Aden, which is now discovered to be composed of long ridges of dark rocks, covered with volcanic scoriæ, from the main body of which several short spurs or mountain ridges extend towards the waters of the bay, leaving between them small plains of naked sand. On one of these small sand-plains are seen the buildings of a public-house, kept for the accommodation of the steamboat passengers; and on others a few scattered temporary buildings of matting and cane, while a group of buildings of the same description, occupied by English officers, crowns a prominent height called by the Arabs, Ras Marbat, and by the English, more significantly, Steamer Point.

Leaving Steamer Point, you proceed by a newly-constructed road, four or five miles along the beach, with the bay on your left-hand, and the mountains on your right, rounding several of the spurs which jut down to the water's-edge, and crossing several intervening sand-plains, and in one case the mountain itself, and thus come to the Pass, as it is called. During the last mile or two, you find that the mountains have become loftier, and rise up scarped and stratified in a high precipitous wall, which you approach obliquely in ascending to the Pass, where a branch of the road passes off at right angles along the base of another series of rocky heights at the head of the bay, in which appear also a number of large insular rocks. At the Pass you enter by an unfinished gate of masonry, guarded by sipohis, into a narrow way, partly natural and partly excavated in the rock, on emerging from which you are ushered of a sudden into the scene of a most extraordinary spectacle. Before you, occupying the level bottom of what seems to be a vast crater, is an Anglo-Indian camp, composed of low buildings of matting and cane, arranged in regular streets, with a few buildings of brick or stone discernible in the distance, and the whole apparently surrounded by towering mountains, which form its sides, and along the summit of which, from distance to distance, you see watch-towers and detached walls of masonry.

This part of Aden is called the Camp. It stretches over the site of the old Arabic town of Aden, which is now lost to the eye in the midst of the numerous *bungalows*, as they are called, or buildings of cane covered with matting, which have sprung up under the auspices of the English.

Descending from the Pass, then, into the Camp, and proceeding on, you come to the former port of Aden. Here, on the south-east side of the promontory, the natural walls of the crater seem to be broken down, so as to admit of immediate access to the sea in this quarter, a part of whose mountain-wall, however, still remaining in the form of a lofty insular rock called Sirah. This islet affords protection to the anchorage-ground of the old port, which, however, is of small capacity, and at the same time it commands the approaches of the sea on this side of Aden.

You pass from Aden to Sirah on the sands at low tide, or in boats at high tide, and clamber up the rough sides of the islet rock to a natural platform, on which is a small battery and a *corps de garde*; and, continuing to ascend, you arrive at a triangular citadel on the very summit of the mountain. Here you are enabled to add to and correct the imperfect knowledge of the localities which you have acquired previously. You discern a great number of mountains, which are all connected together, but branch out in various directions, in the most fantastic manner, sometimes in long ridges, sometimes in short spurs.

Thus are formed a succession of exterior valleys. None of these are wholly enclosed, and some are quite open. Some are very small and others large. In some cases the connexion between the mountains is under water, or covered with beach-sand. And you begin now to doubt whether Aden be in fact situated at the bottom of a crater, or not rather in one of the irregular plains left by the singular formation of the mountain ridges and spurs. To the north-east you perceive the long line of beach which is the continuation of the main coast of Arabia, to which Aden is attached. Looking over the town and camp towards the west, you find the view in that direction wholly cut off by a line of lofty mountains, called Sham-shan, which constitute the highest summits of the promontory of Aden.

From the camp a military road leads up to the heights of Ras Kutum, which stands opposite to Sirah, towards the main land, and forms the recommencement of the natural mountain-wall on this side. This road proceeds along the heights, sometimes on the inner sides towards the camp, and sometimes on the outer side towards the sea, and continues around to the main pass. From a battery, placed at an angle of this road, towards the highest part of the ridge, you see beneath your feet a line of field-works on the outside, running across the sandy isthmus which unites Aden to the main land, and which forms in continuation the beach of the Arabian shore previously seen from Sirah.

Going now out through the pass, and taking the road which I spoke of as branching off to the left in coming to the pass from Steamer Point, you proceed by this road along the head of Back Bay under the lee of a high ridge of rocks, which are separated at one point, so as to allow you to pass through into an open plain beyond, and here you are on the outside of Aden, upon the isthmus which connects it with the main land of Arabia.

If you proceed by sea in front of Aden, you pass by a succession of Capes between Ras Tarshem and Sirah, separated from each other by little inlets, or beaches, which run back to the crotches of the mountains, with the lofty heights of Sham-shan, and the old towers on its summit, overtopping, like a giant sentinel, the whole of the promontory of Aden.

Finally, in order to connect all these separate parts, and to gain thus a clear idea of the *tout ensemble* of Aden, it is necessary to ascend to the top of Sham-shan.

This mountain is one thousand seven hundred and seventy-six feet high. To reach its summit, you leave the camp by an old paved military road, which winds up, zigzag, an acclivity several hundred feet high, and brings you to an extensive table-land, with occasional elevations upon it, over one of which it is necessary to climb in order to reach the immediate foot of Sham-shan.

Objects, previously doubtful, now begin to acquire distinctness; you perceive that all the lower heights, the sides of the mountain-spurs you have passed, and the vast table-land over which you are now proceeding, are alike covered with blackened lumps and fragments of volcanic scoriæ, you are walking continually over the heaved-up cinders of a vast furnace; there is nothing but stones beneath your feet, and those stones are nothing but scoriæ, sometimes in the scraggy form in which fire may be supposed to leave them, but more frequently in angular masses covering miles of surface. The sides of all the lesser mountains, from top to bottom, are thus covered with lumps of fragment and lava. Where indeed the rock beneath is laid open by the passage of mountain torrents, or otherwise, you see that under the heaps or ledges of volcanic tufa are other solid rocks, which form the main body of these lower mountains.

But you perceive that the higher mountains all around have a different appearance, looking as if composed of rough layers of rocks. You distinguish in the distance a winding streak on the face of Sham-shan, which indicates the path by which your ascent is to continue. Making for this, over the uneven surface of the table-land, you come to a narrow ridge or spur, with precipitous sides, at the foot of which another tract of paved military road commences. This road, which is itself a very remarkable work, runs along the narrow back of the ridge for a long distance, sometimes in steps, sometimes in long inclined planes, until you reach the side of the Sham-shan itself, up the face and over the inequalities of which the road proceeds, with but a short interruption, until you attain the summit.

In this last stage of the ascent you have been coming gradually in your mind to certain conclusions concerning the formation of the mountains by which you are surrounded. You are now above the scoriæ-covered ridges and table-lands. You see that from Sham-shan on the one side to Sirah on the other is a space of between two and three miles in length; that the sides of Sham-shan above you are stratified; that a continuous range of stratified rocks proceeds at a great height from Sham-shan towards Sirah on the left, and from Sham-shan towards Sirah on the right; that you are wholly surrounded, except at a small space adjoining Sirah, by a lofty wall of rock, either stratified or disposed in tabular layers; that in their highest parts all these mountains visibly and obviously face inwards, so as to describe a hollow circle or ellipse; that their table or strata, though more or less disabled or dislocated, yet have a general correspondence and symmetry, which it is impossible to mistake; that, indeed, you are within a vast elliptical or circular basin, whose walled sides constitute mountains; that from the inner surface of the walls of this basin, sharp spurs extend inward like imperfect or ruptured radii, upon the back of one of which you had for some time past been; that you are clinging to the inside of that basin; that *if* the camp of Aden be in a crater, it is only in one corner of, and at a lower level than, the main body of the bottom of that crater, which is more than two miles in diameter, and whose walls consist in part of the lofty heights of Sham-shan.

All these things become plain to the sight, on at length gaining the summit of Sham-shan. You stand there, within the walls of an ancient fortress, which crowns the summit, and whose walls of masonry, though broken and thrown down in part, yet show what it once was.

You perceive that you are on the highest point of the promontory of Aden, so as to be able to distinguish not only the configuration of Aden itself, but to embrace in the circle of vision many leagues of the Indian Ocean on the south, and on the other side the mainland of Arabia, with its wide wastes of sand, its few scattered villages, and its distant mountains bounding the horizon. Sham-shan you find, though it be a peak, yet is but a portion of the periphery of a great basin, of which you now see the outside as well as the inside; on the inside scarped and tabled, with some scarped and tabled spurs, radiating inward in convergent lines, but leaving on the whole a vast basin, stretching off southeastwardly towards Sirah; and on the outside, in like manner, scarped and tabled in part, but in part sending out numerous ridges of variable heights, with branch ridges on the right hand and on the left, the longest and highest of which ridges terminates near Ras Tarshein, at the entrance of Back Bay.

Along the summits of this vast basin, from space to space, are small towers and continuing walls of masonry, and tanks, and aqueducts, the remains of the fortifications constructed in the old time by some former possessors of Aden, whose name has perished—

Carent quia vate sacro;

but whose works remain, emulating, in their greatness, those which Nature herself had raised before human passions had come to co-operate with her in changing the face of the earth.

Such is the general geological formation and the superficial aspect of Aden.

To complete which general view, some particular facts need to be mentioned.

At and near Steamer Point you do not find any of the peculiar stratified appearance described. The mountains there consist of the remoter spurs of less comparative elevation, and with sides for the most part covered with lava. In passing from Steamer Point to the Camp, on the last long plain, you first become aware, as I have already mentioned, that the steep ridges which now open on the sight, have a surface seemingly marked in lines, which, for aught that can be distinguished at a distance, arise from differences of colour or other irregularities in the face of the mountain. A closer inspection shows you that these lines are tables or strata; that the alternate strata are of a friable nature, so as to have undergone much degradation from the action of the atmosphere or some other cause, and to be thus broken into hollows, holes, and caves; that some of these layers are horizontal, and that others dip, but that they have no uniformity, or rather no identity of inclination, seeming as if they had either been formed by causes of unequal action, or had been disturbed in their site by subsequent convulsions.

To which is to be added, in further explanation as to the lumps and masses of scoriæ or spongy lava which cover the whole surface of the lower mountains, and the tops of the higher ones, that the ejected matter is all of that colour which denotes basaltic lava; that the rocks ejected are of all forms and sizes, from large angular masses and broken fragments to more spongy lumps, whose surface, while it sometimes decays, yet blackens as it decays; that no slags of glassy lava are seen, nor is there any appearance on the surface of a superficial continuous lava stream.

The more prevalent, although by no means the exclusive, appearance of the rocks, is of a compact, rather than of a granulated or crystalline formation, and there are some ledges of an obviously tufacious structure. I say that the appearance is not exclusively compact; for at the Pass, where the rocks have been blasted, they show a trappean appearance, as they do at sundry places on Back Bay, where the mountain-spurs look as if broken off or cut down near the water, exposing the inferior formation.

Sham-shan is incidentally spoken of as a limestone rock in the only printed account of Aden which I have seen—that published by Captain Haines, who surveyed this coast some years since very thoroughly, and greatly to the interests of nautical and geographical science, and who is now the British Political Agent at Aden. But this intimation, it would seem, is an error. The mountains appear to be wholly volcanic. Couches of shell-limestone occur, which will be referred to hereafter; but these are altogether independent of the original mountains, and obviously to be known as of comparatively recent formation.

In the exposed faces of the rocks along Back Bay, thin veins of pure quartz occur frequently, whether veins of segregation or veins of injection, I will not undertake to say; and buttons, nodules, or tubercles of this mineral are to be found all over the mountains, looking as if dropped here and there upon the rocks. But no metal or other mineral substance of commercial value, I believe, has been discovered at Aden. Even the lime which is used there is made from lumps of coral, which are brought there either expressly for this purpose, or as ballast. But, as already hinted, shell-limestone is to be found there in various places, disposed in ledges or couches around the bases of the mountains, and the process of its continued formation is going on before the eye at all times, in a manner which merits elucidation.

Aden, as part of Arabia, partakes of the peculiar climate of the country, which is nearly destitute of rivers. The climate is pure, clear, and dry. There are no sensible dews by night, and by day a cloudless sun shines forth from the heavens, with the exception of only a few days of brief showers, during the whole course of the year. Unless where springs or other means of irrigation exist, the face of the earth is parched and arid. No such means of irrigation occur among the mountains of Aden. All the fresh-water used there is obtained from deep wells dug in the earth, some of the wells yielding brackish water, and others water strongly impregnated with sulphur. Many remains of old tanks are to be seen at Aden, for collecting rain-water, as it flows down the crotches of the mountains, but they have been neglected, and suffered to fall into decay. At any rate, Aden is comparatively destitute of vegetation; a few stunted trees, shrubs, and wild herbs only being found in the mountains, or in the hollows over which the rain flows for the short period of the year when it visits these thirsty regions. The comminuted earth of these mountains would readily form into soil, if it were possible to give it moisture; but, not having this in sufficient quantities, the tops and sides of the mountains seem to exhibit the appearance now which they have possessed for the uncounted ages elapsed since they first rose out of the earth or the sea. But extensive changes have occurred around their bases. All these changes seem to have sprung from the ocean.

Whether these volcanic mountains were formed under the sea, and then heaved up to its surface? or whether the volcanic action occurred, in the first instance above the surface of the sea? These are questions of theory for others to judge. But the little plains of sand between the bases of the ridges speak for themselves, as manifest products of the sea. On a cursory inspection of these plans, one may not be aware of the nature of the sand. He sees a plain of coarse sand filling the triangular spaces from the seashore to the foot of the hills, with a large quantity of shells and lumps of black stone scattered over its sarface, and does not stop at first to scrutinize the composition of that sand. In proceeding to inspect the bases of the mountains in various places near to the sea, he discerns ledges of superficial rock, with shells and lumps of scoriæ imbedded in it; and on carefully examining this rock, he ascertains that it is composed of shells triturated into sand, mixed with some little earth of the mountains, and containing in it not only lumps of stone, but shells in every stage of their possible condition, from entire ones to fragments in the form of the minutest powder. This induces further investigation, and leads to the ascertainment of a class of curious facts.

Of the various sand-beaches occurring between the successive points of rock formed by the ends of the ridges as they extend out towards the water, by which Aden is almost surrounded, some are on the outside, exposed to the unbroken force of the whole Indian Ocean: others are on the shores of Back Bay, where the sea is nearly land-locked; and others again are in the intermediate state, as on the beach between Ras Tarshein and Ras Marbat, and on the beach of the old port of Aden. On comparing the sand of these respective localities, you find that it is alike composed of broken shells with a very small admixture of foreign matter; that, where the beach is less exposed, the sand is more or less coarse, according to circumstances, and consisting of fragments of shells, obviously seen to be such at the slightest glance; that where the beach is not exposed to the flow and beat of the waves of the ocean, the shells are reduced to the finest possible sand, blown about at the least breath of air, and thrown up in downs as extensive as the nature of the ground will admit; but that in each and every case the sand is composed of broken shells. And accordingly ledges of rock may be found on these beaches, composed, as between Ras Tarshein and Ras Marbat, wholly of more or less fine shell-sand; or, as near the Steamboat bungalow, composed of a conglomeration of sand, scoriæ, and shells. Behind Ras Marbat, the strata dip; and here is an example of strata which, when viewed in front, seem horizontal, but when examined on the side are seen to be inclined. Whenever these ledges contain shells, they are obviously the same shell which now occupy the adjoining waters, and lie scattered along the beach; and these ledges may be seen in every stage of growth, from shell rock, so imperfectly compacted as to crumble in the hand, to shell rock, which only the hardest blow of the hammer can break. And, as these seas abound in shell and coral, here is to be seen the beginning and something of the progress of the existence of lime and limestone.

By putting all these visible facts in relation with one another, we may conjecture with reasonable certainty what was, at a certain time, the condition of these mountains, and some of the changes which they have since undergone. We may suppose that, in some past epoch, Aden and the ocean stood here together in solitary grandeur; both, perhaps, boiling up and foaming with primordial fires—Aden being a rock inlet, wholly surrounded by the ocean, which washed on every side the dark flanks and under-sea foundations of Sham-shan. The ocean at length began to teem with its living inhabitants, which performed their stated functions of reproduction, and then died, leaving their coral and shell exuviæ to collect in their rocky sea-beds, until, by the agitation of the waters, they were broken to fragments through mutual collision, which accumulated, and were thrown up in sand on the edge of the sea, and appeared in little beaches and downs, between the shorter ridges, and, at length, in the lapse of many ages, grew up into the wide plains of sand and of sand-rock which constitute the shores of Aden.

I am very faithfully yours, C. Cushing.

Francis Markoe, Jr., Esq.,
Corresponding Secretary of National Institute.

RICHARD THOMPSON — THE SYDNEY HERALD — AND OURSELVES.

In the *Sydney Morning Herald* of April 18th, 1844, the following unvarnished paragraph appears:

" There is a long article on the Exports of New South Wales, in the COLONIAL MAGAZINE, in which a deal of credit is given to a ' Mr. Thompson, of Port Macquarie,' for having 'embarked very extensively in the speculation of salting beef for export,' and by his success having 'encouraged an extended imitation of his enterprising example.' It is stated, also, that Mr. Thompson's exertions have ' opened a new epoch in the colonial history of our Australasian settlements,' &c., &c. *Who is this Mr. Thompson*, who has thus benefited the colonists? *We have no recollection of having heard of him before*; and yet, as residents, as close observers of the passing events of the day, we should have thought that the sounds of the trumpet of fame would have reached our ears before the reverberation could have been heard in England; but it is often, alas! the fate of genius to be slighted by those who are benefited by its exertions."

In the numbers of the *Herald* published at the commencement of 1842, we find this prècise Mr. Thompson loudly lauded for his enterprising temperament, and interjections, optative moods, and other adjumenta employed to secure auspicious omens on his behalf, as a genuine beef-salting experimentalist. Here then is a plain illustration of the *obliviscor* (we have no recollection) rather than the *recordor* mode of pleading. *Encore.* In the identical *obliviscor* journal, (one of the most valuable, undoubtedly, in the Australian colonies,) of the date of June 2, 1842, this very Mr. Thompson, not a Thompson *ejusdem nominis et speciei*, not merely of the self-same name and nature, but *every inch the same*, like royalty under all circumstances, is thus spoken of as an hydrographer:

" Mr. Thompson's Map of North-Eastern Australia will embrace the coast of the South Pacific, from Farquhar's Inlet in 32° S., to the embouchure of the M'Leay, northward of Crescent Head, in 31°. It will comprise the whole of the County of Macquarie, and will exhibit that singular portion of the table-land known as New England, together with the country to the westward, as far as the Australian Agricultural Company's station on the Peel. It will present all the rivers between the above parallels, including the M'Leay, now for the first time correctly laid down, with its remarkable serpentine windings and its various tributaries, from its confluence with the Apsley, to Tryal Bay, on the coast. The map will also present the immense tract of table-land lately discovered by Mr. Ralfe, and ascertained by that officer to extend in a south-easterly direction from the main mountain range to the head of Yessebah Brook, (a tributary of the M'Leay,) and thence round Wirrikembe to New England. All the ranges and their passes are likewise laid down, together with the stupendous road from the harbour of Port Macquarie to the table-land; and lastly, this map will exhibit all the appropriated lands in the county of Macquarie. Such a map, if even an approximation to correctness, will be a very important document; and as it is to be dedicated to one of the largest landholders in the district, who must be well acquainted with its localities, we presume that he may be considered as, in some measure, guaranteeing its fidelity."

This to us appears something like innate evidence of obliviousness, or of inconsistency, or of mistake. We have no desire to employ foreign aid, nor is it necessary, when the case is so simple; besides, our own feeling for the offender is of the most peaceable and pleasant, shall we acknowledge, grateful kind, also.

But, having demonstrated from premises furnished by the *Herald* himself, that *this here Thompson* is not *a* but *the Thompson*, a few words from contemporaries may be useful, as clearly showing, that we did not make an injurious, mischievous, or mendacious statement by our laudatory remarks on Thompson's colonial labours. *The Sydney Weekly Register*, in its criticism on the opera of Cindrella, (date, Feb. 17, 1844,) says, "The *libretto* has undergone for the present occasion a complete *rifacimento* by Mr. *Richard Thompson*, of the *Australian*, whose fertile pen is equally ready, whether the subject be theatricals or theology—politics or poesy; in each and all of which he has put forth things far from common-place. This arrangement of the dialogue of Cindrella is marked by a style of diction, in which good taste and dramatic skill are predominant." Here again *Richard Thompson* is a name known amongst men. We have not quoted the *Australian's* defence of ourselves *for obvious reasons*, "*nec istis defensoribus egemus*,"—nor have we any regret to express for our misdeeds, beyond what is demanded, for having too warmly applauded colonial patriotism —sympathized with victims of enterprise—and, in so doing, come into collision with the *memory* of an able, honest, and popular journalist. If explanation or exculpation could in any degree promote the objects most dear to the *Herald* and to Ourselves, we should willingly pursue the subject—but it could not, nor should the cause of this *eclaircissement* ever have arisen.

SONNET:

THE EMPEROR OF FRANCE, AND THE KING OF THE FRENCH.

"Look here, upon this portrait, and on this."—SHAKSPEARE.

WHAT pair is this, that Glory's suffrage woo?
Indelibly upon the scroll of fame
She hath already written either name,
For History to judge between the two.
And Fancy's eye forestals with prescience true
The sentence: joying as the fierce acclaim
Which hail'd the conqueror dies, and envious blame
Struck dumb, the man of peace receives his due.
His was renown, who, over Europe roll'd
The tide of war, and hounded armies on;
But lasting praise is his who France doth hold
Curb'd, and the world in quiet.—Mark, you yon,
In rubric cipher this, and that in gold,
The names of ORLEANS and NAPOLEON.

Oct. 13, 1844. C. J. C.

SWANSEA SMELTERS, AND CUBA COPPER-MINES.

The following article, copied from Hunt's Magazine, in its authentic and ambitious form, is entitled to the serious attention of the coal-proprietors, ship-owners, and smelters of South Wales. The Americans are our enterprising competitors in every branch of trade; and the civilized countries of the world, availing themselves of our generosity and free-trade propensities, are acquiring the knowledge of our arts, and employing our ready-made machinery with such effect, that "the cards will beat the card-makers" shortly, if the utmost vigilance be not exerted. As prevention is better than cure, let the British smelters and ship-owners take warning from the facts here put forth, and by determined activity—the maintenance of fair, not exorbitant, prices, as interest and wages—in fact, by a wisely-regulated conduct, prevent the emigration of their long-established, and lucrative, occupation, from the rich coal-fields of Glamorganshire to the shores of North America, now so much nearer to those of England than they were only twenty years since, by the application of steam-power to navigation.

THE COPPER-MINES OF CUBA.

"We were not aware of the commercial importance of the copper-mines of Cuba, until our attention was called to the subject by the letter of George Ditson, Esq., the United States consul at Neuvitas, which we give below. We have since conversed with several gentlemen, familiar with mining in Cuba and our own country, from whom we have gathered many valuable facts; and to George Bacon, Esq., the secretary of the 'Copper Company' of New York, we are indebted mainly for the information embraced in the remarks with which we now introduce Mr. Ditson's letter.

"The quantity of copper ore shipped from Cuba to England, during the year, from 1st July, 1842, to 30th June, 1843, was 28,886 tons of 21 cwt., and the amount for which the ore sold at Swansea, Wales, previously to smelting, was £408,865, or 1,978,896 dollars; from Valparaiso, Chili, and Copiapo, 12,804 tons, which sold for £295,084, or 1,428,206 dollars, and making a total of 3,407,102 dollars, imported into Great Britain from these two sources. The whole amount of copper ore sold in England and Wales, during the same period, of one year, was 7,790,749 dollars; the ore imported from Cuba and the west coast of South America, is, therefore, nearly one-half the amount smelted, or nearly equal in value to the product of the mines of Cornwall and Ireland.

"The vast product of the mines of Great Britain, and the extent of her smelting works, together with the fact that English merchants appreciate the value of copper ore and mines, and are working the mines of Cuba and Chili, give to her the entire control of the copper of the world; the business of smelting, being also in the hands of wealthy capitalists, its value remains steady under all circumstances. The quantity smelted by one house, in the same period, was £478,293. 8s. 5d., or 2,314,940 dollars.

"By reference to the sales of ore, since June 30th, 1843, we find the foreign supply continues steady, and Mr. Bacon entertains no doubt will be found to have increased when the report for the last year is received.

"The whole of this vast amount of copper, which Cuba produces, and a share of that from South America, might readily be transferred to the port of New York. The English companies in Cuba have been anxiously inquiring for a position nearer to their mines, where they might smelt their ores, and avoid the duty in England of £4. 10s. and £6 per ton of copper. No position offers advantages equal to New York; and the business of smelting, if established here, would command the whole ore of the island, English, as well as Spanish and American, beside offering a new branch of trade to South America, from whence our ships now bring large quantities of copper, but no ore, there being no market here for want of a smelting establishment.

"Not the least difficulty exists, except the want of information in relation to the existence of so large a business passing by us, and the courage to invest a few thousand dollars in demonstrating the best method of smelting. The English method is not the best, and would long since have been abandoned, but that the whole is in the hands of five or six houses, who have a vast amount of capital already invested in their works, are subject to no competition, and are able to realize large profits by their present method.

"The mines of Mr. Ditson are situated about twenty-five miles from the port of Neuvitas, near the line of the Neuvitas and Principe railroad, now constructing. Their operations can hardly be said to have commenced—everything is new; the information necessary to the prosecution of mining, to be acquired, shafts to be sunk, machinery to be erected, and the late drought in the island has retarded their operations; yet the company have shipped to England, since their operations commenced, (two or three years since,) about 1,000 tons of ore, yielding from 12 to 20 per cent, and which must have furnished ample means for the prosecution of their business; and having now erected their steam-engine and other machinery, they will be able to increase their product to 100 or 200 tons per month, all of which must go to England, unless his wish, 'that American furnaces require them,' is realized.

"The copper company of New York have recently purchased three mines in the neighbourhood of Mr. Ditson, and are preparing to prosecute the same business. Want of capital is retarding their operations, and, like most *new* projects, it meets with but little encouragement from individuals of capital and influence; should it, however, outlive its difficulties, and, by the establishment of smelting works—a leading object of the company—open a new branch of commerce to New York, and bring only one quarter of the copper ore of Cuba to our market, of the value of half a million of dollars, their efforts, which are now but little known and less appreciated, will be more properly estimated.

"That our readers may be able to form some opinion of the profit of mining, and the value of copper mines in Cuba, we may state, on the authority of Mr. Bacon, that the Royal Santiago Company, at St. Jago de Cuba, realised a net profit of £32,000 from their business, for twelve months of 1843 and 1844, equal to about 50 per cent per annum, upon the capital invested; and that the Cuba Company paid for their mines £480,000, upwards of 2,000,000 dollars.

"A Spanish company are also working mines in the neighbourhood of Mr. Ditson, which is probably one of the richest copper districts in the world, and quite unoccupied. They have shipped to England some hundred tons of ore, through New York; and the mines at Cienfurgos, worked by an American company, also send their ores to England, through the port of New York, several cargoes of which have been forwarded within the last year.

"*Consulate of the United States of America.*

"NEUVITAS, CUBA, June 19th, 1844.

"DEAR SIR:—Aware that you, as well as a great portion of your readers, are deeply interested in all that concerns the commerce of the United States, allow me to present my opinions, along with the many widely-disseminated truths of your invaluable Magazine, upon a very important branch of industry, which has, as yet, unfortunately, received little or no attention in our country—I mean, the smelting of copper ores, which is so productive of revenue to Great Britain.

"Are you aware that there are several American companies in the island of Cuba, who ship the ores of their copper-mines to England, under enormous expenses of duty, freight, &c., for want of purchasers in the United States? Such is the fact. Now, if these ores could be smelted in the States, even at double the sum it costs in Swansea, (which is £2. 10s. per ton, and called return charge,) hundreds and thousands of tons, not only from Cuba, but from South America, would be sent direct to the United States in American vessels, and thus open almost a new channel of commercial advantage, and give to our own shipping that profit of freight they should have, and might have had, years ago, with those various other benefits which have so long been ceded, without a struggle, and almost without a thought, to European energy and enterprise.

"The reason why we could afford to pay twice as much for smelting our ores in America as it costs in England, is, because the other expenses connected with the introduction and sale of it at the latter place, so far exceed what it could possibly cost in the former. The expenses on a cargo of mineral, from the time it leaves New York till it is sold in Liverpool or Swansea, amount to nearly *one-fifth* of its entire value; and if it is shipped direct from Cuba to the latter place, they will exceed even that, as freight is usually from £2. 10s. to £3. per ton. To prove to you the truth of what I have here stated, I beg to present a copy of account sales, rendered to me by my agents in England. (*See subjoined table.*)

"The freight of mineral from this place to New York, for instance, is from five to seven dollars per ton. There is no duty on copper ores introduced into the United States. In sending ores to the States, for smelting, the wastage would be little, compared with what it is by our present and cheapest mode of getting it to Swansea.

"Several copper-mines have recently been opened in this district, and some of them bid fair to be very productive. At the one in which I am interested, I have put up a high-pressure engine—the first steam machinery ever introduced into this province. Mineral appears to be very abundant here, and I shall be delighted to know, when I am again loading American vessels with ores, that American furnaces require them.

"This subject of smelting, at which I have hinted in the above very hasty and imperfect sketch, I shall endeavour to present to our government in a more extended form for its consideration, in order that it may have an eye to the minutest interests of the commerce of the United States, as well as the welfare of its subjects here and in other foreign places.

I have the honour to remain, dear Sir,

Your very obedient servant,

GEORGE DITSON, VICE-CONSUL.

FREEMAN HUNT, ESQ.

Account Sales of Copper Ore received from New York, per Joseph Cunard, *Captain Harrison, and sold here by order, on account and risk of John Simmons & Son, Boston.—Sold at three months' credit.*

1844.		T.	C.	Q.	Lbs.	
March 21. Pile No. 1, weighing		60	10	3	0	
Moisture, 250½-7,000	43 cwt. 1 qr. 8 lbs.	2	15	3	20	
Allowance, 24½ lb. per 21 cwt.	12 " 2 " 12 "					
	20 cwt.	57	14	3	8	

T. C. Q. Lbs.
Or, 54 20 3 0 of 21 cwt. product, 18¾, st'd 90¼
Price £14. 8s. 6d. .... £793 4 .

	T.	C.	Q.	Lbs.	£	s.	d.
Brought forward..................					£793	4	1
1844.							
Pile No. 2, weighed	28	8	3	0			
Moisture, 397½-7,000 .... 32 cwt. 1 qr. 5 lbs. / Allowance, 24¼ lbs. per 21 cwt.... 5 " 3 " 19 "	1	18	0	24			
20 cwt................	26	10	2	4			
T. C. Q. Lbs. Or, 25 5 2 0—21 cwt. product, 19⅛, st'd 90.							
Price, £14. 14s. 0*d*.					371	7	0
					£1,164	11	1

Charges.

	£	s.	d.	£	s.	d.
Insurance, £1,150 c. 25, and 3 per cent, ...	£16	3	6			
Freight, 15, and 5 per cent per ton, 89 tons, 7 cwt., 3 qr., 10 lb.,	70	7	10			
Bond, dock, town dues, and entry,......	5	4	6			
Duty, 16 tons, 10 cwt., 1 qr., 12 lb., £4 10, and 5 per cent premium,	78	0	10			
Rec. weighing, lightering due, baskets, &c., ...	10	5	2			
Yard rent, crushing and delivering 84 tons,...............	33	12	0			
Sampling ex., and assaying,.................	2	5	0			
Int. on charges, 3 months, ...	2	13	10			
Bank com., ¼ per cent, on £1,164 11*s*. 1*d*., ...	2	18	2			
Com., brokage, &c., 4 per cent, ...	46	11	7			
				268	2	5
E. E. Due 24th June, 1844, ...				£896	8	8

"*To the Editor of the Merchants' Magazine.*

"DEAR SIR,—I was much pleased with a letter which appeared in the last number of your excellent periodical, from George Ditson, Esq., Vice-Consul of the United States at Neuvitas, on the subject of the copper-mines of Cuba; suggesting, also, the great benefit which would accrue to the manufacturing, as well as the commercial interests of the country, by the establishment of smelting works in the neighbourhood of New York; in which opinion, I perfectly agree with him.

"As New York is the great emporium of American commerce, it is consequently the port where most of the foreign, as well as American copper ores, are sent, to be shipped to England, for smelting. No better place, therefore, could be selected for the establishment of copper works, than somewhere in this neighbourhood; and, in my opinion, Red Hook Point, near the south end of the Atlantic dock, would be a most eligible location; as there is every facility there for discharging cargoes of copper ore, as well as coal for smelting it, and ample space for the erection of suitable buildings, not only for smelting the ore into cakes, but for drawing the copper into bars, and rolling it into sheets. The establishment of copper works would also give an impulse to *copper mining operations throughout the Union*, as there would then be a ready market for all the American copper ore raised, without sending it to England to be smelted; and, by amalgamating American ores with foreign, better copper, (as to the temper and malleability of it,) could be made, than from one kind of copper ore only. Moreover, the copper made here could be sold cheaper than that which is imported; as the freight and insurance on the ore sent to England, as well as on the manufactured copper sent back again, would be saved—independent of the duty on the ore, (£4. 10s. per ton,) and the other heavy charges upon the importation of it into England. I think these are good and sufficient reasons for the establishment of copper works near New York; and coming, as they do, from one who was formerly engaged as a mineral broker in England, and is *practically acquainted with the modus operandi* of sampling, assaying, roasting, and smelting copper ores, they may be well worthy of the consideration of those who feel interested in the matter. The establishment of such works, independent of the great advantage they would be to the country in a national and commercial point of view, would also be a very profitable investment of capital, for those who might embark in the undertaking; and, hoping soon to see them in operation,

I remain, dear sir, yours, respectfully, J. T. BAILEY.

FREEMAN HUNT, Esq., *Editor of the Merchants' Magazine.*

BRITISH ENTERPRISE—ITS RESULTS AND REWARDS IN SOUTH AMERICA:

TO BE COMPARED WITH THOSE IN OUR BRITISH COLONIES.

[The singular fact, that a ship is at this moment afloat on salt-water, at an elevation of 18,000 feet above the level of the sea, and there carrying on a lucrative traffic, is so little known, that we insert the following brief mention of it, as likely to be read with some interest, as well as from our having, on former occasions, published articles on the history and affairs of the Rio Plata, by the same writer, whose views, therein set forth, appear, from subsequent events and other recent advices, to be just, correct, and comprehensive.]

In the year 1825, the firm of Rundell and Bridge (of London) having entered upon arrangements for the purchase of the gold mines of Tipuani, and the emerald mines on the river Illumani, in Upper Peru, sent a gentleman (Mr. Page) as their agent, to complete the acquisition of the property. The speculation, as regarded the gold-mines, was tolerably successful; but the emeralds found at Illumani proved of inferior quality generally. These mines are situate on the borders of the great Salt-Water Lake of Chuqueta, which is 248 miles in length, and nearly 150 miles in breadth, and 18,000 feet above the level of the sea on the Cordillera of the Andes; its depth, in many parts, is such that it cannot be sounded, and the peculiar blue colour of its waters resembles that of the sea. There are other mining establishments in the same vicinity as the Tipuani and Illumani, belonging to two English gentlemen, (General O'Brien, and John Begg, Esq.,) who are also part owners of those above named. Those of most importance are the copper-mines of Corocora, and the famous silver-mines of Salcedo, at Puno.

The only vegetable productions found in this part of these high regions, are a small red potato, called "Chusina," and a few plants, one of which affords a seed called "Quinaué" much used by the aborigines as an article of food; but on the eastern side of the lake, at a place called Copacavana, and in several of the valleys of Bolivia, there is found an abundance of Indian corn, barley, potatoes, and fruits.

The difficulty of procuring provisions for the considerable number of Indians employed in the mines, suggested the idea of building a vessel for the purpose of communicating with the opposite shore of the great lake; and Mr. Page, Mr. Begg, and General O'Brien, determined to enter upon the attempt, Mr. Page undertaking to superintend the construction of a brig * of 150 tons. He proceeded in the first place to the port of Arica, where he procured the necessary iron-work, rigging, sails, &c., &c., from a condemned ship, which he there met with and purchased. These materials he transported, at vast trouble and expense, to the mouth of the river Apolobamba, where he found timber (roble) of very fine quality, closely resembling English oak.

At the spot where this river falls into the lake, Mr. Page established his dockyard, having engaged a few carpenters and shipwrights at Arica,

* A schooner should have been the construction.

and at the end of two years' labour and perseverance, the brig *Julia* was launched on the waters of the great lake of Chuquita.* The brig subsequently became the property of a gentleman of fortune residing at La Paz; she is chiefly engaged in fulfilling the original objects of her construction —transporting agricultural products, &c., from the valleys of Bolivia to the mining districts of Puna and Lampas, whereby she yields to her owner an amount of profit exceeding anything of her size in any trade or any part of the known world.

General O'Brien, when on his way from Lima to Buenos Ayres, sailed in her over the lake, and was nearly lost on the island of Titicaca† in a severe gale; she was commanded by a Swede, and in every way well found, except that her anchors were not of sufficient weight, owing to the difficulty of conveying over the mountain-tracts of the Andes such as her size required.

Mr. Begg was the first person who projected the application of steam to the navigation of the west coast of South America, and in 1827 caused a steamer to be built, called the *Telica*, which was sent round Cape Horn, but was unfortunately blown up at Paita. The undertakings of these gentlemen were such as had always been deemed impracticable; they carried steam-engines over the Andes, they cut an adit of 2,000 yards through the metallic mountains of Lacaycota, they formed a canal (from the waters of the mines) intersected by nine locks, by means whereof the ore is raised, in flat-bottomed iron boats, more than one hundred feet, to a railroad that conveys it to their mills (trapiches).

Most of these details have been communicated by a gentleman who was present when General Gamarra, president of Peru, effected his escape from General Salaverre, when only a few hundred yards in advance of his pursuers, by embarking hurriedly on board the brig *Julia*, and crossing the lake of Chuquita.

General O'Brien is now resident at the Rio Plata, and owner of one of the finest estates in that country. The eminent and gallant services rendered by him to the cause of independence, and in furthering the prosperity of South America, have caused him to be universally esteemed and respected; even during the present afflicting warfare, in which person and property have suffered, General O'Brien, and his, have gone unscathed. His open hospitality and urbanity of manners, displayed alike to all, have secured for him these considerations, which perhaps but few persons, even in this country, can deservedly boast of.

By decrees of late date, (August,) the Buenos-Ayrean Government had thrown open the trade to the populous and important district of Paraguay, and further permitting the free export of wheat and flour to all parts not

---

* Mr. Page, to whose skill and energy the completion is much indebted, did not live to see it consummated; shortly before the vessel was ready to be launched, he had occasion to go to Arequipa, and there met his death by a very extraordinary accident. On a Sunday evening, as he was walking with H. M.'s consul, (Mr. Crompton,) to see a procession that accompanied a minister of Bolivia on his public entrée, and whilst passing under a balcony, in which were fourteen ladies and gentlemen, the structure gave way, precipitating all into the street, thereby killing Mr. Page, with three other persons, whilst Mr. Crompton escaped with some severe bruises.

† The island of Titicaca is spoken of in the traditionary legends of Peru, as the birth-place of the first of the race of the Incas, Manco Copac.

occupied by the enemy, (*c'est à dire*, the Montevidean party,) for the suppression of whom the Buenos-Ayrean government was making great exertions and preparations; the nature and duties whereof have been set forth in a recent pamphlet by Mr. Mallalieu, published by Blackwood, and in former numbers of your Magazine by G. T. W.

REVIEWS OF NEW BOOKS.

ART. I.—*Our Indian Empire.* By CHARLES MAC FARLANE. 2 vols. small 4to. London: Charles Knight & Co.

The close of this valuable publication would seem to call for some further notice at our hands, from the nature of the subject, notwithstanding our oft-repeated eulogies upon numbers past; and we readily consent to answer the appeal. This part of the work opens with the celebrated Burmese War, and closes with the annexation of Scinde, embracing a period of less than twenty years, yet so full of incident and change, that the terse style of the author alone could have secured the narrative from exceeding the just limits of a readable history. Lord William Bentinck's administration of Indian affairs is impartially related, but his character treated with less admiration than it unquestionably deserves, and undoubtedly enjoys amongst the ablest and most illustrious of his contemporaries. For the evidence of this fact we refer to the eminent individual, one of the wisest men in Europe, now seated on the throne of France, and to our great chieftain, the Duke of Wellington. However, we do not accuse Mr. Mac Farlane of prejudice; our regret only extends to the absence of any special approbation of that virtuous, humane, and enlightened nobleman's conduct. How characteristic of the man was his determined agency in suppressing Suttees!—Another omission in this particular part of "Our Indian Empire" is that of Mr. Buckingham's name. We have not certainly read every single word in the volume before us, but we have actually looked into every page, in vain, however, for the name of one who first called on England to open the trade with India, abolish the commercial monopoly of the Company, and allow free-trade to British subjects with British possessions, at all events—whether such policy might ever be capable of extension to foreign countries or not. We still hope that this indefatigable reformer's name is commemorated in some note, or reference, in the interesting and useful volume before us, for he was, most indisputably, the founder of free-trade with India, and the cause of the amendment in the Company's Charter.

In the recent recall of Lord Ellenborough, the public, recurring to one of their accustomed vulgar errors, conceived that the Court of Directors had exceeded their authority in that act; it will perhaps be acceptable to some of our readers to know the real state of the law on this point.

"On the 27th of May Mr. Grant expressed the satisfaction with which his Majesty's government had learned the termination of the appeal to the ballot in Leadenhall-street. He stated it to be the anxious wish of ministers to accommodate themselves as far as possible to the views and feelings of the Company, and he agreed to increase the guarantee fund to 2,000,000*l*. Other minor points were yielded as requested by the Court of Directors or by the general Court. They had claimed to have the exercise of the same powers as the Company now possessed under their charter. To this Mr. Grant replied, that his Majesty's ministers did not contemplate curtailing or impairing these powers; and that whatever changes parliament might, in its wisdom, see fit to adopt, could, he did not doubt, be made without detriment to the substantial authority of the Company." The Court of Directors had conceived that the government, through the Board of Control, intended to claim and exercise a veto on the recall of governors-general, &c., as exercised by the Court of Directors. On this point Mr. Grant said, "If the words have been inserted in consequence of the hint thrown out in the memorandum that the Board should have a veto on the recall of governors and military commanders in India, I must state that *it is not the intention of his Majesty's ministers to insist on that suggestion.*" Thus the power of recall was left undisturbed in the hands of the Directors."—Vol. ii. p. 350.

We now come to those changes, the separation of the legislative from the commercial duties of the Company—the retention of the former, but abandonment of the latter, to which the literary labours of Mr. Buckingham so materially contributed. The bill for reforming the East India Company having been approved openly by parliament, and further opposition becoming more than vain,—

"On the 28th of August it became law, the royal assent being given to it by commission. The rapidity with which it was carried through parliament was thought as extraordinary as the change which it effected in the character of the Company was extensive. Much of the detail must necessarily be suppressed; but the following is a brief analysis of the principal clauses of the Act 3 & 4 William IV, c. 85.

Section 1. The government of the British territories in India is continued in the hands of the Company until 1854. The real and personal property of the Company to be held in trust for the crown, for the service of India.

2. The privileges and powers granted in 1813, and all other enactments concerning the Company not repugnant to this new act, are to continue in force until April, 1854

3. From 22d April, 1834, the China and tea trade of the Company to cease, and to be opened to all his Majesty's subjects.

4. The Company to close its commercial concerns, and to sell all its property not required for the purposes of government.

9. The debts and liabilities of the Company are charged on the revenues of India.

43. The governor general in council is empowered to legislate for India, and for all persons, whether British or native, foreigners or others, and for all courts of justice, and for all servants of the Company; but he is not to do anything to affect the Mutiny Acts, or the prerogative of the crown, or the authority of parliament, or the constitution or rights of the said Company, or any part of the unwritten laws or constitution of the United Kingdom, whereon may depend the allegiance of any person, or the sovereignty or dominion of the crown over any part of India.

44. If the laws thus made by the governor-general are disallowed by the authorities in England, they shall be annulled by the governor-general.

46. The governor-general in council, without the previous sanction of the Court of Directors, must not make any law or regulation whereby power shall be given to any courts of justice, other than the courts of justice established by his Majesty's charters, to sentence to the punishment of death any of his Majesty's natural-born subjects born in Europe, or the children of such subjects, or which shall abolish any of the courts of justice established by his majesty's charters.

51. This bill not to affect the right of parliament to legislate in future for India.

53. A law commission to be appointed to inquire into the jurisdiction, &c., of existing courts of justice and police establishments, and the operation of the laws.

81. Any natural born subject of England may proceed by sea to any part or place within the limit of the Company's charter having a custom-house establishment, and may reside thereat, or pass through to other parts of the Company's territories to reside thereat.

86. Lands within the Company's territories may be purchased and held by any persons where they are resident.

87. No native, nor any natural-born subject of his Majesty resident in India, shall by reason o his religion, place of birth, descent, or colour, be disabled from holding any office or employment under the government of the Company.

88. Slavery to be immediately mitigated, and abolished as soon as possible.

89. And as the present diocese is of too great an extent for the incumbent thereof to perform efficiently all the duties of the office without endangering his health and life, his Majesty may found two bishoprics, one of Madras and the other of Bombay, with revenues respectively of 24,000 sicca rupees by the year.

94. The Bishop of Calcutta to be metropolitan in India.

112. The island of St. Helena to be taken from the Company and vested in the crown."—Vol. ii. page 353.

Henceforth the native Anglo-Indians were freemen, British-born subjects free to settle in India, and British merchants to share in the commercial benefits of that vast region.

In our past notices of this excellent epitome, we impressed upon the writer and the reader the incalculable value of authorities, references, evidences—without which history is reduced to the level of fable or fiction. Never was fact more clearly demonstrated than in the seventeenth chapter now open before us. The note itself, which we extract, will explain our meaning without the addition of a single remark, beyond this, that Mr. Thornton has omitted to give his authorities, by which omission he leaves his rival, for the present, at all events, in triumphant possession of the field of contest.

"The councils of the inferior presidencies of Madras and Bombay were not done away with. We know not what the Company's servant and historiographer, Edward Thornton, Esq., means by saying in the last volume of his "History of the British Empire in India," which was published only last year, that no council has been appointed for Bengal, and that the executive of that presidency is administered by the governor-general as governor, but without a council. Was not Mr. Macaulay made by the Whig government a fifth member of the Bengal or Calcutta Supreme Council? Did not Mr. Macaulay's successor claim the right of sitting in council on all occasions? And was it not one of Lord Ellenborough's first acts to quote the Act of 3 & 4 William IV. to that gentleman, and to tell him that he had no business to attend the council except when legislative matters were under discussion, when his attendance as a lawyer could not be dispensed with? Will Mr. Thornton inform us how all this could have happened if no council had been appointed for Bengal?"

Lord Auckland's administration, and the miseries that either followed or sprang from it, are too fresh in the recollection of the public to be noticed here: they are feelingly related in Mr. Mac Farlane's pages, and we think faithfully also. Had he quoted an extract from the *Englishman*, itself a quotation from the London *East India Telegraph*, in which the motives of Dost Mohammed were unfolded, and the disasters of Affghanistan plainly foretold, it would have been an interesting, perhaps valuable admonition to statesmen, who repose a blind and infatuated confidence in agents whom they have once selected. Here we must pause, having only space to give the writer's recommendation to the study of Indian history, as one of the best incentives to the reading of his own book, which we do not hesitate to say will and ought to be widely known.

"In order to avoid debatable ground, and for the motives which have been already stated, we conclude our narrative, which we have endeavoured to conduct throughout in a spirit of fairness and impartiality. We shall have done some good if we draw attention to a vast and most important subject, which has been too much neglected, notwithstanding the undeniable fact that every Englishman has an immediate interest in our Indian Empire. The generality of readers have been deterred by the bulk and number of the books written about India, by strange and constantly varying orthographies, and other affectations, and by the too frequently prolix, tedious style of our Anglo-Indian writers, who have made that "harsh and crabbed" which is not so intrinsically. But, as materials, these very books, or many of them, are truly excellent, having been written by men who were themselves actors in the scenes and events they describe, or who passed their lives in a country which is scarcely to be understood without a long residence in it. To the excellence and authenticity of these materials is to be added the interest of a narrative or of a course of events full of the most startling, exciting, and romantic interest, and of the most varied character. One of the best interests of all, or that which arises out of our nationality, is assuredly not wanting: the way in which our empire in the East has been acquired, enlarged, and maintained—making allowance for every fault, blunder, or even crime—reflects the highest honour on the character, the steady perseverance, the policy, and the valour of Englishmen; and never, since the days of Clive down to those of Pollock and Napier, has a more brilliant valour been displayed in any part of the world by British troops than in our Indian Empire and the countries which border upon it. Let it never be forgotten, that when our national greatness and our reputation seemed to be on the decline in Europe, and the glory of our arms was obscured in the West, that reputation and glory shone forth, through the genius of Warren Hastings and the ability and courage of the officers he employed, bright as the morning sun, in the East. And let it ever be remembered that India is the school which has produced some of our most eminent men, and which mainly helped to form the great Captain of the age, the illustrious Wellington."

ART. II.—*Lorimier's Patent Transparent Planes*, for Drawing from Nature or from Models. London: Dobbs, Ackerman, Reeves, Newman, and all Printsellers.

The best, simplest, and most manageable invention, for the correct delineation of objects by persons totally ignorant of the art of drawing, yet invented. A transparent medium, (prepared paper,) black, white, or coloured, is placed at the distance of about ten inches from the eye, and the object viewed through it, the eye being guarded by a fixed sight. Let the operator then sketch with a pencil, which the patentee supplies, the image of the size he finds it depicted on the medium, and his copy will be a faithful representation, in fact, a correct drawing, only reduced in the ratio of the distances of the object and image from the eye. We have ourselves experimented before now, in our pedestrian excursions, with the Camera Lucida, unsuccessfully; that beautiful application of the prism requiring the hand of a tolerable draughtsman: with *Lorimier's* medium we have been eminently successful. The advantages of this portable and simple invention are many and important. The clever draughtsman will carry away an exact copy of his original in a moment of time; the unskilful in that elegant art will furnish his journal with sketches of all scenes of interest and curiosity that have arrested and delighted his attention; from these he may subsequently select choice views, and place the chosen favourites in the hands of an accomplished artist to be translated into finished paintings. Sympathizing more with the tourist and the traveller, we dwell with unmixed pleasure on the facilities afforded by the transparent medium for recording those ideas which the pen is unable to trace; but the inventor, with perfect truth, asserts its meritorious character in economizing the time of architect, engineer, land-agent, and surveyor, designer, engraver, drawing-master, *et hoc genus omne*. Price and portability must not be omitted from the numerous recommendations which we are enabled to offer in favour of the transparent drawing planes

---

ART. III.—*The Young Husband, or Hints to regulate the Conduct of Young Men who have entered, or are about to enter, the Married State.* By ARTHUR FREELING. London: Houlston and Stoneman, Paternoster Row.

Some say wooing is undoing—marrying marring—for where is a good wife to be found?

For fain would I lead a single life,
If I could get me a good wife.

But here lies the puzzle—here the deep river—here the barrier in the highway of happiness. A number of birds fed about a cage, and were rather pleased with their lot so long as they could fly away at their pleasure; but when they were caught, and could not get loose again, although they had the same food, they pined away sullenly at the loss of their liberty, and would not eat again. Many talk too lightly, and act too thoughtlessly, in this particular case made and provided; and, above all, there are many who, having acted inconsiderately, and finding themselves in the gin, have not the knowledge, the resolution, the philosophy, so to improve their circumstances, that their captivity shall prove a very blessing. Such a little mentor as Mr. Freeling's memoranda is the best companion for all so situated.

Levius fit patientiâ quicquid corrigere est nefas, "What can't be cured must be endured," is no bad motto, for there are many who are incompetent, in any case, to govern themselves; and what better can such men do than listen to the admonitions and accept the guidance of a virtuous high-minded woman? Our author treats his subject playfully, pleasantly, philosophically,—commencing with the first steps in the Journey, he advises in the choice of a partner, and proceeds to point out to those already married, how to secure a haven of happiness. The lover will find advantage in consulting these pages, the bridegroom learn the secret of preventing disunion, the father the most effectual means of maintaining it unbroken. Believing that much of the indifference, if not unhappiness, witnessed in married life, arises from a very false estimate of the female mind, not only by worthless, ignorant, and idle husbands, but by men otherwise of excellent education and understanding, we think the author's chapter upon the influence of woman is entitled to the most serious attention. In this the key will be found to unlock the human heart,—here the keystone of that arch of peace which should overshadow, as the bow in the heavens, domestic life, will be plainly seen. Many valuable passages might be extracted for the edification of our readers, but we must dismiss the interesting subject with the following:—

"The influence of a sensible woman is of no ordinary kind, and happy is the man who is thus favoured; not, indeed, that sensible women are more rare than sensible men; but because men are too apt to monopolize the entire sense of the family, (in their own opinion,) to desire the women "to leave the thinking to them,"—to treat women as automatons,—objects rather of amusement than rational beings,—as children or dolls, to be coaxed and made fools of, rather than as equals or friends, bound to one eternity: fellow-sufferers who weep in their misfortunes; as partakers and heighteners of their joys; and as being equally accountable to one God. Others again look on women as the mere slaves of their will—a sort of safety-valve for their spleen, by means of which their ill tempers find vent. Both these characters, I trust, will be far from my reader; but if he should have entertained such erroneous ideas of what woman in her higher moral capacity is, and ought to be, let me entreat him to try for a short time, (and he will then continue to do so,) by kindness and affection to draw forth the hidden treasures from the mind and the heart of his wife: if he have treated her as a mere cipher in his family, let him gradually introduce her to trust and responsibility; if he have treated her as a child, incapable of maturity of mind, let him now make her his confidant, and in the many opportunities for inference which will then occur, he will soon be aware how much he has lost by past neglect; and if he have treated her as a tyrant, if he have crushed the but half-uttered sentiment, if he have satirised her tastes and opinions; if by coldness he have thrown the oft-springing affections back upon her heart, there to wither and to die, or with the wound to rankle and to become gall,—let him try, before it be too late, to restore sufficient confidence to elicit opinion: let him then, by especial gentleness, awaken the dormant affection, and by the warmth of his love perpetuate its flow. The unadulterated love of woman is the greatest boon heaven itself can, in this world, bestow on man."

We remember in Euripides something to this effect, which we shall add at hazard—

"If fitly match'd be man and wife,
No pleasure's wanting to their life."

Art. IV.—*The War of Jehovah in Heaven, Earth, and Hell.* By Thomas Hawkins, Esq., with Illustrations by John Martin. London: Francis Baisler, Oxford Street. 1844.

This is a bold attempt,—an epic poem on the fall of Lucifer, and in the same language, too, that Milton wrote. The author is evidently a scholar, clearly a man of ambition, and possessing withal a degree of courage suited to his high pretensions and immortal theme. A classic elegance, refinement of sentiment, and perfect harmony, pervade all his lines; so that if the choice of his subject shall divide the admirers of his labours, he will yet retain their universal respect. Here terms are employed always, and only, in a poetic meaning, ranged uniformly in a poetic order, and applied to express poetic conceptions. Passing through descriptive passages with much clearness, the author reaches those where his sublimest conceptions, his grand impersonations, are looked for and introduced, and, in some instances, the display of fervid feeling and noble sentiment, that enter into his allegories, are the creations of a soul deeply imbued with poetic powers.

Distributing his poem into nine cantos, the author pursues the model that Homer left for imitation to Virgil, Ariosto, Tasso, Milton, and Klopstock,—varying from all in the single instance of referring to self-existence, which he proves from a consciousness of mental operations, in the opening stanzas of his song.

The subject may be described briefly thus: The universe is summoned, and the crime of Lucifer being stated, he is banished from the skies. Chaos and Space are next personified, one being ruined, but the other incapable of destruction, Lucifer selects the universal area for his battle-field, and there arrays his legions for impious assault upon the heavens. Of the issue of the conflict none can doubt, and the fate of the rebel angels, falling headlong from heaven, the world are prepared to hear; for Homer applies the description of such a fall to Vulcan, and Milton to Satan, in words precisely similar, and even in the exactly same part of the first book of their respective epic poems—

"From morn to eve he fell, a summer's day."

Mr. Hawkins has introduced much new machinery in the management and detail. The spirits of slaughter are conceived with great ability—the description of Lucifer wandering in the boundless realms of space, while the angels of heaven calmly eye his movements, is a passage of immense power, and the employment of the sun as a fiery fortress is remarkably bold and ambitiously imagined.

In pursuing the grand scheme of redemption, the author has exceeded much the limits which his prototype placed to his immortal poem; nor is there anything objectionable in reducing the facts and precepts of the new covenant to a poetic form, any more than those of the ancient. Impressed with this conviction, Mr. Hawkins has made the advent, temptation, and ascension of our Lord the subject of his latter cantos, and there, where the field has not been preoccupied, he is not only more, that is, entirely, original, but his very best passages, and those on which he may be content to rest his fame, are to be found. We take the following at random, but perhaps, if not rather subdued in sentiment and tone, it furnishes a fair specimen of those powers which the poet has exercised in his great poetic narrative:—

Thus these wars
Were finish'd; God his cerule chariot turned
Triumphant back, diffus'd celestial day—
Which brush'd to brightest all the golden zones,
And love omnific: all the glorious gates
Of hallow'd heaven thrown open to receive
The King, the Conqueror, the First-Begot,
And Prince of all powers in Earth and Heaven,
With acclamation all His hasting hosts
Shouting, "Ye Worlds! ye Worlds, join, join with us!
Glory, praise, power, dominion unto Him:
Salvation now is come, O heavens, rejoice
Thou first." They entering sung, "Captivity
Is captive; O thou earth, fear God, and give
To Him the glory: God the King of Saints!
Who shall not fear and glorify thy name?
Thy judgments now are manifest: rejoice,
Prophets and ye Apostles:" thus they sung
Through all the six bless'd heavens that yet the youth
Untainted kept, "O allelula, God
Omnipotent reigneth, and he shall reign
Ever and ever."

The riches of poetry are still yet enriched by the addition of eleven mezzotinto designs by Martin, not inferior to any of that great master's scriptural subjects with which he has adorned the age. The grandeur and simplicity, the singleness and power of this artist's thoughts, as developed in his works, have not been equalled by any contemporary painter of history; and his efforts to illustrate Mr. Hawkins's majestic poem, only affix the bay-leaves more lastingly to his brow.

COLONIAL INTELLIGENCE.

INDIA.—The intelligence from India, though not of a striking nature, is of considerable interest. From Calcutta it relates principally to the new and late governors-general. Sir Henry Hardinge arrived there at eight o'clock in the evening of the 23d of July, and was immediately sworn into his high office. His first act was to continue Mr. Bird as governor of Bengal. On the next and subsequent days he held levees and durbars, and has thus far gained golden opinions from all parties. The most extraordinary criticisms continued to be made on Lord Ellenborough and his acts, which have been characterised as the result of his caprices. Prior to his departure, his lordship was entertained publicly by the officers of the army at Calcutta.

The arrival in Bombay of Sir Henry Pottinger from China, was the signal of great rejoicings. He was welcomed with addresses, and with dinners, balls, &c. The chamber of commerce presented an address, to which his excellency returned a most remarkable answer, in which the late proceedings and negotiations in China are reviewed. This document is worthy of great attention, as placing the question of the opium trade in a fair light.

He embarked at Bombay on the 27th of August, on his return to Europe.

The news from the Punjaub represents that country as a prey to anarchy and confusion, and the lowest intrigues of assassination and plunder by the chiefs. Heera Singh does not appear to be fixed in his power, and expectation was afloat of the great commotions agitating the Seikhs in the month of October next, at the time of the great Hindoo festival of the Dusserah, when all the native states are in the practice of making war against their enemies. The British Indian government is the chief object of the Seikhs' hatred, and, if credit can be given to the rumours current on their frontiers, that spirit of hatred is fomented by intrigues that take their origin from Persia and Russia.

Mahommed, and his infamously notorious son, Akhbar Khan, have formed alliances (the latter a matrimonial one) with Yar Mahomet, the usurper of the sovereignty of Herat: while they are also making arrangements with Heera Singh for aiding the Seikhs in case of a conflict with the British, with a large army, in the hope of conquering and plundering the north of India. These intrigues are well known, and cannot fail to influence the future policy of Sir Henry Hardinge: for, however pledged he may be to avoid a dispute with the Seikhs, circumstances more powerful than his promises are likely to force him into a war.

It is therefore highly probable that Sir Henry Hardinge, like all prudent men, will not wait for an invasion of the British territory, in order to make effective preparations for the approaching emergency.

The rulers of Cabul, Candahar, and Herat, are described as acting with more unanimity than ever known before, and Heera Singh, notwithstanding the difficulties of his government, is eager to side with, and to be supported by, those chieftains. It is, therefore, an absurdity, to suppose that in India the British government can govern by a merely passive system. There is by far more security in the practice of rapid conquests, which awes the natives into submission.

Another report stated that Yar Mahommed had driven away the Persians, who contemplated an attack on this city. It was said also that the Wullee of Khooloom was preparing at the head of a considerable force to invade the dominions of Dhost Mahommed. The cause of the dispute is said to be the abduction of a youth of great beauty, who belonged to Wullee, but whom the Dhost detained since last year, when he came on a visit to Cabul.

In Gwalior there were some intrigues respecting the command of the Jhinsee troops, who had mutinied against their chief, Buleevunt Rao, on account of his great oppressions. It was said that an uncle of the young Maharajah would obtain the command.

Bundlekund was tranquil, and great praise was bestowed on the police batallions, and especially on the portion of them under the orders of major Ferris, for their activity and energy in putting down the disturbances, and arresting the numerous Dacoits that used to infest those districts, before the measures introduced by Lord Ellenborough led to those favourable results.

The succession to the throne of Holkar, at Indore, has been settled by the elevation to it of a son of Bhow Holkar, who had married a daughter of Hurree Rao Holkar. The young Maharajah has assumed the name of Tookajee Holkar, and promises well. He is described as a manly boy, and has conciliated the good will of the people.

Amongst the deaths on the western shores of India dnring July and August may be mentioned those of Mr. W. S. Boyd, C. S.; Dr. Jephson, assistant-surgeon; Rev. M. Valentine, and Captain Halliday, 86th regiment.

The rainy season in the north-west provinces prevented all military movements. It was stated at Agra that Sir H. Hardinge was about to undertake a journey to Allahabad, whither the lieutenant-governor of the north-western provinces was about to proceed in order to meet him. It appears probable that the new governor-general will not content himself until he shall have visited the principal military stations in those provinces. As he is freed from the minor regulations of the government of any of the presidencies, it is highly probable he will carefully examine the details of the army.

The popularity of Sir Henry Hardinge with the military is likely to be increased, as it had been rumoured in India, and as it was said on good authority, that he was empowered to raise new regiments, to add one captain to each of the actual corps, and to reintroduce the punishment of flogging into the native army. This last measure appears to be considered imperative by the generality of the officers, especially since the occurrence of the several mutinies which have latterly disgraced the troops of Madras and Bengal.

China.—The news from China does not come down later than the 21st of June. Great dissatisfaction was expressed at the meddling of the French and Americans in the now settled affairs with China. It is mentioned that Sir H. Pottinger, prior to his departure, had introduced his successor, Mr. Davis, to Keying, when they held a conversation without the aid of an interpreter. This is considered a great advantage. Admiral Sir T. Cochrane had returned from the north, on the 2nd of June. The visit of the French frigate Alcmene to Chusan and Shanghai had occasioned much excitement amongst the Chinese along the coast, so that it was considered eminently desirable that a strong naval force should be kept in the north for the protection of British life and property against the outbreaks of the mob. The American and French men-of-war Brandywine, St. Louis, Cleopatra, and Alcmene, had arrived almost simultaneously in the Chinese waters. At Canton the populace continued very unruly, manifesting, on every occasion that presented itself, a spirit of extreme discontent at the presence of foreigners. An arrow, as a wind-vane, had been placed on the top of the United States' flag-staff, and great umbrage had been taken at this by the Chinese; on what ground is not explained.

Manilla.—Advices have been received to the 1st of June. English bar was in great demand. Segars were very scarce; there will be no more exportations of cheroots from Manilla until the new crop comes in, and that cannot be sooner than eight months. Tonnage scarce, at £3. 10s. to £4 per 20 cwt.

New South Wales.—Accounts have been received from Sydney to the 20th of May, and there is a decided improvement in the general tone of them. Stock was improving in value, sheep having been sold at 5s. and 7s., up to 9s. each, according to age, &c., both at Sydney and Port Phillip, and at 7s. for cash in the latter settlement. There was a prospect, apparently, of a further rise, as the boiling-down system was already leading to an increased demand, and supplying a market for surplus stock. Nevertheless the general state of mercantile affairs at Sydney was not active.

Abstract of the revenue of the colony, exclusively of the district of Port Phillip, for the quarter ending 31st March, 1844, showing the decrease on the revenue of the same quarter of the year 1843. The total revenue for the quarter this year is £61,161 19s. 8d. being a decrease on the same quarter of 1843 of £16,817 7s. 2d. In the duties on spirits imported, there is a decrease of £3,784 13s. 10d.; and on spirits distilled in the colony £790 7s. 6d., on the amount of *ad valorem* duties on goods imported there is a still larger decrease, amounting to £4,067 11s. 10d. The falling off in the tobacco duties amounts to £469 13s. 3d.; and in auction duty and fees for auctioneers' licenses £888 3s. 5d. The decrease in the proceeds of sales of land and town allotments, is £2,901 11s. 6d.; in quit-rents and redemption of quit-rents, £3,503 7s. 6d, In short, the total decrease is £20,332 18s. 2d., while the increase amounts only to £3,515 11s., leaving, as before stated, a net decrease of £16,817 7s. 2d.

The following statement upon the recently arrived immigrants, is from the *Sydney Herald* of May 9th. On inquiry as to the engagements which have been made on board the *Elizabeth* and the *United Kingdom*, we find that of the immigrants by the former, seventeen single women, twenty-four single men, and twelve families have been engaged; and at wages not much lower than the immigrants by previous vessels. There are still on board the *Elizabeth* 107 souls without engagements; these are principally composed of couples with large families, and the parents, in some instances, have refused advantageous offers for their elder children: they labour under the impression that if they should not be engaged by to-morrow, they will be received into the immigrant barracks, but this is a mistaken notion. Their *ten days'* ration time will be up to-morrow (Friday), and they will then have to provide for themselves. Of the *United Kingdom* a similar report may be made. Nearly all the single men and single women have been engaged; but there are between twenty and thirty families, who have been accustomed to agriculture, who are still disengaged. Their time for receiving rations also expires on Friday. We regret to state that, according to the account of the immigration agent, neither of these two ships have been so clean, or apparently kept in such good order, as those immigrant vessels which have preceded them this year.

Port Phillip.—From the Port Phillip journals we are gratified to find that their list of exports are improving with rapidity, and offer satisfactory proof of the energy of the settlers. Beef, tallow, leather, bark, tobacco, and butter, appear, in large quantities, in every outward manifest; and among some miscellaneous consignments we have particularly noticed, 10,000 mutton hams by the *Flying Fish*, for the Hobart Town market. With these gratifying signs of their attention to the best interests of the province, we can excuse their somewhat erratic proceedings in political and social affairs.

On looking to the exports for the last two years, we find that the wool shipped from this port from the 1st October, 1842, to 31st March, 1843, amounted to 2,067,305 lbs.; bark during the same period, 800 tons. For the half-year commencing October, 1843, and ending March, 1844, the wool was 3,284,929 lbs.; the bark 1703 tons—showing an increase on the former of 1,214,624 lbs.; and on the latter of 903 tons. The wool shipped from last March to the 4th instant amounts to 738,821 lbs. The first export of tallow occurred in January, 1841, from which date down to the present month, 204,425 lbs. have been exported from Port Phillip.—*Port Phillip Gazette*, May 11.

Australia Felix.—Sir George Gipps has granted the Jews, resident at Melbourne, a piece of ground on which to build a synagogue.

The supposed forest of cedar between Geelong and Port Phillip, mentioned in the *Observer* of 3d February, turns out to be a species of wood altogether different from any hitherto found in Australia. Messrs. Beavor and Scott, who have lately penetrated to the site of the newly-discovered forest, find it of immense extent, and composed of trees, whose trunks are straight and free from branches to the height of about twenty-five feet, with an average circumference of nine feet. The wood is hard, solid, close-grained, and of a dark-brown colour. Whether or not these trees are identical with those previously seen and reported as cedar, the value of such extensive discoveries of new kinds of timber must afford the greatest encouragement for further research.

The decrease on the last quarter's revenue is £4,558 0s. 3d.; on the year, £13,645 2s. 1d. The deficiency is principally on the duties on spirits. The decrease in the revenue of the colony for the last quarter is £14,195 14. 7d.; for the year it amounts to £49,363 2s. 5½d. If arises from the nonpayment of quit-rents, and the duties on foreign goods imported.

South Australia.—Our papers from Adelaide contain no intelligence of immediate interest, except that South Australia still appears to be gaining ground.—The question of our over-importation of wheat and flour being one likely to cause considerable discussion during the ensuing Session of Council, and one also which involves other inquiries of paramount importance to us all, we think that a comparison of our flour imports with the exports of the same article from the United States last year, will afford subject-matter for serious reflection amongst our settlers, and excite feelings of emulation which we should like to see practically evinced. Our imports of flour during the last year, may be estimated in round numbers, at four thousand tons. The exports from the United States during the same period was 1,516,817 barrels. The following table shows the scale of distribution. England and her dependencies taking considerably more than one half of the whole:

	Barrels.
England	206,154
Scotland	3,830
Gibraltar	19,229
Malta	100
British East Indies	11,857
Australia	7,419
British West Indies	246,465
British Guiana	17,385
Cape of Good Hope	3,570
Honduras	4,699
British American Colonies	377,806
Total to England and her dependencies	898,514
Brazil	282,406
Cuba	69,337
Danish West Indies	42,394
Hayti	36,456
Venezuela	28,796
Buenos Ayres	22,132
Mexico	19,602
Swedish West Indies	15,624
Porto Rico	15,556
Dutch West Indies	14,932
Monte Video	13,327
Dutch East Indies	7,841
Chili	6,478
Texas	6,401
Madeira	5,408
French West Indies	4,739
Manila	3,425

An abstract of the receipts and expenditure of the colonial government of South Australia, for the quarter ending the 31st March, 1844.

The total receipts, including the transfer of £600 from the land account, and £31. 18s. for rents of land temporarily leased, are £7,928. 15s. 8d., and the total expenditure, including £202. 10s. 8d. for the immigration department, is £6,887. 8s. 7d. Showing a balance in favour of the revenue over the expenditure of £1,041. 7s. 1d.

The colonists are, however, labouring under considerable depression, on account of the high rates of wages.

Cape of Good Hope.—From the Cape of Good Hope, under date of July 28th, we learn that the Caffres continued their thefts and outrages; and that the inhabitants were kept in constant alarm, although no general irruption was anticipated. The value of property, owing to the increase of the population, was gradually rising.

St. Helena.—By the latest news from this island, it appears to be the intention of government to make St. Helena a depôt for captured slaves, with a view, we imagine, to their being ultimately shipped to the West Indies as emigrants. The information as to the treatment of those unfortunate Africans who have already been taken there, imperatively demands that a complete alteration of the system, as inhuman as it has been found expensive, should take place, before another of these unhappy people should be sent thither. The schooner which brought the last batch of captured Africans, some six or seven months ago, to the island, was there when the last mail was despatched, with all those who survive, about one half, on board. It appears that they have not been allowed to land; but whether this has arisen from instructions received from the Colonial Office, or whether it results from the mere will of the Governor of the island, was not ascertained. It is said some of those who had previously arrived, and were allowed to land, are half-starved.

It is really sickening to read the accounts which have been submitted to us of the hardships endured by the liberated Africans at St. Helena, previously to their being despatched to the West Indies. It is estimated that about seven thousand Africans have been introduced into St. Helena, a part of whom have been removed to British Guiana, Trinidad, Jamaica, and the Cape of Good Hope; the remainder, a few in number, still continue on the island.

West Indies.—The Jamaica House of Assembly was dissolved on the 26th of August, and the new elections were proceeding. Strange to say, one of the election battle-cries was "Church and State." The weather in Jamaica, and most of the other islands, had been rather favourable for the agriculturists, but great alarm appears to have been excited in most of our West India possessions by shocks of an earthquake, Jamaica, on this occasion, appearing to have escaped. No lives had been lost, nor, although the shocks were of unusually lengthened duration, had there been any destruction of property. At St. Christopher's, on the 17th July, a smart shock was felt about eleven o'clock at night. At about eight o'clock on the same evening, a meteor was seen to the northward and westward, which illumined the whole island for a short period. It is a remarkable circumstance, that a large meteor preceded the great earthquake of the 8th of February last year. On the 30th of August, a smart shock was experienced in George-town, Demerara, about half-past three o'clock in the morning; but it does not appear to have been attended with damage to buildings or loss of life. Coolie immigration, it is thought, will not be favourably regarded by the new House of Assembly, nor encouraged to the extent which parties in the mother-country seem to desire.

It appears that the rumoured intention of Government to lend to the principal West India colonies a million and a half for immigration purposes, has been changed into the settled purpose of presenting to them nearly 13,000 Coolies within the next year—5,000 to Jamaica, 5,000 to British Guiana, and 2,500 to Trinidad.

Trinidad.—It is made the subject of an exceedingly exultant leading article in a Trinidad paper (of September last), that an ice-house has been established for the supply of the natives with delicacies preserved in ice, including meat, fish, vegetables, and fruits.

The Census.—The following are extracts from the census, showing the population of the various West India islands, as taken on the 3rd day of June, 1844.

	Males.	Females.	Total.
Port of Spain district	6,656	8,953	15,609
Western dist.	3,682	3,595	7,277
Toco dist.	290	254	553
Southern dist.	2,353	1,634	3,984
Carapichaima dist.	4,034	3,008	7,042
St. Joseph dist. ..	6,324	6,002	12,326
Eastern dist.	772	590	1,362
Naparima dist. ...	6,593	5,069	11,662
Total........	30,713	29,102	59,815

Barbadoes.—Of the total number of the inhabitants there are 56,004 males, and 66,124 females; showing an excess of 10,190 females. There are 30,005 over 18 years of age employed in agriculture, of which 14,576 are men, and 15,429 women; an excess of 853 in favour of the women. There are 28,125 over 18 years engaged in trade or other business, of whom are 12,348 men, and 15,777 women —an excess of 3,429 women. There are 8,956 persons of both sexes without employment, and 55,112 boys and girls, the latter exceeding the former in number by 430; 19,362 persons living in Bridgetown, and 14,982 in the rural part of the parish. Most perso s are of opinion (and his excellency the governor, in his late speech on opening the Legislature, stated it) that this census falls short of the amount of the population by upwards of 10,000.—*Liberal.*

St. Kitt's.—Shows a total population of 23,177; namely, 10,523 males, and 12,654 females;—of these, 8,797 (of both sexes) are agricultural labourers. The population of Bas'terre, the chief town, is 1,908 males, and 2,785 females, or a total of 4,693.

Grenada.—Shows a total population (including the island of Carriacou, 3,835) of 29,082—namely, 13,804 males, and 15,278 females; of these, the population of the town of St. George is stated at 1,921 males, and 2,476 females—total, 4,397.—*St George's Chronicle.*

Tobago.—Shows a total population of 13,208—namely, 6,152 males, and 7,056 females. Of these, 2,335 males and 2,517 females above the age of 18 years are engaged in agriculture. The population of Scarborough (the chief town) is 605 males, and 869 females,—total, 1,474. A census was taken in January, 1839, when the population was found to be 11,748; thus showing a total increase since that period of about 12 per cent., or an annual increase of 2·2 per cent.—*Tobago Chronicle.*

The entire population of this island and its dependencies, as stated above, amounts to only 27,248, a number far less than was anticipated. On the 31st July, 1834, there were of slaves alone 22,245. being 718 more than the whole of the present black inhabitants. If to this number of 22,245 we add 4,467 for the coloured inhabitants, and as many more for free blacks, together with 1,252 for the white inhabitants, and something for the Charaibs (who are included in the present census), we find that the population in 1834 was about 33,000. Now supposing the deaths from that period to the present to equal the births, the astounding fact is arrived at, that 6,000 labourers have left the island since August, 1838.—*St. Vincent's Chronicle.*

On the 29th of August an earthquake was felt in several of the West Indian islands, including St. Vincent's, Grenada, Trinidad, and British Guiana.

Canada.—Sir Charles Metcalfe had fixed upon his new cabinet, and arrived in Montreal on the 3d of October, to swear the members in. The following are the names:—Hon. William Henry Draper, attorney-general for that part of the province formerly Upper Canada; the Hon. William Morris, receiver-general; Denis Benjamin Papineau, Esq., commissioner of crown lands; James Smith, Esq., Queen's counsel, in and for that part of the province formerly Lower Canada, and attorney-general for the same.

Sir Charles Metcalf, had issued a proclamation calling a meeting of parliament for the despatch of business for the 22nd. This is the first session since the removal of the seat of government to Montreal. Beyond this the Canadian journals contain no news of interest.

The weather in Lower Canada has, it appears, been most unfavourable for the crops, and a niggardly harvest has been the consequence.

Number of emigrants arrived at Quebec from the 24th August to the 7th of September:—

	Cabin.		Steerage.
From England .. .	9	..	132
.. Ireland	4	..	337
.. Scotland	14	..	246
.. Lower Ports .	0	..	0
Total	27	..	715
Previously reported	402	..	17,110
Total	429	..	17,825
To same period last year	691	..	19,151
Decrease in 1844	262	..	1,326

The Royal Exchange.—On Monday, October 28, her most gracious majesty Queen Victoria and his royal highness prince Albert, attended by the lord mayor and corporation, the Gresham committee, and a vast concourse of merchants, bankers, and other influential gentlemen connected with the trade and commerce of the city of London, opened the new Royal Exchange, just completed. Future historians will be enabled to record the erection and inauguration of as many as three Royal Exchanges within the short period of three centuries, and that on two of those occasions the ceremony was graced by the august presence of two youthful queens of Great Britain in person, reigning in their own right on the throne of these realms. Well may we congratulate the citizens of London on the present occasion, that a prince-consort laid the first stone, and that the inauguration was honoured by the presence of a queen-regnant, endeared to her subjects by every sentiment that can stimulate loyalty or excite devotion and attachment.

SOUTH AUSTRALIA.

The following RETURNS, compiled from documents furnished by the Collector of Customs, have been published for general information:—

No. 1.—Return of the Value of Imports into the Province of South Australia, during the Quarters ending 31st December, 1843, and 31st March, 1844.

Quarter ending.	From Great Britain.	From British Colonies.	From other Places.	TOTAL.
	£. s. d.	£. s. d.	£. s. d.	£. s. d.
Dec. 31, 1843....	27,161 1 1	7,910 11 7	366 3 6	35,437 16 2
March 31, 1844..	16,466 18 4	12,183 18 10		28,650 17 2

No. 2.—Return of the Value of Exports from the Province of South Australia, during the Quarters ending 31st December, 1843, and 31st March, 1844.

Quarter ending.	To Great Britain.	To British Colonies.	To other Places.	TOTAL.
	£. s. d.	£. s. d.		£. s. d.
Dec. 31, 1843....	26,792 19 6	5,888 0 6		32,681 0 0
March 31, 1844..	19,201 8 6	8,176 9 0		27,397 17 6

No. 3.—Abstract of Imports and Exports, showing the Amount of Imports for Home-Consumption, and the Amount of Colonial and Foreign Produce exported at the Port of Adelaide, for the Quarters ending 31st December, 1843, and 31st Mearch, 1844.

IMPORTS.	£. s. d.	EXPORTS.	£. s. d.
Quarter ending Dec. 31, 1843.		Quarter ending Dec. 31, 1843.	
Imports	35,437 16 2	Exports, produce of the Colony	28,874 17 6
Imports re exported	3.806 2 6	Imports re-exported	3,806 2 6
Total Imports consumed in the Colony	31,631 13 8	Total Exports	32,681 0 0
Quarter ending March 31, 1844.		Quarter ending March 31, 1844.	
Imports	28,650 17 2	Exports, produce of the Colony	24,136 0 6
Imports re-exported	3,261 17 0	Imports re-exported	3,261 17 0
Total Imports consumed in the Colony	25,389 0 2	Total Exports	27,397 17 6

No. 4.—Return of Shipping Inwards at the Port of Adelaide, South Australia, for the Quarters ending 31st December, 1843, and 31st March, 1844.

Quarter ending.	To Great Britain.		To British Colonies.		To other Places.		Total Tons.	Men.
	No.	Tons.	No.	Tons.	No.	Tons.		
Dec. 31, 1843...	2	687	10	1532	1	99	2318	134
March 31, 1844..	2	780	14	1388			2168	160

No. 5.—Return of Shipping Outwards at the Port of Adelaide, South Australia, for the Quarters ending 31st December, 1843, and 31st March, 1844.

Quarter ending.	To Great Britain.		To British Colonies.		To other Places.		Total Tons.	Men.
	No.	Tons.	No.	Tons.	No.	Tons.		
Dec. 31, 1843...	3	737	7	1106			1843	108
March 31, 1844..	3	1006	15	1653			2659	181

OBITUARY.

Baird, Captain, of the 15th Hussars, on 12th of August, at Bangalore, East Indies.

Bent, Thomas Hamlyn, Esq., Deputy-Commissary-General, formerly stationed at Barbadoes, on 26th of June, at his residence the Lodge, Hillingdon, near Uxbridge, aged 69.

Beresford, Admiral Sir John, Bart., K.C.B., G.C.H., &c., on 2d October, at Bedale, Yorkshire. The deceased admiral entered the navy in the year 1782, and had seen considerable service. He is succeeded in his title by his son, Captain George Beresford.

Caulfield, Lieut. James G., eldest son of Major-General Caulfield, on 21st of September, at Madeira.

Cotton, Major-General, E. R. I, on 3d of Oct., at Etwall Hall, in his 67th year. General Cotton served in the expedition to the Helder in 1799, and in the Mediterranean, Egypt, and the Peninsula, where he was present at the siege of Saragossa and in various other actions. He continued actively employed until 1817, when he retired on the half pay of the 10th Foot. He commenced his military career in the 5th Foot. His Commissions are dated as follow · viz., Ensign, 22d May, 1797; Lieutenant, 11th Oct., 1797; Captain, 9th July, 1803; Major, 4th March, 1807; Lieutenant-Colonel, 4th June, 1813; Colonel by Brevet, 22d July, 1830; and Major-General, 23d November, 1841.

Crawford, Mr. Adam, son of the late John Crawford, Esq., merchant, Leith, Scotland, on 11th April, at Sydney.

Deshon, Lieutenant-Colonel C. J., of her Majesty's 17th regiment, on 31st July, at Aden, East Indies. He was a brave and distinguished soldier, and beloved by the officers and men under his command.

Donegal, his grace the Marquis of, on 5th Oct., at Ormean, Ireland. His lordship, George Augustus Chichester, Marquis of Donegal, Viscount Chichester, and Baron Belfast (Viscount Fisherwick in England) Lieutenant of the county of Donegal, Knight of St. Patrick, &c., was born in 1760, and was consequently in the seventy-sixth year of his age. He is succeeded in his title and estates by his eldest son, the Earl of Belfast, Lieut. of the county of Antrim.

Eustace, Lieutenant-General Henry, late of the Royal Engineers, on 5th Oct., at Geneva. His Commissions were dated as follow:—Lieutenant, 8th May, 1790; Captain, 2d September, 1795; Major, 3d October, 1798; Lieutenant-Colonel, 25th September, 1803; Colonel by Brevet, 1st January, 1812; Major-General, 4th June, 1814; and Lieut.-General, 22d July, 1830.

Grafton, George Henry Fitzroy, fourth Duke of Grafton, on 28th Sept., at Euston Hall, Suffolk, in his 85th year.

Hale, William Amherst, Esq., late Captain in the 52d Light Infantry, in September, at his residence, St. Anne's, Canada.

Hayter, Lady, wife of Sir George Hayter, principal Painter in Ordinary to her Majesty, on 6th October, at Brighton.

Heytesbury, her Excellency the Baroness, wife of the Right Honourable Lord Heytesbury, Lord Lieutenant of Ireland, on 6th October, at Dublin.

Higgins, Colonel Sir Samuel Gordon, K. C. H., Equerry to her Royal Highness the Duchess of Gloucester, on 14th Oct,, at London, in his 74th year.

Hodgson, the Very Rev. R., D. D., Dean of Carlisle, and Rector of St. George's, Hanover Square, London, on 9th October, at Hanover Square, London.

Hoque, Thomas John, Esq., W.S., late of Woodcockdale Cottage, Linlithgowshire, on 27th July, at Chittagong, Bengal.

Jephson, James, M. D., Assistant-Surgeon of the Lunatic Asylum at Colabah, Bombay, on 12th of August, of cholera, at Colabah. "He arrived in India in 1835. Wherever he went —at home or abroad—James Jephson was a general favourite."—*Bombay Times.*

Kepple, William Henry, Esq, late Lieutenant in the 36th regiment, at Fredericton, New Brunswick.

Lewis, Captain Richard, of her Majesty's 45th regiment, on 30th Sept., at Gibraltar.

Moore, Richard, Esq., formerly Major in the 45th regiment, on 2d Oct., at Cheltenham, aged 67 years. He was thirty-five years in active service.

Marlborough, her grace the Duchess of, on 12th October, at Blenheim Park. Her grace was born March 29, 1798, was the eldest daughter of George, eighth Earl of Galloway, and was married to the present Duke on 11th Jan., 1819.

Nicolay, Edmond G., Esq., late Captain in the 29th regiment, and last surviving son of the late Lieutenant-General Sir William Nicolay, on 25th June, at Mhow, East Indies.

O'Reilly, Captain Dowell Knox, of her Majesty's 95th regiment, only son of the late Capt. O'Reilly, Royal Navy, of the Queen's County, Ireland, on 12th August, at Barbadoes.

Thomson, Captain James Eyre, Royal Marines, on the 21st October, at Woolwich, aged 59.

The Stanley Mausoleum.—Died last month, universally condemned, the political career of Lord Stanley. The remains have been interred in the House of Lords.—Punch.

LONDON: FISHER, SON, AND CO., PRINTERS.

FISHER'S

COLONIAL MAGAZINE.

INDIAN EMIGRATION.

FREE LABOUR IN THE MAURITIUS AND ISLE OF BOURBON.

THE abolition of negro slavery in the British Colonies, and the declaration which extinguished apprenticeships *in transitu*, have created a necessity for filling up the void produced in colonial operations by the suppression of forced labour,—and have suggested the project of importing free-labourers from other parts of our empire.

The density of the native Indian population,—the periodic difficulties that arose amongst them, the Hill Coolies, especially, in procuring subsistence, drove whole hordes of labourers from their mountain-homes, down to the principal sea-port and other towns. The leading agriculturists in the Mauritius, becoming cognisant of this periodical migration amongst the Coolies, resolved upon availing themselves of the circumstance, and accordingly invited them to extend their wanderings in search of work to their productive island, which was almost deserted by its enfranchised negroes. The first importation of Coolies took place in 1834, and in the space of five years from that date, no fewer than twenty-five thousand souls, having a proportion between the sexes, of one woman to fifty men, were safely landed, and found ample employment.

We shall now endeavour to submit a brief exposè of the means adopted in the importation and employment of this new class of labourers—the changes it was found necessary to make—the regulations that were established, and the results with which the immigration has been attended, with reference both to the Mauritius and British India. This investigation, supported in every instance by authentic documents, will serve as a guide in examining the condition of the

Isle of Bourbon,—because, their analogous geographical position, similarity of culture and produce, as well as the relation that so recently existed between the Creole proprietor and the negroes, render the cases of these isles identical.

The introduction of Coolies into the Mauritius, from 1834 to 1839, was conducted in the manner, and on the conditions, following:—The Mauritius colonists applied to some commercial house at Calcutta, requesting that they would engage for their service a certain number of Coolies. These establishments again applied to intermediate agents, native Indians, called there *daffadurs*, who carry on a traffic not unlike that of the *marchands d'hommes* attached to the French military service,—or of those whom we denominate contemptuously *crimps* or *kidnappers*,—all which classes of persons, namely, *daffadurs*, *marchands d'hommes*, and *crimps*, then exercise their callings most advantageously for their employers and themselves, when they use the greatest amount of deception and artifice towards their respective victims.

The Coolies were now induced to form engagements and execute contracts with agents, who immediately forwarded the same to the Mauritius colonist, receiving in exchange a very handsome commission. Now, although the word *sale* was most cautiously excluded from all these dealings, the distinction between a bonâ fide *sale* and an *assignment of the contract* is without a difference. By these contracts the Coolies were bound to serve for five years, generally at the rate of five rupees (12 f. 50 c.) per month, exclusive of their maintenance, which amounted to about as much more. At the expiration of their five-years' service, they were entitled to a passage back to India at the Mauritius planter's expense.

It was understood that the Coolies were to be paid six months' wages (30 rupees), in advance, but the *daffadurs*, under various pretexts,—debts said to have been contracted for lodging, support, clothing, and other necessaries,—generally contrived to relieve the poor Coolie of the whole amount, who was consequently obliged to work for six full months without any compensation. This constituted one of the chief causes of complaint and outrage amongst the objects of the spoliation. The Coolie assignment was actually sold to the planter, who, at the period before mentioned, paid sometimes forty Spanish piasters a head, exclusive of the six-months' wages in advance.

Seduced by the enormous profits which they realized, the kidnappers and speculators suffered themselves to be led into the commission of the most culpable practices, for the purpose of procuring a greater number of emigrants; many facts contributing to prove this assertion have been brought before the public. Meetings were now held—petitions addressed to the governor-general of India, to forbid such a scandalous traffic. It was at this precise moment that the price of these Indian contracts attained its maximum, and when the prohibition, which we are about to speak of, was issued, had reached to 100 Spanish piasters, or 543 francs.

In 1839, an Indian legislative act prohibited Coolie emigration, until proper measures could be taken to secure for them an efficacious protection. The consequence of this prohibition was, that the planters paid as much as 100 Spanish piasters to an Indian for one year's service. Sugar, the principal production of the colony, brought from eight to ten Spanish piasters the quintal, the profits realized permitting the master to pay a salary of about twelve piasters per month (exclusive of support), to his workmen.

It was impossible that such high prices could be long maintained, but, want of hands did not permit a reduction. In this difficulty, the Mauritius colonists had recourse to the only measure capable of remedying their grievances; and on the 4th of June, 1840, a general association of planters was formed under the title of "The Mauritius Free-Labour Association."

After this arrangement, the emigration of free-labourers from India, Madagascar, Muskat, and other places, became dependent on the association, by means of intermediate agents appointed by them; and, to fix the necessary expenses, the association solicited the co-operation of government. They sought at the same time, from the English minister, a retraction of the order prohibiting Coolie emigration from India, and by these active steps their efforts were crowned with complete success. An order by the queen in council, dated 15th January, 1842, renewed the permission of Coolie emigration, organized, however, after a system based on the following principles:—

1. The introduction of Coolies, and their return to India, when their term of service had expired, was not to be at the expense of the colonists, or of the association, but of the colony.

2. The emigrant should not form any engagement before his arrival at the Mauritius, where he was at liberty to place himself in whichever service he preferred. The order of the queen in council went so far as to declare every engagement contracted by Indians within forty-eight hours after their disembarkation, as null and void. On the other hand, the colonial law of the Mauritius did not allow a labourer to engage himself for a longer term than one year.

3. Every emigrant was at liberty to return to his country at any time; but, the expenses of his return fell upon himself, if he quitted before the space of five years, without any prejudice to the claims of the proprietor with whom he had contracted an engagement which he did not fulfil.

4. Particular arrangements regulate the treatment of the emigrants on board ship. A height of six feet is required between decks, and a sufficient quantity of wholesome nourishment must be provided for them during their voyage.

5. A special agency is established, to examine into the emigrant's state of health, to ascertain whether he emigrates voluntarily, and whether he is provided with every necessary prescribed by the regulations.

6. Captains of emigrant ships are subject to fine and imprisonment for opposing or neglecting any of these regulations.

7. A protector of emigrants is appointed at the Mauritius to enforce the strict observance of all these regulations.

Indian emigration had been limited to the three ports of Calcutta, Madras, and Bombay, by an act numbered 14, of 1839, emanating from the legislative council of Calcutta. The Indian and the Mauritius governments adopted regulations conformable to the orders issued by the queen in council.

The Mauritius government established a premium, or insurance, of seven pounds sterling for the introduction of an emigrant, man or woman, and the half of that sum for a child: they calculated that this sum would sufficiently compensate those who undertook to import Coolies into the colony. However, the establishment of an insurance, or premium, necessarily opened a wide field for private speculations,—likely, eventually, to produce the very results which government had been most solicitous to avoid.

Secondary agents again took possession of the unfortunate emigrants, and, under the pretext of reimbursing themselves for the expenses incurred in bringing them from the interior to the place of embarkation, absorbed a great part of their future salaries. Arrived at the sea-port, the emigrants next fell into the fangs of speculators, who undertook to secure their passage, obtain the fulfilment of all the required conditions on board, and, forward them expeditiously to the Mauritius.

The public agent at Calcutta endeavours to put the regulations in force, examines the emigrants, ascertains, as far as it is possible for him to do, that their own free will has not been violated ; but, having neither authority nor means to provide for their passage, he is obliged to abandon them to private speculators. These harpies undertake the charge with the sole view of realizing exorbitant profits, and, in order to obtain their object, make themselves acquainted with opportunities of disposing of the emigrants previous to their embarkation.

Although the colonial government neither sanctioned nor even recognized this proceeding, it nevertheless tolerated the exercise. In a country where slavery had just been abolished, and where twenty-five years before a slave-treaty had been publicly and legally made, it was not surprising that men should be found base enough to speculate upon Coolie importation, and endeavour to make it a source of profit. On the arrival of a cargo of Coolies, no one ventured to engage them without first treating with the importer; and this was the way that the object of the order in council for protecting emigrants against the rapacity of speculators in labour was completely eluded. When the Coolies first arrived, and the want of hands was severely felt, the planters paid, exclusive of provisions, which we have already spoken of, the sum of from twenty to twenty-five Spanish piasters to the importer, and that for a man whom the colonial law did not allow to be engaged in their service for longer than a year. The monthly pay of a free-labourer was then fifteen rupees, whilst the latest arrivals only received five rupees a month, support not included; intermediate agents absorbing the other two-thirds of the price-current for labour. The immense profits realized in this traffic, attracted a number of speculators to the same pursuit; and persons arrived in India commissioned to expedite Coolie-emigration. So great was the competition to obtain passages on board emigrant-vessels, that the ordinary price of forty rupees was increased to fifty-five, not including provisions.

Kidnappers took advantage of the competition amongst shipping-agents, in order to enhance, in a still greater proportion, the price of their own services. The remuneration with which they were at first content, was from two to three rupees each emigrant, but when they got the shipping-brokers into their power, they raised their fees to fifteen rupees. Under the reign of a better order of things, one rupee each would have been sufficient reward for secondary agents.

In the years 1840, 1841, and 1842, the frequent returns of Coolies, whose economy had accumulated from 200 to 300 rupees, acted as a powerful stimulant to increased emigration.

Nevertheless, persons well acquainted with the real state of things in India and the Mauritius, had serious thoughts that this traffic in human beings was performed in a manner directly opposed to the intentions of government, and that it must have led to calamitous results. With this impression, they resolved on correcting the error; and on the 22d of June, 1843, through the "land-holders' society," an address was presented to the government of India, (drawn up by Mr. George Thompson,) exposing the system on which this emigration was conducted, as well as the disuse into which the regulations prescribed by government had fallen. It pointed out, in the clearest manner, the most correct means of remedying these abuses.

According to the suggestion of the society, these means consisted in the nomination of a person, in the entire confidence of the Mauritius government, in whose hands should be placed the sole direction of the Coolie-emigration, up to their final delivery to the agents previously established for that purpose. This agent should defray all necessary expenses on account of the colony, but neither receive nor accept a single commission from a private person. The address was graciously received by the lieutenant-governor of Bengal, who promised to call the serious attention of government to the evils pointed out, as well as to the measures recommended for their correction.

An accidental circumstance now contributed an astonishing evidence in favour of the contents of the address. There was a vessel filled with emigrants, lying in the river near the botanic gardens at Calcutta, ready to set sail for the Mauritius. Just as she was getting under weigh, three men jumped over-board, and attempted to reach shore; one was drowned, the two others were rescued by a gentleman, (Mr. Miller,) who happened to be walking in the gardens, to whom they declared that they had been deceived, and that they were seduced on board under false representations, and kept there against their will.

Mr. Miller brought them before a magistrate, who immediately sent two police-officers on board the vessel to tell the Indians, in Mr. Miller's presence, that they were all at liberty to dispose of themselves as they pleased,—that no one had a right to force them to emigrate against their will. The result was, that out of 200, forty-five availed themselves of this opportunity of returning.

This circumstance created a great sensation; but, after the first movement of the philanthropic party, the whole business was allowed to fall into oblivion. Too little attention is paid generally in India to the condition of the poorer classes of people. The declaration of the forty-five Coolies taken by a press-gang, gave a strong tincture of unpopularity to the question of emigration, but no means had been employed to remedy the abuses. Mean time, the fact just related was certainly a dark spot in the series of abuses that revealed the magnitude of an evil, arising entirely from the vices of the commission-system. It was unfair to throw all the fault on the public agent, who, having more than 2,500 emigrants to pass in review during the course of a month, could not examine minutely the wishes of each individual; besides, they all conspired to deceive him, and to hide the truth from him. The kidnappers spared neither trouble nor money to deceive his vigilance. All this resulted from the extraordinary combination of these kidnappers. There lay the source of all the evil; for so long as there were no means of dissolving the combination, the public agents, whatever may have been their number, would find it impossible to counteract the fraud. Their superintendence, therefore, became almost useless.

To attain the object of protecting the Indians at the Mauritius, Mr. Anderson visited Calcutta, in order to concoct with the Indian government means for placing Coolie-emigration on a more moral basis. The consequence was, that all the measures suggested in the address of "the land-holders' society" were adopted, and an act passed by the government of India restricting the emigration of Coolies to the single port of Calcutta, and there only through the medium of an agent belonging to the government of Mauritius, who was appointed by Mr. Anderson and the governor-general in concert. They gave him the necessary means for assisting in the cost of emigration,—enough to buy clothing, utensils, and defray the expenses of the voyage, &c. He was instructed to settle all arrangements for the passage and sea-store of the Coolies, by means of sealed agreements; the stipulated price to be paid to the owners of the transports, after the disembarkation of the Coolies at the Mauritius, according to the prescribed order in council.

This new system was ordered to be put into operation from the 1st of January, 1844, after which the system of premiums or insurances was entirely abolished.

Combinations having been partially suppressed, the transport of emigrants must evidently be conducted on a better footing. Hitherto the premiums of seven pounds sterling had been entirely absorbed by the expenses; according to the new system, it is hoped, that each Coolie arriving at the Mauritius will not cost more than six pounds sterling, including all expenses of agency. The agent himself receives from the company 1,000 rupees per month, or 30,000 francs a year.

In dividing the cost of agency amongst 5,000 emigrants, a number sufficient for the wants of the colony, the average of all expenses for each individual will be as follows:—

	C. R.	Fr.	C.
Passage, with food	40	100	0
Clothing, &c., for the voyage	5	12	50
Expenses before embarkation	10	25	0
Expenses of agency	5	12	50
Total	60	150	0

It may be calculated, that, at the end of 1843, there departed from the three presidencies of India more than 35,000 emigrants; that is to say—

From Calcutta about	16,000
From Madras "	14,000
From Bombay "	5,000
Total	35,000

About an eighth of these were women,—the proportion required by the regulations being at least twelve women to a hundred emigrants.

The want of labourers which the Mauritius experienced was thus amply satisfied; nothing more remained but to replace the loss occasioned by the return of the emigrants to India, and by deaths, and continue the culture of the colony until a development had taken place much more extensive than had hitherto been witnessed, but which would inevitably arrive.

It is probable that the demand for labourers will not exceed 5,000 each year, and that the colonists will be obliged to reject any surplus that may present itself. It is calculated that about 18,000 Coolies at least arrive every month from the interior at Calcutta, without the adoption of any means to draw them thither. Bourbon could recruit several thousand free-labourers, without including in this estimate any contribution from the Mauritius, which might easily be had.

We have said that the regulations required the proportion of twelve women in every hundred emigrants, at least; many motives concur in proving that this proportion is too small. First, the planters wish the women to be engaged in tilling the ground, which is contrary to the usages and ideas of Indians. On the other hand, emigration over the seas was for them an enterprize full of hazard, and those who have performed it paint its dangers and fatigues as so terrible, that few desire to bring their wives along with them.

As to religious prejudices, which have been considered as an insurmountable obstacle to the emigration of women, experience has proved the contrary; and the only real difficulty which has prevented the establishment of Indian families at Mauritius, is, that the colonial law did not grant the Indian husband ample rights over his wife, adultery not being punished there amongst the blacks of the lower classes.

Emigration, facilitated by the allowance of necessary funds for the engagement and transport of labourers, simplified by the suppression of combination amongst the kidnappers, and become less painful to the Indians, by the presence of a great number of women, who partake of their lot,—receives, meantime, its principal encouragement from the difference existing between the wages of India and those paid in the Mauritius, that difference permitting them to realize considerable profit in the colony.

We have before stated, that a free-labourer has a right to receive at least 5 C.R. each month, (his support not included). It is not so in Bengal; the labourer, working near to his home, earns there commouly from $1\frac{1}{3}$ to $2\frac{1}{2}$ C.R. In the distant districts—in the indigo districts, the Coolie earns 3 C.R., always without food, which he is obliged to procure for himself. At Calcutta, wages are as much as $3\frac{1}{2}$ rupees, but the price of subsistence there is more expensive. Food, of the same kind as that which they receive in the Mauritius, costs them $2\frac{1}{2}$ rupees. But they do not work so constantly under the burning sky of India, and less abundant nourishment, therefore, is sufficient for them; so that their expenses are generally about $1\frac{1}{2}$ rupee. As to clothing, their wants are excessively few, and can be provided for at an outlay of three rupees per annum.

The rent of a lodging is a quarter-rupee per month, so that the whole of a Coolie's expenses at Calcutta would not exceed two rupees a month; and this permits them even to economize about eighteen rupees a year, when there is no interruption of employment.

Receipts and Expenses of an Indian Coolie at Calcutta:

Wages (at C.R. $3\frac{1}{2}$ by the month) by the year	...	C.R. 42	C R.
Maintenance (by the month, R $1\frac{1}{3}$) each year	...	...	18
Lodging do. $\frac{1}{4}$ do.	...	...	3
Clothing do. $\frac{1}{4}$ do.	...	...	3
Savings	...	...	18
Balance	...	C.R. 42	42

In the indigo manufactories three rupees a month brought them probably the same profit, which they obtained in working at home near their families; because, in the latter case, although their salary was less, the expenses of support were diminished in an equal proportion.

Europeans in India have generally so little direct intercourse with the lower class of people, that the calculations which they make of their expenses and their profits, can only be looked upon as approximative.

The proper means of obtaining the exact appreciation of the advantages they derive from their present emigration, is to offer them the means of transportation to countries where their work would be useful, and to assure them of a free and easy return, if not *gratis*, to their native country.

As vessels returning eastward from Mauritius to India can afford a passage to a Coolie for twenty rupees, it would suffice to guarantee to him the payment of this sum, in order that he might consider himself free on this point.

All that has been here urged relative to Coolie-emigration to the colony of Mauritius, is applicable to the isle of Bourbon; the relative positions of the colonist and black population does not essentially modify certain considerations here stated. In fact, slavery still existing in the French colony, removes the necessity of introducing free-labourers to the same extent. Meanwhile, this necessity began to arise upon the decisive suppression of the treaty with the blacks, who hitherto filled up the periodical voids in the ranks of the labourers. Besides, for several years back, the attention of the Bourbon planters has been directed to the introduction of Indian Coolies.

Some attempts have been made to form engagements with the Indians on the coast of Coromandel, but, up to the present time, they have proved fruitless; whatever measures have been taken for this object, it is doubtful whether they will ever produce any numerous emigration, unless some great alteration take place in the relationship existing between master and slave in the isle of Bourbon.

The contact of two systems, so much opposed to each other as those of the slave and the freeman, could not continue long, without the one exercising a powerful influence over the other; for, the interest of humanity, as well as the future prosperity of the colony, it is to be desired that the system of slave-labour underwent, as soon as possible, important changes. Unfortunately, the laws which regulate the position of labourers coming from Asia, prove rather a reaction of the system of slavery upon free-trade. They give the Indian an exceptionable position, which does not suit his spirit of independence, and of passive resistance. Instead of considering him as a freeman, whatever colour he may be of, the colonial law of the 25th of December, 1838, which still serves as the basis of the existing relations between planters and free-labourers, and which was made, apparently, with the object of affording guarantees to the latter, subjects them to numerous restrictions, on the whole equivalent to a mitigated slavery. Thus, the Indians could not advance a step without the will of their master. They are under the command of the chiefs of their caste, appointed by the master; they can be punished by this chief at the request of the master.

These conditions ought evidently to be modified; England, who has taken so many precautions to guarantee the safety and protection of these Indian emigrants, in her own colonies, has evidently opposed their introduction, on different conditions, into French establishments. The emancipation so much desired by the blacks, must certainly experience much delay, if this vicious organization of the Indian labour be permitted to continue.

However, one point must be distinctly decided upon. The abolition of slavery in the French colonies is no longer a question of time and opportunity; enlightened by the experience of English-colonial legislation, France is enabled to follow a firmer and safer path. The colony of Bourbon should be made the theatre of the first trial. There are several important motives for this choice.

For instance, an immigration of several thousands of free-labourers, in French vessels, would give more activity and importance to their commerce at Calcutta, or rather to French navigation in the Indian seas. The commerce of Bourbon with Calcutta has for its object the providing of the colony with rice and other necessaries; the number of vessels actually employed in this commerce would be doubled by the transportation of Coolies, because a vessel carrying emigrants, being obliged to have its deck free, can only take on board half a cargo. But that which should especially determine the government to adopt Bourbon as a field of action, in the question of abolishing slavery, is because of its possessing greater facilities of obtaining free-labour, in lieu of the insufficiency of hands that would at first be caused.

The proximity of one of the most populous countries in the universe, being able at all times to furnish robust and clever labourers, capable of enduring the climate of the tropics, admits of preferring Bourbon rather than the Antilles and Guiana, and of accelerating the moment of giving complete freedom to the African population.

To this abundant source, whence labour pours forth into the neighbouring colonies, perhaps at no distant period another more abundant still will be united.

The late events, of which China has been the theatre, seem to announce the opening of great avenues, through which an exuberant population will pour in great floods, over countries richly endowed by nature, but lacking hands for cultivation.

Notwithstanding that the dark and contemptible policy of the Chinese government prevents any emigration of inhabitants from their celestial empire, the overplus of population, according to natural inclination, has been spreading itself already for upwards of a century, into countries abundantly fertile, although sparingly peopled.

The Philippine Islands, the Indian Islands, the Malayan Gulf, Siam, and Cochin China, afford an asylum to those indefatigable labourers and clever workmen. Some attempts for importing Chinese was even tried at the Cape, at St. Helena, and as far as Guiana; but in too scanty proportions to enable us to judge of the results, which a well-organized and regular emigration would produce. The *improved* constant relations, more direct communications, which the new state of things, since the treaty of Nanking, must necessarily open to the Europeans in China, will doubtless admit of carrying away free-labourers upon a more extended scale.

Then will be produced that result which the providential march of events has reserved perhaps for the human race. The black population, crushed and trodden upon on all sides, by other families placed in a more elevated degree in the development of the human species, will disappear from those countries that are subject to the sovereignty of the white races, unless, by an unjustified imprudence, the latter shall become, as at St. Domingo, the victims of a race morally inferior, but who, too long oppressed, became outrageous against the ancient governors.

De Challaye.

EUROPE'S POLICY LIES IN HER PACIFICATION.

GOVERNMENTS that are essentially military will hardly allow the truth of this; but the reasons which, upon the slightest examination, are found to array themselves in favour of this position, are so conclusive, that they can hardly be set aside.

In the first place, nations that are deeply indebted, either to themselves or their neighbours, are not in a condition to wage war. If their rulers are rash enough to engage in it, they do so at the imminent risk and peril of their social prosperity and happiness. Wealth and apparent prosperity may distinguish them; but while large classes of their inhabitants are the victims of privation and comparative penury, in consequence of excessive taxation, the funds necessary to furnish forth the unusual expenses attendant upon a state of war, must be accompanied with deep-felt misery to many.

The nations of Europe are more or less involved in heavy pecuniary liabilities, in consequence of their prodigious struggles to meet the exigencies of the late war. England, although she escaped the severe personal calamities inflicted on so many of them, is still, perhaps, in a pecuniary point of view, the most onerously and permanently afflicted. She is still smarting under the wounds which a long course of warfare, in other times, has superinduced. Shall she not, for a century at least, enjoy an interval which shall recruit her strength, expand her resources, place her trade on a firm and secure basis, and diffuse through her society that abundance and content so essential to her happiness?

Had Europe, for very many centuries of her past history, not been desolated by continual wars, there is little question but that she would sooner have emerged from that barbarism which overspread the nations at the dissolution of the Roman empire. She would sooner have risen to a positive development of mind, and have asserted that ascendancy over the other nations of the earth which she has long since acquired—she would sooner have ripened to an age of literature—she would sooner have become eminent in the investigations of science—in the knowledge of the great secrets of nature—in maritime discovery—in the possession of extensive colonial regions, tending to enrich the mother-country: in all these attainments she would sooner have gained the ascendant, had not war, in most of the periods alluded to, been so much a ruling propensity.

Will any one, indeed, with the evidence of history before him, assert, that Europe, if, for the last two hundred years blessed with profound peace, would not have attained a higher pinnacle of knowledge? that she would not have risen higher in arts, if she had been less addicted to the practice of arms? France and England have each long occupied a place as mediatrix in the councils of Europe. Should not examples of forbearance and good feeling be reciprocally kept up by those who have a supreme voice in the direction of its affairs? They were each bitter sufferers in the late tremendous struggle—but do they not each, at the present moment, possess extensive colonies in the Old and New World, in the due cultivation of which may be opened up mines of wealth, which may confer on their possessors power, and grandeur, and general content, which may repair these wastes?

The repose of the most civilized portions of mankind will be the end and object of the enlightened legislator. The nations of Europe constitute its most civilized portions; and that minister, or that monarch, must ever stand high in the general estimation, who seeks to derive true glory from the tranquillity and happiness of those over whom he rules.

True it is, that wealth seems still to abound in some of the countries of Europe; true it is, that, in England especially, certain individuals or classes can, when required, raise sums to an almost unlimited extent, when tempting investments are presented to them. But, in a trading country, such as Great Britain, there will be always found persons who will embark property to a large extent (sometimes beyond their actual means), in what they consider to be good securities; and, on the other hand, the existence of wealth in certain quarters does not, by any means, always imply either universal prosperity or universal plenty. Privation and even penury may still attend its hundreds of thousands, and excessive taxation may place our commercial intercourse with foreign countries in jeopardy.

France, likewise, has, in consequence of almost perpetual wars for the last century or two, most lavishly expended her blood and treasure. Whether growing out of the unjust ambition of her rulers, or from great national convulsions, the impoverishing effects have been the same, in keeping down the natural or acquired sources of its wealth. These sources of revenue, both of France and England, are vast; what pity it is that they should constantly be *anticipated* by ruinous wars! Alas! why should not two of the most civilized and intellectual nations of the world reciprocally consent, if it be possible, to merge minor differences, and to emulate each other in leading the way to noble pursuits (rather than that of impoverishing and destroying each other) in the paths of glory and of fame? A quarter of a century has of late occurred, in which the noble pursuits of science have superseded those of war, and the reciprocation of arts and human inventions has risen high: why should not the period be indefinitely prolonged?

Both countries stand high in the possession of rich colonies, in a variety of latitudes, and in distant quarters of the globe; both are maritime powers of enterprise and skill; why should the inheritors of exhaustless wealth in soils, and mines, and fisheries, not form a league of perpetual amity with each other? The foreign possessions of these leading powers, in both hemispheres, are noble and extensive. Why should the countries of Europe be made the theatre of war through the contentions engendered by the grasping jealousies of either?

Are there not ample arenas for deriving almost exhaustless revenues in the distant regions, which, either as conquests, or as territorial cessions on the basis of former treaties, remain as an appanage of either crown. Do not their territorial jurisdictions in the Guianas of South America; in the Canadas and their vicinity, including the finest fisheries in the world; in the vast peninsula of India; in the Caribbean seas, furnish them with permanent and still unexplored mines of wealth? Do not the fertile islands lying in the great oceans of our globe which own their allegiance, and the boundless territories of Australia, discovered by the genius of Cook, (alas for England in the matter of Cook! his incalculable services have been repaid by his countrymen with frigid neglect,) and numerous other illustrious navigators, from Dampier and Drake downwards—do not these territorial annexations, which might be turned to higher account in promoting the commerce and the manufactures, and therefore the wealth, of the mother-countries, than they are—offer a higher prize for emulation than perpetuating fire and sword through the nations of civilized Europe? Assuredly they do; for upon the basis of expediency alone, could no other argument be urged, this must be maintained.

We will notice a few points in the civil and military history of Europe, illustrative of this position. Two centuries back, at the famous Peace of Westphalia, Europe enjoyed an interval of repose from the troubles which had so long afflicted her. From the death of Henry the Great of France, in 1610, the war, which had prevailed almost without intermission in Europe, between the Protestants and Catholics, had introduced a state of anarchy fatal to its repose. At the death of that prince, the two great confederacies which divided the greater part of Europe, under the names of the *Evangelical Union* and the *Catholic League*, were not dissolved. Under the Elector of Brandenburgh, and the Duke of Neuburgh, who laid claim to certain sovereignties and jurisdictions, these disputes were renewed, and Europe was plunged anew into the horrors of war.

It has been generally observed that religious wars are carried on with more rancour and animosity than any others. Such was the case in the wars of the League. They were participated in and supported by their adherents, on either side, with a zeal and party-spirit, which does not always animate other causes of dispute. The Bohemians formally deposed Ferdinand the Second, whom they disliked for his tyrannical disposition, and chose Frederick the Fifth, elector palatine, for their king. Frederick was supported by all the continental Protestant princes, except the Elector of Saxony; though he incurred the displeasure of James the First of England, who, however, assisted him with troops against Ferdinand, who, on the other hand, was supported by all the Catholic princes of the empire, with the King of Spain at their head.

Thus was lit up afresh, on the theatre of Europe, the flames of general war, as all the belligerents who had taken up arms under the plea of religion now sided either with Ferdinand or with Frederick. The latter, however, opposed by the House of Austria, was at length compelled to resign his pretensions in favour of his more successful rival. The grand supporter, as he was the most distinguished ornament of the Protestant League, was the great Gustavus Adolphus of

Sweden. Great, as well as good, the character of Gustavus stands higher than that of Henry the Fourth of France—his renowned predecessor in the cause or the triumph of Protestantism, and equally an advocate for civil and religious freedom. The first died a martyr in the cause of liberty of conscience; the last, though a patriot prince, was more the sovereign of expediency, than the uncompromising champion of the Protestant cause. But the first rose higher in the scale of human greatness; to disinterested patriotism he added a high and devoted zeal for the Protestant cause, which he defended with an ardour which perhaps in an equal degree never characterized any prince of Christendom. Heroic to a fault, his zeal in the Protestant cause, joined to a love of military glory, hurried him on in a career of victory; and he perished at Lutzen, in a manner in which few true military heroes would shrink to follow. His great generals, schooled by himself, the Duke of Saxe Weimar, Horne, Banier, Kniphausen, Tortenson, and others, pursued the war for the Protestant ascendancy, with various success, until the unfortunate battle of Nordlingen struck a fatal damp into the minds of those princes who supported the Evangelical Union. Although Banier and the Duke of Saxe Weimar afterwards raised themselves to the highest reputation for military conduct and courage, yet the soul of the heroic king was wanting to the now drooping courage of the confederates. Victorious in the plains of Wisbek and at Rhenfield, there yet wanted an illustrious head to whom they might look with confidence; and the war languished, with no decisive blow struck on either side. Although after the base assassination of Wallenstein, by order of his master, the Imperialists were often defeated by the skill and heroism of the Swedish generals, yet the rare union of illustrious rank with first-rate military talents and Christian magnanimity, was not perhaps to be found even in Christendom.

At length, the Thirty-Years' War, by the general consent of the powers, closed by the peace of Westphalia. Torn, and bleeding, and wearied with continual alarms, from which no permanent good seemed to be derived, while society in its progress was disorganized, and rather retrograded than advanced; Europe, at length, once more listened to the voice of humanity, which her judgment and better feelings inspired, and obtained that repose which her exhausted energies so deeply needed.

The state of Europe, indeed, was such at the celebrated Peace of Westphalia, that an interval of tranquillity seemed essential. Tired with long-continued hostilities, the nations sought to forget for a time, in a well-consolidated peace, the miseries and the evils of war. All ranks of men hailed with eagerness a treaty which, in its basis of pacification, seemed to promise a permanent rest from the toils and alarms of a previous age. If a greater curse cannot be inflicted on nations than to become the seat of war, a general peace, after a long course of hostilities, must be hailed with rapture. A *panacea* was here applied to its recent wounds, and nations, in whom science and the arts had begun to assert their empires, rejoiced in their emancipation from those evils which had so long afflicted them.

But, after the amazing cost of blood and treasure with which this famous treaty had been purchased, what, on the grand aggregate, was gained? The powers of Europe occupied, for the most part, the same position, and were left, as to their political rights and jurisdictions, in a state very similar to that in which they existed at the commencement of the war. On the side of philosophy, no less than of politics, this consideration might read to mankind an important lesson. It has a direct tendency to show, that, after a long-protracted and bloody series of warfare, a general pacification often ensues, which leaves the belligerents precisely in the state, as to territorial possessions, as they were at the commencement of the contest, although weakened in their resources and drained of their population. What, on the great aggregate, is the boon obtained by the immense sacrifices paid by nations as an equivalent for the tears, and groans, and blood of a suffering people—desolated either by the march of armies, or by the iron hand of excessive taxation? Simply this,—that the balance of power, as it previously existed, or pretty nearly so, be again adjudicated and apportioned; and social institutions, which had been disorganized and destroyed, should again assume their pristine state.

An interval of tranquillity again intervened in Europe. The leading powers, finding that nothing of permanent or satisfactory good was to be obtained by a thirty-years' war, were anxious to preserve a treaty, the basis of which, at least, gave them that tranquillity so essential to their political existence. How much it was to be regretted that society could not enjoy a peace, so framed and consolidated, for a longer period! But the restless ambition and warlike propensities of Lewis the Fourteenth effectually prevented such an accomplishment. This despotic monarch, who is destined to figure in history under the name of a generous prince, emulant of glory, a reckless military conqueror, and a gloomy bigot, again blew up the flames of discord, and involved Europe in a general war. This continued with varied fortune to the armies of France, until the Treaty of Aix-la-Chapelle, in 1668, put a temporary stop to the progress of hostilities.

The Peace of Nimeguen, which was consolidated in 1678, offered a more effectual barrier to the ambitious projects of Lewis. That prince, however insatiable of dominion, could not resist the temptation of continually making excursions into the territories of his neighbours, until at length the Great Duke of Marlborough humbled the pride of France, and restored, once more, peace to western Europe. The Triple Alliance, as it was called, between England, Holland, and Sweden, had also opposed an obstacle to the views of Lewis. Sir William Temple, the high-minded courtier of the politically profligate cabinet of Charles the Second, negociated this famous treaty with that incorruptible minister and patriot, De Wit; and this, so far as his sphere and opportunity extended, redeemed his master's honour—already implicated by acts of pusillanimity. But whenever a thirst for domination is found united with ample means and despotic power, the peace of Europe stands endangered; and it was not until the genius of Marlborough had taught the ambition of France, or her sovereign, the memorable lesson of humiliation, that the blessings of permanent peace were again realized by the nations of Western Europe.

The Northern States were not, however, so fortunate; they were soon again to be involved in the calamities of war, with all its train of attendant evils.

Originating in the grasping cupidity, which is sometimes observed to be inherent in nations, to prey upon their weaker brethren, the calamities attendant upon warfare were again opened up, through the wide districts of modern Scandinavia.

Russia, Poland, and Denmark, presuming upon the youth and inexperience of Charles the Twelfth of Sweden, marked him for their prey. Pursuant to this policy, they invaded his dominions, but the young hero quickly showed them that he was not only capable of defending himself, but of making the most severe reprisals. To the two former powers he soon dictated terms of humiliating submission, whilst to the Czar himself the menace of treating with him at Moscow was all but realized. Charles the Twelfth trod a career of victory, which, accompanied as it was by personal heroism, has distinguished few monarchs. But his wars, whilst they extensively desolated the northern countries of Europe, might be said to be essentially the scourge of his own people; in this respect he stands out in unfavourable relief to his predecessor—the no less heroic Gustavus Vasa.

After his disastrous reverse at Pultowa, and his subsequent flight into Turkey, the northern parts of Europe again enjoyed an interval of repose; and, at the grand settlement of affairs at the close of Marlborough's victories, the southern continental nations were, for a considerable period, freed from the scourge of war. Some partial and isolated contests were continually prevailing in some districts; but the great leading powers were not embroiled, and their attendant satellites, ever ready to reflect the policy of their powerful allies, participated in the general tranquillity.

The Peace of Aix-la-Chapelle, a second time, in 1748, introduced a period of tranquillity to the nations of the continent. Arts flourished, and society rejoiced in the prospect of a long interval of cessation from hostilities. But it was not so fortunate. Again the civilized world was doomed to witness the horrors of a general war. A coalition was formed, similar to that which sought to dispossess Charles the Twelfth of his dominions, against Frederick of Prussia, and with pretty similar success. The event, though not fatal to the King of Prussia, was so to the tranquillity of the continental nations engaged in it.

For a lengthened term of years the distractions attendant upon a state of warfare afflicted those countries whose governments sided with the belligerents of either party. More than once did the fortunes of the heroic Frederic appear, to those who had leisure calmly to observe them, to be all but desperate; more than once did the invincible constancy and genius of this extraordinary man turn the tide of affairs, triumph over every misadventure, and lead afresh his armies on to military glory and conquest.

At length, the Imperialists and their allies grew weary of a war, by which they got not even glory, and which was prosecuted at an immense cost of blood and treasure. The exertions, constant and undeviating, by which the allies sought, on the one hand, to crush the

King of Prussia, and the unparalleled defence by which he neutralized their exertions, and hurled defeat upon his enemies, had materially impoverished the finances of the contending powers, and taught them a memorable lesson, which mankind would do well not to despise—that, to nations pretty nearly balanced in resources and valour, few benefits can arise from a protracted contest; while a long series of continued warfare will inevitably superinduce a train of unmitigated evils.

The Treaty of Aix-la-Chapelle had, in 1748, taken for its basis a general confirmation of all the treaties from the famous Peace of Westphalia. The principal stipulations, at that time mutually recognized and entered into, are acknowledged by historians to have been based upon an enlarged recognition of the rights of nations, and to have placed the vested liberties of the belligerents on their former footing.

On the contemplation of these facts, of the prolonged duration and final close of the Seven-Years' War, this reflection will be powerfully excited in the mind, and it cannot be better stated than in the language of a judicious and eloquent historian. He thus speaks:—

"But although the Treaty of Aix-la-Chapelle, all circumstances considered, cannot be deemed unfavourable to the confederates, or by any means an ill-timed measure, it must be lamented that it was the necessary consequence of such a long and fruitless war,—of a war singular in the annals of mankind; by which, after a prodigious destruction of the human species, and a variety of turns of fortune, all parties (the King of Prussia excepted, whose selfish and temporizing policy it is impossible to justify), may be said to have been losers.

"This reflection more particularly strikes us, in contemplating the infatuation of France and GreatBritain; of the former, in lavishing such a quantity of blood and treasure, with a view of giving an emperor to Germany; and of the latter, in neglecting her most essential interests, in withdrawing her attention from Spanish America, and loading her subjects with an immense public debt, in order to preserve entire the succession of the House of Austria; but more especially the folly of both, in continuing the war for several years after the object of it was lost on one side, and attained on the other. Nor can we, as Englishmen, in taking such a survey, avoid looking back with peculiar regret to the peaceful administration of Sir Robert Walpole—when the commerce and manufactures of Great Britain flourished in so high a degree, that the balance of trade in her favour amounted annually, on an average, to four millions sterling."

It is acknowledged that the few years of general peace subsequent to the Treaty of Aix-la-Chapelle, were some of the most prosperous and happy which Europe had known for ages. A free interchange of science, literature, and commerce, produced new views of society, and new inventions of the human mind. England and France, forgetting their past animosities, might be said to vie with each other in promoting the general welfare and interests of both countries.

And such, again, it may be said, was the case after the Peace of Paris in 1763, when a bloody and exterminating war had for seven years spread its desolating effects through some of the finest districts of Europe. Were the nations of Europe in any imaginable way benefited by this extreme trial of strength? No; but it left them weak, exhausted, and indebted to an amount unknown before. Whereas, had that long interval been spent in promoting instead of destroying its tranquillity, higher things might have resulted. Thrice happy might the nations of Europe, after that general pacification, have deemed themselves, could that treaty, with all its defects, have been prolonged! But it was not so to be. As if injustice, fraud, and rapacity had not been sufficiently manifested by some of the nations of Europe in the perpetration of palpable iniquity, a combination of might against right was for the third time in this century formed by some of the more powerful, against a weaker government; and Russia and Prussia, to whom, at length, Austria lent herself a willing accessary, marked the kingdom of Poland for their prey. With true Machiavellian policy, these powers, in defiance of all laws which the tacit consent of all civilized nations have recognized as the bulwarks of their political existence, the dismemberment of Poland was at length accomplished; while the other powers, with most unrighteous apathy, stood passively neutral. The horrors of fire and sword, and extermination, were thus let loose upon a country, in many respects one of the finest of continental Europe—untold miseries inflicted upon its inhabitants, who were thus driven as wanderers to seek refuge wherever the common humanity of mankind would afford it—and the remnant reduced to the humiliating condition of slaves. And thus was the genius of a high-minded people broken, and, in a measure, annihilated, and their share in the intellectual advance of the mind and of science retarded.

The western countries of Europe also were again to be the scene of bloodshed and of warlike devastation, towards the end of the eighteenth century. The French Revolution, that awful and all-ingulfing catastrophe, burst forth like a volcano, and overwhelmed all civilized governments with consternation and dismay. Like a pestilence, it flew to every corner of the land which gave it birth; the frame of general society was disorganized and convulsed, and the wide-spreading wars, to which it quickly gave rise, desolated the ancient monarchies of Europe with a rapidity perfectly unexampled. Almost the entire continent was soon converted into one vast military arena, for the study and practice of arms, and the genius of war sounded the tocsin in every land.

The soils of Europe were perpetually ensanguined by the blood of its population; the labours of the industrious serf were unjustly appropriated to the use of invading or retreating armies—the harvests which industry had sown and cultured, for the hosts of invaders which overran the previously peaceful districts of the Peninsula, of Holland, of Belgium, of Germany, of Russia,—fields of carnage on a frightfully extended scale. Lamentation, and mourning, and woe attended the footsteps of Napoleon, and marked the track of his emissaries, who, like locusts, infested the continental countries. The awful effects of his wicked and vain ambition were traced in the slaughtered millions of his victims—thus realizing, in its most literal sense, the sentiment, that the "Paths of glory lead but to the grave;" and that whilst this glory is gathered by a few, in the shape of honours and renown, large portions of the human race are visited with calamities of more than common magnitude; whilst the achievements of a few ring in the ears of mankind, long-enduring and unmitigated evils are, in various ways, heaped upon the nations who participate in these scenes of devastation and of blood.

If, then, the Peace of 1763 found the nations of Europe labouring under the severe pressure of debt, the peace of 1815, which terminated the most tremendous and bloody war which had ever afflicted them, perhaps, either in ancient or modern times—found the pressure, accompanied, as it was, by an unprecedented weight of taxation, its inseparable and ill-omened attendant, left them still poorer and more exhausted. It will invariably happen also, that at the termination of a long and general war, vast numbers of persons, whose sole profession was fighting, are turned loose on society; and, unable or indisposed to mingle in the painful occupations of citizens, become the drones or the common disturbers of order.

So was it subsequent to the Peace of Paris; so was it immediately after the battle of Waterloo had given new life and breathing to European society, and filled all hearts with new hopes of brighter days. And then the pecuniary affairs of the leading powers were disorganized and embarrassed to an unprecedented extent. Some of them—as Great Britain, burdened with debt, hastily contracted, to meet the extreme exigencies of the times—were placed in a state of financial difficulty. After subsidizing the allied powers to an extent perfectly unparalleled in former periods of history, and stirring up coalitions, both by her example and her negociations, against the common enemy, the condition of England, politically speaking, was one of comparative weakness.

Her resources and her strength were certainly inferior to what they were at the commencement of the war—for these resources were anticipated; and while the fee-simple (so to express it) was applied to existing exigencies, the interests of these vast sums were bequeathed to posterity.

Surely England merited high and honourable treatment at the hands of her allies in the negociations of 1814. Her commerce with all the ports of the world, which had been so mainly instrumental in crushing the continental despot, should have been pre-eminently promoted and assisted.

But it was not admitted to that consideration which it demanded: and the minister plenipotentiary, who, with full powers, represented the crown of England, either through the interest of high Tory principles, which led him to exalt the aristocracy and depress the meaner ranks of citizens; or from a reprehensible wish to gratify foreign potentates by the cession of advantages which ought to have preponderated on the side of Great Britain; or from an inability to grasp the true interest and position of his country; whatever were the causes, England did not reap all the advantages from this treaty which the high rank she then occupied entitled her to expect. But in his negociations, it must be assumed, that England's representative was not guided by that patriotism which led him to view all her relations with an abstract and a high reference to the whole. And if Lord Castlereagh, at Ghent, did not display the high-minded jealousy of his country's interest, as

Sir William Temple once did, at the Hague, (with his kindred spirit, De Wit,) of the honour of his master Charles the Second, it must be assumed that the last proved himself a more honest diplomatist than the profligate court of Charles had a right to expect. Whereas England, at the peace of 1814, might have looked for a more scrupulous diplomatist. But it signifies nothing, at this period, to view these matters in retrospect: our view should be prospective. With the relations and incumbrances which now characterize England, peace, for an indefinite period, is indispensable to her future prosperity. Overwhelmed with debt and taxation, her only chance of rising unscathed through her liabilities is in a period of uninterrupted peace, and in a skilful economy in the direction of her financial resources. And cannot—it is reiterated for the hundredth time—cannot England, which possesses colonies in almost every clime, with the sovereignty of the ocean, so regulate her measures of finance, as will carry her through her difficulties? She may, as has frequently been contended, turn these rich territories to a much higher account—in promoting an increased reciprocity of commerce, in making the produce of soils which own our jurisdiction, more instrumental in supplying the staple of our great manufactories—thus aiding and facilitating our traffic with other countries, by reducing the price of the raw commodity, and enabling us to better compete with those countries who are not so advantageously situated, in the foreign markets. Thus, in the raw article of cotton wool, our colonial advantages might be turned to an increasing account. The cotton manufactories of Great Britain are of the most prominent importance; they constitute a very considerable share of our native commerce.

Any attempt to cheapen the raw commodity should receive due attention. Why could we not grow the whole of our cotton-wool without purchasing of our neighbours, the Dutch and the French? The soils and climate of Guiana have been pronounced fitter for the growth of cotton than the West India islands. Why not appropriate almost the whole of this settlement to the produce of this tropical weed—or, at any rate, materially increase the number of its plantations? The prodigious consumption which the mills of Great Britain annually make of this staple article of their commerce, demands that every facility in the growth and propagation of this invaluable plant should be used. And if the soils of Guiana are more propitious to the growth and high culture of this MATERIAL than those of the Antilles, or the islands bordering on the Gulf of Mexico, a strong reason hence exists why a preference should be yielded to the former as an arena for its propagation. Will not the official authorities of the empire offer facilities for promoting this important object? Will not Lord Stanley, as the colonial organ of the state, promote all reasonable improvements which have a tendency to increase the wealth of that state? After having, some years back, recommended from his seat in parliament a grant to the planters of twenty millions of our money—a grant which, to many not unacquainted with the value of West India estates, appeared a profligate waste of the public money—will he not now, both by the timely application of bounties and otherwise, assist in promoting the revenue? Bounties and restrictions are frequent in some departments of our statistical code, and enacted with little reservation.

It will be said by some (and the truth of the allegation has never been set aside) that the agriculturists—so far as the growing of corn on lands unfitted by nature to produce the article, either in the same quality or abundance which distinguishes the soils of more propitious climes, is concerned—are visited with undue privileges; that they are protected by embargoes, restrictions, and duties which are intended to keep up the price of its produce above its natural, to an artificial standard. This may be a proper boon in favour of the inheritors of the soil, or it may not; but surely no one, in his senses, will contend that one great department or estate of the realm, should be protected, over others at whose expense the indulgence is granted.

Does it not occur to the President of the Board of Trade, or to the Secretary for the Colonies, that the trade of Great Britain—which has borne her so triumphantly through the late struggle, but which, at certain periods, has been, in many of its departments, embarrassed—likewise, occasionally needs a helping hand? Should not those classes of its citizens who, acting upon the inventions of Arkwright and of Watt, and striving to uphold the dignity and wealth of the state, be likewise admitted to equitable privileges, if not to high and honourable notice?

Viewing the question of peace or war on the side of expediency, in the great statistics of Europe, what is to be got by plunging the nations in a general war? Is not everything, on the other hand, to be lost? Let England and France, who may now be said to hold the balance of power in Europe, rather study to improve their high colonial advantages. Rich in maritime possessions, and in a prodigious extent of coasts in various parts of the world, whose fisheries may furnish forth exhaustless springs of wealth,—masters of soils yielding the produce of almost every clime, they may increase in power and in wealth, without seeking perpetually to impoverish each other.

Sir Robert Walpole and Cardinal De Fleury pursued a patriotic policy when they acted upon this principle. They knew how to estimate the blessings of peace; and millions of industrious citizens, in their respective countries, doubtless hailed with gratitude the boon which these ministers conferred upon them. How vast in the scale of true greatness do the names of Gustavus Vasa, and General Washington, rise above that of Napoleon? The first strove to raise their countries to high prosperity and greatness. Hence, to a degree of chivalry, the first Gustavus never ceased to pursue the enemies of his country, until he had re-established its freedom and happiness; he then sheathed his sword, and strove only how to benefit that country by the arts of peace. But the last of these seemed to exist only for blood and carnage. It will be said that he established an imperishable name by his military prowess and skill, and that the hero of Austerlitz, Jena, Friedland, Eylau, Wagram, and Borodino, stands prominent among the heroes of ancient and modern times. But the genius of his name, and the magnitude and celebrity of his conquests, should not blind us to the incalculable evils which have attended his lawless career. His acts are now matters of history, and posterity will know how to estimate them; but the inscription said to be affixed to his statue on the lofty column of Trajan, in the Place Vendôme, towards the latter part of his career, may, perhaps, pass as no extravagant exaggeration of the truth.*

What, then, on a general review of its history, has Europe actually gained by the wars of the last two hundred years? Have they tended to make her more rich, and powerful, and great, among the nations of the world? Has she become happier, risen higher in the scale of science, or more capable of imparting lessons of wisdom to mankind? Certainly not. On the contrary, the reverse of all this has sometimes been the case. When, after the Thirty Years' War, in which the Imperialists under Wallestein held Europe in alarms, the Peace of Westphalia gave the nations tranquillity, universal joy diffused itself throughout Europe. When, after the Seven Years' War under Frederick, peace again lent its healing influence to calm the troubled passions of the belligerent powers, society, oppressed with the intolerable evils which a constant state of warfare superinduced, hailed its termination at the famous Treaty of Paris in 1763. When, in 1814, the allied armies deposed the French usurper, and hurled him from his dominions, one note of universal gratulation prevailed; and society, which had been so long shaken to its very centre, again resumed confidence. Shall the lessons of past experience be altogether lost on the nations of Europe? Will they not see that they have much to lose and little to gain by plunging into a war? Can they not again emulate each other in promoting the higher interests of science? The internal structure of the earth whereon we dwell, for instance, is but little known. Volumes have been written upon the real nature and stratification of our globe beyond its mere superficies, far away from the actual inspection of man.

Theory, embracing splendid pictures of imagination, from the times of Burnet and Woodward, has been propounded to the world, with all the confidence and ingenuity of a fine and amplified fancy; and the present age abounds with scientific geologists, who have brought to their subject a much closer and more patient investigation. But, although the investigators of our day smile at some of the theorists of a former age, as at visionaries and enthusiasts, is there not also much of hypothesis mixed up with *their* assumptions?

The arduous and the accurate researches of the present age, in the process of examining the earth's surface, and the classifying the formations of the secret and wonderful agents which act unseen in the beds and recesses of our planet, no one will disparage or underrate; but it must be recollected, that we have scarcely yet pierced the superficies of the crust or rind of our globe, and therefore are but ill calculated to pronounce concerning its hidden structure. The unfathomed regions which lie far, far beneath those stratified beds, which have as yet been explored by the miner, are utterly unknown to us. Whether

* The inscription was to the effect following:—"Tyrant! if all the blood which you have shed were congregated around you, you might drink without bowing the head." A slaughter on a gigantic scale like his, might, in the opinion of some, earn for its ruthless perpetrator the title of *butcher* of his species.

central fires, or some other element, occupy the unknown spaces of these vast internal regions, is only vague conjecture.

Could not some of the leading powers of Europe, instead of expending their treasures in cutting each others throats, avail themselves of the inventions of a WATT or a DAVY, and pierce through the earth's crust to far greater depths than has ever yet been attempted by the ingenuity of man?

Again: could not the long-talked-of scheme of cutting through the Isthmus of Darien, and connecting the Atlantic with the Pacific, (lately revived by the French,) be made the undertaking of ourselves, as well as our neighbours? We are at least equally concerned in facilitating this junction of the two oceans, as any power in Europe.

In the year 1835 the present writer endeavoured to point out the vast advantages which would accrue from carrying into effect this project. The scheme is not a new one; it has been talked of at various periods, but the measure has never yet been attempted.

The celebrated Humboldt, in 1802, pointed out eight different routs which he esteemed practicable for the communication between the two oceans, but neither of these have ever been acted upon. These were, (to use his own words,) 1st. Riviere de la Paix, et Tacoutche, Tesse; 2d. Rio del Porte et Rio Colorado; 3d. Rio Huallaga, et Huacanco; 4th. Golfe de St. George's et Estero de Aysen; 5th. Rio de Huasacualco et Rio de Chimalapa; 6th. Lac Nicaragua; 7th. Isthme de Panama; 8th. Ravin de la Raspadura, et Embarcadero de Naipi. Of these eight, the preference was given by the present writer to that through the Isthmus of Panama, and the valley through which the river Chagres flows was pointed out as offering an eligible line, by way either of Cruces or Bala Mona. It was, moreover, on the occasion alluded to, strenuously urged upon England not to suffer the honour of such an undertaking to be wrested from her by others. A frigid apathy, however, seemed to pervade our countrymen in this matter; and the French, more enterprising in the cause of science, are now about to profit by our supineness.

Could we not, however, it is asked, still participate in this great undertaking? In the promotion of schemes for facilitating wide-extended commerce, might the nations of Europe thus emulate each other in the cultivation of science and in investigating the greater works of nature; they might devote some part of their treasures at once in furthering the interests of commerce, and raising the sum of human knowledge. And where is the philanthropist who will not place these pursuits before the practice of aggressive warfare—attended with the destruction of social order, and substituting in its room the wholesale slaughter of human kind?

Are the battles of Austerlitz, and Trafalgar, and Waterloo, with their bloody trophies, to be fought in every age, in order to preserve the balance of power, or to please the cupidity of selfish despots?

Is it not rather thrice to be wished that the famous scheme which Henry the Great, had he lived, would, as Sully tells us, have carried into execution for effecting a perpetual peace in Europe—or a similar one—be still made the subject of serious and philosophic attention?

E. P.

Avon House, Wilts, Oct. 27th, 1844.

COLONIAL STATISTICS.

[NEW SERIES.]

NO. IX.—THE ISLAND OF ST. CHRISTOPHER (ST. KITT'S).

History.—Saint Christopher, by the Caribs called *Liemuiga*, or the fertile isle, and known also by the name of *St. Kitt's*, was discovered by Columbus, on his second voyage, 10th Nov., 1493. The island was first settled (by the English) in 1625. In 1623, Captain Warner (afterwards Sir Thomas) settled on the island, "with his son and fourteen Londoners." In 1772, the inhabitants experienced a terrific hurricane, which destroyed £50,000 worth of property.

Extent.—St. Kitt's, or St. Christopher's, is situated in 17° 18′ north latitude, and 62° 40′ west longitude; it is west by north 50 miles from Antigua, N.N.W. 11 miles from Nevis. The extreme length of the island is 19 miles, north-west to south-east; extreme breadth, 6 miles; circumference, 72 miles; extreme altitude, 3,711 feet; area, 68¾ square miles, or 44,000 acres, divided into nine parishes and seven districts, which are named below.

Geography.—The *West India Guide* thus clearly describes the island:—"The beauties of this island have been frequently and justly extolled; although of a mountainous character, and of a similar organic construction to the generality of the Caribbean range, the combination of its parts suggests the idea of elaboration, and it may be said to claim for itself a peculiar conformation. It is of an elongated form, contracted towards the south-east into a long neck, a regular series of mountains running longitudinally through the island, increasing in height, and becoming more compact towards the north-western quarter, where a rude craggy pyramid shoots high above the common masses, inclining its rugged head towards the verge of a capacious crater. A nearly uniform range of country on an inclined plane, and intersected at intervals by deep ravines, generally intervenes between the more precipitous features of the mountains and the sea-coast, presenting a rich surface of cultivation, and a vivid contrast with the more sombre shades of the forests towering above them."

Soil.—The soil is considered to be generally good, chiefly of a dark grey loam, very porous, and well adapted for the sugar-cane, which has been very productive here. Among the numerous fruits of so rich a soil, the *citrus aurantium*, or China-orange tree, (as also the *Seville*,) grows in great luxuriance. The *Shaddock* and "forbidden" fruit is of the citrus tribe; it is dangerous for an European to indulge in eating this delicious but deceitful fruit, without its being duly prepared for the reception of the stomach.

Geology.—The igneous character of the earth is evident; immense strata of volcanic ashes are everywhere observable. Among the mountains in the centre of the island, there is one that contains mines of sulphur, and another in which there is said to be a mine of silver, but, as in the case of the Irish gold mine of yore, the precious metal is not to be obtained without a *quid pro quo* of labour.

In the south-eastern quarter there are several salt-ponds, one of which is upwards of 100 acres in extent.

Climate.—The climate is judged to be very healthy, which is accounted for by the elevation of the land above the sea; the mean temperature on the coast is 80°. The coldest month is February, the warmest August. The bracing quality of the atmosphere distinguishes this from other West India islands.

Rivers.—There are four rivers on the isle; two at Old-road, in the parish of St. Thomas; another at the small village of St. Mary's, (Cayon,) and the fourth at Palmetto-point, Trinity parish; in the low-lands springs are plentiful, but some of their water is too much impregnated with saline particles to be palatable.

The water in common use (as is the case in most of our West India possessions) is rain-water, collected from the houses, preserved in large tanks.

Mountains.—The awful crag of *Mount Misery* shoots slantingly forward over the mouth of a volcanic chasm, like a huge peninsula in the air. It is a most tremendous precipice.

St. Kitt's presents to the eye an irregular oblong figure, through the centre of which runs a regular series of mountains from north to south, in the midst of which stands Mount Misery, 3,711 feet in perpendicular height, and, although evidently of volcanic production, clothed with the finest wood and pasture almost to the very summit. On the west side Brimstone Hill rises gradually from the sea to a height of 950 feet. Monkey Hill is the south termination of a range of great mountains, which increase in height towards the north.

Valley.—The Valley of Basseterre, on the coast of which district the capital is situated, is exquisitely beautiful.

Chief Towns.—These are termed Basseterre, south, (the capital); Sandy Point, west; Cayon, north; Old Road, south. Parishes: St. George, St. Peter, St. Mary, Christ Church, St. John, St. Paul, St. Thomas, St. Anne, Trinity, (Palmetto Point).

"The two principal hotels (says a recent traveller, whose work is quoted in 'Osborne's West India Guide for 1844',) are better houses than are generally to be met with of that class in the West Indies. The *cuisine* is very good, and the bed-rooms airy and clean. There are branches of the West India and Colonial Banks established here." An excellent reading-room is supplied with standard English literature and newspapers: there is a billiard-room also.

Population.—In 1834 the population consisted of 1,612 whites, 3,000 coloured, and 20,660 negroes, forming a total of 25,272. Population in July 1838—free, 4,952 males, 5,483 females; apprenticed, 5,739 males, 6,308 females; total, 22,482.

The amount awarded to St. Christopher's under the Emancipation Act, was 331,630*l.*

Religion—Education.—There are six public schools, and an institution for the support and education of poor and destitute children. A return of the number of churches, &c., dated 1838, is given in the "History of the British Colonies." The colonists support eight valuable livings, and more than a dozen Methodist and Moravian chapels.

Government.—There is a Lieutenant-Governor, Council of Ten, and House of Assembly, (24 members,) with a deputy from Anguilla. The subjoined is a list of the present government-officials: Lieut.-Governor, C. Cunningham, Esq.; President of the Council, W. G. Crooke, Esq.; Chief Justice, &c., J. K. Wattley, Esq.; Registrar of Vice-Admiralty Court, T. Harpur, Esq.; Marshal of ditto, J. G. Pickwood, Esq.; Secretary, &c., T. Harpur, Esq.; Attorney-General, ———; Solicitor-General, R. Claxton, Esq.; Provost-Marshal, N. Hart, Esq.; Treasurer and Post-Master, J. Berridge, Esq.; Collector of Customs, A. Jones, Esq.; Comptroller of ditto, H. King, Esq.; Speaker of the Assembly, A. H. Rawlins, Esq.; Agent in London, J. Colquhoun, Esq., St. James's Place. (It is the duty of the London Agents of the West India settlements to direct attention at home to the political, mercantile, and domestic interests of their different colonial constituencies.)

Commerce.—The chief products are sugar, rum, and molasses. The following is a table of exports of the chief articles of produce to the United Kingdom in the following years:—

	1837.		1838.
Rum	87,380 gallons.	...	65,677 gallons.
Molasses	14,895 cwts.	...	18,488 cwts.
Coffee	605 lbs.	...	80,839 lbs.
Arrow-root	8,290 lbs.	...	16,568 lbs.

We subjoin an account of the exports of sugar from St. Christopher's into the United Kingdom, during each of the eleven years ending with 1841:—

	1831.	1832	1833.	1834.	1835	1836.
Cwts.	101,968	80,602	80,390	105,355	87,614	64,810

	1837.	1838.	1839.	1840	1841
Cwts.	73,270	93,597	135,548	94,390	63,936

The total value of exports from the island in 1836, was 145,703*l.*; imports to the island in the same year, 98,344*l.*

Collective value of imports and exports, 1840—imports, 134,732*l.*; exports, 217,403*l.*

Aggregate annual value of the productions of St. Christopher's, (from parliamentary documents,) 753,528*l.*

Shipping, 1842. { Inwards, 469 ships, of 23,782 tons. / Outwards, 475 ships, of 22,723 tons.

Revenue.—The revenue of 1836 is stated at 4,193*l.*, and the expenditure at 4,372*l.* Expenditure by Great Britain in 1836: civil establishment, 1,970*l.*; ecclesiastical, 136*l.*; total, 2,106*l.* Expenditure, paid by the colony in sterling money, (1836): civil establishment, 2,564*l.*; contingent expenditure, 576*l.*; judicial establishment, 438*l.*; contingent expenditure, 1,554*l.*; ecclesiastical establishment, 2,161*l.* The salary of the president administering the government is 650*l.*, and about 152*l.* in fees.

Wages for Labour.—Domestic, per month, 1842, 1*l.* 0s. 10d.; predial, per day, 1s.; trades, 2s. 1d.

Colonial Arms.—The shield represents a figure, in Spanish costume, (probably Columbus,) standing on the deck of a man-of-war, in the attitude of looking through a telescope, and reconnoitering the land in the distance.

THE SYSTEM OF COLONIAL-CROWN-LAND GRANTING,

THE TRUE SOURCE OF THE DIFFICULTIES WHICH BESET EMIGRATION.

BY A SIXTEEN-YEARS' RESIDENT IN CANADA.*

FROM 1835 to the present time, the settlement actually made in Canada has been comparatively trifling; in 1832 or 1833, emigration was at its height, then fell off, and ceased totally during the disturbance in 1837, 1838, and 1839. Since then it has partially revived, but the laws relative to wild-land valuation have become so unequal, that money, to a considerable amount, is now necessary, as the price is to be in cash at the time of sale. The emigrants of these latter days are mostly of the poorer classes; and if they could not procure money to pay an instalment of one-fifth down, how could they get money to pay the whole price of the land at eight shillings an acre? or the additional valuation of a government agent, whose interest it is to sell the land as high as he can, in order to increase his own per-centage— consequently, though some persons had means, purchased, and became settlers, the number as compared with other periods was trifling and insignificant, and fully warrants the assertion, that the settlement of the country by emigration has been not only checked, but nearly put a stop to. The emigrants of this latter period were, as to general character, poor, and as they found no rest for their feet in Canada as a home, nor work for their hands; they were, like thousands of their predecessors, left without a choice, and went to the States, where of course many of them settled, having friends and connections; others became hewers of wood and drawers of water to Uncle Sam, so long as he had means, or could *shave* John Bull out of means, to pay them. But the aforesaid John, considering that he was shaved too close, and finding that the operator in many cases, not content with the hair, had taken largely of the hide, stopped the supplies; and, moreover, was such a fool as to expose himself, and yet quite *gritty*, (anglicè angry) even at the expense of being laughed at; and though told there was no kind of use in getting *riled* (anglicè rippled) about it, for Sam himself said that John was the darndest fool on earth to say a word about it, having such a chance, from his position in society, that he could shave rings round him, to make up for it; however, John certainly did get riled, though he should not have done so. But he was unaccustomed to doing the business in a public manner; it is true, he tried shaving a little in his own family, as in the case of the emigrant pensioners and half-pay officers; and it may also be true that he has established shaving-shops in all his colonies; but then it is only to keep his own children clean; he has a great abhorrence, poor man of a public shave, his position in society compels him to denounce the doctrine of repudiation as connected with the business, and he stamps, as base rascality, any attempt upon his own pocket.

* Continued from page 607.

He stopped Sam's supplies, and about the same time he was seized with a fit of real munificence; out of mere spite, one would think, to Sam, he determined to cultivate one of his own plantations, and make a nation of it in less than no time; and with this purpose in view, he resolved to expend one million and a half of money in Canada on public works, for the improvement of the country, and encouragement of settlement by emigration. These were great days for Canada; and, no doubt, Mr. Bull's munificence has been, and will be, of great service to the country, in a commercial point of view; and this is perhaps saying as much for it as it deserves. The emigration which was caused was immense, but it was not from the quarter John had anticipated; he merely succeeded in employing Sam's discarded workmen, and, generally speaking, a rough set of fellows they are: the onset of labourers from the United States was tremendous—they fairly stormed the country, and have continued storming since they came. I should say that from ten to twenty thousand indigent people, men, women, and children, were brought into Canada by the sudden announcement, and as sudden execution, of public works, which the British government projected, under the mistaken idea that they would, like the public works of former days, be an assistance to the British emigrant, willing and likely to become a settler in the country. Instead of the emigrant fresh from the land of his fathers, with all the associations of friendship, and feeling, for his home and the institutions of his country, we have thus been inundated with the froth of the emigration of years, the refuse of the multitude from which every thing that had weight had long subsided, from which every thing that had worth was long since separated—in fact, the scum of humanity. Few of these men have the idea of settling, even if they had the ability. The length of their sojourn in the land of liberty is not without its effect, and it is not at all surprising to find anti-British feelings amongst them.

The attempt to promote emigration and consequent settlement by an outlay on public works, has decidedly failed in the only quarter from which it would be desirable or proper to encourage it; indeed, the newly arrived emigrant, supposing him to have land to fall back upon, would still have no business in a place, or on a work, occupied by the rival factions of Cork and Connaught, composed of men who have individually made the tour of the United States, and drank deeply at the fountain of lynch-law and liberty. Let us glance at the benefit which the government thought they could confer on the emigrant, by the plan of affording employment on public works. Unquestionably, it was to enable him to obtain means to further his settlement in the country, to render his condition more stable and secure, and protect him as much as possible from the unfortunate or unforeseen circumstances of difficulty, which might beset his path at the commencement of his labours as a settler; and there is no doubt this end was fully attained by the outlay on the Welland and Rideau canals in former years; for, without doubt, many men, now in affluence, first got the start of their difficulties as early settlers, through their earnings as labourers on those public works. But how were these men situated? had they to work to support their families from day to day—had they nothing to fall back upon—no place, no home to go to in the long winter—nothing earthly to depend upon, but what the morrow might bring forth? No! no! this was not their case; every man had land in those days, free-grants had not gone out of fashion; the families of great numbers of them were upon that land, and had a house over them, and wherewithal to keep body and soul together; at the least, they were not the houseless, homeless, wanderers of the present day; their exertions, as labourers in the construction of works of great benefit to the community, enabled them to turn to account the capital that had been placed in their hands by the government, namely, land; and, from being poor, to become rich, comparatively; from being a weight upon the community, probably rate-receivers at home, to become rate-payers, revenue-payers, and consumers, in the colony. In this way public works were of incalculable benefit to the country: but how does the case now stand? do the public works of the present day assist settlement? No—whoever dreamt of a man earning and procuring as a day-labourer, with perhaps six or seven children hanging on him, the sum of forty pounds in cash, to enable him to purchase one hundred acres of land, in the rear of all settlement, at the established price of eight shillings—what Canadian could imagine it? why, he might live a long life in the country, live well, and in independence, and not see so much money during the whole period. The labourers of the present day cannot become settlers; they must not become possessors either at home or abroad; their poverty is their curse; honesty, industry, privations, and hardships avail them not; they are seemingly too low in the scale of nature even to rank as independent beings; their poverty is, as I say, their curse; and with us, legislation, which ought to protect, is made use of to grind them to the earth. How singular, when we think of Britain's millions of square miles of waste territory teeming with the means of life and wealth, so capable of being made the home of industrious happiness!

John Bull's million and a half is expended, or nearly so, with a double purpose, as he had intended, truly; but one of the results not quite what had been anticipated:—it is true, as to the first purpose, it has opened up the country, it has advanced its general interests, making it as a colony more wealthy in resources; as to the second purpose, *it is true*, it has kept hunger from the bowels of a starving multitude of aliens, emigrants, men who would rather be his foes than his friends to-morrow: has it done more than the act of charity I have just detailed? has it made a settler, or established one? has it enabled these aliens to purchase his land, and become settlers, feigning subjection to his laws, whilst they sought but an opportunity of destroying his power? No, no, it has not done this evil; for whilst, through its means, no British settler, a poor man, could make a permanent home of the country, praise be to God, the mass of vagabonds from Down East, who have eat it up, will also, when the banquet is concluded, be compelled to seek elsewhere a subsistence, and relieve us of their presence. What might have been done with this amount of means, how many hundreds of families might have received assistance from it in their establishment as settlers, if it had been accompanied with that greatest of all boons to the poor man—land! It would not then have been necessary to advertise in the United States for labourers; judiciously expended, at proper times and seasons, it would have afforded an almost unbounded source of relief and assistance to the man who, while he laboured at public works, the effect of the growing greatness of his country, was himself growing with her, in the course which led to independence and wealth; in this way, it might have been made to aid the settlement of from one to five thousand heads of families. Its effect then, as regards healthy emigration, has been of a negative character: the settler who had means, it did not make a labourer of, he did not want its assistance; the emigrant who had no means, it did not make a settler of.

The settlement of Canada by emigration is at a stand-still, none but the monied man can obtain land: now, as a general rule, emigrants are poor; they are not the rich who will leave home and its associations, to begin life in a wilderness; consequently the purchasers are few, and I make little doubt that the purchase of wild crown-land at the present day is chiefly confined to persons who have been long resident in the province, have become wealthy, and are seeking to extend their possessions: the industrious labourer is nearly as well off in either England, Scotland, or Ireland, particularly if he has a family; indeed, I have only to refer to the facts which have occurred, and are daily occurring, upon the St. Lawrence and Welland canals, to prove that the labourers are in pinched and straitened circumstances; there are such immense numbers of them in the country, that the price of labour has fallen, and must continue to do so. As farm-labourers there is but little chance, for, as I have before stated, the country is full of cotters; and I have no doubt of the truth of the assertion I make, that if the crown-lands were thrown open to actual settlers, there are from one to two thousand heads of families, at present in the country as cotters, who would take up land within six months, and thus leave room for others in the capacity of labourers.

In the foregoing pages the reader has a sketch of emigration as it resulted in settlement, combined with remarks which it is hoped will direct his attention to the great source of all, both of good and evil, that abounds in the lengthened period it embraces. That which in the first instance gave Canada a name as a settlement, was crown-grants and protection;—that which has made it a province with a settled frontier of hundreds of miles, and a population of some hundreds of thousands, is the self-same power: to be more particular, That to which Canada owes its great prosperity and wonderful increase, up to 1830, is the action of the crown-land office;—that to which it, in the same period and ever since, owes its greatest curse, wild-land monopoly, is the self-same office, the self-same power. To come down to later times: the source of the misery as well as the welfare of hundreds is the same fountain: It has been the medium of wealth to the speculator;—it has been the medium of suffering and ruin to the unsuspecting half-pay officer, pensioner, and others, who were gulled by its misrepresentations: It has been the medium of establishing a noble fortune for the Canada Land Company, and in some measure of replenishing the provincial treasury;—it has been the medium of plunging thousands into the arms of republicanism, and it is the grinding heavy curse which hangs over the poor industrious emigrant, and gags the energies of the land, depriving us of the assistance that long ere this might have been derived from thousands of our countrymen:

It might have been the means of making us powerful, happy, united in a preponderating British influence;—it might be the ultimate means of our destruction. Let me then call the mind of the reader more particularly to the consideration of this power, so great for either good or evil; let us search for the secret springs which gave it action.

Until 1827, crown land was given to the settler free, or with trifling regulations attached, in the later years of the period, which in nowise retarded settlement, though they failed of their object; namely, compelling settlement on granted lands;—and while we must admit, that up to this period the province received a greater accession in settlement than it has ever proportionally done at any other period, under any other regulations; yet we must look to this long continuance of free grants, for most of the evils which have and do now beset emigration.

Lands, as I have said, were given out with great freedom in the earlier times; United-Empire loyalists received grants of land for themselves to a great extent, and their children were entitled to grants of two hundred acres each, without restriction as to time in the application for it; and thus, up to a very late period, these rights were still under a course of application; and during the whole period in which they have existed, they have been a subject of barter and speculation, causing immense tracts of land to get into the hands of individuals, to the great injury of the general interests of the country. Of a similar character to these, in effect, were the grants of land accorded to the militia-men, who so gallantly served in defence of the province during the last American war of 1812, and the sale of, and application for which, was, like the others, without restriction. Likewise, any man who applied in these times, could get one or two hundred acres of land, whether he in reality intended to become a settler, or not; he had only to state that it was his wish to do so, in order to get the grant; and any influential man, who was brought by circumstances into connection with the government, and did some service or other, was rewarded with two or three thousand acres, or so: the consequence of this course began to appear, in the immense blocks of land which lay, through the settlements, in a state of nature, materially retarding its interests, as the holders could not procure their price, for settlers at the then present time would not buy, even if they had the means, when they could get land as good, for nothing; and thus these lands lay till the settlement of the country gave them a value; and, as I have elsewhere remarked, they were a dead weight upon the settler in their vicinity. However, labour did give them a value, and was fast increasing it; and the farmer, to redeem himself, and as a means in his opinion to check this accumulation in the hands of non-settlers, demanded a tax upon wild lands, which was established; but this measure was so slow in its operation, necessarily so limited in its amount, and withal so improperly managed, that it had no other effect than to change the lands from the hands of those absentees, and others who had omitted or were unable to pay the tax, into the hands of men who were, and thus further to constitute and consolidate the monopoly.

I have shown some of the evil; let us now take a glance at the good which flowed from this system of crown-land granting. I have said that settlement went on rapidly under these regulations; the province was growing rapidly, it was making prodigious strides; the success of one man brought many; emigration showed a steady increase from year to year, which nothing but the demand on the part of the crown, of money for their land, could have checked; and which to the present day would have increased, and kept increasing, if that demand had not been made; and if we look to the class of men who composed the settlers of those days, we find that they were of a character generally distinguished for industry and application, and every quality calculated to make themselves successful, and the country prosperous.

These people came to the country, (with the single exception of the Robinson emigration,) as people should come—without help, without assistance, with a full knowledge of the responsibilities they laboured under: as regarded their families, they knew that they had help in perspective, but by their own exertions they must live to reach it; a beneficent government held out the hand to them, and promised to foster their energies, to guard their interests, and enable them to reap the benefit of their industry; and they had before them examples of others, who, coming to the country similarly poor, similarly circumstanced, had risen to affluence; thus they had the strongest incentives to perseverance; and, with such motives of action in view, for themselves and their families, namely, affluence and independence, what difficulties were too great to be overcome, what restrictions, short of debarring them from the possesion of the soil, could operate against their success?

They did succeed, and are now a living testament of the triumph of industry, as well as a certain indication of what might be effected by a well-regulated system of free grants, and, in numberless instances, a striking proof that poverty is no bar to success, but, on the contrary, if we view it as impelling to action and exertion, it operates as a most powerful assistant. Again, I will repeat an assertion I have before made; namely, that industry and poverty are the best capital a new settler can start with: under the influence of the first, exertion becomes less difficult, and labour light; the second compels exertion, compels labour, compels a close observance of the practical working of things, in order to be enabled to seize every advantage which may offer; in a word, it is the parent of necessity, and necessity is the parent of invention; the want of either one or both of these qualities constituted the rock on which the Robinson emigration split; as a general character, industry was totally wanting among them: and how could men be said to be poor, who lived upon the fat of the land, and had not a thought for the morrow; they fared sumptuously, they knew not how they got to America, they knew not how they got to their land, their energies, if they indeed possessed such, were not called into action in any other way than in exertions to eat as much pork, and beef, and bread as they could—eat, drink, and be merry was the order of the day; their minds were lulled into a state of suavity; they rose up like the ox, and eat, and lay down again, and slept; their day was all sunshine, they never dreamt of a cloud overcasting; and, poor devils, when they did get their eyes opened, by the withdrawal of government support, they found themselves more helpless and miserable than they had ever been in their father-land? Was it at all strange, then, that such men as these did not succeed, was it strange that they should abandon their settlement, and separate east, west, north, and south, in search of a living, and to unlearn the habits which the unfortunate character of their advent in the country had inculcated; as well as to learn the contrary and most essential habit of self-dependence, without which, in the lower walks of life, independence would become an obsolete word, to which no meaning could be attached.

So much for settlements effected by free unrestricted land-granting! there is no doubt the system did good, there is no question but it did evil; it gave a large amount of sound and healthy settlement to the country; it also entailed a curse upon it in more ways than one, it effected settlement in a manner that no other plan could, it placed means at once in the hands of the emigrant, which in ninety-nine cases out of a hundred he could wield by his own unaided exertions, at all events so as to keep far in advance of want; again in almost every case, this gift served to call forth his energies, year by year he added to its value, and went on his course in the almost certain expectance of independence. Its evils were alike great; it promoted and maintained speculation in wild land, to the utter detriment of the general interests of the country, retarding general settlement by diverting the possession of waste land from the crown, and purposes of settlement to the monopolist or speculator; and it was the mainspring, from the action of which resulted that greatest of all evils, wild crown-land valuation. It ceased; as I have said, the last act was that which gave land to an indifferent class, the Robinson emigration, and it gave place to a string of measures which have finally checked the accumulation of wild crown-lands, in the hands of speculators—the grants to the children of United-Empire loyalists, and militia pensioners, have also been commuted and abolished; and thus measures have been adopted, by means of which the crown can retain possession of the wild land as long as they like; but I would beg to remind the reader, that if the great benefit of checking speculation has been brought about by these enactments, it has been at the expense of settlement, which has in a great degree ceased also; nor were these measures at all sudden in their operation, there must have been plenty of time to digest them, for they have extended over a period of upwards of twenty years; so that there is but little excuse afforded to those men who have had the management of our affairs, for not being able to distinguish between a positive evil and a positive good, and legislate in such a way as to prevent the one, while they fostered and encouraged the other.

I have said that the operation of the unrestricted free-grant system was injurious to the country, that it promoted and maintained speculation, retarded general settlement, and was also the source of the greatest evil we labour under namely, crown-land valuation; the investigation of these subjects embraces a wide field, and though I may not be able to go into the matter as fully as might be thought necessary, yet I trust that the few observations I may make will be sufficient to place it in a fair light, and aid the formation of an opinion in the minds of the intelligent. The immense tracts of wild land, held by every man of influence in the country, naturally induced them to cast about in their minds for any possible plan of turning it to account and though their land must, from its situation, and the labour of the surrounding settlement, become more and more valuable every day, as of course in a new country, labour is the foundation of value, and as the country increased from the labour of settlers, so must that value; yet so long as settlement was fostered to such an extent by free grants from the government, or rather so long as free grants existed, they must wait an indefinite time to realize any thing from it—these reflections were much increased, when the country demanded a tax upon wild lands, which lay, as I have said, a drag upon the exertions of the farming class. I am loth to pronounce an opinion upon any set of men, that might be unjust, but I can say what my own opinions and wishes would be likely to be, if I had been in their circumstances, possessed of large tracts of unavailable land, with a threatened tax hanging over it, I would have striven to prevent free grants to settlers, and, instead thereof, have a value put upon wild crown-land, thereby raising my own property nominally to that value at least, and in general bringing me into the market with greater advantage than the crown; for if a man would settle, and must buy, he would be likely to seek situation, and would give me the preference, my land having a value from its contiguity to market and good neighbourhood, and the labour expended in that neighbourhood, whereas the crown value was merely nominal, and not intrinsic: by this course I would fortify myself against the tax.

Now these would be my opinions and wishes; I don't say how much they were acted on by others. The people succeeded in passing a wild-land-tax law in 1820, but as lands were to be permitted to be eight years in arrear before distress for collection, the law did not apparently come into operation till 1828, and lands were not sold under it till 1830, and by that time the waste lands of the crown were from four to five shillings per acre, and consequently the property of every holder of wild lands was increased in the same ratio, as no man was expected to undersell the government, and thus a value was given to lands for the first time, which they did not intrinsically possess. Now there was at this period, independent of the absentee lands owned by persons resident in the province, hundreds of thousands of acres which had in early as well as later days been given out by the government, the owners of which had left the country, and abandoned it; this circumstance, together with the value which government had been prevailed upon to give to wild land, reconciled the speculator to the tax, and, if he had money, gave an opportunity for another haul; he well knew that a great portion of these lands must be sold to pay the tax; he well knew that money was scarce in the country, and consequently that there would be few competitors; and when we consider that the eight-years' tax ranged at about twenty pounds a thousand acres, is it to be wondered that fortunes were made in a day, and the monopoly of wild lands increased tenfold? These were glorious times for the speculator; he got in numberless instances a thousand acres of land for twenty pounds, when the crown price for the same quantity was two hundred and fifty pounds; and he had all the advantages of situation in his favour besides, for, as I have said, these lands lay in the heart of settlements.

Here, then, the motive power was the people in the first instance demanding a tax, which in itself, and the proceedings had upon the law, was just and proper, with this single exception, (a great one certainly,) that the government should have been the purchasers, in fact, should have paid the tax, reassumed the land, and appropriated it to purposes of settlement at once, putting a sufficient price upon it to make a return for the outlay, being guided in such estimate by the value which labour and situation had given it. Again, that the landed interest had a hand in these affairs, it would be in vain to deny; they assisted in no small degree to establish a crown-land valuation, and the tax-law in its first effects was a mine of wealth to them.

Now, as regards the law, it evidently arose out of the free-grant system; no other state than such as was brought about by that system would have rendered it necessary; in a case of general settlement, it could have had no foundation, for in that case individuals would not, through means of the possession of large intervening blocks of land, have reaped the benefit of the labour of the neighbouring settlers, and it would not then be necessary to establish any tax or rate, but such as was contributed in common by every one; but the accumulation of wild lands in the hands of non-settlers had grown to be a crying evil in the land, and such as could be dealt with in no other way than by a tax. The people demanded redress of the grievance under which they laboured; they demanded a tax upon the, to them, unproductive lands of the non-settlers, to enrich whom their labour was expended; they demanded it, to free themselves from the evils which the bad policy of their rulers had entailed upon them; and the institution of it would have been sound policy, if it had been made the means of replacing the government for purposes of settlement again in possession of the land, which unquestionably had been diverted from its original purpose, by falling into the hands of the speculator or non-settler.

The public mind was fully opened to the evils of unrestricted land-granting, and as any course was considered better than one which had led to such results, no fault was found with the adoption of a remedy by the law-makers and influential members of the community, which, as it had no effect upon the then settler, was disregarded by him; he was content if this property paid a tax, and cared not who it belonged to whilst it did so; and besides this, he was given to understand that the operation of the tax-law would most certainly bring the land into the market, and immediate settlement would follow; and thus the landowners were allowed to legislate for themselves, which of course they did, and if they gave the settler a wild-land tax of trifling amount, they took to themselves, as a set-off, wild-land valuation, seeming to lose in the prospect of present gain, all power to estimate the shackles they were forging for future emigrants. These men had enough of waste crown-land, they did not want any more of that article, but sought most anxiously to make what they had available as a marketable matter, and how could this be better done than by putting a price upon wild crown-land, thus checking settlement in that quarter, and drawing it to the channels they had prepared for it?—this extra value of land rendered the tax bearable as far as they were concerned, and as the law appointed that lands should be sold for the tax in the way which I have elsewhere stated, they saw their further benefit in the purchase of what they had given so great a value to, and which from the circumstances of the country they well knew must fall into their hands.

It was about these times, when the birth of this idea of crown-land valuation occurred, that government, no doubt taking into consideration the continual and increasing influx of emigrants, came to the conclusion that it was not, within itself, able to deal with them all, and in this vein being willing to divide the trouble as well as profit of the business, brought, what many (perhaps ignorant) people are pleased to term a curse upon the country, in the shape of the Canada Land Company, at once constituting it the leviathan landholder, and placing it at the head of all monopolies. I am one of those who hold that the settlement of a colony should proceed through the crown alone, that it should not be made a matter of trade or barter, or be conducted on principles of speculation for any other interest than that of the settler and the country. Now I would wish to ask, what has the Canada Company done for the country, that could not have been just as well done by the government? I will say—could it not have been better done by the government, on a more extended scale, and with infinitely less cost to the settlers? for if the crown could deal with the company for eighteen pence or two shillings an acre, is it not reasonable to suppose that it could have dealt with the settler on the same terms, and, by a parity of reasoning, it is right to assume that, by such a course, the settlement of the country would have progressed much more than it has done; for if the company could do what they have effected, holding lands at from five to twenty shillings an acre, it is quite likely the crown would have gone beyond them with less rates, perhaps free grants, and equal exertions; in a word, is it a good principle of Colonial government, to throw up the direction of settlement, and for a mere matter of present apparent gain to hand the emigrant over to the tender mercies of a company whose sole object is to enrich themselves, and procure a large dividend out of the pocket of the emigrant, thereby extracting from him the means that otherwise would go to enrich the country? is it honest, I say, thus to make the poor man a subject of barter, and to enter into, or sanction a scheme, which has for its object making money out of his distresses; did these men enter into this speculation solely with a view to benefit the public, or with a view to make the public the means of benefiting themselves? did they, good-natured souls as they have ever been represented, lavish their attentions upon the country, and their money upon public works, (which they have taken care to let the world know,) without a thought of remuneration, without a thought of self? could they, have had an eye to their pocket in those things? oh, no, they are so disinterested, if you look at the public papers, they will tell you that the company has done wonders for Canada, and laid out enormous sums of money in it, which the public might reasonably suppose came from their own pockets, as there is no talk of their ever having received anything. I ask, with what sense of justice the government could lend themselves to the establishment of such an incubus upon the land, how they could sanction the robbery of the immigrants for private purposes, making public property the medium? I ask, on what principle of justice the government of the day could throw into the hands of these men, not only large tracts of land in the western parts of the province, but also the vacant crown-reserves all over the province, thus bringing the company to every man's door already settled in the country, and making him a means of improving their property, so as to enable them to sell these same crown-reserves for from eight and nine-pence to twenty shillings an acre. I do not dispute the fact, that the Canada Company have expended large sums of money in the country; I do not dispute that they have been anxious to settle their land, for by this means they would raise money, and increase the value of what lay on hand; nor do I think the fact can be disputed, that they have endeavoured to sell their land at as high a price as it would bear, and sought to make all they could by their speculation: and small blame to them for it; but I cannot echo the sentiment as regards the government, which first established the cursed conclave, and then fostered, encouraged, and, I may say, confederated with them to raise the value of their property by high prices on crown-land.

This measure did not take its rise exactly, in free-crown-land granting, but it trod so closely upon its heels, and was so analogous in its effects in many respects, that the resemblance is not to be mistaken; all the private monopoly we before had, was nothing to it; it at one blow shut up millions of acres of the best land in the province from general settlement, and placed it in such a situation, that the labour of individual settlement, must go to aid the government-appointed monopoly in conferring a value upon it, until men possessed of money sufficient to purchase at their appointed price could be found. Monopolies sprung from unrestricted free grants, but we never had anything to equal this one, till free grants had first paved the way by land-valuation, and, when once constituted, its effect was the same as all others. It has now existed nearly twenty years, the public is not in possession of any matter which would go to show that the company has ever lost a fraction by its speculation; and the strongest evidence might be produced to prove that the labour of the poor and rich settlers, from one end of the province to the other, has conferred thousands per cent in value upon their land, and established for them unbounded wealth, which sooner or later must become available to them. The government of the day, no doubt, thought they were doing wonders for the country, when they procured the establishment of this leviathan-monopoly by legislative enactment; but no Canadian of sense could now be got to deny that there is little apparent, future benefit, derivable to the province from an establishment, which, for an indefinite number of years to come, will act as a drain upon the emigrant and the country: the spirit which passed such laws, as established this company, put a price upon wild crown-land, and adopted an absentee-tax law, without a clause of resumption by the government, was such as we might suppose a man to possess, who looked to his own comfort and convenience, while, in attaining it, he left a certain legacy of hardship to his children—it may with truth be termed day-legislation—the legislator's own interest, or that of his friends, was too nearly concerned to permit him to see that the future emigrant had any interest in his proceedings; and the constituent who gave him the power to make laws, did not trouble himself about those whom they were to affect, so long as he himself was clear, and his own ends served thereby—self, self, was the order of the day, and all parties seemed to be agreed that the public weal had nothing to do with their private welfare.

From 1827 to the present time, the crown-office regulations hang on the crooked stem of that departmental tree as thick as blackberries, but it is enough when we say, that the whole end, aim, and object of them is, to make as much money as possible out of the unfortunate sinner who has the ill luck to fall into their meshes; in this period, as I have shown, land was made the means of luring men to their destruction, as in the case of the pensioners, and the means of open and almost undisguised robbery in the case of the respectable emigrants. I have entered elsewhere into a detailed account of the different classes of emigrants, and it will not here be necessary for me to do more than notice the prominent characteristics of the period. As to the government-emigration of the period, in which I class half-pay officers and pensioners, it was, as I have said, in the main a failure, and most disastrous in its individual effects, producing misery and distress at any former period unheard of in the country: of the respectable portion of the settlement of this period it may be said, that when they had the good luck to steer clear of the government, and settle on cleared farms, they did well, and were a great acquisition to the country; on the contrary, where they turned bushwhackers and backwoodsmen, they brought, in numberless instances, misery on themselves, and have not made that progress which would enable them to be classed as good settlers. Of the pensioners I have little more to say; they, too, struggled against difficulties; which they were never calculated to contend with, and under which many of them sunk, whilst the majority of those who have succeeded in establishing themselves are still far behind settlers of other classes, and as a whole it may be said of them also, that they cannot be considered as good and efficient settlers. Of the farming class possessed of means, who came to the country within these years, I have said, that they were a great benefit, and undoubtedly they did do good service to the country as far as settlement was concerned; they seldom bought from the crown, but purchased from individual land-holders, who had lands in eligible situations, and in most cases it was intrinsically worth the money they gave, or very near it: numbers also had means sufficient to purchase cleared farms. These men did good service as far as settlement was concerned; but I cannot help remarking a strong feature of difference between many of them, and those who came to the country in a steamer, under the auspices of the government; they were in a great many instances English and Scotch, and strongly imbued with so-called liberal principles, and in 1837, when a call was made upon the militia of the country, their example as well as their conduct was pernicious—many of them made answer, that they did not owe the government any thing, they were no way indebted to it, they had never received land or any kindness from it, and they would see it d—d before they would turn out to fight for it, let it defend itself—this was not the feeling certainly that brought ten thousand men to Toronto, or on the way, within a few hours of the receipt of information that they were wanted as settlers; the monied farmers were good, and it was in that case a pity their numbers were so limited; in a political point of view, people might be got to say that the country would be better without some of them.

During the whole extent of this period, restrictions upon settlement were every day accumulating, and the value of wild land was forced to its utmost limits. The apparent desire on the part of the government to make settlement general and prevent the accumulation of wild lands in the hands of private individuals; the desire on the part of the people for a tax on wild land; the desire on the part of the holders of lands to have a valuation put on crown-lands, in order to enable them by this means to meet the tax and reap a profit; and lastly, the formation of the Canada company—were the causes which individually and collectively led to the present result; and if it had been possible to have continued the stream of emigration of those early days, and to have increased the means of each and every emigrant in proportion to the amount which would be required from him, and thus enable him to feed the hungry maws of the expectants, all would have gone merry as a marriage-bell; but unfortunately all, or nearly all, has gone wrong. Government did not succeed in making settlement general, for larger quantities of land still got into the hands of private owners from the operation of the tax-law, and the remains of the unrestricted grants of former times, together with the formation of the Canada company. Nor did government, until the last two years or so, effectually stop individual speculation in wild land; for it is only within that period, that the free unrestricted grants which I have elsewhere spoken of were summarily dealt with; but government did succeed in bringing matters to such a pass, that settlement on crown-lands has ceased, and the rapid growth of the country, so apparent from the conclusion of the war to 1830, been suspended.

The people succeeded in their wishes as regards the tax, probably as well under all the circumstances as could be expected; but by the lands being sold to individuals, instead of being reassumed by the crown, they have not reaped the benefits which they sought in the same degree or so soon as they might have done; and the formation of the act was a basis on which to build land-valuation to an extent prejudicial to the best interests of the country. The holders of lands, both the private individual and the Canada company, reaped the full and immediate benefit of a crown-land valuation; and it was impossible to conceive a more prosperous state of things, than existed for a few years in their particular branch of business; they could sell in some cases for twenty shillings the acre, what did not cost them more perhaps than two or three shillings, perhaps not sixpence. What a pity then that times should have changed, what a hardship that the land is still worth the same money; every one says it is *not dear*, yet there is no one to buy it; the Canada company, it is probable, have worn out two or three printing-presses in their endeavours to puff off their commodities, and yet it won't do; they have tried every tack, but the description of people they want won't bite, they seem wide awake to the evils of the present state of things, and within the last year or two have concocted and puffed off a rent scheme, as a means of enlisting in their service the hitherto despised and discarded industrious emigrant; but rent, tithe, and taxes are words of horrible sound and import to any inhabitant of the British isles from all or any of which he is ready to exclaim, Good Lord, deliver us! in fact, it is almost as easy to sell land in Canada, as to rent it. The wild land valuation was in the first instance the making of these men and this company; it enabled them to put a really remunerating price upon land, which in some cases they got, and which, what still remains on hand is worth; but under the present state of things, they must wait the natural increase of the country for a chance to dispose of it, and pay taxes in the mean time, and perhaps the grandson or sons of the present owner or owners may meet with a purchaser. Their property is immense, it is true, it is in land, which is safe, it can't run away; it is easy to find a man in Canada worth from ten to fifty thousand pounds in wild land; but, that cursed tax-law, and the absolute dearth of purchasers, render it necessary to have a small income from some other source, to pay charges; and this is not at all pleasant. So that these gentry are beginning sensibly to feel that they have overshot the mark, in trying to make money too fast; they are beginning to feel the absence of settlement by emigration; and it would not surprise me, if they at length stirred themselves in some endeavour to revive it.

As I have elsewhere remarked, much might be said upon the various subjects depending upon or connected with the crown-land-granting system; but it would be useless for me, in a publication which must necessarily be limited, to attempt to enter so fully into the discussion as might be requisite. I hope enough has been said to show its true character; and that, through its operation, the settlement of by far the largest portion of the emigrants who visit our shores has been effectually put a stop to; they have no portion with us; and, though they are the class of people who possess, (with the single exception of, not only intelligent but cunning, monied men,) the fairest chance of success; and though the emigration of every year is composed of such people in great numbers, who are urged by their necessity, and consequently in most respects better fitted to combat the difficulties of a new settlement, and raise themselves and the country to affluence and prosperity; though these favourable circumstances meet, I say, in the poor but self-acting emigrant, yet we derive no benefit from such people: we have shut them out by actual legislation, and debarred them from the possession of that which would at once benefit both parties, and from the keeping of which no commensurate profit can possibly accrue to us. It is fair to suppose that from 1830 to the present year, the amount of emigrants reported at Quebec would be somewhere between two and three hundred thousand souls; take the medium, and I ask, if, upon reference to the population returns of both years, and making due allowance for the natural decrease and increase, we have increased the population of Canada in an equal proportion? and if the answer is—no, then in that answer lies confirmation of the fact, that settlement does not keep pace with emigration; and thus by the action of the crown-land office, the province is deprived of the full benefit of the emigration which does come, and, instead of a province numbering this day from six to seven hundred and fifty thousand souls, we have about five hundred thousand; and this is not the only view of the matter which may be assumed, for it is reasonable to suppose, from what we have seen in former years, that successful settlement on free grants would have brought at least double the number who did come: and indeed it might fairly be supposed, that the emigration of former years, thirty to fifty thousand would have been at least continued; and if so, the amount would have swelled far beyond anything I have estimated, and thus we would have a province containing a million or more? a diligent comparison and investigation of the population and emigration returns will tend to clear the mist from any man's mind upon these points.

I shall now glance at the remaining difficulties which, in my opinion, beset settlement by emigration: the country, as I have elsewhere stated, is full of cotters and labourers, and consequently labour is cheap, and the farmer derives the benefit; he, as a natural consequence, is quite apathetic as regards the settlement of the country, or, at the least, would wish to retain the advantages which he possesses, and, I have little doubt, would raise his voice against any measure tending to promote settlement, if he thought for a moment it would increase the price of labour, or that a sufficient number of emigrants would not remain to supply the place of those who would take up land. This objection on the part of the farmers could not have much weight, however, and I think there would be but little danger of a scarcity of workmen; for I have no doubt that emigration might be brought to the magnitude of former years, by proper treatment, and without any great loss of time; and numbers of new settlers would seek for work during the period of the year they were at liberty, a new farm on their small scale not requiring their entire labour. To increase emigration, it is only necessary to make settlement prosperous, and afford speedy and safe letter-communication between the colony and the mother-country; one prosperous settler will bring many by his account of his success, it is not necessary for the government to embark in the matter in any other way than to provide emigrants with land, sound advice when asked, and protection: let them, however, do this with all the spirit and good faith they possess, let emigrants find their own way, and if they leap in the dark, they have only themselves to blame for it. A man does not know what difficulties he can contend with till he tries, but let him enter the contest with his eyes open, not blindfolded by promises or false ideas, the product of every other imagination than his own. Let him think for himself! let him act for himself! let him emigrate or not, just as he pleases; and let him feel that if he takes the step, he does it wholly and entirely on his own responsibility. Let the home-government take the part in the affair I have stated, let them make it a national affair if they like, as the fancy seems to run now upon a national scheme of emigration; give it that name, it will do as well as any other, and I can assure them the only stock in trade that is necessary to commence business in this country, is a permanent placard upon the wall of every police-barrack in England, Scotland, and Ireland, stating the precise terms upon which two hundred acres of land in the colonies will be granted, as a free gift to the enterprising emigrant settler.

There is another difficulty to be overcome, the mention of which I have left to the last, though I am far from saying it is the least; there is a strong, and at the present day a powerful, party in the province of United Canada, opposed to immigration; it is the party that passed the capitation-tax in Lower Canada; it is the party that seeks to deprive us of British institutions and the British constitution in Upper Canada: in the one it is anti-British, but aristocratic, in its character; in the other it is anti-British, and republican; they wish for an object common to both; they desire to wrest the country from Britain, or to sicken her of her colonies, and thus induce her to throw them up; it is gall and wormwood to these men to see British influence extending in the country, it is a sore reflection to think that ten or fifteen years' successful settlement of British subjects, imbued with British principles, and a strong love for their father-land, would swamp them, and totally annihilate their interest and influence; and it would hardly be reasonable to expect legislation favourable to immigration, from men holding such principles, and thus I would look for difficulty in the enactment of measures calculated to revive settlement; but this subject merges in politics, I must avoid it.

I have now said as much as the limits of this article will permit, though I am fully convinced, that articles bearing upon the point at issue, and interesting to the public, might be written upon many of the subjects here touched upon. In the rambling and desultory manner which I have pursued, I have endeavoured to set forth, as particularly as possible, what I conceived to be the right and wrong of the case, and it will be a source of great gratification to me indeed, if I find that I have been able to set the various facts I have stated, before the public in such a manner, as to enable them to arrive at sound opinions, entirely independent of my inferences and conclusions. And now to wind up, I shall propose my theories, and produce the panacea, which of course, with me as with others, will cure every thing: the nostrum is simple in the extreme; I am convinced there can be no difficulty in taking it; and there ought to be no difficulty in giving it, for nature has herself prepared the medium.

Free grants to settlers is the burden of my song. I cry to the British government, at home and abroad, but at home in particular, as being the fountain of power, which should check evils and right the wronged. I say, give the poor man land that is of no use to you, it will help him, he will make it valuable, he will make himself wealthy and happy, he will strengthen and support you in honour and opulence; why therefore do you deny him the possession of the soil? why do you cast him off and out, is he not also one of your children? why drive him into the land of the stranger? why make his poverty a curse, why shackle his industry? why press with a heavy hand upon his helplessness? he does not ask for valuables? he does not want you to give him money? he does not want you to give him food? he does not ask for anything which would increase your taxes? he asks merely for what Providence has placed in your hands for his benefit; you are the guardian of his interests, he supplicates for a share of nature's bounty, of nature's blessing, that he may not be an outcast and murderer, he asks for a portion with his people, the granting of which will not infringe upon any man's right? give him, that he may enjoy nature's riches? give him, that he may draw from her bosom sustenance for his little ones, and means to train them in the paths of honesty, industry, loyalty, and affection for his native country. Yes, free grants to settlers, it will not infringe upon any man's right; it will not operate to the prejudice of any loyal British subject; it will raise instead of depress the value of property in the country, inasmuch as it will give an impetus to every branch of business; money will follow in its train, rich men will be induced to go to a country which is making such rapid strides, and where opportunities must occur for profitable investment of capital; it will magnify the resources of the country, and enable it to enter into operations for the development of the gifts that nature has bestowed with such an unsparing hand; such outlays will then be of use, giving employment to settlers, and immigrants intending to settle, and rendering them assistance which they will repay four-fold in their advancement. Yes, free grants to settlers—the operation of this principle would raise up nations of British subjects, preserve to the latest posterity British laws, British rights, and British freedom, and cast a halo of glory round the British name, to be extinguished only when time shall be no more. England can do this; she has territory sufficient, her people are Anglo-Saxons, they have ever been found sufficient for any emergency; she has already made a nation many times as large as herself, and nearly as populous, but it is a nation of strangers to her interests, alien alike in feeling and principle, inimical to her name, inimical to her nature, her antagonist in the field—whether open and avowed, or in secrecy and treachery, her enemy. Yes, to come to the very apex of things, free grants to settlers is the only thing that can preserve the North American colonies to the British crown; upon this subject alone, a book as long as Lord Durham's celebrated nonsensical report, might be written, and proof presented sufficient to demonstrate the truth of what I state; everything in the colony is tending to such a state of things; British interests in Canada received their death-blow in the union-act; they are overwhelmed, they are submerged, and though, like a drowning man, they have made and are making an occasional show at the surface, yet sink they must, and sink they will, unless they are relieved by immigration; the people of British origin are numerous in the country, they are strong, but they are divided; the people of French origin are more numerous, and they are strong, and united with one of the divisions of the others, decidedly not in favour of British interests; though British connection may be on their tongues' end, and loyalty on their lips, their heart is with the stranger.

Free grants to settlers should be on the broad scale of equality to all persons willing to fulfil the conditions; the rich man should not get more than the poor, nor be allowed any advantage; every man should be entitled to the fee-simple of two hundred acres of land, whenever he had satisfied the crown, through its agent or inspector, that he was actually permanently settled, with improvements, or buildings, and a certain quantity of cleared land; and in no case should such deed issue in a shorter space than after two years' actual continued residence. Now if a man cleared, say twenty acres of land, and built a shanty and a good barn, got his deed, and then took it into his head to sell, and abandon it, and leave the country, it is scarcely probable that it would again fall into a state of nature; and on the other hand, it is likely that if he remained in the country long enough to make the improvements I speak of, he would have but little inclination to leave it, and if, he chose to go before they were completed, the crown would reassume the land, and give it to another; in like manner if a man made the land a partial residence only, and did not clear or improve it, or appropriated it to other purposes than that for which it was given, he could get no title for it that would entitle him to continue the misappropriation, and the crown should be empowered by legislative enactment to enter into and repossess the land by a summary process, in order that another person might be placed thereon; giving, however, every chance to the first nominee, if his circumstances warranted it: and in all future sales under the absentee-tax law, the crown should be empowered to redeem the full lots of land which had lain eight years in arrear, and for which, after advertisement, no owner or applicant had appeared; and the same having been sold to pay the taxes, the crown, upon payment of the tax and per-centage after the usual time having expired for such redemption on the part of the owner, should repossess the land, and, affixing a price commensurate with the value of land in the neighbourhood, offer it for actual settlement.

It is time that the besom of destruction should be applied pretty freely, in many cases of laws and ordinances, and in no case would its operation be a greater source of satisfaction and delight than in that Augean repository of rottenness, the crown-land office; and its neighbour and fellow-worker in iniquity, the surveyor-general's department. If one of these should be merged in the other, and that other conducted on different principles, then the crown would effect general settlement, all jobbing in *wild* lands would be at an end: in the course of a little time, I have no doubt, the financial state of the country would be as much changed for the better, as the face of it would be improved; and in lieu of the paltry amount of territorial revenue which now comes to the treasury, there would be an immense increase in the casual, with the prospect of still greater returns every year; the country would soon become the home of thousands, might we not say millions of our countrymen, and the course of time would raise a powerful barrier of strength, as well as feeling, against the encroachments of democracy, and perhaps in future ages disarm of its violence and horrors, the operation of that principle of self-destruction, which is so deeply planted in the United States—universal suffrage, and mob law.

How singular, as I have elsewhere said, that England should have pursued such a policy, with regard to America! how singular that she, the conservator of peace and order, should have fostered and encouraged, in the manner in which she has, republicanism, and rampant democracy, to the utter neglect of her own interests, and her own people! Is the Britain of the present day blind to the shadows of coming events, are the eyes of her statesmen so intensely fixed within the scope of their own time, so bounded by the horizon of their own day or hour, that they have not a thought to bestow on the future; upon the concentrated mass of misery and horror, of which the North American continent must one day be the stage, when the principles of law and order are compelled to enter the arena of public strife with anarchy and confusion, and the tide of its mighty rivers runs crimson with the blood of men;—the day is distant, far, far distant, but is it the less sure? Let the United States be hemmed in by other nations; let her boundaries be contracted, or, what is equally the same as to cause, but must be more disastrous as to consequence, let her people fill the whole continent; give her time to do so; banish every other form of government but her own, give her time,

I say, and when the tide of population rolls back from the shores of the Pacific to the Atlantic, from Labrador to the Gulf of Mexico, when the avenues to power, place, profit, and emolument are crowded as in other countries, if intervening circumstances should not long ere the time I speak of have worked her ruin—then may men look for the working of republican institutions, then will their enduring qualities be tested, and then, we may add, woe to them in that land that see that day!—and if the Britain of future ages has the reflection, that she founded, and established a power, which has counteracted the effects and perhaps curbed and restrained the passions of furious men, it will be a happy one; and the pen of history will bear proud record to the glory of those institutions, which, like her meteor flag, have already braved a thousand years the battle and the breeze, and would thus descend to posterity a blessing and a safeguard.

It may be considered temerity on the part of an unknown colonist, to promulgate opinions upon a subject which has occupied the attention of noble and talented men; but Burke comes to my aid, "I have known, (says that statesman,) and, according to my measure, have co-operated with great men; *and, I have never yet seen any plan, that has not been mended by the observations of those who were much inferior in understanding to the persons who took the lead in the business.*" E. H. C.

THE LATE WILLIAM HUTTMANN.

The fate of genius has often been referred to as one of the many blots on civilized life, and seldom, indeed, with less truth than in the case of the learned individual whose melancholy decease we here deplore. Modest merit, his greatest ornament, was also his greatest injury; and he now ranks amongst those, for whose tomb that laurel was reserved, which should have wreathed his brow. Destined for the labours of a Missionary's life, he had early cultivated Oriental languages, and at a period when no lexicon facilitated the student's efforts, made himself perfect master of the Chinese language, and all its deflections—of the Sanscrit and its numerous dialects; in addition to a familiar acquaintance with Hebrew, Greek, and Latin.

The early death of his father,—limited resources,—unobtrusive manners, combined to frustrate the objects of his young ambition, and, with an habitual philosophy and philanthropy, he now reconciled himself to his lot, and directed all his energies to the care and support of the younger branches of an orphaned family. In 1820 appeared "The Annals of Oriental Literature," in which several papers written by Mr. Huttmann attracted attention, especially those relating to the civil and military state of the Chinese. To the *Asiatic Journal* he also contributed, and an article of his on the culture and preparation of Tea, proved eminently useful to the Tea-growers in our district of Assam. The peculiar nature of his acquirements, the eminence he had now unassistedly attained, recommended him to the notice of the Royal Asiatic Society, to which he was appointed assistant Secretary, and afterwards Secretary to the *Oriental Translation Fund*. These honourable and not unprofitable appointments he continued to hold, until the difficulties in which his luckless connection with a newspaper called *The World* involved him, obliged him to relinquish them.

His life being exclusively literary, his attainments as a linguist, and geographer, of a very high order, he continued to supply articles to various periodicals. Amongst those connected with China, written for this Magazine, his Essay on the Population of that Empire is the most generally known, because so generally quoted, at the date of its appearance, in the leading journals.

Until the conquest of China by British arms, the Chinese language was little cultivated in England, and its knowledge in London was confined perhaps to Mr. Huttmann, and Mr Birch of the British Museum; hence the little pecuniary profit which resulted from its acquisition. But just at the moment when the possessor might have reaped a golden harvest; just when an acquaintance with that symbolic language became an object of surpassing interest, the fruit was snatched from the hand that gathered it. We [illegible], personally, in regret for this admirable scholar and amiable man;—his urbanity, his readiness to impart knowledge, to all who approached him, are well remembered by visiters to the library of the India House; and, in the ranks of London literary labourers, although no person was less equitably rewarded, no absence will be more distinctly felt.

We learn with much regret that the lamented subject of this notice, (who it appears had been twice married) has left seven orphans totally unprovided for; and sympathy will be further awakened in their favour by remembering, that the mother of the three youngest, all under eight years of age, died but a few months before her husband. Few men had less the appearance of over-fatigue than Mr. Huttman; his frame was firmly knit, his mind always clear and vigorous: and, such a constitution at such an age as fifty, might fairly have promised some few years of triumph here—*sed diis aliter visum.*

CORN-FIELDS.

[BY THE AUTHOR OF HOURS OF THOUGHT, OR POETIC MUSINGS.]

"Thou crownest the year with thy goodness, and thy paths drop fatness."

THE loaded fields, now ripe with yellow grain,
That undulates, with waving richness fraught,
'Neath every breeze, that sweeps the bending stalk;
Denotes that harvest has again arrived,
To bless the fruitful land;—and echo joy,
From thousand thankful hearts, spontaneous felt;
And who but owns the rich provision sent,
Sent undeserved, by kindly providence
To man bestowed, too thankless for the grant!
How lowly Cottager, now smiles content,
And should have cause, when such abundance pours
From plenty's fruitful barn:—so lavish spread:
The sun-burnt swain, his shining sickle plies,
And the full sheaf falls heavy from his hand,
Scattering the grain, let fall for gleaners' use;
They round the reapers hang, the boon to catch,
And, Ruth-like, bear the gathered treasure home;
Perchance, an aged parent's eye to cheer,
That glistens more at thought of filial love;
What sight more pleasing to an English breast,
Than fields of British growth, embrowned with corn;
Full-eared, and large, that speak abundant crop;
When fear of short supply is far removed,
And all a farmer's hopes are crowned at once;
Whose barns in prospect sees well stored with wheat:
The sheaves to bind, a busy group attend,
To gather, and dispose, the graceful heap;
While slowly drags along, the creaking wain,
High piled, that groans beneath the precious load;
Such sights enlivening, every where abound
At this glad season of the bounteous year;
And Albion glories, is her son's employ,
To bring her native growth, mature and ripe,
Safe housed in granary, or securely stacked.
But other lands partake the joy, as well
As England's peasant, whom his corn-fields cheer;
So rustic labourer of the German States,
And Poland's breadth of land, 'neath harvest smiles,
With fruitful Spain, that pours her thousands forth
To gather in the produce of her soil;
A rich luxuriance spreads each distant shore.
And far Canadia swells with ripening grain,
While "Harvest Home" resounds through every land,
A joyous and exhilarating sound,
That wafting should man's gratitude bespeak;
If others are unconscious of the gift,
At least, let Britain's thanks! responsive rise,
To heaven!—such meed of praise she owes,
Her flowing fields attest, of waving corn,
Dispersed; thro' length, and breadth, of her rich vales,
In golden seasons, thrice prolific shed,
O'er England's happy Isle! so prosperous blest.

PECKHAM.

REVIEWS OF NEW BOOKS.

ART. I.—*Heath's Book of Beauty*, 1845. Edited by the COUNTESS OF BLESSINGTON. London: Longman & Co. 8vo.

If judgment ripen by maturer years, her ladyship ought to be an accomplished editress, but as she commenced a literary career in the full possession of the gift of taste, the productions of her later years give abundant evidence of tact, talent, and discernment. Thirteen admirable portraits by the chosen amongst our painters, and of the fairest lights in the galaxy of aristocratic beauty, constitute the pictorial attractions of this beautiful volume. Ross's picture of the Baroness le Despenser is one of those works of genius, that, like our architecture and our literature, will mark the state of the arts in the age of its production. His efforts in Mrs. Conyngham's portrait have been less happy, from an ill-chosen attitude, although the design is otherwise faultless; but, possibly the artist may be wholly guiltless of this violation of the posture-master's rule, the employée being sometimes directed to paint to orders in this respect. For its most especial loveliness, its pensive madonna effect, its grace, dignity, and sentiment, we much prefer the frontispiece, the Marchioness of Douro; and yet, above all those witching welcomes, it comes recommended with one dear to every Englishman, the recollection that, in due course of years,—may that course flow slowly on!—the original of this interesting picture will wear the title of Wellington. Oh, lady,—

> Proudly doth England claim thee as her own
> And cherish thee among her dearest daughters,
> And not, sweet lady, for thy sake *alone*,
> But his, who won from Spain's fast-rolling waters,
> The title that thou bearest, and her prayer
> Is still that long thou mayest that title bear.

Art, however, has not triumphed over literature in this field of emulation, for the essays and the poetry, which the noble editress has selected for her gallery, are in every instance characterized by vigour of thought and language. A very delicious scrap might be extracted from the little ballad by an Oxonian, on the *Madonna dell'Acqua*, beginning—

> Oh! lone Madonna, angel of the deep,

if our duty were not restricted to the raising, rather than the satisfying of curiosity,—to the proclamation, not the publication, of those charms that are in reserve for the readers of the Book of Beauty. *The Other Side of the Wall*, a name that casts no shadow of its features before it, is an agreeable tale, founded on fiction that may have been fact, and touching *pointedly* on needlewomen's sorrows, and the "stitches" in the heart to which they are professionally subject. The story displays powers of no ordinary quality,—rather subdued, in some instances, to the level of the light tale they are embarked in, than let loose to contend with passion's whirlwinds, which they need not be apprehensive of encountering. As to needlewomen, the moral should have been carried out further, since undertaken at all,—because much misunderstanding prevails in the public mind, and immense injustice amongst the stitching classes. The object to be accomplished by the humane should be, "more equable distribution of the quantity of work to be performed amongst the hands competent to perform it;" for, under the present unequal division, while clever sempstresses are starving, women of little ability, and ordinary character, are receiving exorbitant prices for their clumsy performances. A registry-office for the residence and references of needlewomen, is the chief desideratum in this business. To return, however, to our subject: Miss Toulmin's enlistment of the feeling for female suffering in her cause, will prove auxiliary to the injured sempstress. "Foiled by Mistake" is an excellent story,—admirably painted, although unaccompanied by an illustration. Was the artist afraid to encounter the bright colouring of the author, or did the editress think an illustration would have been superfluous? It will not spoil the story to quote a few lines, describing the *entrée* of the modern Venuses, and Dianas, and Junos, to "the Judgment of Amherst," in Mrs. Estcourt's drawing-room, premising only, that none but acknowledged beauties were admissible:—

The evening of the party arrived, the beauties began to pour in, all looking as lovely as nature, their milliners, and hair-dressers could make them; chaperons wisely filed off to enjoy cards, and annuals in an adjoining room, and the houris had a clear stage and fair-play. The whole thing, however, proved a failure; it was all light, and no shade; the eye was fatigued with brightness, and longed to rest on some refreshing object: it gave to the beholder more the idea of a scene in a theatrical pageant, or a beautiful collection of wax-work, than of a meeting of "the women of England," of future wives and mothers.

"Neither were the beauties themselves at all in good humour; each had been accustomed to be the star of her own circle, and to look down with a tranquil sense of superiority on the cheeks lacking bloom, and eyes lacking brightness, in her vicinity: now she enjoyed these triumphs no longer,—all were beautiful, some perhaps more so than herself,—and in several cases an admirer, who had hitherto been devoted to one alone, seemed for the first time to find out that there were others as fair or fairer. Have any of my readers been smitten with the vain ambition of collecting a party of wits together at dinner? If they have, and have succeeded in the undertaking, I appeal to them whether the conversation was not far less brilliant and agreeable than when the party was judiciously compiled of wits and common-place people. There can be no enjoyment where there is not ease; and nothing is so destructive to ease as the spirit of competition.

This passage deserves a place in a *perennial*—it contains good wholesome counsel. Could Mrs. Abdy be induced to allow her compositions the just enjoyment of their claims to originality, by omitting to speak so familiarly of the literary stars of our age, as if she well-nigh borrowed from *their works*, or as if they were household words elsewhere as. *chez nous?* This practice is not only unjust to herself, but is wanting in dignity.

Amongst the other fugitive pieces, the most meritorious are "The Affianced Bride" and "Starlight,"—the first a lovely lyric, the second a moral anacreontic. We have not space, while we burn with inclination, to give Mrs. Abdy's Starlight, and Moore's anacreontic version, commencing

"Oh that I were yon spangled sphere," &c.

It would gratify and instruct, to lay two kindred souls for poetry side by side, and contemplate their loveliness. The Book of Beauty must prove personally grateful to the relatives of those whose brilliant portraits adorn its pages,—peculiarly acceptable where opportunities of seeing the great ones of the land are necessarily limited,—and generally welcome wherever a felicitous union of literature and art are appreciated.

ART. II.—*The Drawing-Room Scrap-Book* for 1845. Edited by the Author of "The Women of England." London: Fisher, Son, and Co., Angel Street. Newgate Street.

Constructed on a principle essentially differing from those on which all other annuals depend, this cherished favourite continues to grow upon public affection, and maintain its robustness and beauty unimpaired by years. Containing three times the numerical amount of engravings now habitually allotted to Christmas gifts, many of them before unseen, and all of conspicuous artistic merit, it admits of no competitor as a drawing-room portfolio for the season. In other respects, however, the balance of adjudication remains in the hands of the public, who always, although often it is long deferred, decide impartially on literary claims. But it is not in its including a greater number of plates, and being more varied in character, that the distinguishing feature of this annual consists, its editorship has always been differently arranged. To one hand, one heart, one head, the descriptive and sentimental lyrics of the Scrap-Book seem always to have been entrusted, and, for ourselves, we still return with pleasure to the contemplation of those exquisite verses of L E. L., which illumine the first pages of this her best production. Now to our daily labour. This number of the Scrap-Book opens with Ross's living likenesses of the royal children, the Princess Royal and the Prince of Wales, engraved by Robinson, under all that desire to excel which the interesting subjects must necessarily have created,—Allom's pencil, steeped in power and pleasure, has furnished an affecting little subject for a vignette, and a cloud of witnesses in the cause of art attend them both. David's great historical painting of Belisarius, seated in the highway and asking alms of his ungrateful countrymen, has been engraved specially for this year's Scrap-Book, and, if we mistake not, so has the copy of West's admired design of Alfred sharing his last loaf with the Pilgrim. Amongst other novelties on which we have here fallen, is O'Connell's *speaking* portrait,—a quality borrowed, we suppose, from the original, as characteristic of the man. This, we understand, is the only portrait for which he has sat for the last thirty years; and the fidelity of the likeness has become a subject of very general admiration. Besides the portrait of the Liberator, Sir C. Ross has contributed two exquisite subjects, exquisitely engraved also,—one, the infant Count of Flanders, a grandson of Louis Philippe; the other named, poetically, we imagine, the Morn of Life. But it is less to portrait than to landscape that the purchaser of the Scrap-Book will acknowledge obligation: greater general interest, deeper intellectual indulgence, more real instruction, belong to those groves where Horace and Mæcenas sauntered, beguiling the hours with interchange of thought; those domes that Michael Angelo suspended in the sky,—those areas where myriads of Roman citizens assembled to indulge in scenes of horrible and most merciless carnage. Such scenes as those may be dwelt on with a deeper conviction of utility, and more real intellectual indulgence, probably, than a true and faithful portrait of an illustrious individual, or highly-born dame. However, both tastes are gratified in the volume before us. But, let us not take leave, of these six-and-thirty admirable engravings, without the courage to name our choice. Our feelings hurrying us on so rapidly, in unison with an early-formed judgment, that we feel no hesitation in pronouncing a decision: we ask, therefore, to dwell with melancholy delight on Veit's simply-magnificent composition, "Behold the place where they laid Him."

We do not here enjoy the variety of literary tastes and manners,—differing degrees of excellence in composition and invention, that occur in most other annuals; the literary portion of the Scrap-Book has been from the beginning, and so continues, the distinct performance of an individual, from which praise is to accrue, or censure to be incurred; and it is but reasonable to conclude, that its established popularity has safely secured, for its pages, each editor's best-intentioned efforts. And in this conclusion we are not mistaken. We could bring forth many unanswerable witnesses to the spirit of poetry prevailing in these broad pages, whether the theme be love or liberty; but, not being quite free ourselves, we must submit to the production of a few stanzas only, and these the closing ones of a little sonnet on that glorious passage of the Rhine, called Rheinfels above St. Goar:—

What though the rocks are wild and high,
The hollow caves are still;
There sits a glorious majesty
Enthroned on every hill;
And spirit-voices seem to say,
While pointing to those ruins gray,
"Behold the work of yesterday!"

Yes, beautiful are mountains bold,
And valleys deep and green,
And waves, their crystal course that hold,
Those shadowy banks between;
And but to picture such a scene,
And think it never can grow old,
Is almost bliss enough, I ween.

But, oh! to stand upon that shore,
To watch those very sails pass by,
To trace the sunshine lingering o'er
Some spot 'twere rapture to explore,
And gaze upon that summer sky—
It must not, and it cannot be
That chariot-wheels drag heavily
Through such a scene, so soft—so fair—
With happiness so mirrored there.

We should willingly quote "Amalfi," and "The Secret Thought," either entire or partially, were our hands unchained, for their true poetic feeling, as well as their smooth versification, since, in the latter respect, they are the best compositions in the volume. This year's Scrap-Book may now go forth with little apprehension as to a failure in variety, and none as to literary excellence.

ART. III.—*Historic Annual.* By the Rev. R. CATTERMOLE, B. D. London. Longman, Brown, Green & Brown, Paternoster Row.

This is the second Volume of a valuable, interesting, and highly instructive work, an illuminated history, the continuous publication of which has been suspended by accidental circumstances. The period chosen by the reverend author is the civil wars, or rather the concluding years of the First Charles's reign. Having carefully investigated the different narrations of that calamitous period, steered clear of factious sentiments, and fanatic impressions, he has given to his readers a connected and impartial narration of the contest between Charles and his subjects; the one endeavouring to retain the power of the Crown as entire as he had received it—the other determined upon invading its prerogatives from every quarter. It is a period of our history with which all are familiar, and on which the author could not be expected to have thrown any new light; his only duty was to tell an unvarnished tale, and this has been, with all fidelity, performed. His style evinces no uncommon or elevated powers, but it is uniformly correct, classic, clear, and easy flowing. Few historians, however, have been so powerfully aided, by the accessories that art, in its higher walk, can contribute. Fifteen illustrations, designs of G. Cattermole, co-operate in impressing on the reader's mind the character, date, and circumstances of the most striking events in his history; so that when the author's narrative may have escaped from the memory, the artist's illustration will in all probability retain its hold. Objects of sight and perception are more likely to seize tenaciously on the mind than those of the latter faculty only.

If hyper-criticism, or rather implied censure, were not contrary to our notion of just reviewing, we might indulge in the opportunity of declaiming against Mr. Cattermole's treatment of some of his subjects. Not certainly his calm, dignified portrait of Henrietta interceding for the king; not his startling picture of Cromwell viewing the body of his royal victim—nor the yet better design of Hammond discovering the king's intention to escape from Carisbrook castle—these are perfect in their class. We dislike that whole-length of the king by Vandyke, which he has selected for this series; it is by far the least admirable of all the royal portraits by that great painter. We object to the insertion of a scene styled "The plundering of a Royalist's House," instead of taking some real Brambletye for the subject: apropos of omissions—we have a whole chapter on the Uxbridge Treaty, and, although the very oak-panelled room in which the commissioners sat, still survives in all its primitive beauty, we are not gratified with a little vignette or tail-piece of it. Cromwell by Vandyke is a glorious painting, and admirably engraved by Holl, yet that taste is questionable which gives him the position and circumstances previously conferred upon the portrait of the king by the same artist. It degrades Vandyke in the estimation of posterity to see with what facility he transferred his professional allegiance from a patron to a parricide.

The battle of Naseby and the retreat of Montrose, are of course in the *fumo-tinto*, or smoke colour, and would equally represent any other murderous contest between persons in British costume; they are in the "ex uno disce omnes" manner. The king on his journey to Scotland is an agreeable picture, the subject carefully considered, and poetically treated. The facts of history have been observed in every part of this design. We cannot so entirely concur with the reverend author in his view of the results of this tour in search of the Scotch, our conviction, long since formed, being that, that brave people *did*, most indubitably, *sell* their king, and that the best thing their descendants can do is to plead guilty and promise to sin no more. In the subject of "Pride's Purge," the attention of the artist to costume, architecture, armour, furniture, and all distinctive records of the age, is conspicuous, and we are not without a suspicion, that if art was better understood by society at large, and therefore more fully appreciated, the instruction it conveys would prove more lasting than it now does, more general in its application to different countries, and less liable to be the author of false impressions than the pen of the ablest writers. In every library, therefore, where the history of England occupies a niche, we should recommend Cattermole's annual to be placed beside it—one will excite impressions, the other stamp them on the mind.

ART. IV.—*The Keepsake for* 1845. Edited by the COUNTESS OF BLESSINGTON. London: Longman & Co., Paternoster Row.

The quality of the literature here displayed is not merely characteristic of the educated state of the age, but with more specialty of the higher classes of society. Emanating from the aristocratic order almost entirely, it may be received as an illustration of that eulogy so felicitously paid to our high grades by Moore, "that in English society, the higher you ascend the purer the atmosphere." This compliment, remembering the exquisite lyrist's own origin, does not preclude the possession of talents and cultivation by those less nobly sprung. However, laying aside all such contingencies as rank and fortune, and deciding the case before us on its merits solely, this year's Keepsake is a literary production of a highly meritorious and agreeable character. Less happy in its poetic pieces than in former years, it contains several prose articles that are deserving of a lasting existence from the matured reflections which they embody, and vigour of language employed in expressing them. Nothing can be more stirring, spirited, life-like, and specific than Mrs. Hall's story of the Fair Client. True, we have Glosson's before us, and the villanous lawyer in the *Mendicant*, a forgotten but genuine character also, yet neither are drawn so boldly, and, at the same time, with so little of the really odious in their composition, as Ned Lynch :—

"What can you expect from a petty-fogging attorney?" said Frank. "A great deal," replied the Fair Client; "an amount of costs—a multiplication of falsehoods—a perversion of truth—a perplexing of facts—a discoloration of objects—ruin as the result—ignorance as to common honesty—a proficiency in dishonesty. In short, a combination of evils which no other human being could gather together, by which *he* lives, and *we* die. You have only to tell me that a man is a petty-fogger, and I vanish; and, as to Old Lynch, in addition to his bearing the plague-spot of his 'profession' about with him, smelling of parchments, and looking latitats, he is old and ugly," &c.

Possibly this picture of *sharp*-practice might be retorted by the petty-fogger, for it certainly is somewhat pungent. It would have been a splendid speech for Sir George Stephens to have delivered from the chair, at the recent meeting for the extinction of that class of denounced professionals. Stephanoff's illustration of Ned and his Fair Client is very clever; the old lawyer is an admirable portrait—a face, although of the Iscariot family, familiar to every one. The artist has contrived to give an admirable effect to his design by the juxta-position of beauty and deformity, in the countenances of the lawyer and his client.

The *Island* Bride, a story calculated to give to Englishmen a character they have never forfeited, devotion to the softer sex, is very agreeably told, but belongs solely to the Garrison school. A query suggests itself, therefore, whether it should have been told out of the limits prescribed by the pupils in such cases. Corbould's personification of the Island Bride does not convey any idea of the fevered state of Eliodore's mind under the terror of being overtaken by Demetrius. She seems as tranquil, and placid, and indifferent, as a piece of Parian marble moulded into a form of equal gracefulness. The engravings, thirteen in number, are all worthy of Heath's established name, and the designs are the products of just ambition. We cannot call Lord Byron's saloon in the Moncenigo Palace, Venice, an original, but the correctness and cleverness of the drawing place it in a higher rank than a copy,—it is historical. The richly stuccoed ceiling, walls clothed with silk, a ground, on which are laid the noblest works of Italian art; the rich, and costly, and picturesque decorations, that fill and furnish every corner of this well remembered apartment, augment that undying interest in the history of the ancient grandeur of this city, which every cultivated mind possesses. The reading public and the travelling public are much indebted to Lake Price, the one for information, the other for a delightful help to memory, in his drawing of

That chamber where *he* dwelt, whose presence lent
A mournful interest to each favoured spot
Wherein he rested.

Much pleasure will be afforded by the perusal of "The Glen of the Grave;" the story is told with more than every-day powers of description, and, however it may be ranged amongst entire fictions, every event in it has been realised, repeatedly, during the sanguinary struggle for the recovery of liberty by the Greeks. Warren's accompanying design is good, well drawn, and carefully engraved, but not the most critical moment in the narrative. Why not introduce the Giaour just springing on his hated rival, and giving liberty to the captive maiden, rather than these motionless figures—these dismounted riders. By the bye, the horses' tails (a Turkish term well known) startle us; they protrude from the picture, and appear to have been artificially attached, like those of a certain chief civic functionary's horses, upon his inauguration day. And now, we feel that this tale must be cut off. We have spoken of the fun of Mrs. Hall's story, the feeling of Mr. Simmonds's, to which we may add our admiration of the ability of Wright's "Love Letter," in which one figure, the laughing lady on the sofa, is most happily conceived; and of Hayter's heiress, so gay, glittering, and flooded with light, that, although—

"Oft I turn me from the picture, yet I pause to gaze again."

Amongst the poetic effusions of the Keepsake, "the Wounded Conscript" detained us as firmly as the cruel institutions of his country had once secured his own services. Interest grew as we read—we came to the end—it was too short. Poetry would flush its wings again, if written up to the education of the age.

ART. V.—*The Juvenile Scrap-Book.* Edited by the Author of "The Women of England." London: Fisher, Son, & Co., Angel St. Newgate St.

The Authoress appears to apologize, in her preface, for the gravity of her last year's gift for youth, and informs us of her having now written to the level of her readers' capacities. We not only observe that she has done so, but congratulate her upon the change; although we think that young people are benefited by talking with their elders, as well as by reading works that demand the best exertions of their minds to comprehend entirely. However, all objection is cancelled, by writing explicitly for those whose amusement and improvement are the sole end to be attained. Another ground of cavil, different, but perhaps as well founded, may possibly be raised, to the quality of the plates in this number of the "Juvenile Scrap Book,"—that they are too highly finished, too able in design, too elaborate in composition,—but the same line of defence which we have employed in repelling objections to a graceful and polished literary style, will defeat these senseless enemies of art. Never was the Editress more judicious and happy in her selection of subjects for a Christmas present, than in the volume before us. Thus history is made accessary to literary amusement, in the touching narrative of Cromwell and his favourite Daughter, and in the description of the Castle of Pau, the birth-place of Henri Quatre. Natural phenomena find a grand representation in the wonders of Vesuvius, of which, as well as of many other scenes of the greatest interest, both topographical and classical, in Central Europe, the Editress has herself been an eye-witness—an advantage that contributes freshness and truth to her smooth-flowing narrations of all such scenes. In the story of the "Ambitious Boy," much general information is incorporated with reflections, cursorily made, on the feelings that agitate the youthful mind; and the various ordeals through which young ambition is made to pass, from its first pulsations, till that fervour of the mind subsides in riper years, are significantly portrayed in the engravings of the youthful student and of the aged philosopher. There is an unaffected description in these pages, of the glories of St. Peter's Cathedral at Rome, which will command the respect of those more advanced in years than their intended readers. It puts us in possession of the first impressions which this vast edifice, and sacred monument of art, produced upon a mind calmed by the lessons of philosophy, and regulated by precepts of a still purer atmosphere; they should not, therefore, be lightly valued, nor departed from without a careful analysis.

"All things suitable," is an ancient diverb, and much respected; but it does not signify "all things stationary." Everything, to be healthy, must be progressive; and literature for the child should partake of the onward movement. Nursery-rhymes, tales of ghosts and demons, and fictions of merciless giants, are not profitable; on the contrary, they often prove singularly destructive of youthful intellect and happiness. It is to such literature as Mrs. Ellis's juvenile gift—a literature calculated to unfold the mind of youth, as the sun does the budding flower, and prepare it to receive the broad light of learning, the lofty one of religion—that early attention should be invited. Away then with all such initiatory works, as unprofitable and impossible fictions! let possibility and truth be inculcated from the first, and then it will not be necessary to lop off some branches, or tie down others, in order to reduce the tree to rectitude amongst its fellows. The "Juvenile Scrap-Book" is written for those who are competent to understand a simple sentence; it abounds in amusing narrative, and moral reflections; and, it is enriched with plates of a higher quality than we have ever known in other books of the same description. These seem to be its true and principal features. Amongst the contributing artists, we meet with the names of Lawrence, Daniell;

Prout, and Allom; amongst the engravers, of Goodall, Cousens, and Greatbach. Two subjects attracted our notice more particularly than the others, one the Castle of Pau, which is engraved from a drawing by the Editress during a lengthened residence in the south of France, and is highly creditable to her abilities as a draughtswoman; the other, "Just Come from School," a design by Mr. Allom, the architect, so full of the fire of those days it records, that the Author himself may be supposed to have been but recently emancipated from the chrysalis state.

New Mode of purifying Feathers. Invented by Gilbert & Co., Belle-Sauvage Yard, Ludgate Hill, London.

Those who have had much experience in house-keeping, will not be surprised to learn, that one of the most disagreeable interruptions to their best exertions has at length been conquered. Imperfect modes of curing, or cleaning, feathers for beds and pillows, failing to remove the fœtid odour arising from putrifying animal matter adhering tenaciously to the feather, many excellent beds are sold for half their value, and others are retained at a sacrifice of health, but saving of money. Pillows, or bolsters, filled with feathers not sufficiently purified and disengaged from minute particles of animal matter, are distressingly offensive, and the testimony of eminent physicians is not wanting to show, that such odour is highly dangerous to many constitutions. The process by which Messrs. Gilbert accomplish this very important object to our domestic comfort, is secret, we believe, but successful. It effectually destroys the animalculæ that establish themselves in all such substances, clears away all animal matter, and imparts a degree of elasticity to the feathers, estimated at one-fourth of their bulk in their uncleaned state We have now before us the testimony of a practical philosopher, Dr. Ryan, of the Polytechnic Institution, who, after having examined a certain bulk of feathers, chemically and microscopically, before and after the process of purifying, writes as follows:—

"I am surprised that the attention of the medical profession has not been more fully directed to this important point, for the quantity of insects and animal matter amongst unpurified feathers must have been hitherto a frightful source of disease. Messrs. Gilbert's purified feathers I find to be perfectly free from both inconveniences, nor can I discover any trace of the chemicals employed by them, so that the materials are not only rendered beautifully soft and elastic, but more healthy than new feathers."

From this opinion, so valuable to the patentee or inventor, the advantage, the value, and the necessity for such a process, seem obvious; and it is not the least remarkable circumstance in that certificate, that the analysis appears to have been made upon a collection of old feathers. Dr. Ryan's distinct opinion, unequivocally expressed in the preceding extract, does not require confirmation, nor admit of distrust; yet, to heap up proofs, we may add, that several medical gentlemen, having actually made trial of Messrs. Gilbert's process by sending their old beds to his establishment to be purified, have added their testimony of its efficacy and completeness to that of the learned professor. Amongst the names which we have had submitted to us, we recognized those of surgeons Eland, Dodd, Symes, Wormald, Walker, Duffin, and Dr. Eason. An accession to domestic comforts, involving considerations of health, cleanliness, and economy, and declared to be a sincere discovery, by those most competent to estimate its objects, cannot remain unpatronized by a large proportion of society.

LITERARY NOTICE.

In the press—"Look to the End; or, The Bennets Abroad." By the Author of 'The Women of England.' 2 vols., post 8vo.

To the Editor of the Colonial Magazine.—

Sir,—I have it on good authority for stating that "The Demerara ordinances are disallowed; and that the negro is not to be taken for his provisions." As you have so often and so ably vindicated the cause of the negro, and pointed out the flagrant blundering of the Colonial Office. I am certain that you and your readers will rejoice that, at length, though tardily, justice will be done to the suffering labourers of our West Indian Colonies.

T.

COLONIAL INTELLIGENCE.

INDIA.—The news which was received by the Bombay mail of the 1st of October is not very remarkable, the chief intelligence relates to disturbances in the southern Mahratta country, which has been some time in a disturbed state. Some of the malcontents seized two of the strong hill-forts, where they hoisted the standard of revolt against the Rajah of Kholapore. They consist chiefly of Arab troops, who placed themselves under some bold leaders, and bade defiance to the Rajah and his allies. A force was sent by the British authorities to disperse them. It consisted of 50 artillerymen, and troops, amounting to about 1,200 men, under the command of Colonel Wallace, of the Madras army. An attack is said to have taken place on one of the forts, in which the rebels defended themselves stoutly with their long guns. Some soldiers were wounded on the side of the British, for the hill-forts from their position are difficult of access. The British were subsequently firing and throwing shells into the first fort, which is situate about 25 miles from Belgaum. The other is 18 miles further off.

The Bombay Government was on the alert in making arrangements for having its disposable regiments ready for any emergency that might arise. Lieutenant-Colonel Wyllie, of the 21st Bombay Native Infantry, who had taken his passage by the steamer, was ordered to stop, and join his regiment.

The steamers were in Bombay harbour under orders to be ready to remove troops at a moment's notice. Nothing serious was apprehended, but the Government is acting with prudence in being prepared to meet every difficulty.

Serious riots took place at Surat on the 29th of August, in consequence of the popular dissatisfaction at the increase of the salt-tax from half a rupee to one rupee (2*s*.) per maund of 80lb. Troops were promptly sent there by the Government, and the disturbances ceased. The Supreme Government subsequently ordered, by virtue of instructions from the Court of Directors, that the increased duty should be in the Bombay Presidency only of the sum of one quarter of a rupee (6*d*.) per maund. This arrangement has apparently pacified the people, although there were petitions presented against the tax.

In Scinde tranquillity prevailed, and the health of the troops, with the exception of one or two stations (Sukkur and Shirkarpore,) was very good. The climate in general in September was highly agreeable, and half the prejudices excited against the possession of the Indus by the outcry of some designing persons had vanished. It was even reported that there was an intention of making it an integral part of the Bombay Presidency, and of increasing the Bombay army so as to be able to maintain the British rule in Scinde. There have been blunders committed by the troops there. Captain Mackenzie, at the head of some cavalry, in pursuing the Beloochee robbers, came on a body of armed men; they were said to be ryots, who had gone out to attack the Beloochees. His cavalry cut them to pieces. This fact has been exaggerated, as if the troops did not spare their own friends. Sir Charles Napier was proceeding to Upper Scinde, in order to regulate its affairs on a proper basis. It is reported on good authority, that a committee has been appointed by the Governor-General in council to open the boxes containing the principal part of the jewels taken at Hyderabad, and now lying at Bombay, for the purpose of selecting the most valuable to be returned to the late Ameer of Scinde.

In the Punjab confusion and anarchy prevailed. Heera Singh governed at Lahore, in the name of the young maharajah Dhuleep. He was engaged in collecting a force to combat with his own uncle, Ghoolab Singh, and with the widow of Suchet Singh, the brother of Ghoolab, who was anxious to punish Heera for the late dastardly murder of her gallant husband, Suchet Singh.

There appears to be an apprehension on the British frontiers that some of those conflicting parties will enter the British territory, or that of the protected Sikhs, our allies, where the interference of the British Indian army will become imperative. Notwithstanding the policy of the present governor-general, Sir H. Hardinge, is supposed to be altogether pacific, he, like former British rulers, must conform to circumstances, and be ready to defend or to attack. It was rumoured that Sir H. Hardinge would soon proceed to the north-west, in order to confer with the commander-in-chief of India, who was at Simla, and perhaps even with Sir Charles Napier, the governor of Scinde.

It is useless to disguise from public view the political propriety of the British dominion being established in the Punjab, the possession of which fertile country is necessary to the security of India, as being the chief gate through which all past invaders by land have entered. The country is at present a prey to civil discord, and without any efficient government; for the prime minister and his relatives were the disputants, and the descendant of Runjeet Singh was but a mere puppet in their hands.

The government of Affghanistan, as administered by Dhost Mohammed, was in the usual state of turmoil; conspiracies, revolts, and skirmishes about the revenue kept that chief in continual employment.

The ex-chief of Jeltpore, Pareechut, and his two relatives and chief supporters, Puhlwan Singh and Kummode Singh, both leaders of the rebels who lately kept the Bundelkund districts in a distracted state, had offered to make terms with the British; but after some parleying with the second, the negotiations are said to be broken off, to the dissatisfaction of the troops, who are likely to be harassed in chasing those bandits and their followers through the mountainous districts.

The new rulers at Gwalior, although appointed under the British, are busied in peculations, and in oppressing the ryots and zemindars subject to them.

The object of those rulers being to gather money as soon as they can, they care not about the means they use for that purpose. It was thought that the British authorities would have to compel them to adopt another course. The unfortunate Christians who were formerly employed by the Gwalior government, having been turned adrift, were in great distress, and a subscription had been raised for their relief, under the protection of the lieutenant-governor of the North-Western provinces.

There was considerable excitement in Bombay relative to the approaching trial of Aloo Paroo, one of the heads of the Bunder gang, and who is accused of being involved in the burning of the Belvedere ship. His trial was fixed for the 7th of October. He had been arrested at Jinjeera, a small island 80 miles south of Bombay, where he lay concealed for some months, but he was surrendered by the Rajah on the requisition of the Bombay government.

Mr. W. W. Bird, the oldest member of the Supreme Council, who for some time past has filled the office of deputy-governor of Bengal, takes his departure by the Hindostan. He is succeeded in council by Sir G. Pollock, who is now on his way down to the Presidency; and it is generally believed that the governor-general will resume the duties of the Bengal government.

Mr. Justice Burton and lady had arrived at Madras on the 27th of August.

At the Presidency, everything has been characteristically flat and uninteresting. Nothing has happened to awaken us from the pleasant drowse into which we are accustomed to fall during the rainy season. The departure of the old Governor-General created a little sensation; the arrival of the new Governor-General has created none. His ways are the ways of quietness; he has afforded society no topics of conversation, the press no themes of discussion: he has made no promises — issued no threats; displayed no over-weening desire to be considered a *sub-junta*; but has been placidly looking about, and leaving people to discover by his acts, as they develop themselves, what is the nature of the policy he purposes to pursue. So far, so well. There is every reason to be hopeful of a good steady administration; during which affairs will settle down into a fit state for the cultivation of the arts of peace. We regret to learn the death of Lieutenant Mackintosh, late Aide-de-Camp to Lord Ellenborough, and subsequently in charge of the Mysore princes. The gallant officer died from the effects of fever. Captain M'Lean succeeds the deceased lieutenant in charge of the Mysore princes.

As Sir Henry Hardinge was proceeding in his customary drive on Saturday morning, the progress of the carriage was stopped by a native, running up to it, hanging on by the mane of one of the horses, and vociferating a supplication to his Excellency for his clemency and protection. One of the aides-de-camp, who was with Sir Henry, had the fellow removed, and handed him over to the police, where he remained in confinement all Saturday, and, perhaps, is so detained up to this moment. From subsequent inquiries it appeared, that the poor man is a native of Joudpore, and has travelled on foot all the way from that distant part of the country, for the purpose of getting certain grievances redressed. He complains of having been subjected to some cruel measures of oppression by the zemindar on whose lands he is a ryot. To obtain redress he has been induced to traverse so many hundred miles. He reached Calcutta a few days ago, and presented, as he says, a petition to the governor-general to look into his case and protect him from the oppression of his zemindar; but not getting any reply to that petition, with all his money exhausted, and himself left in a state of starvation in this place, he resorted to the mode of importunity which has earned him a safe lodgment in the police lock-up.—*Bengal Hurkaru*, Sept. 16.

"Our commercial operations have

during the past month been characterized by their usual languor at this period of the year. The last mail, bringing the news of the alteration in the sugar duties, has caused a considerable derangement in that trade, and has created great anxiety amongst the principal speculators in the article, who must now calculate on heavy losses. It is expected that many bills drawn against such consignments will be returned, and the operations of the money market are consequently much disturbed. The East India Company has announced that its operation in exchange for the ensuing season will be limited to £800,000 sterling. This is the first time that the Court of Directors has yielded to the strong expression of public opinion as to the publication of its financial measures, and the concession is now only made by halves. Lord Ellenborough intended to abolish the purchase of private bills in this market altogether, and to substitute for it draughts by the East India Company in London for the whole amount annually required. The Court of Directors have not thought proper to carry this suggestion into effect, but it is not probable that they will be able to continue their present mode of operating much longer. The indigo crop may now be considered as certain not to fall below 140,000 maunds, and may perhaps somewhat exceed this quantity. It is understood that the crop in Java will not exceed 25,000 maunds, but that the quality, owing to the attention now paid to it, will be considerably better than in former years. A report just published by the Agricultural Society of Calcutta will put an end to the expectations of those who thought that India might rival China in the tea trade. It appears, on the evidence of the most experienced cultivator in Assam, that tea cannot be grown at less than 1s. a pound on the average of years, and this without reckoning any of the expenses of bringing to market. It can, therefore, never compete with the produce of China, not even in this country."

China.—Our advices from China are to the 29th of July from which we learn that disturbances had again taken place at Canton. The English last year repaired the walls of the Company's garden, which had been broken down at the fire in 1842. They put on a gate, and were in the habit of walking, playing at quoits, and otherwise amusing themselves. On the 15th of July the Chinese endeavoured to force themselves into the garden, but were opposed. Upon this they threw brickbats, and broke down the gate, compelling the Englishmen to take refuge in a boat, in which they made their escape to the Consulate. On the following evening a party of Chinese went armed with brickbats, and attempted to take possession of the other garden. Resistance being offered, they commenced an indiscriminate attack upon all the foreigners who came within their reach. Several American gentlemen immediately armed themselves, and drove them from the front of the factories. Still continuing to throw brickbats, they were fired upon, and one man killed, and another wounded in the arm, which ended the affair for the day. The English and American Consuls applied to the Chinese authorities for a sufficient force to protect the factories, and a message was sent to the American man-of-war at the Bogue to request assistance. Intelligence of the 28th informs us that no further rioting had taken place, nor was any likely to occur at present, though it was quite certain that the authorities at Canton were either unable or unwilling to adopt measures sufficiently vigorous to check the riotous disposition of the commonalty.

The *Friend of China* contains some correspondence which has taken place between the principal British merchants resident at Canton and Her Majesty's Consul at that place. The merchants complain, first, of the unprotected state of that port, and request that a vessel of war may be forthwith stationed there, in lieu of the Wolverine lately removed. They next request to be allowed to occupy and build upon the ground on which the former factories stood, and which is at present under the control of Her Majesty's Superintendent of Trade. They likewise complain of the annoyance which they suffer from the Chinese mob, and request that these ruffianly intruders may be prevented from infringing upon their liberties. In the absence of a British man-of-war, the British and foreign residents have been indebted to Captain Tilton, of the United States' frigate St. Louis, for protection. The American ambassador, Mr. Cushon, has negotiated a treaty on the same terms as Sir Henry Pottinger's, but has obtained a slight concession in the duties on lead, which the Americans expect to supply in large quantities from their western territories.

Exchange was heavy at 1 10½, or a small fraction above, at 10 months' date.

Commercial matters in China were dull. Cotton yarn continued depressed as before. The iron market was over-supplied. Opium was firm, being supported by the smallness of the supply. In rice prices had given way. In tea very little doing. The second and third crops are said to have been destroyed by the late rains. Rate of exchange on London, at six months' sight, 4s. 3d. per dollar; Government bills, at 30 days' sight, 4s. 10d., in little request. Freight to London and Liverpool, £3 per ton of 50 feet.

New South Wales.—Sydney papers to the 14th of July have arrived, which give a return of the revenue of New South Wales, exclusive of Port Philip, for the quarter ending the 30th of June. From this it appears, that the gross receipts were £71,832 against £82,129 in 1843, showing a decline of £10,297. Prices for all articles of consumption continued low, and the markets are not reported to be in a better condition. Great hopes are, however, expressed of a revival of business when the export trade should set in; and from the estimates given in the papers, there is every reason to expect that tallow will before long become an almost equal staple with wool. The decline in the import trade had raised serious apprehensions respecting the sufficiency of freightage for the produce in course of shipment for England; for, what with a good clip of wool, an increased manufacture of tallow and hides, and the ores received from the mines opened in South Australia and New Zealand, it was supposed that the homeward tonnage before the close of the season would be found to a considerable extent inadequate for the purpose of the export trades. The return of the several banks had been published, and these, *prima facie*, showed a healthy state of business. The late arrival of emigrants, being for the most part the description of persons employed in agriculture, had been speedily cleared, and the majority found good employment. Portland Bay is spoken of as a very rising place, and the Government were about to encourage emigration thither, it having of late contributed largely to the Crown-Land revenue.

In the legislative council at Sydney on the 13th of June, Sir T. L. Mitchell moved an address to his Excellency the Governor, praying for returns of the number of whites and of aborigines who had been killed by collision with each other in the southern district. He regretted deeply that so little progress has yet been made in ameliorating the condition of the aboriginal natives, and inducing a more friendly disposition towards the white settlers. He feared the ill-feeling, however, was on the increase, and that the vast sums which had been expended in protectorates and other schemes had been utterly thrown away on the banks of the Glenelg and Murray, where those hostile tribes were located, even among the richest lands in the colony, and if half the money had been spent in forming agricultural settlements here, he thought the dreadful evil he complained of would have been much lessened.

The Colonial Secretary regretted as much as possible the collisions which took place between the whites and the aborigines. The Government was most anxious to civilize and Christianize the natives, and would willingly adopt any suggestions which might bring about so desirable an end. He feared, however, some difficulty might arise in furnishing the returns, particularly of the blacks killed, which he did not think could be a true one.

The motion was then agreed to.

Mr. Windeyer had much pleasure in hearing the Colonial Secretary speak in terms of such sympathy towards the aboriginal natives, as it would, he was sure, lead to a satisfactory explanation of the causes on which he had occasion to found his present motion, namely a return of all correspondence between the Colonial Secretary's office and the Bathurst Hospital, relative to the case of a native boy named Jemmy Maning. It appeared that this boy was met in the bush by a naval officer, labouring under a complication of diseases, which could be cured only by hospital treatment. The surgeon had the lad removed to the Bathurst Hospital, and when in that institution sent to the Government to know how the expenses were to be defrayed; the reply of his Excellency was, "that he'd got no money." He thought, in a case like this, with a Government professing sympathy with the natives, and where a reserve of 15 per cent. on the territorial revenue was made for the protection of the natives, that it was a little out of character to say of its acts, that instead of the relief that had been offered him, this unfortunate boy should have been left to die like a dog in the bush.

After a few words from the Colonial Secretary, stating that the application for the expense had come to a wrong quarter, but promising to furnish the returns, the motion was agreed to.

Port Philip.—From Port Philip it appears that the manufacture of tallow by boiling down sheep was increasing rapidly —not far short of 50,000 sheep had been boiled down at Sealong (Port Philip) in about ten months.

Tahiti.—Later accounts have been received from the Society Islands by way of the United States, from which it appears that there has been another battle between the French and the natives, in which great numbers of the latter have been butchered by their well-armed and well-disciplined assailants. Louis Philippe's new officer of the Legion of honour, Captain Bruat, is, we suppose, the hero of this new slaughter. The Fishguard English frigate has conveyed Queen Pomare to the Island of Bolabola.

Estimated statement of the ways and means required to meet the expenditure of the year 1845, exclusively of that chargeable on the revenue arising from crown lands.

Head of Revenue.	Sydney.	Port Philip.	Total.
Customs:—	£.	£.	£.
Duties on spirits imported	60,000	27,200	87,200
Duties on tobacco	36,000	8,360	44,360
Ad valorem duty on foreign goods imported	30,000	1,650	31,650
Miscellaneous	4,000	1,700	5,700
Post-office	16,000	3,100	19,100
Duties on colonial spirits	13,000	......	13,000
Publicans' licenses	18,000	4,950	22,950
Auction Duties	5,300	1,050	6,350
Tolls and ferries	4,900	100	5,000
Fees of public offices	25,800	7,200	33,000
Interest on public moneys	500	250	750
Assessment on stock, and fees and fines collected by commissioners of crown lands	12,500	8,000	20,500
Miscellaneous receipts	4,000	230	4,230
	225,500	53,750	279,250

The abstract of the revenue for the quarter ended the 30th June, again exhibits a falling off, as compared with the corresponding quarter of last year; but we are glad to perceive that the decrease is by no means so considerable as in several preceding abstracts. The decrease (not including Port Philip) on the quarter ended 30th June, 1843, compared with the same quarter of the previous year, was £15,144, or 15½ per cent.; the decrease on the quarter ended 31st December, 1843, was £15,280, or 20½ per cent.; whilst the decrease on the quarter just expired was only £10,296, or 12¼ per cent. This fact bears out the hope expressed by the governor in his speech at the opening of the council, that the revenue had nearly reached the lowest point of declension, when it might be expected to rally.—*Sydney Herald.*

Australia.—The following extracts relative to the prices paid for various commodities and kinds of labour, are from a letter written from Australia, of the 16th of August, to a gentleman at Fife in Scotland; and the information will no doubt be interesting to our readers:—

"The country is far from being in a good state for any class of men, with the exception of the sheep-farmers, who are making fortunes rapidly. Oats are now selling at from 2s. to 3s. per bushel. Wheat from 2s. 6d. to 4s. Potatoes from 30s. to £2 per ton. The four-pound loaf, from 5d. to 7d. Tea is from 1s. 6d. to 4s. per pound. Flour is from £9 to £13 per ton. Sugar is from 1½d. to 4d. per pound in the country. Brandy, gin, and whisky are still at 1s. per glass. Mutton is from 1½d. to 2d. per pound. Beef the same. In regard to sheep and cattle, a new system has been commenced here of melting the fat down for tallow, which, however strange it may appear, has increased their value to a great extent. Previous to this scheme being put in operation, sheep were sold as low as 1s. per head, and cattle at 12s., but at the present moment sheep realize from 8s. to 10s., and cattle from £2 10s. to £4. Colonial butter is about 10d. per pound. The butter exported from Ireland to this place is perfectly unsaleable. Cheese is generally sold at 10d. per pound. Clothing is now selling in proportion with everything else. Moleskin trousers from [illegible]s. to 14s. per pair. Striped shirts from 2s. 6d. to 4s. each. Flannel shirts from 5s. to 8s. each. English light boots from 8s. to 10s. per pair; and colonial from 12s. to 14s. What the price of leather is I do not know, but it is considered the best trade in the country. Wages at present are very low. Shepherds from £15 to £18 per annum. Carpenters from £20 to £25, and their victuals. Blacksmiths have from 20s. to 30s. per week, and their board costs them from 12s. to 15s. Shoemakers from 8s. 6d. to 10s. 6d. Women servants £10 per annum. You may give my best respects to every person, whom you know, who intends to come out here, and tell them that it is my opinion that, if they can live at home at all, they are just as well off as we are in this place. If they have less money, they have more domestic comfort, for that is a complete stranger amongst us."

The abstract of the census had been published in the official *Gazette*. The grand total is 17,366, and of these 9,526 are males, 7,670 females; the sex of the remaining 170 at Kangaroo Island and Mount Gambier not having been given.

The following is an analysis, in the *Register*, of the abstract of the receipts and expenditure of the Colonial Government of South Australia, for the quarter ending the 31st March, 1844:—

"The total receipts, including the transfer of £300 from the land account, and £31 15s. for rents of land temporarily leased, are £7,325 15s. 3d., and the total expenditure, including £282 10s. 8d. for the emigration department, is £6,565 8s. 7d.

"According to the statement, the surplus revenue of the quarter is £1,041 7s. 1d., a state of things, which ought not, under the present circumstances of the colony, for one moment to be tolerated. True, the licenses for the past quarter amounted to £1,640, and this source of revenue will not be available to the same extent until the corresponding quarter of the next year; but even admitting all that can be claimed on this score, the colonists have no right to be taxed for a surplus revenue, and especially, when any one, by casting his eye down the items of expenditure, can see, at a glance, that they might at once be reduced from thirty to fifty per cent, without any infliction of the least injustice."

There has been a further postponement of the Government Debentures in lieu of the bills for outstanding claims.

Swan River.—From Swan river it is stated that the colonists were turning their attention to the cultivation of the vine most sedulously, and ere long the exports of wine, of a quality far superior to the Cape, is a matter of certainty.

New Zealand.—By the last accounts received from New Zealand, the news is not of prominent interest. The tribes were quiet and peaceable, but the conduct of the agents of the Land Company is said to be anything but calculated to secure harmony between them and the natives. The Government surveys were not concluded at the latest date.

We augur ill of Captain Fitzroy's government, from his reply to the Memorial of the Settlers at Nelson. It shows at least an inclination to consult the claims of the natives, which have been practically disregarded in the whole system pursued under his predecessors. Of course when he says that they are entitled to the protection of British law, he means in their property as well as their persons. We may therefore look for some change in the power of disposing of the lands. At present they cannot sell, or, what amounts to the same thing, the Government will not recognize a native title to lands if transferred directly by them to British subjects. This must be altered, or the idea of their possessing the rights of British subjects is a farce.

His Excellency has taken precisely the same view of the melancholy catastrophe, which the colonists call the massacre of Walroa that we did some time since. There could be no doubt that the whole body engaged on that occasion were acting illegally, and that the natives were justified in resistance precisely as Englishmen would have been under the same circumstances. That the result was fatal, we must regret, but the principal parties certainly provoked it by their folly. In fact thy despised too much the strength and spirit of their antagonists, under the idea too prevalent that a savage has no right to resist the encroachments of his superiors, the whites.

At the same time that we approve of the spirit of his Excelleney's proclamation, we cannot conceal the fact that his future course is beset with difficulties from the rival pretensions of the different races, the arrogance of our own countrymen, and the independence, spirit, courage, and determination of our new fellow-subjects;—partly too from their ignorance and contempt of European prowess, guaranteed by their success.

Cape of Good Hope.—Cape Town papers to the 19th of September, according to which the frontier Boers were complaining of the inadequacy of protection, and the repeated infringements of the Caffres, notwithstanding the treaties entered into with the local government. The Dutch farmers, it would appear, lay much of the blame arising from aboriginal aggression to the ready access the natives have had to fire-arms and ammunition in the way of trade with the British, and they seem to consider that the Boers have been misrepresented here as persons who were only desirous of exterminating the original possessors of the soil, for their own exclusive advantage. A meeting had been held of the Dutch farmers on the frontier, at which these feelings were strongly expressed, the late murder of one or two of their number having called them together to give their opinion on the subject. An active investigation was being made into the circumstances of these atrocities, and the Lieutenant-Governor had so disposed his military force in the neighbourhood as to command the movements of the tribes within a certain distance of the frontier, and trace the guilty parties, if they were within the range of his district. The Boers are described as having attended the meeting well-armed, and several of them came from a great distance to be present at the debate. In other respects the news by this arrival is of no great importance. Sandilla appears to be a chief most amicably disposed towards the British, and within his district he had desired the presence of the military to crush and disband the native depredators. The muderers of De Lange, the Boer farmer, had been discovered and surrendered to justice, Sandilla at the same time ordering 60 head of cattle found in their possession to be given up to the widow. From Natal the advices are favourable, and the progress of affairs in that part of Africa are stated to be of the most satisfactory description. Captain Smith was to be presented with a valuable sword, as the reward for his exertions in that part of the country. The trading prospects of the Cape are alluded to as steadily increasing, and those of Algoa Bay present a remarkable feature in the business of the colony.

The consideration of the Estimate of Revenue and Expenditure for 1845, was concluded on Thursday last, and the Estimate Ordinance was published the next day in the *Government Gazette*, authorizing an Expenditure for the year 1845 of £172,179. 10s. 3d.

Of this amount, £10,000 has been allowed, to provide for Immigration to this Colony, from the United Kingdom; and a sum of £10,653. 18s. for Miscellaneous services,—of which latter the particulars will be published in the next *Government Gazette*. We hear, however, that a grant of £1000 towards the erection of a Light House at Cape L'Aghulas and £4,000 for the same purpose at Cape Receif, are included in the above Miscellaneous.

The consideration of the Estimate has been preceded by a communication, made by the Secretary to Government, of the state of the public debt of this Colony, from which it appears that from the 1st of June 1843 up to the 17th of May last, a sum of £131,086 has been paid towards the redemption of the Government Promissory Notes,—of the balance, £10,000 still unredeemed, £1,800 are in the Treasury, and £8,200 still outstanding and unredeemed.

The satisfaction which must necessarily be felt at the settlement of a debt, long and warmly disputed, is much diminished, by the springing up of another debt, which during the last year, was never spoken of, nor perhaps known to exist, viz.: a sum of £51,803 for capital and interest due to the Home Government, and the East India Company.

In 1822 severe storms having occasioned great damage throughout the colony, the Home Government is said to have advanced to this colony, a sum of £35,000 called the "*Storm Fund*," which together with interest thereon, unpaid, would at this time amount to £38,493.

The debt to the East India Company is said to have arisen from a loan to this colony in 1827, originally to an amount of £18,750, but on which a balance is still due of £2,359. 15s.

These two sums, together with a sum of £20,950 borrowed on debentures, for the redemption of the Government promissory notes, during the last year, constitutes a public debt still unpaid of £61,803, which the Secretary to Government proposes to pay off, without trenching upon the *ordinary* Colonial Revenue, in the following manner:—

"We are able," says he, "to provide for the payment of this debt without trenching upon the ordinary colonial revenue. In the first place, I must mention that £10,000 of the Storm Fund debt was paid off to the officer in charge of the Commissariat Department, on the 18th instant, thus reducing your debt to £51,803. In the next place, you must bear in mind that I have already shown you that you have uncollected claims to the extent of £55,"60. But of this sum I am of opinion that about 10,000l. are irrecoverable. On the other hand, I calculate on raising, this year, by the sale of land under the new regulation, by the redemption of quit-rents and by surplus revenue, 10,000l. If I am correct in this, you will have 55,960l. to pay off 51,803; and that having been done, you will not owe one shilling."

Mr. Advocate Cloete, however, was of opinion that the debt to the Home Government should not be regarded as a mere debtor and creditor account, but that on public grounds, the exertions which the Colony has made to redeem the Government Promissory Notes, and the sacrifices of the Caffre War, ought to be considered tantamount to an extinguishment of the debt. He therefore gave notice that he would at the close of the discussion on the Estimates propose to solicit Her Majesty to consider the repayment of the original sum of £35,000, as a satisfactory adjustment of the whole claim; which proposition Mr. Ebden promised to second.

We trust Mr. Advocate Cloete will not fail to bring forward his intended resolution, for the purpose of ascertaining Her Majesty's views on that head.—*Cape Town Journal.*

Mauritius.—Mauritius papers to the 31st of August have arrived; but, beyond complaining of the scarcity of silver, occasioned by the necessity of paying the labourers in cash, they contain nothing worth especial notice. The paper circulation of the island was at a heavy discount, and hence the difficulty experienced with respect to specie payments. Amongst the remedies suggested was one, that the banks should sell their draughts on India at a reasonable rate, and thus get a supply of Company's rupees, which, when taken at a proper exchange, would be a more extended metallic currency. The Government in this, as in all other cases, is upbraided for not giving proper assistance in alleviating the wants of the inhabitants. The labourers who find employment in the Mauritius are notorious for being a class of persons who hoard their wages throughout their servitude, mainly with a view of returning to their own country (either India or Africa); and thus, in a certain measure, may the scarcity be accounted for. The latest *Price Current* quotes treasury-bills on London at 4 to 5 per cent. premium, and private bills 6 per cent. discount. The rate of discount on commercial paper was 9 to 12 per cent. per annum.

West Indies.—The Governor of Jamaica had issued his proclamation for the assembling of the new legislature, and proceeding to business on the 15th of October. The convocation of the house thus early was attributed to the measures taken in England with respect to immigration from India. The West India body in this country having guaranteed the cost of sending 5000 Coolies to Jamaica during the approaching season, the opinion of the House of Assembly upon the scheme was required, as also upon the proposition to raise a loan in England, with the guarantee of the Government, of half a million sterling for carrying on such immigration in future.

Since the year 1818, there has not occurred such a dreadful visitation at Montego bay as was witnessed on the 5th instant, (October.)

The following is a list of the vessels and other property destroyed:—The schooner Africanus and the Rachel, the property of Captain Bates, completely wrecked; four boats, the property of Captain Bates; the schooner Exertion, and the sloop Isabella, the property of Mr. J. G. Jump; the sloop Siszia, the Wave, and the Mary, the property of Captain Selley; the sloop Magna Charta, the property of Captain Brown and Son; the sloops Hunter and Tom Smith, the property of Messrs. Watson and Mowat; the sloop Glassinia, the property of Mr. Peter Watson; a sloop boat, the property of James C. Hart and Co.; a schooner boat, Mr. D. Levy; a lighter, Mr. Garth; a lighter, Mr. Manderson; a lighter, Captain Heslop; a lighter, Mr. Thompson; a lighter, Messrs. Watson and Mowat. A large number of small boats and canoes, and Mr. Lindo's bathing-house, a considerable quantity of lumber, staves, heading - boards, and scantlings, the property of Mr. J. G. Jump, washed off from Gun-point-wharf. Several wharfs are considerably injured.

On Wednesday afternoon last, the 16th of October, a frightful conflagration took place at Demerara, (the work of incendiaries,) which continues to rage up to the moment that we are now writing. The first property that fell a prey to the infatuation, or the fanaticism, of the incendiaries, was Uitkomst, the property of Mr. C. J. Visser, one of the resident planters. After desolating Uitkomst, the fire kept on its course in a direction due west towards the head of the canal, next threatening with destruction Java, the fine property of Messrs. Murray, Brothers, and Co., of this colony and Liverpool. It next proceeded to a third estate, bordering Java on the west, the De Kinderen, once the well-cultivated property of Mr. Revers, the entire of which it has laid waste. From De Kinderen the flames successively traversed plantations Mon Bijou and Two Brothers, both coffee properties, committing the most dreadful havoc on them; and by accounts received from the canal up to a late hour yesterday evening, were every hour expected, as they had then become quite irresistible, to invade the next estate to the west, Vreed-en-Vrindschap. Nothing but heavy rain, of which there are not the least symptoms, can, we fear, save the whole of the northern, and by far the most valuable, bank of the canal, from its centre to its head, from complete destruction.—*Georgetown Gazette.*

It appears from the *Royal Gazette* of George-town, British Guiana (October 4), that the Court of Policy of that island, to whom had been referred by the Colonial Secretary certain grave charges against Mr. T. Bagot, late acting colonial registrar, had resolved that the charges had been proved, and that he be not retained in or restored to any office.

The Island of Cuba was, on the 2d of October, visited with a most terrific hurricane, which continued, however, only a few hours, passing over without doing much damage from that time until the morning of the 4th.

On the morning of the 4th it commenced raining, and continued so during the day. The wind at first blew right from N. E., veering afterwards to E.; and at dusk it became a calm. At this time the thermometer was at 19 of Reaumur. It began to blow at 8 p.m., and also rained. At 9 and 10 p. m., the wind blew a hurricane, and increased during the whole night, with occasional flashes of lightning, accompanied with great destruction of property in the city of Havannah

The principal damage to the houses was sustained in the suburbs, but scarcely a house escaped without injury.

The *Courrier Français* states, that since the sixteenth century 161 earthquakes have been experienced in the West Indies —viz., in the 16th century 1; 17th, 9; 18th, 43; 19th, 108; of which 12 were in January, 9 in February, 11 in March, 11 in April, 10 in May, 10 in June, 7 in July, 15 in August, 17 in September, 25 in October, 14 in November, and 10 in December; 32 in winter, 31 in spring, 39 in summer, and 41 in autumn.

CANADA.—Advices from Canada and the United States, arrived at Liverpool, on Saturday Nov. 23, bringing Montreal papers of the 4th inst., and Toronto of the 5th. The total return of the election in favour of the governor-general, is stated at 42 against 27 radicals, with 4 doubtful, making a total of decided election of 73, and the whole number is 84. This we think is decisive, Sir Charles Metcalfe has presented £100 in aid of the funds of the Montreal temperance society.

A serious riot is reported to have taken place in Quebec on the occasion of an Irish procession in honour of the liberation of O'Connell. Some parties having refused to illuminate, their dwellings were attacked, they fired from the windows, and several of the assailants were wounded.

The following is the state of the Montreal markets, up to the 2nd of November.

Ashes, both descriptions in good demand; pots readily find buyers at 24s. 3d., and pearl at 24s. 6d. to 24s. 9d. Shipping parcels of pots could not be obtained this morning under 24s. 6d., and several large lots have changed hands at that price.

Flour, Canada fine, is taken for consumption here, and for Quebec account, at 23s. 6d. to 24s. 6d. per barrel, while United States commands 25s. 3d. to 25s. 6d.

Grain, Upper Canada wheat is worth 4s. 9d. to 4s. 10d. per 60lb., and peas 2s. 6d. to 2s. 7d.

Exchange, the banks draw on London at 11½ to 11¾ per cent. premium; the latter rate was paid this morning for £5,000. Draughts on New York are 1½ to 2 per cent.

Freights, for ashes, to Liverpool and the Clyde, the rate is 35s. to 37s. 6d.; and, for flour, 4s. 6d. to 5s., but we cannot learn that any flour is now being shipped to Great Britain.

Throughout Canada we have tidings of the near approach of winter.

Canal of Panama.—A canal across the isthmus which connects North and South America has always been looked upon as a thing of great importance. Puerile efforts to cut a canal have long been made from time to time by individuals or companies, but nothing has been done, and probably nothing will be done until it is made a national business. It seems to us that the great nations particularly interested in the matter should at once unite in the enterprise, cut the canal, and declare it under the same laws which regulate the open ocean; and even more than that, making it neutral water under all circumstances. America, England, France, and Russia, could accomplish the undertaking at small cost, and we should expect would all readily unite for the purpose, if it were but proposed. No Government could more properly lead in this enterprise than our own. Why should it not be brought before Congress at the approaching session? As to the constitutional power of Congress to appropriate money for the purpose—if nothing better can be found, let it go under the power to "regulate trade," to "coin money," or to "do whatever may be necessary" for the establishment of "post-offices and post-roads." It is, at any rate, a proper matter for the great nations to agree about, fixing some plan by which it may be accomplished.—*New York Journal of Commerce.*

United States.—Letters and papers from New York are up to the 9th of Nov. the intelligence is ample and important. The contest for the Presidency, esteemed so doubtful, is decided—we may almost say unexpectedly—in favour of Mr. James K. Polk, foremost in whose policy are the annexation of Texas to the United States, the support of the institution of slavery, and, to use his own words, "such a tariff for revenue as will yield a sufficient amount to the treasury as will defray the expenses of Government, economically administered." Other questions are likewise involved in this decision given by the citizens of the United States—the bank question, the distribution of the surplus revenue, affecting the repudiating States, Native Americanism, and other minor matters. According to the *New York Herald*, the tariff may be somewhat modified at the next session, though it never can be essentially altered; no bank, no distribution, can take place for the present; new negotiations may be opened for the annexation of Texas, but as the Senate will be Whig for two years at least, nothing can be done effectually as regards that matter for some time to come. This journal regards the Whig party as utterly and for ever disbanded, and conceives that on their ruins will spring up the American Republicans.

In another article it reviews the effect of the election upon the repudiating States in respect of the settlement in the negative of the question of distributing the surplus revenue among the States—a measure of great importance both to this country and to the United States; and considers it a result most fortunate for the character of the country and the prospects of the stockholders, as compelling them to depend solely upon themselves in order to redeem their character. It conceives that a moral feeling will now be awakened throughout the Union, which will operate so powerfully as to lead to the adoption of an honest and upright course. Why this reformation in moral feeling is to be, we are not informed. The triumph of Mr. Polk is a triumph of the South over the North, and opens a vast field for speculative opinions; but the time has not arrived for commencing them. He was 49 years of age on the 2nd of November.

As soon as the result of the Presidential election was known, Texas bonds rose, nominally, 15 to 20 per cent, while United States stocks were depressed.

The following official return from the Treasury Department of the receipts into and expenditure from the Treasury during the quarter ending the 30th of

September last will be interesting. They are as nearly ascertained as can be:—

	Dollars.	Cents.
From Customs, about	10,750,000	0
From lands, about, ...	450,000	0
From miscellaneous sources	25,500	0
	11,225,500	0

The expenditures for the same period were—

On account of the Civil List, miscellaneous and foreign intercourse		1,411,052 05
On account of the army	1,245,682 75	
On account of the Indian department	907,968 76	
On account of the fortifications ..	200,627 24	
On account of the pensions	923,717 50	
		2,277,996 25
On account of the navy		1,906,206 89
On account of the interest of public debt, ...		81,404 62
On account of the reimbursement loan of 1841		284,600 0
On account of the reimbursement and interest on Treasury notes		322,584 61
		7,233,844 42

Thus the receipts, over and above the expenditure, amount to within a few dollars of being nearly four millions for one quarter of the year. It was considered a very satisfactory state of things.

The revenue collected at the port of New York during the month of October as 1,334,675 dol. 43c.

The first steam-vessel ever despatched from the United States for any parts beyond the Cape of Good Hope had sailed from New York on the 4th. It was the steam-propeller Midas.

France.—The usual annual report of the commercial movement of France, has been published for the year 1843. From this it appears that the commerce of France with her colonies and with foreign powers, has embraced, during the year 1843, merchandise to the amount of 2,179,000,000f., divided into imports, 1,187,000,000f., and exports 992,000,000f.

The following is a statement of loans contracted in France for the last thirty years:—

Years.	Amount.	Rate per Ct	Negociated at fr.	c.	Produce. fr.
1815	3,600,000	5	61	23	35,863,200
1816	6,000,000	5	57	26	69,763,800
1817	669,755	5	59	16	7,924,035
1817	30,000,000	5	57	51	345,025,000
1818	14,925,500	5	66	50	197,909,400
1818	12,313,433	5	67	—	165,000,090
1821	407,912	5	87	7	7,000,000
1821	12,514,220	5	85	55	214,118,301
1823	23,114,516	5	89	55	413,980,981
1830	3,134,950	4	102	7	80,000,005
1831	7,142,858	5	84	—	120,000,014
1832	7,614,213	5	98	50	150,000,000
1841	—	3	78	52½	150,000,000
		Total			1,956,623,939

HOME INTELLIGENCE.

Local Rates and Taxes.—Of the yearly total levy of £12,000,000, sterling for "local rates and taxes" in England and Wales, £10,750,000, are raised in England; of that, above 30 per cent are upon houses, and 52 per cent or £6,000,000 are levied upon (£30,500,000, sterling as net value or rental of) land in cultivation, comprising 25,500,000 acres of cultivated land. The Report or Local Taxation says—"This burden was so intolerable as in some places to throw land out of cultivation." These local rates extend over above 14,000 parishes, and engage above 180,000 persons in their collection and expenditure, which the Poor Law Commisioners (report) recommend should be placed in their hands! On 27 English railways, 1,200 miles in length, and averaging 12,000 acres, the statistics (taking the actual figures on six months of 1843 as a guide) are as follows:—For one year, gross receipts, above £5,000,000; working expenses, £1,500,000; interest on loans, &c., £750,000; Government duty of 5 per cent, £161,081; local rates and taxes, £111,000, (besides, tithes, land and assessed taxes, &c.) leaving only £2,000,000 for dividend, which was subject to some deductions, the income tax being about £60,000. The yearly assessment to the poor-rate of those 27 railways was £555,000, being an average of £48 an acre, and a yearly payment of £9. 2s. per acre (at 4s. in the pound) towards local rates for a quantity of land, which, as such, averaged less than £8,000 assessed value, or 15s. per acre, and would have paid (at 4s. per acre) less than £2,400. Every year the traffic and the taxation increase. There are above 2,000 miles of railways now in work, with a capital of above £100,000,000; another 1,000 miles in progress of formation, and another 1,000 to be applied for next session. This enormous difference in local taxation arises from including the profits of the railways and their trade—a principle from which canals, Irish, Scotch, and continental railways, are exempt. This contribution is, besides that to £5,000,000 of tithe (the commutation increasing it from £3,500,000, under the old law, and a portion of which was never recovered), £1,250,000, of land tax and sewers, assessed, and state taxes, &c., and for which and all other taxes the poor rate assessment is the guide.—*Railway and Land Taxation.*

Exports to China.—The demand for China (according to letters from Manchester) is, at the present moment, prodigious for shirtings. The export in this article alone will, it is said, exceed that of last year by 1,500,000 pieces.

OBITUARY.

Allen, Richard, Esq., Registrar of the Court of Requests, on the 16th July, at Sydney, New South Wales, aged 44 years.

Begbie, Clarence, son of John Begbie, Esq., of Camberwell, senior ensign of the 1st Madras Native Infantry, on 29th August, at Secunderabad, aged 22, in consequence of injuries sustained the day previous through a fall from his horse.

Champain, John, Esq., third son of the late John Champain, Esq., of London, on 12th June, at West Martland, New South Wales.

Cochrane, Rear-Admiral, on 16th November, at Bathford, the seat of his brother, at an advanced age. The admiral, when commanding the "Kingfisher," sloop, captured a French privateer of fourteen guns and one hundred men; was present and rendered important service in the action off St. Domingo.

Dallas, Lieutenant Henry, 98th regiment, on 25th July, at Hong-Kong, China.

Dance, Colonel Sir Charles Webb, K.H., on the 13th November, at Bar House, near Taunton, in the 59th year of his age.

Dunne, General Edward, in November, at his seat in Queen's County, Ireland, in his 83d year. The deceased had rendered particular service during the rebellion in Ireland in 1798. His commissions were dated as follows:—Ensign, September 9, 1780; Lieutenant, May 24, 1784; Captain, February 28, 1785; Major, September 30, 1791; Lieut.-Colonel, December 31, 1793; Colonel, Jan 26, 1797; Major-General, September 25, 1803; Lieutenant-General, July 25, 1810; and General, July 19, 1821.

Dyett, Lieutenant Malcolm R., Royal Navy, on 6th November, at London.

Greenwell, Major-General Sir Leonard, K C.B., and K.C.H., on 11th November. The deceased general, who was third son of the late Mr. Joshua Greenwell, of Kebblesworth, was born in 1781.

Gunton, Henry, Esq., late Captain in her Majesty's 50th regiment of Foot, on 15th July, at Keshnaghur, near Paramatta, New South Wales.

Haining, Captain James, of the 3d West India regiment, formerly of the 65th foot, on 23d July, at Sierra Leone, aged 39 years. Whilst in South America, Captain Haining volunteered and travelled along with Dr. Schomberg, for the Geographical Society, in order to explore the unknown regions to the interior of the Guianas.

Jenkins, John Edward, Esq., of her Majesty's 31st regiment of foot, eldest son of John Jenkins, Esq., surgeon, of Gosport, and of the East Suffolk light infantry, on 24th August, at Umballa, East Indies.

Macdonogh, Montague, Esq., late of the 4th or King's Own regiment of foot, on the 12th Nov., at Boulogne-sur-Mer, aged 48.

Nicolls, Commander Jonathan, Royal Navy, on 19th November, at Coleraine, in his 62d year.

Ottley, Captain Osbert Davenport, of the 1st Bombay European regiment of fusileers, on 19th September, at Lallee, near Ahmedabad, East Indies, aged 37.

Ram, Komul Sen, the dewan or treasurer of the Bengal bank, died in the early part of August, at Calcutta. Of the native gentlemen who have raised themselves to eminence in the native society of Calcutta, by the acquisition and distribution of wealth within the present century, Ram Komul Sen will be freely acknowledged as the most remarkable. Others have risen from equal obscurity to greater wealth, but none have been more distinguished for their intellectual attainments. There is scarcely a public institution in Calcutta of which he was not a member, and which he did not endeavour to advance by his individual exertions. He was one of the chief instruments in the establishment of those institutions which have diffused European science among the natives, and so greatly raised the tone of native society.—*Friend of India*, Aug. 15.

Ross, the Rev. William H., M.A., on the 7th August, at Calcutta.

Saye and Sele, the Right Hon. Lord, on 13th November, in the 76th year of his age. He is succeeded in his title and estates by his only son the Hon. William Twisleton Fiennes, who was born in April, 1798.

Scotland, Thomas, Esq , eldest son of John Scotland, Esq., of Glen Douglas, Roxburghshire, on 10th July, at Macao, China.

St. John, the Hon. General Frederick, on 19th November, at Chailey. This remarkable general officer was the second son of Frederick, second Viscount Bolingbroke, and brother of the late and uncle to the present Viscount. He was born on the 20th of December, 1765, and entered the army in August, 1799; at the time of his death he was the senior general in the army, with the single exception of Sir G. Nugent, Bart. He served with much distinction in India under Lord Lake.

Udny, Charles Grant, Esq., Bengal Civil Service, on 3d November, at London, aged 38.

Western, the Right Hon. Lord, on 4th Nov., at Felix Hall, Essex, in his 78th year.

Whitmore, Charles, Esq., of the Bengal Civil Service, on 19th August, near the Neilgherry Hills, aged 36.

Wilkinson, Charles, eldest son of Edward Wilkinson, Esq., of Regent's-Park, London, on 23d September. He was crossing the St. Lawrence, Canada, with three companions, when a violent tornado burst upon them, and all perished.

Wilson, Captain William Thomas, of the 58th regiment of Bengal Native Infantry, on his return from Europe to join his corps, on 3d August, near Dinapore. He was the son of Major-General Thomas Wilson, C.B., of the Hon. East India Company's Service.

LONDON: FISHER, SON AND CO., PRINTERS

Lightning Source UK Ltd.
Milton Keynes UK
UKHW020212091118
331957UK00012B/1600/P

9 780483 273948